Sex Matters

The Sexuality and Society Reader

THIRD EDITION

Mindy Stombler

Dawn M. Baunach

Elisabeth O. Burgess

Denise Donnelly

Wendy Simonds

Elroi J. Windsor

Georgia State University

D1456025

Allyn & Bacon

Boston   Columbus   Indianapolis   New York   San Francisco   Upper Saddle River
Amsterdam   Cape Town   Dubai   London   Madrid   Milan   Munich   Paris   Montreal   Toronto
Delhi   Mexico City   Sao Paulo   Sydney   Hong Kong   Seoul   Singapore   Taipei   Tokyo

Publisher: Karen Hanson
Editorial Assistant: Courtney Shea Ball
Marketing Manager: Kelly May
Production Supervisor: Patrick Cash-Peterson
Manufacturing Buyer: Debbie Rossi
Cover Administrator: Joel Gendron
Cover Designer: Stefan Kjartansson
Editorial Production and Composition Service: Omegatype Typography, Inc.

Photo Credits: p. 46, David Hiller, courtesy of the Kinsey Institute; p. 93, Ed Cunicelli; p. 154, Charles Harrington, Cornell University Photography; p. 386, Eng-Beng Lim; p. 466, Margaret Benes.

Library of Congress Cataloging-in-Publication-Data

Sex matters : the sexuality and society reader / [edited by] Mindy
Stombler . . . [et al.].—3rd ed.
      p. cm.
  Includes bibliographical references and index.
  ISBN-13: 978-0-205-61061-7 (pbk.)
  ISBN-10: 0-205-61061-7 (pbk.)
  1. Sex—Social aspects. 2. Sex—Social aspects—United States. 3. Sex in popular culture—United States. 4. Sex customs—United States. I. Stombler, Mindy.
  HQ16.S46 2010
  306.7—dc22

                                      2009022937

10 9 8 7 6 5 4 3 2 1 EB 13 12 11 10 09

Allyn & Bacon
is an imprint of

www.pearsonhighered.com

ISBN 10: 0-205-61061-7
ISBN 13: 978-0-205-61061-7

In loving memory of Chet Meeks (1973–2008).
Here's hoping the afterlife is full of sinful pleasures.
If not, please come back. Actually, just come back.

Contents

Preface

We live in a sex-saturated society. We hear of sex drive, sex toys, sex machines, sex slaves, sex scandals, sex gods, sex crimes, and sexaholics. Sex permeates every aspect of our lives from advertising to politics to our relationships with others. Yet we rarely consider the historical, legal, and cultural contexts of sexuality. Many people take the current state of sexual attitudes and practices in our society for granted, as if they are natural and thus unchangeable. Understanding contemporary sexual matters requires considering how sexuality varies across time and place and how it is modeled, molded, and even manipulated by those around us. Consider, for instance, the influence of social contexts as you read the following scenarios:

- Imagine that you've chosen to have sex for the first time. How do you know what to do? How do you plan on pleasing your partner? Yourself? Do you turn for guidance to books or magazines, pornographic videos, or the wall of the public bathroom? What makes you excited? Nervous? Will you practice safe sex?

- Imagine that you and your partner do things together that you've never heard about before but make you feel transported, ecstatic, or orgasmic. Or imagine you feel nothing much during your encounters or that you feel disgusted or that you're not even sure if you have "had sex." Imagine that you want to stop but your partner won't. What would you do? Whom would you tell?

- Imagine that you and your partner are the same sex. Would you feel comfortable showing affection in public? Can you imagine a cultural context in which you wouldn't have to worry about others' reactions? Can you imagine how dating someone of the same sex might be beneficial to you?

- Imagine that an evening of partying ends in an unplanned one night stand. You or your partner become pregnant. Would you see the pregnancy as something to celebrate? To ignore? To hide? To terminate? Would your family and friends share your feelings? Would their reaction be the same if

you were 15 or you were 45? What if your partner were much older or younger than you? Or of a different race, ethnicity, or religion?

- Imagine that you've made a careful decision to refrain from sexual activity. What circumstances might compel such a decision? Would it be hard to maintain your resolve? Or imagine, by contrast, that you've sought out as much sexual activity as you can find. Either way, who would support your decision to be celibate or sexually adventurous? Who might challenge it? How would these responses be different, depending on your age, your gender, or your social status?

Sexuality and Society

If you vary the time, the place, or the cultural setting of the scenarios, you'll find that your feelings, the decisions you would make, and the reactions of those around you will probably change. These variations occur because the social norms governing sexual behavior are continually in flux. Other social factors, such as your religious beliefs, level of education, economic status, ethnicity, gender, and age, influence sexual activity and its meaning. All of the following are influenced by society: what counts as a sex act, how often we have sex, what is considered erotic, where we have sex, the age when we begin having sex, with whom we have sex, what we do when we are having sex, how often we desire sex, our reasons for having or avoiding sex, whether we pay others or get paid for sex, and whether we coerce our sexual partners. Although often characterized as a purely biological and often uncontrollable phenomenon, sex is, in fact, social. The readings we have selected portray sex as a social issue influenced by culture, politics, economics, media, education, medicine, law, family, and friends.

Sex Matters

Our title reflects the content of the book in two ways. First, we have included research articles and essays on a variety of sexual matters. Second, the title supports our assertion that sex, and the study of sexuality, *matters*. There is much to learn about sexuality. Despite the prevalence of sexual matters in public life and the media, as well as its private significance, scholars researching sexuality have difficulty getting institutional and financial support. Funding agencies, politicians, and many academics do not take sexuality seriously.

Yet the study of sexuality is burgeoning, as evidenced by the proliferation of courses on sexuality in colleges and universities throughout the United States. This book applies social theory and methods to the study of sexuality. Thus, research-oriented articles dominate our collection. This empirical focus is enhanced in each chapter by the Spotlight on Research feature, which profiles the work of ten sex researchers. Each of these interviews echoes the fact that sex really does matter.

Themes of This Book

Each of our chapters highlights the dual themes of social construction and social control. In other words, society—composed of social institutions and the individuals within them—constructs our understanding of sexuality and influences our behaviors, attitudes, and sexual identities. The readings illustrate that some social institutions and some members of society have more power to control and define a society's sexual agenda than others. At the same time, social control is usually met with social resistance, and we offer readings that feature examples of successful individual and cultural resistance to societal expectations and oppression.

Chapter 1, "Categorizing Sex," explores how society constructs sexual categories. We challenge readers to question what should count as having sex, a topic with wide-ranging legal and health implications. Readings on intersexuality and transsexuality encourage us to consider the viability of our current categories of "male" and "female," what it takes to change one's sex, and who controls sex assignment and reassignment. Other readings question current methods of categorizing sexual orientation and sexual identity. What does it mean to be straight, gay, lesbian, or bisexual? Is sexual identity a matter of behavior, erotic attraction, or self-

definition? What role does community play in the construction of our sexual identities? Although existing categories can be helpful for understanding commonalities, they also collapse a wide variety of experiences and feelings into inflexible and essentialized divisions. As the readings show, sexual categories vary across societies, cultures, and time.

Chapter 2, "Investigating Sexuality," presents historical and contemporary sex research and theory and considers ethical, political, and methodological issues involved in conducting sex research. The readings introduce the unique challenges of conducting sex research. The association of sex with privacy creates a level of anxiety and reluctance among would-be research participants that is unmatched in other areas of research. For example, the cultural unwillingness to see adolescents as sexual beings discourages parents from allowing minors to participate in sex research. Differing religious teachings on sexuality add to the controversial nature of sex research. The protest efforts of fundamentalist religious groups have successfully limited governmental support of art, health, and research programs that involve sexuality. Furthermore, because sexuality has historically been viewed as too trivial to merit social research, funding agencies are reluctant to support sex research.

Chapter 3, "Representing Sex," presents a variety of interpretations of the ways that U.S. culture depicts sexualities and sexual activities. For example, media (books, songs, magazines, videos, Internet, etc.) both reflect and create ideas about sexuality. Cultural representations of sexuality affect viewers or readers in a variety of ways by telling powerful stories about appropriate sexual activity and what happens to individuals who deviate from cultural expectations. Cultural representations tell us about who we are, where we've been, and where we're going. The critical perspectives presented in the readings demonstrate the varieties of possible interpretations of these representations.

Chapter 4, "Learning about Sex," describes the diverse sources of education about sexuality and examines how these sources shape people's sexual practices and identities. The readings explore how young people are socialized to understand sex and sexuality. Ironically, although talking (or even thinking) about sex may be considered inappropriate, the articles indicate that from a young age we all absorb many sexual messages. Young people learn appropriate and inappropriate sexual behaviors and attitudes from their families, peers, churches, schools, and the media. These messages about sexuality are often used to control sexual behavior, and the degree and methods of social control are tied to a person's gender, sexual orientation, class, race, and culture.

Chapter 5, "The Sexual Body," addresses how we eroticize bodies, body parts, and bodily functions and explores how notions of the erotic can encourage us to manipulate our bodies. Societal discourse both celebrates and stigmatizes the body and its functions. What is sexy about a person's body? Most people can come up with distinct body types or features that are appealing or unappealing to them. Yet these ideas about what is sexy and what is not are culturally constructed. For example, some people use surgery to craft "sexier" bodies, whereas others' life-saving surgeries challenge norms about bodily function and sexuality. Cultural constructions of the sexual body also function as a form of social control—shaping how we feel about our own bodies, framing our interactions with others, and even forcing us to manipulate our bodies, both voluntarily and involuntarily, to meet cultural expectations. The articles in this chapter explore many traditional ideas about sexuality that emphasize the gendered and racialized nature of the sexual body.

Chapter 6, "Sexual Practices," examines how people behave sexually. As you read the articles in this section, think about how social norms, laws, religion, families, friends, and partners influence our sexuality and shape our behavior. Also, think about the tremendous diversity in sexual practices reflected in these articles. These readings cover a range of sexual practices such as national patterns of sexual behavior, monogamy, the "down low," interracial sexuality, and kinky sex. Although how we enact our sexuality varies tremendously, these readings demonstrate what can happen when we vary from expected and accepted ways of acting sexually. Finally, these articles also remind us that sexuality is important from the cradle to the grave; regardless of our age, we remain sexual beings.

Chapter 7, "Sexual Disease," illustrates how society treats sexually transmitted infections—commonly called *sexually transmitted diseases* (STDs)—quite differently from other communicable diseases. Sexu-

ally transmitted infections (STIs) are the only major group of diseases categorized by their method of transmission, rather than by their symptoms or the parts of the body they affect. People infected with STIs are stigmatized, creating a shield of secrecy in which some people deny to themselves that they have an STI, fail to tell their partners, and avoid seeking treatment. The stigma and perceptions of risk surrounding STIs affect the resources that the government and medical agencies opt to dedicate to fight them. For example, when AIDS was first discovered, it was seen as a "gay" or "African" disease and received little attention. In spite of intense efforts by gay activists, AIDS was considered a national emergency only when it began infecting white, middle-class heterosexual Americans. Regardless of how much we learn about sexually transmitted infections, fears associated with them continue to be a powerful tool in the control of sexuality.

Chapter 8, "Social Control of Sexuality," illustrates how sexuality is managed and directed by forces both internal and external to individuals. Whereas much research on sexuality emphasizes individual responsibility, in this section we explore the social factors that influence sexual attitudes and behaviors. Social institutions such as the law, medicine, and education control sexual behavior through systems of rewards and punishments. Interpersonal interactions further constrain sexual choices through means such as harassment and labeling. This chapter explores how the mechanisms of social control are often turned against certain groups and how the social control of sexuality is a powerful weapon of oppression. Some selections highlight how social control is a two-way street, with the forces of control and resistance in constant conflict.

Although people like to think of sex as an intimate—and ideally pleasant—activity, it can be used as a weapon of violence and control to humiliate, degrade, and hurt. The readings in Chapter 9, "Sexual Violence," deal with various types of sexual assault, rape of sex workers, date or acquaintance rape, the rape of men, rape on campus, and rape during war. The articles presented in this section also illustrate the diversity of sexual violence. Although women are the primary targets of sexual violence, no group is exempt. Sexual violence cuts across all social categories. The articles presented here contain graphic and appalling information: it is our hope that readers will not simply be shocked, but rather become motivated to take steps toward ending sexual violence.

Chapter 10, "Commercial Sex," explores the commodification of sexuality. Despite numerous laws regulating the sale of sexual services, it continues to be both a profitable business and a source of abuse. We address the tensions between the freedom to express sexuality through commercial avenues and the exploitation and control of sexuality through its sale. The readings examine who profits financially from the sex industry, who works in the sex industry, and who consumes its products.

Acknowledgments

Revising this book for the third edition was a challenge and a treat. We would like to thank Karen Hanson, Courtney Shea Ball, and the other folks at Allyn and Bacon. Thanks also to the team at Omegatype for their wonderful job on the production of this book. It was a joy working with you. Thanks to Stefan Kjartansson for the fun and inventive sex-positive cover we love so much! We also extend our thanks to the following reviewers who helped shape the book: Barbara J. Denison, Shippensburg University; Tiffany Guidry, University of Arizona; and Kassia Wosick-Cornea, UC-Irvine.

We are grateful to the researchers and scholars who took time out of their busy schedules to be interviewed for the Spotlight on Research features. Their dedication to the field of sex research, their humor in the face of monetary and political challenges, and their willingness to share personal experiences make us optimistic about the future of sex research. We want to thank the authors who wrote original pieces for the third edition. Their contributions make the book bigger and better (not that size matters . . .).

We edited this book in an incredibly supportive environment. Our colleagues in the Department of Sociology at Georgia State University provided unequivocal support for "Team Sex." The department, and particularly chair Donald Reitzes, provided a great deal of practical support by providing graduate student assistance and expense money. Of course this supportive department could not function, nor could Team Sex, without the assistance of Quanda Miller, Selma

Poage, and Dracy Blackwell. We received crucial assistance from Kirstin McMillen. We appreciate Elizabeth Cavalier and Amanda Jungels's efforts to compile this book's wonderful instructor's manual as well.

Thanks to our families and friends for their encouragement and support. In particular, Mindy would like to thank her ten-year-old son, Moey Rojas, for the scintillating conversations about sex (the non-coital sex talk was especially interesting), her parents Lynne and Milton Stombler, and her partner Nate Steiner (they don't come any more loving and supportive). Dawn thanks Jeff Mullis and their four cats. Elisabeth appreciates the support of Leila Burgess-Kattoula, Ehsan Kattoula, and the rest of her family and friends. Denise truly values her friends and family near and far for their love, patience, and never-ending diversions, especially her gorgeous granddaughters, Aurora and Emilia. Wendy thanks Jake and Ben Simonds-Malamud, Gregg Rice, and Bumble and Hinky Simonds for their sweetness. Elroi thanks Aly Windsor for her femme ingenuity and supportive queer insights.

We would be remiss if we did not acknowledge that we have done this revision in spite of the deaths of loved ones, divorce and breakups, depression, the demands of infants and children of all ages, neurotic pets, an increasing variety of chronic conditions, minute raises, the horrible Atlanta traffic, the sad state of the world, and the general futility of it all! But we have hope that the political climate has changed and will offer us a more sex-positive America.

This book would not have been possible without our dedicated and discerning undergraduate students, graduate students, and writing consultants. We appreciate their letting us know their favorite readings, for fearlessly voicing their opinions, and for asking tough questions.

This project is truly an example of collaborative feminist work. With Mindy Stombler as the team's "dominatrix," and the constant mutual support among all team members, creating this book often felt more like fun than work. Not only did we enjoy meetings, but our frequent loud laughter provoked the insane jealousy of our colleagues at Georgia State. We hope you have as much fun reading this book as we had putting it together.

About the Contributors

The Editors

Mindy Stombler, Ph.D., is a senior lecturer of sociology at Georgia State University. Her research interests include the construction of collective identity in fraternity culture, focusing on black and white fraternity little sister programs and gay fraternities. Her research on gay fraternities examines how men negotiate the dual identities of being gay and being Greek and how men in gay fraternities reproduce hegemonic masculinity. Her latest research project examines power relations and oral sex.

Dawn M. Baunach, Ph.D., is an associate professor of sociology at Georgia State University. Her research interests include inequality and stratification, gender and sexuality, work and occupations, and social demography. She is currently studying various sexual attitudes and behaviors, including gay marriage, sexual fluidities, sexual prejudice, and sexual disclosure.

Elisabeth O. Burgess, Ph.D., is director of the Gerontology Institute and an associate professor of sociology at Georgia State University. Her research interests focus on changes in intimate relations over the life course, including involuntary celibacy, sexuality and aging, and intergenerational relationships. In addition, Dr. Burgess writes on theories of aging and attitudes toward older adults.

Denise Donnelly, Ph.D., is an associate professor of sociology and senior faculty associate for the advancement of women at Georgia State University. Her research interests include involuntary celibacy, services to battered women, culturally competent approaches to ending violence, peace in Northern Ireland, and race and gentrification.

Wendy Simonds, Ph.D., is a professor of sociology at Georgia State University. She is author of *Abortion at Work: Ideology and Practice in a Feminist Clinic* (Rutgers, 1996) and *Women and Self-Help Culture: Reading between the Lines* (Rutgers, 1992), coauthor with Barbara Katz Rothman of *Centuries of Solace: Expressions of Maternal Grief in Popular Literature* (Temple, 1992), and coauthor with Barbara Katz Rothman and Bari Meltzer Norman of *Laboring On: Birth in Transition in the U.S.* (Routledge, 2007). She is currently working on a project entitled *Queers on Marriage.*

Elroi J. Windsor, M.A., is a doctoral candidate in the department of sociology at Georgia State University. His current research focuses on surgical body modification and the disparate regulation of its transgender and cisgender consumers.

The Authors

John Archer is a professor and the research coordinator in the school of psychology at the University of Central Lancashire in Preston, Lancashire of the United Kingdom.

Elizabeth A. Armstrong is an associate professor and the director of undergraduate studies in the department of sociology at Indiana University in Bloomington.

Alison Bain is an associate professor of geography at York University in Ontario, Canada.

Elizabeth Bernstein is an assistant professor of women's studies and sociology at Barnard College, Columbia University in New York City.

Mattilda Bernstein Sycamore (www.mattildabernsteinsycamore.com) is the author, most recently, of *So Many Ways to Sleep Badly,* and the editor of *Nobody Passes: Rejecting the Rules of Gender and Conformity* and *That's Revolting! Queer Strategies for Resisting Assimilation.*

Kathleen A. Bogle is an assistant professor of sociology and criminal justice at La Salle University in Philadelphia.

Heather Boonstra is a senior public policy associate in the Alan Guttmacher Institute's Washington, D.C. office.

Keith Boykin is the editor of *The Daily Voice,* a host of the BET television show *My Two Cents,* a New York Times bestselling author, and a frequent political commentator on CNN and MSNBC.

Allan M. Brandt is the Amalie Moses Kass Professor of the History of Medicine and the Dean of the graduate school of arts and sciences at Harvard University in Cambridge, Massachusetts.

Virginia Braun is a senior lecturer of psychology at the University of Auckland in New Zealand.

Barbara G. Brents is an associate professor of sociology at the University of Nevada, Las Vegas.

Vern L. Bullough was, before his death, a distinguished scholar, author, and professor emeritus in the history department at California State University in Northside.

Elizabeth Cavalier is a doctoral candidate in the sociology department at Georgia State University.

Centers for Disease Control and Prevention is one of the thirteen major operating components of the Department of Health and Human Services, which is the principal agency in the U.S. government for protecting the health and safety of all Americans and for providing essential human services.

Anjani Chandra is a researcher at the Centers for Disease Control and Prevention.

Greta Christina is editor of the "Best Erotic Comics" annual anthology series. She has written and edited several other books, and has contributed to numerous magazines, newspapers, and anthologies. She lives in San Francisco with her wife, Ingrid. She blogs at gretachristina.typepad.com.

Patricia Hill Collins is an author and distinguished professor of sociology at the University of Maryland in College Park.

David W. Coon is a professor in the college of nursing and health care innovation at Arizona State University in Phoenix.

Robert Darby is an independent scholar and cultural historian with an interest in the history of sexuality and sexual medicine.

Michelle Davies is a senior lecturer in the school of Psychology at the University of Central Lancashire in Preston, Lancashire of the United Kingdom.

Clive M. Davis is a professor emeritus of psychology at Syracuse University in New York.

Phillip W. Davis is an associate professor of sociology at Georgia State University in Atlanta.

Kathleen Dolan is an associate professor of sociology at North Georgia College and State University in Dahlonega.

Cynthia Enloe is a research professor of international development and social change at Clark University in Worcester, Massachusetts.

Loree Erickson is a community organizer and porn star academic at York University in Toronto.

Jeffrey Escoffier writes on sexuality, gay history and politics, and social theory and has taught history and politics of sexuality at Universities of California at Berkeley and Davis, Rutgers University, and the New School University.

Amy M. Fasula is a researcher at the Centers for Disease Control and Prevention.

Elizabeth Fee is chief of the history of medicine division of the National Library of Medicine at the National Institutes of Health and professor of history of medicine in the School of Medicine at Johns Hopkins University in Baltimore, Maryland.

April L. Few is an associate professor of human development at Virginia Polytechnic Institute and State University in Blacksburg.

Katherine Frank is a honorary research fellow of sociology at the University of Wisconsin in Madison and an adjunct faculty member of the College of the Atlantic in Bar Harbor, Maine.

John H. Gagnon is a distinguished professor emeritus of sociology at the State University of New York in Stony Brook.

Ina May Gaskin is the executive director of the Farm Midwifery Center in Summertown, Tennessee.

Nicola Gavey is an associate professor of psychology at the University of Auckland in New Zealand.

M. Alfredo González is an urban and medical anthropologist, and a long-time HIV activist living in New York City. He has done research in New York City, South Florida, the Dominican Republic, and Rio de Janeiro in Brazil.

Judith Gordon was, before her death, a nursery school teacher and journalist.

Sol Gordon is a professor emeritus of child and family studies at Syracuse University in New York and former director of the university's Institute for Family Research and Education.

Jamison Green is an author, educator, and consultant specializing in transgender and transsexual social, legal, and healthcare issues and policy.

Gary Greenberg has been a practicing psychotherapist for 25 years; he is affiliated with the Human Relations Counseling Service in New London, Connecticut.

Nora Ellen Groce is the Leonard Cheshire Chair of Disability and Inclusive Development in the department of epidemiology and public health at University College London.

Kate Haas is a lawyer living in California.

Laura Hamilton is a graduate student in the department of sociology at Indiana University in Bloomington.

Chong-suk Han is an assistant professor of sociology at Temple University in Philadelphia.

Heather Hartley was, before her death, an associate professor of sociology at Portland State University in Oregon.

Kathryn Hausbeck is an associate professor of sociology and senior associate dean for graduate studies and academic affairs at the University of Nevada, Las Vegas.

Jo Jones is a researcher at the Centers for Disease Control and Prevention.

Amanda M. Jungels is a doctoral student in the department of sociology at Georgia State University.

Marni Kahn is a doctoral student in the department of sociology at Georgia State University.

Suzanne Kessler is a professor of psychology and dean of the School of Natural and Social Sciences at the State University of New York in Purchase.

Laura Kipnis is a professor in the radio-television-film department at Northwestern University in Evanston, Illinois.

David M. Latini is an assistant professor in the Scott Department of Urology at Baylor College of Medicine in Houston, Texas, and the Houston Center for Quality of Care and Utilization Studies at the Michael E. DeBakey VA Medical Center.

Edward O. Laumann is the George Herbert Mead Distinguished Service Professor of Sociology at the University of Chicago.

Alice Leuchtag is a freelance writer, social worker, counselor, college instructor, and researcher.

Jacob Levenson is an adjunct faculty member of the journalism school at Columbia University in New York City.

Meika Loe is an associate professor of sociology and anthropology and the women's studies program at Colgate University in Hamilton, New York.

Lenore Manderson is the Hillel Friedland Fellow in the School of Public Health at the University of the Witwatersrand and a professor in the School of Psychology, Psychiatry and Psychological Medicine at Monash University in Australia.

Naomi B. McCormick was a distinguished teaching professor of psychology at the State University of New York in Plattsburgh, a fellow with the American Psychological Association, and a fellow and past president of the Society for the Scientific Study of Sexuality.

Kirsten McLean is a lecturer in sociology in the School of Political and Social Inquiry at Monash University in Melbourne, Australia.

Glenn J. Meaney is a master's candidate in the department of psychology at Wilfrid Laurier University in Ontario, Canada.

Chet Meeks was, before his death, an assistant professor of sociology at Georgia State University in Atlanta.

Melinda Miceli is an associate professor of sociology at the University of Hartford in Connecticut.

Robert T. Michael is the Eliakim Hastings Moore Distinguished Service Professor Emeritus at the Harris School of Public Policy at the University of Chicago.

Stuart Michaels is assistant director of curriculum and development and chair of undergraduate studies of the Center for Gender Studies at the University of Chicago.

Kim S. Miller is a researcher at the Centers for Disease Control and Prevention.

Lisa Jean Moore is a professor of sociology and women's studies and the coordinator of gender studies at Purchase College of the State University of New York in Purchase.

William D. Mosher is a demographic statistician at the National Center for Health Statistics.

Joia S. Mukherjee is medical director at Partners in Health, director of the Institute for Health and Social Justice, and assistant professor of medicine at Harvard Medical School and the Brigham and Women's Hospital in Boston, Massachusetts.

Jeffery S. Mullis is a senior lecturer of sociology at Emory University in Atlanta, Georgia.

Adina Nack is an associate professor of sociology at California Lutheran University in Thousand Oaks.

Joane Nagel is a university distinguished professor of sociology at the University of Kansas in Lawrence.

Catherine Jean Nash is an associate professor of geography at Brock University in Ontario, Canada.

Amy Palder is a visiting instructor of sociology at Georgia State University.

C. J. Pascoe is an assistant professor of sociology at Colorado College in Colorado Springs.

Rebecca F. Plante is an associate professor of sociology at Ithaca College in New York.

Scott Poulson-Bryant is a founding editor of *Vibe* magazine.

June Machover Reinisch served as director of the Kinsey Institute and professor in the department of psychology and psychiatry at Indiana University from 1982 until 1993. Upon her retirement she was named director emerita and member of the Kinsey Institute Board of Trustees.

Dorothy E. Roberts is the Kirkland & Ellis Professor at the Northwestern University School of Law, with a joint appointment as a faculty fellow at the Institute for Policy Research.

Susan Rose is a professor of sociology at Dickinson College in Carlisle, Pennsylvania.

B. J. Rye is an associate professor of psychology and sexuality, marriage, and family studies and the director of sexuality, marriage, and family studies at St. Jerome's University at the University of Waterloo in Ontario, Canada.

Stephanie A. Sanders is a professor of gender studies and associate director of The Kinsey Institute at Indiana University in Bloomington.

Teela Sanders is a senior lecturer of sociology at Leeds University in the United Kingdom.

Carmine Sarracino is a professor of English at Elizabethtown College in Pennsylvania.

Kevin M. Scott is the director of the English education program at Elizabethtown College in Pennsylvania.

Steven Seidman is a professor of sociology at the State University of New York in Albany.

Amy C. Steinbugler is a visiting assistant professor of sociology at Dickinson College in Carlisle, Pennsylvania.

Dionne P. Stephens is an assistant professor in the departments of psychology and African diaspora studies at Florida International University in Miami.

Karen Sternheimer is a lecturer of sociology at the University of Southern California in Los Angeles.

Brian Sweeney is an assistant professor of sociology and anthropology at Long Island University, C.W. Post Campus, in Brookville, New York.

Melissa Travis is a graduate student in sociology at Georgia State University in Atlanta.

Jayne Walker is a former research student in the school of psychology at the University of Central Lancashire in Preston, Lancashire of the United Kingdom.

Donna Walton is a certified cognitive behavioral therapist, motivational speaker, and founder of LEGG Talk, Inc.

Jane Ward is an assistant professor of women's studies at the University of California in Riverside.

Jeffrey Wiener is a researcher at the Centers for Disease Control and Prevention.

chapter 1

Categorizing Sex

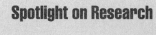

An interview with . . .

Raewyn Connell

Raewyn Connell, B.A. (Melb), Ph.D. (Syd), holds a University Chair in the University of Sydney. She is a Fellow of the Academy of Social Sciences in Australia, a recipient of the American Sociological Association's award for distinguished contribution to the study of sex and gender, and of the Australian Sociological Association's award for distinguished service to sociology in Australia. Her book *Masculinities* (1995) is the most cited research publication in this field. More recently, she has opened up questions about the relations between masculinities and neoliberal globalization, showing her concern to understand both large-scale social structures and personal experience, and the power that people have when acting together.

What led you to begin studying sexuality?

First, wonder. I learnt early on that sexuality was a vehicle of repression, privilege and power. That was shown by campaigns against patriarchy, rape and the objectification of women's bodies; in another way it was shown by Freud and the post-Freudians. But I also learnt that sexuality was an arena of liberation, joy and human solidarity. That was seen in positive views of women's sexuality and it was shown by gay liberation and the new left generally. How could both be true? I think I have made a few steps towards finding out.

Second, fear. When the HIV/AIDS epidemic appeared, it was recognized, especially in the gay community, that only social action could halt the devastation. With support from intelligent politicians (there are some!), government funding was channelled into sexuality research in Australia. I was one of the team who set up the country's main social science research programme on sexuality, in this moment.

How do people react when they find out that you study sexuality?

"Oh, that's very nice, dear. Would you like some more tea?" Most people take it in their stride. I research other things as well as sexuality, so I guess I'm likely to be seen as a general-purpose sociologist rather than as a sex fiend. Issues about sexuality often arise in a wider context: for instance, my research interviews about masculinity naturally included some talk about sexuality, but also about work, education, etc.

Sometimes, when a person is invited to join a study, they respond "Why me?"—meaning, what could possibly be interesting about such an ordinary person as they are? There is a simple answer: everyone's experience is of value, and if the research is to be democratic, we need every sort of person to be involved. By "democratic," I mean research that is part of society's self-knowledge—not part of the secret knowledge gained by the rich and powerful, such as market research.

What ethical dilemmas have you faced in studying sexuality?

Anyone who does close-focus interviewing on such issues will hear some terrible stories about abuse, exploitation and suffering. I have wondered if I should become a whistle-blower, or if I needed to offer counselling and comfort; neither is easy to do from the position of a researcher. I have had the bad experience of learning that some creep was calling people on the telephone, pretending to be from my university, and asking for intimate details of sex life (our research team did not do telephone interviews).

But I think the major ethical dilemma about sexuality research is who gets to use it. Most research is published in venues where only specialists, policy-makers and university students get to read it. For the mass audience, bullshit pretending to be research is pumped out by talk shows and pop psychology best-sellers. How can good research be circulated to the people who need it—without falling into the hands of pornographers or right-wing fanatics? Part of our answer was to feed research results directly into community education campaigns, setting up dialogue between researchers and educators.

What do you think is most challenging about sexuality?

Understanding the contradiction between sexual repression and exploitation, on the one hand, and sexual pleasure and mutuality, on the other. Understanding how sexuality can be both completely embodied, really a matter of sweaty bodies, and also completely social, really a matter of learning, culture, interaction and social structure. Understanding the links, and disconnections, between sexuality and gender. Coming to terms in my own life with contradictory desires, changing situations, mistakes, loss and grieving. Coming to terms with joy. Learning how to reach out to people in an arena where one is so vulnerable.

Why is sex research so important?

Well, some sex research is not! I don't think the counting of orgasms or abstracted surveying of opinions and information matters very much. We have been there, done that, and it wasn't much use. However, good quality sex research—which is hard to do, and takes imagination and patience—is important for several reasons. It is necessary for informed practice to make human life safer, richer and more creative. It is needed to help stop the worldwide HIV/AIDS epidemic, which has horrifying effects in Africa and is growing to a formidable scale in south Asia right now. A thorough, research-based understanding of sexuality is essential for good sex education—which in most school systems, we do very badly. Sex education also occurs outside schools; for instance a key issue is education about safe pregnancy and childbirth, especially among the billion or so people in the world living in absolute poverty. Finally, knowledge about sexuality is an important part of humanity's self-knowledge, our understanding of the human condition and our collective fate.

If you could teach people one thing about sexuality, what would it be?

That sexuality is intricately linked with other parts of social life. Sexuality has to be understood, researched, and for that matter enjoyed, in this light. When we leap into bed we are bringing a whole society and culture with us—for good and for ill. Conversely, we can't understand most aspects of human life (gender, class, development, creativity . . .) without including sexuality. Sexual practices and sexual experiences are points of connection between social structures as well as between individual lives.

Is there anything else that you'd like to add?

Lots! But read the texts. Above all, I would say to students, try walking a mile in someone else's shoes. Try to understand the inner logic of a form of sexuality that is different from your own. Trace out the fears, hopes and transformations that someone in a different country, class, race, religion or gender might experience.

Are We Having Sex Now or What?

Greta Christina

When I first started having sex with other people, I used to like to count them. I wanted to keep track of how many there had been. It was a source of some kind of pride, or identity anyway, to know how many people I'd had sex with in my lifetime. So, in my mind, Len was number one, Chris was number two, that slimy awful little heavy metal barbiturate addict whose name I can't remember was number three, Alan was number four, and so on. It got to the point where, when I'd start having sex with a new person for the first time, when he first entered my body (I was only having sex with men at the time), what would flash through my head wouldn't be "Oh, baby, baby you feel so good inside me," or "What the hell am I doing with this creep," or "This is boring, I wonder what's on TV." What flashed through my head was "Seven!"

Doing this had some interesting results. I'd look for patterns in the numbers. I had a theory for a while that every fourth lover turned out to be really great in bed, and would ponder what the cosmic significance of the phenomenon might be. Sometimes I'd try to determine what kind of person I was by how many people I'd had sex with. At eighteen, I'd had sex with ten different people. Did that make me normal, repressed, a total slut, a free-spirited bohemian, or what? Not that I compared my numbers with anyone else's—I didn't. It was my own exclusive structure, a game I played in the privacy of my own head.

Then the numbers started getting a little larger, as numbers tend to do, and keeping track became more difficult. I'd remember that the last one was *seventeen* and so this one must be *eighteen,* but then I'd start having doubts about whether I'd been keeping score accurately or not. I'd lie awake at night thinking to myself well, there was Brad, and there was that guy on my birthday, and there was David and . . . no, wait, I forgot that guy I got drunk with at the social my first week at college . . . so that's seven, eight, nine . . . and by two in the morning I'd finally have it figured out. But there was always a nagging suspicion that maybe I'd missed someone, some dreadful tacky little scumball that I was trying to forget about having invited inside my body. And as much as I maybe wanted to forget about the sleazy little scumball, I wanted more to get that number right.

It kept getting harder, though. I began to question what counted as sex and what didn't. There was that time with Gene, for instance. I was pissed off at my boyfriend, David, for cheating on me. It was a major crisis, and Gene and I were friends and he'd been trying to get at me for weeks and I hadn't exactly been discouraging him. I went to see him that night to gripe about David. He was very sympathetic of course, and he gave me a backrub, and we talked and touched and confided and hugged, and then we started kissing, and then we snuggled up a little closer, and then we started fondling each other, you know, and then all heck broke loose, and we rolled around on the bed groping and rubbing and grabbing and smooching and pushing and pressing and squeezing. He never did actually get it in. He wanted to, and I wanted to too, but I had this thing about being faithful to my boyfriend, so I kept saying, "No, you can't do that, Yes, that feels so good, No, wait that's too much, Yes, yes, don't stop, No, stop that's enough." We never even got our clothes off. Jesus Christ, though, it was some night. One of the best, really. But for a long time I didn't count it as one of the times I'd had sex. He never got inside, so it didn't count.

Later, months and years later, when I lay awake putting my list together, I'd start to wonder: Why doesn't Gene count? Does he not count because he never got inside? Or does he not count because I had to preserve my moral edge over David, my status as the patient, ever-faithful, cheated-on, martyred girlfriend, and if what I did with Gene counts then I don't get to feel wounded and superior?

Years later, I did end up fucking Gene and I felt a profound relief because, at last, he definitely had a number, and I knew for sure that he did in fact count.

Then I started having sex with women, and, boy, howdy, did *that* ever shoot holes in the system. I'd always made my list of sex partners by defining sex as penile-vaginal intercourse—you know, screwing. It's a pretty simple distinction, a straightforward binary system. Did it go in or didn't it? Yes or no? One or zero? On or off? Granted, it's a pretty arbitrary definition, but it's the customary one, with an ancient and respected tradition behind it, and when I was just screwing men, there was no compelling reason to question it.

But with women, well, first of all there's no penis, so right from the start the tracking system is defective. And then, there are so many ways women can have sex with each other, touching and licking and grinding and fingering and fisting—with dildoes or vibrators or vegetables or whatever happens to be lying around the house, or with nothing at all except human bodies. Of course, that's true for sex between women and men as well. But between women, no one method has a centuries-old tradition of being the one that counts. Even when we do fuck each other there's no dick, so you don't get that feeling of This Is What's Important, We Are Now Having Sex, objectively speaking, and all that other stuff is just foreplay or afterplay. So when I started having sex with women the binary system had to go, in favor of a more inclusive definition.

Which meant, of course, that my list of how many people I'd had sex with was completely trashed. In order to maintain it I would have had to go back and reconstruct the whole thing and include all those people I'd necked with and gone down on and dry-humped and played touchy-feely games with. Even the question of who filled the all-important Number One slot, something I'd never had any doubts about before, would have to be re-evaluated.

By this time I'd kind of lost interest in the list anyway. Reconstructing it would be more trouble than it was worth. But the crucial question remained: What counts as having sex with someone?

It was important for me to know. You have to know what qualifies as sex because when you have sex with someone your relationship changes. Right? *Right?* It's not that sex itself has to change things all that much. But knowing you've had sex, being conscious of a sexual connection, standing around making polite conversation with someone while thinking to yourself, "I've had sex with this person," that's what changes things. Or so I believed. And if having sex with a friend can confuse or change the friendship, think how bizarre things can get when you're not sure whether you've had sex with them or not.

The problem was, as I kept doing more kinds of sexual things, the line between *sex* and *not-sex* kept getting more hazy and indistinct. As I brought more into my sexual experience, things were showing up on the dividing line demanding my attention. It wasn't just that the territory I labeled *sex* was expanding. The line itself had swollen, dilated, been transformed into a vast gray region. It had become less like a border and more like a demilitarized zone.

Which is a strange place to live. Not a bad place, just strange. It's like juggling, or watchmaking, or playing the piano—anything that demands complete concentrated awareness and attention. It feels like cognitive dissonance, only pleasant. It feels like waking up from a compelling and realistic bad dream. It feels like the way you feel when you realize that everything you know is wrong, and a bloody good thing too, because it was painful and stupid and it really screwed you up.

But, for me, living in a question naturally leads to searching for an answer. I can't simply shrug, throw up my hands, and say, "Damned if I know." I have to explore the unknown frontiers, even if I don't bring back any secret treasure. So even if it's incomplete or provisional, I do want to find some sort of definition of what is and isn't sex.

I know when I'm *feeling* sexual. I'm feeling sexual if my pussy's wet, my nipples are hard, my palms are clammy, my brain is fogged, my skin is tingly and super-sensitive, my butt muscles clench, my heartbeat speeds up, I have an orgasm (that's the real give-away), and so on. But feeling sexual with someone isn't the same as having sex with them. Good Lord, if I called it sex every time I was attracted to someone who returned the favor I'd be even more bewildered than I am now. Even *being* sexual with someone isn't the same as *having* sex with them. I've danced and flirted with too many people, given and received too many sexy, would-be-seductive backrubs, to believe otherwise.

I have friends who say, if you thought of it as sex when you were doing it, then it was. That's an interesting idea. It's certainly helped me construct a coherent sexual history without being a revisionist swine: redefining my past according to current definitions. But it really just begs the question. It's fine to say that sex is whatever I think it is; but then what do I think it *is*? What if, when I was doing it, I was *wondering* whether it counted?

Perhaps having sex with someone is the conscious, consenting, mutually acknowledged pursuit of shared sexual pleasure. Not a bad definition. If you are turning each other on and you say so and you keep doing it, then it's sex. It's broad enough to encompass a lot of sexual behavior beyond genital contact/orgasm; it's distinct enough *not* to include every instance of sexual awareness or arousal; and it contains the elements I feel are vital—acknowledgment, consent, reciprocity, and the pursuit of pleasure. But what about the situation where one person consents to sex without really enjoying it? Lots of people (myself included) have had sexual interactions that we didn't find satisfying or didn't really want and, unless they were actually forced on us against our will, I think most of us would still classify them as sex.

Maybe if *both* of you (or all of you) think of it as sex, then it's sex whether you're having fun or not. That clears up the problem of sex that's consented to but not wished-for or enjoyed. Unfortunately, it begs

the question again, only worse: now you have to mesh different people's vague and inarticulate notions of what is and isn't sex and find the place where they overlap. Too messy.

How about sex as the conscious, consenting, mutually acknowledged pursuit of sexual pleasure of *at least one* of the people involved. That's better. It has all the key components, and it includes the situation where one person is doing it for a reason other than sexual pleasure—status, reassurance, money, the satisfaction and pleasure of someone they love, etc. But what if *neither* of you is enjoying it, if you're both doing it because you think the other one wants to? Ugh.

I'm having trouble here. Even the conventional standby—sex equals intercourse—has a serious flaw: it includes rape, which is something I emphatically refuse to accept. As far as I'm concerned, if there's no consent, it ain't sex. But I feel that's about the only place in this whole quagmire where I have a grip. The longer I think about the subject, the more questions I come up with. At what point in an encounter does it *become* sexual? If an interaction that begins nonsexually turns into sex, was it sex all along? What about sex with someone who's asleep? Can you have a situation where one person is having sex and the other isn't? It seems that no matter what definition I come up with, I can think of some real-life experience that calls it into question.

For instance, a couple of years ago I attended (well, hosted) an all-girl sex party. Out of the twelve other women there, there were only a few with whom I got seriously physically nasty. The rest I kissed or hugged or talked dirty with or just smiled at, or watched while they did seriously physically nasty things with each other. If we'd been alone, I'd probably say that what I'd done with most of the women there didn't count as having sex. But the experience, which was hot and sweet and silly and very, very special, had been created by all of us, and although I only really got down with a few, I felt that I'd been sexual with all of the women there. Now, when I meet one of the women from that party, I always ask myself: Have we had sex?

For instance, when I was first experimenting with sadomasochism, I got together with a really hot woman. We were negotiating about what we were going to do, what would and wouldn't be ok, and she said she wasn't sure she wanted to have sex. Now we'd been explicitly planning all kinds of fun and games—spanking, bondage, obedience—which I strongly identified as sexual activity. In her mind, though, *sex* meant direct genital contact, and she didn't necessarily want to do that with me. Playing with her turned out to be a tremendously erotic experience, arousing and stimulating and almost unbearably satisfying. But we spent the whole evening without even touching each other's genitals. And the fact that our definitions were so different made me wonder: Was it sex?

For instance, I worked for a few months as a nude dancer at a peep show. In case you've never been to a peep show, it works like this: the customer goes into a tiny, dingy black box, kind of like a phone booth,

puts in quarters, and a metal plate goes up; the customer looks through a window at a little room/stage where naked women are dancing. One time, a guy came into one of the booths and started watching me and masturbating. I came over and squatted in front of him and started masturbating too, and we grinned at each other and watched each other and masturbated, and we both had a fabulous time. (I couldn't believe I was being paid to masturbate—tough job, but somebody has to do it . . .). After he left I thought to myself: Did we just have sex? I mean, if it had been someone I knew, and if there had been no glass and no quarters, there'd be no question in my mind. Sitting two feet apart from someone, watching each other masturbate? Yup, I'd call that sex all right. But this was different, because it was a stranger, and because of the glass and the quarters. Was it sex?

I still don't have an answer.

Would You Say You "Had Sex" If . . . ?

**Stephanie A. Sanders and
June Machover Reinisch**

. . . The current public debate regarding whether oral sex constitutes having "had sex" or sexual relations has suffered from a lack of empirical data on how Americans as a population define these terms.[1,2] The data reported here were originally collected in 1991 for their relevance to sexual history information gathering and to specifically examine the need for behavioral specificity to avoid possible confusion.[3] These findings also serve as an indication of attitudes regarding definitions of having "had sex" among college students [at a large Midwest State university] assessed prior to current media publicity about this issue. . . .

Almost everyone agreed that penile-vaginal intercourse would qualify as having "had sex." Approaching this level of common perspective and yet importantly different is the fact that while 81% of participants counted penile-anal intercourse as having "had sex," 19% did not. In contrast, few individuals considered deep kissing (nearly 2%) or breast contact (nearly 3%) as having "had sex" with a partner. . . . Approximately 14% to 15% indi-

cated that manual stimulation of the genitals (either given or received) would constitute having "had sex." Only 40% indicated that they would say they had "had sex" if oral-genital contact was the most intimate behavior in which they engaged (60% would not). For the behaviors less frequently included as having "had sex," men were slightly more likely to incorporate them into the "had sex" category. . . .

Among the behaviors assessed, oral-genital contact had the most ambivalent status. Overall, 60% reported that they would not say they "had sex" with someone if the most intimate behavior engaged in was oral-genital contact. Additionally, we found evidence of belief in "technical virginity." Compared with others, those who had experienced oral-genital contact but had never engaged in penile-vaginal intercourse were less likely to consider oral-genital contact as having "had sex." . . .

The virtually universal endorsement of penile-vaginal intercourse as having "had sex" in contrast with the diverse opinions for other behaviors highlights the primacy of penile-vaginal intercourse in American definitions of having "had sex." The lack of consensus with respect to what constitutes having "had sex" across the sexual behaviors examined herein provides empirical evidence of the need for behavioral specificity when collecting data on sexual histories and identifying sexual partners.

NOTES

1. *The Starr Report Referral to the United States House of Representatives Pursuant to Title 28, United States Code §595(c).* Available at: http://icreport.house.gov/icreport. Submitted by the Office of the Independent Counsel, September 9, 1998.

2. Baker, P., Marcus, R. Experts scoff at perjury loophole proposed for Clinton. *Washington Post.* August 15, 1998:A6.

3. Reinisch, J. M., Sanders, S. A., Ziemba-Davis, M. The study of sexual behavior in relation to the transmission of human immunodeficiency virus: caveats and recommendations. *Am Psychol.* 1988;43:921–927.

Source: Sanders, Stephanie A. and June Machover Reinisch. 1999. "Would You Say You 'Had Sex' If . . . ?" *Journal of the American Medical Association* 281: 275–277. Reprinted by permission. © 1999 American Medical Association.

Who Will Make Room for the Intersexed?

Kate Haas

Introduction

Between 1.7 and 4% of the world population is born with intersex conditions, having primary and secondary sexual characteristics that are neither clearly male nor female.[1] The current recommended treatment for an infant born with an intersex condition is genital reconstruction surgery to render the child as clearly sexed either male or female.[2] Every day in the United States, five children are subjected to genital reconstruction surgery that may leave them with permanent physical and emotional scars.[3] Despite efforts by intersexed people to educate the medical community about their rejection of infant genital reconstruction surgery, the American medical community has not yet accepted the fact that differences in genital size and shape do not necessarily require surgical correction.[4]

Genital reconstruction surgery may involve removing part or all of the penis and scrotum or clitoris and labia of a child, remodeling a penis or creating a vaginal opening.[5] While the initial surgery is typically performed in the first month of a child's life, genital reconstruction surgery is not only performed on infants.[6] Older children may be subjected to multiple operations to construct "functional" vaginas, to repair "damaged" penises, and to remove internal sex organs.[7] Personal accounts written by intersexed adults indicate that some children have been subjected to unwanted surgery throughout their child-

hood and teenage years without a truthful explanation of their condition.[8]

Genital reconstruction is rarely medically necessary.[9] Physicians perform the surgeries so that intersexed children will not be psychologically harmed when they realize that they are different from their peers.[10] Physicians remove external signs that children are intersexed, believing that this will prevent the child and the child's family from questioning the child's gender.[11] However, intersexed children may very well feel more confused about their gender if they are raised without any explanation about their intersex condition or input into their future treatment options.[12] The medical community's current practice focuses solely on genital appearance, discounting the fact that chromosomes also affect individuals' gender identities and personalities.[13]

Operating on children out of a belief that it is crucial for children to have genitals that conform to male/female norms ignores the fact that even the best reconstruction surgery is never perfect.[14] Genital reconstruction surgery may result in scarred genitals, an inability to achieve orgasm, or an inability to reproduce naturally or through artificial insemination.[15] The community-held belief that an individual's ability to engage in intercourse is essential, even without orgasm or reproductive capability, seems to govern the decision to perform genital surgery on many otherwise healthy, intersexed children.[16]

Despite the intersex community's rejection of genital reconstruction surgery, no U.S. court has examined the legality of performing these operations without the individual child's consent.[17] By contrast, Colombian courts have heard three such cases and have created a new standard for evaluating a parent's right to consent to genital reconstruction surgery for

From "Who Will Make Room for the Intersexed?" by Kate Haas (2004), *American Journal of Law and Medicine* 30(1): 41–68. Reprinted by permission of the American Society of Law, Medicine and Ethics.

their minor children.[18] In response to the Colombian rulings and pressure from intersex activists, the American Bar Association recently proposed a resolution recommending that physicians adopt the heightened informed consent procedures required by the Colombian Constitutional Court decisions.[19]

This Article questions whether genital reconstruction surgery is necessary in the Twenty-first Century. [The next section] discusses the history and current preferred "treatment" for intersex conditions. . . . [The following sections analyze] the protection that current U.S. law could provide to intersexed children [and explore] how international law may influence decisions regarding the treatment of intersexed children.

A History of Collusion: Destroying Evidence of Ambiguous Genitals

The term "intersex" is used to describe a variety of conditions in which a fetus develops differently than a typical XX female or XY male.[20] Some intersexed children are born with "normal" male or female external genitals that do not correspond to their hormones.[21] Others are born with a noticeable combination of male and female external features, and still others have visually male or female external characteristics that correspond to their chromosomes but do not correspond to their internal gonads.[22] Individuals who are considered intersexed may also be born with matching male chromosomes, gonads, and genitals but suffer childhood disease or accident that results in full or partial loss of their penis.[23] The loss of a penis may lead physicians to recommend that a boy be sexually reassigned as female.[24] Although the conditions differ, the commonality of intersexed people is that their gonads, chromosomes, and external genitalia do not coincide to form a typical male or female.[25] The current American medical treatment of intersexuals is to alter the individual's internal and external gonads to sex them as either clearly male or clearly female.[26]

Medical "treatment" of intersexuals has only been practiced in the United States since the 1930s.[27] During that period, the medical community determined that intersexed people were truly male or female but had not fully developed in the womb.[28] Hormone treatments and surgical interventions were meant to complete the formation of an intersexed adult into a "normal" man or woman.[29] By the 1950s, physicians were able to identify most intersex conditions at birth and began operating immediately on intersexed children to eliminate any physical differences.[30]

Prior to the treatment of intersexuality in the United States, intersexed Americans were treated as either male or female according to their dominant physical characteristics.[31] This strict male/female delineation is not used in all countries though. Other cultures have treated intersexuals differently, either as a third sex, neither male nor female, or as natural sexual variations of the male or female sex.[32] Alternatively, some societies still accept intersexed people without clearly defining their sex at birth.[33]

For instance, within small communities in the Dominican Republic and Papua New Guinea, there is a hereditary intersex condition known as 5-alpha reductase deficiency that occurs with a relatively high frequency.[34] This condition causes male children to be born with very small or unrecognizable penises.[35] During puberty, the children's male hormones cause their penises to grow and other secondary male sexual characteristics to develop.[36] Most of these children are raised as girls and begin living as men when they reach puberty.[37] These communities have accepted these intersexuals without genital reconstruction surgery.[38] In the United States, however, a child with the same condition would likely be surgically altered at birth, raised as a girl and treated with hormones to prevent the onset of male physical development.[39]

Genital reconstruction surgery became standard practice in the United States through the efforts of John Money, a Johns Hopkins University professor.[40] Money introduced the theory that children are not born with a gender identity, but rather form an understanding of gender through their social upbringing.[41] He based this theory on early research done with intersexed children who were surgically altered at birth and raised as either male or female.[42] Money's research found that children who were born with exactly the same genetic makeup and physical appearance fared equally well when raised as either females or males. He concluded that chromosomes did not make any difference in gender differentiation, and that children could be successfully reared as either sex irrespective of their anatomy or chromosomal make-up.[43] Money attempted to prove his theory by demonstrating that a "normal" male child could be successfully raised as a female with Bruce Reimer.[44]

In 1972, Money made public his experimental sex reassignment surgery on a twenty-two-month-old male child named Bruce Reimer who had been accidentally castrated during a routine circumcision.[45] The doctor who examined Reimer shortly after the accident believed that he would be unable to live a normal sexual life as an adolescent and would grow up feeling incomplete and physically defective.[46] Money's solution was to perform a sex change operation on baby Bruce and to have his parents raise him as a girl named Brenda. During Brenda's childhood, Money removed all of "his" internal reproductive organs. As Brenda approached puberty "she" was given female hormones to trigger breast development and other female secondary characteristics.[47] By removing Brenda's gonads, Money destroyed Brenda's reproductive capability. However, Money believed that by changing Brenda's sex, he would make it possible for her to engage in intercourse and marry.[48]

Early reports of Money's experiment claimed that the operation was successful and that Brenda was a happy, healthy girl.[49] Money's research was published throughout the world, convincing doctors that gender was a societal construct, and therefore intersexed children could be raised unconditionally as either male or female.[50] He believed that the only way to ensure that both the family and the child would accept the child's gender was if the child's genitals looked clearly male or female. Based on this theory, babies born with ambiguous genitals or small penises and baby boys who were accidentally castrated were surgically altered and raised as females.[51] Similarly, children born with mixed genitalia, gonads, and chromosomes were surgically altered to fit the definition of a "normal" male or female.[52] Following U.S. lead, other countries also began to practice routine genital reconstruction surgery on intersexed infants.[53]

Despite the widespread use of genital reconstruction surgery, there is no research showing that intersexuals benefit psychologically from the surgery performed on them as infants and toddlers.[54]

No follow-up studies were ever done on adult intersexuals who underwent genital reconstruction surgery as children.[55] In the late 1980s, researchers attempting to disprove Money's gender identity theory began searching for Brenda, the subject of Money's highly publicized research.[56] The boy who was raised as a girl was now living as a man and had changed his name to David.[57] In 1997, Milton Diamond and Keith Sigmundson published an article rebutting the results of Money's famous gender research.[58] The publicity caused by Diamond and Sigmundson's article led to a biography of Reimer by John Colapinto. When Colapinto interviewed Reimer in 1997, Reimer admitted that he had always been certain that he was not a girl, despite being deceived by his doctor and his family.[59]

Reimer suffered emotional duress at all stages of his development, despite the corrective surgery that was meant to make him "normal." In his biography of Reimer, Colapinto describes the painful experiences that Reimer suffered throughout his childhood and teenage years.[60] During her childhood, Brenda did not fit in with her peers and felt isolated and confused.[61] As early as kindergarten, other children teased Brenda about her masculinity and failure to adopt "girl's play."[62] Although her kindergarten teacher was not initially told of her sex change, the teacher reported realizing that Brenda was very different from other girls.[63]

In addition to her failure to fit in socially, Brenda was constantly reminded that she was different by her parents and Dr. Money. During her visits to Johns Hopkins, Money would often force her to engage in sexual role-play with her twin brother in order to enforce that she was a girl and he was a boy.[64] Her genitals were scarred and painful as a child and she hated to look at them.[65] She became suspicious that something terrible had been done to her, primarily due to the frequent doctor's visits with John Money. During these visits, Dr. Money and his associates questioned Brenda about her genitals and her gender identity.[66] Rather than enforcing her gender identity, the medical intervention compounded the trauma caused by her medical condition.

One particularly traumatic procedure inflicted on intersexed children was not discussed in the biography of David Reimer. Intersexed children who have artificially created vaginas must undergo vaginal dilation procedures throughout their early childhood.[67] In order to ensure that the newly created vaginal opening does not close up, the child's parents must insert an object into the child's vagina on a daily basis.[68] This procedure has sexual implications that may be emotionally traumatic for many children.

As a teenager, Reimer rejected his assigned sex and refused to take his female hormones. He reported engaging in typically male behavior throughout his teens. He dressed as a male, chose a trade school for mechanics, and even began urinating standing up.[69] When Reimer's parents finally told him that he was born male, he immediately chose to adopt a male identity and changed his name to David.[70] He had a penis constructed and implanted, and underwent breast reduction surgery to rid himself of the breasts developed through estrogen therapy.[71] There is no procedure that can replace the gonads that were removed as part of Reimer's sex reassignment surgery. There is also no cure for the deception that he experienced upon learning that his parents and doctors had lied to him about many aspects of his life.[72] The trauma of learning about his condition caused David to attempt suicide on several occasions.[73]

[David's] story reads as a happy ending to many people. However, David could have avoided the gender dysphoria, loss of reproductive capability, and many years of therapy that resulted from genital reconstruction surgery. These experiences are not atypical in the intersexed community. According to many intersexed activists, the comfort of being raised in a clear gender role does not outweigh the pain of deception or the physical side effects associated with the surgery.[74]

Despite the emotional and physical scars that people like David Reimer face from genital reconstruction surgery, the majority of American physicians continue to encourage early childhood surgery.[75] In some cases, physicians have insisted on performing genital reconstruction surgery on teenagers without their consent.[76]

In 1993, an intersexed activist named Cheryl Chase began a support and advocacy group for intersexed adults called the Intersex Society of North America ("ISNA").[77] Chase was born with a large clitoris, which was removed when she was an infant.[78] When she was eight years old, her internal gonads were removed without her knowledge or consent.[79] Because of the surgery, she is no longer capable of having her own children or obtaining orgasm.[80] Today, Chase and other advocates are vocal about their hope for a moratorium on the invasive treatment of intersexed children.[81]

ISNA members have contributed significantly to the debate over genital reconstruction surgery by providing personal insight into the effects of surgery on intersexed adults. As of the late 1990s, more than 400 intersexed individuals from around the world contacted ISNA and recounted stories similar to Ms. Chase's.[82] According to ISNA, sex change operations and genital normalizing surgeries should not be performed on children until the child has the ability to consent personally to the operation.[83]

At this point, there is insufficient proof that intersexed adults who are not operated on [fare] any worse than intersexed adults who have had genital reconstruction surgery as children.[84] The only research that has been done on intersexed adults who have not been surgically altered also comes from John Money. In the 1940s, prior to his well-known study on Reimer, Money interviewed many intersexed adults about their gender identity and upbringing.[85] To his surprise, he found that intersexed adults who had not undergone genital reconstruction surgery had a gender identity comparable to other adult males and females.[86] Unfortunately this research was done as part of Money's doctoral thesis and was never published. . . . [87]

Making Room for Intersexuals in the United States

The United States does not currently provide any procedural protection for intersexed children. In the United States, doctors are not required to receive the consent of intersexed children before performing genital reconstruction surgery.[88] Neither are parents routinely given sufficient information to make an informed decision on their child's behalf.[89] Currently, the United States lacks even the standard for informed consent. . . . [90]

Thus far, there has been no legal challenge brought on behalf of intersexed children in the United States. Intersexed adults who have inquired about suing their doctors for performing genital reconstruction surgery that altered their gender have met resistance.[91] Intersexed adults have been told that because the doctors followed standard medical practice when they performed the surgery, the doctors are not liable for medical malpractice.[92]

. . . [T]he U.S. Constitution does not have specific provisions protecting a child's right to bodily integrity. However, the Constitution has been interpreted to protect privacy rights, including the right to marry and reproduce, and the right to bodily integrity generally.[93] Common law also provides some protection for children when there is no "informed" consent, or when a parent's consent or lack of consent to medical treatment is found to be contrary to the child's best interest.[94] In addition to case law supporting the need for informed consent and the best interest of the child, there are recent federal and state statutes protecting female children from genital mutilation.[95] Thus, while no intersexed Americans have successfully sued a physician or hospital for conducting early genital reconstructive surgery, they may have grounds to sue based on female genital mutilation laws, the constitutional right to privacy and lack of informed consent by their parents.

Constitutional Protection for Intersexuals: Leaving Room for an Open Future

The U.S. Constitution protects individuals from overreaching government power through the Fourteenth Amendment, which states "No state shall make or enforce any law which shall abridge the privileges or immunities of citizens of the United States, nor shall any state deprive any person of life, liberty, or property, without due process of law. . . ."[96] The U.S. Supreme Court has interpreted the Fourteenth Amendment as protecting individuals from government action that infringes upon certain "fundamental rights" considered "implicit in the concept of ordered liberty."[97]

The Supreme Court has found that the right to bodily autonomy, the right to choose whether or not to reproduce, the right to marry, and the right to make decisions about how to raise children are all fundamental privacy rights.[98] The government may not violate a person's liberty by infringing any of these rights without first proving in a court of law that there is a compelling state interest that must be served, and that the method that the government is using is narrowly tailored to achieve a compelling governmental interest.[99]

Historically, children have not been accorded the same constitutional rights as adults. A child's parents and the government are allowed to restrict some rights that would be held fundamental for an adult.[100] The Supreme Court has also recognized a fundamental right to family privacy, according parents a high degree of respect regarding decisions they make about their child's upbringing.[101] This includes the choices parents make regarding their children's medical care.[102] Despite the Fourteenth Amendment right to family privacy, the parents' rights must be weighed against the children's rights to be protected against harm. The doctrine of parens patriae articulates the government's interest in protecting the rights of vulnerable individuals from harm.[103]

The doctrine of parens patriae allows the government to interfere with parents' choices about how to raise their children when the children may be harmed because of the parents' actions or inactions.[104] Generally, the government interferes with parental decisions under laws prohibiting parental abuse or neglect.[105] In the case of intersexed children, the government may have reason to override the parents' decision to perform surgery if the surgery would harm the child. . . .

Bodily Integrity: If It Works, Don't Fix It

Included in the Fourteenth Amendment right to privacy is the right to bodily autonomy, which protects individuals from intrusion by the government into their health care decisions.[106] This right includes the right to choose to forego medical treatment, even if foregoing treatment may result in death.[107] For the most part, children are not accorded the right to choose medical treatment or to choose to forego medical treatment without parental consent, despite the fact that it has been found to be a fundamental right.[108] The reason that parents are allowed to consent for children is that a child may not be able to understand fully the consequences of their own consent because of their age or inexperience.[109]

There are several exceptions to the rule requiring parental consent to treatment. . . . These exceptions take into account the fact that parents do not always act in their child's best interest, and a child may suffer abuse or psychological harm if required to seek parental consent to certain treatments. The right to choose whether or not to undergo genital reconstruction surgery should be an exception to the general rule allowing parental consent to treatment of minors. Genital reconstruction surgery is a personal choice that children should be allowed to make on their own in certain circumstances, or, at a minimum, in conjunction with their parents. It is difficult for many children to learn about their intersexuality. However, it is also hard for children to learn to cope with pregnancy, drug addiction, mental illness, or their HIV positive status. In contrast to intersex conditions, all of the above medical conditions are free of parental consent requirements under certain circumstances.

Genital reconstruction surgery is arguably the ultimate infringement of an individual's bodily autonomy. Genital reconstruction surgery can cause a child significant psychological and physical harm.[110] For these reasons, parents should not be allowed to make the decision to alter surgically their child's genitals without the child's consent absent clear and convincing evidence that it is in the child's best interest. If the state participates by allowing the procedure to be performed at a state hospital or by ordering the procedure over the child's objection, then there may be a constitutional violation of the child's right to bodily autonomy under the Fourteenth Amendment.

Reproduction: Gonads Cannot Be Replaced

The right to choose whether or not to reproduce is a fundamental right and, accordingly, certain restrictions are placed on the government's right to interfere with decisions bearing on reproduction.[111] For example, all minors regardless of age have the right to seek an abortion without undue burden from the state, though the state may act to ensure that a woman's decision is informed.[112] Therefore, even when state law requires minors to receive parental consent before seeking an abortion, minors are permitted a judicial bypass, allowing them the right to prove to a court that they are mature enough to make the decision to have

an abortion without parental consent.[113] Children may also have the right to seek contraception, treatment for pregnancy, and childbirth without parental consent.[114]

Because reproduction is a fundamental right, parents are limited in their ability to consent to sterilization procedures for their children. Generally, sterilization is raised in the context of a parent who wants to sterilize a handicapped child to protect the child from the harm of a dangerous pregnancy. If there is an objection made by the child or an advocate for the child, then a court cannot order the procedure against the child's objections without affording the child due process.[115] The child must be appointed an independent guardian *ad litem,* and receive a fair trial at which the court must determine by clear and convincing evidence that the operation to remove the child's gonads will be in the child's best interest.[116]

As with all people, some intersexed adults do not have the ability to reproduce even without genital reconstruction surgery.[117] Others will retain their full reproductive capacity even after the surgery is performed.[118] However, some intersexuals have the ability to reproduce either naturally or artificially and are denied that right by the removal of their gonads and other reproductive organs. For those children whose gonads are removed to complete their physical transformation, their fundamental right to reproduce has been violated. For example, a child born with male chromosomes and sexed at birth as female will have her gonads removed, thus, effectively sterilizing her. . . .

Marriage: Determining Gender Determines Sexuality

Genital reconstruction surgery may inhibit or completely interfere with a child's fundamental right to marry. . . . In 1993, several gay couples challenged the prohibition against same-sex marriages under the Hawaii Constitution.[119] The Hawaii Supreme Court ruled in favor of the plaintiffs and allowed the first gay couples to marry legally.[120] In reaction to the ruling, the Hawaii state legislature immediately amended their own constitution to prohibit same-sex marriages.[121] The federal government reacted to the first gay marriages by passing the Defense of Marriage Act, which allows states to refuse to recognize same-sex marriages that are legally valid in another state.[122] Given that 3% of the world population does not fit into a clearly defined sex and still engage in marriage and child birth, it would be wise to re-think this prohibition.

However, given the laws as they currently stand, genital reconstruction surgically defines an intersexed person as male or female, thus, prohibiting them from marriage to a person of their "same" gender. Intersexuals are in a unique position before they undergo genital reconstruction surgery because they can petition the court to change their legal gender from female to male or male to female without having to undergo a sex change operation. They must prove that they are intersexed, that they have unclear genitals, and that they identify as the opposite sex, and their birth certificate may be altered.[123]

Once an intersexed person has undergone genital reconstruction surgery making his or her genitals clearly male or female, he or she cannot then choose to change his or her birth certificate without having a second round of surgeries performed.[124] For example, if a child born with male chromosomes or mixed chromosomes is surgically assigned a female gender at birth, that individual would be prohibited from marrying a female later in life without first undergoing another sex change operation.[125] In this case, if the initial gender reconstruction surgery had not been performed, this person would be considered a male, not a homosexual female, and thus would have a fundamental right to marry.

By choosing a gender for the child and performing reconstruction surgery at birth, the doctors may be infringing on an individual's ability to marry as an adult. The imposition of additional surgery to change their assigned sex would add such high financial and emotional costs on the individual that it may prohibit some, otherwise qualified, intersexuals from marrying.

Taking a First Step: Informing Parents That Their Child Is Intersexed

Physicians must receive informed consent from all patients before they treat them for any medical condition.[126] If physicians fail to obtain informed consent from their patients, they may be liable for medical malpractice.[127] Under the informed consent doctrine, a patient may even choose to refuse life saving treatment after weighing their treatment options.[128] The informed consent doctrine originated in the tort doctrine of battery, which includes intentionally touching a person in a way that they find harmful or offensive.[129] The surgical removal of part or all of a child's genitals must only be done after receiving informed consent or it may be considered battery.

Absent a recognized exception allowing children to consent to their own medical treatment, parents will generally be allowed to give or withhold consent for medical treatment on behalf of their children. In the United States, genital reconstruction surgery is not currently a procedure that children are allowed to consent or object to without their parents' participation. For informed consent to be valid, the parents must be informed of the nature and consequence of their child's medical condition, as well as the various treatment options available. . . .

[P]arents of intersexed children are not given enough information to make a truly informed decision about their child's treatment.[130] Some parents are not told that their child is intersexed, but instead that their child is a girl or boy with "unfinished" genitals that the doctor will repair with surgery.[131] Physicians may also tell the parents that their baby will have "normal" genitals after surgery.[132] Surgery may make the child's genitals look more clearly male or female, but it will also leave scarring and possibly diminish sexual functions.[133] Generally, more than one surgery is needed to alter completely the genital appearance, and the average number of surgeries is three or more.[134] Surgery and check-ups will continue through the child's early years and may be extremely stressful for the child and his or her parents.[135]

Additionally, parents must understand that while surgery will make intersexed children look more similar to their peers, it will not change their chromosomes. Even with hormone therapy, many intersexed youth will endure gender dysphoria.[136] They may feel confused about their gender despite having genitals that look clearly male or female. Intersexed adults may decide that their assigned gender is not their gender of choice. This might prompt the desire for additional, more complicated surgeries to perform a complete sex change operation.[137] Most of these facts are not presented to the parents of intersexed children at the time that they approve genital reconstruction surgery.[138] If parents are encouraged to consent to surgery without being told of the risks and side effects, their consent is not truly informed. . . .

Genital Mutilation: Equal Protection for Intersexed Children

Intersex children may also have a claim for medical malpractice based on violation of the law prohibiting female genital mutilation.[139] In 1996, Congress passed the Criminalization of Female Genital Mutilation Act.[140] Five states have also individually criminalized female genital mutilation.[141]

The process of removing or altering the genitalia of intersexed children is a form of genital mutilation as defined by the statute.[142] The law prohibits anyone from authorizing or performing an operation on a female child to remove all or part of her genitals for other than health reasons.[143] The statute explicitly covers ritual circumcisions, even if the child herself believes in the religious or cultural significance of the procedure.[144] In section 116(c), the law specifically states that no account shall be taken of the effect of any belief that has led the person or their family to demand the operation.[145] This Act holds the physician liable even if the family believed that the operation would be in the child's best interest and it was standard practice in their ethnic or religious community.[146]

According to the Act, the only way that genital operations can be legally performed on female children in the United States is if the doctor can show that under section 116(b)(1), it is necessary for the health of the person on whom it is performed. . . . [147]

When an intersexed child is operated on to normalize his or her genitals, it is also part of a cultural tradition. Parents want their child to look like other children in Western countries, or as close to "normal" as possible.[148] In some Native American cultures, India, the Dominican Republic, and Papua New Guinea, intersexed people are accepted in society and occupy a specific cultural and social position.[149] In those cultures it would not be considered beneficial to the child to alter the child's genitals.

In the United States, intersexed children are operated on in order to make them look like other children who are not intersexed. Although some medical conditions might endanger intersexed children and therefore make the operations beneficial, this is not usually the case.[150] Most doctors who agree with genital operations for intersexed children claim that the surgery is necessary to protect their mental health.[151] However, no studies have been done that support the question of whether or not genital reconstruction and hormones actually protect the mental health of the patient any better then counseling and education. . . . [152]

The congressional findings on the practice of female genital mutilation in the United States are particularly relevant to the issue of genital surgery on intersexed children. In particular, Congress found that female genital mutilation harms women both physically and psychologically.[153] They found that the practice violates both federal and state constitutional and statutory laws.[154]

The damaging physical and psychological effects of genital reconstruction surgery are identical to the effects of ritual female circumcision. In both cases, the surgery may result in pain, scarring, and the inability to achieve orgasm.[155] Congressional findings that females should not be subjected to the loss of any part of their genitalia for cultural reasons is directly applicable to intersexed children.

The Act indicates that parents do not have the right to give consent to nonessential genital surgery and doctors do not have the right to perform such surgery even if it will make the children assimilate with their ethnic and religious community.[156] The statute only applies to female children.[157] If taken as such, the statute may violate equal protection.[158] However, the Act does not define "female" by genetic make-up or external characteristics. Arguably, most intersexed children fall under one definition of "female" or another. Thus, intersexed children who have their clitoris reduced or other genital parts removed seem to have a strong claim of assault under the Female Genital Mutilation Act.

Sexual Diversity and the International Community

The United States should consider international standards for the treatment of children when considering the legality of genital reconstruction surgery.

One of the main standards by which to judge the international consensus on children's rights is the Convention on the Rights of the Child.[159] The United States was one of only two United Nations member countries that did not sign the Convention on the Rights of the Child.[160] Despite the fact that the United States has not signed the Convention, it is an internationally accepted standard that should be considered by U.S. healthcare practitioners.

The Convention recognizes the rights of children independent of their parents by allowing them to veto parents' decisions on issues of health, education, and religious upbringing.[161] The Convention specifically states that a child should have input into all decisions affecting him or her.[162] Because the decision to alter a child's genitals will forever change the course of the child's life, particular care should be taken to involve the child in this decision.

The second international agreement that is relevant to the treatment of intersexuals is the Nuremberg Code, signed by the United States after World War II.[163] The Nuremberg Code prohibits countries from conducting experimental medical treatments on patients without their express informed consent.[164] Since genital reconstruction surgery has only been in practice during the last thirty years and no studies have been done to prove the procedure's effectiveness, critics argue that genital reconstruction surgery is still experimental.[165] If the procedure is an experimental procedure, then the level of consent required should be higher.

Other countries look to the U.S. medical establishment in developing standards of care.[166] It is important for intersexed children around the world that doctors within the United States make a concerted effort to provide parents and children with all available knowledge regarding intersex conditions before making the recommendation to perform genital reconstruction surgery.

Conclusion

. . . [F]uture legal decisions in the United States and abroad should prohibit hospitals from performing childhood genital reconstruction surgery when it is not medically necessary. The current insistence on genital "normalizing" surgery can be explained by our society's obsession with physical appearance and our fear of people who are "different."[167] However, as the Americans with Disabilities Act and other anti-discrimination laws integrate more and more people with different physical characteristics and abilities, society will begin to accept physical differences as a natural and positive part of being human.[168] At the point that our society makes room for the intersexed through laws prohibiting gender reassignment surgery and unnecessary genital reconstruction surgery on children, then people will begin to acknowledge the existence of intersexuals. When faced with the fact that 3% of the population has chromosomes, genitals, and sexual characteristics that are different, teachers will need to modify sex education courses. Ideally, children will learn that every individual has unique sexual characteristics that help make up their gender identity and sexual preference. Through open discussions of growth and sexual development, intersexed children will learn that they are not alone, and others will learn that intersexuality is a common condition that may effect someone they know.[169]

NOTES

1. Anne Fausto-Sterling, Sexing the Body: Gender Politics and the Construction of Sexuality 51 (2000) (reporting that 1.7% of the population may be intersexed); Julie A. Greenberg, *Defining Male and Female: Intersexuality and the Collision Between Law and Biology,* 41 ARIZ. L. REV. 265, 267 (1999) (reporting that Johns Hopkins sex researcher John Money estimates the number of people born with ambiguous genitals at 4%). Historically, people with intersex conditions were referred to as "hermaphrodites" but this word has been rejected as embodying many of the misperceptions and mistreatment of intersexed people. Raven Kaldera, *American Boyz Intersexuality Flyer,* at http://www.amboyz.org/intersection/flyerprint .html (last visited Mar. 27, 2004).

2. Hazel Glenn Beh & Milton Diamond, *An Emerging Ethical and Medical Dilemma: Should Physicians Perform Sex Assignment Surgery on Infants with Ambiguous Genitalia?,* 7 MICH. J. GENDER & L. 1, 3 (2000); Fausto-Sterling, *supra* note 1, at 45; see *infra* note 4.

3. Emi Koyama, *Suggested Guidelines for Non-Intersex Individuals Writing About Intersexuality and Intersex People,* at http://isna.org/faq/writing-guidelines.html (last visited Mar. 27, 2004). *But see* Beh & Diamond, *supra*

note 2, at 17 (estimating the number of sex reassignments in the United States at 100 to 200 annually).

4. Kishka-Kamari Ford, *"First Do No Harm"—The Fiction of Legal Parental Consent to Genital-Normalizing Surgery on Intersexed Infants,* 19 YALE L. & POL'Y REV. 469, 471 (2001).

5. Fausto-Sterling, *supra* note 1, at 61–63.

6. *Id.* at 45; Ford, *supra* note 4, at 471; Sentencia No. SU-337/99 (Colom.), *available at* http://www.isna.org/Colombia/case1-part1.html (last visited Mar. 27, 2004) [hereinafter Ramos]. There are currently no published English translations of the three Colombian cases referred to in this Article. E-mail from Cheryl Chase, founding director of Intersex Society of North America ("ISNA") (Mar. 19, 2002) (on file with the author).

7. Fausto-Sterling, *supra* note 1, at 62, 84–85.

8. *Id.* at 84. Fausto-Sterling recounts the story of a twelve-year-old intersexed girl named Angela Moreno who lost her ability to orgasm after having her enlarged clitoris removed without her consent. She was told that she had ovarian cancer and was going to have a hysterectomy performed. Later she discovered she never had ovaries. Instead, she had testes that were also removed during the procedure. *Id.*

9. *Id.* at 63–65; Ford, *supra* note 4, at 476–77.

10. Fausto-Sterling, *supra* note 1, at 63–65; Ford, *supra* note 4, at 476–77. According to Ford, "medical professionals admit that it is the psychosocial problem of intersex that makes it an emergency." *Id.*

11. Fausto-Sterling, *supra* note 1, at 64–65; Beh & Diamond, *supra* note 2, at 51.

12. *See* Fausto-Sterling, *supra* note 1, at 84; Beh & Diamond, *supra* note 2, at 2; John Colapinto, As Nature Made Him: The Boy Who Was Raised as a Girl 143–50, 212–13 (2000). In his book, Colapinto vividly describes the gender dysphoria and sexual confusion of David Reimer, a boy raised as a girl after his penis was destroyed during a botched circumcision. *Id.* at 143–50. This biographical account of Reimer's life was written with the cooperation and participation of Reimer himself who sat for more than 100 hours of interviews and allowed the author access to all of his confidential files and medical records. *Id.* at xvii. Colapinto also discusses other children who have suffered extreme gender dysphoria growing up without being informed of their condition. One fourteen-year-old girl described in the book dropped out of high school and threatened suicide if she could not have reconstructive surgery to make her a boy. Testing revealed that she was intersexed, having male chromosomes and female external genitalia. *Id.* at 212.

13. Colapinto, *supra* note 12, at 32; Fausto-Sterling, *supra* note 1, at 46. Fausto-Sterling cites Johns Hopkins researcher John Money, "From the sum total of hermaphroditic evidence, the conclusion that emerges is that sexual behavior and orientation as male or female does not have an innate, instinctive basis." *Id.*

14. Fausto-Sterling, *supra* note 1, at 85–87.

15. *Id.* at 58, 80, 85–87.

16. *Id.* at 57–58. Doctors consider a penis adequate if, as a child is able to stand while urinating and, as an adult is able to engage in vaginal intercourse. *Id. See also* Ford, *supra* note 4, at 471 (stating the "penis will be deemed 'adequate' at birth if it is no less than 2.5 centimeters long when stretched").

17. Ford, *supra* note 4, at 474.

18. Julie A. Greenberg & Cheryl Chase, *Colombia's Highest Court Restricts Surgery on Intersex Children,* at http://www.isna.org/colombia/background.html (last visited Mar. 27, 2004) (synthesizing in English the three Colombian cases to which this Article will refer).

19. E-mail from Alyson Meiselman, Liaison Representative of NLGLA (Aug. 19, 2002) (on file with author). The American Bar Association ("ABA") resolution was proposed by the International Law and Practice Section regarding surgical alteration of intersexed infants. The memorandum was drafted for the ABA Commission on Women in the Profession. *Id.* The resolution will be voted on by the House of Delegates at the August 2003 ABA meeting in San Francisco, California. E-mail from Alyson Meiselman, Liaison Representative of NLGLA (April 29, 2003) (on file with author). A draft of the proposed resolution is available at http://www.kindredspiritlakeside.homestead.com/P_ABA .html (last visited Mar. 27, 2004).

20. Fausto-Sterling, *supra* note 1, at 36–39, 48–54.

21. *Id.*

22. *Id.* at 48–54. The most common forms of intersexuality are: Congenital Adrenal Hyperplasia, which affects children with XX chromosomes and is otherwise referred to as "female pseudo-hermaphrodite;" Androgen Insensitivity Syndrome, which affects children with XY chromosomes and is also referred to as "male pseudo-hermaphrodite;" Gonadal Dysgenesis, which predominantly affects children with XX chromosomes; Hypospadias, which affects children with XX chromosomes; Turner Syndrome, which affects children with XO chromosomes and causes these children to lack some feminine characteristics such as breast growth and menstruation; and Klinefelter Syndrome, which affects children with XXY chromosomes and causes these children to lack some external male characteristics. *Id.*

23. *Id.* at 66.

24. Beh & Diamond, *supra* note 2, at 3; *see* Colapinto, *supra* note 12, at 32.

25. Fausto-Sterling, *supra* note 1, at 51.

26. *Id.* at 56–63; Beh & Diamond, *supra* note 2, at 3.

27. Fausto-Sterling, *supra* note 1, at 40.

28. *Id.*

29. *Id.*

30. *Id.* at 44–45.

31. *Id.* at 40.

32. *Id.* at 33.

33. *Id.* at 109. For example, the Dominican Republic and Papua New Guinea acknowledge a "third type of child," however, they still recognize only two gender roles. *Id.*

34. *Id.*

35. *Id.*

36. *Id.*

37. *Id.*

38. *Id.*

39. *Id.*

40. Colapinto, *supra* note 12, at 39. Colapinto quotes Dr. Benjamin Rosenberg, a leading psychologist specialized in sexual identity, as saying, "Money was 'the leader—the front-runner on everything having to do with mixed sex and hermaphrodites. . . . " *Id.*

41. *Id.* at 32–35; Ford, *supra* note 4, at 471.

42. Colapinto, *supra* note 12, at 32.

43. *Id.* at 32–35.

44. *Id.* at 50, 67–68, 70.

45. *Id.* at 65. John Money presented the case at the annual meeting of the American Association for the Advancement of Science on December 28, 1972.

46. *Id.* at 16.

47. *Id.* at 131.

48. *Id.* at 50. Money envisioned Brenda marrying a man and engaging in vaginal intercourse. *Id.*

49. *Id.* at 65–71.

50. *Id.* "The twins case was quickly enshrined in myriad textbooks ranging from the social sciences to pediatric urology and endocrinology." *Id.* at 70.

51. Ford, *supra* note 4, at 471–73; Beh & Diamond, *supra* note 2, at 3.

52. Ford, *supra* note 4, at 471; Beh & Diamond, *supra* note 2, at 3.

53. Colapinto, *supra* note 12, at 75.

54. Summary of Sentencia No. SU-337/99 (Colom.), at 4 [hereinafter Ramos Summary] (on file with author). The Colombian Court asked for follow-up studies on intersexed children and was not able to obtain any. *Id.*; Colapinto, *supra* note 12, at 233–35. There have been several cases of genetic

males raised as females that were not followed until recently. *Id.* at 273–75; *see also* Fausto-Sterling, *supra* note 1, at 80–91 (providing statistics and personal accounts of intersexuals who received surgery during childhood).

55. Ramos Summary, *supra* note 54, at 4.

56. Colapinto, *supra* note 12, at 208–09. Milton Diamond, an outspoken opponent of John Money put out an advertisement searching for Brenda in the 1980s. With the help of Keith Sigmundson, he tracked down the subject of Money's famous study. *Id.* at 199, 208–09.

57. *Id.* at 208.

58. *Id.* at 214. The article was published in the *Archives of Pediatrics and Adolescent Medicine* in March 1997. *Id.*

59. *Id.* at 216.

60. *Id.* at 60–63, 145–50.

61. *Id.*

62. *Id.* at 60–63.

63. *Id.* Due to Reimer's negative behavior at school, she was referred to a guidance counselor in the first grade. Brenda's parents then allowed her doctor to speak with her guidance counselor and her teacher about her condition. *Id.* at 63–64.

64. *Id.* at 87.

65. *Id.* at 92.

66. *Id.* at 80.

67. Ramos Summary, *supra,* note 54, at 9; Kaldera, *supra* note 1.

68. Kaldera, *supra* note 1.

69. Colapinto, *supra* note 12, at 190–95.

70. *Id.* at 180–85.

71. *Id.* at 184.

72. *Id.* at 267. The Reimer family moved after Brenda's sex change operation and her parents created stories about other parts of their family history in order to hide the truth from her. *Id.* at 100–01, 106, 267.

73. *Id.* at 188.

74. *Id.* at 218–20; Alice Dreger, *Why Do We Need ISNA?,* ISNA News, May 2001, *at* http://isna.org/newsletter/may2001/may2001.html. Because of the private nature of the topic many intersexed adults are hesitant about talking of their experiences. *Id.*; Fausto-Sterling, *supra* note 1, at 85. The ISNA website provides links to personal accounts written by intersexed adults, press releases, medical information, and other resources.

75. Fausto-Sterling, *supra* note 1, at 45–50.

76. *Id.* at 84.

77. *Id.* at 80; Intersex Society of North America, ISNA News, Feb. 2001, *at* http://isna.org/newsletter/feb2001/feb2001.html.

78. Fausto-Sterling, *supra* note 1, at 80.

79. *Id.*

80. *See Id.* at 81; ABCNews.com, *Intersex Babies: Controversy Over Operating to Change Ambiguous Genitalia,* Apr. 19, 2002, at http://abcnews.go.com/sections/2020/DailyNews/2020_intersex_020419.html; Colapinto, *supra* note 12, at 217–18.

81. Colapinto, *supra* note 12, at 220.

82. *Id.* at 218.

83. *Id.* at 220; Intersex Society of North America, ISNA's Amicus Brief on Intersex Genital Surgery, Feb. 7, 1998, *available at* http://isna.org/colombia/brief.html.

84. Colapinto, *supra* note 12, at 233–34; Fausto-Sterling, *supra* note 1, at 94–95.

85. Colapinto, *supra* note 12, at 233–35.

86. *Id.* at 234. The study included interviews with ten intersexed adults who had not been operated on as infants. The study found that genital appearance only plays a small part in a person's formation of gender identity.

87. *Id.*

88. Beh & Diamond, *supra* note 2, at 38–39.

89. Ramos Summary, *supra* note 54, at 4.

90. Glenn M. Burton, *General Discussion of Legal Issues Affecting Sexual Assignment of Intersex Infants Born with Ambiguous Genitalia,* § IIG, *at* http://www.isna.org/library/burton2002.html (last visited Mar. 27, 2004).

91. Beh & Diamond, *supra* note 2, at 2.

92. *See* Helling v. Carey, 519 P.2d 981, 983 (Wash. 1974). A physician may be negligent even if they follow customary medical practice. *Id.; see* Burton, *supra* note 90, § IIA. Burton writes that the American Board of Pediatrics added an addendum to their 1996 recommendation for early surgical intervention acknowledging the recent debate over infant genital reconstruction surgery. *Id.*

93. Loving v. Virginia, 388 U.S. 1, 12 (1967) (holding that the right to marry is fundamental); Skinner v. Oklahoma, 316 U.S. 535, 541 (1942) (holding that the right to reproduce is fundamental); Rochin v. California, 342 U.S. 165, 172–73 (1952) (holding that the right to bodily integrity is fundamental).

94. *See* Parham v. J.R., 442 U.S. 584, 606–07 (1979) (holding that a parent can involuntarily commit a minor child for mental health treatment as long as the treatment is determined to be in the child's best interest by an independent medical determination). The Court stated that there should be an independent examination to determine that parents were not using the hospital as a "dumping ground." *Id.* at 598. *See also In re* Rosebush, 491 N.W.2d 633, 640 (1992) (recognizing the best interest standard applies for determining whether life saving treatment should be provided for a minor child against the parent's wishes).

95. *E.g.,* 18 U.S.C. § 116 (2000).

96. U.S. Const. amend. XIV, § 1.

97. Gideon v. Wainwright, 372 U.S. 335, 342 (1963).

98. Washington v. Glucksberg, 521 U.S. 702, 720 (1997); Planned Parenthood of Southeastern Pa. v. Casey, 505 U.S. 833, 851 (1994) ("Our law affords constitutional protection to personal decisions relating to marriage, procreation, contraception, family relationships, child rearing, and education." (citing Carey v. Population Services International, 431 U.S. 678 (1977))).

99. *Washington,* 521 U.S. at 721 ("The 14th Amendment 'forbids the government to infringe . . . 'fundamental' interests at all, no matter what process is provided, unless the infringement is narrowly tailored to serve a compelling state interest.'" (quoting Reno v. Flores, 507 U.S. 292, 302 (1993))).

100. *Casey,* 505 U.S. at 899. Although the Court reaffirmed that women have a constitutional right to seek an abortion without undue burden, a state may require minors to seek a parent's consent for an abortion provided that there is an adequate judicial bypass procedure. *Id.* In an earlier case, the Supreme Court stated "our cases show that although children generally are protected by the same constitutional guarantees against governmental deprivations as are adults, the State is entitled to adjust its legal system to account for children's vulnerability and their needs for 'concern, . . . sympathy, and . . . paternal attention.'" Bellotti v. Baird, 443 U.S. 622, 635 (1979).

101. Lassiter v. Dep't of Social Services of Durham County 452 U.S. 18, 39 (1981); *see* Wisconsin v. Yoder, 406 U.S. 205, 232–34 (1972); Pierce v. Society of Sisters of the Holy Names of Jesus and Mary, 268 U.S. 510, 534–35 (1925); Meyer v. Nebraska, 262 U.S. 390, 399 (1923).

102. Parham v. J.R., 442 U.S. 584, 602–04 (1979) ("The fact that a child may balk at hospitalization or complain about a parental refusal to provide cosmetic surgery does not diminish the parents' authority to decide what is best for the child.").

103. *Id.* "The court is not without constitutional control over parental discretion in dealing with children when their physical or mental health is jeopardized." *Id.* at 603. "The parent's interests in a child must be balanced against the State's long-recognized interests as parens patriae." Troxel v. Granville, 530 U.S. 57, 88 (2000). *See also* Prince v. Massachusetts, 321 U.S. 158 (1944). In *Prince,* the Supreme Court examines the parents' right to have their child distribute religious material on the street. *Id.* The Court allowed the state to limit parent's power in this regard stating, "Parents may be free to become martyrs themselves. But it does not follow they are free, in identical

circumstances, to make martyrs of their children before they have reached the age of full and legal discretion when they can make that choice for themselves." *Id.* at 170.

104. Elizabeth J. Sher, *Choosing for Children: Adjudicating Medical Care Disputes Between Parents and the State,* 58 N.Y.U. L. Rev. 157, 169–70, 170 n.57 (1983); Jennifer Trahan, *Constitutional Law: Parental Denial of a Child's Medical Treatment for Religious Reasons,* 1989 Ann. Surv. Am. L. 307, 309 (1990). Trahan has divided the medical neglect cases into three categories: those where the child's death is imminent; those where there is no imminent harm; and those where the child is endangered but death is not imminent. *Id.* at 314–15. In most cases, courts will interfere when death is imminent and where the child is endangered even where death is not imminent. However, when there is no risk of imminent death, the parent's religious rights and privacy rights are weighed against the state's parens patriae rights. *Id. See also In re* Richardson, 284 So.2d 185, 187 (1973) (denying parents' request to consent to son's kidney donation for the benefit of his sister where it was not found to be in the son's own best interest).

105. Child Abuse Prevention and Treatment Act of 1996, Pub. L. No. 93–247, 88 Stat. 4 (codified in sections of 42 U.S.C. §§ 5101–5116i (2000)); Adoption and Safe Families Act of 1997, Pub. L. No. 105–89, 111 Stat. 2117 (1997); *see Lassiter,* 452 U.S. at 34 (citing various statutes in support of decision to uphold a termination of parental rights).

106. Rochin v. California, 342 U.S. 165, 172–73 (1952).

107. Cruzan v. Director, Mo. Dep't of Health, 497 U.S. 261 (1990).

108. Parham v. J.R., 442 U.S. 584, 603 (1979); Lawrence Schlam & Joseph P. Wood, *Informed Consent to the Medical Treatment of Minors: Law & Practice,* 10 Health Matrix 141, 142 (2000); *see* Andrew Popper, *Averting Malpractice by Information: Informed Consent in the Pediatric Treatment Environment,* 47 DePaul L. Rev. 819 (1998).

109. Schlam & Wood, *supra* note 108, at 147–49.

110. Fausto-Sterling, *supra* note 1, at 81.

111. Eisenstadt v. Baird, 405 U.S. 438, 453 (1972). The Court stated that it is the right of the individual to decide "whether to bear or beget children." *Id.*

112. Planned Parenthood of Southeastern Pa. v. Casey, 505 U.S. 833, 899–901 (1994).

113. Planned Parenthood of Central Mo. v. Danforth, 428 U.S. 52 (1976); Bellotti v. Baird, 443 U.S. 622 (1979).

114. *Casey,* 505 U.S. at 833 (abortion); Carey v. Population Serv. Int'l, 431 U.S. 678 (1977) (contraception); *see also* Schlam & Wood, *supra* note 108, at 166.

115. Estate of CW, 640 A.2d 427 (Pa. Super. Ct. 1994).

116. *Id.; see In re* Guardianship of Hayes, 608 P.2d 635 (Wash. 1980). In limited circumstances, parents can consent for their incompetent children to be sterilized to protect them from harmful pregnancies. *Id.* at 638. However, there are strict procedural guidelines that the court follows before allowing parental consent. *Id.* at 639. The following guidelines must be followed: (1) the child must be represented by a disinterested guardian ad litem; (2) the child must be incapable of making her own decision about sterilization; and (3) the child must be unlikely to develop sufficiently to make an informed judgment about sterilization in the foreseeable future. *Id.* at 641. Even after the court establishes the listed criteria, the parent or guardian seeking an incompetent's sterilization must prove by clear, cogent, and convincing evidence that there is a need for contraception. *Id.* First the judge must find that the individual is physically capable of procreation. *Id.* Second the judge must find that she is likely to engage in sexual activity at the present or in the near future under circumstances likely to result in pregnancy. *Id.* Finally the judge must determine that the nature and extent of the individual's disability, as determined by empirical evidence and not solely on the basis of standardized tests, renders him or her permanently incapable of caring for a child, even with reasonable assistance. *Id.*

117. Reproductive rights will not be infringed for those intersexed children who are incapable of producing sperm or eggs or who do not have a functional uterus.

118. Reproductive rights will also not be infringed for intersexed children who have clitoral reduction surgery and do not have their gonads or uterus removed.

119. Baehr v. Lewin, 852 P.2d 44 (Haw. 1993); Baehr v. Miike, No. 91–1394, 1996 WL 694235 (Haw. Cir. Ct. Dec. 3, 1996).

120. *Lewin,* 852 P.2d at 67.

121. Haw. Const. art. 1, § 23; *see also* Baehr v. Miike, No. 91–1394, 1996 WL 694235 (Cir. Ct. Haw. Dec. 3, 1996). The Hawaii Constitution was amended by voter referendum shortly before the decision was rendered in *Baehr v. Miike.* David Orgon Coolidge, *The Hawai'i Marriage Amendment: Its Origins, Meaning and Fate,* 22 U. Haw. L. Rev. 19, 82, 101 (2000).

122. Defense of Marriage Act, 28 U.S.C. § 1738C (1996).

123. Lynn E. Harris, *Born True Hermaphrodite, at* http://www.angelfire.com/ca2/BornHermaphrodite (last visited Mar. 27, 2004). The Superior Court, County of Los Angeles, granted the two-part request of Lynn Elizabeth Harris, Case No. 437625, changing the name and legal sex on her birth certificate from Lynn Elizabeth Harris to Lynn Edward Harris, and from female to male, respectively. *Id.*

124. *See In re* Estate of Gardiner, 22 P.3d 1086 (Kan. Ct. App. 2001). Most court cases discussing the legality of changing birth certificates, names or gender identification only consider chromosomes as one factor in determining a person's legal gender. *Id.* The main factor that courts consider is the genitalia of the individual requesting a legal change of status. *Id.* In this case involving a male to female transsexual, the court discusses intersex conditions extensively in explaining the difficulty in determining legal gender. *Id.*

125. Burton, *supra* note 90, § IIIC. Burton cites Littleton v. Prange, 9 S.W.3d 223 (Tex. App. 1999). In *Littleton v. Prange,* a male to female transsexual legally changed her birth certificate to female and married. 9 S.W.3d at 224–25. However, the court found that she was not a legal spouse because she was born male and thus was unable to sue for the wrongful death of her husband. *Id.* at 225–26.

126. Cruzan v. Mo. Dep't of Health, 497 U.S. 261, 269 (1990). "This notion of bodily integrity has been embodied in the requirement that informed consent is generally required for medical treatment. Justice Cordozo, while on the Court of Appeals of New York, aptly described this doctrine: Every Human being of adult years and sound mind has a right to determine what shall be done with his own body; and a surgeon who performs an operation without his patient's consent commits an assault, for which he is liable in damages." *Id.*

127. *Id.*

128. *See Id.* at 279.

129. *See* Washington v. Glucksberg, 521 U.S. 702, 725 (1997).

130. Beh & Diamond, *supra* note 2, at 47–48.

131. Fausto-Sterling, *supra* note 1, at 64–65.

132. Beh & Diamond, *supra* note 2, at 47; Ford, *supra* note 4, at 483–84.

133. Ford, *supra* note 4, at 483.

134. Fausto-Sterling, *supra* note 1, at 86.

135. Ford, *supra* note 4, at 485.

136. *Id.* at 484.

137. *Id.*

138. *See* Beh & Diamond, *supra* note 2, at 48–52.

139. 18 U.S.C. § 116 (2000).

140. *Id.*

141. Bruce A. Robinson, *Female Genital Mutilation in North America & Europe, at* http://www.religioustolerance .org/fem_cira.htm (last updated Jan. 22, 2004). "FGM has . . . been criminalized at the state level in California, Minnesota, North Dakota, Rhode Island, and Tennessee." *Id.*

142. 18 U.S.C. § 116.

143. *Id.*

144. *Id.*

145. *Id.* § 116(c).

146. *Id.* § 116.

147. *Id.* § 116(b)(1).

148. Fausto-Sterling, *supra* note 1, at 48, 51.

149. *Id.* at 109.

150. *Id.* at 52, 55, 58. Intersexed children with Congenital Adrenal Hyperplasia may develop problems with salt metabolism, which could be life threatening if not treated with cortisone. *Id.* at 52. Some intersexed babies may have an increased rate of urinary tract infections possibly leading to kidney damage. *Id* at 58.

151. Beh & Diamond, *supra* note 2, at 46; Fausto-Sterling, *supra* note 1, at 58.

152. Ramos Summary, *supra* note 54, at 4; Kaldera, *supra* note 1, at 4.

153. 18 U.S.C. § 116.

154. Pub. L. No. 104–208, div. C, § 645(a), 110 Stat. 3009–709 (1996) (codified as amended at 18 U.S.C. § 116 (2000)). "The Congress finds that—(1) The practice of female genital mutilation is carried out by members of certain cultural and religious groups within the United States; (2) the practice of female genital mutilation often results in the occurrence of physical and psychological health effects that harm the women involved; (3) such mutilation infringes upon the guarantees of rights secured by Federal and State law, both statutory and constitutional; (4) the unique circumstances surrounding the practice of female genital mutilation place it beyond the ability of any single State or local jurisdiction to control; (5) the practice of female genital mutilation can be prohibited without abridging the exercise of any rights guaranteed under the first amendment to the Constitution or under any other law; and (6) Congress has the affirmative power under section 8 of Article 1, the necessary and proper clause, section 5 of the fourteenth Amendment, as well as under the treaty clause, to the Constitution to enact such legislation." *Id.*

155. Fausto-Sterling, *supra* note 1, at 85–86.

156. See 18 U.S.C. § 116.

157. *Id.*

158. Craig v. Boren, 429 U.S. 190, 197–98 (1976). Equal protection claims brought on the basis of gender must meet intermediate scrutiny; thus, the government must show that there is a legitimate state interest in treating the sexes differently, and that this statute is substantially related to a legitimate government interest. *Id.*

159. *Convention on the Rights of the Child,* G.A. Res. 44/25, U.N. GAOR, 44th Sess., Supp. No. 49, at 167, U.N. Doc. A/44/49 (1989), *available at* http://www.un.org/ documents/ga/res/44/a44r025.htm.

160. *Id.* The other country that did not sign the convention was Somalia. *See* Office of the United Nations High

Commissioner for Human Rights, *Status of the Ratification of the Convention on the Rights of the Child* (Nov. 4, 2003), *available at* http://www.unhchr.ch/html/menu2/6/crc/treaties/status-crc.htm.

161. *Convention on the Rights of the Child, supra* note 159.

162. *Id.*

163. *Trials of War Criminals Before the Nuremberg Military Tribunals Under Control Council Law No. 10 (1946–1949)* [*Nuremberg Code*], *available at* http://www1.umn.edu/humanrts/instree/nuremberg.html [hereinafter *Nuremberg Code*]; Grimes v. Kennedy Krieger Institute, Inc. 782 A.2d 807 (2001). This case discusses experimental research on children in the United States without informed consent. *Id.* at 811. The court in that case stated, "The Nuremberg Code is the most complete and authoritative statement of the law of informed consent to human experimentation. It is also part of international common law and may be applied, in both civil and criminal cases, by state, federal and municipal courts in the United States." *Id.* at 835 [internal quotations omitted]. The court refers to the text of the Nuremberg Code to support its conclusion that the consent to the research was invalid, "The voluntary consent of the human subject is absolutely essential. This means that the person involved should have legal capacity

to give consent; should be so situated as to be able to exercise free power of choice, without the intervention of any element of force, fraud, deceit, duress, over-reaching, or other ulterior form of constraint or coercion; and *should have sufficient knowledge and comprehension of the elements of the subject matter involved as to enable him to make an understanding and enlightened decision.*" *Id.*

164. *Nuremberg Code, supra* note 162.

165. In *Ramos,* the court explores the experimental nature of the surgery and its possible violation of the Nuremberg Code. Ramos Summary, *supra* note 54, at 6.

166. Colapinto, *supra* note 12, at 75.

167. Cf. Ryken Grattet & Valerie Jenness, *Examining the Boundaries of Hate Crime Law: Disabilities and the 'Dilemma of Difference,'* 91 J. Crim. L. & Criminology 653 (2001) (exploring the susceptibility of minority groups to hate crimes).

168. Americans with Disabilities Act of 1990 [ADA], 42 U.S.C. § 12101, (2000). The ADA was enacted in the face of discrimination against individuals with disabilities in all areas of life. *Id.* The purpose of the ADA is to ensure inclusion of individuals with disabilities in employment, education, public accommodations, and government services. *Id.*

169. Fausto-Sterling, *supra* note 1.

Defining Genitals: Size Does Matter

Suzanne Kessler

The size of an infant's genitals is important to physicians who "manage" the sex assignment of intersexed infants. In her book entitled *Lessons from the Intersexed,* Suzanne Kessler explores how physicians use size to determine the appropriateness of genitals:

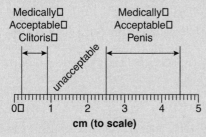

Ranges of Medically Acceptable Infant Clitoral and Penile Lengths

"How big must a clitoris be before physicians decide it is too large? . . . In spite of there being a table of standards, physicians are more likely to refer to the average clitoris in food terminology, such as a pea or a small bean. In general, medical standards do not allow clitorises larger than .9 centimeters (about 3/8 of an inch). . . . When is a penis too small? In general, medical standards permit infant penises as small as 2.5 centimeters (about one inch) to mark maleness, but usually not smaller. [Boys with penises smaller than 2.5 centimeters may be reassigned as girls based on the assumption that] a male infant needs a penis of a certain size in order to be accepted by family and peers. [The figure shown here] indicates standard clitoral and penile lengths for infants, revealing that intermediate area of phallic length that neither females nor males are permitted to have."

Source: Kessler, Suzanne, *Lessons from the Intersexed,* copyright © 1998 by Suzanne J. Kessler. Reprinted by permission of Rutgers University Press.

Sex and the Trans Man

Jamison Green

I've been asked to speak to thousands of college students, professionals, and corporate staff members on the subject of transsexualism and I've found that audience members are frequently confused [about] the difference between transgender and transsexual. I use the words transgender and transsexual to describe specific human behaviors or conditions: transgender means "across gender" and it describes people whose sex and gender identity or expression are not aligned the way most people experience themselves as male or female. Many people have the ability to break gender boundaries and function outside of the stereotypes that generally define men and women. Transgender people may appear androgynous, whether they choose to do so or whether their appearance or characteristics are involuntary, or they may have the ability to express more than one gender, like some cross-dressers or drag performers can do. Some transgender people feel that the best way for them to manage their gender variance is to medically (and legally, if possible) change their sex. I (and most medical authorities) call this subset of transgender people transsexual people. This is the category to which I belong.

I was transgendered as a child and young adult. I was born with a female body, but the spirit that informed that body was masculine, so much so that, as a child, even when I was wearing a dress people couldn't tell what sex I was. I thought I should have been born male, but people expected me to be a girl, so I did the best I could without completely erasing my personality. So for a long time people thought I was a "tomboy," and that I would "grow out of it;" but I knew I was different. I knew I wasn't really a

girl, but I didn't know how to express that to other people around me without sounding like I didn't think very highly of women. On the contrary, I thought girls and women were wonderful; I just didn't know how I could possibly become one, in spite of my female body. I tried to just be a human being with a female body, but the older I got, the less comfortable I felt having people perceive me as something in between.

Not all transgender or transsexual people have experiences that are identical to mine, a man born with a female body (alternatively labeled a female-to-male—or FTM—transsexual, or trans man). And I believe that people who are either natively "in-between" or who choose to live an androgynous life should be free to do so. No one should be forced to change his or her sex; but for some people, changing their sex is a necessary process if they are to make personal progress in their life.

It took me until I was well into my thirties before I figured out that it was actually possible to change one's sex from female to male, and to gather the courage to do it. In those days (the early 1980s), there was very little information available about surgical sex reassignment, and every step of the way felt like an experiment. One of the first things I noticed when I began to take testosterone was a tremendous increase in libido about a week after my first injection. Testosterone does several things to one's body: causes body and facial hair growth, activates genes for male-pattern baldness (if present), increases red blood cells, increases serum (blood) cholesterol, increases muscle density, causes the vocal cords to thicken (and changes the voice), changes the texture of the skin, increases metabolism (makes one feel warmer and increases perspiration), changes body odor, can contribute to weight gain if proper diet and exercise are not maintained, and causes the genital organs to increase in size (in some individuals, the clitoris can become the size of a small penis, with a glans and coronal ridge and erectile tissue that nearly doubles its size on arousal). Most of these changes take place over a period of months or even years (every body is different), but in most female-to-male transsexual people, increased libido is the first change they perceive. I thought it felt pretty good myself!

Some people wonder how going through surgical sex reassignment changes your sexual orientation. Sexual expression is, in large part, reactive; that is, it is dependent upon who is one's partner or "object choice." Certainly, one can have sexual interests that are never expressed because of inhibition, lack of opportunity, or deliberate (or unconscious) repression. This is true for anyone. There's a theory (but no large scale studies have ever been done on this topic to prove the theory) that FTM transsexual people are sexually attracted to women. Some theorists have even conjectured that trans men are simply homophobic lesbians, or women who feel that only men should be able to love women, so if they love women they must be men. It's probably possible to find some trans men who feel this way, but not all trans men who are attracted to women are so constrained by social convention. There are definitely trans men who are attracted to men, too, just like there are very feminine women who are attracted to other very feminine women, and masculine men who are attracted to masculine men. It's important to realize that a lot of assumptions people make about how gender expression indicates sexual orientation are simply logical errors caused by heterocentrism, something (very much like racism or sexism) that many people don't even realize they use to filter their social observations.

One of the remarkable things that I've found is that people's sexual orientation and sexual expression can actually change in ways that are unexpected and surprising. Because of the number of people who have transitioned (both FTM and MTF, or from male-to-female) who have told me about changes in their sexual orientation that they were not expecting to happen, I have to conclude that human beings do not have control of their own sexual orientation. One example from among my acquaintances is the trans man who started life as a heterosexual woman who

anticipated that once he transitioned to a male body he would simply be a gay man. However, it didn't turn out that way: he found that he didn't really like gay men, and he kept finding himself attracted to women (and women were making advances toward him, too!). Another example is the trans man who was a committed lesbian who seemed to have a lot of resentment toward men who, surprisingly, became a gay man once he could completely express his masculinity through a male body. Ironically, this man, like many trans men, has never had genital reconstruction. He manages to engage in gay male sex without having a penis. How does he do that? He does it creatively, and erotically, with a full command of his masculine self-expression. The idea that you have to have a penis to be a man—gay *or* straight—is another fallacy. We don't always think through the logic of our assumptions about sex, gender, or sexuality.

Some trans people have a strong need to have their genitals match their gender, though, and that is no better or worse than not caring whether your gender and genitals line up the way people expect. There should not be a value judgment about whether anyone is more real than anyone else because their genitals are a certain shape or size. In an enlightened society, there is no reason to judge people on this, or any other, physical basis. For those trans men who require genital reconstruction, there are several technical options, each of which has advantages and drawbacks. The least expensive technique, called metaoidioplasty (sometimes spelled metoidioplasty), involves using the inner labia and clitoral hood to "finish" the testosterone-elongated clitoral shaft along the underside, and raising it about one centimeter upward on the body so it is in a more penile position and can better extend forward when erect. This process retains full erotic sensation and the ability to achieve erection through engorgement of the native erectile tissues, but also results in a penis that is relatively small, usually from two to four inches in length when erect. Another issue to consider is that while techniques are advancing, urinary extension through the penis may still result in painful and expensive complications. The most technically advanced (and expensive) alternative that can create a penis of a moderately realistic size uses muscle tissue from (usually) the forearm,

which can be disfiguring. This alternative also requires implants to achieve erection, and the penis
never changes size, even on arousal. A scrotal sac is
formed from the labia majora, which is homologous
tissue (technically, the same tissue that forms the
scrota), and the testes are prosthetic implants that do
not produce sperm. So when trans men who have had
genital reconstruction have orgasm, they do not ejaculate through the penis. They may have some fluid
emission upon orgasm from the glands that remain
inside the opening of the vagina, which in most cases
is constricted or completely closed off. So when it
comes to constructing penises, if size matters, erectile
capacity suffers. That's the trade-off. Either way,
trans men can have very interesting bodies.

Hormones, in particular, definitely have an effect
on the nature of one's orgasm. And that is the only
generalization it is safe to make about trans men's
sexual response: hormones do change it. There is
usually an increase in libido, or interest in sexual expression, but the type of stimulation one prefers may
change, or the ability to have multiple orgasms
may change. In my case, before taking testosterone I
required very little stimulation and would have multiple orgasms. Once I started taking testosterone, I began to enjoy increased stimulation for a longer period
of time, and I have one orgasm, and that's that for at
least an hour. Another friend of mine had exactly the
opposite experience: prior to taking testosterone he
would only have a single orgasm, but once he started
his hormonal transition he found he was capable of
multiple orgasms. Many trans men find themselves
more interested in using sex toys like dildos and vibrators, or experimenting with different modes of
sexual expression such as sadomasochism or
bondage and discipline, but this can depend, too, on
the interests of their partner(s). Many trans men have
very conventional sexual lives, and feel no need to experiment. Every body is different! Some trans men
who have vaginas enjoy the experience of vaginal

penetration, while others who still have them may ignore them completely. And some trans men do not
have vaginas, depending on whether they have had
genital reconstruction, and how that reconstructive
surgery was done. For the most part, those trans men
who have had genital surgery retain erotic sensation
and orgasmic capacity, though the type of stimulation
they enjoy will usually change somewhat. How it
changes is such an individual matter that it is impossible to describe.

Sex for trans men is as rich and varied and diverse
as sex can be for any other type of person. For each of
us, whether we are trans or non-trans, the way or ways
in which we manifest our gender, our gender identity,
and/or our sexual orientation is an individual matter
that is a blend of factors, including our family, our
culture, our biology—including our hormones, our instincts, our personality, our social experience/history,
and our beliefs and expectations.

One other question people frequently ask about
sex for trans people is this: is sex better as a man or
as a woman? My answer is, first of all, because of
my transgender status, I don't think I ever experienced sex the way most women do. I didn't experience myself as a woman, and I never had missionary
position sex with a man. I enjoyed sex with women,
and my female partners often told me that they experienced me as a man sexually, even though they knew
I had a female body. But the real answer to the question is that sex is better when you are connected to
your body. For me, once I had a male body, I was
more fully present in my body, and I can say that I
have really enjoyed sex better in this body. The best
sex isn't dependent on being a man or a woman. The
size or shape of your genitals (or your partner's!)
aren't what make sex good; what makes for good
sex is being present in your body, really engaging
with another person, and consciously giving and
receiving sexual energy and pleasure. That's what's
important.

Straight Dude Seeks Same: Mapping the Relationship between Sexual Identities, Practices, and Cultures

Jane Ward

In January of 2005, I discovered the following personal ad in the Casual Encounters section of Craigslist Los Angeles, an online community bulletin board:

> *Let's Stroke It Together NOW! All (Str8) Guys to Str8 Porn, Hot:*
> *I have done this now about 20 times and it never fails to amaze me how hot it can get. Nothing gay here at all, just two guys, watching hot porn, stroking until just before the point of no return and stopping. It hits the ceiling when we finally pop. Something about two guys stroking it together touches most guys and they feel comfortable after about 3 minutes, then it's heaven. Testosterone city!*

When I read this ad for the first time, I was at a meeting with queer feminist colleagues, all of whom, including myself, marveled at the suggestion that the ad was anything but gay. At best, we imagined that this man was sexually repressed; at worst, we imagined his life "in the closet" and the pain caused by so much internalized homophobia. Yet as we scanned through three days of Craigslist postings, we discovered dozens of similar ads in which straight men were soliciting sex with other men.

The ads point to the complex and often seemingly contradictory relationship between sexual identities, sexual practices, and sexual cultures. Is there really "nothing gay here at all"? What are the social and political stakes of arguing that there is or isn't something gay about sex between straight-identified men? And why were my friends and I (as queer) so invested in owning a cultural space that is so decidedly intent on identifying with heterosexuality? Metrosexuality discourses and television shows such as *Queer Eye for the Straight Guy* have inundated us

with knowledge about the pairing of heterosexual sex and ostensibly queer culture (Miller 2005). However, sociological knowledge about how same-sex sexuality lives and flourishes within "heterosexual culture" has generally been limited to the study of total institutions, such as prisons and the military, in which heterosexual sex is presumably unavailable (Kaplan 2003, Schifter 1999). In response to these questions and the lack of sociological research that engages them, I decided to conduct a small pilot study of the "STR8 dude" community on Craigslist in order to explore a different side of queer heterosexuality—gay sex for the straight guys, or what I call "dude sex." Research assistants and I collected and coded 118 Craigslist ads in which straight-identified men solicited sex with other men.[1] The findings of the study point not only to the ways in which heterosexuality is constructed and authenticated among men who have sex with men, but also to the limitations of current sociological analyses of these kinds of sexual relationships. Despite the temptation to view the men who post on Craigslist as closeted or to invoke other ideas about repressed homosexuality, I emphasize here the theoretical and political importance of reading their ads as they wish them to be read—as one among myriad manifestations of *heterosexuality*.

Like Blackness in the 19th century, homosexuality is often implicitly subject to a one-drop rule, in which any same-sex sexual experience muddies the waters of heterosexuality at best, and marks one as either an open or repressed homosexual, at worst. Even to the extent that we allow for the identity "bisexual," this identity is also frequently suspect as a form of repressed homosexuality (Hutchins and Ka'ahumanu 1991). On the one hand, the one-drop system maintains heterosexual privileges by policing the boundaries of heterosexuality and homosexuality and ensuring that the smallest indiscretion can become cause for harassment, isolation, or violence. Even those carefully prescribed social contexts in which we allow heterosexuals to engage in queer transgression, presumably without being severely stigmatized (e.g., adolescent boys "experimenting," college women making out at parties for male onlookers) are accompanied by shame and self-doubt that can only be assuaged by disclaimers about developmental theories or drunkenness. On the other hand, to "own" all same-sex sexuality as queer terrain has also been a useful political strategy for the lesbian and gay movement, and one that has been supported by scholarship on sexuality. From Kinsey's (1948) sexual identity scale to Adrienne Rich's (1980) lesbian continuum, many theorists of sexual identity have asserted that almost *everyone* engages in some form of same-sex desire and practice, and that variation is largely a matter of degree or quantity. Continuum models of sexual identity lay the groundwork for resisting the gay/straight binary, yet do so by illustrating that many people who call themselves "straight" might actually be closer to the gay end of the continuum. In the end, it appears we are all invested, for different reasons, in calling as many people and behaviors "gay" as possible, a practice that leaves the gay/straight binary intact.

As Eve Sedgwick explains in *Epistemology of the Closet* (1992), the notion of "the closet" implies a real or essential "gay self" that is waiting to be revealed. It implies some truth of sexuality that exists outside of the social process of its naming and confession. Similarly, continuum models of sexuality tend to rank people as more or less gay or straight based on the quantity of their same-sex desires and practices, overlooking the social context in which sexuality is given form and shape. Are straight women who "get it on" when they get drunk at parties "more gay" than lesbian couples I know who, for many reasons, rarely ever have sex anymore? Are the straight dudes on Craigslist "more gay" than a man who comes out in his late 50s and spends several years finding a sexual partner? According to social constructionist theory, it is difficult to answer these questions because

homosexuality and heterosexuality do not refer to essential aspects of the self or some quantifiable set of sexual practices, but to the culturally and historically specific language used to explain and regulate sexuality (Almaguer 1993, Blackwood and Wieringa 1999, Fausto-Sterling 2000, Foucault 1978, Seabrook 1999). In other words, gay and straight are what we decide they are, and how we make these decisions varies across time and place.

Gay Sex versus Dude Sex

The erotic culture of dude sex highlights the ways that "gay" and "straight" cannot be reduced to sexual practice, especially in a time when the queer eye (aesthetic tastes, fashion, and the ability to make a fine risotto) is marketed for mass consumption. In contrast with the logic that gay and straight are opposite ends of a behavioral and gender-based binary, the STR8 dudes who post on Craigslist view "gay" as a *chosen* identity that is not particularly linked to *who* is having sex, or *what* sexual acts are involved. Instead, being gay is about *how* sex is done. Among STR8 dudes, "gay" is a *cultural* phenomenon with which one can identify or disidentify, a form of gender expression, and a community affiliation—*not* a description of one's sexual practice. In a clever turn, STR8 dudes on Craigslist assert that it is willingness to consume queer culture that makes others queer—and conversely, it is commitment to the symbols of heterosexual masculinity that keeps them straight. The following ads, representative of dozens of others, illustrate how STR8 dudes authenticate their heterosexuality while soliciting sex with other men.

STR8 for STR8 Dudes:
I'm STR8 looking to mess around with another STR8 dude from time to time. Discreet and looking for more than one time hook-time hookups so if you respond, have the balls to follow through with this ad and meet up.

STR8 Bud Smoke-n-Stroke (420):
Any other hot straight dudes wanna smoke out, kick back and jack off to some hot porn? Like to kick it with another bro and work out a load together? . . . We'll just be jacking only—no making out, no touching, no anal bullshit. And smoking out!!!

STR8 Drunk Dude Looking to Get Off:
Hi there, Looking to lay back, have some beers, etc. and watch some STR8 porn this evening. I'm 5.10, brown hair, brown eyes white dude.

Authentic heterosexuality is established in part by demonstrating one's disinterest in presumably gay activities ("anal bullshit"), as well as one's interest in hyper-masculine activities. STR8 dudes are often drunk or stoned, they watch heterosexual porn, and they maintain a clear emotional boundary between them that draws upon the model of adolescent friendship, or the presumably harmless, "proto-sexual" circle jerk.[2] Reference to "being buddies" and "having the balls" to have sex with another dude also helps to reframe dude sex as a kind of sex that bolsters, rather than threatens, the heterosexual masculinity of the participants. Only those who are "man enough" will want dude sex or be able to handle it. Yet what is perhaps the most important evidence of heterosexuality provided by STR8 dudes in their posts, and at the heart of STR8 dudes' culture of desire, is the discursive presence (and yet literal absence) of women in their sexual encounters. Unlike in similar websites for gay men, women are a central part of STR8 dudes' erotic discourse. In some cases, women are referenced as acceptable or preferable but unavailable sex partners, reinforcing that dude sex is an insignificant substitute for "real" sex:

> *Laid back STR8 guy seeks same for j/o [jerk off] buddy:*
> *Easygoing STR8 Caucasian male seeks same—looking for a buddy to stroke with who enjoys STR8 porn and sex with women but who is cool and open minded. I'm not gay but do like to show off and have done some bi stuff in the past. Interested in jerk off only. I'm in shape and attractive, and this is no big deal to me. Don't have girlfriend right now and wanted to get off today so hit me back if interested.*

In an alarming number of other cases, violence against women is advertised as a central part of the sexual encounter. STR8 dudes explain that while masturbating together, they will talk about women's bodies and imagine sex with women. The desire to act out the gang rape of a woman is also common, although not always explicit, such as in the following ad:

Whackin Off to Porn:
STR8 porn. Gang bang. STR8, bi-curious masculine white guy lookin for a masculine guy. Get into stroking bone with a bud, talkin' bout pussy and bangin' the bitch.

While the phrases "gang bang" and "bangin' the bitch" are used in this ad, it is unclear who the object of the gang bang will be. In most ads, heterosexual porn and *talk* about women's bodies serves the function of incorporating the objectification of women into dude sex. In a few ads, however, such as the following, women were represented by blow-up dolls that dudes would have sex with in lieu of an available woman.

> *Any Straight/Bi Guys Want to Help Me Fuck My Blow-up Doll???:*
> *Come on guys . . . we can't always pick up the chick we want to bone right??? So let's get together and fuck the hell out of my hot blow-up doll. Her mouth, her pussy, and her ass all feel GREAT. Just be cool, uninhibited, horny, and ready to fuck this bitch. It's all good here. . . .*

In some cases, women are invited to observe dude sex, yet even in these cases, it is the sex between the two STR8 dudes that is the event. While women are present in the encounter, they reinforce the heterosexuality of the men involved, even as their role is clearly voyeuristic and ancillary:

> *Wanna Bang a STR8 Dude in Front of His Girl:*
> *This is a fantasy of mine, and hey it's new years, why not? I'd like to bang a STR8 guy in the ass in front of his chick. I'd even bang a STR8 dude 1 on 1 if you want. I'm not into guys that sound/act like chicks. I'm really not into guys, I just think it's kinky/hot to do this.*

The link between dude sex and the gang rape of women suggests that we may read dude sex as a sexualized form of (heterosexual) male bonding that is facilitated by misogyny and violence against women. Gang rapes, not typically viewed as homosexual sex, nonetheless involve men cheering on and witnessing the orgasms of other men. Like in the Craigslist ads, women's bodies are the objects of violence, while the expression of agentic sexuality occurs among and between the men involved. This pattern suggests that dude sex is a sexual and often violent expression of heterosexual masculinity and heterosexual culture, quite distinct from gay male culture in which miso-gyny typically manifests as the invisibility, rather than the objectification, of women (Ward 2000). Marilyn Frye (1983), in her analysis of drag queens, argues "What gay male affectation of femininity seems to be is a serious sport in which men may exercise their power and control over the feminine, much as in other sports. . . . But the mastery of the feminine is not fem-inine. It is masculine." Similarly, we might consider that while dude sex makes use of and masters homo-sexual sex, this deployment of homosexual sex in the service of heterosexuality is not homosexuality. It is heterosexuality, or, to be more accurate, it is hetero-sexual culture. Indeed, there may be "nothing gay here at all."

Gay Men Pretending to Be Straight?

In her recent book *Black Sexual Politics* (2004), Patricia Hill Collins examines the subculture of men on the DL (down low)—Black men who have sex with men but don't identify as gay or bisexual and are typically married or have girlfriends. Benoit Denizet-Lewis, the journalist who first wrote about the down low phenomenon in the *New York Times Magazine,* describes the DL as a reaction to the (white) racializa-tion of gay male culture. Denizet-Lewis (in Collins 2004, p. 173) explains: "Rejecting a gay culture that they perceive as white and effeminate, many Black men have settled on a new identity, with its own vo-cabulary and customs and its own name: Down Low. There have always been men—Black and white—who have had secret sexual lives with men. But the creation of an organized, underground subculture made up of Black men who otherwise live straight lives is a phenomenon of the last decade." Men on the DL also meet in specialized websites and chat rooms, and like the STR8 dudes on Craigslist, they neither identify as gay nor wish to participate in gay male culture. While Denizet-Lewis suggests that the DL culture is a response to a racial system in which ho-mosexuality is perceived as a "white thing" and Black masculinity is linked to fatherhood, it's important to note the existence of other Black identities, such as "same-gender loving," that simultaneously take pride in same-gender relationships *and* Blackness by

rejecting the centrality of whiteness in gay culture.[3] In other words, being on the DL is not the only way to have sex with men while asserting one's Blackness; instead, it reflects a particular desire to participate in Black hyper-masculinity, relationships with women, and heterosexual culture.

Yet Patricia Hill Collins consistently reads men on the DL as closeted and gay, referring to them as "a new subculture of gay men" and arguing that, "for men on the DL, masculinity that is so intertwined with hyper-heterosexuality renders an openly gay identity impossible" (p. 207). While I agree with Collins' con-tention that the DL identity reflects a particularly complex positionality informed by race, gender, and sexual desire, I want to complicate the suggestion that men on the DL are closeted gay men who cannot come out because they are constrained by homopho-bia and racism. Such arguments obscure the processes through which Black men *do* assert nonheterosexual identities even in the face of homophobia and racism, as well as obscure the authentic pleasure that DL men take in heterosexual culture, heterosexual identity, and relationships with women.

Recent analyses of men on the DL reflect the temp-tation to invoke the closet as a means of understanding all same-sex sexuality that is not willing to call itself "gay" (see also King 2004). In part this is due to the ideology of the contemporary lesbian and gay rights movement, in which many queers themselves assert basic rights based on the premise that sexual identity is biologically determined and just waiting to be dis-covered, revealed, outed. Seduced by this logic my-self, my first reaction to the STR8 dudes' ads was to perceive the men who wrote them as closeted gay men, and my second reaction was to perceive them as "real" gay men pretending to be straight in order to satisfy a fetish for "real" straight men. After hearing from many gay male friends about their desire to se-duce straight men, I became attentive to the possibil-ity that the Casual Encounters section of Craigslist might be a place in which gay men seduce one another by posing as straight. While the vast majority of the ads gave no indication of familiarity with gay culture, and generally expressed disdain for it, some posts seemed to hold the tell-tale signs of "undercover" gay men, such as the following:

Do You Like Stroking Your Dick with Another STR8 Guy? I Got STR8 Porn!:
Looking to host in West LA, laid back, chill watchin extremely hot porn, all kinds. Pullin' out your cock when you get your woody, start playing with it more, take off your clothes and watch porn jackin all the way, watchin your buddy or buddies get horned up and on fire. The testosterone is in the air, you see him rapidly jerkin and stopping, you do the same thing, for however long it feels good. Looking at him stroke is hot for you, the same for him. Finally you can't hold back, he can't either, he shoots right before you and seeing his dick surt [sic] all that cum makes your orgasm all the more intense. THE RULES ARE THERE ARE NO RULES!!! GAY GUYS THIS IS PROBABLY NOT YOUR CUP OF TEA, no clones, baseball capped generic guys here, real guys, real passion, real woodies.

While the long and indulgent description of the sex itself is somewhat distinct from the other more minimalist and emotionless ads, what brought my attention to this post was the reference to "clones," "cup of tea," and "real passion." The latter are simply language choices that seemed out of sync with the macho tenor of the other ads, however the reference to "clones"—a queer insider term popular in the 1970s to describe straight-acting gay men—suggests an intimate familiarity with gay male culture. Ironically, the very expression of desire for "real" straight men (and not straight-acting gay men) is what casts suspicion on the authentic heterosexuality of this STR8 dude. In other words, what is suspicious in this ad is neither the sex it describes, nor the meaning it attributes to the sexual encounter. Instead it is the cultural reference to queer worlds of knowledge that makes me think that, indeed, there is "something gay" in this particular ad!

Conclusions: The Significance of Culture

Academic discussion regarding the social construction of sexual identities often revolves around whether we might privilege sexual practice as the unit of analysis, or whether scholars of sexuality are better served by focusing our attention on the meanings and identities that social actors assign to sexual practices. In the Casual Encounters section of Craigslist, neither sex itself nor the self-identifications of the men who post

there are useful guides for delineating the boundaries of queer and non-queer, or establishing political alliances with queer stakeholders. From a queer perspective, to de-queer the sex described on Craigslist is to give up the epistemological pleasure of self-righteous knowing, owning, outing, and naming. In the face of homophobia and heterosexism, the self-righteous pleasure of honing one's "gaydar" is one of few queer luxuries. Yet this study suggests that de-queering various forms of same-sex sexuality may be a quicker route to queer liberation than one that builds solidarity around sex acts. Instead, shared *culture*—including aesthetic preferences, a sense of collective identity, and participation in a community of resistance—may better help us determine whom we "own" as queer scholars and activists. While I am not inclined to want to swell the ranks of heterosexuals or argue that fewer people engage in same-sex desire than we think, this study does point to the theoretical and political usefulness of disowning or "sending back home" (to heterosexual culture) the STR8 dudes who have the "balls" to have sex with one another.

Such a project accomplishes three important interventions. First, this analysis invites us to give name to new identities and practices that aren't predicated on the idea of essential, hidden gayness, and that demonstrate the multiplicity and richness of queer as well as heterosexual sexual expressions. Building upon Sedgwick's call to transcend theories of the closet, which privilege and reify sexual practices, we may then map same-sex sexuality across identities, cultures, and space.

Second, what are straight and gay if not sexual practices? I suggest we view these distinctions as primarily sociocultural categories, or cultural spheres that people choose to inhabit in large part because they experience a cultural fit. Some men like to have sex with men in the bathrooms of gay bars after dancing to techno music, others like to have sex with men while watching straight porn and talking about bitches. Because the only thing these experiences have in common are sex acts between men, we might view heterosexuality, then, as a system of erotic relations and a cultural experience that appeals to people who choose to be straight. Conversely, we might view queerness as a system of erotic relations and a cultural experience that appeals to people who choose to be queer.

Lastly, where is the power in this analysis and what does this mean for the queer movement? In social movement context, redefining queer and non-queer as cultural affiliations implies that queer "rights" serve to protect not everyone who engages in same-sex sexuality, but all those who are excluded from, and alienated by, hegemonic STR8 culture—gender freaks, all kids in gay-straight alliances, all people who are or are willing to be part of this thing we call "gay." Such an approach refuses biological determinism, the essentialism of the closet, and distinctions between "us" and "them" rooted in the gay/straight binary. But perhaps more importantly, if it's not same-sex sexual practices that bind us, we must examine and take responsibility for the cultural spheres that we produce. Queer culture becomes not simply the outgrowth of resistance to oppression—although it certainly is this—but an available repertoire of aesthetic distinctions, personal preferences, and comforts we call home: dyke haircuts, techno music, drag shows, queer jokes, leather, and so on. To view queerness as constitutive of these pleasures, as opposed to some agreed upon set of rights linked to sexual practices, will keep queerness intact regardless of movement gains or losses.

NOTES

The research described in this article was supported by an Investigator Development grant to the author from the Wayne F. Placek Fund of the American Psychological Foundation.

1. This pilot study was approved by the Internal Review Board at the University of California, Riverside. Research assistants and I collected and coded 118 ads, which represented all of the ads placed during a nine-day period (from January 6 through January 15, 2005) in which straight-identified men solicited sex with other men. We collected and coded ads until we determined that we had coded enough ads to identify the primary and recurring discursive methods used by STR8 dudes on Craigslist to construct and authenticate their heterosexuality.

2. While many ads focus on masturbation, 65% of ads coded in this study expressed desire for, or openness to, oral or anal sex.

3. Same-gender loving is a concept created by and for black men and women in same-gender relationships. The term has been embraced as one that rejects the white origins of the identities "gay" and "lesbian," and focuses more on the practice and culture of "loving" people of the same gender. See www.fobrothers.com, "a reference-based online community for the same-gender loving black man."

REFERENCES

Almaguer, Tomás. 1993. "Chicano Men. A Cartography of Homosexual Identity and Behavior." In Abelove, Barale & Halperin (eds.) *The Lesbian and Gay Studies Reader.* New York: Routledge.

Blackwood, Evelyn and Saskia Wieringa. 1999. *Female Desires and Transgender Practices across Cultures.* New York: Columbia University Press.

Collins, Patricia Hill. 2004. *Black Sexual Politics: African Americans, Gender, and the New Racism.* New York: Routledge.

Fausto-Sterling, Anne. 2000. In *Sexing the Body: Gender Politics and the Construction of Sexuality.* New York: Basic Books.

Foucault, Michel. 1978. *The History of Sexuality: An Introduction.* New York: Vintage Books.

Frye, Marilyn. 1983. "Lesbian Feminism and Gay Rights." In *The Politics of Reality: Essays in Feminist Theory.* New York: Crossing Press.

Hutchins, Loraine and Lani Ka'ahumanu (eds.). 1991. *Bi Any Other Name: Bisexual People Speak Out.* New York: Alyson Publications.

Kaplan, Danny. 2003. *Brothers and Others in Arms: The Making of Love and War in Israeli Combat Units.* New York: Harrington Park Press.

King, J. K. 2004. *On the Down Low: A Journey Into the Lives of "Straight" Black Men Who Sleep With Men.* New York: Broadway.

Levine, Martin. 1998. *Gay Macho: The Life and Death of the Homosexual Clone.* New York: New York University Press.

Miller, Toby. 2005. "A Metrosexual Eye on Queer Guy." *GLQ: A Journal of Lesbian and Gay Studies.* Volume 11, Number 1, pp. 112–117.

Rich, Adrienne. 1980. "Compulsory Heterosexuality and Lesbian Existence." *Signs: Journal of Women in Culture and Society.* Volume 5, Number 4, pp. 631–660.

Schifter, Jacobo. 1999. *Macho Love: Sex Behind Bars in Central America.* New York: Harrington Park Press.

Seabrook, Jeremy. 1999. *Love in a Different Climate: Men Who Have Sex With Men in India.* New York: Verso.

Sedgwick, Eve Kosofsky. 1992. *Epistemology of the Closet.* Berkeley: University of California Press.

Ward, Jane. 2000. "Queer Sexism: Rethinking Gay Men and Masculinity." In Peter Nardi (ed.) *Gay Masculinities.* Thousand Oaks, CA: Sage Publications.

Gay by Choice? The Science of Sexual Identity

Gary Greenberg

When he leaves his tidy apartment in an ocean-side city somewhere in America, Aaron turns on the radio to a light rock station. "For the cat," he explains, "so she won't get lonely." He's short and balding and dressed mostly in black, and right before I turn on the recorder, he asks me for the dozenth time to guarantee that I won't reveal his name or anything else that might identify him. "I don't want to be a target for gay activists," he says as we head out into the misty day. "Harassment like that I just don't need."

Aaron sets a much brisker pace down the boardwalk than you would expect of a doughy 51-year-old, and once convinced I'll respect his anonymity, he turns out to be voluble. Over the crash of the waves, he spares no details as he describes how much he hated the fact that he was gay, how the last thing in the world he wanted to do was act on his desire to have sex with another man. "I'm going to be perfectly blatant about it," he says. "I'm not going to have anal intercourse or give or receive any BJs either, okay?" He managed to maintain his celibacy through college and into adulthood. But when, in the late 1980s, he found himself so "insanely jealous" of his roommate's girlfriend that he had to move out, he knew the time had come to do something. One of the few people who knew that Aaron was gay showed him an article in Newsweek about a group offering "reparative therapy"—psychological treatment for people who want to become "ex-gay."

"It turns out that I didn't have the faintest idea what love was," he says. That's not all he didn't know.

He also didn't know that his same-sex attraction, far from being inborn and inescapable, was a thirst for the love that he had not received from his father, a cold and distant man prone to angry outbursts, coupled with a fear of women kindled by his intrusive and overbearing mother, all of which added up to a man who wanted to have sex with other men just so he could get some male attention. He didn't understand any of this, he tells me, until he found a reparative therapist whom he consulted by phone for nearly 10 years, attended weekend workshops, and learned how to "be a man."

Aaron interrupts himself to eye a woman in shorts jogging by. "Sometimes there are very good-looking women at this boardwalk," he says. "Especially when they're not bundled up." He remembers when he started noticing women's bodies, a few years into his therapy. "The first thing I noticed was their legs. The curve of their legs." He's dated women, had sex with them even, although "I was pretty awkward," he says. "It just didn't work." Aaron has a theory about this: "I never used my body in a sexual way. I think the men who actually act it out have a greater success in terms of being sexual with women than the men who didn't act it out." Not surprisingly, he's never had a long-term relationship, and he's pessimistic about his prospects. "I can't make that jump from having this attraction to doing something about it." But, he adds, it's wrong to think "if you don't make it with women, then you haven't changed." The important thing is that "now I like myself. I'm not emotionally shut down. I'm comfortable in my own body. I don't have to be drawn to men anymore. I'm content at this point to lead an asexual life, which is what I've done for most of my life anyway." He adds, "I'm a very detached person."

It's raining a little now. We stop walking so I can tuck the microphone under the flap of Aaron's shirt pocket, and I feel him recoil as I fiddle with his button. I'm remembering his little cubicle of an apartment, its unlived-in feel, and thinking that he may be the sort of guy who just doesn't like anyone getting too close, but it's also possible that therapy has taught him to submerge his desire so deep that he's lost his motive for intimacy.

That's the usual interpretation of reparative therapy—that to the extent that it does anything, it leads people to repress rather than change their natural inclinations, that its claims to change sexual orientation are an outright fraud perpetrated by the religious right on people who have internalized the homophobia of American society, personalized the political in such a way as to reject their own sexuality and stunt their love lives. But Aaron scoffs at these notions, insisting that his wish to go straight had nothing to do with right-wing religion or politics—he's a nonobservant Jew and a lifelong Democrat who volunteered for George McGovern, has a career in public service, and thinks George Bush is a war criminal. It wasn't a matter of ignorance—he has an advanced degree—and it *really* wasn't a psychopathological thing—he rejects the idea that he's ever suffered from internalized homophobia. He just didn't want to be gay, and, like millions of Americans dissatisfied with their lives, he sought professional help and reinvented himself.

Self-reconstruction is what people in my profession (I am a practicing psychotherapist) specialize in, but when it comes to someone like Aaron, most of us draw the line. All the major psychotherapy guilds have barred their members from researching or practicing reparative therapy on the grounds that it is inherently unethical to treat something that is not a disease, that it contributes to oppression by pathologizing homosexuality, and that it is dangerous to patients whose self-esteem can only suffer when they try to change something about themselves that they can't (and shouldn't have to) change. Aaron knows this, of course, which is why he's at great pains to prove he's not pulling a Ted Haggard. For if he's not a poseur, then he is a walking challenge to the political and scientific consensus that has emerged over the last century and a half: that sexual orientation is inborn and immutable, that efforts to change it are bound to fail, and that discrimination against gay people is therefore unjust.

But as crucial as this consensus has been to the struggle for gay rights, it may not be as sound as some might wish. While scientists have found intriguing biological differences between gay and straight people, the evidence so far stops well short of proving that we are born with a sexual orientation that we will have for life. Even more important, some research shows that sexual orientation is more fluid than we have come to think, that people, especially women, can and do move across customary sexual orientation boundaries, that there are ex-straights as well as ex-gays. Much of this research has stayed below the radar of the culture warriors, but reparative therapists are hoping to use it to enter the scientific mainstream and advocate for what they call the right of self-determination in matters of sexual orientation. If they are successful, gay activists may soon find themselves scrambling to make sense of a new scientific and political landscape.

In 1838, a 20-year-old Hungarian killed himself and left a suicide note for Karl Benkert, a 14-year-old bookseller's apprentice in Budapest whom he had befriended. In it he explained that he had been cleaned out by a blackmailer who was now threatening to expose his homosexuality, and that he couldn't face either the shame or the potential legal trouble that would follow. Benkert, who eventually became a writer, moved to Vienna, and changed his name to Karoly Maria Kertbeny, later said that the tragedy left him with "an instinctive drive to take issue with every injustice." And in 1869, a particularly resonant injustice occurred: A penal code proposed for Prussia included an anti-sodomy law much like the one that had given his friend's extortionist his leverage. Kertbeny published a pamphlet in protest, writing that the state's attempt to control consensual sex between men was a violation of the fundamental rights of man. Nature, he argued, had divided the human race into four sexual types: "monosexuals," who masturbated, "heterogenits," who had sex with animals, "heterosexuals," who coupled with the opposite sex, and "homosexuals," who preferred people of the same sex. Kertbeny couldn't have known that of all his literary output, these latter two words would be his only lasting legacy. But while homosexual conduct had occurred throughout history, the idea that it reflected fundamental differences between people, that gay people were a sexual subspecies, was a new one.

Kertbeny wasn't alone in creating a sexual taxonomy. Another anti-sodomy-law opponent, lawyer Karl Heinrich Ulrichs, proposed that homosexual men, or "Uranians," as he called them (and he openly considered himself a Uranian, while Kertbeny was coy about his preferences), were actually a third sex, their attraction to other men a manifestation of the female soul residing in their male bodies. Whatever the theoretical differences between Ulrichs and Kertbeny, they agreed on one crucial point: that sexual behavior was the expression of an *identity* into which we were born, a natural variation of the human. In keeping with the post-Enlightenment notion that we are morally culpable only for what we are free to choose, homosexuals were not to be condemned or restricted by the state. Indeed, this was Kertbeny and Ulrichs' purpose: Sexual orientation, as we have come to call this biological essence, was invented in order to secure freedom for gay people.

But replacing morality with biology, and the scrutiny of church and state with the observations of science, invited a different kind of condemnation. By the end of the 19th century, homosexuality was increasingly the province of psychiatrists like Magnus Hirschfeld, a gay Jewish Berliner. Hirschfeld was an outspoken opponent of anti-sodomy laws and championed tolerance of gay people, but he also believed that homosexuality was a pathological state, a congenital deformity of the brain that may have been the result of a parental "degeneracy" that nature intended to eliminate by making the defective population unlikely to reproduce. Even Sigmund Freud, who thought people were "polymorphously perverse" by nature and urged tolerance for homosexuality, believed heterosexuality was essential to maturity and psychological health.

Freud was pessimistic that homosexuality could be treated, but doctors abhor an illness without a cure, and the 20th century saw therapists inflict the best of

modern psychiatric practice on gay people, which included, in addition to interminable psychoanalysis and unproven medications, treatments that used electric shock to associate pain with same-sex attraction. These therapies were largely unsuccessful, and, particularly after the Stonewall riots of 1969—the clash between police and gays that initiated the modern gay rights movement—patients and psychiatrists alike started questioning whether homosexuality should be considered a mental illness at all. Gay activists, some of them psychiatrists, disrupted the annual meeting of the American Psychiatric Association for three years in a row, until in 1973 a deal was brokered. The APA would delete homosexuality from its *Diagnostic and Statistical Manual of Mental Disorders* (DSM) immediately, and furthermore it would add a new disease: sexual orientation disorder, in which a patient can't accept his or her sexual identity. The culprit in SOD was an oppressive society, and the cure for SOD was to help the gay patient overcome oppression and accept who he or she really was. (SOD has since been removed from the DSM.)

The APA cited various scientific papers in making its decision, but many members were convinced that the move was a dangerous corruption of science by politics. "If groups of people march and raise enough hell, they can change anything in time," one psychiatrist worried. "Will schizophrenia be next?" And their impression was confirmed when the final decision was made not in a laboratory but at the ballot box, where the membership voted by a six-point margin to authorize the APA to delete the diagnosis of homosexuality. It may be the first time in history that a disease was eliminated by the stroke of a pen. It was certainly the first time that psychiatrists determined that the cause of a mental illness was an intolerant society. And it was a crucial moment for gay people, at once getting the psychiatrists out of their bedrooms and giving the weight of science to Kertbeny and Ulrichs' claim that homosexuality was an identity, like race or national origin, that deserved protection.

Three decades later, at least one group is still raising hell about the deletion: the National Association for the Research and Therapy of Homosexuality (NARTH), an organization founded by Charles

Socarides, a psychiatrist who led the opposition to the 1973 APA vote . . .

But the men of NARTH (nearly all the 75 attendees are white men) aren't spewing nearly as much hellfire and brimstone as I expected. They do seem to hug a lot—many reparative therapists are ex-gay themselves, and, someone explains, part of being ex-gay is learning to be same-sex affectionate without being same-sex sexual—and maybe some of those hugs last a little too long, but it's mostly like every other convention: bad coffee, worse Danish, dry-as-dust lectures . . .

Some gay rights lawyers point out that whatever biology's role in sexual orientation, it should not be legally paramount. The Supreme Court has ruled that the immutability of a group's identifying characteristics is one of the criteria that entitle it to heightened protection from discrimination (and some cases establishing gay rights were decided in part on those grounds), but, according to Suzanne Goldberg, director of the Sexuality and Gender Law Clinic at Columbia Law School, there's a far more fundamental reason for courts to protect gay people. "Sexual orientation does not bear on a person's ability to contribute to society," she notes. "We don't need the science to make that point." Jon Davidson, legal director of Lambda Legal, agrees, adding that if courts are going to ask about immutability, they shouldn't focus on biology. Instead they should focus on how sexual orientation is so deeply woven into a person's identity that it is inseparable from who they are. In this respect, Davidson says, sexual orientation is like another core aspect of identity that is clearly not biological in origin: religion. "It doesn't matter whether you were born that way, it came later, or you chose," he says. "We don't think it's okay to discriminate against people based on their religion. We think people have a right to believe whatever they want. So why do we think that about religion and not about who we love?"

[Sean] Cahill [former director of the National Gay and Lesbian Task Force Policy Institute]—who says he doesn't think he was born gay—points out that even if it is crucial for public support, essentialism has a dark side: the remedicalization of homosexuality, this time as a biological condition that can be treated. Michael Bailey, a Northwestern University

psychologist who has conducted some of the key studies of the genetics of sexual orientation, infuriated the gay and lesbian community with a paper arguing that, should prenatal markers of homosexuality be identified, parents ought to have the right to abort potentially gay fetuses. "It's reminiscent of eugenicist theories," Cahill tells me. "If it's seen as an undesirable trait, it could lead in some creepy directions." These could include not only abortion, but also gene therapy or modulating uterine hormone levels to prevent the birth of a gay child.

Psychology professor Lisa Diamond may have the best reason of all for activists to shy away from arguing that homosexuality is inborn and immutable: It's not exactly true. She doesn't dispute the findings that show a biological role in sexual orientation, but she thinks far too much is made of them. "The notion that if something is biological, it is fixed—no biologist on the planet would make that sort of assumption," she told me from her office at the University of Utah. Not only that, she says, but the research—which is conducted almost exclusively on men—hinges on a very narrow definition of sexual orientation: "It's what makes your dick go up. I think most women would disagree with that definition," she says, not only because it obviously excludes them, but because sexual orientation is much more complex than observable aspects of sexuality. "An erection is an erection," she says, "but we have almost no information about what is actually going on in terms of the subjective experience of desire.". . .

Diamond cautions that it's important not to confuse plasticity—the capacity for sexual orientation to change—with choice—the ability to change it at will. "Trying to change your attractions doesn't work very well, but you can change the structure of your social life, and that might lead to changes in the feelings you experience." This is a time-honored way of handling unwanted sexual feelings, she points out. "Jane Austen made a career out of this: People fall in love with a person of the wrong social class. What do you do? You get yourself out of those situations.". . .

Which isn't all that different from what they say at NARTH—that people like Aaron who hate the gay lifestyle and don't want to be gay should leave the gay bars, do regular guy things with men, and put themselves in the company of women for romance. And indeed the NARTHites know all about Diamond's work. "We know that straight people become gays and lesbians," NARTH's outgoing president Joseph Nicolosi told the group gathered in Orlando. "So it seems totally reasonable that some gay and lesbian people would become straight. The issue is whether therapy changes sexual orientation. People grow and change as a result of life experiences, especially personal relationships. Why then can't the experience of therapy and the relationship with the therapist also effect change?" Diamond calls this interpretation a "misuse" of her research—"the fluidity I've observed does not mean that reparative therapy works"—but what is really being misused, she says, is science. "We live in a culture where people disagree vehemently about whether or not sexual minorities deserve equal rights," she told me. "People cling to this idea that science can provide the answers, and I don't think it can. I think in some ways it's dangerous for the lesbian and gay community to use biology as a proxy for that debate.". . .

NARTH is perfectly positioned to exploit [Americans' confusion about sexuality] by arguing that sexual orientation can be influenced by environmental conditions, and that certain courses are less healthy than others. That's how NARTHites justify their opposition to extending marriage and adoption rights to gay people: not because they abhor homosexuality, but because a gay-friendly world is one in which it is hard for gay people to recognize that they are suffering from a medical illness.

Of course, in deploying medical language to serve its strategic interests, NARTH is only following the lead of Kertbeny and Hirschfeld, the original gay activists, and their modern counterparts who, despite minimizing the importance of biology, resort to scientific rhetoric when it suits their purposes. "People can't try to shut down a part of who they are," says Sean Cahill. "I don't think it's healthy for people to change how their body and mind and heart work."

But medicine, which is what we rely on to tell us what is "healthy," will always seek to change the way people's bodies and minds and hearts work; yesterday's immutable state of nature is tomorrow's disease to be cured. Medical science can only take its cues from the society whose curiosities it satisfies and whose confusions it investigates. It can never do the heavy political lifting required to tell us whether one way of living our lives is better than another. This is exactly why Kertbeny originated the notion of a biologically based sexual orientation, and, to the extent that society is more tolerant of homosexuality now than it was 150 years ago, that idea has been a success. But the ex-gay movement may be the signal that this invention has begun to outlive its usefulness, that sexuality, profoundly mysterious and irrational, will not be contained by our categories, that it is time to find reasons other than medical science to insist that people ought to be able to love whom they love.

Hiding in the Closet? Bisexuals, Coming Out and The Disclosure Imperative

Kirsten McLean

The process of coming out—of revealing a gay, lesbian or bisexual identity to others—is considered one of the key events in the development of an integrated and healthy homosexual and bisexual identity. Sexual identity development models view coming out as a milestone event which often occurs as one of the last stages that needs to be overcome before one settles, happily, on a homosexual or bisexual identity. As well as this, narratives about coming out position disclosure as an ideal stage of developing a positive and healthy sexual identity. For bisexual men and women, however, coming out is a complex process that involves revealing not just that one is attracted to the same sex, but that one is also, or still, attracted to the opposite sex. In this article I use empirical evidence gathered from interviews with bisexual men and women to argue that coming out is not always a straightforward process that can be simply understood as an essential part of living with a non-heterosexual identity. On the contrary, for bisexuals the decision about whether to come out is influenced by several factors not often taken into account in sexual identity development models and coming out narratives, such as the numerous stories told in biographies, anthologies, interviews, and in the media (Plummer, 1995: 82). I also contend that the disclosure imperative that idealizes coming out as part of living with a non-heterosexual identity may not necessarily be appropriate for bisexual men and women.

The Research

This article draws on in-depth interviews with 60 Australian bisexual men and women aged between 21 and 66 years of age. Participants were recruited via advertisements for volunteers distributed through bisexual networks and online bisexual communities in Australia. The sample were mostly Australian-born, living in urban, east coast areas of Australia, were well educated, and 60 percent were under the age of 30. The interview covered issues such as self-identity; coming out; relationships with partners, friends, family; and participation in gay, lesbian and bisexual communities. Most interviews were approximately two hours long, and all were done by telephone or face-to-face. The data for this article [draw] on participants' stories about their experiences of coming out to others, and their feelings about living with a bisexual identity—and the difficulties and challenges they faced in doing so. All participants quoted herein have been assigned pseudonyms to protect their identities.

Coming Out and Its Role In The Sexual Identity Narrative

For the most part, coming out is seen as a positive step in the process of being gay, lesbian or bisexual; to some, it is the "most momentous act in the life of any gay and lesbian person" (Plummer, 1995: 82). The importance of coming out is reinforced by the many narratives that detail the stories of those who have come out as gay, lesbian and bisexual, and about the difficult, but rewarding, process of coming out. Such stories encourage others to come out, despite the pain of doing so, in order to live a more "honest" life. . . .

The idealization of coming out constructs a binary of disclosure that positions coming out as "good," as it enables the healthy development of sexual identity, and positions non-disclosure as "bad." A good example of this is the use of the phrase "hiding in the closet" to describe non-disclosure. As such, there is a disclosure imperative attached to living as gay, lesbian or bisexual, and one's level of commitment to a sexual identity is often measured by how "out" one is to loved ones and in everyday life. . . .

The disclosure imperative, however, ignores the complex factors attached to identity development and identifying as gay, lesbian or bisexual. Sexual identity development models and coming out narratives fail to acknowledge that identity development, in the first instance, may be rather more complex than simply realizing one is "different" and then disclosing this fact to others, and that coming out may not necessarily be the ideal situation for many people. These discourses also do not adequately capture the difficulties of living with a sexual identity that is considerably misunderstood, such as bisexuality. . . .

Coming Out as Bisexual

In my research, the bisexual men and women interviewed were selective about the people they chose to tell, and about the necessity of coming out in the first place. They demonstrated low levels of disclosure of their bisexuality to others—particularly to parents, siblings and some friends. . . . The seeming reluctance of bisexuals to come out, however, may be a strategy for managing a bisexual identity, rather than simply a refusal or unwillingness to come out, an issue I return to below.

Understanding Bisexuality

One of the problems in looking at the coming out process for bisexuals is that there are multiple meanings attached to bisexuality. For some people who identify as bisexual, it involves both emotional and sexual attractions to both men and women; for others it may be only emotional or sexual attractions to one gender. Bisexuality may involve only sexual experiences with one gender but emotional and sexual experiences and relationships with the other. Some of the other types of bisexuality identified in the literature include *historical*, where a "person who lives a predom-inantly hetero- or homosexual life but in whose history there are either bisexual experiences and/or fantasies" (Klein, 1993: 21); *sequential*, where a person has sequential relationships with both men and women, but with only one person at a time; *concurrent*, involving relationships with both men and women occurring at the same time; *episodic* and *temporary*, both incorporating brief encounters with the same or opposite sex while living mainly as heterosexual or homosexual; *experimental*, where a person experiments once with bisexuality but soon returns to their former sexual identity; and *situational*—such as in the prison system (Klein, 1993: 20–21). The myriad meanings of bisexuality make it rather difficult to explain what identifying as bisexual means and reinforces the lack of understanding of bisexuality in the social world.

This is complicated by the fact that bisexuality is often understood as equal attractions to both men and women: according to Weinberg et al., the word "bisexual" itself implies a need for similar degrees of sexual experience with both genders, and similar degrees of attraction (1994: 145). However, the assumption that bisexuals are "equally erotically disposed to one gender or the other" (Blumstein and Schwartz, 1977: 32) may be inaccurate. In fact, very few bisexual people have equal levels of attraction and equal amounts of sexual experience with both sexes (Zinik, 1985: 15). . . . Instead, there is great diversity in the sexual attractions, emotional attractions, sexual experiences and relationships of bisexual men and women. Therefore trying to describe a typical bisexual—and typical bisexual sexual attractions and experiences—is difficult. . . .

In my research, the belief that bisexuals are equally attracted to both men and women was evident when Megan, a 33-year-old bisexual woman, said that she felt she could not come out properly until she had more experience with women, reinforcing the idea that to be bisexual one must have equal, or at least similar, experiences with both men and women, at the same time highlighting the difficulties of coming out as bisexual:

Having a girlfriend could have raised my "credibility." I feel I lack a certain street cred because of my lack of experiences with women. I think I need a girlfriend to really come out.

Bisexuality is also often constructed as a "hybrid" identity, composed of a heterosexual component and a homosexual component, combined together in the one person. In this way, bisexuality is constructed as consisting of "two 'halves' forcibly glued together to make an ungainly and necessarily unstable whole" (Heldke, 1997: 175). References to bisexual people as being "half homosexual and half heterosexual," or to bisexuality as consisting of two sides or components, reinforce this construction of bisexuality. This assumes that bisexual men and women can switch off or switch on the different parts of their sexuality according to context—for example, when mixing in the heterosexual world, bisexual men and women can only relate to that world as heterosexual, and hide their same-sex attractions and experiences, or when mixing in the gay and lesbian world, bisexual men and women will only relate to that world as if they were gay or lesbian, thus hiding their opposite-sex attractions and experiences. This idea came up in interviews, as evidenced by these quotes:

It's difficult because it's not something you can talk about to everyone. You often have to hide some information from people—like that you've met a woman from the personals. (Olivia, age 26)

At work I have to leave out bits of my life when discussing attractions—I can be a participant in conversations about attractions to men, but not about attractions to women. (Tracey, age 25)

From these quotes it is clear that some bisexuals feel compelled to hide particular aspects of their identities, instead presenting themselves as either heterosexual or homosexual according to context. This has a significant impact on the recognition of bisexuality as a legitimate sexual identity category, reinforcing a continued lack of understanding of bisexuality. This can then create considerable anxieties amongst bisexual people that, if they do come out, their sexuality will not be well understood by those they are disclosing it to. As a result, many bisexuals may not come out at all.

(Mis)Representing Bisexuality

The myriad meanings attached to bisexuality explain, in part, the difficulties associated with coming out as bisexual. While society has come to grips, at least to some degree, with what it means to be gay or lesbian, there is less understanding of what it means to be bisexual. As a result, not only are there multiple understandings of bisexuality itself, there is also a range of inaccurate stereotypes of bisexuality as well. These include the belief that bisexuality is not a real sexual identity but that bisexuals are instead "in transition" to a gay or lesbian identity—that it is a stage (Rust, 1995: 65), or that bisexuals are "in denial" about their "true" sexuality (homosexuality). In terms of coming out, some claim that bisexuals lack the courage to come out as gay or lesbian (Weinberg et al., 1994: 117) or that they are confused or undecided about their sexual orientation. It has also been said that bisexuals refuse to come out as gay or lesbian in order to maintain heterosexual privilege (Israel and Mohr, 2004: 121). In addition, stereotypes of bisexuals as untrustworthy, overtly promiscuous, sexually indiscriminate beings who will have sex with "anything that moves," as needing two lovers at once (a man and a woman) to be "truly" satisfied, or as unable to be monogamous (Israel and Mohr, 2004: 122) also exist.

As a result, it can be rather difficult to come out to others as bisexual, particularly if one is concerned that the recipient of this information may only understand it in terms of one or more stereotypes. For the participants who did come out, many experienced reactions that reflected some of the many stereotypes of bisexuality. One young bisexual woman, Amanda, commented on the construction of bisexuality as a stage, or a transition to homosexuality:

Once she [ex-girlfriend] decided she was a lesbian, she assumed bisexuality would be a stage for me like it was for her. When I said I still identified as bi later, she saw that as me being confused, less together—even a little immature. (Amanda, age 26)

Another young woman, Lauren, also talking about a previous lesbian relationship, was considered indecisive by her partner simply because she identified as bisexual. She said:

She couldn't stand it, was not happy about it at all. She felt bisexuals are unable to make decisions, and that they are not part of the lesbian and gay community. She said I was not self-aware; that I didn't know how to relate to her, and that I couldn't be trusted. (Lauren, age 27)

Furthermore, two participants noted the stereotype of bisexuals as "in transition" or "in denial" when talking about coming out to others in their lives:

My ex-girlfriend knew about the fact I had identified as gay before we got together. Towards the end of the relationship she kept insisting I was really gay. I tried to tell her that when I was with her I wasn't thinking about boys and that I thought I was bi. But she still didn't believe me. . . . I haven't told my father because it would probably mean to him that I was heterosexual after all—he would probably think I've been "won over" by women. I hate that idea that all a gay man needs is the "love of a good woman." (Shaun, age 22)

My Mum is really sex negative and I think she was more shocked about having to come to terms with her daughter having a sexuality. Seven or eight months ago she told me she has come to terms with my "lesbianism." (Lauren, age 27)

For Shaun and Lauren, their bisexuality was interpreted instead as meaning "really gay" or "really lesbian." These and the previous quotes highlight the difficulties participants experienced when coming out as bisexual to others. Not only were participants faced with misleading stereotypes of bisexuals as untrustworthy, in denial or in transition to homosexuality, but their bisexual identity was dismissed by those they had come out to. Not only does this reinforce the difficulties attached to coming out as bisexual, it also highlights the invisibility of bisexuality as a valid and legitimate sexual identity.

Several participants had chosen not to come out to certain people because they harboured significant fears that their bisexuality would be misunderstood or misrepresented, especially if they were also married. The dilemmas faced by married bisexuals are highlighted in this quote by Celeste, a 25-year-old bisexual woman:

I haven't told the rest of my friends, they just wouldn't understand. I would have to defend myself, and my marriage—they would judge me. They wouldn't disown me but would ask me if I wasn't in love with my husband any more. I suspect one friend is very homophobic. I find it very frustrating that I can't tell them, especially when they have conversations in front of me and I can't say anything when they say stuff about homosexuality and things like that. . . . Because I am married I have a

role to play as a wife and future mother. I'm not sure my parents would cope with what others would say about my marriage. If I wasn't married and I told them it would be easier because they wouldn't have to deal with others' reactions to it. I worry about having to explain how it works, being bi and married. (Celeste, age 25)

The assumption that bisexuality equals promiscuity or non-monogamy has permeated popular thinking about bisexuality, fuelled by stereotypes that bisexual people need to have simultaneous relationships with both men and women to be truly satisfied. Given the expectations of monogamy and commitment within marriage, it is perhaps reasonable for some married bisexuals to have concerns that their marriages would be viewed differently, or negatively, if others knew they were bisexual, even if they were monogamous within that marriage.

Very few of the participants in this research had permanent multiple partners. However, some of those participants in relationships with more than one partner noted the "dual" difficulty of coming out as bisexual when it also entailed the disclosure of non-monogamy to others. Concerned they would be perceived as "cheating" on their primary partner, or be accused of promiscuity, they tended to keep both their bisexuality and their non-monogamy or other partner to themselves. The stereotype of the promiscuous bisexual convinced some that secrecy about their bisexuality and non-monogamy was better than accusations of infidelity and deceit.[1]

The stereotypes of bisexuality that make coming out as bisexual difficult are also reinforced when bisexuals, if they do not disclose their bisexuality, are assumed to be either heterosexual or homosexual. This was a common assumption participants felt was being made about them, in a variety of contexts, as these female participants argued:

I feel it's a juggling act. I'm feeling less positive about the whole situation, because it's hard to meet other bi people. I can join lesbian groups but they assume you're a lesbian and if you pipe up and tell them you're bi they get agro [hostile]. (Megan, age 33)

If you're bisexual and a parent everyone assumes you're straight. People still don't understand bisexuality—and I can't come out to the parent's group I'm in because of this. (Diana, age 35)

The hardest thing is assumptions that I'm straight. When I'm with a male partner, I'm assumed to be straight. When I'm with a female partner, I'm assumed to be lesbian. (Vicki, age 26)

The misrepresentation of bisexuality as a number of stereotypes, the belief that bisexuals are either in denial and in transition to homosexuality, and assumptions that bisexuals are either heterosexual or homosexual, highlight the complexities faced by bisexual men and women when deciding whether or not to come out. Confronted with the possibility of these judgments, some bisexual men and women make the decision to not come out to avoid the pain and anguish of rejection or misunderstandings about their bisexuality.

Continued Uncertainty and the Complexity of Coming Out

The third factor that makes coming out as bisexual difficult relates to the final stage of the bisexual identity development model proposed by Weinberg et al. in which they claim that bisexuals often feel "continued uncertainty" after settling on a bisexual identity (1994: 34).[2] . . . In this instance, coming out is particularly difficult if a person is not entirely sure of their sexual identity, or if they are plagued with continuing doubts about the reality of emotional and sexual attractions and experiences. For example, a bisexual woman who may doubt that her bisexuality is the "right" or "correct"[3] identity to describe her attractions and/or experiences may postpone coming out until she is more certain of the strength of her bisexuality. . . .

This continued uncertainty makes it rather difficult to come out as bisexual, not only because it means harbouring considerable doubts and anxieties about being bisexual, but also because those doubts and anxieties are compounded by having to explain bisexuality, or having to justify certain attractions and experiences. For example, Alicia, a 27-year-old bisexual woman said:

I feel it's an "equally cursed and equally blessed" thing. I find it difficult in the sense that I have to explain to people about it. (Alicia, age 27)

The continued uncertainty felt by many bisexuals was also evident when two other females spoke of feelings that their identity was made up of two separate sides that were sometimes in conflict:

I feel like I have a split identity, because bisexuality isn't a concrete identity. It's frustrating because I know people think I'm heterosexual and there's no space for me to be anything other than this. (Justine, age 27)

Because I'm monogamous in my current relationship it's easy for the outside world to see me as heterosexual, and that frustrates me because I need to keep reminding people I'm not heterosexual. You also have to deal with the fact that when you are with gay men or lesbians, you have to ignore your heterosexual side, and when you're with heterosexual people you have to ignore your gay/lesbian side. (Karina, age 38)

Both of these participants conveyed their awareness that some of the many meanings of bisexuality, such as the construction of bisexuality as a hybrid identity, can reinforce feelings of continued uncertainty about being bisexual. Furthermore, it can be seen that, for many participants, concerns about the validity of their bisexuality continued, despite participants having settled on a bisexual identity and after coming out to many others around them. Such continued uncertainty indicates the difficulties many face when living with a bisexual identity, and living in a world where bisexuality is significantly misunderstood. And if continued uncertainty is something that many bisexuals face, then this can intensify the difficulties many bisexuals face when making the decision whether or not to come out.

Strategies of Selective Disclosure: The Bisexual Coming-Out Experience

For bisexuals living in a society in which bisexuality is not easily understood, and in which bisexuality is misrepresented in a number of ways, it is very difficult to come out as bisexual. For these reasons, bisexuals have mixed experiences of coming out and, for many, the choice of selective disclosure is often the path most travelled. In this respect, selective disclosure is a deliberate choice made in a climate that leaves little room for the articulation of a bisexual identity. Many bisexuals often have significant fears and concerns that coming out as bisexual will be more difficult than not coming out, and that keeping their bisexuality a secret from some people around them is actually the more straightforward option. As a result, bisexual men and women develop a number of strategies to manage coming out, strategies which normally involve some sort of selective disclosure. The first of these is "testing the waters."

Testing the Waters

While others have described the method of "testing the waters" as a means to gauge reactions of others to their bisexuality by telling some family members before others—for example, siblings before parents (see George, 1993; Weinberg et al., 1994), for my participants, "testing the waters" meant hinting or making suggestive comments about their same-sex attractions without any specific reference to bisexuality. Hinting about same-sex attractions was often seen as a better alternative than fully disclosing their bisexuality, and was used to test whether a full disclosure of bisexuality would be successful in the future. Two of the young bisexual women I interviewed said:

I haven't told any of my friends outwardly. I made a couple of jokes about giving up on men and taking up with girls but they were only jokes. (Rachel, age 23)

I have kind of told one of my brothers. I didn't really tell him I'm bi, rather it was more about making comments about thinking women are cute, kind of agreeing with his comments about women. Now it's normalized in my conversations with him, but he didn't say anything much about it. . . . I haven't actually come out [to my parents] but made a comment to them about women and the possibility of a "Miss Right." Mum was a bit nonplussed, and said "It's your decision," but I don't think she's comfortable with it. She has made almost too much effort to say she would accept her children whatever choice they make. My father makes comments about me "swinging both ways" and being "AC/DC." I think these comments are pretty tacky, although I know he's trying to be hip and trendy. They are probably both hoping it's all talk and no action. (Alex, age 29)

The last quote by Alex highlights the dilemma faced by some of the younger participants about coming out as bisexual to their family. While they were happy to joke about the possibility of same-sex attractions, they were more reluctant to admit they had

actually adopted a bisexual identity. This leads some bisexual men and women to choose not to come out, despite indications it will or might be accepted, at least to some degree, as the comments by Alex's father above demonstrate. . . .

Sometimes In, Sometimes Out: The "Disclosure Necessity"

Another method used by participants to manage the coming out process was to make the decision only to come out by necessity. As such, participants practised selective disclosure in many facets of their lives—amongst family and friends, amongst work colleagues and in particular social contexts. . . .

The decision only to come out selectively, or to use what I term the "disclosure necessity," was evident when I asked the participants in my research about their general level of openness about their bisexuality. Overall, the participants were only selectively out to other people around them, such as workmates or acquaintances. For example, three participants said:

The only people that know are my counsellors—the women I've had contact with see me as lesbian. Everyone else sees me as straight. (Margaret, age 41)

I'm only open when necessary. I'm not open to my friends at all. I live a life of mainly secrecy. (Steven, age 55)

I don't hide it, but being married I don't have to be open and people assume I'm straight. In professional work circles I hide it because I deal with senior management and I don't want to add anything into the equation that may adjust their perceptions about me, I have to look credible with experience and authority to back me up. (Matthew, age 30)

What is interesting about this last quote is the degree to which many bisexual men and women believe bisexuality is seen as a non-legitimate or non-credible sexual identity in wider society. Often this meant that participants lived by a guiding principle of being prepared to be open to others about their bisexuality, but often only if they felt that the information would be received well. . . .

Rather than coming out as bisexual and maintaining one public sexual identity, this means that many bisexual men and women use a strategy of developing a number of different "personas" to use in different contexts. In my research, many participants either passed as heterosexual or let assumptions of heterosexuality go unchallenged. For some, mixing in gay and lesbian circles meant often playing the part of being gay or lesbian if people did not know they were bisexual. Very few challenged assumptions about heterosexuality or homosexuality in these situations; instead, maintaining a heterosexual or gay/lesbian persona was seen as necessary to protect themselves from judgment, discrimination and conflict with others. This means that many bisexual men and women maintain up to three distinct "personas" depending on the context: a heterosexual one, a bisexual one—if they have come out as bisexual—and, sometimes, a gay or lesbian one. . . .

The strategies used by bisexuals to manage disclosure, either by testing the waters or disclosure by necessity, indicates that not coming out is not simply a matter of "hiding in the closet." Rather, the use of these strategies, as well as the development of several "personas," demonstrates a concerted effort by many bisexual people to manage coming out in a way that suits them best, rather than following prescribed models of how coming out should be both managed and expressed.

Conclusion

With coming out popularized as a significant event in the development and maintenance of a non-heterosexual identity, it is no surprise that there is great importance attached it. The decision about whether or not to come out created a great deal of anxiety for many participants. They felt that the potential loss of the love and support of others if they did not react well to the news was reason enough to not come out as bisexual. They attached enormous fears about coming out to family members, some friends and others around them, and believed these people would have great difficulty accepting their bisexuality.

Participants' fears about the reactions of others to coming out as bisexual emphasize the difficulties faced by bisexual men and women in choosing who to tell and who not to tell. As a result, the participants in my research were not open about their bisexuality.

Less than one-third of participants (14) described themselves as "generally" open about their sexuality, and very few said they were completely "out" to everyone in their life. Instead, participants were very careful about revealing their bisexuality to people and sometimes only did so if someone directly asked them. They maintained a very private bisexual identity while at the same time admitting, often with some guilt, to passing as heterosexual in many contexts. This passing, however, was motivated by a significant fear that people would not understand their bisexuality, or would misconstrue it as something else. Hiding specific details about their lives was seen as a more preferable option than being cut off from loved ones or ostracised in other personal situations, and provided something of a safety net that protected them from the pain of being misunderstood, hurt or rejected by loved ones.

What these findings reveal is that bisexual coming out cannot simply be understood as a matter of coming out, or not coming out. Instead, understanding the decisions made by bisexual men and women to come out or not requires consideration of the factors that make coming out as bisexual especially difficult. As many of these factors exist at a broad societal level—such as the myriad meanings and stereotypes attached to bisexuality—they are very tricky to shift and negotiate. Moreover, the continued uncertainty bisexual people experience makes coming out an especially problematic decision if feelings of confusion or conflict persist. My research has found that full disclosure may not be the most important part of living with a bisexual identity for many bisexual men and women.

To construct coming out as an imperative for all non-heterosexuals is to ignore these factors, and to claim that a person who has not come out is lacking, dishonest or not empowered is to ignore the complexities of both identity development and coming out itself. The disclosure imperative is particularly problematic for bisexuals in that it assumes that, while coming out is fraught with fear and anxiety for most people, these fears and anxieties can be overcome. For many bisexuals, the fears and anxieties are compounded by a strong belief that bisexuality is either not well understood or is misunderstood, and are further compounded by the continued uncertainty that appears to be common in those who identify as bisexual, meaning that non-disclosure is often seen as the better alternative.

NOTES

1. Despite the stereotypes of bisexuals as deceitful and sexually promiscuous, many bisexuals in open or non-monogamous relationships demonstrate a commitment to honesty, communication and negotiation within these relationships. For a more detailed discussion of these issues, see McLean (2004).

2. This is not to say that some gay men and lesbians do not also feel uncertain after settling on a gay or lesbian identity. Weinberg et al. (1994), however, identified *continued uncertainty* as significant in the lives of many bisexuals interviewed for their research.

3. Of course, this assumes that there is a "right" or "correct" way to identify as bisexual. I do not propose to argue this: instead, the belief that there is a "right" or "correct" way to identify as bisexual leads many bisexual people to question their bisexuality if they feel they do not "fit" the bisexual label, which contributes to continued uncertainty.

REFERENCES

Blumstein, P. and P. Schwartz (1977) "Bisexuality: Some Social Psychological Issues," *Journal of Social Issues* 33(2): 30–45.

George, S. (1993) *Women and Bisexuality.* London: Scarlet Press.

Heldke, L. (1997) "In Praise of Unreliability," *Hypatia* 12(3): 174–82.

Israel, T. and J. Mohr (2004) "Attitudes towards Bisexual Women and Men: Current Research, Future Directions," pp. 119–34 in R. Fox (ed.) *Current Research on Bisexuality.* New York: Harrington Park Press.

Klein, F. (1993) *The Bisexual Option,* 2nd edn. New York: Harrington Park Press.

McLean, K. (2004) "Negotiating (Non)Monogamy: Bisexuality and Intimate Relationships," pp. 85–97 in R. Fox (ed.) *Current Research on Bisexuality.* New York: Harrington Park Press.

Plummer, K. (1995) *Telling Sexual Stories: Power, Change and Social Worlds.* London: Routledge.

Rust, P. (1995) *Bisexuality and the Challenge to Lesbian Politics.* New York: New York University Press

Weinberg, M., C. Williams and D. Pryor (1994) *Dual Attraction: Understanding Bisexuality.* New York: Oxford University Press.

Zinik, G. (1985) "Identity Conflict or Adaptive Flexibility? Bisexuality Reconsidered," pp. 7–19 in F. Klein and T. Wolf (eds) *Bisexualities: Theory and Research.* New York: Haworth Press.

Investigating Sexuality

An interview with...

Julia R. Heiman

Julia R. Heiman, Ph.D., a leader in the field of sex research, is the sixth director of The Kinsey Institute for Research in Sex, Gender, and Reproduction at Indiana University, Bloomington. Heiman, who joined the university on June 1, 2004, is also a professor in the Psychological and Brain Sciences Department with a joint appointment in the Psychiatry Department in the IU School of Medicine in Indianapolis.

So, to start off the interview, what got you interested in the study of sexuality in the first place?

In 1971, in the early stages of my graduate career, I was working for the summer with a professor named James Geer, who was a faculty member in the Psychology Department at Stony Brook. He had been studying emotions such as fear and their psychophysiological components for many years. Masters and Johnson's sexual treatment book, Human Sexual Inadequacy, _had just been published. Dr. Geer was interested in figuring out if there was something there that psychophysiologists should study, and basically gave me the choice of doing something in the fear research area or in the sexuality research area. I picked sexuality [because] at the time almost no one else in the lab_ *(except Ray Rosen) was working on it while several people were working on fear research. That started my whole interest in the psychophysiology of sexuality. Jim Geer, along with an engineer named George Sintchak, developed the vaginal photoplethysmograph, and that allowed the physiological measurement of sexuality to be a possibility. This meant that a study that looked at a combination of social, psychological, and physiological variables could be done. I did the second study using the vaginal photoplethysmograph. This was a comparison between men and women's [sexual] responses that became my dissertation. To this day, I remain interested in those basic questions—the subjective and physical experience of sexuality—what that means to people in terms of their problems and health, and to our understanding of humanity. So, some of the reason that I got into sexuality research was my own doing, and a great deal of it was timing of persons and events that made it possible.*

How do you tell people that you study sexuality? How do they react?

Well, that's an interesting question, and it varies, as you can imagine. If I am talking to other social or psychosocial researchers, they're usually interested and usually wondering how sexuality studies might relate to their own work. As you go to some of the other disciplines, it varies. Some people think it's quaint, while others think it's odd. Some think it's not quite science. If you tell the general public, they can have reactions all over the place. They can feel like, "Well, that's a little strange," or they can feel like, "Oh well, that allows me to ask you every single question I ever had about sexuality. I'd better start right now!" But, in general, if you as a person doing sexuality research are comfortable with it, interested in it, and feel it's important, most people will pick up on that, and they'll want to know more.

Of the projects that you've done over your academic career, which was the most interesting, and why?

I would say those projects that surprised me or didn't turn out quite the way I expected were the most interesting. For example, when we looked at differences between genders in patterns of [sexual] responding, we didn't find that many. Another instance would be the study I did on adding romantic content to erotic content in films. There were few differences in arousal when the romantic content was added. Sexual content was what made people aroused. The fact is that sexual response is pretty robust, and the tendency is to respond. Another thing that I found very, very interesting is that the more important data, when you are talking about sexuality, concerns variability rather than similarity. Means (averages) are fine, but when you have a group—for example women responding to sexual fantasy—there is a mean, but the interesting information is really that responses go from very weak to very strong. This focus on variability was introduced by Alfred Kinsey, and contains an important message about our sexuality. That doesn't mean that all variability is always healthy, but it does mean that variability is part of the human condition when it comes to sex.

What are the biggest ethical dilemmas that you've faced? Could you tell us about one particularly thorny dilemma, and how you solved it?

There are certain kinds of film content that I, though I see the legitimacy of showing it, am hesitant to use. For instance, showing people a really aggressive rape scene and getting their reactions to it can make them worried or anxious. I think this type of work needs to be done in order to understand and treat problematic sexual behaviors, but you have to make sure that you are studying it in the most serious and careful way possible, so as not to harm the participants. Sometimes the only way we can study difficult and unpleasant topics is by studying difficult and unpleasant topics. But, you need to be extremely alert to ethical considerations, and make sure that you have someone else (such as the Institutional Review Board) look over and approve your protocols. You also need to be careful about your own sensitivities about what is ethical, and make sure that you are fully informing respondents of risk, and giving them every possible opportunity to decide whether or not to participate, and not communicating biases inadvertently.

What are the most challenging things about studying sexuality?

I think of several aspects. For one, measurement continues to be a struggle. Looking for new methods that might better measure what we are interested in. There are lots of mediocre measures available. We have to acknowledge the weaknesses of the measures, and make sure we agree with why they should be used, or take the time to develop new ones of our own. Another issue is seriously working across disciplinary lines and incorporating different disciplinary perspectives. Political sensitivity is another issue. Sex research is so politicized that even though individual researchers may not consider themselves to be political, the topic is, and you may have to deal with—or at least be very careful with—these issues. Finally, I think we need to find better ways to translate our research to the general public so they can understand and benefit from it.

What's it like being the Director of the Kinsey Institute?

What is most stimulating is that the Institute is an extremely unique and unusual and truly interdisciplinary gathering place. [In addition to those studying the psychological and physiological aspects of sexuality], we have people coming in who are scholars of history or gender, and they find things to work on in our archives. We have a huge collection of manuscripts and materials, art and photography, and they use these to do scholarly studies of various aspects of sexuality. Of course, we also have people doing ongoing empirical studies, developing new ideas and grants. All of this makes the Institute alive and vibrant. One of the important things for the field of sexuality is to have a place like the Kinsey Institute where interdisciplinary research can take place. It has a history that goes back more than fifty years and that has survived a lot of controversy. You wouldn't expect a place like the Kinsey Institute to be in such a conservative state [Indiana], and yet the atmosphere here works well for sex research ideas.

How have things changed since the Kinsey film came out?

I was coming into this job just as the Hollywood feature film, Kinsey, *was about to be launched, and our focus was being prepared for how we were going to handle the publicity and the media—especially if it was negative. On balance, the reaction has been more positive than negative. There were no disasters that happened as a result of the film. We did get attacked by a small group that is very anti-sex research—that will say anything to discredit sexuality research—and they campaigned in some cities. As the movie gained attention, we kept the website open and answered questions. We also went around to various cities and presented the film and talked about where sex research is today. We made a number of new contacts and new friends. We seem to have a lot more supporters now as a result.*

OK, a final question—if you could teach people one thing about sexuality, what would that be?

Oh, not just one! How about a multi-part answer? First, I think we need to understand what influences sexual feelings and desires and behaviors, because it's really part of understanding what humans are about. Second, it is important to understand what your own sexuality is about and how it changes over time. There is a lot of room for variability without it being a problem or difficulty for one's self or others. Every culture decides for itself what is normal and abnormal, but to act like the variation in sexuality should not be there, or can be eliminated, is probably naïve. Finally, how do we help citizens develop a concept of sexual health that fosters respect for body and person?

—Interviewed by Denise Donnelly

Alfred Kinsey and the Kinsey Report

Vern L. Bullough

The more I study the development of modern sexuality, the more I believe in the importance and significance of Alfred Kinsey. Although his research was on Americans, it came to be a worldwide source of information about human sexuality and set standards for sex research everywhere. In America and much of the world, his work was a decisive factor in changing attitudes toward sex. Within the field of sexuality, he reoriented the field, moving it away from the medical model and medical dominance, to one encompassing a variety of disciplines and approaches. In short, his work has proved revolutionary.

To understand what Kinsey wrought, one must look at the field of sexuality when Kinsey began his studies. One must also look briefly at Kinsey as an individual to understand his accomplishments.

Sex Research, 1890–1940

The modern study of sexuality began in the nineteenth century, and these early studies were dominated by physicians. It was assumed that since physicians were the experts on body functions, they should be the experts regarding sexual activities. In a sense, this was a divergence from the past, when sexuality had been regarded almost entirely as a moral issue. And although there were still moral issues involved, physicians were also judged as qualified to speak on these

issues as well. Although few physicians had any specialized knowledge on most sexual topics, except perhaps for sexually transmitted diseases, this did not prevent them from speaking with authority on most aspects of human sexuality.

Havelock Ellis, one of the dominant figures in promoting sexual knowledge in the first third of the twentieth century, said that he sought a medical degree primarily because it was the only profession in which he could safely study sex. Inevitably, most of the so-called experts were physicians. Equal in influence to Ellis was Magnus Hirschfeld, another physician. Both Ellis and Hirschfeld compiled what could be called sexual histories, as Kinsey later compiled. Ellis, however, acquired almost all of his histories from correspondence of volunteers and, as far as I know, never interviewed anyone. Hirschfeld, later in his career, compiled many case histories based on interviews, but early on he depended mainly on historical data and personal knowledge. Unfortunately, Hirschfeld used only a small portion of his data in his published books, and before he could complete a comprehensive study of sexuality, his files were destroyed by the Nazis (Bullough, 1994).

Although some of the data physicians reported about sex was gathered from their own practices, these were usually interpreted in terms of traditional views and were supplemented by historical materials or reports of anthropologists to increase their authenticity. Simply put, most physicians writing about sex were influenced more by the zeitgeist of the time rather than by any specialized base of knowledge. A few early physician investigators, such as the American obstetrician Robert Latou Dickinson (Dickinson & Beam, 1931, 1934), had over 1,000 case studies, but most had only a handful. As the twentieth century progressed, the ordinary physician probably was regarded as the easiest available authority on sex, but most of the medical writings on sexual topics came from psychiatrists, particularly those who were psychoanalytically trained (Bullough, 1997). Unfortunately, even the most comprehensive sex studies undertaken by psychiatrists, such as that of George Henry, were flawed by the assumptions of the investigators interpreting data. For example, they assumed that homosexuals were ill. Moreover, whether the answers to their questions were valid for determining differences with heterosexuals is uncertain, as there was a lack of any comparative study of heterosexuals (Henry, 1941).

Still, assumptions about medical expertise remained. When the Committee for Research in the Problems in Sex (CRPS), the Rockefeller-funded grant-giving body operating under the umbrella of the National Research Council, began to explore the possibilities of carrying out surveys of sexual behavior, they first sought out physicians. For example, Adolf Meyer of Johns Hopkins University was commissioned to complete a study of attitudes of medical students, but failed to complete his work. The only social scientists funded in the first 20 years of the CRPS were psychologists, although anthropological consultants and members of other fields provided occasional input. Lewis Terman, for example, was given funds to carry out studies on attitudes toward sex and marriage. Though his and similar studies were valuable, they depended on questionnaires rather than interviews to gather their data (Terman, Buttenweiser, Ferguson, Johnson, & Wilson, 1938), and the sexual part of their studies was secondary to other interests. Even though one of the major reasons the CRPS had been created in 1921 was to complete such general studies, the committee members were either unwilling or unable to find a person to carry out this kind of study. I suspect that the first factor was more important than the second: There is considerable evidence to indicate that the committee members were uncomfortable with studies on actual sexual behavior and much preferred to fund what might be called bench (i.e., laboratory-based) scientists to social scientists. I should add that this attitude was not shared by the Rockefeller Foundation or John D. Rockefeller, Jr.: both funded other survey projects

dealing with sex, including that of Katherine Bement Davis (1929).

Funding for research projects when Kinsey began his work operated much more according to an old-boy network than it does today. There was little advertisement of fund availability and individuals were invited to apply, had to be nominated to apply, or had to have a connection. Certain universities and individuals dominated the disbursement of the money available. To an observer [today] examining most of the research grants given for sex research, the relationships look almost incestuous.

Unfortunately for the committee, sex activity could not be studied exclusively in the laboratory or even in the field by observing animals or gathering historical data. There had been nongrant-supported popular studies of sex, but their samples were not representative and the questionnaires were poorly designed. Moreover, in keeping with its reliance on academia, the committee seemed reluctant to give its imprimatur to individuals conducting such studies. What was needed was a person willing to blaze new trails, dispassionately examining sex without the preconceived notions of most of the physicians then involved in writing about sex. The qualified individual or individuals needed an academic connection, preferably one with an established reputation for scientific studies.

Kinsey Comes on the Scene

It was in this setting that Kinsey entered the scene. He was the right person at the right time; that is, a significant amount of money was available for sex research and there was an interest within the CRPS for some general kind of survey of American sex behavior. Who was Kinsey?

In terms of overall qualification, Kinsey's best asset was that he was a bench scientist, a biologist with a Ph.D. from Harvard, and an internationally known expert on gall wasps. But he was also a broad-based scientist. Unlike most research scientists today, who often are part of a team, researchers in the 1930s in the United States were self-dedicated and carried a major teaching load. Kinsey, for example, simultaneously taught general biology, published two editions of a popular introductory general biology text, two editions of a workbook, and a general text on methods in biology, and carried out major research. His entry into sex seems to have been serendipitous, taking place after he had completed his studies on gall wasps. Professors at the University of Indiana had discussed the possibility of an introductory cross-discipline course on marriage, then a topic beginning to receive some attention in academic circles. Kinsey was not only involved in such discussions but took the lead. In 1938, he was invited to coordinate and direct the new course on marriage and family. As a sign of the time, the course was taught by an all-male faculty from a variety of disciplines, including law, economics, sociology, philosophy, medicine, and biology.

Before the appearance of courses on marriage and family, the academic discussion of human sexuality had been confined to lectures in the hygiene-type courses that had been established on many campuses in the second decade of the twentieth century, largely through the efforts of the American Social Hygiene Association. The approach to sex of these hygiene classes was quite different from that of the marriage and family courses, as they generally emphasized the dangers of sexually transmitted diseases and masturbation. In a sense, these hygiene-type courses were conceived to preserve sexual purity, whereas the sexual portions of marriage and family courses provided information, following the outlines of the better sex manuals of the time.

Kinsey went even further in his discussion of sexuality than the sex-positive marriage manuals, and soon clashed with Thurman Rice, a bacteriology professor who had written extensively on sex, primarily from the point of view of eugenics. For many years, Rice had delivered the sex lectures in the required hygiene course, where the males were separated from the females when he gave his lectures. Kinsey deliberately had not included Rice in his recruited faculty, which probably furthered Rice's antagonism. Rice was typical of an earlier generation of sex educators in that he considered moral education an essential part of sex education. He believed and taught that masturbation was harmful, condemned premarital intercourse, and was fearful that Kinsey's course on marriage was a perversion of academic standards. For example, he charged Kinsey with asking some of the

women students about the length of their clitorises. To show that his accusations were based on more than gossip, Rice demanded the names of students in Kinsey's class so that he could verify such classroom voyeurism. Rice opposed Kinsey's questioning of students because he believed that sexual behavior could not and should not be analyzed by scientific methods because it was a moral topic, not a scientific one. Rice's perspective thus was perhaps typical of the hygiene approach to sex.

Kinsey had probably been doing at least some of the things that Rice mentioned because he had approached sex as a taxonomist—as one interested in classifying and describing—as a dispassionate scientist and not as a reformer or politician. In a sense, he was a political innocent. He believed that science could speak for itself, and he criticized his faculty colleagues who took any kind of political stand. He refused to join organizations that he felt had any kind of political agenda, including the Society for the Scientific Study of Sexuality (SSSS) in its early years.

There is, however, much more to Kinsey's interest in sex than the dispassionate scientist. In his personal life, he was not inhibited about body functions. Even before starting his course on marriage, he had sought information about the sex life of his students. His openness about sex (see Jones, 1997: 1997a) was what Rice objected to.

It might well be that when Kinsey began teaching the sex course, he was undergoing a kind of midlife crisis, feeling that he had come to know all he wanted to know about gall wasps and needing to explore new fields. Sex to him represented an unexplored new field where comparatively little was known, and where there was much information to be gleaned. He began his study as he had that of gall wasps: finding out what was known and, in the process, building up a personal library of serious books on sex (hardly any of these had found their way into university libraries) and reading extensively. He also sought first-hand information by questioning his students about topics such as their age at first premarital intercourse, frequency of sexual activity, and number of partners.

All this gave fodder to Rice and his allies, including a number of parents who, perhaps at Rice's urging, complained about the specific sexual data given in the course and particularly about questions that Kinsey asked of his students. The president of the university, Herman Wells, a personal friend of Kinsey who had appointed him coordinator of the course, counseled him and gave him two options: to continue to teach the course and give up some of his probing of student lives, or to devote more time to his sex research and not teach the course. Because Kinsey had already begun to extend his interviews off campus, the answer was perhaps inevitable. Although Kinsey continued to teach courses in biology, his load was reduced, and much of his life came to be devoted to sex research.

Because Kinsey was already well connected to the scientific establishment, his initial efforts to study sex received encouragement from the CRPS. He received an exploratory grant from them in 1941, during which time he would be evaluated as to suitability for a larger grant. George W. Corner, a physician member and later the chair of the CRPS, visited Kinsey as one of the grant investigators to determine whether Kinsey deserved further funding. He was tremendously impressed and reported that Kinsey was the most intense scientist he had ever met. He added that Kinsey could talk about little besides his research. According to Corner (1981), Kinsey was an ideal person for a grant to study sex:

> He was a full professor, married with adolescent children. While carrying on his teaching duties in the zoology department he worked every available hour, day and night, traveling anywhere that people would give him interviews. He was training a couple of young men in his method of interviewing. Dr. Yerkes and I submitted separately to his technique. I was astonished at his skill in eliciting the most intimate details of the subject's sexual history. Introducing his queries gradually, he managed to convey an assurance of complete confidentiality by recording the answers on special sheets printed with a grid on which he set down the information gained, by unintelligible signs, explaining that the code had never been written down and only his two colleagues could read it. His questions included subtle tricks to detect deliberate misinformation. (p. 268)

Important to the continuation of the grant was the support of the university administration and its president, which Kinsey received despite sniping by some fellow faculty members such as Rice and others who regarded Kinsey's interest in sex with suspicion. As Corner's reference to Kinsey's family indicates, the committee wanted to make certain that the researcher had no special agenda except, perhaps, to establish some guides to better marriages. Kinsey satisfied them on this account and was well aware that any indication otherwise might endanger his grant. Thus, his own sex life remained a closed book, only to be opened by later generations of scholars (Jones, 1997). The CRPS came to be so committed to Kinsey that by the 1946–1947 academic year, he was receiving half of the committee's total budget.

Before the interviews stopped with Kinsey's death, about 18,000 individuals had been interviewed, 8,000 by Kinsey himself. Kinsey strongly believed that people would not always tell the truth when questioned about their sexual activities and that the only way to deal with this was through personal interviews in which the contradictions could be explored. He did not believe that self-administered questionnaires produced accurate responses: He regarded them as encouraging dishonest answers. He also recognized that respondents might lie even in a personal interview, but he provided a variety of checks to detect this and believed his checks were successful. Subjects were usually told that there were some contradictions in their answers and were asked to explain them. If they refused to do so, the interview was terminated and the information not used. Kinsey was also aware of potential bias of the interviewer. He sought to overcome this bias by occasionally having two people conduct the interviews at different times and by relying mainly on four interviewers, including himself, to conduct the study. If there was a bias, it came to be a shared one. The questions, however, were so wide-ranging that this too would limit much of the potential for slanting the data in any one direction. Following taxonomic principles, he wanted to gather data from as many subjects as possible, and he hoped initially to conduct 20,000 interviews and later to conduct 80,000 more. He did not live to achieve this. Before he died, the funding sources had dried up for such research, and other methods based on statistical sampling grew more popular.

What Kinsey Did

Kinsey's major accomplishment was to challenge most of the assumptions about sexual activity in the United States. In so doing, he aroused great antagonism among many who opposed making sexual issues a matter of public discussion and debate. One reason for the antagonism is that he brought to public notice many sexual practices that previously had not been publicly discussed. Although Kinsey prided himself as an objective scientist, it was his very attempt to establish a taxonomy of sexual behaviors—treating all activities as more or less within the range of human behavior—that got him into trouble. Karl Menninger, for example, said that "Kinsey's compulsion to force human sexual behavior into a zoological frame of reference leads him to repudiate or neglect human psychology, and to see normality as that which is natural in the sense that it is what is practiced by animals" (quoted in Pomeroy, 1972, p. 367).

Most sex researchers today accept the fact that total objectivity in our field is probably impossible. Some of Kinsey's difficulty resulted from his belief that he could be totally objective. He did not realize that the way he organized his data sometimes could challenge his objectivity, even though the organization seemed logical. For example, Kinsey developed a seven-point bipolar scale, which was one of the standard methods of organizing data in social science research at that time. He did not trust people's self-classification as homosexual or heterosexual. Therefore, he decided that regardless of how they might have classified themselves, the only objective indicator that he could use was to define sex in terms of outlet—namely, what activity resulted in orgasms.

In most seven-point scales, the extremes are represented by 0 and 6 (or by 1 and 7, depending upon the number with which the scale starts). Most people tend to respond using the middle of the scale. When one rates heterosexual orgasm as 0 and homosexual orgasm 6, a logical decision in terms of taxonomy, he in effect weights the scale by seeming to imply that exclusive heterosexuality is one extreme and exclusive homosexuality the other. Although his data demonstrated that far more people were identified as exclusively heterosexual than as any other category, his

scale also implied that homosexuality was just another form of sexual activity, something that I think Kinsey believed was true. For his time and place this was revolutionary. His discussion of homosexuality and its prevalence resulted in the most serious attacks upon him and his data (Kinsey, Pomeroy, & Martin, 1948).

Kinsey was a trailblazer, openly and willingly challenging many basic societal beliefs. It was not only his dispassionate discussion of homosexuality that roused controversy, but also his tendency to raise questions that society at that time preferred to ignore. In his book on males, for example, he questioned the assumption that extramarital intercourse always undermined the stability of marriage and held that the full story was more complex than the most highly publicized cases led one to assume. He seemed to feel that the most appropriate extramarital affair, from the standpoint of preserving a marriage, was an alliance in which neither party became overly involved emotionally. Concerned over the reaction to this, however, he became somewhat more cautious in the book on females. He conceded that extramarital affairs probably contributed to divorces in more ways and to a "greater extent than the subjects themselves realized" (Kinsey, Pomeroy, Martin, & Gebhard, 1953, p. 31).

Kinsey was interested in many different sexual behaviors, including that between generations (i.e., adults with children or minors). One of his more criticized sections in recent years is the table based on data he gathered from pedophiles. He is accused of not turning these people over to authorities, although one of the major informants was already serving time in jail for his sexual activities when interviewed. Kinsey gathered his data wherever he could find it, but he also reported on the source of his data. His own retrospective data tended to show that many individuals who experienced intergenerational sex as children were not seriously harmed by it, another statement that got him into trouble.

Kinsey is also criticized for his statistical sampling. Although his critics (even before his studies were published) attempted to get him to validate his data with a random sample of individuals, he refused on the grounds that not all of those included in the random sample would answer the questions put to them and that, therefore, the random sample would be biased. It is quite clear that Kinsey's sample is not random and that it overrepresents some segments of the population, including students and residents of Indiana. Part of the criticism, however, is also due to the use and misuse of the Kinsey data without his qualifications. This is particularly true of his data on same-sex relationships, which are broken down by age and other variables and therefore allowed others to choose the number or percentage of the sample they wanted to use in their own reports.

Another assumption of American society that Kinsey also challenged was the asexuality of women. This proved the issue of greatest controversy in his book on females. A total of 40% of the females he studied had experienced orgasm within the first months of marriage, 67% by the first six months, and 75% by the end of the first year. Twenty-five percent of his sample had experienced orgasm by age of 15, more than 50% by the age of 20, and 64% before marriage. On the other hand, he also reported cases in which women failed to reach orgasm after 20 years of marriage. In spite of the controversies over his data on orgasms, it helped move the issue of female sexuality on to the agenda of the growing women's movement of the late 1960s and the 1970s, and to encourage further studies of female sexuality.

In light of the challenges against him, Kinsey ignored in his writings what might be called sexual adventurers, paying almost no attention to swinging, group sex, and alternate lifestyles such as sadism, masochism, transvestism, voyeurism, and exhibitionism. He justified this neglect by arguing that such practices were statistically insignificant. It is more likely that Kinsey was either not interested in them or not interested in exploring them. He was also not particularly interested in pregnancy or sexually transmitted diseases. However, he demystified discussion of sex insofar as that was possible. Sex, to him, was just another aspect of human behavior, albeit an important part. He made Americans and the world at large aware of just how big a part human sexuality played in the life cycle of the individual and how widespread many kinds of sexual activities were.

Kinsey was determined to make the study of sex a science, a subject that could be studied in colleges much the same way that animal reproduction was, with succeeding generations of researchers adding to the knowledge base. He succeeded, at least in the long run. He had a vision of the kind of studies that still needed to be done, some of which were later done by his successors at Indiana and elsewhere, but he himself died before he could do them and the funds dried up.

Another of his significant contributions was to establish a library and to gather sources about sexuality from all over the world. He blazed a trail for future sex researchers: The library he established at Indiana University served as an example that helped many of us to persuade other university libraries to collect works from this field. Although there are now several impressive collections of this kind in the country, Kinsey's collection is still tremendously important.

In sum, Kinsey was the major factor in changing attitudes about sex in the twentieth century. His limitations and his personal foibles are appropriately overshadowed by his courage to go where others had not gone before. In spite of the vicious attacks upon him during his last few years of life, and the continuing attacks today, his data continue to be cited and used (and misused). He changed the nature of sexual studies, forced a reexamination of public attitudes toward sex, challenged the medical and psychiatric establishment to reassess its own views, influenced both the feminist movement and the gay and lesbian movement, and built a library and an institution devoted to sex research. His reputation continues to grow, and he has become one of the legends of the twentieth century.

REFERENCES

Bullough, V. L. (1994). *Science in the bedroom: A history of sex research.* New York: Basic Books.

Bullough, V. L. (1997). American physicians and sex research. *Journal of the History of Medicine, 57,* 236–253.

Corner, G. W. (1981). *The seven ages of a medical scientist.* Philadelphia: University of Pennsylvania Press.

Davis, K. B. (1929). *Factors in the sex life of twenty-two hundred women.* New York: Harper.

Dickinson, R. L., & Beam, L. (1931). *A thousand marriages.* Baltimore: Williams and Wilkins.

Dickinson, R. L., & Beam, L. (1934). *The single woman.* Baltimore: Williams and Wilkins.

Henry, G. (1941). *Sex variants: A study of homosexual patterns* (2 vols.). New York: Hoeber.

Jones, J. H. (1997, August 2 & September 1). Annals of sexology: Dr. Yes. *New Yorker,* pp. 99–113.

Jones, J. H. (1997a). *Kinsey: A Public/Private Life.* New York: Norton.

Kinsey, A., Pomeroy, W., & Martin, C. (1948). *Sexual behavior in the human male.* Philadelphia: Saunders.

Kinsey, A., Pomeroy, W., Martin, C., & Gebhard, P. (1953). *Sexual behavior in the human female.* Philadelphia: Saunders.

Pomeroy, W. B. (1972). *Dr. Kinsey and the Institute for Sex Research.* New York: Harper and Row.

Terman, L., Buttenweiser, P., Ferguson. L., Johnson, W. B., & Wilson, D. P. (1938). *Psychological factors in marital happiness.* New York: McGraw-Hill.

Survey of Sexual Behavior of Americans

Edward O. Laumann, John H. Gagnon,
Robert T. Michael, and Stuart Michaels

Most people with whom we talked when we first broached the idea of a national survey of sexual behavior were skeptical that it could be done. Scientists and laypeople alike had similar reactions: "Nobody will agree to participate in such a study." "Nobody will answer questions like these, and, even if they do, they won't tell the truth." "People don't know enough about sexual practices as they relate to disease transmission or even to pleasure or physical and emotional satisfaction to be able to answer questions accurately." It would be dishonest to say that we did not share these and other concerns. But our experiences over the past seven years, rooted in extensive pilot work, focus-group discussions, and the fielding of the survey itself, resolved these doubts, fully vindicating our growing conviction that a national survey could be conducted according to high standards of scientific rigor and replicability. . . .

The society in which we live treats sex and everything related to sex in a most ambiguous and ambivalent fashion. Sex is at once highly fascinating, attractive, and, for many at certain stages in their lives, preoccupying, but it can also be frightening, disturbing, or guilt inducing. For many, sex is considered to be an extremely private matter, to be discussed only with one's closest friends or intimates, if at all. And, certainly for most if not all of us, there are elements of our sexual lives never acknowledged to others, reserved for our own personal fantasies and self-contemplation. It is thus hardly surprising that the proposal to study sex scientifically, or any other way for that matter, elicits confounding and confusing reactions. Mass advertising, for example, unremittingly inundates the public with explicit and implicit sexual messages, eroticizing products and using sex to sell. At the same time, participants in political discourse are incredibly squeamish when handling sexual themes. . . . We suspect, in fact, that with respect to discourse on sexuality there is a major discontinuity between the sensibilities of politicians and other self-appointed guardians of the moral order and those of the public at large, who, on the whole, display few hang-ups in discussing sexual issues in appropriately structured circumstances. . . .

The fact remains that, until quite recently, scientific research on sexuality has been taboo and therefore to be avoided or at best marginalized. While there is a visible tradition of (in)famous sex research, what is, in fact, most striking is how little prior research exists on sexuality in the general population. Aside from the research on adolescence, premarital sex, and problems attendant to sex such as fertility, most research attention seems to have been directed toward those believed to be abnormal, deviant, criminal, perverted, rare, or unusual, toward sexual pathology, dysfunction, and sexually transmitted disease—the label used typically reflecting the way in which the behavior or condition in question is to be regarded. "Normal sex" was somehow off limits, perhaps because it was considered too ordinary, trivial, and self-evident to deserve attention. To be fair, then, we cannot blame the public and the politicians

"Survey of Sexual Behavior of Americans" by Edward O. Laumann, John H. Gagnon, Robert T. Michael, and Stuart Michaels, in *The Social Organization of Sexuality: Sexual Practices in the United States,* edited by Patricia A. Adler and Peter Adler (2000). University of Chicago Press. Reprinted by permission.

entirely for the lack of sustained work on sexuality at large—it also reflects the prejudices and understandings of researchers about what are "interesting" scientific questions. There has simply been a dearth of mainstream scientific thinking and speculation about sexual issues. We have repeatedly encountered this relative lack of systematic thinking about sexuality to guide us in interpreting and understanding [our] many findings. . . .

In order to understand the results of our survey, the National Health and Social Life Survey (NHSLS), one must understand how these results were generated. To construct a questionnaire and field a large-scale survey, many research design decisions must be made. To understand the decisions made, one needs to understand the multiple purposes that underlie this research project. Research design is never just a theoretical exercise. It is a set of practical solutions to a multitude of problems and considerations that are chosen under the constraints of limited resources of money, time, and prior knowledge.

Sample Design

The sample design for the NHSLS is the most straightforward element of our methodology because nothing about probability sampling is specific to or changes in a survey of sexual behavior. . . .

Probability sampling, that is, sampling where every member of a clearly specified population has a known probability of selection—what lay commentators often somewhat inaccurately call random sampling—is the sine qua non of modern survey research (see Kish 1965, the classic text on the subject). There is no other scientifically acceptable way to construct a representative sample and thereby to be able to generalize from the actual sample on which data are collected to the population that that sample is designed to represent. Probability sampling as practiced in survey research is a highly developed practical application of statistical theory to the problem of selecting a sample. Not only does this type of sampling avoid the problems of bias introduced by the researcher or by subject self-selection bias that come from more casual techniques, but it also allows one to quantify the variability in the estimates derived from the sample. . . .

Sample Size

How large should the sample be? There is real confusion about the importance of sample size. In general, for the case of a probability sample, the bigger the sample, the higher the precision of its estimate.[1] This precision is usually measured in terms of the amount of sampling error accruing to the statistics calculated from the sample. The most common version of this is the statement that estimated proportions (e.g., the proportion of likely voters planning to vote for a particular candidate) in national political polls are estimated as being within ± 2 or 3 percent of the overall population figure. The amount of this discrepancy is inversely related to the size of the sample: the larger the sample, the smaller the likely error in the estimates. . . .

In order to determine how large a sample size for a given study should be, one must first decide how precise the estimates to be derived need to be. To illustrate this reasoning process, let us take one of the simplest and most commonly used statistics in survey research, the proportion. . . . For example, what proportion of the population had more than five sex partners in the last year? What proportion engaged in anal intercourse? With condoms? Estimates based on our sample will differ from the true proportion in the population because of sampling error (i.e., the random fluctuations in our estimates that are due to the fact that they are based on samples rather than on complete enumerations or censuses). If one drew repeated samples using the same methodology, each would produce a slightly different estimate. If one looks at the distribution of these *estimates,* it turns out that they will be normally distributed (i.e., will follow the famous bell-shaped curve known as the Gaussian or normal distribution) and centered around the true proportion in the population. The larger the sample size, the tighter the distribution of estimates will be.

This analysis applies to an estimate of a single proportion based on the whole sample. In deciding the sample size needed for a study, one must consider the subpopulations for which one will want to construct estimates. For example, one almost always wants to know not just a single parameter for the whole population but parameters for subpopulations such as men and women, whites, blacks, and Hispanics, and younger people and older people. Furthermore, one is usually interested in the intersections of these various breakdowns of the population, for example, young black women. The size of the interval estimate for a proportion based on a subpopulation depends on the size of that group in the sample (sometimes called the *base "N,"* i.e., the number in the sample on which the estimate is based). It is actually this kind of number that one needs to consider in determining the sample size for a study.

When we were designing the national survey of sexual behavior in the United States for the NICHD [National Institute of Child Health and Human Development], we applied just these sorts of considerations to come to the conclusion that we needed a sample size of about 20,000 people . . .

First, let us consider the cooperation or response rate. No survey of any size and complexity is able to get every sampling-designated respondent to complete an interview. Individuals can have many perfectly valid reasons why they cannot participate in the survey: being too ill, too busy, or always absent when an effort to schedule an interview is made or simply being unwilling to grant an interview. While the face-to-face or in-person survey is considerably more expensive than other techniques, such as mail or telephone surveys, it usually gets the highest response rate. Even so, a face-to-face, household-based survey such as the General Social Survey successfully interviews, on the average, only about 75 percent of the target sample (Davis and Smith 1991). The missing 25 percent pose a serious problem for the reliability and validity of a survey: is there some systematic (i.e., nonrandom) process at work that distinguishes respondents from nonrespondents? That is, if the people who refuse to participate or who can never be reached to be interviewed differ systematically in terms of the issues being researched from those who are interviewed, then one will not have a representative sample of the population from which the sample was drawn. If the respondents and nonrespondents do not differ systematically, then the results will not be affected. Unfortunately, one usually has no (or only minimal) information about nonrespondents. It is thus a challenge to devise ways of evaluating the extent of bias in the selection of respondents and nonrespondents. Experience tells us that, in most well-studied fields in which survey research has been applied, such moderately high response rates as 75 percent do not lead to biased results. And it is difficult and expensive to push response rates much higher than that. Experience suggests that a response rate close to 90 percent may well represent a kind of upper limit.

Because of our subject matter and the widespread skepticism that survey methods would be effective, we set a completion rate of 75 percent as the survey organization's goal. In fact, we did much better than this; our final completion rate was close to 80 percent. We have extensively investigated whether there are detectable participation biases in the final sample. . . . To summarize these investigations, we have compared our sample and our results with other surveys of various sorts and have been unable to detect systematic biases of any substantive significance that would lead us to qualify our findings at least with respect to bias due to sampling.

One might well ask what the secret was of our remarkably high response rate, by far the highest of any national sexual behavior survey conducted so far. There is no secret. Working closely with the NORC [National Opinion Research Center] senior survey and field management team, we proceeded in the same way as one would in any other national area probability survey. We did not scrimp on interviewer training or on securing a highly mobilized field staff that was determined to get respondent participation in a professional and respectful manner. It was an expensive operation: the average cost of a completed interview was approximately $450.

We began with an area probability sample, which is a sample of households, that is, of addresses, not names. Rather than approach a household by knocking on the door without advance warning, we followed NORC's standard practice of sending an advance letter, hand addressed by the interviewer, about a week before the interviewer expected to visit the address. In this case, the letter was signed by the principal investigator, Robert Michael, who was identified as dean of the Irving B. Harris Graduate School of Public Policy Studies of the University of Chicago. The letter briefly explained the purpose of the survey as helping "doctors, teachers, and counselors better understand and prevent the spread of diseases like AIDS and better understand the nature and extent of harmful and of healthy sexual behavior in our country." The intent was to convince the potential respondent that this was a legitimate scientific study addressing personal and potentially sensitive topics for a socially useful purpose. AIDS was the original impetus for the research, and it certainly seemed to provide a timely justification for the study. But any general purpose approach has drawbacks. One problem that the interviewers frequently encountered was potential respondents who did not think that AIDS affected them and therefore that information about their sex lives would be of little use.

Gaining respondents' cooperation requires mastery of a broad spectrum of techniques that successful interviewers develop with experience, guidance from the research team, and careful field supervision. This project required extensive training before entering the field. While interviewers are generally trained to be neutral toward topics covered in the interview, this was especially important when discussing sex, a topic that seems particularly likely to elicit emotionally freighted sensitivities both in the respondents and in the interviewers. Interviewers needed to be fully persuaded about the legitimacy and importance of the research. Toward this end, almost a full day of training was devoted to presentations and discussions with the principal investigators in addition to the extensive advance study materials to read and comprehend. Sample answers to frequently asked questions by skeptical respondents and brainstorming about strategies to convert reluctant respondents were part of the training exercises. A set of endorsement letters from prominent local and national notables and refusal conversion letters were also provided to interviewers. A hotline to the research office at the University of Chicago was set up to allow potential respondents to call in with their concerns. Concerns ranged from those about the legitimacy of the survey, most fearing that it was a commercial ploy to sell them something, to fears that the interviewers were interested in robbing them. Ironically, the fact that the interviewer initially did

not know the name of the respondent (all he or she knew was the address) often led to behavior by the interviewer that appeared suspicious to the respondent. For example, asking neighbors for the name of the family in the selected household and/or questions about when the potential respondent was likely to be home induced worries that had to be assuaged. Another major concern was confidentiality—respondents wanted to know how they had come to be selected and how their answers were going to be kept anonymous.

Mode of Administration: Face-to-Face, Telephone, or Self-Administered

Perhaps the most fundamental design decision, one that distinguishes this study from many others, concerned how the interview itself was to be conducted. In survey research, this is usually called the *mode* of interviewing or of questionnaire administration. We chose face-to-face interviewing, the most costly mode, as the primary vehicle for data collection in the NHSLS. What follows is the reasoning behind this decision.

A number of recent sex surveys have been conducted over the telephone. . . . The principal advantage of the telephone survey is its much lower cost. Its major disadvantages are the length and complexity of a questionnaire that can be realistically administered over the telephone and problems of sampling and sample control. . . . The NHSLS, cut to its absolute minimum length, averaged about ninety minutes. Extensive field experience suggests an upper limit of about forty-five minutes for phone interviews of a cross-sectional survey of the population at large. Another disadvantage of phone surveys is that it is more difficult to find people at home by phone and, even once contact has been made, to get them to participate. . . . One further consideration in evaluating the phone as a mode of interviewing is its unknown effect on the quality of responses. Are people more likely to answer questions honestly and candidly or to dissemble on the telephone as opposed to face to face? Nobody knows for sure.

The other major mode of interviewing is through self-administered forms distributed either face to face or through the mail.[2] When the survey is conducted by mail, the questions must be self-explanatory, and much prodding is typically required to obtain an acceptable response rate. . . . This procedure has been shown to produce somewhat higher rates of reporting socially undesirable behaviors, such as engaging in criminal acts and substance abuse. We adopted the mixed-mode strategy to a limited extent by using four short, self-administered forms, totaling nine pages altogether, as part of our interview. When filled out, these forms were placed in a "privacy envelope" by the respondent so that the interviewer never saw the answers that were given to these questions. . . .

The fundamental disadvantage of self-administered forms is that the questions must be much simpler in form and language than those that an interviewer can ask. Complex skip patterns must be avoided. Even the simplest skip patterns are usually incorrectly filled out by some respondents on self-administered forms. One has much less control over whether (and therefore much less confidence that) respondents have read and understood the questions on a self-administered form. The NHSLS questionnaire (discussed below) was based on the idea that questions about sexual behavior must be framed as much as possible in the specific contexts of particular patterns and occasions. We found that it is impossible to do this using self-administered questions that are easily and fully comprehensible to people of modest educational attainments.

To summarize, we decided to use face-to-face interviewing as our primary mode of administration of the NHSLS for two principal reasons: it was most likely to yield a substantially higher response rate for a more inclusive cross section of the population at large, and it would permit more complex and detailed questions to be asked. While by far the most expensive approach, such a strategy provides a solid benchmark against which other modes of interviewing can and should be judged. The main unresolved question is whether another mode has an edge over face-to-face interviewing when highly sensitive questions likely to be upsetting or threatening to the respondent are being asked. As a partial control and test of this question, we have asked a number of sensitive questions in both formats so that an individual's responses can be systematically compared. . . . Suffice it to say

at this point that there is a stunning consistency in the responses secured by the different modes of administration.

Recruiting and Training Interviewers

We firmly believed that it was very important to recruit and train interviewers for this study very carefully. In particular, we worried that interviewers who were in any way uncomfortable with the topic of sexuality would not do a good job and would adversely affect the quality of the interview. We thus took special steps in recruiting interviewers to make it clear what the survey was about, even showing them especially sensitive sample questions. We also assured potential recruits that there would be no repercussions should they not want to work on this study; that is, refusal to participate would not affect their future employment with NORC. None of these steps seemed to hinder the recruitment effort. In general, interviewers like challenging studies. Any survey that is not run of the mill and promises to be of current public relevance is regarded as a good and exciting assignment—one to pursue enthusiastically. In short, we had plenty of interviewers eager to work on this study. Of course, a few interviewers did decline to participate because of the subject matter.

The Questionnaire

The questionnaire itself is probably the most important element of the study design. It determines the content and quality of the information gathered for analysis. Unlike issues related to sample design, the construction of a questionnaire is driven less by technical precepts and more by the concepts and ideas motivating the research. It demands even more art than applied sampling design requires.

Before turning to the specific forms that this took in the NHSLS, we should first discuss several general problems that any survey questionnaire must address. The essence of survey research is to ask a large sample of people from a defined population the *same set of questions*. To do this in a relatively short period of time, many interviewers are needed. In our case, about 220 interviewers from all over the country collected the NHSLS data. The field period, beginning on 14 February 1992 and ending in September, was a time in which over 7,800 households were contacted (many of which turned out to be ineligible for the study) and 3,432 interviews were completed. Central to this effort was gathering comparable information on the same attributes from each and every one of these respondents. The attributes measured by the questionnaire become the variables used in the data analysis. They range from demographic characteristics (e.g., gender, age, and race/ethnicity) to sexual experience measures (e.g., numbers of sex partners in given time periods, frequency of particular practices, and timing of various sexual events) to measures of mental states (e.g., attitudes toward premarital sex, the appeal of particular techniques like oral sex, and levels of satisfaction with particular sexual relationships).

The basic problem in writing a questionnaire thus becomes the construction of a formal protocol that combines the specific wording of questions as well as instructions and skip patterns that allow the interviewer to take all the respondents over the same material. As much as possible, each respondent should be asked the same questions in the same words and in the same order since variations in wording and order are known to affect the responses that one gets (cf. Bradburn, Sudman, et al., 1979; Groves 1989). There are two ways to approach this problem. One approach is to make the questionnaire very simple, treating each question as a separate summary statement that can be answered independently of all other questions. This is what one must do in a self-administered questionnaire. It is also almost always the practice in questionnaires that focus on attitudes.

The problem that we faced in writing the questionnaire was figuring out how best to ask people about their sex lives. There are two issues here that should be highlighted. One is conceptual, having to do with how to define sex, and the second has to do with the level or kind of language to be used in the interview.

Very early in the design of a national sexual behavior survey, in line with our goal of not reducing this research to a simple behavioral risk inventory, we faced the issue of where to draw the boundaries in defining the behavioral domain that would be encom-

passed by the concept of sex. This was particularly crucial in defining sexual activity that would lead to the enumeration of a set of sex partners. There are a number of activities that commonly serve as markers for sex and the status of sex partner, especially intercourse and orgasm. While we certainly wanted to include these events and their extent in given relationships and events, we also felt that using them to define and ask about sexual activity might exclude transactions or partners that should be included. Since the common meaning and uses of the term *intercourse* involve the idea of the intromission of a penis, intercourse in that sense as a defining act would at the very least exclude a sexual relationship between two women. There are also many events that we would call sexual that may not involve orgasm on the part of either or both partners.

Another major issue is what sort of language is appropriate in asking questions about sex. It seemed obvious that one should avoid highly technical language because it is unlikely to be understood by many people. One tempting alternative is to use colloquial language and even slang since that is the only language that some people ever use in discussing sexual matters. There is even some evidence that one can improve reporting somewhat by allowing respondents to select their own preferred terminology (Blair et al., 1977; Bradburn et al., 1978; Bradburn and Sudman, 1983). Slang and other forms of colloquial speech, however, are likely to be problematic in several ways. First, the use of slang can produce a tone in the interview that is counterproductive because it downplays the distinctiveness of the interviewing situation itself. An essential goal in survey interviewing, especially on sensitive topics like sex, is to create a neutral, nonjudgmental, and confiding atmosphere and to maintain a certain professional distance between the interviewer and the respondent. A key advantage that the interviewer has in initiating a topic for discussion is being a stranger or an outsider who is highly unlikely to come in contact with the respondent again. It is not intended that a longer-term bond between the interviewer and the respondent be formed, whether as an advice giver or a counselor or as a potential sex partner.[3]

The second major shortcoming of slang is that it is highly variable across class and education levels, ages, regions, and other social groupings. It changes meanings rapidly and is often imprecise. Our solution was to seek the simplest possible language—standard English—that was neither colloquial nor highly technical. For example, we chose to use the term *oral sex* rather than the slang *blow job* and *eating pussy* or the precise technical but unfamiliar terms *fellatio* and *cunnilingus*. Whenever possible, we provided definitions when terms were first introduced in a questionnaire—that is, we tried to train our respondents to speak about sex in our terms. Many terms that seemed clear to us may not, of course, be universally understood; for example, terms like *vaginal* or *heterosexual* are not understood very well by substantial portions of the population. Coming up with simple and direct speech was quite a challenge because most of the people working on the questionnaire were highly educated, with strong inclinations toward the circumlocutions and indirections of middle-class discourse on sexual themes. Detailed reactions from field interviewers and managers and extensive pilot testing with a broad cross section of recruited subjects helped minimize these language problems.

On Privacy, Confidentiality, and Security

Issues of respondent confidentiality are at the very heart of survey research. The willingness of respondents to report their views and experiences fully and honestly depends on the rationale offered for why the study is important and on the assurance that the information provided will be treated as confidential. We offered respondents a strong rationale for the study, our interviewers made great efforts to conduct the interview in a manner that protected respondents' privacy, and we went to great lengths to honor the assurances that the information would be treated confidentially. The subject matter of the NHSLS makes the issues of confidentiality especially salient and problematic because there are so many easily imagined ways in which information voluntarily disclosed in an interview might be useful to interested parties in civil and criminal cases involving wrongful

harm, divorce proceedings, criminal behavior, or similar matters.

NOTES

1. This proposition, however, is not true when speaking of nonrandom samples. The original Kinsey research was based on large samples. As noted earlier, surveys reported in magazines are often based on very large numbers of returned questionnaires. But, since these were not representative probability samples, there is no necessary relation between the increase in the sample size and how well the sample estimates population parameters. In general, nonprobability samples describe only the sample drawn and cannot be generalized to any larger population.

2. We ruled out the idea of a mail survey because its response rate is likely to be very much lower than any other mode of interviewing (see Bradburn, Sudman, et al., 1979).

3. Interviewers are not there to give information or to correct misinformation. But such information is often requested in the course of an interview. Interviewers are given training in how to avoid answering such questions (other than clarification of the meaning of particular questions). They are not themselves experts on the topics raised and often do not know the correct answers to questions. For this reason, and also in case emotionally freighted issues for the respondent were raised during the interview process, we provided interviewers with a list of toll-free phone numbers for a variety of professional sex- and health-related referral services (e.g., the National AIDS Hotline, an STD hotline, the National Child Abuse Hotline, a domestic violence hotline, and the phone number of a national rape and sexual assault organization able to provide local referrals).

REFERENCES

Blair, Ellen, Seymour Sudman, Norman M. Bradburn, and Carol Stacking. 1977. "How to Ask Questions About Drinking and Sex: Response Efforts in Measuring Consumer Behavior." *Journal of Marketing Research* 14: 316–321.

Bradburn, Norman M., and Seymour Sudman. 1983. *Asking Questions: A Practical Guide to Questionnaire Design.* San Francisco: Jossey-Bass.

Bradburn, Norman M., Seymour Sudman, Ed Blair, and Carol Stacking. 1978. "Question Threat and Response Bias." *Public Opinion Quarterly* 42: 221–234.

Groves, Robert M. 1989. *Survey Errors and Survey Costs.* New York: Wiley.

Kish, Leslie. 1965. *Survey Sampling.* New York: Wiley.

Doing It Differently: Women's and Men's Estimates of Their Number of Lifetime Sexual Partners

Mindy Stombler and Dawn M. Baunach

A recent national survey of sexual practices found that men report having more than three times as many sexual partners as women over the course of their lifetimes (Davis, Smith, and Marsden 2006). Theoretically, heterosexual men's and women's estimates should be the same because for each new female partner a man adds to his "lifetime account," a woman adds a new male partner to her "lifetime account." The discrepancy between women's and men's estimates remains even when researchers define *sexual partners* very specifically and account for possible sampling problems (such as undersampling female sex workers). What explains the gender gap in claims people make about numbers of sexual partners?

One possibility is that women and men misrepresent their number of lifetime sexual partners to others. Our society tends to hold a double standard regarding the sexual behavior of women and men. Men who have a great deal of sexual experience generally are not subject to shame (and in some circles their behavior is lauded), whereas women with "too many" lifetime partners are stigmatized. Attempts to give interviewers the socially approved response (called *social desirability bias*) may lead women to intentionally underreport their numbers or men to inflate theirs.

Another possibility is that people misrepresent their behaviors to themselves. If women discount partners for whom they feel little affection, such partners could slip from memory, thereby erroneously lowering their reported lifetime account. Women and men also rely on different estimation strategies. Women tend to enumerate (actually count), whereas men tend to give rough estimates (Brown and Sinclair 1999; Weiderman 1997). Weiderman (1997) notes a clear tendency for men reporting larger numbers of lifetime sexual partners to choose numbers that end in 0 or 5. Men prefer "round" numbers rather than exact counts.

The number of sexual partners that women and men report does become more similar when researchers shorten the time frame for estimation to the past year or the past five years (see the table below), indicating that both men and women estimate more accurately over a shorter period of time. In addition, the cultural meaning that we attach to our accumulated lifetime number of sexual partners carries more weight than, say, the number of partners we might have in a year. Taking the double standard into account, it might be in women's best interest to carefully consider their number of lifetime sexual partners and in men's best interest to round up.

| | MEAN NUMBER OF SEXUAL PARTNERS | | RATIO |
	Women (n = 1,325)	*Men (n = 1,005)*	*Men: Women*
Last Five Years	1.94	4.02	2.07
Last Year	.88	1.58	1.80

Source: General Social Survey, 2006.

REFERENCES
Brown, Norman R., and Robert C. Sinclair. 1999. "Estimating number of lifetime sexual partners: Men and women do it differently." *The Journal of Sex Research*, 36: 3 (292–297).

Davis, James Allan, Tom W. Smith, and Peter V. Marsden. 2006. *General Social Surveys, 1972–2006: Cumulative Codebook.* Chicago: National Opinion Research Center.

Weiderman, Michael. 1997. "The truth must be in here somewhere: Examining the gender discrepancy in self-reported lifetime number of partners." *The Journal of Sex Research*, 34: 4 (375–386).

Racism and Research: The Case of the Tuskegee Syphilis Study

Allan M. Brandt

In 1932 the U.S. Public Health Service (USPHS) initiated an experiment in Macon County, Alabama, to determine the natural course of untreated, latent syphilis in black males. The test comprised 400 syphilitic men, as well as 200 uninfected men who served as controls. The first published report of the study appeared in 1936 with subsequent papers issued every four to six years, through the 1960s. When penicillin became widely available by the early 1950s as the preferred treatment for syphilis, the men did not receive therapy. In fact on several occasions, the USPHS actually sought to prevent treatment. Moreover, a committee at the federally operated Center for Disease Control decided in 1969 that the study should be continued. Only in 1972, when accounts of the study first appeared in the national press, did the Department of Health, Education, and Welfare halt the experiment. At that time seventy-four of the test subjects were still alive; at least twenty-eight, but perhaps more than 100 had died directly from advanced syphilitic lesions. In August 1972, HEW appointed an investigatory panel which issued a report the following year. The panel found the study to have been "ethically unjustified," and argued that penicillin should have been provided to the men.

This article attempts to place the Tuskegee Study in a historical context and to assess its ethical implications. Despite the media attention which the study received, the HEW *Final Report,* and the criticism expressed by several professional organizations, the experiment has been largely misunderstood. The most basic questions of *how* the study was undertaken in the first place and *why* it continued for forty years were never addressed by the HEW investigation. Moreover, the panel misconstrued the nature of the experiment, failing to consult important documents available at the National Archives which bear significantly on its ethical assessment. Only by examining the specific ways in which values are engaged in scientific research can the study be understood.

Racism and Medical Opinion

A brief review of the prevailing scientific thought regarding race and heredity in the early twentieth century is fundamental for an understanding of the Tuskegee Study. By the turn of the century, Darwinism had provided a new rationale for American racism. Essentially primitive peoples, it was argued, could not be assimilated into a complex, white civilization. Scientists speculated that in the struggle for survival the Negro in America was doomed. Particularly prone to disease, vice, and crime, black Americans could not be helped by education or philanthropy. Social [Darwinists] analyzed census data to predict the virtual extinction of the Negro in the twentieth century, for they believed the Negro race in America was in the throes of a degenerative evolutionary process.

The medical profession supported these findings of late nineteenth- and early twentieth-century anthropologists, ethnologists, and biologists. Physicians studying the effects of emancipation on health concluded almost universally that freedom had caused the mental, moral, and physical deterioration of the

From "Racism and Research: The Case of the Tuskegee Syphilis Study" by Allan Brandt. © The Hastings Center. Reprinted by permission. This article originally appeared in the Hastings Center Report, Vol. 8, No. 6 (1978).

black population. They substantiated this argument by citing examples in the comparative anatomy of the black and white races. As Dr. W. T. English wrote: "A careful inspection reveals the body of the negro a mass of minor defects and imperfections from the crown of the head to the soles of the feet. . . ." Cranial structures, wide nasal apertures, receding chins, projecting jaws, all typed the Negro as the lowest species in the Darwinian hierarchy.

Interest in racial differences centered on the sexual nature of blacks. The Negro, doctors explained, possessed an excessive sexual desire, which threatened the very foundations of white society. As one physician noted in the *Journal of the American Medical Association,* "The negro springs from a southern race, and as such his sexual appetite is strong; all of his environments stimulate this appetite, and as a general rule his emotional type of religion certainly does not decrease it." Doctors reported a complete lack of morality on the part of blacks:

> Virtue in the negro race is like angels' visits—few and far between. In a practice of sixteen years I have never examined a virgin negro over fourteen years of age.

A particularly ominous feature of this overzealous sexuality, doctors argued, was the black males' desire for white women. "A perversion from which most races are exempt," wrote Dr. English, "prompts the negro's inclination towards white women, whereas other races incline towards females of their own." Though English estimated the "gray matter of the negro brain" to be at least a thousand years behind that of the white races, his genital organs were overdeveloped. As Dr. William Lee Howard noted:

> The attacks on defenseless white women are evidences of racial instincts that are about as amenable to ethical culture as is the inherent odor of the race. . . . When education will reduce the size of the negro's penis as well as bring about the sensitiveness of the terminal fibers which exist in the Caucasian, then will it also be able to prevent the African's birth-right to sexual madness and excess.

One southern medical journal proposed "Castration Instead of Lynching," as retribution for black sexual crimes. "An impressive trial by a ghost-like kuklux

klan [sic] and a "ghost" physician or surgeon to perform the operation would make it an event the "patient" would never forget," noted the editorial.

According to these physicians, lust and immorality, unstable families, and reversion to barbaric tendencies made blacks especially prone to venereal diseases. One doctor estimated that over 50 percent of all Negroes over the age of twenty-five were syphilitic. Virtually free of disease as slaves, they were now overwhelmed by it, according to informed medical opinion. Moreover, doctors believed that treatment for venereal disease among blacks was impossible, particularly because in its latent stage the symptoms of syphilis become quiescent. As Dr. Thomas W. Murrell wrote:

> They come for treatment at the beginning and at the end. When there are visible manifestations or when harried by pain, they readily come, for as a race they are not averse to physic; but tell them not, though they look well and feel well, that they are still diseased. Here ignorance rates science a fool. . . .

Even the best educated black, according to Murrell, could not be convinced to seek treatment for syphilis. Venereal disease, according to some doctors, threatened the future of the race. The medical profession attributed the low birth rate among blacks to the high prevalence of venereal disease which caused stillbirths and miscarriages. Moreover, the high rates of syphilis were thought to lead to increased insanity and crime. One doctor writing at the turn of the century estimated that the number of insane Negroes had increased thirteen-fold since the end of the Civil War. Dr. Murrell's conclusion echoed the most informed anthropological and ethnological data:

> So the scourge sweeps among them. Those that are treated are only half cured, and the effort to assimilate a complex civilization driving their diseased minds until the results are criminal records. Perhaps here, in conjunction with tuberculosis, will be the end of the negro problem. Disease will accomplish what man cannot do.

This particular configuration of ideas formed the core of medical opinion concerning blacks, sex, and disease in the early twentieth century. Doctors generally discounted socioeconomic explanations of the state of black health, arguing that better medical care could not alter the evolutionary scheme. These assumptions provide the backdrop for examining the Tuskegee Syphilis Study.

The Origins of the Experiment

In 1929, under a grant from the Julius Rosenwald Fund, the USPHS conducted studies in the rural South to determine the prevalence of syphilis among blacks and explore possibilities for mass treatment. The USPHS found Macon County, Alabama, in which the town of Tuskegee is located to have the highest syphilis rate of the six counties surveyed. The Rosenwald Study concluded that mass treatment could be successfully implemented among rural blacks. Although it is doubtful that the necessary funds would have been allocated even in the best economic conditions, after the economy collapsed in 1929, the findings were ignored. It is, however, ironic that the Tuskegee Study came to be based on findings of the Rosenwald Study that demonstrated the possibilities of mass treatment.

Three years later, in 1932, Dr. Taliaferro Clark, Chief of the USPHS Venereal Disease Division and author of the Rosenwald Study report, decided that conditions in Macon County merited renewed attention. Clark believed the high prevalence of syphilis offered an "unusual opportunity" for observation. From its inception, the USPHS regarded the Tuskegee Study as a classic "study in nature,"[1] rather than an experiment. As long as syphilis was so prevalent in Macon and most of the blacks went untreated throughout life, it seemed only natural to Clark that it would be valuable to observe the consequences. He described it as a "ready-made situation." Surgeon General H. S. Cumming wrote to R. R. Moton, Director of the Tuskegee Institute:

The recent syphilis control demonstration carried out in Macon County, with the financial assistance of the Julius Rosenwald Fund, revealed the presence of an unusually high rate in this county and, what is more remarkable, the fact that 99 per cent of this group was entirely without previous treatment. This combination, together with the expected cooperation of your hospital, offers an unparalleled opportunity for carrying on this piece of scientific research which probably cannot be duplicated anywhere else in the world.

Although no formal protocol appears to have been written, several letters of Clark and Cumming suggest what the USPHS hoped to find. Clark indicated that it would be important to see how disease affected the daily lives of the men:

The results of these studies of case records suggest the desirability of making a further study of the effect of untreated syphilis on the human economy among people now living and engaged in their daily pursuits.

It also seems that the USPHS believed the experiment might demonstrate that antisyphilitic treatment was unnecessary. As Cumming noted: "It is expected the results of this study may have a marked bearing on the treatment, or conversely the non-necessity of treatment, of cases of latent syphilis.". . .

Selecting the Subjects

Clark sent Dr. Raymond Vonderlehr to Tuskegee in September 1932 to assemble a sample of men with latent syphilis for the experiment. The basic design of the study called for the selection of syphilitic black males between the ages of twenty-five and sixty, a thorough physical examination including x-rays, and finally, a spinal tap to determine the incidence of neuro-syphilis. They had no intention of providing any treatment for the infected men. The USPHS originally scheduled the whole experiment to last six months; it seemed to be both a simple and inexpensive project.

The task of collecting the sample, however, proved to be more difficult than the USPHS had supposed. Vonderlehr canvassed the largely illiterate, poverty-stricken population of sharecroppers and tenant farmers in search of test subjects. If his circulars requested only men over twenty-five to attend his clinics, none would appear, suspecting he was conducting draft physicals. Therefore, he was forced to test large numbers of women and men who did not fit the experiment's specifications. This involved considerable expense since the USPHS had promised the Macon County Board of Health that it would treat those who were infected, but not included in the study. Clark wrote to Vonderlehr about the situation: "It never once occurred to me that we would be called upon to treat a large part of the county as return for the privilege of making this study. . . . I am anxious to keep the expenditures for treatment down to the lowest possible point because it is the one item of expenditure in connection with the study most difficult to defend despite our knowledge of the need therefor." Vonderlehr responded: "If we could find from 100 to 200 cases . . . we would not have to do another Wassermann on useless individuals. . . . "

Significantly, the attempt to develop the sample contradicted the prediction the USPHS had made initially regarding the prevalence of the disease in Macon County. Overall rates of syphilis fell well below expectations; as opposed to the USPHS projection of 35 percent, 20 percent of those tested were actually diseased. Moreover, those who had sought and received previous treatment far exceeded the expectations of the USPHS. Clark noted in a letter to Vonderlehr:

> *I find your report of March 6th quite interesting but regret the necessity for Wassermanning [sic] . . . such a large number of individuals in order to uncover this relatively limited number of untreated cases.*

Further difficulties arose in enlisting the subjects to participate in the experiment, to be "Wassermanned," and to return for a subsequent series of examinations. Vonderlehr found that only the offer of treatment elicited the cooperation of the men. They were told they were ill and were promised free care. Offered therapy, they became willing subjects. The USPHS did not tell the men that they were participants in an experiment; on the contrary, the subjects believed they were being treated for "bad blood"— the rural South's colloquialism for syphilis. They thought they were participating in a public health demonstration similar to the one that had been conducted by the Julius Rosenwald Fund in Tuskegee several years earlier. In the end, the men were so eager for medical care that the number of defaulters in the experiment proved to be insignificant.

To preserve the subjects' interest, Vonderlehr gave most of the men mercurial ointment, a noneffective drug, while some of the younger men apparently received inadequate dosages of neoarsphenamine. This required Vonderlehr to write frequently to Clark requesting supplies. He feared the experiment would fail if the men were not offered treatment. . . .

The readiness of the test subjects to participate of course contradicted the notion that blacks would not seek or continue therapy.

The final procedure of the experiment was to be a spinal tap to test for evidence of neuro-syphilis. The USPHS presented this purely diagnostic exam, which often entails considerable pain and complications, to the men as a "special treatment." Clark explained to Moore:

> *We have not yet commenced the spinal punctures. This operation will be deferred to the last in order not to unduly disturb our field work by any adverse reports by the patients subjected to spinal puncture because of some disagreeable sensations following this procedure. These negroes are very ignorant and easily influenced by things that would be of minor significance in a more intelligent group.*

The letter to the subjects announcing the spinal tap read:

> *Some time ago you were given a thorough examination and since that time we hope you have gotten a great deal of treatment for bad blood. You will now be given your last chance to get a second examination. This examination is a very special one and after it is finished you will be given a special treatment if it is believed you are in a condition to stand it. . . .*
>
> *REMEMBER THIS IS YOUR LAST CHANCE FOR SPECIAL FREE TREATMENT. BE SURE TO MEET THE NURSE.*

The HEW investigation did not uncover this crucial fact: the men participated in the study under the guise of treatment.

Despite the fact that their assumption regarding prevalence and black attitudes toward treatment had proved wrong, the USPHS decided in the summer of 1933 to continue the study. Once again, it seemed only "natural" to pursue the research since the sample already existed, and with a depressed economy, the cost of treatment appeared prohibitive—although there is no indication it was ever considered. Vonderlehr first suggested extending the study in letters to Clark and Wenger:

At the end of this project we shall have a considerable number of cases presenting various complications of syphilis, who have received only mercury and may still be considered untreated in the modern sense of therapy. Should these cases be followed over a period of from five to ten years many interesting facts could be learned regarding the course and complications of untreated syphilis.

"As I see it," responded Wenger, "we have no further interest in these patients *until they die.*" Apparently, the physicians engaged in the experiment believed that only autopsies could scientifically confirm the findings of the study.

Bringing the men to autopsy required the USPHS to devise a further series of deceptions and inducements. Wenger warned Vonderlehr that the men must not realize that they would be autopsied:

There is one danger in the latter plan and that is if the colored population become aware that accepting free hospital care means a post-mortem, every darkey will leave Macon County and it will hurt [Dr. Eugene] Dibble's hospital.

The USPHS offered several inducements to maintain contact and to procure the continued cooperation of the men. Eunice Rivers, a black nurse, was hired to follow their health and to secure approval for autopsies. She gave the men non-effective medicines— "spring tonic" and aspirin—as well as transportation and hot meals on the days of their examinations. More important, Nurse Rivers provided continuity to the project over the entire forty-year period. By supplying "medicinals," the USPHS was able to continue to deceive the participants, who believed that they were receiving therapy from the government doctors. Deceit was integral to the study. When the test subjects complained about spinal taps one doctor wrote:

They simply do not like spinal punctures. A few of those who were tapped are enthusiastic over the results but to most, the suggestion causes violent shaking of the head; others claim they were robbed of their procreative powers (regardless of the fact that I claim it stimulates them).

Letters to the subjects announcing an impending USPHS visit to Tuskegee explained: "[The doctor] wants to make a special examination to find out how you have been feeling and whether the treatment has improved your health." In fact, after the first six months of the study, the USPHS had furnished no treatment whatsoever.

Finally, because it proved difficult to persuade the men to come to the hospital when they became severely ill, the USPHS promised to cover their burial expenses. The Milbank Memorial Fund provided approximately $50 per man for this purpose beginning in 1935. This was a particularly strong inducement as funeral rites constituted an important component of the cultural life of rural blacks. One report of the study concluded, "Without this suasion it would, we believe, have been impossible to secure the cooperation of the group and their families."

Reports of the study's findings, which appeared regularly in the medical press beginning in 1936, consistently cited the ravages of untreated syphilis. The first paper, read at the 1936 American Medical Association annual meeting, found "that syphilis in this period [latency] tends to greatly increase the frequency of manifestations of cardiovascular disease." Only 16 percent of the subjects gave no sign of morbidity as opposed to 61 percent of the controls. Ten years later, a report noted coldly, "The fact that nearly twice as large a proportion of the syphilitic individuals as of the control group has died is a very striking one." Life expectancy, concluded the doctors, is reduced by about 20 percent.

A 1955 article found that slightly more than 30 percent of the test group autopsied had died *directly* from advanced syphilitic lesions of either the cardiovascular or the central nervous system. Another published account stated, "Review of those still living reveals that an appreciable number have late complications of syphilis which probably will result, for some at least, in contributing materially to the ultimate cause of death." In 1950, Dr. Wenger had concluded, "We now know, where we could only surmise before, that we have contributed to their ailments and shortened their lives." As black physician Vernal Cave, a member of the HEW panel, later wrote, "They proved a point, then proved a point, then proved a point."

During the forty years of the experiment the USPHS had sought on several occasions to ensure that the subjects did not receive treatment from other sources. To this end, Vonderlehr met with groups of local black doctors in 1934, to ask their cooperation in not treating the men. Lists of subjects were distributed to Macon County physicians along with letters requesting them to refer these men back to the USPHS if they sought care. The USPHS warned the Alabama Health Department not to treat the test subjects when they took a mobile VD unit into Tuskegee in the early 1940s. In 1941, the Army drafted several subjects and told them to begin antisyphilitic treatment immediately. The USPHS supplied the draft board with a list of 256 names they desired to have excluded from treatment, and the board complied.

In spite of these efforts, by the early 1950s many of the men had secured some treatment on their own. By 1952, almost 30 percent of the test subjects had received some penicillin, although only 7.5 percent had received what could be considered adequate doses. Vonderlehr wrote to one of the participating physicians, "I hope that the availability of antibiotics has not interfered too much with this project." A report published in 1955 considered whether the treatment that some of the men had obtained had "defeated" the study. The article attempted to explain the relatively low exposure to penicillin in an age of antibiotics, suggesting as a reason: "the stoicism of these men as a group; they still regard hospitals and medicines with suspicion and prefer an occasional dose of time-honored herbs or tonics to modern drugs." The authors failed to note that the men believed they already were under the care of the government doctors and thus saw no need to seek treatment elsewhere. Any treatment which the men might have received, concluded the report, had been insufficient to compromise the experiment.

When the USPHS evaluated the status of the study in the 1960s they continued to rationalize the racial aspects of the experiment. For example, the minutes of a 1965 meeting at the Center for Disease Control recorded:

> *Racial issue was mentioned briefly. Will not affect the study. Any questions can be handled by saying these people were at the point that therapy would no longer help them. They are getting better medical care than they would under any other circumstances.*

A group of physicians met again at the CDC in 1969 to decide whether or not to terminate the study. Although one doctor argued that the study should be stopped and the men treated, the consensus was to continue. Dr. J. Lawton Smith remarked, "You will never have another study like this; take advantage of it." A memo prepared by Dr. James B. Lucas, Assistant Chief of the Venereal Disease Branch, stated: "Nothing learned will prevent, find, or cure a single case of infectious syphilis or bring us closer to our basic mission of controlling venereal disease in the United States." He concluded, however, that the study should be continued "along its present lines." When the first accounts of the experiment appeared in the national press in July 1972, data were still being collected and autopsies performed.

The HEW Final Report

HEW finally formed the Tuskegee Syphilis Study Ad Hoc Advisory Panel on August 28, 1972, in response to criticism that the press descriptions of the experiment had triggered. The panel, composed of nine members, five of them black, concentrated on two issues. First, was the study justified in 1932 and had the men given their informed consent? Second, should penicillin have been provided when it became available in the early 1950s? The panel was also charged with determining if the study should be terminated and assessing current policies regarding experimentation with human subjects. The group issued their report in June 1973.

By focusing on the issues of penicillin therapy and informed consent, the *Final Report* and the investigation betrayed a basic misunderstanding of the experiment's purposes and design. The HEW report implied that the failure to provide penicillin constituted the study's major ethical misjudgment; implicit was the assumption that no adequate therapy existed prior to penicillin. Nonetheless medical authorities firmly believed in the efficacy of arsenotherapy for treating syphilis at the time of the experiment's inception in 1932. The panel further failed to recognize that the entire study had been predicated on nontreatment. Provision of effective medication would have violated the rationale of the experiment—to study the natural course of the disease until death. On several occasions, in fact, the USPHS had prevented the men from receiving proper treatment. Indeed, there is no evidence that the USPHS ever considered providing penicillin.

The other focus of the *Final Report*—informed consent—also served to obscure the historical facts of the experiment. In light of the deceptions and exploitations which the experiment perpetrated, it is an understatement to declare, as the *Report* did, that the experiment was "ethically unjustified," because it failed to obtain informed consent from the subjects. The *Final Report's* statement, "Submitting voluntarily is not informed consent," indicated that the panel believed that the men had volunteered *for the experiment.* The records in the National Archives make clear that the men did not submit voluntarily to an experiment; they were told and they believed that they were getting free treatment from expert government doctors for a serious disease. The failure of the HEW *Final Report* to expose this critical fact—that the USPHS lied to the subjects—calls into question the thoroughness and credibility of their investigation.

Failure to place the study in a historical context also made it impossible for the investigation to deal with the essentially racist nature of the experiment. The panel treated the study as an aberration, well-intentioned but misguided. Moreover, concern that the *Final Report* might be viewed as a critique of human experimentation in general seems to have severely limited the scope of the inquiry. The *Final Report* is quick to remind the reader on two occasions: "The position of the Panel must not be construed to be a general repudiation of scientific research with human subjects." The *Report* assures us that a better designed experiment could have been justified:

> It is possible that a scientific study in 1932 of untreated syphilis, properly conceived with a clear protocol and conducted with suitable subjects who fully understood the implications of their involvement, might have been justified in the pre-penicillin era. This is especially true when one considers the uncertain nature of the results of treatment of late latent syphilis and the highly toxic nature of therapeutic agents then available.

This statement is questionable in view of the proven dangers of untreated syphilis known in 1932.

Since the publication of the HEW *Final Report,* a defense of the Tuskegee Study has emerged. These arguments, most clearly articulated by Dr. R. H. Kampmeier in the *Southern Medical Journal,* center on the limited knowledge of effective therapy for latent syphilis when the experiment began. Kampmeier argues that by 1950, penicillin would have been of no value for these men. Others have suggested that the men were fortunate to have been spared the highly toxic treatments of the earlier period. Moreover, even these contemporary defenses assume that the men never would have been treated anyway. As Dr. Charles Barnett of Stanford University wrote in 1974, "The lack of treatment was not contrived by the USPHS but was an established fact of which they proposed to take advantage." Several doctors who participated in the study continued to justify the experiment. Dr. J. R. Heller, who on one occasion had referred to the test subjects as the "Ethiopian population," told reporters in 1972:

> I don't see why they should be shocked or horrified. There was no racial side to this. It just happened to be in a black community. I feel this was a perfectly straightforward study, perfectly ethical, with controls. Part of our mission as physicians is to find out what happens to individuals with disease and without disease.

These apologies, as well as the HEW *Final Report,* ignore many of the essential ethical issues which the study poses. The Tuskegee Study reveals the persistence of beliefs within the medical profession about the nature of blacks, sex, and disease—beliefs that had tragic repercussions long after their alleged "scientific" bases were known to be incorrect. Most strikingly, the entire health of a community was jeopardized by leaving a communicable disease untreated. There can be little doubt that the Tuskegee researchers regarded their subjects as less than human. As a result, the ethical canons of experimenting on human subjects were completely disregarded.

The study also raises significant questions about professional self-regulation and scientific bureaucracy. Once the USPHS decided to extend the experiment in the summer of 1933, it was unlikely that the test would be halted short of the men's deaths. The experiment was widely reported for forty years without evoking any significant protest within the medical community. Nor did any bureaucratic mechanism exist within the government for the periodic reassessment of the Tuskegee experiment's ethics and scientific value. The USPHS sent physicians to Tuskegee every several years to check on the study's progress, but never subjected the morality or usefulness of the experiment to serious scrutiny. Only the press accounts of 1972 finally punctured the continued rationalizations of the USPHS and brought the study to an end. Even the HEW investigation was compromised by fear that it would be considered a threat to future human experimentation.

In retrospect the Tuskegee Study revealed more about the pathology of racism than it did about the pathology of syphilis; more about the nature of scientific inquiry than the nature of the disease process. The injustice committed by the experiment went well beyond the facts outlined in the press and the HEW *Final Report.* The degree of deception and damages have been seriously underestimated. As this history of the study suggests, the notion that science is a value-free discipline must be rejected. The need for greater vigilance in assessing the specific ways in which social values and attitudes affect professional behavior is clearly indicated.

NOTES

1. In 1865, Claude Bernard, the famous French physiologist, outlined the distinction between a "study in nature" and experimentation. A study in nature required simple observation, an essentially passive act, while experimentation demanded intervention which altered the original condition. The Tuskegee Study was thus clearly not a study in nature. The very act of diagnosis altered the original conditions. "It is on this very possibility of acting or not acting on a body," wrote Bernard, "that the distinction will exclusively rest between sciences called sciences of observation and sciences called experimental."

EDITOR'S NOTE

On May 16, 1997, President Bill Clinton apologized to the participants in the Tuskegee Study. He acknowledged that the U.S. government had done "something that was wrong—deeply, profoundly, and morally wrong."

Sexuality and Social Theorizing

Denise Donnelly, Elisabeth O. Burgess,
and Wendy Simonds[1]

Introduction

Many of us don't think of sexuality and theorizing as two things that go together, but theories can be very useful in helping us understand sexuality. Theories are simply ways of viewing and organizing the world and of making sense of what happens. Sociologists use theories to understand, explain, predict, question, or change social behaviors and trends. Theories about sex vary dramatically across time and place, and reflect the social and moral thinking of the day.

In addition to helping us understand the history and context of sexuality, theories also provide explanations for sexual attitudes and behavior: why there are differences in how people think about sex or how people behave sexually, how societal norms and laws regarding sex arise and are enforced, and how and why change takes place. Sexuality is important in most of our lives, yet many people don't understand it, are uncomfortable talking about it, and don't know where to go to get their questions answered. Sexuality theories can provide explanations and answers, but no one theory is appropriate for addressing all questions and concerns about sexuality. Thus, we are especially interested in the ways in which sociological theories help us understand the social construction and social control of sexuality.[2]

We'll begin by reviewing what some early thinkers (called sexologists) had to say about sexuality. Then, we'll examine the utility of sociological theory for studying sex, and end with some current theories, questions, and challenges. As you'll see, theories about sexuality are constantly offered, challenged, revised, and rejected. Throughout the reading, we'll be asking "What relevance does theory have for helping us understand the social construction and control of sexuality?"

Laying the Groundwork: The Sexologists

We're probably all familiar with Sigmund Freud, sometimes called "The Father of Modern Psychoanalysis," who felt that sexuality was a driving force in human behavior (Freud [1938] 1995), but there were other important early thinkers as well. For example, at the end of the nineteenth century (prior to most of Freud's work), Richard von Krafft-Ebing ([1871] 1965) cataloged types of sexual deviance, and later on, Havelock Ellis (1942) pondered the differences between normal and abnormal sexuality and appealed for tolerance of a wide array of sexual behaviors.[3]

Freud, the most theoretical of the early sexologists, based his observations on the people he treated, who were mainly wealthy Victorians. Freud believed that sex was a basic drive that motivated most people, and that sexuality was formed early in life. He theorized that, as toddlers, young boys fell in love with their mothers (the "Oedipus complex") and that young girls fell in love with their fathers (the "Electra complex"). He suggested that each wanted the same-sex parent out of the way. He introduced the terms "penis envy" and "castration anxiety," arguing that young girls envied boys' penises, and that young boys were anxious about keeping theirs, for they feared that their fathers would castrate them to win the rivalry over their mothers. According to Freud, in order to resolve these issues and become healthy heterosexual adults, children had to learn to identify with their same-sex parents. Freud also made many controversial statements about women's sexuality, including his supposition that women have two types of orgasms (clitoral and vaginal), with the vaginal being superior, and that recollections of sexual abuse are simply the fantasies of neurotic young women who fantasize about their fathers and crave excitement in their lives.[4]

Some of the ideas of Freud and his contemporaries may seem very outdated by today's standards, but these sexologists still influence the ways in which scholars think about sexuality and the ways therapists treat sexual problems. The work of these early sexologists resisted the social control of sexuality by challenging state and religious definitions of normal and abnormal sexual practices and contributed to the social construction of sexuality by openly discussing sexual variability, the origins of homosexuality, and the relation of women to sexuality. While their perspectives may lack the social and historical sophistication of later theories, their ideas have persisted through the years.

In the United States during the mid-twentieth century, the study of sexuality shifted from theorizing to research. Using models drawn from the biomedical sciences, researchers such as Alfred Kinsey (Kinsey, Pomeroy, and Martin 1948; Kinsey, Pomeroy, Martin, and Gebhard 1953) and William Masters and Virginia Johnson (1966; 1970), provided an empirical base for testing the ideas and theories of earlier scholars. Although they were primarily researchers, their findings have influenced the ways in which Americans think about sexuality today.[5]

The Contributions of Twentieth-Century Sex Researchers to Sexual Theorizing

Alfred Kinsey is probably the best known of the twentieth-century sex researchers. His curiosity about human sexuality led him and his team to survey 12,000 Americans and to write *Sexual Behavior in the Human Male* (1948) and *Sexual Behavior in the Human Female* (1953). His books created a huge controversy and were even banned in some areas. This negative publicity increased the visibility of his work, exposing his ideas on sexuality to hundreds of thousands of average Americans. He challenged the conservative ways in which sexuality was constructed by documenting the range of sexual practices among Americans and discussing numerous taboo topics including female orgasm, masturbation, and homosexuality. Moreover, Kinsey argued that "normal and ab-

normal" and "good and bad" were labels created to control sexuality. He illustrated the wide diversity in sexual expression in the United States and noted the discrepancies between public standards for sex and private expressions of sexuality. The research of Kinsey and his peers raised questions about the theories of Freud and the early sexologists, and laid the groundwork for more recent theories such as postmodernism and queer theory, which we discuss later.[6]

From the mid-sixties to the mid-eighties, Masters and Johnson (1966; 1970) further challenged social constructions of sexuality by observing volunteers engaging in masturbation and coitus in their labs, while hooked up to monitors. Although their samples were not representative, their data and theories on human sexual response are still used by clinicians today.[7] For example, they demonstrated that the clitoris is the seat of the orgasm (in direct contradiction to Freud's earlier theorizing) and documented similarities and differences in male and female sexual response. Masters and Johnson also argued that couples' sexual problems were not caused by neuroses or disorders, but instead resulted from poor communication, marital conflict, or a lack of information. Their findings greatly influence the ways in which both scholars and the general public think about and theorize sexuality today by questioning prior theories and providing an empirical basis for many of our later theories.

Sociological Theories and Sexuality

Our discussion of theorizing about sexuality will focus on differences between "traditional" sociological theories and those—such as feminism and postmodernism—that emerged in reaction to these perspectives. Traditional sociological theories include structural functionalism, conflict theory, symbolic interactionism, and exchange theory. Although most classical sociological theory (written in late nineteenth and early twentieth centuries) did not explicitly address issues of sexuality, those who wrote on the subject usually did so within the context of marriage, emphasizing the social control of intimate relations. For instance, Marx ([1888] 1978) and Durkheim ([1897] 1979) analyzed the regulatory practices of marriage, while Max Weber called sexual love "the greatest irrational force of life" ([1915] 1958: 343). Weber saw religious forces as seeking to diminish love's power through regulation—again, referring to marriage. Other lesser-known theorists of this era, such as Marianne Weber, Charlotte Perkins Gilman, and Anna Julia Cooper, examined marriage as a gendered form of social control over sexuality.

Structural-functionalism, or systems theory,[8] strongly influenced social thought and policy in the post-World War II years. According to structural functionalists, society was organized into parts (or structures), each of which had a specific function to fill. When each was performing its function, the system would run smoothly. In families, for example, men were supposed to be wage earners and administrators, while women were supposed to be housewives, mothers, and caretakers. The structural functionalists argued that things worked best when each person knew her or his role and stuck to it (Parsons and Bales 1955). Regarding sexuality, they argued that men were "naturally" the aggressors, and were always ready and willing to have sex, while women were "naturally" more reticent and submissive, and had to be coaxed into sexual situations. Men continually pushed the boundaries, while women constantly enforced them. Women had "pure" natures, while men were more experienced sexually, and expected to be "worldly." According to structural functionalism, the system functioned best only when heterosexuals married, had children together, and raised them in two-parent families. From this traditional perspective, sociologists viewed homosexuals and others who did not fit into the nuclear family model as "dysfunctional" or "deviant." Examples include Albert J. Reiss's writing on street hustlers (1961), and Laud Humphreys's ethnographic exploration of sex in public restrooms (1970).

Structural-functionalism and deviance theories dominated sociology and influenced the social construction and control of sexuality into the 1970s. Social movements—for civil rights, sexual rights, women's rights, and gay/lesbian rights—led to questioning of the status quo, and eventually raised questions that led to theoretical change. What about men who weren't sexually aggressive or promiscuous, and

women who were? Were they really "dysfunctional" as the theory suggested, or were they simply part of a normal range of behaviors (as Kinsey's analysis indicated)? Was the system really running smoothly, or was it simply supporting the largely white, male, middle-class status quo? Where did single mothers, people of color, gays and lesbians, and those who enjoyed nonmarital sex fit in? Because of these questions, sociological theorizing about sexuality took several turns.

Conflict theorists (Buss and Malamuth 1996; Eisenstein 1978) argued that the systems surrounding marriage, family, and sexuality were not running smoothly at all, and that the norms of the day were oppressive to many people. Anyone who fell outside a very narrow range of behaviors was penalized and often ostracized as well. At best, these nonconformists were considered deviants, and punished with social stigma. At worst, they were arrested, jailed, institutionalized, or even killed because of their sexuality. In many states, this social control extended to laws against having sex with someone of the same sex, someone of a different racial or ethnic group, or someone to whom you were not married (D'Emilio and Freedman 1997).

Conflict theorists also asked questions about sexual rights and freedoms and examined how arrangements of the day (such as marriage) were benefiting some people (men), while hurting others (women) (Eisenstein 1978). They questioned the status quo and pushed for social change, arguing that as long as sexual practices were conducted between consenting adults, they shouldn't be considered dysfunctional, abnormal, or illegal; and that current sexual arrangements were in need of examination and, potentially, elimination. Contemporary applications of conflict theory are also evident in global and political economy approaches to sexuality (Altman 2001) that examine "how economic and political transformations have shaped sexual experiences, identities, politics, and desires" (Gamson and Moon 2004: 56).[9]

While conflict theorists challenged norms, systems, and stability, they often neglected any examination of the interpersonal level. Indeed, not all people wanted to be "freed" from conformity and stability, and some stayed in sexual relationships because of love and commitment, despite elements of institutional oppression (Simmel 1964). And while the conflict theorists explained change very well, they sometimes lacked explanations for stability. On the whole, conflict theories did a better job of explaining structural and systematic sexual oppression than they did of explaining individual behaviors. In contrast, symbolic-interaction and exchange theories—which we review next—emphasized the individual level of analysis.

Symbolic interaction theorists were less concerned with social structures and institutions, and more concerned with how individuals interacted sexually (Plummer 2003). These theorists examined the meanings attached to sexual behaviors and how behavior changes based on interactions with others (Goffman 1959). Symbolic interaction helps explain the social construction of sexuality—why people interpret others as they do, why misunderstandings occur, and how individuals form opinions about themselves as sexual beings. However, because the symbolic interaction theorists focus on microlevel interactions (between dyads or small groups), they tend to underestimate the role of social institutions and structures in controlling sexual behavior.

One theory that emerged from the symbolic interactionist perspective was social constructionist theory (Berger and Luckmann 1966). Proponents of this perspective argued that through interaction, individuals create shared meanings that are reinforced by norms, laws, and social institutions. Social construction theory helps us understand why people label some components of sexuality "right" and others "wrong," and why there is so much pressure to conform to sexual norms (Plummer 2003).

Another direction taken by symbolic interaction theory was sexual scripting theory (Gagnon and Simon 1973; 1987). These theories, based on an acting analogy (Goffman 1959), suggest that humans have scripts for sexual behavior that tell us who to be attracted to, how to behave sexually, and even how to feel about our sexual experiences. Sexual scripts exist on the social level, the interpersonal level, and the individual level. Cultural scripts are contained in the broader norms of a society and define what is legal or illegal, permissible or not permissible. Interpersonal

scripts tell us how to act with partners and how to respond to certain situations, while individual (or intrapsychic) scripts influence how we view ourselves and evaluate our sexuality.

Taking a slightly different perspective, exchange theorists argued that sexuality was in many ways a transaction or trade. Unlike the structural functionalists who focused on maintaining stability, the exchange theorists posited that relationships are only stable so long as people feel they are getting a fair deal (Thibault and Kelly 1967). If the balance tilts too far in their partner's favor, they may withhold sex, have an affair, begin using pornography, or even withdraw from the relationship entirely in an attempt to tip the balance of power back in their own favor (Donnelly and Burgess 2006). One early exchange theorist was Waller (1938), who suggested that in a heterosexual relationship, women exchange their looks, youth, and sexuality for a man's status, money, and security. The couple bargain with each other—and the one who has the least interest in continuing the relationship has the upper hand. Much popular wisdom contained in "self-help" books (such as Robin Norwood's 1990 book, *Women Who Love Too Much*) is still based on these notions.

Critics of exchange theory point out that like conflict theory, it strips the role of love, emotion, and sacrifice from understanding romantic and sexual relationships. Exchange theorists assume that individuals act in rational, utilitarian ways (attempting to maximize rewards and minimize costs), and that they are always motivated by self-interest. Moreover, they assume that value can be attached to all aspects of a relationship, and that people actually measure the quantity and quality of sexual interactions. A final critique of this theory is that, like symbolic interaction, it pays little attention to the larger social context in which exchanges take place.

In sum, traditional sociological theories tended not to place sexuality at the center of their theorizing, but rather addressed sexuality within the context of families, couples, relationships, and deviance. While these theories may help us understand the social control and construction of sexuality, they tend to describe, rather than question, existing social arrangements. Challenges to these ways of thinking about sex often came from other disciplines and from countries outside the United States.

Challenges and Alternatives to Traditional Sociological Theorizing

With the emerging sexual freedom of the 1970s, sexual research and theorizing became less taboo. Although it was still marginal to most of mainstream sociology, some theorists began to place sexuality at the center of their inquiries. These new perspectives challenged sociologists' silence with regard to issues of sex and sexuality and pushed the boundaries of traditional social sciences. Although they posed a wide variety of questions, we focus on those asked by three groups: feminists, postmodernists, and queer theorists. These theorists draw on ideas and explanations from a variety of disciplines across the humanities and social sciences. While it is impossible to address all the contributions of these three theoretical perspectives, we will introduce a few of the key themes for understanding the social construction and control of sexuality. First, we'll examine the challenges posed by feminist theories.

By feminist theory, we mean a variety of (often competing) perspectives, or feminisms.[10] At the heart of these perspectives is the idea that patriarchal (male-run) societies are oppressive to women, and that women must have both freedom and choice if they are to contribute to society and become fully participatory adults. Feminists identify "the personal as political," meaning that the troubles women face as a result of sexism are not simply individual private issues (such as an abusive male partner), but rather part of a larger public problem (domestic violence) best solved through political change (Weedon 1999). Three key contributions of feminist theory include feminist discussions of the gendered nature of sexuality; heterosexuality as a form of social control; and the notion of intersectionality.

First, feminists question the ways in which sexuality has been constructed, and note that these constructions favor men in a variety of ways. At the intersection of gender and sexuality, for example, they point out that men control women's sexuality by defining it in masculine and heterosexual terms (Rich 1980). All women are presumed to be heterosexual, men are presumed to be the initiators of sex, and the sex act itself is defined in terms of male performance (Tiefer 1995). Traditionally, "sex" meant that a man inserted his penis into a woman's vagina, and other forms of sexuality were seen as "not quite sex." When the man ejaculated, "sex" was over. Moreover, feminists questioned the usefulness of the very categories we use for sex and gender, illustrating that gender itself is a social construction and that using biological essentialist arguments[11] about "women's natural place" is also a means of social control (Elshtain 1981; Epstein 1988).

Feminist theory about sexual violence, such as rape and sexual harassment, explored how violence is a tool of social control by men, and pointed out that restrictions on abortion, birth control, and sexual expression were oppressive to women and denied them choice (Brownmiller 1976; Kelly 1988; Russell 1998). Some feminists (Dworkin 1987; 1989; MacKinnon 1989) theorized that because of the power differentials between men and women, all heterosexual sex had an element of force behind it. They saw heterosexual sex and rape as existing on a continuum, with the common element being male control of female sexuality. In contrast, a coalition of sex-positive feminist theorists campaigned for the recognition of women's agency in sexuality, and began to organize groups such as dancers and prostitutes into professional unions and organizations (see Nagle 1997).

A second strand of theory emerged from the work of lesbian feminists who theorized that the institution of heterosexuality and restrictive notions about "normal" sexuality limit what counts as sexual. Adrienne Rich (1980) argued that heterosexuality is central to patriarchy and, thus, not a choice but rather a form of social control of women. Moreover, she theorized that there is not a clear distinction between lesbians and heterosexual women but instead argued women's experiences can be understood on a lesbian continuum. This continuum describes the range of women's experiences with other women, including identifying with them, bonding with them, and sharing sexual experiences.

As feminism promised to give "voice" to women, many asked "whose voice?" For example, Gayle

S. Rubin (1984) argued that feminist theories of sex must account for the oppression of all sexual minorities, not just women. She posited that the state and other social institutions reinforce an erotic hierarchy that defines "normal" sexual behavior, emphasizing heterosexual, marital, monogamous, vanilla sex,[12] and demonizing other sexual practices. Not always popular with mainstream feminists, these theories drew on many of the same ideas as postmodern and queer theories that we discuss later.

Marginalized groups of women, such as women of color, poor women, women with little or no formal education, and women from non-Western nations, argued that the majority of feminist theorizing ignored their standpoints and assumed that white middle class women's experiences represented everyone (hooks 1981; 1984; Lorde 1984; Moraga and Anzaldúa 1983; Mohanty, Russo, and Torres 1991). For example, African American feminist theorists (sometimes called "womanists") argued that while white women may suffer because of their gender status, the color of their skin gives them privilege to be protected sexually and depicted as virginal or pure. In contrast, black women have been seen as sexually accessible and their history has been one of rape and exploitation by both white and black men (Davis 1983; Hill Collins 2004; hooks 1984; Wyatt 1997).

Initially, critics of white feminist thought focused primarily on racial differences, arguing that the standpoint of African American women was ignored in feminist theorizing, but eventually sociologists such as Patricia Hill Collins (1991; 2004) pointed out that intersectionality—the ways in which a *variety* of statuses and characteristics intersect—needed to be taken into account when thinking about female sexuality. Intersectionality theory contended that not only does one's race affect the ways sexuality is experienced and perceived, but so does one's class, age, ability, sexual orientation, and nation. Essentially, there can be no single perspective on black women's sexuality, poor women's sexuality, or the sexuality of women in non-Western nations.

While feminists critiqued the gender order, postmodernists questioned the usefulness of grand theories to explain the social world and wondered whether it was meaningful to search for universal, all-encompassing truths about society.[13] They argued that there was no "right" way of seeing or describing the world, and that no two people shared the same reality. They posited that ideas about right and wrong and good and bad had no inherent meanings, but were simply social constructions that had emerged from modern society. They questioned the concept of modernity itself, and wondered if modern society, with its emphasis on science, positivism, and progress, was really beneficial to humanity.

Moreover, the postmodernists recommended that we not take the social order at face value, but instead work to deconstruct existing structures (such as language, law, or sexuality) by examining their various components (such as history, discourse, and interaction). In contrast to earlier theorists, postmodernists emphasized that the power to control and construct sexuality does not lie with one central entity (such as government), but is constantly negotiated by a variety of ways of talking or thinking about a topic, coming from a variety of groups (such as religion, activist movements, or the legal system).

Applying these ideas to sexuality, postmodern theorists argued that sexuality has been produced in socially and culturally specific ways. Michel Foucault (1978) examined the construction of sexuality by analyzing a variety of discourses and sexual practices. In the *History of Sexuality,* he rejected "the repressive hypothesis" that blamed the Victorians for the shame and guilt that people in many Western societies felt about sexuality, and instead examined the influence of the scientific discourse on these constructions of sexuality. He rejected the dominant belief that modern industrial societies, such as the Victorians, "ushered in an age of increased sexual repression" (49). Rather, he argued that multiple sources of power (for instance, religion, medicine, education, law) dominated our understandings of sexuality and sought to manipulate sexual attitudes and practices according to their own (often very profitable) agendas. He went on to say that scientific disciplines, such as psychology and medicine, control sexualities, but while they inform us, they also dominate us. Individuals internalize the norms set by scientists, and monitor their own behavior in an effort to conform to the scientific constructions of sexuality.

Postmodern perspectives have appealed to a wide variety of scholars, and some feminist postmodernists felt that feminism and postmodernism could be complementary. For example, both groups questioned concepts such as objectivity, universality, and reason, claiming that what is considered objective in a given culture at a particular time in history reflects the interests of those in power. Moreover, both feminists and postmodernists have worked to avoid the tendency to construct theories based on the experiences of privileged groups of women (Flax 1990; Nicholson 1990).

Although the deconstruction of modern ideas about sexuality is a useful theoretical exercise, critics maintain that it is more of an intellectual exercise than an explanatory framework. They note that while postmodernism critiques and deconstructs modernity and objectivity, it suggests no alternatives and provides no agenda for social change. While postmodern perspectives have gained some acceptance in sociology (Mirchandani 2005), the larger contribution of this perspective has likely been its influence on queer theory.

Drawing on the energy of the gay and AIDS movements of the 1980s and the academic perspectives of postmodernism, feminism, and gay and lesbian studies, queer theorists (Seidman 1996; Stein and Plummer 1996; Sullivan 2003) challenged the identities seen as normative and natural in our culture, insisting they were instead, "arbitrary, unstable, and exclusionary" (Seidman 1996: 11).[14] For example, queer theorists argued that sexuality is structured as a "binary opposition" (meaning that our culture has constructed heterosexuality and homosexuality as opposites), with heterosexuality given the label of good and homosexuality the label of bad or immoral. These labels are then used for social control, as evidenced by the passage of laws against same-sex marriage and adoption. Additionally, focusing on some identities and not others silences or excludes the other experiences. Part of the queer theorists' project is to continually question and deconstruct current beliefs about sexual, gender, and sex identities. By questioning binary social categories such as male or female, masculine or feminine, and heterosexual or homosexual, queer theorists demonstrate how these sexual categories and identities are actually fluid and

not necessarily natural. Rather, they argue that current categorizations of sexuality, gender, and sex are tied to power, and that some institutions and groups have more power to define what is sexually acceptable than others do. Queer theorists believe transsexuals, the intersexed, and those immersed in drag culture are boundary crossers, challenging rigid categories of sex, gender, and sexual identity (c.f. Butler 1990; Currah 2001).

When they speak of "queering" sexuality, queer theorists are not talking about making everyone gay or lesbian. Instead, they are questioning (or "queering") existing sexual arrangements that privilege heterosexual, coupled, monogamous adults. This queering reveals the biases our ideas are constructed on, and demonstrates how certain groups benefit from current constructions of sexual identities. In general, queer theorists argue that it is important to separate the sexual behaviors that people participate in from the moral judgments of those with power in a society.

For all its contributions to sexuality theory, queer theory does not appeal to everyone and some scholars question its usefulness for sociological inquiry. For instance, Namaste (1996) and Green (2002) question the explanatory power of queer theory and argue that their focus on the abstract ignores the social realities of real sexual beings. Furthermore, Gamson and Moon (2004) debate the value of queer theory for addressing traditional sociological problems such as systems of oppression, and suggest that contributions of social theories, such as intersectionality and political economy, are more useful for sociological research.

Feminists, postmodernists, and queer theorists challenge the boundaries on which much of sexual theorizing takes place, while also building on some aspects of earlier theories and ideas. The common thread among the theories presented in this section is that current arrangements are socially constructed and must be questioned. They posit that old ideas about sexuality may not be useful or relevant, and indeed act as a form of social control—silencing, excluding, and even harming groups of people.

As you might imagine, these theories are confusing to many students, and aren't necessarily that popular with "mainstream" society. Most people take existing structures (institutions, norms, and conventions) surrounding sexuality at face value, and rarely think to question (or deconstruct) them. People assume that existing patterns of behavior exist because that is what works best for society, and that to go against these rules, beliefs, and norms would be to invite chaos. Even when people violate these widely held prohibitions, such as the ones against premarital sex or adultery, they often still feel that as a whole, these rules benefit society. Moreover, these norms are upheld and enforced by social institutions such as religion, family, education, the legal system, and the economy. To question them feels—and may well be—dangerous.

Can Theory Help Us Understand Sexuality?

So, back to our original question—can social theories help us understand sexuality? We think so. Although each of the theories presented here is based on a different assumption and operates at a different level, they all provide us with ways of understanding the sexual behavior of individuals and groups, the development of social norms, and the underpinnings of social policies regarding sexuality. These theories invite us to ask interesting questions and to push the boundaries of our knowledge. The most liberatory theories, in our view, are the ones that reject notions of normalcy, resist moralizing, and question biological or essentialistic views of sexual behavior. Rather than providing answers, such theories delight in muddying the waters and raising new questions. Will we ever have a theory that explains all aspects of sexuality? Probably not. But by theorizing about sex, we broaden our understandings of ourselves and of the world around us. And, it very well may be that the most interesting parts of sexuality are in the questions, not in the answers!

NOTES

1. The authors would like to thank Mindy Stombler and Dawn M. Baunach, who were integral in defining the structure and content of this article and providing valuable perspectives on theory and sexuality and essential editorial advice. In addition, we acknowledge the assistance of Elisabeth Sheff, Elroi Windsor, Elizabeth Cavalier, Amy Palder, Robert Adelman, and Chet Meeks, who read earlier versions of this article and participated in numerous theoretical debates on sexuality.

2. By social construction we mean the process by which people create ideas, meanings, categories, and values through interaction. Social control refers to a system of rewards and punishments intended to control or influence others' behavior.

3. The field of sexology and the scientific study of sexuality emerged in the late nineteenth century. Sigmund Freud, Richard von Krafft-Ebing, and others were integral to the development of sex research and our understanding of sexuality. These scholars and others in the late nineteenth and early twentieth centuries were trained in the medical profession and, thus, approached issues of sexuality using a medical model. The ideas of these early sex researchers contributed to our theoretical understanding of sexuality in more ways than we can discuss in this essay. For more on the history of sex research see Bullough (1995), and for classic writings of this era see Bland and Doan (1998) and Barreca (1995).

4. The latter was a revision to his earlier theory. Initially, he believed that sexual abuse was real, but because of his colleagues' disbelief, Freud revised his theory and marked his patient's recollections of child sexual abuse down to "fantasy."

5. For more on Kinsey, see Reading 7 in this book. For additional information on sex research during the twentieth century see Ericksen (1999) and Bullough (1995).

6. During the first half of the twentieth century several other researchers conducted sex surveys of specific populations, including Katherine Bement Davis's research on female sexuality (1929) and Evelyn Hooker's work on male sexuality (1956; 1957; 1958), and expanded our understanding of sexual variation and the social construction of sexual deviance.

7. Teifer (1995) provides a thorough critique of Masters and Johnson's sample and their findings about the human sexual response cycle.

8. For many scholars, the distinction between these theories is the level of analysis. Structural-functionalism addresses the structural or societal level of analysis and systems theory explores the microlevel issues of families and individuals.

9. See also Altman (2004).

10. Additionally, the term *feminism* covers theory, belief systems, and political action. Many times it is difficult to distinguish among them because the boundaries between academic perspectives and practices are not always clear.

11. Biological essentialism argues that women are naturally different from men because of their ability to become

mothers, and that these differences mean that women are better suited to certain roles and men to others.

12. *Vanilla sex* refers to standard heterosexual practices, and excludes such variations as sadomasochism (BDSM), fetish, and kink.

13. The ideas of postmodernism and poststructuralism are intertwined and trace their roots to French philosophers such as Foucault (1978) and Lyotard (1984). As with feminism, there are many variations and conflicting perspectives on these theories. In this article we are focusing on postmodernism.

14. Like the feminists and postmodernists, queer theorists do not always agree or even acknowledge the same texts. In addition to Foucault, discussed previously, Judith Butler (1990; 1993) and Eve Sedgwick (1990) produced works widely acknowledged to be central to queer theory. In this article we emphasize sociological interpretations of queer theory.

REFERENCES

Altman, Dennis. 2001. *Global Sex.* Chicago: University of Chicago Press.

Altman, Dennis, 2004. "Sexuality and Globalization," *Sexuality Research & Social Policy.* 1:63–68.

Barreca, Regina, ed. 1995. *Desire and Imagination: Classic Essays in Sexuality.* New York: Meridian.

Berger, Peter L. and Thomas Luckmann. 1966. *The Social Construction of Reality.* New York: Doubleday.

Bland, Lucy and Laura Doan, ed. 1998. *Sexuality Uncensored: The Documents of Sexual Science.* Chicago: University of Chicago Press.

Brownmiller, Susan. 1976. *Against Our Will: Men, Women, and Rape.* New York: Bantam Books.

Bullough, Vern. 1995. *Science in the Bedroom: A History of Sex Research.* New York: Basic Books.

Buss, David M. and Neil Malamuth. 1996. *Sex, Power, Conflict: Evolutionary and Feminist Perspectives.* London: Oxford University Press.

Butler, Judith. 1990. *Gender Trouble: Feminism and the Subversion of Identity.* New York: Routledge.

Butler, Judith. 1993. *Bodies that Matter: On the Discursive Limits of "Sex."* New York: Routledge.

Currah, Paisley. 2001. "Queer Theory, Lesbian and Gay Rights, and Transsexual Marriages." In *Sexual Identities, Queer Politics* (pp. 178–199), edited by Mark Blasius. Princeton, NJ: Princeton University Press.

Davis, Angela Y. 1983. *Women, Race, & Class.* New York: Vintage Books.

Davis, Katherine Bement. 1929. *Factors in the Sex Life of Twenty-Two Hundred Women.* New York: Harper.

D'Emilio, John D. and Estelle B. Freedman. 1997. *Intimate Matters, Second Edition.* Chicago: University of Chicago Press.

Donnelly, Denise and Elisabeth O. Burgess. 2006. Involuntary Celibacy in Long-Term Heterosexual Relationships. Unpublished Manuscript.

Durkheim, Emile. [1897] 1979. *Suicide: A Study in Sociology.* New York: Free Press.

Dworkin, Andrea. 1987. *Intercourse.* New York: Free Press.

Dworkin, Andrea. 1989. *Pornography: Men Possessing Women.* New York: Dutton.

Eisenstein, Zillah. 1978. "Developing a Theory of Capitalist Patriarchy and Socialist Feminism." *Capitalist Patriarchy and the Case for Socialist Feminism,* by Zillah Eisenstein. New York: Monthly Review Press.

Ellis, Havelock. 1942. *Studies in the Psychology of Sex, Volumes 1 and 2.* New York: Random House.

Elshtain, Jean Bethke. 1981. *Public Man, Private Woman.* Princeton, NJ: Princeton University Press.

Epstein, Cynthia Fuchs. 1988. *Deceptive Distinctions: Sex, Gender, and the Social Order.* New Haven, CT: Yale University Press and Russell Sage Foundation.

Ericksen, Julia A. 1999. *Kiss and Tell: Surveying Sex in the Twentieth Century.* Cambridge, MA: Harvard University Press.

Flax, Jane. 1990. "Postmodern and Gender Relations in Feminist Theory." In *Feminism/Postmodernism* (pp. 39–63), edited by Linda J. Nicholson. New York: Routledge.

Foucault, Michel. 1978. *The History of Sexuality: An Introduction, Volume 1.* New York: Vintage Books.

Freud, Sigmund. [1938] 1995. *The Basic Writings of Sigmund Freud.* Translated by A. A. Brill. New York: Modern Library.

Gagnon, John H. and William Simon. 1973. *Sexual Conduct: The Social Sources of Human Sexuality.* Chicago: Aldine.

Gagnon, John H. and William Simon. 1987. "The Sexual Scripting of Oral Genital Contacts." *Archives of Sexual Behavior* 16:1–25.

Gamson, Joshua and Dawne Moon. 2004. "The Sociology of Sexualities: Queer and Beyond." *Annual Review of Sociology* 30:47–64.

Goffman, Irving. 1959. *The Presentation of Self in Everyday Life.* New York: Anchor.

Green, Adam Isaiah. 2002. "Gay but not Queer: Toward a Post-Queer Study of Sexuality." *Theory and Society* 31:521–545.

Hill Collins, Patricia. 1991. *Black Feminist Thought: Knowledge, Consciousness, and the Politics of Empowerment.* New York: Routledge.

Hill Collins, Patricia. 2004. *Black Sexual Politics: African Americans, Gender, and the New Racism.* New York: Routledge.

Hooker, Evelyn. 1956. "A Preliminary Analysis of Group Behavior of Homosexuals." *Journal of Psychology* 42:217–225.

Hooker, Evelyn. 1957. "The Adjustment of the Male Overt Homosexual." *Journal of Projective Techniques* 21:18–31.

Hooker, Evelyn. 1958. "Male Homosexuality in the Rorschach." *Journal of Projective Techniques* 23:278–281.

hooks, bell. 1981. *Ain't I a Woman: Black Women and Feminism.* Boston: South End Press.

hooks, bell. 1984. *Feminist Theory: From Margin to Center.* Boston: South End Press.

Humphreys, Laud. 1970. *Tearoom Trade: Impersonal Sex in Public Places.* Chicago: Aldine.

Kelly, Liz. 1988. *Surviving Sexual Violence.* Boston: Cambridge University Press.

Kinsey, Alfred C., Wardell B. Pomeroy, and Clyde E. Martin. 1948. *Sexual Behavior and the Human Male.* Philadelphia: Saunders.

Kinsey, Alfred C., Wardell B. Pomeroy, Clyde E. Martin, and Paul H. Gebhard. 1953. *Sexual Behavior and the Human Female.* Philadelphia: Saunders.

Krafft-Ebing, Richard von. [1871] 1965. *Psychopathia Sexualis: A Medico-Forensic Study.* Translated by Harry E. Wedeck. New York: Putnam.

Lacan, Jacques. [1972–1973] 1998. *On Feminine Sexuality: The Limits of Love and Knowledge.* Translated by Bruce Fink. New York: Norton.

Lyotard, Jacques. [1979] 1984. *The Postmodern Condition: A Report on Knowledge.* Translated by G. Bennington and B. Massumi. Minneapolis: University of Minnesota Press.

Lorde, Audre. 1984. *Sister Outsider: Essays and Speeches.* Trumansburg, NY: Crossing Press.

MacKinnon, Catherine A. 1989. *Toward a Feminist Theory of the State.* Cambridge, MA: Harvard University Press.

Marx, Karl. [1888] 1978. "Manifesto of the Communist Party." In *The Marx-Engels Reader, Second Edition* (pp. 469–500), edited by Robert C. Tucker. New York: W. W. Norton.

Masters, William H. and Virginia Johnson. 1966. *Human Sexual Response.* Boston: Little, Brown.

Masters, William H. and Virginia Johnson. 1970. *Human Sexual Inadequacy.* Boston: Little, Brown.

Mirchandani, Rekha. 2005. "Postmodernism and Sociology: From Epistemological to Empirical." *Sociological Theory* 23:86–115.

Mohanty, Chandra Talpade, Ann Russo, and Lourdes Torres. 1991. *Third World Women and the Politics of Feminism.* Bloomington: Indiana University Press.

Moraga, Cheríe and Gloria Anzaldúa. 1983. *This Bridge Called My Back: Writings by Radical Women of Color.* New York: Kitchen Table/Women of Color Press.

Nagle, Jill, ed. 1997. *Whores and Other Feminists.* London: Routledge.

Namaste, Ki. 1996. "'Tragic Misreadings': Queer Theory's Erasure of Transgender Subjectivity." In *Queer Studies: A Lesbian, Gay, Bisexual, and Transgender Anthology* (pp. 183–203), edited by Brett Beemyn and Mickey Eliason. New York: New York University Press.

Nicholson, Linda J., ed. 1990. *Feminism/Postmodernism.* New York: Routledge.

Norwood, Robin. 1990. *Women Who Love Too Much.* New York: Pocket Books.

Parsons, Talcott and Robert F. Bales. 1955. *Family, Socialization and the Interaction Process.* Glencoe, IL: Free Press.

Plummer, Ken. 2003. "Queers, Bodies, and Postmodern Sexualities: A Note on Revisiting the 'Sexual' in Symbolic Interaction." *Qualitative Sociology* 26:515–530.

Reiss, Albert J., Jr. 1961. "The Social Integration of Queers and Peers." *Social Problems* 9:102–120.

Rich, Adrienne. 1980. "Compulsory Heterosexuality and Lesbian Existence." *Signs: Journal of Women in Culture and Society* 5:631–660.

Rubin, Gayle S. 1984. "Thinking Sex: Notes for a Radical Theory of the Politics of Sexuality." In *Pleasure and Danger: Exploring Female Sexuality* (pp. 267–319), edited by Carole S. Vance. New York: Routledge.

Russell, Diana. 1998. *Dangerous Relationships: Pornography, Misogyny, and Rape.* Thousand Oaks, CA: Sage.

Sedgwick, Eve. 1990. *Epistemology of the Closet.* Berkeley: University of California Press.

Seidman, Steven, ed. 1996. *Queer Theory/Sociology.* Malden, MA: Blackwell Publishers.

Simmel, Georg. 1964. *Conflict and the Web of Group Affiliations.* New York: Free Press.

Stein, Arlene and Ken Plummer. 1996. "'I Can't Even Think Straight': 'Queer' Theory and the Missing Sexual Revolution in Sociology." In *Queer Theory/Sociology* (pp. 129–144), edited by Steven Seidman. Oxford, UK: Blackwell.

Sullivan, Nikki. 2003. *A Critical Introduction to Queer Theory.* New York: New York University Press.

Thibaut, J. and H. Kelley. 1967. *The Social Psychology of Groups.* New York: John Wiley & Sons.

Tiefer, Leonore. 1995. *Sex Is Not a Natural Act and Other Essays.* Boulder, CO: Westview Press.

Waller, Willard Walter. 1938. *The Family: A Dynamic Interpretation.* New York: Dryden.

Weber, Max. [1915] 1958. "Religious Rejections of the World and Their Directions." In *From Max Weber: Essays in Sociology* (pp. 323–362), edited by H. H. Gerth and C. Wright Mills. New York: Oxford University Press.

Weedon, Chris. 1999. *Feminism, Theory, and the Politics of Difference.* Oxford, UK: Blackwell.

Wyatt, Gail Elizabeth. 1997. *Stolen Women: Reclaiming Our Sexuality, Taking Back Our Lives.* New York: John Wiley and Sons.

Sexing Up the Subject: Methodological Nuances in Researching the Female Sex Industry

Teela Sanders

Despite the interdisciplinary accounts of the sex industry, apart from some reflective revelations (for instance by Hart, 1998; Hubbard, 1999a; Maher, 2000; Melrose, 2002; O'Connell Davidson, 1998; O'Neill, 1996; Sharpe, 2000; Shaver, 2005) researchers have been reluctant to report on the methodological demands of this topic. These pieces of work highlight the importance of reflexivity in the researcher process—a research account that is aware that the researcher is of the world being studied and therefore should be included in the process of analysis.... This article explores the methodological challenges that question existing procedural boundaries and push the parameters of the qualitative method as the subject becomes increasingly sexual. Drawing on my own ethnography in the indoor prostitution markets (see Sanders, 2005a), this article reflects mostly on research into female adult consensual prostitution but will refer to other aspects of the non-contact sexual services such as pornography and erotic dancing.

Stumbling at the First Hurdle: Ethics Committees

Much of what has been written about the ethics of fieldwork and the sex industry focuses on what happens in the field. Yet increasingly, one of the first stumbling blocks for the researcher (especially students) is gaining approval for the project from the internal institution's ethics committee. With these

regulatory bodies becoming an increasing part of funding applications and university bureaucracies, having a vague plan and heading into the field is becoming less of an option. Anecdotally it can be said that ethics committees have treated the sex industry as a problematic area of inquiry, which can sometimes result in projects failing at this initial stage. An example from [Mattley] (1997) demonstrates how funding research into prostitution continues to be stifled by stigma and excluded by research councils. This [section] teases out three familiar areas of suspicion that are charged at those wanting to research sex work: the methods employed, the setting of the fieldwork and concerns for the reputation of the institution.

Methodological concerns are often raised at ethics committees when the method of inquiry is based on an ethnographic style that places informality at the heart of the data collection. Invariably this method requires lengthy periods of observation, interviews that can take the form of informal conversations and other methods that are unorthodox in the minds of positivist thinkers. As a result committees can query the validity of the methods, whether enough information will be collected and the quality of the data. For instance, in situations where interviews cannot be taped, data collection relies on fieldnotes and memory, which raises questions about how information can be accurately recorded. In addition, as Shaver (2005) documents, researchers in the sex industry are constantly struggling with the unknown size and boundaries of the population, leading to queries of sample representation. Covert methods have also been adopted in sex work research highlighting the difficulties of informing all parties that are being observed, often for the sake of access and at the request of sex workers and managers. Ethics committees are

From "Sexing Up the Subject: Methodological Nuances in Researching the Female Sex Industry" by Teela Sanders, *Sexualities* 9(4), 449–468. © 2006 Sage Publications.

usually hostile to covert methods as they can appear unethical and potentially dangerous for the researcher. Stereotypes and misunderstandings about the research setting exacerbate these generic concerns about the methods often employed when studying the sex work field.

The setting, whether it is a "red light district," crack house or illegal brothel, is often the focus of concern raised by ethics committees. Is this the correct environment for research to be conducted, or for a student to be initiated into the research culture? Questions of danger always arise because of stereotypes that link prostitution to criminality, especially drug-related crimes. Associations between HIV, drug-injecting sex workers, vicious and violent male pimps and the sex work setting all surface with the prospects of researching the sex industry. Fuelled by assumptions about the type of people who organize and work in the sex industry, as well as the men that buy sex, the researcher is expected to take extra precautions when assessing participants and fieldsites. In addition, the routines that the researcher will be expected to engage in usually entail long hours in fairly unknown or secluded locations, often late at night, and sometimes alone.

The danger that the researcher is exposed to is a central concern of officials, but this can sometimes be a disguise for more pressing anxieties about the reputation of the institution. As a postgraduate student my own research (which was originally based on an internet survey of the sex work community) was scrutinized by the senior officials in the university before it was vetoed as an unacceptable area of inquiry and methodological design (see Sanders, 2005b). Behind this decision was apprehension related to preserving the reputation of the university and concerns about media headlines that linked students to the seedy underworld environment in the name of completing a doctorate. . . .

However, there are solutions to these ethical trials. The plethora of successful work in this field, using both ethnographic and more mainstream methods, is a testament to the appropriateness of the sex industry as a fieldsite. The general literature that explains the limitations of informed consent in all circumstances and the acceptability of covert inquiry within an ethical framework that prioritizes the anonymity of those

being studied, can be used to demonstrate the feasibility of the design. There are few horror stories reported (this does not mean that researchers have not experienced some difficult and vulnerable situations), and good quality accounts of ethnography explain the basic rules of engagement such as finding a gatekeeper that acts as a protector (Hart, 1998: 55; O'Connell Davidson and Layder, 1994). Therefore, it can be demonstrated that despite common conceptions, there are regulators (health workers, sauna owners, police, key informants) in the sex industry that researchers can align themselves with in order to stay out of trouble and learn the local scene.

In addition, researchers in this field can rely on the professional codes of practice promoted by the subject discipline that set out procedures, obligations and expectations of the research process (for example the British Sociological Association produces guidelines for its members). Often universities have their own codes of etiquette, which can include safety procedures when researchers are working alone or at night for instance. Basic safety checks such as never meeting people alone in private, always in a public place, letting a third party know of your whereabouts and checking in after the session has ended, are assurances that go a long way to maintaining safety (see Shaver, 2005: 302 for a thorough account of safety procedures for sex work researchers). The potential dangers and strong stereotypes associated with the sex industry are issues that researchers have to confront before the project gets off the ground. Although this means that research designs are perhaps over scrutinized and charged with queries that expect more insight from the novice researcher, this encourages the researcher to be reflective even at this initial stage. Thinking ahead to foreseeable problems, having a set of plan "B's" if the initial methods fail, and taking time out of the fieldwork to reassess are good practice in an intense and volatile environment.

Access and Acceptance into the Sex Industry

For the researcher, the legal status of prostitution and the actual environment are the key considerations when planning the access route. Prostitution is often located outside a legitimate legal framework or even where the sex industry is legitimate, there are always issues of stigma and deviancy to consider. The different environments that facilitate street and off street prostitution offer some peculiarities (for a lengthy discussion see Shaver, 2005). On the street, the environment is vulnerable, as women mainly work at night, in deserted and unlit industrial areas, in an economy that can be linked to other forms of acquisitive crime. Indoors, although not usually characterized by the violence and vulnerabilities of the street scene, the premises of illegal brothels may be well known but getting a foot in the door is a difficult prospect—especially if the researcher is a woman. Owners, managers and workers are suspicious of unknown inquirers, and women who enter the building are normally looking for work (i.e. competition) or are spying for the opposition. Rarely has it been reported that a researcher has introduced herself or himself to sex workers without a third party mediating the initial introductions.

To side-step these closed environments researchers use various gatekeepers to overcome initial hostilities. Some access routes have been outside the sex work environment. For example the criminal justice system (prisons, bail hostels, courts, probation service and so on) or sexual health and welfare services have traditionally been a successful introduction route to women and men involved in prostitution. Specific sex work outreach projects (see Cooper et al., 2001) have been the most prolific gatekeepers, as their established and trusted ties with street workers and indoor establishments provide researchers with the opportunity to prove their credibility. Hubbard (1999b: 233) explains four principles that must be demonstrated to outreach projects and sex workers to achieve success in the negotiation phase. First, the investigator must establish how the research will produce knowledge to help reduce stigma surrounding prostitution; second, that the researcher has an insight into the reality of prostitution and the circumstances in which sex is sold; third, a recognition that prostitution is a legitimate form of work; and fourth, a belief that health and safety risks should be minimized for sex workers. However, as Melrose (2002: 340) documents, securing access through sexual health projects

is not straightforward. This route can be met with refusal because of concerns that the research will demand too much time from the project, disagreement with the premise of the research or the worry that their clients are "over-researched" or exploited. . . .

Accessing Private and the Public Lives

Once access to sex establishments or sex workers has been achieved, researchers then negotiate whether the research will be conducted in either the working environment or in the private lives and spaces of the sex workers. Despite the difficulties of the prostitution environment, research is often conducted in the working spaces of the commercial sex exchange. By striking "research bargains" and "exchanges" that involve giving out condoms, sterile needle equipment and hot drinks on the street, researchers have been able to observe successfully how the street markets operate. . . . A combination of methods (usually a mixed approach that includes observations and interviews) appears to be a successful recipe for data collection. . . .

Entering the private worlds of women who are involved in activities that are largely disapproved of presented additional ethical issues. On the few occasions I was permitted into the private worlds of participants I would often be asked to collude with the secrecy stories that sex workers had constructed to hide their money-making activities. I would have to pretend I was a colleague from the office, or an acquaintance whilst I chatted to a participant's husband, or was invited to stay for tea with the children. An example of the role-playing that I describe in the next section shows how it is an essential tool in the field.

Making Sense of the Sexual Field

When actually doing research in the sex industry where the exchange of sexual services, bodily functions and flesh-to-flesh contact is the everyday trade, the reality of research cannot avoid these characteristics. Although there are similarities with other illicit economies, the setting of the sex industry is unique because the combination of studying sex and money in a illegal arena affects how the research is executed, the dilemmas for the researcher and the immediacy of making decisions in the "sexual" field. For those who are unaware, a typical sauna or brothel can be characterized by televisions showing hardcore pornography, pornographic magazines, sex toys, domination equipment, a menu of sexual services on offer, an explicit photographic gallery of the women who are available and other sex paraphernalia. This environment can be distasteful at best but is often violently shocking and disturbing.

The sexual subtext of the environment is impossible to escape as participants are in their work clothes (which usually consists of very little), buying into the fantasies that tempt customers to part with their cash (see Sanders, 2005c). The physical sexual environment is not the only sexualized element to the fieldwork setting. Men are constantly wandering into the premises and engaging in a set of negotiations with the receptionist (maid) and then (often in private) with the sex worker. Men linger in the communal lounge while they wait for a worker to finish her current client, idling the time away by flicking through a pornographic magazine or watching graphic images on the screen, before they are called to the shower room and finally the specifically chosen bedroom, until, 30 minutes later they come out the other side, £60 lighter. This routinization of the sexual negotiation is a process with which the observer becomes familiar (and perhaps desensitized) and after several sessions of data collection, the process of negotiating sexual services becomes part of the momentum of the fieldwork. . . .

My own experiences of being in the sexual field of the sauna and brothel involved two other methodological nuances that at the time became routinized yet had an intrinsic effect on the way in which information was collected, my role in this foreign arena and establishing rapport with participants. First, as my role in the sauna was overt to the sex workers but, at the request of the managers, the clients were unaware of my researcher status and I was often propositioned by interested customers. Men would assume I was another worker or a new member of the team and would make propositions and innuendo that had to be managed. Initially flustered, embarrassed and uncomfortable, I soon adopted strategies to deflect their requests: I

would either pretend I was "fully booked," a friend of a worker or a sexual health professional, switching between these roles depending on how confident I felt at the time and the amount of back up I had from those around me. Ultimately, role-playing became a necessity in the field, especially where a delicate "research bargain" existed that required keeping my researcher status anonymous to one party while others were aware of the investigation.

Second, the majority of the fieldwork in the indoor sex work venues was conducted amongst women who were semi-naked for most of the time. For instance, my interviews with Beryl, a 39-year-old mother of four who had worked in a range of sex markets for 20 years, took place in the 30-minute slot she allocated each day as her "preparation time" before she welcomed her first customer. In this time Beryl was showering, shaving, applying make-up, styling her hair, putting on lingerie and at the same time answering my questions. It became natural to see women naked as they changed from one outfit to another, were flitting between bathroom and bedroom or needed a hand squeezing into a particular costume. These situations were non-sexualized and non-erotic as the women conducted their behaviour in a professional matter-of-fact manner, relegating luxurious lingerie or kinky outfits to the function of a work uniform. Participants approached their work and ultimately the display of their bodies in an entirely pragmatic, de-sexualized and business-like manner with no sense of shame, embarrassment or vulnerability. Explaining their trade as a combination of physical, sexual and emotional labour, the role of the body and their sexuality was afforded different meanings in the context of a money-making economic exchange.

What Is Participant Observation in the Sex Industry?

The ethnographic method in the sex work arena brings into question what participation means, and whilst there are those that maintain "going native" jeopardizes the professional status of the researcher (Hart, 1998: 55), others have used complete participation as the key to the insider status. For example, Wahab (2003: 629) describes how she not only conducted observations in strip clubs but decided to engage in the sex work venue. Encouraged by her participants who insisted that to really understand the job it had to be lived, Wahab took part in a peep show as a dancer, immersing herself in the context of the culture. . . .

Like the familiar debates in qualitative social science inquiry (see Labaree, 2002), the insider–outsider dilemma is a point of negotiation, confusion and reflection for the researcher in the sex work setting. Rarely are researchers' identities clearly defined as only "information gatherers." In the spirit of transparency, researchers interested in sex work qualify their intentions and character which often means blurring the roles and boundaries that other types of research and methods have the luxury of maintaining. . . .

Pleasures and Dangers of the Research Process

One account of my fieldwork experience in the sex work setting could read as a list of uncomfortable moments, scary confrontations, mistakes that led to insults, embarrassments, treading on toes and appearing unprofessional and out of my depth. Another positive account could reflect the strong bonds and lasting friendships I built with key informants, idling time away putting the world to rights, and sharing our histories, hopes and expectations. This section will reflect on some of the contrasting experiences of dangers and pleasures when conducting research in the sex work environment, highlighting the complexity of the method and the necessity of investing oneself in the process.

The practical challenges of doing research in the field have been discussed in relation to dangerous fieldwork settings or sensitive topics of inquiry (Ferrell and Hamm, 1998; Lee, 1995; Sharpe, 2000). . . . In the sexual field, despite the advantages of collecting different types of live data when immersed in the working environment, there are inherent dangers for researchers who operate in illegal environments that are isolated. Several researchers describe how they have met with opposition from potential participants, other hustlers on the street and territorial pimps who

take issue with a researcher on their patch (see O'Neill, 1996). . . . Sometimes obvious risks are expected when working with populations at the margins of society, but, as I describe later, the emotional risks of such work are often unknown when the research is designed. Other hazards in the field make sex work a tricky subject for the well-intended researcher. Researchers have been mistaken for plain clothes police (see Barnard, 1992: 145; Sharpe, 2000: 366), journalists (Sanders, 2005b), or accused of spying for rival competitors (Lever and Dolnick, 2000)—all of which add extra hurdles to achieving safety, credibility and, of course, a sample! . . .

The Emotional Toil of Data Gathering

The emotional effort needed to research sex work is stark in both the pragmatics of the fieldwork and the efforts needed to dissect, reflect and understand the researcher's own position in a complex social activity. What Melrose (2002) calls the "labour pains" of researching sensitive areas like prostitution are often given little attention as the researcher is expected to apply emotional labour to manage the feelings of others as well as their own responses. Although not always the case, informal conversations and taped interviews with women who work in prostitution can involve the disclosure of disturbing and unpleasant data consisting of tales of exploitation, abuse, violence, desperation, drug use and hopelessness.

Melrose, like others (Miller, 1997; O'Connell Davidson and Layder, 1994: 216–7; Sharpe, 2000: 365), documents how stories provoke feelings of anger, rage and despair both in the data collection phase and again in the analysis stage. In a current project with men who buy sex from female sex workers, such feelings of anger and contempt have been a consequence of listening to the other side of the story. In a minority of cases, as interviewees have left my office I have felt pure rage at their misogynist attitudes and belief that if they buy the services of a sex worker then they can do as they please. It is difficult to understand or accept these experiences as research but maintaining a professional attitude and response to people who incite such negative feelings is the only reason why the project has not been shelved.

The dangers of the sexual field are not only related to the physical safety of the researcher as the emotional investment in the endeavour is significant and needs to be reflected upon and managed. At times the field relations with participants can prove to be very intense. To bridge the scepticism and doubts held by potential participants the researcher knowingly or unknowingly enters into a degree of self-disclosure. . . . Participants always wanted to know why I was interested in sex work and whether I could be tempted or indeed had the guts to sell sexual services for money. Such curiosity could not be ignored and a natural process of self-disclosure and identification became an integral part of how field relations were secured. I recall this process as natural rather than manipulative because it was not a chore to engage in in-depth conversation with the participants as I shared many experiences with them. Yet although disclosure brought me closer to the women, this self-investment also opened up vulnerabilities and concerns about keeping my private life protected from the demands of the fieldwork setting and the public academic eye. At the same time, having to do some personal soul searching also made me confront my stereotypes and prejudices about sexuality and lifestyles. Not something that is generally written into the research design.

The intensity of the research does not necessarily decrease as time lapses between the fieldwork and the safety of the academic corridors. In processes of self-reflection, what was experienced cannot be fully understood until the "after" phase of the data collection, writing up and dissemination (see Roberts and Sanders, 2005). It is in the after phases that the journey can be considered as a whole, the mistakes highlighted and good practice recognized as worthy of repeating or sharing with peers. It is also in the "after" phase that there are dilemmas about whether we make our academic careers off the backs of the people who have supplied the material. Making a successful academic career through permanent positions, book contracts and promotions from the experiences of those in the sex industry brings added suspicions of exploitation. The information used to make that career is based on experiences of individuals involved in what some consider an immoral or inhumane exchange of sex for money, or an institution that exists

as a prop for patriarchy and wider unequal power structures that subjugates women. . . . Collaborative research partnerships that work alongside informants, offering directorship and control to those who are normally subjected to the research process is a step towards reducing the exploitative nature of social science research. . . .

Concluding Comments

Despite its criticisms and dwindling application, here I have argued that there is great value in small-scale ethnographic research, especially collaborative in nature, into the sex industry that is concentrated both in time and space. Yet at every stage there are hurdles and challenges, often from within the institution as questions are posed by ethics committees of the appropriateness and feasibility of the sex industry as a worthy topic of study. Sex work research diverges from institutional patterns and accepted paths of information gathering, transgressing expectations of the types of group that are worthy of research or will produce useful knowledge (Pyett, 1998). In addition, the nature of the sex work environment and the political issues surrounding prostitution demand that the researcher make personal investment (such as self disclosure) into the research process. The demands of emotional labour on the researcher are complex and intense. Researchers have to confront hostile and volatile environments that need to be managed with care, making skills in negotiation, conflict management, role playing and keeping quiet an essential part of the fieldwork tool-kit.

The challenges do not stop as the researcher leaves the field. The writing up process demands considerable reflection on all aspects of the fieldwork and decisions have to be made about what to reveal and what to confine to the fieldwork diary. Continually promoting research into sex work, tirelessly applying (and re-applying) for funding and pushing to disseminate findings amongst the decision-makers is also part of the methodological challenges that face those committed to this important social issue. Pragmatics aside, to advance the theoretical arguments and knowledge regarding the nature and place of prostitution in contemporary life, research needs to be directed at wider issues relating to the politics of gender and social issues. O'Neill (2001: 187) suggests some of these wider social issues such as the feminization of poverty, violence and abuse in the home, and routes into sex work such as homelessness and leaving care are intrinsically linked to finding out more about prostitution. Researchers have the responsibility not to produce more of the same but to address the questions and areas that are often pushed to one side, constantly rejected by funding bodies and appear to be in discord with national political objectives. As Shaver (2005: 307) comments, challenges to stereotypes and the victimization of sex workers needs to be implicit in the methods that are employed to produce knowledge about these groups. If there is to be any advancement in the sociology of sex work, separate aspects of the industry should not be studied in isolation, and female sex workers should not remain the only focus of investigation.

REFERENCES

Barnard, M. (1992) "Working in the Dark: Researching Female Prostitution," in H. Roberts (ed.) *Women's Health Matters,* pp. 141–56. London: Routledge.

Cooper, K., Kilvington, J., Day, S., Ziersch, A. and Ward, H. (2001) "HIV Prevention and Sexual Health Services for Sex Workers in the UK," *Health Education Journal* 60(1): 26–34.

Ferrell, J. and Hamm, M. S. (1998) *Ethnography at the Edge: Crime, Deviance and Field Research:* Boston. MA: Northeastern University Press.

Hart, A. (1998) *Buying and Selling Power: Anthropological Reflections on Prostitution in Spain.* Oxford: Westview Press.

Hubbard, P. (1999a) *Sex and the City. Geographies of Prostitution in the Urban West.* Aldershot: Ashgate.

Hubbard, P. (1999b) "Researching Female Sex Work: Reflections on Geographical Exclusion, Critical Methodologies and 'Useful' Knowledge," *Area* 31(3): 229–37.

Labaree, R. (2002) "The Risk of 'Going Observationalist': Negotiating the Hidden Dilemmas of Being an Insider Participant Observer,' *Qualitative Research"* 2(1): 97–122.

Lee, R. (1995) *Dangerous Fieldwork.* London: Sage.

Lever, J. and Dolnick, D. (2000) "Clients and Call Girls: Seeking Sex and Intimacy," in R. Weitzer (ed.) *Sex for Sale,* pp. 85–100. London: Routledge.

Maher, L. (2000) *Sexed Work: Gender, Race and Resistance in a Brooklyn Drug Market.* Oxford: Oxford University Press.

Mattley, C. (1997) "Field Research with Phone Sex Workers," in M. Schwartz (ed.) *Researching Violence Against Women,* pp. 146–58. London: Sage.

Melrose, M. (2002) "Labour Pains: Some Considerations on the Difficulties of Researching Juvenile Prostitution," *International Journal of Social Research Methodology* 5(4): 333–51.

Miller, J. (1997) "Researching Violence Against Street Prostitutes," in M. Schwartz (ed.) *Researching Sexual Violence Against Women,* pp. 144–56. London: Sage.

O'Connell Davidson, J. (1998) *Prostitution, Power and Freedom.* London: Polity.

O'Connell Davidson, J. and Layder, D. (1994) *Methods, Sex and Madness.* London: Routledge.

O'Neill, M. (1996) "Researching Prostitution and Violence: Towards a Feminist Praxis," in M. Hester, L. Kelly and J. Radford (eds) *Women, Violence and Male Power,* pp. 130–47. London: Open University Press.

O'Neill, M. (2001) *Prostitution and Feminism.* London: Polity Press.

Pyett, P. (1998) "Doing it Together: Sex Workers and Researchers," *Research for Sex Work,* 1. URL (accessed June 2006): http://hcc.med.vu.nl/artikelen/pyett.htm

Roberts, J. M. and Sanders, T. (2005) "'Before, During and After': Ethnography, Reflexivity and Pragmatic Realism," *Sociological Review* 53(2): 294–313.

Sanders, T. (2005a) *Sex Work. A Risky Business.* Cullompton, UK: Willan.

Sanders, T. (2005b) "Researching the Online Sex Work Community," in C. Hine (ed.) *Virtual Methods in Social Research on the Internet,* pp. 66–79. Oxford: Berg.

Sanders, T. (2005c) "It's Just Acting: Sex Workers' Strategies for Capitalising on Sexuality," *Gender, Work and Organization* 12(4): 319–42.

Sharpe, K. (2000) "Sad, Bad And (Sometimes) Dangerous To Know: Street Corner Research With Prostitutes, Punters and the Police," in R. King and E. Wincup (eds.) *Doing Research on Crime and Justice,* pp. 362–72. Oxford: Oxford University Press.

Shaver, F. (2005) "Sex Work Research: Methodological and Ethical Challenges," *Journal of Interpersonal Violence* 20(3): 296–319.

Wahab, S. (2003) "Creating Knowledge Collaboratively with Female Sex Workers: Insights From a Qualitative Feminist and Participatory Study," *Qualitative Inquiry* 9(4): 625–42.

Challenges of Funding Sex Research

Mindy Stombler and Amanda M. Jungels

Getting funding for sex research has always been challenging. In the 1950s, Alfred Kinsey and his colleagues lost funding from the Rockefeller Foundation following publication of their controversial report on women's sexuality. More recently, the National Health and Social Life Survey (1994)—the closest we've come to a national sexual "census"—lost federal funding following opposition by Representative William Dannemeyer and Senator Jesse Helms. The researchers were forced to dramatically reduce the scope of their project, after conservatives in Congress lobbied against funding sexuality research.[1] Other grant-seekers report that they find themselves in a very defensive position. According to James Wagoner, president of Advocates for Youth, "For 20 years it was about health and science, and now we have a political ideological approach. . . . Never have we experienced a climate of intimidation and censorship as we have today."[2]

In 2003, there was a strong Congressional effort to block the funding of four National Institutes of Health (NIH) grants. These grants had already been judged as outstanding by peer scientists in an independent review process. The grants called for research on sexual risk taking and its link to sexual arousal, the sexual habits of older men, Asian sex workers, and sexual and gender identity among American Indians. Conservative politicians argued that the government had no business funding such inappropriate topics. Efforts to block the funding were narrowly defeated by two votes in the House.[3] Although some scientists will continue to apply for large government grants, others are becoming increasingly discouraged and are turning to alternative sources. Aside from the federal government, sources for funding sex research include a handful of private institutions and universities, whose resource pools are often more limited.[4] This lack of available funding reduces the scope of the sex-related research projects that do get carried out. For example, a recent extensive sex survey conducted by the CDC (see the box in Chapter 6 entitled "Sexual Behavior and Health") had to cap its sample at age 44, ignoring the sexual behaviors of the older generation that brought us the sexual liberation movement. [5]

As conservative politicians fight to reduce funding available for sex research, researchers feel pressured to focus on topics for which funding is available, such as pharmaceutical research. This trend necessarily narrows the breadth of researchable topics to those connected to potential profit making. Geoffrey Miller, a psychologist, claims that his research on kissing (why couples kiss less the longer they remain involved) is valuable for society but not necessarily fundable: "kissing could help couples rejuvenate a marriage and reduce divorce rates . . . but it's less threatening and more profitable to study orgasms."[6] In fact, Mark Schwartz of the Masters and Johnson clinic claims that the survival of the study of sexual behavior is a result of the HIV/AIDS epidemic and the development of Viagra "because the pharmaceutical companies suddenly became very interested in the fact that they can make huge amounts of money off the genitals."[7] Leonore Tiefer, a sex researcher interviewed in Chapter 5, cautions sex researchers about their over reliance on pharmaceutical money, insisting it contributes to a medical model of sexuality where all sexual problems can be fixed with a pill.[8]

Following the AIDS crisis and the public's concern with teen pregnancy rates, researchers who studied sexually transmitted infections (STIs) and reproductive health had a decent chance of being funded. But today, even these researchers have their share of challenges. Recently scientists who study HIV/AIDS and other STIs claim they have been warned by government officials to avoid the use of certain key words in their grant applications. Grants that include terms like "sex workers," "men who sleep with men," "anal sex," "needle exchange," "prostitute," "gay," "homosexual," and "transgender" are rumored to face additional scrutiny in an already fiercely competitive arena.[9] Ironically, this self-censorship of controversial terms has made it harder to assess whether funding has declined for sex research, as it is difficult to determine what researchers are actually studying when they submit disguised or re-framed research proposals.[10]

In addition to reframing how they present their research proposals to funding sources, researchers must tackle the issue of how to present their research results to the media: issues of inaccurate, politicized, sensationalized or misused findings are common concerns for sex researchers.[11] While controversy generates publicity for the researchers and the media outlets, it can also "threaten funding, result in restrictive policies, and lead to negative consequences for the individual or the field."[12] This fear of reprisal has led some researchers to avoid appearing in the media to report findings at all.

Frustrated by the increasing interference of politicians, researchers—and even federal agency directors—have been fighting back. For example, scientists from a range of disciplines have formed the Coalition to Protect Research (CPR), an organization "committed to promoting public health through research [and promoting the idea that] sexual health and behavior research is essential to providing a scientific foundation for sound public health prevention and intervention programs."[13] Organizations like this and the Society for the Scientific Study of Sexuality (SSSS) call for politicians to respect the scientific peer review process and to actively fund sex research. Some researchers, particularly those targeted by the Congressional effort to block NIH funding in 2003, have been reinvigorated by the controversy brought on by their research, wearing it as a "badge of honor," insisting that they will continue to do sex research, even if they must engage in self-censorship to do so.[14]

NOTES

1. Senator Helms and Representative Dannemeyer were also leaders in the successful effort to de-fund the American Teenage Study, a project designed to study "patterns of adolescent sexual and contraceptive behavior and the cause of these patterns" (106). In Udry, J. Richard. 1993. "The Politics of Sex Research." *The Journal of Sex Research* 30 (2):103–110.

2. Navarro, Mireya. 2004. "Experts in Sex Field Say Conservatives Interfere with Health and Research." *The New York Times.* July 11.

3. McCain, Robert Stacy. 2003. "Sex and Child Health: Critics Wonder Why NICHD Funds Studies." *The Washington Times:* A02.

4. American Experience: Kinsey, Online Forum, Day 2. February 15, 2005. Retrieved December 12, 2005 from www.pbs.org/wgbh/amex/kinsey/sfeature/sf_forum_0215 .html.

5. Hunter, Jennifer. 2005. "Sex Study Spurns Generation of Love." *Chicago Sun-Times.* October 5:63.

6. Clark, Justin. 2005. "Sex: The Big Turnoff." *Psychology Today.* Jan/Feb.

7. Clay, Rebecca. 2003. "Sex Research Faces New Obstacles." *APA Online.* Retrieved December 12, 2005 from www.apa.org/monitor/apr03/obstacles.html.

8. Tiefer, Leonore. 1995. *Sex Is Not a Natural Act and Other Essays.* Boulder, CO: Westview Press.

9. Goode, Erica. 2003. "Certain Words Can Trip up AIDS Grants, Scientists Say." *The New York Times.* Section A, Column 6, National Desk: 10.

10. Kempner, Joanna. 2008. "The Chilling Effect: How Do Researchers React to Controversy?" *PLoS Medicine* 5(11) 1–8.

11. McBride, Kimberly R., Stephanie A. Sanders, Erick Janssen, Maria Elizabeth Grabe, Jennifer Bass, Johnny V. Sparks, Trevor R. Brown, Julia R. Heiman. 2007. "Turning Sexual Science Into News: Sex Research and the Media" *Journal of Sex Research* 44 (4): 347–358.

12. Ibid.

13. Ibid.

14. Coalition to Protect Research (CPR). Retrieved December 16, 2005 from www.cossa.org/CPR/cpr.html.

chapter 3

Representing Sex

Spotlight on Research

An interview with . . .

Joshua Gamson

Joshua Gamson, Ph.D., is Professor of Sociology at University of San Francisco. His research and teaching focus on the sociology of culture, with an emphasis on contemporary Western commercial culture and mass media, social movements, and the history, theory, and sociology of sexuality. He is the author of *Claims to Fame: Celebrity in Contemporary America* (California, 1994); *Freaks Talk Back: Tabloid Talk Shows and Sexual Nonconformity* (Chicago, 1998); and *The Fabulous Sylvester: The Legend, The Music, The Seventies in San Francisco* (Henry Holt, 2005).

What led you to begin studying sexuality?

I didn't know it at the time, but studying sexuality began for me as part of what some scholars have called "identity work." I was a 23-year-old graduate student at UC Berkeley, and I'd decided it was time to figure myself out a bit better, and a big part of that seemed to be figuring out my sexuality a bit better. I knew that the Bay Area was a great place to do that, given the history of sexual subcultures—gay ones, especially— but somehow I didn't want to just take myself out exploring. So I decided to study it, come at my personal life from the outside in, as it were. When I had a statistics paper to do, I made it about public opinion about homosexuality, for instance. When I took a graduate seminar in participant observation research, I eventually decided on a field site that would get me into San Francisco, among gay and lesbian people: the AIDS activist group ACT UP. That turned into a very rewarding research experience, and to do it I had to teach myself some of the literature on sexuality-based social movements, so it fed my head. But it also fed my identity. That work moved me into a part of the gay community that I liked, felt comfortable in, and identified with; it helped me see myself as gay, and to actually experience gayness without shame or apology. It was a case of personal identity leading to intellectual pursuit and then back to personal identity. That back and forth continues to this day.

How do people react when they find that you study sexuality?

It depends on which people are doing the reacting, I suppose. Back when I started, my more senior colleagues would generally seem mystified, as if they couldn't quite figure out what there was to study about sexuality. Some, I'm certain, didn't and still don't think it's a legitimate area of study, but I think a lot of people just didn't know how to have a conversation about studying sexuality. That's rarely the case any more, partly because over the last decade the field has become much more established and much less marginalized in sociology—and partly because sexuality has been such a significant political and public policy focal point. Younger people seem to think it's kind of cool that I study sexuality, or cool that there is such a field of study. Then there are always those who want to joke about how much fun the "research process" must be.

Which of your projects have you found most interesting? Why?

My two book projects were the most interesting to me, for sure. The book on TV talk shows, Freaks Talk Back, *was interesting to me for a whole slew of reasons. I found it really interesting to investigate how the everyday production routines—the kinds of things talk show producers think about, talk about, worry about, and do all the time to get a show made—affected LGBT topics. Usually, when scholars and activists talk about "cultural visibility," they have only a vague sense of what kinds of institutional and organizational processes shape that visibility, and I felt like I was pushing past that vagueness. I was also really interested in the experiences of guests, and learned a lot about sexuality politics from that—in particular, the internal struggle over who best represents "gayness," which is very much a class-based divide. I became very interested in how complicated media visibility was for sexually-stigmatized and gender-nonconforming populations: How gay and lesbian respectability was shored up on the shows by demeaning or stereotyping transgender and bisexual guests; how the exposure of class and race diversity among LGBT populations only really came about through the extraordinarily exploitative, confess-accuse-pull hair kind of shows, like* Springer. *Media visibility has really changed since then, but that project tuned me in to dynamics of gay visibility I still see all around me.*

My most recent book, The Fabulous Sylvester, *was interesting in a whole other kind of way. It's a sort of combination biography (of the 1970s openly gay, sometimes cross-dressing, African American disco star, Sylvester) and cultural history (of San Francisco's gay subcultures, in which Sylvester lived and through which he rose to fame; and of AIDS, from which Sylvester died). So it was interesting partly because it was a different sort of project, more narrative and less analytical scholarly. It was interesting to me because it put me into contact with Sylvester's life and friends, and his story is just beautiful, and beautiful largely because his sexuality was such an integrated part of who he was—he was never closeted, and he suffered quite a bit for that, but he eventually became an international disco star by putting gay "fabulousness" to music, while refusing to be reduced to, or by, sexuality, and by never apologizing for being gay and sexual. I also loved delving into 1970s gay liberation cultures, which were so creative and novel and important, and which have been largely lost to AIDS, assimilation, and fear.*

What ethical dilemmas have you faced in studying sexuality?

I haven't really experienced ethical dilemmas, frankly. I'm not studying sexual behavior, and I've never studied covert sexual populations, so I've never had concern about revealing things that might hurt the subjects. I always tell people I'm a researcher, and give them the option of not participating, or of participating without having their name used, and sometimes people take me up on that. When I'm interviewing, they always have the option of having me turn off the tape recorder. The closest I've come to an ethical dilemma is in dealing with the question of how what I write might be used by others, such as journalists or policymakers who have an anti-gay agenda—which is, of course, totally out of my control. I don't think I've ever made a decision to censor myself for fear that the wrong people would use it in a way that damages those to whom I'm loyal and allied, but I certainly am careful how I frame and phrase things.

What do you think is the most challenging thing about studying sexuality?

The most challenging thing for me is that it's a constantly moving target. Again, I don't study sexual behaviors, but instead sexual identities, movements, politics, cultures, and cultural representations. One can easily be at the end of a project and find the phenomenon entering some radically different new phase, so that one has to be ready to always rethink and revise. (Maybe that's one of the reasons I enjoyed doing the Sylvester book, since it was more historical.) Media visibility is a good example: Ten years ago, when I finished the talk show book, the issue was still that LGBT people were mainly invisible on television or restricted to narrow stereotypes; the issues now, after Ellen, Will and Grace, Queer as Folk, The L Word, Queer Eye, *and so on, are quite different. The talk show study, over the course of just a few years, went from being a statement about the limits and paradoxes of LGBT media visibility to being an account of a historical moment. A study of same-sex marriage laws now, to take another example, is going to face the same sort of difficulty; things are changing so rapidly in legislation and law related to sexuality. That's not an insurmountable challenge, and I'd rather study something that is active and volatile than something inert. But sexual cultures and politics don't stand still for their snapshot.*

Why is it important to do sex research?

Most basically, because sex is an important part of human existence, and it's been so smothered by shame and negativity that there's still plenty that's not well understood. Although it hasn't always been the case, and I suspect won't be forever, sexuality has also become a significant basis for people's identities and self-understandings, and it affects their life chances and life paths in various ways—where they wind up living, what kinds of jobs they can and can't get. And sexuality is one of several significant bases of social inequality, and therefore is a very significant arena of politics. These are things that need to be understood, both just because more knowledge is better than less, and because sexualities research can help us figure out what needs to be changed and how to change it—the research can inform the pursuit of social justice.

If you could teach people one thing about sexuality, what would it be?

That it's both more significant and less significant than it's been made out to be: Sexuality is not just a phenomenon of nature, and not just "personal," but a phenomenon of society, and political; at the same time, at the root of all of this politics is just sex, just the fun and sometimes funny things people do with their bodies, together and alone.

—Interviewed by Denise Donnelly

Hip Hop Honey or Video Ho: African American Preadolescents' Understanding of Sexual Scripts

Dionne P. Stephens and April L. Few

African American preadolescents' beliefs about female sexuality differ in meaning and sexual behavior values when compared to preadolescents in other racial/ethnic groups (Sterk-Elifson 1994; Wyatt 1997). . . . Across preadolescent and adolescent female populations, African Americans experience the highest rates of HIV/AIDS transmission, gonorrhea, herpes, syphilis, multiple partners, unplanned pregnancy, non-voluntary intercourse, sexual abuse, and earliest ages of sexual onset (Centers for Disease Control [CDC] 2000). Among males aged 12–18, the rates of sexual activity and sexually transmitted diseases are highest among African Americans, followed by Latinos and Euro-Americans (CDC 2000).

Unfortunately, while many of these findings provide important behavioral outcome information, they are commonly drawn from research designs and questions that ignore race and intraethnic variations in beliefs and attitudes about sexuality (Benda and Corwyn 1998; McLoyd 1998). This is because there is a tendency for researchers to normalize Euro-American adolescents' experience, and it is against these conceptualizations of appropriate behaviors that other populations are compared (Few et al. 2003; Wiederman et al. 1996).

This study identifies how meanings about sexuality are developed by African American preadolescents through an examination of sexual scripts identified by Stephens and Phillips (2003). Sexual scripts are

schema used to categorize norms regarding appropriate sexual beliefs and behaviors. Stephens and Phillips believed African American preadolescents have developed sexual scripts specific to and reflective of African American popular culture. These scripts include: the Diva, Gold Digger, Freak, Dyke, Gangster Bitch, Sister Savior, Earth Mother, and Baby Mama.

In this study, we argue that these sexual scripts do exist and that they identify ways in which African American preadolescents gave meaning and value to African American female sexuality and corresponding behavioral outcome expectations. Further, we believe these scripts are influential in African American preadolescent decision-making processes regarding sexual activity and behaviors. . . .

African American Sexual Scripts

There is a body of literature that provides a foundation for examining sexual scripts in African American populations. These narrative studies focus on iconographic images of African American womanhood—the promiscuous Jezebel, asexual Mammy, breeding Welfare Mama, controlling Sapphire and emasculating Matriarch (cf., Collins 2000; Guy-Sheftall 1990). However, few researchers have empirically examined the relevance of these images in African American preadolescent sexual risk-taking processes today. . . .

Insiders to Hip Hop culture know that this phenomena encompasses a deep understanding of diverse cultural expressions, such as body language (e.g. Frith 1996), language usage (e.g. Smitherman 1997), clothing styles (e.g. Kim 2001), value and belief systems (e.g. Baker 1992), racial/ethnic identity (e.g. Ro 1996; Rose 1992; Rubio 1993), and general

From "Hip Hop Honey or Video Ho: African American Preadolescents' Understanding of Female Sexual Scripts in Hip Hop Culture" by Dionne P. Stephens and April L. Few (2007), *Sexuality and Culture*, 11, 48–69. Reprinted with kind permission of Springer Science and Business Media.

behavioral expectations (e.g. Henderson 1996; Venable 2001) than the music can convey alone. Hip Hop culture's music is reflective of a very specific African American youth experience that began in the early 1980s reflecting their anger and fears about their present lives and unknown futures (Ransby and Matthews 1995; Smitherman 1977; Williams 1992).

Although the music began as an underground and often highly political art form, it was quickly appropriated and depoliticized by mainstream culture within the prevailing business climate of the late 1980s (Chuck 2001; Cutler 1999; Henderson 1996; Wahl 1999). Caught in the conflict were the images of young African American women whose relation to both the White mainstream and the emerging Hip Hop culture were being re-defined and re-negotiated. Neocolonialism has framed these new relationships among African American women, the music industry, the White mainstream, and Black youth culture. Neocolonialism within this [reading] refers to corporations and dominant group's influence over another marginalized populations, areas or sectors by economic, language, cultural and political means rather than by the traditional colonialist methods of military-political take-over and direct control (Nkrumah 1965; Sartre 2001; Suret-Canale 1988; Young 2001). For African American youth, they experience [these] indirect control aspects of Hip Hop cultural life, including art, theatre, cinema and television. We believe that a new media elite that may include White or Black men or women in positions of power have recolonized the Black female body.

We cannot, however, characterize Black women as mere victims of a neocolonizing process; this would overstate their lack of agency. Black women . . . have vitally shaped the discourse about themselves and their sexuality. What is particularly unique about the contemporary climate is the fact that African American youth, including young, African American women, have more influential power in the construction of their own cultural symbology (Rose 1994; Kitwana 2003). Yet, we cannot overlook that the self-definitions produced by this group are, sadly, far from devoid of the remnants of racism and sexism.

Hip Hop music videos are the most accessible providers of these sexual script frameworks. Music videos have emerged as some of the most popular genre of television programming among preadolescents. Hip Hop is the most popular genre of music shown on two of the most widely viewed channels among preadolescents and young adults—Black Entertainment Television (BET) and Music Television (MTV). Through clothing, camera address, and visual images, women in Hip Hop videos are depicted as having both great sexual power and sexual desires (Brown 2000; Roberts 1996; Stephens and Few 2007). The projected sexual scripts not only work to reinforce stereotypical beliefs of viewers living in predominately White communities who have little contact with members of other racial or ethnic groups (Heaton and Wilson 1995; Stephens and Phillips 2005), but also serve as representation[s] of how African American preadolescent women are expected to view themselves.

Current Incarnations: The New Stereotypes

From the Hip Hop foothold of African American culture, [unique sexual scripts such as] the Diva, Gold Digger, Freak, Dyke, Gangster Bitch, Sister Savior, Earth Mother, and Baby Mama (c.f. Stephens and Phillips 2003) . . . emerged. In some ways, these scripts are contemporary manifestations of older stereotypes of Black womanhood—the Jezebel, Sapphire, Welfare Mama, and Matriarch. In this section, we describe the socially located characteristics of each script.

The *Diva* is characterized as being pretty based on Westernized standards of beauty (namely long straightened hair, light skinned, and having a slender build). Middle-class in its projection, the Diva script is commonly applied to women who appear independent yet select partners that primarily [bolster] social status and [provide] companionship. Her sexuality is framed from a traditional view of power in relationships, such that males are viewed as central to defining who she is, although not necessary to get what she needs (Stephens and Phillips 2003).

Where trading social status for sex describes the Diva, it is the *Gold Digger* who uses sex to gain material and economic rewards (Jones 1994). *Gold Diggers* are aware that sexuality may be used to barter for basic needs (e.g. purchasing groceries, paying rent, or an electric bill) or leisure items (e.g. pedicures, new clothing, or vacations). But, if a woman decides to [forgo] financial gains and only seeks to satisfy her own sexual desires, she is labeled a *Freak*. The Freak is a "bad girl" who gains male attention through an overt sexual persona. She appears sexually liberated, empowered, and seeks sex solely for physical satisfaction, not for a relationship. A debate rages over [whether] the Freak reflects a true persona of sexual empowerment, or if she is simply reinforcing and falling victim to male desires about female sexuality.

In contrast, women who choose not engage in sexual acts with men and enter relationships exclusively with women are referred to as *Dykes*. Within this frame, heterosexuality is viewed as the natural emotional and sexual inclination for women, and those who go against this are seen as deviant, pathological or as emotionally and sensually deprived (Lorde 1984; Pharr and Raymond 1997). This script is commonly associated with women who appear to be . . . self-determined with a strong locus of control. No matter what her true sexual orientation is, she confronts men when disrespected or threatened. Clearly, the tensions around this script are about the strength that these women are able [to] project without incorporating the sexual desires of men.

Gangster Bitches are associated with women who live in the same squalid, poverty-stricken, drug-infested, violent environments that have traditionally focused on the "endangered African American male" in popular imagination for the past decade (Hampton 2000). The Gangster Bitch's focus is on survival, and men are partners in this endeavor. They are not expecting long-term love from men. They have become emotionally hardened in that sex is viewed as a means to release stress and to feel good for that moment (Campbell 1991; Sanchez Jankowski 1991). Sexuality, then, not only becomes a tool to please men, but to prove their loyalty to them.

The *Sister Savior* script decrees that sex is to be avoided because of the moral issues it poses within a religious context. She projects a demure, moral, obedient attitude, particularly toward men, that reflects African American religious institutions' foundation in a tradition of patriarchy that often places women in submissive and oppressed positions (Brown Douglas 1999; Grant 1992; Hoover 1993). Their sexual decision-making information is often framed using fear tactics, not a holistic understanding (Brown Douglas 1999; Wyatt 1997).

The *Earth Mother* script appears to have a more developed sense of self as expressed through an Afrocentric political and spiritual consciousness that is obviously part of their everyday discourse and worldview. Traditional views of beauty are openly challenged by the Earth Mother's beauty expectations and ideals embedded within an Afrocentric framework. They are less sexualized as men tend to be intimidated by Earth Mothers (Amber 2001); this reality also decreases their pool of eligible interested partners.

Once an illegitimate child is born, the *Baby Mama* script is enacted. Her title aptly and wholly describes this woman's role—she is basically the mother of a man's baby and nothing more. This attitude reflects popular beliefs that the Baby Mama purposely becomes pregnant so that she could maintain a relationship while making the biological father financially indebted to her or to keep a part of him (Aaron and Jenkins 2002). The Baby Mama is assumed to desire her former or current sexual partner so much that she will sacrifice all other life plans to have his baby (Aaron and Jenkins 2002; Wyatt 1997, p. 131). The Baby Mama uses all—including unethical—ploys to achieve her desire to attain the status of mother and/or a relationship.

Relationship to Behavioral Outcomes

While these scripts are widely recognized, empirical research assessing their existence and impact on decision-making processes has not been conducted. Some preliminary research indicates, however, sexual behaviors may be [influenced] by images of African American female sexuality in the media . . . (Stephens and Few 2007). In one study, African American female adolescents who watched films with African American women engaging in sexually explicit behaviors were found to (a) be approximately twice as likely to have multiple sex partners, (b) have more frequent sex, (c) not use contraception during last intercourse, (d) hold negative attitudes toward condom use, (e) [test] positive for chlamydia, and (f) . . . have a strong desire to conceive (Wingood et al. 2001). African American female adolescents who had greater exposure to Hip Hop videos with high levels of sexual content were twice as likely to have had multiple sexual partners, and 1.5 times more likely to have a sexually transmitted disease (Wingood et al. 2003). Gillum (2002) investigated the link between stereotypic images of African American women and intimate partner violence and found that a large percentage of African American men endorsed stereotypic images of African American women. Endorsements of the images, in turn, were positively related to justification of violence against women.

Unfortunately, these studies do not specifically identify or examine . . . frameworks of sexuality through sexual scripting or the ways in which scripts give meaning to sexual behavioral norms for this population. This study sought to fill this void by clearly assessing the existence of sexual scripts as a framework for African American female sexuality. To explore these phenomena, we examined the following research questions about African American preadolescents' consumption of sexual messages in Hip Hop culture.

1. What role do images of women [in] Hip Hop culture play in transmitting information about African American female sexuality?
2. How do these values and beliefs inform sexual-decision making processes and potential behavioral outcomes?

Methods

. . . This study used purposeful sampling, which involved identifying participants who might give the most comprehensive and knowledgeable information about female sexual scripts in African American youth culture. Seven male and eight female African American preadolescents aged 11–13 participated in the study. Data [were] gathered from both [genders] as the frameworks for African American female preadolescent sexual scripts are informed through heterosexual relationship expectations.

Participants resided in a large southeastern college town and were recruited from an after school program targeting working and lower class families. All attended public middle schools and had resided in the community all their lives. None of the participants were currently involved in a romantic or sexual relationship. The

majority had never experienced any form of intimate sexual activity (i.e., hugging, kissing, or dry humping the opposite sex). All self-reported never [having experienced] sexual intercourse. Only four boys and two girls indicated that they had ever kissed or "made out" with a member of the opposite sex. None of the participants reported currently being involved in an intimate relationship . . . although several discussed having "boyfriends" or "girlfriends" in the past.

. . . Three data collection techniques were used: (1) semi-structured focus group interviews, (2) written feedback documentation, and (3) researcher notes. These multiple sources of data were collected in order to triangulate the data and to confirm emergent themes and inconsistencies in the data.

The focus groups coincided with the open period of the after-school programming schedule. The boys and girls were interviewed in a private classroom on separate days. . . .

In addition, each participant was given a handout with an image of a female Hip Hop artist who personified the sexual scripts identified by Stephens and Phillips (2003). . . . Participants listed beliefs about these scripts as they related sexual behaviors and attitudes from the perspective of (a) themselves, (b) their African American female cohort, and (c) their African American male cohort. The scripts were introduced individually, so that participants were not made aware in advance of what scripts were being discussed. . . .

Characteristics of the eight sexual scripts were used as markers to analyze the data. The researchers triangulated interview transcripts, participant feedback, and entries from the researchers' notes in order to identify and confirm inconsistencies, salient issues, and patterns. Reissman's (1993) levels of representation model guided continuing attempts through analysis to represent and interpret data.

Findings

African American Sexual Scripts

Each of the eight sexual scripts identified by Stephens and Phillips (2003) were recognized by the participants in this study. Their centrality in participants' daily lives was evident in two ways: (a) self-reported frequent consumption of the scripts, and

(b) self reported frequent usage of the sexual scripts' labels. In terms of usage, participants were immediately familiar with the labels presented to them. There was never a need to clarify the meaning of the terms [used] to classify each script.

The participants acknowledged that these scripts were encountered on a daily basis as they embraced their "passion"—Hip Hop culture. They continuously listened to it throughout their day. Both female and male preadolescents felt it was an integral part of their daily lives, taught them things about life, and gave them a perspective on their role or position in society.

> **Tracy:** I love Hip Hop. I love it. I listen to it [every day], all day. When I hear it. . . . (hitting a beat on table, laughter). I love it. All day long I listen to it.
> **Keisha:** It's about us, you know. It's about being in America and how [African American kids] are.
> **Tyrone:** Yeah, yeah, it's good. It tells you what's going on. I love watching videos to see all the cars and stuff . . . you know what I mean? To see how others live, you know.

Due to this continuous consumption of Hip Hop, there was congruency in the definitions and meanings associated with each by both male and female participants. Because the labels of the sexual scripts were drawn from the language of Hip Hop culture, their meanings were widely disseminated. Participants referenced songs that used these terms and shared the accompanying lyrics that gave definitions of their meanings. Only the word Dyke was unfamiliar to these participants, although they understood the meanings and behaviors associated with this script. The Dyke script is understood as overtly masculine and the Dyke's preference for same-sex intimate relationships were viewed as undesirable. The participants later discussed this further in the context of sexual behaviors.

Beyond the labels, the participants were able to easily identify examples of the sexual scripts enacted by others who embrace Hip Hop culture. These participants readily sang out lyrics from songs and identified artists that represented each script. Furthermore, through these associations, they were able to articulate their feelings and share the meanings they gave to these sexual scripts. They, in turn, would give

real life examples of peers who they felt re-enacted key cues associated with these scripts. Two female preadolescents shared:

> **Leesa:** I see it all the time at school . . . One girl got in trouble for wearing a top like Tweet [Hip Hop artist]. She thinks she look like her and she tries to act, dress so she can be her. She think she's like the Diva, right?
> **Pam:** Everyone wants to look like Beyonce because she's seen as pretty and sexy. Like in the "Survivor" video—she looked strong in those [army fatigues] but still pretty . . . Yeah, [female peer] wore something like that to school but she didn't look anything like [Beyonce].

For these participants, music videos provided the most visible evidence of sexual script existence and the sexual behaviors associated with them. As demonstrated by the quotes below, gender expectations about sexuality are created through projections of acceptable male and female roles.

> **Shawn:** [Hip Hop artist] Snoop is a pimp. You see all 'dem girls he's got going off on him in [the music video]. You saw that video? Those girls were all over him . . . freaks all over him. Yeah, Snoop ran all that.
> **Susan:** You see the Freak a lot in videos—she is always in the videos.
> **Nicole:** No, there is the Diva. [Hip Hop artist] Ashanti is a Diva.
> **Tamika:** But she is like a leader and everyone like her.
> **Crystal:** Yeah, people don't really like [Freak persona] Lil' Kim.
> **Susan:** She's good . . . she has good songs. But she's not really respected. Boys want to sleep with her but not be with her long term.

Through this visual and audio forum, a hierarchy of desirable and undesirable scripts and associated behaviors are established. This gendering of behaviors and expectations expressed through sexual scripts was made evident in the dialogues with these preadolescents.

Sexual Behaviors

. . . It was found that both male and female preadolescents were able to give examples of sexual behaviors associated with each script by quoting from Hip Hop songs. However, this did not necessarily mean they had an accurate understanding of what those behaviors entailed or knew the correct terminologies.

> *Keisha:* Well, Freaks also like to have oral sex.
> *Pam:* What is oral sex? (giggling)
> *Tamika:* It's when you blow on the guy's . . . thing.

The second key issue was the actual behaviors, and more specifically, the value and meanings given to these behaviors. For example, kissing, hugging or cuddling were acceptable and not viewed as being associated with sex. In fact, sexual intercourse (specifically penile/vaginal penetration) and oral sex were the only two behaviors that these preadolescents defined as "sex." Sexual scripts that were perceived as including these behaviors were viewed as promiscuous and negative.

These frameworks of sexual knowledge shaped beliefs about sexual behaviors. The less sexualized the script, the less sexual risk the woman was assumed to present in terms of health and reputation. Sister Saviors and Divas were described as the most "clean" and healthy. Further, they were seen as the least likely to engage in sexual acts or do so only with select male partners. Male preadolescents believed that these were women who would not put them at risk for acquiring sexually transmitted diseases. Furthermore, these two scripts were described as being "good girls" and deserving of respect. To have sex with these women, deferential sexual advances were required. Female preadolescent responses agreed with assessments made by male preadolescents:

> *Anthony:* [Divas] generally they don't have sex a lot.
> *Curtis:* I basically think that they are good and clean.

In contrast, both female and male preadolescents labeled Freaks as "easy," meaning they had no inhibitions about engaging in sexual activity. It was felt across all groups that males would not have to put any effort into convincing those associated with this script to have sex. Freaks were referred to as dirty, and required the usage of condoms as a means of protecting male partners from catching sexually transmitted diseases. Moreover, both female and male preadolescents reported that by freely engaging in sexual acts with men, sexually aggressive women willingly put themselves at risk for negative reactions and behavioral outcomes.

> *Wayne:* They want sex whatever it takes and whatever happens is fine. They like stripping, they show their body—they don't care.
> *Pam:* I say that girls think Freaks are hos [whores].
> *Tamika:* They are bitches, they are whores.
> *Keisha:* Yeah, they walk into that.

. . . [In contrast,] the male desire for sex was reported as being innate and central to heterosexual relationships. . . . [Girls] expected that boys or men would seek sexual interactions wherever and whenever they could. In fact, when discussions about male promiscuity arose, there was a greater level of acceptance in both female and male responses.

In reality, male preadolescents were willing to have sex with all the scripts except the Baby Mama and Dyke. The lack of interest in the Baby Mama was related to age and her desire to have children. Male preadolescents noted she has "babies with no daddy" and possibly "several daddies." They viewed this script as being applicable to mature women who were more sexually experienced:

> *Shawn:* She is older and will give it up, though she might have diseases.
> *Wayne:* If they had sex one time, they can have it more than one time later probably.

Male preadolescents were willing to engage in sexual relations with a Baby Mama and even acknowledge they "would go out with them," but not in this phase of their development. The fact that she was raising a child indicated maturity and a level of sexual experience they had not yet reached.

The attitudes toward Dykes' sexual behaviors were related to issues of morality and lack of knowledge. It was clear that these participants' homophobic attitudes were shaped by a lack of information about same-sex relationships. . . . They would reference issues of morality, stating that same-sex sexual behaviors were prohibited by the church, and were against what was "natural" human behavior. Male preadolescents appeared to be less disturbed by the Dyke script; five said that men would "get with them" with the belief that it could lead to a threesome with another woman. Female preadolescents were more negative in their assessment of the Dyke script, referring to them as "gayfers" and their behaviors as "nasty" in their notes. However, their reasons for why women might enact these scripts were diverse.

> **Researcher:** So why do women become dykes then?
> **Nicole:** Because they can't get a man. Because they can't get a man.
> **Crystal:** Like she said because they can't get a man and maybe they think that women are prettier. Because there are some beautiful people out there.
> **Leesa:** They might not want to get pregnant by men so. . . . So it is safer to be with women. You never know.
> **Susan:** I think a dyke is. . . . I mean I don't think that it is right to be one, because if we're supposed to be with another woman then we would.

Although these participants all stated that they had never been sexually active, they reported that these scripts could influence younger children and sexually active preadolescents. They believed it was important to address the behaviors in these scripts as a means of negotiating sexual relationship dynamics.

Discussion

. . . These preadolescents made it clear that Hip Hop was important to them; they actively sought to consume or express aspects of it [every day]. The centrality of Hip Hop to these participants ensures their daily observations of these sexual scripts. Still, Hip Hop is a vast culture with a matrix of meanings and values.

Studies examining risk prototypes and stereotypes may shed light on why this finding was reached. Research indicates that adolescents are generally very aware of and continuously develop social group identities, known as prototypes, within their social settings (Simmons and Blyth 1987; Skowronski and Carlston 1989). These serve as guides for categorizing behaviors and people associated with them (Chassin et al. 1984; Feit 2001). Adolescents then realize that by engaging in the behavior, they are likely to be identified as being a member of a definable group or clique. For example, "typical" smokers or drinkers, "nerds," or "jocks." In this sense, accepting a prototype is part of

the process through which individuals develop frameworks for understanding social hierarchies and networks in their social contexts.

Participants' recognition of the eight sexual scripts may also be explained by stereotyping research that has shown African American preadolescents have a greater awareness of racial stereotypes than their Euro-American peers (Crocker and Major 1989; McCreary et al. 1996). As such, we assert that the acceptance and knowledge of sexual scripts, as frameworks for behavior within a specific racial context, are important for understanding the social structure of Hip Hop culture and African American preadolescent sexuality. . . . More specifically, these sexual scripts were shown to be central for the development of conceptual frameworks of appropriate gender, race, and sexuality attitudes that help individuals negotiate their roles in African American youth culture.

. . . [T]hese scripts are also embedded within a framework of patriarchy, which includes the accumulation of material wealth and sexual conquest. The traditions of Hip Hop are embedded in a male culture; it is a space that was developed and initially controlled by men (Phillips et al. 2005; Smitherman 1977; Stephens and Phillips 2005). Women's entrance was not readily accepted and still requires negotiation of male values and attitudes toward women. This reality was particularly evident in music videos where, for example, women are typically depicted as having great sexual desires, which they can only quench by being degraded for male pleasure (Brown 2000; Morgan 2002; Roberts 1996). Males, in contrast, are more often presented as having agency and control of their contexts in this male defined space (Iwamoto 2003; Kitwana 2003; Morgan 2002; Stephens and Phillips 2003). As a result, women are less likely to be depicted as individuals; rather they serve as backdrops with a focus on select body parts for male consumption. It is common in videos to have multiple women vying for one man's attention through the use of highly sexualized verbal and non-verbal cues (Stephens and Few 2007; Stephens and Phillips 2003).

Participants were particularly aware of these projections and spent a considerable amount of time discussing their existence in various popular videos. Through these visual forums, concrete examples of the eight sexual scripts were made evident. Furthermore, they illustrated the culture and these preadolescents' views regarding female sexuality. Although music videos are primarily a vehicle to promote particular artists and songs, this study supported prior assertions by Hip Hop culture researchers that videos reflect the content of the music, exposing the beliefs, attitudes, and behaviors of those consuming them (Farley 1999; Roberts and Ulen 2000; Rose 1994; Smart Young 2002). . . .

Both within Hip Hop culture and the broader society, men are normally viewed as the aggressors seeking sex, while women are gatekeepers resisting male overtures (e.g., Carpenter 2001a, b; Jackson 1996; Lichtenstein 2000). Frameworks embracing these traditional scripts of female sexuality were found to dominate beliefs of participants in this study. Most notable were the normalization of heterosexuality and the celebration of female virginity.

Virginity has long been ascribed a high value for women in most cultures. Preserving female virginity until marriage is still celebrated, although not the norm, in the United States (c.f. Carpenter 2001a, b). Among these participants, virginity or low levels of sexual activity were viewed as positive for women; none of the female preadolescents identified themselves as sexually active and were not embarrassed about this. These values given to virginity (and in turn, promiscuity) directly informed attitudes about appropriate and healthy female sexual behaviors. For example, participants noted that sexual scripts that did not appear to assert sexuality (i.e., Sister Savior, Diva) were "safe" in terms of sexual risk. Both male and female preadolescents stated in their written notes that women enacting these scripts were sexually "clean" and "no condoms" were needed when engaging in sexual intercourse.

This observation reinforces prior research on college students that had found that the appearance of partners ("She doesn't look sick" or "She is too good looking to have AIDS") and familiarity with the partner ("I know them and the type of person they are") causes them to underestimate their AIDS risk and need to use condoms (Malloy et al. 1997). Lichten-

stein (2000) similarly found that African American young women engaged in unsafe sex at first intercourse because their male partners said that neither would put them in jeopardy for sexual health risks (i.e., STDs) due to her virginity.

These female preadolescents relied upon stereotypic gender norms regarding female sexual passivity to guide their decisions. As in other studies (Dantzker and Eisenman 2003; Reiss 1967; Stephens and Few 2007; Werner-Wilson 1995), none of these preadolescent females endorsed a permissive or casual attitude toward sexual behaviors. The hypersexual sexual script challenged the "good girl" model of sexual behaviors that African American young women are usually socialized to accept (Fullilove et al. 1993; Windham 1995; Wyatt 1997). These female preadolescents responded to women's interest in sexual pleasure as threatening to both themselves and the sexually empowered female. General cultural level sexual scripts portray unemotional and casual sex as negative for women. For our female participants, rejection of negative sexual scripts appeared to reflect the acceptance of traditional gender roles. If the goals of sexual desire for women entail interpersonal and romantic involvement (Regan and Berscheid 1996), being seen as promiscuous endangers these goals, particularly if men prefer partners with moderate sexual experience.

The negotiation of the balance between being promiscuous and virginal was evident when the Baby Mama script was considered. The presence of a child clearly indicated that these women had already engaged in sexual intercourse. However, some male preadolescents noted that they "may date" a Baby Mama in the future. It was felt that the degree of her sexual activity was important to consider. If the Baby Mama had multiple "baby daddies" or several male friends, then she was not an acceptable, sexually "safe" or "good" girl for sexual intercourse. However, if she appeared to have had just one child within confines of a committed relationship, she was still a potential sexual partner.

It is important to note that only heterosexual frameworks of sexuality were viewed as acceptable. Anything beyond these behaviors was viewed as promiscuous and abnormal. This observation was made particularly evident during discussions about the sexual behaviors associated with the Dyke script. Despite the fact that the Dyke is not a feminine or sexually wild script, she was still not viewed as sexless. Rather, her sexuality, in terms of engaging in same-sex intimate behaviors, was stereotyped by participants as repulsive, abnormal, and contrary to African American cultural norms. Their comments reflect findings from prior research on compulsory heterosexuality in African American communities (e.g., Chideya 1993; Lewis 2003; Smith 1994). This belief system fits with the frameworks about homosexuality embedded in African American youth culture. Hip Hop artists know that declaring one's sexual identity—if it is not a typical straight one—is a huge risky personal decision that can have social, political, as well as financial and career repercussions (Coker 1999; Iwamoto 2003; Outlaw 1995; Venable 2001). These influences clearly extended to the participants in the study, particularly the female preadolescents, who expressed negative attitudes and intolerance toward the Dyke script sexual behaviors. As was found among men in prior research, the male preadolescents in this study shared the same resistance to accepting this sexual script, yet still found the potential of engaging in female–female–male sex alluring enough to lessen their rejection of women who appeared to follow this sexual script (e.g., Jackson 1997; Odih 2002; Rehin 2003).

Clearly, the acceptability of female sexual desire is inextricably linked to male expectations, beliefs, and goals. Essentially, a woman's sexual identity is shaped not only by her own behaviors, but the appraisals and evaluations of others viewing her actions. For example, female participants expressed that women who appeared to desire sexual pleasure may suffer rejection from a potential Black male partner.

Cultural ideas about appropriate gender behaviors were further reinforced when preadolescent females suggested and accepted the belief that males would have sex with any woman who was willing. . . . The possibility of men engaging in sexual relations with women who followed even the most vilified sexual scripts was not viewed as problematic. Instead any negative projection may lay with the woman who allowed a man to have sex with her. Hence, women are constructed to be the gatekeepers while men are the conquerors of sexuality. This finding supports prior research that has shown African American women are commonly socialized to be "good" and nonsexually aggressive, while promiscuity among men is accepted, if not encouraged, through parental messages (Adimora 2001; Fullilove et al. 1993).

These double standard messages regarding male–female sexuality "rules" do not provide women with the skills and attitudes required to negotiate sexual practices effectively (Gomez and Marin 1996). When preadolescent females are presented primarily as objects of male desire rather than sexual agents in their own right, the cultural script of women as sexually powerless is perpetuated and ignores their possible experience of desire (Fine 1988). However, there is also debate that questions the legitimacy of the projection of female . . . self determination in those sexually aggressive scripts. It is suggested that these scripts do not represent a position of empowerment as they just recreate male desire. Marriott (2000) asks us to consider: Are women projected as the subversive manipulators or the ones being manipulated? Are they exploitative in their own right, or complicit in their own exploitation? These questions are an important concern for forthcoming research to consider, especially given that male preadolescents in this study were the only ones to note that some women may "just want to have sex." Clearly, researchers examining sexual behaviors need to be conscious of and integrate understandings of how gender expectations and desires for both men and women can inform behavioral outcomes. Sexual scripts provide a context for this examination.

Implications for Research and Practice

The usage of sexual scripts for understanding sexual risk behaviors does inform research about the simultaneous influence of gender and race with sexual meanings. Given this, intervention programs and projects about sexuality should acknowledge and integrate discussions about sexual scripts. Unique cultural messages that influence these decision-making processes must be acknowledged to achieve positive, healthy behavioral outcomes (Benda and Corwyn 1998; Irvine 1994). As the scripts were found to be immediately recognized by African American preadolescents, it is possible they will experience a sense of comfort discussing sexuality through these frameworks. These preadolescent[s] may feel empowered by being able to actively deconstruct sexual meanings and values with minimal guidance using these scripts. Furthermore, for African American female preadolescents, discussions using sexual scripts can provide a safe forum to engage in explicit talk about sexuality. Like a child abuse survivor pointing to an anatomically correct doll to talk about his or her victimization, female preadolescents can look at pictures of women who represent certain scripts to discuss their understanding of sexuality and expectant behavioral outcomes. A doll or a photograph can allow individuals to step "outside" of themselves to communicate ideas, feelings, or values about a specific topic. Preadolescent African American females require tools, such as these sexual scripts, to help visualize and identify sexual behaviors within a specific gender and racial context. Scripts provide an innovative, accessible way for both participants and researchers to understand the dynamic evolution of African American female preadolescent sexuality.

Conclusion

. . . These findings provide unique insights into African American preadolescent attitudes about sexuality. Data collected at this phase of the life span is of particular importance, given that the average age of sexual onset among African American preadolescents is 13 (CDC 2000). Thus, the responses of our participants provided information about the beliefs and attitudes of those on the cusp of potential sexual initiation.

REFERENCES

Aaron, S. J., & Jenkins, R. R. (2002). Sex, pregnancy, and contraception-related motivators and barriers among Latino and African-American youth in Washington, D.C. *Journal of Sex Education, 2,* 5–30.

Adimora, A. A., Schoenbach, V. J., Martinson, F. E., Donaldson, K. H., Fullilove, R. E., & Aral, S. O. (2001). Social context of sexual relationships among rural African Americans. *Sexually Transmitted Diseases, 28*(2), 69–77.

Amber, J. (2001). The pick up. *Essence, 31*(12), 147–148.

Baker, H. A. (1992). You cain't trus' it: Experts witnessing in the case of rap. In G. Dent (Ed.), *Black popular culture* (pp. 132–128). Seattle: Bay Press.

Benda, B., & Corwyn, R. F. (1998). Race and gender differences in theories of sexual behavior among rural adolescents residing in AFCD families. *Youth and Society, 1,* 59–88.

Brown, J. D. (2000). Adolescents' sexual media diets. *Journal of Adolescent Health, 27,* 35–40.

Brown Douglas, K. (1999). *Sexuality and the Black church: A womanist perspective.* Maryknoll, NY: Orbis Publishing.

Campbell, A. (1991). *Girls in the gang.* Cambridge, MA: Basil Blackwell, Inc.

Carpenter, L. M. (2001a). The ambiguity of "having sex": The subjective experience of virginity loss in the United States. *Journal of Sex Research, 38,* 127–139.

Carpenter, L. M. (2001b). The first time/Das erstes mal: Approaches to virginity loss in U.S. and German teen magazines. *Youth & Society, 33,* 31–62.

Centers for Disease Control (2000). *2000 Adolescent health chartbook.* Atlanta: Centers for Disease Control.

Chassin, L., Presson, C. C., Sherman, S. J., Corty, E., & Olshavsky, R. W. (1984). Predicting the onset of cigarette smoking in adolescents: A longitudinal study. *Journal of Applied Social Psychology, 14*(3), 224–243.

Chideya, F. (1993). How the right stirs black homophobia. *Newsweek, 122,* 16, 73.

Chuck, D. (2001). Essay: The sound of our young world. *Time Magazine, 153,* 5, 66.

Collins, P. (2000). *Black feminist thought: Knowledge, consciousness and the politics of empowerment* (2nd ed.). New York: Routledge.

Coker, C. H. (1999). Total disclosure. *Vibe, 10,* 136–138.

Crocker, J., & Major, B. (1989). Social stigma and self-esteem: The protective properties of stigma. *Psychological Review, 96,* 608–630.

Cutler, C. (1999). Yorkville crossing: A case study of Hip Hop and the language of a White middle class teenager in New York City. *Journal of Sociolinguistics, 3*(4), 428–442.

Dantzker, M. L., & Eisenman, R. (2003). Sexual attitudes among Hispanic college students: Differences between males and females. *International Journal of Adolescence and Youth, 11,* 79–89.

Farley, C. J. (1999). Music: Hip Hop nation. *Time Magazine, 153,* 5, 54–64.

Feit, M. N. (2001). Exposure of adolescent girls to cigar images in women's magazines, 1992–1998. *American Journal of Public Health 2001, 91,* 286–288.

Few, A., Stephens, D., & Rouse-Arnette, M. (2003). Sister-to-sister talk: Transcending boundaries in qualitative research with Black women. *Family Relations, 52,* 205–215.

Fine, M. (1988). Sexuality, schooling and adolescent females: The missing discourse of desire. *Harvard Educational Review, 58,* 29–53.

Frith, S. (1996). *Performing rites: On the value of popular music.* Cambridge: Harvard University Press.

Fullilove, M. T., Fullilove, R. E., Hayes, K., & Gross, S. (1993). Black women and AIDS prevention: A view towards understanding the gender rules. In M. Berer (Eds.), *Women and HIV/AIDS: An international resource book* (pp. 212–217). London: Pandora.

Gillum, T. L. (2002). Exploring the link between stereotypic images and intimate partner violence in the African American community. *Violence Against Women, 8,* 64–87.

Gomez, C. A., & Marin, B. V. (1996). Barriers to HIV prevention strategies for women. *The Journal of Sex Research, 33,* 355–362.

Grant, J. (1992). Black women and church. In G. Hull, P. Bell Scott & B. Smith (Eds.), *All the women are White, all the Blacks are men, But some of us are Brave.* New York, NY: The Feminist Press.

Guy-Sheftall, B. (1990). *Daughters of sorrow: Attitudes toward Black women, 1880–1920 (Black women in United States history, Vol. 11).* New York: Carlson.

Hampton, D. (2000). Flick: Girls interrupted. *Vibe,* June/July, 169–170.

Heaton, J. A., & Wilson, N. L. (1995). *Tuning in trouble: Talk TV's destructive impact on mental health.* New York: Jossey-Bass.

Henderson, E. L. (1996). Black nationalism and rap music. *Journal of Black Studies, 26,* 308–340.

Hoover, T. (1993). Black women and the churches: Triple jeopardy. In J. H. Cone & G. S. Wilmore (Eds.), Black theology: A documentary history, Volume One, 1966–l979 (pp. 293–303). Mary Knoll, NY: Orbis Books.

Irvine, J. M. (1994). Cultural differences and adolescent sexualities. In J. M. Irvine (Ed.), *Sexual cultures and the construction of adolescent identities* (pp. 3–28). Philadelphia: Temple University Press.

Iwamoto, D. (2003). Tupac Shakur: Understanding the identity formation of hyper-masculinity of a popular hip-hop artist. *Black Scholar, 33,* 44–50.

Jackson II, R. L. (1997). Black 'manhood' as xenophobe. *Journal of Black Studies, 27,* 731–751.

Jackson, S. (1996). The social construction of female sexuality. In S. Jackson & S. Scott (Eds.), *Feminism and sexuality: A reader* (pp. 62–73). New York: Columbia University Press.

Jones, L. (1994). *Bullet proof diva: Tales of race, sex, and hair.* New York: Double Day.

Kim, S. (2001). Style council. *Vibe,* 206–210.

Kitwana, B. (2003). *The hip hop generation: Young Blacks and the crisis in African American culture.* New York: Basic Civitas Books.

Lewis, G. B. (2003). Black-White differences in attitudes toward homosexuality and gay rights. *Public Opinion Quarterly, 67,* 59–79.

Lichtenstein, B. (2000). Virginity discourse in the AIDS era: A case analysis of sexual initiation aftershock. *NWSA Journal, 12,* 52–70.

Lorde, A. (1984). *Sister outsider: Essays and speeches by Audre Lorde.* Freedom, CA: Thee Crossing Press.

Malloy, T. E., Fisher, W. A., Albright, L., Misovich, S. J., & Fisher, J. D. (1997). Interpersonal perception of AIDS risk potential of persons of the opposite sex. *Health Psychology, 16,* 480–486.

Marriott, R. (2000). Blowin' up. *Vibe,* 125–132.

McCreary, M., Slavin, L., & Berry, E. (1996). Predicting problem behavior and self-esteem among African-American adolescents. *Journal of Adolescent Research, 11,* 194–215.

McLoyd, V. C. (1998). Changing demographics in the American population: Implications for research on minority children, adolescents. In V. C. McLoyd & L. Steinberg (Eds.), *Studying minority adolescents: Conceptual, methodological and theoretical issues* (pp. 167–182). Mahwah: Lawrence Erlbaum.

Morgan, J. (2002). The war on girls: Sex, lies and videos. *Essence, 2,* 120–124.

Nkrumah, K. (1965) *Neo-colonialism: The last stage of imperialism.* London: Thomas Nelson and Sons.

Odih, P. (2002). Mentors and role models: Masculinity and the educational 'underachievement' of young Afro-Caribbean males. *Race, Ethnicity, & Education, 5,* 91–106.

Outlaw, P. (1995). If that's your boyfriend (he wasn't last night). *African American Review, 29,* 347–351.

Pharr, S., & Raymond, S. G. (1997). *Homophobia: A weapon of sexism.* New York: Chardon Press.

Phillips, L. D., Reddik-Morgan, K., & Stephens, D. P. (2005). Oppositional consciousness within an oppositional realm: The case of Feminism and Womanism in rap and hip hop, 1976–2004. *Journal of African American History, Special Issue-Hip Hop History: Past, Present and Future, 90*(3) 19–32.

Ransby, B., & Matthews, T. (1995). Black popular culture and the transcendence of patriarchal illusions. In

B. Guy-Sheftall (Ed.), *Words of fire: An anthology of African American feminist thought* (pp. 526–536). New York: The New Press.

Rehin, G. (2003). A question of manhood: A reader in U.S. Black men's history and masculinity, "Manhood Rights": The construction of Black male history and manhood, 1750–1870/A Question. *Journal of American Studies, 37,* 335–338.

Regan, P. C., & Berscheid, E. (1996). Beliefs about the state, goals, and objects of sexual desire. *Journal of Sex and Marital Therapy, 22,* 110–120.

Reiss, I. (1967). Response to Coleman's comments on premarital sexual permissiveness. *The American Journal of Sociology, 72,* 558–559.

Reissman, C. K. (1993). *Narrative analysis qualitative research methods.* Thousand Oaks: Sage.

Ro, R. (1996). *Gangsta: Merchandising the rhymes of violence.* New York: St. Martin's Press.

Roberts, R. (1996). *Ladies first: Women in music videos.* Jackson: University of Mississippi Press.

Roberts, T., & Ulen, E. N. (2000). Sisters spin talk on hip hop: Can the music be saved? *Ms. Magazine, 10,* 69–74.

Rose, T. (1992). Black texts/Black contexts. In G. Dent (Ed.). *Black popular culture.* (pp. 132–128). Seattle, WA: Bay Press.

Rose, T. (1994). *Black noise: Rap music and Black culture in contemporary America.* New York: Wesleyan University Press.

Rubio, P. (1993). Crossover dreams: The 'exceptional White' in popular culture. *Race Traitor, 2,* 68–80.

Sanchez Jankowski, M. (1991*). Islands in the street: Gangs and American urban society.* Berkeley, CA: University of California Press.

Sartre, J. P. (2001). *Colonialism and neocolonialism.* New York: Routledge.

Simmons, R. G., & Blyth, D. A. (1987*). Moving into adolescence: The impact of pubertal change and school context.* New York: Aldine.

Skowronski, J. J., & Carlston, D. E. (1989). Negativity and extremity biases in impression formation: A review of explanations. *Psychological Bulletin, 105,* 131–142.

Smart Young, T. (2002). One to watch: Sanaa Hamri, video director. *Essence Magazine, 2,* 84.

Smith, N. (1994). Homophobia: Will it divide us? *Essence, 25,* 128–129.

Smitherman, G. (1977). *Talkin' and testifyin'.* Detroit: Wayne State University Press.

Smitherman, G. (1997). The chain remain the same. *Journal of Black Studies, 28,* 3–26.

Stephens, D. P., & Few, A. L. (2007). The effects of images of African American Women in Hip Hop on early adolescents' attitudes toward physical attractiveness and interpersonal relationships. *Sex Roles: A Journal of Research, 56,* 251–264.

Stephens, D. P., & Phillips, L. D. (2003) Freaks, gold diggers, divas and dykes: The socio-historical development of African American female adolescent scripts. *Sexuality and Culture, 7,* 3–47.

Stephens, D. P., & Phillips, L. D. (2005). Integrating Black Feminist thought into conceptual frameworks of African American adolescent women's sexual scripting processes. *Sexualities, Evolution and Gender, 7*(1), 37–55.

Sterk-Elifson, C. (1994). Sexuality among African American women. In A. S. Rossi (Ed*.), Sexuality across the life course* (pp. 99–126). Chicago: The University of Chicago Press.

Suret-Canale, J. (1988). *Essays on African history: From the slave trade to neocolonialism.* London: Hurst.

Venable, M. (2001). A question of identity. *Vibe,* 98–106.

Wahl, G. (1999). I fought the law, and the cold won: Hip hop in mainstream. *College Literature, 26,* 98–113.

Werner-Wilson, R. J. (1995). Predictors of adolescent sexual attitudes: The influence of individual and family factors. *National Council on Family Relations Annual Meeting.* Portland, Oregon.

Wiederman, M. W., Maynard, C., & Fretz, A. (1996). Ethnicity in 25 years of published sexuality research: 1971–1995. *Journal of Sex Research, 33,* 339–342.

Williams, S. A. (1992). Two words on music. In G. Dent (Ed.), *Black popular culture.* (pp. 164–172). Seattle: Bay Press.

Windham, Y. (1995). Good girls do not do it. *Vital Signs, 11,* 30–31.

Wingood, G. M., DiClemente, R. J., Harrington, K., Davies, S., Hook, E. W., & Oh, K. (2001). Exposure to x-rated movies and adolescents' sexual and contraceptive-related attitudes and behaviors. *Pediatrics, 107,* 1116–1120.

Wingood, G. M., DiClemente, R. J., Bernhardt, J. M., Harrington, K., Davies, S. L., Robillard, A., & Hook, E. W. (2003). A prospective study of exposure to rap music videos and African American female adolescents' health. *American Journal of Public Health, 93,* 437–440.

Wyatt, G. (1997). *Stolen women: Reclaiming our sexuality, Taking back our lives.* New York: Wiley Books.

Young, R. (2001). *Postcolonialism: An historical introduction.* Oxford: Blackwell.

Geisha of a Different Kind: Gay Asian Men and the Gendering of Sexual Identity

Chong-suk Han

Introduction

Shortly before midnight, bodies gyrate to ear-numbing music on a small wood-paneled dance floor on the third level of R-Place, a local gay bar. The rhythmic pump from refrigerator-sized speakers high above on rafters, urge patrons to, "get on off of your feet." As naked torsos bump and grind, scent of cigarettes and alcohol linger in the air. The already small dance floor, tucked neatly into the rear corner, is even more crowded than usual due to the presence of a small, plastic, K-Mart variety kiddie-pool occupying key, center-floor, property. Yet, as oddly out of place as such paraphernalia might be, patrons dance easily and freely around it, almost unconscious of its presence; or at least, unwilling to acknowledge the awkwardness of its mere existence. For those moving in synch to the music, and to those observing the movement of bodies from the sidelines, the small tub and the gold-painted bar that rises out of it and reaches nearly up to the ceiling, is a familiar sight. These are the props required for one of the most staple of entertainments at gay bars around the country, the wet underwear contest.

To these same patrons, the participants in the competition are also a familiar bunch, a cast of characters predictably representing that which is widely valued and desired in the gay community. Young, thin, and overwhelmingly white, the contestants mirror the images found on gay billboards and magazine covers. Deviations from the formula are met with sympa-

thetic laughter or outright disdain. An older man, whose appearance may be frail but is nonetheless full of life, is met with hoots of encouragement. An obese man is confronted with verbal mocks. "That is so gross," I hear someone yell behind me. Making no attempt to lower his volume, the same voice yells out, "What *is* he thinking?" Whether tolerated or castigated, those deviating from the formula never "win." There isn't much room for diversity in this arena, and none seems to be encouraged with a prize.

If the visual image of the "winners" represents what is physically valued and desired in the gay community, their actions represent what is desired behaviorally. Each "performance" is a display of masculinity. Contestants flex muscles, saunter across the floor, and proudly display their manhood for the participants to see. One contestant who just finished 100 crunches—because "the guy with the best abs usually wins"—before coming on stage told me, "you never wear boxers, it doesn't show it off." Apparently, the bigger the "display," the bigger the cheers, and bigger the likelihood of winning. Here, like in many other arenas of contemporary gay life, femininity is discouraged.

Even the most cursory read through gay personal ads, makes the emphasis on "masculinity" blatantly clear. "Straight acting," is a marketing gimmick. In fact, if "straight acting" is a plus for those advertising themselves, "no femmes," is an equally striking warning to potential suitors that femininity is not desired. In this arena of gay life, men are to be men. "If I wanted to fuck a girl, I would find one," a young gay man told me regarding his desire for a "real" man. According to Levine, this hypermasculinization of the gay male image, thus gay male desire, can be traced to "the gay male world of the 1970s and 1980s

From "Geisha of a Different Kind" by Chong-suk Han (2006), *Sexuality & Culture*, 10, 2006, 3–28. Reprinted with kind permission from Springer Science and Business Media.

[that] catered to and supported this hypermasculine sexual code." As a response to the stigmatized "sissies" that defined what it meant to be gay, the "gay clone" came to represent a hypermasculine image for the gay community. "[The gay clones] butched it up and acted like macho men," Levine wrote, "the manliest of men" (1998: 7). Stereotypical images of effeminate gay men still exist, to be sure. However, most of these representations seem to be found in media outlets geared toward heterosexual consumption. When found within gay media, these images seem to represent a form of camp, where gender boundaries are actively challenged for the sake of entertainment value. More importantly, not only is there a "preference" for masculinity within the gay community but also a strong anti-effeminate bias (Taywaditep, 2001).

Yet, here, in the mecca of masculinity, or at least the visual display of it, one racial group of gay men occupies a predominantly feminine space. If the performances of the white contestants are a reflection of the desire for, and expectation of, masculinity, the performances of all-too rare Asian contestants are a reflection of expected femininity. On this particular night, the lone Asian contestant stands quietly waiting among the other contestants for his turn in the tub. While waiting in line, he is noticeably shy, half hiding behind a larger, muscular white contestant. When his name is called, he blushes and shrinks further behind his human shield until the MC coaxes him onto the "stage." While being [led] into the pool, the Asian contestant continues his "performance," giggling with one hand over mouth and feigning hesitation. Where "real" men pushed their way into the pool, the Asian man is pushed into it. Yet, once in the pool, his performance becomes vividly sexual. Hips gyrate and legs fly into the air as the contestant simulates a lone sex act with the giant pole. Whereas the white contestants thrust into the pole, taking the "dominant" position of inserter, the Asian contestant pushes his ass up against it, in the submissive role of receiver.

"Damn," one of his friends yells out, "I knew *she* would tear it up!"

Another friend answers, "You know it." Despite the initial display of hesitation, despite having to be "forced" into the pool, and despite what appeared to

be an overly shy demeanor, the spectators *expected* a sexualized performance. To his friends, and many watching the performance, the "unexpected" turn of events was nothing but expected.

Constructing Gender, Sexuality, and Race

Gender theorists have long argued that gender is a social construction. Butler (1990) maintains that rather than merely being constructed, gender is also performed and it is these performances that give meaning to gender and gender identities. As such, gender is not something we are born with, instinctively knowing how to behave within its confines, but a learned identity reinforced by behaviors thrust onto us by societal expectations of "appropriate" gender behavior. . . .

Much like scholarship on gender, scholarship from queer theorists has also maintained that "queerness" is never just about sexual acts. . . . Gay identities—like gender identities—are formed and negotiated through a wide range of social interactions within the confines of our social positions that we occupy in society and the influences that we take from it, that defines what it means to be "queer" (Vance, 1995). Thus, "being" queer is not merely about our choice of sexual partners but is intimately tied to our sense of self that we continuously perform when we are in public in order to make sense of our sexual identities. . . .

Sexual acts, even outside of sexual identity, are also marked by domination and subordination. During intercourse, it is the penetrating partner who "possesses" the penetrated partner (Dworkin, 1987). Not surprising then, the "receiving" partner in gay intercourse is seen as the passive, submissive, "feminine" actor while the penetrating partner is seen as the active, dominant, "masculine" actor. As such, gender roles are performed and reinforced even during the intimate act of sexual intercourse.

Likewise, students of race have often pointed to the social construction of race and have documented how "race"—rather than a primordial fact—is a socially constructed illusion rooted deeply in time and place (Omi & Winant, 1994). What it means to be a member of a racial category is often contested and changed. During interactions, meanings surrounding race are constantly negotiated and re-negotiated, thereby changing what is meant by "racial" minorities all together. While much less has been written about how race is performed in public, Steele and Aronson (1998) [argue] that racial expectations are often reinforced through personal behaviors.

Yet examining the life experiences of those who are simultaneously gendered, sexed, and raced is never as simple as engaging an additive analysis. Rather, the intersections of race and sexuality form new identities separate from the individual racial and sexual identities that they represent (Nagel, 2003). More importantly for our discussion, not everyone experiences racial, sexual, and gendered categorizations in the same way. Within these categories also lie subcategories. Often a member of the subcategory also inhabits a subcategory of yet another category. Members within these multiple categories do not simply experience being "raced" along with being "gendered." Rather, people who are raced, gendered, and sexualized, experience unique societal pressures specifically because they are raced, gendered, AND sexualized. Gay Asian men do not simply feel racial and sexual oppression but are oppressed in unique ways and experience unique identity issues precisely because they are gay, Asian, and "male."

In this [reading], I examine how gay Asian men have been constructed in the Western, mostly American, imagination and how that construction has affected the development of a gay Asian male identity. It should be noted that "gay Asian men" encompasses a large group of people from different cultural, historical and social backgrounds. Cultural and historical norms regarding homosexual acts and homosexual identities are different in different parts of Asia. However, as Espiritu (1992) points out, identity formation for Asian Americans in the United States are more a reflection of common experiences they found within Western borders than the discrepant histories and cultures of their homelands. Thus, I am more interested in factors that have contributed to how gay Asian men come to make sense of themselves within "Western" borders. As such, my discussion is limited to Asian men who live within "Western" borders, particularly

the United States. Within this narrative, by "Asian" men, I mean those with ancestral roots in East and Southeast Asia (including the Philippines). While West and South Asians have also been influenced by similar historic projects of racial formation discussed by Omi and Winant (1994), their "Western" experience is sufficiently different enough to warrant a different discussion (Shankar and Srikanth, 1998).

Historic Construction of Asian "Masculinity"

The West thinks of itself as masculine—big guns, big industry, big money—so the East is feminine—weak, delicate, poor . . . but good at art, and full of inscrutable wisdom—the feminine mystique . . . . I am an Oriental. And being an Oriental, I could never be completely a man.

—Song Liling in David Henry Hwang's *M. Butterfly*

According to Said, "The Orient was almost a European invention, and had been since antiquity a place of romance, exotic beings, haunting memories and landscapes, remarkable experiences" (1978: 1). But rather than a method of describing the "Orient," along purely "romantic" lines, orientalist discourse acted as a "political vision of reality whose structure promoted the difference between the familiar (Europe, the West, 'us') and the strange (the Orient, the East, 'them')" (Said, 1978: 43) that acted to promote the domination and superiority of all that was "West" against all that was "East." The orientalist project also had the consequence of homogenizing vastly different cultural groups with different views, regarding not only appropriate gender roles but homosexual acts, and placing them all under the umbrella of the "oriental."

That is, what it "means" to be Asian, from a Western perspective, is an entirely constructed image, largely based on Western "expectations" of what is normal and what is "foreign." As such, images painted about what it means to be "Asian" often focus on stereotypical, one dimensional portrayal[s] of Asians and Asian Americans who are nearly always presented as one in the same despite divergent histories, cultural backgrounds, and points of origins. These types of portrayals, then, present gay Asian men, and all other Asians, as being a "certain" way, a way that is distinctively different from the "West," one dimensional, and, fundamentally foreign. But more importantly, as being "inferior." By doing so, it portrays Asian and Asian Americans as being interchangeable with each other. In the Western imagination, all Asians come to be represented by the singular image of the "oriental" despite their points of origin or current locations.

Perpetuating this mirage of Western superiority, orientalist discourse took on a distinctively gendered tone. Within this narrative were the messages of the feminized Asian male body. Hinging on this masculine superiority of the West, Asian bodies, both male and female, were painted with feminine brushstrokes. . . . Even in today's media, Chen notes that "Asian men are rarely portrayed as anything other than housekeepers, waiters, or ruthless foreign businessmen" (1996: 68).

This distinction, particularly useful as a means of justifying the "masculine thrust" on the Asian continent by European colonial powers, became an easy way to maintain hierarchical relations even within Western borders.

For Asian men, the discourse of domination focused largely on the "feminine" East opposed to the "masculine" West. Historic projects that have hindered Asian American family formations and excluded Asian men from the "masculinized" labor market of the "West," have simultaneously produced an image of Asian men that has both racial and gendered implications. . . . [P]opular media portrayals further emasculated Asian and Asian American men until they, "[were] at their best, effeminate closet queens like Charlie Chan and, at their worst, [were] homosexual menaces like Fu Manchu" (Chan et al., 1991: xiii). . . .

Asian men have also been portrayed as being more "traditional" and "conservative" when it comes to sex, while being portrayed as meek asexual houseboys or as sexual deviants (Hamamoto 1994). While the stereotypes of Asian men being sexual deviants and sexual conservatives may seem contradictory, they both serve the purpose of emasculating Asian men in a process that Eng [2001] calls "racial castration."

According to Fung [1996], this desexualization of Asian men helps neutralize concerns regarding a rapidly reproducing racial class and thus eases the mainstream's fear of a growing "yellow peril," eager to dominate Western locations. If Asian men are not "true" men, capable of sexuality—thus, sexual reproduction—they become less threatening to Western minds. . . .

Even when presented as masculine "heroes" by the dominant culture, Asian men continue to be denied sexual prowess. For example, in the blockbuster movie, *Romeo Must Die,* the main "hero" of the film, played by Jet Li, makes no romantic connection with the female lead. When compared to the other films in the action movie genre using the "damsel in distress" formula, the omission of a sexual relationship (implied or explicit) between the male "hero" and the female lead is striking. On a similar thread, the popularity of Jackie Chan in a string of American mainstream films has yet to land him a girl. Instead, his role seems to be limited to playing the comedic sidekick to a male lead who does get the girl (*Shanghai Noon*) or to a female lead who is not the least bit interested in him romantically (*The Tuxedo*). Also, it is important to note that the roots of their "heroic" acts are based on "ancient" and "mysterious" Eastern ways that continue to shroud Asian men under the veiled cloak of orientalism. As such, "Asian men are not able to fulfill their role as 'real men' because they are 'weak,' 'passive,' and 'eunuch-like'" (Chen, 1996: 68).

Representations of Gay Asian Men

Given the long standing racial feminization of Asian men in western discourse, looking at samesex sexuality for gay Asian men involves more than looking at homosexual acts *per se,* but also at the intersections of race, gender, and sexuality and the way that racial and sexual categories have been created for them (Leong 1996). For example, in *Immigrant Acts,* Lowe (1996) points out that nineteenth and twentieth century immigration policies including exclusion lead to the formation of a racialized and gendered Asian male subject. Lowe stresses the judicial processes that led to the demasculinization of

Asian male immigrants through a legal process that led to the inability of Asian men to form heterosexual unions due to immigration laws that barred the arrival of Asian women and anti-miscegenation laws that forbade Asian men from marrying non-Asian women. Left without potential life-partners, Asian men lived in predominantly male communities, forever condemned to a life of bachelorhood. Also, limited career opportunities due largely to restrictions on Asian labor left them with little options other than traditionally "feminine" occupations such as laundry workers, cooks, and domestics. Western notions of appropriate dress also added to the feminization of Asian men whose full pants and long queues (in the example of Chinese American men) led to further feminized view of this group (Chen, 1996).

Thus, conceptions of sexual identity for gay Asian men in the United States is intimately tied to the same processes that led to Asian Americans being racialized, feminized, and marginalized by the mainstream. While heterosexual Asian men have been able to function within the growing Asian American community with various degrees of success, gay Asian men continue to be marginalized both by the dominant society and their respective Asian American communities. More importantly, the 1965 Immigration Law that favored family reunification also helped heterosexual Asian men by allowing them to bring their wives from Asia or return to Asia to find wives. Not only are gay Asian men marginalized, they are made invisible by a new process of racial formation—stressing Asian American "family" values and perpetuating the model minority image for Asian Americans—that simply denies the existence of gay Asian Americans (Leong 1996). Mainstream discussions about Asian Americans often focus on their traditional and family values—two arenas dominated by heterosexist discourse. If Asian men are torchbearers for these values, they simply cannot be gay. At the same time, studies on sex and (homo)sexuality have largely ignored racial minorities in their discussions.

Not surprising then, gay Asian men are virtually non-existent in the gay media as well. Reading through gay publications, it is almost as if no gay Asian men exist outside of the "fantasy cruises" to the "Orient." As Cho notes:

> The pain of being a gay Asian, however, is not just the pain of direct discrimination but the pain of being negated again and again by a culture that doesn't acknowledge my presence. . . . Not only did I have to deal with the question of sexual invisibility as a gay man, there was also the issue of racial invisibility (1998: 2).

When portrayed at all, they are often presented in the feminized "other" to a masculinized white male. For example, a recent ad by Servicemembers Legal Defense Network (SLDN), as a part of their "Let Them Serve" ad campaign which appeared in *The Advocate, Genre,* and other numerous gay and lesbian publications around the country, shows a gay Asian male attempting to provide comfort to what is implied to be his white male lover. In the ad, the Asian male is looking lovingly at his partner with his hands resting gently on his partner's shoulder while his partner is looking solemnly away. The caption which reads, "let him serve," is meant to convey the message that the "masculine" white male is prevented from serving bravely in the armed forces, a fact which dismays him greatly. It is the white male who is the "soldier" while the Asian male is the spouse who stands lovingly beside him during his time of need for feminine emotional support. . . .

When gay Asian men are the objects of gay publications, such as in the magazine *Oriental Guys,* the most famous publication among what Hagland (1998) calls the "rice queen magazines," in reference to "rice queens," non-Asian gay men who prefer Asian sex partners, they are "portrayed as an exotic but ultimately pliant sexual creature whose sexuality is directed outward toward the [gay white male]." Within the context of these magazines, which are produced by white men and meant for white male consumption, descriptions of Asian men take on a noticeably orientalist tone. Hagland quotes one passage from the magazine describing a gay Asian male:

> Jamie is playful and mischievous. There is a boy still playing inside . . . Jamie is proud. He knows his heritage and his roots. . . . He is a rare blend. Tenderness and strength. Playful innocence and unexpected wisdom. . . . He exemplifies exactly what is most enticing and mysterious about all of Asia itself (1998: 278).

The description of Jamie, written by Victor Davis, illustrates how gay Asian men are viewed through the lens of gay white male desire. First, Jamie is both a child and an adult, possessing both "playful innocence and unexpected wisdom." The Asian "child" is to be dominated by white male adult but is also capable of providing the implied sexual "enticement" of the "East." The infantilization of Asian men is not new to gay publications but is a long standing practice of orientalist discourse describing Asian men. As a "child," the feminized Asian male is not capable of achieving the maturity required of adults, much in the way that women are also not capable of achieving "adulthood" (Lim, 1994). Also, he is both tender and strong, taking on an androgynous trait. It is this exotic mysticism that is most noticeable about Asia, and by extension Asian men. Not surprisingly, knowing "his heritage and roots" is important to the white male. As one gay white man told me regarding his preference for newly immigrated men:

> The [Asian guys] who were born here, or even grew up here, are too pushy and demanding. Too much like *American* guys. I think the guys who just got here are more polite and respectful, they have a better understanding of their culture (emphasis added).

It is not simply a phenotype that this man finds attractive but "cultural" traits that he believes some Asian men possess that others do not. It is his desire for someone who is "polite and respectful" that drives his sexual quest. As such, the attraction is not based entirely on physical traits but on an orientalized vision of what someone who "knows his heritage and his roots" is able to provide.

Gay Asian men don't fare much better in American hardcore pornography. As Fung (1991) notes, Asian men are used only as the vassals which fulfill the white males' sexual desires. Within the context of video pornography, it is the white male who is at the center of attention, who is the target of desire, and the "active" partner in sexual intercourse. Asian men, simply provide the "props" required for the white male to reach sexual climax. Ultimately, gay Asian men are nothing but, "feminized bottoms who serve white studs with their asses" (Browning, 1994: 196). In print pornography, white men are often shown full-frontal, while Asian men are shown mostly from the back (Hagland, 1998). Clearly, it is the white male cock (manhood) that is desirable as opposed to the Asian male, whose most desirable attribute is his ass (womanhood). For example, Leong quotes a letter written to *Oriental Guys* where the reader gushes:

> *The image of Sakoi, the handsome Thai adonis featured in this issue (no. 13, 1994) took my breath away. To me he epitomizes that tantalizing fusion of androgynous beauty and potent masculinity, that set Asian males apart. . . . The buns shot is a real prick teaser, firm rounded buns and hairless scrotum, leading ones eye to the centre of ones desire . . . (1996: 13).*

To this reader, and based on the inclusion of this particular letter by the editors of the magazine, many other readers, the "centre of ones desire" when it comes to Asian men is the "buns."

Because gay Asian men are racialized and gendered, their predicted role performance involves becoming the "feminine" counterpart to the "masculine" gay white male. Much like the way that women are "rewarded" for playing the feminine role, gay Asian men are "rewarded" by the dominant gay community for performing their prescribed gender roles. Because being with a gay white man is seen by gay Asian men as being favorable to being with other men of color, they learn to behave in the ways that will allow them to be desirable to white men. Writing for the Gay Asian Pacific Support Network, Jason Chang notes:

> *Most of the gay Asians I knew would only date white guys, and most of us just accepted this as the norm. But as I looked more deeply into the phenomenon, I was astonished by how widespread it was, at just how huge a percentage of gay Asian men were attracted only to white men. I thought of how my gay Asian friends and I accepted dates from Caucasian men we weren't even attracted to, just so we could have a white partner (2001: 58).*

Moreover, he goes on to write:

> *I started noticing that in gay magazines and newsweeklies, almost every personal ad placed by a "GAM" (gay Asian male) was for a "GWM" (gay white male). . . . It wasn't just that gay Asian men were mainly looking for Caucasian partners, it was also that many were*

strongly, viscerally opposed to ever dating another Asian (2001: 59).

Unfortunately, for gay Asian men, being with a white partner often means acting the part of the feminine, mysterious, and submissive sexual "other." A gay Vietnamese American social worker told me:

I did a small mini-experiment in a gay chat room. I posted two profiles, they were exactly the same, except on one, I put that I was Asian and on the other, I didn't put a race. I was going to say "white"—but I didn't want to lie. Well, the guys who responded to the profile without my race started with something like, "hi" or "what's up?" [The] guys who responded to my profile that said "Asian" were much more aggressive. They said, something like, "Do you like to be fucked?" But the most interesting thing is, the guys who didn't know I was Asian would negotiate about being a top or bottom. The guys who knew I was Asian would automatically assume I was a bottom and if I told them that I wasn't, they would stop the conversation right away.

In the context of this performance, gay Asian men are limited in their ability to question the sexual actions of the dominant white partner or to negotiate a sexual role for himself. Rather, he is expected to take on the role that is prescribed to him if he wants the "prize" of white male companionship. In fact, David Henry Hwang argues that within gay Asian/white relationships:

The Asian virtually always plays the role of the "woman"; the [white male], culturally and sexually, is the "man". . . . [Gay Asian men] would be taunted with phrases which implied they were "lesbians" if they dated other Asian men. (1986: 98)

So ingrained is the feminine gender role among gay Asian men that dating another Asian man would be akin to lesbianism, where two women enter into a mutually romantic and sexual relationship. Hagland also notes the lesbianization of intra-Asian male coupling. According to Hagland:

The intra-Asian coupling portrayed [in gay porn] is constructed largely by Caucasians for their own gratification: the Asians, whether constructed in fictional narrative or choreographed in pornographic video and film, perform for the "gaze" of the GWM much as the

"lesbians" in heterosexual pornography perform in the genre of "fake lesbianism" (1998: 285).

Much like the "fake lesbians" in straight-male pornography, the sexual act is not performed for their satisfaction but for that of the voyeur. As such, the implication is that they would not "normally" be engaging in such acts but do so in order to please the white male. Likewise, when I asked one gay Asian man why he does not date other Asian men, he told me, "It would be like dating my *sister* (emphasis added)." Also, for some gay Asian men, femininity becomes a strategy for attracting "masculine" white men. Manalansan describes a Filipino cross-dresser in New York City who favors "exotic" *nom de plumes* such as "Suzy Wong" or "Nancy Kwan," who specifically targets men who are attracted to "beautiful, oriental" cross-dressers rather than "compete in the hypermasculine, gym-oriented world of mainstream gay life," (1996: 54) where nobody would give him a second look due to his "slight build." Feminization also means that gay Asian men have little control over who they date. Even in gay bars, gay Asian men seem to play the role of the "woman" waiting to be chosen. As Cho recalls about his days at a gay bar:

While white men cruised looking for their prey, most Asians stood back, lined up against the wall like beauty pageant queens waiting to be chosen. . . . With all the attention focused on white guys, I instinctively knew that as a gay Asian, I rarely had the power to choose and would always be the one chosen (1998: 3).

Again, the pursuit of white male companionship limits the opportunities for gay Asian men to choose, pursue, and conquer the sexual targets of their choice. Instead, they are led into the submissive position of waiting to be chosen and being grateful for the opportunity. . . .

Discussion

In *Black Skin, White Masks,* [Frantz Fanon] describes how stereotypical images can lead to a "consciousness of the body that is solely a negating activity" for blacks (1967: 110). According to [Fanon], negative stereotypes perpetuated by the dominant culture are internalized by blacks and leads to the devaluation of the black body. In the process, blacks come to favor white bodies and begin to associate all positive things with whiteness while associating all negative things with blackness. [Fanon's] work on internalized racism (1967) along with theories of internalized colonialism (Memi, 1965) also provides important insights to how the dominant discourse is internalized by subaltern groups. Thus, when gay Asian men internalize these stereotypes, they also internalized the corresponding expectations, leading them to perform them in much the way that gender is performed. In a classic case of "self-fulfilling prophecies," expectations about performances can actually lead to behavior (Berger et al., 1985; Steele and Aronson, 1998). If gay Asian men are expected to perform certain roles, and many gay Asian men expect to perform them, many gay Asian men will act in accordance with these expectations.

Sadly, many gay Asian men seem to have accepted the stereotypes presented to them by the dominant gay community. For example, in his article, "Using chopsticks to eat steak," Kent Chuang quotes a young gay Asian man as stating:

> There [in Europe] we [Asians] are considered exotic. The Europeans treat us like special people, like a real woman. They buy us dinner and drinks and even drive us back to the hotel (emphasis added) (1999: 34).

Not only are they exotified by gay white men, gay Asian men also tend to exotify themselves. By doing so, gay Asian men further alienate themselves from, and marginalize themselves in, the mainstream gay community.

In addition, Asian men themselves have also bought into the gay western notion of what is desirable. Ayers explains that:

> The sexually marginalized Asian man who has grown up in the West or is western in his thinking is often invisible in his own fantasies. [Their] sexual daydreams are populated by handsome Caucasian men with lean, hard Caucasian bodies (1999: 91).

Mirroring this sentiment, gay Asian men who recently appeared on a local cable access television show in Seattle aptly titled, "Rice Queens" all indicated a preference for "blonde, blue-eyed, masculine

guys." Not surprising then, Phua and Kaufman (2003) found that gay Asian men were the most likely among all racial groups to indicate a preference for "only" white men in internet personal ads. While 31% of gay Asian men explicitly indicated "white only" in their personal ads, only 8% indicated "Asian only" as their preference with none explicitly preferring another race. Also, in a survey of gay Asian men in San Francisco, Choi and her colleagues (1995) found that nearly 70% of gay Asian men indicate a preference for white men. This high percentage is particularly telling given that within gay Asian communities, San Francisco is seen as a mecca for "sticky rice," Asian men who prefer to date other Asian men. If even in this mecca, the vast majority of Asian men prefer to date white men, anecdotal evidence suggests that the percentage is much higher in other locales. More damaging to the gay Asian population is that most of these men seem to be competing for the attention of a limited number of "rice queens" (Ayers, 1999). Other writers also note this phenomenon. Chang (2001) notes that it is this competition for a limited number of white men who prefer Asian men that leads to gay Asian men viewing each other as competitors rather than compatriots. This competition hinders the formation of a unified gay Asian community and further acts to splinter those who should be seen as natural allies.

In addition, gay Asian men report feeling inadequate within the larger gay community that stresses a Eurocentric image of physical beauty (Ayers, 1999; Choi et al., 1998; [Chuang,] 1999). Given these feelings of inadequacy, gay Asian men may suffer low levels of self-esteem and actively pursue the company of white men in order to feel accepted by the gay mainstream. In addition to seeking the company of white men over that of other Asian men, the obsession with white beauty leads many gay Asian men to reject all aspects of themselves as Asian. For example, Chuang writes about how he tried desperately to avoid anything related to his Chinese heritage and his attempts to transform his "shamefully slim Oriental frame . . . into a more desirable western body." (1999: 33)

Sadly, when gay Asian men are deeply integrated into the dominant gay community, they are more likely to be exposed to these stereotypes and, in turn, these stereotypes are more likely to influence them. While no empirical study about gay Asian male socialization into the dominant gay community yet exists, Carrier and Magana (1992) found that for gay Mexican American men, sexual behavior was influenced by their level of socialization into the gay "white" majority and their enculturation into the Mexican community. . . . As gay Asian men begin to learn the "rules" of conduct within the gay community, they learn that they are not likely to find a white male partner unless they can provide for the orientalized fantasy. Thus, they internalize these stereotypes and learn to perform them in gay interactions.

Rather than simply affecting their self-esteem and choice of partners, the gendered racialization of gay Asian men within the gay community has larger consequences. For example, Wilson and Yoshikawa (2004) point out that social discrimination faced by gay Asian men within the gay community can lead to detrimental results in their health and well-being, particularly when it comes to HIV risk behaviors. In addition, the "feminine" role adopted by gay Asian men may lead to a higher vulnerability to same-sex domestic abuse for gay Asian men, especially for those with white partners (Poon, 2000).

According to Walters (1998), the development of healthy group and self identities among members of oppressed groups, including the facilitation of the pressures of the dominant society with the competing demands of their own ethnic, racial, and sexual communities, can lead to psychological well-being for gays and lesbians of color. In her work, she finds that gay Native Americans who are more enculturated into Native American communities are better equipped to handle the emotional stress of being gay in a gay white community. O'Donnell et al. (2002) found a similar pattern within gay Latino men. In their study, gay Latino men who were better attached to their ethnic communities were much less likely to engage in unprotected anal intercourse than those who were not connected to their Latino communities. Clearly, the behavioral "demands" placed on gay Asian men due to their racialized and gendered position within the larger gay community, if added to a lack of enculturation into their respective

Asian American communities, is likely to hinder the development of healthy group and self identities for this group.

REFERENCES

Ayers, T. (1999). China doll: The experience of being a gay Chinese Australian. In P. Jackson and G. Sullivan's (Eds.) *Multicultural queer: Australian narratives.* New York: Haworth Press, Inc.

Berger, J., Wagner, D., & Zelditch, M. (1995). Expectation states theory: Review and assessment," in *Status, rewards, and influence.* J. Berger and M. Zelditch (Eds.). San Francisco, CA: Jossey-Bass.

Browning, F. (1994). *The culture of desire: Paradox and perversity in gay lives today.* New York: Vintage Books. Butler, J. (1990). *Gender trouble: Feminism and the subversion of identity.* New York: Routledge.

Carrier, J.M., & Magana, J.R. (1992). Use of ethnosexual data on men of Mexican origins for HIV/AIDS prevention program. *The time of AIDS.* G. Herdt & S. Lindenbaum (Eds.). London: Sage.

Chan, J., Chin, F., Inada, L., & Wong, S. (Eds.) (1991). *The big Aiiieeeee! An anthology of Chinese American and Japanese American literature.* New York: Meridian.

Chang, J. (2001). The truth about GAM. *aMagazine.* February/March. 58–60.

Chen, C.H. (1996). Feminization of Asian (American) men in the U.S. mass media: An analysis of The Ballad of Little Jo. *Journal of Communication Inquiry 20*(2): 57–71.

Cho, S. (1998). *Rice: Explorations into gay Asian culture and politics.* Toronto: Queer Press.

Choi, K.H., Coates, T.J., Catania, J., et al. (1995). High HIV risk among gay Asian and Pacific Islander men in San Francisco. *AIDS 9:* 306–307.

Choi, K.H., Yep, G.A., & Kumekawa, E. (1998). HIV prevention among Asian and Pacific Islander American men who have sex with men: A critical review of theoretical models and directions for future research. *AIDS Education and Prevention, 10* (Suppl A): 19–30.

Chuang, K. (1999). Using chopsticks to eat steak. In P. Jackson & G. Sullivan's (Eds.) *Multicultural queer: The Australian narratives.* New York: Haworth Press, Inc.

Dworkin, A. (1987). *Intercourse.* New York: Free Press.

Eng, D. (2001). *Racial Castration: Managing Masculinity in Asian America.* Durham, NC: Duke University Press.

Espiritu, Y. (1992). *Asian American Pan-Ethnicity.* Philadelphia, PA: Temple University Press.

Fanon, F. (1967). *Black Skin, White Masks.* New York: Grove.

Fung, R. (1996). Looking for my penis. *Asian American sexualities.* R. Leong (Ed.). New York: Routledge.

Hagland, P.E.P. (1998). "Undressing the oriental boy": The gay Asian in the social imagination of the gay white male. *Looking queer: Body image and identity in lesbian, bisexual, gay and transgender communities.* D. Atkins (Ed.). New York: Harrington Park Press.

Hamamoto, D. (1994*). Monitored Peril: Asian Americans and the Politics of TV Representation.* Minneapolis, MN: University of Minnesota Press.

Hwang, D. (1986). *M. Butterfly.* New York: Plume Books.

Leong, R. (1996). Home bodies and the body politic. *Asian American sexualities.* R. Leong (Ed.). New York: Routledge.

Levine, M. (1998). *Gay macho: The life and death of the homosexual clone.* New York: New York University Press.

Lim, S. (1994). Gender transformations in Asian/American representations. *Gender and Culture in Literature and Film East and West: Issues of Perception and Interpretations.* N. Masavisut, G. Simson, & L. Smith (Eds.). Honolulu, HI: University of Hawaii Press.

Lowe, L. (1996). *Immigrant Acts.* Durham, NC: Duke University Press.

Manalansan, M. (1996). Searching for community: Filipino gay men in New York City. *Asian American sexualities.* R. Leong (Ed.). New York Routledge.

Memi, A. (1965). *The colonizer and the colonized.* Boston, MA: Beacon Press.

Nagel, J. (2003). Race, ethnicity, and sexuality: *Intimate Intersections, Forbidden Frontiers.* Oxford: Oxford University Press.

O'Donnell, L., Agronick, G., Doval, A., Duran, R., Myint-U, A., & Stueve, A. (2002). Ethnic and gay community attachments and sexual risk behaviors among urban Latino young men who have sex with men. *AIDS Education and Prevention, 14*(6): 457–471.

Omi, M., & Winant, H. (1994). *Racial formation in the United States.* New York: Routledge.

Phua, V., & Kaufman, G. (2003). The crossroads of race and sexuality: Date selection among men in internet "personal" ads. *Journal of Family Issues 24*(8): 981–994.

Poon, M.K. (2000). Inter-racial same-sex abuse: The vulnerability of gay men of Asian descent in relationships with Caucasian men. *Journal of Gay and Lesbian Social Services, 11*(4): 39–67.

Said, E. (1978). *Orientalism.* New York: Vintage Books.

Shankar, L.D., & Srikanth, R. (1998). *A part, yet apart: South Asians in Asian America.* Philadelphia, PA: Temple University Press.

Steele, C., & Aronson, J. (1998). How stereotypes influence the standardized test performance of talented African American students. *The Black-White Test Score Gap.* C. Jencks and M. Philips (Eds.). Washington D.C.: Brookings Institute.

Taywaditep, K.J. (2001). Marginalization among the marginalized: gay men's anti-effeminancy attitudes. *Journal of Homosexuality 42*(1): 1–28.

Vance, C. (1995). Social construction theory and sexuality. *Constructing masculinity.* M. Bergre, B. Wallis, & S. Watson (Eds.). New York: Routledge.

Walters, K. (1998). "Negotiating conflicts in allegiances among lesbians and gays of color: Reconciling divided selves and communities," in *Foundations of social work practice.* G. Mallon (Ed.). New York: Harrington Park Press.

Wilson, P., & Yoshikawa, H. (2004). Experiences of and responses to social discrimination among Asian and Pacific Islander gay men: Their relationship to HIV risk. *AIDS Education and Prevention 16*(1):68–83.

Gay-for-Pay: Straight Men and the Making of Gay Pornography

Jeffrey Escoffier

Situational homosexualities emerge when heterosexually-identified individuals encounter institutional settings that permit or reward homosexual behavior. Simon and Gagnon's (Gagnon and Simon 1973; Simon and Gagnon 1986) theory of sexual scripts allows us to understand situational sexualities as the result of interplays among stereotyped social cues, prescribed role-playing, enabling social conditions, and the converging intra-psychic motivations of participating individuals. Both the norms that regulate sexual behavior and the enabling social conditions that elicit and permit homosexual conduct from heterosexually-oriented participants can be activated using sexual scripts that circulate throughout the culture. Cues and social roles are embedded in culturally available scenarios, while the enabling conditions are often those material circumstances (prisons, barracks, economic need, drug use, or porn studio) that limit or exclude the supply of potential heterosexual sex partners (Escoffier 1999). In contrast to its use in the 1940s and 1950s, I distinguish situational sexuality from sexual behavior as governed by the individual's sexual identity which, over the course of his life, is constantly forged, reinforced, interrupted and reconfigured within and through culture and history.

In many cases, sexual scripts are situationally specific. The "situation," in part, emerges from the characteristics (gender, race, age) of the potential population of sex partners which constrain or normalize a sexual repertoire not normally chosen by the situated

From "Gay-for-Pay: Straight Men and the Making of Gay Pornography" by Jeffrey Escoffier (2003), *Qualitative Sociology* 26: 531–555. Reprinted with kind permission from Springer Science and Business Media.

individual. Albert Reiss's classic essay "The Social Integration of Queers and Peers" explored a form of homosexual prostitution that took place between young men ("peers") who did not "define themselves either as hustlers or as homosexuals" and homosexual men ("queers") who performed fellatio upon them (Reiss 1961, p. 102). Reiss found that certain norms governed the sexual transactions that occurred between the young men and homosexuals, the most important that it be undertaken "solely as a way of making money: sexual gratification cannot be actively sought as a goal in the relationship." Another was that the transaction between them "must be limited to mouth-genital fellation. No other sexual acts are tolerated" (ibid.). Reiss also found that the young men defined someone as homosexual "not on the basis of homosexual *behavior,* but on the basis of participation in the homosexual *role,* the 'queer' role."

In this article I examine the homosexual activities of a group of men whose primary sexual identities are not gay, yet who regularly perform in gay pornographic videos. These men are widely known in the porn industry and among spectators as "gay-for-pay," the implication being that they would not engage in homosexual conduct were they not paid to do so. Of course, there are many explanations for such behavior. I will argue that this group of men exemplifies "situational homosexuality." There is no irrefutable evidence establishing these men as *really* straight or *actually* gay but in denial. However, all sexual conduct in the video porn industry is to one degree or another an example of situational sexuality inasmuch as the performers are often required to engage in sexual acts for monetary compensation that they would not otherwise choose to perform and with partners for whom they feel no desire.

The Gay Porn Industry: Identity Politics and Markets

Since the late 1960s, the pornography industry in the United States has grown rapidly. While there is little reliable information about its size or annual revenues, experts estimate that the "adult entertainment" industry—which includes "XXX" videos and DVDs, Internet porn, cable and satellite porn, peep shows, phone sex, live sex acts, sex toys, and porn magazines—takes in somewhere between eight and ten billion dollars per year. That is comparable to Hollywood's annual domestic ticket sales or the annual revenues of professional sports. Again, while there are no reliable estimates, the gay market represents a significant portion of this amount—probably from ten to twenty-five percent (Antalek 1997a; Rich 2001; Thomas 2000).

Until the early 1970s male homosexual pornography was produced and distributed under "black market" conditions. The first commercial male pornographic films were probably made in the late 1960s, but they were few in number (Waugh 1996). Only after the gay movement had gained momentum were companies formed explicitly to produce gay male pornography. The production and distribution of commercial gay pornography took off between 1970 and 1985. Initially, gay pornographic movies were made by amateur filmmakers, and to some degree, many of the films made in this period represented an expression of the filmmaker's own newly "liberated" homosexuality—this was especially true for many of the performers. This development also reflected the liberating effect of the sexual revolution: during the same period, straight erotic films, such as *I Am Curious (Yellow), Deep Throat, The Devil in Miss Jones* and *Last Tango in Paris,* often played in mainstream movie houses. Wakefield Poole's gay *Boys in the Sand* opened in 1973, followed shortly by Jerry Douglas's *Back Row* (1974) and, like straight erotic movies, both films played in mainstream movie houses.

After 1985, production of gay pornography entered a new period in which video technology and extensive ownership of VCRs lowered its cost and made pornography more accessible. It became inexpensive

and easy to rent. The new technology also enabled pornography to be viewed privately and at home. The AIDS crisis reinforced the privatized experience, some viewers turning to video porn out of fear of engaging in homosexual activities.

Moreover, starting in the mid 1980s, the gay market developed into a lucrative and dynamic growth sector for many industries, supplying specialty consumer goods to satisfy the aesthetic, social and sexual preferences of homosexuals. The commercial development of gay male pornography also benefited greatly from the growth of the gay market and urban gay communities by supplying erotic images to a growing number of self-accepting gay men. This demand helped shape the business in a number of ways: the standards of physical attractiveness, the repertoire of sexual acts, the production values, and the narrative conventions closely reflected the prevailing attitudes of gay male consumers.

In the early days of gay commercial pornography, it was difficult to recruit performers because homosexual behavior was still highly stigmatized and production was illicit. The performers were frequently recruited by the filmmakers (who were primarily gay) from among friends, casual sexual partners and boyfriends (Douglas 1996a). There was no pre-existing network or agents to recruit performers for gay pornographic films. . . .

Today, the gay pornography industry has a highly developed infrastructure of production companies, distribution networks and technical services, as well as agents and scouts for performers. If the first phase (1970–1985) in the development of commercial gay pornography attracted primarily gay men as performers, the second phase (post-1985) began to attract performers who did not identify as gay or homosexual. One contributing factor is that male performers were better paid in the gay pornography industry than in the straight side of the business. Given the heterosexual focus of straight pornography and the primarily male audience, the industry's female performers are better paid than most of the male performers. The prolific director Chi Chi Larue estimates the number of straight men in gay pornographic videos to be sixty percent. I suspect that this is on the high side, or it may merely reflect her selection of performers for her own work. By the mid 1980s, there was active recruiting of performers by scouts, photographers and others who work in the gay segment of the industry.

The Spectator of Gay Pornography: Documentary Illusion and Identity Effects

Pornography probably has a more significant role in the life of gay men than it does among comparable groups of heterosexual men. Gay men often turn to gay pornography for cultural and sexual validation. As film critic Richard Dyer has noted, gay pornography contributes to the education of desire—it provides knowledge of the body and of sexual narratives, and examples of gay sexuality and of sexuality within a masculine framework. Since most gay men have become adults without having been socialized in the social and sexual codes of their communities, pornography can contribute to that as well (Dyer 1992).

The pleasure and sexual excitement that viewers of porn experience depend, to some degree, on the patterns of social and sexual interactions (i.e., the narratives, cues and symbols) that circulate in the larger culture (Kipnis 1996; Loftus 2002). The gay spectator's psychological response to the fictive world of pornography and sexual fantasy—the symbolic conditions of sexual arousal—and the everyday life of social roles, values and social structures is mediated by the ideological and social developments of the gay community; not only do psycho-social elements predominate in the organization of the pornographic materials, but both the immediate social context and wider social environment also influence the sexual response to pornography (Gagnon and Simon 1973, pp. 260–265). Gagnon and Simon, in their analysis of pornography, show that an individual's fantasy life and his capacity for sexual arousal is significantly influenced by cultural context and historical situation. For example, in gay porn condoms are widely used (for many years they have appeared in almost all videos) for anal intercourse, in sharp contrast to their virtual absence in heterosexual pornography. Some gay men find that they are not aroused by the sexual action in "pre-condom" era movies, made before the discovery of AIDS—in this way the ideological and social context clearly influence the potential for sexual excitement.

In the case of video pornography, its effectiveness stems from its ability to satisfy the viewer's expectation that the sex is plausibly "real" in some way—a pornographic film or video is a "document" of sexual pleasure, of successful arousal and orgasm. The viewer's sexual arousal presumes the suspension of *disbelief* in pornography's fictional character. A "documentary illusion" exists in the photographic pornographic genres, which promise to enact certain sexual fantasies and certify them through the "authenticity" of *erections* (although some significance may be lost with the increased use of Viagra and other drugs) and *orgasms*. The psychological as well as the ideological power of pornography is achieved through this certification of sexual fantasy by its "documented" sexual conclusions—visibly displayed orgasms (Patton 1988, pp. 72–77; Williams 1989, pp. 93–119; Barthes 1986).

Viewers' responses and reviews of porn videos often minimize the genre's ambiguous expectations between fantasy/fiction and real sex. The sexual acts portrayed must seem genuinely exciting to the performers in order to arouse the viewer (they must be realistically credible), while also representing fantasies that invoke the culture's sexual scenarios. Reviewers sometimes will stress the "realness." "Ultimately what viewers want to see," one reviewer writes, "is guys *having* sex, not actors *pretending* to have sex. A few times there were some moans and some 'Oh, yeah, fuck me!' that sounded like typical porno soundtrack, but other than that this all seemed very authentic" (Foxxe 1999). . . .

Pornography's *identity effects* are enunciated through the genre's dominant semantic and syntactical conventions: the "standard" narrative sequence (kissing, oral sex, rimming, anal intercourse) of sexual acts, a convincingly energetic performance and, most importantly, the *erections* and visible *orgasms* that authenticate (and narratively close the scene) the embodied forms of homosexual desire. Operating within the "documentary illusion" the erections and the orgasms putatively "prove" to a gay male spectator that these "sexually desirable, masculine, and energetic performers" are *really* gay—thus affirming the gay male identity. An individual video may often deviate from these generic expectations, either through failure to provide a credible performance or by offering new or creative sexual variations.

In addition to its identity effects, gay male porn also has a somewhat paradoxical "hetero/masculinist effect," in which the generic conventions that consolidate and reinforce gay male identity coexist with frequent representations of "straight" men engaging in homosexual acts. In this way gay porn reinforces the incongruity between male homosexual desire—stigmatized, abject—and the heterosexual dominance of the masculine regime of desire. It serves to situate homosexual *desire* within masculine territory irrespective of heterosexual or gay identities (Pronger 1990, pp. 125–176). Thus, the widespread employment of straight performers in gay pornography intensifies the contradiction between *gay male identity* and *homosexuality without identity,* conferring legitimacy on homosexual *behavior* independent of gay identity.

The creation of a market for gay pornography relies upon the cultural and economic significance of gay identities, and not—however widespread it may be among males—homosexual desire (Bronski 1984, pp. 166–174; Burger 1995; Harris 1997; Chasin 2000). Its expansion into other identity markets continues to reflect a significant trend in the gay pornography business, hence the growing number of videos targeting various demographic or sexual audiences— Latinos, black men and other gay men of color, the leather, S/M and bear subcultures, and all sorts of sexual specialties like spanking, uniforms and other fetishisms (Suggs 1999).

The central ambivalence between *identity* and *behavior* in gay male porn frames the reactions of spectators to—along with their libidinal investments in—porn "stars" (Dyer 1979, pp. 17–19). The gay men who buy or rent and view a video expect the sexual pleasure portrayed to be "authentic" enough to produce an orgasm. For the most part, the orgasm affirms the sexual act leading up to it and contributes to the viewer's own sexual arousal (Patton 1988; Williams 1989). But if the performer isn't gay, then the potential "meaning" of the orgasm is ambiguous. It can mean that orgasm is "acted" (or dramatically

fabricated in some sense—"It's really only a heterosexual orgasm!"), or it can mean that even a straight man experienced an orgasm from sex with a man— this is one of the central ambiguities of gay porn (Pronger 1990, pp. 125–154). It potentially undermines the viewer's willingness to suspend disbelief in the fictional aspect of the porn video. Thus, while every pornographic movie made for a gay male market manifestly performs at least two tasks—to sexually stimulate its viewers and, in some way, to affirm their sexual identity—it may also perform a third and more contradictory task: to provide evidence of *homosexuality without identity* (Bech 1997, pp. 17–84). It may do so either narratively, through the inclusion of scenes portraying straight men having credible sex with gay men, or by employing "known" heterosexual (gay-for-pay) performers to credibly represent gay male sexuality.

The Theory of Sexual Scripts

. . . Gagnon and Simon introduced a thoroughgoing conception of sexual behavior as a learned process, one that is possible not because of instinctual drives or physiological requirements, but because it is embedded in complex social scripts that are specific to particular locations in culture and history. Their approach stressed the significance of individual agency and cultural symbols in the conduct of our sexual activities. . . . No previous theorists of sexuality had interpreted sexual behavior as so completely social. They redefined sexuality from being the combined product of biological drives and social repression into an arena of creative social initiative and symbolic action. . . . In their theory they argue that individuals utilize their interactional skills, fantasy materials and cultural myths to develop "scripts" (with cues and appropriate dialogue) as a means for organizing their sexual behavior (1973; Simon and Gagnon 1986).

Sexual arousal and the performance of sexual acts frequently depend upon the meanings and cues of the social and cultural context. In fact, human sexual behavior is organized by structured expectations and prescribed interactions that are coded like scripts. The theory of sexual scripts as formulated by Gagnon and Simon provides a useful analytical framework for exploring the dynamics of sexual performance in pornographic production. Scripts are metaphors for the narrative and behavioral requirements for the production of everyday social life. In their theory of sexual scripting, Simon and Gagnon (1986) suggest that these "scripts," with cues and appropriate dialogue, which are constantly changing and which reflect different cultural groups, circulate in societies as generic guidelines for organizing social behavior. They distinguish three distinct levels of scripting: *cultural scenarios* provide instruction on the narrative requirements of broad social roles; *interpersonal scripts* are institutionalized patterns in everyday social interaction; and *intrapsychic scripts* are those that an individual uses in his or her internal dialogue with cultural and social behavioral expectations (ibid., pp. 98–104). For example, interpersonal scripts help individuals to organize their self-representations and those of others to initiate and engage in sexual activity, while the intrapsychic scripts organize the images and desires that elicit and sustain an individual's sexual desire. Cultural scenarios frame the interpersonal and intrapsychic scripts in the context of cultural symbols and broad social roles (such as race, gender or class) (Goffman 1976).

Thus the making of pornography, like other forms of sex work, relies upon the learned sexual responses of its participants—much of the sexual behavior shown in pornography is a display of situational sexuality. However, unlike other forms of sex work, gay pornography as a representational genre, which often implicitly reflects as well as affirms an *identitarian* agenda, is explicitly marketed to self-identified gay men. However, the gay male pornography industry routinely recruits men who do not identify as gay or homosexual to perform in gay videos. In addition, non-gay-identified men frequently have used their work in gay pornography to launch lucrative careers as escorts. Nevertheless, the fact that industry gossip about sexual orientations circulates constantly demonstrates how important these issues are to the industry's operation as well as to the audience's response (for examples of this kind of fan discourse see the forums at www.atkol.com). In gay pornographic videos, the ability of actors who are self-defined and otherwise behaviorally heterosexual to perform homosexual

acts, maintain erections (both while penetrating or being penetrated) and have orgasms provides the opportunity to explore the construction of situational homosexuality on the gay pornography set.

One distinctive characteristic of video pornography is that it is a dramatic fabrication of sexual activity that also requires demonstrations of "authentic" sexual signs, that is, erections and orgasms. The dramatic fabrication is achieved not only by the performers enacting sexual scenes but also by elaborate editing and montage of the filmed sexual acts themselves. Usually the filming of a sexual scene requires many takes, stops and starts, and requires the performers to regain their erections. The maintenance and refreshing of erections—"wood" in the industry vernacular—is a constant preoccupation of video pornographers.

The gay pornography business, through its employment of men who are heterosexual or who do not self-consciously identify as gay, provides straight actors with social conditions that enable situationally specific sexual behavior. The pornography industry supplies (1) the social and physical space where these sexual activities can take place; it provides (2) other actors who expect to engage in sexual activities with one another; and it offers (3) narratives of sexual activities that invoke the culturally available sexual scripts that elicit and activate the filmed sexual activities. Pornographic video production is obviously a "situation" in which sexual activity can take place: it provides access to sexual experiences for its participants (Simon and Gagnon 1986, pp. 104–107).

Gay-for-Pay as a Porn Career: Constructing the Persona

It is common practice that when anyone enters the porn industry they adopt a stage name—a *nom de porn*—by which they will be known to viewers. This protects the performer's privacy despite what is often a very visible public presence. In addition to taking the *nom de porn,* the performer must create his "character" as a performer. This persona is a "career script" through which the performer integrates traits of personality, physical characteristics and sexual performance style.

The new "porn star" fashions himself from the cultural myths and social roles that define male sexuality or violate masculine roles, or that affirm homosexual desire or draw upon ethnic or racial beliefs. Performers must obviously also draw upon their "intrapsychic" fantasies and beliefs. Thus one performer may create his persona as the aggressive, dirty-talking "top" (the one who penetrates). In Rod Barry's case, his persona enables him to play the military man having sex in the barracks, a white trash hillbilly who fucks his cousin Seth but who won't kiss (they are "fucking cousins, not kissing cousins"), or a man who, in his first scene as a "bottom" (the one who is penetrated), "aggressively" urges on the man who tops him (Escoffier 2000). Another performer might create his persona as an exclusive top, a man with a large penis and a man who never kisses—elements drawn from sexual scripts, from both cultural scenarios and intrapsychic fantasies or fears.

Whatever his sexual preferences, when any man seeks employment in gay pornographic video production he must justify his choice from a number of perspectives. Participation in gay pornographic video production is, to some degree, a socially stigmatized activity (especially for those who do not identify as gay), not only because it is a form of sex work and because most people believe that public sexual performance negatively affects those who participate in it, but also because homosexuality is still a stigmatized form of sexuality. Thus, every new entrant into the porn business must give himself *permission* to engage in it (Simon and Gagnon 1986, pp. 109–110; Abbott 2000). Men who identify as heterosexual wanting to work in the gay porn industry must overcome the standard presumption that only gay men would want to perform in gay pornographic films. Obviously, the description of these performers as "gay-for-pay" presumes that the permission they require is primarily economic. But economic permission is often entangled with other reasons, such as curiosity or latent homosexual fantasies, such as in the following example:

> Um, well, I was straight before I found out about gay videos, but I was a straight person with, like, thoughts and feelings. And through my twenties, they got real

strong. I almost thought I would try to have an interlude or a contact with a man. I thought about it, yeah, I was, like, one of those straight-curious types. But then I got into gay video, and I decided I can simultaneously make money and fulfill a fantasy. The money's a perfect way to justify going into the sexual world. I guess I consider myself formerly straight and now I'm sexually bi with a lifestyle of straight (Paul Morgan, in Spencer 1998).

Permission for some performers can come from surprisingly odd sources. One performer, who had "danced" in local Latino gay bars in Jackson Heights in New York City, gave one of the more unusual forms of permission:

> *Interviewer:* How did you get started in this business?
> *Tiger Tyson:* I just went in and did the video Tiger's Brooklyn Tails about two years ago. It turned out very successful. I didn't know I was going to become this whole character.
> *I:* Did making films come naturally?
> *TT:* It was something new, being that I'm bisexual. You could say I lost my virginity on video . . .
> *I:* You haven't bottomed on film. Would you?
> *TT:* No, never. I would probably turn into a little punk . . . I wouldn't feel right being on the bottom.
> *I:* Do you now date guys?
> *TT:* No. Actually I'm engaged. She's very supportive . . . I met her at Magic Touch while I was dancing for gay men, and she knows all about the videos. My mother is even supportive . . . that's why I don't bother to think I'm doing something wrong. If my mother doesn't feel disgraced, I feel good about it (Straube 1999).

Dancing or stripping in gay bars, as Tyson's story suggests, is a common way of entering the world of gay porn, where other dancers or agents will scout for producers of gay videos (De Marco 2002). But many of the young straight men who enter the gay porn industry develop their permission to engage in homosexual activity in a video by using a surprisingly limited number of "scripts." One of the most common narratives that gay-for-pay performers tell of their entry into the industry is the story of responding to a modeling ad or the approach of a recruiter who misleadingly offers to set up a photo shoot that turns out to be a nude photo shoot or porn audition. Brian Estevez, who worked in the industry in the late 1980s, gives this account of his recruitment:

> **Brian Estevez:** *They wanted to see my whole body . . . and I thought: "What the fuck is this?" . . . At that point, I began to wonder what was going on and what the deal was. I turned to the old guy and said, "You told me modeling. What is this shit?" He then told me that these guys had big companies and that they made movies. I told him I didn't want to do movies—and then he started talking money and I swear . . . I don't know . . . I guess money manipulated me . . . I didn't want to do it!*
>
> **Interviewer:** *And then the next step?*
>
> **BE:** *. . . and I went ahead, even though I'm very straight to this day.*
>
> **I:** *Now about being straight . . .*
>
> **BE:** *. . . You know, I grew up very straight—never had any homosexual tendencies.*
>
> **I:** *You didn't connect it in any way to sexual pleasure?*
>
> **BE:** *I didn't get any sexual stimulation from it. Even to this day, even in a sexual act, even if I have a hard-on and everything—I still didn't connect it to "Wow, this feels good."*
>
> **I:** *And yet you started in films as a bottom?*
>
> **BE:** *Well, I didn't have a lot of choice.*
>
> **I:** *I'd think a straight boy would be a bit put off—that being a top would be more logical . . . more straight.*
>
> **BE:** *I know—and that's how I felt. I'd much rather be a top, and in my later movies I didn't bottom anymore. It's just when they manipulated me into the business, they manipulated me into being a bottom. They told me that I wasn't big enough or buff enough to play a top role, so I was labeled a bottom—a small, hot guy who gets dick up his ass. After a few times around, I said, "Fuck it—I'm not doing that anymore."*
>
> **I:** *Was the fact that you were doing it eating away at you?*
>
> **BE:** *[quietly] Yeah—being a top would have been easier on my ego.*
>
> **I:** *Did you enjoy it while it was happening?*
>
> **BE:** *No, I didn't, because suddenly, out of nowhere, I was taking these big, hot monster dicks up my ass. It wasn't pretty (Richards 1991).*

Estevez's construction of permission to perform in gay porn involves a series of disclaimers: "I'm very straight to this day," "I didn't get any sexual stimulation . . . even if I have a hard-on," and "I didn't have a lot of choice [to bottom]." Elaboration of permission

and the construction of a persona often go hand-in-hand. Estevez's account illustrates this when he explains that "they manipulated me into being a bottom. They told me that I wasn't big enough or buff enough to play a top role, so I was labeled a bottom—a small, hot guy who gets dick up his ass . . . being a top would have [been] easier on my ego." Eventually, he refused to bottom, and in his later videos he only topped. However, it is clear from the permission Estevez gives himself and his ambivalence about the roles he performs in gay pornography that his persona is fashioned from other socially prevalent sexual scripts. Particularly noteworthy is his need to disclaim the evidence of erections as signifiers of sexual pleasure in a publication for gay men.

Constructing a persona is an important step for any new entrant in the gay industry, but for the straight performers it is probably the most important step. Gay men can rely to some extent on their private sexual personalities. For the heterosexual man, constructing a persona becomes the basis for navigating the demands of directors, agents, interviewers and audience members, and provides a foundation for determining what sexual acts and roles he will perform. In part, the persona is the self-conscious construction of a "personal" sexual script that draws on the individual's intrapsychic script as well as on grand cultural scenarios. The persona is a sort of sexual resume which the actor constructs around the kind of permission that he gives himself for entering the gay pornography business, but it is also based on the image that he wishes to project of who he is as a sexual performer. The persona is what sociologist Erving Goffman has called (following certain vernacular uses) a "front": ". . . that part of the individual's performance which regularly functions . . . to define the situation for those who observe the performance" (1959, pp. 22–30). The actor's porn persona consists of a hodgepodge of beliefs about gender, sexuality, identity, acceptable sexual scripts that he may engage in, and his repertoire of acceptable sexual acts. Thus the actor's porn persona is a "situational sexual identity" that is constructed to be used within the confines of a porn career and the gay porno business. The persona is important because it enables the performer to have a self-concept that gives him permission to engage in homosexual activity and thus to sustain a credible sexual performance, to have erections and to produce orgasms.

Once the actor has his porn persona, he will use it to negotiate auditions, interviews with the press, street encounters with fans and, most importantly, performances. He will use the persona to answer questions about why he started doing gay pornography (e.g., "I'm in it for the money"), his sexual orientation, his physical assets as a sexual performer (muscles, penis size, a "fuckable" ass), those particular sex acts he will or won't do, and to limit who is cognizant of his career in gay porn, and to provide plausible excuses for any failure to turn in credible performances. Another aspect of a porn persona is whether the actor engages in professionally related activities like escorting or dancing. Usually, people in the industry—agents, directors or journalists—help new entrants develop their porn personas. Often, industry insiders inject a more palpable "marketing spin" into a new actor's persona. Insiders also supply standard terms like "top," "bottom" or "versatile" for roles involving anal intercourse, or more complex terms like "sex pig," "trade" or "straight bottom" to characterize the actors' porn performances.

When a gay-for-pay performer successfully conveys sexual pleasure, fans begin to question the performer's sexual orientation. Frequently a performer will concede that he is in fact bisexual. Describing himself as sexual is at least as common:

> *Interviewer: Obviously, you think of yourself as heterosexual . . .*
> *Rod Barry: [interrupting] I wouldn't say "heterosexual." I'd say "sexual."*
> *I: What's the difference between being sexual and bisexual?*
> *RB: I think bisexual means you're a switch-hitter, you like it both ways. Sexual is you like an orgasm and you don't care how you get it . . . (Douglas 1998a).*

Porn personas are intentionally constructed to facilitate work in the porn industry, but they often reflect intrapsychic investments. Rod Barry's description of himself as "sexual" may be more than a justification or permission to engage in homosexual sex. Over the course of his career he has insistently characterized himself as "sexual" or even "omni-sexual" rather than gay or bisexual: "Don't call me gay. Don't call me

straight. Don't call me bisexual. Just call me sexual. I can cater to anybody . . . a gay male, a transsexual, or a female," he proclaimed in another interview (Antalek 1997b). He suggests a sexuality for himself that encompasses a wide range of "object choices" and roles (top or bottom); his image may embody an emerging style of masculine sexuality, one envisioned by Foucault: "What these signs and symbols of masculinity are for is not to go back to something that would be on the order . . . of machismo, but rather to invent oneself, to make oneself into the site of production of extraordinarily polymorphous pleasures" (Escoffier 2000; Foucault quoted in Halperin 1995, pp. 89–90).

Virtually every actor who makes a name for himself as a top is challenged to bottom at some point in his career. Rod Barry, a former Marine and one of the top gay-for-pay porn stars in the late 1990s, was frequently asked if he would bottom. He always replied, "Where's the bucks?" The decision to bottom is justified in many ways but, like other aspects of the persona, involves repackaging symbolic resources, social roles and culturally available sexual scripts:

> *I: Was "getting fucked" a big step or just another step?*
> *RB: Another step. Obviously, it's a big step, because in the industry, everybody makes a big deal out of it . . . That day was, to me, like any other day. Except for the fact that I was "getting fucked" . . . It's different from what I was doing, but it's just like any other day at the office.*
> *I: Did you feel that you were playing a feminine role at that moment?*
> *RB: No. No. No. And if you watch the movie, I don't think so, because I'm an aggressive top and I was also an aggressive bottom, playing the same way, like reaching around and grabbing his ass and pulling him: "Do it right!" (Douglas 1998a)*

Barry's performance as a bottom was very favorably reviewed by fans and critics. In a review in *Manshots*, director Jerry Douglas wrote: "Either Barry is one hell of an actor or he does delight in bottoming . . . his pleasure seems downright palpable. His energetic response to the rutting, the sparkle in his eyes, his joyous grin, and his rockhard erection all confirm that he is indeed as exciting a bottom as he is a top" (Douglas 1998c, pp. 38–39). . . .

The longer their porn careers, the more actors are under pressure to revise their personas, to expand their repertoire of sex acts, and to put themselves into new situations in order to avoid becoming too predictable, and therefore boring to their fans. An integral dynamic of the porn industry, and for many forms of sex work, is a steady pressure for "fresh meat." . . . Most porn actors are aware of this retrogressive dynamic and try to develop a career strategy for their post-porn careers. Some leave the industry and go into other careers or businesses. Some work behind the scenes in porn, while others increasingly rely on escorting or some other form of sex work— which usually just stretches out the retrogressive dynamic over a longer period. Some performers will try to hold onto their fans by expanding their sexual repertoire—they will bottom or do a gang bang picture. But this progression usually leads to lower budget productions as well. "One interesting thing about this business," director Kristen Bjorn observed, "is that the longer you are in it, the less money you are paid. Once you are an old face, and an old body, forget it. You're through as far as your popularity goes" (De Walt 1998). . . .

Wood and Money Shots: Sexual Performance as Work

. . . While porn actors, like other sex workers, may exclude certain activities from their repertoire, their sexual behavior is governed by the demands and constraints of the video production context. Heterosexual actors in gay pornography must necessarily engage in homosexual sex acts. However, in the context of video production, three other factors help to define their sexual activities. One is the constant interruption of the homosexual activities in which they engage. A second is the use of various forms of heterosexual pornography—such as straight porn magazines or hetero porn videos shown on television monitors on the sidelines—as aids in maintaining their erections and stimulating orgasm. Third is post-production and editing, which result in the illusion of an "authentic" sexual performance. The finished movie is the combined product of the credible sexual performances of the actors, the director's skill in motivating and preparing the actors to perform the sexual acts filmed, and the success of post-production editing in sustaining the credibility and coherence of the sex portrayed and minimizing any discrepancies between the actors' personas and their sexual performances.

For the straight actor in gay pornography, it is the on-set performance of homosexual acts that defines his ability to successfully manage the situationally specific sexual demands. Many of these heterosexual actors claim that their first sexual encounter with another man was on the set of a gay porn video. Thus, even before his first homosexual experience, a straight actor must choose his repertoire of sexual acts. Certainly his most significant decision is whether or not he will engage in anal intercourse as a top or as a bottom. The repertoire of sex acts is very much a part of the actor's development of his porn persona. The shaping of his persona is dependent on those sexual scripts—those that exist in the culture at large, his own intrapsychic ones or those he can imagine in his everyday life—in which he is able to invest his energy. Thus, for the straight actor, there is a continuum from the "trade" role, where the actor refuses all "gay" sex roles or reciprocity, to that of "sex pig," where he engages energetically in all aspects of sexual activities, to the "straight bottom" role, in which the straight actor engages primarily as a bottom.

The trade role is the gay porn role in which the actor "presumably" can maintain the most distance from the stigma of being labeled as homosexual but, ironically, the straight bottom is a role that allows the performer to demonstrate that he is not aroused even though he is being penetrated—QED he is not gay. The straight bottom, since he does not even need to produce an erection, requires even less of a libidinal investment than does an actor with a trade persona. However, the straight bottom role may also be adopted when an actor doesn't have the confidence or ability to maintain an erection in order to anally penetrate his co-star. One such performer, Tim Barnett, during an interview questioning his choice of roles, responded:

> ***Interviewer:*** *Since you were relatively new to male-male sex . . . did you lay out any rules? . . . Was the whole menu of what you [were] going to do discussed, or was it just "You're going to bottom"?*

Tim Barnett: I think it was more or less discussed when I came out [to Los Angeles].

I: The scene was filmed around what you were willing to do?

TB: Right. And I'm very versatile . . .

I: Was there ever any question . . . whether you would top or if it would be a flip-flop?

TB: . . . They wanted me to top Greg or do a flip-flop, and it just never came about . . . I just don't know if I'm comfortable enough with the sex yet that I would be a top.

I: It's easier to be a bottom.

TB: It's a lot easier to be a bottom (Douglas 1996b).

Despite the relative "ease" of bottoming, the *1996 Adam Gay Video Directory* (Anonymous 1996) was, nevertheless, critical of Tim Barnett's performances: "Tim is a big beefy blonde who just loves to get fucked. Unfortunately, he enjoys giving his co-stars pleasure so much he rarely has time to maintain his own erection." (Here the reviewer maintains the public pretense of Barnett's libidinal investment, attributing his lackluster performance to his focus on giving pleasure to his co-stars.) Even gay actors, like straight actors, may have difficulties staying hard while being penetrated. That can be ignored, if they project some form of libidinal engagement. Without any erections or effective engagement a straight bottom cannot give a credible performance.

Once the actor decides on the acts he is willing to perform, the major practical issue is the enactment of a credible performance of sexual acts. As I have already mentioned, heterosexual actors often use straight porn magazines, straight videos on monitors or "fluffers" (performers who fellate the actor off-camera) to help themselves achieve erections. Tim Barnett, the straight bottom quoted above, was asked if he used the person he was playing opposite to or if he drew on his own private world to get himself aroused. The actor answered: "Both. It really depends who it is. I really like my nipples played with, and sometimes the other person will be the kind of person I'd like to have playing with my nipples. A lot of times I'll use a magazine" (Douglas 1996a).

Another adaptation is the development of what might be called a "professional" work ethic on the porn set. Still photographer Greg Lenzman discusses one such actor:

Usually, with the gay-for-pay, there are certain things they will not do or they don't have that energy. But there are some exceptions. Rod Barry, who started off more as a straight—I think he's now moved on to a lot of stages in his video career . . . [H]e will give all for his shoots and is very supportive of other performers. He's a joy to work with on a set, and you just know you're going to have a good scene with Rod Barry. The scene with Rod bottoming for the first time was just like an evolution (Douglas 1998b).

Dirk Yates, the director-producer who discovered Rod Barry, concurred:

He seemed pro from the first day I met him . . . He did twenty-nine scenes in a year. He started right off the bat. And I believe the guy's straight—maybe I'm wrong—but I've never seen such a performer. He would never turn you down on anything (Lawrence 1999).

To porn video viewers, an important element is the sexual chemistry of the performers. It is unclear how often this is really the performers' chemistry or the result of editing and post-production work. How do performers who are not gay manage to project the sexual appeal needed to attract viewers? Gay-for-pay performer Rod Barry insists that "porno is all about energy" (Douglas 1998a).

Kristen Bjorn, probably the most successful contemporary director of gay porn, has made a series of videos using predominantly performers who do not identify, in any sense, as gay or homosexual (Jamoo 1997). While most of his actors are Latin American and European (and therefore from societies with different "sexual scripts"), they nevertheless have a large following of American gay men. Both Bjorn and his assistant director, who goes by the name of "the Bear," have discussed the desirability of using straight actors many times. In one interview, the Bear notes:

. . . Straight men usually have less of a problem getting erections for still photography as well as video. I believe that they are better prepared to come to work knowing that sexual energy must come from themselves through fantasy, memories, erotic magazines, etc. Gay men often come to work thinking that their work is going to be a realization of a sexual fantasy that they have had for a long time. When they realize that they are not in control of the sexual activity, partners, and duration, they

become detached and often bored with it and one another. When a gay model is turned on to another model, it can be great to film. In many cases the models are not that excited by each other, especially after four full days of filming the same sex scene. As one model put it at the end of a scene, "That was the longest trick that I ever had!" Once a gay model has decided that he is not sexually interested in the other models, it seems most difficult to bring him into the action and get him aroused. Straight boys don't seem to be as dependent upon the excitation of the other models nor as concerned whether or not they are exciting their partners. But when a gay model perceives that he is not arousing his partner, as often happens in scenes that involve gay and straight models together, it can make him feel insecure with himself. This affects his ability to get erections and ejaculate. Straight models are not as sensitive to the stimuli that can make or break a gay model's performance (Bear 1999).

The dynamics between gay men and straight actors is another important factor in the production of credible homosexual performances. Homophobic attitudes on the part of a straight actor often undermine the necessary "sexual chemistry." Gay actors often complain about working with straight performers. As the Bear notes, gay men are much more sensitive to the sexual chemistry between themselves and the straight actors. The identity issue frequently surfaces in gay men's assessment of working with heterosexual actors. Tommy Cruise, who explicitly identifies as a bisexual and as a bottom, comments:

One of the things I hate is working with straight guys, because if they're not attracted to me, then I don't like it. People say, "What is your favorite guy like?" It doesn't matter as long as they like me. That turns me on. If someone wants to fuck me really bad, that just turns me on—because they want me. Don't ask me why, I don't really know. That's what does it for me. It's not very enjoyable for me when I'm with a straight guy. A lot of straight guys, they don't even want me touching them. I'm like, "Why are you even in the business?" I've only worked with two straight guys who were okay—and one of them actually blew my mind. He was the strangest dude I ever saw. He was like, "Okay, time to get a hard-on." Boom, he'd get a hard-on. It's like he's standing there like a friggin' robot. "Okay, time to come." Boom, he comes. He was so on-cue, it was kind of freaky, but he was so good to work with (Douglas 1999).

Cruise's remarks point to the importance of the straight actor's attitude towards gay men and homosexuality, in addition to his intrapsychic need for his sexual partners to find him attractive. Buddy Jones, a gay man who has performed in several Kristen Bjorn movies, found it enjoyable to work with a straight actor. He reported:

. . . It was a turn-on working with a straight boy . . . who was eating my ass and sucking my dick. And he was really good at that, especially the rimming. I was concerned about turning him on while he was fucking me, because I was really turned on. I thought that in his mind he was just working. But then his hard cock was up my ass and his hot cum shot all over me, and it kind of made me wonder if he was really enjoying it (Bear 1999).

One gay man, Eric Hanson, who performs primarily as a top, says that his favorite co-star is "straight bottom" Kurt Stefano: ". . . He has a great persona about him. I think it's the straight thing going on with him. Straight-acting guys are a total turn-on" (Adams 1998).

By itself, the porn persona is not sufficient for the successful management of sexual performances. . . . Getting wood and producing orgasms are merely the certifying components of sexual performances in pornographic movies. Porn actors must convincingly play the roles of men engaged in sex in other ways in order to sustain a credible homosexual performance. As one porn actor after another iterates in interviews throughout the gay press and pornography magazines, making porn is hard work (no pun intended).

The Camera Frame: Sexual Scripts and Video Production

. . . For straight performers, the gay porn video set provides highly structured access to homosexual activity. It is a social space dense with sexual cues (Simon and Gagnon 1986, pp. 105–107). Video production organizes the space (both physical and social) where sex will take place. But the making of pornography necessarily invokes the culture's generic sexual scenarios—the sex/gender scripts; racial, class and ethnic stereotypes; the dynamics of domination and submission; and various reversals and transgressions of these codes. Porn video scripts utilize these cultural and symbolic resources. These culturally significant symbolic codes help mobilize the actor's private desires and fantasy life in the service of the video's sexual narrative.

The making of a porn video requires not only the performance of real sexual acts but also the simulation of a coherent sexual "narrative." Real sex acts are usually performed, but the video representation of them is more coherent than the actual sexual activity being filmed. The shooting of any sexual scene is made up of an apparently simple sex act photographed from several different perspectives. In fact, the performed act is interrupted many times to arrange shooting angles and lighting and to allow the actors to "get wood"—to regain their erections.[1] For example, the cameraman crawls under actors fucking doggie-style, then shoots them from above to show penetration of the ass, then from behind the active party to catch yet another penetration shot of the hard penis going in and out. Then the "money shots" (shots of the actors ejaculating) of all the performers in the scene have to be choreographed, often at the end of many hours of filming. The actors may need help of various kinds to help them ejaculate—heterosexual porno magazines, porn videos on monitors, or manipulation by one of their co-actors such as biting their nipples, inserting a finger in their anus, or kissing them. Thus a 15-to-20-minute sexual scene that the viewer sees is edited and patched together, with soundtrack added, from footage shot over a six or seven hour period. . . .

Ultimately, it is the director's choreography of sexual performances and the effectiveness of the editing process that give pornography its quality as an idealization of sexual performance. Whatever shortcomings commercial pornography exhibits—the repetitiveness of sexual activities, inadequate performances (flaccid erections, lackluster orgasms, bored actors) and shoddy production values—they are exacerbated by the idealization that pornography as a medium promotes. . . .

The director uses the porn actor's persona as the raw material for the sexual plot when choreographing the sexual combinations. Of course, sometimes actors can't successfully manage the persona that they want to project. For example, if a straight performer whose persona presents him as "trade" (i.e., he will not perform oral sex, allow himself to be penetrated, or kiss) can't get an erection, making him unable to penetrate the performer assigned to play bottom, then he and the director must negotiate some modification in order to have a credible sex scene. If he isn't fired and replaced, the actor with the "trade" persona may have to perform outside his persona—perform oral sex or agree to bottom—in order to get paid. In the last couple of years, Viagra has helped in achieving and maintaining erections, but there are still numerous other problems involving an actor's ability to live up to his persona and perform credible sex.

Conclusion

The making of gay male pornography provides an interesting example of the dynamics of situational homosexuality. Since performing in pornography is a kind of sex work, the performers' sexual conduct is a specific response to their customers' preferences and does not represent the preferred sexual responses of the performer. In other words, the sex that is performed is that for which the customer is willing to pay (Adams 1999, pp. 102–121).

In gay pornography, the participants have had to develop a "persona" or "front" (a *nom de porn,* sexual histories, a repertoire of sex acts) to negotiate the social demands they must contend with as sexual participants. Like any front, it is more manageable if it is, to some degree, consistent with biographical attributes of the participant. But the persona also provides the performer with a way of invoking the potential cultural scenarios and sexual scripts that are compatible with his intrapsychic scripts (Goffman 1959). The production process of gay pornography creates a *situation* that enables straight men to engage in homosexual sex for money. It is a highly organized commercial space that supplies sex partners, symbolic resources and other erotic stimulants, and a video production technology that can produce coherent and credible sexual narratives and images.

The *identitarian* expectations of gay spectators shape both the making of a pornographic video and their interpretations of the sexual performances. It is commonly presumed that when an actor in a pornographic video has an erection while being penetrated he must be gay. In contrast, I have argued that credible homosexual performance, whether or not it sexually arouses the performer, can take place without conscious identification as a homosexual person or even without spontaneous preference for homosexual forms of activity. Situational homosexualities emerge when heterosexually identified individuals encounter situations that enable or reward homosexual behavior.

Situational homosexuality is socially constructed sexuality. All sexual performance is fundamentally situational and does not always result in long-lasting social psychological commitment to any one form of sexual activity. It is a process that draws on both *intrapsychic scripts* and *cultural scenarios* and integrates them into the *interpersonal scripts* of everyday social life. The theory of sexual scripts presumes that sexual performance is not about discovering and pursing one's intrapsychic desires (the presumptive core sexual self), but about defining and constructing scenarios of desire using cultural scenarios and negotiating interpersonal situations (Gagnon and Simon 1973; Foucault 1997). The men who work in the gay porn industry—whether gay, straight or "sexual"—must all construct scripts in order to perform. In this way they are no different from any person engaging in sexual activity—since all sexual performance is situational.

NOTES

1. This has changed to some degree since the introduction of Viagra in 1998. Regaining erections is now much quicker.

REFERENCES

Abbott, S. A. (2000). Motivations for pursuing an acting career in pornography. In R. Weitzer (Ed.), *Sex for sale: Prostitution, pornography and the sex industry* (pp. 17–34). New York: Routledge.

Adams, J. C. (1998). The Adams report, www.radvideo.com/news/adamhans.html.

Adams, M. (1999). *Hustlers, escorts, porn stars: The insider's guide to male prostitution in America.* Las Vegas: The Insider's Guide.

Anonymous (1996). Current performers: Tim Barnett. In *1996 Adam Gay video directory* (pp. 7–8). Los Angeles: Knight Publishing.

Antalek, J. (1997a). Porn in the USA. *Q San Francisco,* October/November (http://qsfmagazine.com/9711/index.html).

Antalek, J. (1997b). Porn in the USA: Rod Barry. *Q San Francisco,* October/November (http://qsfmagazine.com/9711/index.html).

Barthes, R. (1986). The reality effect. In R. Barthes (R. Howard [Trans.]), *The rustle of language* (pp. 141–148). New York: Hill and Wang.

Bear (1999). Interview with Buddy Jones. *Manshots,* 11 (pp. 30–33, 80).

Bech, H. (1997). *When men meet: Homosexuality and modernity.* Chicago: University of Chicago Press.

Bronski, M. (1984). *Culture clash: The making of Gay Sensibility.* Boston: Alyson.

Burger, J. R. (1995). *One-handed histories: The erotopolitics of gay male video pornography.* Binghampton: Harrington Park Press.

Chasin, A. (2000). *Selling out: The gay and lesbian movement goes to market.* New York: St. Martin's Press.

De Marco, J. R. G. (2002). The world of gay strippers. *The Gay and Lesbian Review,* 9, March/April (pp. 12–14).

De Walt, M. (1998). The eye of Kristen Bjorn. *Blueboy,* January (pp. 52–55).

Douglas, J. (1996a). Jaguar Productions: Interview with Barry Knight and Russell Moore. *Manshots,* 8, Part 1: June (pp. 10–15); Part 2: August (pp. 10–15, 72).

Douglas, J. (1996b). Interview with Tim Barnett. *Manshots,* 8, February (pp. 30–33, 72–73).

Douglas, J. (1998a). Interview with Rod Barry. *Manshots,* 10, June (pp. 53–57, 72–73).

Douglas, J. (1998b). Behind the camera: Interview with Greg Lenzman. *Manshots,* 10, August (pp. 10–15, 81–82).

Douglas, J. (1998c). *Beach buns* (review). *Manshots,* 10, November (pp. 38–39).

Douglas, J. (1999). Interview with Tommy Cruise. *Manshots,* 11, October (pp. 66–71, 78–79).

Dyer, R. (1979). *Stars.* London: British Film Institute.

Dyer, R. (1992). Coming to terms: Gay pornography. In R. Dyer, *Only entertainment* (pp. 121–134). London: Routledge.

Escoffier, J. (1999). Non-gay identified: Towards a post-identitarian theory of homosexuality. Paper presented at the annual meeting of the Eastern Sociological Society, March 6.

Escoffier, J. (2000). Dirty white guy: Rod Barry's career from Marine to porn star. Unpublished paper.

Escoffier, J., & Spieldenner, A. (1998). Assessing HIV prevention needs for immigrant men who have sex with men (MSM) in New York City. Grand Rounds, HIV Center for Clinical and Behavioral Studies, Columbia University, School of Public Health, New York, April 30.

Foucault, M. (1997). Sex, power and the politics of identity. In M. Foucault (P. Rabinow [Ed.]), *The essential works of Michel Foucault, 1954–1984, volume I: Ethics, subjectivity and truth* (pp. 165–173). New York: The New Press.

Foxxe, A. (1999). Home bodies. *Unzipped,* August 31 (p. 40).

Gagnon, J. H., & Simon, W. (1973). *Sexual conduct: The social sources of human sexuality.* Chicago: Aldine.

Goffman, E. (1959). *The presentation of the self in everyday life.* New York: Doubleday Anchor.

Goffman, E. (1974). *Frame analysis.* New York: Harper & Row.

Goffman, E. (1976). *Gender advertisements.* New York: Harper & Row.

Halperin, D. (1995). *Saint Foucault.* Cambridge: Harvard University Press.

Harris, D. (1997). The evolution of gay pornography: Film. In D. Harris, *The rise and fall of gay culture* (pp. 111–133). New York: Hyperion.

Jamoo (1997). *The films of Kristen Bjorn.* Laguna Hills: Companion Press.

Kipnis, L. (1996). How to look at pornography. In L. Kipnis, *Bound and gagged: Pornography and the politics of fantasy in America* (pp. 161–206). New York: Grove Press.

Lawrence, D. (1999). *The Dirk Yates collection: Adam Gay video erotica.* Los Angeles: Knight Publishing.

Loftus, D. (2002). *Watching sex: How men really respond to pornography.* New York: Thunder's Mouth Press.

Patton, C. (1988). The cum shot—three takes on lesbian and gay sexuality. *OUT/LOOK,* 1, (pp. 72–77).

Pronger, B. (1990). *The arena of masculinity: Sports, homosexuality and the meaning of sex.* New York: St. Martin's Press.

Reiss, A. (1961). The social integration of queers and peers. Social *Problems,* 9, (pp. 102–120).

Rich, F. (2001). Naked capitalists. *The New York Times Magazine,* May 20, (pp. 51–56, 80–81, 92).

Richards, R. W. (1991). Interview with Brian Estevez. *Manshots,* 3, (pp. 53–58,79).

Simon, W., & Gagnon, J. (1986). Sexual scripts: Permanence and change. *Archives of Sexual Behavior,* 15, 97–119.

Spencer, W. (1998). Interview with Paul Morgan. *Manshots,* 10, December, (pp. 52–57, 72–73).

Stoller, R. J. (1991). *Porn: Myths for the twentieth century.* New Haven: Yale University Press.

Straube, T. (1999). Porn profile: Tiger Tyson. *HX,* May 14, (p. 68).

Suggs, D. (1999). The porn kings of New York. *Out,* June, (pp. 85–89).

Thomas, J. A. (2000). Gay male video pornography: Past, present and future. In R. Weitzer (Ed.), *Sex for sale: Prostitution, pornography and the sex industry* (pp. 49–66). New York: Routledge.

Waugh, T. (1996). *Hard to imagine: Gay male eroticism in photography and film, from their beginnings to Stonewall.* New York: Columbia University Press.

Williams, L. (1989). *Hard core: Power, pleasure and the "frenzy of the visible."* Berkeley: University of California Press.

What We Know about Pornography

Clive M. Davis and Naomi B. McCormick

What Is Pornography?

The word pornography derives from a Greek word meaning writing about prostitutes. Although there is no widely accepted modern definition, the common element in all definitions is that the material is sexually explicit. Controversy revolves around whether specific depictions are art or smut, good or bad, innocuous or harmful. People often label as pornographic material that violates their own moral standards and use the terms artistic or erotic for sexual materials they find acceptable.

Pornography must be distinguished from obscenity. Obscenity is a legal term identifying material that has been judged by the courts to have violated specific statutes pertaining to sexually explicit material. Central to these statutes is whether the material violates community standards of acceptability and whether it involves minors. Thus, many books, movies, and even advertisements that are acceptable today could have been judged obscene earlier in our history.

The Effects of Exposure to Sexually Explicit Material

Since the 1960s, research has been conducted to assess the effects of exposure to sexually explicit material. Primary attention has been paid to commercially produced materials intended to generate sexual arousal and/or activity in adult audiences. Three components have been of principal interest: (a) the degree of explicitness, (b) whether the material also contains aggression, and (c) whether it depicts women in demeaning and degrading ways. . . .

Reactions

People vary in response to sexual materials: Some react negatively to all depictions, whereas, others find at least some material acceptable and arousing. Materials that are liked produce more positive emotions and greater sexual arousal than those that are disliked, for both sexes. Nonetheless, sexual arousal may occur even when people are mildly offended. Men tend to respond more positively to the more hard-core and male-dominated material; women tend to react more negatively to this material.

Individuals who hold authoritarian beliefs and have conservative social and religious attitudes tend to experience more sex guilt and react more negatively to explicit materials. Even if they do experience arousal, they judge the material to be undesirable.

Hypermasculine men tend to hold more negative and sexist attitudes toward women. They also are likely to believe that women respond positively to dominant, aggressive men. These men react more positively to scenes of sexual aggression and degrading portrayals of women. Most people, both men and women, respond negatively to this type of material.

Changes in Sexual Attitudes and Sexual Behavior

Repeated exposure generally increases tolerance of explicit material and to the behaviors depicted, except for those who start out with negative attitudes. Those who are aroused by the material are likely to engage in sexual acts, such as masturbation or coitus, within a few hours of exposure. Repeated short-term exposure results in increased disinterest and satiation, but after a period of no exposure, the impact is regained.

Attitudes toward Women and Aggressive Behavior

For obvious ethical, moral, and legal reasons, researchers have not conducted experiments to determine whether exposure to material in which high levels of sexual explicitness and violence are both present leads to increased sexual violence. They have, however, looked at whether men with a history of such exposure are more likely to have committed sex crimes. Sex offenders tend to come from restrictive and punitive home environments. Compared to nonoffenders, they have had more undesirable experiences during childhood, including heightened exposure to sexual and physical abuse. Some offenders have had more exposure to explicit materials than other men, but early exposure alone does not increase the risk of becoming a sex offender.

In controlled laboratory research, individuals have been exposed to material containing (a) both aggression and explicit sex, (b) only aggression, and (c) only the sexual material. The results suggest it is exposure to aggression that triggers aggressive behavior. Exposure to sexual material alone does not increase aggression toward women. For most people, aggression and sex are incompatible. For a small percentage of men predisposed to aggression toward women, however, combining sex and aggression does stimulate arousal and aggressive responses.

The impact of exposure to sexist, demeaning material depends on the person's pre-existing attitudes. Under some conditions, those predisposed to negative views become more calloused and accepting of these negative views.

Is Pornography Harmful?

The answer is complex: "It depends." For those who believe that anything fostering more permissive attitudes toward sexuality or that even viewing others engaging in sexual acts is morally wrong, then exposure to explicit sexual material is clearly unacceptable. Others, however, believe that there is nothing wrong with permissive attitudes and being stimulated by explicit materials. Indeed, materials depicting consensual activity have been used in beneficial ways by therapists and educators to reduce anxiety and to improve sexual knowledge, and by individuals and couples to enhance their sexual pleasure. . . .

Exposure to material that contains sexist or violent depictions can promote undesirable attitudes and behaviors. Increased censorship, however, will not be effective in addressing the problems, for three reasons. Firstly, censorship is most often directed toward only the most sexually explicit material, leaving the much more problematic sexist and violent content of R-rated material untouched. Secondly, censorship would not end sexual exploitation or violence. The roots of those behaviors are far deeper in the culture. Sexist, sexually explicit material is more a symptom than a cause of female subordination and sexual violence. Finally, restrictions beyond the existing obscenity laws and protection for minors would create numerous other problems in a free, democratic society. Few sexual scientists judge the evidence as warranting additional restrictions.

RECOMMENDED READINGS

Davis, C. M., & Bauserman, R. (1993). Exposure to sexually explicit materials: An attitude change perspective. *Annual Review of Sex Research,* 4, 121–209.

Donnerstein, E. L., & Penrod, S. (1987). *The question of pornography: Research findings and policy implications.* New York: Free Press.

Fisher, W. A., & Barak, A. (1991). Pornography, erotica, and behavior: More questions than answers. *International Journal of Law and Psychiatry,* 14, 65–83.

McCormick, N. B. (1994). *Sexual salvation: Affirming women's sexual rights and pleasures.* Westport, CT: Praeger.

Source: Davis, Clive M. and Naomi B. McCormick. "What Sexual Scientists Know . . . : About Pornography." *What Sexual Scientists Know* 3(1). Reprinted by permission of the Society for the Scientific Study of Sexuality.

Out of Line: The Sexy Femmegimp Politics of Flaunting It!

Loree Erickson

I'd like to tell you a story, which as it turns out, is in fact at least three related stories.

Story One: A Day Like Any Other Day

One day, which really could be any day, I left my house in a rather good mood. I had found a lovely patch of sunshine to sit in while I waited for the bus. Soon I was joined by another bus rider who stood about four or five feet away from me. In a minute or two another person passed by with no real difficulty, but found it necessary to grumble at me while passing that I should have "parked [my] car" (more appropriately called a wheelchair) elsewhere as I was blocking the sidewalk. I wasn't blocking anything. The person who was waiting with me was shocked that this other person had made such a rude, ableist comment. I was not surprised. Nor was I surprised by the message behind his words, which was: *You are in the way. You and "your car" are taking up too much space.* I just let it go and waited. I was relieved when the bus that arrived moments later was accessible, and was a bit surprised when the other person waiting stepped to the side to allow me on, rather than rushing/pushing past me—as many people tend to do, making the bus more difficult to navigate.

As I waited for the driver to ready the bus, the person who had been waiting with me looked at the step of the bus and then to my power wheelchair and asked if I needed help. I simply replied that the bus has a ramp. Behind this sort of well-intentioned query is the everpresent assumption that I am in need of help. I get this also when I am sitting somewhere waiting to meet a friend. People just come up to me and ask if I am okay.

As the bus pulled away, I was thinking about how back-to-back these moments were when I heard a loud shrill voice from the back of the bus, "you're *amazing*!" I freeze. "The way you just whipped that little cart of yours right in that spot." I ignore it, too tired after three ableist encounters in ten minutes to offer any witty comebacks in response, and too angry to feel like educating anyone.

These three encounters are not isolated or individual experiences. Sadly, they are common and systemic. These three moments only tell us some of what disability means, how it appears, and how it is done. Disabilities, and many associated experiences, are often reduced to essentialized biomedical[1] limitations or malfunctions of certain bodies. Disability can more accurately be described as a process enacted through social relations. While the term disability appears to describe bodies and how they act/move/inhabit/sense/think/exist/communicate, the label carries the weight of how these bodies are deemed inferior to other bodies through illusory, arbitrary, and compulsory social and economic standards designed to enable certain ways of being over others. Disability is a complex, intersectional, cultural, and fluid constellation of experiences and constructs.

While this is *my* story of systemic ableism, it is not—and could not be—every story of systemic ableism. My story is reliant on my particular embodiment and cultural context, which includes, but is not limited to, physical disability, whiteness, with a high level of education. As a thirty-something-year-old, queer femmegimp who lives below the poverty line, I am marked by a unique interplay of identities. Disability never appears in isolation; it is always interrelated with a matrix of other marginalities and privileges. Systemic ableism manifests based on other marginalities (race, other experiences of disability, class, gender, and beyond).

The encounters in the story above tell something about how people make sense of my body: both the anxieties they project onto it and the simultaneous erasures they enact. These are moments among many where the relations of power reveal themselves. For example, the idea that people take up "too much space" underscores the notion that some people are worthy of occupying space and others are not—and is reminiscent of other sociohistorical practices of isolation and segregation. In *Reading and Writing Disability Differently*, Tanya Titchkosky writes, "The meaning of disability is composed of conflicts of inclusion and exclusion as this intersects with our ordinary ways of recognizing people . . . or not." (2007: 6)

Story Two: Why I Became a Porn Star

Disabled people are often imagined as being in the way; unimportant; in need of help; or called "inspirational" for doing ordinary things. Disabled people are imagined as less capable than or not as good as "normal" people (a problematic term as well). All of these attitudes simultaneously bolster and create policies and practices that propagate the association of disability with undesirability. We see this in state-sponsored practices of funding and mandating institutionalization via incarceration in prisons, psychiatric wards/hospitals, group homes, and nursing homes over community based support; immigration policies using racist, capitalist, and ableist definitions of who counts as [a] desirable citizen; in historic and contemporary eugenic ideals (affecting marginalized bodies and minds of all varieties), "lives not worth living" rhetoric and consequent denial of medical treatment to those deemed unworthy; as well as welfare and disability income programs that keep us impoverished and hungry.

The same structures that impact other areas of our lives, creating an overwhelming climate of devaluation, also regulate our sexual lives.[2] From forced and coerced sterilization to institutional surveillance that limits privacy, there are multiple systems that pathologize, control, and punish the sexual explorations and expression of disabled people. Common paternalistic

assumptions hypersexualize and/or portray disabled people as hypervulnerable. This damaging ideology is used to justify segregation. Disabled people—all people—need affirming resources, sex-positive information, and ways to realize their sexual potentials. Anti-sex laws in many U.S. states criminalize certain sexual activities that may be preferred ways for some disabled people to experience pleasure and express desire.

Disabled people are also often subjected to medical and psychological gawking that objectifies, stigmatizes, and pathologizes our experiences of our bodies, including our minds (Blumberg, 1994). Many children who are born with or acquire their disabilities early on are told directly and indirectly to not expect to have a family or anyone ever romantically love them (*Willing and Able: Sex, Love and Disability*, 2003). Disabled people experience the cumulative effects of this extensive system of desexualization every day.

People have begun organizing around this site of oppression as honestly and effectively as we have for other issues of access and justice. There are many particular barriers associated with this type of organizing and it is often deprioritized. In part, this is because there has been a disconnection between sexuality and other needs. It can be argued that one should focus more on needs such as housing, adequate attendant care, employment, transportation, and the like. However, this omission of sexuality ignores how profoundly interconnected all of these aspects of our lives are. Another part of the struggle to include sexuality as an organizing goal requires us to challenge the way sex operates in Western society. We learn to associate shame with sex. We are surrounded by images that convey a very narrow definition of sex and of desirable bodies. We learn we are not supposed to talk about sex. This framing of normative desire is larger than life and does not make room for a whole range of enjoyable experiences and possibilities. When sex is thought of a bountiful playground for the relatively few who can approximate the illusory ideals of the desirable body (skinny, white, able-bodied, rich, etc.), then sex, desire, and pleasure for the rest of us remains relatively invisible. Sex and sexual expression are also often dismissed as frivolous "wants" rather than fundamental aspects of humanity. This is especially true for people with disabilities.

Felt as a personal and private emotion, shame is spun to internalize, naturalize, and individualize many of the oppressions mentioned above as well as others. As Abby Wilkerson argues, "shame is not so much a psychological state of individuals as such (even though it may shape individual subjectivity), but rather a socially based harm which oppressed groups are subject to in particular ways . . . Shame is deployed as a 'political resourc[e] that some people use to silence or isolate others'" (Wilkerson, 2002: 45). I would like to expand this idea to include how shame is used not only as a tool of social control to isolate us from each other, but to keep us from accessing those very parts of ourselves, our bodies, our desires, and our experiences (usually wrapped up in our differences from that illusory ideal mentioned earlier) that hold the most potential for change by offering us a different way of being in the world.

Rather than hide away, deny, and ignore those very sites of the deepest shame, we must not only embrace them and learn from them, we need to *flaunt* them.

What better way to flaunt conventions of sexuality than by making porn? Pornography is surrounded by shame. We feel shame for watching, enjoying it, making it, and buying it. The content of porn also often instills shame in us. We can feel badly for not living up to certain standards (both in terms of not fitting the mold of which bodies are seen as beautiful and in terms of not measuring up in regards to sexual prowess and skills). There is porn that demeans our identities and experiences and replicates oppressive power dynamics. Porn is complex, multifaceted— and yes—powerful. Rather than attempt to regulate and control it, which only drives it more underground and into the hands of those with privilege, we need to follow in the work of sex-positive feminists and explore the many benefits that pornography made from such alternative perspectives have to offer (Erickson, 2007).

This all may seem an unlikely beginning to porn stardom. By making queercrip porn I moved out of line and took the "queer" and "wonky" path to place new stories within reach. I took this path to open up new possibilities and imaginings.

My journey began in a progressive sex shop in San Francisco in 2000; I was looking at an issue of *On Our Backs,* a lesbian porn magazine, featuring an article on sex and disability. I was so excited—until I opened to the article. There was *one* picture of someone in a wheelchair with someone sitting on their lap kissing them. This one picture—the only image combining sex and disability I had found up to that point in my life—was inverted, so the image was obscured and barely recognizable. I wanted to see bodies that looked and moved and felt like mine represented in the exciting, but clearly still problematic, queer sexual culture. I wanted to see something that reflected my desires! I wanted to know that desiring people like me was possible. I resolved then and there to become a porn star.

I began with a series of photos and in the summer of 2006, I made a short film called *want. want* weaves together sexually explicit images with everyday moments and scenes of the ableist world. It works to get people hot *and* poses an insightful, complex, honest, and sexy image of disability and gender transgressive bodies. *want* was clearly wanted. It won several awards, and continues to screen internationally at numerous film festivals, conferences, and workshops.

I wouldn't be making porn right now if I weren't so pissed off. I would not be making porn if I hadn't struggled for most of my life to be recognized as a sexy and sexual being, or if the world wasn't so fucked up. But making porn is one of the best things I've ever done. On a political level it allowed me to make a movie that would not only offer a moment of recognition of how sexy queercrips could be, but also a way to tell others how I wanted to be seen. Making this video allowed me to take up space and reconceptualize what is sexy.

Personally, it was an amazing experience—and not just because of all the really great sex. The three of us (my co-star, the video artist, and I) created a space of comfort, beauty, respect, and desire. To be able to share that with others is truly remarkable. That day was one of the first times in my life that I truly felt wanted for exactly who I am. The first time was with my first lover. Unfortunately, experiences like these are rare for many people. Despite the sheer joy of the day—I must have been smiling for days afterward—it took me a while to work up the nerve to watch the video footage. I was afraid that what I might see would allow all those stories I was trying to erase to reemerge and pollute my experience of that day. While there were some bits that were hard to watch, it turned out to be not so bad—and kind of hot. I could see that I was sexy. I still feel that pull of doubt, but I am building up a whole host of stories, salacious stories, to counter the other ones.

Story Three: Being a Porn Star is Hard Work

Before this turns into a simple story of overcoming adversity, I would like to complicate things a bit. "Flaunting it" is not without its difficulties, but it does help to loosen up the knots a bit and free up more space for imagining. Our bodies, identities, desires, and experiences have multiple meanings, and thus, we need multiple stories. We need stories of love, lust, and other stuff. We need the success stories and the stories of pain and frustration. We also need stories about the work that stories being told about us, *without* us, do. These stories still inform our stories. We also need to look at the work that our stories do. Here are some stories that attempt to do that work.

Mainstream porn uses a series of conventions to shape the discourse of what is considered sexy. As I mentioned earlier, we can feel shame for not measuring up to these standards. Despite my politics, while editing, I found myself tempted to recreate those standards. I wanted to edit out the messy stuff, the very things that made this particular porn different. Wouldn't leaving in these sites of shame make it so that we wouldn't have to feel bad that when we don't fall seamlessly into bed with our hair splayed out perfectly on the pillow? I've seen other porns that do this; they show pauses for gloves and lube, the negotiation process: "try moving my leg here," or "I like this," or "touch me here." How powerful would it be to show that when we fell back or slipped, it didn't ruin anything? We just kept going. Then I realized that, within the constellation of power relations, I had somewhat contradictory aims. How far could I go toward a new vision of sexy and still be recognized as sexy? How far could I go away from that standard

referent and not be discounted as too different or have my film written off as a fetish film? If, as Foucault contends, we can never get outside of power, then how do we create something new without reinforcing oppressive ideologies? In the end I compromised; I showed bits of both.

Despite all the recognition, there are also times of misrecognition. I find these particular moments quite revealing. They are useful not just in highlighting how difficult it can be to unlearn conceiving of only certain bodies as desirable, but also what possibilities there are for bodies to take. A perfect example of this is how people assume that my co-star and I are lesbians. I only have space to offer partial explanations here. Some of this assumption is explained by normative readings of gender which argue that a certain tone of voice implies a corresponding gender or that a dildo is a dildo, when sometimes what may appear to some as a dildo is someone's cock. Another explanation is that representations of genderqueer boy/femmegimp love are still rare, leaving many to not even realize that these experiences and identities are imaginable. I am also interested in thinking through what work it does to read the film and thus the identities and bodies portrayed in the film as lesbian. I am often either seen as straight or a lesbian, this is more complicated and interesting than I can really take up here, but both readings (straight or lesbian) erase the desiring of gender-transgressive bodies (both his and mine). This assumption also presumes that desire occurs along heteronormative binary axes of gender and sex and sexuality. In addition, the way that disabled people are often denied agency contributes to a lack of recognition of subversively performed gender expression. Hot boy/femme lovin' action must be made unintelligible, yet again, to keep certain bodies and desires in line.

The first time I screened *want* at a festival, during the Q and A section, one of the other directors commented that "eventually your chair just faded away and you were just a hot girl getting fucked." For this viewer, this was meant as praise: the all too familiar "I was so hot he forgot I was in a wheelchair" compliment. I was not fulfilling the asexual poster-child stereotype that he views as being what disability *is*; and thus, disability and hot sexiness could not exist as simultaneously. So in his viewing he made what he considered to be the less desirable bit disappear. But, my wheelchair will not just fade away; when I am hot I am still disabled. I feel it is important to mention here that I had to win an obnoxious email argument about why my screening had to be held in an accessible theatre to make the exchange even possible. And sorry, no, you can't keep your little bubble of queer sex-positivity or the locations of said activities exactly the same and include me. The alignment of the inaccessible location of the event and his ablest views of hotness are not accidental.

Films like mine are unsettling as well as productive. What is made possible in the moments where we recognize being out of line, being crooked, being variant, as red smoking hot? This is especially true when being *in* line means hiding the parts that *don't* fall in line, so that we never feel fully recognized. As already discussed, shame is a panoptical device used to urge bodies toward assimilation and normalcy. In my life, the many ways not having the privilege of hiding certain sites of shame has been complicated and in some ways hard, but it has also opened up new possibilities and ways of being-in-the-world. In *want* I show myself as a body that is explicitly sexual and also needs intimate daily personal care. Bodies that cannot or do not hide their interdependence, needs, and leakiness as well as others do, have faced a long history of violence, discrimination, and desexualization. Being regarded as a dependent body is certainly one of the major ways that disabled bodies have been cast as undesirables. I wanted to bring these two supposedly disparate parts of me together because I am certain that disability will never be fully desirable until notions of dependency and care are reworked. I also wanted to show how adopting a non-traditional model of meeting my care needs through a collective of people has not only enabled my sexual expression, but opened up a space for so much more. The mutuality of these caring relationships contributes to new ways of being-in-the-world-with-others.

In the article "Loving You Loving Me: Tranny/Crip/Queer Love and Overcoming Shame in Relationships," Samuel Lurie states, "being desired, trusting that, reciprocating that cracks us open" (2002: n.p.). Remaining open and vulnerable is scary because of shame, past hurts (both systemic and interpersonal), and the very real chance of harm, but it is also hard because it means we have to tell new stories. We have to tell stories that contradict the omnipresent chorus that tells us that we are not good enough to be wanted. These stories can be hard to tell because they can sometimes be hard to believe, but they need to be told because in their telling, they make change possible. As Eli Clare argues:

> *Never are we seen, heard, believed to be the creators of our own desires, our own passions, our own sexual selves. Inside this maze, the lives of queer crips truly disappear. And I say it's time for us to reappear. Time for us to talk sex, be sex, wear sex, relish our sex, both the sex we do have and the sex we want to be having. I say it's time for some queer disability erotica, time for an anthology of crip smut, queer style. Time for us to write, film, perform, read, talk porn. I'm serious. It's time* (Clare, 2002: n.p.).

I screened *want* at a queer conference in Massachusetts; afterward, a young woman with a disability thanked me for my video and told me she had never had a romantic relationship. She said before that moment she had never even thought it was a possibility for her. So while my story tells many stories, there is most definitely a love story or two in there that are also stories of resistance and systemic change.

NOTES

1. The term biomedical here is used to encompass biological, psychological, intellectual and medical practices and praxis not acting as interrelated systems.

2. This is true of many experiences of marginalization. An easy comparison is made when looking at laws regarding marriage in the prohibition of interracial marriages, same-sex marriages, and so on.

REFERENCES

Blumberg, L. (1994). Public Stripping. In B. Shaw (Ed.). 77–81. *The Ragged Edge: the Disability Experience from the Pages of the First Fifteen Years of The Disability Rag.* Lousiville, KY: Advocado Press.

Clare, E. (2002). *Sex, Celebration, and Justice: A Keynote for QD2002.* Paper presented at the Queer Disability Conference, San Francisco, CA.

Erickson, Loree. (2007). Revealing Femmegimp: Sites of Shames as Sites of Resistance for People with Disabilities. *Atlantis: A Journal of Women's Studies* 32(1).

Lurie, S. (2002). *Loving You Loving Me: Tranny/Crip/ Queer Love and Overcoming Shame in Relationships*. Retrieved July 15, 2004, from www.bentvoices.org

Titchkosky, Tanya. (2007). *Reading and Writing Disability Differently: The Textured Life of Embodiment*. Toronto: University of Toronto Press.

Wilkerson, A. (2002). Disability, Sex Radicalism, and Political Agency. *NWSA Journal, 14*(3), 33–57.

Willing and Able: Sex, Love and Disability, SexTV Documentary, 2003.

The Porning of America

Carmine Sarracino and Kevin M. Scott

How has porn changed the way we see one another and ourselves? How has it altered our personal relationships and our sexual behavior? How has it changed the social order? How has it shaped our individual identities, and our national identity? To begin to answer these questions, we need to have some understanding of the development of pornography in America.

Growth of the Porn Runt

Nathaniel Philbrick's *In The Heart of the Sea: The Tragedy of the Whaleship Essex* (2000) tells about a surprisingly sexually active religious sect in colonial America: the Quakers living off the coast of Massachusetts on Nantucket Island. In this community, where men were at sea hunting whales for long periods of time, sometimes even years, it was an open secret that the women had learned to pleasure themselves. Their journals contain opaque references to their masturbatory activities, including code words for dildos, such as *he's at homes*. In 1979, homeowners remodeling a house in the historic district of Nantucket found a six-inch dildo made of clay.

Still, examples of what might be considered porn from seventeenth- and eighteenth-century America are rare, and consist mainly of cheaply printed pamphlets, called chapbooks, containing smutty jokes, lewd drawings, and cartoons.[1] The chapbooks were produced surreptitiously, bought for a penny or two, and passed around among males.

Unlike the Nantucket Quakers, the Puritans, the largest group of earliest settlers, kept their secret sex lives, if they had them, secret. And yet, as we will show, the Puritans figure importantly in the construction of the American idea of pornography.

Despite the stereotype of them as austere and sexually repressed, the Puritans were quite sexually active. Recent scholars, for instance, have examined the records of births, deaths, and marriages in various colonies and discovered that quite often the date of a first child's birth was less than nine months from the time of the parents' marriage. This may well have been a result of the practice of bundling, in which prospective couples were allowed to sleep in the same bed, typically in the home of the young woman's parents, provided they were individually restrained in garments or separated by a board. Unsurprisingly, many young people found their way around these obstacles and into each other's embrace. Also, remarriage after the death of a spouse often happened quickly, without the observance of what many today would consider a proper period of mourning. One cannot help wondering whether the later marriage had originated as a liaison of some sort.[2]

But the reason we connect the Puritans with pornography has to do with their religious condemnation of sexuality as sinful and satanic, and the denial (whether hypocritical or not) of their own sensual nature, which they constantly tried to hold in check. . . .

Pornography, as it grows and strides across America over the mid-nineteenth and twentieth centuries, and then dominates American culture at the turn of the new millennium, typically has an essentially Puritan point of view on sensuality and sex. The vocabulary of the typical Internet porn site could be written by one of Nathaniel Hawthorne's *Scarlet Letter* Puritans: Sex is *sinful! Nasty! Naughty!* The only difference in this regard between the Puritans and the pornographers is that from the same starting point they go not merely in different, but in opposite, directions. Porn revels in what Puritanism rejects.

In the world of porn, sex is dirty, the women are sluts—but unlike what happens in the world of Puritanism, in porn all restraints are off. . . . The immensely popular contemporary series of porn films called *Girls Gone Wild* is a Puritan nightmare come horribly, horribly true. . . .

From the Civil War to Celebrity Culture: Porn Comes Into Its Own

In all the changes wrought by the Civil War, from the earthshaking to the trivial, the oddest may be this: the War Between the States marked the beginning of the pornography industry in America.[3]

In the middle of the nineteenth century, for the first time, it became technologically possible to cheaply and quickly produce multiple prints of a photograph. And just when this happened, the Civil War separated hundreds of thousands of men and boys from their wives and sweethearts. For most of them it was their first time away from home. They were lonely and bored in camps. The words *horny* and *hooker* came into widespread usage.[4]

Photographs of all kinds were important to the soldiers. In the pockets of their frock coats they carried ambrotypes of their loved ones. They mailed home small calling cards, called *cartes de visite,* showing themselves photographed in uniform, wielding Colt revolvers and bowie knives. And deep down in their haversacks, or under the straw mattresses of their winter quarters, they hid stereoscopic photos of seductive women. When viewed through a special holder, two side-by-side photographic images transformed into the three-dimensional form of a girl clad only in see-through gauze, or brazenly lying with her legs spread. The popular *carte de visite* had a prurient incarnation: a prostitute's nude form occupied the space normally reserved for the image of the gallant soldier.

It did not take long for some to spot a market opportunity, however illicit. Young men may have been horny before the war, but they were spread thinly across a nation of farms. Now they were amassed in camps, by the thousands and tens of thousands, away from the prying eyes at home that would certainly have prevented them from trafficking in pornography via the mail. Companies such as G. S. Hoskins and Co. and Richards & Roche in New York City sent out flyers and catalogs to the soldiers, detailing their offerings: photographs of Parisian prostitutes; condoms and dildos; even miniaturized photographs that could be concealed in jewelry such as stickpins, and that, when held close to the eye, revealed a couple engaged in a sex act.

Despite the sea of catalogs that were printed, only a handful survive. From time to time field commanders "cleaned up camp" and built bonfires with the copious material. No doubt countless more after the war fell victim to former soldiers' pangs of conscience or to the fear that a family member might happen upon them. *In The Story the Soldiers Wouldn't Tell: Sex in the Civil War,* Thomas P. Lowry reviews five catalogs, including one that ended up in the National Archives because a Capt. M. G. Tousley wrote to President Lincoln complaining of the obscene catalogs and thought to include a sample. We don't know whether Lincoln ever saw the catalog, but it is droll to imagine him, in those darkly serious days, paging through "mermaids wearing only mist and foam," and "The Temptation of St. Anthony," showing the "naked charms" of the seductresses, and "Storming the Enemy's Breastworks," in which a Northern soldier quite literally assaults the breasts of a Southern belle.

A new industry had been created, and a lot of money was changing hands. So much obscene material was passing through the mail that the Customs Act of 1842, which contained the first federal antiobscenity legislation, was strengthened in 1857. In 1865, in an attempt to check the flood of pornography triggered by the Civil War, a federal statute prohibited the use of the mail to ship obscene books and pictures. After the war, alarmed moralists led by the zealous crusader Anthony Comstock, who was truly obsessed with stamping out smut, passed the Comstock Act of 1873, making it illegal to trade in "obscene literature and articles of immoral use." As Walter Kendrick notes in The *Secret Museum: Pornography in Modern Culture,* Comstock himself, in 1874, reported seizing and destroying in a two-year period 134,000 pounds of "books of improper character" as well as 194,000 pictures and 60,300 "sundries" such as "rubber articles."

Those who today look to legislation, or to a moral crusade, as the best means to limit if not eliminate pornography, would do well to recall Comstock's relentless, but ultimately futile, efforts. Attorney General Edwin Meese and his Commission on Pornography, convened about a hundred years after Comstock's campaign (the commission's final report was issued, and almost immediately ignored, in 1986), could have saved time and energy had it recalled that earlier zealot's failure.

And zealot he certainly was. Comstock, who was not above using false names and even disguises to investigate obscene materials, pursued wrongdoers with the tenacity of a pit bull. He drove one offender, W. Haines, a surgeon by training who became rich producing more than three hundred obscene books, to suicide.

Before Haines, an Irishman, appeared on the scene, America had only imported from Europe, but not produced, obscene books. Haines changed all that. By 1871 he was selling one hundred thousand such books a year. The night before he killed himself, Haines received a message: "Get out of the way. Comstock is after you. Damn fool won't look at money." In later years Comstock, who would blush at an indelicate photograph, boasted about the suicide, which he regarded as a victory over the forces of evil.

But neither the criminalization of obscenity in 1865 nor Comstock's obsessive crusade killed off pornography. Another war, the Great War, was not far on the horizon, and it would once again concentrate huge numbers of lonely, horny men—and with photographic and printing technologies further advanced, offer them an improved, more enticing product.

Porn's birth weight had been low, and the runt was pushed into the dark alleys of American life. But there it thrived. By the end of the twentieth century, it had emerged mature and powerful—son of the European curators' Frankenstein. Widely known if not respected, it had corporate offices in New York, Chicago, and Los Angeles. Its annual earnings at the turn of the twenty-first century were estimated at $10 billion to $14 billion. . . .

From the Civil War until recent times, pornography was marginalized and stigmatized. Lately, though, it has moved from the edges to the mainstream of American culture. But more than that—and far more importantly—it has now become the dominant influence shaping our culture.

Porn spread beyond a particular segment of the population—soldiers at war—and began to enter the mainstream of American culture via early porn films variously known as blue movies, stag movies, and smokers. These were typically anonymous productions, and the participants were often, like outlaws, masked. Not only were they not like us, they were, visually, the opposite of us: we show our faces and hide our genitals; they hid their faces and showed their genitals.

Further, the individuals who appeared in these short movies (fifteen to twenty minutes long) were not "acting" in any sense. The women were usually prostitutes, photographed performing sexual acts with their johns.

But by the turn of the twenty-first century the outlaws had become entertainers, celebrities even, acting in scripted movies. Many of these porn stars were so familiar to so many Americans that a sophisticated and highly regarded exhibit of their portraits, the XXX exhibit, could be shown in a major art gallery. Rather than misfits and deviants, then, they had become, in about a hundred and fifty years, people like you and me. They had become like us and we in tam had come to imitate the way they dressed, talked, and behaved sexually. Our identities merged to such a degree that what had been marginalized and stigmatized became instead the norm.

"She's Gonna Look Just Like A Porn Star!"

Dr. 90210 is a reality television show on the E! network featuring patients undergoing plastic surgery. A recent show was typical of the offerings.

"Heather Ann," an attractive, self-employed beautician in her twenties, was about to receive breast implants. As she was sedated in preparation, she expressed anxiety about undergoing surgery to her mother and boyfriend.

Then the cameras followed Dr. Robert Rey, a Harvard Medical School graduate, as he deftly inserted implants to enlarge Heather Ann's breasts. Camera cutaways showed the patient's mother and boyfriend fidgeting and chatting nervously throughout the procedure. Finished, Dr. Rey cleaned up and went to the waiting room. He assured Heather's mother and boyfriend that everything had gone very well, adding: "She's gonna look just like a porn star!" They beamed back at him.

Even as a joke—a lighthearted comment to break the tension—we cannot imagine anything comparable from a doctor speaking to a patient's family members much before the mid-1990s, by which time porn had been destigmatized for most Americans. Dr. Rey did not know the mother and boyfriend well, but well enough to surmise that neither was, say, a Christian fundamentalist. For the most part, only religious extremists and the elderly (who tend to think of porn in terms of its earlier, stigmatized incarnations) would now take offense at the easygoing comparison of a daughter or girlfriend with a porn star.

Porn stars, like celebrities in general, had become not only culturally accepted but even objects of emulation, as exemplified by popular books published in 2004 and 2005, *How to Make Love Like a Porn Star,* by Jenna Jameson, and *How to Have a XXX Sex Life,* by "the Vivid Video stars," eight performers well known in the industry—all functioning now as educators of a public eager to learn their sex secrets. So destigmatized had the term become that girls and young women playfully sported T-shirts emblazoned with the words PORN STAR.

The release of the porn film *Deep Throat* in 1972 would be a pivotal event in the cultural changes that permitted Dr. Rey his icebreaker. But the mainstreaming of porn actually began in those innocent days of the 1950s, with Hugh Hefner and *Playboy* magazine.

Before *Playboy* started publication in 1953, porn was low-rent. As we have seen, the earliest pornography in seventeenth- and eighteenth-century America consisted of ribald tales badly printed and shabbily bound. Through the nineteenth century and most of the twentieth, pornography was typically printed on cheap paper, featuring grainy photographs of prostitutes and their johns. Prostitutes were depicted as desperate women—alcoholics and drug addicts, victimized by brutal pimps. The marginalization of the women and men in the photographs was evident in the illegal, seedy-looking presentations of porn and the underground nature of the porn industry.

The communications theorist Marshall McLuhan famously said, "The medium is the message." On its simplest level this complex understanding may be applied to *Playboy's* presentation of soft-core pornography. The "message" in the medium of the cheap catalogs sold to Civil War soldiers, for instance, was: *Here are deviants, losers, engaged in sinful, taboo, illicit—but tempting! exciting! sexual behavior. Want to take a peek?* (While of course allowing the partaker to remain on the other side of the line separating darkness from light.)

Shame—the shame of poverty, of transgression, the shame of the outsider—was in a sense encoded into the early presentations of pornography. Shame inhibits identification. We don't want to see as "ourselves" those who are socially, morally, and legally stigmatized.

Hefner, however, imitated prestigious magazines such as *The Saturday Evening Post* and *The New Yorker* in the quality of paper and sophisticated formatting and graphics he used, publishing only the best writers and photographers. Most importantly, he featured seminude and nude photographs of "the girl next door"—an All-American girl who, in a typical profile, enjoyed long walks on the beach, playing the guitar, and sharing a candlelit bottle of wine with a special someone.

The principal element in the mainstreaming of porn is that it enters the world that the readers/viewers themselves inhabit or would like to inhabit. It must enter their actual or desired reality in order for them to identify with it. . . . The playmates were, in their own way, as distant from the men and women who read *Playboy* as the catalog hookers were from the farm boy soldiers marching to Gettysburg.

Through *Playboy,* however, pornography (albeit soft core) not only detached itself from the negative associations of earlier porn, but also in fact attached itself to the polar opposite of those negatives. If earlier porn inhibited individuals' readiness to identify with losers, *Playboy,* on the contrary, made them feel like the affluent, smart, informed winners they aspired to be.

Within this elevation of the social context of pornography, in 1972 *Deep Throat* took porn movies in an entirely new direction, much as *Playboy* had done for print porn. *Deep Throat* abandoned the stag movie format, and instead starred an actress, billed as Linda Lovelace, along with a supporting cast. Instead of the twenty-minute length of the traditional 8 mm stag movie, it ran about an hour and a half. And—wonder of wonders—it was actually scripted, with characters and a plot (of sorts), as well as all the sex expected of a blue movie. It was, in other words, in all its basic elements a Hollywood movie, but with the added feature of plenty of graphic sex.

To say that the movie is a cultural milestone (as has become fashionable since the release of the 2005 documentary *Inside Deep Throat*) does not exaggerate its significance. Top celebrities—the likes of Frank Sinatra, Mike Nichols, and Sammy Davis Jr.—not only admitted watching the film, but raved about it. (The documentary features such intellectual luminaries as Gore Vidal, Norman Mailer, and Camille Paglia, with cameos by the political satirist Bill Maher and Hugh Hefner.) From a financial point of view, the movie was an unprecedented blockbuster: shot for around $24 thousand, it has grossed perhaps as much as $600 million in worldwide revenues from an audience estimated at 10 million viewers. In the industry of pornography, nothing like it had ever been seen—or probably even imagined.

What explains *Deep Throat*'s acceptance and cultural assimilation? Although not billed as a porn comedy, the film adopts a goofy comic tone right from the outset. The camera follows Linda Lovelace walking along the docks in Miami, and getting into her car as credits roll and a sound track plays. For a couple of minutes the camera watches over her shoulder from the backseat as she drives (a somewhat eerie shot for those who know that the actress was involved in three serious car wrecks, the third fatal in 2002, when she was fifty-three. In fact, camera angles were carefully planned in *Deep Throat* to avoid showing a scar on her abdomen that had resulted from an earlier accident.)

When Linda arrives home, she finds her mother in the living room, legs spread over a chair, enjoying cunnilingus. Well, sort of enjoying: in addition to its silliness, a tone of ennui pervades the film. Her mother, for instance, languidly lights a cigarette, tilts up the head of her busy partner, and asks, "Mind if I smoke while you're eating?" The sound track plays "Taking a Break from the Mundane."

The structure of the film is simple, consisting of typical 8 mm sex loops, without dialogue but with musical accompaniment, interspersed with a plot based on a nutty premise: Linda learns from a Dr. Young, a psychiatrist, that the reason she cannot achieve orgasm is that her clitoris is in her throat. Concluding her gynecological examination, he announces, "No wonder you hear no bells, you have no tinkler!" During the exam, the sound track consists of a dirty version of Mickey and Sylvia's well-known "Love Is Strange."

One more example of the slapstick humor that characterizes the film: Dr. Young consoles Linda, "Having a clitoris deep down in the bottom of your throat is better than having no clitoris at all." "That's easy for you to say," she objects. "Suppose your balls were in your ear?" He is momentarily flummoxed, until a lightbulb pops on over his head: "Well, then I could hear myself coming!"

Humor, even lame humor, is disarming. From a propagandistic point of view, the makers of *Deep Throat* had stumbled onto a mass-market presentation of porn that would assist its acceptance, its normalization.

First, the opening credits announced, "Introducing Linda Lovelace As Herself" We had an actress, then, rather than the prostitute of a typical 8 mm stag movie, but she was "playing herself"—an ordinary, attractive young woman—someone we might know. Once the movie begins, the humor takes over and in effect tells us to lighten up, not to take it seriously. Ifs just entertainment, dizzy and raunchy, like some weird, X-rated *I Love Lucy.*

It worked. The star, Linda Lovelace, appeared in an extensive photo layout by Richard Fegley in *Playboy* in April 1973, and the next month on the cover of *Esquire* magazine dressed in a polka-dot dress modestly buttoned to the white wing collar and wearing white gloves—a send-up of the girl next door, but the girl next door nevertheless.

Hidden beneath the appearance of an ordinary young woman starring in a new kind of porn film, however, lay an altogether different reality—one representative, in fact, of "old porn." Linda Susan Boreman, "Linda Lovelace," was a former prostitute who had appeared in such 8 mm stag movies as *Dogarama* (also known as *Dog Fucker*) in 1969, and *Piss Orgy* in 1971. Her husband/manager, Chuck Traynor, had forced her—often at gunpoint, she later claimed—to perform in the stag movies and in *Deep Throat.* Add to this submerged reality the heavy use of hard drugs by Linda, her husband, and others in the movie, along with mob involvement (mainly financial, but some theaters were reportedly strong-armed into featuring *Deep Throat*), and the film seems quite far afield indeed from mainstream American culture's notions of acceptability.

Still, the crucial step had been taken: Linda Lovelace presented herself in some important ways as "one of us." She was, after all, the star of a kind of movie we recognize as legitimate: one that plays in theaters, not in the back rooms of smoky mens clubs, features attractive actors in a narrative that defused its illicit subject matter with a comic outlandishness, had a sound track and rolled credits, and was viewed and praised by well-known and respected figures. As film critic Richard Corliss pointed out in a March 29, 2005, *Time* online article, "That Old Feeling: When Porno Was Chic," even comics such as Johnny Carson and Bob Hope, cultural icons in 1972, made jokes about *Deep Throat,* conferring a kind of blessing on the film, tacitly legitimatizing it and its place in the world.

The film was quickly followed by another in 1972, *Behind the Green Door.* In it, Marilyn Chambers was in fact billed as "the All-American Girl." Chambers (who would in 1975 marry Chuck Traynor, divorced from Linda Lovelace) was indeed so all-American looking that just as *Behind the Green Door* was released, Ivory Snow soap flakes put out a newly designed box featuring a photo of a mother holding her baby. The mother was none other than Marilyn Ann Briggs, otherwise known as Marilyn Chambers, the suddenly famous porn star. Procter and Gamble abashedly withdrew the box design.

Like *Deep Throat, Behind the Green Door* imitated the Hollywood movie and contained a hip sound track, an important element in getting the audience to identify with the characters in the film. Again, to paraphrase McLuhan, an audience does not so much listen to a sound track as put it on, bathe in it. A sound track of hits feels familiar and comfortable, making everything associated with it more familiar and comfortable.

These two movies from 1972 launched the porn movie industry as we know it today, catapulting its stars to celebrity status and playing to larger and larger audiences of men and women, especially through the addition of video (and later DVD) rentals and sales.

Beginning in the early 1970s, then, it became increasingly easy to acquire porn without buying it under the counter or from a shady character on a street corner. One could simply go to the neighborhood theater or, beginning in the 1980s, to a hotel or motel with in-room pay-per-view. In the 1990s, of course, porn would come right to your home through cable offerings such as Vivid, the Spice Channel, and the Playboy Channel. In these ways, the acquisition of porn has become quick and easy, a critical step in its destigmatization.

But the story of the mainstreaming of pornography, with its shaping influence on American life and culture, is more complex and subtle than simply the evolution of the pornographic movie industry. If *Deep Throat* took porn films in a totally new direction by imitating Hollywood, and by drawing on girl-next-door and all-American stereotypes, soon enough Hollywood and ordinary people would in turn begin imitating porn.

In the same year as *Deep Throat* and *Behind the Green Door,* Marlon Brando starred in Bernardo Bertolucci's *Last Tango in Paris,* which transgressed the limits of traditional Hollywood treatments of sex, even containing an infamous "butter scene" of anal penetration. But the film was controversial, and not in any sense mainstream. It was originally unrated, then later rated NC-17.

Fast-forward to the mid-1990s, however, and a Hollywood movie could now deal with explicit sex, including such taboos as anal sex. The celebrated film

Leaving Las Vegas (1995), for instance, contained these lines delivered by the prostitute Sera (played by Elisabeth Shue) to Ben Sanderson (Nicholas Cage): "So for five hundred bucks you can do pretty much whatever you want. You can fuck my ass. You can come on my face—whatever you wanna do. Just keep it outta my hair, I just washed it."

It is impossible to imagine those lines ever finding their way into a Hollywood movie without the decades of porn films preceding it. Later in the movie, Sera is anally gang-raped, and we see her nude in the shower (an overhead shot) with blood washing down her legs and into the drain. The film was regarded as somewhat risqué, but not seriously controversial. It was rated R. In fact, Elisabeth Shue was nominated that year for an Academy Award for Best Actress for her role as Sera, and Nicholas Cage won the Oscar for Best Actor.

If Hollywood had been transformed by porn (a character like Sera could not have existed in a movie of the 1950s, 1960s, or even the 1970s), so had the audience. Only an audience in a sense made ready by the kind of porn films that *Deep Throat* pioneered would accept such language and images in a Hollywood movie.

Softening the Contours

Two films from the 1970s and early 1980s—*Pretty Baby* (1978) and *Blame It on Rio* (1984)—are instructive in showing the major role that Hollywood played in normalizing pornography, thereby increasing its power to influence and eventually dominate American culture. . . .

In much the same way that Hugh Hefner glamorized soft-core pornography through the sophistication of *Playboy* as a physical artifact, [in *Pretty Baby*] Louis Malle took on a subject that had only been dealt with in the most taboo kinds of hardcore pornography—child pornography and child prostitution—and made his treatment not only acceptable but admirable. . . .

Although the film is indeed about a misfit photographer, . . . it nevertheless also plays to the prurience of the audience, which is viewing what would in other less-normalized contexts be regarded (and perhaps even prosecuted) as child pornography. But the film distances itself from child pornography by first of all being *about* child prostitution, and then further distances itself because it clearly does not in any sense endorse prostitution, and in fact presents us with the pathos of a prostitute who is sexy, savvy, and also enjoys playing with her very first doll. . . .

So *Pretty Baby,* in 1978, after the era of *Deep Throat* and other Hollywood-like porn movies, could present the topic of child-as-sex-object in candid and graphic ways that, by contrast, Stanley Kubrick's *Lolita* could not dare in 1962. In Kubrick's movie, a nude scene of Sue Lyon as Lolita was so unthinkable it was never even proposed by Vladimir Nabokov, who wrote the screenplay, or Stanley Kubrick, who directed. Lolita and Humbert Humbert (James Mason) were not allowed even to kiss, let alone display any kind of sexuality—as later they would in the 1997 remake of *Lolita* starring Jeremy Irons and Dominique Swain.

Two years after [starring in] *Pretty Baby,* Brooke Shields was back on the screen in *The Blue Lagoon,* again nude, now as an early teen (both fictionally and in fact). Just as *Deep Throat* opened a door for other porn movies to crowd through, so *Pretty Baby* opened a farther door for the unabashed portrayal of children as sex objects, frequently partnered with adults. . . .

In 1980 Brooke Shields moved offscreen to star in ads for Calvin Klein jeans. The most famous of these showed Shields slightly bent over (presumably having just pulled on a pair of jeans) beginning to button her enticingly open blouse, with the tag line: "Nothing comes between me and my Calvins." She was now fifteen years old and a familiar sex symbol in America and overseas as well. A teenager functioning as a sex symbol had by now become, culturally speaking, accepted as normal—thanks in large part to the barrier-breaking influence of pornography (such as *Deep Throat*) on Hollywood mainstream movies.

The contours of the taboo had been sufficiently softened that, by the 1980s, children as sex objects had become culturally familiar in movies, on television, and in advertisements—with all sorts of offshoots. For instance, beauty pageants for very little girls—five or six, and even younger—swelled into a multimillion-dollar industry of local, regional, and national competitions involving highly paid consultants and coaches, clothing designers, makeup specialists, and so on. Arguably, the winner of these pageants is the child who most successfully combines adult sexuality with childlike innocence. (The most well known of such child beauty queens, of course, is Jon Benét Ramsey, who was murdered in 1996.)

Calvin Klein's use of children as sex objects continued in the 1990s with an ad campaign featuring children in highly sexualized situations. When rumors began circulating that he was being investigated on charges of the sexual exploitation of children, he began pulling the ads in August 1995. Sexualized children, however, continued to appear in ads, movies, and on television. Consider, for instance, the Olsen twins.

Mary-Kate and Ashley Olsen have become a brand name. After the twins turned eighteen, in June 2004, they took over control of their corporation, Dualstar Entertainment Group, a company that brings in over a billion dollars a year and has made each of the twins worth a reported $137 million. The twins first gained fame as the character Michelle Tanner on the sitcom *Full House,* starting their acting careers at less than a year old. The show ran for eight years, so the country watched them grow up nearly from their birth. . . . More than any other single popular-culture figure, the twins, for over a decade, determined what tweeners could aspire to. And while Dualstar has always marketed the twins as wholesome American girls, their popularity has grown, in significant part, due to the steady porning of Mary-Kate and Ashley. Whether the marketing of the twins intentionally adopted the imagery of porn or whether the online porn community merely appropriated the twins, they became the fuel for an online porn engine that combined pedophilia and kiddie porn with twin and sister porn. . . .

The imagery of the Olsens began to change as they entered puberty. With increasing frequency, they were photographed in clothing that was tight and revealing but still maintained, if only marginally, their persona as sweet and wholesome girls. As they moved through their teen years, these photographs steadily grew more sensual, culminating in photo shoots for Allure and Rolling Stone in the spring of 2004, before their eighteenth birthdays.

The increasing sexuality of the twins and their marketing during their teen years paralleled their increased presence online. "Olsen twins" became a phrase that, if Googled, led to cloaked porn sites. The porn community was so aware of the sexual allure of the twins that it used their names as a "Google-beater," including the words "Olsen twins" on their sites, which otherwise had no Olsen content, simply to increase hits—a strategy that assumes that a high percentage of people looking for Olsen twin information would be happy to find themselves landing on a porn site. Other porn sites, many of them dedicated to celebrity shots, have entry sites that simply list the names of the most famous female celebrities intermixed with keywords like "boobs naked nude sex hot" in order to capture web searches. "Olsen twins" is always on the list.

"Twin tracker" websites were sprinkled throughout the Internet in the years leading up to the twins' eighteenth birthdays, with reverse clocks counting down to the very minute when they would be "legal." The twins were such a porn commodity that they became the subject of a porn community debate online—is it okay to Photoshop the heads of underage women onto the bodies of performing porn stars, as was common? The community was split on the issue, but the simple fact of the discussion demonstrates the unspoken assumption that the Olsen twins were fit subjects of sexual interest.

Though the porn community was undeniably fascinated with the Olsen twins, it is not clear whether the twins, or their management company, were colluding in their online porn popularity in order to heighten their mainstream popularity or profitability. Yet it is hard to imagine that their agent or manager could have been unaware of the uses to which the online porn community was putting the twins' images. *Playboy's* "Twins and Sisters" site includes women in trademark Olsen poses, though the Olsens appear clothed. In shot after shot, the public was presented with images of the twins leaning in toward each other, faces and mouths close, as if about to kiss. Caught by paparazzi on red carpets, the twins would snap into their standard pose, Mary-Kate's arm around Ashley's hip, Ashley's arm around Mary-Kate's neck (or vice versa). It is a pose that forces their torsos tantalizingly close, and the ease with which they assumed their positions showed how well coached and practiced they were.

The porning of the Olsen twins reached its height in the *Allure* and *Rolling Stone* articles, which essentially announced their legal status—a "Hey, we'll be legitimate sex objects next month!" message. The *Rolling Stone* article, which acknowledged the latent pedophilia of their marketing campaign by headlining them as "America's Favorite Fantasy," included images of the twins draped over each other in clearly erotic poses. The cover showed them leaning toward each other, their hands pulling at clothing and touching in a way clearly evocative of twin porn.

The signature photo for the *Allure* article showed the twins—still underage—in an unabashed sexual embrace, breasts together, mouths open in porn-pose ecstasy, their hands sliding into each other's clothing. The article, which emphasized their essential youth and innocence, also discussed whether they would ever do nude scenes ("Probably not"), the suggestiveness of the photo shoot ("If everybody knew we were straddling each other . . . oy vey . . . All those dirty old men out there . . ."), and an anecdote about Mary-Kate using her finger to "slowly, firmly" remove some excess lip gloss from Ashley's lip and "slowly smear[ing] it on her own, slightly open mouth."

On one level, certainly, the twins consented to the articles in order to ease their movement into more mature careers, but the stories were also explicit acknowledgments of the porned sexualization of children. One *Rolling Stone* photo combined both messages, their youth and their sexuality, by putting them in the clothing of little girls dressing up, but with highly sexualized makeup and hairstyles, and with Ashley pulling a pearl necklace through her puckered lips—the kind of imagery dirty old men would find fascinating.

Not only are children, such as the Olsen twins, sexualized, they are also targeted as consumers of sexually charged products. *Playboy,* for example, has marketed a *Playboy* skateboard, a *Playboy* snowboard, and a pink Bunny tracksuit. The target market for such products is supposed to be eighteen- to twenty-five-year-olds, but reportedly Playmate Pink glitter cream and Bunny Pink lipstick are big hits with preteen girls.

Sexually revealing clothing, sometimes called the stripper look or slutwear, is specifically target-marketed to children as well as adults. In 2002 Abercrombie & Fitch, for example, began selling thongs in its stores catering to children, with the words EYE CANDY and WINK WINK printed on them. Thongs are also available with Simpsons and Muppets characters. . . .

In June 2005 a spokesperson for Sony Computer Entertainment announced that it "could not stop" software makers from producing and marketing pornographic discs for the PlayStation Portable game console, most of whose users are children. Almost 3 million of these handheld consoles, which Sony introduced in March 2005, had been delivered to Japan and the United States by June of that year. Two pornographic filmmakers had discs on the market by July, and several more followed shortly after.

At the same time, July 2005, the video game industry changed the rating of the very popular Grand Theft Auto: San Andreas, from M for mature to AO, adults only. After initial denials, Take-Two Interactive Software, makers of the game, which plays not only on PCs but also on Xbox and PlayStation 2 consoles, acknowledged that scenes of pornographic sex had indeed been programmed into the game, and could be unlocked through an Internet download, called a mod (short for *modification*) in the gaming community.

By the 1980s, not only had children become thoroughly sexualized in movies, advertisements, and marketing, but something more general had begun to occur: the sexualization of just about everyone, regardless of age or status in society.

In other words, if we ask how porn has shaped us, how it has affected how we see ourselves and one another, one answer is that we are coming to see ourselves and one another in sexual terms first and foremost, regardless of age, and regardless as well of marital, professional, or social status. Like Heather Ann with her sexier breasts—*Everyone a porn star*! . . .

In the real world of America in the early years of the twenty-first century, everyone—from professional athletes to teachers to the president of the United States—is seen in sexual terms. A national online site allowing students to rate college professors, for instance, includes the possibility of adding a special symbol, a chili pepper, to the male or female professor's rating if he or she is "hot." And for those who are hot, student comments often focus more on the professor's allure and on sexual fantasies than on his or her attributes as a teacher.

The most compelling example of such universal porning occurred during the presidency of Bill Clinton. Details of the president's sex life, which were publicly revealed during his impeachment, included an initial encounter with an intern that could have come right out of a porn script. An attractive young woman snaps the waistband of her thong at the president of the United States. Like someone playing "Mister President" in a porn film, the real-life president eagerly responds to this come-on by engaging in oral sex with the young intern in the Oval Office. In one session, she masturbates with a cigar for his titillation. In another—well, we all saw the movie.

A number of polls indicated a pattern in the responses of Americans. Young people in high school and college (who view porn as entertainment and casual sexual encounters as a norm) were mainly amused by it all. Older Americans, especially those over fifty, who still attached stigma to porn, were shocked.

By 2008, however, it had become difficult to imagine anyone being truly shocked by real-life examples of "right out of a porn movie" sex. Let's consider just the most famous of recent scandals involving older male politicians and younger—sometimes very much younger—females and males.

- In 1974 Representative Wilbur Mills (D-Ark.) was found to be having an affair with a young stripper named Fanne Foxe, aka "the Argentine Firecracker," who jumped into the Tidal Basin in Washington, D.C., when police pulled over their car.
- In 1983 the House Ethics Committee censured Representatives Dan Crane (R-Ill.) and Gerry Studds (D-Mass.) for having had sexual relationships with seventeen-year-old pages, Crane with a female, Studds with a male.
- In 1988 former senator Gary Hart's relationship with actress/model Donna Rice derailed his presidential bid.

- In 1989 Stephen Gobie, the former gay lover of Barney Frank (D-Mass.), admitted having operated a male prostitution ring out of the congressman's apartment.
- In 2001 the U.S. senator Garry Condit (D-Calif.) admitted to an affair with missing and presumed dead Chandra Levy, a young woman in her twenties, ending his political career—because of his casual response to her disappearance rather than the affair.
- In 2006 Representative Mark Foley (R-Fla.) resigned from Congress when it was revealed that he had been sending "dirty e-mails" to teenage House pages.
- In 2007 Senator Larry Craig (R-Idaho) plead guilty to disorderly conduct after being caught in a police sting operation investigating lewd acts in a Minneapolis airport men's public restroom. Craig had been widely considered a "family values" conservative.

Politics was only one source of scandals involving sex between older, more powerful adults and young partners. Religion and education were two other similarly tainted institutions.

- In 1987 Jim Bakker, a televangelist reportedly bringing in a million dollars a week in donations from followers, confessed to a sexual liaison with a young woman, Jessica Hahn (who later appeared nude in Playboy). That scandal was followed by a spate of similar stories involving celebrity ministers caught in sexual transgressions, the most famous of which, in the following year, 1988, was Jimmy Swaggart, who wept his confession to a national audience.
- Beginning in 2002 and extending through the next few years, reports proliferated of hundreds of Catholic priests who had molested and raped young boys and girls. Bishops who simply moved the offending priests from one diocese to another as the crimes were brought to their attention had in effect, it turned out, protected serial rapists.
- In 1996 a thirty-six-year-old schoolteacher, Mary Kay Letourneau, gained notoriety when her sexual relationship with one of her sixth-grade students, a thirteen-year-old boy, became known. Her

case was soon followed by innumerable others involving male and female high school and middle school teachers having sex (and sometimes, like Letourneau, having children) with their teenage and even preteen students.

We could go on. To see just how jaded we have become by such events, try telling someone a made-up story about having just seen a news report in which a respected individual (choose anyone in the public eye) was reported having sex with someone unlikely (make it as outlandish as you want). There may be some surprise, some heads may shake in disgust, but it's a good bet that people will accept the story as true.

Our readiness to believe almost any example of sexual pairing, however outrageous, is fueled by the fact that we are exposed not only to sensational anecdotes (which though significant are usually atypical) but also to instances of sex being infused into mainstream culture everywhere we look. Let us catalog some examples of this cultural porning, just to sample the field:

- World Wrestling Federation mixed tag team matches, which receive heavy television coverage, can only be described as soft-core porn, featuring unsubtle double entendres in the pre-match challenges and taunts ("I'm gonna slam her ass!"), and scantily clad men and women in clearly sexual positions (in their male-female and female-female pairings) during the match.
- Female athletes have become increasingly sexualized, and even marketed in soft-core formats for their sexuality rather than their athletic prowess. Anna Kournikova, for example, never a top singles professional tennis player, nevertheless became a media darling, receiving more attention than better players simply because of her sex appeal and her willingness to flaunt it. In a way, she set the pattern (seminude/nude, highly suggestive calendars and posters, advertisements, appearances in movies) that other female athletes, both professional and amateur, now must follow.
- High school cheerleaders have so dramatically sexualized their routines, often bumping and grinding like strippers, that in one recent instance, a state congressman in Texas, Representative Al

Edwards, proposed legislation that would put an end to "sexually suggestive" performances at high school athletic events and other extracurricular competitions.
- Dirty dancing has gotten even dirtier. At the turn of the nineteenth century, waltz partners were thought by some alarmed moralists to be mimicking sexual intercourse. Imagine what they would make of contemporary "grinding," and "freaking," popular forms of dancing in which the female bends over and presses her buttocks against the pumping groin of her partner.
- Nude calendars have become commonplace. Beginning on a large scale in the 1990s, groups of all sorts, usually connected with charities or not-for-profit organizations, began publishing such calendars as a fund-raising ploy. One of the most well-known featured the Australian women's soccer team, the Matildas, in 1999. A dedicated website lists hundreds of nude calendars for sale, consisting of photos of amateur, volunteer models ranging in age from early twenties to senior citizens, raising money for athletic teams, theatrical companies, volunteer fire fighters, and disease research. These calendars range from depictions of naked grannies holding kittens and puppies (raising money for animal shelters) to buff male rugby players, clearly conveying the message: *Everyone a porn star!*

And the list goes on. Porn chat rooms, for example, abound on the Internet. Such spaces invite ordinary people to participate in the creation of pornography, mainly in the form of "cybering," having imagined sex, in real time, with a partner or partners in the room. The participants, who often admit that they are simultaneously masturbating, describe in detail what they are "doing" with the other (or others), how they are responding, and so on. These "performances," to describe them that way, are sometimes enhanced with webcams for one or both (or all) participants to view. Further enhanced with voice, the results can be quite complex and sophisticated, even indistinguishable from the offerings of professional porn websites.

Chatropolis, a site with both free and pay options, advertises itself as one of the largest and most active chat sites on the Web, offering about 230 chat rooms, most with a maximum capacity of twenty-five people. Not all rooms are full all the time, but if, let's say, on average, half the number of possible chatters are online, that means about three thousand are in Chatropolis at any given moment. Chatters come and go throughout the day and night, however, sometimes merely changing rooms within the site, but also logging in fresh, so the total number of chatters on this one site alone in the course of a day is huge, certainly in the thousands, perhaps even the tens of thousands.

One Chatropolis room is called "Legal Today." Another, at the other end of the age spectrum, is "Perverted Old Men." Still another links the extremes of age, "Across the Generations." Some rooms cater to phone sex, such as "Call Me." Others to sexual preferences, such as "Analopolis."

Thousands of such chat sites (free and pay, large and small) are available on the Internet. For years Yahoo, for instance, offered hundreds of rooms with cam and voice options, many exclusively pornographic— "PA Girls for Sex," for example, and many others, such as user rooms (rooms created by users) focusing on specific sex acts and fetishes, particular sexual orientations, such as bi and lesbian, and so on.[5] Even an unscientific, thumbnail approximation, then, would conservatively find millions of Americans of all ages in such chat rooms—all in this together—every day. . . .

The Amateurs Take Over

If it is true, as we have suggested, that not only has porn become mainstream but that the mainstream has become porned, it would follow that porn produced by professionals would merge with a new kind of porn created by secretaries, bakers, nurses, auto mechanics, housewives, schoolteachers—ordinary people from the mainstream of American society who, à la Timothy Greenfield-Sanders, have come to see porn stars as like themselves, and who therefore see themselves as like porn stars. And indeed this is exactly what we do find.

Throughout the 1980s and 1990s, "amateur" porn movies were produced in great quantity, created by and large by professionals who employed unknown porn actors billed as amateur performers. Since the

turn of the millennium, however, as digital video cameras and cell phones with video capability have enabled people to record their own sexual activities and post the results via their computer on a dedicated website, there has been a skyrocketing increase in true amateur porn. The number of such websites (such as Private Porn Movies, YourAmateurPorn, and Best Home Sex) is growing exponentially. Even websites that are not specifically for amateur porn become such sites de facto, because some members use their webcams on these sites to broadcast themselves masturbating or having partnered sex.

It may well be the case that true amateur porn is the future of porn in America. And to say this is perhaps to announce the end of porn. Because just as it is true that if everything in the world were blue there would be no word *blue,* when blue movies are everywhere, there are no more blue movies.

The final result of the porning of America, then, may well be the end of the recognition of porn as something separate from the mainstream. Pornography will have shrunk to porn and porn further shrunk away altogether, disappearing because it can no longer be distinguished from what we see everywhere around us on the Internet (on innumerable amateur sites, in chat rooms, on MySpace, Craigslist, Stickam, and so on), on cable television, in movies, magazines, advertisements, music videos. Porn will have become our cultural wallpaper.

NOTES

1. The following books, from which we draw in this chapter, provide a detailed examination of the early history of pornography in the West: Walter Kendrick's *The Secret Museum: Pornography in Modern Culture* (New York: Viking, 1987); Isabel Tang's *Pornography: The Secret History of Civilization* (London: Channel 4 Books, 1999); and Julie Peakman's *Mighty Lewd Books: The Development of Pornography in Eighteenth-Century England* (Houndmills, Basingstoke, U.K., and New York: Palgrave Macmillan, 2003).

2. Certainly these facts have a social and historical underpinning. A Puritan couple typically observed a long betrothal, and so were in effect "married" before the formal ceremony. And life in the colonies was so tenuous, and death rates so high, that survival itself required speedy

remarriage to maintain the necessary production rate of off-spring. Our point here is simply that the Puritans had unde-niably active sex lives.

3. The best study of prostitution and pornography in the Civil War, from which we have drawn some examples of period pornography, is Thomas P. Lowry's *The Story the Soldiers Wouldn't Tell: Sex in the Civil War* (Mechanics-burg, Pa.: Stackpole Books, 1994). Lowry, an MD, also has some chilling descriptions of venereal diseases and their of-ten ghastly treatments.

4. The word *hooker* has been traced to General Joseph "Fighting Joe" Hooker, who permitted prostitutes to encamp near the soldiers on the theory that it was better for soldiers to deal with boredom and release pent-up energy with pros-titutes than to get drunk, fight, and gamble. Another theory on the origin of the term is that prostitutes used to fall into step with prospective clients and "hook" an arm through the arm of the male.

5. In the summer of 2005, Yahoo shut down the user rooms because of allegations that the sites were being used for child pornography. Initially, they were unclear about whether such rooms might be reopened, with some correc-tive modifications, but as of this writing they have not reappeared.

chapter 4

Learning about Sex

Spotlight on Research

An interview with . . .

Ritch C. Savin-Williams

Ritch C. Savin-Williams, Ph.D., is chair and professor of human development at Cornell University in Ithaca, New York. His research centers on the psychological strength, resiliency, and well-being of same-sex attracted youth and the sexual development of youth of all sexualities. He is author of *The New Gay Teenager* (Harvard University Press, 2005), *"Mom, Dad, I'm Gay": How Families Negotiate Coming Out* (American Psychological Association, 2001), *". . . And Then I Became Gay": Young Men's Stories* (Routledge, 1998), and the co-editor of *The Lives of Lesbians, Gays, and Bisexuals: Children to Adults* (Harcourt Brace College Publishing, 2001).

What led you to begin studying sexuality?

My interest in adolescent development centers on the promotion of resiliency, strength, and coping skills of youth. I am less interested in what places youth at risk as I am in what gives them the ability to do well. Clearly, sexual development during adolescence has been a taboo topic for researchers, except insofar as it is a medical, social, or political problem. For example, we know a lot about unsafe sex, but little about the meaning or significance of sexuality for an adolescent's enjoyment of daily life or conception of the future. We know a lot about the whats and whens of sexual intercourse but little about other sexual behaviors such as kissing and oral-genital contact. Contraception, pregnancy, sexually transmitted diseases, number of sex partners, and the linkage of vaginal-penile intercourse to clinical and social problems are common topics of sex researchers; sexual desire, pleasure, physical and emotional intimacies, the meaning of sex, what is sex, and sexual minorities are uncommon. I want to help promote the positive aspects and complexity of sexuality for adolescent development.

Which of your projects have you found most stimulating?

The most fun I have had are the intensive, in-depth interviews I have conducted with over 350 young men and women of all sexualities during the past decade. These youth willingly shared their sexual histories with honesty and insight that humbled me. Their developmental sex trajectories have been so divergent from my own that it was as if I was privy to a new experience of growing up. Their thrilling and, at times, heart-wrenching stories about growing up in the 1990s and now in the 2000s have convinced me that we must hear their stories. In particular, listening to the lives of same-sex attracted young women were remarkably awe-inspiring and persuaded me that they are the most resilient, healthy, spirited group of youth I had ever encountered. During this past year I have undertaken a new project to hear the sexual lives of young men, most of whom identify as straight. I can't wait to tell the unknown worlds of the young straight male.

What have you found most challenging about studying sexuality?

The most challenging aspect of my work has been convincing adult authorities to end the silence about adolescent sexuality, showing them that it is "okay" to ask youth about their sexual development. Many adults are incredibly anxious about sexuality and they project that discomfort onto younger cohorts. My task is to let adolescents speak for themselves; I am merely a conduit and translator, and occasionally an interpreter of their lives.

Why is it important to do sex research with adolescents?

We know a considerable amount about many aspects of adolescents' lives. Their sexual development is the last frontier. The silence and the medicalization of their sexuality must end so that those youth who are embarrassed about their sexuality, who do not feel "normal," and who spend far too many hours chastising themselves for "unpure" thoughts and behavior can be freed from these constraints to live normal, happy lives.

What ethical dilemmas have you faced in your research with adolescents? How did you resolve them?

University review boards demand parental permission for inclusion of their under-18 child in behavioral research. Few U.S. parents want us to ask their children about their sexuality. One approach is to retrospectively ask over-18 youth about their sexual histories. This skirts one dilemma but compounds another—we aren't listening to the sexual lives of adolescents as they live them. So much has transpired in the sexual development of adolescents prior to age 18. Second, sometimes gaining parental permission places youth at-risk for parental censure or chastisement, such as when sexual-minority youth want to talk about their lives but have not yet disclosed their sexuality to their parents. Making this case to university review boards has allowed me to interview 16 and 17 year olds—but even this resolution appears to imply that at age 16—but not before—a young person becomes capable of making a decision to share her sexual history.

How do people react when they find out that you study sexuality?

Envy and disbelief.

If you could teach people one thing about sexuality, what would it be?

Sex is to enjoy and add meaning to one's life.

—Interviewed by Denise Donnelly

The Death of the Stork:
Sex Education Books for Children

Wendy Simonds and Amanda M. Jungels

Why Not the Stork?

You may say, "Isn't it easier and less embarrassing to tell them about the stork?" There are several reasons. . . . Even if he doesn't suspect anything at 3, he is surely going to find out the truth or the half-truth when he's 5 or 7 or 9. It's better not to start him off wrong and have him later decide that you're something of a liar. And if he finds out that you didn't dare tell him the truth, it puts a barrier between you, makes him uneasy. He's less likely to ask you other questions later, no matter how troubled he is (Spock and Rothenberg, 1992: 511).

> *"Does it feel good when a mommy and daddy make a baby?" he asked.*
>
> *Joey's father answered, "It feels very nice, especially since you're able to be so close to someone you love."*
>
> *"Hey," Joey said in an excited voice, "maybe sometime you two can show me how you do it."*
>
> *Joey's parents smiled and laughed, but Joey knew it was a nice laugh and they weren't making fun of him.*
>
> *"Joey, when a mommy and daddy make love, it's private, just something for the two of them," said Joey's father.*
>
> *"Well, when can I do it? When can I make a baby?"*
>
> *"When you get older, Joey," said Joey's mother. (Brooks and Perl, 1983)*

This hokey conversation from *So That's How I Was Born!,* a sex education book aimed at preschoolers, exemplifies the sort of sexual honesty Spock and Rothenberg prescribe advising against the stork story. And certainly everyone believes that honesty is the best policy. But there's more than one way to be honest, and there are multiple truths about sexuality. We educate kids based on our perceptions of social reality, often without questioning norms to which we've grown accustomed. We also educate kids without knowing we're doing it—with offhand remarks or behaviors that we're not aware they notice. When we do intend to teach, we can now select from a variety of texts designed to help us. Parents may choose sex education books because doing so gets them off the hook altogether from discussing sex with their kids, or they may use the books as supplementary material. Several of these books have introductory notes to parents instructing them about instructing their kids. Sex education books for children both represent and shape cultural ideologies about children, sexuality, and procreation.

In the U.S., teaching sex to children in any form seems to induce cultural anxiety and controversy. An early sex-ed pamphlet addressed to teens by Mary Ware Dennett, *The Sex Side of Life: An Explanation for Young People* (1919), was deemed obscene under the Comstock Law in 1922, which banned sending any materials related to sexuality, contraception, or abortion through the U.S. mail (see Moore, 2007 and Solinger, 2005 for more complete historical discussions). This decision was overturned on appeal in 1930; the ruling stated: "an accurate exposition of the relevant facts of the sex side of life in decent language and in manifestly serious and disinterested spirit cannot ordinarily be regarded as obscene" (cited in Solinger, 106). Sex-ed books gained legal respectability on shaky grounds. What, after all, constitutes "accuracy"? Who decides what the "facts" are and which of them are "relevant" to children? Authors, since this time, have continually asserted their credibility by presenting themselves as *scientific* authorities on what morally constitutes "accurate" "facts" about "sex."

In this reading, we discuss recent sex-ed books for children. In our research, we found no books about sex targeted to young children published before the late 1960s. Publishers apparently began to perceive young children as a market for this sort of didactic material as a result of a particular combination of cultural forces that together promoted resistance to authority and more openness about sexual matters in the late 1960s and early 1970s: the student movement, the feminist movement, the gay rights movement (all of which are indebted to the Civil Rights movement); hippie subculture; the so-called sexual revolution; and the human potential movement (promoting psychological growth techniques and practices). Advice books on sexuality for adults also flourished during this time (e.g., see Ehrenreich and English, 1986; Simonds, 1992), and sex education programs proliferated in U.S. public schools (Moran, 2000). The notion that children should be educated about sex before adolescence developed as cultural views of adolescents *as* sexual became accepted by educators and doctors. Thus, adolescents were in need of sexual education—especially regarding management and control. Moran describes the development of these ideas, beginning at the turn of the twentieth century (2000). Patton (1996) writes that the way in which we now conceive of adolescence is "as a time of turmoil between a period of innocence (childhood) and one of accomplished identity and safety (adulthood)" (75). So how do we present sexuality to innocents to prepare them for impending turmoil?

In order to consider this didactic medium systematically and sociologically, we examined all the androgynous (not addressed specifically to one gender) non-religious picture books about sex geared toward young children currently in print and available through Amazon.com in 2008, sex ed books for older kids, and advice books for parents regarding talking with children about sex. In all, we surveyed fourteen books for young children, seven for adolescents, and eleven for parents. (These books are arranged by category in the bibliography.) Our sample spans 40 years; the earliest is a 1979 reprint of a 1968 book, and the most recent book was published in 2008.

These books, taken together, address a loose set of problems parents face in their presumed desire to present a variety of complex, baggage-laden topics to children in an understandable way without feeling deeply uncomfortable in the process. Talking about sexuality and childbearing with children creates a multifaceted dilemma. Parents are, in essence, attempting to create openness about a range of topics they may feel unable to be truly open about. First there is the issue of deterrence: How can parents present sexuality without making it seem too appealing? Second, how ought adults avoid frightening children with all the ways that sexual encounters and their outcomes can be painful, even horrible? How should parents balance a desire not to frighten with the goal of offering them information that might protect them from sexual dangers and unintended consequences (sexual predators, rape, sexually transmitted diseases, teen pregnancy, abortion, not to mention heartbreak)? Fourth, how can parents deal with, acknowledge, respond to evidence of, and instruct them about their own sexuality? And fifth, how do adults teach children appropriate contexts for expressions of sexuality?

What are appropriate contexts, after all? In this rest of this essay, we look at how authors of sex-ed books for children and advice books for parents contextualize sexuality. These books reify (and occasionally resist) heteronormative, gendered, and medicalized sociosexual conventions through an examination of five general topics: procreative/sexual anatomy; procreative sex; childbirth; managing childhood sexuality; and alternatives to procreative sex. Our primary focus is on the books for young children; we supplement this discussion of these books with interpretations of the books for older children and for parents.

Changing Bodies

In sex books for young and older kids, authors foreground the primary discussion of procreative sex with brief anatomy lessons. They equate biological sex with gender: There are people with penises and people with vaginas, and this is what makes them boys or girls. Eventually, boys and girls grow up into men and women and make babies together utilizing these parts. Laurie Krasny Brown and Marc Brown (1997) preface their presentation of genital difference with a litany of ways in which boys and girls *may* be different (clothes, hairstyles, playing styles, emotions). After each example they write that the difference is "sometimes, but not always" evident. Harris (2006) has a similar discussion (including that "girls play with dolls and teddy bears! And so do boys!" and "boys have very big and strong muscles. So do girls!"), but also concludes that boys and girls are "not all that different" (12–13).

Despite claims of similarity, divergent anatomy is central in these discussions of difference: "Actually the only sure way to tell boys and girls apart is by their bodies. If you're a boy, you have a penis, scrotum, and testicles. If you're a girl, you have a vulva, clitoris, and vagina" (11–12). This text appears alongside illustrations of a naked boy and girl, with labeled body parts. The cartoon girl proclaims, "Look! Our bodies are more alike than different!" Harris and Emberley (1999) include a similar picture, with the text "Most parts of our bodies . . . are the same and look quite the same whether we are female or male. . . . The parts that are different are the parts that make each of us a female or a male" (10). Occasionally, authors omit the clitoris from their depictions of girls' bodies, as in Saltz's (2005) book *Amazing You,* or describe girls' sex organs as if they are somehow based on boys' sex organs. For example, in a description of sexual arousal in girls, Foster (2005) describes the elongation of the clitoris as an example of how, "in some ways, a female's clitoris is like a male penis" (29). In the book *Boys, Girls and Body Science,* Hickling (2002) frames her discussion of sexual development with the device of a teacher interacting with elementary-aged students; these students present their ideas about sexual development and the teacher redirects them along the "correct" path. For instance, a student asks whether "girls have balls," and the teacher responds that "girls have two ovaries inside their abdomen and they are sort of like balls" (np). Early fetal development begins with undifferentiated female internal sex organs, not male parts. So, in actuality, "balls" are like ovaries, not vice versa. Yet authors' language tends to centralizes boys' bodies, and to make girls' bodies secondary and/or deviant.

Authors do not mention the possibility of not being able to tell bodies apart easily, nor do they broach the topic of gender identity that doesn't "match" genitalia, nor do they question the bifurcated social constructs of girl and boy, man and woman. As Joey's mother says in *So That's How I Was Born!* (Brooks and Perl, 1983), "a boy's body isn't better than a girl's body and a girl's body isn't better than a boy's. They're just different from the time they're born and each is special in their own way." In this way, authors proclaim gender difference as essential (rooted in dimorphic biological sex), while also contradictorily claiming the difference doesn't matter. Perhaps introducing sex and gender ambiguity and fluidity would confuse kids. The majority of babies are born genetically dimorphous, after all, and most people appear to grow up relatively comfortable with socially constructed gender divisions. Yet in other cases, it is not the frequency of a phenomenon that determines whether authors will present it; some of these books include discussions of occurrences at least as infrequent as intersexuality or gender-bending identities (e.g., multiple births, home births, adoption), apparently without worrying about the confusion these mentions might cause. Authors seek to demystify some social practices but leave others untouched, and in so doing appear to take most cultural norms for granted.

To cite another example, the vast majority of illustrations and photographs of children and their families in these books only show racially alike families. Though the majority of those pictured are white, illustrators and photographers include children and adults interacting with each other across racial boundaries. In the original version of this reading, written in 2001, there was only one clear depiction of an interracial family (Smith and Wheatley, 1997, 14). Harris and Emberley (1999) had a few illustrations that *might* have been interracial family groups. In 2008, only Harris continued to include these images in her work: her book *It's Not the Stork!* for preschool-aged children depicts and discusses families in a multitude of ways, including foster, adoptive, blended, gay and lesbian, and intergenerational families (2004; 2006); one of the families depicted may be a gay, interracial family. Harris also presents interracial families in the birthing section, with women of color giving birth, accompanied by white fathers (2004, 42). In her book for older children, Harris again depicts interracial intimacy (2006, 55–56). While other authors do discuss different family forms (adoptive, foster, and intergenerational), and also present and promote multicultural interactions among people; no others depict or discuss interracial intimacy.

Making Love and Making Babies

Children do, indeed, ask their parents "Where did I come from?" or "How are babies made?" Thus, many parents find themselves working backward from baby (or pregnancy) to heterosexual sexuality. We suspect that if children initiate conversations about sexuality apart from procreation many parents don't know what to do or say, so they may end up in the procreation story because it's easier for them to deal with than sexuality on its own.

Sexual information conveyed in the books for young children tends to be vague, to reinforce heteronormativity, and to represent penile–vaginal intercourse as the only example of sexual activity in which men and women engage. Sometimes authors omit the act altogether, as in Joanna Cole's *How You Were Born* (1993) and Alastair Smith's *How Are Babies Made?* (1997).

In a woman's body are egg cells. The egg cell is round. It does not have a shell like a chicken's egg. In a man's body are sperm cells. The sperm cells have long tails and can swim. When a sperm and an egg join together, they form a special cell that can grow into a baby. (Cole, 1993, 19)

How does the baby start? A tiny sperm from the man's body has to join up with a little egg from the woman's body. (Smith, 1997, 5)

When authors do discuss penile–vaginal intercourse, they describe it as pleasurable and functional for both men and women, and portray it taking place within the context of loving relationships:

Sexual intercourse may seem gross or nice, scary or funny, weird or cool—or even unbelievable to you. But when two people care for each other, sexual intercourse is very loving. Kids are much too young to have sexual intercourse. (Harris and Emberley, 1999, 29)

When a woman and a man who love each other go to bed, they like to hug and kiss. Sometimes, if they both want to, the man puts his penis in the woman's vagina and that feels really good for both of them. Sperm come

out through the man's penis. If one tiny sperm meets a tiny egg inside the woman's body, a baby is started, and the man and woman will be the baby's parents. (Gordon and Gordon, 1992)

None of the authors writing for young children describes orgasm, though clearly they present the emission of sperm as momentous. Eggs and sperm are personified in gendered ways; Lisa Jean Moore writes: "There is a preponderance of narratives describing the exceptionalness of the one sperm that gets to fertilize the egg. Other than primping and batting eyes to be attractive to the sperm, eggs typically are passive" (2007, 62). Authors depict sex cells as engaged in analogous romances to those of their producers.

The reason for sex in these books is parenthood. Brooks and Perl (1983) label the lovers "mommy" and "daddy" before the fact, thus presenting sex as predicated on this goal of future parenthood:

*One of the ways a mommy and daddy show they love one another is by hugging each other very close. In bed, they can get really close when a daddy puts his **penis** inside the special opening between a mommy's legs which is called a **vagina**. The sperm comes out of the daddy's penis and goes into the mommy's vagina, and then the sperm meets the egg and a baby starts. (Brooks and Perl, 1983)*

Andry, Schepp, and Hampton's *How Babies Are Made* (1979) and Baker's *The Birds and the Bees* (1990) are more lackluster than the others in their descriptions of procreative sex:

The sperm, which come from the father's testicles, are sent into the mother through his penis. To do this, the father and mother lie down facing each other and the father places his penis in the mother's vagina. Unlike plants and animals, when human mothers and fathers create a new baby they are sharing a very personal and special relationship. (Andry, Schepp, and Hampton, 1979)

When men and women mate, the penis becomes stiff and is inserted into the vagina, which has become larger and moist, ready to receive it. (Baker, 1990)

These authors make heterosex sound like a cross between directions for putting together a bookcase and a recipe for baking a cake. (Imagine the seductive dialogue: "Hey baby, I have some sperm I'd like to send you through my penis! May I insert it?" "Oh yeah, my vagina is large and moist, ready to receive!")

Many books present humans' procreative method after first laboriously introducing habits of other plant and animal species. This approach makes sex seem natural and scientific. "By relying on science, these children's books bolster their contents as being objective and truthful" (Moore, 2007, 51). Andry, Schepp, and Hampton (1979) interestingly sever this naturalistic connection with other living things, separating humans out by insisting on our emotional superiority ("unlike plants and animals . . ."). They want to show that sex is more than just the casual rubbing together of stamens and pistils. The experts writing for parents endorse grounding sex in satisfying long-term connection between adults. For instance, Spock and Rothenberg (1992) advise, "Parents shouldn't ever let the anatomical and physiological explanation of sex stand alone but always connect it with the idealistic, spiritual aspects" (509).

Our favorite among the books for young children is Babette Cole's *Mommy Laid an Egg OR Where Do Babies Come From?* (1993). Cole uses humor throughout the book, both in the prose and in her illustrations, which mix a cartoon family together with raucous, childlike stick-figure drawings. The book begins with the cartoon parents misinforming their children, "some babies are delivered by dinosaurs," "you can make them out of gingerbread," and "sometimes you just find them under stones." The children respond with laughter, and say "what a bunch of nonsense!" They proceed to instruct their parents about procreative sex, all the while pointing to their crude comical illustrations.

> **Girl:** *"Mommies do have eggs. They are inside their bodies."*
> **Boy:** *"And daddies have seeds in seed pods outside their bodies. Daddies also have a tube. The seeds come out of the pods and through the tube."*
> **Girl:** *"The tube goes into the mommy's body through a hole. Then the seeds swim inside using their tails."* (Cole, 1993)

On the page where the boy proclaims "here are some ways. . . mommies and daddies fit together,"

Cole illustrates his words with childlike drawings of the mommy and daddy cavorting in a variety of imaginative positions while linked at the crotch, including holding balloons, bouncing on a big ball (labeled "space hopper"), and lying on a skateboard. These are raunchy yet clean, because they are children's drawings (and do not depict genitalia, only breasts). The language is crude in a childish way, yet the botanical allegories don't seem embarrassingly goofy, just goofy in a fun way. Sex seems fun for once—not just a pleasant sperm-delivery arrangement. Why else would the participants wear party hats? Yet, at the same time, this language of "fitting together," which recurs in several books, reinforces the notion that heteronormative, procreative sex is natural and right.

In the six books for young children that include illustrations of sexual encounters (the other seven do not depict the act), the man is on top in three (Baker, 1990; Harris and Emberley, 1999; Andry, Schepp, and Hampton, 1979), and the man and woman are side by side in two (Gordon, Gordon, and Cohen, 1992). The copulators are all under the covers except in Baker's drawing (which is decidedly unrevealing despite the nudity of the illustrated characters).

Having Babies

The next step after procreative sex in all of these books is pregnancy and birth. After a brief discussion of the growth of the fetus and changes in the mother's body, authors tell how babies are born. They depict childbearing as wonderful, a job to be done together by a mommy and a daddy (who cheers her on). Many authors tell the story of birth from the point of view of the baby, which is apparently the perspective with which they imagine child readers will identify. Authors do not discuss pain in childbirth, although Cole (1993) comes close, referring to contractions as "sharp twinges called labor pangs" (30). Authors portray labor as a biological (muscular) activity, as hard work that a woman does, or both. Birth is described as awesome and wonderful for the parents.

Marc Brown (Brown and Brown, 1997) and Michael Emberley (Harris and Emberley, 1999) both depict women in the lithotomy position (on their backs, with feet in stirrups) surrounded by masked and gowned people. The daddies are also decked out in medical garb, though in Emberley's drawing he doesn't wear a mask. Laura Krasny Brown (1997) writes "When a baby is ready to be born, muscles in the mother's womb begin to tighten and relax, tighten and relax, helping her push out the baby. In most births, the baby comes out the vagina, which stretches to let it pass through" (28). Similarly, the text accompanying Emberley's drawing says:

> When a baby is about to be born, the muscles in the mother's uterus begin to squeeze tight. This is called "labor." "Labor" is another word for "work." A mother's muscles work very hard to push and squeeze the baby out of the uterus and into the vagina. Then the mother's muscles push and squeeze the baby's body through the vagina. The vagina stretches wide as the baby's soft, wet, and slippery body travels through it. (Harris and Emberley, 1999, 56–57)

Even though these authors' descriptions of labor and birth sound like they might have been written by midwives, they tend to depict medical management of the process as normal. Four of the eighteen authors mention alternatives to hospital birth, but none depicts it. Joanna Cole (1993) writes: "Your mother and father went to the hospital or childbirth center where you were to be born. If you were born at home, then the doctor or midwife came to your house" (31). The photographs accompanying this text show couples in more casual hospital or birth center settings than the settings depicted in the other books, but none are at home. Sol and Judith Gordon write: "Some babies are born at home. But most women like to go to the hospital for the birth of their baby" (1992). This text is accompanied by a drawing of a woman lying in the lithotomy position in a hospital, a masked woman birth attendant standing between her legs holding a screaming baby up for her (and us) to see. We are positioned behind and above the woman's head, watching the baby come out from her vantage point, but we can also see her face, and she looks happy. We rarely see a vaginal view of birth except in Cole's (1993) child drawing, which shows a baby sticking out of a round-blob mother

and saying "Hello Mommy!" Harris (2004) depicts both a vaginal view of birth and a woman in the lithotomy position in the same set of illustrations (63). All other illustrations show babies mediated by medical personnel in medical settings both during and after birth.

As mentioned, authors writing for young children often seek to present labor and birth from the baby's perspective—these authors tend to present the birthing process as both fun and exciting. In *Boys, Girls and Body Science* (Hickling, 2005), Nurse Meg describes to a class of elementary students how the birthing process happens. This dialogue is accompanied by a picture of a woman in the lithotomy position who appears serene and peaceful—if not unconscious:

> "But what would happen if you kept squeezing on a balloon?" asked Meg.
> "It would pop," said Nicholas.
> "That is exactly what happens," said Meg. "After a few hours, the water bag breaks and the water comes pouring out of the mum's vagina and makes it all wet and slippery, just like a water slide. So, the first water slide that you ever had was the day you were born when you came slip-sliding down your mum's vagina."
> All the children loved the water slide story and made swooshy noises as they waved their arms around.

Harris (2006) uses the same "balloon" analogy in a much more effective way, explaining that a pregnant woman's uterus does *not* pop because her uterus and skin are stretchy—"like a balloon." This response is an excellent example of how an analogy can be used to explain a phenomenon to a young child in a way that is correct, yet understandable to the child.

Teaching about Touching

A few of the sex books for young children explicitly address children's sexuality within the context of danger. Brown and Brown (1997) and Harris and Emberley (1999) attempt to differentiate between touching that is "okay" and "not okay"—that is, between masturbation and sexual abuse. Brown and Brown (1997) write:

> Touching and rubbing your genitals to feel good is called masturbation. Some of us try this; some of us

don't. However, it's best to do this private kind of touching off by yourself.

Touching others is just as important. . . . If someone doesn't want to be touched, then respect his or her wishes—don't do it! . . . Everyone needs good touches to feel loved and happy. . . . But no one has the right to touch you in a way that feels wrong or uncomfortable.

If you don't like the way someone touches you, speak up and tell him or her to stop. If that doesn't work, tell your mom or dad or another grownup. Your body belongs to you, and you should say who touches it! (16–19)

Harris (1999) goes into more detail about both masturbation and abuse, and like Brown and Brown, the discussion of masturbation leads into the issue of abuse. The Browns differentiate between self-touches that feel good, touches from others that *are* good, and those that feel wrong or are somehow dislikable. Harris (1999) makes the same points, and goes into more detail about contentiousness over masturbation: "Every family has its own thoughts and feelings about masturbation. . . . Some people and some religions think it's wrong to masturbate. But most doctors agree that masturbation is perfectly healthy and perfectly normal, and cannot hurt you or your body" (69). Doctors apparently have the last word and validating authority on the subject. This is ironic, given that well into the twentieth century, sex educators backed up denouncements of masturbation as pathological with medical authority. (See Conrad and Schneider, 1992, 180–181, on nineteenth-century conceptualizations of masturbation as disease; and Moran, 2000, 57, on lasting sex educational prohibitions.)

Harris next defines touches that are not okay: "But if any person touches any part of your body and you do not want them to, say "STOP!". . . . Sexual abuse happens when someone touches the private parts of a person's body and does NOT have the right to do that" (1999, 70). Harris acknowledges that sexual abuse is "always wrong," that it "can hurt" or "feel gentle," and thus, that it can be "very confusing" (70). He advises, like the Browns, that children tell someone they trust if they experience sexual abuse, and reassures readers that it is "NEVER your fault" (70–71).

Kleven's book *The Right Touch* (1997) is one of the few children's books we found that discusses only sexual abuse, and no other sexual education topics. In this book, a mother tells her son the story of the attempted sexual abuse of a young girl by a neighbor. The text is accompanied by Bergsma's illustrations of "whimsical, elfin-like people" (np) that seemed too cute to us for this topic. Kleven portrays child abuse as potentially everywhere: "grown-ups, babysitters, and bigger kids" can be abusers. Child readers are urged to be self-protective at all times. The mother in the story says, "no one has the right to touch private parts of your body without a good reason, not even Dad or me" (Kleven, 1997). How a child determines what constitutes a "good reason" is not clear. Kleven asserts that many children in bad-touch-situations-in-the-making have "warning feelings" when "things are not safe" (1997). This position suggests to readers that knowing how to recognize a sexual predator is innate and universal: so if one fails to escape danger, one is somehow to blame.

One book that describes masturbation in an overtly positive way is Bell's *Changing Bodies, Changing Lives* (1998). Bell writes that "having masturbated helps you enjoy lovemaking more," and gives descriptions of how boys and girls masturbate (1998, 83). In addition, Bell provides advice for what to do "if you don't have orgasms and want to," and addresses the pressure that many teenagers, especially girls, feel about orgasms:

It is not surprising that girls and women have orgasms less easily than boys and men do. First, there's anatomy. A boy can't miss his penis. He touches it several times a day . . . most boys discover masturbation, and it is pretty easy for them to figure out how to do it. But a girl's clitoris, and certainly her vagina, are more hidden. Also, she may be taught as a child not to touch her genitals.

Then there is sex education, or lack of it. Most girls are never taught that they have a clitoris and what it is and does. Since orgasm usually depends at least in part on a girl's clitoris getting stimulated, not knowing about your clitoris can make orgasms pretty hard to have.

Third, girls in general are brought up to be less accepting and proud of their sexuality than boys are. This is part of the double standard. A teenage boy finds that his sexual adventures are usually tolerated or even encouraged. A girl, however, is told she must be the one to say, "No!" and hold off a boy's sex drive. She rarely hears about her own sex drive. So it can be hard for her to let her sexual responses flow freely, and let go enough to have an orgasm. . . .

But for both girls and boys, feeling that you have to have orgasms to be a "liberated" person can add to the confusions and pressures that many of us feel about sex. Try not to let yourself feel pressured to come.

Authors writing for older kids and parents all discuss masturbation and sexual abuse in similar terms to those utilized by those writing for young children. They describe masturbation as normal and generally healthy; they describe sexual abuse as always dangerous.

Books for teens tend to combine the topic of sexual abuse with discussions of rape (Basso, 2003; Bell, 1998). Bell discusses the "sexual script" that occurs because the "man is 'supposed' to be dominant, to be sexually powerful and demanding. The woman, on the other hand, is 'supposed' to be coy and shy and passive, to lead men on but not let them get 'too far' " (1998, 128). She argues that girls have to learn to "give straightforward messages. Boys have to learn to believe what girls are saying. It is important to say yes *only* when you mean yes; and to really mean no when you say no" (1998, 129).

Basso addresses the issue of dealing with sexual scripts, but in a slightly different, less clear manner: when "your mouth is saying one thing and your body language is saying another, your partner may become confused" (2003, 218). He lays out a table of poorly matched body language and verbal messages ("'Stop!' + smile = He/she is just playing") and a table of well-matched body language and verbal messages ("'Stop!' + serious or angry look on your face = I don't want you to do that") (1998, 218–219). Here, if an individual sends "mixed messages," then s/he should not be surprised if her/his partner continues to pressure her/him for sex. Unlike Bell, Basso does not discuss how "peer pressure" might devolve into a date rape scenario. Despite the gender-neutral framing of the "information" in this table, it is clear from Basso's extended discussion of danger and risk-taking that rape victims are girls and women, and that rapists and potential rapists are boys and men.

Basso discusses date rape and stranger rape in a way that infantilizes women and reinforces heteronormative sexual scripts. His definition of rape seems only to include those cases that include physical harm, verbal threats, or limited capacity due to drugs or alcohol (2003, 233). Even though Basso argues that, "it doesn't matter what a female wears, says, or does, there is never any excuse for rape" (234), and that, "ladies, you are free to wear anything you want any way you want, and you can act any way you want" (237), he contradicts these statements, outlining several scenarios in which young women inadvertently place themselves at risk. Here is just one example:

You wear a short, tight skirt and loose blouse that shows off some cleavage . . . Your message: I'm being fashionable and wearing something that is in style. Male interpretation: She's sexy! She wants me to see her breasts because she wants to have sex with me. (237)

Young women are advised to be careful about what they wear; to know their dancing might be interpreted as sexually provocative; and to avoid casual touches to avoid sending the wrong message to their dates. Boys are advised that they are responsible for their actions "regardless of the situation or condition" (i.e., intoxication) (239). Boys are told that, "when a female says no, she means no. Although the female may have led you on, she has every right to change her mind, and you must honor her decision" (234). Basso continues with a bizarre analogy, in which he compares committing rape to a getting ticketed for speeding:

It's like driving a shiny red Corvette with a racing stripe down the side. Suddenly a police officer pulls up behind you, flashes her/her lights and gives you a speeding ticket. Is it fair to get a speeding ticket just because you're driving a shiny red Corvette? Just because a female dresses a certain way doesn't mean she should be treated a certain way based on YOUR assumptions. Of course, comparing rape to a speeding ticket is like comparing a nuclear explosion to a firecracker—rape is a devastating crime. (234).

Well, the good news is, "you can avoid the embarrassment of being arrested as a rapist" if you just drive your date home and behave responsibly. (240)

Basso clearly identifies with male readers. Beyond the offensive analogy, we are troubled by the message that what a boy should seek to avoid is the "embarrassment of being arrested as a rapist," rather than *being* a rapist.

In childhood, inappropriate sexual touching and sexual activity is *never* okay, no matter who does it, and no matter the context. In adolescence, the messages become mixed: inappropriate sexual touching and sexual activity is usually not all right, unless you confused your partner—then, can you blame them? Didactic presentations of boundaries become mired in a discourse of thwarted or dangerous desires for boys and provocative yet (rightfully) reluctant girls. We find Basso's gendered messages about date rape especially troubling; ultimately, he places the responsibility for control of sexual limits on young women, and implicitly blames girls when boys feel "led on." It is not possible that a girl might pressure a boy to have sex or attempt to rape him. Same-gender situations are notably absent in all these discussions.

In contrast to the warnings they issue about abusive sex, authors describe "sex play" between children as generally harmless. Westheimer acknowledges only that this occurs among boys, writing: "Sometimes groups of boys will masturbate together. There's nothing wrong with doing this in privacy" (53). In books for parents where masturbation and sex-play are discussed, the goal seems to be allaying parents' fears of impending gayness or sexual excessiveness (non-normativity). Regarding solitary masturbation, Eyre and Eyre (1998) and Spock and Rothenberg (1992) warn against too much of this good thing. Spock and Rothenberg discuss what they call "excessive masturbation," never specifying how often is too much. They do attempt, after raising this specter, to keep parents calm:

> It's important for parents to know that the fear that something will happen or has happened to the genitals is one of the most common causes of excessive masturbation in young childhood. To tell such children that they'll injure themselves makes matters worse. To tell them that they're bad and that you won't love them any more gives them a new fear. (504)

Even as they introduce this behavior as abnormal, Spock and Rothenberg (1992) reassure parents that sexual exploration is natural, writing:

> I think that whatever your personal beliefs or feelings, you should avoid threatening or punishing your children when they reveal their natural sexuality. . . . It's important to try to say something about how normal and universal the activity is. It's good for children to feel they can ask their parents about sex. (506)

This seemingly conflicting advice could be confusing to parents, especially those who have themselves been brought up by parents who disapproved of masturbation.

In a prescripted dialogue between a father and a son who asks "Is masturbation bad?" (meant to be helpful for parents seeking to initiate discussion with their kids) the Eyres (1998) propose replying: "Everyone at least experiments with it. But it can be a problem if it becomes a habit or happens too often" (105). The father then advises the son to "think about how beautiful and awesome it can be with the beautiful and special wife you'll have someday. . . . If you try to do this, you won't feel like masturbating as often, and when you do, at least you'll be thinking about the best kind of sex that will happen someday with your wife" (106). The Eyres propose monogamous married sex as an anti-erotic fantasy to *curb* boys' sexual urges. With a similar weird twist, Maxwell (2008) warns that "obsessive masturbation to only one kind of stimulation" can lead to "difficulty reaching orgasm within a relationship" (58). She claims to have seen this in her practice as a clinical psychologist, but admits that, "there is no current research to support that this is the case with most men" (58). Thus, she urges parents to talk to their children (read: boys) about porn. She proclaims, "Demeaning pictures or pictures that promote dominance of one person over another, can, over time, train a person to respond only to that form of stimulation" (58–59). All authors who write about sexual urges and danger in children stress that they are natural or normal, even as they coach parents about how to best protect, contain, constrain, and train these desires in socially desirable ways.

Words You May Have Heard

Authors of sex books for young children tend to limit discussion of sexual issues to procreative sex, and occasional mentions of masturbation and child abuse. Authors of sex books for adolescents all cover masturbation and sexual abuse, but beyond this they tend to discuss sexual diversity (anything other than penile–vaginal intercourse) in a very limited way. For instance, Westheimer offhandedly mentions anal and oral sex in her section on AIDS: "some people think they can avoid AIDS by practicing anal intercourse (putting the penis in the anus) or oral sex (putting it in the mouth). They are dead wrong" (Westheimer and deGroat, 1998:74).

Throughout these books, authors depict loving sexual relationships between men and woman as normative. When they do discuss alternatives—gayness, lesbianism, and bisexuality (transgenderedness is discussed only by Lefkoff [2007])—they treat them with a liberal touch, yet cordon these topics off into short sections of their own. These authors advocate tolerance, but are careful to avoid endorsing or advocating nonheterosexual activities. The following are examples of discussions of "homosexuality" from two books for teens and one for adults (set up as a prescribed parental response to a child's question):

> *Some people prefer to have sexual experiences with persons of their own sex. They are called homosexuals. Most boys and girls have homosexual thoughts occasionally. Some even have homosexual experiences. This doesn't mean that they are homosexual. The people properly called homosexual are those who, as adults, have sexual contacts only with persons of their own sex. . . . Some people enjoy sexual relations with both sexes throughout their adult life. They are called bisexuals. Modern psychologists no longer see homosexual or bisexual behavior between consenting adults as a disorder. (Gordon and Cohen, 1992, 28)*

Why Are Some People Straight and Others Gay?

Psychologists do not really know what causes a person's sexual preferences. Some believe that whether a person is straight or gay depends on experiences in early childhood. Others think homosexuality might be an inherited, or built-in preference. . . .

Is Homosexuality a Sickness?

No. People used to believe that homosexuality was a form of mental illness, but now psychiatrists say that it is not. Homosexuality is just one way people can express love.

Can Homosexuals Choose Not to Be Gay?

Homosexuals can choose not to practice homosexuality. . . . But for most gay people, it is probably not possible to choose how they feel inside and which sex they are attracted to. (Cole and Tiegreen, 1988, 75)

Is It Bad to Be a Homosexual?

We don't think so, but that's one of those questions that different people have different opinions about. Some people think that you should only have sexual relations with a person of the other sex, and that anybody who doesn't choose to do that is not doing the right thing. In this family we agree with the scientists and doctors who say that a homosexual is just different from a heterosexual, but not bad or sick or strange. Certain people who don't approve of homosexuals are sometimes very cruel to them, so many homosexuals are hurt and tend to be very private about their personal lives. That's too bad, we think, because it's very hard and sad to have to hide that you love someone. (Calderone and Ramey, 1982, 87)

Even as they attempt to advocate openmindedness, authors frame sexual nonconformity as deviant by using the clinical term *homosexual*, by discussing lesbian/bisexual/gay sexuality via questions that are pointedly negative, and by emphasizing that it was once officially pathological. By consistently presenting medicine as the arbiter of the current non-pathology of "homosexuality," authors do not question medical authority or effectively critique its past homophobia. Calderone and Ramey's discussion of homophobia, although disapproving, also presents it as a valid point of view. They describe "some people" who think that only straight sex is "the right thing." Authors denounce cruelty and violence, but do not usually explicitly denounce homophobic beliefs; often they take this stance in the name of respect for religious orthodoxy. Maxwell writes, in this vein:

> *I don't address issues of homosexuality in public schools because I embrace the principle that respecting diversity means respecting those parents whose religious convictions are opposed to homosexuality. . . . I*

also tell them [kids] that no religion has ever supported humiliating, disrespecting, or harming another human being and that the word "gay" should never be used as a put-down, not even as a "joke." (2008, 65)

Here, Maxwell grants homophobia credibility as long as it is religiously-based; she also likens being gay to being persecuted for one's religious identity, presumably to elicit empathy for victims of homophobia from religious readers. This is a fine line to be walking, indeed.

The Eyres (1998) are the only authors among our sample who are *overtly* homophobic. They discuss "homosexuality" in one paragraph (which precedes a paragraph on AIDS), saying "we shouldn't judge a person who is gay, but it can be a sad situation because it doesn't allow for the birth of children or for the kind of family that a heterosexual couple can have" (97). In contrast, a few authors do actually denounce homophobia, usually by explaining that gayness is "not a choice" (Levkoff, 2007, 89), and then proclaiming that, anyway, discrimination is morally wrong:

There has never been a reason to treat people with disrespect. Homophobia is as bad as any other type of hatred—including racism and religious persecution. People should be judged according to their character, not who they sleep with. (Levkoff, 2007, 90)

We must teach our children tolerance so that some other child's life is not made miserable by name-calling, harassment, or violence. We must teach tolerance so our kids know that any question they have about sexual orientation is okay and that we love them for who they are. (Schwartz and Capello, 2000, 186)

Some people disapprove of gay men and lesbians. Some even hate homosexuals only because they are homosexuals. Usually these people know little or nothing about homosexuals, and their views are based on fears or misinformation, not facts. People are often afraid of things that they know little or nothing about. (Harris, 2004, 18)

Even advocates of respect for sexual diversity tread with a great deal of caution, and in so doing, undercut their affirmation of gayness in children. Many of the authors writing for older kids and adults seek to reassure readers that nonheterosexual urges and experiences might well be transitory. Though the

categories they introduce have the same essential ring to them as gender does in the books for young kids, authors recognize some flux on the road to a permanent sexual identity. But because authors explain that eventually sexual identity (straight, gay, lesbian, bisexual) is permanent, this changeability often comes across as an experimentation phase.

Are you homosexual? It's difficult to know. Some people don't figure out if they're gay or straight until their late teens or their twenties. Having a crush on, or even kissing or touching, someone of your own sex does not necessarily mean that you're gay. (Westheimer, 1993, 54)

Because there are so many negative ideas in our society about being gay, young people may panic if they have any feelings or daydreams about people of their own sex. Yet most of them will not end up being gay. Naturally, a small percentage will—about five to ten percent. . . . But most will not. They are simply going through a stage of growing up. (Cole, 1988, 76)

[A] child's sex experimentation at an early or late age has no bearing on his or her sexual orientation. . . . Usually they don't think of their same-sex play as homosexual. But . . . some children end up very worried that because they want to touch a friend of the same sex, or already have, that means they're gay. It doesn't. And it's normal—all the varieties of sex play among kids are normal. (Morris, 1984, 85)

Most of the books addressed to parents offer advice about what parents should do if they think their kids aren't straight. Ratner and Chamlin (1985) pose the hypothetical question, "Will my son's love of 'dressing up' lead to homosexuality?" And they respond, "No. Many parents discourage boys from playing 'dress-up' and 'house,' but at certain ages, certainly preschool, it's appropriate. Preschoolers actively assume many different roles" (35). They imply that at a certain age, gender-bending will—and should—straighten out. Spock and Rothenberg (1992) imply this as well, saying "When parents think that their little boy is effeminate or their little girl too masculine, they may worry that the child will grow up to be a homosexual or lesbian. In fact, the majority of such children will grow up to be heterosexual" (52). However, they then recommend therapy for a boy who wants to play with girls and dolls, and who wants to wear dresses ("I would assume that something had gotten mixed up in his identification"), as well as for a girl who plays "only with boys" and is "**always** unhappy about being a girl" (52). A girl who prefers to play with boys and who "occasionally" wishes she were a boy, "but also [enjoys] playing with girls" does not concern them (52).

Levkoff is the only author among those writing to parents who discusses the social construction of gender and of sexual identity, and she endorses parental acceptance of all forms of self-expression among kids. At the same time, she presents parental emotional responses to a child's coming out as gay (there is no discussion of parental response to transgenderedness) as almost entirely unpleasant: "It can be an emotionally challenging time. . . . Most people speak of grief and mourning, as if they have lost a loved one. . . . It is natural and it will pass. What we hope is that these turbulent and complex feelings will bring you, in the end, to acceptance. But it isn't an easy road" (2007, 99).

Harris and Emberley (1999) are the only authors of books for young children who explore alternatives to heterosexuality, and they, along with Levkoff, are the only authors in our sample who explain that love and sexual behavior can be multifaceted without invoking the past pathologizing or current acceptance of medical experts: "There are lots of kinds of love—like love between a parent and child, love between friends, love between kids, love between teenagers, and love between grownups. There can be love between a female and a male, or a male and a male, or a female and a female" (Harris and Emberley, 1999, 31). They go on to explain the terms homosexual, heterosexual, gay, lesbian, bisexual and straight, and proclaim "A person's daily life—having friends, having fun, going to work, being a mom or dad, loving another person—is mostly the same whether a person is straight or gay." This text appears with an illustration of a possibly interracial gay male couple and their two kids eating dinner (32). Authors seek to promote harmony across difference by positing that difference is overshadowed by commonalities among people, regardless of sexual identity.

So What Should We Tell the Kids?

First let us sum up what we *do* tell the kids in the discourse of these didactic books: that the central focus of sexuality is procreative penile-vaginal intercourse; that this form of sexuality is "natural" and good; that participants should be monogamous adults; and that proper sexual expression is based in love and enacted in private. Many authors writing for older kids and adults do acknowledge other sorts of sexual behavior, but these discussions are limited and not integrated into presentations of what is clearly the main event. Nonheterosexual activities are marginalized. The books can be seen as precursors to school-based sex education programs, which increase the focus on dangers, often advocate abstinence, and are notoriously heterosexist and devoid of discussions of gendered or sexual power dynamics (e.g., see Irvine, 2004; Luker, 2007; Raymond, 1994; Watney, 1991).

When do we tell children that some sex is amazing, some is lovely, some is dull, some becomes repugnant in retrospect, and some is horrible while it's happening? When do we tell them about its potential variety and variability? When do we expose children to a peerlike level of sexual honesty in which we speak to them of the intensity of desire, the fickleness of lust, the pain of rejection? Or do we simply not venture this far into the murky depths of sexuality? Do we just let them find out whatever they'll find out by themselves from people we can only hope will not hurt them or mess up their lives? All the while, we must bear in mind that something we say to them today could be the impetus for therapy later. What truths, warnings, and recommendations do we dare to communicate? In short, our task is absurd and impossible the more we ponder it, yet most of us would agree that to say nothing would be worse than to make some kind of attempt.

So we're back where we started, with Spock and Rothenberg's (1992) admonition against the stork, in favor of the truth. There is no absolute truth about sexuality, so we have to decide what and how we want to discuss sexuality with our children. Sex education books for children and parents are generally a step in the right direction, and are certainly better than nothing, in our view. But they are not as comprehensive or critical or political as they could be.

Imagine sex education books that would present gender and genitals as socially constructed; sexuality could then more easily be conceived by young readers as taking place on a continuum rather than as written in stone. Imagine books that present sex as not only the cause of procreation but also as recreational, as indeed it is for most people engaged in it most of the time. Imagine books that present sexual activities other than penile–vaginal intercourse as satisfying and good for body and soul (or even just for body!). Imagine sex educational books that would acknowledge and contest power dynamics based on gender and sexual categories—books that would urge children to interrogate, rather than reify, these categories. Imagine the sex lives that might develop out of such an antifoundational foundation. Would you buy these books for your children?

REFERENCES

Sex Books for Young Children

Andry, Andrew, Steven Schepp, and Blake Hampton (ill.). 1979 (1968). *How Babies Are Made.* Boston: Little, Brown.

Baker, Sue. 1990. *The Birds and the Bees.* Swindon, Bologna, New York: M. Twinn.

Brooks, Robert, and Susan Perl (ill.). 1983. *So That's How I Was Born!* New York: Aladdin.

Brown, Laura Krasny, and Marc Brown. 1997. *What's the Big Secret?: Talking about Sex with Girls and Boys.* Boston: Little, Brown.

Cole, Babette. 1993. *Mommy Laid an Egg OR Where Do Babies Come From?* New York: Chronicle Books.

Cole, Joanna, and Margaret Miller (photo.). 1993 (1984). *How You Were Born.* New York: Mulberry.

Davis, Jennifer, and Laura Cornell (ill.). 1997. *Before You Were Born: A Lift-the-Flap Book.* New York: Workman.

Gordon, Sol, Judith Gordon, and Vivien Cohen (ill.). 1992 (1974). *Did the Sun Shine before You Were Born?: A Sex Education Primer.* Amherst, NY: Prometheus Books.

Harris, Robie H. and Michael Emberley (ill.) 2006. *It's Not the Stork! A Book about Boys, Girls, Babies, Bodies, Families and Friends.* Cambridge, MA: Candlewick Press.

Harris, Robie H., and Michael Emberley (ill.). 1999. *It's So Amazing!: A Book about Eggs, Sperm, Birth, Babies, and Families.* Cambridge, MA: Candlewick Press.

Hickling, Meg, and Kim La Fave (ill.) 2002. *Boys, Girls and Body Science.* Maderia Park, British Columbia, Canada: Harbour Publishing Co. Ltd.

Kleven, Sandy, LCSW and Jody Bergsma (ill.). 1997. *The Right Touch: A Read Aloud Story to Help Prevent Child Abuse.* Bellevue, Washington: Illumination Arts.

Saltz, Dr. Gail, and Lynne Cravath (ill.). 2005. *Amazing You! Getting Smart about Your Private Parts.* New York: Penguin Group USA.

Smith, Alastair, and Maria Wheatley (ill.). 1997. *How Are Babies Made?* London: Usborne Publishing.

Sex Books for Older Children

Basso, Michael J. 1998. *The Underground Guide to Teenage Sexuality.* Minneapolis, Minnesota: Fairview Press.

Basso, Michael J. 2003. *The Underground Guide to Teenage Sexuality, 2nd Edition.* Minneapolis, Minnesota: Fairview Press.

Bell, Ruth. 1987. *Changing Bodies, Changing Lives.* New York: Random House.

Cole, Joanna, and Alan Tiegreen (ill.). 1988. *Asking about Sex and Growing Up: A Question-and-Answer Book for Boys and Girls.* New York: Beech Tree.

Foster, Lorri. 2005. *Let's Talk about S-E-X, 2nd Edition.* Minnetonka, MN: Book Peddlers.

Gordon, Sol, and Vivien Cohen (ill.). 1992 (1977). *Facts about Sex for Today's Youth.* Amherst, NY: Prometheus Books.

Harris, Robie H., and Michael Emberley (ill.) 2004. *It's Perfectly Normal: Changing Bodies, Growing Up, Sex and Sexual Health.* Cambridge, MA: Candlewick Press.

Westheimer, Ruth, and Diane deGroat (ill.). 1998 (1993). *Dr. Ruth Talks to Kids: Where You Came From, How Your Body Changes, and What Sex Is All About.* New York: Aladdin.

Sex Books for Parents

Berkenkamp, Lauri, and Steven C. Atkins. 2002. *Talking to Your Kids about Sex from Toddlers to Preteens: A Go Parents! Guide.* Chicago: Nomad Press.

Calderone, Mary S., and James W. Ramey. 1982. *Talking with Your Child about Sex: Questions and Answers for Children from Birth to Puberty.* New York: Random House.

Eyre, Linda, and Richard Eyre. 1998. *How to Talk to Your Child about Sex.* New York: Saint Martin's Griffin.

Levkoff, Logan. 2007. *Third Base Ain't What It Used to Be: What Your Kids Are Learning About Sex Today—and How to Teach Them to Become Sexually Healthy Adults.* New York: New American Library.

Maxwell, Sharon. 2008. *The Talk: What Your Kids Need to Hear from YOU about Sex.* New York: Avery.

Morris, Lois B. 1984. *Talking Sex with Your Kids.* New York: Simon and Shuster.

Ratner, Marilyn, and Susan Chamlin. 1985. *Straight Talk: Sexuality Education for Parents and Kids 4–7.* New York: Viking.

Richardson, Justin, and Mark A. Schuster. 2003. *Everything You Never Wanted Your Kids to Know about Sex (But Were Afraid They'd Ask).* New York: Three Rivers Press.

Roffman, Deborah M. 2002. *How'd I Get in There in the First Place?: Talking to Your Young Child about Sex.* New York: Perseus Publishing.

Schwartz, Pepper, and Dominic Cappello. 2000. *Ten Talks Parents Must Have With Their Children about Sex and Character.* New York: Hyperion.

Spock, Benjamin, and Michael B. Rothenberg. 1992 (1945). *Dr. Spock's Baby and Child Care.* New York: Pocket Books.

Other Sources

Conrad, Peter, and Joseph W. Schneider. 1992. *Deviance and Medicalization: From Badness to Sickness.* Philadelphia: Temple University Press.

Ehrenreich, Barbara, and Diedre English. 1986. *ReMaking Love: The Feminization of Sex.* Garden City, NY: Anchor Press/Doubleday.

Irvine, Janice. 2004. *Talk about Sex: The Battles over Sex Education in the United States.* Berkeley: University of California Press.

Luker, Kristin. 2007. *When Sex Goes to School: Warring Views on Sex and Sex Education Since the Sixties.* New York: WW Norton.

Moran, Jeffrey P. 2000. *Teaching Sex: The Shaping of Adolescence in the 20th Century.* Cambridge, MA: Harvard University Press.

Moore, Lisa Jean. 2007. *Sperm Counts: Overcome by Man's Most Precious Fluid.* New York: NYU Press.

Patton, Cindy. 1996. *Fatal Advice: How Safe-Sex Education Went Wrong.* Durham, NC: Duke University Press.

Raymond, Diane. 1994. "Homophobia, Identity, and the Meanings of Desire: Reflections on the Cultural Construction of Gay and Lesbian Adolescent Sexuality." In *Sexual Cultures and the Construction of Adolescent Identities,* edited by Janice M. Irvine. Philadelphia: Temple UP.

Simonds, Wendy. 1992. *Women and Self-Help Culture: Reading between the Lines.* New Brunswick, NJ: Rutgers University Press.

Solinger, Rickie. 2005. *Pregnancy and Power: A Short History of Reproductive Politics in America.* New York: NYU Press.

Watney, Simon. 1991. "School's Out." In *Inside/Out: Lesbian Theories, Gay Theories,* edited Diana Fuss (pp. 387–401). New York: Routledge.

What Do I Say to My Children?

Sol Gordon and Judith Gordon

Sex educators Sol Gordon and Judith Gordon stress the importance of being an askable parent in their book Raising a Child Responsibly in a Sexually Permissive World.[1] *Here are their responses to some of the most frequently asked questions:*

When Should I Tell?

The answer is simple: It is time to tell whenever the child asks. If you are an askable parent, your children may come to you with questions about sex from the time they are two or three years old. Young children's questions are sometimes nonverbal. For example, a child may constantly follow you into the bathroom. To encourage them, you could say, "It looks like you're wondering about something—can I guess what it is?"

Some shy children might ask no questions at all, even of the most askable parents. If your child hasn't raised sexuality-oriented questions by age five, you should start the conversation. Read a book with your child. Tell him or her about a neighbor or a relative who is going to have a baby. While it's fine on occasion to make analogies to animals, do not concentrate on them in your explanations. People and animals have very different habits.

How Explicit Should I Be?

Make it a point to use the correct terminology. Avoid such childish expressions as "pee-pee" or "wee-wee.". . . [P]arents can be explicit without overstating the case or feeling compelled to describe sexual relations to a child who hasn't yet grasped much more basic ideas. It is also wiser to say at the start that a baby has its beginning in the mother's uterus, not the stomach, because a child's imagination can easily picture the fetus being mixed up with the food.

Is There Such a Thing as Giving Too Much Sex Education Too Soon?

Parents worry a great deal about whether they can "harm" their children with "too much" information or by telling their children things that they won't understand. Let us state again that despite the protests of a few "experts," knowledge is not harmful. It does not matter if the child doesn't understand everything you say. What counts is that you are an askable parent. If the child can trust you not to be rigid or hostile in your response or to give misinformation, he or she will ask you questions and use you as a source of wisdom and guidance. . . .

What about Embarrassing Questions in Public?

Children have a great knack for asking the most delicate questions in the supermarket or when special guests have come to dinner. The best approach, no matter how embarrassed you are, is to tell the child that he or she has asked a very good question; if you still have your wits about you, proceed to answer it then and there. In most cases, your guests will silently applaud. If you feel you can't answer the question right away, it is very important to praise the child for asking and to state specifically when you will discuss it. In general, it is better to risk shocking a few grown-ups than to scold or put off your own child.

NOTES

1. Gordon, S., and Gordon, J. 2000. *Raising a Child Responsibly in a Sexually Permissive World,* Second Edition (pp. 43–46). Holbrook, MA: Adams Media.

Fear of Sex: Do the Media
Make Them Do It?

Karen Sternheimer

When I was twelve I did something I never had done before: I snuck into an R-rated movie. My friend and I told our parents we would be seeing a PG film playing at the same complex and bought tickets for that movie, so when they dropped us off and later picked us up they would have no idea. When the lights went down we walked into another theater to see *Young Doctors in Love,* which promised to feature a racier version of our favorite daytime soaps.

In spite of feeling that any minute an usher would appear and kick us out, it seemed remarkably easy to enter this forbidden zone. But aside from a few more four-letter words, the movie was no different than any television show I'd seen except it was longer. This of course did not stop us from embellishing what we saw when we returned to school on Monday. I was finally part of the group who had seen an R-rated movie, and for a day that felt good.

My story is not unique, of course. At one point most young people take a peek behind the iron curtain of adulthood. Knowledge about sex is often kept from children as long as possible, considered the final frontier separating adults from children. It is a hard-fought battle that is almost never won by adults, in part because sex permeates our media culture. Sex becomes associated with maturity and with status largely because adults define it that way and our popular culture appears to be obsessed with sex. It only makes sense

for young people to be curious, and media culture threatens to satisfy all sorts of sexual curiosities.

Sex is feared almost as much as violence, and the belief that sexuality in media culture will increase teen sexual activity is quite common. . . . Horror stories of teen promiscuity make the media rounds to demonstrate the popular hypothesis that kids now are morally depraved (note stories about equally promiscuous adults aren't considered newsworthy) and imply the media are at fault. Has media culture created a sex-crazed generation? While yes may be the simple answer, this [reading] critically assesses common beliefs about media, youth, and sex and demonstrates that the relationship between the three is more complex than we are often told. As we will see, changes in economics and demographic shifts during the past century have driven changes in sexual attitudes and behavior. But sexuality has always been part of coming of age, and parents have always felt anxious about this passage. The declining ability of adults to control children's sexual knowledge has created a high level of fear and that fear is often focused on popular culture. When we take a closer look at how young people make sense of sexuality in media, we see that they are not simply influenced by popular culture, but use sexual representations to create identity and status within their peer groups.

Teenage Sex: New Media, New Mores?

While attending a seminar about issues concerning contemporary youth, a man who appeared to be in his early to mid-fifties said with certainty, "People didn't have sex before marriage back when I was a kid. It just wasn't done." He was very sure of himself and it was clear he wanted to set the younger expert straight. "You weren't there," he told her. "Now things are totally different. Kids today just don't have the same morals."

I wasn't there either, but then again neither was he. The time he spoke of did not exist. The history he remembers is likely television and film history. On that count, he would be right. It just wasn't done—on TV.

Sexual behavior steadily changed throughout the twentieth century. During the "good old days" adults shared many of the same fears that today's parents have, that young people were engaging in behavior they never did at their age, and that kids today have too much freedom and not enough sexual restraint. Chances are, if history is any indicator, in about fifty years people will look back at today as an age of innocence too. When it comes to young people and sexuality, the past has always seemed more innocent because it is viewed through the lens of nostalgia.

Sexuality in media has always been a cause for concern. Film content in the 1920s reflected changes in sexual mores, featuring Rudolph Valentino's passionate kissing and sometimes even female nudity. Hollywood's early stars created scandals just like those in our own era; their wild parties, frequent failed marriages, and sex scandals made conservative groups weary. Movies were a new source of influence that religious leaders feared would bypass the family, school, and religion in importance in young people's lives. Politicians and the Catholic Legion of Decency called for government censorship. Instead, the new film industry guaranteed self-regulation by what came to be known as the Hays Office, led by prominent political figure Will Hays, to monitor movie content and ensure it met the standards of a new code, formally implemented in 1934.[1] As the country took a more conservative turn at the end of the 1920s, the Hays Office restricted film content to what was deemed "wholesome entertainment." This included censoring any content that appeared to criticize "natural or human" laws so as not to incite "the lower and baser element" of American society.[2] Rules governing film production were overtly racist—no interracial relationships were allowed—and any criticism of the status quo was interpreted as a violation of the "moral obligation" of the entertainment establishment. An extremely reactionary ideology of filmmaking was justified in the name of preserving children's "innocence."

The Hays Code dominated film production until 1966. In an attempt to compete with the rise of television, films started presenting sexuality more frankly beginning in the 1960s, particularly as European "New Wave" films by directors like Federico Fellini and Jean Luc Godard helped redefine movies as art. Twenty years later, cable television and videos brought more sexually explicit programming into the home. Sex has become another product of contemporary society, circulating more rapidly and difficult to control and regulate because highly sexualized images attract attention and profit. Adults now have less control over what young people know about sex, which blurs the perceived distinction between adults and children.

Popular culture *is* different today than in the past and provides an easy (but ultimately misguided) answer to explain social changes. We didn't arrive here on the coattails of television or movies; popular culture incorporates and reflects societal issues and values, many of which some people find objectionable. Instead of targeting attention solely on popular culture, we need to first understand the social context of sex in twentieth and twenty-first century America.

New Century, New Meanings

During a discussion in my juvenile delinquency course a student once volunteered that he was sure teen sex is much more prevalent now than ever before. "We don't hear about teenage pregnancy being a problem during colonial times or anything," he noted.

There is some truth to this statement, particularly because "teenagers" as we now think of them did not exist until about one hundred years ago. Colonial "teens" were likely to be regarded as adults with full familial and economic responsibilities. . . . [C]ross-cultural and historical studies have not found adolescence as we know it to have existed in all societies, suggesting the teenager is more of a social than biological creation.[3] Thus, it is hard to compare the teenagers of today with those of the past. This new phase of life emerged as the outcome of industrialization and the diminished necessity for people in their teens to join the labor force. Previously, the group we now know of as teenagers often functioned as adults:

they worked instead of attending school and may have been married with children. The time before adulthood steadily lengthened throughout the twentieth century, as did the gap between sexual maturity and marriage. Socially and sexually we expect teenagers today to function partially as adults and partially as children. The roles and expectations of adolescents today are far different from their counterparts a hundred years ago.

New Sexual Freedom

It is nearly impossible to understand changes in dating rituals without considering the economic context. Courtship began to change with the rise of industrialization and was marked by the gradual decrease of adult control. In rural life work was concentrated in the home, so supervision of courtship was much simpler: a suitor might call on a potential mate at her home with parents or chaperones very close by. Industrialization led to the growth of cities and took adults away from the home for longer periods of time. The possibility for supervision decreased, as did the amount of space a family might have had in which courtship could take place. Dating thus moved from the parlor to the public sphere, and progressively became more of an independent pursuit with less family intervention. Highly populated cities offered more anonymity and the expansion of suburbs following World War II created even more space for young people to congregate away from adults. The new affluence of the postwar era brought more leisure time for teens, and teenagers could do what they wanted with less fear of getting caught or punished. Economic changes led to higher rates of high school and college attendance, which increased separation between adults and young people. . . .

The 1950s economic boom created the possibility for many people to experience youth as a time of leisure, while a generation before teens were much more likely to be in the labor force. Young people were likely to have fewer responsibilities than their parents had before them, and childhood and adolescence were increasingly seen as time for fun.[4] Dating became associated with recreation rather than procreation, as the search for a spouse became a more distant concern. . . .

[T]echnological changes created more freedom for young people. The widespread availability of electricity at the beginning of the twentieth century enabled nightlife to emerge away from the family home, and the automobile became an important part of American dating. Courtship grew even more difficult to monitor, as having a car provided more privacy, opportunities for sexual experimentation, and the ability to travel even farther from parental supervision. Drive-in restaurants and movies as well as lovers' lanes are examples of semi-private settings where teens went to be away from parental supervision.

Contrary to nostalgia, premarital sex did occur before the so-called sexual revolution of the 1960s; it was the *reaction* to premarital sex that changed. In mid-century, for instance, if sex resulted in pregnancy, it was more likely to remain secret through a quick marriage, a forced adoption, or, for the affluent perhaps, an abortion disguised as another medical procedure.[5] The main difference now is that we are more likely to acknowledge both premarital sex and teen pregnancy compared with in the past, and it is certainly talked about in public forums and in the news media. Teenage girls today are less likely to be pressured into early marriage and more likely to have access to birth control.

Premarital sex and pregnancy have always been part of the contemporary social landscape. . . . Yet we still often hope that people who are sexually mature don't engage in sexual behavior before socially defined adulthood, if not marriage. A full 72 percent of adults responding to the 1998 General Social Survey agreed that teen sex before marriage is "always wrong," yet a large proportion of people engage in sex before their teen years end.[6] In all likelihood many in the survey had premarital sex themselves, but help build a generation gap by insisting teens do as we say, not as we did.

Asexual Children?

Movies, daytime soap operas, talk shows, and the Internet are often filled with sexualized imagery. If only children were not exposed to so much so soon, popular thinking goes, they would maintain their "innocence" instead of becoming sexually active. . . .

Adults often attempt to deny the importance of sexuality within childhood, because to do otherwise is kind of scary. After all, America was largely founded by Puritans. Sexual innocence serves as a major marker in the way our society presently defines children and distinguishes them from adults. Interestingly, the term "adult" tends to connote sexuality rather than responsibility. "Adult" books and "adult" films indicate sexual content, not emotional maturity. We like to believe that knowledge of sex represents the last remaining dividing line between childhood and adulthood.

But does it really?

Sexual exploration is and has been a big part of childhood, but perceptions of how parents should deal with sexually curious children have shifted during the past century.[7] Before World War II, American child-rearing practices reflected the belief that controlling children's behavior could prevent any "inappropriate" sexual exploration. In the postwar era the influence of Sigmund Freud and Benjamin Spock altered perceptions about sexuality and childhood. Both Freud and Spock considered children inherently sexual, so sexual curiosity was natural, even necessary for healthy development. Unlike the prewar notion that control created a well-adjusted child, postwar advice urged parents to avoid shaming their children lest a fixation develop. Parents were encouraged to provide information about sex, a major shift from prewar practices.

Starting in the early 1970s a backlash against the new openness began.[8] The 1960s tends to get the credit for being a time of sexual freedom, but actually the 1970s was the time when much experimentation happened. This new sexual openness led to fears that a more accepting approach to childhood sexuality had gone too far, that the lack of discouragement in early childhood led to less restraint against premarital sex. But think back to your own "facts of life" talk, if your parents had one with you. If it was anything like mine, it was tense and embarrassing for all parties involved—certainly not a pep talk. Concerns about parents' being "too open" blamed behavioral changes on the availability of information and did not take into account the demographic, economic, and political changes of the twentieth century. Our contemporary

ambivalence about sexuality was born, as were complaints that the media make them do it. Today American adults want young people to be both psychologically healthy and sexually restrained, which is why we are at best ambivalent about providing children with information about sex; sex education now is often just abstinence education.

Sexuality, as much as adults may like to convince themselves otherwise, is not only a part of adulthood and adolescence but also a part of early childhood. We often dismiss things like childhood crushes as innocent puppy love, but the reality is that the development of sexual identity is an important component of childhood. Instead of young people simply learning about sex in the media and then acting on what they watch, preteens and teens try to make sense of what they see in the context of their other experiences. Seeing all these images of sex does not necessarily mean that children interpret them by having sexual intercourse, but instead that coming to terms with sexuality in popular culture and their lives is a major part of adolescence and preadolescence as well.

A Tale of Two Studies

A 2001 Kaiser Family Foundation study of sex on television is a great example of the traditional American approach to understanding sex, youth, and media.[9] The study received a great deal of media attention because it follows the conventional wisdom that there is even more sex on TV than ever, presumed to be a potential danger to youth. This study's assumptions are in direct contrast to a 1999 British study that received no American media attention. The British study critically examines how children make sense of representations of sexuality and romance on television.[10] Comparison of these two studies reveals our tendency to underestimate youth and overstate the power of popular culture.

Assumptions of the Kaiser Study

While the authors of this study insist that television is not the most important factor in sexual socialization, television is the main focus of their study. Researchers analyzed over a thousand television programs, counting incidents they deemed sexual in nature,[11]. . . yet they interviewed no young people to ascertain how they actually interpret these messages. This method isolates meaning from the context of both the program and the audience, a problem the researchers don't seem to be worried about. Additionally, this study broadly defines sexual messages to include flirting, alluding to sex, touching, kissing, and implication of intercourse. When the incidents get boiled down into statistics, hugs and handholding appear the same as more explicit representations of sex. . . .

The researchers seem to presume that young viewers will be heavily influenced by television, completely negating young peoples' ability to interpret media images on their own.[12] The authors presume that media are an important source of information about sex for teens, but media sources are not where young people get most of their knowledge. Within the report, authors noted that only 23 percent of teens say they learn "a lot" about pregnancy and birth control from television, while 40 percent have "gotten ideas on how to talk to their boyfriend or girlfriend about sexual issues" from media.[13] We focus on media when other sources are clearly more important because media is the feared spoiler of innocence—it is always there for us to credit with social influence and enables us to overlook the complexity of the history of sexuality and social change. . . .

[T]he authors note almost as an aside that many teens feel they do not get enough information about sex from parents or teachers. Rather than focusing on this point, we belabor the media issue. We fear that popular culture is filling the void that nervous adults have created and beg Hollywood to teach kids about sex more responsibly. Here's an idea: how about we initiate a dialogue about sex ourselves, where young people are not just preached to but heard. We ought to stop whining about what young people shouldn't know and start dealing with what they *do* know. . . .

The authors cite the risky sexual behaviors some adolescents engage in to support the need for their research, but they fail to provide real context.[14] In emphasizing negative behaviors, important statistics get buried. Prime example: the majority of teens under fifteen (80 percent of girls and 70 percent of boys) reported *not* being sexually active.[15] Most of those

sexually active reported using condoms, yet the authors of the Kaiser Family Foundation report chose to invert these statistics to tell the negative story. Dangerous behavior is of course important to examine, but perhaps the biggest problem here is that we focus on adolescent risk and fail to put it in the context *of adult* behavior. For instance, the 1998 General Social Survey found that just 20 percent of adults used condoms during their last sexual encounters. By ignoring adults within the media-sex panic we pathologize teen behavior even if it is consistent (or even better than) that of adults.[16]

In sum, this study found that sexual content (as the researchers define it) on television rose from a similar study two years before, but so what? We are left with no information about how young people actually interpret and make sense of these programs. It is important that we find out how young people interpret sexual images in advertising, music, and television in their context, and in their own words. If we are so concerned about teen sexuality we need to talk with them, not just about them, to learn more. The British study did just that.

Talking "Dirty"

Initiating conversations about sex with children is not just frowned upon, in some situations it is considered morally questionable or even illegal. Likewise, providing sex education in schools is frequently the subject of fierce debate. Maybe that's why studies like the one conducted by the Kaiser Family Foundation only focus on television. Talking about sex is considered indecent where children are concerned, enabling us to maintain the illusion that they can be separated from the rest of the world.

No doubt, this is why the British authors chose a provocative title for their study. . . . "Talking Dirty: Children, Sexual Knowledge and Television" was published in the journal *Childhood* in spring 1999 with no American fanfare. Not surprising, considering that the authors challenge our assumptions about childhood and sexuality at every turn. First, the authors critique the belief that television is responsible for the loss of childhood "innocence" and argue it is best to find out what children *do* know rather than continue to focus on what adults *want* them to know.

To that end, the researchers were more concerned with how the children they studied made sense of the programs they watched, and how they understood the content in the context of their own lives. Unlike the Kaiser Family Foundation study, . . . these researchers were interested in how children negotiated their social roles as children dealing with a subject that is regarded off-limits for them. The research team sought to find out what the children knew and how they made sense of it on their own terms, avoiding value judgments in the process.

Secondly, in contrast with traditional views that we need only pay attention to teenagers when it comes to sex, these researchers talked with six-, seven-, ten-, and eleven-year-olds in small groups, asking them to talk about what programs they liked and disliked. Children were then asked to sort a list of program titles into categories, which enabled researchers to see how the children defined adult content compared with programs that the kids considered appropriate for children, teens, or general audiences. Sex itself was not brought up by researchers but by the children, often used by the kids to define adult programs.

Researchers found that although most children felt that programs with romantic themes were "adult" shows (like *Ricki Lake* and *Blind Date*), the ten- and eleven year-olds were quite familiar with these programs and others like them. Kids reported that adult shows were appealing because they knew that they were supposed to be off-limits. . . . [T]he authors of the *Childhood* study note that claiming interest or knowledge of an "adult" program elevates one's status amongst peers. It was not uncommon for some kids to claim knowledge of a show when they clearly hadn't seen it. Other research has found similar results when studying children's interest in horror films; the more restrictive rating the film earned, the greater mark of status kids attained by watching.[17]

Gender was also central in identifying children's interest in the television programs discussed. The younger boys in particular were likely to deny any interest in shows with kissing or romantic themes. That was "girl stuff," which they wanted no part of. The authors also observed that children feigned shock or disgust about romantic scenes, a response common amongst preadolescents in adult company.

Rather than advance the narrow view that sexual content does something *to* children, this research informs us that it is used *by* children to build peer connections and to make sense of sexuality from a safe distance. Children use adult themes from television to try to demonstrate adult-level competence and knowledge. The researchers concluded that neither television nor audiences "hold anything approaching absolute power. Television obviously makes available particular representations and identities. . . . In defining and debating the meanings of television, readers also claim and construct identities of their own."[18]

In my own research with high school students, I found that sexuality in media is used differently depending on the context: in groups comprised of mostly males, sexuality was collectively defined as the celebration of women as objects, while mainly female groups tended to challenge the objectification of women's sexuality.[19] . . . Interestingly, boys in predominantly female groups tended to agree with their female classmates that [an] ad's use of a scantily clad woman was offensive. The teens I studied clearly demonstrate how the meaning of popular culture is created collectively in the context of peer culture, a negotiation process that goes way beyond simple cause-and-effect.

As the above example demonstrates, sometimes the way people talk about sexuality is a way to bolster their status among their friends. Rather than only criticize the quantity of sexual images in the media, providing more opportunities for young people to critically discuss these images is a way to better understand underlying beliefs about sex and gender. Young people use media imagery in their struggle to fit in with each other while developing individual identities. They also try to fit into the larger society, where issues of sex, gender, and power are deep seeded.

Sexuality and Children's Culture

Several recent American studies demonstrate the importance of sexuality within elementary and middle school children's peer groups. Traditionally, studies of children have focused only on social and cognitive development, or on how close kids are to being like adults. However, recent sociological thinking has sought to understand children as creators of their own experiences who need to be understood in their own contexts without only considering them adults in the making.[20] Rather than devise surveys to get answers to the questions adults think are important, these researchers immersed themselves into the daily experiences of children's lives. . . .

These studies detail that young people may borrow issues from adult culture and from the media, but children's culture does not completely emerge from either.[21] Instead, an interactive negotiation process takes place as children seek acceptance and status from their peers. While popular culture is an important part of this undertaking, it is not the all-powerful force many adults fear.

Adults tend to view children as imitators, sponges who soak up the language, behavior, and attitudes of the world around them. But sociologists Patricia and Peter Adler studied children's peer groups for eight years and concluded that we need to recognize the power of preadolescent peer culture. According to their research, children negotiate individual identities while striving to maintain status amongst peers, and sexual themes are interwoven into this process. Adults somehow fail to acknowledge (or remember) that curiosity about sexuality is a big part of growing up.

In her study of elementary school students, sociologist Barrie Thorne discusses how games like "kiss and chase" demonstrate that children are actively involved in the construction of their own sexuality.[22] We might deem this sort of behavior "innocent child's play," but that would ignore how children themselves define their experiences. I can remember the excitement of chasing a boy I liked; of course I had no clue what I'd do if I caught him. Thorne details how children's play incorporates heterosexual meanings into everyday occurrences and shapes male-female interactions. Accusing someone of "liking" a student of the other sex is used to police boundaries between genders. . . . Also, popular rhymes ("Susie and Bobby sitting in a tree, K-I-S-S-I-N-G") amongst girls highlight the importance of romantic connections within children's games.

Children use popular culture to negotiate meanings from the world around them within their peer groups. . . . In a study of middle school students, researchers found that sexually explicit scenes from movies are often repeated in peer groups in order for the storyteller to solidify his or her rank in the group.[23] . . .

[Y]oung people are not simply influenced by popular culture, they negotiate meaning within the context of their friends and within the larger structure of social power. There *is* a problem when boys must adopt very narrow versions of masculinity to fit in. But if we were to somehow totally succeed in keeping children away from these sorts of films, or even do away with all such representations of sexuality in popular culture, we will have done nothing to address the real issue. The media did not initiate women's objectification, but we see it most clearly there. Popular culture is where we see reflections of power and inequality. It is naïve to think that the next generation only reproduces this shallow form of sexuality because they see it in movies or on TV. They are part of a society where gender inequality is replicated in many social institutions, including education, religion, government, and economics. Our popular culture shows us some of the ugly realities of our society and we focus on media as if that's where these realities originate. . . .

The Danger of Innocence

The myth of childhood innocence is not simply a benign fantasy, it can be a dangerous one. First of all, it does not match the reality of children's experiences. Secondly, sexually curious or sexually knowledgeable kids are . . . considered damaged, spoiled, and robbed of [their] rightful "childhood" when in fact their knowledge may stem from sexual abuse.[24]

Clinging to the notion of childhood innocence serves to further entice those who exploit children. . . . Abusers are often titillated by innocence, which our cultural construction of childhood unconsciously supports. . . . [W]e must . . . reevaluate how our culture unwittingly contributes to this eroticized definition of childhood innocence.[25] Even though most of us are not pedophiles and do not directly harm children, the insistence on children's inherent innocence can create danger for children. . . .

Adding to the confusion is the manner in which innocence is eroticized, particularly within girls and women. . . . Virginity has served as a sexual commodity for centuries, increasing female value on the marriage market in the past and fueling male fantasies in the present. . . . Innocence serves as a sexual marker denoting increased desirability, reflecting the traditional gender order where women's passivity and lack of experience are prized and reproduce patriarchal power. Beauty pageants are a good example of the contradictions between innocence and sexuality projected onto the female child's body. While young girls in pageants are made to look like women, women are encouraged to look like girls.[26] The teenage female body is fetishized as the ideal against which adult women are measured.

Our culture creates and reinforces inconsistencies, asking us to see children as pure and untainted by the adult world when in fact sexuality is part of the human experience. This of course does not mean people of all ages ought to engage in sexual intercourse, but instead that we must recognize that self-awareness, curiosity, and some knowledge of sex are a part of childhood. When we acknowledge that media alone do not create curiosity and knowledge about sex, we begin to recognize the complexity of children's experiences. Our anxiety is rooted in the fear that adults cannot control children's knowledge or identities. One of the ways our culture defines childhood is the absence of knowledge of sex, yet its presence in popular culture serves as a reminder that our ideal childhood is merely an illusion. While adult guidance is useful to help young people navigate this terrain, we must also recognize that sexuality is partially rooted in peer culture, which by definition excludes adults.

More Promiscuous Than Ever?

Just as sexuality seems like a new invention for each generation of teens, the fear of teen sexuality is renewed in each adult generation. . . . Teenage sex is frequently associated with irresponsibility, disease, promiscuity, and unwanted pregnancy. We claim that teens have trouble controlling themselves due to "raging hormones," implying that adolescents are ruled by sexual impulses. Ironically, we blame powerful forces

of nature for shaping teen behavior, yet at the same time we condemn young people for this allegedly biological and natural behavior. Meanwhile, we ignore the majority of teens who are responsible or do not engage in sex, and we don't stereotype promiscuous adults as hormone-crazed animals. When it comes to young people and sex, we tend to hear only the negative side of the story. We hear about the kid who makes a sex video and shows all of his friends. The teens frequently on tabloid-style talk shows speak freely of their ample sexual experience. . . . Chastity just isn't dramatic.

Consequently, a false impression exists, created in part by media culture, that young people are sexually out of control at earlier and earlier ages. Even teens themselves think their peers are having sex more than they really are. A survey conducted by the National Campaign to Prevent Teen Pregnancy found that more than half of teens overestimated the percentage of their classmates who are sexually active.[27] Sociologist Mike Males dispels such faulty perceptions in *The Scapegoat Generation: America's War on Adolescents*. Based on his analysis of public health statistics, Males found:

Between 1970 and 1992 there was just a 7 percent rise in the number of junior high school aged boys claiming to have had sex and a 6 percent rise amongst girls;[28]

Adult men (aged nineteen to twenty-four) are far more likely than teen boys to father children born to teenaged girls;[29]

Adult men, not teenaged boys, are most responsible for spreading HIV and other sexually transmitted diseases to girls;[30]

For 40 percent of girls under fifteen who report being sexually active, their *only* sexual experience was rape.[31]

In addition, Males points out that we must consider any claims of sexual activity with skepticism. In spite of the belief that teens now are far more sexually active than adolescents of previous generations were, any data must be analyzed through the context of the sexual mores of the time. Simply put, people are more likely to *under-report* behavior that is considered deviant and more likely to *over-report* behavior that they perceive as elevating their status amongst peers. The fact that claiming sexual experience is treated differently now than fifty years ago makes accurate comparisons difficult. While boasting may be a factor, we must also consider that surveys rarely distinguish between forced and consenting sex. The small proportions of young teens who report having had sexual experiences quite possibly have been victims of sexual abuse.

The second and third points made above highlight the inadequacy of the term "teenage sex." We overlook the role adults, particularly adult males, play in teen pregnancy and the spread of sexually transmitted diseases. Adult men are responsible for seven out of ten births to girls eighteen and younger.[32] Also, because the HIV infection rate for teen girls is so much higher than for teen boys (a whopping disparity of 8 to 1), it is unlikely that teen boys are responsible for a large proportion of new cases.[33] . . .

Nonetheless, politicians and public health officials try to steer this conversation away from adults and onto teens. In Males' analysis, he found that the teen birth rate can be predicted not by changes in media or pushes for abstinence, but by adult birth rates and poverty rates.[34] It is far easier to blame media than to study the effects of poverty. Studying poverty is dangerous: we uncover structural problems that can't be blamed on individuals; we find reasons to question the viability of our current economic policies. It is much easier to simply charge poor people with personal failure without examining why the link between teen motherhood and poverty is so strong.[35] We let policymakers off the hook and give the media bashers something to complain about.

We are all too eager to point out the bad behavior of a few teenagers and hold them up as symbolic of an entire generation. Imagine if we saw a story on the news about a child molester followed by a commentary on how the middle-aged generation is completely without moral grounding. Of course this would never happen—we would say the molester was a sick individual, different from the rest of us. Yet we never afford young people this same explanation. Teens are accused of participating in risky sexual behavior, allegedly coaxed by sex in media. Adults tend to ignore the fact that a large proportion of young people report

very little or no sexual experience, but instead focus on those that do.[36] We also hear very little about the fact that the teen birth rate has been steadily *falling* since 1990 and that the teen abortion rate fell 39 percent between 1994 and 2000.[37]

Finally, and perhaps most significantly, we overlook the role of sexual abuse in the discussion about teens and sex. For many young people, sex is not a choice they have made but it was forced upon them. Adolescents who have been sexually abused as children are also far more likely to engage in riskier sexual practices in the future.[38] Rather than focus so heavily on popular culture leading to sexual activity, we see that *adult* behavior must be taken to task. We need to pay more attention to adults who impregnate, infect, and sexually abuse children and adolescents. They are the problem here, not the media.

Why Lie?

So how is it that in a society that claims to put young people first, we ignore the good news and highlight the risky behavior of a few? The answer is by no means simple, but one that has become a recurring theme in the way our society has treated disempowered groups. Immigrants, racial ethnic minorities, women, and the poor at varying times in history have been perceived as sexually out of control and in need of tighter social restraint. . . . In the next section we will see the parallels between the treatment of young people now with historical perceptions of immigrants, racial ethnic minorities, women, and the poor.

Fear, Sex, and Social Control

It is difficult to think of sexuality as anything but personal and individual, but the way we understand sex is socially constructed. Sexuality is a central site where struggles over social power take place.[39] The regulation and control of sexuality have served as ways to maintain dominance over disempowered groups. One such power struggle in the United States has emerged following demographic shifts of the past hundred years. Historically, fears that the population is becoming less Protestant and less white have led to attempts to control the reproduction of immigrant and nonwhite groups. This has been accomplished by policies promoting sterilization, removing girls from their families if juvenile courts believed they were likely to engage in sex, and, more recently, demonizing mothers of color.[40] Due to this fear, during the early part of the century white women's pregnancies were encouraged, and their access to birth control and abortion was restricted. So while sexuality is personal, the uses and meanings attached to the practice are decidedly social and linked with broader systems of power.

No Sex As a Weapon

The sexuality of groups perceived to be a threat is labeled dangerous and serves to legitimate public policies that restrict members' behavior. Many African-American men were lynched by whites allegedly protecting white women's virtue; black male sexuality came to be defined as a threat to the racial order. Miscegenation laws were enacted for much the same reason. They were created to prevent a union of a non-white man and a white woman, but were certainly not enforced when slave owners fathered the children of black slave women. This double standard reveals how the dominant group maintains power by controlling the sexuality of the "other." . . .

Measures like California's Proposition 187, which sought to restrict undocumented immigrant children from obtaining an education or medical care, represent the same kind of logic, that our society just cannot afford any more of "those" children. Contrast the "welfare queen" diatribe to the personal and corporate outpourings to multiple-birth families that have five, six, even seven children at once, which they cannot afford. These families appear on news magazine programs and talk shows to speak of their multiple blessings, while policymakers and pundits rail against the huge cost of other people's children. Concerns about promiscuity, pregnancy, and disease have served as a way for dominant groups to assert control over those whom they feel threatened by, whether the threat is real or imagined.

Gender (Dis)order

In addition to changes in demographics we have been experiencing shifts in the gender order that are closely linked with sexuality. Historically, abstinence has been a female burden, with girls and women supposedly responsible for regulating male sexuality. The social control of women has been secured in recent history by policing female sexuality. . . . Women who enjoyed sex were viewed as deviant and considered threats. Even when women's desire ceased to be considered a medical problem, sexual gratification was defined as a socially undesirable quality, one that might reduce a woman's chances for marriage. This was of course a serious threat in a time when women's wages rarely enabled them to live independently. Women were socially and economically constrained by the need for male financial support, as well as by the fear of unplanned pregnancy.

The threat of rape has historically been used to keep women from public spaces, supported by the practice of humiliating rape victims in court and not acknowledging marital rape. Women's sexuality has been a double-edged sword: a woman's worth has been tied to her appeal to men, yet rape has historically been blamed on women for being too appealing. The threat of sexual violence, even if not carried out, serves to limit women's movement and freedom.

In recent decades the widespread availability of birth control and shrinkage in the wage gap between men and women have created more personal freedom for women. But the old sexual double standards, that male sexuality is natural and female sexuality is a threat, are still alive in our fears about teens and sex. Concerns about teens' sexual activity reflect shifts in the gender order: attempts to control teen sexuality tend to focus on girls, on pregnancy, on girls' self-esteem and body image, but usually leave male sexuality out of the conversation. . . . So why is *female* sexuality so frightening?

Teenage girls are considered a threat when they seek to become more than just sexual objects—when they act as sexual *agents* we worry. . . . American society still expects girls to hold the keys to chastity, but at the same time they are held up as the ideal form of female desire. Open any fashion magazine and chances are good a teenage girl will be pouting back at you. We see this representation of teenage girls in many forms of popular culture, but it certainly does not originate there; its history lies in our tendency to value women who are young and sexually available for men. Rather than only blaming media culture for this representation of teenage girls, we need to take a closer look at the nature of power, sex, and gender in contemporary American society. Underneath fears of teens having sex are concerns about the changing meaning of gender.

The Genie Is Out of the Bottle

Societal shifts spurred by economic changes have altered American life, which has made it more difficult to monitor teens. Knowledge of or engagement in sex reveals that the illusion of innocence cannot be sustained, no matter how hard adults may try. Censoring media will not work, nor will less than complete and honest sex education.[41] This includes dealing with the reality of how sexual content is used and understood by young media audiences. No matter how much we may want to turn back the clock we can't. Teen sexuality *is* a threat: it destroys the unsustainable myth that adults can fully control young people's knowledge or their actions. The media are an easy target, but not the root cause of the changes in the attitudes and practice of sexuality in the twenty-first century.

As we have seen, changes throughout the twentieth century have provided young people with the means to become more independent from their parents, rendering their behavior far harder to control. Generally adults look at this as a sad reality, one that will inevitably lead to the breakdown of social order and the decline of American society.

Adults need to recognize that teenagers cannot be fully controlled, nor should this be our goal. . . . [I]nstead we must acknowledge that teenage sexuality is not new nor is it necessarily the threat that adults believe it to be. Education that helps young people deal with the realities of sexuality is needed, beyond doom-and-gloom scare tactics. Most centrally, adults need to let go of the illusion that childhood innocence can be maintained through ignorance. We have to begin by understanding how young people make sense of sex, both in media and in their lives.

Rethinking Media, Youth, and Sexuality

Sex on TV, in movies, and on the Internet scares lots of adults. Representations of sex in media expose the reality that childhood does not and cannot exist in a separate sphere from adulthood. Ironically, we use sex as the ultimate dividing line between childhood and adulthood, the line in the sand that adults try so hard to maintain and young people try so hard to cross. We define sex as a ticket to adulthood, so we should not be surprised when teens do, too. . . . Sex in popular culture reminds us that we cannot sustain the lengthened version of childhood we have idealized since the mid-twentieth century. The realities of sex dispel myths about childhood and media remind us such myths cannot be upheld.

We often associate changes in sexual behavior with changes in media. Historical shifts are difficult to see and understand, while media are by nature visible and always trying to grab our attention. And yes, frank exploration of sexuality is more prominent in popular culture now than it was at mid-century. But sexuality within popular culture has changed in conjunction with other social changes. Media are not the sole cause, but a messenger, jumping into the social conversation about sex, not starting it. To paraphrase Syracuse University's Robert Thompson's explanation, media do not push the envelope; they merely open the envelope that has been sitting under our noses.[42]

That being said, we should not ignore representations of sexuality in media. They provide useful clues about power and privilege and can launch greater exploration of contested meanings of both sexuality and gender. Rather than seek to censor, we should study media representations to analyze the taken-for-granted nature of relationships and sexuality in our culture. But instead of using these representations for cultural criticism, we often condemn the images and fail to critically challenge what they represent. If we really are concerned about the meanings young people make from such images, we ought to encourage people to critically address them, not simply call for self-censorship.

The truth is there aren't *enough* representations of sex in popular culture: not enough exploration of the depth of emotion that comes with sexual intimacy and not enough representations of regular-looking bodies.[43] Depictions of sex in media offer a prime opportunity to open up important discussions about gender and power within society as well. Of course, if we could have conversations like this there wouldn't be so much fear about sex in media in the first place. Instead of fearing the "negative effects" of sex in media and demanding that it go away, we need to keep learning about how young people make sense of sex in both media and in their lives.

We can choose to cling to old fears and old ways of thinking and try and make ourselves believe in the whimsical myth of innocence. Of course, that will leave us complaining from here to eternity, because the fear is based on faulty beliefs about both media and children. On the other hand we can get real and try to better understand how young people make sense of what they do know, rather than bemoaning *that* they know. The choice is ours: we can either try in vain to put the genie back into the bottle or open our eyes and create a deeper level of understanding of both media and youth.

NOTES

1. Lyn Gorman and David McLean, *Media and Society in the Twentieth Century: A Historical Introduction* (New York: Blackwell, 2003), pp. 36–40.

2. The Motion Picture Production Code, 1930.

3. James E. Cote and Anton L. Allahar, *Generation on Hold: Coming of Age in the Late Twentieth Century* (New York: New York University Press, 1994), Chapter 1.

4. For further discussion see Martha Wolfenstein, "Fun Morality: An Analysis of Recent American Child-Training Literature," in *The Children's Culture Reader,* ed. Henry Jenkins (New York: New York University Press, 1998), p. 199.

5. Rickie Solinger, "Race and 'Value': Black and White Illegitimate Babies, 1945–1965," in *Feminist Frontiers,* fourth edition, eds. Laurel Richardson, Verta Taylor, and Nancy Whittier (New York: McGraw-Hill, 1997), p. 282.

6. National Opinion Research Council, General Social Survey (NORC: University of Chicago, 1998). www.icpsr.umich.edu-GSS-index.html.url.

7. Henry Jenkins, "The Sensuous Child: Benjamin Spock and the Sexual Revolution," in *The Children's Culture Reader,* ed. Henry Jenkins (New York: New York University Press, 1998), p. 209.

8. Jenkins, ibid., p. 225.

9. Kaiser Family Foundation, "Sex on TV," full report online: www.kff.org/contentl2001/3087SexOnTv.pdf.

10. Peter Kelley, David Buckingham, and Hannah Davies, "Talking Dirty: Children, Sexual Knowledge and Television," *Childhood* 6, no. 22 (1999): 221–242.

11. This study replicated a previous study of sex on television by analyzing 1,114 programs from the 1999–2000 season. Authors sought to address whether the frequency of what they defined as sexual messages were increasing, how sexual messages are presented, and whether the risks and responsibilities of sex are portrayed.

12. For discussion about how audiences create varying meanings from texts and are not simply manipulated by messages, see: David Morley, *Television, Audiences and Cultural Studies* (New York: Routledge, 1992); John Fiske, *Understanding Popular Culture* (London: Routledge, 1989); and Ien Ang, *Living Room Wars: Rethinking Audiences for a Postmodern World* (London, Routledge, 1996).

13. Kaiser Family Foundation, ibid., p. 1.

14. Kaiser Family Foundation, ibid., p. 1.

15. Alan Gutmmacher Institute, *Facts in Brief Teen Sex and Pregnancy,* 1999 (online: [www.agi-usa.org]).

16. Mike Males, *Framing Youth: Ten Myths About the Next Generation* (Monroe, Maine: Common Courage Press, 1999), Chapter 6.

17. Julian Wood, "Repeatable Pleasures: Notes on Young People's Use of Video," in *Reading Audiences: Young People and the Media,* ed. David Buckingham (Manchester: Manchester University Press, 1993), p. 184.

18. Kelley et al., 238.

19. Karen Sternheimer, "A Media Literate Generation? Adolescents as Active, Critical Viewers: A Cultural Studies Approach" (Ph.D. dissertation, University of Southern California, 1998).

20. For elaboration on this concept, see: William Corsaro, *The Sociology of Childhood* (Thousand Oaks, Calif.: Pine Forge Press, 1997), Chapter 1. Alan Prout and Allison James, "A New Paradigm for the Sociology of Childhood? Provenance, Promise, and Problems," in *Constructing and Reconstructing Childhood,* eds. Allison James and Alan Prout (London: Falmer Press, 1997), pp. 7–33. Patricia A. Adler and Peter Adler, *Peer Power: Preadolescent Culture and Identity* (New Brunswick, N.J.: Rutgers University Press, 1998), introduction.

21. Corsaro discusses the concept of "interpretive reproduction" in Chapter 2 of the work listed above. He argues that children do not merely reproduce adult culture but reinterpret it to fit their own experiences.

22. Barrie Thorne, *Gender Play* (New Brunswick, N.J.: Rutgers University Press, 1993).

23. Donna Eder, Catherine Colleen Evans, and Stephen Parker, *SchoolTalk: Gender and Adolescent Culture*

(New Brunswick, N.J.: Rutgers University Press, 1995), pp. 83–102.

24. Jenny Kitzinger, "Who *Are* You Kidding? Children, Power, and the Struggle Against Sexual Abuse," in *Constructing and Reconstructing Childhood,* eds. Allison James and Alan Prout (London: Falmer Press, 1997), pp. 165–189.

25. For further discussion see James R. Kincaid's provocative book, *Child-Loving* (New York: Routledge, 1992).

26. Giroux discusses beauty pageants in "Stealing Innocence: The Politics of Child Beauty Pageants," in *The Children's Culture Reader,* ed. Henry Jenkins (New York: New York University Press, 1998), p. 277.

27. Results of the National Campaign to Prevent Teen Pregnancy as reported by Lisa Mascaro, "Sex Survey: Teach Teens To Just Say No," *Daily News,* April 25, 2001, p. N1.

28. Mike Males, *The Scapegoat Generation: America's War on Adolescents* (Monroe, Maine: Common Courage Press, 1996), p. 46.

29. Males, ibid., pp. 47–48.

30. Males, ibid., p. 52.

31. Males, ibid., p. 56.

32. Males, ibid., p. 48.

33. Males, ibid., p. 51.

34. Mike Males, *Framing Youth: Ten Myths about the Next Generation* (Monroe, Maine: Common Courage Press, 1999), pp. 214–215.

35. In *Framing Youth,* pp. 182–188 Males discusses the connections between poverty and early pregnancy. He argues that underlying fears of teenage pregnancy is fear of young people of color, and that focusing only on pregnancy enables us to avoid talking about race and class. He concludes it is easier to demonize teen mothers and popular culture than to understand why teen pregnancy is so much more likely amongst the poor. The middle-class privileges many Americans take for granted often do not apply to this disadvantaged group, who are less likely to benefit from public education and whose economic prospects, even *without* children, are rather grim. In sum, Males argues that the teens most at risk of becoming pregnant are the same ones we demonize as we refuse to acknowledge the economic and social challenges they face *prior* to becoming parents.

36. Statistics supporting this point from the Centers for Disease Control and Prevention can be found in the introduction of: Dale Kunkel, Kirstie Cope-Farrar, Erica Biely, Wendy Jo Maynard Farinola, and Edward Donnerstein, *Sex on TV: A Biennial Report to the Kaiser Family Foundation 2001* (Menlo Park, Calif.: Kaiser Family Foundation, 2001).

37. Alan Gutmmacher Institute, *Trends in Abortion in the United States, 1973–2000,* 2003.

38. See Debra Boyer and David Fine, "Sexual Abuse as a Factor in Adolescent Pregnancy and Child Maltreatment," *Family Planning Perspectives* 24 (1992): 4–11.

39. See Michel Foucault, *The History of Sexuality Volume 1: An Introduction* (New York: Vintage, 1980).

40. For a discussion of this practice in the beginning of the twentieth century see Steven Schlossman and Stephanie Wallach, "The Crime of Precocious Sexuality," in *Juvenile Delinquency: Historical, Theoretical and Societal Reaction to Youth,* second edition, eds. Paul M. Sharp and Barry W. Hancock (Englewood Cliffs, N.J.: Prentice-Hall, 1998), pp. 41–62. Immigrant girls were often considered delinquent if juvenile courts believed they were *likely* to engage in sex— no proof of actual behavior was necessary.

41. See Debra Haffner, *Beyond the Big Talk: Every Parent's Guide to Raising Sexually Healthy Teens* (New York: Newmarket Press, 2001). Also see Deborah Roffman, *Sex & Sensibility: The Thinking Parent's Guide to Talking Sense About Sex* (Reading, Mass.: Perseus, 2001).

42. Closing speech delivered at the National Media Education Conference in Colorado Springs, Colo., 1998. Thompson noted that television programs tend to be at least a decade behind in terms of presenting social changes. For instance, in spite of the social turbulence of the 1960s, television programs did not reflect the changing social climate until the 1970s.

43. For further discussion, see Naomi Wolf, *The Beauty Myth: How Images of Beauty Are Used Against Women* (New York: Anchor Books, 1991).

In the Trenches: LGBT Students Struggle with School and Sexual Identity

Melinda Miceli

The activism that ultimately led to the [Gay-Straight Alliance (GSA)] movement was set in motion when scattered small groups of gay, lesbian and bisexual high school students started to think and speak about themselves in ways that transcended the common cultural and academic understandings of their lives. Prior to the mid-1980s, it was almost as if they did not exist. Although they were clearly walking through the hallways and sitting in the classrooms, they were invisible to school officials, academics, and most of the general public, because of the belief that the age of "realization" of a gay or lesbian identity came later in life. This "fact" erased the possibility from the minds of experts that self-aware, and certainly self-identified, LGBT students were populating the nation's schools. In pop-cultural images, too, homosexuality was presented as a personal struggle entered into in college or the early years of an attempted heterosexual marriage, not on the varsity team or at the prom. Any fragmented images of LGBT adolescents that filtered through this veil were tortured, depressed, shame filled, and confused.

Emerging from this quagmire at the end of the 1980s and through the 1990s in increasing numbers were a few self-identified, self-assured and outspoken LGBT teenagers who wanted a place in their schools. In the face of limited information, school officials were, at first, generally shocked that these stu-

dents existed (and some chose to continue to deny their existence) and then tried to address their needs in the ways that this information suggested. As this chapter will show, what was advised did not meet the needs of many students. These students understood their experiences in very different terms and knew that what needed to be addressed and changed was the very structure and culture of schools, and not their sexual identity. This wisdom and the courage to articulate it became the driving force behind the efforts to establish GSAs.

How Service Providers, the Public, and School Officials Viewed LGBT Youth

. . . With a few notable exceptions,[1] not much was written about LGBT youth until 1989. The 1989 Department of Health and Human Services' report on gay youth suicide broadened the concern among some psychologists, counselors, teachers, and others working with teenagers. This concern resulted in a small but significant surge in research projects on this population from the fields of psychology and education.[2] The report, because it was issued by a government agency and was given a considerable amount of publicity, also prompted a surge of more news stories on the problems and struggles of gay youth.[3] Generally, these were written as tragic stories about the pain of growing up gay, or heroic stories of overcoming the odds.

What virtually all of these accounts of LGBT youth have in common is an emphasis on the developmental challenges they face. Whether the specific emphasis is placed on the risk of suicide, drug and alcohol abuse, homelessness, or harassment and abuse at home or school, the accounts portray these youth as individuals struggling to develop into happy and healthy adults. This focus on developmental problems is a result of the general ways researchers and the public understood both groups—adolescents and gays and lesbians. Adolescence is an important time for physical, emotional, and identity development, therefore, the processes and stages of this development are often the focus of research and public discourse on this population. From the late 1970s to the late 1980s, researchers sought to also understand homosexuality as a developmental process. Some of these researchers, largely from the fields of psychology and social psychology,[4] delineated developmental stages that, they argued, individuals pass through on the way to forming and coming to terms with their inherent homosexual identity. It is not surprising, then, that those who wished to investigate, understand, and assist gay adolescents focused much of their attention on the developmental problems they may face and turned to these models for assistance. By the late 1980s, the academic understandings of sexual identity in most disciplines had moved past the rather simplistic and essentialist developmental models in favor of more complex social, historical, and cultural analyses.[5] However, it is clear in reading the research and literature on LGBT youth that dominated through the mid to late 1990s that these more sophisticated academic theories of sexual identity had not filtered through to those working with these students.

How Developmental Models Inform the Literature on LGBT Youth

Homosexual identity development models have heavily influenced most research and cultural understandings of LGBT youth.[6] I use the framework of these models to critique the concepts and analysis they employ and to trouble the knowledge and meanings they have produced. In my critique, I interweave the self-reports of LGBT students to illustrate the influence of these meanings on their interpretation of their experiences. The stages of personal struggle generalized in identity formation models, to the extent that they loosely exist, are significantly influenced by the socially produced stereotypes of LGBT people that have become institutionalized in public

schools. The words of students themselves provide empirical evidence to the assertion that public schools are powerful forces systematically shaping these experiences.

Learning the Meaning of Sexual Identity

The literature on developmental models suggests that individuals become consciously aware of their homosexual identities at an average age range of 19–21 for males and 21–23 for females.[7] More current research on gay and lesbian youth suggests that this average age may be considerably lower today.[8] Although no definitive age range is given, some experts hypothesize that the range is now 15–18 for males and 17–20 for females. I interviewed only self-identified lesbian, gay, and bisexual youth ages 14–20, therefore, the age at which they realized their sexual orientation was generally younger than either of these estimates.[9]

The literature states that awareness of sexual orientation is closely followed by a period of "identity confusion." This is a period in which the individual struggles to understand what same-sex attractions mean about who they really are. In other words, their otherwise "normal" identity is shaken by these emerging feelings and they must reassess their identity. I found that what at first seemed like personal confusion was highly contingent upon the messages the youth received from their social environment. For the youth I spoke with, there was a significant relationship among awareness of their sexual/affectional feelings, "identity confusion," and their interaction with the institution of public education. Sometimes such a connection was obvious and immediate in response to my initial question, "When did you first begin to realize that you might be gay?"

> "When I was younger I had a lot of really close girlfriends and I use to really like them, but never really thought about it because . . . In middle school I had millions of boyfriends, but everyone did. And I guess I didn't really . . . When it first started I was like, 'No! No!' you know. But I guess I didn't really say it out loud to myself until my sophomore year of high school; I've known though."
>
> —Becca, bisexual Jewish female, age 18[10]

"I guess junior high. You know? Like the whole puberty thing . . . When girls start talking about boys and stuff and sexual stuff. Then, I guess it just seemed like I didn't feel like all those girls did so something must be wrong with me. So, basically, I just tried to act like them, you know, talk about boys with them and stuff."

—Chloe, gay biracial female, age 20

In these responses, and many others like them, it is obvious that students mark their thinking about their sexual identity in relationship to the stage they were at in school. This indicates that, in some way, school was significant to their experience of these emerging feelings. In what way it was significant was less immediately clear. . . .

For instance, after Chloe gave the above response to my initial question about when she began to realize she was gay, I asked, "When did you know what those feelings you had meant? Did you come out at an early age?" She replied,

"No. . . . Once I realized that it was a wrong or a bad thing to feel, I tried to make myself stop. I told myself I didn't really feel that way and never talked to anyone about it. When I was a kid I knew that I really liked girls, friends and teachers, but I didn't think it was a bad thing. So I didn't try to hide it or anything, and it wasn't a secret. But once I realized it was a bad thing, it became this secret I had to keep and something that I had to fix about myself."

This statement reveals several things about the significance of the relationship between Chloe's "self-realization of sexual orientation" and school. She reports having feelings of affection for other females from an early age, and this was neither something that troubled her nor anything she felt compelled to hide. However, when she entered junior high school, with its environment of normative heterosexuality heightened by "the whole puberty thing," she learned that her feelings for other females could be labeled as homosexual. She was given the messages that this was "a bad thing to feel," that this made her different from her peers, and that she should keep this part of herself a secret and try to be like everyone else. The meaning of the messages she received from other students and the school environment was that heterosexuality was the only accepted and reinforced

feeling and behavior. The force of these social norms defined her feelings as a discreditable stigma, manipulated her into believing that there was something wrong with her, and coerced her into taking on behaviors that would serve to hide or "closet" that part of herself. They also informed her that these same-sex feelings made her a specific *type* of person, which socially marked her as someone who would be the target of ostracism.

Analyzing Chloe's experience in this manner is different in several respects from the way that this situation is usually understood in the literature on homosexual identity development. If we were to apply the analysis used in that literature, we might read her actions as merely personal reactions to the self-hatred caused by her same-sex attractions that she believes are wrong. I argue, however, that the empirical evidence strongly supports an analysis of Chloe's behavior as an active or *reactive* strategy to cope with others' definitions of her feelings and the social forces around her that are hostile to that part of herself. This process, which much of the previous literature describes as an intra-psychic, personal, and staged journey of self-acceptance, is actually a social process—a process constructed by social and structural definitions and categorization of individuals' same-sex feelings and behaviors. Social and cultural definitions of sexual identity, which stigmatize and define homosexuality as unnatural and abnormal, shape and condone negative reactions to LGBT people. Importantly, these same definitions also serve as the base of information out of which LGBT people come to understand and define themselves.

Much of the psychological, counseling, and popular literature on LGBT individuals portrays them as struggling to develop a relatively positive definition of themselves *despite* their "sexual orientation." However, it is more accurate to view them as individuals battling with the social forces that *define* their feelings as an essential and problematic identity. This is further illustrated by Chloe's statement: "I mean, I'm not upset about it or anything, I'm not unhappy that I'm gay . . . but . . . I don't know. I guess I feel a little left out of the world."

Statements like these were made repeatedly by the youth I interviewed. Frequently, they expressed a deep understanding that it was not their feelings that were inherently wrong or deviant. It was, instead, the social world that created the difficulties associated with being LGBT. As Rick stated about realizing that he was bisexual, "It was just like the initial shock of like the first day and then I was over it. But like everybody else had a problem dealing with it. That was the problem, and that fucked me up." In relation to school, Rick stated, "When I was at school I was always on edge. It affected me as far as how I would deal with people, you know, or I didn't deal with people at all. And because I couldn't, nobody could know the truth, otherwise I would die." Rick reported that he perceived his school as a place where harassment of LGBT students took place often and generally went unpunished by teachers or school administrators. The "truth," that he was not heterosexual, was not a threat to Rick's (and other LGBT students') self-concept. Rather, this "truth" was a threat to the normative heterosexuality of the school, and this threat put him in danger of abuse, which, in this context, was often condoned as justifiable punishment.

"Acceptance": A Setup for Failure

Overwhelmingly, journal articles and books targeted at school counselors, social workers, teachers and administrators communicate to them that the heart of the problems experienced by LGBT students is low self-esteem. That body of literature, like the homosexual identity development models that inform it, presumes that same-sex attractions are inherently unacceptable to the individual causing self-esteem-related problems. In these assertions there is little distinction made between one's perception of oneself and the judgment enforced by one's environment. This de-emphasizes the reality that some individuals do not have to work to accept themselves, and yet still find it unacceptable that they are deemed intolerable by society. In fact, according to these models, an essential step in the developmental process is for the homosexual individual to "accept" the socially defined, structurally ingrained, and institutionally enforced stigma of homosexuality. Also, and somewhat of a contradiction in logic, these models take for granted that "self-acceptance" is fully achievable

within a society in which homosexuality is so thoroughly defined as unacceptable. Such complexities are not critically addressed in these developmental models or in the research on LGBT youth that has been informed by them. It is important to note that such complexities have now been addressed by a large and growing body of academic theory and research, but, in the early days of LGBT activism, these understandings had not yet been used to inform the emerging research on gay youth.

The concept of "acceptance" is an important one in LGBT students' lives. However, it is important in ways that are distinctly different from those outlined in the previous literature. In group meetings as well as individual interviews, the students spoke of problems with being accepted for who they are in school, at home, and in public, because they were LGBT. They also spoke of *self-acceptance*. Acceptance was something that they worried about losing and actively sought out from those they loved as well as from the social world that surrounded them.

The degree to which the LGBT youth I spoke with felt they received acceptance from others varied depending on what group of people they were referring to—the general school environment, teachers, peers, family, gay and lesbian communities, the general public, etc. The degree to which they accepted their same-sex feelings as a positive part of their own identity also seemed to vary largely in relation to their experiences with external social factors. In other words, the factors of self-acceptance and acceptance from others form a reciprocal relationship. The level of tolerance that students receive from others and from their environments influences their self-acceptance; and an individual student's level of self-acceptance influences the degree to which she/he seeks out, or worries about, the approval of others. Two major themes emerged in relation to the concept of "acceptance." The first is that, for LGBT students, school is overwhelmingly not a place of acceptance, but rather, it is a place where they feel uncomfortable, fearful or worried, and often hated. The second is that not receiving acceptance and having to worry about acceptance causes these students to have feelings of frustration and anger throughout their school experience.

I'm not good at being around kids, you know, people at school. . . . I am really confident outside of school, but once I'm in school I don't feel confident. It's really hard to feel confident at school, I feel uncomfortable.

—Vincent, gay white male, age 16

It's something that is more comforting to know that [my new] high school is not afraid to talk about gay and lesbian issues. It's comforting to know that I can wake up in the morning and not think, am I going to call in sick or am I just going to lie. I can just go to school and feel comfortable, you know, today is going to be a good day. I can wake up at eight o'clock in the morning and say I'm gay and feel good about it. I don't have to worry, ok who's going to say what to me today, when I get to school what's my locker going to look like. In gym class—oh god, do I skip or do I go and risk being tortured. So, it's easier for me now to walk around with my head held high, that's something that I can do now.

—Mike, gay biracial male, age 17

These statements illustrate that the way many LGBT students feel about themselves is conditionally based on their school environment. Vincent reports that his level of self-confidence drops as he enters school walls. Mike's statement illustrates the impact that both a homophobic and an accepting school environment can have on a LGBT student's life. The majority of students I spoke with reported that school made them feel uncomfortable, unaccepted, isolated, angry, or afraid.

The narrative told by traditional homosexual identity models, and much of the literature on youth that is informed by them, positions "self-acceptance" as a crucial step toward the achievement of a relatively tolerable and contented life for a homosexual individual (relative to that of heterosexuals). On the one hand, this can be read as a positive narrative in opposition to other past scientific, medical, and some contemporary religious discourses that see the future for the LGBT individual as one of misery unless they change, cure, or repress their feelings. On the other hand, it can be read as a narrative that inescapably sets the LGBT individual up for failure. It makes acceptance an accomplishment that *individuals* must work to achieve if they are to be content in a society in which non-acceptance of

homosexuality is intertwined with cultural messages, institutions, and structures. This assures that acceptance is, at worst, impossible and, at best, a continuous struggle. By stressing *self-acceptance,* and submitting to the ideology that social stigmatization is justifiable, the onus is fully on the individual. It is the individuals' failure to accept themselves as LGBT that is presumed to cause the difficulties they encounter, and society is absolved.

"Coming Out": A Socially Produced Narrative of Shame and Liberation

The concept of acceptance, both from others and of self, is talked about in the literature as part of the identity-development process that builds up to the "coming-out" process. This is basically a procedure through which homosexual individuals learn self-acceptance of their stigma and the social limitations that this stigma places on them, and how to make decisions about where and to whom to reveal this discreditable feature of themselves. The terms "coming-out" and "the closet," have become a large part of the cultural discourse about gay and lesbian people. Coming-out stories and narratives of "self-discovery" are now common types of pop-cultural accounts of the lives of gay people. As a result, many people feel that, to understand a gay person, they need to know when the person "knew" he or she was gay, if the person is "in" or "out" of the "closet," and why.[11] The youth I interviewed are no exception to this. They often used the language of the "coming-out" discourse to describe their own and others' experiences. Issues of coming out—to do it or not to do it, how to do it, who to tell and who not to tell, negative and positive results of, the safety or danger of, etc.—were some of the most prevalent themes in the support group meetings I attended and the interviews I conducted.

The decision to come out or to hide in the closet is generally not based on a level of self-acceptance. It is, however, largely based on their perception of the social circumstances in which they find themselves.

I was out to some of my close friends and I hinted about it to others and was not at all out to others. It depended on how much I thought I could trust them or how I thought they would react to it. . . . I'm still afraid to be out in public and be with other gay people, to have people know that I'm gay. I don't want to get hurt or have anyone make judgments about me or anything.

> —Ani, gay white female, age 18

It would be like suicide to come out at my high school. It is worse than the backwoods. It is such a small town and so conservative. In the eighteen years that I've lived there I've never known anyone who was gay and out there.

> —Luke, gay white male, age 18

These LGBT students discern that it is not their acceptance of homosexuality that is most important to coming out, but rather other individuals', the institution's, or society's level of acceptance of homosexuality that will affect their experiences when and if they decide to come out. . . .

Well, I came out when I was fifteen, to my family and a few close friends. But I was still in high school and didn't come out to everybody. I had people come up and ask me after rumors started flying around. I would still say no, you know, I'm straight or whatever. [laughs] I didn't want to get my butt kicked. I live in a small town.

> —Rick, bisexual biracial male, age 18

These students' decisions to reveal or to not reveal their same-sex attractions to others is based on an assessment of the costs and benefits, punishments and rewards, and danger and safety associated with such an action.

I'm out and nobody really bothers me. I have been out since I was fifteen and it hasn't really been a major thing. Everyone knows who I am and that I am gay and they don't really bug me much. Then again, I'm the kind of person who thinks that it's better to be who you are. I couldn't stand not being what I am. If people can't deal with it then fuck 'em—that's their deal, not mine. I mean I don't go around announcing to everyone that I am gay, but if they ask me I tell them and I don't censor myself for anyone. . . . If they can't deal with it then that's their shit, not mine. I don't have time for it and I won't deal with it.

> —Warren, gay white male, age 16

I tried at first to hide that I was gay, I tried really hard to act like everyone else, and to just kind of be invisible. It didn't work though, because people could just tell, like they said by the way I talked and walked and stuff, they

could just tell I was gay, and they made fun of me and threw stuff at me and hit me in the halls, no matter how much I kept denying it. So, finally I just admitted it, because I was so tired of it, but the abuse just got worse.

> —Andy, gay white male, age 16

As the preceding statements evidence, many social factors are involved in this "coming out process" for LGBT students. For example, Ani, Luke, and Rick all perceived their school environments to be risky places to be LGBT. Based on this evaluation of their surroundings, they felt fearful of others' judgments of them and of the punishment that might accompany these judgments. For Warren, the potential risks of such judgments were outweighed by what he felt to be the cost of "censoring himself." For Andy, neither decision—to hide or to come out—could spare him from the judgment and punishment associated with being outside of the heterosexual norm of his high school. In these assessments, the students conclude that institutions of public education are dangerous places in which to come out, to be found to be, or be suspected of being gay, lesbian, or bisexual. Therefore, some choose to hide this part of themselves at school while others choose to reveal it. Regardless of the choice made, all students first assessed the relative safety or danger of their school environment.

Sexual Identity Labels: The Paradox of "Self-Definition"

According to the literature on homosexual identity development models, an individual's acceptance and situational use of the label gay, lesbian, or bisexual is a sign of successful and mature homosexual identity formation. Therefore, discomfort with these labels is taken to be a sign of a personal difficulty with self-acceptance. The developmental models, and the theoretical perspective of symbolic interactionism that informs them, take the meaning of these labels for granted. They do not discuss or analyze the social construction of these labels, the "natural" binary of heterosexual and homosexual that these labels reinforce, or the compulsion to categorize people within them.

In contrast, other theoretical perspectives argue that the terms and conditions on which sexual identity labels are based, and the very concept of labeling, result from the power of scientifically and socially produced meanings of sexual identity.[12] These identity categories are used as social controls of individual behaviors and as structured enforcement of the normative dominance of heterosexuality. Many of the LGBT students spoke about sexual identity labels as categories and definitions that they felt were being forced upon them.

The use of sexual identity labels was, at times, the subject of debate at the weekly support group meetings. When I interviewed youth individually, it was revealed that many found labeling to be personally frustrating, because they felt pressured to define and categorize their "true sexual identity."

> It depends on who I'm talking to . . . I say that I'm bisexual to people that I think are closed-minded. . . . It seems like a more acceptable term. So, I guess I think that people will be more willing to accept that, or won't get as freaked out if I say that as they would if I said that I was lesbian. . . . I don't think that any term is really an accurate description of who I am. It makes me uncomfortable to use them and, you know, all that it means to people. Like, people make assumptions about it—like it's sexual or disgusting or whatever. . . . but to other people, like my closer friends, I say that I am a lesbian.
>
> —Ani, gay white female, age 18

> I use the term gay, if I use any term at all. . . . I don't like the term lesbian. It's like too technical or something. It sounds like a disease or a different species or something.
>
> —Emily, gay white female, age 16

These statements provide examples of how many of the students make the choice of how and when to label themselves. Many do this not based on their definition, understanding, or tolerance of their attractions, but rather on their perception of the meanings that *others* have attached to these labels of sexual identity. Generally, the students had little problem with self-acceptance. However, they did have anxiety about "coming out" and about the pressure they felt to choose a label and define their sexual identity.

> I don't understand why I have to label myself anything. I'm just Adam. If somebody asks me if I'm gay I'll say yes, but why do I have to go around calling myself anything? Being gay is just a small part of who I am. It happens in my bedroom, not on a big screen in the street. It

doesn't affect anyone. I'm just like everybody else, I like to go to the movies and dinner and talk with my boyfriend. I don't want anything radical and I don't want to talk about it to everyone I meet. I mean, yeah I want rights like everybody else and the legal right to marry, you know, that stuff's really important. But, it's not radical.
>
> —Adam, gay white male, age 19

The students who respond to labels in this way demonstrate a knowledge that these terms have social meanings beyond being only a simple description of their attractions, and that these meanings are, more often than not, beyond their ability to define for themselves. They are generally uncomfortable with using these labels, which they feel do more to take away their ability to fully define and express themselves to others than to assert their identity.

> I don't use any label really. Except at group where you kind of are expected to say something. Then I guess I say gay. . . . I'm not ashamed of it or anything. I just don't like . . . I don't go around announcing it to everyone. I don't really think that it is anyone's business.
>
> —Carol, gay white female, age 17

. . . Statements like these illustrate social factors, *not* personal problems of acceptance. It is evidence of their knowledge of and anger at the ways in which others perceive the meaning of these labels and in the way such labels may be used by others to place limits on who they can be. Some of the LGBT students I interviewed took an active approach to try to define themselves outside of the definitional boundaries of these sexual identity categories.

> I use the word dyke because I don't like the word lesbian. I think when people say it, it's like lesss-bee-ann [slow and drawn out]. Like it sounds really old and . . . I don't know. I'm young and . . . Ever since I've been out no one's ever used the word dyke against me in a bad way. And so . . . I've been called lesbo and I've been called other things having to do with lesbian. So, I prefer not to use it because it has negative meaning to me. . . . Dyke is a really powerful word, and it seems like an active word. Because when people say the word dyke, people stop and listen. And nobody stops to listen when you say lesbian. Ever. It's just like, 'O.K. Whatever. You mean you're gay, right?'
>
> —Janice, gay white female, age 19

Not straight. Because . . . I don't like heterosexuals and I don't like homosexuals, and for me each are incorporated in my thoughts. . . . Just things that I don't like that go along with each trait that I don't like. I don't like, extremely flamboyant people. . . homosexuals especially. . . . And I don't like . . . jock-ass heterosexuals . . . hardcore heteros. Basically they piss me off. . . . I consider myself bi . . . I can go either way. [I: Why don't you use that label?] Because I'm not generic. (laughs) Pretty much that's it. I don't like labels.

—Rick, bisexual biracial male, age 18

Statements like these reveal an awareness of the shaping force of sexual identity categories on these students' lives—setting the definitional terms for who they are and who they can potentially be. They also evidence the possibility of fostering a positive identity and "self-acceptance" without simultaneously passively accepting the social, structural, and institutional meanings of homosexuality. Many LGBT students are actively trying to forge an identity for themselves that rejects the stigma forced on them by society and that moves beyond the definitional limitations of sexual identity categories.

Most of the research on and writing about LGBT youth has been focused largely on the negative aspects of "growing up gay," addressing and analyzing only the negative variables and outcomes of their experiences. The motivation for such an approach was benevolent, hoping that documenting the suffering, problems, and risks involved with being a gay teenager would lead to the development of services and resources to address their needs. . . . [T]his focus on the sufferings of LGBT youth has brought such resources and services. However, what was missed by this focus on problems was an understanding of adolescents who have successfully avoided or transcended many of the negative experiences and outcomes associated with being LGBT, and an understanding of the factors that contributed to their success. Many LGBT teens are indeed struggling and in need of assistance. However, if effective solutions are to be found, it is crucial for researchers, school officials, social service workers, and the general public to understand the social and institutional factors that contribute to these negative experiences.

Students have been well ahead of researchers and those seeking to develop services to meet their needs. The teenagers who pioneered the GSA movement were the first to understand the institutional forces putting LGBT students at risk and to have a vision of the direction that effective change should take. . . . The assertions of positive, self-assured sexual identities and student rights served as the catalyst for a social movement and for cultural transformations in images of what it is to be a LGBT teenager.

NOTES

1. e.g., Dennis and Ruth 1986; Hunter and Schaecher 1987; Martin and Hetrick 1988; Remafedi 1987.

2. e.g., Herdt 1989; Harbeck 1992, 1994; Cook and Herdt 1991; Herdt and Boxer 1993; DeCresenzo 1994.

3. e.g., Due 1995; Woog 1995; Chandler 1995; Hayes 1991.

4. e.g., Cass 1979, 1984; Troiden 1979, 1988, 1989.

5. e.g., Foucault 1976, 1980; Seidman 1995, 1996, 2002; Bravmann 1996; Irving 1994; Warner 1991.

6. e.g., Hetrick and Martin 1987; Herdt and Boxer 1993; DeCresenzo 1994; Walling 1996.

7. ibid v.

8. ibid i, ibid ii.

9. Of course, because my sample was non-random, no generalization can be made as to the age range of "sensitization" for the LGBT population as a whole.

10. All names have been changed to protect the anonymity of those I interviewed. I use the sexual identity label that each respondent prefer to use in describing themselves.

11. Seidman (2003) *Beyond the Closet*. New York: Routledge.

12. e.g., Foucault 1976; McIntosh 1968; Seidman 1994; Gamson 1996.

REFERENCES

Bravmann, S. (1996), "Postmodern Queer Identities." 333–361 in *Queer Theory/Sociology*, Steven Seidman (Ed.). Cambridge, MA: Blackwell.

Cass, V. C. (1979), "Homosexual Identity Formation: A Theoretical Model." *Journal of Homosexuality* 10:77–84.

Cass, V. C. (1984), "Homosexual Identity: A Concept in Need of Definition." *Journal of Homosexuality*, 9:105–126.

Chandler, K. (1995), *Passages of Pride*. Los Angeles, CA: Alyson Books.

Cook and Herdt. (1990), "To Tell or Not to Tell: Patterns of Self-Disclosure to Mothers and Fathers Reported by Gay and Lesbian Youth." in *Parent and Child Relations Across the Lifespan,* Pillemer, K. and K. McCartney (Eds.). New York: Oxford University Press.

DeCrescenzo, C. (Ed.) (1994), *Helping Gay and Lesbian Youth: New Policies, New Programs, New Practice.* Binghamton, NY: Harrington Park Press.

Dennis, D. I. and Ruth, E. H. (1986), "Gay Youth and the Right to Education." *Yale Law and Policy Review,* 4:445–455.

Due, L. (1995), *Joining the Tribe: Growing Up Gay and Lesbian in the '90s.* New York: Doubleday.

Foucault, M. ([1976] 1990), *The History of Sexuality Volume 1: An Introduction.* New York: Vintage Books.

Foucault, Michel (1980), *Power/Knowledge: Selected Interviews and Other Writings, 1972–1977.* Translated by C. Gordon, L. Marshall, J. Mepham, K. Soper. New York: Pantheon Books.

Gamson, Joshua (1996), "Must Identity Movements Self-Destruct? A Queer Dilemma." In Steven Seidman (Ed.). *Queer Theory/Sociology:* 395–420. Cambridge, MA: Blackwell.

Harbeck, K. (1994), "Invisible No More: Addressing the Needs of Gay, Lesbian, and Bisexual Youth and Their Advocates." *High School Journal,* special edition: 170–180.

Hayes, W. (1991), "To Be Young and Gay and Living in the '90s." *Utne Reader,* March/April, pp. 94–100.

Herdt, G. (Ed.) (1989), *Gay and Lesbian Youth.* New York: Harrington Park Press.

Herdt, Gilbert and Andrew Boxer (1993), *Children of Horizons: How Gay and Lesbian Teens Are Leading a New Way Out of the Closet.* Boston, MA: Beacon Press.

Hunter, J. and Schaecher, R. (1987), "Stresses on Lesbian and Gay Adolescents in Schools." *Social Work in Education,* 9 (3):180–190.

Irving, J. ([1994] 1996), "A Place in the Rainbow: Theorizing Gay and Lesbian Culture." 213–240 in *Queer Theory/Sociology,* Steven Seidman (Ed.). Cambridge, MA: Blackwell.

Martin and Hetrick (1988), "The Stigmatization of the Gay and Lesbian Adolescent." *Journal of Homosexuality,* 16:163–183.

McIntosh, M. ([1968] 1996), "The Homosexual Role" 33–40. In *Queer Theory/Sociology,* Steven Seidman (Ed.). Cambridge, MA: Blackwell.

Remafedi, G. (1987), "Homosexual Youth: A Challenge to Contemporary Society." *JAMA,* July 10, 258.

Seidman, S. (1995), "Deconstructing Queer Theory or the Under-Theorization of the Social and the Ethical." 116–140 in *Social Postmodernism: Beyond Identity Politics,* Steven Seidman and Linda Nicholson (Eds.). Cambridge, UK: Cambridge University Press.

Seidman, S. (1996), "Introduction." 1–29 in *Queer Theory/Sociology,* Steven Seidman (Ed.). Cambridge, MA: Blackwell.

Seidman, Steven (2002), *Beyond the Onset. The Transformation of Gay and Lesbian Life.* New York: Routledge.

Troiden, R. R. (1979), "Becoming Homosexual: A Model of Gay Identity Acquisition." *Psychiatry,* 42:362–373.

Troiden, R. R. (1988), *Gay and Lesbian Identity: A Sociological Analysis.* New York: General Hall.

Troiden, R. R. (1989), The Formation of Homosexual Identities. *Journal of Homosexuality,* 17:43–73.

Walling, D. R. (Ed.). (1996), *Open Lives, Safe Schools: Addressing Gay and Lesbian Issues in Education.* Bloomington. In Phi Delta Kappa Educational Foundation.

Warner, M. (1991), "Fear of a Queer Planet." *Social Text,* 9 (14): 1–17.

Woog, D. (1995), *School's Out: The Impact of Gay and Lesbian Issues on America's Schools.* Boston, MA: Alyson.

Sexual Risk and the Double Standard

for African American Adolescent Women

Amy M. Fasula, Kim S. Miller, and Jeffrey Wiener

The disproportionate rates of HIV/AIDS for Black women in the United States are staggering (CDC, 2005), and young Black women are at particularly high risk. In 2002, AIDS was the leading cause of death for Black women of ages 25–34 (Anderson & Smith, 2005), and many of these women were likely infected as adolescents or young adults. In addition, 13- to 19-year-olds have the highest proportion of AIDS cases among females (43%) (CDC, 2004). The primary mode of HIV transmission for adolescent and adult women of all race and ethnicity categories is through unprotected heterosexual contact (CDC, 2005).

These trends highlight the critical need to develop new intervention strategies that address young Black women's HIV risk in their heterosexual interactions more effectively. We need to create innovative approaches to HIV prevention that speak directly to the lived experiences of Black women in their intimate relationships with men. Furthermore, such prevention efforts need to begin early in the sexual socialization process, before sexual behaviors have begun and sexual scripts have already taken hold. In order to develop such early, socially relevant HIV interventions, we need to gain a richer understanding of Black girls' sexual socialization as it relates to heterosexual risk.

One aspect of sexual socialization relevant to sexual risk reduction is the sexual double standard

(SDS). Under this social norm, males are afforded more freedom and power than females to engage in and direct heterosexual interactions, which may limit young women's ability to fully control their sexual risk reduction behaviors (Connell, 1987; Holland, Ramazanoglu, Sharpe, & Thomson, 2004; Tanenbaum, 2000; Tolman, 2002). Parents, particularly mothers, play a key role in adolescents' sexual socialization (Downie & Coates, 1999; Miller, Kotchick, Dorsey, Forehand, & Ham, 1998; Nolin & Petersen, 1992; Rosenthal & Feldman, 1999) and mother-adolescent sexual discussions have positive effects on reducing adolescent sexual risk (DiIorio, Kelley, & Hockenberry-Eaton, 1999; Fasula & Miller, 2006; Miller, Levin, Whitaker, & Xu, 1998; Whitaker, Miller, May, & Levin, 1999). Therefore, in this [reading], we qualitatively explore the SDS in African American mothers' sexual messages to sons and daughters, specifically in terms of daughters' sexual risk reduction.

[Adolescents'] gender is a factor in mother-adolescent sexual discussions. Mothers are more likely to talk to daughters, are more comfortable talking with daughters (DiIorio, Hockenberry-Eaton, Maibach, Rivero, & Miller, 1996), and talk about a wider range of topics with daughters than with sons (for a review see DiIorio, Pluhar, & Belcher, 2003). The reasons mothers put more emphasis on daughters' sexual socialization may be related to their identification and comfort in talking with same-gender children about sexual topics and the increased social and physical sequelae of pregnancy and STDs for females.

Ironically, however, in mothers' attempts to protect daughters from negative sexual health outcomes they often reinforce an SDS that may limit daughters'

From "The Sexual Double Standard in African American Adolescent Women's Sexual Risk Reduction Socialization" by Amy M. Fasula, Kim S. Miller, and Jeffrey Wiener (2007), *Women & Health, 46*(2/3), 3–21. The Haworth Press, reprinted by permission of the publisher (Taylor & Francis, http://www.informaworld.com).

sexual agency and risk reduction preparedness (DiIorio et al., 1999; Downie & Coates, 1999; Espiritu, 2001; Nolin & Petersen, 1992; O'Sullivan, Meyer-Bahlburg, & Watkins, 2001). For example, in a study with African American mothers and adolescents, topics discussed by mothers and fathers emphasized consequences of STDs, HIV and condom use more for sons, and normal development and abstinence more for daughters (DiIorio et al., 1999). Similarly, Levin and Robertson (2002) found that ethnic minority mothers were more accepting of sons than of daughters carrying condoms, even when mothers thought their son or daughter was sexually active. This paradoxical situation in which mothers believe daughters to be sexually active, yet do not want them to carry condoms pointedly illustrates the dangers the SDS sets up for young women.

These findings suggest that it is of critical importance to women's HIV prevention efforts to understand how the SDS specifically affects daughters' sexual risk reduction socialization. . . .

In this study we examined gender differences and SDS patterns in African American mothers' messages to 15- to 17-year-old sons and daughters about sexual topics. In particular, we focused our analyses on mothers' messages related to sexual risk reduction. . . .

Methods

The data for this study were taken from a larger study, the Family Adolescent Risk Behavior and Communication Study (FARBCS). FARBCS was a cross-sectional study with Black and Hispanic mother-adolescent dyads which examined the effects of individual, family, peer, and environmental factors on adolescent risk reduction behaviors. . . . Of these, 907 . . . mother-adolescent dyads were successfully interviewed—259 Black dyads in Montgomery and 172 in the Bronx. . . .

Mother and adolescent were interviewed separately, with the mother's interview conducted, when possible, before the adolescent interview. . . .

To create the sample for the current analyses, we started with the 431 dyads in which the adolescent

self-identified as Black. To control for potential effects of mother's race, we then excluded 67 dyads in which the mother did not self-identify as Black, leaving a sample of 364 dyads. Next, to focus our analyses on the SDS, we included only dyads that reported SDS attitudes in the closed-ended data. Attitudes about adolescents having sex, having many partners, and getting pregnant/getting someone pregnant were determined by mothers' and adolescents' responses (never ok, sometimes ok, always ok) to questions such as "What do you think about male [female] teenagers your age having sex?" Adolescents were also asked about their perceptions of the mother's attitudes (e.g., "What does your mother think about male [female] teenagers your age having sex?"). If either the mother or the adolescent indicated that any behavior was more acceptable for males than for females, the dyad was included in the study analyses. Of the 364 Black dyads, 35% held at least one SDS, for a final sample of 129 dyads. . . .

Results

Sample Characteristics

The majority (65%) of the mother-adolescent dyads were from Montgomery, AL. . . . Mothers were typically between 35 and 44 years of age (66%); education attainment of mothers in the sample ranged from less than a high school diploma (16%) to a college degree or above (16%); the majority were employed outside of the home either full-time (54%) or part-time (15%); and 43% were married at the time of the interview. Most mothers attended religious services at least one to two times per month (71%). Nearly all of the mothers were the biological parent of the participating adolescents (92%), and they had on average four children, including the participating adolescent. All of the dyads self-identified specifically as African American.

The age of the adolescents at the time of the interview ranged from 14 to 17 years, with a mean of 15 years. Mother-daughter dyads comprised 53% of the sample. The majority of sons (85%) reported ever engaging in intercourse, whereas the majority of mothers perceived their son (51%) not to be sexually active. . . . For daughters, 37% reported ever engaging in intercourse although only 27% of mothers thought their daughter was sexually active.

Qualitative Results

Our analyses revealed one overarching theme and four sub-themes related to the SDS and mothers' sexual risk reduction socialization. The primary theme was the "clean" and "dirty" girl dichotomy. The sub-themes were: (1) sexual guidance for sons, conflict and controls for daughters; (2) discouraging daughters' sexual risk reduction preparedness; (3) challenges to passive condom preparation for daughters; and (4) proactive condom preparation for sons.

The Clean and Dirty Girl Dichotomy

In mothers' sexual risk reduction messages, the gender ideology of the "good" and "bad" girl dichotomy, which stigmatizes female sexual knowledge and experience, intersects with disease prevention to create the clean and dirty girl dichotomy. In discussions with sexually active and non-sexually active sons about avoiding STDs and HIV, a consistent theme emerged of mothers categorizing women as clean and dirty, and some used disparaging terms such as "slutty" or "scaliwags" to define safe and unsafe female partners. For example, the mother of a sexually active son said, "[I told my son to use condoms] whether or not he thought that the girl was clean. . . . " And a sexually active son stated "[My mother told me that to prevent HIV] . . . use a condom if you're gonna have sex. Don't bring a slutty girl in the house. . . . " In addition to such statements, several mothers warned their sons that pretty women can also be dirty. For example, a mother of a sexually active son stated, "I told him that appearance says nothing, she can be the prettiest girl in school and infect everyone on the football team. . . . "

Although mothers of both sons and daughters warned their adolescents, "You never know" if a person is infected, none of the mothers labeled males as "good or bad," "clean or dirty" or "handsome but dirty." The ways mothers tried to protect daughters from being labeled dirty or their discomfort with their daughters' sexual development based on this aspect

of the SDS ran through each of the following sub-themes.

Sexual Guidance for Sons, Conflict and Controls for Daughters. Conflict and controls over sexual issues consistently recurred in the mother-daughter data, for both sexually and non-sexually active daughters. Some mothers and daughters argued about the highly charged issues of sex and pregnancy. A number of these arguments, however, occurred because daughters were not allowed to date or have a boyfriend, or they argued about talking to boys. For example, a sexually active daughter stated, "[The reoccurring arguments with my mother are] mostly about boys. She doesn't want me to have a boyfriend." Half of the daughters restricted from dating or talking to boys were already sexually active.

In contrast, it was rare for mothers and sons to report reoccurring arguments about sexual issues. Of those that did, the majority were about sex and pregnancy, rather than dating or talking with girls. In fact, the data suggested that when mothers noticed sons taking an interest in girls, rather than triggering arguments, they often used these events as the impetus for discussions to help guide their sons about sexuality. For example, a mother of a sexually active son stated, "[The sexual discussions with my son start because] a lot of girls call the house for him and I just tell him to be careful and take precautions." And a mother of a non-sexually active son stated, "[The sexual discussions with my son start] 'cause I care and I want him to know. Sometimes I overhear them telling about what girls they've gone to bed with."

Discouraging Daughters' Sexual Risk Reduction Preparedness. Following this restrictive stance toward daughters' sexual guidance and preparation, some mothers overtly discouraged their daughters (but never sons) from obtaining safe sex methods. Mothers often told both sons and daughters that abstinence from sex was the only way to protect themselves from negative sexual outcomes. In nearly half of these messages to daughters, however, the mothers went one step further and told their daughters not to obtain other forms of protection, such as birth control pills or condoms. As the mother of a non-sexually active daughter stated, "[I told my daughter that] no birth control method is foolproof. I did not specify one over another. I told her that she did not need it and not to participate in the school programs where birth control is distributed. . . . " The following quote from a sexually active daughter illustrated the paradox these messages created for sexually active daughters' prevention efforts: "[My mother said] that if I wanted to be on birth control it was for people that slept around. She says the best way to prevent pregnancy is to not have sex."

Challenges to Passive Condom Preparation for Daughters.   Some mothers did encourage their daughters to obtain, carry, and use condoms if they had sex—although these messages were more common for sons than for daughters. Some mothers' messages even ran counter to the SDS and explicitly challenged a passive female role in condom use. These messages, however, revealed a perception by mothers that there were social norms that promoted shame and passivity for female condom preparation and use. In these messages mothers told daughters "not to be ashamed to provide her own condoms," and not to depend on the man for condoms. Neither the link between condoms and shame nor messages of "don't depend on the woman for condoms" came up in the sons' data.

Proactive Condom Preparation for Sons.   Condom skills and access are important aspects of condom preparation. Mothers in this study were consistently more proactive in providing sons with these resources than either sexually active or non-sexually active daughters. In particular, mothers commonly reported that they provided their sons with condoms. A mother of a sexually active son illustrated a typical example, "I bought [my son] some [condoms], gave him permission to buy some for himself and asked his father to have a talk with him." Additionally, condoms were part of pubertal socialization and skills development for some non-sexually active sons. For example, a mother of a non-sexually active son provided him with condoms after his first wet dream. Another explained, "[My son and I have] talked about condoms. I gave him packages

of them that told how to use them on the back. I told him he need to use them to ask me and I'll get them for him."

In contrast to the way condoms were encouraged, provided, and treated as part of the "facts of life" for sons, mothers of even sexually active daughters were more removed from the process of providing their daughters with condom protection. Only one mother told her daughter that she would buy her condoms when she was ready to have sex; two gave their daughters permission to obtain condoms at school; and none reported giving their daughter condoms.

Discussion

The study findings illustrated how the SDS affects the content and process of mothers' sexual risk reduction socialization for sons and daughters. Mothers typically took a proactive approach with sons and a neutral or prohibitive approach with daughters regarding sexual risk reduction. Mothers used sons' sexual interest as impetus for sexual guidance. They often encouraged sons to carry and use condoms, and some provided sons with condoms. However, daughters' sexual interest often resulted in restrictions and arguments; mothers did not provide daughters with condoms, and some explicitly discouraged daughters' sexual risk reduction preparedness. Previous research on adolescent sexual development and risk help contextualize how mothers' SDS messages and this neutral or prohibitive approach to daughters' sexual risk reduction socialization may affect their ability to protect themselves from sexual risk.

Similar to previous research, the good girl and bad girl dichotomy was an overarching theme related to young women's sexuality (Fullilove, Fullilove, Haynes, & Gross, 1990; Gilmore, DeLamater, & Wagstaff, 1996; Hutchinson, 1999; Tanenbaum, 2000; Wilkins, 2004). Under this ideology, it is considered deviant, even unnatural, for girls and women to experience and express sexuality, thus girls and women are considered good or bad based on their perceived knowledge and experience of sexuality (Eyre, Hoffman, & Millstein, 1998; Fullilove et al., 1990; Hutchinson, 1999; Tanenbaum, 2000; Wilkins, 2004). For young women undergoing their sexual development, this asexual message is likely to result in an underdeveloped sense of themselves as a sexual being (Fullilove et al., 1990; Thompson, 1995; Tolman, 2002; Tolman & Brown, 2001).

Without a strong sexual self, young women are likely to deny the possibility or the experience of sexual desire, which can create barriers to actively developing attitudes about how, when, and why they would or would not engage in sexual behaviors (Holland et al., 2004; Thompson, 1995; Tolman, 2002; Tolman & Debold, 1994). This sexual denial reduces young women's agency in their sexual decisions (Holland et al., 2004; Monahan, Miller, & Rothspan, 1997; Nolin & Petersen, 1992; Thompson, 1990; Tolman, 2002; Tolman & Debold, 1994; Whitley & Schofield, 1986).

In addition, this aspect of the SDS is deeply embedded in the heterosexual romance script in which males are supposed to pursue sex and females are supposed to resist and say no, whether they want to have sex or not (Muehlenhard, 1988; Muehlenhard & McCoy, 1991). Under this scenario women are left to act as "gatekeepers" and merely respond to men's actions rather than take an active role in their sexual encounters (Campbell, 1995; Fine, 1988; Hartley & Drew, 2001; Holland et al., 2004; Muehlenhard, 1988; Muehlenhard & McCoy, 1991; Tolman, 1996). Without strong grounding in their own sexuality, young women are likely to put the sexual decision-making power into the hands of their male partners, thereby limiting their ability to ensure safe sexual behaviors (Wingood & DiClemente, 1998).

In these data, the good girl-bad girl dichotomy was transformed by the threat of STDs and HIV into categorizing young women as clean or dirty. This transformation added another layer to the social stigma of the bad girl by defining her not only as deviant, but also dangerous and diseased. Furthermore, the theme of pretty but dirty introduced suspicion that any girl may be dirty. The challenges mothers made to this aspect of the SDS also revealed the shame associated with being deemed dirty and the passive role females are expected to take in condom preparation.

This need for young women to distance themselves from the dirty girl image can have detrimental effects on their sexual risk behaviors. The deliberate

planning necessary to ensure safe sex is in direct conflict with the idea that good girls don't have sex (Hillier, Harrison, & Bowditch, 1999; Holland et al., 2004; Wight, 1992). Condoms in particular run counter to the good or clean girl image because condom use is often associated with sexual promiscuity and disease (Dahl, Darke, Gorn, & Weinberg, 2005; Loxley, 1996). The social stigma of being labeled dirty or the shame of providing condoms was apparent in the data and revealed the intense conflict that condoms present for young women. Thus, those women who see themselves as good and clean, and want to avoid being labeled as dirty by partners or others are likely to avoid planning for and using condoms (Gilmore et al., 1996; Holland et al., 2004; Tolman, 2002).

In addition to the way the SDS affects young women's sexual risk behaviors, the study findings suggested that the SDS limits the effectiveness of daughters' sexual risk reduction socialization. Most striking were the reports of mothers explicitly prohibiting daughters from obtaining condoms or birth control. This theme powerfully illustrated how the SDS can transform mothers' concern for daughters' sexual health into messages and socialization processes that can actually put daughters at risk. The findings from a recent longitudinal study highlight the potential detrimental effects of such messages for sexually active daughters. Sexually active daughters' perception that their mothers disapproved of them having sex predicted lower contraception use one year later (Sieving, Bearinger, Resnick, Pettingell, & Skay, 2007).

The theme of restrictions and arguments about dating and sexuality for daughters follows along this prohibitive approach to protecting daughters' sexual health. Instead of creating an environment for open and safe dialogue and guidance about sexuality, this approach may encourage daughters to keep their sexual experiences secret (O'Sullivan et al., 2001), thereby creating missed opportunities to promote sexual risk reduction at critical times in their transition to sexual activity. This environment of conflict, secrecy, and missed opportunities has important implications for daughters' sexual risk.

Mothers' lack of openness, comfort, and rapport in parent-adolescent sex discussions is associated with greater adolescent sexual risk behaviors (Dutra, Miller, & Forehand, 1999; Fasula & Miller, 2006; Kotchick, Dorsey, Miller, & Forehand, 1999; Whitaker et al., 1999). In addition, risk reduction messages are more effective if they are given before adolescents become sexually active (Kirby, Barth, Leland, & Fetro, 1991; Miller, Levin et al., 1998). For instance, in a study using the full FARBCS data, mothers talked to sons about condoms earlier than daughters and these condom discussions predicted adolescent condom use at first and subsequent intercourse—but only if the discussion happened prior to sexual debut (Miller, Levin et al., 1998). Furthermore, adolescents' lack of condom use at first intercourse was associated with a 20-fold decrease in the likelihood of future regular condom use (Miller, Levin et al., 1998).

Finally, even when mothers encouraged their daughters to obtain, carry, and use condoms their sexual guidance was abstract and removed. Positive attitudes and encouragement for sexual risk reduction behaviors are essential, but not sufficient to ensure condom use. Daughters still need to seek out condom skills, knowledge, and access before they can use them correctly.

Thus, under the ideology of the SDS, mothers' sexual socialization is likely to be less effective in helping their daughters learn to avoid sexual risk and more likely to deny their daughters the agency they need to prevent negative sexual outcomes. Teaching adolescents to delay sexual intercourse has a great deal of merit. However, when it is done by making them less knowledgeable about their own sexuality, promoting male privilege and female passivity, and limiting risk reduction skills and access, it does not adequately equip young women to take control of their sexual experiences. Furthermore, it can create critical missed opportunities to help daughters establish behaviors that can set the stage for a lifetime of healthy sexual behaviors.

In contrast to the neutral and prohibitive approaches for daughters, mothers' sexual risk reduction socialization for sons outlines an ideal comprehensive, proactive approach to ensuring sons' sexual health. First, mothers used "teachable moments" in their sons' sexual development to open a dialogue for relevant, information- and skill-based sexual discussions. Condoms were introduced early in their pubertal development, so that sons could develop attitudes and expectations about sexuality that included safer sex practices. And mothers reduced one of the critical steps necessary for condom use—they provided sons with direct access to condoms.

Public Health Implications

. . . At the individual level, adolescent sexual guidance programs can provide young African American women with the knowledge and skills to identify and communicate their own sexual needs, and help them feel that it is empowering, rather than shameful, to be in command of their own sexuality. For both male and female youth, they can also illuminate and challenge SDS expectations, and encourage heterosexual scripts that emphasize open communication, mutual respect, and responsibility between partners.

At the familial level, public health initiatives can support African American families through group-level interventions where parents can come together, share their stories, and gain support from one another. Given the importance of religion in this sample, it may be particularly useful for parents to connect with other parents in their religious organizations. In such supportive environments, parents can explore their own SDS attitudes, learn about the negative implications of the SDS, and develop the confidence and tools to talk to their sons and daughters about sexuality without reinforcing the SDS. Programs should also emphasize that the SDS already puts daughters at a disadvantage for sexual risk reduction preparation. To counteract these negative effects on daughters' sexual risk reduction it is even more important that parents provide them with comprehensive, proactive sexual risk reduction socialization.

Finally, the study findings revealed that daughters in particular may receive incomplete sexual risk reduction socialization at home. Thus, community-level programs can fill critical gaps in providing young women with the information, encouragement, and resources they need to protect themselves from HIV and other negative sexual health outcomes.

REFERENCES

Anderson, R. N., & Smith, B. L. (2005). Deaths: Leading causes for 2002. *National Vital Statistics Reports, 53*(17).

Campbell, C. A. (1995). Male gender roles and sexuality: Implications for women's AIDS risk prevention. *Social Science Medicine, 41*(2), 197–210.

CDC. (2004, 7/31/06). HIV/AIDS surveillance in adolescents and young adults (through 2004). Retrieved 1/11/07, 2007, from http://www.cdc.gov/hiv/topics/surveillance/resources/slides/adolescents/index.htm

CDC. (2005). *HIV/AIDS surveillance report, 2004. Vol. 16.* Atlanta: US Department of Health and Human Services. Centers for Disease Control and Prevention.

Connell, R. W. (1987). *Gender and power: Society, the person and sexual politics.* Stanford: Stanford University Press.

Dahl, D. W., Darke, P. R., Gorn, G. J., & Weinberg, C. B. (2005). Promiscuous or confident? Attitudinal ambivalence toward condom purchase. *Journal of Applied Social Psychology, 35*(4), 869–887. doi:10.1111/j.1559 1816.2005.tb02150.x

DiIorio, C., Hockenberry-Eaton, M., Maibach, E., Rivero, T., & Miller, K. S. (1996). The content of African American mothers' discussions with the adolescents about sex. *Journal of Family Nursing, 2*(4), 365–382.

DiIorio, C., Kelley, M., & Hockenberry-Eaton, M. (1999). Communication about sexual issues: Mothers, fathers, and friends. *Journal of Adolescent Health, 24*(3), 181–189.

DiIorio, C., Pluhar, E., & Belcher, L. (2003). Parent-child communication about sexuality: A review of the literature from 1980–2002. *Journal of HIV/AIDS Prevention & Education for Adolescents & Children, 5*(3/4), 7–32.

Downie, J., & Coates, R. (1999). The impact of gender on parent-child sexuality communication: Has anything changed? *Sexual and Marital Therapy, 14*(2), 109–121.

Dutra, R., Miller, K. S., & Forehand, R. (1999). The process and content of sexual communication with adolescents in two-parent families: Associations with sexual risk-taking behavior. *AIDS and Behavior, 3*(1), 59–66.

Espiritu, Y. L. (2001). 'We don't sleep around like white girls do': Family, culture, and gender in Filipina American lives. *Journal of Women in Culture and Society, 26*(2), 415–440. doi:10.1086/495599

Eyre, S. L., Hoffman, V., & Millstein, S. G. (1998). The gamesmanship of sex: A model based on African American adolescent accounts. *Medical Anthropology Quarterly, 12*(4), 467–489.

Fasula, A. M., & Miller, K. S. (2006). African-American and Hispanic adolescents' intentions to delay first intercourse: Parental communication as a buffer for sexually active peers. *Journal of Adolescent Health, 38*(3), 193–200. doi:10.1016/j.jadohealth.2004.12.009

Fine, M. (1988). Sexuality, schooling, and adolescent females: The missing discourse of desire. *Harvard Educational Review, 58*(1), 29–53.

Fullilove, M. T., Fullilove, R. E., III, Haynes, K., & Gross, S. (1990). Black women and AIDS prevention: A view towards understanding the gender rules. *The Journal of Sex Research, 27*(1), 47–64.

Giltnore, S., DeLamater, J., & Wagstaff, D. (1996). Sexual decision making by inner city black adolescent males: A focus group study. *Journal of Sex Research, 33*(4), 363–371.

Hartley, H., & Drew, T. (2001). Gendered messages in sex ed films: Trends and implications for female sexual problems. *Women and Therapy, 24*(1/2), 133–146. doi:10.1300/J015v24n01_16

Hillier, L., Harrison, L., & Bowditch, K. (1999). 'Never-ending love' and 'blowing your load': The meanings of sex to rural youth. *Sexualities, 2*(1), 69–88.

Holland, J., Ramazanoglu, C., Sharpe, S., & Thomson, R. (2004). *The male in the head: Young people, heterosexuality and power* (second ed.). London: The Tufnell Press.

Hutchinson, J. F. (1999). The hip hop generation: African American male-female relationships in a nightclub setting. *Journal of Black Studies, 30*(1), 62–84.

Kirby, D., Barth, R., Leland, N., & Ferro, J. (1991). Reducing the risk: Impact of a new curriculum on sexual risk-taking. *Family Planning Perspectives, 23,* 253–263.

Kotchick, B. A., Dorsey, S., Miller. K. S., & Forehand, R. (1999). Adolescent sexual risk-taking behavior in single-parent ethnic minority families. *Journal of Family Psychology, 13*(1), 93–102.

Levin, M. L., & Robertson, A. A. (2002). Being prepared: Attitudes and practices related to condom carrying among minority adolescents. *Journal of HIV/AIDS Prevention & Education for Adolescents & Children, 5*(1/2), 103–121. doi:10.1300/J129v05n01_07

Loxley, W. (1996). 'Sluts' or 'sleazy little animals'? Young people's difficulties with carrying and using condoms. *Journal of Community & Applied Social Psychology, 6*(4), 293–298.

Miller, K. S., Kotchick, B. A., Dorsey, S., Forehand, R., & Ham, A. Y. (1998). Family communication about sex: What are parents saying and are their adolescents listening? *Family Planning Perspectives, 30*(5), 218–235.

Miller, K. S., Levin, M. L., Whitaker, D. L., & Xu, X. (1998). Patterns of condom use among adolescents: The impact of mother-adolescent communication. *American Journal of Public Health, 88*(10), 1542–1544.

Monahan, J. L., Miller, L. C., & Rothspan, S. (1997). Power and intimacy: On the dynamics of risky sex. *Health Communication, 9*(4), 303–321.

Muehlenhard, C. L. (1988). 'Nice women' don't say yes and 'real men' don't say no: How miscommunication and the double standard can cause sexual problems. *Women and Therapy, 7*(2–3), 95–108.

Muehlenhard, C. L., & McCoy, M. L. (1991). Double standard/double bind: The sexual double standard and women's communication about sex. *Psychology of Women Quarterly, 15,* 447–461.

Nolin, M. J., & Petersen, K. K. (1992). Gender differences in parent-child communication about sexuality. *Journal of Adolescent Research, 7*(1), 59–79.

O'Sullivan, L. F., Meyer-Bahlburg, H. F. L., & Watkins, B. X. (2001). Mother-daughter communication about sex among urban African American and Latino families. *Journal of Adolescent Research, 16*(3), 269–292.

Rosenthal, D. A., & Feldman, S. S. (1999). The importance of importance: Adolescents' perceptions of parental communication about sexuality. *Journal of Adolescence, 22*(6), 835–851.

Sieving, R., Bearinger, L., Resnick. M. D., Pettingell, S., & Skay, C. (2007). Adolescent dual method use: Relevant attitudes, normative beliefs and self-efficacy. *Journal of Adolescent Health, 40*(3), 275.e215-275.e.222.doi: 10.1016/j.jadohealth.2006.10.003

Tanenbaum, L. (2000). *Slut!: Growing up female with a bad reputation.* New York: Perennial.

Thompson, S. (1990). Putting a big thing into a little hole: Teenage girls' accounts of sexual initiation. *The Journal of Sex Research, 27,* 341–361.

Thompson, S. (1995). *Going all the way: Teenage girls' vales of sex, romance, and pregnancy.* New York: Hill and Wang.

Tolman, D. L. (1996). Adolescent girls' sexuality: Debunking the myth of the urban girl. In N. Way (Ed.), *Urban girls: Resisting stereotypes, creating identities* (pp. 255–271). New York: New York University Press.

Tolman, D. L. (2002). *Dilemmas of desire: Teenage girls talk about sexuality.* Cambridge, MA: Harvard University Press.

Tolman, D. L., & Brown, L. M. (2001). Adolescent girls' voices: Resonating resistance in body and soul. In R. K. Unger (Ed.), *Handbook of the psychology of women and gender* (pp. 133–155). New York: John Wiley & Sons, Inc.

Tolman, D. L., & Debold, E. (1994). Conflicts of body image: Female adolescents, desire, and the no-body body. In S. Wooley (Ed.), *Feminist perspectives on eating disorders* (pp. 301–317). New York: The Guilford Press.

Whitaker, D. J., Miller, K. S., May, D. C., & Levin, M. L. (1999). Teenage partners' communication about sexual risk and condom use: The importance of parent-teenager discussions. *Family Planning Perspectives, 31*(3), 117–121.

Whitley, B., & Schofield, J. W. (1986). A meta-analysis of research on adolescent contraceptive use. *Population and Environment, 8,* 173–203.

Wight, D. (1992), Impediments to safer heterosexual sex: A review of research with young people. *AIDS Care, 4*(1), 11–21.

Wilkins, A. C. (2004). Puerto Rican wannabes: Sexual spectacle and the marking of race, class, and gender boundaries. *Gender and Society, 18*(1), 103–121. doi:10.1177/0891243203259505

Wingood, G. M., & DiClemente, R. J. (1998). Partner influences and gender-related factors associated with non-condom use among young adult African American women. *American Journal of Community Psychology, 26*(1), 29–51. doi:10.1300/J013v46n02_02

Going Too Far?

Sex, Sin and Social Policy

Susan Rose

"What if I want to have sex outside of marriage?" "I guess you'll just have to be prepared to die."

—*No Second Chance*

The United States leads the industrialized world in teen pregnancy, abortion and sexually-transmitted disease rates—and in legislating and funding abstinence-until-marriage programs as social policy. It also stands out as the only industrialized country still embroiled in a debate about whether creationism should be taught in public schools. These issues help reveal the dynamic interplay between religion and politics in the United States. In examining the role and power of conservative religious groups in shaping domestic and foreign policy, this paper focuses on the issues of reproductive and sexual health, education and family—and the impact they have on young people. . . .

[T]his study presents a comparative analysis of Danish and U.S. approaches to family planning, reproductive health and sexuality education. . . . The case of Denmark is informative because the rates of teen pregnancy and attitudes towards sexuality 50 years ago were not much different than those in the United States. Since the 1970s, however, Denmark has taken a much more pragmatic approach to teen sexuality and sex education. Although Danish and American teens tend to have similar patterns of sexual debut and activity, Danish teens have much lower rates of teenage pregnancy, abortion and sexually transmitted diseases (STDs). . . . Today the dominant

Danish discourse about sexuality and reproductive rights is strikingly different from the dominant discourse in the United States—not because Danes are by nature or nationality "just more open" about sex and Americans "just naturally more prudish"—rather, the debates over sexuality and reproductive rights and responsibility are rooted in different religious, political, economic and community orientations.

Abstinence-Until-Marriage Programs in the United States

Since 1996, nearly $1 billion in state and federal funding has been allocated for abstinence-only education despite a lack of evidence supporting the effectiveness of this approach (Hauser 2004; Kirby [1997] 2000; Manlove et al. 2004; "New Studies" 2005; "Sex Education" 2002; "Waxman Report" 2004). . . .

Despite the declining teen pregnancy rates during the 1990s, 34 percent of teenage girls get pregnant at least once before they reach age 20, resulting in more than 850,000 teen pregnancies a year—the vast majority of which are unintended. At this level, the United States has the highest rate of teen pregnancy in the fully industrialized world. Roughly 9 million new STIs also occur among teenagers and young adults in the United States annually (Children's Defense Fund 2004; Henshaw 2004; "New Studies" 2005). By law, abstinence-only programs must have as their "exclusive purpose, teaching the social, psychological and health gains to be realized by abstaining from sexual activity." While this is a desirable option for young people, it is also problematic for many. By promoting abstinence-only education that omits complete, medically accurate information, U.S. policy ignores research, public opinion and the experience of other countries about what actually works to prevent teenage pregnancy and STIs.

The Waxman Report (December 2004), which examined school-based sex education curricula, concluded that many young people are receiving medically inaccurate or misleading information, often in direct contradiction to the findings of government scientists. Since 1999, several million children ages 9 to 18 have participated in the more than 100 federally-funded abstinence programs. After reviewing the 13 most commonly used curricula, Congressman Waxman's staff concluded that two of the curricula were accurate but 11 others . . . contain unproved claims, subjective conclusions or outright falsehoods regarding reproductive health, gender traits and when life begins (Connolly 2004; see also "Texas Teens Increased Sex After Abstinence Program" 2005; Waxman 2004).

In May 2002, the House of Representatives passed H.R. 473, the Personal Responsibility, Work and Family Protection Bill, which renewed funding of abstinence-only programs at the level of $50 million a year for the next five years. While there was opposition to the bill by many, including Rep. Lois Capps (D-Calif.) who argued that "abstinence programs are exaggerating the failure rate of condoms" and using "terror techniques to keep teens from having sex," the bill passed . . . with committee Republicans arguing that "it would be impossible to agree on what information is medically accurate."

Americans Teaching Fear

In abstinence-until-marriage materials, sex is often equated with death, disease and danger, fear surfaces as the primary message and tactic used to persuade young people to steer clear of sex before or outside of marriage. The abstinence-only video, "No Second Chance," used for middle-school Sex Respect audiences, juxtaposes discussions of having sex outside of marriage with images of men dying from AIDS. In "No Second Chance," an evangelical sex educator compares sex outside of marriage—not to the all-American game of baseball—but to playing Russian Roulette. She tells a classroom of young people that: "Every time you have sex, it's like pulling

the trigger—the only difference is, in Russian Roulette, you only have one in six chances of getting killed." When one boy asks, "what if I have sex before marriage?" he is told, "Well, I guess you'll just have to be prepared to die. And you'll probably take with you your spouse and one or more of your children." James Dobson's organization, Focus on the Family, distributes "No Second Chance" and its companion, "Sex, Lies, and the Truth." Both have been widely used in public, as well as Christian, schools throughout the United States (Kantor 1994; Mast 1983; "Teaching Fear" 1996). According to the organization's website (1999–2005), "Sex Respect" is now being used in 50 states and 23 countries.

Founder and president of the National Abstinence Clearing House in Sioux Falls, South Dakota, Leslie Unruh uses snakes to teach about STDs and the dangers of using condoms. "As she uncoils her nest of rubber vipers: Herbie Herpes, Wally Wart, Hester Hepatitis, Albert AIDS, Lucy Loss of Reputation—and don't forget—poor Pregnant Peggy Sue, she tells young people about the risks of sex before marriage." (Sternberg 2002). "Condoms," she says, "are overrated. 'We tell them condoms won't protect your heart, that latex won't stop human papilloma virus.'" (See also Brody 2003; quoted in Sternberg 2002.) Another abstinence-only curriculum, *Abstinence Works: A Notebook on Pre-Marital Chastity,* invokes the image of Mother Teresa (Driscol 1990). Displayed on its 1990 cover is a picture of Mother Teresa on one side and a picture of a skeleton on the other. Surrounding them in bold italics are the words:

> *Today I set before you Life or Death, Blessing or Curse. Oh, that you would Choose Life that you and your children might Live.*
>
> *—Deuteronomy 30:19*

Leslie Kantor, former director of the SIECUS Community Advocacy Project, conducted an extensive content analysis of abstinence-only sex-ed programs produced and promoted by Christian Right groups that are used in public schools. She concluded:

> *These programs omit the most fundamental information on contraception and disease prevention, perpetuate*

medical misinformation, and rely on religious doctrine and images of fear and shame in discouraging sexual activity.

Given this introduction to sexuality in increasing numbers of public schools across the United States (Dailard 2000; Landry et al. 1999), how are young Americans conditioned to think about and negotiate their own and others' sexuality? Once they marry—if they choose to marry—how will they deal with their sexuality and the sexuality of their spouses? Even within the context of a heterosexual marriage, how are such negative—even terrifying images—suddenly transformed? And what about those who do not live within the confines of a heterosexual marriage; those who are gay, lesbian or transgendered: or those who find themselves without a partner, be it through death, divorce or never marrying? Where should the lines between private belief and public policy be drawn?

The Religious Right represents some 10 percent of the adult American population. Their concerns about teenage sex and teen pregnancy clearly resonate with a larger public, but their solutions do not. Their influence on social policy is disproportionate to their numbers; the vast majority of the American public is supportive of sex education. A 2004 report on "Public Support for Comprehensive Sexuality Education" indicates that 93 percent of parents of junior high school students and 91 percent of parents of high school students believe it is very or somewhat important to have sex education as part of the school curriculum.[1] And young people? Eighty-two percent of adolescents ages 15–17 and 75 percent of young people ages 18–24 want more information on "how to protect yourself from HIV/AIDS and other STDs," "the different types of birth control that are available," and "how to bring up sexual health issues such as STDs and birth control with a partner" (Hoff 2003: pp. 70–71 and 111–112).

The electorate likewise shows support for comprehensive sexuality education: 63 percent of voters said they were more likely to vote for a candidate who supports comprehensive sex education, while only 10 percent of engaged voters supported abstinence-until-marriage programs in public schools ("Mobilizing Support" 2002). While 30 percent of American adults

agree with the statement "the federal government should fund sex education programs that have 'abstaining from sexual activity' as their only purpose," 67 percent of adults agree with the statement that "the money should be used to fund more comprehensive sex education programs that include information on how to obtain and use condoms and other contraceptives" (*Sex Education in America* 2000: 7). Although 28 percent of American adults agreed that "providing information about how to obtain and use condoms and other contraception might encourage teens to have sexual intercourse," 65 percent of adults believed that "not providing information about how to obtain and use condoms and other contraception might mean more teens will have unsafe sexual intercourse" (*Sex Education in America* 2004:22).

Even conservative Christians tend to support comprehensive sex education. A 1999 survey showed that 8 in 10 conservative Christians supported comprehensive sex education in high schools and 7 in 10 supported it in middle schools (Survey of America's Views 1999). Former President and CEO of SIECUS for 12 years and current president of "The Religious Institute on Sexual Morality, Justice and Healing," Deborah Haffner agrees, arguing that the majority of evangelicals support comprehensive sex education that includes abstinence as an option.[2]

In spite of millions of dollars in funding, to date, there are no sound empirical data that indicate that abstinence-only programs are effective; in fact, there have been very few evaluation studies of abstinence-until-marriage programs (Kirby 2001; Manlove 2004; "New State Evaluations" 2004). Empirical data also suggest that to the degree that an effect of comprehensive sex education has been identifiable, it has been found to *postpone* initiation of sexual intercourse; reduce the frequency of intercourse and number of sexual partners; increase the use of contraceptives; and reduce pregnancy rates among teens (Kirby [1997]; 2001; Schorr 1998; "Teaching Fear" 1994). Why, then, do abstinence-only approaches appeal to many politicians and policy-makers, even when the majority of Americans support comprehensive sex education? What are the consequences of implementing abstinence-only approaches compared with comprehensive sex education that includes abstinence as a reasonable and often desirable option? No one is debating whether abstinence should be presented as a viable option and reasonable choice. What critics are questioning is how *abstinence-until-marriage* programs came to masquerade as *education* in public schools. . . .

International Consequences: From Domestic to Foreign Policy

[R]ecent actions to limit reproductive health reveal the ways in which the United States is retreating from its own previous position and that of its traditional allies around the world (LaFranchi 2004). On his first day in office in January 2001, President Bush reimposed the "global gag rule" that had been instituted by President Reagan in 1984 and revoked by President Clinton in 1993. Imposing the United States' position on the abortion practices of other countries, however, reflects neither U.S. law nor U.S. public opinion. It also significantly impedes women's access to family planning and contraceptive services by prohibiting U.S. family planning assistance to hospitals and health clinics in developing countries that also provide abortions or abortion-related information (Cohen 2001).

At the U.N. Children's Summit in May 2002, U.S. Health Secretary Tommy Thompson argued for the teaching of abstinence as the preferred approach to sex education. According to a CBS World News report, "The three-day conference was long on rhetoric about the sanctity of childhood but short on consensus. Delegates at a U.N. session on children haggled . . . over a final declaration with the United States, the Vatican and Islamic states in favor of sexual abstinence and against any hint of abortion for adolescents" (Ireland 2002; U.N. Children's Summit Hits Snag 2002). Susan Cohen, writing for the Guttmacher Institute, reported that: "The United States delegation, siding with the Sudan, Iran, and Iraq" (and sliding perilously close to Bush's "evil axis"), "both stupefied and angered the European (EU) and Latin American delegations which finally voted against the U.S. position." Adrienne Germain,

president of the International Women's Health Coalition, bluntly stated:

This alliance shows the depths of perversity of the [U.S.] position. On the one hand, we're presumably blaming these countries for unspeakable acts of terrorism, and at the same time we are allying ourselves with them in the oppression of women.

—*quoted in Cohen 2002*

In its closing statement at the summit, the EU delivered a strong rejoinder to the United States. "Young people should be empowered to make appropriate and safe choices about their sexual behavior.". . .

Likewise, in the seven-day Asian and Pacific Population Conference held in Bangkok in December 2002, the American delegation engaged in an acrimonious debate with all of the other countries over abortion, sex education and methods of birth control (Dao 2002). . . . Rejecting proposals by the Bush Administration, 32 Asian nations reaffirmed the historic agreement reached at the 1994 International Conference on Population and Development (ICPD). They also agreed on an action plan to advance reproductive and sexual health and rights across the region (Caucus for ICPD 2002; Statement by Obaid 2002; "U.S. Fails to Block" 2002).

"It is sad to see the U.S. move from being a leader on these issues, to that of a minority voice," said Ninuk Widyantoro of the Women's Health Foundation in Indonesia:

Sexual and reproductive health is one of the most important social issues of the millennium. We know that the U.S. delegation does not even represent the views of the majority of the American people. The current U.S. administration is being held hostage by an extreme conservative minority with little regard for the health, welfare and freedoms of women. . . . We hope that in the future, U.S. delegations . . . will more accurately represent the humanitarian values of the women and men of their nation.

—*quoted in Dao 2001*

Such positions have distanced the United States even further from the worldwide consensus on reproductive and sexual health issues that the United States had once been instrumental in shaping. . . .

Cross-National Data on Teen Sexual Behavior

The United States leads the industrialized world in its high rates of teenage pregnancies, abortions and STDs. Although the U.S. *teen pregnancy rate* has decreased during the past decade, it is still nine times higher than that of the Netherlands, nearly five times higher than in Germany, and nearly four times higher than the rate in France. The *teen birth rate* is also much higher in the United States, nearly 11 times higher than in the Netherlands, nearly five times higher than the rate in France, and nearly four times higher than in Germany.[3] The *teen abortion rate* is nearly eight times higher in the United States than in Germany, nearly seven times higher than in the Netherlands, and nearly three times higher than in France (Feijoo 2001). Much higher rates for HIV, syphilis, gonorrhea and chlamydia likewise distinguish the United States (Darroch et al. 2001; Feijoo 2001).

Cross-national studies reveal that differential rates in teen pregnancy are influenced by cultural attitudes towards and education about sexuality, the accessibility of health care and contraception, the relationship between religion and politics, and the degree of economic inequality (Jones et al. 1996). With one of the highest rates of infant mortality, child death, child poverty and economic inequality between rich and poor in the industrialized world, the United States is not faring well (Brouwer 1998; Henshaw 2004; Kids Count 2000; "New Studies" 2005; Shapiro 1992; Singh et al. 2000; *State of America's Children* 2004). Rather than deal with these complex and interrelated issues, however, U.S. policy too often addresses teen pregnancy as an isolated social problem and increasingly advises young girls to *"just say no."*

Just Say No

Abstinence-only advocates advise young people to not have sex; their aim, however, is to curtail sexual activity for anyone not in a heterosexual marriage. Uneasy about teen sexuality, homosexuality, the increase in out-of-wedlock births, and the erosion of the patriarchal, nuclear family, they emphasize the dangers of sex and the hazards of sexual relationships outside of marriage (Gallagher 1999). Fear rather than affirmation, rejection rather than acceptance, and denial rather than knowledge about sexuality tend to dominate abstinence-only materials, and serve as a chilling effect on contemporary American research and social policy.

For example, in 1987 a number of institutes . . . supported a proposal by Edward Laumann, et al., to undertake an ambitious study of sexuality in America. Scientists . . . "wanted more general studies of sexuality to then examine such issues as teen pregnancy, sexual dysfunction and child abuse." But soon after the contract was awarded, the researchers noted that (America's) "national squeamishness about sex" began to emerge (Michael et al. 1994: 27; Nussbaum 1997). Government officials in particular were squeamish about the inclusion of questions about masturbation—evidenced also in the forced resignation of former U.S. Surgeon General Jocelyn Elders for using the M-word (masturbation). Political battles followed. . . . As a result, the researchers conducted the study through private money; the sample was reduced from 20,000 to 3,500 adults, and no one under the age of 18 was included in the sample (Boonstra 2001; Nussbaum 1997:225). . . .

In contrast to the current U.S. trends in legislating abstinence-only policies, Denmark—and many other countries both in the industrialized and developing world—continue to implement more comprehensive research and sex education programs, believing that it is important to inform and educate young people about sexuality and contraception. They believe that adolescents have a right to information (Alford 2005).

Attitudes toward Teen Sexuality in the United States and Denmark

Case Study: The United States

Since the 1960s, Religious Right political groups have waged a campaign against the teaching of comprehensive sex education in public schools. . . . Phyllis Schafly, head of the conservative Eagle Forum, went as far as to argue that exposing children in public schools to sex ed may constitute child abuse

(1985). Their position was clear: any discussion about sex belonged in the home, not in the schools.

By the 1980s, however, it was clear that the Religious Right was having little success in removing sex education from the schools.[4] As a result, conservative Christian groups shifted strategies and began to promote "abstinence-only" programs in the public schools. . . . Through a range of educational materials, videotapes and promotional advertising, they have effectively promoted curricula that teach fear and withhold vital information about prevention of AIDS and teen pregnancy.

Programs such as "Sex Respect," "Facing Reality" and curricula developed by Teen Aid initially . . . received federal Title XX funding through the Adolescent Family Life Act (AFLA). . . . The state and federal money used to fund "Sex-Respect" was essential, according to a writer for the *Conservative Digest:*

> . . . the Adolescent Family Life Act was written expressly for the purpose of diverting [federal] money that would otherwise go to Planned Parenthood into groups with traditional values. This noble purpose has certainly been fulfilled here.
>
> —quoted in (Teaching Fear 1994: 11)

While rates of pregnancy, AIDS and other sexually transmitted diseases remain alarmingly high among America's youth, opponents of sex education have become increasingly successful in censoring vital, life-saving information that has proven effective in dealing with these problems (Kantor 1994).

Beyond Sex: Teaching Traditional Gender Roles

Central to the sex ed debate is the Religious Right's attempt to preserve patriarchy and to privilege men's rights over women's rights and parental rights over children's rights (Bendroth 1993; Hawley 1994; Howland 1997; Marty and Appleby 1999; Riesebrodt 1993). The idea of equality between men and women is threatening to many advocates of abstinence-only policies. Not only are they working to prevent sex before or outside of marriage, they are also fighting to preserve the traditional, patriarchal family. The pro-marriage movement goes hand-in-hand with this

(Gallagher 1999; Stacey 2002) as does the promotion of old-fashioned gender-role norms.

As one reads through the abstinence-only materials, one finds an old and mixed message. It is the story of sex as the tale of predator and prey—and women, beware. Men are considered to be sexual beings, who beyond a certain point, cannot hold back. Therefore, women must. . . .

The Religious Right's concern about sex and sexuality focuses on issues regarding social order and control—especially over women's bodies and desires. The adage that "good girls don't" but "real boys do" continues to engender the double-standard that defines male and female in opposition to one another, although many of the abstinence-only curricula are pushing for abstinence for all pre-marrieds. This framework, however, reveals contradictions. From a conservative Christian perspective, humans are not animals (which is at the crux of the evolution-creation debate), rather they stand only a little lower than the angels. Yet, they are also seen as no different from animals driven by sexual instincts: once aroused, there is no turning back. These distinctions sound very familiar because they are part of the "sexual wisdom" of American culture that goes well beyond the confines of conservative Christian thinking. . . .

The renewed efforts to undermine sex education are not just about sex; they are part of a broader challenge to public education which centers around parents' vs. children's and states' rights.

Gender and Sexual Politics of the Religious Right

The attempts of the Religious Right in the United States to preserve parental rights over those of children's rights reveal the kind of hostility directed towards women and children. In his critique of the Fourth World Conference on Women, Gary Bauer, president of the Family Research Council, wrote that feminists wanted "to enshrine the 'rights' of adolescents to information and medical services where sex and AIDS were concerned, without 'interference' from parents" and that although, "parents rights were not completely overruled, they were subordinated to 'the best interests of the child.'" Moreover, "these radical women are trying to achieve greater equality between women and men in economic and political spheres, so that women can better support their families and children" (Bauer 1995). . . .

Different Discourses: The Danish Approach

The dominant Danish discourse about sexuality and reproductive and teens' rights is strikingly different from the dominant discourse in the United States (Adolescent Sexual Health 2001; see also Heins 2001; "Sexuality Rights" 1995). In Denmark, the rights of adolescents to sexual and reproductive information and choice are framed within the context of a *social democracy* and have been embedded in Danish legislation since 1966. . . .

> *Denmark became the first country in the world to grant young people, regardless of age, access to contraception and contraception counseling. . . . It's about human rights: in order for you to act responsibly, you have to have choices—government or parents or whoever the decision makers are cannot demand responsible behavior of teenagers or of the population if they don't give them an opportunity to make their own choices based on sufficient information. . . . We have developed an enabling environment for young people to support themselves in the process of making their sexual identity and realizing themselves as becoming adults—and sexuality is an important part of becoming an adult. . . . Young people have the right to ask and they have a right to be met with respect . . . they shouldn't be let down, they should be supported. (Rasmussen, 1998)*

Rasmussen also argued that progressive social policies recognizing adolescent sexuality have not promoted promiscuity.

> *From the outside, (it seems that) we in Denmark have the most liberal system of adolescent sexual and reproductive health and rights. Seen from the inside, however, we don't tend to think that we have a very liberal system. We tend to think that we have a very practical and pragmatic approach to the fact that young people do start having sexual relations somewhere in their teens. In Denmark, actually rather late: around 16.7 for boys and even 16.9 for girls, and it really hasn't changed very much over time. And 80 percent of young people use contraception at first intercourse. That may not be enough but it's a very favorable situation. (See also Knudsen 1999.)*

Historically, dominant Danish attitudes towards sexuality were not so different from mainstream American ones (Centerwall 1995; "Sexual Rights" 1995). Within the past three decades, however, we find Danes much more open about sexuality and contraceptive use than Americans (David et al. 1990). The Danish government has mandated the teaching of comprehensive sex education as part of the general school curriculum. These programs tend to be quite pragmatic and straightforward, without being graphic, which is hard for many Americans to envision.

One of the sex ed videos used in elementary schools, "Where Do Babies Come From," is a cartoon-animated video that presents four children talking, laughing and giggling with one another as they share questions and information about where babies come from. Covering female and male anatomy, menstruation, intercourse and birthing, the video presents a lot of information in a very funny yet direct way. When I showed this to my college class, students said that it was the best—the most informative and the funniest—"documentary" they had ever seen on sex education. The video demystifies sex and invites the audience to laugh with the children and couple, who are loving, affectionate—and yes—sexual with one another. The message reflects the reality that kids are curious and have lots of questions, that talking about sex can be both embarrassing and fun, and that it's as much about feelings, caring and love as it is about biology.

Young People's Perspectives

Individual interviews and co-ed classroom and small-group discussions (both same sex and co-ed) with approximately 100 Danish and 300 American teens revealed significant differences in how they spoke about sexuality and relationships. The Danish teens tended to talk about sex in terms of mutual pleasure and responsibility whereas the American teens tended to speak in terms of performance and achievement (as in "feeling inadequate if they didn't *achieve* orgasm"). When asked when "no means no," both Danish boys and girls were quite clear: "when someone says no, that means no." Their language did not assume that the male was the predator and the female the prey who was the one pressured into having sex. For example, one 15-year-old boy in the presence of his male and female classmates said:

> If I don't feel like it, then I want that to be OK. If my girlfriend doesn't like something, well then we try something else. If one of us doesn't want to, then we find another way. Or we go for a walk.

A 15-year-old girl in the same class commented:

> If a girl says no and she really means yes, well then she's the one who misses out—she could have said yes if she wanted to.

In discussions with American teenagers, there was much less consensus. Deciding when "no meant no" was seen as a very confusing judgment call, and there was greater tolerance for—or at least more willingness to not speak out against—sexually aggressive behavior. In the American classrooms, those who came right out and said "if someone says no, that means no" were in the minority. Typically there would be a prolonged conversation about whether a person (always assumed to be a female) was clear in her own mind, whether she really meant no when she said no, how forcefully or frequently she said no, whether she was giving double messages either verbally or non-verbally, what the girl was wearing, and how she was acting when she said no. The same ambivalence or confusion was expressed in small-group discussions and individual interviews as well.

The discourse among American teenagers also was gendered in ways that the Danish discourse about sexual responsibility and responsiveness was not. In the American context, only females were referred to as saying "no" or being ambivalent about having sex; not once was the male pronoun used to speak of someone saying "no." When it came to talking about women's ambivalence, the discussion often led to girls and women being untrustworthy rather than confused or conflicted about what they wanted, or their being unclear in their expression of what they did and did not want. The blame for *mis*communication was placed, as much by other women as by men, on the female. Often the conversation in the American classroom would fall back on: "I have known girls who tease men;" ". . . who say no when they mean yes;" "You can't blame the guys." "If the girl teases a guy,

then she has to be ready to get what she gets." "After a certain point, you can't expect a guy to just stop." In the Danish context, both male and female teenagers put responsibility on the individual to say what he or she meant, and they held the individual responsible for *his or her* actions (including contraceptive choices). In the American context, more responsibility and blame was placed on the female especially if something went wrong. . . .

This seemed to be much less of a quandary for the Danish girls interviewed. While some of them had sex that was not particularly pleasurable, they were less likely to have experienced unwanted or forced sex and much more likely to know what they wanted and didn't want. They also were much less likely to confuse love and sexual desire. For the Danish young people and their parents, it was OK to have sex with someone once you turned 16 or 17. Validation did not depend on how much you were in love with the other person, but how responsible you were in making decisions. Becoming sexual was considered a part of normal development, of growing up.

> Love is such a strong word. I have a boyfriend and I care about him. We're having sex and that's OK with my parents. They know. They just want us to be protected. He can sleep over at my house. But, I can't say I love him. Love and hate are such strong words. My parents, and my sisters and my brother—I love them. I've known them all my life. But my boyfriend, I've only known him a few months. We need to know each other more. It should be really deep when you say that.
>
> —17-year-old Danish girl

> I really love my boyfriend. So I think it's OK I'm having sex with him. But if my parents caught me, they would kill me!
>
> —17-year-old American girl

Lene, the Danish girl, takes love quite seriously. It is not a word to be thrown about easily. Sex, on the other hand, is not a big deal. It's fun, but you need to take care to use protection so you don't get AIDS or an infection. Elena, the American girl emphasizes love. Because she's in love, it's OK to have sex. Elena is both sincere and adamant when she says, "I really love my boyfriend," but then she leans forward and whispers, "But if my parents caught me, they would kill me. If they knew, it would be all over. I don't know why they can't understand how much we love each other."

Another striking contrast between the Danish and American teenagers was their attitude towards alcohol and sex. While the American teenagers reported that they or their friends often drink in order to lower their inhibitions to have sex, the Danish teenagers believed that alcohol and sex were not a good match. A small group of 15- to 17-year-old Danish girls commented:

> It ruins it if you're drunk I think. If the boy's very drunk he can't get it up. He can't get [an] erection and that ruins it a lot. So I think you shouldn't do it if you're drunk. And you forget the condom if you're drunk. It's easier to have good sex if you're not drunk.

A 15-year-old boy concurred,

> If you're drunk, you can't do it very well and it doesn't feel as good. If I really like a girl, I don't drink before we have sex.

The Danish girls were also more open in talking about sexuality, communication and intimacy:

> But I think you have to be comfortable. If you feel totally comfortable and safe with the person, you do more things. So I think you can have sex and all, but the more safe and the more comfortable you get with the person the more wild the things get the more open you get with your boyfriend.
>
> —16-year-old Danish girl

. . . What both Danish and American young people emphasized was their desire for more information and discussion about feelings, emotions and relationships. They wanted more communication with their parents and teachers. Many of them faced problems at home: a parent's alcoholism, abuse, depression that often made that communication difficult.

For example, Laura, an American 14-year-old girl shared her story just after attending an abstinence-only assembly at her rural school in central Pennsylvania. . . .

> My Mom got pregnant when she was 16 and had to really struggle. Then when my older sister got pregnant at 16, my Mom was really angry. She wouldn't talk to her

about sex or getting pregnant; and she doesn't talk to me. She just yells and tells me "not to do it." You can't have a reasonable conversation with her about it. And now it's really crazy at home with my sister's baby, and everyone crying and screaming. It's nuts. I think we need to know more about sex not less.

Laura felt left in the lurch both at home and at school when it came to sex education. The school counselor who sat in with us agreed: "They deserve more—better." Both American and Danish teenagers wanted parents and teachers to trust them more, respect them more, and teach them more. They believed they needed more, rather than less, information, but it was the American teenagers who pointed to the number of their friends, sisters or school mates who had gotten pregnant as proof. . . .

Adolescent Rights as Human Rights: The Danish Case

. . . Since the 1960s, with the activism of the labor, women's, and disabilities' movements, young people's rights were also recognized and given a more prominent place in Danish society.

> *During the '60s, the Danish Welfare Society . . . realized that young people were equal members of society and should share the same benefits of belonging to society as adults. If we want people to behave responsibly, we have to give them the chance to . . . The government saw the benefits of this—if you give them (young people) the option, you can also demand that they behave responsibly.*
>
> *—Rasmussen*

This was a recurrent theme in interviews with teachers, as well as with sex educators and professionals working in the area of reproductive health. Bjarne Rasmussen, AIDS-Secretariat at the Frederiksberg Hospital . . . explained in a 1998 interview:

> *It's important not to cheat young people. . . . To be honest in sexual education, especially in the schools because if the young people find out that you are cheating them, they won't believe you later on. It's very, very important to get a discussion going. It's important to make the young people understand that they make their own choice. They must make an active choice and say 'I want to use contraception' or 'I don't want to use*

contraception' because they have made the choice and they are involved.

Conclusion

Who then is going too far? The Danes in providing information or the Americans in withholding information? While the onset of sexual activity for Danes is similar to that of Americans, both averaging around 16.7 years, Danish teenagers are more likely to use contraception and are much less likely to get pregnant, have an abortion or contract a sexually transmitted disease. There are also proportionately fewer Danish 11 to 14 year olds who have been engaged in sexual activity (B. Rasmussen [1997] 1998). . . .

In the American context, special interest groups vie for power and often have disproportionate influence. This is the case with sexuality education and reproductive health in general. Numerous mainstream organizations, including medical, government, and religious agencies, are supportive of comprehensive sexuality education. Many signed a letter to President Bush stating that they "are committed to responsible sexuality education for young people that includes age-appropriate, medically accurate information about both abstinence and contraception, [and] urge [him] to reconsider increasing funding for unproven abstinence-only-until-marriage programs."[5] And while new bills are being introduced to better support comprehensive sexuality education, at the moment, abstinence-only programs continue to dominate the agenda.

Abstinence-only proponents not only provide medical misinformation and promote fear and ignorance, they also fail to plan, fund, and implement effective social policy that could more effectively curb teen pregnancy and the spread of STDs—and provide better economic, educational, and health opportunities for all young people. Experts on teen pregnancy and child welfare . . . convincingly argue that teen pregnancy is less about young girls and their sex lives than about restricted horizons and the boundaries of hope. Yet, the Religious Right continues to blame the "fallen girl/woman," the feminization of men, the decline of two-parent families, homosexuality, and the media for the ills of our society rather than economic and structural forces that perpetuate inequality between men and women, and between the enriched and impoverished classes. In the battle over sexuality and choice, it's girls' and women's bodies, lives, and livelihoods that are all too often sacrificed—blamed, marginalized and held accountable for creating the problem of teen pregnancy. . . .

[F]amily planning, reproductive and sexual health, and economic well-being are vital concerns for individuals, communities, and nations. The United States which is the only country that legislates and funds abstinence-only-until marriage programs in public schools, also leads the world in its high rates of teenage pregnancies, abortions, and STDs. Moreover, abstinence-only-until-marriage programs have been taught for over two decades and yet there is still no peer-reviewed research that proves it is effective.[6] While rates of pregnancy, AIDS, and other sexually transmitted diseases remain alarmingly high among America's youth and people in the developing world, opponents of sexuality education and reproductive health are trying to censor vital information and services both at home and abroad.

The Religious Right has not achieved its agenda, but it has produced a chilling effect on comprehensive sexuality education. . . . In the interest of all children, as well as family well-being, we need to take seriously a broad-based approach to both social problems and social policy that is based on empirical evidence and a recognition of the pluralistic society in which we live. This is what democracy is all about. In the final analysis, rather than having gone too far, the United States has not gone nearly far enough in providing reliable information, education and health care to our children.

NOTES

1. Only 4 percent of parents of junior high school students and 6 percent of parents of high school students believe sexuality education should not be taught in school ("Public Support" 2004).

2. Personal communication, January 2005.

3. Adolescent child-bearing is more common in the United States (22 percent of women reported having a child before age 20) than in Great Britain (15 percent), Canada

(11 percent), France (6 percent) and Sweden (4 percent). And the differences are even greater when comparing births to younger teenagers. A greater proportion of U.S. teenagers did not use contraception at either the first or most recent intercourse (25 percent and 20 percent respectively) than that reported in France (11 percent and 12 percent), Great Britain (21 percent and 4 percent), Sweden (22 percent and 7 percent) (Adolescent Sexual Health 2002; Darroch et al. 2001; Feijoo 2001; Jones et al. 1996; "Teenage Sexual and Reproductive 2001).

4. This fieldwork included classroom observations; class, small group, and one-on-one interviews with teenagers; and interviews with parents, teachers, and sex educators. In the case of the Central Pennsylvania School, 240 9th through 12th graders also filled out surveys in the week following the abstinence-only assemblies sponsored by Heartbeat Community Services. This number included all those in one of four health classes or a quarter of the high school population.

5. In 1981, a national poll indicated that 70 percent of parents favored sex-ed programs in the public schools; a 1985 poll showed 75 percent of adults approving sex-ed in the public high schools, with 52 percent approving of such programs in grades 4 through 8; most respondents also believed that programs should cover a wider range of topics, including teaching about birth control, the biology of reproduction, the nature of sexual intercourse and abortion ("Teaching Fear" 1994).

6. Studies conducted by Johns Hopkins researchers . . . indicate the effectiveness of sexuality education programs in delaying the age at first intercourse, increasing the use of contraception, and reducing pregnancy rates among teens. Researchers found no significant association between taking a course in sexuality education and being sexually active . . . (Schorr 1988; "Teaching Fear" 1994).

REFERENCES

Allord, S., N. Cheetham and D. Hauser. 2005. *Science and Success in Developing Countries: Holistic Programs That Work to Prevent Teen Pregnancy, HIV & Sexually Transmitted Infections.* Washington, D.C.: Advocates for Youth.

Bendroth, Margaret Lamberts. 1993. *Fundamentalism and Gender, 1875 to the Present.* Yale University Press.

Boonstra, Heather. 2004. "Abstinence-Promotion and the U.S. Approach to HIV/AIDS Prevention Overseas." *Issues in Brief.* The Alan Guttmacher Institute.

Brouwer, Steve. 1998. *Sharing the Pie: A Citizen's Guide to Wealth and Power.* Henry Holt & Co.

Children's Defense Fund. 2004. "Children's Defense Fund Blasts Withholding of Report on Hunger." Press Release: Oct. 24.

Cohen, Susan. June 2001. "Global Gag Rule: Exporting Antiabortion Ideology at the Expense of American Values." *The Guttmacher Report on Public Policy,* 4(3).

Connolly, Ceci. 2004. "Some Abstinence Programs Mislead Teens, Report Says." *Washington Post,* December 2, A01.

Dailard, Cynthia. April 2000. "Fueled by Campaign Promises, Drive Intensifies to Boost Abstinence-Only Education Funds." *The Guttmacher Report on Public Policy,* 3(2).

Dao, James. 2002. "Over U.S. Protest, Asian Group Approves Family Planning Goals." *New York Times,* December 18.

Darroch, Jacqueline, Singh Susheela, Jennifer J. Frost and the Study Team. November/December 2001. "Differences in Teenage Pregnancy Rates Among Five Developed Countries." *Family Planning Perspectives,* 33(6). The Alan Guttmacher Institute.

David, H. A., J. M. Morgall, M. Olser, et al. 1990. "United States and Denmark: Different Approaches to Health Care and Family Planning." *Studies in Family Planning,* 21:1–19.

Driscoll, Patricia. 1990. *Abstinence Works: A Notebook on Pre-Marital Chastity.* Womanity Publications.

Gallagher, Maggie. 1999. *The Age of Unwed Mothers Is Teen Pregnancy the Problem? A Report to the Nation.* New York: Institute for American Values. (http://www.americanvalues.org/Teen.PDF).

Hauser, Debra. 2004. Five Years of Abstinence-Only-Until-Marriage Education: Assessing the Impact. Washington, DC: Advocates for Youth.

Hawley, John, editor. 1994. *Fundamentalism and Gender.* Oxford University Press.

Heins, Marjorie. 2001. *Not in Front of the Children.* Hill & Wang.

Henshaw, S. K. 2004. *U.S. Teenage Pregnancy Statistics with Comparative Statistics for Women Aged 20–24.* New York: The Guttmacher institute.

Hoff, Tina, et al. 2003. *National Survey of Adolescents and Young Adults: Sexual Health Knowledge, Attitudes, and Experiences.* "National Survey of Adolescents and Young Adults: Sexual Health Knowledge, Attitudes, and Experiences." Henry J. Kaiser Family Foundation.

Howland, Courtney, editor. 1999. *Religious Fundamentalisms and the Human Rights of Women.* St. Martin's Press.

Ireland, Doug. May 27, 2002. "US and Evil Axis—Allies for Abstinence." *The Nation.*

Jones, Elise, et al. 1996. *Teenage Pregnancy in Industrialized Nations.* Yale University Press.

Kantor, Leslie. August/September 1994. "Attacks on Public School Sexuality Education Programs: 1993–94 School Year," *SIECUS Report.*

Kirby, Douglas. 1997. *No Easy Answers: Research Findings on Programs to Reduce Teen Pregnancy.* Washington, D.C. National Campaign Prevent Teen Pregnancy.

———. 2001. *Emerging Answers: Research Findings on Programs to Reduce Teen Pregnancy.* Washington, DC: National Campaign to Prevent Teen Pregnancy.

Knudsen, Lisbeth. 1999. "Recent Fertility Trends in Denmark." *Report 11.* Danish Center for Demographic Research.

Landry, D. J., L. Kaeser and C. L. Richards. 1999. Abstinence promotion and the provision of information about contraception in public school district sexuality education policies. *Family Planning Perspectives* 31(6):280–286.

LaFranci, Howard. 2004. "On Family Planning, U.S. vs. Much of the World: De-emphasis of Contraception Runs Contrary to Global Goals." *Christian Science Monitor.* March 30.

Manlove, Jennifer, Angela R. Papillio and Erum Ikramullah. September 2004. "Not Yet: Programs Designed to Delay First Sex Among Teens." Washington, DC: National Campaign to Prevent Teen Pregnancy.

Marty, Martin, and Scott Appleby (eds.). 1993. *Fundamentalisms and Society,* Vol 2. University of Chicago Press.

Mast, Coleen Kelly. 1977. "Sex Respect: The Option of True Sexual Feeling," *Student Handbook* (rev. ed.) 7. 90, Bradley, IL: Respect Incorporated.

Michael, Robert T., John H. Gagnon, Edward O. Laumann and Gina Kolata. 1994. *Sex in America: A Definitive Survey.* Little, Brown.

"Mobilizing Support for Sex Education: New Messages and Techniques." 2002. New York: The Othmer Institute of Planned Parenthood of NYC.

"New State Evaluations Show Federally Funded Abstinence-Only Programs Have Little Effect." September 27, 2004. Washington, D.C.: Advocates for Youth.

"New Studies Signal Dangers of Limiting Teen Access to Birth Control Information and Services: Researchers and Medical Experts Urge New Congress and State Legislatures to Heed Data." January 18, 2005. Media Release. New York: The Guttmacher Institute.

No Second Chance. Jeremiah Films.

Nussbaum, Martha. 1997. *Cultivating Humanity: A Classical Defense of Reform in Liberal Education.* Harvard University Press.

"Public Support for Comprehensive Sexuality Education." 2004. *SIECUS Fact Sheet.* (www.siecus.org/pubsfact/fact0017.htm)

Rasmussen, Bjarne. 1997. "Young People's Sexual Behavior," *Danish National Survey and Report.* AIDS Sekretariat, Frederiksberg Hospital, Denmark.

Rasmussen, Bjarne. June 1998. AIDS Sekretariat, Interview with the author.

Rasmussen, Nell. June 1998. Director of the Danish Family Planning Association, Copenhagen, Interview with author.

Riesebrodt, Martin. 1993. *Pious Passion: The emergence of modern fundamentalism in Iran and the United States.* University of California Press.

Schafly, Phyllis, editor. 1985. *Child Abuse in the Classroom.* Crossway Books.

Sex Education in America: A View from Inside the Nation's Classrooms. 2000. Menlo Park, CA: The Kaiser Family Foundation.

Schorr, Lisbeth. 1988. *Within Our Reach.* Anchor Press.

"Sex Education: Politicians, Parents, Teachers, and Teens." Issues in Brief. The Alan Guttmacher Institute. (www.agi-usa.org/pubs/ib_2–01.html)

Sex Respect Website (http://www.sexrespect.com/ProgramOrig.html).

Shapiro. 1992. *We're Number One.* Vintage Books.

Singh, Susheela and Jacqueline E. Darroch. 2000. "Adolescent Pregnancy and Childbearing: Levels and Trends in Developed Countries." *Family Planning Perspectives.* 32(1).

Stacey, Judith. July 9, 2001. "Family Values Forever." *The Nation.*

State of America's Children 2004. Children's Defense Fund.

Sternberg, Steve. 2002. "Sex Education Stirs Controversy." *USA Today.* July 11.

Survey of America's Views on Sexuality Education. 1999. Washington, DC: SIECUS and Advocates for Youth.

"Teaching Fear: The Religious Rights' Campaign Against Sexuality Education." 1996. People for the American Way. (http://www.pfaw.org/pfaw/general/default.aspx?oid=2025&print=yes&units=all).

"Texas Teens Increased Sex After Abstinence Program." January 31, 2005. Houston: Reuters.

"UN Children's Summit Hits Snag." May 10, 2002. (Reuters) CBS World News.

"U.S. Fails to Block Consensus at Bangkok Population Conference." 2002. International Women's Health Coalition. Posted Tuesday, December 17. (http://www.iwhc.org/index.cfm?fuseaction=page&pageID).

The Waxman Report. December 2004. "The Content of Federally Funded Abstinence-Only Education Programs." Prepared for Rep. Henry A. Waxman. U.S. House of Representatives Committee on Government Reform. Minority Staff Special Investigations Division. (http://www.democrats.reform.house.gov/Documents/20041201102153–50247.pdf).

Preventing STIs

Heather Boonstra

In his [2004] State of the Union address . . . , President Bush expounded on the dangers that young people face from exposure to sexually transmitted infections (STIs). "Each year, [millions of] teenagers contract sexually-transmitted diseases that can harm them, or kill them, or prevent them from ever becoming parents," he said. His prescription was simple: "We will double federal funding for abstinence programs, so schools can teach this fact of life: Abstinence for young people is the only certain way to avoid sexually-transmitted diseases.". . .

As teenage pregnancy rates have continued to fall, STIs have largely replaced pregnancy in the drive for funding for abstinence-only education programs. Social conservatives dismiss sexual risk reduction strategies as ineffective. Instead, they advocate a risk elimination approach: a clear and simple message that the best means of preventing STIs is to avoid risk altogether.

STIs in Perspective

[E]stimates published in the January/February 2004 issue of *Perspectives in Sexual and Reproductive Health* show that nearly 19 million new STIs occurred in the United States in 2000. Although they make up only a quarter of the sexually active population, young people aged 15–24 account for nearly half of new infections. This is not surprising, as most young people are not yet in a long-standing, stable relationship. According to the U.S. Census Bureau, 78% of 20–24-year-olds in 2000 had never been married.

With the exception of HIV, STIs are not new; the diseases or their manifestations have been recognized for decades, even centuries. The impact of STIs on people's lives varies widely. At one end of the spectrum is HIV, which still must be considered inevitably fatal, although new drug regimens are helping many people with HIV/AIDS live longer. Many of the most common STIs, however, are either harmless or can be treated and cured. . . .

Preventing STIs

Social conservatives' solution to the problem of STIs is simple: Young people should simply abstain from all sexual activity until they are married to a disease-free spouse. Organizations such as Focus on the Family and the Medical Institute for Sexual Health say we must stop promoting condoms, which are known to have high failure rates in actual use. Instead, they say we should be promoting abstinence, which is 100% effective, 100% of the time.

If the president's proposal to double funding for abstinence-only education is adopted, the federal government will spend almost a quarter of a billion dollars in the fiscal year beginning October 1 to promote abstinence for all unmarried people.* In accordance with the requirement that these programs have abstinence promotion as their "exclusive purpose," they may include instruction about the failure rates of condoms and other forms of contraception, but they may not provide any information about contraceptive methods that could be construed as promoting contraceptive use. The Bush proposal is sparking hope among abstinence-only proponents who are a key component of the president's political base of support. "This is a president who's finally putting his money where his mouth is," said LeAnna Benn, a pioneer in the abstinence-only movement, to the *Washington Times.* Benn went on to say that what is needed now is for abstinence-friendly government officials to structure grant programs so that an abstinence network can be built to match the powerful family planning network.

Meanwhile, . . . social conservatives hope that a warning label on condoms will dissuade people from having sex, but public health experts are skeptical. Because in the real world, abstinence can and does fail ("Understanding 'Abstinence': Implications for Individuals, Programs and Policies," *TGR,* December 2003, page 4), a more comprehensive and nuanced approach is needed, they say. "There is no magic bullet," says Ralph DiClemente, a researcher at Emory University who has been studying HIV prevention among adolescents. "That's why young people need a 'menu' of interventions, including information about condoms. There is no moral justification for withholding information or, worse yet, discouraging individuals from adopting behaviors that could save their life." Theresa Raphael, executive director of the National Coalition of STD Directors, agrees. "While abstinence is a public health message that we can all support, it cannot be the only message," she says in a February 5, 2004, press release. "Public health officials are obligated to dwell in the real world and support an approach . . . that reflects how Americans actually live."

Public opinion data have consistently shown that while American adults want abstinence to be promoted to young people, they also want those young people to have information about contraception and condom use.

According to a 2003 poll conducted by NPR, the Kaiser Family Foundation and Harvard's Kennedy School of Government, 93% of adults support instruction in school-based sex education programs about waiting to have sexual intercourse until marriage. At the same time, overwhelming proportions also support giving teens information on how to use and where to obtain contraceptives (86%), how to put on a condom (83%) and how to get tested for HIV and other STIs (94%).

Even conservatives cannot avoid the inescapable conclusion that most Americans do not support abstinence-only sex education. According to a Heritage Foundation analysis of a survey conducted earlier this year by Zogby International for Focus on the Family, "Some 75 percent of parents want teens to be taught about both abstinence and contraception." . . .

* Author's Note: FY05 funding for abstinence-only education was $167 million. In FY06, it was $176 million. The president requested $204 million for FY07 and promised to increase funding to $270 million by the end of his administration.

Source: "Comprehensive Approach Needed to Combat Sexually Transmitted Infections Among Youth" by Heather Boonstra (2004), *The Guttmacher Report on Public Policy 7*(1), 3–5. Reprinted by permission.

chapter 5

The Sexual Body

Spotlight on Research

An interview with . . .

Leonore Tiefer

Leonore Tiefer, Ph.D., is clinical associate professor of psychiatry at the New York University School of Medicine in New York City and has a private practice in sex therapy and psychotherapy in Manhattan. Recently, Dr. Tiefer has become internationally known as the primary spokesperson for a movement that challenges the medicalization of women's sexual problems by the pharmaceutical industry (for more information, see www.fsd-alert.org). Both the Society for the Scientific Study of Sexuality and the Association for Women in Psychology selected her for their Distinguished Scientific Career Awards in 2004.

What led you to begin studying sexuality?

I see sexuality as one of the most interesting and complex topics in all of academia. In the 1960s, I majored in psychology and in psychology grad school (UC Berkeley) I was at first attracted to the subject of learning and conditioning. But after two years of research on learning in rats I felt bored, and I became more interested in physiological psychology—the study of the biological bases of behavior. Frank Beach had a very active research group studying mating behavior in rodents and dogs, and although at that time (he changed later) he wouldn't fund women grad students to work in his lab, he allowed us to do experiments and participate in seminars. I studied hamster sexuality for my dissertation and then directed an animal lab for seven years in my first academic job. BUT, and this is a big but, I began to question the value of animal research on sexuality when the women's liberation movement (now called "second wave") hit me in the 1970s. After a sabbatical working with human sexuality issues, I decided I was really interested in sexuality, but that I wasn't suited to animal work and I doubted its ultimate significance. I re-specialized as a clinical psychologist specializing in sexuality. I also studied the new work in sexuality emerging from women's and gay and lesbian studies. Feminist politics combined with my biological and psychological background provided a well-rounded view of sexuality.

How do people react when they find that you study sexuality?

Usually they express political opinions first (about abortion or porn or sex ed), and ask personal questions about their own sexual life second. I have learned that no matter how strong the opinions, most people feel undereducated when it comes to sexuality and appreciate the opportunity to talk with an "expert." Ironically, however, my "expert" opinion is that sexuality is complicated and my answers to their questions usually involve more variables than they had anticipated.

Which of your projects have you found most interesting? Why?

I had the opportunity to participate in a monthly New York intellectual seminar on sexuality that lasted 11 years (1982–1993). Participants were journalists, writers, political activists, and a wide range of humanities professors. I was the only "official" sex expert. Members presented papers on topics ranging from gays in World War II to Picasso's sojourn in Barcelona to histories of food to "dirty" postcards. You cover a lot of ground in 11 years! The seminar always focused on how these various cultural events arose from and affected sexuality. The seminar completely changed my idea of what kind of thing sexuality was—from a biopsychological aspect of individual experience to a socially constructed ever-changing sociocultural phenomenon. This consciousness changing occurred slowly. Standards of evidence were completely different than in my psychological training and the topics taxed my general knowledge base (World War II? Barcelona?). But, when, slowly and gradually, I finally got it that sex was constructed differently within groups, generations, genders, religions and regions, my eyes were permanently opened in a way few conventionally trained sexologists can understand.

What ethical dilemmas have you faced in studying sexuality?

I became an activist against the medicalization of sexuality after Viagra was approved in 1998. I saw corporations taking advantage of people's lack of education about sexuality to promote drugs with marginal benefits and various dangers. It made me angry to see few other sexologists resisting the financial opportunities and propaganda of the pharmaceutical industry, but I have found many allies in public health, women's health, investigative journalism, and health reform. My ethical dilemma has occurred because throughout my years of activism, I have continued my clinical private practice doing sex therapy. People come to me for help with their personal sexual problems and I have to put their concerns and perspectives first, and refrain from lecturing or moralizing about the things that are on my mind. On occasion I even recommend that someone try one of the new sex drugs because in his or her individual case they might be helpful, even though I believe that for society at large they are the very opposite. Even when I think a person's problem has been caused by all the exaggerated public relations claims about the new drugs, I don't ever say, "I told you so." That's not my role as a clinical psychologist.

What do you think is the most challenging thing about studying sexuality?

The subject is very complicated, and many professionals and academics are unwilling to read widely outside their primary field. I think to be a good sexologist you have to be somewhat well versed in psychology, physiology, sociology, anthropology, history, law, religion, media studies, and gender studies.

Why is it important to do sex research?

It's important to do good sex research, but it's a waste of time to do foolish or trivial sex research. Good quality research, qualitative research, especially, can help shed light on topics many areas of society want to be hidden in darkness. Ignorant people can be shamed, guilt-tripped, and manipulated, and they raise ignorant children. Our media-saturated world requires an informed public, and good sex research is part of the information base essential in modern culture. For example, many states in the U.S. now have grossly uninformed laws about the dangers of "sex offenders" and are punishing people far too harshly for minor offenses. Ambitious politicians manipulate an ignorant public. The same thing happens with sex education or new contraceptive methods. The public is easily scared into taking a repressive position because they are uninformed. Movies and TV (and drug ads) promote ecstatic sex, but the public lacks the knowledge to assess these images. Good sex research will narrow the gap.

If you could teach people one thing about sexuality, what would it be?

As the title of my book says, I believe that "Sex Is Not a Natural Act." At least in the twenty-first century it's not. Everything about sex is the result of cultural influences and totally saturated with cultural meaning. Madison Avenue has hyped the pleasures and right-wing values have hyped the dangers—and, oddly, both insist that sex is a "natural" result of evolution (or God)—and that learning, practice, reading, reflection, conversation, and research are unnecessary. I believe just the opposite.

Is there anything else you'd like to add?

Every college and university should have a Department of Sexuality Studies. At the present time it is impossible to get the kind of multidisciplinary education I think every sexologist needs. You have to do it all on your own. As a consequence, few sexologists are well trained. Such departments would employ sexuality scholars who would generate interesting new theory and research. I wish I could be in such a department.

—Interviewed by Denise Donnelly

The G-Spot

and Other Mysteries

Elisabeth O. Burgess and Amy Palder

Is there a G-spot? One common question about female sexuality is whether there is a localized place in the vagina, often referred to as the G-spot, which causes especially pleasurable sensations when stimulated. The G-spot, or Grafenburg spot, was named for Dr. Ernst Grafenburg, a German gynecologist who first described this spot in 1950. Although Grafenburg often is credited with discovering this spot, descriptions of sensitivity in a specific area of the vagina can be found across cultures and historical periods (Sevely & Bennett, 1978; Ladas, Whipple, & Perry, 1982). Yet, contemporary sexologists disagree about the significance of the G-spot and its prevalence in the female population. Those in support of the G-spot claim that it is either a bundle of nerves, possibly representing the root of the clitoris, or a gland, or series of glands, that produces lubrication. Those who believe the G-spot is a myth argue that there is no anatomical evidence that it exists.

Over the past two decades, the G-spot has gained widespread acceptance by the mass media. Numerous articles on sexual pleasure in the popular press, self-help literature, and on the Internet describe the G-spot and provide instructions on using it for sexual pleasure (for instance, Cass, 2007; Hicks, 2006; Paget, 2004; Solot & Miller, 2007; Sundahl, Ladas, & Sprinkle, 2003; and Winks, 1998). These readings frequently cite the book *The G-spot and other recent discoveries about human sexuality* (Ladas, Whipple, & Perry, 1982) as evidence that all women have G-spots. Ladas et al. (1982) reported that the G-spot is located through deep pressure to the anterior vaginal wall. These researchers and other colleagues argue that this spongy mass, about the size of a quarter and the shape of a bean, can be found about halfway up the anterior (or belly) side of the vagina. The mass

becomes more rigid or identifiable when a woman is sexually aroused (Perry & Whipple, 1981; Zaviacic, Zaviacicova, Holoman & Molcan, 1988; Zaviacic & Whipple, 1993). According to self-reports, the G-spot produces orgasms that are "more intense" and "full body" orgasms than other female orgasms (Davidson, Darling, & Conway-Welch, 1989; Ladas et al., 1982; Perry & Whipple, 1981). Ladas et al. (1982) report that in a study supervised by Perry and Whipple, a medical professional was able to locate a G-spot in each of over 400 female volunteers (p. 43). Because Ladas et al. found that all women in their study had G-spots, they explain that women who have not been able to locate their G-spot are either not sufficiently aroused or not using the proper technique to locate it.

Yet, while many women believe the G-spot exists, not all women have heard about the G-spot and many women have not found their own G-spot. A survey of over 1000 women found that although 85.3% of the women surveyed believed that a sensitive area existed in the vagina, only 65.9% reported having such an area (Davidson et al., 1989). This survey also found that angle of vaginal entry, position of vaginal intercourse, and a woman's degree of emotional involvement with her partner affected her ability to orgasm from being stimulated in this area. Because traditional sexual positions such as the "missionary position" fail to stimulate the anterior wall of the vagina, women who explore other sexual practices such as manual stimulation from a partner or vibrator may be more likely to discover a G-spot (Ladas et al., 1982).

In contrast, some researchers strongly dispute the existence of the G-spot. Alzate and colleagues (Alzate & Hoch, 1986; Alzate, 1985) argue that the walls of the vagina are sensitive to touch, but there is no specific area in the vagina that produces orgasm.

These authors also argue that there is no anatomical evidence of a G-spot and critique previous research for using small clinical samples and anecdotal evidence. In a recent review of the literature on the G-spot, Hines (2001) calls it a myth and goes on to say that "the widespread acceptance of the reality of the G-spot goes well beyond available evidence" (p. 361). Other prominent sex researchers, including Masters and Johnson, do not discuss the G-spot or an especially sensitive area in the vagina but instead focus on the clitoris as the locus of female orgasms (Masters & Johnson, 1966).

Some feminist researchers also dispute the existence of the G-spot, but for different reasons. These scholars fear that the "discovery of the G-spot" and subsequent emphasis on vaginal orgasms support Freudian notions about the female orgasm and privilege heterosexual male-centered models of sexuality. These authors emphasize the clitoris as the primary location of the female orgasm and sexual empowerment for women (Ehrenreich, Hess, & Jacobs, 1987; Gerhard, 2004). Other feminist researchers believe that, because of cultural preferences about (hetero) sexual behavior, many women prefer to view the vagina as an important location of orgasmic response. These scholars recognize that orgasm is not merely a physiological response but it is also an emotional and psychological response to sexual stimuli and, as such, orgasms centered in the vagina should not be ignored (Hite, 1976; Schneider & Gould, 1987). However, if such a spot does exist, even supporters such as Ladas (2001) argue that it is harmful to think of the G-spot as the holy grail of female sexuality. In a critical review of the discourse of female orgasm, Tuana (2004) argues that this false dichotomy of clitoral and vaginal orgasm ignores the perspective that the majority of the clitoris is internal (see also Moore & Clarke, 1995; O'Connell, Sanjeevan & Hutson, 2005). Moreover, Tuana finds that some models of female anatomy that do include the G-spot ignore the feminist argument for a perineal sponge which is located between the posterior wall of the vagina and the rectum and also can become engorged during sexual stimulation. In sum, regardless of the politics of measuring and defining female genitalia, the female body contains many potential erogenous zones.

Whether individuals find stimulation of these locations pleasurable depends on the social context, the expertise of their partner, and personal preference.

Do women ejaculate? Another common debate about the sexual body is whether women ejaculate. For centuries, erotic literature and sex research has alluded to the elusive female orgasm that results in a squirt of liquid from the woman (Belzer, 1981; Sevely & Bennett, 1978). Contemporary researchers disagree as to where it comes from, what it is, and whether it is something that all women are capable of releasing.

Most often associated with G-spot stimulation, female ejaculation is the release of fluid through the urethra at the climax of an orgasm. One common concern about female ejaculation is whether the fluid is urine, a result of incontinence, or whether it is similar to male ejaculate. Self-reports indicate that this fluid is different from urine in smell, consistency and color (Davidson et al., 1989; Belzer, 1981; Taormini, 2000). Chemical analyses of female ejaculate have been less conclusive. While Goldberg et al. (1983) found the expelled fluid to be chemically similar to urine, numerous other clinical studies argue that the consistency of this fluid is significantly different from urine (Addiego, Belzer, Moger, Perry, & Whipple, 1981; Belzer, Whipple, & Moger, 1984; Wimpissinger, Stifter, Grin, & Stackl, 2007; Zaviacic, Zaviacicova, Holoman & Molcan, 1988). Additionally, a recent study concluded that women who reported experiencing female ejaculation are not more likely to experience urinary problems than women who do not report ejaculation (Cartwright, Elvy, & Cardozo, 2007). Regardless of these findings, without larger samples of ejaculate, it would be difficult to reach any definitive conclusions.

A related controversy associated with female ejaculation concerns the source of the fluid. The most common theory is that the Skene's glands, which surround the urethra, secrete fluid into the urethra that is then ejaculated upon orgasm. Researchers who support this theory argue that female ejaculate may have a different consistency, at different times, for different women. In addition, reported rates of ejaculation among women vary from 10% to over 50% (Ladas et al., 1983; Bullough, David, Whipple, Dixon, Allgeier, Rice, & Drury, 1984). Only a few women report ejaculating fluid with every orgasm. Although manipulation of the G-spot is not required to produce female ejaculation, women who experience pleasure or orgasms through stimulation of the G-spot are more likely to report experiencing ejaculation (Davidson et al., 1989). Either way, by focusing solely on chemical components of the fluid, researchers are ignoring the role this event plays in sexual satisfaction.

Female ejaculation also has become the subject of several self-help sexuality books and sexuality workshops. According to an article by Taormino (2000), female ejaculation was the subject of one of the workshops at the 2000 Michigan Womyn's Festival. After the workshop, several women participated in the "First Annual Ejaculation Contest," competing in categories such as "speed," "distance," "quantity," and "best single handed job." While reports based on nonclinical trials do not receive scientific approval, the nature of this contest helps to alter negative stigma associated with female ejaculation.

There are several important implications of this research on female ejaculation. Because female ejaculation is not a widely known phenomenon, women who experience the expulsion of fluids frequently feel shame or anxiety (Davidson et al., 1989). Many women, particularly those who are uncomfortable examining the fluid, assume that any release of fluid is urine and a sign of urinary incontinence. In some cases women may seek and receive medical treatment for urinary incontinence when this is not, in fact, the problem. If women were aware that the expulsion of fluid was a normal and healthy bodily function, they would feel free to enjoy a pleasurable event rather than perceiving themselves as deviant (Cartwright, Elvy & Cardozo, 2007; Winton, 1989).

REFERENCES

Addiego, Frank, Edwin G. Belzer, Jill Comolli, William Moger, John D. Perry, & Beverly Whipple. 1981. Female Ejaculation: A Case Study. *The Journal of Sex Research,* 17, 13–21.

Alzate, Heli. 1985. Vaginal Eroticism: A Replication Study. *Archives of Sexual Behavior,* 14, 529–537.

Alzate, Heli, & Zwi Hoch. 1986. The "G-Spot" and "Female Ejaculation": A Current Appraisal. *Journal of Sex and Marital Therapy,* 12, 211–220.

Belzer, Edwin G. 1981. Orgasmic Expulsions of Women: A Review and Heuristic Inquiry. *The Journal of Sex Research,* 17, 1–12.

Belzer, Edwin G., Whipple, Beverly, & William Moger. 1984. On Female Ejaculation. *The Journal of Sex Research,* 20, 403–406.

Bullough, Bonnie, Madeline David, Beverly Whipple, Joan Dixon, Elizabeth Rice Allgeier, & Kate Cosgrove Drury. 1984. Subjective Reports of Female Orgasmic Expulsion of Fluid. *Nurse Practitioner,* 9, 55–59.

Cartwright, Rufus, Susannah Elvy, & Linda Cardozo. 2007. Do Women with Female Ejaculation Have Detrusor Overactivity? *Journal of Sexual Medicine, 4*(6), 1655–1658.

Cass, Vivienne. 2007. *The Elusive Orgasm: A Woman's Guide to Why She Can't and How She Can Orgasm.* New York: Marlowe & Company.

Davidson, J. Kenneth, Carol A. Darling, & Colleen Conway-Welch. 1989. The role of the Grafenburg Spot and Female Ejaculation in the Female Orgasmic Response: An Empirical Analysis. *Journal of Sex and Marital Therapy,* 15, 102–120.

Ehrenreich, Barbara, Elizabeth Hess, & Gloria Jacobs. 1986. *Re-Making Love: The Feminization of Sex.* New York: Anchor Books.

Gerhard, Jane. 2004. The Politics of the Female Orgasm. In M. Stombler, D. M. Baunach, E. O. Burgess, D. Donnelly, & W. Simonds. (Eds.). *Sex Matters: The Sexuality and Society Reader* (pp. 213–224). Boston: Allyn & Bacon.

Hicks, Donald L. 2006. *Unleashing Her G-Spot Orgasm: A Step-by-Step Guide to Giving a Woman Ultimate Sexual Ecstasy.* Berkeley, CA: Amorato Press.

Hines, Terence M. 2001. The G-Spot: A Modern Gynecological Myth. *American Journal of Obsterics and Gynecology,* 185, 359–362.

Hite, Shere. 1976. *The Hite Report: A Nationwide Study of Female Sexuality.* New York: Dell.

Goldberg, Daniel C., Beverly Whipple, Ralph E. Fishkin, Howard Waxman, Paul J. Fink, & Martin Weisberg. 1983. The Grafenberg Spot and Female Ejaculation: A Review of Initial Hypotheses. *Journal of Sex and Marital Therapy,* 9, 27–38.

Ladas, Alice. 2001. Review of *Secrets of Sensual Lovemaking* and *The Good Vibrations Guide. Journal of Sex Education and Therapy, 26,* 150–151.

Ladas, Alice, Beverly Whipple, & John Perry. 1982. *The G-Spot and Other Recent Discoveries about Human Sexuality.* New York: Plenum.

Masters, W. H., & V. E. Johnson, 1966. *Human Sexual Response.* Boston: Little, Brown.

Moore, Lisa Jean & Adele E. Clarke. 1995. Clitoral Conventions and Transgressions: Graphic Representations in Anatomy Texts, c. 1900–1991. *Feminist Studies, 21*(2), 255–301.

O'Connell, H. E., K. V. Sanjeevan, & J. M. Hudson. 2005. Anatomy of the Clitoris. *The Journal of Urology,* 174, 1189–1195.

Paget, Lou. 2004. *Orgasms: How to Have Them, Give Them, and Keep Them Coming.* New York: Broadway Books.

Perry, John D., & Beverly Whipple. 1981. The Varieties of Female Orgasm and Female Ejaculation. *SIECUS Report.*

Schneider, Beth E. & Meredith Gould. 1987. Female Sexuality Looking Back into the Future. In Beth B. Hess & Myra Marx Ferree (Eds.), *Analyzing Gender: A Handbook of Social Science Research* (pp. 120–153). Newbury Park, CA: Sage.

Sevely, J. L. & J. W. Bennett, 1978. Concerning Female Ejaculation and the Female Prostate. *The Journal of Sex Research,* 14, 1–20.

Solot, Dorian, and Marshall Miller. 2007. *I Love Female Orgasm: An Extraordinary Orgasm Guide.* New York: Marlowe & Company.

Sundahl, Deborah, Alice Ladas, and Annie Sprinkle. 2003. *Female Ejaculation and the G-Spot: Not Your Mother's Orgasm Book*! Alameda, CA: Hunter House, Inc.

Taormini, Tristan. 2000. Pucker Up. *Village Voice* (September 5) *45*(35), 130.

Tuana, Nancy. 2004. Coming to Understand: Orgasm and the Epistemology of Ignorance. *Hypatia,* 19(1), 194–232.

Winks, Cathy. 1998. *The Good Vibrations Guide: The G-Spot.* San Francisco: Down There Press.

Wimpissinger, Florian, Karl Stifter, Wolfgang Grin & Walter Stackl. 2007. The Female Prostate Revisited: Perineal Ultrasound and Biochemical Studies of Female Ejaculate. *Journal of Sexual Medicine,* 4(5), 1388–1393.

Winton, Mark A. 1989. Editorial: The Social Construction of the G-Spot and Female Ejaculation. *Journal of Sex Education and Therapy,* 15, 151–162.

Zaviacic, Milan, Alexandra Zaviacicova, Igor Karol Holoman, & Jan Molcan, 1988. Female Urethral Explusions Evoked by Local Digital Stimulation of the G-Spot: Differences in the Response Patterns. *The Journal of Sex Research,* 24, 311–318.

Zaviacic, Milan, & Beverly Whipple. 1993. Update on the Female Prostate and the Phenomenon of Female Ejaculation. *Journal of Sex Research, 30,* 148–151.

Hung: A Meditation on the Measure of Black Men in America

Scott Poulson-Bryant

Allow me to introduce myself.

My name is Scott and I am a black man in America. I've never done hard time. I've never been arrested. I don't have any kids. I know I'm invisible to many, but I also know that I'm highly visible to more.

I've been told that I am a success story.

I like to think that I measure up.

I'm a suburban kid. I was educated at an Ivy League university that at the time was dubbed the "hot college" because everyone wanted to go there. I've had some success in the Manhattan media world, and don't they say that if you can make it in New York, New York, you can make it anywhere? . . . I live in NYC in the summer and Miami's South Beach in the winter, because I want to and because I can. I've had successful relationships, and I love my parents and my parents love me.

Sure, I like to think that, in the grand American rat race that is life, I measure up.

But even with a laundry list of accomplishments that makes my résumé attractive, there are still days when I go to the gym and I get out of the shower and wrap my towel close around me, because I am a black man, and for a black man I just may not—in the swinging-dick sense of the words—"measure up."

That's because, you see, I'm what people call a grower and not a show-er. In other words, my soft hanging dick is not the monster of Mapplethorpean proportions that draws looks of wonder and awe. Of course many men are growers rather than showers, but that doesn't mean I'm not still conscious of it. Partly because I'm a man—and men are concerned about those things—but also partly because I am a black man.

In other words, I should be hung like a horse. I should be the cock of the locker-room walk, singing and swinging and getting merry like every day is, for hung brothers, Christmas.

But I'm not. I guess I could spend the last few seconds of my shower doing my own fluff job, spanking little Scott into some semierect state that speaks more to the size of my actual sex-ready self. But would it be worth it? To let that towel fly free just in case I get some stares from the dudes lining the room, stepping into their own boxers and briefs and bikinis? Of course it would be worth it, because I am a black man and black men are hung like horses. I'm not. So what kind of black man am I?

But here's the thing. I don't want to measure up in the locker room. I don't want to be the stereotype. I don't want to be Mister Myth, because if I am, then I'm just a dick; the big dick in the locker room; the recipient of the real, live, guy-on-guy penis envy no one talks about; the guy white boys hate yet want to be; the brother other black dudes recognize as representative of their gender; the stone-cold stud with a dick of doom. I think of black-man dick and I think that once upon a time we were hung from trees for being, well, hung. The sexual beast, the loin-engorged predator, the big-dicked destroyer not just of pure pristine white women but also of white men's sense of themselves. That's where black men have found themselves, culturally speaking: hung. Strung up from trees; lynched to protect the demure pureness of white women; dissed to soothe the memory sin of slave-raping white masters; castrated to save the community from the sexual brutality black men trail behind them like a scent—the scent of the stereotypical boogeyman created by the fears of a nation. And I don't want anything to do with that ugly American history, the stereotypes that have been created to control me—do I?

Hell yeah, my inner ear tells me, I do. Fuck history. Let's be real here: Who doesn't want to have the biggest dick in the room?

Speaking of history, here's a flashback, my own first history lesson, if you will.

The place: Providence, Rhode Island. The time: spring 1986, my sophomore year in college.

I'm dancing at the RISD Tap Room, a smoky second-floor dive just down the hill from Brown University, a sorta rathskeller hangout for the artsy students who attend the Rhode Island School of Design and the local beer drinkers who love them. I'm dancing, like I said, a plastic cup of beer in my hand, a baseball cap on my head, wearing a cotton Oxford shirt and a pair of Levi's

jeans. I'm sorta buzzed and I want a cigarette. I look around for a smoker. . . .

There's one, a white girl in a plain T-shirt with a bushy crown of brown curls, nodding her head to the synthesizer beat of Depeche Mode while she sits at a bruised-up little wooden table behind me and my crew. She smiles at me and holds open the soggy red-and-white box of Marlboros sitting on the table among the cups of beer. I take a cig. She flicks her Bic. I lean in to light the smoke. Before I can pull away, she says, "You are so cute." And I say, "Thanks," and start dancing again. By the time the next record starts, she's standing next to me, dancing next to me, sustaining eye contact with a vengeance.

We dance. We talk. We laugh. Her name is Kelly and she's from Michigan and she was a student in Providence but she's dropped out to work and "experience life." She asks me at one point, apropos of, it seems to me at the time, nothing, "What size shoe do you wear?" I look down at my Nikes, wondering where that question came from, and that's what I say to her: "Where does that question come from?" She shrugs and smiles and says, "I just noticed, that's all. Then again, you are a big guy." We dance some more. And drink some more beer. And laugh some more. By the time she's grinding against me, to a song that doesn't exactly require any sort of grinding, I'm beginning to see the light. This girl wants me. She wants me bad. Here I was, dancing and drinking in the RISD Tap Room, feeling cooler than cool, a Brown sophomore in Levi's and a button-down shirt, dancing with a white girl to the guitar strains of the Cure, and she wants to bed me. Not that I went out looking for it—which, when you're a well-raised young black man like me, is what you tell yourself when a white girl comes on to you.

When you're a well-raised young black man like me the voice in your inner ear sometimes sounds like your dad, your dad who grew up in the South in the forties and fifties, who knew what it was like to live life on the front lines of the constant battle for black male respect. When you're a well-raised young black man like me, you check yourself when a white girl's dangling the come-on, and you wonder what it is about you that made her seek you out. Are you just black enough to nab a white chick? Or are you, like she says, just a cute guy who likes to dance and smoke in the Tap Room because the Tap Room is the cool place to be?

Cut to Kelly's off-campus apartment . . . there is no door to Kelly's room, just some Indian-type fabric hanging across the doorway, blowing in the slight breeze from the open window near her bed.

We're done, me and Kelly. I'm a little new to this, this meeting, a strange girl and going to her spot and getting some ass. I'm also new to sex with white girls. I didn't do it in high school and the only girl I'd fooled around with at Brown was a black chick who, I'd later find out, didn't really want to be with dudes anyway. But we're done, me and Kelly, and we're lying there, twisted in the sheets, sweating, postorgasmic, passing a cigarette between us like we're in some French New Wave movie.

She turns to me, reaches down, and touches my dick. And she smiles. "That was really good," she says. And then she says, "I thought you'd be bigger than you are."

I look down at myself, turn to her, and shake my head. "So did I."

Which was true.

"Why?" I ask her.

"Because you're black," she replied. "Black guys have big penises."

I didn't know what to say to that. Inside, I felt this sudden explosion of self-doubt. Partly because I'd had a cousin who'd explained to me when I was a kid that if you have a little dick, you're not a man. I knew I didn't have a little dick, but apparently I didn't measure up to expectations, for myself and this chick at least. So this is what happens when you fool around with white girls? Later a buddy of mine, upon hearing this story, says yes, it is, telling me, "You got White-Girl-ed."

Which in his mind meant I'd been dragged home with Kelly because I was black, because she was white, and because she was experiencing a little of what Spike Lee would soon popularize as Jungle Fever.

See, White-Girl-ed meant that I hadn't been out there trolling to bed a white chick. White-Girl-ed meant that I hadn't *had* to go out there trolling for a white chick. I didn't have to, my buddy explained, because there were enough of them out there trolling for us, for black men, for the big black dick of their fantasies, for the big black dick they had probably been warned their whole lives against seeking out. And why was that exactly? The flip side of fantasy, the other side of desire, was the distorted fun-house-mirror image of black men as objects of fear; the myth of the black man as the big-dicked beast, always on the lookout for vulnerable white girls and eager to purloin them of their purity, had been so culturally enforced that trolling for white girls was pointless: endowed

with the enduring myth of sexual aggressor, demonized by it though we may be, black men only end up being more attractive to them.

"White people believe in myths," he said. "They have to, or else they couldn't exist. Nor could we," he added, "in their eyes, at least."

This was the beginning of an education for me, an education in the twisted ways in which race and sex rage through American culture, fanning the flames that are constantly charring the walls of America, the place James Baldwin called "this burning house of ours." Sure, I'd seen *Roots*. Sure, I knew my black history, all the names and dates and events that built the totems of black pride that defined my community and myself. I'd been educated in the ways of white folks, about the hurtling inevitability of racism rearing its ugly head, even in a world where some of my best friends were white. I'd even heard my father's words about dating white women, about the very real possibility of some white people (and some black people) taking issue with such behavior. I'd heard all that.

What I didn't have was any insight into the potential for self-discovery that occurs when all the discordant strands of lessons I'd learned were braided into one big cohesive lesson. Because it wasn't only Kelly's bold forthrightness that bothered me, her "white" way of making me feel "black" when all I was trying to be was a guy. I was also bothered by my response to what she'd said to me. For me, through all the lessons learned up to then, there had never been an intersection of race and sex before I'd lain down with the white chick in Providence. I'd risen from her bed a changed man.

"So did I." That had been my response to her statement. "So did I," as in: I agree, I thought I'd have a bigger dick, too. There was shame in that response but also a nagging question, as in: Why the shame? What had seeped into my consciousness about my emotional self that could be so affected by a quantitative judgment about my physical self? I partly knew the answer to that. The same cousin who'd told me about the lack of masculinity that came with a little dick had also once told me—when I was about thirteen—that eight and a half inches was average. And I *knew* I wasn't packing an eight-and-a-half-inch dick, and since I was probably about to stop growing, I never *would* be packing an eight-and-a-half-inch dick. I thought of myself as damaged and I was ashamed of it. Of course some of this also had to do with my thorough lack of sexual experience. I had no idea what women wanted and I had no idea whether I'd be able to satisfy them with whatever size dick I had. I'd had sex before but I was, essentially, an emotional virgin. And an idiot, truth be told, still carrying around my cousin's Guide to Sex in my teenaged brain.

I ultimately had to figure out that my cousin's lectures to me were all about us being guys. Black guys, yes, but guys nonetheless. Now I had my experience with Kelly and my college buddy's White-Girl-ed education to add a race element to that. What was it about my "guyness" that was truly supposed to be defined by my "blackness"?

More sex with Kelly didn't exactly answer all the questions I suddenly had—except one: that I wasn't the first black guy she'd slept with. More sex with Kelly did, however, change both my sexual and racial relationship to her. I knew now that I was a "black" guy having sex with a "white" woman. And there was something actually liberating about that. All the cards were on the table and there was nothing political or cultural to bluff through anymore. The well-raised young black guy in me didn't behave in such a well-raised way when we got together two more times. Somehow I'd figured out that even if I didn't have the huge black penis of her fantasy I could still fuck her like I did. We were louder, rougher, tougher, blacker. We never met each other's friends. We only screwed like animals in the room with the Indian-print cloth across the door. She thought I'd be bigger and so had I. But it was enough for both of us. Because, I suppose, at the end of the day, in the sweaty, postcoital silence poked through with cigarette puffs, we both sort of suspected about my dick what James Baldwin had written in *Just Above My Head:* "It was more a matter of its color than its size . . . its color was its size."

Ultimately, when the sex had run its course, when I'd gone my way and she'd gone hers—sexually satisfied on her part, a little mortified on mine—my sexual education was in full swing.

The discovery that I could be affected by someone else's devotion to culturally prescribed mythology; that I could actually want to maintain the myth, yet tug against the very pull of it; that I would have to live up to my own expectations as well as the misplaced expectations of others—this was my sexual revolution. It was everything I'd gone to college for. It was the beginning of my desire to want to understand "desire," to find the place where we transcended the usual stereotypes, yet carried them around with us like stowed luggage we knew we'd have to deal with but wouldn't have to look at during the whole trip. I'd been somebody's black buck before I knew that that's what she'd wanted me to be. Yet, just like she'd expected and just like I'd wanted to, I'd turned her out—she'd certainly come back for more. I could be ashamed of one of those roles, and still live to brag about the other to my friends.

Come to find out I wasn't the only brotha who'd experienced this—definitely not there at Brown, there in Providence—aptly named, looking back. *Providence,* as defined by *The American Heritage Dictionary:* "Care or preparation in advance; foresight."

My history lessons would be informed by the present-tense discussions of life with my black brothers, other young black guys like me caught up in similar circumstances, trying to make history while we found ourselves caught up in American history's far- and long-reaching web. We shared the eternal conflict of "measuring up"—balancing the burden of the white stereotype with the complicated desire to maintain the myth, to grow up from the Bigger Thomas within, yet stay on speaking terms with the Dolomites we yearned to be.

Source: From "Hung: A Meditation on the Measure of Black Men in America" by Scott Poulson-Bryant, copyright © 2005 by Scott Poulson-Bryant. Used by permission of Doubleday, a division of Random House, Inc.

The Sorcerer's Apprentice:

Why Can't We Stop Circumcising Boys?

Robert Darby

People have always eaten people,
What else is there to eat?
If the Juju had meant us not to eat people
He wouldn't have made us of meat.

—Flanders and Swann, "The Reluctant Cannibal"

The pediatrician spent hours resuscitating and assessing the injuries of a boy who had been born unable to breathe, without a pulse, and with a broken humerus and depressed skull fracture resulting from a difficult forceps delivery. He then visited the mother, whose first question was "When can he be circumcised?" Such a sense of priorities indicates the privileged place of male circumcision in modern America and highlights the difficulties in explaining what Edward Wallerstein has called "the uniquely American medical enigma." Why does routine circumcision persist in the United States long after it has been abandoned in the other English-speaking countries that originally took it up? Despite critical statements from the American Academy of Pediatrics and the College of Obstetricians and Gynecologists in 1971, 1975, 1978, 1983, 1989, and 1999, the operation is still performed on well over half of all newborn boys.

The U.S. experience contrasts with that of the other countries in which routine circumcision had once been common. In Britain, the procedure was widely recommended in the 1890s, reached its peak of popularity in the 1920s (at a rate of about 35 percent),

declined in the 1950s, and all but disappeared by the 1960s. In Australia, the incidence of circumcision peaked at over 80 percent in the 1950s, but it declined rapidly in the 1980s after statements by pediatric authorities. Today it stands at about 12 percent. The Canadian pattern is broadly similar, though the decline was slower until the late 1990s, when rates fell sharply. In New Zealand, the procedure was nearly universal between the wars, but fell so precipitately in the 1960s that now fewer than 2 percent of boys are circumcised. We thus face a classic puzzle of comparative sociology: Why did routine circumcision arise in the first place? Why only in Anglophone countries? Why did it decline and all but vanish in Britain and its dominions? Why does it survive in the United States?

Nobody has firm answers to these questions. The rise of circumcision was associated with the "great fear" of masturbation and anxiety about juvenile sexuality; the misidentification of infantile phimosis (the naturally nonretractile state of the juvenile foreskin) as a congenital abnormality; the puritan moralities of the nineteenth century; dread of many incurable diseases, especially syphilis, and the rising prestige of the medical profession, particularly surgeons, leading to excessive faith in surgical approaches to disease control and prevention. Most of these features were common to all European countries, however, and the factors which provoked the Anglophone [pattern] remain obscure. . . . The fall of circumcision in Britain was associated with other medical advances, especially the discovery of antibiotics, the decline of anxiety about masturbation, concern about complications and deaths, and the development of a more positive attitude toward sexual pleasure. In 1979, an editorial in the *British Medical Journal* attributed much of the trend to a better understanding of normal anatomical development and the consequent disappearance of fears about childhood phimosis.

The same editorial contrasted the British case with the situation in the United States, where the majority of boys were still circumcised, and many doctors (despite the AAP statement) defended the procedure with some vehemence. It offered no suggestions as to why the experience of the two leading Anglophone powers diverged so sharply after the 1940s, but clues may be found in the relatively low incidence of circumcision in Britain, its concentration among the upper classes, and the fact that even at the height of its popularity it was a minority practice that lasted scarcely more than two generations. In the United States, generous medical insurance policies after World War II allowed more families to take advantage of surgical procedures, and the introduction of Medicaid in the 1960s permitted even the poor to enjoy many of the same services as the rich. The practice thus came to affect the vast majority of U.S. males and to endure for more than two generations, with the result that there were soon few doctors and parents who were familiar with the normal (uncircumcised) penis and thus knew how little management it needed. In Britain, there were always doctors and relatives who had not lost touch with the way things used to be. In my research on Britain and Australia, I found that routine circumcision began as a doctor-driven innovation, became established in the medical repertoire, spread rapidly, and then declined slowly as doctors ceased to recommend it. Since parents had absorbed the advice of the generation before and many fathers had been circumcised themselves, they continued to ask for it. The fundamental reason for the circumcision of boys is a population of circumcised adults.

The American situation remains puzzling: Why has a custom initiated by our Victorian forebears prospered so mightily in the age of medical miracles? Some doctors blame parents for demanding circumcision, while parents accuse physicians of suggesting and even urging the operation, and of not warning them about risks and possible adverse effects. Critically minded doctors call for "the organized advocacy of lay groups . . . rather than the efforts of the medical profession," while others object to the interference of

"outsiders" in what they insist is a strictly clinical matter. Wallerstein felt that the practice continued because "medical and popular literature abounds in serious errors of scientific judgment," with the result that the medical profession is reluctant to take a firm or united stand. Although few think there is any real value in circumcision, and many regard it as cruel and harmful, doctors seem mesmerized by the force of parental demand and social expectation. Like the sorcerer's apprentice in *Fantasia,* they watch helplessly as the waters mount, waiting for the master magician to return and restore normality.

There has been remarkably little research into this problem. Circumcision is a highly controversial subject, but most of the debate is over whether it should be done, not on why the practice continues; those who defend it regard it as an unproblematic hygiene precaution or at least a parent's right to choose, and often become annoyed when critics ask them to justify it. Discussion of the issue is hampered by uncertainty as to the incidence of routine circumcision, its social distribution, and the reasons parents want it or agree to have it done. There has certainly been a significant decline in the incidence of circumcision in the United States since the 1970s, but it has been neither steady nor uniform across the country. The rate fell from 85 percent of newborns in the 1970s to 60 percent in 1988, rose again to 67 percent in 1995, then fell slightly to 65 percent in 1999—the last year for which authoritative figures are available. But given the AAP's critical statement in 1999, another substantial reduction might be coming. The incidence of circumcision varies significantly by region, and nearly all the observed reduction has occurred in the West, particularly in California, where the rate fell from 63 percent in 1979 to 36 percent in 1999. In the Northeast, the rate remained constant at about 65 percent over the same period, while in the Midwest and South it actually increased—from 74 to 81 percent and 55 to 64 percent, respectively.

Other variations are found on the basis of ethnic origin and education level. When Edward Laumann and colleagues analyzed data from the National Health and Social Life Survey (covering men aged 18–59) they found that while 81 percent of whites were circumcised, the figure was only 65 percent for blacks and 54 percent for Hispanics. Whereas 87 percent of men whose mothers were college graduates were circumcised, the figure for those whose mothers did not complete high school was only 62 percent. Laumann also found that circumcision was less common among conservative Protestants, but noted that all these differences shrank as the sample got younger, suggesting a trend toward homogeneity. We can thus say that circumcision is rarer among blacks and Hispanics (though more common than it was), and that the same is probably true among non-Muslim Asians, among the less educated, and in the western states. But we cannot know which of these is the decisive variable; it may be that blacks, Hispanics, and Asians tend to be less educated than whites and also to be concentrated in the South and West.

Preventive circumcision has always been an experimental and controversial surgery, never endorsed by the medical profession as a whole. Given the uncertainty of its benefits, the high risk of harm, and the significance of the organ being so dramatically altered, you might expect a few ultranervous adults would elect to have it done to themselves but not for millions to inflict it on their babies. These days only a few diehards seriously believe that circumcision in infancy confers compelling health benefits, and nobody suggests that the practice continues because the inhabitants of Indiana are healthier than those of California or because Americans in general are healthier than the populations of countries where the practice is rare. Indeed, readily available statistics suggest the opposite. Although per capita health spending is vastly greater in the United States than anywhere else, health outcomes on such key indicators as infant mortality, life expectancy, and the incidence of Sexually Transmitted Diseases (STDs) are significantly worse in the United States than in comparably developed countries where most men retain their foreskins. Far from circumcision being a protection against STDs, as often claimed, Laumann found that circumcised men had more STDs, both bacterial and viral, than the uncut, and the United States has the highest incidence of HIV infection of any country in the developed world except Portugal.

If American health outcomes are no better than those of noncircumcising countries, why does this "health precaution" survive on a mass scale? Robert Van Howe suggests seven lines of inquiry: (1) the foreskin is the focus of myths, misconceptions, and irrationality affecting the medical profession and public alike; (2) a lack of respect for the rights and individuality of children; (3) a contrasting exaggerated respect for the presumed sensibilities of religious minorities who practice circumcision for cultural reasons; (4) the reluctance of physicians to take a firm stand against circumcision and to refuse parental requests; (5) a bias in American medical journals, which tend to favor articles with a pro-circumcision tendency; (6) a failure to subject circumcision to the normal protocols for surgery, such as the need for informed consent, evidence of pathology, and proof of prophylactic benefit; and (7) strong financial incentives to perform the operation, which is generally covered by medical insurance.

To these suggestions might be added the role of the armed forces. During the two world wars, the U.S. military made a concerted effort to circumcise servicemen because it believed this would make them less susceptible to venereal disease. Military discipline forced men to submit to a procedure they would not otherwise have agreed to, and thousands of men were circumcised in their late teens and early 20s. When they returned home and became fathers, doctors began asking whether they wanted their sons circumcised. Remembering the ordeal that they or their buddies had endured from the operation as adults, many said yes, thinking it would avoid the need to do it later when the pain was thought to be worse than in infancy. With two generations circumcised, the foreskinned penis became rare, and few men had the personal experience to refute the rumors told about it.

The importance of financial incentives has been stressed by a number of critics. In their analysis of Medicaid funding, Amber Craig and colleagues found that low and declining rates of circumcision correspond to regions where the procedure is not funded, notably in California, which dropped coverage in 1982. Even more striking is their finding that the higher the rebate, the higher the incidence of circumcision—vivid proof of the power of market signals. Nor do the advantages of circumcision—for doctors—end there. Despite optimistic claims that the rates of injury and death are low, there has never been an adequate assessment of long-term complications, and they are certainly more frequent than most people think. The dirty little secret in pediatric surgery is that badly performed circumcisions, causing discomfort or poor cosmetic outcomes, often necessitating repeat operations and repair jobs, are common; one attorney who specializes in medical malpractice reports that some urologists see at least one such case each week. In this way the division of professional labor ensures that the benefits of circumcision are spread far beyond the original doctors: their mistakes provide work for many colleagues and the disasters add lawyers to the equation.

Yet physicians may not be the major beneficiaries. In the age of biotechnology and tissue engineering, human body parts have a high market value, and baby foreskins are prized as the raw material for many biomedical products, from skin grafts to antiwrinkle cream. The strongest pressure for the continuation of circumcision may not be from doctors or parents at all, but from the hospitals that harvest the foreskins and sell them to commercial partners.

Lack of unanimity and conviction among the medical profession has been stressed by Lawrence Dritsas, who attempts to deconstruct the AAP's unwillingness to make a firm recommendation and its corresponding tactic of throwing the burden of decision onto parents. He quotes an article that offered this explanation:

> *"We are reluctant to assume the role of active advocacy (one way or the other) because . . . the decision is not usually a medical one. Rather, it is based on the parents' perceptions of hygiene, their lack of understanding of the surgical risks, or their desire to conform to the pattern established by the infant's father and their own societal structure."*

He translates this to mean that circumcision is irrational but that, contrary to the usual protocol, "parental wishes become sufficient, while medical necessity, normally a guiding rule for the surgeon's knife, takes a back seat." Dritsas contrasts this hands-off approach with the AAP's ethically based rejection of female genital mutilation (where the possibility of a health benefit is not even entertained). In its position statement on informed consent the AAP says, "Providers have legal and ethical duties to their child patients to render competent medical care based on what the patient needs, not what someone else expresses. . . . The pediatrician's responsibility to his or her patient exists independently of parental desires or proxy consent." Except, it seems, when it comes to male circumcision.

Dritsas is genuinely puzzled by the glaring contradictions in AAP policy and explains them in terms of medical culture and the apprenticeship model of professional training, which does not encourage students to question authority. "For a physician to cease performing circumcisions represents a condemnation of past practice and an admission of error," he writes, and nobody holding the power of life and death wants to be seen as doing that. The doctors are thus in much the same position as the parents themselves, whose unconsidered assumption that the baby will be circumcised is an expression of the authority of their grandparents' physicians who convinced prior generations that it was the thing to do. Dritsas criticizes the stance of the AAP as reminiscent of the response of Pontius Pilate when confronted with the problem of what to do with Jesus. In his view, what they are really saying is that, "as scientific doctors, we find ourselves unable to recommend or deny this procedure; therefore, you will decide, and we shall be your scalpels." This sort of abdication of responsibility contrasts with the proactive stances of pediatric bodies in Britain, Australia, New Zealand, and, most forcefully, Canada, which have seen it as their duty not only to discourage parents from seeking circumcision but, in the end, to refuse to perform the operation.

There must be an explanation for these national differences. The medical profession is not an independent force; its members are subject to the same social pressures that shape the beliefs and condition the actions of everybody else. Several recent commentators have thus argued that circumcision should not be seen as a medical issue at all but as an expression of social norms. At a superficial level this has long been known. In the 1950s Dr. Spock urged circumcision because it would help a boy to feel "regular," and pediatricians since then have noted that "entrenched tradition of custom is probably the greatest obstacle faced by those who would decrease the number of circumcisions done in this country." But it is only recently that the sociological aspect of the question has received serious attention. In a comprehensive survey of the history of modern circumcision and the debate over its "advantages," published in 2002, Geoffrey Miller shows in brilliant detail how late Victorian physicians succeeded in demonizing the foreskin as a source of moral and physical decay. Acting as "norm entrepreneurs" they "reconfigured the phallus," transforming the foreskin from a feature regarded as healthy, natural, and good into one feared as polluted, chaotic, and bad. The incessant quest for novel associations between the foreskin (often expressed as "lack of circumcision") and nasty diseases is a tribute to the lasting success of their enterprise.

As a legal scholar, Miller is surprised at the law's indifferent or often supportive attitude toward what one might expect it to regard as an assault, or at least a mutilation, but he points out that the law is an expression of the surrounding culture and cannot be expected to be too far ahead of prevailing norms. Even so, he considers routine circumcision in the mainstream community to be on the way out. Although still normative, it is in decline and edging toward the critical halfway mark, or "tipping point," where the incidence can be expected to fall precipitously as parents come to believe that their children will now face stigma if they are circumcised. Like foot-binding in China or wife-beating in nineteenth-century Britain, a widely accepted social convention is "likely to collapse as the culture reaches a 'tipping point' and turns against the practice." The increasingly desperate search for new health reasons to circumcise—urinary tract infections (1985), HIV AIDS (1989), and cervical cancer in potential future partners (revived in 2002)—may delay the process, but cannot permanently halt it.

Sarah Waldeck offers a subtle analysis of how norms contribute to a person's behavioral cost-benefit calculations, how the desire to have a child circumcised fits into this assessment, and thus why parents continue to seek it. She is particularly interested in the "stigma" supposedly attached to the uncircumcised penis in a society where most males are cut, and she considers the role of the popular media in perpetuating a stereotype of the foreskin as somehow disagreeable. She also notes that few parents have any clear reasons for wanting their sons circumcised and produce them only when challenged. The most common justifications turn out to be the supposed need to look like the father or peers and not to be teased in the proverbial locker room. If "health benefits" are mentioned at all, they enter as an afterthought or when other arguments fail. Waldeck still subjects the medical case to scientific, legal, and ethical scrutiny, and finds it inadequate to justify the removal of healthy body parts from nonconsenting minors. She concludes with a thoughtful discussion of how the American norm might be changed and suggests three specific strategies: requiring parents to pay for the procedure; requiring doctors who perform the operation to use effective pain control; and tightening the informed-consent process.

As a celebrated German-Jewish philosopher once observed, "The tradition of all the dead generations weighs like a nightmare on the brains of the living." When preventive circumcision was introduced in the late nineteenth century, concepts of medical ethics, informed consent, therapeutic evidence, and the cost-benefit trade-off were rudimentary. Neither the morality nor the efficacy of the procedure was seriously debated, nor was there any study of its long-term consequences; it became established in the medical culture of Anglophone countries by virtue of the authority of its early promoters. No matter how many statistics-laden articles get published in medical journals, circumcision cannot shake off the traces of its Victorian origins. It remains the last surviving example of the once respectable proposition that disease could be prevented by the preemptive removal of body parts, which, though healthy, are thought to be a weak link in the body's defenses. In its heyday, this medical breakthrough, described by Ann Dally as "fantasy surgery," enjoyed wide esteem and included excisions of other supposed foci or portals of infection, such as the adenoids, tonsils, teeth, appendix, and large intestine. Few doubted that if the doctor thought you were better off without any of these, it was your duty to follow his orders.

Because there was no real debate about the propriety or efficacy of preemptive amputation as a disease-control strategy when it was first introduced, those who wanted to remove healthy body parts from children were able to throw the burden of proof onto their opponents. Instead of the advocates having to demonstrate that the gain outweighed the loss, it was up to the doubters to prove that the loss outweighed the gain. The consequence is that what should have been a debate about the introduction of preventive circumcision in the 1890s has turned into a debate about its abolition a century later. Miller and Waldeck are probably right to argue that circumcision will not die out until the uncut penis becomes an acceptable—perhaps the preferred—option. But the transformation of attitudes will not seem so improbable, nor is the task of effecting it so daunting, if we remember that there is no need to invent a new norm, merely to restore the sensibility that governed the Western world before the late nineteenth century. In the 1870s, when Richard Burton remarked that Christendom "practically holds circumcision in horror," the observation was ceasing to be true, but it was certainly the case before Victorian doctors reconfigured the phallus and bequeathed a thorny problem to their successors.

(*Note on terminology:* In this article "circumcision" or "routine circumcision" means circumcision of normal male minors in the absence of any medical indication or valid religious requirement, on the decision of adults, and without the consent of the child.)

RECOMMENDED RESOURCES

*Lawrence Dritsas. "Below the Belt: Doctors, Debate and the Ongoing American Discussion of Routine Neonatal Male Circumcision." *Bulletin of Science and Technology* 21 (2001):297–311. A brief analysis of the uncertainties, contradictions, and disagreements among American medical professionals.

*Geoffrey Miller. "Circumcision: Cultural-Legal Analysis." *Virginia Journal of Social Policy and the Law* 9 (2002):497–585. Miller shows how Victorian medical men transformed popular images of the penis and set routine circumcision in motion.

Robert Van Howe. "Why Does Neonatal Circumcision Persist in the United States?" In *Sexual Mutilations: A Human Tragedy,* ed. Marylin Milos and George Denniston (Plenum, 1997). A discussion of the main factors behind American exceptionalism.

*Sarah Waldeck. "Using Circumcision to Understand Social Norms as Multipliers." *University of Cincinnati Law Review* 72 (2003):455–526. A searching analysis of routine circumcision as a cultural phenomenon.

*Edward Wallerstein. "Circumcision: The Uniquely American Medical Enigma." *Urologic Clinics of North America* 12 (1985): 123–32. Why doctors and parents prefer health faddism to biological evidence.

Items marked with an asterisk are available online at the Circumcision Information and Resource Pages website: http://www.cirp.org/library.

Female Genital Cutting

Elisabeth O. Burgess

Cultural norms regarding physical attractiveness, sexual appeal, chasteness, and/or marriageability often encourage the manipulation of women's and girls' bodies. These issues are evident in many times and places. Manipulation of the female body falls on a continuum from clothing, hairstyles, and make-up on one end, to surgical procedures at the other extreme. It also includes techniques such as breast enhancement surgery, hymen restoration (to "reinstate" virginity), and labia slimming or plumping. Some bodily manipulations are "elective," while others are externally imposed on girls and women by parents and caregivers. One of the most extreme forms of bodily manipulation is female genital cutting.

Female genital cutting (FGC) is the current name for a variety of practices that involve the cutting of female genitalia. These practices have been called everything from *female circumcision* to *female genital mutilation.* The naming of these procedures is meaningful because each carries a value judgment (Walley, 2002; Davis, 2004) and serves to "other" African or non-Western women (Njambi, 2004). The term *circumcision* brings to mind male circumcision (See Darby, Reading 23) and, thus, encourages us to view the procedure as medicalized and less severe in scope. In contrast, to call it *female genital mutilation* suggests that the intent is to harm or torture women. To better represent the problem and consequences of this procedure, many health activists, researchers, and policy makers have adopted the term *female genital cutting,* which allows for more culturally sensitive discussion of the topic and acknowledges the diversity of practices (James and Robertson, 2002).

The World Health Organization (2000a; 2000b) identifies four types of FGC:

1. Removal of part or all of the clitoris.
2. Removal of clitoris and labia minora (also known as *clitoridectomy* or *excision*).
3. Removal of the clitoris, labia minora, and labia majora (also known as *infibulation*). The wound is stitched or covered until it heals. Sometimes a foreign object is placed in the wound to leave a place for the flow of urine and menstrual blood.
4. Other procedures that alter the genitals include, but are not limited to, cauterization, burning, and piercing.

Although rates of FGC are difficult to measure, the World Health Organization (2000a) estimates that between 100 and 140 million girls and women have undergone some variation of FGC, and approximately 2 million girls are at risk of FGC each year. Infibulations are the most severe form of FGC, and represent approximately 15 percent of all cases. While all types of FGC pose health risks, such as infection, infibulation is particularly hazardous. The severity of the surgery and unsanitary conditions often lead to medical complications including infertility; infection; difficulties with urination, menstruation, and childbirth; and even death (World Health Organization, 2000b). If the wound heals properly, the resulting scar tissue and size of the opening may require deinfibulation (tearing or cutting of the scarred tissue) for sexual activity or childbirth. In most cases women are reinfibulated after childbirth (World Health Organization, 2000b; Walley, 2002).

Although the majority of genital cutting occurs in Africa, it also occurs in some parts of Asia and the Middle East.[1] Moreover, FGC has occurred in other times and places. In the Victorian Era, some European and American doctors used clitoridectomy as a cure for masturbation and nymphomania (Sheehan, 1997; Walley, 2002) and Chase (2002) argues that contemporary surgery on intersexed infants[2] is also a form of genital cutting.

In Africa, older women or midwives commonly perform genital cutting procedures on young girls.[3] The cultural belief is that FGC will ensure that girls remain virgins, thus making them desirable brides, and that uncut genitals are unclean and offensive. Also, many men believe that FGC of a female partner enhances male sexual pleasure (James and Robertson, 2002). Some cultures perform FGC as communal initiation rites for girls at puberty. After undergoing the procedure, girls are welcomed into the community of women, often receiving gifts and gaining social status (James and Robertson, 2002; Njambi, 2004). Although some girls risk their lives by leaving their families in an effort to avoid genital cutting,[4] other girls see these ceremonies, which may combine FGC with other rites of passage, as bonding experiences that enhance life-long solidarity (James and Robertson, 2002; Walley, 2002; Njambi, 2004).

Human rights organizations, including UNICEF, the World Health Organization, the United Nations Population Fund, Amnesty International, and numerous feminist organizations condemn FGC and define it as a violation of civil rights, favoring its elimination (World Health Organization, 2000a; Kalev, 2004). As a result, rates of FGC have decreased in some areas and numerous African women and men are working to eradicate FGC (Robertson, 2002). The World Health Organization provides training for nurses, midwives, and health care workers in order to increase awareness of health problems that arise from the practice of FGC (World Health Organization, 2001). In contrast, some FGC-practicing communities favor continuing the less severe FGC practices as long as they are carried out under medical supervision in sanitary conditions.

NOTES

1. It is also important to recognize that FGC is not the only or even necessarily the most important health and body issue facing women in Africa or the developing world (Robertson, 2002; Njambi, 2004).

2. See Reading 2 by Haas for more on intersexuality.

3. Although infants and adult women may undergo FGC, the majority of cases are girls aged 4 to 10 (Leonard, 2000).

4. Over the past several decades there have been several well publicized cases of women and girls seeking asylum to avoid FCG for themselves or their daughters. (See Njambi, 2004, for a critique of media coverage of these cases.) In many cases, these girls are cut against their will. In other cases, male and female peers ostracize uncut girls.

REFERENCES

Chase, Cheryl. 2002. "'Cultural Practice' or 'Reconstructive Surgery'? U.S. Genital Cutting, the Intersex Movement, and Medical Double Standards." Pp. 126–151 in Stanlie M. James and Claire C. Robertson. (Eds.) *Genital Cutting and Transnational Sisterhood: Disputing U.S. Polemics.* Chicago: University of Illinois Press.

Davis, Kathy. 2004. "Responses to W. Njabi's 'Dualism and Female Bodies in Representations of African Female Circumcision: A Feminist Critique': Between Moral Outrage and Cultural Relativism." *Feminist Theory, 5* (3), 305–323.

James, Stanlie M. and Claire C. Robertson. 2002. "Introduction: Reimagining Transnational Sisterhood." Pp. 5–15 in Stanlie M. James and Claire C. Robertson. (Eds.) *Genital Cutting and Transnational Sisterhood: Disputing U.S. Polemics.* Chicago: University of Illinois Press.

Kalev, Henriette Dahan. 2004. "Cultural Rights or Human Rights: The Case of Female Genital Mutilation." *Sex Roles, 51,* 339–348.

Leonard, Lori. 2000. "Interpreting Female Genital Cutting: Moving beyond the Impasse." *Annual Review of Sex Research, 11,* 158–190.

Njabi, Wairimu Ngaruiya. 2004. "Dualism and Female Bodies in Representations of African Female Circumcision: A Feminist Critique." *Feminist Theory, 5* (3), 281–303.

Robertson, Claire C. 2002. "Getting beyond the Ew! Factor: Rethinking U.S. Approaches to African Female Genital Cutting." Pp. 54–86 in Stanlie M. James and Claire C. Robertson. (Eds.) *Genital Cutting and Transnational Sisterhood: Disputing U.S. Polemics.* Chicago: University of Illinois Press.

Sheehan, Elizabeth A. 1997. "Victorian Clitoridectomy: Isaac Baker Brown and His Harmless Operative Procedure." Pp. 325–334 in Roger L. Lancaster and Miceala di Leonardo. (Eds.) *The Gender Sexuality Reader: Culture, History, Political Economy.* New York: Routledge.

Walley, Christine J. 2002. "Searching for Voices: Feminism, Anthropology, and the Global Debate over Female Genital Operations." Pp. 17–53 in Stanlie M. James and Claire C. Robertson. (Eds.) *Genital Cutting and Transnational Sisterhood: Disputing U.S. Polemics.* Chicago: University of Illinois Press.

World Health Organization. 2000a. "Fact Sheet, Number 241: Female Genital Mutilation." Retrieved January 15, 2006, from www.who.int/mediacentre/factsheets/fs241/en.

World Health Organization. 2000b. "A Systemic Review of Health Complications of Female Genital Mutilation Including Sequelae in Childbirth." Retrieved January 15, 2006, from www.who.int/mediacentre/gender/other_health/en/systreviewFGM.pdf.

World Health Organization. 2001. "Female Genital Mutilation, The Prevention and the Management of the Health Complications: Policy Guidelines for Nurses and Midwives." Retrieved January 15, 2006, from www.who.int/reproductivehealth/publications/rhr_01_18_fgm_policy_guidelines/index.html.

Fixing the Broken Male Machine

Meika Loe

The quest for manhood—the effort to achieve, demonstrate, and prove masculinity—is rooted deep in American history, starting at least with the nineteenth century's self-made man.[1] But in the early twenty-first century, when gender equity is believed to be increasingly achievable and men are no longer the sole family breadwinners, male power and control are no longer assured. Scholars specializing in masculinity studies have had much to say about male confusion in the roughly thirty years preceding Viagra. Attempts to understand and locate "masculinity in crisis" are varied and incomplete, but crucial to an understanding of the success of the Viagra phenomenon.[2] . . .

Today, a new and profitable masculine recovery movement is being generated with the aid of a pharmaceutical drug, and the male body is reemerging as a site for confidence and control. . . . Now, millions of men turn to Viagra to reclaim something they lost. . . . [T]his . . . is a silent movement, forged by individuals who may be vaguely aware of other men pursuing "recovery" of potency confidence, and "life" at the same time. But for most of the participants, the recovery process is too personal and too stigmatizing to discuss.

The silence, privacy, and relative invisibility of this movement proved difficult for a sociologist wanting to talk with Viagra consumers. Many times I asked myself, Where do those who are wanting to recover their potency "hang out," besides in doctors' offices? This question was difficult to answer and left me feeling sympathy for the men who wanted an answer to the same question. Where did men turn who wanted to talk with other men about their experiences with ED or Viagra? In the end, the communities I found that are built around the experience of erectile dysfunction and recovery were support groups and internet chat rooms. The majority of men featured in this chapter were members of male support groups or ED-themed internet chat rooms when they agreed to talk with me. What emerges is a discussion of bodies in need of "fixing."

Male Bodies in Need of Fixing

In the late twentieth century, masculinities scholars began to write about the connections between manhood and men's bodies. Australian social scientist R. W. Connell wrote, "True masculinity is almost always thought to proceed from men's bodies."[3] Sander Gilman's work revealed how "aesthetic surgeries" such as penile implants can help in the achievement of masculinity. And sociologist Michael Kimmel suggested that the realms of health and fitness have replaced the workplace in the late twentieth century as the next major testing ground for masculinity, where body work inevitably becomes a "relentless test."[4] But few masculinity scholars have taken a critical perspective on current theories of the body as a machine or as a surface imprinted with social symbolism.[5] Likewise, limited scholarship on male sexual bodies suggests that sexuality, particularly heterosexuality, is a proving ground for masculinity.[6]

Only recently have researchers, particularly feminist social scientists, begun to expand their inquiries to include the medicalization of male bodies.[7] Since Viagra's release, a small number of women social scientists have written about the ways in which this product promises to reinforce "phallocentrism" or, in

From "Fixing the Broken Male Machine" by Meika Loe, from *The Rise of Viagra: How a Little Pill Changed Sex in America* (2004, 62–93). New York University Press. Reprinted by permission.

my words, "erect the patriarchy."[8] In other words, some are concerned that a product like Viagra may hinder ongoing efforts for gender equality. Others are concerned about the new commodification of masculinity and the related proliferation of mass insecurity around manhood.[9] Additionally, medical sociologists Marco and Fishman have written about Viagra's potential for liberatory or disciplinary effects.[10] In contrast, most male scholars who study masculinity have yet to fully take up the question of the new medicalized male body or, more specifically, the Viagra body.[11]

How have men themselves responded to this newfound medical attention? In the following pages, medical professionals and patients use the language of "trouble" and "repair" as they grapple with "deficient" body parts, the concept of manhood, and medical diagnoses. In the process, they expose as constructs that which we take for granted; they imagine their bodies as machines, and they use Viagra as a tool for fixing their broken masculinity. And finally, they discover that Viagra not only solves problems but sometimes produces them as well.[12]

A Problematic Package

Several years after Viagra's debut, I had a fascinating conversation with a doctor and his long-time patient about sexual dysfunction. Upon hearing about my research, a man I will call Gray had volunteered to help by bringing me to talk to the only expert he knew on Viagra, his doctor.[13] Dr. Bern, an internist in private practice in his seventies, and Gray, a retired business owner in his eighties, had a fifty-year history together.[14] As we sat in Dr. Bern's office in Los Angeles, California, discussing my research project, both men tried to convince me that masculinity was intimately tied to penile functioning.

> *Dr. Bern:* You see, sexual dysfunction in males is peculiar. I'm sure if someone is a paraplegic and can't walk he would feel psychologically deprived. But beyond the great obvious lack—people who don't see or hear as well, they don't feel like they have lost their manhood, you see. I must tell you, and I'm not a psychiatrist, but I think it is far more preva-

lent in males than it would be in females. The fact that if women don't have sexual gratification . . . It isn't that they don't miss it, but they don't have the psychological burden that males seem to have. Maybe it's a throwback to the time when the caveman went and dragged a woman out on his shoulder.
>
> *ML:* So sexuality is integral to male identity?
>
> *Gray:* Absolutely! [My wife and I] talked about it for a long time—well, a couple of weeks before the [prostate] operation itself. We talked about it's possible we may not be able to have sex because the apparatuses they had out didn't necessarily work. So you could go for the rest of your life without having sex. And [the doctor] is so right. You feel part of your manhood is gone.[15]

Doctor Bern uses an evolutionary example to construct contemporary male sexuality as overt, desirous, assertive, and central to masculinity, in contrast to femininity, which is passive and nonsexual. Manhood is seen as the ability to have sexual control of and desire for women. Most importantly, though, Dr. Bern and Gray agreed that the trouble associated with erectile dysfunction involves the psychological burden of the loss of manhood. Most of my male interview subjects, both consumers and practitioners, were in agreement on this point. If the penis is in trouble, so is the man.

> You probably wouldn't understand it—it's a big part of manhood. Ever since you're a little boy growing up that's a part of your masculinity. And whether it's right or wrong, and however you deal with it—that's, well, I'm dealing with it and I seem to be okay. If a man gets an erection, or the boys in the shower compare each other, that's your masculinity. A lot of men don't like to admit it. (Phil, fifty-four years old, white, heterosexual, insurance broker)[16]

> [Viagra] makes my penis larger, length and widthwise, and that's inherent to the macho thing of men. With impotence, I felt like part of my manhood has been lost. (Byron, seventy years old, white, heterosexual, unknown occupation)[17]

After many of these conversations, I began to see that for men like Byron, Phil, and Gray, gender and sexuality may be difficult to separate out. Masculinity requires sexuality, and vice versa.[18] In contrast, femininity has traditionally been constructed in opposition to masculinity and, thus, sexuality.[19] What these men were telling me was that sexuality, or "erectile health," is compulsory for men, integral to achieving and maintaining manhood. (Implicit here is the requirement that heterosexual desire is compulsory for men.) Or as Australian cultural critic Annie Potts would put it, in a phallus-centered world, "Every man must pump up for phallocracy."[20]

While men may not discuss their masculinity problems openly with a doctor, the comments above and Viagra's recent block-buster success are representative of a new global concern for the "broken," or impotent, male. Some social scientists have argued that gender is "accomplished" in daily life through our interactions with others. In other words, we perform and interactively "do" masculinity or femininity through our appearance, body language, tone of voice, etc. Following this logic, the "accomplishment" of masculinity is situated, to some extent, in erectile achievement.[21] Fixing the "male machine" and ensuring erectile functioning, for the patients quoted above and countless others, is a way to ensure masculinity. Just as some social scientists have argued that cosmetic surgery is institutional support for women to successfully accomplish and "do" femininity,[22] Viagra can be seen as a biotechnological tool used to ensure masculinity by fixing the broken male machine.

The Poorly Functioning Male Machine

As Donna Haraway first argued in her ground breaking essay the "Cyborg Manifesto," we are all "cyborgs." A cyborg is a hybrid creature composed of both organism and machine who populates a world ambiguously natural and crafted.[23] Think of Arnold Schwarzenegger in *The Terminator,* for example. Today, most medical language about the body reflects the overlap between humans and machines. Medical texts regularly describe bodies using mechanical terminology such as "functioning" and "maintenance." In her research into twentieth-century understandings of health and the body, anthropologist Emily Martin found that the human body is commonly compared to a disciplined machine. Like a machine, the body is made up of parts

that can break down.[24] Similarly, Elizabeth Grosz argued that in a postmodern world, the body is treated as a mechanic structure in which components can be adjusted, altered, removed, and replaced.[25] Illness, then, refers to a broken body part. Fixing this part ensures the functioning of the machine. The metaphor of the body as a smoothly functioning machine is central to the way Viagra has been presented. In this [reading], you will see how doctors and patients use mechanical metaphors to make sense of body and gender trouble, or "broken" masculinity.

Such industrial metaphors are used regularly by Viagra spokesperson Irwin Goldstein, who is known for describing erectile functioning as "all hydraulics" and suggesting that dysfunction requires rebuilding the male machine. Following this metaphor, common treatment protocols for erectile dysfunction center on treating the penis, the broken part, separately from the body, the machine. In the new science of sex, penile dysfunction can be measured in a variety of ways: degree of penile tumescence (rigidity), penetrability (ability to penetrate the partner), sustainability of erection, and satisfaction with performance. These measures are figured into Pfizer-distributed "sexual health" scales and questionnaires. While they may not always do so, doctors are encouraged by Pfizer sales representatives to use these resources and to center their sexual health discussions with patients around erectile performance, asking patients to rate their erections in terms of penetrability, hardness, maintenance, and satisfaction levels.

For Pfizer, the focus is on treating the dysfunctional penis. Emphasis is on "optimal" or "maximal" performance—rigidity and sustainability of the erection—which means that anything less than such performance constitutes erectile dysfunction. . . .

Likewise, in the world of science, Goldstein has written that "submaximal rigidity or submaximal capability to sustain the erection" is another way of understanding erectile dysfunction.[26] In other words, "maximal" erectile rigidity and longevity are normal and expected. This understanding of the penis as dysfunctional and fixable (even perfectible) is exemplified in the following statements by two white men in their fifties; Dr. Curt, a urologist in a medical clinic, and Chuck, a heterosexual architect.

What I do is say [to patients complaining of erectile dysfunction], "Tell me about the erections. When you were twenty years old let's say they were a ten, rock hard. Where would they be now on a scale from one to ten?" So I give them some objectible [sic] evidence that they can give me. They'll say, "Oh, now it's a two." A lot of guys say it's now a seven or eight. I say, "Can you still perform with a seven or eight?" They say, "Yeah, but its not as good as it was." (Dr. Curt, urologist in medical clinic)[27]

I'd say as far as functioning sexually, I'm probably at 70 percent. I just can't get hard enough to penetrate. Everything works but the erection. If I were to rate my erectile functioning prior to surgery, with now, I'd say it's at 75 percent. It will never be back to 100 percent, I know that. So I'm somewhat satisfied. And the doctors always tell me that this is a long process, and that I need to be patient about getting back to functioning. So I'm in a wait-and-see mode. (Chuck, fifty-three years old, white, heterosexual, architect)[28]

Many patients who are currently looking for treatment for erectile dysfunction inhabit the in-between, "mild ED" arena (in terms of performance rankings from one to ten) and appear to be concerned with restoring their "machine" to a "normal" level of functioning. Despite Chuck's focus on "getting back to functioning," sexual standards have changed, I believe in part as a response to Viagra, and now "normal" is often not enough.[29]

It is important to point out that while many of these discussions are focused on the penis, they may also reflect expectations about normal manhood and aging. As we have learned, to be normal sexually means being normal in terms of gender, and vice versa. Also implicit in these pursuits of "normality" is a sense of denial and rejection of bodily change and perhaps aging. Thus, Chuck may be just as focused on "getting back to" manhood and youth as he is on "getting back to" normal sexual functioning.

Trouble with Normal

In some cases, Viagra is used by heterosexual and homosexual men who feel that normal penile functioning is not good enough, and extra-normal functioning is now the goal. While these men claim they do not "need" Viagra, they are more satisfied with their performance when they do use it.[30] In the quotations below, Viagra consumers Will and Stanford imply that the pre-Viagra penis is slow, unpredictable, and uncertain, and, thus, problematic.

[I was] totally surprised in my ability to stay erect without effort and the ability to repeatedly snap to attention. Amazing effect. Sorta magical in a way. (Will, fifty-three years old, white, homosexual, program coordinator)[31]

I noticed that if I get titillated [after using Viagra], then the penis springs to attention. Not atypically. But more facile. It's easier. I don't know if it takes less time. It's more convincing. It's not like maybe I'll get hard and maybe I won't. It's like "Okay, here I am!" (Stanford, sixty-five years old, white, heterosexual, counselor)[32]

For Will and Stanford, the Viagra body may be preferable to the natural body because it is consistent and predictable. While rigidity is the goal, part of optimal penile performance is to appear flexible; thus, the Viagra body is, in part, a flexible body.[33] According to . . . Emily Martin, flexibility is a trait cherished and cultivated in all fields, including health.[34] In *Flexible Bodies,* Martin shows how the healthiest bodies in the postmodern era are disciplined machines that also exhibit current cultural ideals such as flexibility, fitness, and elasticity. Viagra can be used as a tool to achieve this ideal elastic body—a body that is always "on call."

Interestingly, the Viagra body is both flexible and controlled, in contrast to the cultural stereotype of men as virile and "out of control." Whereas women have historically been called upon to regulate and control male (mostly teenage) hypersexuality, men are now able to regulate, as well as empower, their bodies with the help of a pill. For Stu, the "on-call" Viagra penis will consistently respond when it is needed, whereas the "natural" body is unpredictable, and therefore unreliable.

Erections are a lot more temperamental than people are willing to admit. But we have this image of masculinity and expectations of male sexuality as being virile and always ready to go and be the conqueror. And I think that this pill allows people to finally live out that myth (laughs). That was one of the things I had to learn early on is that I had irrational expectations of sexuality. And that men don't have big erections every time they want to, usually, and that to believe that one did was to set oneself up for disappointment. (Stu, thirty-six years old, white, homosexual, student)[35]

As Stu points out, Viagra exposes the flawed "natural" body and enables a man to achieve mythic, powerful, and controlled masculinity. By appearing "natural," the Viagra body can easily replace the problematic body in order to avoid the inevitable disappointment. In this way, the Viagra body exists somewhere between artificial and natural, and even beyond to super-natural levels.

For many, the promise of Viagra is the fact that it can deliver "optimal" results, pushing the consumer beyond his own conceptions of "normal" functioning. In this way, Viagra comes to be seen as a miracle cure because it not only "fixes" the problem but also makes it "better." Below, Viagra is described as an enhancement drug. . . .

> It's pretty amazing if you can take a pill and get a better erection. Or even an erection . . . [Viagra is] the first type of medication like this, and for it to work, I mean, is it a wonder drug? Well maybe some of the antibiotics maybe, or diabetes drugs—those are wonder drugs. But in the sexual area, you could say in terms of sexual activity and all of that, yeah, it's a wonderdrug. (Dr. Tobin, urologist in private practice)[36]. . .

> The entire world relies on drugs simply because they work, or solve—or help—physical conditions. Why is Viagra any different if it is able to extend—excuse the pun—the full and most zestful part of being human? (Will, fifty-three years old, white, homosexual, program coordinator)[37]

As the voices above reveal, doctors and patients tend to collaborate in imagining Viagra as a magic bullet that can "extend" the realm of "normal" and push people to the next level: extranormality, or superhumanness. By pushing the boundaries of erectile function, performance, and sexuality, Viagra sets new standards and, ironically, marks countless male bodies as in need of repair. Consequently, millions of men are now convinced that their sexual and masculine performance can be improved with Viagra.

Viagra to the Rescue?

Viagra can also come to the rescue for men who feel that they are not quite masculine enough. While culture, the media, the economy, or relationships can be a source of "male crisis," such factors are complicated to fix. However, when the problem is located solely in the individual body and treated as a physiological dysfunction, the repair can seem easier. Even clinical psychologists, who acknowledge that the trouble can be psychological, social, or relational, may join medical practitioners in seeing Viagra as a tool for regaining body function and repairing confidence and masculinity. Viagra, as a recent biotechnological innovation and medical treatment, represents progress on the path towards health and freedom.

Some consumers take Viagra hoping to restore or supplement not only "natural" physiological function but also "normal" masculinity and heterosexuality.[38] Others choose not to use Viagra, claiming that Viagra is more problem than solution in that it can produce an artificial and uncontrollable body. This section will reveal how patients and doctors grapple with medical solutions, the promise of Viagra, and the necessity of repairing broken male bodies and masculinities.

In an era of advancing sexual medicine, patients and doctors now collaborate in their judgments about successful medical solutions.[39] Both may agree that Viagra will enhance or fix gender, sexuality, and maybe even health and aging. . . .

Other doctors and consumers construct their own, sometimes counterhegemonic or contrary meanings about medicine and sexual dysfunction. This may mean reframing what is problematic and in need of treatment or redefining popular conceptions of what is "normal" and "natural." Below, I illustrate how the growing relationship between sexuality and medicine becomes accepted, and how the repair of broken sexual bodies becomes associated with quick and efficient medical solutions, to the point where such solutions are taken for granted by all involved. In the process, ideologies about what is natural versus artificial, functional versus dysfunctional, and excessive versus deficient are used to make sense of the troubled and fixable body.

Medicalization, or the increased treatment of previously nonmedical problems with medicines, is generally viewed as an inevitable feature of our contemporary lives. Medical professionals like Drs. Pellis . . . and Redding do not question what they see as the forward march of medical science. Instead, these practitioners tend to embrace this push towards new knowledge, solutions, and healthier bodies as beneficial, inevitable, and unstoppable.

> It started a long time ago. Sexuality is a mind/body connection. Even Freud said it; one day there will be medical solutions to sexual problems. So he foresaw it as inevitable. (Dr. Pellis, psychiatrist in medical clinic)[40] . . .

> It's true—science is getting to that point. [Doctors are] better able to help the body in ways it can't help itself. We don't know what else the medications do—just what they do do. But as with guns or anything, it is a tool, and the more medications that come out, the less the coincidence of stigma around mental health seems to occur. (Dr. Redding, psychotherapist in private practice)[41]

As science enables doctors to help "when bodies can't help themselves," medical solutions are increasingly normalized and accepted, and their professions are legitimated. Even among mental health practitioners such as Dr. Redding, quoted above, medications can be seen as "tools" to help professionals do their jobs and cut through the stigma of mental health work.

Then again, for some medical professionals who don't write prescriptions or who work outside of the current medical system, medicalization is a force to be reckoned with. Drs. Blackwood [and] Bern . . . find themselves becoming defensive as they witness their previously accepted ideas about health and treatment slowly become outmoded.

> Everything is medicalized, and HMOs vote in favor of medication over therapy. I think it's a travesty. I find it very disturbing. (Dr. Blackwood, psychologist in private practice)[42]

> I happen to be a therapeutic nihilist. I'm a firm believer that the less medicine you take for anything, the better off you are. That doesn't mean I won't use medication. But I don't run and jump in areas. (Dr. Bern, internist in private practice)[43]

. . . These doctors take issue with a health care system and a culture that creates and validates expanding

medicine. . . . Such contrary voices appear deviant in a world that generally embraces medical science as unquestioned progress, and even as the path towards health and freedom.[44]

More often than not, medical professionals and journalists couch the discovery and availability of Viagra in the language of scientific progress. After a barrage of Pfizer promotion, media attention, "scientific" reporting on the high prevalence of erectile dysfunction, and the clear popularity of Viagra after its debut in 1998, the medical professionals I interviewed are generally convinced that ED is a "major public health concern" and that Viagra is a "magic bullet" treatment.[45] Employing discourses of scientific advancement, most medical practitioners construct Viagra as a vast improvement over previous treatments for erectile dysfunction, which are now constructed as risky, painful, expensive, time consuming, and complicated. Viagra's success comes in part from this construction as the biotechnological answer to erectile dysfunction that promises the most freedom, simplicity, and expedience, due to its convenient pill form. . . .

> It has really helped a lot of people. I've seen some great successes. And it's certainly much easier to do than the other alternatives—penile injections, prostheses, all of these vacuum devices. The alternatives are all more complicated than simply popping a pill. (Dr. Loud, urologist in private practice)[46]

> Viagra is really great because it is just a pill and as long as it works it's great. And you don't have to stick needles in, or use cumbersome equipment. . . . Instead of going to see a counselor and spending a lot of money and time on a problem that may not necessarily get better with psychotherapy—this way you take a pill and get better. (Dr. Cummings, urologist in medical clinic)[47]

For . . . [Drs. Loud] and Cummings, simply "popping a pill" is constructed as quick, easy, and painless— not nearly as threatening as the other options: chemicals delivered through needles, equipment hooked up to the body, or months of counseling. This sentiment is shared with consumers like Thom and Scott, who have tried other available options for treating sexual dysfunction, such as pumps and psychological counseling.

[The vacuum pump] is difficult from a standpoint. . . . It's all the apparatuses, the preparation, and even with the constriction ring which is basically like a tourniquet, I still could not hold a firm enough erection for penetration. So it just didn't work for that effect. It's really tough because it takes all the spontaneity out of it. (Thom, fifty-three years old, white, heterosexual, engineer)[48]

Viagra is so popular in my belief because it cuts out the "middle man" as it were . . . all the psycho-sexual counseling that one would have to go through in order to get to the root of the problem. I know what my problem is without some psycho babbler telling me! It's lack of confidence in the size of my penis! (Scott, thirty-seven years old, Welsh, heterosexual, manager)[49]

Thom and Scott are among the millions of men who like Viagra for its spontaneity and ease. Medical solutions have been so successful that sometimes devices and pharmaceuticals appear to be the only options for treatment. Ricardo, a sixty-one-year-old Mexican-American consumer of Viagra, says he's tried every type of treatment and considered every gadget available, seemingly unaware that alternatives to prescription treatments exist (e.g., therapy).[50] "I've tried everything. There's a gadget for everything. . . . Don't forget, years ago we didn't have any of this. I'm really okay—I finally ended up with a pump that works. I tell everybody, 'Man, I'm back!'"[51] Ironically, with recent "advances" in medical technology, the production of seemingly straight-forward and accessible treatments, the availability of medication online, and direct-to-consumer advertising, consumers are finally free to cut out the "middle man"—the therapist, doctor, or health-care practitioner—and just get what they need, quickly and easily. In fact, with the push towards health-care efficiency and insurers' reticence to cover counseling, I have been told that referrals to therapists to treat the psychological dimensions of ED have decreased substantially.[52]

Medicine continues its forward march, impacting bodies and lives in such a way as to blur the line between what is real and what is man made. This tension between "the natural" and "the artificial" is a common theme in my conversations with others about Viagra. Pfizer's most crucial selling point (after constructing a widespread need for Viagra) involves convincing consumers that Viagra not only is the easiest treatment to use but also is as close to "natural" as one can get. A 1999 Pfizer ad reads, "Achieve erections the natural way—in response to sexual stimulation." Not only is a pill simple and efficient, but Viagra enables the body to work normally and "naturally." Following Pfizer's lead, medical professionals construct Viagra as restorative, moving men smoothly and easily from dysfunction to "normal functioning."[53]

These are distraught, angry, guilty people. . . . We're just trying to restore them to normal. Or just get them to some functioning—to relieve personal distress. (Irwin Goldstein, urologist in sexual dysfunction clinic)[54] . . .

Generally, there's a need for this stuff. Many medications inhibit sexual functioning. And people with diabetes tend to need it. Viagra seems to work quite naturally. And it's selling like crazy. (Long, chainstore pharmacist)[55]

According to those quoted above, Viagra can be understood as a medical treatment for dysfunction, which can restore and relieve distressed and deficient people and bodies. Like these medical professionals, I felt for the men I spoke with, many of whom had admitted their concerns only to their doctors (amazingly not even to their partners) and to me.[56] These men wondered if they were "normal" but suffered in silence because of the shame they associated with their bodies, and because of the lack of close friendship networks to turn to for support.[57] For these men, admitting to impotence (even to themselves) was like conceding that they were no longer young or masculine in a culture that conflates these identities with sexuality and sexual health. Thus, the project of restoring "normal functioning" cannot be divorced from the achievement of "normal masculinity." In this way, both patients and doctors construct Viagra not only as a treatment for erectile dysfunction but also as a pill that restores masculinity.

Viagra: A Dose of Masculinity

"Erectile performance," or achievement of an erection with the potential to penetrate and ejaculate, is central to the "accomplishment" of heterosexual masculinity, according to medical definitions of erectile functioning. By defining terms in this way, medicine is actively shaping what is permissible and ideal in terms of gender roles.[58] Male roles and expectations are clearly laid out in Pfizer's 2000 definition of erectile dysfunction; in a brochure designed for doctors ED is described as "the consistent inability of a man to achieve and/or maintain an erection sufficient for satisfactory sexual performance." We are left to assume that successful masculine performance requires a specific and successful penile performance, involving consistency, achievement, and satisfaction. Is this really the case?

In my conversations with male consumers, I asked if Viagra could be seen as a masculinity pill of sorts. Most affirmed this idea, reiterating the link among erections, potency, and masculinity. Below, it is apparent that white, heterosexual, male consumers ranging from twenty-seven to seventy-five years of age have literally bought into the idea of a masculinity pill.

> **ML:** Is Viagra a masculinity pill?
> **Fred:** (He laughs.) I can't argue with that. Without it you aren't much of anything.
> **ML:** What do you mean?
> **Fred:** If you have an impotency problem to any degree, you look for something to help it with, or you abstain completely. If they feel like this is a masculinity problem, I guess they are right. (Fred, seventy-five years old, white, heterosexual, retired Marine)[59] . . .

> Viagra to me is a miracle pill! It does boost confidence as well as other things! I suppose it can be called a masculinity pill, for without an erection, I believe that my masculinity is somewhat diminished! (Scott, thirty-seven years old, Welsh, heterosexual, manager)[60] . . .

According to these men, Viagra can be seen as a treatment for lost, "diminished," troubled, or incomplete masculinity. As Fred mentioned above, impotence reveals that a man is "not much of anything." Over and over in my interviews, in the face of erectile difficulty or even deficiency, male consumers cast themselves as incomplete, or "half a man." Taking a dose of Viagra allows men to be "whole" again. . . .

However, even for "complete" men, Viagra appears to offer an "extra boost" of masculinity. In the quotations below, both patients and practitioners describe how men use Viagra to enhance their masculinity—to construct themselves as studs and supermen. Interestingly, these medical professionals acknowledge the fact that patients may not be "sexually dysfunctional" before taking Viagra but may just be curious about having a "better" erection.

> Some men, like [my] older clients, used [Viagra] just for that extra hardness. They could always get an erection, but [they would say] "I'm sixty-five and it just don't work like it used to." So they might be a little softer. So they'd use it just to harden things up. So they just felt like studs. (Dr. Pemel, sexual health practitioner in private practice)[61]

> It's the superman complex. It's that "faster, shinier, bigger" sort of thing. Men feel they've gotta do/have this: the new TV, the car, and the latest products. You know by the numbers that not all the guys getting [Viagra] have erectile dysfunction. (Wilshore, pharmacist)[62]

> I am not a macho type at all, but Viagra certainly has made me feel more masculine and sexy at sixty! (Pal, sixty years old, white, heterosexual, retired court administrator)[63]

Practitioners also work to perpetuate the relationship between "complete" manhood and "normal" erectile function. Erectile health equals healthy and complete masculinity to many consumers and practitioners. A man who is dysfunctional may be constructed as castrated, lacking a penis, and/or lacking manhood. For example, conference programs for the 1999 conference on "The Pharmacologic Management of Erectile Dysfunction"—underwritten by several pharmaceutical companies with Pfizer as the largest donor—showed on the outside page a profile of a man cut in half who becomes whole on the inside page where "objectives for treatment" were listed. . . .

When erectile functioning decreases, confidence and sense of masculinity tend to disappear as well, and the body reveals this loss in its posture. Below, Bob, a black heterosexual barber in his sixties, and Pemel, a white forty-something sexual health practitioner, shared with me how the image of a "shrinking" man conveys the way erectile dysfunction can visibly take its toll.[64] As I flipped through Bob's booklet, "Keys to Great Sex for Men over Fifty," I showed him the first page, which reads in large letters, "YOUR PENIS SHRINKS 19.8% AS YOU GET OLDER," part of an ad for testosterone treatment. I asked if he believed this.

> Yes, that's what prompted me [to buy the treatment]. Oh yeah, you wake up in the morning and you know something is different. Reading this stuff makes you more aware of what is happening. After taking stuff, there is a difference, a change. (Bob, sixty-two years old, black, heterosexual, business owner)[65]

> This whole thing psychologically, men being impotent, it's just devastating. It just affects so much. Testosterone levels. The ability to produce muscle in our bodies. I mean, men just shrink when they just don't have a strong erection. So it's interesting. Not that they become waifs, but . . . in the cases I've seen once they start to have more erections, they are more interested, hormonally things are flowing, testosterone is being produced more, and they are kind of feeling bigger and bulkier and more manly in many ways. (Dr. Pemel, sexual health practitioner in private practice)[66]

Here, the norm for males is to be big and bulky, not shrinking and diminutive. This theme of loss came up frequently in conversations with practitioners and consumers, although expressed and constructed in various ways. Many times loss of erectile function is seen as a death. Social scientist Annie Potts, in a critical commentary on "The Hard-On," reminds us that the experience of "the fallen flesh"—or the limp penis causing the body to appear desexed, soft (feminine), and powerless—is a common male horror story because it feminizes the body, rendering the person unidentifiable as a man.[67] . . .

[Other men] literally compared erectile dysfunction to death. For them, Viagra is constructed as a tool for restoring not only masculinity but also "life" itself.

> Sexual dysfunction is no joke. These people have horrible lives, they may lose their relationships, and they come in a fairly desperate condition. Some say they'd rather be dead. Both men and women. And their lives are destroyed. They have nowhere to turn. They are not themselves. All of that. (Irwin Goldstein, urologist in sexual dysfunction clinic)[68]

> I'm fifty-five and for some reason I just didn't seem to feel like I was alive and well like I was when I was twenty years old. And you know, I thought that shouldn't be so because that's not the way it is. I've never talked to

anybody about that situation, so I told my doctor. For some reason or other I said I'd like to try something to see if I'm still alive or not. And so anyway he says, "Do you want to try this Viagra?" I say I don't like drugs or anything artificial. Maybe my time is over and that should be the end of that. But then I tried [Viagra]. (Joel, fifty-five years old, white, heterosexual, unknown occupation)[69]

. . . For most of these consumers, an active, erect penis symbolizes normal health, masculinity, and sexuality. A limp penis or absence of virility appears to symbolize death of the body as well as of manhood. To capture this disinterest in life that comes with erectile failure, Pfizer has chosen the tag line "Love Life Again" to sell its product.

As we have seen, for both male consumers and (usually male) practitioners, communicating about pain, loss, and concerns associated with sexual problems can be difficult, embarrassing, and heavily laden with metaphor, myth, and shame.[70] Phrases such as "it's over" and "I'm no longer alive," along with labels such as "shrinking," "eunuch," and "incomplete" reveal male discomfort with discussing sexuality and convey the degree of importance erectile functioning plays in men's sense of self, masculinity, and health. These men visit doctors with their complaints to investigate ways to fix their selves, their manhood, and their health. In the process, patients look to practitioners and those around them to provide a rationale for their troubles. . . .

Repair = Trouble

Not all consumers buy into the techno-fix model. Some consumers commented that although Viagra may promise bodily repair or enhancement, it can actually cause more trouble than it's worth. In this section, consumers indicate that Viagra creates problems, not solutions. For Joel and Don, Viagra is constructed as techno-trouble, rendering the male body increasingly out of control.

> I don't ever want to try [Viagra] again. The thing about it is, the side effects could be very dangerous for someone a little older than I am. Because you do end up with palpitations. Your body is just not your body. So if [your functioning is] not normal, I think it's better to just let it

go at that. Or make pills that are much, much weaker. But I wouldn't recommend it for anybody. (Joel, fifty-five years old, white, heterosexual, unknown occupation)[71]

I have tried it. I went a long time and the bottom line is I don't like it. It hasn't done me any good and it had a harmful side effect—heart-burn and indigestion. I'm a little fearful of it. I'm a healthy guy and I don't take any maintenance medicines of any kind. My system seems to be functioning nicely. I think I'll just leave it alone. (Don, sixty-seven years old, white, heterosexual, retired fire captain)[72]

As we saw earlier, some men see Viagra as a tool to create the ideal flexible body. For other consumers, Viagra may produce a body that is overly rigid and inflexible. For them, the Viagra effect is "unnatural" and uncontrollable, and consequently undesirable for both Dusty, a homosexual student, and Stanford, a heterosexual counselor in his sixties.

Well, I also didn't like it because it was unnatural. Like you were hard and you stayed hard. And I also didn't like the fact that it guaranteed things would be sexual until you weren't hard. I didn't like the idea of being forced into being sexual. You can't do anything nonsexual when you are on it. So basically it guarantees that the entire period you are on it is going to be sexual. (Dusty, seventeen years old, white, homosexual, student)[73]

The idea that I thought was hilarious at first—that erection that won't go away—is not hilarious at all. In fact it happens and sometimes endangers one's life. (Stanford, sixty-five years old, white, heterosexual, counselor)[74]

For Stanford and, Dusty, Pfizer's Viagra tag line, "Love Life Again," is inappropriate. Instead of regaining an appreciation for life, these men see Viagra as dangerous or even deadly. While priapism or death can occur in rare instances of Viagra use, and even Pfizer admits that Viagra is not for everyone, neither Stanford nor Dusty experienced real bodily danger while taking Viagra. Nonetheless, both take Viagra seriously, remaining cautious and seeming to prefer the natural way to the artificial alternative.

Rather than lose control of their bodies or experience trouble through repair, some men construct alternatives to the pharmaceutical quick-fix model, accepting their bodies as they are or just "leaving it alone." Despite overwhelming evidence that Viagra is associated with the production of normal and/or mythic masculinity, men like Ollie and Joel work hard at reconstructing masculinity as separate from "erectile health." They insist that heterosexual masculinity can be achieved without the help of Viagra or consideration of erectile potential.

Oh no, if you don't feel like a man before you take the pill, you're not a man anyways. No, you have to know where you're at. If you have a little misfunction, that's minor. But you have to be a man before you go through that. It's not a macho pill. (Joel, fifty-five years old, white, heterosexual, unknown occupation)[75]

I've talked to a lot of different men about this. Some cannot live without sex. They feel their sex makes them the man that they are. And I'm not sure how important that is to me. I'm a man anyways. It's about self-esteem. What do you think about yourself to begin with? (Ollie, sixty-four years old, black, heterosexual, printer)[76]

For many, Viagra fits perfectly in a society that is known for pushing the limits of normal. Some men are critical of American culture and Viagra's role in perpetuating the endless pursuit of the quick fix. Hancock and Miles warn of a hedonistic, money-driven, artificial world, where there is a pill for everything. For them, Viagra exists in this world as a crutch or bandaid solution to larger social problems.

We are willing to take the latest thing that is fast and painless. Also, Americans seem to think happiness is their birthright. They take Viagra to become better, happier. And supermen. All that stuff about self-worth, image, and sex life, it's what people want. . . . And maybe those guys who think they need Viagra just need to chill out and reduce stress in their lives. It's about lifestyle modification more than anything, I think. Maybe we are too lazy and it just takes too long. We want something to work fast. (Hancock, sixty-nine years old, white, heterosexual, retired teacher)[77]

I think there is a gross overuse of drugs for happiness and well-being. Feeling depressed, get a script for a mood enhancer . . . feeling tired, get a pill for energy . . . want to have better sex, get some blue magic. What about the age-proven solution of removing or reducing the problems or stress factors affecting your life and then seeing if pharmacological agents are still needed? (Miles, forty-five years old, white, heterosexual, paramedic) [78]

Here, Miles and Hancock construct society as drug-infused, producing individuals who are dependent upon pills for health and happiness. They, along with Stu and Ollie, are critical of corporate and biotechnological attempts at constructing needs, desires, and easy markets for products.

> How do I express this? This is a . . . capitalist hegemony of our emotions. We live in a state of anomie, or at least we are told that we do, and we're also told what to do about it. Have you seen these commercials? I have files of "The Paxil Christmas" that I cut out of a magazine. This young college-aged woman in a family Christmas portrait and it says, "You can go home this year and have a good time. Paxil." Paxil and Prozac and Zoloft—that's what it was. They ran these ads and marketed them to different age groups and they are telling us what the problem is—creating a problem—and they give us a solution. We all have anxieties and relationship issues, and they do this to make it look like the way to solve your relationship issue is to take Paxil. The way to deal with your crazy family is to take Paxil. That way you don't have to address the relationship issues, substantive issues. I have a big problem with that. (Stu, thirty-six years old, white, homosexual, student)[79]

> I think everything we do nowadays is overblown. I just see that society is just driving us crazy, making us jump through hoops and do things we really don't need to do. So a drug for everything . . . I think they—or not they, but the way things are set up, is to make you want to do things. Even if you don't want to do it, you are driven if you pay attention to what's going on. I'm not that kind of person. I won't let you do me that way. You won't be able to drive me that way. I just don't believe in it. (Ollie, sixty-four years old, black, heterosexual, printer)[80]

These men are clearly critical of Viagra's potential to enforce social and gender ideals. They refuse to "buy into" mythic masculinity, and they see through the problematic language used to describe medical progress as well as so-called widespread public health crises. In this way some men do resist and reframe masculinity, biotechnology, and medical science in ways that make sense to them. Rather than construct their bodies as troubled, with Viagra as a technofix or magical solution, these consumers see Viagra as problematic, contributing to larger social problems. These skeptical voices, however, are easily drowned out by the overwhelming chorus of those who sing Viagra's praises.

Masculinity, Biotechnology, and Resistance

At the turn of a new century, the desire to "fix" and "erect" male sexuality and power in a male-dominated society appears to be strong. This desire is perhaps a reaction to the gains of women's liberation and sexual empowerment, and as some of the men I spoke with pointed out, we are also living in a time of self-help movements, expanding medicalization, great social change, and personal crisis. Today it is not uncommon to hear about American social problems such as "male betrayal," the "malaise among men," and the "masculinity crisis." Just as Betty Friedan warned against women "buying into" their own victimhood in the 1960s, so now it is argued that men are buying into commercially packaged manhood in many forms, including "amped-up virility" and "technologically-enhanced supermanhood."[81]

When Lewis Carroll wrote *Alice's Adventures in Wonderland* in 1865, the idea of an ingestible tonic that would answer Alice's wishes and make her "grow large" was a magical, fantastical fantasy. Today, we all inhabit this magical reality, surrounded and tempted by endless products packaged in promises of personal transformation. This is the era when the "magic bullet" for sexual energy, confidence, and masculinity comes in the form of a pill. Today, so-called lifestyle drugs of all types are available to anyone with access to the internet and a credit card. And Americans have a newly transformed relationship with biotechnology, one that goes beyond "healing" to "transforming" and "fixing" bodies with the help of reproductive technologies, hormones, implants, surgeries, and other technological innovations.

Today, enhancement technologies are not just instruments of self-improvement or even self-transformation—they are tools for working on the soul.[82] The new player in this enhancement tale is the man who has been told he is sick. With Viagra, a highly successful masculine empowerment campaign is underway, centered around a new, late-twentieth-century tool, a magic blue pill that promises to produce and enhance male "magic wands." The doctor's tools are now turned back on the doctor himself. The male body is constructed as in need of repair, and is a new site for medical and biotechnological innovation and healing. With health and fitness as the new testing ground for masculinity, Viagra enters doctors' and patients' worlds, envisioned as cutting-edge biotechnology and used, I argue, as a cultural and material tool in the production and achievement of "true" manhood. Then again, Viagra can lead to male confidence without even being ingested. One of my informants told me that he purchased Viagra at a time of intense sexual insecurity with a partner but hasn't had a chance to use it. He is hoping that just having it around will make him a more self-confident lover. Others echoed this idea, that simply pills in the medicine cabinet was enough of an assurance.

The implications of constructing the male body as sexually potent, or as a technologically enhanced machine, can be both hurtful and helpful, as medical professionals, Viagra consumers, and their partners have discovered. Here I think of a friend's lesson about the importance of antidepressants: "You can't start a revolution if you're so depressed you can't get out of bed!" Similarly, during the course of this research, practitioners told me that their patients would not be attentive to their partners' sexual needs or desires if they were insecure or paralyzed by their own. Thus Viagra enabled them to be more confident and attentive to themselves as well as to their partners. In this way, it is important to acknowledge that prescription drug use has the potential to enable broad social change.

Nonetheless, social historian Lynne Luciano warns,

> Medicalizing impotence lures men into believing there is a standard for erections to which they must adhere. By quantifying the normal erection—it has to be just hard enough to achieve penetration and last long enough to achieve ejaculation—medicalization forces men to conform to its specifications for masculinity. The results are twofold: first, men, like women, have their sexuality and desirability linked to physical parameters; second, emotion, sexual technique, and the role of one's partner are rendered insignificant. By making the erection the man, science isn't enhancing male sexuality, but sabotaging it.[83]

Like Luciano, many social theorists have recently expressed concern with the state of manhood in America. Sexologist and practicing therapist Wendy Stock points out that to focus on male bodies as Viagra-infused, finely tuned, flexible machines perpetuates a detached, unemotional masculinity. She comments, "Although a common cultural male fantasy is to be able to function like a machine, as the sexual equivalent of the Energizer Bunny, both men and women may lose something if medical interventions allow us to function without the necessity of emotional connection. Is the ability to perform like a sexual machine desirable, individually or on a cultural scale?"[84] Similarly, feminist journalist and social commentator Susan Faludi warns of a "performance culture . . . where people are encouraged to view themselves as commodities that are marketed and fine-tuned with chemicals, whether it's Viagra or Prozac or Botox injections."[85]

Despite such warnings, sexual medicine continues to expand, as experts and marketers find ways to understand and treat a wider and wider range of sexual troubles for men and women. At a major international conference on sexual dysfunction in 2003, definitions and treatments for "rapid ejaculation" and "delayed ejaculation" were being discussed and finalized. For women, delay or absence of orgasm, arousal, or desire is cause for medical intervention. Insurers also intervene, by setting rules about who has access to sexual health treatments, and how many. Meanwhile, performance anxiety will only grow as the definition of "normal" sexuality and masculinity narrows. As sexual medicine gets more and more commonplace, what will be the ramifications for those who don't follow medical protocol? For those who have little interest in sexuality, or in medical models of sexuality? Lynne Luciano poses similar questions, with no clear answers:

> What happens to a man or woman who doesn't want to take drugs to enhance sexuality, who is content to age without the benefit of pills and potions? How far are we willing to go in our public discourse about how much sex is enough, and what constitutes good sex, and how central a role sex should play in relationships? Medical advances and healthier lifestyles offer men hope for longer and more potent sex lives than at any other time

in history. But expectations are likely to continue to out-pace reality. Not even Viagra can guarantee sexual success for all men, all the time. What it can guarantee is a continuing moral and ethical debate.[86]

The individual stories in this [reading] add up to what I see as a larger, disturbing story about the pressures and requirements for being fully male in American society, and even worldwide. Are we doing our men a service in the Viagra era? As the doctors and patients that I interviewed and quote in this [reading] reveal, Viagra can and is being used to enforce and perpetuate an ideal masculinity. In this way consumers collaborate with medical professionals and pharmaceutical companies in an attempt to understand and fix "broken" bodies. Perhaps of more interest, my data also reveal the struggle with the necessity for the Viagra-enhanced body, and what that struggle represents. As men negotiate their relationship to this product, mainstream ideas about sexuality, masculinity, and health are both reinforced and redefined in important ways. For example, some men insist that "doing" masculinity does not require sexual performance. Others are critical of a society that increasingly promotes and depends upon biotechnology for achieving health and happiness. They have their own ideas about manhood, medicalization, and biotechnology that may or may not fit with Pfizer's. In general, this chapter reveals men complicating manhood by constructing not only corporate corporealities[87] but also "various and competing masculinities" in the Viagra era.[88] As most of us do, the men I spoke with are constantly negotiating social and cultural pressures to be healthy, young, sexual, and in control.

For Pfizer, fixing the broken male machine is supposed to be a simple process with the help of Viagra. The men in this [reading] suggest otherwise, pointing out that the bodily "repair" process, the man, and the culture he belongs to are all more complex than Pfizer may acknowledge.

NOTES

1. Michael Kimmel, *Manhood in America: A Cultural History* (New York: Free Press, 1996).

2. In the 1970s and 1980s, gender scholars began to complicate and problematize normative (and thus prescriptive) white, heterosexual "hegemonic masculinity." For more on hegemonic masculinity, see Robert Connell, *Masculinities* (Berkeley: University of California Press, 1995). Michael Messner, *The Politics of Masculinities: Men in Movements* (Thousand Oaks, CA: Sage Publications, 1997) argues that a singular, reductionist, unified masculinity does not reflect a society in which "at any given moment there are various and competing masculinities." Responding to feminist scholarship, early masculinities scholars argued that patriarchy forces men to oppress themselves and other men. Such scholars inspired many inquiries into male competition, power struggles, and self-objectification. Joseph Pluck's *The Myth of Masculinity* (Cambridge: MIT Press, 1981) suggested that hegemonic masculinity and the promotion of unattainable ideals caused men to experience "sex role strain" in trying to attain the unattainable. In this way, Pluck sparked an interest in male confusion and "crisis" related to out-of-date, inflexible, contradictory, turn-of-the-century sex roles. Similarly, Lynne Segal, in *Slow Motion: Changing Masculinities* (London: Virago, 1990) warned that lived masculinity is never the seamless, undivided construction it becomes in its symbolic manifestation. She argued that in the late twentieth century, masculinity was not in crisis per se, but it was less hegemonic than before. While contemporary, increasingly visible and complicated masculinities can exist in tension with potentially outdated roles and expectations, this tension can also lead to confusion about manhood and how to "do" it.

3. Connell, *Masculinities,* 45.

4. Kimmel, *Manhood in America,* 332

5. Connell proposes his own model, the "body-reflexive" model, in which the social relations of gender are experienced in the body and are constituted through bodily action. See Connell, *Masculinities,* 60–64.

6. See, for example, Susan Brood, *The Male Body: A New Look at Men in Public and Private* (New York: Farrar, Straus, and Giroux, 1999); Marc Faseau, *The Male Machine* (New York: Dell, 1975); Kimmel and Messner, *Men's Lives;* and Michael Kimmel, *Manhood in America.*

7. See, for example, Annie Potts, "The Essence of the Hard-On," in *Men and Masculinities* (3:1, 2000): 85–103. Also see Leonore Tiefer, "The Medicalization of Impotence: Normalizing Phallocentrism," *Gender and Society* (8, 1994): 363–77, and *Sex Is Not a Natural Act and Other Essays* (San Francisco: Westview Press, 1995).

8. See, for example, Potts, "The Essence of the Hard-On"; Tiefer, *Sex Is Not a Natural Act;* Lynne Luciano, *Looking Good: Male Body Image in Modern America* (New York: Hill and Wang, 2001); and Barbara L. Marshall, "'Hard Science:' Gendered Constructions of Sexual Dysfunction in the 'Viagra Age,'" *Sexualities* (5:2, 2002):131–58.

Phallocentrism refers to the phallus, a male organ that symbolizes power and control.

9. See, for example, Bordo, *The Male Body.*

10. Laura Mamo and Jennifer Fishman, "Potency in All the Right Places: Viagra as a Technology of the Gendered Body," *Body and Society* (7:4, 2001): 13–35.

11. A very limited cohort of scholars, primarily historians, has written about how white men's heterosexual bodies have been normalized and naturalized and, in rare cases, pathologized. See Bordo, *The Male Body.* Also see Vern Burlough, "Technology for the Prevention of 'les maladies produites par la masturbation,'" *Technology and Culture* (28:4, 1987): 828–32; and Kevin Mumford, "Lost Manhood Found: Male Sexual Impotence and Victorian Culture in the United States," *Journal of the History of Sexuality* (3:1, 1992). Kevin Mumford explores how male impotence was medicalized, constructed, and cured historically. Starting from advertisements promising male virility and vigor, Mumford traces the "crisis of masculinity" along with modernization and the changing American conceptions of male sexuality and masculinity from the 1830s to the 1920s.

12. All names have been changed to protect the identity of my informants. The twenty-seven male consumers I spoke with are a self-selected group who responded to the interview requests I made through internet postings, newspaper advertisements, practitioner referrals, senior-citizens organizations, personal contacts, and prostate cancer support-group meeting announcements. Those consumers who volunteered for an interview generally had experience with Viagra and had an interest in sharing this experience because it had affected their lives in some way (good or bad). A group of men from a post-prostate-surgery support group agreed to speak with me over the phone under conditions of anonymity and confidentiality about their experiences dealing with surgery-induced ED. Interestingly, all had tried Viagra, and none had had any "success" with it, a fact that turned several of the interviews into "ranting" sessions, which rendered visible how emotionally invested these consumers were in Viagra's promise. Of the twenty-seven male consumers I spoke with, all but two had tried Viagra, and half of these discontinued using Viagra after the initial trial because of unsatisfactory response or preference for a different product. This "take rate" is representative of the larger population of Viagra users nationally; Pfizer's research has shown that over half of those who receive a prescription for Viagra do not request a refill.

13. In addition to being the only Viagra expert known to most men, their doctors are the only person most men feel comfortable talking to about their sexual problems.

14. I also spoke with twenty-two medical practitioners. Six of the twenty-two medical professionals I spoke with are female; sixteen are male. Eight are acclaimed experts in sexual medicine, regularly publishing and delivering lectures on female sexual dysfunction.

15. Dr. Bern, interview with author, tape recording, California: August 2000.

16. Phil, phone interview, tape recording, May 2000.

17. Byron, phone interview, tape recording, May 2000.

18. In *The Male Body,* Susan Bordo explores the link between masculinity and the phallus throughout Western history from Roman phallic gods to St. Augustine's "lustful member" to John Bobbitt's detachable penis to Clinton's not-so-private parts (24–25). Bordo argues that for as long as we can remember, the phallus has embodied our cultural imagination, symbolic of power, permission, defiance, and performance. Annie Potts adds that medicine and sexology produce and perpetuate the idea that an erect penis signifies "healthy" male sexuality—a destructive form of hegemonic masculinity that "ignores the diversity of penile pleasures" (89).

19. The idea that female sexuality can only be awakened by (or responsive to) the male was popular in marriage manuals of the early twentieth century and currently exist in medical discourse about female sexual dysfunction. . . .

20. Potts, "The Essence of the Hard-On," 98. Potts argues that we need an expansive view of male sexuality that need not rely on phallic ambitions. This would require a rethinking of penis power, "a relinquishment of this organ's executive position in sex," and an "embrace of a variety of penile styles: flaccid, erect, and semiflaccid/semierect" (100).

21. For more on gender as an accomplishment, see Candace West and Don Zimmerman, "Doing Gender," *Gender and Society* (1, 1987): 125–51; and Candace West and Sarah Fenstermaker, "Doing Difference," *Gender and Society* (9:1, 1995): 8–38. Also see West and Fenstermaker, *Doing Gender: Doing Difference* (New York: Routledge, 2002).

22. See, for example, Diane Dull and Candace West, "Accounting for Cosmetic Surgery: The Accomplishment of Gender," *Social Problems* (38:1, 1991): 54–71; and Kathy Davis, *Reshaping the Female Body: The Dilemma of Cosmetic Surgery* (New York: Routledge, 1995).

23. Donna Haraway, *Simians, Cyborgs, and Women: The Reinvention of Nature* (New York: Routledge, 1991): 149.

24. See Emily Martin, *Flexible Bodies* (Boston: Beacon Press, 1994).

25. Elizabeth Grosz, *Space, Time, and Perversion: Essays on the Politics of Bodies* (New York: Routledge, 1995): 35.

26. See any of Goldstein's coauthored reports in the *International Journal of Impotence Research,* volumes 10, 11, 12, and 15.

27. Dr. Curt, interview with author, tape recording, California: August 2000.

28. Chuck, phone interview, tape recording, May 2000.

29. Differing markedly in age, health, and reason for using Viagra (and, less markedly, in race, occupation, and sexual orientation), my sample is representative of a diversity of Viagra users. Pfizer identifies its largest market as "men over forty years of age." Pfizer Pharmaceuticals, Inc., *Patient Summary of Information about Viagra,* Fact Sheet, 1999, 2000; and *Uncover Ed,* Pfizer Informational Brochure, March 2000. In my sample of male consumers, diseases, medications, and surgeries were the most frequently cited reasons for trying Viagra. Ten of the twenty-seven male consumers I interviewed experienced erectile difficulties after undergoing prostate surgery. Others blamed erectile dysfunction on age (four), diabetes (one), heart problems (one), and medications (two). Three consumers cited psychological (self-esteem) factors as the main cause of their erectile difficulties. Perhaps of most interest is the significant number of interviewees who denied they had erectile dysfunction (seven), and instead explained that they used Viagra as an assurance or enhancement drug. Pfizer does not officially acknowledge or discuss this population of Viagra users in its promotional or training information, although these users may fall into the "mild ED" and "psychological and other factors" categories.

30. Nora Jacobson found this to be the case with breast implants in her book *Cleavage: Technology, Controversy, and the Ironies of the Man-Made Breast* (New Brunswick, NJ: Rutgers University Press, 2000). Some have suggested that gay males are a ready market for the "enhancement" uses of Viagra, including several of my gay interview subjects. But both gay and straight men in my interview pool expressed interest in the enhancement uses of Viagra.

31. Will, interview with author, tape recording, California: September 2000.

32. Stanford, interview with author, tape recording, California: August 2000.

33. Previous treatments for ED included a liquid injected directly into the penis, which would produce an erection for several hours (Caverject). Viagra is constructed as a superior treatment due to its simple delivery (as a pill) and production of a penis that will wait to become erect until the user is ready.

34. See Martin, *Flexible Bodies.*

35. Stu, interview with author, tape recording, California: October 2000.

36. Dr. Tobin, phone interview, tape recording, May 2000.

37. Will, Ibid.

38. Potts, in "The Essence of the Hard-On" (94), reminds us that the true mark of therapeutic success is restoration of "phallic manhood."

39. This idea comes from Riessman, "Women and Medicalization: A New Perspective," *Social Policy* (14:1, 1983).

40. Dr. Pellis, interview with author, tape recording, California: May 2000.

41. Dr. Redding, interview with author, tape recording, California: May 2000.

42. Dr. Blackwood, phone interview, tape recording, May 2000.

43. Dr. Bern, Ibid.

44. Peter Conrad and Joseph Schneider, *Deviance and Medicalization: From Badness to Sickness* (London: Mosby, 1980); and Riessman, "Women and Medicalization."

45. See Edward Laumann, A. Paik, and R. Rosen, "Sexual Dysfunction in the United States: Prevalence and Predictors," *JAMA* (281:6, 1999): 537–44. . . .

46. Dr. Loud, interview with author, tape recording, California: August 2000.

47. Dr. Cummings, interview with author, tape recording, California: August 2000.

48. Thom, phone interview, tape recording, May 2000.

49. Scott, e-mail interview, e-mail transcript, May 2000.

50. There is a long-standing struggle between therapists and practitioners to locate the source of erectile dysfunction and treat either physiological or psychological manifestations of the problem.

51. Ricardo, phone interview, tape recording, August 2000.

52. Barbara L. Marshall, "'Hard Science.'"

53. Viagra competitor Enzyte is an over-the-counter product that offers "natural male enhancement," which seems to put Viagra in the "unnatural" (synthetic) category.

54. Irwin Goldstein, phone interview, tape recording, November 2000.

55. Long, interview with author, tape recording, California: October 2000.

56. I never expected to be a stand-in for consumers' doctors. In these cases where consumers asked for advice, I awkwardly assured them that I was not an expert on ED, but judging from my interviews with other male consumers, their experiences sounded normal. If the side effects they mentioned sounded potentially dangerous (like heart palpitations or trouble breathing), I advised them to contact their doctors as soon as possible.

57. Interestingly, several of the men I spoke with, primarily those who had undergone prostate surgery, felt more of a stigma associated with incontinence than with impotence. This is yet another area where millions of men suffer in silence.

58. See Janice Raymond, *Transsexual Empire: The Making of the She-Male* (New York: Atheneum, 1994).

59. Fred, phone interview, tape recording, August 2000.

60. Scott, Ibid.

61. Dr. Pemel, interview with author, tape recording, California: August 2000.

62. Wilshore, interview with author, tape recording, California: May 2000.

63. Pal, email interview, e-mail transcript, August 2000.

64. Bordo, in *The Male Body,* argues that in a culture where "big and bulky" represent male ideals, "shrinkage" is feared, as evidenced in popular culture *(Seinfeld, Boogie Nights,* etc.).

65. Bob, interview with author, tape recording, California: August 2000.

66. Dr. Pemel, Ibid.

67. Potts, "The Essence of the Hard-On," 96.

68. Irwin Goldstein, Ibid.

69. Joel, interview with author, tape recording, California: October 2000.

70. Relationship experts have described this "delicate dance" that couples do when they are dealing with situations like sexual dysfunction. Without open communication between partners, the fear of "failure" can lead to avoidance and alienation, which can only exacerbate the problem.

71. Joel, Ibid.

72. Don, Ibid.

73. Dusty, interview with author, tape recording, California: August 2000.

74. Stanford, Ibid.

75. Joel, Ibid.

76. Ollie, phone interview, tape recording, May 2000.

77. Hancock, phone interview, tape recording, May 2000.

78. Miles, e-mail interview, e-mail transcript, August 2000.

79. Stu, Ibid.

80. Ollie, Ibid.

81. Quoted in Susan Faludi, *Stiffed: The Betrayal of the American Male* (New York: Morrow, 1999): 602.

82. See Carl Elliott, *Better Than Well: American Medicine Meets the American Dream* (New York: Norton, 2003): 53.

83. Luciano, *Looking Good,* 165.

84. Wendy Stock and C. Moser, "Feminist Sex Therapy in the Age of Viagra," in *New Directions in Sex Therapy: Innovations and Alternatives,* P. Kleinplatz, ed. (New York: Brunner-Routledge, 2001): 27.

85. P. J. Huffstutter and Ralph Frammolino, "Lights! Camera! Viagra! When the Show Must Go On, Sometimes a Little Chemistry Helps," *Los Angeles Times,* July 6, 2001, A1.

86. Luciano, *Looking Good,* 204.

87. I have Michael Kimmel to thank for helping me come up with this term.

88. This phrase is borrowed from Michael Messner's *Politics of Masculinities.*

In Search of (Better) Sexual Pleasure:
Female Genital "Cosmetic" Surgery

Virginia Braun

In this [reading], I explore the role of "sexual pleasure" in accounts of female genital "cosmetic"[1] surgery (FGCS). FGCS procedures are some of the newest to become popularized in the arsenal of surgical and other cosmetic procedures aimed at transforming the (female)[2] body in some way. My classification of genital surgery as FGCS does not include surgery for transsexual or intersex people,[3] nor is it "female genital mutilation" (FGM).[4] Procedures for (cosmetic) genital alteration include: labiaplasty/labioplasty (labia minora reductions), labia majora "augmentations" (tissue removal, fat injections), liposuction (mons pubis, labia majora), vaginal tightening (fat injections, surgical tightening), clitoral hood reductions, clitoral repositioning, G-spot "amplification" (collagen injected into the "G-spot," which swells it significantly), and hymen reconstruction (to restore the *appearance* of "virginity").

Like cosmetic surgery generally, FGCS can be seen as both *surgical* practice and *cultural* product (see Adams, 1997; Fraser, 2003) and practice (Haiken, 2000). Dubbed the "designer vagina," FGCS has received considerable media attention in recent years. Headlines range from the sensational—"I've saved my sex life" (M30)[5]—to the serious—"Designer vagina service a first for NZ" (N10). There is an apparent increase in the popularity of FGCS.... By some accounts, this increasing popularity is due, at least in part, to media coverage.

The material practice of FGCS, and women's participation in it, are enabled within particular sociocultural (and technological) contexts which render certain choices possible, and locate cosmetic surgery as a solution (K. Davis, 2003). The contexts of women's ongoing, widespread, and increasingly specific, body dissatisfactions (Bordo, 1997; Sullivan, 2001), ongoing negative meanings around women's genitalia (Braun and Wilkinson, 2001, 2003), and women's engagement in a wide range of body modification practices—such as hair removal (Toerien and Wilkinson, 2004)—cohere to render women's genitalia a viable site for surgical enhancement....

In this [reading], I focus specifically on the issue of (female) sexual pleasure in accounts of FGCS. Female sexual pleasure appears as a central concern, mirroring a broader socio-cultural shift towards the "eroticization of female sexuality" (Seidman, 1991: 124) with women's sexual pleasure located as central in (hetero)sex (e.g. Braun et al., 2003; Gordon, 1971) and beyond. . . . This increased attention to pleasure has also resulted in an increased attention to the body and sexual technique (Seidman, 1991), with possible concurrent increases in feelings of sexual inadequacy (Hart and Wellings, 2002). I will show that the story of FGCS is, at least in part, a story of the (legitimate) search for (better) female sexual pleasure, and argue that this functions not only to legitimate, and promote, FGCS, but also to reaffirm particular models of desirable sexual bodies and practices.

Theorizing and Researching FGCS

This [reading] is part of a broader project on FGCS which analyses data drawn from two datasets: media accounts and surgeon interviews. The research is situated with a (feminist) social constructionist framework (Burr, 1995; Tiefer, 1995, 2000; White et al., 2000), which theorizes language and social representations as an integral part of the production of social (and material) realities for individuals, as well as producing possibilities for individual practices. Sexuality is thus a material, but always social, practice (Connell, 1997; Jackson and Scott, 2001). . . .

My convenience sample was located primarily through Google searches using terms like "designer vagina" and "labiaplasty," and through surgeon websites. . . . My [media] analysis in this [reading] focuses on the [data from 31] print [magazines]. . . .

24 surgeons were contacted and invited to take part in semi-structured interviews, with 15 agreeing. . . .

FGCS and Female Sexual Pleasure

Women's sex lives or their sexuality was often reported to be impeded in some way, with pre-operative genitalia:

Extract 1: Woman's Day Magazine, NZ, 2004

Amanda was utterly miserable. She no longer enjoyed sex with Russell, the husband she adored, and on those rare occasions when they made love, Amanda would insist they switch off the lights. (M30)

In this and other extracts, general pre-surgical sexual "impediments" were noted. In addition, specific causes of such sexual impediments were identified in many accounts:

Extract 2: male plastic surgeon, UK

S1: what comes in more and in my practice it is not—quite often it's not purely cosmetic but there are functional complaints with the labia the size of the labia too . . . for example . . . it can be painful during intercourse because the labium keeps going in and out with every thrust.

Although physical pain was often discussed, the *psychological* response to genital morphology was frequently highlighted as the crux of the problem which "hampered" or "ruined" their sex life:

Extract 3: male plastic surgeon, NZ

S6: I think most . . . of the women that I've dealt with have thought that this was a real impediment to

sexual enjoyment . . . not so much from their point of view but from their partner's point of view . . . if they were worried about their partner not liking whatever they could see or . . . touch or whatever then they felt tense themselves . . . and so the enjoyment of everything goes (spiralling) . . . down. . . .

Extract 4: Cosmopolitan Magazine, AUS/NZ, 1998

Sarah, a 27-year-old secretary is a case in point. Throughout puberty, she thought her vaginal lips were too long and was embarrassed by one that hung lower than the other.

"They ruined my sex life," she recalls. "I never felt confident during sex—I felt like a freak. I'd never let anyone see me naked." (M1)

Extract 5: New Woman Magazine, AUS, 2003

. . . the biggest problem was sex. I've been with my boyfriend since I was 15 but I always felt self-conscious when we made love. I'd engineer positions so that he'd always be behind me and couldn't see my vagina, and I'd never have oral sex because I couldn't bear him seeing me up close. (M20)

The psychological problems invoked to explain a (pre-surgery) sexual impediment included embarrassment, self-consciousness, lack of confidence, and shame. The inclusion of such concepts fits with Frank's (2003) observation of an "inflation of the language of pain" around medicine to include such psychological concepts. In my data, this negative psychological response to *appearance* often resulted, via other psychological responses like anxiety or self-consciousness, in an inability to "receive" oral sex from a male partner, an account which fits with women's reports of various genital anxieties, particularly around oral sex (Braun and Wilkinson, 2003; Reinholtz and Muehlenhard, 1995; Roberts et al., 1996). Women's reports of genital anxiety reflect a range of negative sociocultural representations of women's genitalia (Braun and Wilkinson, 2001), and it seems some women "live these [negative] cultural meanings in their embodiment" (Roberts et al., 1996: 119). However, my concern is not just about women's embodiment, as psychology here provides the "moral justification" (Frank, 2003) for cosmetic surgery to alleviate this distress.

While *impeded* sexual possibilities and pleasures were central in media and surgeon accounts of why women might choose to have FGCS, *increased* sexual pleasure as an outcome of surgery was the main area in which sexual pleasure was discussed. FGCS, in a variety of forms, was represented as increasing sexual pleasure. The *aim* of sexual enhancement was often explicitly stated in the titles of magazine articles about FGCS—"THE G-SHOT . . . plastic surgery for your orgasm" (M22)—and in the setting up of media stories:

Extract 6: New Woman Magazine, UK, date unknown

Would you go under the knife to improve your sex life? These four women did. (M29)

Extract 7: Marie Claire Magazine, UK, 2000

What are the reasons for surgery? Firstly, to improve their sex lives. (M4)

Extract 8: Marie Claire Magazine, US, 2000

Some women are going under the knife to change the appearance of their genitals, while others are having surgery in the hopes of better orgasms. (M3)

In some, the possibility of increased sexual pleasure was initially framed with mild scepticism:

Extract 9: Cosmopolitan Magazine, AUS/NZ, 1998

Doctors [in the US] claim to be able to boost women's sexual pleasure, taking them to previously uncharted erotic heights. And their secret weapon in the quest for sexual ecstasy? The scalpel. (M1)

Extract 10: Marie Claire Magazine, UK, 2000

The sales pitch being that sexual gratification of the female is diminished if friction is lost because of a slack vagina, so this procedure tightens up your bits and helps you reach orgasm. (M4)

Extract 11: FQ Magazine, NZ, 2004

Will sex be mind-blowing once you've been trimmed or tightened? Well, the jury is still out. (M31)

Any initial scepticism in reporting the doctors' "claim" that the operations "supposedly increase sexual pleasure" (M3) was typically not reiterated in most media accounts of surgical results and patient experiences, or in surgeon accounts. Instead, overwhelmingly, increased pleasure was noted:

Extract 12: Cleo Magazine, NZ, 2001

Feedback from patients suggests their sex lives have improved enormously. (M7)

Extract 13: male urologist, AUS

S7: I've known women who are mono-orgasmic to become multiply orgasmic as a result.

All procedures, even ostensibly cosmetic ones such as labiaplasty, were frequently framed as being "successful" in terms of increased sexual pleasure:

Extract 14: Cosmopolitan Magazine, AUS/NZ, 2004

I am no longer embarrassed to be naked and my sex life has improved because I'm more confident. (M23)

Extract 15: Company Magazine, UK, 2003

I was so thrilled with my new vagina, Dan and I "tried it out" after just four weeks. What a difference—it was like my whole sex life was beginning again. Suddenly I discovered how amazing oral sex could be, because I could finally relax and be myself during sex. I didn't have to worry about my boyfriend seeing me naked. (M18)

In these extracts, improved sexual function was identified as a key outcome of "cosmetic" procedures. In Extract 15, psychological changes post-surgery allowed the woman to experience cunnilingus. Surgery reportedly expanded women's sexual repertoires. However, such reports continue to situate heterosex within the bounds of normative heterosexuality, through the suggestion that certain sexual acts (cunnilingus) can only be engaged in, and enjoyed, by either or both partners, within a very limited range of female genital aesthetics. This aesthetic is one where the labia minora do not protrude beyond the labia majora—a youthful, almost pre-pubescent aesthetic, and one often associated with, and derived from, the "unreal" vulvas displayed in heterosexual male-oriented pornography (see Adams, 1997; S. W. Davis, 2002). This was explicitly noted:

Extract 16: Shine Magazine, AUS/NZ, 2001

A lot of women bring in Playboy, show me pictures of vaginas and say, "I want to look like this." (M5)

The genital produced is one in which diversity is replaced with conformity to this particular aesthetic, a "cookie cutter" (I25) genital. FGCS becomes a practice of changing women's diverse bodies to fit a certain (male-oriented) aesthetic of what women's genitals *should look like,* if they are to engage in cunnilingus (or other sexual activities). With male (hetero)sexuality continuing to be constructed as *visual* (e.g. Moghaddam and Braun, 2004), with desire based on the aesthetic, such accounts reinforce a traditional model of male sexuality, and female sexuality alongside it. FGCS effectively becomes surgery to change bodies to fit, and to enable certain sexual practices, through psychological/emotional changes enabled by bodily transformation. A pathologization of "large" labia minora has a long history, and a long association with perceived sexual "deviance" (S. Gilman, 1985; Terry, 1995). FGCS appears to offer a surgical process for subsequently passing—to oneself, as well as others—as "sexy" or just as "normal" (see K. Davis, 2003).

In these accounts, sexual pleasure occupies a status of almost unquestioned good. . . . There are "cultural expectations that each individual has a right and a duty to achieve and give maximum satisfaction in their sexual relationships" (Nicolson, 1993: 56). FGCS is framed as a viable means to achieve this. A key question to consider, however, is what (female) sexual pleasure is being offered:

Extract 17: Cosmopolitan Magazine, AUS/NZ, 1998

Four months after the operation, Kate claims to be enjoying the best sex of her life . . . "removing the excess fat has made me much more easily aroused. Now I achieve orgasm easily and often." (M1)

Extract 18: New Woman Magazine, AUS, 2003

"The G-Shot procedure is all about maximising sexual pleasure for women. By injecting a fluid made up partly of collagen we can increase the G spot to three or four times its normal size, so it's easier to stimulate.

"The effects last about four months and my patients tell me how even something as gentle as yoga is giving them orgasms!" (M20)

Extract 19: New Woman Magazine, UK, date unknown

What a result though! All I have to do is think about sex and I can feel my G spot react. Even during my spinning class I can feel the bike seat pressing on it—and I have

to pretend I'm just enjoying the workout! I've also had my first ever multiple orgasm and it was great. (M29)

The conception of "sexual pleasure" for women was typically synonymous with orgasm—or multiple-orgasm. By prioritizing orgasm over other forms of sexual pleasure, such accounts work to reaffirm an orgasm imperative (Heath, 1982; Potts, 2000). Orgasm was framed, a-contextually, as positive—the possibility of orgasm in non-sexual situations was identified not negatively (as, for instance, impeding the woman's ability to partake in exercise without fear of orgasm), but rather positively. Typically, orgasm was framed in unequivocally positive ways:

Extract 20: Cleo Magazine, NZ, 2003

Rosemary is promised about four months of orgasmic delights . . . having heard about the G-Shot through a friend who raved about her endless climaxes, Rosemary had no hesitation in handing over US$1850 for a dose of heightened pleasure. (M22)

Therefore, the accounts of pleasure in heterosex—and it typically *was* heterosex—presented in the data failed to offer any radical questioning of orgasm as the pinnacle of sexual pleasure and achievement (Jackson and Scott, 2001; Potts, 2000). "Better" sex typically meant orgasmic sex (or, sometimes, simply more sex), and more (and better) sex was inherently framed as good. By locating orgasm as so central to women's sexual pleasure, other ways in which sex could be more pleasurable—e.g. more fun, more intense, more relaxed, more intimate—were relegated to second place, if any, behind orgasm. This affirms what Seidman (1992: 7) has identified as a "new tyranny of orgasmic pleasure."

Although physical changes, such as an enlarged G-spot or tighter vagina, were often identified as resulting in increased pleasure, *psychological* elements were also highlighted as key in explanations for increased sexual pleasure, post-surgery:

Extract 21: male plastic surgeon, UK

S1:   when you feel better about what you look like down there if you feel happier with the cosmetic aspect of . . . yourself of your genitalia then you are more relaxed in the bedroom . . . and a lot of patients report back to me that they do feel better and therefore have better sex because . . . they're less embarrassed. . . .

Extract 22: Flare Magazine, CA, 1998

What does work, according to Angela, is the boost in self-esteem that stems from feeling sexually confident. "I spent years not feeling good about myself and my sexuality," she says. "I started to retreat from my husband. I tried to avoid him sexually because every time we tried, it was disastrous."

It all gets back to the psychosexual response, says Dr Stubbs. (M26)

Extract 23: Shine Magazine, AUS/NZ, 2001

My sex life has improved so much since the operation— we have more sex now than we've ever had. I'm much more into my boyfriend and now that I'm tighter, I'm much more confident about initiating sex. Even better, my boyfriend is enjoying sex with me more, as there's much more stimulation for him, too. (M5)

In these extracts, the psychological was invoked as an essential ingredient in the production of female pleasure, and, indeed, situated as a primary reason this surgery was effective in producing increased sexual pleasure for women. . . .

Extract 23 is relatively unusual in that increased male sexual pleasure was noted. Women were the primary focus in accounts of sexual pleasure, with comparatively little discussion of male sexual pleasure. This is not surprising, as cosmetic surgery is necessarily often framed as "for oneself" rather than for others (see Fraser, 2003). Where male sexual pleasure was referred to, it was often positioned as secondary to, or less important than, female sexual pleasure. For instance, Extract 23 situates her boyfriend's increased sexual pleasure as secondary to her pleasure, as an added bonus, something that makes it "even better.". . .

Overall, the prioritizing of female sexual pleasure and general lack of discussion of male sexual pleasure work to construct FGCS as something that is in the (sexual) interests of women, rather than in the sexual interests of (heterosexual) men. Through current accounts, FGCS is effectively constructed as a liberatory action for women—it produces sexual pleasure, which is, socioculturally, almost mandatory for women—rather than a capitulation to unreasonable patriarchal demands on women's bodies. However, while FGCS offers (apparent) empowerment to individuals who have it, albeit within a limited range of options, it simultaneously reinforces oppressive

social norms for women (see Gagne and McGaughey, 2002; Gillespie, 1996; Negrin, 2002).

FGCS: Normative Heterosexuality, Generic Bodies, and Generic Pleasures

The central role that (female) pleasure plays in accounts of FGCS is revealing in terms of contemporary discourses of (hetero)sexuality and what it could/should mean to be a woman in the West today. Women's sexual pleasure—or ability to orgasm—appears as a central concern for women, and indeed for society. The account is almost exclusively one where, sexually, women should be comfortable in their bodies and should be able to enjoy sex—and the more sex, and sexual pleasure, the better. Women are represented as (inherently) entitled to sexual pleasure, and indeed, inherently, (hetero)sexual. That *these* women are not sexually "liberated," sexually "satisfied," or, even, as sexually satisfied as other people appear to be, is, at least in part, what is "wrong" with their preoperative genitalia. In this sense, accounts of FGCS and women's sexual pleasure fit squarely within a discourse of liberal sexuality (Hollway, 1989), and even, within some feminist discourse around the importance of equality in sex (see Braun et al., 2003). It also affirms an imperative for "more and better sexual gratification" (Hart and Wellings, 2002: 899), by whatever means possible.

However, the construction of female sexual pleasure in relation to this surgery fails to challenge the bounds of normative heterosexuality. First, sexual pleasure was often (although not exclusively) framed as being derived through coitus, particularly in the case of vaginal tightening, and the sexual pleasure that is derived was typically orgasmic. In this sense, it can be seen to be (at least in part) a practice of designing bodies to fit certain sexual practices, rather than designing sexual practices to fit bodies. We then have to ask whether it is so different from the "love surgery" of the now disgraced Dr. James Burt, who surgically altered women's genitalia to make them more amenable to stimulation during coitus (Adams, 1997). As Adams (1997: 64) noted, such surgeries "make women conform to traditional heterosexual values." The same criticism applies to FGCS: the sexual "freedom" that is being produced is a freedom to enjoy sex within a very limited frame of reference.

Moreover, at the same time as it constructs the legitimate female body as an orgasmic one, it reinforces this "ideal" as something not all women necessarily (easily) achieve (without surgery). So sexual pleasure, through orgasm, is simultaneously situated both as what most women can/should do and as a current impossibility for some women. The very construction of FGCS as surgery to enhance or enable orgasm fits with an ongoing construction of a woman's orgasm as difficult to achieve, in contrast to a man's inevitable one (Jackson and Scott, 2001; Moghaddam and Braun, 2004). Moreover, although couched in terms of liberation of women (to a "full" enjoyment of sex), rather than pathology, the framing of FGCS as a solution to "sub-par" sexual pleasure on the woman's part decontextualizes sex, locating any deficiency in the woman's body/mind, and offering an individualized solution. In this way, FGCS fits within a broadening medicalization of sexual behaviour (Hart and Wellings, 2002; Tiefer, 1997), which, Tiefer (1997: 112) has argued, has "only reinforced a limited script for heterosexual sexual life."

These points raise the question of the generic versus the particular. The idea of a surgical "fix" or enhancement of (lack of) sexual pleasure locates sexual pleasure at the level of the *individual* body, rather than in relation to a "fit" between bodies/people and the practices they are engaged in. In this sense, the sexual enhancement of the body is framed as generic sexual enhancement, regardless of with whom, and how, one might be having sex. This framing disregards the particularities of sex, with different partners, with different practices, for different purposes, and, indeed, in different moods, modes, and venues. Sex, sexual pleasure, and even sexual desires vary hugely according to this range of contextualizing variables. Accounts of FGCS not only fail to account for this, but actually work to promote the idea of generic sexual pleasure as possible.

The context of consumer culture provides another angle from which to examine public discourse around FGCS. Bordo's (1997: 42) analysis identifies that a consumer system "depends on our perceiving ourselves as defective and that will continually find new ways to do this." Media accounts that demonstrate a "cure" to

some problem for women can be seen to also contribute to the creation of that problem in the first place. FGCS, and media coverage of it, have the potential to produce consumer anxiety (S. W. Davis, 2002). One item commented that media coverage had "taken a very unusual phenomena and concocted a new "embarrassing problem" that could get readers squinting nervously at the privates" (M28). In the case of labiaplasty, then, there is the potential that "a brand-new worry is being created" (S. W. Davis, 2002: 8). In these accounts, the appearance and sexual function of women's genitalia are rendered *legitimately* problematic and sub-optimal; this part of the body is legitimately commodified, and positioned as "upgradeable" (see Negrin, 2002). More than this, these media have the potential to construct the very nature of problems and their *solutions,* simultaneously. Both the problem of aesthetically "unappealing" genitalia and the desire for better sex have a ready worked-up solution—surgery.

While FGCS might seem relatively arcane, a form of cosmetic surgery very few women would access, and one that is unlikely to become popular, the surgeons I interviewed indicated that media coverage seems to increase demand for their services. This fits with Kathy Davis' (2003: 134) observation that media coverage of new surgical interventions "seduc[es] more individuals to place their bodies under the surgeon's knife" (see also Wolf, 1990). The history of other cosmetic procedures does nothing to dispute this concern. Indeed, as Haiken [1997] has commented in her history of cosmetic surgery, individual change can often be "easier" than social change. . . .

The appearance of FGCS raises important questions about the alteration of the body in the pursuit of pleasure, which I have only started to address. If media coverage can contribute to the nature of, and legitimate, a "new" problem for women, with a ready-made surgical solution, we need to continue to act as "cultural critics" (Bordo, 1993), and question the assumptions on which such surgery rests, and the models of sexuality, bodies, and practices it promotes.

NOTES

1. My classification of these surgeries as "cosmetic" is not necessarily the way surgeons or the women themselves

would classify them. Some of these surgeries are primarily (or exclusively) done for functional reasons, and even where cosmesis is prioritized, the notion that surgery is purely cosmetic is challenged through diverse accounts of "functionality."

2. Although cosmetic surgery is increasingly popular among men, it is important to retain some sense of the gendered context in which cosmetic procedures originated and became popularized, such that women were (and continue to be) the primary consumers of cosmetic surgery (see K. Davis, 2003, for a discussion of the limitations of "equality" analyses in relation to cosmetic surgery).

3. The techniques might be the same or similar in some instances. At a more theoretical level, the practices around the construction of "normal" genitalia through FGCS are, like other genital surgeries, part of the ongoing social, and material, construction of (gendered) genital meaning and appearance. Moreover, an inappropriately "masculine" appearance/perception of their genitalia was one of the reported reasons some women desired FGCS. The constructed genitalia tend to display *more* gendered genital difference (bigger penises, tighter vaginas, smaller labia minora). So while much cosmetic surgery can be seen to produce the surgical "erasure of embodied difference" (K. Davis, 2003: 133), the one difference that is promoted, rather than erased, in FGCS is "gendered" (genital) difference.

4. A comparison between these western practices and FGM was rarely mentioned in the data, and a focus on notions of "free choice," purported low risk to health, and likely increased sexual pleasure, all rhetorically constructed FGCS as inherently *different* to FGM. However, Manderson and colleagues (Allotey et al., 2001; Manderson, 1999) point to contradictions between how FGM and FGCS are treated in the West (see also S.W. Davis, 2002; Essen and Johnsdotter, 2004; Sheldon and Wilkinson, 1998).

5. Quotations from data are coded by letter and number: S = surgeon; M = magazine; N = news media; I = Internet material other than "Internet magazines." Numbers were applied sequentially across each data source, starting from 1. In the surgeon extracts, material in parentheses (like this) indicates a best guess as to what was said at that point on the tape.

REFERENCES

Adams, A. (1997) "Moulding Women's Bodies: The Surgeon as Sculptor," in D. S. Wilson and C. M. Laennec (eds) *Bodily Discursions: Gender, Representations, Technologies,* pp. 59–80. New York: State University of New York Press.

Allotey, P., Manderson, L. and Grover, S. (2001) "The Politics of Female Genital Surgery in Displaced Communities," *Critical Public Health* 11: 189–201.

Bordo, S. (1993) *Unbearable Weight: Feminism, Western Culture, and the Body.* Berkeley: University of California Press.

Bordo, S. (1997) *Twilight Zones: The Hidden Life of Cultural Images from Plato to O.J.* Berkeley: University of California Press.

Braun, V., Gavey, N. and McPhillips, K. (2003) "The 'Fair Deal'? Unpacking Accounts of Reciprocity in Heterosex," *Sexualities* 6(2): 237–61.

Braun, V. and Wilkinson, S. (2001) "Socio-cultural Representations of the Vagina," *Journal of Reproductive and Infant Psychology* 19: 17–32.

Braun, V. and Wilkinson, S. (2003) "Liability or Asset? Women Talk about the Vagina," *Psychology of Women Section Review* 5(2): 28–42.

Burr, V. (1995) *An Introduction to Social Constructionism.* London: Routledge.

Connell, R. W. (1997) "Sexual Revolution," in L. Segal (ed.) *New Sexual Agendas,* pp. 60–76. New York: New York University Press.

Davis, K. (2003) *Dubious Equalities and Embodied Differences: Cultural Studies on Cosmetic Surgery.* Lanham, MD: Rowman and Littlefield.

Davis, S. W. (2002) "Loose Lips Sink Ships," *Feminist Studies* 28: 7–35.

Essen, B. and Johnsdotter, S. (2004) "Female Genital Mutilation in the West: Traditional Circumcision versus Genital Cosmetic Surgery," *Acta Obstetricia et Gynecologica Scandinavica* 83: 611–13.

Frank, A. W. (2003) "Connecting Body Parts: Technoluxe, Surgical Shapings, and Bioethics." Paper presented at the *Vital Politics* Conference, London.

Fraser, S. (2003) *Cosmetic Surgery, Gender and Culture.* Houndmills: Palgrave Macmillan.

Gagne, P. and McGaughey, D. (2002) "Designing Women—Cultural Hegemony and the Exercise of Power Among Women Who Have Undergone Elective Mammoplasty," *Gender and Society* 16: 814–38.

Gillespie, R. (1996) "Women, the Body and Brand Extension in Medicine: Cosmetic Surgery and the Paradox of Choice," *Women and Health* 24(4): 69–85.

Gilman, S. (1985) *Difference and Pathology: Stereotypes of Sexuality, Race and Madness.* Ithaca, NY: Cornell University Press.

Gordon, M. (1971) "From an Unfortunate Necessity to a Cult of Mutual Orgasm: Sex in American Marital Education Literature 1830–1940," in J. M. Henslin (ed.)

Studies in the Sociology of Sex, pp. 53–77. New York: Appleton-Century-Crofts.

Haiken, E. (1997) *Venus Envy: A History of Cosmetic Surgery.* Baltimore, MD: The Johns Hopkins University Press.

Haiken, E. (2000) "The Making of the Modern Face: Cosmetic Surgery," *Social Research* 67: 81–93.

Hart, G. and Wellings, K. (2002) "Sexual Behaviour and its Medicalisation: in Sickness and Health," *British Medical Journal* 324: 896–900.

Heath, S. (1982) *The Sexual Fix.* New York: Schocken Books.

Hollway, W. (1989) *Subjectivity and Method in Psychology: Gender, Meaning and Science.* London: Sage.

Jackson, S. and Scott, S. (2001) "Embodying Orgasm: Gendered Power Relations and Sexual Pleasure," in E. Kaschak and L. Tiefer (eds) *A New View of Women's Sexual Problems,* pp. 99–110. New York: The Haworth Press.

Manderson, L. (1999) "Local Rites and the Body Politic: Tensions Between Cultural Diversity and Universal Rites," paper presented at the *Sexual Diversity and Human Rights: Beyond Boundaries* conference, Manchester, July.

Moghaddam, P. and Braun, V. (2004) "'Most of us Guys are Raring to go Anytime, Anyplace, Anywhere': Male (and Female) Sexuality in *Cosmopolitan* and *Cleo,*" Manuscript under submission.

Negrin, L. (2002) "Cosmetic Surgery and the Eclipse of Identity," *Body and Society* 8: 21–42.

Nicolson, P. (1993) "Public Values and Private Beliefs: Why do some Women Refer Themselves for Sex Therapy?" in J. M. Ussher and C. D. Baker (eds) *Psychological Perspectives on Sexual Problems: New Directions in Theory and Practice,* pp. 56–76. London: Routledge.

Potts, A. (2000) "Coming, Coming, Gone: A Feminist Deconstruction of Heterosexual Orgasm," *Sexualities* 3: 55–76.

Reinholtz, R. K. and Muehlenhard, C. L. (1995) "Genital Perceptions and Sexual Activity in a College Population," *Journal of Sex Research* 32: 155–65.

Roberts, C., Kippax, S., Spongberg, M. and Crawford, J. (1996) "'Going Down': Oral Sex, Imaginary Bodies and HIV," *Body and Society* 2(3): 107–24.

Seidman, S. (1991) *Romantic Longings: Love in America, 1830–1980.* New York: Routledge.

Seidman, S. (1992) *Embattled Eros: Sexual Politics and Ethics in Contemporary America.* New York: Routledge.

Sheldon, S. and Wilkinson, S. (1998) "Female Genital Mutilation and Cosmetic Surgery: Regulating Nontherapeutic Body Modification," *Bioethics* 12: 263–85.

Sullivan, D. A. (2001) *Cosmetic Surgery: The Cutting Edge of Commercial Medicine in America.* New Brunswick, NJ: Rutgers University Press.

Terry, J. (1995) "Anxious Slippages Between 'Us' and 'Them': A Brief History of the Scientific Search for Homosexual Bodies," in J. Terry and J. Urla (eds) *Deviant Bodies: Critical Perspectives on Difference in Science and Popular Culture,* pp. 129–69. Bloomington: Indiana University Press.

Tiefer, L. (1995) *Sex is Not a Natural Act and Other Essays.* Boulder, CO: Westview Press.

Tiefer, L. (1997) "Medicine, Morality, and the Public Management of Sexual Matters," in L. Segal (ed.) *New Sexual Agendas,* pp. 103–12. New York: New York University Press.

Tiefer, L. (2000) "The Social Construction and Social Effects of Sex Research: The Sexological Model of Sexuality," in C. B. Travis and J. W. White (eds.) *Sexuality, Society, and Feminism,* pp. 79–107. Washington, DC: American Psychological Association.

Toerien, M. and Wilkinson, S. (2004) "Exploring the Depilation Norm: a Qualitative Questionnaire Study of Women's Body Hair Removal," *Qualitative Research in Psychology* 1: 69–92.

White, J. W., Bondurant, B. and Travis, C. B. (2000) "Social Constructions of Sexuality: Unpacking Hidden Meanings," in C. B. Travis and J. W. White (eds) *Sexuality, Society, and Feminism,* pp. 11–33. Washington, DC: American Psychological Association.

Wolf, N. (1990) *The Beauty Myth.* London: Vintage.

The Pleasures of Childbirth

Ina May Gaskin

Is childbirth always painful? Although at first thought it might seem easy to answer this straightforward question with a loud and unequivocal yes, the truth is less simple. It is true that many women who have given birth more than once answer in the affirmative. But I have given birth four times without pain or medication, so my answer is not always. There are exceptions, and from them we can gain important insights about labor and birth.

I am far from being alone in saying that birth is not always painful. In fact, under the right circumstances and with good preparation during pregnancy, labor and birth can even be pleasurable for many women. How do I know? I have worked as a midwife for over thirty years, and many of the women I have attended have told me so. I have been with them during these ecstatic experiences, virtually all of which occurred in women who took no pain-numbing medication. Just as compelling, my own body has informed me.

Let's start by looking at some of the written evidence that exists. Numerous reports of painless birth have been gathered over the last couple of centuries by missionaries, travelers, soldiers, and doctors. Ezra Stiles, an early American clergyman and educator, wrote during the period of 1755 to 1794: "I have often been told that a pregnant Squaw [sic] will turn aside and deliver herself, and take up the Infant and wash it in a Brook, and walk off" (Vogel cited in Speert, 1980, p. 1).

Judith Goldsmith, a modern-day writer, has gathered many reports from European observers of various cultures. Among them is the following account of Guyanese women of South America in 1791: "When on the march an Indian is taken with labor, she just steps aside, is delivered, wraps up the baby with the afterbirth and runs in haste after the others. At the first stream that presents itself she washes herself and the infant" (1990, p. 2). Another seemingly painless birth was that noted by a visitor to the island of Alor, near Java, who witnessed six births without seeing a mother show real signs of pain. Sweat and soft groans were noted, but each of the six women gave birth easily (2). Livingston Jones, a visitor among the Tlinget people of Alaska, remarked: "The vast majority of Tlinget women suffer very little and some not at all, when their children are born. They have been known to give birth while sleeping" (cited in Goldsmith, 1990, p. 2).

Giving birth while sleeping! How can this be? As unusual as this seems, it can and does occasionally happen. Dr. Alice Stockham describes a doctor's account of a birth that took place in 1828:

On his arrival he found the house in the utmost confusion, and was told that the child had been born before the messenger was dispatched for the doctor. From the lady herself he learned that, about half an hour previously, she had been awakened from a natural sleep by the alarm of a daughter about five years old, who slept with her. This alarm was occasioned by the little girl feeling the movements, and hearing the cries of an infant in bed. To the mother's great surprise, she had brought forth her child without any consciousness of the fact. (1890, p. 3)

Stockham's book *Tokology,* published late in the nineteenth century, quoted a world traveler who said, "I know of no country, no tribe, no class, where childbirth is attended with so much pain and trouble as in North America" (1890, p. 11). She believed that the reputed better performance of peasant or indigenous women in birth was largely due to their superior physical vigor from a healthy diet and regular exercise. European-American women could have healthy births, too, she argued, adding:

I attended a neighbour of mine in four different confinements. I never was able to reach her before the birth of the child, although I lived only across the street, and, according to her injunctions, always kept my shoes "laced up." She sent for me, too, at the first indication of labor. There was always one prolonged effort and the child was expelled. (1890, p. 15)

Another lady patron had two children without a particle of pain. With the first she was alone with her nurse. During the evening she remarked that she felt weary and believed that she would lie down. She had been on the bed no more than twenty minutes when she called to her nurse, saying: "How strangely I feel! I wish you would see what is the matter," when to their astonishment the child was already born. (1890, p. 3)

Even though it is possible to find an occasional reference in U.S. medical textbooks of the nineteenth and twentieth centuries to women of "civilized" cultures giving birth with little or no apparent pain, such accounts are usually the exception rather than the rule. In general, childbirth pain is viewed to be severe and intrinsic to the process of labor and birth. Even in texts written during the nineteenth century, when anesthetics and analgesics were not yet a normal feature of care giving, there is little recognition that childbirth pain can vary tremendously according to the position adopted (or required) by the mother during labor and birth.

In one of the exceptional works, *Labor among Primitive Peoples,* published in 1883, Dr. George Engelmann made a huge contribution by synthesizing knowledge drawn from obstetrics, cultural anthropology, and massage therapy. Renowned as an accomplished biologist, archaeologist, and anthropologist, he corresponded regularly with a long list of scholars and explorers who also studied the medical practices of people who still lived according to "primal" ways. His book supports the general observations about the greater ease of birth-giving among indigenous women compared with their "civilized" sisters.

To Engelmann, the short, comparatively easy labors of women who lived in cultures untouched by civilization could be explained by several factors. He noted that these women typically led active lives right up to the time they went into labor. But his correspondence with physicians who knew about indigenous ways of giving birth convinced him that it was not just exercise during pregnancy that made birth easier for indigenous women. He thought their behavior in labor

was at least as important a factor. Unlike European-American women, who stayed in their beds during the last weeks and months of pregnancy and in labor, indigenous mothers moved about freely and adopted various positions, many of them upright, during the different stages of labor. There was no supposedly superior class of women in these societies to sanction practices and positions that were obstetrically fashionable, and there was no prudery, so they behaved according to instinct. Equally important, the clothing they wore during pregnancy did not hamper free movement or full expansion of the lungs. The comfortable and practical clothes of indigenous women contrasted sharply with the clothing styles of prosperous civilized women of the nineteenth century, a period when corsets with whalebone or steel stays were typically worn laced so tightly that women wearing them sometimes suffered displacement of their kidneys, liver, and other organs. Fainting was common among corset-wearers because tight lacing kept them from breathing deeply.

To his great credit, Engelmann was one of the few North American doctors who took the view that civilized women had something to learn from women who were more in tune with nature. He was very frank about his opinion that women whose connection with their instincts had not been altered by civilization were far more able to give birth without complication, protracted labor, or unbearable pain, and that physicians, as well as European-American women, had much to learn from them. "The savage mother, the Negress, the Australian or Indian, still governed by her instinct, is far in advance of the ordinary woman of our civilization," he emphasized (1883, p. xvii).

Nineteenth-century feminist philosopher and writer Elizabeth Cady Stanton regarded pregnancy as a natural state rather than an illness, and she knew from her own experience that labor and birth could be painless. Instead of accepting physicians' advice to stay in bed from the seventh or eighth months of pregnancy until a month after giving birth, she kept on with her usual work until she went into labor with each of her seven children. She felt that confinement (restriction of movement by clothes or social custom) was the cause of women's difficult labors, as well as their numerous postpartum ailments. After the birth of her fifth child, she wrote:

> *I never felt such sacredness in carrying a child as I have in the case of this one. She is the largest and most vigorous baby I have ever had, weighing twelve pounds. And yet my labor was short and easy. I laid down about fifteen minutes and brought forth this big girl. I sat up immediately, changed my own clothes, put on a wet bandage, and after a few hours' repose sat up again. Am I not almost a savage? For what refined, delicate, genteel, civilized woman would get well in so indecently short a time? Dear me, how much cruel bondage of mind and suffering of body poor woman will escape when she takes the liberty of being her own physician of both body and mind? (1971, p. 4)*

Probably the best-known physician in the twentieth century to study the riddle of pain in childbirth (at least, in the English-speaking world) was Dr. Grantly Dick-Read. He included the story of the first pain-free birth he ever witnessed in *Childbirth without Fear* because it amazed him enough to change forever the way he thought about childbirth. The birth in question took place in the Whitechapel district of London around 1913. Despite the fact that the mother was laboring in the poorest of hovels, with the rain pouring in through a broken window, Dick-Read remarked on the atmosphere of "quiet kindliness" in the room. The only note of dissonance during the entire experience stemmed from his attempt to persuade the laboring woman to let him put the chloroform mask over her nose and mouth as the baby's head was being born. Dick-Read (1972) wrote:

> *She, however, resented the suggestion, and firmly but kindly refused to take this help. It was the first time in my short experience that I had ever been refused when offering chloroform. As I was about to leave some time later, I asked her why it was she would not use the mask. She did not answer at once, but looked from the old woman who had been assisting to the window through which was bursting the first light of dawn; then shyly she turned to me and said: "It didn't hurt. It wasn't meant to, was it, doctor?" (p. 5)*

For months and years after that experience, Dick-Read thought about the woman's question and eventually came to realize that "there was no law in nature and no design that could justify the pain of childbirth" (1953, p. 39). Later experience in World War I in foreign lands gave him chances to witness many more apparently painless births. The sum of all these experiences plus his own battlefield experience of terror and loneliness led him to articulate his theory of why some women experience pain in birth while others do not. "It slowly dawned on me that it was the peacefulness of the relatively painless labor that distinguished it most clearly from the others. There was a calm, it seemed almost faith, in the normal and natural outcome of childbirth," he wrote (1953, p. 34).

Dick-Read was the first physician to write about birth as a spiritual experience and to discuss fear as a major contributing factor to pain in childbirth. He wrote that the pain of what he called "cultural childbirth" was caused by a combination of fear and muscle tension caused by ignorance of the birthing process, isolation during labor, and uncompassionate care received in hospital labor and delivery wards.

Remember the soft groans mentioned earlier, in reference to a Javanese birth that took place in the nineteenth century? It is worth noting that the only way one could write about orgasm during that period of U.S. history was to allude to soft moans or groans. By the 1970s times had changed, and a new group of people began to weigh in on the topic of painless birth: women who, in the tradition of Elizabeth Cady Stanton, had given birth themselves and had something to say about their experience. Among them were Raven Lang (1972), Jeannine Parvati Baker (1974), and myself (1975). Not only did these writers mention painless birth, they also mentioned the phenomenon of orgasm during labor or birth.

Since the appearance of these books, virtually nothing has been written on this subject. When I began hearing from young women that many were opting for elective cesarean as a way avoiding pain during labor and birth, I began to wonder why so many writers and childbirth educators never mentioned the possibility of it. Is it so rare that they simply can't conceive of it, or do they wish to avoid raising women's expectations given that many women would still experience pain even if they knew that orgasm was a possibility? I began asking young women if they had ever heard of women having ecstatic labors and births and found that most hadn't.

Curious about how many women I could find who had orgasmic experiences in labor or birth, I decided to conduct a small survey among some close friends. Of 151 women, I found 32 who reported experiencing at least one orgasmic birth. That is 21 percent—considerably higher than I had expected. Most of the women had their babies on The Farm (the community in Tennessee where my colleagues and I have been practicing midwifery for over a quarter-century), but interestingly, some said the orgasm occurred during a hospital birth. I have included some of the women's comments below, as they perhaps shed some light on what factors are present when women have birth experiences such as these. (I have changed the women's names out of respect for their privacy.)

Julia: I had an orgasm when I had my fourth child. It happened while I was pushing. We went to the hospital after I had been "stalled" at nine centimeters for a while, attempting a home birth with some midwives who made me nervous. I no sooner got inside the door than I began having overwhelming urges to push that baby OUT!!! I orgasmed as she was being born. They just barely got me onto the delivery table in time for her birth, but I was oblivious to all that because it was feeling so good to get her out.

Margaret: I had a cosmic union orgasm, a bliss-enhanced state. In a way, this has had a permanent effect. I can still go to that place.

Vivian: Being in labor felt like work; but giving birth, the actual process of passing the baby's entire body out of my womb (which did happen quite quickly), was indescribably incredible, particularly the first time.

Marilyn: My last birth was very orgasmic in a sustained sort of way, like I was riding on waves of orgasmic bliss. I knew more what to expect, was less afraid, and tried to meet and flow with the energy rather than avoid or resist as I had the first time. The effect was probably mostly psychological in that it gave me tremendous satisfaction just to have accomplished such a difficult passage safely. I felt great for months afterward, which helped me feel positive about myself in general. This, in turn, affected how I felt about myself sexually. I also think that, for me, learning to let go and let my body take over in labor (as opposed to thinking about it with my mind all the way through!) helped me tap into a part of me I never

knew before and helped me feel more willing to let go while making love.

Janelle: Giving birth was like pre- and post-orgasm by the second or third birth but did not contain the pulsation felt at climax. Being in tune with rushes [contractions], pushing, deeply relaxing in between was a very sexual and powerful experience but higher than orgasm, because orgasm can seem more self-gratifying and is short-lived. Giving birth is such a spiritual experience, so miraculous, you are very in tune with God and seeing the divinity in everyone that the sexual part is not that important. You are totally immersed in selfless love and so the blissful and sexual feelings are a byproduct, a gift of allowing your body to do what it knows how to do while your consciousness is very expanded.

Paula: I have been pondering this question for some time. I have always felt that labor and birth were like one big orgasm. The contractions were like waves of pleasure rippling through the body. I only found the final few centimeters of dilation as extremely strong and slightly less pleasurable. But I felt like labor and birth were/are a continuous orgasm. I can't say that it is like the orgasm experienced during sexual intercourse, where I find myself being engulfed and lost in the wave of orgasm. The type I experienced during labor and birth was a more all-consuming feeling that required more of my attention than that experienced during sex. However, I do feel that it is an orgasm. The birth itself is very orgasmic as the baby comes through the birth canal—extremely pleasurable and rewarding.

Maria: I had to think about this one for a few days. At first I thought "no," but there certainly were sensations in the first stage during dilation that were incredibly intense when Ted would kiss me or I would bury my face in his neck during a rush. I did not have a particularly hard time during the first stage of any of my births and remember enjoying the birthing process for the most part. The general excitement, rushes of energy, and all the touching were very pleasurable. The sensations weren't the same as an orgasm exactly, but when the rushes would end, the total splash-out [relaxation] was very similar to how I feel after orgasm now (which I call the wet-noodle effect). For me, however, the second stage was another story. I remember not liking that part because of the intense stinging of the tissue stretching. I always thought I was weird since I liked the first stage and couldn't really get into the second stage.

Anyway, it goes without saying that good energy rushes are enjoyable and, even though I don't know if my inner muscles were twitching rhythmically or not, having a baby was the greatest energy sweep ever. I think it is very probable that it is much larger than an orgasm rush, or certainly different. One other thing I think might be true—I think it is possible that I hadn't perfected the art of having superorgasms back then when I was so young and having the babies. Since then, over the years, I have become quite good at it, so I'm not sure if that lack of experience could have kept me from experiencing some of those sensations during labor and birth.

Some of the women described, instead of orgasm, a euphoria that had some similarities to the bliss they associate with sexual pleasure.

Elayne: I didn't have an orgasm, but I felt a little bit like it when I had my first baby. And that was only at the transition shortly before pushing. For a moment I felt like [I do] . . . shortly before orgasm—being high, having pain, and being afraid [of] what's coming next. And I felt all this at the same time.

Alicia: No, I can't say I would describe the experience as "orgasmic." Rather, it was "euphoric." To say it was orgasmic would describe the experience in almost a base way. Rather, it was spiritual.

Nanette: I wouldn't say I experienced orgasm either in labor or giving birth. However, I would say the sensation of out-of-controlledness (!) was comparable. My sister says that giving birth was "like" the biggest orgasm ever—but only "like" it—so it sounds like a qualitative difference. I remember you telling me that my brain had migrated to my pelvic area, which was where it was needed, and I think you were right—the births of all three children are a delightful blur that was so much just being there and experiencing it with my body and not my head.

To conclude, I'll speak from personal experience. It is easier to reach orgasm if one is not feeling violated, angry, frightened, distracted, or goal-oriented. I'm sure that it is easier when there is no one shouting at you when and how to push or counting. As I mentioned earlier, I haven't encountered any reports of orgasm in women who had received pain medication. Orgasm is more possible if one is touched in just the right way—at the right place, the right pace, the right amount of pressure, and the right time. The challenge for women and their caregivers during birth is to come up with a system of pregnancy preparation and birth care that is not inimical to orgasm during labor and birth.

REFERENCES

Baker, Jeannine Parvati. 1974. *Prenatal Yoga & Natural Birth.* Berkeley, CA: North Atlantic Books.

Dick-Read, Grantly. 1953. *Childbirth without Fear* (2nd revised edition). New York: Harper & Row.

Engelmann, George. 1883. *Labor among Primitive Peoples.* St. Louis, MO: J. M. Chambers & Co.

Gaskin, Ina May. 1977. *Spiritual Midwifery.* Summertown, TN: The Book Company.

Goldsmith, Judith. 1990. *Childbirth Wisdom from the World's Oldest Societies.* Brookline, MA: East-West Health Books.

Lang, Raven. 1972. *The Birth Book.* Palo Alto, CA: Genesis Press.

Stanton, Elizabeth Cady. 1971. *Eighty Years and More: Reminiscences of Elizabeth Cady Stanton 1815–1987.* New York: Schocken.

Speert, Harold. 1980. *Obstetrics and America: A History.* Chicago: American College of Obstetricians and Gynecologists.

Stockham, Alice. 1890. *Tokology.* Melbourne, Australia: Butler & Tanner, Frome and London.

Vogel, V. J. 1970. *American Indian Medicine.* Norman: University of Oklahoma Press.

Boundary Breaches: The Body, Sex and Sexuality after Stoma Surgery

Lenore Manderson

Introduction

Intimacy and privacy constellate not only specifically around sexual acts, but also in the most general ways the body itself. People with bodily anomalies, and their sexual partners, are particularly aware of the contradictions of the body and its exposure in intimate acts when the body and its imperfections are exposed. Absent body parts and various bodily dysfunctions complicate individuals' social and sexual lives. People with bodies that are changed dramatically and irrevocably after surgery must similarly adapt, and in doing so must re-negotiate their bodies as a sexual canvas. The difficulty of this adaptation has been highlighted in literature on the social and sexual impact of breast, gynaecological and to a lesser degree, testicular cancer, when surgery has included mastectomy, vulval excision or the removal of a testis (Schultz, Van de Wiel, Hahn, & Bouma, 1992; Andersen, 1994; Gilbar, Steiner, & Atad, 1995; Lalos & Eisemann, 1999; Anllo, 2000; Fobair et al., 2001; Lagana, McGarvey, Classen, & Koopman, 2001; Joly et al., 2002; Schultz & Van de Wiel, 2003; Gurevich, Bishop, Bower, Malka, & Nyhof-Young, 2004). But body image and sexuality are also affected by other surgery. In this [reading], the surgical change is the creation of a stoma, an artificial opening on the side of the abdomen. Surgery to close or remove the urethra or anus (and/or rectum) can result from several serious conditions; following surgery, elimination and other bodily practices become highly managed acts.

From "Boundary Breaches: The Body, Sex, and Sexuality after Stoma Surgery" by Lenore Manderson, *Social Science & Medicine,* 61, 405–415. Copyright © 2005. Reprinted with permission from Elsevier.

Around one in 1000 people in the developed world, depending on the country and its medical services, have a stoma. The surgery is undertaken for a number of conditions, some congenital, such as anorectal or urethral malformations, and others due to disease or other reasons for failure to function: bladder cancer, spinal cord injuries, colorectal cancer, an intestinal blockage or internal injury, inflammatory bowel disease or an intestinal abscess. Inflammatory bowel diseases such as ulcerative colitis or Crohn's disease are universally severe and incapacitating, circumscribing individuals' professional and personal lives. These have no predictable prognosis and no options for control or cure; surgery is necessary to ease the symptoms and improve quality of life. For other diseases such as cancer, stoma surgery can be life-saving.

In surgery, the bowel or bladder is diverted to empty through an opening (stoma) in the abdomen. The stoma permits the attachment of a changeable, watertight bag that fills with urine or [feces] and is emptied manually. Some people are able to dispense with the bag and instead are able to irrigate on a routine basis and wear a small stomal cap over the stoma. With ulcerative colitis, the surgery may be temporary, with an anastomosis performed later to preserve the anal sphincter and normal intestinal patterns, thereby also improving social and sexual functioning and quality of life (Bigard, 1993; Oresland et al., 1994; Damgaard, Wettergren, & Kirkegaard, 1995). Many people do not have this option, however, and must continue to use a stoma and bag, or a stoma, plug and irrigation.

An important and ongoing tension exists for people who, on an everyday basis, have to deal with their bodies as objects, caring for the stoma, preventing lesions and infections, changing bags and so on. The tension is both to establish a routine such that the stoma does not intrude in everyday life, and despite the artificial management of [feces] and/or urine, to establish an illusion of normalcy. Individuals' sense of themselves, and others' perceptions of them, are informed by presumptions of a link between the physical body and the self (Manderson, 2000), and managing a stoma impacts on self-image and sexual/social relationships (Klopp, 1990; Cohen, 1991; Gloeckner, 1991). Individuals need to separate self from substance—the subject (the "real" self) from the object (body-with-stoma). The challenge for many is to establish, or re-establish, a sense of identity unrelated to the body, so that they are recognised for "themselves," despite and apart from the barrier to this that their non-conforming body might present. Some people are able to make this first step without difficulty, and for them, the problem lies in others' difficulty in doing this. Others find it more difficult. Reluctance to discuss the nature of the surgery is influenced by cultural ideas of delicacy and aesthetics in relation to changed bodies and body functions. The particular difficulty for individuals with a colostomy or ileostomy is the link with defecation, sensory and cultural aversions to [feces], and the need therefore to reconcile or manage potential and actual experiences of disgust. Miller reflects on how the idiom of disgust consistently invokes *sensory* experience: of being "too close" to the object of disgust, and of having to smell it, see it, and touch it (Miller, 1997). Disgust is a visceral emotion; so is lust. Hence the contradictions for those who must reconcile sexuality and their stoma.

Background

As noted, stoma surgery is conducted for a variety of chronic and acute conditions. Inflammatory bowel diseases and chronic bladder problems are particularly prevalent, and cause considerable anxiety and depression, often in combination with and exacerbated by pain and reduced energy (Sewitch et al., 2001; Smolen & Topp, 2001). The physical [effects] of these diseases, their unpredictability, and the importance for individuals of organizing around their bodily needs, impact on family and interpersonal relationships, work, the social environment and leisure (Cuntz, Welt, Ruppert, & Zillessen, 1999; Peake, Manderson, & Potts, 1999; Hjortswang et al., 2003; Peake & Manderson, 2003). Given the psychological, social and physical impact of such conditions, surgery is often the preferred treatment (Casellas, Lopez-Vivancos, Badia, Vilaseca, & Malagelada, 2000). For people diagnosed with cancer, stoma surgery offers remission of disease and extended life expectancy.

Post-surgery, increased control over the body (as for inflammatory bowel disease or urinary incontinence) and over disease progression (for cancer) usually offers people enhanced quality of life, less anxiety and higher self-esteem (McLeod & Baxter, 1998; Rauch, Miny, Conroy, Nyeton, & Guillemin, 2004). Adjustment to the post-surgical body is not unproblematic, however (Follick, Smith, & Turk, 1984; Sahay, Gray, & Fitch, 2000). The continued impact of cancer diagnosis arguably explains the differences in outcome among individuals following stoma surgery. Cancer survivors, in particular, must cope with a variety of physical problems and psychological difficulties associated with continuing sense of loss of control and uncertainty of prognosis (Schag, Ganz, Wing, Sim, & Lee, 1994; Little, Jordens, Paul, Montgomery, & Philipson, 1998). For example, men and women who had surgery for bladder cancer had greater difficulties than those who had had surgery for incontinence or bladder dysfunction in terms of sexual and social activities (see Nordstrom & Nyman, 1991; Nordstrom, Nyman, & Theorell, 1992). Nevertheless, all people who have had stoma surgery must learn to use a bag and care for the stoma, prevent skin inflammation and excoriation, manage accidental leakage and overcome fear of leakage, and overcome embarrassments related to sound and smell. They must also adapt to a changed body image that may have profound impact on their psychological wellbeing, and social and sexual identity (Kelly, 1992). Routine management practices impact on self-esteem, and by virtue of its location, the stoma presents explicit problems for intimacy (Weerakoon, 2001; Carlsson, Bosaeus, & Nordgren, 2003).

The relationships between abject bodies and personhood, implied in the cases of incontinence and stoma surgery, raise interesting questions in relation to mind/body. In understanding the cognitive leaps that individuals post-surgery must make to adapt to body change, it is important—and not necessarily easy—for individuals to separate the body and mind; to insist, contra contemporary philosophical and ethical theorizing (Grosz, 1994; Kempen, 1996; Burkitt, 1998; Switankowsky, 2000), that body and mind are separate, and that while the self is embodied, personal worth cannot be determined on this basis. Individuals' relationships to their own bodies and their relationships with others, social membership and sexual identity, are informed by such suppositions—that the individual is normal, and that the self is other than the abject body. Little qualitative research has been undertaken on bowel disease and stoma surgery that would allow us to explore these issues. Even qualitative papers focus on the experience of illness rather than its embodiment, and slide over the subjective experience of the stoma and sexuality. Little and colleagues, e.g., observe that "(w)e live with taboos—bowel movements, menstruation, sexuality—which we do not usually discuss" and note that a colostomy "brings reminders of bodily functions that we know and never discuss" (Little et al., 1998, p. 1489).

In this [reading], men and women's experiences of adapting to a stoma are explored. As noted already, the presence of a stoma and taboos relating to elimination complicate the establishment and maintenance of intimate relationships. An interrogation of discomfort related to the stoma draws attention to the disease that informs individuals' attitudes to bladder and bowel dysfunction, and more generally, to diseased and disordered bodies.

Methods

The data on which this [reading] is based were collected as part of a larger, ongoing study on body change, chronic disease, disability and social inclusion. Thirty-two participants responded to a research note placed in *Ostomy Australia,* a national journal provided three times a year to all Australians (26,000) who receive government-subsidized stoma supplies.

Unstructured interviews were conducted with 18 of these people in three states at their choice of venue, usually their home. Because interviews were lengthy (2–5 h), several were conducted over two sessions to allow for full accounts of illness, surgery and subsequent experiences. All interviews were tape-recorded and transcribed for thematic analysis. In addition, 14 people whose area of residence made personal interviewing difficult responded to questionnaires which collected basic demographic and medical data and elicited their experiences of diagnosis, surgery, adjustment to the stoma, and its ongoing impact. In response to the open-ended questions, people often wrote extensive narratives; some wrote more than once as new ideas came to them. Some also elaborated on their responses verbally, using a cassette tape sent to them for this purpose; these tapes were transcribed and treated as interview texts for the purpose of identifying dominant themes. In this [reading], interview extracts and written comments are attributed to interviewees or respondents using pseudonyms selected by them. Quotes are taken from a select number of respondents who were most articulate, but their experiences and perspectives were shared by other participants.

All participants were Australian-born or immigrants who were English-language speakers. Thirty-four percent (11) were male; 66 percent (21) female, ranging in age from 24 to 82 years at the time of the interview (mean age 45 years). At the time of first surgery, 75 percent (24) were married or living in a de facto relationship; four divorced after the stoma and three established new partnerships, and so when they participated in the research, 71 percent of respondents had partners with whom they lived. Seventy-eight percent had children (median 2, range 1–4). Consistent with the general Australian population, all had at least some secondary schooling; 50 percent had a tertiary education or post-graduate qualifications. Approximately 31 percent (10) were in professional or managerial positions, and six only were involved in full-time home duties at the time of surgery. At the time of interview or return of questionnaire this had changed dramatically, primarily because of the interval between surgery and study participation. The majority had had stoma surgery more than

5 years prior to interview with a range from 6 months to 42 years. During the study, 50 percent of participants were working at home or retired. This diversity makes generalization difficult, but as is common in qualitative studies, the purpose of the research—and this [reading]—was to explore the diversity of experiences and perceptions, not to seek associations.

Data from questionnaire returns, cassettes, letters and interviews were supplemented and triangulated by articles, letters and biographic accounts published in *Ostomy Australia,* and by participation and observation of local meetings and national conferences of voluntary associations for people with stomas, and professional conferences of stoma therapists; these provided insight into the interpersonal and wider social issues that face people with stomas and provided a measure of validity and reliability to the data from interviewees and questionnaire respondents.

Adapting to Change

Loss of bodily control over body waste, Isaksen (1996, 2002) argues, places individual identity and human dignity at risk. Incontinence and surgery to correct this, or surgery to prevent the spread of disease, can subvert notions of adulthood, and while surgery can be liberating, it can also strip individuals of autonomy and inhibit their ability to live productive and fulfilling lives. Individuals find meaning in their corporeal as well as their social, emotional and intellectual selves. This is challenged by surgery as well as illness. Participants were clear about the advantages of surgery, including "improved quality of life" for those whose lives had previously been circumscribed because of incontinence and those for whom surgery was life saving. Others reflected that they were now able to maintain "constant, acceptable weight," felt physically healthier and stronger, had developed positive coping skills, and relative to what they had expected, were pleased with how the stoma looked.

But these advantages did not negate the disadvantages. A number spoke of their discomfort with the appearance of the stoma ("I was revolted when I saw photos showing the red lips well after I had adjusted to my surgery"). Some reported a loss of control over

their weight, found "waste removal a challenge," had to manage constant bowel movements, had difficulty passing gas, had problems with noise, had excoriation around the stoma, and had slight [fecal] soiling. Others found it hard to accept the bag as permanent, were distressed by scarring, and found it extremely difficult to adjust to changed body appearance. One participant, e.g., reflected on the powerfulness of her image of a "hanging bag" and spoke at length of the difficulties: "Do people see the bag? Do I smell? Can they hear the plastic rustle?" (Lorraine). Research participants recounted that they were reassured by their physicians that "sex would not be a problem as (partners) would not be turned off by the bag." And many, but not all, people found that family and friends were supportive. When one interviewee learnt that she would have "a thing hanging off (her) stomach," she told her partner to "go, go and get a life," and "just pushed him right out of (her) life." After surgery, she withdrew almost entirely from social life and for 10 years, from her early 30s to her early 40s, she rarely went out and had no intimate relationships:

> It was like going through a grieving period for about 5 years. I didn't want to know about it (the stoma) . . . I just hated myself; there is no other way of describing my feelings. I just was beside myself. It is just the fact that you have got something hanging off your stomach that is full of weight . . . this thing hanging there, that I would just like to rip it off and throw it away, you know, if I could. It is all to do with body image, isn't it? How does one overcome this? (Babaloo).

When she was 42, this participant established an intimate relationship. Her partner at the time of the interview makes jokes about the bag, and assures her that the stoma "doesn't make any difference." However, she is profoundly embarrassed by the bag and avoids him seeing her naked. Dimity similarly reported that her husband had been "absolutely wonderful and he says he doesn't even notice the bag and everything else," but she reflected that she can feel it and knows it is there, and her husband's joint role as nurse and lover disproves to her his lack of awareness. As she explained, if you can give your partner an enema and clean her up after a burst bag or an "accident," how can you ignore it? Dana recounted that her husband said that "he didn't care at all about her stoma or various related accidents. He just says, 'Okay, let's change the sheets. You go and hop in the shower and I'll wash the clothes.'" But because of her self-consciousness, she did not think she would be able to develop another sexual relationship were he not around.

Men as well as women often reported their partners were fairly matter-of-fact about spillage and leaks, but they were no less embarrassed and uncomfortable: "Well, we're really good, I'm more freaked about it than she is I think. In a way she's very good. And she says she's not into body image, which I like to believe. I have my own problems with the thing because well, I'll tell you, it's so painful for me" (Phoenix). Others were less sanguine. Gary, e.g., reflected on the difficulties he faced in adjusting to a permanent colostomy bag, and watching what he drank and ate; he spoke of his embarrassment with distended bags, smell and noise: "I feel like a baby when I have to take spare clothing bags, wipes, creams, and deodorizers when I go out." As these participants pointed out, post-surgery as well as in illness, individuals with limited bladder or bowel control to an extent are repositioned as child-like, at times needing the kind of care provided to a child and dependent in ways contradictory to constructions of adulthood and adult social relations. Incontinence and dependence on others for assistance in the event of loss of control contradicts internalized ideas of autonomous adulthood and adult sexuality. Occasional leakage, concerns about bodily appearance and self-consciousness were compounded for those whose friends or family were not supportive or who treated the individual, after surgery, as if still sick. . . .

Disguise and Discomfort

For many men and women who participated in this study, incontinence of the bladder or the bowel leads to feelings of depression and loneliness, as well as presenting practical dilemmas that impose a social and emotional burden—the need to manage the environment by identifying where toilets and change rooms are located, arranging for supplies if planning a lengthy trip, carry pads and/or changes of clothing, and so on (Peake et al., 1999; Fultz & Herzog, 2001;

Peake & Manderson, 2003). While stoma surgery reduces the risk of accidents and so dilutes the anxiety of risk of exposure as incontinent, it does not eliminate the risk, and people with stomas continue to be mindful of their bodies. In sex, people who are incontinent must monitor their bladder and bowel, controlling their bodies while at the same time desiring to be submerged in and free from bodily consciousness. Dimity spoke of being self-conscious with her husband because of the multiple ways that her body might reveal itself: "he could feel through my skin impacted [feces] or something. Those kinds of things, I mean even if there was no smell or no sound, that he would touch my stomach." And Babaloo:

> Basic things like, if you have sex, is there a risk of the stoma coming off, I mean the bag coming off, or will it hurt you? I mean internally, by losing your rectum, are you the same person internally? What effect will it have to have a penis pressing against the walls of your vagina when there is no rectum? And if you have got that vigilance there as well, and this affects sexual response . . . you are lying on the bed and half of you is on auto-pilot and the other half of you is thinking, hang on, is the bag still safe, or, oh yuk, I can hear it go gurgle, gurgle or squish, squish?

The bag is always an intruder. Dimity reflected that many people . . . coped with "all the other bits," but they didn't cope "in the bedroom." Many were especially fearful that the bag would be noisy, smell or come off. Such exposure is a risk regardless of whether a partner (or any other) knows about the stoma. Pleasurable sex, idealized, is about being able to lose control, but people can only lose control when they are confident their bodies are in control in the first place. Like Babaloo, Dimity emphasized this when she spoke of her inability to "let go" and [lose] control for sexual pleasure, following as well as before surgery:

> When we first went to bed, I was like, I used to have to hang on, I was literally clenched because of fear, like I never knew if I was going to be letting off wind or something more than that and it took me a long, long time to feel comfortable.

People are advised by counsellors and stoma therapists "to get around it and be creative." While a number of people were curious about the extent of creativity—the degree to which others might incorporate the stoma into love-making, for instance—for most people, the stoma was unsightly, to be protected and kept secret, and the bag was potentially so intrusive that creativity was unimaginable. It is not only the physical breach of the boundary—smell, sound or leak—but also the presence of the bag as a container of abject fluid and solid that strips a moment of its sensual potential. Breaches in bodily control have the potential to undermine the sexual relationship, and so in establishing sexual relations, people need to reconstruct privacy and dignity, and preserve the notion of bodily aesthetics in the process. Both men and women with stomas often had a strong sense of being sexually unattractive, even if in other respects their social life was enhanced following surgery (Bjerre, Johansen, & Steven, 1998). Those without partners when they had surgery had to disclose to potential sexual partners, and were often deeply self-conscious. Individuals found it difficult to sexualize a body that is also a defecating/urinating body, when the two images are so visibly confused, as Perdita explained:

> You can actually see through (the bag), and you can see what's in it and especially when it comes to sexual relations with male/female, whoever the ostomate may be, they find it very hard to come to terms with this.

Most research participants were comfortable about having a stoma, if at all, only with their own or other children such as nieces or nephews, extending their general willingness to talk about body functions to small children to include their own abject bodies. Mia, for instance, was simply amused by her 3-year-old niece's fascination when she emptied her bag, and she was happy for the child to go with her to the toilet, "Because she's a child and she's not going to judge me. She doesn't see that as being, you know, freaky different. She says, 'Cool.' Yeah, cool different kind of thing, so . . . ". Christine's grandchildren similarly took great interest in her stoma: "They would find me in the bathroom and would watch 'the procedure' while continuing a conversation and asking questions." The ease of men and women with stomas in this context was essentially no different to people's

general comfortableness in bathing and using the toilet in front of small children. With adults, however, self-consciousness governed comportment or the etiquette of body practice. Warwick commented that although his libido had diminished due to radiation and chemotherapy, his relationship with his wife was also affected by the fact that he had a hernia and had a bag "filled with [feces]," noisy and needing to be emptied every three hours. In his words, she was not "sympathetic: she finds the bag repulsive and does not like the sight of my hernia or my body." Further, as already noted, few women were comfortable being seen naked, with or without the bag, by their partners:

> He certainly hasn't seen it (the stoma) naked or anything like that. He respects my privacy, he doesn't push the issue. He doesn't badger me to see it, or anything like that. You know, he doesn't walk in—I mean, when I'm in the shower, or—because he knows that it would make me uncomfortable and make me angry (Mia).

Many participants reflected on the importance of disguising the stoma and bag to avoid obvious confrontation. Mia, again, explains this:

> It's really not a sexy thing to see, so that's probably why I don't want him to see because we—I mean, if we have a sexual relationship. With my family—I don't know. I'm sure they wouldn't think anything of it, but . . .
>
> Is it the stoma itself that you think is not sexy, or . . . ? It's definitely the [feces] in the bag. The stoma itself, it wouldn't worry me in the slightest. It's the fact that I shit in a bag. And I carry it around with me all the time.

Dana wore a cover around her abdomen to protect the stoma and bag, and her partner shared her view that it was better to wear it "because it's more secure;" he, as well as she, felt more comfortable because it protected against possible leakage and reduced awkward noise. Ted was divorced because his wife "couldn't handle looking at him" with his bag on. When he wanted to start another relationship, he searched for something to disguise the bag, "a cover or cummerbund or something" that would make his appearance "much more appealing to the opposite sex" than looking at the bag with its contents. In bed, Babaloo always wore a nightgown around her abdomen, and addressed at length her frustration about finding feminine and sexy underwear to cover and protect the bag; on several occasions she sent away for garments that proved to be "preposterous" and decidedly "unsexy." This was a recurrent complaint. Phoenix found the idea of a cummerbund silly:

> About the only time I've ever worn a cummerbund was way back when I was doing ballroom dancing and a more ridiculous piece of equipment I've never come across, I mean, what's wrong with a belt. But prancing into bed with a cummerbund, I just feel like a bloody Christmas present or something. You're trying to hide this thing, but what do you do, draw attention to it with a bloody cummerbund.

Sex and Sexiness

Values relating to bodily parts and sexual repertoires are relevant in any context, as well as in relation to physical disability, and the most rigid interpretations of these inform illiberal notions of the right to desire, to be desired and to be sexually active. Part of disgust, Miller argues, "is the very awareness of being disgusted, the consciousness of itself" (1997, p. 8). Disgust is a visceral response which, provoked by [fecal] waste, urine, associated odours and sounds, is accompanied by culturally constructed ideas of danger of contamination and defilement. However, the feeling of disgust is produced for the owner of the body, the source of that which is disgusting, by the conflation of material and symbol. This is equally so for others in contact with the producing body if not the matter itself. In a sexual relationship, therefore, both individuals—the owner of the problematic body and his or her partner—must find ways to set aside reactions of disgust, and so put [feces], farts, rumblings and smells out of mind, both by ignoring obvious embodied reminders of the stoma (such as the bag), overlooking minor intrusions, and making light of occasional crises that threaten to replace lust with disgust and sex with hygiene. The tacit and sometimes explicit recognition of this dilemma between lust and disgust influences individual comportment in sex as well as in more public moments in everyday life:

> All my friends know about my stoma and I am quite comfortable talking to strangers about it. My husband won't even look directly at it, especially when I am

catheterizing, not because he thinks it ugly but he disappears when I [am] having a cannula sited. Our relationship hasn't altered, not our sex life. He doesn't "cringe" if he touches the bag on my tummy when we make love; it is just as if it wasn't there (Christine).

The participants in this study commonly had extensive histories of ill health, diagnoses and medical tests before surgery, followed by the abnegation of the body and associated periods of depression. In consequence, many had lengthy periods of sexual inactivity, and sometimes doubted their ability to be responsive: "I had no idea whether I would or whether I wouldn't or whether I would still have the same sensations. I think I have, probably not as quite as intense, but I don't have a big problem with that . . . if you are not testing out the muscles in the interim then if nothing else, you are starting out from a little lack of use" (Babaloo). Lynette similarly reflected on the difficulty of coping with an intimate relationship: "For the record, I just backed off. Also, I have noticed that I tend to be much quieter or sedate in larger social settings. I think it may be that I don't feel overtly confident."

Bodily surveillance, including body emissions and the appearance of the body and the bag, were for many people complicated by other health concerns, which compounded libidinal response. Dimity reflected on how constant pain, nausea, antidepressants, fear of accidents, fear of additional pain from intercourse, and tiredness probably all contributed to her not feeling sexy, and to worrying about this fact:

> There is just no desire. I have virtually no sexual desire what so ever. We have sex. We should have sex. My husband is always saying to "touch me, or kiss me, or . . ." and I just think, "Oh, I am supposed to be doing that" because I feel literally nothing, which is terrible. I am 28. You know, I should be enjoying it. That is the whole thing you know, we don't have to worry about pregnancy, or diseases. This should be a time when it is fantastic, but no . . . I mean there is no desire, no nothing there, and there hasn't been, probably for 2 years. I mean, any sort of chance of developing a fabulous sex life has sort of been diverted into feeling and being sick.

Mia shared this view, relating her inability to feel sexual to quite simple, material things, such as clothing:

I see girls wearing hipsters, or something like that. I'd like to wear those, or a—tight—something swingy, something like that. I mean, part of feeling sexy, I think, is feeling sexy in what you wear. And when you're wearing big baggy pants, it doesn't make you feel sexy in your own mind. So I'm really lucky in that my fiancé tells me, you know, every day that I'm beautiful and things like that.

Some partners had difficulty regaining desire or feeling erotically towards the partner with a stoma, as indicated earlier; the sight, sounds, odours and occasional contact with the stoma and/or its contents destroyed any possible desire and its exploration. Gertrude reflected on her husband:

I am thinking about sex and I don't know how I will go on that. I thought I had better heal a bit more. My husband has very low libido anyway unfortunately, but it came in handy for this present time. I knew there was always a reason for everything. But I am soon going to be through this and then the old problem of his low libido will be back. That is his problem, not mine.

Some older men and women were no longer sexually active and stoma surgery had little effect on this. Faith, for instance, over a 15-year period had cervical cancer, a hysterectomy, an appendectomy, ileostomy, a urostomy, and finally, her vagina was removed. Her husband had had major heart surgery, and as she explained it:

Well, his heart didn't allow (sex), so that was the end of it. It doesn't worry me, no. But up until I got sick and before my husband got sick, we have a good sex life. But then it's just passed, because we're both on heavy medication and that's it.

For several partners, however, the conflated roles of lovers and carers complicated intimacy. Isaksen (1996) suggests that care work is always structured by bodily taboos related to elimination, the management of incontinence, and specific body parts. Reactions of disgust or distaste are tabooed and techniques of distancing develop. He is writing of the professional distanciation of paid carers; in intimate relationships a different kind of distancing takes place. As noted earlier, some interviewees reported that their partners were able to be pragmatic, making light of noise, dismissing occasional leaks as unfortunate accidents to minimize embarrassment, and quickly running baths and changing bed clothes as the need arose. However, not all partners were able to adjust to these transposed roles as carers and lovers. Ian, for instance, cares for his wife when required, cleaning her when bags burst, bathing her and changing sheets. But this has been at the cost of a sexual relationship. His wife Sara explains his sexual withdrawal from her as over-determined because his mother also had a stoma; she feels that he oscillates between caring for her as if she were a child and as if she were his elderly mother. Neither the child nor the mother can also be his sexual partner. Gertrude's husband similarly adapted to her stoma by placing her in the position of child. Since her surgery, he has been comfortable being in the bathroom when she changes a bag, although he would never enter the bathroom previously if she were on the toilet and was never comfortable discussing bowel movements:

My husband makes me laugh because before, he was always very self-conscious about being on the toilet, and if I went in or if I left the door (of the toilet) open he would sigh and huff and all that sort of thing . . . and now he will walk in on me, just emptying my bag out and start cleaning his teeth and walk out because he will say "Well, that smell is a bit over powering at times" and I say to him "well, you wouldn't have come near me with a barge pole if I had been going to the toilet the normal way," and he went "Oh yeah," Because it is a completely different concept, he doesn't really consider that as bad as sitting on the toilet and doing a poo.

Gertrude and her husband no longer have a sexual relationship: his comfortableness about the stoma occurred as he withdrew from her sexually, and she feels that his role as carer gave him permission to do so. He has explained to her his sexual disinterest otherwise—that she is "too fat" for him to find her desirable. She reflects: "The stoma has helped me to realise that it is not me, it is him, and so I just continue on my way . . . "

The accounts of how stoma surgery affects sexuality provide a bleak picture, therefore, although stomal surgery was not inevitably problematic, not all individuals had negative experiences consequently, and many were able to overcome boundary breaches. Several who had surgery following extended periods of incontinence, often with pain and infection, reported a significant improvement in their quality of life and had no regrets. Many who had a colostomy, ileostomy or urostomy following diagnosis of cancer were relieved that surgical intervention was possible and were pragmatic about their treatment choices. In addition, people were able to negotiate, and to overcome embarrassment and discomfort to varying degrees.

Although individuals hold onto specific notions of body function and boundary, therefore, social notions of boundaries are elastic, influencing the diversity of sexual repertoire (e.g., with respect to anal and oral sex), and allowing intimacy even if the boundaries overlap and body control is unpredictable. Two cases provided illustrations of this. Perdita's marriage broke down after her colostomy for colorectal cancer. She divorced; after 10 years of abstinence (pre- and post-marriage and operation), she commenced a new relationship. "I knew that there would be somebody out there who would want me one day and I would deal with the colostomy when it happened. I didn't worry about it. I couldn't afford to anyway because stress is your worst enemy when you've had cancer." Perdita told her new lover about her stoma on their way to bed. Others find a way of diversion when the materiality of the stoma and the abject body intervened in sex. Vanessa, who had an ileostomy after years of suffering from Crohn's disease, maintained that neither she nor any of her "various partners over the 20 years since the surgery" had had a difficulty with the bag. If anything, she claimed it was "a novelty which can be ignored," although she also reflected that a leaking bag could be a "pest" if a leak occurred or the bag burst in someone else's bed, as once happened when the bag "flew off" in the height of passion. She described one particular relationship she had with a war veteran who had lost both his legs, and in doing so she illustrates how humour and the inherent comedy of coupling operate to dilute the potential of shame, embarrassment and humiliation. She illustrates too how a sexual relationship of any kind requires its participants to relax the rules of etiquette and establish trust in order for intimacy to take place. In writing down her experiences for this study, she checked with him [about] his views of the

relationship and reported to me in a second letter: "We made an amusing sight in bed and understood each other very well. We had a short conversation on the topic of my bag and his lack of legs! He said it has/had never worried him and he equates his legs with my bag!"

Concluding Remarks

Control of bodily functions is a passage to and precondition of conventional adulthood. Sexual negotiation and autonomy, too, is informed by constructions of adulthood. For many men and women, the sense of self as a valued adult and as a sexual being was threatened not only by the illness that led to surgery, but also by the lived experience of having a stoma. The permanent loss of continence also challenges others in relation to them, as evident in the ways that men and women narratively position partners in supporting and accommodating them after surgery, and express their concern about placing excessive demands on them. Not all couples stay together, and in some cases, as discussed, separation occurs on the initiative of the person with the stoma. In other cases, husbands and wives leave their partners, illustrating the difficulties both for the person at the centre of the bodily crisis, and for those nearest to him or her, in adjusting to dramatic, unforeseen and undesirable changes to the body. Partnership crises illustrate also how difficulties related to the stoma, and the increased need of the person with the stoma for psychological, physical and often financial support, compound other conflicts and tension. Partners who stay in the relationship but cease sexual relations reinforce for the person with the stoma fears of the loss of physical desirability. Spouses and lovers who stay and maintain sexual relations play a major role in reaffirming the adult status and desirability of their partners post-surgery.

The self-selection of participants in this study raises questions about the generalizability of findings, and the ability to which the data might be interpreted and extrapolated to other populations, particularly given that most research points simply to the positive outcomes of individuals following stoma surgery. However, research conducted to date has relied primarily on psychometric instrumentation and has not provided individuals with the freedom to explore the complex issues that they face following surgery (e.g., Northouse, Mood, Templin, Mellon, & George, 2000). In this study, individuals did include the positive aspects of having a stoma—most emphasized improved quality of life—but at the same time, they reflected on the difficulties of adjustment to the stoma and new bodily disruptions. Given the cultural background of participants, the discussion on sexuality after stoma therapy pertains particularly to Australians, although arguably it might be extended to other contexts. It is significant, of course, that stoma surgery is most common in industrialized country settings, but taboos relating to fecal material and acts of elimination are near universal. Further research is required to understand how individuals negotiate their bodies and interact with sexual partners after stoma surgery in other cultural and social settings.

An awareness of these difficulties has implications in terms of patient care and advice. A number of authors have drawn attention to the psychological distress that affects this group of people, and consequently the importance of the care provided to assist adaptation and outcome (Sahay et al., 2000; Sewitch et al., 2001, 2002; van der Eijk et al., 2004). In Australia and the United Kingdom, a stoma therapist or stoma therapy nurse provides patients with assistance in adjusting. Concerns about health status, and specifically about the stoma, appear to depend on the disease state preceding the surgery and the ability of the patient to adapt to the changes. The data presented in this study suggest, in addition, that adaptation is not simply about professional/patient interaction, nor about interaction of the person with a stoma and his or her partner. Cultural attitudes to the body, body image and sexuality play an important role in individuals' ability to adjust to body change. Miller (1997, p. xi) maintains that "(l)ove bears a complex and possibly necessary relation to disgust" involving "a notable and non-trivial suspension of some, if not all, rules of disgust" for pleasure to be possible. As reflected in the experiences of men and women with stomas, sexual pleasure requires that various physical bodily boundaries and social inhibitions be suspended, and that the transgressions of boundaries be negotiated.

REFERENCES

Andersen, B. L. (1994). Surviving cancer. *Cancer, 74*(4), 1484–1495.

Anllo, L. M. (2000). Sexual life after breast cancer. *Journal of Sex and Marital Therapy, 26*(3), 241–248.

Bigard, M. A. (1993). Functional results of ileal pouch-anal anastomosis. *Annales De Chirurgie, 47*(10), 992–995.

Bjerre, B. D., Johansen, C., & Steven, K. (1998). Sexological problems after cystectomy: bladder substitution compared with ileal conduit diversion—a questionnaire study of male patients. *Scandinavian Journal of Urology and Nephrology, 32*(3), 187–193.

Burkitt, I. (1998). Bodies of knowledge: beyond Cartesian views of persons, selves and mind. *Journal for the Theory of Social Behaviour, 28*(1), 63–82.

Carlsson, E., Bosaeus, I., & Nordgren, S. (2003). What concerns subjects with inflammatory bowel disease and an ileostomy? *Scandinavian Journal of Gastroenterology, 38*(9), 978–984.

Casellas, F., Lopez-Vivancos, J., Badia, X., Vilaseca, J., & Malagelada, J. R. (2000). Impact of surgery for Crohn's disease on health-related quality of life. *American Journal of Gastroenterology, 95*(1), 177–182.

Cohen, A. (1991). Body image in the person with a stoma. *Journal of Enterostomal Therapy, 18,* 68–71.

Cuntz, U., Welt, J., Ruppert, E., & Zillessen, E. (1999). Inflammatory bowel disease, psychosocial handicaps, illness experience and coping. *Psychotherapie Psychosomatik Medizinische Psychologie, 49*(12), 494–500.

Damgaard, B., Wettergren, A., & Kirkegaard, P. (1995). Social and sexual function following ileal pouch-anal anastomosis. *Diseases of the Colon & Rectum, 38*(3), 286–289.

Fobair, O. H. K., Koopman, C., Classen, C., Dimiceli, S., Drooker, N., Warner, D., Davids, H. R., Loulan, J., Wallsten, D., Goffinet, D., Morrow, G., & Spiegel, D. (2001). Comparison of lesbian and heterosexual women's response to newly diagnosed breast cancer. *Psycho-Oncology, 10*(1), 40–51.

Follick, M. J., Smith, T. W., & Turk, D. C. (1984). Psychosocial adjustment following ostomy. *Health Psychology, 3*(6), 505–517.

Fultz, N. H., & Herzog, A. R. (2001). Self-reported social and emotional impact of urinary incontinence. *Journal of the American Geriatrics Society, 49*(7), 892–899.

Gilbar, O., Steiner, N., & Atad, J. (1995). Adjustment of married couples and unmarried women to gynecological cancer. *Psycho-Oncology, 4*(3), 203–211.

Gloeckner, M. (1991). Perceptions of sexuality after ostomy surgery. *Journal of Enterostomal Therapy, 18,* 36–38.

Grosz, E. (1994). *Volatile bodies: toward a corporeal feminism.* Bloomington: Indiana University Press.

Gurevich, M., Bishop, S., Bower, J., Malka, M., & Nyhof-Young, J. (2004). (Dis)embodying gender and sexuality in testicular cancer. *Social Science & Medicine, 58*(9), 1597–1607.

Hjortswang, H., Jarnerot, B., Curman, B., Sandberg-Gertzen, H., Tysk, C., Blomberg, B., Almer, S., & Strom, M. (2003). The influence of demographic and disease-related factors on health-related quality of life in patients with ulcerative colitis. *European Journal of Gastroenterology & Hepatology, 15*(9), 1011–1020.

Isaksen, L. W. (1996). Unpleasant aspects of corporeality. *Sociologisk Forskning, 33*(2–3), 71–86.

Isaksen, L. W. (2002). Toward a sociology of (gendered) disgust—images of bodily decay and the social organization of care work. *Journal of Family Issues, 23*(7), 791–811.

Joly, F., Heron, J. F., Kalusinski, L., Bottet, P., Brune, D., Allouache, N., Mace-Lesec'h, J., Couette, J. E., Peny, J., & Henry-Amar, M. (2002). Quality of life in long-term survivors of testicular cancer: a population-based case-control study. *Journal of Clinical Oncology, 20*(1), 73–80.

Kelly, M. (1992). Self, identity and radical surgery. *Sociology of Health & Illness, 14*(3), 392–415.

Kempen, H. J. G. (1996). Mind as body moving in space—bringing the body back into self-psychology. *Theory & Psychology, 6*(4), 715–731.

Klopp, A. L. (1990). Body image and self-concept among individuals with stomas. *Journal of Enterostomal Therapy, 17,* 98–105.

Lagana, L., McGarvey, E. L., Classen, & Koopman, C. (2001). Psychosexual dysfunction among gynecological cancer survivors. *Journal of Clinical Psychology in Medical Settings, 8*(2), 73–84.

Lalos, A., & Eisemann, M. (1999). Social interaction and support related to mood and locus of control in cervical and endometrial cancer patients and their spouses. *Supportive Care in Cancer, 7*(2), 75–78.

Little, M., Jordens, C. F. C., Paul, K., Montgomery, K., & Philipson, B. (1998). Liminality: a major category of the experience of cancer illness. *Social Science & Medicine, 47*(10), 1485–1494.

Manderson, L. (2000). The gendered body: negotiating social membership after breast and gynecological cancer surgery. *Psycho-Oncology, 9*(5), S20.

McLeod, R. S., & Baxter, N. N. (1998). Quality of life of patients with inflammatory bowel disease after surgery. *World Journal of Surgery, 22*(4), 375–381.

Miller, W. I. (1997). *The anatomy of disgust.* Cambridge, MA: Harvard University Press.

Nordstrom, G., Nyman, C. R., & Theorell, T. (1992). Psychosocial adjustment and general state of health in patients with ileal conduit urinary-diversion. *Scandinavian Journal of Urology and Nephrology, 26*(2), 139–147.

Nordstrom, G. M., & Nyman, C. R. (1991). Living with a urostomy—a follow-up with special regard to the peristomal-skin complications, psychosocial and sexual life. *Scandinavian Journal of Urology and Nephrology, Supplementum, 138,* 247–251.

Northouse, L. L., Mood, D., Templin, T., Mellon, S., & George, T. (2000). Couples' patterns of adjustment to colon cancer. *Social Science & Medicine, 50*(2), 271–284.

Oresland, T., Palmblad, S., Ellstrom, M., Berndtsson, I., Crona, N., & Hulten, L. (1994). Gynecological and sexual function related to anatomical changes in the female pelvis after restorative proctocolectomy. *International Journal of Colorectal Disease, 9*(2), 77–81.

Peake, S., & Manderson, L. (2003). The constraints of a normal life: the management of urinary incontinence by middle aged women. *Women and Health, 37*(3), 37–51.

Peake, S., Manderson, L., & Potts, H. (1999). Part and parcel of being a woman: female urinary incontinence and constructions of control. *Medical Anthropology Quarterly, 13*(3), 267–285.

Persson, E., Severinsson, E., & Hellstrom, A. L. (2004). Spouses' perceptions of and reactions to living with a partner who has undergone surgery for rectal cancer resulting in a stoma. *Cancer Nursing, 27*(1), 85–90.

Rauch, P., Miny, J., Conroy, T., Nyeton, L., & Guillemin, F. (2004). Quality of life among disease-free survivors of rectal cancer. *Journal of Clinical Oncology, 22*(2), 354–360.

Sahay, T. B., Gray, R. E., & Fitch, M. (2000). A qualitative study of patient perspectives on colorectal cancer. *Cancer Practice, 8*(1), 38–44.

Schag, C. A. C., Ganz, P. A., Wing, D. S., Sim, M. S., & Lee, J. J. (1994). Quality-of-life in adult survivors of lung, colon and prostate-cancer. *Quality of Life Research, 3*(2), 127–141.

Schultz, W. C. M. W., & Van de Wiel, H. B. M. (2003). Sexuality, intimacy, and gynecological cancer. *Journal of Sex and Marital Therapy, 29*(1), 121–128.

Schultz, W. C. M. W., Van de Wiel, H. B., Hahn, D. E. E., & Bouma, J. (1992). Psychosexual functioning after treatment for gynecological cancer: an integrative model, review of determinant factors and clinical guidelines.

International Journal of Gynecological Cancer, 2(6), 281–290.

Sewitch, M. J., Abrahamowicz, M., Bitton, A., Daly, D., Wild, G. E., Cohen, A., Katz, S., Szego, P. L., & Dobkin, P. L. (2001). Psychological distress, social support, and disease activity in patients with in flammatory bowel disease. *American Journal of Gastroenterology,* 96(5), 1470–1479.

Sewitch, M. J., Abrahamowicz, M., Bitton, A., Daly, D., Wild, G. E., Cohen, A., Katz, S., Szego, P. L., & Dobkin, P. L. (2002). Psychosocial correlates of patient–physician discordance in inflammatory bowel disease. *American Journal of Gastroenterology,* 97(9), 2174–2183.

Smolen, D. M., & Topp, R. (2001). Self-care agency and quality of life among adults diagnosed with inflamma-tory bowel disease. *Quality of Life Research,* 10(4), 379–387.

Switankowsky, I. (2000). Dualism and its importance for medicine. *Theoretical Medicine and Bioethics,* 21(6), 567–580.

van der Eijk, I., Vlachonikolis, I. G., Munkholm, P., Nijman, J., Bernklev, T., Politi, P., Odes, S., Tsianos, E. V., Stock-brugger, R. W., & Russel, M. G. (2004). The role of quality of care in health-related quality of life in patients with IBD. *Inflammatory Bowel Diseases,* 10(4), 392–398.

Weerakoon, P. (2001). Sexuality and the patient with a stoma. *Sexuality and Disability,* 19(2), 121–129.

chapter 6

Sexual Practices

An interview with . . .

Elisabeth Sheff

Dr. Elisabeth Sheff is an assistant professor in the Department of Sociology at Georgia State University in Atlanta, Georgia. Her areas of specialty are gender, deviance, family, and sexuality, all of which culminate with her focus on families of sexual minorities. In her longest-running study, Sheff has followed a group of polyamorists for eight years and is currently collecting the third wave of data from these participants. Another of Sheff's studies focuses on the intersections between participants and practices of polyamory and kink/BDSM, and the impact of Internet communications on both communities.

What led you to begin studying sexuality?

When I was 23, I fell head over heels in love with a man who told me he wanted to have a non-monogamous relationship, which terrified me. We discussed it for several years and I became, if not more open to it, at least less freaked out by the idea. Eventually I heard a National Public Radio interview with Ryam Nearing, the (then) editor of Loving More, a magazine about polyamory. She was talking about exactly what he had been advocating, and it turned out that there was a group meeting in my area. I tend to intellectualize things that frighten me, hoping that if I can understand them then I will be better able to cope with them. Initially approaching the group as a "civilian" interested in learning about polyamory as it was relevant to my own life, I became increasingly interested the community as a whole and ultimately did my doctoral research on mainstream polyamorous communities in the Western United States. So, I guess you could say that I started studying sexuality because it scared me!

How did that lead to the research you do today?

My research focuses on two groups of sexual minorities, polyamorists (polys) and kinksters. Polyamorists are people who openly conduct sexual and affective relationships with multiple partners. Kinksters are people who identify as kinky, many of whom are involved in BDSM. BDSM is the abbreviation for Bondage/Domination or Discipline/ Sadism or Submission/Masochism, a sexual style and category of relationships based on enjoyment of a wide variety of sensations, especially pain. Many kinksters negotiate an exchange of personal power in which (most often) one agrees to submit to the other, with one taking the role of "top" (dominant) and the other the role of "bottom" (submissive).

I find studying the variety of relationships and complexity of interactions fascinating. Participants in my research construct some of the most interesting, creative, and well thought out relationships I have ever seen. They are articulate and say some remarkable things that challenge me to think about sexual and social interactions in new ways. It is most striking how "normal" polyamorous and kinky people are—they are your accountant, orthodontist, neighbor, or friend. There is no way to tell from the outside who is or is not having multiple partner relationships and/or kinky sex.

How do people react when they find out that you study sexuality?

The vast majority of people react fairly positively to hearing about my research. Sometimes it just blends into the conversation, and is neither ignored nor problematized. At other times, it becomes the main topic of the conversation, and people often ask thoughtful questions about how to deal with issues such as jealousy, parenting, managing complex relationships, and where people sleep in poly relationships. These discussions often spur people to tell me about their own relationships and attitudes towards sexuality, which often proves quite interesting.

Occasionally I get negative reactions about my specific topics of study. Polyamory sometimes makes people uncomfortable. I think this is probably because virtually everyone has at some point felt attracted to different people (even if not at the same time), so everyone has the potential to be non-monogamous. Our society negatively sanctions this type of relationship, so we often think that non-monogamy is "bad" or "wrong." Obviously many people will not act on feelings of attraction to others when they are in monogamous relationships, but the threat of that possibility can be very uncomfortable for some people. Kink/BDSM relationships and practices may seem strange to some people, and they either want more details about exactly what they find so shocking, or they seem uncomfortable and change the subject.

Rarely, I get an inappropriately titillated response from people, usually men, who assume that I do everything I research and seem to want, or even ask, me to do it with them, or at least let them watch!

What do you do when this happens?

I let them know that I keep my personal life and my research separate, and that it would be unethical to mix the two! I also let them know that I prefer to pick my own partners and practices without being pressured into uncomfortable situations.

What do you think is most challenging about studying sexuality?

That many people see sexuality as a global identity—so much so that it obscures other aspects of sexual minorities' lives. In other words, one's sexual identity becomes the identity that people focus on and supersedes all other identities—so that one is a gay, kinky, or poly parent, a gay/kinky/poly student, or a gay/kinky/poly employee—not just a parent, student, or employee.

I study relationships between people who are sexual non-conformists. They may have multiple partners, family members who are polyamorous, and/or unconventional sexual practices. Other than questions about who is involved and how it affects their relationships, I don't tend to ask people the specifics about how they have sex. So, in a way, I am not a sex researcher at all, I am a relationship researcher. But because my research populations are sexual minorities, I am seen as a "sex researcher" in a way that people who study (ostensibly) monogamous, heterosexual, dyadic relationships are not viewed as "(hetero)sex(ual) researchers."

Why is sex research so important to do?

To educate people about the variety of sexual relationships and practices which exist and help combat fear borne of ignorance. Some people fear those that are different and want to regulate or punish them, even though what they do in their own bedrooms has little impact on the rest of their lives. For example, people often assume that children raised in polyamorous or kinky families are being harmed and should be removed from the home, when in reality, parental sexual practices have little to do with one's ability to parent. In fact, children in polyamorous families—instead of having one or two concerned parents—may have three, four, or more! Both the kids and adults tell me that these extra adults have a very positive impact on the kids' lives because it means the children get so much attention.

If you could teach people one thing about sexuality, what would it be?

The most important thing I would emphasize is communication around consent. To effectively discuss consent, you have to talk about what is going to happen. That means exploring possibilities, setting boundaries, and (ideally) discussing which kinds of safer sex practices you will use. All of this communication could prevent some rapes, reduce the spread of sexually transmitted infections, and possibly even help people to address power issues in their relationships because true consent cannot be granted under coercion. Finally, expressing what they want might enable people to have more fulfilling sex lives, which I think is a good thing!

The Pursuit of Sexual Pleasure

B. J. Rye and Glenn J. Meaney

Sex and sexuality are surprisingly difficult terms to define. In one sense, sex can be seen as a collection of behaviors related directly or indirectly to stimulation of the genitals; our bodies then respond to this stimulation with a reflex that is pleasurable and tension-releasing (i.e., orgasm). This . . . definition does not, however, provide much insight into the role that sexuality plays in our lives. Rather, sexuality can be thought of as an institution defined by shared social meaning that is constructed around the simple stimulation of genitals; sex, in this sense, is what we make it (e.g., DeLamater & Hyde, 1998; Foucault, 1976/1978). At the individual level, human sexuality is subjective and represents how we experience and express ourselves as sexual beings. At a cultural level, sexuality can be constructed to serve a variety of needs: sex is a means of procreation, an intimate bonding ritual, even a form of social control (Foucault, 1976/1978; Hawkes, 1996; Weeks, 1981). For some, sex is work (e.g., prostitution, "spousely duty"). For others, sex is play. . . . [T]his [reading] will focus on the "playful" aspect of sex. In particular, we will discuss the more physical gymnastics involved in the pursuit and attainment of *sexual pleasure*—"sex for fun." We hope to show how pleasure is a primary motivator for sexual activity and how social constructions of sexuality are built around this fundamental desire for sexual pleasure. . . .

Our perspective on sexual pleasure is constructed from a review of mainly Canadian and U.S. literature concerning sexual activity and sexual behavior. We supplement this review from our own ongoing survey of Canadian university students. . . . We . . . focus our discussion on a very North American version of the pursuit of sexual pleasure.

The Pursuit of Sexual Pleasure

What Is Sexual Pleasure?

Broadly defined, sexual pleasure involves the positive feelings that arise from sexual stimuli (Abramson & Pinkerton, 1995). Sexual pleasure may result from a variety of activities that involve sexual arousal, genital stimulation, and/or orgasm. . . . While it may seem self-evident, people are more likely to engage in sexual behaviors they consider pleasurable than sexual behaviors that they find less pleasurable (Browning et al., 2000; Pinkerton et al., 2003).

It is seldom overtly stated, but sexual pleasure is very important in our society. Achieving sexual arousal and orgasm is significant enough to people that manuals of sexual technique have been compiled—such as the venerable *Kama Sutra* (trans., 1994), *The Joy of Sex* (Comfort, 1972), and *Sex for Dummies* (Westheimer, 1995). There are university courses, television shows (e.g., *The Sex Files,* Colby, 2006), web sites (e.g., www.sexualityandu.ca), sex stores, and shows (e.g., *The Stag Shop,* see www.stagshop.com; *The Everything to Do with Sex Show,* see www .everythingtodowithsex.com) devoted to human sexuality and the attainment of the highest level of sexual satisfaction possible. Clearly, people have a great interest in sexual pleasure. This pleasure can be pursued in many forms—and can occur in solitary and/or partnered contexts. Perhaps the simplest sexual activities are those in which an individual can engage alone, such as masturbation and sexual fantasy.

From "The Pursuit of Sexual Pleasure" by B. J. Rye and Glenn J. Meaney, *Sexuality & Culture,* 11, 28–51. © 2007. Reprinted with kind permission from Springer Science and Business Media.

Solitary Sex

Fantasy

Sexual fantasy has the appeal of being the safest form of sexual enjoyment: One can fantasize any time, one can have total control, and there are no (direct) consequences (Doskoch, 1995). Sexual fantasy is difficult to research, especially because it is difficult to define exactly what constitutes fantasy (see Byrne & Osland, 2000). Leitenberg and Henning (1995: 470) define sexual fantasy as "almost any mental imagery that is sexually arousing or erotic to the individual." Byers and colleagues (Byers, Purdon, & Clark, 1998; Little & Byers, 2000; Renaud & Byers, 1999) prefer the term *sexual cognitions,* which may have positive or negative connotations. Sexual thoughts can take many forms, some of which may not be pleasurable to the individual. . . .

The great majority of men and women engage in sexual fantasy, either as an activity by itself (i.e., daydreaming), or in conjunction with other sexual activities, including masturbation and partnered sex. For example, when asked "how often do you think about sex?", 97% of men and 86% of women responded with a few times a month or more (Laumann et al., 1994). In terms of content, men seem more likely to have explicitly sexual fantasies (Ellis & Symons, 1990), to imagine themselves in positions of dominance (Byers, Purdon, & Clark, 1998; Hsu et al., 1994), to see themselves as the "doer," (Byers, Purdon, & Clark, 1998; Knafo & Jaffe, 1984) and to fantasize about multiple partners (Ellis & Symons, 1990). Women tend to have more emotional and romantic fantasies and to see themselves in positions of submission (Hsu et al., 1994; McCauley & Swann, 1978). Lesbians and gay men tend to have fantasies similar to heterosexual women and men, respectively, except that they typically imagine same-sex partners (Hurlbert & Apt, 1993; Keating & Over, 1990; Masters & Johnson, 1979; Robinson & Parks, 2003). In general, people report a wide variety of content in sexual fantasy. People who have more sexual fantasies tend to have fewer sexual problems and report more sexual satisfaction than people who have fewer fantasies (Byrne & Osland, 2000; Leitenberg & Henning, 1995). . . .

Renaud and Byers (1999) found that all of their New Brunswick university student sample reported having had sexual thoughts at some time. Both men and women reported more positive than negative thoughts, with men reporting more of both positive and negative thoughts. Participants reported a wide variety of content in sexual thoughts. . . . Little and Byers (2000) [found that] . . . [p]eople often enjoyed having sexual fantasies while in public places, and people in committed relationships were not more likely to evaluate sexual thoughts as negative. Our survey of Ontario students enrolled in an introductory sexuality course (1999–2006) indicated that 63% of women and 78% of men—who have had sex—fantasize while engaging in sexual activity with a partner. Our students fantasize in greater numbers (98% of men; 93% of women) during masturbation—sexual self-stimulation.

Masturbation

Historically, masturbation has been stigmatized and associated with immorality and pathology, but it is quickly gaining respect as a common and healthy sexual activity (Coleman, 2002). A recent survey of American university students (Pinkerton et al., 2002) found that about two-thirds of the women and almost all of the men reported masturbating at least once. Both genders reported frequent masturbation in the past three months. People masturbated more if they perceived social norms in support of this behavior (Pinkerton et al., 2002). More sexually active people masturbated more often, indicating that masturbation is not a substitute for other sexual activity (also see Davis et al., 1996).

Men tend to masturbate fairly uniformly whereas women tend to have more varied masturbation techniqes from woman-to-woman (see Masters & Johnson, 1966). There were no gender differences in reasons for masturbating: the majority of men and women stated that they masturbated to relieve sexual tension and the second most commonly cited reason was for physical pleasure (Laumann et al., 1994). . . . Of all sexual behaviors, masturbation seems most clearly motivated by pleasure, or at least, release of tension. . . .

Partnered Sexual Activity

A common North American sexual script suggests that we have a shared idea about the sequence of partnered sexual behaviors that proceeds from kissing and touching ("petting" above the waist) to more intensive touching ("petting" below the waist or manual stimulation of the genitals) to oral sex to genital-to-genital contact to vaginal or anal intercourse (Gagnon & Simon, 1987; Laumann et al., 1994; McKay, 2004). Of course, there are a multitude of variations on this script and many behaviors have been omitted from this generic description. In almost all cases, kissing is a starting point.

Kissing

Kissing is a very common behavior with same-sex and other-sex couples reporting that they usually kiss when they have sex (Blumstein & Schwartz, 1983). In a U.S. study of university students, most (96%) had "dry" kissed someone and a large majority (89%) reported having "French-kissed" (i.e., kissed with open mouths). Ninety-one percent (91%) of men and 95% of women who participated in our human sexuality student survey indicated that they were experienced French-kissers, as well. A representative study of Canadian youth found that about a third to half of seventh-grade students, approximately two-thirds of ninth-grade students, and about eight out of ten eleventh-grade students reported engaging in "deep, open-mouth" kissing (Boyce et al., 2003). It should be noted that, while kissing is generally considered an erotic activity in North American society, it is not considered erotic in all cultures (Harvey, 2005). When kissing is considered erotic, however, it is often a precursor to petting (kissing, of course, may accompany petting).

Touching

Petting is a rather odd term for sexually touching another person—usually interpreted as meaning in the genital region. This is also known as mutual masturbation or being masturbated by a partner. This is a common behavior amongst university students . . . (Browning et al., 2000; Pinkerton et al., 2003). . . . Over a third of seventh-grade students, about two-thirds of ninth-grade students, and eight out of ten

eleventh-grade students indicated that they had engaged in "touching above the waist at least once." The incidence of hand-genital contact was less common—with about a quarter to a third of seventh-grade students, slightly over half of ninth-grade students, and about three quarters of eleventh-grade students responding yes to "touching below the waist at least once" (Boyce et al., 2003). Mutual masturbation is a common sexual behavior and being masturbated by one's partner tends to be ranked as highly pleasurable relative to some other sexual behaviors (Pinkerton et al., 2003). Another form of touching is oral sex: sexual stimulation of the genitals by mouth.

Oral Sex

People frequently engage in oral sex. Recent national surveys in the U.S. indicated that a large majority of adult men (79–85%) have had oral sex performed on them (called fellatio) while many women (73–83%) have received oral sex (called cunnilingus) (Laumann et al., 1994; Mosher, Chandra, & Jones, 2005). About 90% of adults have had oral sex (Mosher et al., 2005). This has changed somewhat since the Kinsey surveys (1949, 1953) which indicated that about 60% of men and women had engaged in oral sex. Our survey of sexuality students indicated that between 80% and 85% of women and men had performed and received oral sex. Not surprisingly, oral sex is becoming more common among Canadian adolescents, as well (Boyce et al., 2003; McKay, 2004).

There is an emerging literature where researchers and lay people alike discuss adolescent oral sex as an activity on the rise as a "substitute" for intercourse—as this helps prevent pregnancy, reduce STIs risk, and maintain "virginity" (Barrett, 2004; McKay, 2004). Mosher and others (2005) found that just over 10% of teenagers (15–19 years old) have had oral sex without intercourse with about 55% of all teens having had oral sex. . . . [E]ducators and researchers consider this to be a natural increase as oral sex rates have increased for adults, as well (Barrett, 2004; McKay, 2004). One of the major reasons why youth engage in oral sex is that it is fun and pleasurable (Barrett, 2004). Similarly, university students ranked receiving oral sex as the second most pleasant activity after vaginal intercourse (Pinkerton et al., 2003).

Penis-in-Vagina Intercourse

Pinkerton and others (2003) found that penis-in-vagina intercourse was rated as the most pleasurable sexual activity (as did Laumann et al., 1994). This is a behavior in which almost all adults have engaged at least once (Laumann et al., 1994; Mosher et al., 2005; Wellings et al., 1994). In terms of U.S. university students, around 80% have had vaginal intercourse (Browning et al., 2000; Pinkerton et al., 2003). Our sample of Canadian sexuality students had slightly fewer men indicating that they have had vaginal intercourse (75%) compared to women (79%). Most of these students (40–45%) had their first intercourse between the ages of 16–18 years; this is congruent with the representative survey of Canadian youth finding that between 40–46% of eleventh-grade students have had intercourse at least once (Boyce et al., 2003).

While there are *many* different positions for intercourse, there are four "basic" positions: man-on-top ("missionary"), woman-on-top, side-by-side, and rear entry ("doggie style"). Each position has certain "advantages." For example, the woman-on-top position is good when a man has poorer ejaculatory control, allows the woman to control sexual positioning and rhythm, and allows greater accessibility to the clitoris (a key organ to female sexual pleasure). The man-on-top is the recommended position when a couple is trying to become pregnant. Rear entry is good when a woman is pregnant or when particularly deep penile insertion is desired. . . . While vaginal intercourse is considered pleasurable by most people, a substantial minority of people also report enjoying anal sex.

Anal Sex

Anal sex can take different forms. There is penis-in-anus intercourse whereby a man inserts his penis into the rectum of his partner. As the anus has no natural lubrication, a sterile lubricant gel is recommended (e.g., Astroglide, K-Y Jelly) so as to reduce the likelihood of trauma to the anus (e.g., tearing tissue, damaging sphincters). It is recommended that the inserter wear a condom. Because anal intercourse typically involves some tearing of the tissue, there is a direct route for pathogens into the blood stream, making this a very efficient route for HIV transmission and other STIs. It is important that the penis be washed after anal intercourse and prior to any further genital contact. For example, if a man removes his penis from the anus and inserts it into the vagina, various bacteria can be transferred to the vagina.

Anilingus or "rimming" is oral stimulation of the anus. Again, because of the presence of bacteria and possibly other STI pathogens (e.g., gonorrhea, hepatitis), it is prudent to use a barrier (e.g., cut a condom up the side or use a dental dam). Some people enjoy digital stimulation of the anus by having fingers or the hand inserted in the anus during sexual arousal.

Anal intercourse is not as commonly performed as the other sexual activities discussed thus far. A representative U.S. sample found that roughly a third of adults have had anal sex (Mosher et al., 2005). . . . About one-fifth to a quarter of university students in two U.S. samples reported ever having experienced anal intercourse (Browning et al., 2000; Pinkerton et al., 2003). In our sexuality student survey, about one-fifth reported having had anal intercourse. Laumann and others asked their participants if they had experienced anal sex *in the past year* and approximately 5–10% had experienced anal sex that recently. Finally, Laumann and others posed an interesting set of questions to their participants about how "appealing" a variety of sexual behaviors were. When asked about various forms of anal sex, between 1% and 5% of people rated anal contact as 'very appealing' (including stimulating a partner's anus, having anus stimulated by a partner's finger, and anal intercourse).

Techniques of Same-Sex Couples

A substantial minority of people are lesbian, gay, or bisexual (LGB; Laumann et al., 1994). A recent representative U.S. survey found that around 8–10% of adults identified as LGB (Mosher et al., 2005). About 9% of men and 6% of women in our human sexuality class self-identified as LGB. One does not need to be LGB to engage in same-sex behavior;

6% of men and 11% of women indicated that they have had a same-sex sexual partner in their lifetime (Mosher et al., 2005). Laumann and others (1994) found that about 3% of men and women rated having a same-gendered sexual partner as "very appealing."

Same-sex couples tend to engage in similar sexual behaviors as other-sex couples including kissing, hugging, mutual masturbation, oral stimulation, and penetrative sex (Blumstein & Schwartz, 1983; Masters & Johnson, 1979). Male couples sometimes engage in interfemoral intercourse; this is where one man thrusts his penis between the thighs of the other man. Female couples may engage in tribadism whereby "two women rub their vulvae together to stimulate each other's clitoris to orgasm" (Wikimedia Foundation, 2006; also see Caster, 1993) or, there may be mons-to-thigh stimulation. Other-sex couples also engage in this non-penetrative genital-to-genital stimulation (Kinsey et al. [1953] call this apposition; "dry humping" is a more common, but less sophisticated, description).

Masters and Johnson (1979) observed and compared the sexual behaviors of same-sex couples to other-sex couples and found differences in arousal *techniques* rather than sexual behaviors. In general, the same-sex couples tended to "take their time" in comparison to opposite-sex couples. That is, Masters and Johnson characterized heterosexual couples as more "performance oriented"—oriented toward the penis-in-vagina act—in contrast to the same-sex couples, who engaged more in pleasure-seeking throughout the sexual encounter. There were no differences between heterosexual and homosexual people of the same gender in terms of masturbation techniques.

Spicy Sex

Thus far, we have discussed relatively common sexual activities. There are practices that are not necessarily common or usual but that are pleasurable for many people. . . . [I]t is important to remember that uncommon does not equal pathological. Most sexual behaviors can be placed on a continuum from healthy (e.g., having a mild or strong preference) to pathological (e.g., when the behavior/object becomes a necessity or a substitute for a human relationship; see Hyde, DeLamater, & Byers, 2006). Spicier activities

may be an indication of the importance of sexual pleasure. While many of the "vanilla" techniques are quite pleasurable, they are often socially scripted, and are cheap and easy in which to engage. More "spicy" techniques may require creative thought, monetary expense, or even travel plans. The trouble that people are willing to go through for the "spicier" activities might indicate that these are primarily pleasure-seeking activities.

Sex Toys

"Sex toys" are devices that people use to enhance their sexual pleasure (e.g., vibrators, dildos) and, while sex toys have been around for years (in the late 1800s, early 1900s as "medical devices"; see Maines, 1999), people have become more open about discussing sex toys perhaps because of popular media portrayals (e.g., *Sex and the City,* King, Chupack, Melfi, Bicks, Raab, et al., 2006; *The L Word,* Chaiken, Golin, & Kennar, 2006) and books and stores devoted to sex toys (e.g., Venning & Cavanah, 2003). . . . In our survey of human sexuality students, about a third of women had experience with a "mechanical aid" compared to 8% of men. This is quite different from the representative survey of American adults which found less than 1 in 20 (< 5%) of men and women rated vibrator/dildo use as appealing (Laumann et al., 1994). Laumann and others found that the more educated women in their sample found vibrator/dildo use the most appealing—education may impact attitudes toward sex toy use.

Davis et al. (1996) conducted a study of women who use vibrators. . . . The results suggested that many of the women . . . found that clitoral-vibrator stimulation usually triggers an orgasm, they used their vibrators on a variety of sexual sites (clitoral, vaginal, and anal), and in a variety of ways (circular motion, up/down, or back/forth). Most (80%) of the sample used the vibrator during partnered sex—sometimes with the partner watching the woman use the vibrator while sometimes the partner held the vibrator for the woman. Women, who were lesbian and were more likely to, reported being younger when they first used a vibrator and were slightly more likely to use a vibrator with a partner than were bisexual or heterosexual women.

Sexually Explicit Material

Use of erotica—sexually explicit depictions—is also a relatively common aid in autosexual or partnered sexual activity. Erotic materials are broad-ranging and may include books, magazines, videos/DVDs, live shows (e.g., exotic dancers), telephone sex, and cybersexuality (e.g., sex in chat rooms, webcam sex). Laumann and others (1994) found that as many as one out of five men used some form of erotic materials when fantasizing/masturbating while fewer women did (as many as one out of ten). These researchers asked about the appeal of "watching other people do sexual things" (which might be interpreted as erotica or, alternatively, voyeurism) and found that 5% of men and 1% of women found this activity sexually appealing. In the human sexuality student survey, a majority of men and women had favorable attitudes toward erotic materials, although there was a gender difference such that men were more favorable than women were.

Online sexual activities have increased in recent years. . . . A . . . study of people who use the Internet indicated that 80% of participants used the web for sexual purposes. Of those people, about a third had engaged in "cybersex." Cybersex was defined as "when two or more people are engaging in sexual talk while online for the purposes of sexual pleasure and may or may not include masturbation" (Daneback, Cooper, & Månsson, 2005: 321). This cybersex most commonly took the form of a sexual encounter in a "chat room" with the second most popular medium being instant messenger-type programs.

Sexual Internet activities are probably on the rise because of the fact that these materials are affordable, readily available, and can be accessed anonymously (Cooper, McLoughlin, & Campbell, 2000). The Internet allows people with uncommon sexual proclivities to both find and support others with similar interests. As well, the Internet offers users the opportunity to experiment with new behaviors in a relatively safe setting, satisfy curiosity, and seek out new information. While there has been a substantial discussion of "Internet sex addiction," sexually compulsive Internet users typically already have a history of unconventional sexual practices (i.e., diagnosable paraphilias, risky sexual activity). Many people who are recreational users of online sexual material spend less than an hour per week, on average, visiting sexual websites (Cooper et al., 1999).

Sadomasochism

Sadomasochism (S&M) is a term that collectively describes a variety of sexual behaviors which may involve the administration of pain (e.g., use of clothespins/clamps, hot wax, spanking), deliberate humiliation (e.g., use of a gag, face slapping), physical restriction (e.g., handcuffs, chains), and hypermasculine activities (e.g., cockbinding, watersports, rimming) that are experienced as pleasurable by both partners (Alison, Santtila, Sandnabba, & Nordling, 2001; Sandnabba, Santtila, & Nordling, 1999). The S&M scene typically involves fetishistic elements such as leather clothing and whips, and ritualistic activity such as bondage. S&M has been characterized as fantasy-oriented and role-playing scripted behavior. . . .

[T]here is a distinct subculture of psychologically well-adjusted individuals who engage in S&M activities—many of whom belong to S&M "clubs" (Alison et al., 2001; Sandnabba et al., 1999). Partners in S&M activities described here refer to consenting S&M participants. People who have participated in research studies about the S&M subculture have been found to be well-integrated into society in general as they tend to be highly educated and earn high incomes (Alison et al., 2001; Mosher & Levitt, 1987; Sandnabba et al., 1999). Most of these people report engaging in S&M activities occasionally and in non-S&M sexual activities frequently—which indicates that the S&M activities were not part of a "diagnosable paraphilia" (Sandnabba et al., 1999). Most of the information known about S&M involves men; it is sometimes difficult to obtain adequate samples of women within the S&M subculture (Mosher & Levitt, 1987; Sandnabba et al., 1999). In a study of men, Sandnabba and colleagues (1999) found the most common S&M behaviors to include (in order): oral sex, bondage, wearing leather outfits, flagellation (e.g., whipping), anal intercourse, rimming, handcuffs, and the use of chains, dildos, and verbal humiliation; at least 70% of all of the men interviewed participated in each of these behaviors. The most popular role-play for heterosexual men was master/slave (for Mosher & Levitt's, 1987, sample, too) while, for gay men, the most common role-play was a "uniform scene" (e.g., police officer and arrestee).

Although we do not know how many people practice S&M, we do know that people fantasize about and/or have a sexual response to S&M activities. . . . While S&M fantasies appear to be fairly common, we do not know how many people act upon these fantasies.

Sex on Vacation

There is a phenomenon that has recently begun to be documented whereby people travel for the purpose of obtaining sex outside of their community. Much of this literature has focused on heterosexual men who travel to areas such as the Caribbean or Southeast Asia for sexual gratification. While most of these men do not view themselves as engaging prostitution services, the transactions are clearly a form of commercialized sex. Researchers and theorists in this area actually find that sex tourists of this sort tend to be racist, sexist, and believe in their own Western cultural superiority over the people in these Third World locales (O'Connell Davidson & Sánchez Taylor, 1999).

Heterosexual women are also sex tourists who "purchase" the sexual services of local men (e.g., Cabezas, 2004; Herold, Garcia, & DeMoya, 2001). Sánchez Taylor's (2001) study of single women vacationing at resorts in the Dominican Republic and Jamaica, approximately a third, had engaged in sexual relations with local men; this was significantly more new sexual contacts compared to single women vacationing in Europe. Over half of the women with "vacation" sex partners had remunerated the sex partner in some way (e.g., cash, gifts). These women did not view themselves as being consumers of prostitution services despite the economic element to their relationship; rather, they tended to characterize these sexual behaviors as "holiday romances." However, the men tend to be in lower socioeconomic positions (e.g. "beach boys," hotel workers), often live in poverty, and earn a living though various forms of "hustling." Interviews with the men indicated that they do not conceptualize themselves as prostitutes or sex trade workers but they acknowledge that they reap financial and material benefits from entering into a series of fleeting sexual relationships with female tourists. These men even have strategies to assess which women are likely to be the most "generous" (Sánchez Taylor, 2001).

A different type of sex tourism is popular with university students who are on vacation. This involves having casual sex with a relative stranger while on spring break. By *relative stranger,* researchers mean that the individual has met the sexual partner while on vacation and typically known the sex partner for 24 hours or less. . . . Matika-Tyndale and colleagues (. . . 1997; 1998) found that approximately 16% of students vacationing in Daytona Beach had engaged in sexual intercourse with a new casual partner (this excludes those traveling with their boyfriend/girlfriend). Almost half (46%) reported "fooling around in a sexual way" with a new partner; this involved sexual activity excluding intercourse. In the spring break subculture, sexual norms are more permissive than what is expected "back home" (. . . Mewhinney, Herold, & Maticka-Tyndale, 1995). Having a partner "back home" did not seem to deter vacationers from having casual sex; one-fifth to one-quarter of people who were currently in a relationship had intercourse with a casual partner while they were on vacation.

It seems that being on vacation—away from the social constraints of "home"—creates a subculture of sexual permissiveness whereby one can have sex for solely the purpose of having sex (e.g., for fun, to "let loose"). As one student characterized casual sex during spring break vacation: "It is generally expected . . . to have a great time and that includes having sex" (Mewhinney et al., 1995: 278). There are similar destinations that are known for tourist-tourist casual sex such as Ibiza and Cap d'Azur that cater to nonstudents populations (O'Connell Davidson & Sánchez Taylor, 1999). The fact that some will go through so much trouble for the purpose of having sex lends credence to the unspoken value we place on sexual pleasure. The pursuit of sexual pleasure can be seen clearly, not only in sex tourism, but in the multi-faceted behaviours we have chosen to call "spicy" sex.

Spicy sex encompasses a diversity of behaviors, many of which we have *not* discussed (e.g., group sex and swinging, other commercialized sex, cross-dressing, etc.). What is interesting about these diverse behaviors is that, while not popular with everyone, people who engage in these behaviors tend to find a social group who are supportive of the activities (e.g., fantasia parties for those who have an interest in sex toys, S&M clubs, online chat groups devoted to various sexual acts). It is possible that when there is a supportive social network for the "spicy" sexual behavior, people will be more comfortable with their "less common" sexual behavior (see Kutchinsky, 1976, Sandnabba et al., 1999). . . .

What Can We Conclude about Sexual Pleasure?

What is sexually pleasurable is in the eye of the beholder. "Sex" and "sexual pleasure" are very much "social constructions" in that certain attitudes, behaviors, and activities are considered taboo. Societal norms exert a great deal of social control over what is "acceptable" sexuality. In Western society dominated by Christian values, there is a tendency to view the pursuit of sex for pleasure's sake as hedonistic; for example, a person who has casual sex tends to be viewed negatively (Parrinder, 1996). The pleasure of sex for a particular person depends not entirely on attaining orgasm but on the context and psychological state of the individuals involved (Mah & Binik, 2005). How a person has internalized the cultural messages about various aspects of sexuality will have a profound impact on the person's experience of sexual pleasure. For example, if sex is seen solely as a means of procreation—a strongly Christian perspective (Parrinder, 1996)—there may be great guilt associated with feeling pleasure if one engages in sexual behavior solely for pleasure purposes. Similarly, when sex is fundamental to the maintenance of a long-term relationship, it can become an obligatory duty (see Hawkes, 1996, . . . for a discussion). In both cases, sex can become a matter of performance-pressure and anxiety.

In the eighteenth and nineteenth centuries, sex was officially defined in terms of the social and interpersonal functions it fulfilled; there was little mention of sex as a pleasurable experience (or, if so, it was pleasurable only for men). When attention was drawn to the sexual pleasure of women (somewhat ironically, by the work of Freud), social forces constrained that pleasure to marriage. People seeking sexual pleasure outside of marriage were labeled as "deviant" (Hawkes, 1996). Our current societal views on sexual pleasure have their roots in our Victorian history of sex negativity and the subsequent need to "quell" or control a dangerous instinct (Foucault, 1976/1978; Weeks, 1981, 1986).

Current North American attitudes toward sexual pleasure run the gamut from "only for procreation" to "okay when in love or when dating" to "anything goes." While there is no consensus, sex with love or in the context of a committed relationship tends to be deemed as more acceptable and changes in attitudes toward sex tend to relate to concurrent changes in sexual behavior (Barrett et al., 2004). Views about sexuality and sexual pleasure are constantly changing (DeLamater & Hyde, 2003). Enhanced discussions about sexual pleasure will occur as our society incorporates an increasingly positive perspective on sexual pleasure into the existing sexual scripts (Gagnon & Simon, 1987). This positive view of sexual pleasure will need to be incorporated into scripts at all levels: the intrapersonal (i.e., self-acceptance of sex for personal pleasure), the interpersonal (i.e., acceptance of one's partner(s), friends, family, etc. as enjoying sex for pleasure reasons), and finally, the overarching cultural scripts (i.e., schemas for the sexuality of men, schemas for the sexuality of women, environments that reinforce rather than punish the concept of sexual pleasure for pleasure's sake).

While the social discourse surrounding sexuality will continue to evolve and to complicate the meanings attached to sexuality, the avoidance and guilt associated with sexual pleasure seems to be lessening. In fact, a new discourse appears to be arising that specifically and explicitly emphasizes the often-lost pursuit of sexual pleasure (McKay, 2004; Abramson & Pinkerton, 1995). This pursuit, in itself, can become a source of enlightenment spurred by the realization of simple, physical pleasures associated with human sexuality. The dark side of sexuality will continue to exert its influence, of course, in the specters of sexual harassment, sexual coercion, stalking, paraphilias, and related phenomena. . . . But, an acceptance of sexual pleasure would open avenues for personal satisfaction that will, hopefully, serve as a safeguard against such negative outcomes.

REFERENCES

Abramson, P. R., & Pinkerton, S. D. (1995). *With pleasure: Thoughts on the nature of human sexuality.* New York: Oxford University Press.

Alison, L., Santtila, P., Sandnabba, N. K., & Nordling, N. (2001). Sadomasochistically oriented behavior: Diversity in practice and meaning. *Archives of Sexual Behavior, 30*(1), 1–12.

Barrett, A. (2004). Oral sex and teenagers: A sexual health educator's perspective. *Canadian Journal of Human Sexuality, 13*(3/4), 197–200.

Barrett, M., King, A., Lévy, J., Maticka-Tyndale, E., McKay, A., & Fraser, J. (2004). Canada. In R. T. Francoeur & R. J. Noonan (Eds.), *The Continuum complete international encyclopedia of sexuality* (pp. 126–181). New York: Continuum.

Blumstein, P., & Schwartz, P. (1983). *American couples.* New York: Morrow.

Boyce, W., Doherty, M., Fortin, C., & MacKinnon, D. (2003). *Canadian youth, sexual health and HIV/AIDS study.* Toronto, ON: Council of Ministers of Education.

Browning, J. R., Hatfield, E., Kessler, D., & Levine, T. (2000). Sexual motives, gender and sexual behavior. *Archives of Sexual Behavior, 29*(2), 135–153.

Byers, S., Purdon, C., & Clark, D. A. (1998). Sexual intrusive thoughts of college students. *Journal of Sex Research, 35*(4), 359–369.

Byrne, D., & Osland, J. A. (2000). Sexual fantasy and erotica/pornography: Internal and external imagery. In L. T. Szuchman & F. Muscarella (Eds.), *Psychological perspectives on human sexuality* (pp. 283–305). Toronto, ON: Wiley.

Cabezas, A. L. (2004). Between love and money: Sex, tourism, and citizenship in Cuba and the Dominican Republic. *Signs: Journal of Women in Culture and Society, 29*(4), 987–1015.

Caster, W. (1993). *The lesbian sex book.* Boston, MA: Alyson.

Chaiken, I., Golin, S., & Kennar, L. (Producers) (2006). *The L word* [Television series]. Showtime.

Coleman, E. (2002). Masturbation as a means of achieving sexual health. *Journal of Psychology and Human Sexuality, 14*(2/3), 5–16.

Colby, C. (Producer). (2006). *The sex files* [Television series]. Discovery Channel.

Comfort, A. (1972). *The joy of sex: A gourmet guide to love making.* New York: Simon & Schuster.

The complete kama sutra: The first unabridged translation of the classic Indian text (A. Daniélou, Trans.). (1994). Rochester, VT: Rock Street Press.

Cooper, A., McLoughlin, I. P., & Campbell, K. M. (2000). Sexuality in cyberspace: Update for the 21st Century. *CyberPsychology & Behavior, 3*(4), 521–536.

Cooper, A., Putnam, D. E., Planchon, L. A., & Boies, S. C. (1999). Online sexual compulsivity: Getting tangled in the net. *Sexual Addiction & Compulsivity: The Journal of Treatment and Prevention, 6*(2), 79–104.

Cooper, A., Sherer, C., Boies, S.C., & Gordon, B. (1999). Sexuality on the Internet: From sexual exploration to pathological expression. *Professional Psychology: Research and Practice, 30*(2), 154–164.

Daneback, K., Cooper, A., & Månsson, S.-A. (2005). An Internet study of cybersex participants. *Archives of Sexual Behavior, 34*(3), 321–328. *The dark side of sexuality* (n.d.). Retrieved April 22, 2006 from http://www.sju.ca/courses/course.php?course=408&id=29&ad=10&dir=sexuality

Davis, C. M., Blank, J., Lin, H.-Y., & Bonillas, C. (1996). Characteristics of vibrator use among women. *Journal of Sex Research, 33*(4), 313–320.

DeLamater, J. D., & Hyde, J. S. (1998). Essentialism vs. social constructionism in the study of human sexuality. *Journal of Sex Research, 35*(1), 10–18.

DeLamater, J. D., & Hyde, J. S. (2003). Sexuality. In J. J. Ponzetti, Jr. (Ed.). *International encyclopedia of marriage and family, Volume 3.* (2nd ed.) (pp. 1456–1462). New York: Macmillan/Thomson Gale.

Doskoch, P. (1995, September/October). The safest sex. *Psychology Today, 28,* 46–49.

Ellis, B. J., & Symons, D. (1990). Sex differences in sexual fantasy: An evolutionary psychology approach. *Journal of Sex Research, 27*(4), 527–555.

Foucault, M. (1978). *The history of sexuality: Vol. 1. An introduction.* (R. Hurley, Trans.). New York: Pantheon. (Original work published 1976)

Gagnon, J. H., & Simon, W. (1987). The sexual scripting of oral genital contacts. *Archives of Sexual Behavior, 16*(1), 1–25.

Harvey, K. (2005). *The kiss in history.* Manchester: Manchester University Press.

Hawkes, G. (1996). *A sociology of sex and sexuality.* Philadelphia, PA: Open University Press.

Herold, E., Garcia, R., & DeMoya, T. (2001). Female tourists and beach boys: Romance or sex tourism? *Annals of Tourism Research, 28*(4), 978–997.

Hsu, B., Kling, A., Kessler, C., Knapke, K., Diefenbach, P., & Elias, J. E. (1994). Gender differences in sexual fantasy and behavior in a college population: A ten-year replication. *Journal of Sex and Marital Therapy, 20*(2), 103–118.

Hurlbert, D. F., & Apt, C. (1993). Female sexuality: A comparative study between women in homosexual and heterosexual relationships. *Journal of Sex and Marital Therapy, 19*(4), 315–327.

Hyde, J. S., DeLamater, J. D., & Byers, E. S. (2006). *Understanding human sexuality* (3rd ed., Canadian). Toronto, ON: McGraw-Hill Ryerson.

Keating, B. A., & Over, R. (1990). Sexual fantasies of heterosexual and homosexual men. *Archives of Sexual Behavior, 19*(5), 461–475.

King, M. P., Chupack, C., Melfi, J., Bicks, J., Raab, J., et al. (Producers). (2006). *Sex and the city* [Television series]. New York: HBO.

Kinsey, A. C., Pomeroy, W. B., & Martin, C. E. (1949). *Sexual behavior in the human male.* Philadelphia, PA: Saunders.

Kinsey, A. C., Pomeroy, W. B., Martin, C. E., & Gebhard, P. H. (1953). *Sexual behavior in the human female.* Philadelphia, PA: Saunders.

Knafo, D., & Jaffe, Y. (1984). Sexual fantasizing in males and females. *Journal of Research in Personality, 18*(4), 451–462.

Kutchinsky, B. (1976). Deviance and criminality: The case of voyeur in a peepers' paradise. *Diseases of the Nervous System, 37*(3), 145–151.

Laumann, E. O., Gagnon, J. H., Michael, R. T., & Michaels, S. (1994). *The social organization of sexuality: Sexual practices in the United States.* Chicago, IL: University of Chicago Press.

Leitenberg, H., & Henning, K. (1995). Sexual fantasy. *Psychological Bulletin, 117*(3), 469–496.

Little, C. A., & Byers, E. S. (2000). Differences between positive and negative sexual cognitions. *Canadian Journal of Human Sexuality, 9*(3), 167–179.

Mah, K., & Binik, Y. M. (2005). Are orgasms in the mind or the body? Psychosocial versus physiological correlates of orgasmic pleasure and satisfaction. *Journal of Sex and Marital Therapy, 31*(3), 187–200.

Maines, R. P. (1999). *The technology of orgasm: "Hysteria," the vibrator, and women's sexual satisfaction.* Baltimore, MD: Johns Hopkins University Press.

Masters, W. H., & Johnson, V. E. (1966). *Human sexual response.* Boston, MA: Little, Brown.

Masters, W. H., & Johnson, V. E. (1979). *Homosexuality in perspective.* Boston, MA: Little, Brown.

Maticka-Tyndale, E., & Herold, E. S. (1997). The scripting of sexual behaviour: Canadian university students on spring break in Florida. *Canadian Journal of Human Sexuality, 6*(4), 317–328.

Maticka-Tyndale, E., Herold, E. S., & Mewhinney, D. (1998). Casual sex on spring break: Intentions and behaviors of Canadian students. *Journal of Sex Research, 35*(3), 254–264.

McCauley, C., & Swann, C. P. (1978). Male-female differences in sexual fantasy. *Journal of Research in Personality, 12*(1), 76–86.

McKay, A. (2004). Oral sex among teenagers: Research, discourse, and education. *Canadian Journal of Human Sexuality, 13*(3/4), 201–203.

Mewhinney, D. M., Herold, E. S., & Maticka-Tyndale, E. (1995). Sexual scripts and risk-taking of Canadian university students on spring break in Daytona Beach, Florida. *Canadian Journal of Human Sexuality, 4*(4), 273–288.

Mosher, C., & Levitt, E. E. (1987). An exploratory-descriptive study of a sadomasochistically oriented sample. *Journal of Sex Research, 23*(3), 322–337.

Mosher, W. D., Chandra, A., & Jones, J. (2005). Sexual behavior and selected health measures: Men and women 15–44 years of age, United States, 2002. *Advance data from vital and health statistics, no. 362.* Hyattsville, MD: National Center for Health Statistics.

O'Connell Davidson, J., & Sánchez Taylor, J. (1999). Fantasy islands: Exploring the demand for sex tourism. In K. Kempadoo (Ed.), *Sun, sex, and gold: Tourism and sex work in the Caribbean* (pp. 37–54). Oxford: Rowman Littlefield.

Parrinder, G. (1996). *Sexual morality in the world religions.* Oxford: One-world.

Pinkerton, S. D., Bogart, L. M., Cecil, H., & Abramson, P. R. (2002). Factors associated with masturbation in a collegiate sample. *Journal of Psychology and Human Sexuality, 14*(2/3), 103–121.

Pinkerton, S. D., Cecil, H., Bogart, L. M., & Abramson, P. R. (2003). The pleasures of sex: An empirical investigation. *Cognition and Emotion, 17*(2), 341–353.

Renaud, C. A., & Byers, E. S. (1999). Exploring the frequency, diversity, and content of university students' positive and negative sexual cognitions. *Canadian Journal of Human Sexuality, 8*(1), 17–30.

Robinson, J. D., & Parks, C. W. (2003). Lesbian and bisexual women's sexual fantasies, psychological adjustment, and close relationship functioning. *Journal of Psychology and Human Sexuality, 15*(4), 185–203.

Sánchez Taylor, J. (2001). Dollars are a girl's best friend? Female tourists' sexual behaviour in the Carribean. *Sociology, 35*(3), 749–764.

Sandnabba, N. K., Santtila, P., & Nordling, N. (1999). Sexual behavior and social adaptation among sadomasochistically-oriented males. *Journal of Sex Research, 36*(3), 273–282.

Venning, R., & Cavanah, C. (2003). *Sex toys 101: A playfully uninhibited guide.* New York: Fireside.

Warren, W. K., & King, A. J. (1994). *Development and evaluation of an AIDS/STD/Sexuality program for Grade 9 students.* Kingston, ON: Social Program Evaluation Group, Queens University.

Weeks, J. (1981). *Sex, politics, and society.* New York: Longman.

Weeks, J. (1986). *Key Ideas: Sexuality* (P. Hamilton, Series Ed.). London: Tavistock.

Wellings, K., Field, J., Johnson, A. M., & Wadsworth, J. (1994). *Sexual behavior in Britain: The national survey of sexual attitudes and lifestyles.* London: Penguin.

Westheimer, R. K. (1995). *Sex for dummies.* Chicago: IDG Books Worldwide.

Wikimedia Foundation (2006). Tribadism. Retrieved February 26, 2006 from http://en.wikipedia.org/wiki/Tribadism

---

Sexual Behavior and Health

William D. Mosher, Anjani Chandra, and Jo Jones

This [box] provides reliable national estimates of some basic statistics on certain types of sexual behavior, sexual orientation, and sexual attraction for men and women 15–44 years of age, based on data collected in the United States in 2002. The data are relevant to public health concerns, including efforts to prevent HIV and other sexually transmitted infections, and to demographic and social concerns such as birth and pregnancy rates among teenagers. The data are from the 2002 National Survey of Family Growth (NSFG), and are based on 12,571 in-person interviews with men and women 15–44 years of age.

Highlights of Findings

Teens

- At ages 15–19, about 12 percent of males and 10 percent of females had had heterosexual oral sex but not vaginal intercourse. . . . This percent drops to 3 percent for both males and females at age 22–24, when most have already had vaginal intercourse. . . .

Adults—heterosexual activity

- Among adult males 25–44 years of age, 97 percent have had sexual contact with an opposite-sex partner in their lives; 97 percent have had vaginal intercourse, 90 percent have had oral sex with a female, and 40 percent, anal sex with a female. Among women, the proportions who have had sexual contact with an opposite-sex partner were similar.

- Males 30–44 years of age reported an average (median) of 6–8 female sexual partners in their lifetimes. Among women 30–44 years of age, the median number of male sexual partners in their lifetimes was about four. The findings appear to be similar to previous surveys conducted in the early 1990's.

Same-sex activity

- Three percent of males 15–44 years of age have had oral or anal sex with another male in the last 12 months (1.8 million). Four percent of females had a sexual experience with another female in the last 12 months. . . .

- The proportion who had same-sex contact in their lifetimes was 6 percent for males and (using a different question) 11 percent for females. . . .

- About 1 percent of men and 3 percent of women 15–44 years of age have had both male and female sexual partners in the last 12 months. . . .

Sexual orientation

- In response to a question that asked, *"Do you think of yourself as heterosexual, homosexual, bisexual, or something else?"* 90 percent of men 18–44 years of age responded that they think of themselves as heterosexual, 2.3 percent of men answered homosexual, 1.8 percent bisexual, 3.9 percent "something else," and 1.8 percent did not answer the question. . . . Percents for women were similar. . . .

Sexual attraction

- Survey participants were asked if they were sexually attracted to males, to females, or to both. Among men 18–44 years of age, 92 percent said they were attracted "only to females," and 3.9 percent, "mostly" to females. Among women, 86 percent said they were attracted only to males, and 10 percent, "mostly" to males. The percentage attracted "mostly to males" was 3 percent in a survey conducted in 1992, compared with 10 percent in the 2002 NSFG.

Selected health measures

- 29 percent of men who have ever had male-male sexual contact were tested for HIV (outside of blood donation) in the last year, compared with 14 percent of men with no same-sex sexual contact.
- 17 percent of men who ever had male-male sexual contact had been treated for a non-HIV sexually transmitted infection (STI), compared with 7 percent of those who had never had male-male sexual contact.
- Among men 15–44 years of age who had at least one sexual partner in the last 12 months, 39 percent used a condom at their most recent sex. Among never married males, this figure was 65 percent, compared with 24 percent of married males. Among males who had ever had sexual contact with another male, 91 percent used a condom at their last sex, compared with 36 percent of men who never had sex with another male.

Source: Mosher, William D., Anjani Chandra, and Jo Jones. 2005. "Sexual Behavior and Selected Health Measures: Men and Women 15–44 Years of Age, United States, 2002." *CDC Advance Data from Vital and Health Statistics* 362 (September 15). Available at www.cdc.gov.

What's a Leg Got to Do with It?

Donna Walton

What's a leg got to do with it? Exactly what I thought when, during a heated conversation, a female rival told me I was less than a woman because I have one leg.

Excuse me. Perhaps I missed something. How could she make such an insensitive comment about something she had no experience with? Was she some expert on disabilities or something? Was she, too, disabled? Had she—like me—fought a battle with cancer that cost her a limb? For a split second, my thoughts were paralyzed by her insensitivity. But, like a defeated fighter who returns to the ring to regain victory, I bounced back for a verbal round with Ms. Thang.

I am woman first, an amputee second and physically challenged last. And it is in that order that I set out to educate and testify to people like Ms. Thang who are unable to discern who I am—a feisty, unequivocally attractive African-American woman with a gimpy gait who can strut proudly into any room and engage in intelligent conversation with folks anxious to feed off my sincere aura.

It is rather comical and equally disturbing how folks—both men and women—view me as a disabled woman, particularly when it comes to sexuality. They have so many misconceptions. Straight women, for example, want to know how I catch a man, while most men are entertained with the idea that because I have one leg sex with me must be a blast.

I have even been confronted by folks who give me the impression that they think having sex is a painful experience for me. Again, I say, What's a leg got to do with it?

For all of those who want to inquire about my sexual prowess but dare not to, or for those who are curious about how I maintain such positive self-esteem when life dealt me the proverbial "bad hand," this story is for you. But those who have a tough time dealing with reality probably should skip the next paragraph because what I am about to confess is the gospel truth.

I like sex! I am very sexual!! I even consider myself sexy, residual limb and all. You see, I was a sexual being before my leg was amputated 19 years ago. My attitude didn't change about sex. I just had to adjust to the attitudes of others.

For example, I remember a brother who I dated in high school—before my leg was amputated—then dated again five years later. The dating ended abruptly because I realized that the brother could not fathom the one-leg thing. When he and I were home alone, he was cool as long as we got hot and bothered with my prosthesis on. However, whenever I tried to take off my artificial leg for comfort purposes, he immediately panicked. He could not fathom seeing me with one leg.

I tried to put him at ease by telling him Eva's story from Toni Morrison's novel *Sula*—that "my leg just got tired and walked off one day." But this brother just could not deal. He booked.

On the other hand, my experiences with lesbians have varied; they don't all book right away, but some have booked. Not all are upfront with their feelings 'cuz women are socialized to be courteous, emotional, and indirect, sparing one's feelings. Instead, some tend to communicate their discomfort with my missing limb in more subtle ways. For example, one lesbian I dated did not want to take me out to bars, clubs and other social settings. My lop-sided gait was an embarrassment, and the fact that I use a cane garnered unwanted attention for her. Behind closed doors, she did not have any problems with it. How we would be perceived by trendy lesbians was her main concern.

Conversely, I have had positive experiences with lesbians as well. For instance, I have dated and been in love with women who have been affirming and supportive while respecting my difference. My wholeness has been shaped by all of these experiences. Without hesitation, I can now take off my prosthesis, be comfortable hopping around on one-leg and the sex . . . is still a blast.

How does a woman with one leg maintain such a positive self-esteem in a society where people with disabilities are not valued? Simply by believing in myself. I know you're saying, "That sounds much too hokey." But as I said earlier, this is the gospel truth.

I was 19 years old when my leg was amputated. I was diagnosed with osteogenic sarcoma, bone cancer. During the first five years after my surgery, concentrating on other folks' perceptions of me was the least of my concerns. I was too focused on beating the odds against dying. You see, I was given only a 15% chance of survival—with spiritual guidance and support from my family—I had made the very difficult decision to stop taking my chemotherapy treatments. Doctors predicted that, by halting the dreadful chemotherapy, I was writing my own death certificate. However, through what I believe was divine healing, my cancer was eradicated.

Before this cancerous ordeal, I was not strong spiritually, and my faith was rocked when my leg was amputated because I thought I was to keep my leg. At the time, I could not see past the physical. After my amputation, I was preoccupied with the kinds of crippling thoughts that all the Ms. Thangs of the world are socialized to believe: that I was not going to be able to wear shorts, bathing suits or lingerie; that my womanness was somehow compromised by the loss of a limb.

If you have a disability and are in need of some fuel for your spirit, check out any novel by Toni Morrison (*Sula* is my favorite because of the one legged grandmother, Eva) or Khalil Gibran's *The Prophet*. These resources helped me build self-esteem and deal with my reality.

Ultimately, building positive esteem is an ongoing process. To that end, I am currently producing a motivational video that will outline coping strategies for female amputees.

No matter what your disability or circumstance, you cannot give in to a defeatist attitude. When you do, your battle is lost. There is a way of fighting back. It is called self-esteem.

Believe in yourself, and you will survive—and thrive.

Source: Walton, Donna. "What's a Leg Got to Do With It?" *Health Quest Magazine* 3: 51–52. Reprinted by permission of *Health Quest Magazine,* www.healthquestmag.com.

Against Love: A Treatise on the Tyranny of Two

Laura Kipnis

Love is, as we know, a mysterious and controlling force. It has vast power over our thoughts and life decisions. It demands our loyalty, and we, in turn, freely comply. Saying no to love isn't simply heresy; it is tragedy—the failure to achieve what is most essentially human. So deeply internalized is our obedience to this most capricious despot that artists create passionate odes to its cruelty, and audiences seem never to tire of the most deeply unoriginal mass spectacles devoted to rehearsing the litany of its torments, fixating their very beings on the narrowest glimmer of its fleeting satisfactions. . . .

Ever optimistic, heady with love's utopianism, most of us eventually pledge ourselves to unions that will, if successful, far outlast the desire that impelled them into being. The prevailing cultural wisdom is that even if sexual desire tends to be a short-lived phenomenon, "mature love" will kick in to save the day when desire flags. The issue that remains unaddressed is whether cutting off other possibilities of romance and sexual attraction for the more muted pleasures of mature love isn't similar to voluntarily amputating a healthy limb: a lot of anesthesia is required and the phantom pain never entirely abates. But if it behooves a society to convince its citizenry that wanting change means personal failure or wanting to start over is shameful or simply wanting more satisfaction than what you have is an illicit thing, clearly grisly acts of self-mutilation will be required.

There hasn't always been quite such optimism about love's longevity. For the Greeks, inventors of democracy and a people not amenable to being pushed around by despots, love was a disordering and thus preferably brief experience. During the reign of courtly love, love was illicit and usually fatal. Passion meant suffering: the happy ending didn't yet exist in the cultural imagination. As far as togetherness as an eternal ideal, the 12th-century advice manual "De Amore et Amor is Remedio" ("On Love and the Remedies of Love") warned that too many opportunities to see or chat with the beloved would certainly decrease love.

The innovation of happy love didn't even enter the vocabulary of romance until the 17th century. Before the 18th century—when the family was primarily an economic unit of production rather than a hothouse of Oedipal tensions—marriages were business arrangements between families; participants had little to say on the matter. Some historians consider romantic love a learned behavior that really only took off in the late 18th century along with the new fashion for reading novels, though even then affection between a husband and wife was considered to be in questionable taste.

Historians disagree, of course. Some tell the story of love as an eternal and unchanging essence; others, as a progress narrative over stifling social conventions. (Sometimes both stories are told at once; consistency isn't required.) But has modern love really set us free? Fond as we are of projecting our own emotional quandaries back through history, construing vivid costume dramas featuring medieval peasants or biblical courtesans sharing their feelings with the post-Freudian savvy of lifelong analysands, our amatory predecessors clearly didn't share all our particular aspirations about their romantic lives.

We, by contrast, feel like failures when love dies. We believe it could be otherwise. Since the cultural expectation is that a state of coupled permanence is achievable, uncoupling is experienced as crisis and inadequacy—even though such failures are more the norm than the exception.

As love has increasingly become the center of all emotional expression in the popular imagination, anxiety about obtaining it in sufficient quantities— and for sufficient duration—suffuses the population. Everyone knows that as the demands and expectations on couples escalated, so did divorce rates. And given the current divorce statistics (roughly 50 percent of all marriages end in divorce), all indications are that whomever you love today—your beacon of hope, the center of all your optimism—has a good chance of becoming your worst nightmare tomorrow. (Of course, that 50 percent are those who actually leave their unhappy marriages and not a particularly good indication of the happiness level or nightmare potential of those who remain.) Lawrence Stone, a historian of marriage, suggests—rather jocularly, you can't help thinking—that today's rising divorce rates are just a modern technique for achieving what was once taken care of far more efficiently by early mortality.

Love may or may not be a universal emotion, but clearly the social forms it takes are infinitely malleable. It is our culture alone that has dedicated itself to allying the turbulence of romance and the rationality of the long-term couple, convinced that both love and sex are obtainable from one person over the course of decades, that desire will manage to sustain itself for 30 or 40 or 50 years and that the supposed fate of social stability is tied to sustaining a fleeting experience beyond its given life span.

Of course, the parties involved must "work" at keeping passion alive (and we all know how much fun that is), the presumption being that even after living in close proximity to someone for a historically unprecedented length of time, you will still muster the requisite desire to achieve sexual congress on a regular basis. (Should passion fizzle out, just give up sex. Lack of desire for a mate is never an adequate rationale for "looking elsewhere.") And it is true, many couples do manage to perform enough psychic

retooling to reshape the anarchy of desire to the confines of the marriage bed, plugging away at the task year after year (once a week, same time, same position) like diligent assembly-line workers, aided by the occasional fantasy or two to help get the old motor to turn over, or keep running, or complete the trip. And so we have the erotic life of a nation of workaholics: if sex seems like work, clearly you're not working hard enough at it.

But passion must not be allowed to die! The fear— or knowledge—that it does shapes us into particularly conflicted psychological beings perpetually in search of prescriptions and professional interventions, regardless of cost or consequence. Which does have its economic upside, at least. Whole new sectors of the economy have been spawned, with massive social investment in new technologies from Viagra to couples' porn: capitalism's Lourdes for dying marriages.

There are assorted low-tech solutions to desire's dilemmas too. Take advice. In fact, take more and more advice. Between print, airwaves and the therapy industry, if there were anyway to quantify the G.N.P. in romantic counsel, it would be a staggering number. Desperate to be cured of love's temporality, a love-struck populace has molded itself into an advanced race of advice receptacles, like some new form of miracle sponge that can instantly absorb many times its own body weight in wetness.

Inexplicably, however, a rebellious breakaway faction keeps trying to leap over the wall and emancipate themselves, not from love itself—unthinkable!—but from love's domestic confinements. The escape routes are well trodden—love affairs, midlife crises— though strewn with the left-behind luggage of those who encountered unforeseen obstacles along the way (panic, guilt, self-engineered exposures) and beat self-abashed retreats to their domestic gulags, even after pledging body and soul to newfound loves in the balmy utopias of nondomesticated romances. Will all the adulterers in the audience please stand up? You know who you are. Don't be embarrassed! Adulterers aren't just "playing around." These are our homegrown closet social theorists, because adultery is not just a referendum on the sustainability of monogamy; it is a veiled philosophical discussion about the social contract itself. The question on the table is this: "How much renunciation of desire does society demand of us, versus the degree of gratification it provides?" Clearly, the adulterer's answer, following a long line of venerable social critics, would be, "Too much."

But what exactly is it about the actual lived experience of modern domestic love that would make flight such a compelling option for so many? Let us briefly examine those material daily life conditions.

Fundamentally, to achieve love and qualify for entry into that realm of salvation and transcendence known as the couple (the secular equivalent of entering a state of divine grace), you must *be* a lovable person. And what precisely does being lovable entail? According to the tenets of modern love, it requires an advanced working knowledge of the intricacies of *mutuality.*

Mutuality means recognizing that your partner has needs and being prepared to meet them. This presumes, of course, that the majority of those needs can and should be met by one person. . . .

Meeting those needs is the most effective way to become the object of another's desire, thus attaining intimacy, which is required to achieve the state known as psychological maturity. (Despite how closely [it] reproduces the affective conditions of our childhoods, since trading compliance for love is the earliest social lesson learned; we learn it in our cribs.)

You, in return, will have your own needs met by your partner in matters large and small. In practice, many of these matters turn out to be quite small. Frequently, it is the tensions and disagreements over the minutiae of daily living that stand between couples and their requisite intimacy. Taking out the garbage, tone of voice, a forgotten errand—these are the rocky shoals upon which intimacy so often founders.

Mutuality requires *communication,* since in order to be met, these needs must be expressed. . . . What you need is for your mate to understand you—your desires, your contradictions, your unique sensitivities, what irks you. (In practice, that means what about your mate irks you.) You, in turn, must learn to understand the mate's needs. This means being willing to hear what about yourself irks your mate. Hearing is not a simple physiological act performed with the ears, as you will learn. You may think you know

how to *hear,* but that doesn't mean that you know how to *listen.*

With two individuals required to coexist in enclosed spaces for extended periods of time, domesticity requires substantial quantities of compromise and adaptation simply to avoid mayhem. Yet with the post-Romantic ideal of unconstrained individuality informing our most fundamental ideas of the self, this can prove a perilous process. Both parties must be willing to jettison whatever aspects of individuality might prove irritating while being simultaneously allowed to retain enough individuality to feel their autonomy is not being sacrificed, even as it is being surgically excised.

Having mastered mutuality, you may now proceed to *advanced intimacy.* Advanced intimacy involves inviting your partner "in" to your most interior self. Whatever and wherever our "inside" is, the widespread—if somewhat metaphysical—belief in its existence (and the related belief that whatever is in there is dying to get out) has assumed a quasi-medical status. Leeches once served a similar purpose. Now we "express our feelings" in lieu of our fluids because everyone knows that those who don't are far more prone to cancer, ulcers or various dire ailments.

With love as our culture's patent medicine, prescribed for every ill (now even touted as a necessary precondition for that other great American obsession, longevity), we willingly subject ourselves to any number of arcane procedures in its quest. "Opening up" is required for relationship health, so lovers fashion themselves after doctors wielding long probes to penetrate the tender regions. Try to think of yourself as one big orifice: now stop clenching and relax. If the procedure proves uncomfortable, it just shows you're not open enough. Psychotherapy may be required before sufficient dilation can be achieved: the world's most expensive lubricant.

Needless to say, this opening-up can leave you feeling quite vulnerable, lying there psychically spread-eagled and shivering on the examining table of your relationship. (A favored suspicion is that your partner, knowing exactly where your vulnerabilities are, deliberately kicks you there—one reason this opening up business may not always feel as pleasant as advertised.) And as anyone who has spent much time in—or just in earshot of—a typical couple knows, the "expression of needs" is often the Trojan horse of intimate warfare, since expressing needs means, by definition, that one's partner has thus far failed to meet them.

In any long-term couple, this lexicon of needs becomes codified over time into a highly evolved private language with its own rules. Let's call this couple grammar. Close observation reveals this as a language composed of one recurring unit of speech: the interdiction—highly nuanced, mutually imposed commands and strictures extending into the most minute areas of household affairs, social life, finances, speech, hygiene, allowable idiosyncrasies and so on. From bathroom to bedroom, car to kitchen, no aspect of coupled life is not subject to scrutiny, negotiation and codes of conduct.

A sample from an inexhaustible list, culled from interviews with numerous members of couples of various ages, races and sexual orientations:

You can't leave the house without saying where you're going. You can't not say what time you'll return. You can't go out when the other person feels like staying at home. You can't be a slob. You can't do less than 50 percent of the work around the house, even if the other person wants to do 100 percent more cleaning than you find necessary or even reasonable. You can't leave the dishes for later, load them the way that seems best to you, drink straight from the carton or make crumbs. You can't leave the bathroom door open—it's offensive. You can't leave the bathroom door closed—your partner needs to get in. You can't not shave your underarms or legs. You can't gain weight. You can't watch soap operas. You can't watch infomercials or the pregame show or Martha Stewart. You can't eat what you want—goodbye Marshmallow Fluff; hello tofu meatballs. You can't spend too much time on the computer. And stay out of those chat rooms. You can't take risks, unless they are agreed-upon risks, which somewhat limits the concept of "risk." You can't make major purchases alone, or spend money on things the other person considers excesses. You can't blow money just because you're in a bad mood, and you can't be in a bad mood without being required to explain it. You can't begin a sentence with "You always. . . . " You can't begin a

sentence with "I never. . . . " You can't be simplistic, even when things are simple. You can't say what you really think of that outfit or color combination or cowboy hat. You can't be cynical about things the other person is sincere about. You can't drink without the other person counting your drinks. You can't have the wrong laugh. You can't bum cigarettes when you're out because it embarrasses your mate, even though you've explained the unspoken fraternity between smokers. You can't tailgate, honk or listen to talk radio in the car. And so on. The specifics don't matter. What matters is that the operative word is "can't."

Thus is love obtained.

Certainly, domesticity offers innumerable rewards: companionship, child-rearing convenience, reassuring predictability and many other benefits too varied to list. But if love has power over us, domesticity is its enforcement wing: the iron dust mop in the velvet glove. The historian Michel Foucault has argued that modern power made its mark on the world by inventing new types of enclosures and institutions, places like factories, schools, barracks, prisons and asylums, where individuals could be located, supervised, processed and subjected to inspection, order and the clock. What current social institution is more enclosed than modern intimacy? What offers greater regulation of movement and time, or more precise surveillance of body and thought, to a greater number of individuals?

Of course, it is your choice—as if any of us could really choose not to desire love or not to feel like hopeless losers should we fail at it. We moderns are beings yearning to be filled, yearning to be overtaken by love's mysterious power. . . .

Exchanging obedience for love comes naturally—after all, we all were once children whose survival depended on the caprices of love. And there you have the template for future intimacies. If you love me, you'll do what I want—or need, or demand—and I'll love you in return. We all become household dictators, petty tyrants of the private sphere, who are, in our turn, dictated to.

And why has modern love developed in such a way as to maximize submission and minimize freedom, with so little argument about it? No doubt a citizenry schooled in renouncing desire instead of imagining there could be something more would be, in many respects, advantageous. After all, wanting more is the basis for utopian thinking, a path toward dangerous social demands, even toward imagining the possibilities for altogether different social arrangements. But if the most elegant forms of social control are those that came packaged in the guise of individual needs and satisfactions, so wedded to the individual psyche that any opposing impulse registers as the anxiety of unlovability, who needs a soldier on every corner? We are more than happy to police ourselves and those we love and call it living happily ever after. Perhaps a secular society needed another metaphysical entity to subjugate itself to after the death of God, and love was available for the job. But isn't it a little depressing to think we are somehow incapable of inventing forms of emotional life based on anything other than subjugation?

Asexuality

Melissa Travis

We live in a society that assumes all adults are interested in good sex. However, some people just don't want to have sex (even good sex)! This feeling of indifference toward sexual activity is called *asexuality*. While some researchers see asexuality as a disorder needing treatment or a passing phase is a person's life, sex researchers tend to see asexuality as a distinct and non-pathological sexual identity that, like other sexual identities, has the potential to change over time (*Contemporary Sexuality* 2005).

Comprising about one percent of the population, men and women who identify as asexual express no sexual attraction for other individuals (Bogaert 2004),[1] yet they have the same varied emotional and intimate needs as sexually oriented individuals (AVEN 2009). For example, many asexual people have romantic attraction to others, but do not act to consummate their relationships with sex. Other asexual individuals have no romantic attraction or sex drive. While some asexual individuals engage in sex to please partners, they feel apathetic and uninterested during sex. If they see a sexual encounter in a movie, they are not necessarily offended or disgusted, they simply remain erotically unmoved by it. A small number of asexual individuals may feel repulsion toward sexual activity (AVEN 2009).

Asexuality is not the same as anti-sexuality (having guilt, shame, or other negative opinions about sexual practices). Yet some asexual individuals find it easier to pretend to be sexual to the others because their absence of sexual feelings is so misunderstood (AVEN 2009). They are especially frustrated by professionals who label their feelings as "sexual aversion disorder," disregarding asexuality as a legitimate sexual identity (*Contemporary Sexuality* 2005).

While asexual individuals may not be interested in having sex, some enjoy friendships that contain intimate connections such as cuddling, sleeping in the same bed, massage, and other tender or affectionate interactions. Some, like Paul and Amanda Cox, even get married and enjoy lasting sexless romantic relationships (Cox 2008). They enjoy the snuggling, cuddling, kissing and other emotional intimacy that comes from sharing and being close to each other, just without the sex. Even with their indifference towards sexual activities, asexual people can also develop jealous feelings toward their friends or partners who are engaged in sexual relationships with someone else such as when an asexual individual is in a sexless romantic partnership and their partner goes outside the relationship for sexual fulfillment (AVEN 2009).

Individuals who identify as asexual may join asexuality advocacy groups such as the Asexuality Visibility and Education Network (AVEN) to discuss their identities and give each other support (Bergenson 2005). Support for asexuality includes advising those involved in a relationship with someone who desires sex and offering consolation to those who are alone but wish for non-sexual relationships. There are many online advocacy and support groups where asexual individuals engage in discussions, support, and advice for asexual lifestyles. Such groups also work to educate researchers who believe that asexuality is a disorder or sex researchers who simply reject the idea of asexuality by insisting that everyone is a sexual being (*Contemporary Sexuality* 2005). Asexual individuals are still in the process of defining their group identity in such organizations. While groups such as AVEN continue to articulate the asexual sexual orientation, one concept is clear: individuals who identify as asexual lack desire for sexual activity with other individuals and find no sexual attraction to others. Though they can have romantic attachments, and can usually function sexually, asexual individuals generally prefer not to have sex.

NOTE

1. From a probability sample of over 18,000 participants drawn from British households. Anthony Bogaert (2004: 284) found that 1.05% of respondents (aged 16–59) "reported that they had never felt sexual attraction to anyone at all." He described these respondents as "asexual."

REFERENCES

AVEN. 2009. *Asexual Visibility and Education Network*. Taken from the World Wide Web January 14, 2009. http://www.asexuality.org/discussion

Bergenson, Laine. 2005. "Asexual Healing." *Utne Reader* 128: 22–23.

Bogaert, Anthony. 2004. "Asexuality: Prevalence and Associated Factors in a National Probability Sample." *The Journal of Sex Research* 41: 279–287.

Contemporary Sexuality. 2005. Vol. 39, No. 11: 1–5.

Cox, Paul. 2008. *The Guardian for America*. Taken from the World Wide Web September 17, 2008. http://www.guardian.co.uk/lifeandstyle/2008/sep/08/relationships.heathandwellbeing

"Reclaiming Raunch"? Spatializing Queer Identities at Toronto Women's Bathhouse Events

Catherine Jean Nash and Alison Bain

Introduction

It's a Thursday evening at a private party at Club Toronto on Mutual Street just south of Toronto's gay village. Beneath a rainbow awning outside a converted Victorian redbrick house, a queue of women stretches along the sidewalk. At 8:45 p.m. the queue begins to move forward. Volunteer security guards in yellow shirts and headsets check I.D. before letting women purchase tickets that gain them entrance into a women-only bathhouse event called the Pussy Palace.

Behind a heavy black door, buzzed open for each patron, a volunteer sits on a stool and hands out a clean, white towel to each guest. Music pulsates loudly from a turntable set up beside a fake fireplace in a red painted lobby. Lesbian porn plays on a widescreen TV beside the entrance to a faux-Grecian outdoor pool. On the pool deck, women, in different stages of dress and undress and some in different stages of transition from female to male and male to female, claim plastic deck chairs and sunbeds while others play in the pool. A cupid game is set up on the wall of the lifeguard station. Women line up to have numbers playfully written on their bodies. These women will check back later to see if anyone has left a message for them.

Another exit off of the pool deck leads to a hot tub. In the steamy red glow of a glassed changing room, women [peel] off clothes and step into the bubbling water. A notice on the wall of the changing room lists where different Pussy Palace services can be found: temple priestess and portraits, 333; g-spot room, 444; dancers, outside room 222; massage, 3rd floor; cupid game, 2nd floor; dungeon space, 4th floor, breast play, 3rd floor, top of stairs; food, 2nd floor; and sling room, 222.

On the second floor, under the bright lights of a chandelier, two leather-backed armchairs are set up for lap dancing. Volunteer dancers sift through discarded lingerie strewn on the floor and pull on their outfits of choice before each dance. To their left is the locker room. In here, women, who have brought outfits to change into, swap street clothes for combinations of leather, rubber, lace, mesh and cotton. Further along the corridor, a deaf volunteer sells cold water and pop, and oversees a table of finger food. A wide, wooden-banistered staircase leads up. With each new floor the lighting is dimmer and the hallways narrower. There are mirrors everywhere; reflections distort, disorient and startle.

Most of the doors on the third floor are closed. The musky scent of essential oils wafts from beneath a door that has a sign-up sheet for sexual counselling with a "temple priestess." Around the corner, a room is set up for erotic massage. The rest of this floor contains a labyrinth of small rooms. Those rooms not yet in use have clear plastic waste disposal bags draped over their door handles. A sliver of light beneath doors suggests occupancy; and the occasional gasp or moan of pleasure confirms it. Other doors are wide open, the turquoise plastic mattress covers of the single beds exposed and piles of crumpled linen and screwed-up toilet paper on the floor.

Up the final flight of stairs to the fourth floor, the air is close. There is hardly room to squeeze by the

From "'Reclaiming Raunch'? Spatializing Queer Identities at Toronto Women's Bathhouse Events" by Catherine Jean Nash and Alison Bain, *Social & Cultural Geography*, 2007, 8, 47–62, Routledge, reprinted by permission of the publisher (Taylor & Francis Group, http://www.informaworld.com).

door marked "g-spot" where a young woman in a white bikini with soft pink rabbit ears ushers patrons in. Further along the corridor, the floor of the sado-masochism room is sticky underfoot. A black vinyl-covered straight-backed bench provides seating. Two women dressed in black leather wield whips and direct scenes that use the floor to ceiling chains. Out the back door of this attic dungeon the fire escape descends again to the pool deck below.

Pussy Palace events, like the one described above, began in the fall of 1998 and have been held on an irregular basis once or twice a year since then. The inaugural Pussy Palace, Canada's first women-only bathhouse event, was attended by over 350 women. The organizers of the Pussy Palace event interpret their high attendance figures as indicative of an untapped desire in Toronto's queer women's community for spaces supportive of uninhibited, casual and playful sexual encounters. These women's bathhouse events are a new form of women's sexualized social space that, as of yet, has gone unexamined in scholarly literature.

In North American gay male culture, the bathhouse is more than just a building, a space or an "event." It can be interpreted as a sexual sanctuary, a safe-haven, a second-home to some, a hiding place to others. For over a century, bathhouses have functioned in North American cities as places for men to engage in same-sex activity. . . . The bathhouse holds a highly regarded place in historical socio-political lexicons depicting the distinctive gay male culture of Western cities, yet it is no longer exclusive to gay men (Dangerous Bedfellows 1996; Hocquenghem 1978; Hodges and Hutter 1974; Jeyasingham 2002; Leap 1999). Women, as our Toronto case study demonstrates, are developing a bathhouse culture of their own.

For the Toronto Women's Bathhouse Committee (TWBC), the Pussy Palace events are expressly political projects, designed to contest preconceived ideas about women's gendered and sexualized selves—"reclaiming raunch," as one of the organizers put it, for women and their sexual expression. More specifically, the TWBC takes issue with what they regard as the deleterious impact of a particularly inflexible and restrictive version of lesbian feminist ideologies on

the ability of women, and lesbians in particular, to experience the full range of sexual and gender expression. Accordingly, the committee seeks to undo the perceived "damage" wrought by these ideologies through the "queering" of spaces—that is, through the establishment of locations that provide the opportunity to experience alternative sexual practices and behaviours. In so doing, the TWBC has grappled with challenging questions about: what "queering" spaces actually means in policy and practice; the politics and power relations inherent in sexualized space; and the contested nature of body, gender, and sexual identity formation and interaction.

In this [reading], we examine both the possibilities and the problems evoked in the TWBC's creation of a particular form of "queer" sexualized space. We argue that the process of "queering space," is neither a neutral nor an uncontested process. This is especially the case given that the TWBC deploys a particular definition of "queer" that paradoxically opens up a space of liberating sexual possibility but also disciplines gendered and sexualized identities. This paradox of simultaneous liberation and constraint, in turn, raises broader questions about the political and social implications of queer politics and practices which needs more critical and self-conscious reflection. This [reading], . . . critically examin[es] queer identities and spaces. . . .

Our research project is informed by the current geographical work on the production of gendered and sexualized urban spaces. Feminist geographers, in particular, have argued for a spatialized understanding of the constitution of social identities (gender, sexuality, "race," age, ability) and hierarchical social relations (e.g. Duncan 1996; McDowell 1999). . . . [S]pace and identity are linked in the fluid constitution of sexualized and gendered selves (Bell and Valentine 1995; Bouthillette 1997; Lauria and Knopp 1985; Rothenberg 1995; Valentine 1993a, 1993b, 1995). Our consideration of the constitution of women-only bathhouse space is attentive to the ways in which sexuality and gender are constituted (un)intentionally within that space. . . .

[B]athhouse events represent an attempt to reformulate space so as to provide for the opportunity to experience alternative behaviours and practices through which new identities, in this case queer identities, can come into being. . . .

[T]he TWBC seeks to create a space that fosters behaviors that challenge not only the heteronormative prohibitions on women's gendered and sexual expression but also long-standing lesbian feminist proscriptions on lesbians' sexual and gendered expressions of identity. . . .

While it is clear that the TWBC is striving to create a queer space . . . when women transgress gay male space and appropriate gay male sexual norms to produce queer space, they . . . challenge essentialist lesbian subjectivities and sexual practices, and disrupt fixed understandings of gendered and sexualized selves. . . .

Queer Beginnings: The Pussy Palace

. . . In the spring of 1998, the owner of "Come As You Are," a women's sex shop who had attended a women's bathhouse event in Seattle, met with friends . . . to discuss the possibility of organizing a similar event. . . . [T]he . . . non-profit Toronto Women's Bathhouse Committee (TWBC) was born with a mandate to address what the original organizers saw as the serious lack of institutional spaces for women to develop a "sexual imagination, literature, techniques, art or knowledge" (Dhanani and Fong 1998: 21). Committee members approached several Toronto bathhouse owners to use their facilities for women-only events. Only one institution, Club Toronto, agreed. . . .

Behind the Scenes of Queer Eroticism: Feminism in Practice

The TWBC positions their agenda firmly within a feminist framework and regards their endeavours as politically transformative for women. Their main goal has been to challenge what they regard as the debilitating effects of what they term "1980s lesbian feminist politics" as well as what they regard as wider mainstream prohibitions against women's sexual expression. In formulating an alternative sexual and gendered identity the TWBC uses the label "queer," and draws on particular conceptualisations of class

and gay male sexual experience to describe the sexual behaviours or practices they seek to encourage. Accordingly, the committee seeks to challenge a perceived gendered code of sexual passivity among women by "queering" women's sexualities and genders through a particular spatial strategy: the bathhouse event.

Defining Queer Sexuality: Lesbian Feminism, Gay Men and Class

. . . [The TWBC's] self-appointed mandate is to open up the possibility for non-monogamous and casual sexual practice in order to break down the constraints imposed in an earlier historical era. . . . TWBC uncritically positions gay male casual sexual activities (e.g. public cruising and bathhouse sex) as the standard of sexual freedom to which women should aspire. This includes the ability to have multiple partners and to practise sadomasochism and alternative sexual practices previously eschewed by lesbian feminists as wrong or personally damaging.

The TWBC also argues that because women have not had the sexual freedom to explore their sensual worlds, they have not developed "the same institutions as gay men have for anonymous sex" including spaces such as the bathhouses and the cultural cues and practices facilitating sexual activity in other public spaces (Dhanani and Fong 1998: 21). One of the goals of the TWBC is to create an institutional basis that encourages women to engage in more casual sexual expression not only in the bathhouse events but in public spaces such as parks and bars as well as private house parties and clubs. Having the opportunity to actually use gay male bathhouse space, designed specifically for the experience of casual sex, was seen as central to the TWBC's goal of creating alternative practices and institutional spaces.

In formulating an alternative view of what lesbian sexuality should encompass, the TWBC has embraced a stereotypical view of working-class sexuality as coarse, common, vulgar, lustful and uninhibited— attributes deemed appropriately "raunchy." Staging the bathhouse events at what was described as a "grungier" club used by older "street boys" and a more working-class clientele, was deliberate in terms of celebrating working-class sexuality. With a "hamster cage" odour, sticky floors, peeling paint and a run-down appearance, Club Toronto was understood to communicate a particular queer sexual identity. . . .

Defining Queer "Women": The Politics of Transgenderism

The TWBC embraces spatial "queerness" by billing the Pussy Palace as a queer women's event and a queer women's space. Accordingly, within the queer space of the bathhouse, the TWBC encourages people to explore, experiment or play with gender, and to challenge the rigidity of gender categories, stereotypes, norms and expectations. The TWBC does not take a bio-determinist view of gender nor does it assume that women are biologically female. Instead, the TWBC has broadly positioned the category "woman" in a gender continuum that includes biological females, as well as transgendered people who are non-operative, pre-operative or post-operative. As such, it does not expect people's gendered self-presentation (the ways in which they act, dress or live) necessarily to correspond directly with behaviours habitually associated with the genitalia they possess (Armstrong 2004). The inclusion of male-to-female (MTF) and female-to-male (FTM) transsexuals originally, however, elicited much debate. The central conundrum being that the body could no longer be regarded as fixed yet it became unclear how to delimit the boundaries of "woman" for the purposes of admitting gender-ambiguous persons into a women-only space. Much anxiety centered on how maleness might be expressed in a sexualized space where semi-naked people identify as women yet may possess male genitalia. In the end, an invitation to transgendered women was nonetheless included in the advertisement for the first Pussy Palace event. A founding organizer sketched out some of the dilemmas and the goodwill involved in discussing transgendered women:

> We had to have discussions about what the policy on trans-women was. What are we doing? And what does trans-woman mean? Those were interesting discussions. In the end, we just went: 'trans-women were welcome'. We didn't know what that was going to mean. We didn't necessarily know how we were going to deal with those reactions. We just knew that that was the right thing to do. (Julia, 5 December 2003)

Yet, then and now, TWBC members hold different ideas about transgendered women. As a committee they did not completely work through what it might mean to invite people into a space that while queer, was also politically marked as belonging to women.[1]

At the first bathhouse, several transgendered women reported transphobic experiences whereby spaces emptied upon their arrival and direct and indirect comments were made: "So, like, are you the token fag?"; "Are you an honorary woman for the night? A friend of the committee?"; "He must work here"; "Don't you know that this is a women's bathhouse?"; "Is *that* a man?" (Saleh 1999: 7). Reactions centred on recognizing biological markers of maleness in what is billed as a women's space. Paradoxically, there seemed to be a greater appreciation of masculinity in FTM transgendered bodies as "dyke boys" and butches than in MTF bodies. As a member of the security team explained: "A lot of the women that are there have more trouble with folks that are transitioning from male to female than the reverse because I think that there's this idea that the female to male is almost on a continuum of masculinity in a female body" (Joss, 1 April 2004).[2] Interestingly, in the queer women's community, where transitioning is increasingly common, FTMs are more highly regarded as sexual partners than MTFs, not only for the reason that Joss suggests, but also because attraction to an FTM can operate through a reconfiguration of the butch–femme binary. As Hemmings (2002) explains, many FTMs learn to express their sexual desire as butches in lesbian communities, and they are therefore, more easily welcomed.

Eventually, word of transphobic experiences filtered back to the TWBC, inspiring diversification of the committee through recruitment of a MTF with strong ties to the trans-community and an ability to act as a consultant on transgender issues. Upon joining the committee, she undertook a survey of the trans-community's impressions of the Pussy Palace. The survey results demonstrated the need for a more overt statement of the inclusiveness of the bathhouse events and inspired the development of a transgender policy circulated to participants prior to an event and posted on the Pussy Palace website:

Transsexual/transgendered women and trans-men are welcome at the Pussy Palace, as are all women in our community, and as such they must be treated with respect by other participants at the Pussy Palace. If you are uncomfortable with their presence or cannot guarantee you will treat them with respect, it is better if you don't attend . . . This is non-negotiable. Anyone harassing women who are trans will be asked to leave.[3]

Initially, however, the policy did not embrace trans-men. It was, only when a FTM who had attended events while transitioning confronted committee members about the policy's non-inclusiveness that the wording was changed. . . . [T]he committee concluded that: "Trans men have always been a part of our community. We're not going to start excluding them now. End of discussion" (Carolyn, 5 May 2004). Given the prevelance of butchness and "female masculinity" more generally, the committee determined that FTMs and MTFs, in whatever stage of transition, should be welcomed. While some lesbian women were (and are) concerned about the masculinization of lesbian culture, others argue that "because there's a lot of women that are transitioning to become something other than a woman, it's unavoidable—you have to spread your mind open to the idea of men in your community and women that associate with them aren't as huge of a demon" (Jan, 5 June 2004).

Despite developing a trans-friendly policy and creating spaces designed to encompass alternative sexual practices, the TWBC cannot control desire:

> You know, they can't make people hit on each other and they can't make sure that everybody's having a great time, but they can create the space where that's a possibility. And it takes some damn fucking brave trans-women to show up in that space and to use it as their own, and to really politicize women. And that's what's happened. (Joss, 1 April 2004)

For queer space to generate the queer identities envisioned by the TWBC, desire must be multi-directional and multi-faceted. Yet desire in the Pussy Palace remains conditioned by more traditional constructions of gendered and sexualized identities. It is the traditional "butch–femme" binary expressed in biologically female bodies that is must commonly displayed in the "queer" spaces of the "women's" bathhouse.

There are FTMs and MTFs present, but they do not represent the majority of participants, nor do they occupy the most central and visible spaces. Ironically perhaps, one can question how "transgressive" a space may actually be when it does little to break down the classical binary categories of gender. In the present case, the women's bathhouse events seems to simply reassert an understanding of gender as the various performances of the traditional masculine and feminine and does little to undermine or support alternative understandings that are radically undermining or subversive.

Conclusions

With each reincarnation of the Pussy Palace, the Toronto Women's Bathhouse Committee attempts to constitute what they define as a "queer" women's bathhouse culture that challenges a lesbian feminist de-sexualization of lesbianism, and that facilitates and embraces "other" bodies and genders. The TWBC sees itself as embracing an "erotic-positive" (Kinsman 1996) "prosex feminism" (Calitia 2003) that emphasizes: the value of pleasure; the importance of a woman's right to control her own body; the expansion of choice and consent in people's erotic lives; and the acceptance of contradictions within communities and individuals. For the TWBC, a prosex feminism attempts to foster an inclusive atmosphere where lesbians, gay men, transgendered people, sex workers and other sexual minorities share a common "queer" space. . . .

While queer may ostensibly be about the rejection of categories, identities and subject positions, the practice or enactment of queer at the bathhouse seems to be about the creation of more and equal opportunities to act out various formulations of classic masculinity and femininity rather than the dismantling of these constructs all together (Jeffreys 2003).

The bathhouse events also raise difficult questions about the constitution and availability of material and symbolic spaces where lesbian identities and ways of being can be expressed. . . . [T]he advent of a queer politics has resulted in a loss of lesbian space, both geographically and intellectually. Lillian Faderman (1997: 226) notes, for example, that queer women "now seem to have given up entirely a *conceptual* space for themselves as lesbians in adopting the term and the concept 'queer'" (emphasis added). Further, there is a case to be made that so-called "queer dykes," through their privileging of gay male culture and their dismissal of lesbian feminism, have contributed to the accelerated loss of material lesbian social and cultural spaces as well with the closure of women's bookstores, coffee houses, bars and clubs (Case 1997; Jeffreys 2003). . . .

The experience at the TWBC events demonstrates that while queer spaces are often presented as progressive, inclusive and tolerant, these same spaces may be exclusionary or limiting despite efforts at openness. The way in which the TWBC puts "queer" into a spatialized practice demonstrates how queering space is a process through which identities and spaces are disciplined, bounded and defined. The TWBC utilizes a definition of "queer" that draws on gay male sexual practices, involves a specific understanding of working-class sexuality and allows for the inclusion of transgendered bodies. In so doing, the TWBC creates a space in which certain expressions of gendered and sexualized identities are valorized and others are discounted. In particular, certain forms of female masculinity are celebrated and the identity of "lesbianness" because of its association with monogamy, domesticity and emotion is rejected. . . . While the goal of queering of space is laudable in its celebration of difference, its vague current usage by the TWBC imposes its own sets of marginalizations that flatten out identities that have made many lives meaningful.

NOTES

1. For example, the name of the event, Pussy Palace, is not necessarily trans-inclusive as not all trans-people have genital surgery and possess a "pussy."

2. Several authors have written about the erasure of femmes and femme-phobia within lesbian culture and history (Harris and Crocker 1997, Rugg 1997).

3. <www.pussypalacetoronto.com> (accessed 24 August 2004).

REFERENCES

Armstrong, J. (2004) The body within: the body without. *Globe & Mail* 12 June: B4.

Bell, D. and Valentine, G. (eds) (1995) *Mapping Desire: Geographies of Sexualities.* London and New York: Routledge.

Bouthillette, A.-M. (1991) "Vancouver's lesbians," in Ingram, G. B., Bouthillette, A.-M. and Retter, Y. (eds) *Queers in Space: Communities/Public Places/Sites of Resistance.* Seattle, WA: Bay Press, pp. 213–232.

Calitia, P. (2003) *Sex Changes: Transgender Politics* (second edition). San Francisco: Cleis Press.

Case, S.-E. (1997) "Toward a butch-feminist retro-future," in Heller, D. (ed.) *Cross Purposes: Lesbian Feminists and the Limits of Alliance.* Bloomington: Indiana University Press, pp. 205–220.

Dangerous Bedfellows (1996) *Policing Public Sex.* Boston: South End Press.

Dhanani, Z. and Fong, T. (1998) Wet & Wild, *Xtra!* 10 Sep.: 21.

Duncan, N. (1996) *BodySpace: Destabilizing Geographies of Gender and Sexuality.* London and New York: Routledge.

Erderman, L. (1947) Afterword, in Heller. H. (ed.) *Cross-purposes: Lesbians, Feminists and the Limits of Alliance.* Bloomington: Indiana University Press, pp. 221–229.

Harris, L. and Crocker, E. (1997) "Bad girls: sex, class, and feminist agency," in Harris, L. and Crocker, E. (eds) *Femme: Feminists, Lesbians and Bad Girls.* London and New York: Routledge, pp. 93–102.

Hemmings, C. (2002) *Bisexual Spaces: A Geography of Sexuality and Gender.* London and New York: Routledge.

Hocquenghem, G. (1978) *Homosexual Desire.* London: Alyson and Busboy.

Hodges, A. and Hutter, U. (1974) "With downcast gays: aspects of homosexual self oppression," in Gross, L. and Woods. J. D. (eds) *The Columbia Reader on Lesbian and Gay Men in Media, Society and Politics.* New York: Columbia University Press, pp. 551–561.

Jeffreys, S. (2001) *Unpacking Queer Politics.* Cambridge: Polity Press.

Jayasingham, D. (2002) "'Ladies' and 'gentleman': location, gender and public sex," in Francis, K. E. and Chedgzoy, M. P. (eds) *Queer Place: Sexuality and Belonging in British and European Contexts.* Burlington. VT: Ashgate, pp. 79–88.

Kingsman, G. (1996) *Regulation of Desire: Sexuality in Canada,* second edition. Montreal: Black Rose Books.

Lauria, M. and Knopp, L. (1985) "Towards an analysis of the role of gay communities in the urban renaissance." *Urban Geography* 6: 152–169.

Leap, W. (ed.) (1999) *Public Sex/Gay Space.* New York: Columbia Press.

McDowell, L. (1999) *Gender. Place and Identity.* Minneapolis: University of Minnesota Press.

Rothenburg, T. (1995) "And she told two friends': lesbians creating urban social space," in Bell, D. and Valentine, C. (eds) *Mapping Desire: Geographies of Sexualities.* London and New York Routledge, pp. 166–181.

Rugg, R. A. (1997) "How does she look?" in Harris, L. and Crocker, E. (eds) *Femme: Feminists, Lesbians, and Bad Girls.* London and New York: Routledge, pp. 175–189.

Saleh, T. (1999) "Transfixed in (lesbian) paradise." *WillyBoy* 7:5–9.

Valentine, G. (1993a) "(Hetero)Sexing space: lesbians perceptions and experiences of everyday places," *Environment and Planning D: Society and Space* 11: 395–413.

Valentine, G. (1993b) "Negotiating and managing multiple sexual identities: lesbian time-space," *Transactions of the Institute of British Geographers* 18: 237–248.

Valentine, G. (1995) "Queer country: rural lesbian and gay lives," *Journal of Rural Studies* 11: 113–122.

The Hookup Culture on Campus

Kathleen A. Bogle

What does it mean to hook up? Consulting a dictionary won't help, since most dictionaries do not even include an entry on hooking up.[1] Even college students have trouble articulating a definition. My exchange with Tony, a senior at State University, demonstrates the uncertainty.

KB: Define hooking up.

Tony: Taking someone home and spending the night with them. I mean intercourse is probably like a big part of it, but I think if you take someone home and hook up, then that's hooking up.

KB: So, could hooking up mean just kissing?

Tony: Yeah.

KB: What does it usually mean?

Tony: Having sex.

KB: So most people you know when they say "hooking up" they are having sex with somebody?

Tony: Yeah (hesitantly) . . . it depends who the person is, like I can read my friends like really, really easily. Like if my one roommate says he "hooked up," that means he brought a girl and home and this, that and the other thing. . . . But, like if other kids tell me they hooked up, you got to ask, not pry into their life, but it could mean a lot of things.

KB: What do you mean when you say it?

Tony: When I say "hooked up"? [I mean] that I took someone home.

KB: But, [you are] not necessarily explaining what happened?

Tony: Right, I don't like to kiss and tell (laughs).

Collectively, the 51 college students and 25 recent graduates I spoke to were able to convey the meaning of hooking up as well as the norms for following the hook up script. However, as individuals they were often unsure whether the specific way they used the term reflected how the student body in general used it. As Tony pointed out, the meaning of hooking up depends on who you ask.

Despite the confusion over the term, college students at both of the Catholic and State-affiliated universities I studied indicated that "hooking up" was widely used on campus to refer to intimate interaction, which could involve kissing, sexual touching, oral sex, or sexual intercourse.[2] Although the people I talked to may have used the term somewhat differently, they consistently identified hooking up as the dominant way for men and women to get together and form potential relationships on campus. This does not mean that everyone on campus engages in hooking up; but students do consider it to be the primary means for initiating sexual and romantic relationships. Among those least likely to participate in hooking up are: racial minorities, students who are *very* religious and those who are already in exclusive, committed relationships (who therefore have no need to be looking for new partners). Most other students participated in hooking up, albeit to varying degrees.

Defining Hooking Up

Some students, like Tony, favor the idea that hooking up generally refers to "having sex;" (i.e., penile–vaginal intercourse) however, many students that I talked to indicated that when they say hooking up they are referring to something less than intercourse. Some students use hooking up to refer to "just kissing" or "making out." Others said hooking up involves "fooling around" beyond kissing, which includes sexual touching on or underneath clothing.

Still others suggested that hooking up means "everything but" intercourse, which translated to include kissing, sexual touching, and oral sex. Most students acknowledged that different people use the term differently. In fact, many students were already familiar with the term "hooking up" from high school. Their previous exposure to hooking up added to the confusion because the definition they used in high school did not always match their college classmates' use of the term. Thus, you cannot be sure precisely what someone means when he or she reports having "hooked up" unless you ask a follow-up question to see how much sexual activity took place. Nevertheless, some students feel they know their close friends well enough to know what they mean when they say it (i.e., their group has a shared meaning of the term). This is the case with Faith University Senior, Trent.

> *KB:* Define hooking up.
> *Trent:* Kissing.
> *KB:* So, if someone did more than kissing then it's not hooking up?
> *Trent:* It is, but I don't know. Yeah, like hooking up in one sense is like you hook up with a girl and if you're hooking up with someone and it happens a few times, then I guess whatever happens, happens.
> *KB:* Could hooking up mean sex?
> *Trent:* Nah.
> *KB:* So, it's different than sex?
> *Trent:* Yeah.

In another conversation with Kyle, a Senior at State University, he offered the following.

> *KB:* How would you define hooking up?
> *Kyle:* Just kissing and maybe a little groping.
> *KB:* Hooking up isn't sex?
> *Kyle:* No. I know a lot of other people define it differently.
> *KB:* So some people say it and it might mean sex?
> *Kyle:* Yeah. None of my friends would. But I have heard it used that way.
> *KB:* So if someone says they hooked up you don't know what they mean, you just know it is something sexual?
> *Kyle:* Yeah. It involves that. But not sex, everything but sex.

> *KB:* Oral sex could be hooking up?
> *Kyle:* Yeah.

Lisa, a Sophomore at State University, had this to say:

> *KB:* Can you define hooking up?
> *Lisa:* I don't know, anything from kissing to having sex.
> *KB:* So, it could mean intercourse, it could mean to kiss someone?
> *Lisa:* Well, usually if it's a good friend and we're talking about it, they'll tell me if they had sex, but if they say "hooking up" it could mean anything from, in my opinion, kissing to having sex.

Clearly, the term hooking up does not have a precise meaning; it can mean kissing, sexual intercourse or any form of sexual interaction generally seen as falling in between those two extremes.

The ambiguous nature of the term hooking up should not be surprising. During the well-publicized scandal of 1997 between former President Bill Clinton and Monica Lewinsky, the public debated what it means to say "have sex" or "have sexual relations" after the President emphatically declaimed, "I did not have sex with that woman," only to have DNA tests confirm the presence of semen on her clothing. Still, Clinton and his supporters argued that his statement was truthful if one only defines sex as penile–vaginal sexual intercourse. However, much of the American public scoffed at this narrow definition, favoring a broader definition of sex, which would encompass sexual touching and oral sex. What was interesting about this debate was how views on the subject broke down along generational lines. Researchers found that members of the younger generation were more likely to agree with then President Clinton's contention that oral sex did not really "count" as having sex with someone.[3] Perhaps then it is not surprising that the more recent term, "hooking up," does not have a universally agreed upon meaning either.[4]

Several students I spoke to alluded to the confusion over what the term hooking up meant. This may stem from regional variation in usage or even more localized variation between high schools. As Kim, a Sophomore from Faith University puts it:

KB: You mentioned hooking up a minute ago. How would you define that?

Kim: (Laughs) That's kind of funny actually because at home, like in Virginia, hooking up is like more than kissing, but not all the way. And so I would come here and I would hear people, like my friends, say: "I hooked up with this guy and this guy." And I was just thinking: "These people are crazy that they would do that with that many people!" But then I just found out this year that here hooking up [sometimes means] just kissing or making out with a guy at a party.

Even more confusion was generated when college students were discussing hooking up with someone from a different generation. For instance, some female students mentioned that problems arose when they called home to fill their mothers in on what was going on with "guys" at college. Gloria, a Freshman at State University, told her mother that she had been hooking up and this revelation created some panic on the other end of the telephone.

KB: Do people you know [ever] use the term hooking up to refer to sex?

Gloria: I've never heard that. But my Mom saw on the news that hooking up meant oral sex and I always tell my Mom "I hooked up with this guy and he was so nice." I tell her that all the time. And she called me after that news session [and said] "What does hooking up mean?" Because I was telling her I [hooked up with] . . . Billy and Joe and Rob. I was like: "No, just kissing." I guess I never heard it [used] for having sex.

KB: You said [previously hooking up referred to] fooling around?

Gloria: Right. Fooling around is not having sex, but [it can be] like oral sex.

Interestingly, Gloria's definition of what it means to have sex does not include having oral sex. Many of the students I spoke to noted the distinction between sex and oral sex. This provides further evidence that there may be generational differences in perceptions of what counts as sex.[5] Adding to the confusion are media references to hooking up that portray only the most risqué scenarios of hooking up, when in reality students use the term to encompass a much broader range of sexual behavior.

It is likely that there is another reason for the ambiguous nature of the term hooking up. When students say: "I hooked up," they leave the details of the encounter to the listener's imagination. Both men and women may have reasons to intentionally be vague. Men, who often want to feign more sexual experiences than they actually have, can say they hooked up and hope the listener infers *more* than actually happened sexually.[6] Women, on the other hand, who may want to protect their reputations, can say they hooked up and hope the listener infers *less* than what actually happened sexually.[7] When students speak to their close friends, they may know what each other means when they say the term or they may feel close enough to ask a follow-up question on the subject. However, for those who are not friendly enough with the speaker to warrant knowing more intimate details, someone can simply say "I hooked up" and leave it at that. This does not imply that interested parties will not resort to other means to find out what really happened. However, such parties will have to rely on second-hand accounts and rumors to satisfy their curiosity.

Clearly, hooking up is a vague term when it comes to finding out what happened sexually between two people. However, there are several other defining features of the script for hooking up, beyond the sexual aspects, which were largely understood by college students in my study across the board. College students recognize hooking up as the pathway to a potential romantic relationship, yet a hook up does not guarantee *any* commitment beyond when the encounter takes place. After hooking up, someone can opt to ask for the other's phone number or can try to make plans to meet somewhere in the future, but most students indicated that this is not the most common outcome. Instead, students said that the most likely outcome of any particular hook up encounter is "nothing," which means not hearing from the person again unless you coincidentally see him/her out at another social event and decide to hook up again. Although most hook up encounters do not lead to an ongoing romantic relationship, the possibility is there. For many students I spoke to, particularly women, they often hoped that a hook up would evolve into some version of a relationship. Therefore, all hook up encounters cannot be characterized as "casual sex" or "one-night stands" when often one of the parties is hoping for it to lead to "something more" and, at least some of the time, it does.

What Ever Happened to Dating?

The script for how college students become sexually intimate has dramatically changed from the dating script, which dominated campuses throughout the U.S. from the 1920s through the mid-1960s.[8] The college students I interviewed said that they do not date in the traditional sense of the term.[9] Additionally, the alumni I spoke to confirmed that they did not go out on formal dates during their college years. College students do not initiate romantic relationships by asking one another out to dinner or a movie with the hope that something sexual might happen at the end of the evening. Thus, the dominant cultural/sexual script for most of the twentieth-century (i.e., asking someone out for a date as the first stage toward finding an intimate partner) is no longer being used by most college students in my research. The following excerpts from my interviews with Emily (Sophomore, Faith University), Joseph (Senior, Faith University), Lisa (Sophomore, State University) and Jen (Junior, State University), illustrate the point that the current script on campus does not begin with dating. These comments were typical of both male and female students at State and Faith University.

KB: Do you know any students that date?
Emily: Like date?
KB: That go out on dates.
Emily: (Laughs). Umm, no. (Laughs). I would say like if you have a boyfriend, maybe you'll go out, but I don't know, I think that's so out, like a culture from like my parents' time that would ask each other out and stuff like that.
KB: So, the people you know don't do that at all?
Emily: No.

KB: When you look around at your friends, do a lot of people go on dates?
Joseph: Once they're actually boyfriend and girlfriend, I see them going out. But I usually don't see anybody with the approach of saying: "Do you want to go out?"

KB: Would you say that students date?
Lisa: Hmmm . . . not really, I don't think they really do that much. I don't know anyone who, that's what is really weird too when you were asking about how people get together in college, they just don't really do that [date]. At least, I don't know anyone who goes on dates.
KB: Have you gone on a date since you've been at State?
Lisa: I mean with my boyfriend now, but not before.
KB: Not before?
Lisa: No, not at all. I mean, nobody ever asked me [on a date]. I had boys that I liked or whatever, but it was never like that, we would just hang out or go to a party or whatever. None of my girlfriends have ever been on dates either since we've been here [at school].
KB: What do you envision when you hear the term "date"? What do you picture that to look like?
Lisa: I don't know, going to a movie and dinner or something, something where it's just the two of you. It doesn't necessarily have to be that [movie and dinner], that's just the typical thing, but like something that just the two of you are doing by yourselves.

KB: Would you say that students at State University date?
Jen: No.
KB: What do you envision when I say date?
Jen: I think about somebody picking you up, bringing you flowers (laughing), taking you out to dinner and maybe a movie.
KB: And students here don't do that?
Jen: No.
KB: Has anyone asked you on a date since you've come to State?
Jen: No.
KB: And none of your friends here have [gone on dates]?
Jen: I mean they've been asked out on dates I guess but it's *after they've been hooking up with the person* . . . I haven't gone out on a date here [at State University] (emphasis added).

In Jen and Lisa's response to the question on whether students date, they refer to a key issue. College students in my research recognize what the dating script is, but they do not follow it in the traditional sense because a date is no longer the mechanism for college students to find potential partners. It is rare for students to engage in behavior that resembles a tradi-tional date (e.g., a pair going to dinner or a movie to-gether) unless they are *already* in an exclusive rela-tionship. As Jen alludes to, the pathway to becoming a couple, where going on a date might occur, begins with hooking up.

The terms "date" and "dating" are still used on college campuses today, but they are used far less fre-quently than during the dating era and they often do not have the same meaning they once did. Today, the term date is used to refer to a) going out alone with someone who you are already in a serious relation-ship with or b) the person you take to a formal dance. However, neither of these scenarios is very common because going on dates is not the centerpiece of the college campus social life that it once was.[10] Yet the term dating is also used by some students inter-changeably with "seeing each other," "talking" or "hanging out" to refer to hooking up on an on-going basis with someone who you have some form of con-tact with between hook up encounters. According to the men and women I spoke to, students in this type of relationship would rarely, if ever, go out to dinner or the movies or any other public place to spend time alone together. Thus, college students' use of the term "dating" does not reflect the traditional meaning of the term.

Dating vs. Hooking Up

Hooking up and dating are fundamentally differ-ent. Each carries its own set of norms for behavior and although there is some overlap, there are several critical distinctions. During the dating era, men initi-ated invitations to go out on dates.[11] The script for a date followed many widely-recognized conventions. The man was supposed to contact the woman to ask for a date in advance, giving her at least several days notice; he was responsible for planning an activity for the date, such as going to dinner or a movie, as well as picking the woman up and driving (or walking) her home. Given that the man was responsible for the ini-tiation and planning of the date, he had to pay for any expenses.[12]

By contrast, hook up encounters generally occur at the culmination of a night of "hanging out" among a large group of friends and classmates at a campus party or local bar. Either the man or woman can initi-ate the interaction, but in either case cues would be non-verbal. College students said that you can "just tell" when someone wants to hook up by their eye contact, body language, attentiveness, etc. Neither the man nor the woman is responsible for the expenses incurred during the evening. In most cases, the only expense would be alcohol and college students usu-ally pay their own way or may buy "a round" of drinks for their friends.

Alcohol also seems to play a more central role in facilitating the hook up script than it did in the dating era.[13] In fact, alcohol is not only available at campus social events that culminate in hook up encounters, but it is often consumed by one or both parties in-volved in the hook up.[14] Many students, like Larry, a Senior at Faith University, believe that drinking alco-hol lowers their inhibitions thereby making a hook up possible.

> *Larry:* Sometimes it's just something that happens, like you have something to drink and you just feel this sudden attraction for someone and they feel this at-traction for you and it just happens and it ends after that.

Without alcohol as a social lubricant, it is unlikely that college students would be able to signal interest in a hook up and deal with the potential for rejection inherent to this script. This "need for alcohol" may account for the increasing role that "partying" has played in the social lives of college students over the past several decades.[15] Thus, alcohol use and alcohol-centered events (e.g., campus parties) play a critical role in making hook up encounters possible.

Another difference between hooking up and dat-ing is that the timing and meaning of sexual activity has changed. When the dating script dominated cam-pus life, college men and women went on dates first and then, in some cases, became sexually intimate with one another. Through dating, pairs could get to know each other better or build a relationship by spending time together as well as facilitate potential sexual interaction.[16] College men used to ask women to go on dates with the hope that something sexual, such as necking or petting, might happen at the end of the date. In the hooking up era, this sexual norm is reversed. College students, following the hook up script, become sexual first and then *maybe* someday go on a date. In fact, going on a traditional style date is likely to happen only if the two partners progress to the point of deciding to become an exclusive couple (i.e., boyfriend/girlfriend) as reflected in Lee, Marie, and Jack's responses.

> **KB:** Would you say that students go on dates? What do you see around you? What is the most common?
>
> **Lee:** Most common is just hooking up. I don't really see people go out on dates that often, unless they are [already] in a relationship. (Freshman, Faith University)

> **KB:** Would you say that students date or they go on dates?
>
> **Jack:** (Pauses) Some. Like the ones that have gotten into serious relationships, yes. They'll go out to dinner . . . but everyone else it's just: "I'll meet you at this party" or "I'll meet you at this bar." (Sophomore, Faith University)

Hooking up is the first step; going to dinner or a movie or any other typical one-on-one date happens much later or not at all for the majority, who never reach the point of a full-fledged relationship. Therefore, hooking up reverses the traditional "date first, sex later" formula that governed intimate relationships on college campuses from the 1920s through the mid 1960s.

Moreover, in the dating era, the sexual norms dictated that the degree of sexual intimacy would increase between partners over time. Or, as a couple became increasingly committed, sex would escalate.[17] The hooking up script does not require a correlation between sexual intimacy and relationship commitment. A hook up can include anything from kissing to sexual intercourse between partners, even on the first encounter. In fact, many students indicated that they were more likely to "go further" during a hook up encounter if they did not have strong feelings for their partner or when they believed turning the hook up into a relationship was unlikely. Consider the following excerpt from my interview with Marie, a senior at State University.

> **Marie:** [If] I know I kind of like this person, [then] maybe [I won't do] anything [sexually] because I

want this person to respect me and maybe not just look at it as a hook up. Because I feel like when you sleep with somebody, then they tend to look at you as just a hook up.

> **KB:** If you like someone, you would be less sexual with [him]?
>
> **Marie:** Hmm-hmm, yeah.

Jen, a junior at State University, echoed Marie's opinion.

> The more that I like somebody the more I *don't* want to have sex with them. . . . And I can kind of tell when someone tries to have sex with [me] right off the bat or that night I just feel like it's not really showing respect. I feel like when you really like somebody they're not going to try [to have sex immediately] because they have respect for you. (emphasis added)

Violet, a junior at State University, said she would recommend not hooking up with someone at all if you have genuine feelings for him.

> **Violet:** I think you learn that if you hook up with somebody it is probably just a hook up and nothing is going to come of it. And if you have any invested feelings in someone, I wouldn't hook up with him at a party drunk. But if you are a freshman you go into it thinking: "I am going to have a good time, drink and talk to the person I want and when I am drunk I can really say what I want to say." . . . And I think that when you get further in school . . . you learn that things aren't always the way that you would think that they'd be.
>
> **KB:** So would you say that freshmen girls would think that a hook up might turn into something [relationship-wise] and girls that are sophomores, juniors and older would realize that that is not the case?
>
> **Violet:** Yes.

Importantly, Marie, Jen and Violet were juniors or seniors at the time of their interview. Thus, they had had many opportunities to learn how the hook up script works in college. It seems likely, as Violet suggests, that many young women are less aware of these norms, particularly during freshmen year. Thus, less experienced college women may be sexual with someone with the hope that such behavior will lead to a relationship; they may not suspect that their sexual availability decreases their chances of having the man pursue a relationship. One quantitative study confirmed what the upper-class women I spoke to believed; that is, 49% of college students who engaged in sexual intercourse during a hook up encounter said they never saw the person again.[18] Indeed, members of the campus culture, both men and women, had to *learn over time* the rules of the hook up script.

Conclusion

According to my research, the "date" is no longer the centerpiece of college social life. Instead of dating, college students today socialize with large groups of friends and classmates and pair off to hook up. Hooking up is its own script, with its own norms for how to meet, get together, become sexually intimate, and manage the potential formation of relationships. Although students are aware of these norms, many of them also felt that they had to learn them over time. The ambiguity of the term "hooking up" adds to the confusion students feel when trying to judge what is "normal" or appropriate when trying to form a sexual or romantic relationship. Discovering that a relationship is not a probable outcome of a hook up encounter was difficult for some (usually women) whom often wanted "something more," but felt powerless to get what they want. Those unhappy with the hook up script had to come to terms with the lack of clear alternatives for forming sexual and romantic relationships, especially for those whose social life revolved around campus.

The lack of clear alternatives to hooking up was underscored at the end of each interviewee when I posed the question: "If you could paint an ideal scenario of how you would meet and get together with someone, how would it be?" Many of the college students I spoke to struggled with that question; however one commonality among the answers I heard was that students wished they could be "friends first" with someone or at least "get to know" someone before anything sexual happened. Consider this response from Liz, a freshman at Faith University.

> *Liz:* Well I guess . . . seeing them at a party or something and having a nice conversation, realizing that

we have something in common or that we seem to hit it off. And then um, like maybe he would get my number and then we'd talk or I would see him on campus or something. And then we would hang out the next weekend and see where it went from there. I don't like jumping into things because that always ends up bad I feel like.

> *KB:* Why do you think it does?

> *Liz:* Because you don't give it a chance to become friends with someone or you don't really know someone [if you hook up with him right away]. I think that's what happened to me in the beginning [of this year] because we just jumped into it so fast and . . . we're just starting now to like become like real friends . . . Of course we were friends before, but it was more on like a physical level and now that it's backed off [and we don't hook up as often anymore] it's kind of like upsetting. Like I feel bad for myself you know, that I let that happen. Like, I don't want to be like that. I don't want to just like meet someone and jump right into something because it doesn't give it enough like . . . like um . . .

> *KB:* The time to develop the friendship aspect?

> *Liz:* Yeah, yeah things just like, yeah. I don't know, and when things fizzled with that person it was like: "What are you left with?"

Although the college students I spoke to seemed to accept that the hook up culture is the dominant system on campus for meeting sexual or romantic partners, many students struggled with disappointment when they failed to get what they want from a hook up or series of hook up encounters. It is not that my interviewees objected to hooking up per se; rather, many of them were bothered by how often they, like Lisa, were left wondering: "What are you left with?"

NOTES

1. Most dictionaries do not include an entry on [hookups] or hooking up where the definition refers to a form of sexual interaction. This omission includes many dictionaries focused on slang terms or sexual terminology. An exception is Eble's (1996) book on slang among college students. In a study on the use of slang terminology among students at the University of North Carolina from the 1970s to 1990s, Eble found the term "hooking up," defined as "to

find a partner for romance or sex" or "to kiss passionately," to be commonly used since the mid-1980s.

2. In this chapter, I will often refer to "college students"; however, most of my interviewees were white, heterosexual, traditional-aged college students. My sample was further limited to the two universities I studied (i.e., one large state school; the other a smaller faith-based Catholic school) on the East Coast. Since the interviewees were not chosen via probability sampling, the results cannot be generalized to all college students nationwide.

3. Stepp 2003.

4. See Bogart et al. (2000) for a discussion on college students' interpretations of what scenarios count as "sex." See also Sanders and Reinisch (1999) on the debate about what counts as "sex." . . .

5. Notably, oral sex has become an increasingly common part of the sexual script for young heterosexuals over the last several decades. For a complete discussion of this change in sexual practice and its implications see Gagnon and Simon (1987) and Laumann et al. (1994).

6. This point is confirmed by Carpenter's (2005) work on the meaning assigned to virginity loss. Specifically, she found that men often perceive virginity as a "stigma" that they strive to hide from friends and have to get rid of as soon as possible.

7. Research on hooking up has shown that there is a sexual double standard where women can get a bad reputation if they are perceived as hooking up "too often" or with "too many" partners (Bogle 2008; Glenn and Marquardt 2001).

8. Bailey 1988; Waller 1937.

9. This finding is consistent with Glenn and Marquardt's (2001) national study on college women.

10. Bailey 1988; Waller 1937.

11. Bailey 1988.

12. Bailey 1988.

13. Bailey 1988.

14. The crucial role that alcohol plays in facilitating hooking up has been documented by other researchers as well. According to Glenn and Marquardt: "a notable feature of hook ups is that they almost always occur when both participants are drinking or drunk" (2001: 15). Similarly Paul et al. found "the overwhelming majority of hook up experiences included alcohol use by both partners" (2000:85).

15. Moffatt, 1989; Strouse, 1987.

16. Bailey 1988.

17. Bailey 1988; Whyte 1990.

18. Paul, McManus, and Hayes 2000.

REFERENCES

Bailey, Beth L. 1988. *From Front Porch to Back Seat: Courtship in Twentieth-Century America.* Baltimore: The Johns Hopkins University Press.

Bogart, Laura M., Heather Cecil, David A. Wagstaff, Steven D. Pinkerton, and Paul R. Abramson. 2000. "Is it 'sex'? College students' interpretations of sexual behavior terminology." *Journal of Sex Research* 37: 108–116.

Bogle, Kathleen A. 2008. *Hooking Up: Sex, Dating, and Relationships on Campus.* New York: New York University Press.

Carpenter, Laura M. 2005. *Virginity Lost: An Intimate Portrait of First Sexual Experiences.* New York: New York University Press.

Eble, Connie. 1996. *Slang and Sociability: In-Group Language among College Students.* Chapel Hill: University of North Carolina Press.

Gagnon, John H., and William Simon. 1987. "The Sexual Scripting of Oral Genital Contacts." *Archives of Sexual Behavior* 16: 1–25.

Glenn, Norval, and Elizabeth Marquardt. 2001. *Hooking Up, Hanging Out and Hoping for Mr. Right: College Women on Dating and Mating Today.* An Institute for American Values Report to the Independent Women's Forum.

Laumann, Edward, John H. Gagnon, Robert T. Michael, and Stuart Michaels. 1994. *The Social Organization of Sexuality: Sexual Practices in the United States.* Chicago: University of Chicago Press.

Moffatt, Michael. 1989. *Coming of Age in New Jersey: College and American Culture.* New Brunswick, NJ: Rutgers University Press.

Paul, Elizabeth L., Brian McManus, and Allison Hayes. 2000. "Hookups: Characteristics and Correlates of College Students' Spontaneous and Anonymous Sexual Experiences." *The Journal of Sex Research* 37: 76–88.

Sanders, Stephanie, and June Machover Reinisch. 1999. Would you say you "had sex" if . . . ? *Journal of the American Medical Association* 281: 275–277.

Stepp, Laura S. 2003. January 19. The Buddy System: Sex in High School and College: What's Love Got to Do With It. *The Washington Post.*

Strouse, Jeremiah S. 1987. "College Bars as Social Settings for Heterosexual Contacts." *Journal of Sex Research* 23: 374–382.

Waller, Willard W. 1937. "The Rating and Dating Complex." *American Sociological Review* 2: 727–734.

Whyte, Martin K. 1990. *Dating, Mating, and Marriage.* New York: Random House.

Visibility as Privilege and Danger:
Heterosexual and Same-Sex Interracial Intimacy

Amy C. Steinbugler

Introduction

In "Thinking Sex," a pivotal essay from the 1984 volume, *Pleasure and Danger,* Gayle Rubin argues that sexuality is organized into systems of power that reward some individuals and activities while suppressing others. Describing this "sex hierarchy" as privileging particular types of sexual behavior and corresponding lifestyles, Rubin differentiates "good, normal, natural" sexuality which is heterosexual, monogamous, procreative, same-generation, vanilla, in private, and so on, from "bad, abnormal, damned" sexuality that includes homosexual, unmarried, promiscuous, non-procreative, casual, cross-generational or sadomasochistic sex. Rubin (1984) argues that those who practice "good sexuality" are rewarded with respectability, legality and mobility while those who practice "abnormal sexuality" suffer disreputability, criminality and restricted mobility. Yet Rubin omits a dimension which in the United States has long structured perceptions of sexual conduct—interracial sexuality. Interracial sexual relations, especially between African-Americans and Whites, have been restricted and criminalized in the United States, while monoracial . . . heterosexuality is legally, politically and socially sanctioned.[1] . . .

[N]ot only [is] Rubin's omission . . . significant, but . . . her failure to include race as central to her theoretical frame has profound implications for the

way we conceptualize sexuality. Ignoring racial difference in intimate relations, Rubin neglects the fundamental manner in which racial hierarchies have structured and regulated sexual behaviors and identities.[2] . . .

While it is notable that in 1984 Rubin overlooked interraciality in theorizing sexual hierarchy, more striking perhaps is that 20 years later a systematic empirical analysis of interracial sexuality has not been undertaken. Intersections of race and sexuality have been meticulously theorized . . . and interraciality has been examined from postcolonial and historical perspectives . . . yet sexuality scholars have not produced sustained empirical research examining heterosexual and queer interraciality.[3] . . .

In the United States the racial–sexual boundaries that have historically been most strictly and violently upheld are those between African-Americans and Whites. During 300 years of chattel slavery a pernicious double standard existed regarding interracial sexual relations. Slave owners, by virtue of their racial, political and economic power were able to take sexual license with enslaved women, and cloak these violations in silence and denial (Davis, 1983; James, 1996; Collins, 2000). To evade culpability for this abuse, Whites constructed African-American women as overly sensual, lustful and rapacious, possessing such excessive sexuality that even the most strong-willed, reasonable White man eventually succumbed. In contrast, Black men might be murdered and castrated for even the slightest suspicion of intimacy with a White woman. The myth of the Black rapist was used to justify the lynching of thousands of Black men in the late 19th and early 20th centuries (Wells, 1997 [1892]). . . .

Visibility as a Form of Heterosexual Privilege

Within a heterosexual paradigm, presumptions of heterosexuality infuse the social world. Heterosexuality prescribes what is proper intimacy (Rich, 1980), who is a proper citizen (Evans, 1993; Richardson, 2000), and what is a proper family (Donovan et al., 1999; Weeks et al., 2001). . . . Paradoxically, the naturalization of heterosexuality ensures its simultaneous visibility and invisibility in social identities and social spaces—heterosexuality is "invisibly visible" (Brickell, 2000). As a normative category, heterosexuality is invisible as such, yet heterosexual intimacy is overtly visible in social spaces. . . .

Cohen argues that multiple identities—including race, gender and class—limit the entitlement and status individuals receive from "obeying a heterosexual imperative" (1997: 442). Carbado (2000: 117) suggests a list of 44 heterosexual privileges[4] acknowledging the safety of being visibly heterosexual in public spaces in a US context. He asserts that an important element of heterosexual privilege is that a man and a woman can comfortably express affection in any social setting, even a gay one, without wondering whether kissing or holding hands will render them vulnerable to violence. Carbado highlights the ease through which heterosexual couples may navigate social spaces, assuming that they will be recognized as a couple and that no violence will stem from this recognition. His list demonstrates that visibility may be one of the most fundamental heterosexual privileges. Yet for Carbado the hypothetical heterosexual couple, while not necessarily White, is implicitly monoracial. Research suggests that Carbado's list of privileges may not hold true for heterosexual interracial couples (Rosenblatt et al., 1995; Dalmage, 2000; Childs, 2001; Hildebrandt, 2002).

Same-Sex Intimacy: "Up from Invisibility"?

While research on heterosexuality casts visibility as an unspoken privilege, sexuality scholars proclaim a rise in visibility among gays and lesbians in the United States (Dow, 2001; Battles and Hilton-Morrow, 2002; Shugart, 2003). . . . [S]cholars of media and culture turn a critical eye to the influx of gays and lesbians into mainstream culture, announcing an "era of visibility" (Walters, 2001: xvi). Elements of this "explosion of gay visibility" include news coverage of gay-related issues, gay sport stars and rockstars, gay TV characters, gay cartoon characters, gay entrepreneurs, gay days at theme parks, a gay MasterCard and even a gay beer, Triangle Brew (Walters, 2001). Yet media representations of gays and lesbians continue to reflect a particular gay demographic—mostly White, mostly male, mostly middle, upper-middle class (Gross, 2001: 4), and implicitly monoracial.

Simultaneously, media scholars admit a significant disjunction between lived experiences and cultural representation. . . . Because heterosexuals have been established as a *socially* inscribed class and gays and lesbians as a *sexually* inscribed class, queer sexuality is relegated to private realms and out of the public eye (Richardson, 1996).[5] "When gay people engage in behaviors allowed for heterosexuals (such as holding hands and kissing), they make public what society has prescribed should be private. They are accused of flaunting their sexuality and thereby are perceived as deserving or even asking for retribution, harassment or assault" (Herek, 1992: 95). . . .

[Scholars] argue that for "non-heterosexuals," "the simple pleasures of everyday life" are constrained by knowledge of a persistent stigma about non-heterosexuality (Weeks et al., 2001: 184). The result is a constant need to "self-monitor," continually assessing the amount of risk they will take to keep safe on the streets and in their homes (2001). Using interview data from the same project, Donovan et al. suggest that even as non-heterosexuals live in constant vigilance, they also experience a lack of recognition and validation for their relationships. These respondents express a desire for fuller citizenship as a way of protecting, affirming and removing the stigma from their lives (1999: 699). Indeed, risks associated with visibility and frustrations associated with invisibility are simultaneous experiences in the lives of same-sex couples. . . .

Interracial Intimacy: In/visibility and Racial Difference

. . . When examining the relationship between visibility and sexuality, . . . scholars have continued to assume sexual relationships are monoracial. The problems with such an assumption are threefold. First, presuming monoraciality ignores the rapidly increasing number of interracial relationships in the United States.[6] Second, analyzing interracial sexual relationships allows us to see how racial difference may disrupt heterosexual privileges and further marginalize lesbians and gay men. Lastly, the violent history associated with interracial sexuality in the United States may create a difficult social environment that both heterosexual and same-sex interracial couples must navigate.

Given that the United States has been persistently haunted by the specter of interracial sexuality, little is known about how these couples experience visibility or invisibility in public spaces. Assumptions of monoraciality dominate literature on heterosexuality while relationships between White and Black men or White and Black women remain desperately undertheorized. How does this history of violence surrounding interracial heterosexuality in the US mediate the everyday visibility of interracial couples? How do queer interracial couples navigate social spaces dominated by presumptions of heterosexuality and monoraciality? . . .

Research Methodology

Data for this analysis comes from 16 interviews conducted with a nonrandom sample of eight Black/White interracial couples in Philadelphia and New York City in 2004. . . . [F]our were heterosexual and four were same-sex couples. Of the heterosexual couples, two involved a Black man and a White woman and two involved a Black woman and a White man. Of the same-sex couples, two couples were gay and two were lesbian. This research focuses only on Black/White couples. . . .

Heterosexual Interraciality: Seen and Unseen

Moments of Dislocation

A recurring experience in the narratives of interracial couples is their *visual dislocation* in public settings, e.g. while waiting in line at a food counter or a restaurant. If they are not holding hands or being physically affectionate, in a crowd of people they are assumed by the quick glances of strangers to be unrelated. Almost every couple I spoke to—regardless of sexuality—had one of these stories to tell. The significance of these instances to the couples themselves varied from indifference to annoyance and anger. For instance, Vera, a 33 year-old White woman, who has a 12-year-old White daughter, Becky, from a previous marriage and a 6-month-old daughter, Kaya, with her Black husband, Kalvin, relays her frustration at not being recognized as a family.

> We'll be next to each other [in line] and the clerk will say, "Can I help you, sir?" or something like that. Just assuming we are not together, even though we all maybe standing there together and it may be all four of us standing there together. The people just assume that you're not with this person because he is not White.

On some occasions, these disconnections provoked ire. Warren, a 28-year-old White man, voiced his resentment at the persistent inability of strangers to see himself and his Black wife Nakia as together, while allowing that he may possess heightened sensitivity.

> **Warren** For instance [we're] waiting in line for a deli and she pays and they're like, "Can I help you?" I'm like, "I'm with her. Don't you get that?" Why would I stand so close to her? People look at you, like you're not [together]. It happens all the time.
> **ACS** How do you feel when that happens?
> **Warren** Well it pisses me off. I mean small things . . . a small thing like that pisses me off. I don't understand the ignorance, but maybe I would react the same way. Because you never know who is with who or what. So maybe I'm the one that is oversensitive.

In a society in which both living and social spaces are racially segregated[7] the infrequency of interracial intimacy may render these strangers' oversights understandable or seemingly unremarkable. Persons in monoracial relationships may sometimes experience such misunderstandings. Yet the persistent and cumulative nature of these small events in the everyday lives of interracial couples is meaningful to these respondents. While these instances may not convey outright hostility or aggression, . . . they do affirm the marginal or outsider status of interracial intimacy, underscoring the normative status of monoracial intimacy and the invisibility of closeness across racial lines.

Moments of Visibility

Though heterosexual interracial couples feel invisible in particular situations, in others they endure prolonged stares or comments. The sexual–racial configuration of the couple—a White woman with a Black man versus a Black woman with a White man—had a lot to do with when and how they felt conspicuous in public settings. When I asked Kalvin, a 30-year-old Black man married to Vera, a White woman, whether they get noticed as an interracial couple, he dryly explains strangers' stares.

> I think they are more star-stuck because I am an incredibly handsome man and my wife is remarkably beautiful. That's the way I look at things. You have to kind of hypnotize yourself to believe why those people are staring at you.

Kalvin's reference to hypnosis reflects the constancy of the looks and stares he and Vera receive when they are out to eat, at the mall, or at a baseball game. I ask him *who* tends to stare.

> I think, in my opinion the Black race is more vocal. The Black women are upset because this White woman came and took one of their men, one of their good brothers . . . You'll see the dirty looks from some of the Black women, who are sitting in a group of Black women (*mimics their sighs*). You'll see them stare you up and down, and I'll grab my wife and kiss her or something. I'll give them a show if they want. It doesn't matter to me.

Kalvin's comments reveal that he is quite used to the disapproval he encounters from Black women and is

not threatened by it. Similarly, Scott, a 32-year-old Black man, interprets the reactions he gets from Black women as "disapproval" or "dismissal," though he attempts to shrug them off. His White partner, Tamara, who is 30, has a more difficult time with the hostility she perceives.

> I feel very threatened by Black women because I feel like they're looking at me like I've taken one of their men.

As Tamara continues, it appears that she does not fear physical retaliation but feels both concerned and frustrated by the sexual and racial politics that surround her relationship with Scott.

In addition to the displeasure they saw in the faces and comments of Black women, heterosexual couples consisting of a Black man and a White woman experienced more serious and physically aggressive threats from White men, and in one instance, a White woman. Both couples had experienced verbal confrontations involving racial slurs and threats of violence. Scott described an experience he had while dating a White woman in Greece three years before he met Tamara. While walking with his then-girlfriend through the crowded streets of a little town at 9 o'clock on a warm night in August, he was attacked by five "neo-Nazi skinheads." The attackers chased him through the streets and eventually beat him nearly to death with railroad-ties. Though Scott prides himself on not living in fear of another attack, he remains vigilant and hyperaware in public settings. Incidents of physical violence were uncommon among my respondents, but most couples had a few frightening stories they carried with them.

Black women in relationships with White men received a different manner of attention and their experiences of visual dislocation appeared more typical. Moments of heightened visibility were less common, but they did occur. Warren, a 28-year-old White man, explains that when he is out with his wife, Nakia, a 29-year-old Black woman, the most common reaction they get is from Black men.

> ***Warren*** [We had] problems as an interracial couple . . . We would get a lot of troubled comments from a lot of Black men.
> ***ACS*** What would they be likely to say?

Warren They'd be like, "Whoa, sister what are you doing with this guy?" I mean it was never—on occasion once or twice was it Black women. At least not
outspoken it wasn't White people. The most outspoken was Black men who did not like the fact that you
could—a White man could have one of their Black
sisters. They definitely did not like that. It wouldn't
be a problem for a Black man, if a brother has a
White woman. That's cool. The other way it doesn't
work.

Warren was able to recall a few instances where he and
Nakia had been antagonized by Black men, but those
altercations never resulted in physical threats. . . .

[T]he experiences of these interracial couples suggests a more nuanced connection between race, sexuality and visibility. Interraciality serves to disrupt
the workings of heterosexual privilege in two ways.
First, couples report numerous experiences of visual
dislocation, moments where they are rendered visibly
separate from each other by strangers who do not recognize interracial intimacy. Second, when their intimacy is acknowledged by others—often precipitated
by physical displays of affection—it is sometimes
met with hostility or aggression. In addition, the extent to which these couples are "seen" differently by
Blacks and Whites illustrates the relevance of race to
the operation of heterosexual visibility.

Same-Sex Partners:
Invisible Intimacy?

Like the heterosexuals I spoke to, gay and lesbian couples also discussed being in line together in
a deli or grocery store and being approached for assistance separately by the counter clerk or cashier.
Yet these couples also experienced a much deeper,
more acute sense of visual dislocation in public
places.

Both gay and lesbian couples explain their own assumption unless they are holding hands or being
physically demonstrative, strangers often will not recognize their partnership. When I asked Thad, a 46-
year-old White man, whose Black partner of seven
years is 28, whether he thinks people recognize him
and Lucas as a couple, he pauses and takes a deep
breath. "You know, I don't really think about that a

lot. But if I do think about it, I would assume, no. I
would think that they wouldn't. I would think they
would look at us and go 'What are those guys doing
together?'" Leslie, a 37-year-old White woman
who's been with her Black partner, Sylvia, for seven
years explains what she sees as people's inability to
recognize interracial intimacy in almost any form.

> I think, it's really sad, but I think that people think it's so
> unusual for people of different races to have any kind of
> intimate relationship, even a friendship, that people
> don't consider it, you know. And like that's why de-
> pending on where we are I feel like Sylvia's work-
> friend, that people are like, "Oh, who's this random
> White woman that's with you?" Like it doesn't occur to
> people that we could be close—even if we weren't
> lovers—that we could be important to each other in that
> way that you might want to say hello to both of us.

For Leslie this lack of recognition is most troubling
when it comes from men who approach Sylvia when
the two of them are walking on the street.

> A lot of times I feel invisible and particularly with men
> who will walk—if we're together—they'll walk straight
> up to her on the street and start talking to her without even
> making any eye contact or looking at me in any way. So I
> feel like when men pick her out like I'm invisible com-
> pletely. Which is really gross, it's a gross feeling.

Francine, a 23-year-old Black woman, also experiences forward gestures by men when she's with her
22-year-old White partner, Kap. But unlike the story
Leslie related, these advances are made while
Francine and Kap are walking down a street holding
hands.

> Kap and I were talking about this last night, or a cou-
> ple nights ago, about why we think people don't recog-
> nize us as a couple . . . or why men hit on me when
> she's with me. And so she was like, "You know what?
> They wouldn't do that if I were a Black man." And I
> was like "You're right . . . and if you were a Black
> dyke, they would probably still hit on me, but not
> as much." But because of who she is they do hit on me
> . . . I'm talking about Black men hitting on me, be-
> cause that's usually who hits on me. Um, so, I guess
> that's like the way that they interact with us differently
> because we're interracial—the fact that they don't read
> us as a couple or that they don't respect that even if
> they do read us as a couple.

Francine's continual experience of being approached by men in front of her White female partner exemplifies the ways that queer interracial relationships become invisible in certain public spaces. Her assertion that men would not approach her if Kap were a Black man reflects her sense that monoracial heterosexuality is seen as legitimate. Her suggestion that if Kap were a Black lesbian, she might still be "hit on," but "not as much" shows that even when queer intimacy is acknowledged, it is often disrespected.

Sylvia, a Black lesbian, reports that this disrespect sometimes comes in the form of insults hurled by passers by. Describing an experience she and her White partner Leslie had in their old New York neighborhood that was both racially mixed and had a sizable lesbian population, she explains

> There was one night we were going out and we were holding hands, two blocks from our house maybe . . . and this family—what looked like a family a woman and maybe three or four kids, who'd I say were all under the age of ten, Black family, I don't know where they were from—they were coming towards us and as they passed us one of the boys in the back screamed out "Dyke!" . . . And the mother's just walking and like keeps [walking] her family around the block.

In sum, lesbian and gay interracial couples in this study possess a much stronger sense than heterosexual respondents that their relationship is "invisible" to others in non-queer spaces. These couples violate both US conventions of monoraciality and of heterosexuality and many Americans are not conditioned to recognize romantic intimacy outside of these conventions. Yet when their connection is recognized, it comes with the risk of verbal abuse. . . .

Managing Visibility

For both the heterosexual and same-sex interracial couples I interviewed, tensions surround visibility. Feeling as if they are visually dissociated from each other in public places can be a taxing and tedious experience. Yet for many there is danger in being perceived as sexual partners. Apparent from respondents' narratives is that couples anticipate hostile reactions in particular public contexts, and

often self-police or regulate their behavior so as not to draw unwelcome attention.

Almost every gay or lesbian respondent expressed feelings of cautious restraint in spaces they did not perceive to be queer or accepting of non-heterosexual identities.

Many relayed an increased sense of comfort and safety, and a greater inclination to be physically affectionate in queer spaces, whether it be a bar or club, or a gay area or neighborhood. . . .

We can consider the constant self-awareness and self-regulation in which most queer interracial couples, and some heterosexual couples engage as a process of "working" one's identity (Carbado and Gulati, 2000). This work takes the form of deciding when it is safe to show physical affection and what forms of affection will be permissible. Interracial couples often do significant amounts of identity work as proactive defense.

Importantly, this self-monitoring suggests visibility and invisibility are not states of being but ongoing processes in which queer interracial couples often (and heterosexual interracial couples sometimes) engage. . . . While—depending upon the skin tone and appearance of each partner—their racial difference may be apparent, without physical contact like hand-holding or hugging their sexual intimacy may be invisible. Johnson has argued that in public same-sex couples are often expected to "pass" as heterosexual friends instead of same-sex lovers, "a performance of heterosexuality that is particularly oppressive for gays and lesbians since it involves self-policing and self-regulating the most 'innocent' forms of sexual affection" ([Lassey and Tharinger,] 2002: 328). . . . Because many queer interracial couples are unable to perform monoraciality in public spaces, there may be even greater pressure to pass as heterosexual friends. To simultaneously transgress norms of heterosexuality and monoraciality is to violate the basic tenets of the US heterosexual paradigm.

Becoming and Unbecoming Interracial: The Social Geography of Visibility

Across categories of sexuality, gender and race, respondents emphasized the importance of locality—

street block, neighborhood, borough, city, geographic region or even nation—in their perceptions of visibility and recognition. When I ask Warren, a 28-year-old White man, about his experiences with his Black wife Nakia in New York City, his response reflects an attunement to the social landscapes of individual neighborhoods.[8]

> Yeah I think 80% of the city we feel comfortable in, especially Manhattan, even all the way to Washington Heights, which is Harlem. There are certain parts where you might feel a bit more uncomfortable. I think a place like this is just perfect . . . It's kind of what you would look for because people are nice, people are open. You're just a regular old couple, there is no interracial in the couple, you're just a couple and people look at you like that. It's not like, 'Oh they're different. That's interesting.' . . . What I'm saying is that you just kind of blend in and you're just a couple. I think maybe if we go to Harlem and go to 105th [street] and walk around hand in hand, we're not just a couple; we're suddenly becoming an interracial couple. We can go to certain parts in Brooklyn that are either predominately White or Jewish Orthodox, or predominately Black you suddenly become this interracial couple again. It's because the environment changes, not because you change.

 . . . [H]is own neighborhood . . . includes enough other interracial couples that he does not feel particularly conspicuous walking hand in hand with Nakia. In other neighborhoods, however, that are predominantly Black or predominantly White, they "become" an interracial couple. Thus his sense of his own visibility as part of an interracial couple is intricately tied to the social geography of his city.

While Warren describes the social terrain of a single metropolitan area, Mabel, a 43-year-old Black woman, who has been with her husband, Hank, for 13 years, described to me her heightened awareness of her visibility when she is away from Philadelphia with her family. Every summer she and Hank take their three children to his family's cottage on Cape Cod for two months. She describes being more "attuned" in Cape Cod because "there are hardly any African-Americans."

For queer couples, the sexual environment of social landscapes was particularly important. As discussed earlier, gay and lesbian respondents felt less compelled to manage their visibility in queer spaces. Racial difference, however, does not disappear within queer spaces and must be negotiated by interracial partners. For couples that desire and can find racially diverse queer spaces, this experience can be positive. When I asked Sylvia, a 29-year-old Black lesbian, how it felt to be an interracial couple in a queer space, she explains

> There are ways I'm like it's totally normal and in some ways more normal to be an interracial queer couple . . . I don't know but I think like in some ways when you feel outside of your community it's easier to connect with someone.

In New York City Sylvia and Leslie are able to go to queer spaces that are racially mixed. Diverse racial atmospheres are important in order for each of them to feel comfortable. For couples in Philadelphia, gay and lesbian spaces are often racially segregated and diversity can be elusive.[9]

For Francine, a queer Black woman, being in a "people of color queer space" is extremely important for her, but it's not something she feels she needs to share with her partner, Kap.

> Like Black dyke bars in Philly. They are not spaces for White people. There are no White people in those spaces. So first of all it would be like totally inappropriate for me to bring her. And then second of all, I wouldn't, I wouldn't feel comfortable because, like it would just be so random if I brought a White person into the space. And also, it's really important to me to have um, people of color of spaces that are like for people of color where I can go and be a person of color without my White girlfriend. And she's really appreciative of that . . . So I think it's important to make that distinction though cause you know saying "queer spaces" isn't really, I know I've said it a hundred times, isn't an adequate description. Especially in Philadelphia, because the queer worlds are very segregated.

Francine spends most of her social life in queer spaces, some of which are Black and some of which are White. While those spaces often allow her and her partner, Kap, to feel "safe" and "recognized," their racial dynamics can make her feel hypervisible as part of an interracial relationship.

Conclusion

. . . [B]y implicitly constructing same-sex couples as monoracial, scholars fail to consider the extent to which heterosexuality and White supremacy together saturate public spaces to render queer interraciality profoundly invisible. By analyzing interracial narratives of visibility and invisibility, I have offered a critique of the monoracial bias of sexuality research. I conclude with three important points. . . .

While heterosexual interraciality may be privileged relative to queer interraciality, heterosexual respondents in this study shared numerous experiences of invisibility as well as experiences of heightened visibility in which they had been verbally or physically threatened because the race of their sexual partner did not conform to norms of heterosexual monoraciality. That White supremacy in the US proscribes legitimate sexual behavior even among heterosexuals underscores the extent to which heterosexuals are a *sexually* as well as socially inscribed class. . . . While moments of visual dislocation frustrate both heterosexual and queer interracial couples, recognition of sexual intimacy can invoke the possibility of verbal or physical violence. At times interracial couples must therefore "manage" their visibility (Lasser and Tharinger, 2003) by "passing" as heterosexual friends (Johnson, 2002). Conditioned to anticipate possible hostility in public spaces, queer respondents engaged in this identity work more frequently than did heterosexual respondents. . . . I argue that locality is intricately tied to issues of visibility and invisibility. . . . [R]acial dynamics inhere to sexual landscapes, structuring permissible sexual behaviors and identities. Public spaces are not simply heterosexual or queer, they are imbued with assumptions about proper racial intimacy. . . .

[T]he nexus of racial difference and sexual intimacy is not only a productive site for examining visibility, but crucial terrain from which to theorize intersectionality, privilege, and marginalization.

NOTES

1. As Rubin (1984) points out, the only adult sexual behavior legal in every state is the placement of the penis in the vagina in wedlock. At the time Rubin wrote her essay, this had only been true for 17 years, since *Loving* v. *Virginia* legalized interracial marriage across the US in 1967.

2. Special thanks to France Winddance Twine for emphasizing the necessity of such a critique.

3. A notable exception to this point is Ruth Frankenberg's (1993) *White Women, Race Matters* in which Frankenberg interviews White heterosexual and queer women involved in interracial relationships, discussing the intersectionality of racial difference and sexual intimacy.

4. Carbado's list can be seen as in conversation with Peggy McIntosh's work on White privilege (1988).

5. There is debate abound this point. Boykin (1996) suggests that "Heterosexual orientation has become so ingrained in our social custom, so destigmatized of our fears about sex, that we often fail to make any connection between heterosexuality and sex." Carbado (2000) argues that the socially constructed normalcy of heterosexuality is not the result of a "desexualization" but rather the sexualization of heterosexuality as normative and natural.

6. In 2002, the Census reported 1,674,000 heterosexual interracial marriages (2.9% of all heterosexual marriages). Of these, Black–White interracial marriage accounted for 24% of all interracial marriages (US Census, 2003).

7. With a dissimilarity index for African-Americans of 0.810, New York City, where Warren and Nakia live, was the third most racially segregated city in the nation (US Census, 2002). The index of dissimilarity for African-Americans in Philadelphia in 2000 was 0.720, ranking Philadelphia the twelfth most segregated city in the nation (US Census, 2002).

8. According to the 2000 US Census, New York City is 45 percent White, 27 percent Black and 27 percent Hispanic (of any race).

9. There is no official index with which to measure the racial segregation of queer spaces. The racial composition of Philadelphia in 2000 is 45 percent White, 43 percent Black and 9 percent Hispanic (of any race).

REFERENCES

Battles, K. and Hilton-Morrow, W. (2002) "Gay Characters in Conventional Spaces: *Will and Grace* and the Situational Comedy Genre," *Critical Studies in Media Communication* 19(1): 87–105.

Boykin, K. (1996) *One More River to Cross: Black and Gay in America.* New York: Doubleday.

Brickell, C. (2000) "Heroes and Invaders: Gay and Lesbian Pride Parades and the Public/Private Distinction in New Zealand Media Accounts," *Gender, Place and Culture* 7(2): 163–78.

Carbado, D. (2000) "Straight Out of the Closet," *Berkeley Women's Law Journal* 15: 76–124.

Carbado, D. and Gulati, M. (2000) "Working Identity," in *Cornell Law Review.* 85: 1259–1308.

Childs, E. C. (2001) "Constructing Interracial Couples: Multiple Narratives and Images," unpublished dissertation: Fordham University.

Cohen, C. J. (1997) "Punks, Bulldaggers and Welfare Queens: The Radical Potential of Queer Politics?" *GLQ* 3: 437–65.

Collins, P. H. (2000) *Black Feminist Thought: Knowledge, Consciousness and the Politics of Empowerment.* London: Routledge.

Dalmage, H. M. (2000) *Tripping on the Color Line: Black–White Multiracial Families in a Racially Divided World.* New Brunswick, NJ: Rutgers University Press.

Davis, A. Y. (1983) *Women, Race and Class.* New York: Vintage Books.

Donovan, C., Heaphy, B. and Weeks J. (1999) "Citizenship and Same Sex Relationships," *Journal of Social Policy* 28(4): 689–709.

Dow, B. J. (2001) "*Ellen,* Television, and the Politics of Gay and Lesbian Visibility," *Critical Studies in Media Communication* 18(2): 123–40.

Evans, D. T. (1993) *Sexual Citizenship: The Material Construction of Sexualities.* London: Routledge.

Frankenberg, R. (1993) *White Women, Race Matters: The Social Construction of Whiteness.* Minneapolis: University of Minnesota Press.

Gross, L. (2001) *Up from Invisibility: Lesbians, Gay Men and the Media in America.* New York: Columbia University Press.

Herek, G. M. (1992) "The Social Context of Hate Crimes: Notes on Cultural Heterosexism," in G. M. Herek and K. T. Berrill (eds.) *Hate Crimes: Confronting Violence Against Lesbians and Gay Men.* London: Sage.

Hildebrandt, M. D. (2002) "The Construction of Racial Intermarriage: A Comparison of the Effects of Gender, Race, Class and Black Ethnicity in the Daily Lives of Black/White Couples," unpublished dissertation: Columbia University.

James, J. (1996) *Resisting State Violence: Radicalism, Gender and Race in US Culture.* Minneapolis: University of Minnesota Press.

Johnson, C. (2002) "Heteronormative Citizenship and the Politics of Passing," *Sexualities* 5(3): 317–36.

Lasser, J. and Tharinger, D. (2003) "Visibility Management in School and Beyond: A Qualitative Study of Gay, Lesbian and Bisexual Youth," *Journal of Adolescence* 26: 233–44.

McIntosh, P. (1988). "White Privilege and Male Privilege: A Personal Account of Coming to see Correspondences through Work in Women's Studies," Working Paper 189: Wellesley Collage Center for Research on Women.

Rich, A. (1980) "Compulsory Heterosexuality and Lesbian Existence," *Signs: Journal of Women in Culture and Society* 5(4): 631–60.

Richardson, D. (1996) "Heterosexuality and Social Theory," in D. Richardson (ed.) *Theorising Heterosexuality.* Philadelphia, PA: Open University Press.

Richardson, D. (2000) *Rethinking Sexuality.* London: Sage.

Rosenblatt, P. C., Karis, T. A. and Powell, R. D. (1995) *Multiracial Couples: Black and White Voices.* New York: Sage.

Rubin, G. (1984) "Thinking Sex: Notes for a Radical Theory of the Politics of Sexuality," in C. Vance (ed.) *Pleasure and Danger: Exploring Female Sexuality.* London: Routledge.

Shugart, H. A. (2003) "Reinventing Privilege: The New (Gay) Man in Contemporary Popular Media," *Critical Studies in Media Communication* 20(1): 67–91.

US Census Bureau (2002) "Residential Segregation for Blacks of African Americans in Large Metropolitan Areas: 1980, 1990 and 2000," *Racial and Ethnic Residential Segregation in the United States: 1980–2000, Table 5-4.*

US Census Bureau (2003) "Children's Living Arrangements and Characteristics: March 2002," *Annual Demographic Supplement to the March 2002 Current Population Survey, Current Population Reports, Series P20-547.*

Walters, S. D. (2001) *All the Rage: The Story of Gay Visibility in America.* Chicago, IL: University of Chicago Press.

Weeks, J., Heaphy, B. and Donovan C. (2001) *Same Sex Intimacies: Families of Choice and Other Life Experiments.* London: Routledge.

Wells, I. B. (1997 [1892]) "Southern Horrors: Lynch Law in all its Phases," in J. J. Royster (ed.) *Southern Horrors and Other Writings: The Anti-Lynching Campaign of Ida B. Wells, 1892–1900.* Boston, MA: Bedford Books.

Latinos On da Down Low

M. Alfredo González

Saturday Night in El Bronx

That Saturday night of February 2001, Michael and I went to hang out to a South Bronx club not far from where I lived in upper Manhattan. We knew each other for almost 20 years and lately, we had to set up formal dates to catch up with each other. After being frisked for weapons and paying admission, we entered a room packed with tough-looking Black and Latino young men. Michael looked at me with curiosity and asked, "you've been here before, Alfredo?" "Yeah; twice," I responded. "And, are you sure this is a gay club?" "Of course," I answered more interested in checking out the scene. Michael was puzzled by the total indifference that greeted us and the aloof-looking crowd pulsating to the rhythm of rap music. "Let me ask," he said and went to one of the security guys by the door. Michael grew up in the Lower East Side and to me, he is the quintessential New Yorker: bold and assertive. He is the kind of guy that would not flinch at asking "is this a gay club" once he is already in it. "Alright, let's check our coats," he said as he returned persuaded.

Michael preferred the larger dance floor upstairs. The house music, the mirror balls, and the dancing styles made it more gay-identifiable. *Caushun,*[1] "The *Gay* Rapper," was the star of that night's show. I could not make out all the words in his rhyme, but three were clear: "I swallowed it." Next to us stood a tall, masculine and handsome young Latino in oversized pants and a basketball tank top bouncing to the beat. Michael, the Latino chaser, turned to him and

From "Latinos On da Down Low: The Limitations of Sexual Identity in Public Health" by M. Alfredo Gonzalez, *Latino Studies,* 5, 25–52. Copyright © 2007, published by Palgrave Macmillan. Reprinted by permission from Macmillan Publishers Ltd.

asked him, "Do you swallow it?" (Did I mention he was bold?) The guy turned to us with a big smile and replied: "No, I eat it."

That night, I believed we had gone to a gay dance club that local young men attended because it played the music they liked, because it was located close to where they lived, or because they were as bored with the downtown scene as I was. Six months later I realized Michael's doubts that night, had merit: two articles, one by Kai Wright in the *Village Voice,* and another by Malcolm Venable in *Vibe,* discussed African American and Latino men who had sex with men *on the down low* (i.e. on the sly, undercover), but did not identify as Gay (Venable, 2001; Wright, 2001; Denizet-Lewis, 2003). These journalistic accounts listed the South Bronx club as a meeting place for men *on the low* (Trebay, 2000), and reported that some of them may be having sex with women who ignored their homosexual practices (Venable, 2001). They were characterized as interested in rap music and marked masculine demeanor in their sex partners and themselves (Trebay, 2000; Venable, 2001; Wright, 2001).

The articles on the *down low* published in the popular press describe young men unfazed by the tension between their non-normative sexualities and their otherwise conventional Black and Latino working-class male identities. At the core of their secrecy, is their refusal to politicize their intimacy, that is, to adopt a public gay identity.[2] While the literature on same-sex practices among African Americans lists religion as a paramount deterrent of sexual expression, men on the *down low* do not cite choosing between *right* and *wrong* as a dilemma. Like the broad smile of our "handsome Latino" in the South Bronx club suggests, the young men quoted in these articles do not seem to experience guilt for rejecting Judeo-Christian strictures. Their quandary is not ethical but socio-cultural. They would not flout age-, race-, and class-sanctioned masculinities: gay is not an option; Hip-Hop is.

In one of the first articles on the *down low,* Guy Trebay second-guessed these men's enjoyment of rap music, a genre widely depicted as homophobic and misogynistic (Trebay, 2000). Other articles in the popular press, relate the growing HIV infections among young *men-who-have-sex-with-men* (MSM), to the reluctance of men *on the low,* to identify as gay (Ballard, 2001; Suggs, 2001; Wright, 2001), and link their reportedly bisexual practices to the upsurge of HIV infections among women of color (Ballard, 2001; Edwards, 2001; Venable, 2001; Wright, 2001).[3] The *down low debate* has the necessary ingredients to sell: concealed non-normative sexualities, a subaltern genre of expressive culture (Hip-Hop), a pandemic caused by a sexually transmitted agent, *innocent victims* (heterosexual women), and a population often accused of misbehavior (men of color). Although in this discussion men of the *DL* never speak on their behalf, Kai Wright calls the initial flurry of articles "the great down low debate" (2001). . . .

The initial reports focused on youth, linking life *on the down low* to Hip-Hop culture's *hypermasculine* stance (Trebay, 2000; Venable, 2001; Wright, 2001). The connection of the term *down low* with youth of color was consistent with linguistic assessments that place it emerging in the early 1990s among young African Americans (Green, 1998). Thus defined, the notion of the *down low,* although charged with moral and racial implications . . . delineates the sexual identity and behavior of a population, at a specific historical moment.

The sensationalist possibilities of expanding the rubric to all bisexual Black men who keep their men-loving activities to themselves, regardless of age or microcultural niche, proved too tempting, and soon the term *down low,* was applied liberally. In *Essence Magazine,* Tamala Edwards wrote that the *down low* was not just youthful sexual exploration, a common interpretation of bisexuality (Muñoz, 2004), but an established feature in the lives of some adult Black men (Edwards, 2001). Scotty R. Ballard, of *Jet Magazine,* argued that their refusal to identify as "gay" prevents these men from heeding prevention messages directed to the gay

community. Health experts speculated that "some of those on the down low apparently learned the lifestyle in prison, then began dual lives after being released," wrote Ballard (2001), showing that for some people, the *down low* connotes crime and urban pathology.

Criticism also came from the *gay* community. In February 2000, Guy Trebay asked from the pages of the *Village Voice,* "Homo-thugz? Doesn't everybody know that [H]ip-[H]op hates faggots?" Men-loving men "dancing to music that in certain cases may advocate their demise," bewildered Mr. Trebay. Although there are socially responsible rappers (Marable, 2002), Trebay voiced the widespread gay resentment against homophobic rap lyrics. The irony was that young men *on the low* seemed to have guilt-free sex lives, in great measure as result of the sex education the gay movement imparted. Yet, in refusing gay identity, they undermined the political hypothesis that "[*Gays*] are everywhere."

In sum, in the *down low* debate, the rage caused by the alleged bisexuality of men of color, contrasted with the historical silence on white men's bisexuality (Mukherjea and Vidal-Ortiz, 2002). In spite of the possibility of there being a continuum between "*DL* fashion" and strict sexual concealment (Gordon, 2002), press reports on *down low* sexualities were treated as monolithic and unquestionable truths . . . Although most press descriptions of the *down low* included young Latino men, Latino/a HIV workers and communities have eluded the discussion.

This [reading] is an exploration of the *down low* as an emergent MSM sexual identity/culture that defies . . . reliance on MSM political and sexual identities (i.e. gay identity). . . . By analyzing the phenomenon of the *down low* mainly in terms of masculinity, and by discussing the relevant literature and examining texts from the Internet, this [reading] will attempt to show that gender and sexual identities are informed by race and class, and also by history and politics, yet not necessarily sexual politics. Additionally, this [reading] will portray the *down low* as a Latino issue.

First, I will define the term as it is used in the English dialect of African American youth, and in its extended use as a subject position in sexuality. I will then argue that socially located masculinities separate the *down low* from normalized gay identities. Then, with descriptions and texts from Internet sites, and with an analysis of the South Bronx club, I will discuss Latino men's participation in this sexual culture, and the role of masculinity in the *down low*. I will conclude by examining the ethnographic record on Latin American male sexualities to illustrate a critique of static models of sexual systems, and in search of sexual traits congruent with *down low* sexualities. . . .

Down Low?

For Jonathon Green, the term *down low* emerged during the 1990s among African Americans as an adjective meaning *covert* or *secretive*. The acronym *DL* means *keep secret* or *hidden* for teenagers in the United States, and for African Americans means *in a clandestine or sneaky manner*. Green relates the adjective *down low* to the noun *low down*, which means *privileged information*, or *intimate details* (Green, 1998). . . . Geneva Smitherman defines *DL* as *something kept very quiet and secretive, and done on the sly*, and exemplifies it with verses from R. Kelly's song "Down Low": *nobody has to know/Let's just keep it on the down low* (Smitherman, 2000[1994]). Paul Baker's *Fantabulosa: a Dictionary of Polari and Gay Slang* published in London, defines *DL* as the initials of *down low*, and an adjective in African-American slang referring to Black *men who appear heterosexual in public, but have gay sex* (Baker, 2002). This designation, packed with cultural gloss-overs, places *down low* within the focus of this [reading], sex between men. I will use it in a narrower fashion: sex between younger men that identify with Hip-Hop culture.

Latinos [and] Hip-Hop

. . . In this [reading], I will use the term *Latino* for its political and public health significance, but also to acknowledge how the US experience molds Latino lives and cultures. Fellowship with African American communities is part of that experience, and the development of Hip-Hop youth culture (rapping, breaking, DJing) as a social class and ethno-racial-specific artistic expression, is a product of it.

The birthplace of rap is, with certainty, New York City's South Bronx. In this racially mixed working class neighborhood, African American and Latino, or more specifically, Nuyorican youth gave birth to this expressive genre in the context of block and house parties (Lipsitz, 1994; Ards, 1999; Flores, 2000; Rivera, 2001, 2003). Latino rappers have been as political as their African American counterparts. . . .

Keepin' it real, the grounding and foremost principle guiding rap artists' lives and cultural production, denotes steady commitment to inner-city social conditions, history, peoples, and moral and political values, even in the face of financial success (Basu, 1998). The transformation of Hip-Hop into a gendered expression of cultural capital, authenticates for Black [and Latino] youth, their ethno-racial identities and sense of community beyond sexuality (Gordon, 2002; Clay, 2003). Understanding the ethos of Hip-Hop as cultural capital within an economy of scarcity, explains their efforts to express same sex desire (often a negative value in the US), in ways that do not undermine the *realness* of Black and Latino identities. Investing non-normative sexuality in gay identity and community, threatens the cultural capital of ethno-racial identity (Clay, 2003), and implies confronting the racial and class bias of gay communities (Hemphill, 1991, xix, 1992, 40; Chung et al., 1996; Mangaoang, 1996; Díaz, 1998, 124–126). . . .

[The] men [in this study] have an interest in the contemporary expressive cultures of Latino and Black youth, a preoccupation with symbols of masculinity, an apparently "guilt free" sexuality but also, a determination to observe pervading societal homophobia. This cultural logic should not be pathologized but understood as a representation of a historically specific socio-cultural position. This [reading] aims at such understanding and to erode the broad rush to conclusions that has characterized the discussion of this topic.

Sexual and Ethno-Racial Identities in Cyberspace

The growing availability of computers and Internet communication has facilitated the development of virtual social interaction. Norms and rules to inhabit specific cyber environments and to address topics of common interest, organize these interactions.

Anthropologists have studied them for more than a decade (Wilson and Peterson, 2002) and call them "cybercultures" (Escobar, 1996, 112). . . . *[C]yberculture* remains a major focus of present-day anthropological inquiry, and the research strategy to study these real or imagined communities, such as *cybercommunities* centered on sexual interests ("netsex") like *down low* systems, is *cyberethnography* (Marshall, 2003).

Popular press accounts of men *on the down low,* mention public websites nested in networks of electronic communication, as their virtual meeting places. In the anonymity of the Internet, a man *on the DL* can deflect cultural markers of gayness, and meet and arrange sexual encounters ("hook-up") with other men away from gay venues (Venable, 2001; Denizet-Lewis, 2003).

Using keywords such as "down low" in a web search, anyone can locate websites where these men exchange messages and express their sexual agency. Often, website managers apply Hip-Hop's alternative word spelling to the texts posted, so the homophones of keywords (*phine, thugz, boi, boiz*) can also produce results. The sites' names may combine words that evoke sexuality, sex appeal, or physical features (*sexxi, nutting, ballers, hottest, big, bulky, lean*), or name the expected racial and/or ethnic identity of group members (*black, niggah,*[4] *nikka, latin, latino, blatino*[5]). To demarcate the groups' geographical scope and improve their *hook-up* quotient, their sobriquets may include a region, city, or city neighborhood. The free Internet groups welcoming, or aimed to men *on the down low* that I found, declare this intent in a section written by the groups' founders, usually called "group description" in their "home page" (the public façades of websites).

Latinos are an active part of this virtual sexual scene, and it is not odd to find evidence of this. . . . For example, the now defunct group *"NYC Down Low Latinos,"* included them in its name. Sites from large urban centers, typically name Latino and African American ethnicities side by side with references to *DL* sexualities. Clear stipulations about the group's membership ethno-racial constitution are not rare, and it is also common that Internet sites for men of color are closed to European American men. Yet, on occasion, bans are not phrased in terms of social

categories but in terms of preferred and unacceptable cultural expressions. . . .

The detailed enumeration of "desired" and "intolerable" personal traits indicates the group managers' cultural sophistication, and their awareness of the effects that enforcing these rules would have on the composition of the organization. Since the interactions of this group's members would not be face-to-face, it is easy to create false identities in cyberspace. The only opportunity to effectively enforce these rules would be in occasional parties. It is obvious that the purpose of this strict behavioral code is not to regulate behavior and membership, but to inspire self-policing in the group's members.

> This group is dedicated to Philly and South Jersey niggas (black, latino, asian, even white if you down like that) 18–35 yrs. old who are trying to hook up with other niggas on the low. All members must list their ages and location in their profiles or you will be deleted. Spammers, Feminine niggas, and niggas who ain't down with Hip-Hop, Football, Basketball, and Playstation 2 are NOT welcome here. But if you a thugged out[6] nigga who mack[7] bitches but still looking for niggas to kick it[8] with on the low, then this is your spot. Holla!

The first and the last sentences of the paragraph claim the group for sexualities "on the low." The descriptive blurb adds that the "niggas" who can join may include "latino" and "even white if [they] are down like that." The group's ethnic and racial *open door policy* has restrictions.

Upper and lower age boundaries are instituted at the outset. Legal concerns compel commercial and non-for-profit Internet sex sites to prevent minors from joining by setting bottom age limits. The upper age restriction buttresses the youth of the group's membership. . . .

The absence of mention of preferred body types in this *group description,* suggests that fitness may not the major aim of its age regulation. Instead, allusions to a musical form cultivated by Black and Latino youngsters, two kinds of team sports (involving physical contact), and a popular second generation video game console that hosts sports, fight, and war simulation programs, substitute the physical attractiveness requirement. In assembling an "interests list" as a tableau of traits desired in potential sex group members, its managers delineate a cultural gestalt of the *down low*. I turn now to an examination of this open window into these men's sexual conception.

There are two components of note in this *group description,* that appear also in other Internet *down low*-related materials: avoidance of words that may refer directly to body parts or sexual acts, and the identification and allusion to "surrogate arenas" as means of describing complex gender or sexual subject positions. I call *surrogate arenas,* realms of sociocultural practice significantly marked by one or more social structures. Naming these *surrogate arenas,* or the association of their name with the social location of the person doing the naming, evoke specific subject positions with enough vigor to make superfluous their description. In consequence, *surrogate arenas* are means to refer to social locations by proxy, and thus demarcate an all encompassing cultural gestalt. In this particular case, *surrogate arenas* tacitly stand for gender, race, ethnicity and social class. . . .

Since the group is a (cyber)space for sexual *hook ups,* what qualifies *Hip-Hop, Football, Basketball,* and *Playstation 2* to be requirements for membership is not their esthetic value or their recreational promise. Instead, these leisure activities and forms of expressive culture, have gendered symbolic contents enriched by social class, race, age, and ethnic connotations. Making them membership qualifications is a simple way to screen for multiple variables. Another practical advantage of this procedure is that the combination of these interests conveys a more precise identity profile than the intersection of individual conceptions of gender, class, race, age, and ethnicity. A common identity outline may be an effective means of threading together the elusive sense of community in cyberspace.

Freddy's Challenge

I did not come across many personal messages by *DL* Latinos addressing what being *on the down low* means for them. Although Latinos may be reticent to engage in group discussions, they are members of Internet groups for men in the *down low* that welcome their ethnicity, as well as of those that ignore it. Latinos may identify explicitly in their posted messages, may include references to their ethnicity in their screen names,[9] or may use Spanish words in either messages or screen names.[10] The *down low* sexualities of Latinos have to be inferred from the inclusion of those two words, or the acronym *DL* in their screen names. References to the *down low* have become fashionable, so these markers are not enough proof of a man's sexuality. There are few postings in which the writer admits to be *on the low,* and even less of these messages seem posted by Latinos. Yet, some allow us into the way of thinking of these men.

The following message was posted on November 2002, by an Internet user whose screen name included the word *boricua*. The posting was delivered in a *linguistic texture* associated with Hip-Hop writing. In it, the writer referred to his ethnicity, collapsing race and skin color . . . including his place of residence and physical characteristics, and expressing interest in meeting other [marijuana]-smoking men *on the low.*

> what up . . . i'm a wite skin puerto rican from the Bronx . . . i'm on the low . . . looking for a kat that is on the loww too . . . lookin for those thugged out kats . . . if your friends and family know how you get doen [sic] then you aint on the low . . . all my blunt heads holla . . . me: 6ft brown hair-eyes 173lbs

This posting stands out because the writer did not limit himself to his interest in meeting a man *on the low.* Instead, he went on to provide his definition of it, so that those who opened their sexuality to friends or family would not approach him.

The message was included in a reply by another Latino, a man of African descent who lived in Brooklyn. He used as screen name the same name in his e-mail address and his public profile,[11] an uncommon practice even among openly *Gay* men. I will call him *Freddy Santana. Freddy* was not responding to arrange a *hook up* with *wite skin puerto rican from the bronx,* but to mention his experience of sexual openness, and to question with disdain, the wisdom of being *on the down low:*

*shit i get more respect from everybody who knows [how]
I get down cuz of da way I act and that i can hold my
own, ain't scared to let a nigga know what times it is
and still hang with da hoods from ENY[12] to Da Bronx.
most peeps get intimidated by da way I look, so I guess
I don't have to be scared of what peeps think. if dat's U,
more power to U. can't live like dat. if U can't get/earn
UR respect from being who U are and holdin it down,
what kind of respect can U get?*

Occasionally, men in the Internet question those on
the *down low* in this way. Like in this case, most often, the questioning is ignored and that ends the exchange. *Wite skin*'s posting, and *Freddy*'s remark,
were peculiar in the presentation of their sexualities
and their selves.

One man preferred to conceal his sexual interest in
men, and the other bragged about his openness. *Wite
skin,* was "looking for a kat . . . on the low too," and
clarified what he meant by defining of what he did
not: " . . . if your friends and family know how you
get doen [sic] then you aint on the low . . . " To that,
Freddy opposed his rugged sexual frankness: "ain't
scared to let a nigga know what times it is." To establish firmly for *wite skin,* or any reader, the superiority
of his sexual philosophy, he ended with a rhetorical
question: "if U can't get/earn UR respect from being
who U are and holdin it down, what kind of respect
can U get?"

These men's clashing views on the disclosure of
their non-normative sexualities were couched in
analogous masculinities. *Wite skin puerto rican* did
not ask from his sex partners what he did not offer, so
he searched for a "kat that is on the loww" . . . like
him . . .

Freddy questions the merits of the *down low* as a
sexual strategy, but hardly disguised beneath, he is
challenging *wite skin*'s ghetto citizenship. And it is
he who better attains the politics-laden goal of tracing
his ethos to the inner-city environment. The linguistic
style of both messages denotes urban youth culture.
Freddy and *wite skin* place themselves within New
York City's Black and Latino working-class neighborhoods, but only *Freddy* construes his milieu as an
emblem of masculinity. He links his life in the inner-
city, and the respect he gets from "da hoods," to his
fierceness: "I guess I don't have to be scared of what

peeps think." He makes a strong case against *the
closet* without using that phrase, or calling himself
Gay. The respect he gets from the *niggas* who know
how he *gets do[w]n,* evokes Philippe Bourgois' informants (1996), rather than gay liberation's. *Niggas*
respect him because if they do not, they have to fight
him, and apparently, *Freddy* cuts a daunting figure.

Wite skin initiated the exchange, so his message
lacks the benefit of the rebuttal that *Freddy*'s had. His
message was addressed to the membership of their
netsex cybercommunity at large, so he presents his
masculinity within a sexual frame. *Wite skin*'s search
for a *kat on the loww . . . too,* conveyed that he had sex
with men but he was not *Gay.* He ensures the privacy
of his sexual life so his more public gender, should
not be considered a gay masculinity. To express how
serious he was about gender he announced the standard of *down lowness* his potential suitors should observe: "if your friends and family know how you get
doen . . . then you aint on the low." *Wite skin* does not
open himself to a physical challenge. Instead, he
shuts his masculinity behind the seal of secrecy.

There is not enough material in these two messages to make major assertions about how Latinos in
New York City achieve their sexual identities. *Freddy*
and *wite skin* seem to have enough material to actual-
ize their sexual desire within the terms of the cultural
milieu of their birth and rearing. Although for this
achievement, they may not have had to ride the sub-
way downtown, over the past three decades, Lesbian
and Gay lives have become increasingly present and
demystified in the USA's popular culture and [men
like] *Freddy* and *wite skin* . . . may have received
clues from this presence. There may be also emerging
alternatives in sexual identity politics for certain populations. Even though the data in this [reading] cannot fully support either statement, it is better suited to
underscore the significance of race- and class-in-
formed gender in the approach to same-sex sexuality
of certain groups of working-class Black and Latino
young men like *Freddy* and *wite skin.*

Sexin' the Boogie Down

My motivation in inviting Michael to visit a South
Bronx club was to spend time with an old friend near

home, outside New York City's gay neighborhoods. In my prior visits to that club, I did not give much thought to its characteristics. I thought the club was different because the neighborhood was different. I was accustomed for example, to being frisked for weapons upon entering a night club, so I did not consider the ritual peculiar. It assured me that I would not encounter lethal violence inside, but a body search on someone not used to it, could imply lethal violence. The procedure was a deterrent measure hinting at the surrounding neighborhood and the club's patrons, which was unusual at the gay clubs downtown.

The decoration of the locale did not mark it as a gay or men-loving men's space. Since it was rented for private gatherings on weeknights, it did not bear features that could relate it to any specific group or community. That night, the patrons provided the character the club lacked. The young age, and the ethnic and racial make up of the crowd packing the first floor, was in step with the rap music it danced to. The great number of men spoke of their sexual interests, but their attitude puzzled Michael. They were serious, apparently unconcerned about other men. Their eyes converged on a spot right ahead but past the room's walls.

The manner these young men inhabited a sexuality-marked space, was unlike that of patrons at other gay clubs Michael and I had visited: not many smiled; very few talked; and most strikingly, there were no signs of flirting, cruising, or other sexual innuendo. Had the crowd been gay, at least a few of the men would have greeted our arrival with their eyes. (Even a cursory look would have sufficed to place us in the *interesting* or *uninteresting* categories of the mental catalogue of a handful of men.) A gathering of young *Gay* men in a gay recreational space on a Saturday night, like a similar group of heterosexual men and women in a comparable space and night of the week, would not be without some sexual intrigue. The presence of a few women, and the lack of exhibitions of competitive masculinity, like at a cockfight, conveyed a subtler homosocial message. The attitude of the men at this South Bronx club announced resoundingly "straight," but the men to women ratio, the dancing, and the fact that it was Saturday night, communicated, "not straight."

Although most of the information the press disseminated about the *down low* could not be corroborated without meeting the men the journalists interviewed, successive visits to the South Bronx club as a participant observer, confirmed Venable's (2001) assertions about its distinctive ambiance. Even though only a survey of sexual identity and behavior could establish the clientele's thoughts about their sexuality, and with whom they shared their intimacy, that club was visibly different from a gay dance venue.

Other substantial differences were the music and the self-presentation of the patrons: playing non-stop rap music is not a strategy to get a Gay crowd dancing. Even in the upstairs dance floor, rap tunes were heard more often than in a gay nightclub. The dress and hair styles of the customers followed a youth-of-color esthetic sense. More conventionally trendy young Gay men sport a subdued version of this style. The music of the Bronx club, and the attire of its patrons, evoked a point of reference outside mainstream gay communities.

Another distinctive feature of the gathering was the aloofness of its collective ethos. However minimal, the possibility of meeting new friends is one motivation to attend a nightspot, and this cannot happen without some form of self-expression. Emotional display, genuine or otherwise, is a major communication "currency of exchange" in leisure social settings. At the South Bronx club, young men projected indifference. Of course, this may say more about my inability to identify emotional expressions than about their apathy toward contact.

Although the decoration of the larger dance floor upstairs was dull . . . the combination of four features delivered its gay-identifiable quality. Its mirror balls evoked the 1970s *disco* music that agonized longest at gay dance clubs. The DJ played *house* music, which succeeded *disco,* retaining its *ecstasy-through-dance* principle. The dancing was more playful, creative and personal. The swaggering of the patrons was slightly less studied than in the Hip-Hop room, and this allowed me to recognize some flirting.

Caushun, The Gay Rapper, was a slim Black man in his twenties with a lilt in his voice that set him apart from standard rappers. The club's clients responded to his act with full attention and swaying bodies. The refrain of his rap—*I swallowed it*—was the extroverted utterance of their sexual silences. No one's sensibility seemed hurt by the lyrics. The attitude of the handsome Latino to our right, whom I shall call *Pepe,* typified the response of the crowd: his body followed the rhythm; his hands deep in his pants' pockets accentuated his masculine demeanor; and his eyes on the stage revealed his interest in the performance. *Pepe* only looked away from *Caushun* to answer Michael's provocative question. "Do you swallow it?" Parting his lips in a dazzling smile and narrowing his eyes mischievously, *Pepe* raised the stakes. "No, I eat it," he answered displaying amused comfort.

Our interaction ended there, so it is impossible to assess if *Pepe* "ate it" *on the down low* or with the knowledge of those close to him. I know though, that on that night, most if not all HIV prevention messages directed to his age and ethnic group, were not coded with the gender and cultural values he and the other men at the club displayed. Had he gone that night to a club in a gay ghetto, *Pepe* would have been bombarded with unsafe sex warnings, and free condoms would have found their way to the back pocket of his enormous jeans. To do that, *Pepe* may have had to relinquish his preferences in music, peers, and the way of being a man. Most importantly, to contemplate going downtown he would have had to think himself Gay, if he did not. No other population has been asked to travel any physical, cultural, and psychological distances to encounter HIV prevention efforts. . . .

The publicity of the "*down low* debate," has begun to inspire HIV education campaigns targeting *Pepe* and his peers. However, they do not yet counterweight the media's myopic criminalization of *down low* sexualities.

Latinos and the Logic of the Down Low

Reports of men who have sex with men without publicly acknowledging gay identity have hit a sensitive chord in US society. Finding out that they had a way to refer to their sexuality (*down low*) simplified its discussion, but it suggested this was a self conscious community with some degree of organization.

The possibility that these men were having sex with women triggered a wave of AIDS panic. It reawakened the stigma once attached to "risk groups" long after HIV transmission was reconceptualized in terms of risk behaviors. Men who hide their same-sex or bisexual sexualities predate the first reports of the AIDS epidemic, so what is the basis of this newfound concern?

There are two new elements in this controversy. Since the Stonewall riots LGBT communities have become more visible, and the idea that same-sex sexualities should be understood in terms of LGBT identities has become a truism. The legal and political achievements of the LGBT movement have provided a degree of normalcy to the lives of people who otherwise might have lived as pariahs, but also made it easier to identify "sexual danger" as the number of closeted men and women decreased. Almost synchronically, in blighted US urban neighborhoods, Black and Latino youngsters introduced a complex political and esthetic movement: Hip-Hop. A branch of this cultural vanguard, rap music, became dangerous as its verses reflected the oppression of their communities, sprinkled with misogynous and homophobic statements. The mythical mantle of the dark skinned, lower class, sociopath—once on the back of Black Power soldiers—was bestowed onto male rappers, now regarded as most likely to overthrow the government, or at least, give the establishment some headaches.

Since Black and Latino young men are at the center of the *down low* controversy it is easy to compound the historical sexual danger they represent with the cultural danger Hip-Hop evokes. Their refusal to publicize their stigmatized sexual practices by adopting a stigmatized sexual identity defeats the ["]power["] of heterosexuality to prevent HIV causing resentment and anger. Although the first journalistic reports about the *down low* included young Latinos (Trebay, 2000; Venable, 2001), they quickly faded from the discussion in favor of a focus on African Americans. Like the ostrich, the Latino community working on HIV prevention sticks its head in the ground mumbling *eso es cosa de negros.*[13] Is it really? Are we not *negros* also? If we accept that certain Latino groups, namely Chicanos and Nuyoricans, share a great deal and live in close contact with African Americans, are there any specifically Latino cultural features that provide fertile ground for the development of down low sexualities? . . .

The Sexual Predicament of the Immigrant

Latinos in the US are marked by their linguistic and migratory experiences but also by their exposure to the dominant European American, as well as other cultural groups (Díaz, 1998, 129–136). The comradeship of African American communities and leadership in the Civil Rights Movement, other struggles for equality, as well as local and regional politics, influenced the creation of a single Latino identity and the development of its political protagonism. Blacks and Latinos occupy comparable subaltern positions from which their voices and opinions cross-fertilize. Hip-Hop is an example of a joint endeavor in popular culture. The discussion of *down low* sexual practices should not omit this close connection.

Determining factors of this proximity are the geographical location and the length of time people of different Latin American nationalities have spent in the US. Some Latino groups have closer historical, racial, and geographical links to African Americans than others. Puerto Ricans and African Americans in New York City are an instance of that social and political closeness (Rivera, 2003).

The study of Latino sexualities in the US has to take into account their rank in the racial and socioeconomic hierarchies (Díaz, 1998, 113–127). Like other immigrants before them, most Latin Americans in the US originate from the working and peasant classes of their countries of origin. With the exception of the first wave of [Cuban] immigrants, whose financial assets in the US were established before they fled the revolution, the limited cultural capital of Latin American migrants (Bourdieu, 1977), and the needs of the US labor market, predetermine their insertion in the poorer end of the working-class.

The phenotype of most US Latinos reflects the African and indigenous ancestry of Latin America's lower classes. The racial characteristics and class origin of Latino populations impinge on their location within the US' social structure, and racial system. Their condition as "workers," is the connective tissue between their social position in the US and their ancestry and prior class situation. Latinos' class position also marks their insertion into the US' gay communities and social imaginaries, which they enter not as "comrades," or potential "lovers," but in a range of subaltern roles encoded by national, ethno-racial, and class markers. Just as race does, social class molds sexual experience (Healy, 1996; Gluckman and Reed, 1997; Raffo, 1997; González, 2001). A sensible appraisal of Latino *DL* sexualities should not neglect to look into the roles of class, and the major characteristics of the Latin American sexual/gender system in the development of sexual identities.

The Sex/Gender Baggage

Ethnographic works on Latin American sexual systems abound, but the same is not true about US Latino male sexualities (Parker and Cáceres, 1999). . . .

The ethnographic literature on sexuality and gender in Latin America [asserts] that . . . socialization on these matters starts early in life, and that men have to follow a strict path in expressing their masculinities (Parker, 1991, 59–64; Lancaster, 1992, 41–44; Carrier, 1995, 3–4; Melhuus and Stølen, 1996). During this process, men must exhibit traits that go from bravery to sexual prowess (Parker, 1991, 43–49; Lancaster, 1992, 273–274; Carrier, 1995, 3–21; Gutmann, 1996, 235–236). Failure to fulfill gender scripts, generates doubts about sexual preference (Parker, 1991, 45; Lancaster, 1992, 274). Men are defined not only in contrast to women, but above all, in opposition to subordinated masculinities such as the *maricón* or *faggot* (Connell, 1995, 78).

Héctor Carrillo and Alfredo Mirandé affirm that social class is a factor in how far, and in which way men may stray from the norm in asserting and adopting the masculinity styles. However, for Latin American men in general, avoiding the stigma of homosexuality is a compelling motivation to fulfill gender prescriptions (Mirandé, 1997; Carrillo, 2002; see also Cáceres, 1998; Fuller, 1998). Acquiring gender traits and skills (to talk and walk "like a man," to be courageous, and to bond with *real men*), before becoming sexually active, ensures a young man's peers he is no *maricón,* and improves his chances of becoming a *real man* later on (Parker, 1991, 45; Carrier, 1995, 6–7; Gutmann, 1996, 16–19; Fuller, 1998, 60). Once he obtains the credentials of manhood, his sexuality is expected to follow suit, becoming a real man in his equals' eyes.[14]

This gendering process is not infallible. In my experience, the usual privacy of sexual acts limits peers' ability to assess them. In describing their sexual performance, young men can embellish, correct, or fabricate their accounts (see also Cáceres, 1998, 160). Sexual preference is elicited from verbal declarations or from failure or refusal to follow masculine scripts. Thus, masculine Latino homosexuals can trick the sexual/gender system, avoid stigma, and *pass.*

In light of these depictions of the constrains and possibility for cultural resistance within the Latin American sex/gender system, it is not implausible that a young Latino on the *DL,* like *wite skin,* may be motivated to keep his sexuality under wraps, and trick a sex/gender system that destines him to be stigmatized. He may realize that the *faggot, cochón, maricón,* and even the *Gay man,* are defined/identified through their public presentation. Latino/as in the United States, in observing the gay community's hypermasculine culture (the cowboy, the construction worker, the leather-man, etc.), have gathered sufficient proof that gender and sexuality need not overlap. Their anxiety about non-normative sexualities may have decreased through the work of the LGBT movement, yet they may feel that "Gay" has race, class, and gender implications distant from Latino social, political, and cultural locations (D'Emilio, 1983; Weeks, 1986; Maskovsky, 2002; González, 2004).

Global Identities

. . . The United States' "mainstream" gay community and movement are greatly informed by white middle class style and socio-cultural priorities. One marked disparity between Latino/as and the white middle class in the US is the different weight and expectations placed on the "individual" *vis-à-vis* "family" and/or "community" (Carrier, 1995, 3–10). For many Latino/as "to come out of the closet" implies

making hard choices that prioritize the individual over the communal self. It should not be surprising that some may decide to keep their sexuality on the *down low,* propping up their masculinity on Hip-Hop culture, and retaining full membership in their ethnic group (Díaz, 1998, 89–111).[15] Rejecting gay identity does not mean, for Latinos, relinquishing a political life, as their community of birth provides them a platform and agenda from which to propel themselves as political subjects in equality struggles.[16]

The Down Low as Wake Up Call

Public health efforts should not attempt to herd Latino/as toward a gay or *queer* identity, but should learn instead about their worldviews and design preventive strategies that resonate with them. This effort should include a careful consideration of the socioeconomic, geographic, historical, political, and cultural contexts of sexuality (González, 2001; Muñoz, 2001). . . . This effort should be sensitive to social class, race, gender, and to the imprints left on Latino cultures by their coexistence with other ethno-racial, class, gender and sexual groups. Likewise, the terms "gay" or "MSM" should be enriching analytic tools, and not generic categories muddling with ethnocentric assumptions the specificity of the sexual lives and identities discussed (Meyer, 2001, 856).

Recent reports of the Centers for Disease Control indicate that minorities remain at high risk for contracting HIV. Latino/as remain overrepresented among those with HIV, and MSMs continue to comprise a considerable portion of the HIV epidemic (Wolitski *et al.,* 2001). The number of young men infected sexually, suggests that we need new strategies to engage in a prevention dialogue those now at the onset of their sexual lives. In the 1980s, the Latino community reacted with hesitation to the HIV epidemic. Sexual taboos and disagreements about appropriate strategies to contend with drug use, slowed the progression of the community's response from denial, to debate, to action against the ravages of AIDS. By the 1990s, Latino/as developed wide-ranging and sophisticated strategies to contend with the unique profile of the epidemic in their communities, including, among others, the challenge of serving undocumented immigrants and overcoming linguistic barriers.

The emergence of *down low* sexualities is a new development in HIV prevention. The magnitude of the phenomenon, its possible relationship to unsafe sexual practices, and its role in the increasing rates of HIV infection among Latinas and Black women, remain to be assessed. Whether young men on the *down low* represent a concrete social phenomenon, or are just a fad, their actual or imagined readiness to dispense with gay identity reflects a new sexual sensibility in this population. The cultural connotations of a group marked by race, ethnicity, class, and expressive culture make the *down low* both, a problem, and the means to solve it. Confronting the challenge of providing HIV-related services to this young population opens opportunities for public health to learn from the process. Helping young men *on the low* prevent HIV transmission is both a duty and a gateway into the sexualities of the 21st century.

Cultural features and social location increase the probability that Latino/as are part of this trend. To think Latino/as are protected by their cultural distance from their neighbors is not only wrongheaded, but could have dire consequences. As in politics, we should recognize our allies and join them in struggling for the health of our youth. Yet, five years after the eruption of the *down low debate* in the headlines of the press, the silence of Latino/as, implies this is somebody else's problem.

The experience of gender, ethnic, sexual, and class identities will never be static. New strengths and vulnerabilities will emerge and vanish at every step. The task of updating our understanding of HIV infection risk, and the ideological scaffolding that supports it, will never be finish[ed].

NOTES

1. Pronounced as "caution."
2. They give the impression to be fully aware of the *mismatch* between their sexualities and their public personas, and test the limits of the journalists' naïveté with declarations of unlawful masculinity (Venable, 2001).
3. The CDC has reported in 2002 that HIV-related deaths remain a major cause of death among young and middle age minorities (CDC, 2002a). In 2000, 19% of new AIDS cases were reported among Latinos while they were 13% of the total national population (CDC, 2002b). The Young Men Study Phase I found that among MSM between 15 and 22 years of age in seven US cities, Latinos had an HIV prevalence of 6.9%. Preliminary results from Phase II (23–28 years old) indicate a prevalence of 14% for the same population (MMWR, 2001). Men who have sex with men continue to account for the largest group of HIV infections which indicates that new prevention strategies are needed as younger populations become sexually active (CDC, 2002c).
4. The Internet source *Urban Dictionary* (www.urban dictionary.com), was used for words that have not made it yet into "slang dictionaries." It uses contributors' definitions, and site's visitors can give "thumbs up" or "thumbs down" to signal their agreement. A contributor screen-named *THE TRUTH*, refers to the late rapper Tupac Shakur's definition of *nigga:* "NIGGER—a Black man with a slavery chain around his neck. NIGGA—a Black man with a gold chain on his neck," ([www.urbandictionary.com/define.php?term=nigga&r=f]).
5. *platanoluva:* "An abbreviation for 'black & Latino' used most commonly by young urban *Gay* men of color; 2. A person, place, or thing that is Afro-Latino," (www.urban dictionary.com/define.php?term=blatino&r=f).
6. *Carl Willis:* "Adj. Presenting the outward appearance of one's identification with urban ghetto culture through affected attitudes, mannerisms, language, or dress," ([www.urbandictionary.com/define.php?thugged+out&r=f]).
7. *reyflyinfury619:* "(verb) To hit on, flirt with, or seduce a female by using verbal or sometimes physical means of persuasion," (www.urbandictionary.com/define.php?term=mack&r=f).
8. *me:* "getting your game on, trying to get with a person," (www.urbandictionary.com/define.php?term=kick+it&r=f).
9. Latino, Latin, lat, ltn, Blatino (Black Latino), Rican, Puerto Rock, Chicano, cholo, etc.
10. Papi, chulo, caliente, vato, etc.
11. If his e-mail were, let's say Freddy_Santana@electronicnetwork.com, his screen name would be *Freddy_Santana.*
12. East New York is a Brooklyn area with a reputation of being tough and dangerous like the Bronx.
13. "That's a Black thing."
14. He could lose his standing later in life if he is unable to emerge triumphantly from other tests that life will put to him such as being able to support his family, keeping his female companion from sleeping with other men, etc. (Parker, 1991, 47–49; Valdés and Olavarría, 1998, 33–34).

15. For instance, Aponte-Parés (2001) documents the geographical and political distance of *Queer* Latinos in New York City from mainstream Latino and gay communities.

16. In a study of a largely white cohort of MSM that compared those living in four "gay ghettos" to others living elsewhere, Mills et al. (2001) found that the "ghetto"-based men were more likely to embrace a gay or queer identity and to be involved in the gay community. The other men were less likely to have a gay identity but had not abdicated community involvement and were active in the "non-gay" community. The latter could be compared to men on the *DL* that may find compelling reasons to preserve their full membership in their communities of birth by keeping their sex lives on the *down low*.

REFERENCES

Aponte-Parés, Luis. 2001. "Outside/In: Crossing Queer and Latino Boundaries." In *Mambo Montage: The Latinization of New York,* eds. Agustín Laó Montes and Arleen Dávila, 263–286. New York: Columbia University Press.

Ards, Angela. 1999. "Rhyme and Resist: Organizing the Hip-Hop Generation." *The Nation* 269(4, July 26–August 2): 11–14.

Baker, Paul. 2002. *Fantabulosa: A Dictionary of Polari and Gay Slang.* New York: Continuum.

Ballard, Scotty. 2001. "Why AIDS is Rising among Black Women." *Jet*, July 23.

Basu, Dipa. 1998. "What Is Real about 'Keeping It Real'?" *Postcolonial Studies* 1(3): 371–387.

Bourdieu, Pierre. 1977. "Cultural Reproduction and Social Reproduction." In *Power and Ideology in Education*, eds. Jerome Karabel and A. H. Halsey, 487–511. New York: Oxford University Press.

Bourgois, Philippe. 1996. *In Search of Respect: Selling Crack in El Barrio.* New York: Cambridge University Press.

Cáceres, Carlos. 1998. "Jóvenes Varones en Lima: Dilemas y Estrategias de Salud Sexual." In *Masculinidades y Equidad de Género en América Latina,* eds. Teresa Valdés and José Olavarría, 158–174. Santiago de Chile, Chile: FLACSO-Chile.

Carrier, Joseph. 1995. *De los Otros: Intimacy and Homosexuality Among Mexican Men.* New York: Columbia University Press.

Carrillo, Héctor. 2002. *The Night Is Young: Sexuality in México in the Time of AIDS.* Chicago: University of Chicago Press.

CDC. 2002a. Young People at Risk: HIV/AIDS among America's Youth. Divisions of HIV/AIDS Prevention, March 11.

CDC. 2002b. HIV/AIDS among Hispanics in the United States. Divisions of HIV/AIDS Prevention, March 11.

CDC. 2002c. Need for Sustained HIV Prevention among Men who Have Sex with Men. Divisions of HIV/AIDS Prevention, March 11.

Chung, Cristy, Aly Kim, Zoon Nguyen, Trinity Ordona and Arlene Stein. 1996. "In Our Own Way: a Roundtable Discussion." In *Asian American Sexualities: Dimensions of the Gay and Lesbian Experience,* ed. Russel Leong, 91–99. New York and London: Routledge.

Clay, Andreana. 2003. "Keepin' It Real: Black Youth, Hip-Hop Culture, and Black Identity." *American Behavioral Scientist* 46(10, June): 1346–1358.

Connell, Robert. 1995. *Masculinities.* Berkeley: University of California Press.

D'Emilio, John. 1983. "Capitalism and Gay Identity." In *Powers of Desire: The Politics of Sexuality,* eds. Ann Snitow, Christine Stansell and Sharon Thompson, 100–113. New York: Monthly Review Press.

Denizet-Lewis, Benoit. 2003. "Double Lives on the Down Low." *New York Times Magazine,* August 3.

Díaz, Rafael M. 1998. *Latino Gay Men and HIV: Culture Sexuality, and Risk Behavior.* New York: Routledge.

Edwards, Tamala. 2001. "Men Who Sleep with Men (AIDS Risk to African American Women)." *Essence,* October, p. 76

Escobar, Arturo. 1996. "Welcome to Cyberia: Notes on the Anthropology of Cyberculture." In *Cyberfutures: Culture and Politics on the Information Superhighway,* eds. Ziauddin Sardar and Jerome R. Ravetz, 111–137. New York: New York University Press.

Flores, Juan. 2000. *From Bomba to Hip Hop: Puerto Rican Culture and Latino Identity.* New York: Columbia University Press.

Fuller, Norma. 1998. "La Constitución Social de la Identidad de Género entre Varones Urbanos de Perú." In *Masculinidades y Equidad de Género en América Latina*, eds. Teresa Valdés y José Olavaría, 56–68. Santiago de Chile, Chile: FLACSO-Chile.

Gluckman, Amy and Betsy Reed, eds. 1997. *Homo Economics: Capitalism, Community and Lesbian and Gay Life.* New York: Routledge.

González, M. Alfredo. 2001. "USA Poverty, Globalization and 'Men Who Have Sex with Men.'" Paper presented at the American Ethnological Society Annual Meetings, McGill University, Montreal, Canada, May 3–6.

González, M. Alfredo. 2004. "Sexuality and Love in the Lives of Homeless Men in New York City." Ph.D. dissertation, Graduate Center and University Center, CUNY.

Gordon Jr., William. 2002. "The Real 'Down Low': Hip Hop Culture Producing Queer Identities." Paper presented at the American Anthropological Association Annual Meetings, New Orleans, November 22–24.

Green, Jonathon. 1998. *The Cassell Dictionary of Slang.* London: Cassell.

Gutmann, Mathew. 1996. *The Meanings of Macho: Being a Man in Mexico City.* Berkeley: University of California Press.

Healy, Murray. 1996. *Gay Skins: Class, Masculinity and Queer Appropriation.* London: Cassell.

Hemphill, Essex. ed. 1991. *Brother to Brother: New Writings by Black Gay Men.* Boston: Alyson.

Hemphill, Essex, 1992. *Ceremonies.* New York: Plume.

Lancaster, Roger. 1992. *Life Is Hard: Machismo, Danger, and the Intimacy of Power in Nicaragua.* Berkeley, Los Angeles and Oxford: University of California Press.

Lipsitz, George. 1994. *Dangerous Crossroads: Popular Music, Postmodernism, and the Poetics of Place.* New York: Verso.

Marable, Manning. 2002. "The Politics of Hip Hop—Part Two of Two." *The Free Press,* February 4. http://www.freepress.org/columns/display/4/2002/489.

Mangaoang, Gill. 1996. "From the 1970s to the 1990s: Perspectives of a Gay Filipino American Activist." In *Asian American Sexualities: Dimensions of the Gay and Lesbian Experience,* ed. Russel Leong, 101–111. New York: Routledge.

Marshall, Jonathan. 2003. The Sexual Life of Cyber-Savants. *Australian Journal of Anthropology* 14(2): 229–248.

Maskovsky, Jeff. 2002. "Do We All 'Reek of the Commodity'? Consumption and the Erasure of Poverty in Lesbian and Gay Studies." In *Out in Theory: the Emergence of Lesbian and Gay Anthropology,* eds. Ellen Lewin and William L. Leap, 264–286. Chicago: University of Illinois Press.

Melhuus, Marit and Kristi A. Stølen, eds. 1996. *Machos, Mistresses, Madonnas: Contesting, the Power of Latin American Gender Imagery.* London: Verso.

Meyer, Ilan. 2001. "Why Lesbian, Gay, Bisexual and Transgender Public Health." *American Journal of Public Health* 91(6): 856–859.

Mills, Thomas C., Ron Stall, Lance Pollack, Jay P. Paul, Diane Binson, Jesse Canchola and Joseph A. Catania, 2001. "Health-Related Characteristics of Men who Have Sex with Men: a Comparison of those Living in 'Gay Ghettos' with those Living Elsewhere." *American Journal of Public Health* 91(6): 980–983.

Mirandé, Alfredo. 1997. *Hombres y Machos: Masculinity and Latino Culture.* Boulder, Colorado: Westview Press.

Morbidity and Mortality Weekly Report. 2001. HIV Incidence among Young Men Who Have Sex with Men—Seven U.S. Cities, 1994–2000, Morbidity and Mortality Weekly Report, 50(21): 440–444.

Mukherjea, Ananya and Salvador Vidal-Ortiz. 2002. "Figuring Race Masculinity and Perversion: Interrogating the Elision of White Bisexuality to Black 'Down Low' as Identifiable HIV Risk Factors." Paper presented at the Society for the Study of Social Problems Annual Meetings, Sexuality on the Edge section, Chicago.

Muñoz, Miguel. 2001. The Organization of Sexuality of Bisexually Active Latino Men in New York City, Ph.D. dissertation, Mailman School of Public Health, Columbia University.

Muñoz, Miguel. 2004. "Beyond 'MSM': Sexual Desire among Bisexually-Active Latino Men in New York City." *Sexuality* 7(1): 55–80.

Parker, Richard. 1991. *Bodies, Pleasures and Passions: Sexual Culture in Contemporary Brazil.* Boston: Beacon Press.

Parker, Richard and Carlos Cáceres. 1999. "Alternative Sexualities and Changing Sexual Cultures among Latino American Men." *Culture, Health & Sexuality* 1(3): 201–206.

Raffo, Susan, ed. 1997. *Queerly Classed: Gay Men and Lesbians Write about Class.* Boston, MA: South End Press.

Rivera, Raquel Z. 2001. Hip-Hop, Puerto Ricans, and Ethnoracial Identities in New York. In *Mambo Montage: the Latinization of New York,* eds. Agustín Laó-Montes and Arlene Dávila, 235–261. New York: Columbia University Press.

Rivera, Raquel Z. 2003. *New York Ricans from the Hip Hop Zone.* New York: Palgrave Macmillan.

Smitherman, Geneva. 2000[1994]. *Black Talk; Words and Phrases from the Hood to the Amen Corner,* Revised Edition. Boston: Houghton Mifflin Company.

Suggs, Donald. 2001. "The Gospel According to St. Rufus." *Poz Magazine* May: Vol. 70, 28–31.

Trebay, Guy. 2000. "A Gay Hip-Hop Scene Rises in the Bronx: Homo Thugz Blow Up the Spot." *Village Voice,* February 8.

Venable, Malcolm. 2001. "A Question of Identity." *Vibe Magazine.* July: 98–106.

Weeks, Jeffrey. 1986. *Sexuality.* London: Tavistock.

Wilson, Samuel M. and Leighton C. Peterson. 2002. "The Anthropology of Online Communities." *Annual Review of Anthropology* 31: 449–467.

Wolitski, Richard J., Ronald O. Valdiserri, Paul H. Denning and William C. Levine. 2001. "Are We Headed for a

Resurgence of the HIV Epidemic Among Men who Have Sex with Men?" *American Journal of Public Health* 91(6, June): 883–888.

Wright, Kai. 2001. "The Great Down Low Debate: A New Black Sexual Identity May Be an Incubator for AIDS." *Village Voice*, June 12.

10 Things You Should Know about the DL

Keith Boykin

It's coming again. Get ready for a new round of news stories about the down low. It started [in 2004] with a wave of media hype and sensationalism designed to scare black women about men on the DL. But now . . . it's important to separate fact from fiction in this delicate conversation.

Almost everything we've been told about the down low in recent years is wrong. That's why I've put together a quick list of ten things everyone should know about the down low.

1. The down low is just a black version of "the closet."

The down low is popularly used to refer to men who have sex with men but do not identify as gay or homosexual. Maybe you've heard that concept before. Long ago, we called it "the closet." The term "down low" is just a new way of describing a very old thing, but it's the hot new buzz word of the moment.

2. The down low is not new.

The phrase itself may be new, but the practice is as old as history. Men have been secretly sleeping with men since the beginning of time. And married men have been doing the same thing. The only thing new is what we call it.

3. The down low is not just a black thing.

When Jim McGreevey, the governor of New Jersey, announced [in 2004] that he had cheated on his wife with another man, no one bothered to make the obvious point—Governor McGreevey had been on the down low. When white men do it, we call it what it is and move on. When black men do the same thing, we want to pathologize it. Therein lies a double standard.

4. The down low is not simply a gay thing.

The term "down low" entered the mainstream of black popular culture in the early 1990s. In 1993, Salt-n-Pepa recorded a song called "Whatta Man" that mentioned the down low. In 1994, TLC recorded a song called "Creep"

about a woman on the down low. In 1995, Brian McKnight recorded his song, "On the Down Low," about a woman named Maxine on the DL. Then in 1996 and 1998, R. Kelly recorded not one, but two songs about the down low.

We laughed about it when it was a heterosexual thing, but suddenly we became alarmed when we "discovered" that gay and bisexual men were on the down low too. There's another double standard. In reality, the down low is simply about cheating, whether heterosexual, homosexual or bisexual.

5. The down low is not the cause of the black AIDS epidemic.

In 2003 (the last year in which we have full CDC data available) there were more than 7,000 black female AIDS cases reported in the United States. Out of that number, only 118 reported "sex with a bisexual male" as the method of exposure. That's just 1.6 percent of all black female AIDS cases. Believe it or not, there are other ways to get infected besides having sex with a man on the down low. Many women are also becoming infected through injection drug use, sex with an injection drug user, and sex with a heterosexual (not down low) man.

Focusing on the down low misleads women to think that the down low is a health threat instead of HIV. That's a serious mistake. A man on the down low who is HIV negative cannot pass the virus to you, but a straight man who is not on the down low could easily give you HIV if he is infected with the virus. The down low does not cause AIDS. HIV causes AIDS.

6. The down low discussion is a distraction from the real issues.

All the time we've spent sensationalizing the down low in the past few years is time we could have spent talking about solutions to the AIDS epidemic in our communities.

On an individual level, we need to encourage men and women to exercise personal responsibility. On an institutional level, we need to mobilize our churches, fraternities, sororities and civic organizations so they can provide reliable safe sex information, HIV testing, and nonjudgmental counseling. And on a public policy level, we need to talk about free testing facilities, needle exchange programs, condoms in prison, targeted AIDS prevention funding, resources for low-income people living with AIDS, and safe sex education in public schools. That's the dialogue we should be having.

7. There are no "signs" to tell if a man is on the down low.

There are going to be a lot of people out there trying to tell you how to find out if your man is on the DL. Don't waste your time. The whole point of the down low is that these are people who do not want to be detected. The moment you come up with a "guidebook" to give you some warning signs is the moment when men on the down low will devise new strategies to elude you.

8. Becoming a "down low detective" is not the answer.

Log onto various Internet web sites about the down low, and you'll find lots of information about how to spy on your partner. Sure, you could hire a private investigator to follow him around when he goes to work, but what does that say about your relationship? If you do suspect something is fishy, you may be in for a shocking surprise. Your man may be cheating on you—with another woman!

A better solution is to confront the homophobia in our community that contributes to the down low. If we want to stop the down low, then we need to create a climate where men (and women) don't feel the need to be on the down low in the first place. Then we won't have as many men who feel forced into fake relationships to keep the parents, friends and nosey neighbors out of their lives.

9. Demonizing men on the down low will not make them straight.

One popular response to the down low is to demonize all down low men as villains. That may make us feel a little better for a moment, but it won't change the reality of who they are. In fact, demonizing men on the down low is more likely to push these men further into denial about their sexuality. People often ask, "Why don't these men simply come out and say they're gay?" That's a good question, but as long as we keep demonizing homosexuality, don't expect any mass confessions to happen anytime soon.

10. Stereotyping women as victims will not keep them safe.

Much of the discussion about the down low recently has portrayed women as "victims" of black men. Framing the issue this way disempowers women from the ability to protect themselves, reinforces negative stereotypes about black men and encourages an unhealthy battle of the sexes in the black community.

The media machine behind the down low business (and it is a business) has tried to exploit women's fears about the DL in order to make a quick buck. But fear is not the answer. Education is. Knowledge is power, and all women and men need to know the truth.

Source: Boykin, Keith. 2005. "10 Things You Should Know About the DL." www.keithboykin.com. Reprinted by permission.

Sexual Spanking,
the Self, and Deviance

Rebecca F. Plante

The . . . activity described in this [reading] is . . . called erotic spanking. The focus is on spanking in a sexualized context, as a form of sexual discipline, not as corporal punishment. Erotic spanking is generally regarded as a form of bondage/domination and sadomasochism; spankings may be done over clothing, undergarments, or on the bare buttocks. The purpose of erotic spanking is for the emotional and sexual gratification of either or both parties. This kind of spanking is exactly the kind pop music star Madonna sang about: "Treat me like I'm a bad girl, even when I'm being good to you, I don't want you to thank me, you can just spank me. Mmm" (Madonna & Leonard, 1990). This is spanking as an erotic punishment, as part of fantasy scenes of misbehavior, but not as part of a wider array of sadomasochistic activities.

The research highlights the activities of a group of heterosexual men who like to spank consensual heterosexual women. Several questions frame this research. How do "sexual minorities" understand and make sense of their socially stigmatized sexual interests? How do they mitigate the effects of stereotypical and negative sexual scripting? And what is the larger social context for a type of sexual conduct that might appear, at first glance and for the average audience, to be the province of only a few individuals? . . .

This [reading] is an attempt to describe several aspects of erotic, sexual(ized) spanking. Social context provides a lens through which participants situate their sexual interests. Participants know about broader cultural narratives and constructions of "normal," and are aware that their interests are often stigmatized and defined as deviant. . . . [T]hey work to redefine deviance via several strategies and techniques for neutralizing stigma. They collect and share pop cultural references to sexualized spanking and suggest that most people are interested in spanking but simply do not know it. The participants in this research also differentiate themselves from sadomasochistic practitioners, defining themselves as solely interested in "the bottom," or the buttocks, and in fantasies and scenes specifically involving the erotic tableau of a man spanking a woman.

This [reading] focuses on a party attended by the group of heterosexual men and women referred to above, that is, primarily men who wished to spank women and women who wished to be spanked by men. . . .

"Self Stories": The Context
of Sexualized Spanking

. . . [T]he need for research on . . . spanking is related to the usual questions: . . . "Why does someone have this deviant sexual interest?" Really the question should be, "Why does anyone have the sexual interests he/she has, whether those interests are 'mainstream' or outside the mainstream?"

To begin to answer the latter question, it is useful to consider the sociological and cultural scripting of sexuality. Gagnon and Simon (1973) first advanced the idea of sexual scripts, the sociological blueprints that shape our sexual interests. Scripts specify the who, what, where, when, why and how of sexualities and sexual practices. Scripts can be cultural, subcultural, interpersonal, or intrapsychic. Intrapsychic scripts include the stories we tell ourselves, our memories, our internal rehearsals; we develop intrapsychic, or mental,

From "Sexual Spanking, the Self, and the Construction of Deviance" by Rebecca F. Plante (2006), *Journal of Homosexuality,* 50, 59–79.

scripts based on cues from culture, subculture, and interactions. Interpersonal scripts develop primarily from interactions we have with others. Subcultural scripts would include discourses, ideologies, and expectations at the local or small-group level, e.g., according to ethnic or religious group. Cultural scripts include discourses, ideologies, and expectations at the national level.

Standard cultural scripts do not include such things as sexualized spanking. Rather, the standard script eroticizes the basics of (hetero)sexual activity: kissing, breast fondling, genital stimulation, and penile-vaginal intercourse (Laumann, Gagnon, Michael, & Michaels, 1994). How then would someone adapt this basic cultural script? How would an individual with a larger cultural context for sexuality expand the script to include sexualized spanking? And how does one adapt the script to include an attribute that is potentially stigmatizing?

Stigma is defined as an attribute that is discrediting to an individual's self (Goffman, 1963). Those interested in spanking can be said to have a discreditable stigma, or one that can be hidden. Goffman wrote, "Even where an individual has quite abnormal feelings and beliefs, he is likely to have quite normal concerns and employ quite normal strategies in attempting to conceal these abnormalities from others" (p. 131). Awareness of a stigmatizing condition requires impression management, to determine to whom the attribute will be revealed, with the goal of maintaining control over the discreditable attribute. The two "coping mechanisms" most applicable to this research are acceptance of the attribute, and overt rejection of the dominant norms that compel the discrediting in the first place. Some of this norm rejection can be seen when a spanking aficionado implies that everyone is actually interested in spanking (we just may not know it yet).

Brekhus described another form of rejection of dominant norms. He suggests, "Minority subcultures . . . develop oppositional constructions that parody the 'sexual mainstream'" (1996, p. 513). One strategy is to label those who do not engage in radical sex as "vanilla." The implication is that those with "mainstream" sexual interests are conformist, bland, uninteresting, and unadventurous, representing the lowest common denominator of sexualities (Taylor & Ussher, 2001). Turning the mainstream into a negatively-labeled population enables the sexual radical to reject standard cultural scripting, thus normalizing the self. This is a fairly straightforward form of stigma management.

One strategy for rendering the sexual self is to construct a story describing its attributes, tracing its history, and locating it within the nexus of cultural sexual scripting. . . . The stories that spanking aficionados construct are patterned and do describe the nature of the interest, its genesis, and the normalization techniques the individual employs. But it is worth noting that nearly all sexual stories . . . address how the actor fits him or herself into broader social contexts.

In describing postmodern sexualities, Simon noted the tendency to essentialize sexualities of all forms, locating them within genes or innate tendencies (1996). The culturally-motivated interest in essentializing is linked to the social construction of acceptable and unacceptable sexual practices. Simon said, "Once the normal is constructed, its explanation organizes our understanding of all other variations by moving us to conceive of all other outcomes as violations or variations of the logic of the normal" (p. 14). So spanking is viewed within this context as a violation of the normal, thus requiring an explanation of how and why the interest develops. . . .

[F]or those interested in sexual spanking, the construction of the self relies on cultural contexts and recognition of the reality of stigma. There are "vanilla" cultural scripts providing the foundation for identity development, wherein aficionados see that their interests deviate from the narrowly-rendered norms. To address these stigmatizing interests, individuals must develop coping strategies and design culturally and subculturally meaningful "sexual stories." The spanking aficionados' stories that follow address the management of external stigma and provide a script for stigmatizable behavior within the group.

Methods

Participants and Fieldwork

This research describes fieldwork with participants in a loosely-organized group of consensual adults interested in sexual spanking. . . . Because of the sensitivity of the topic, participants are described as generally as possible. Since this research included observation, it is appropriate to explicitly situate the author in the fieldwork. Access to the group occurred via a key informant, Jim, a longtime member of the "scene." After meeting at a professional conference, we had had many general, nonsexual conversations before he mentioned that he had always been interested in spanking. . . . Jim was aware that my interests were solely research-related. . . . I never led him on or misrepresented myself to gain access. . . . All research was confined to observation only.

Jim provided access to a complex and dynamic community of spanking aficionados. The fieldwork included spanking parties, discreetly held in small-town hotels on floors far from hotel traffic, formal interviews and casual conversations, and observations of private scenes between two people. Supplemental research included reading spanking stories, spanking newsletters and magazines. Participants' toy boxes were examined, replete with paddles, straps, hairbrushes, and whips. The research ultimately expanded to include other aspects of the larger world of sadomasochism. This led to observations in sex clubs, scanning of Web sites, interviews with those who incorporate SM into their sexual activities, and visits to commercial ventures, such as Boston's "Fetish Fair." Analysis of the local context of spanking is enhanced by an understanding of the larger context of sexual radicals. The fieldwork took place in Boston, New Hampshire, metro New York, New Jersey, and Atlanta, beginning in 1993 and ending in 2000.

Similarly to SM practitioners, men outnumbered women at this party almost three to one (Brame, Brame & Jacobs, 1993). Most of the approximately 50 attendees were from the East Coast, were between the ages of 30 and 70, and were white-collar professionals. All but one of the attendees were Caucasian. Not all attendees participated in formal and informal interviews; however, about 25 did.

Spanking Stories and Strategies of Neutralization

The narratives offered by the participants to explain or situate their interests in spanking are strikingly similar to narratives offered by others who

adapt standard cultural sexual scripts. Men who like to spank said that they had had this interest for as long as they could remember. . . . Women who like to be spanked said that it took them many years to realize that they were interested. . . . The men tended to essentialize their interests while the women tended to locate them in interpersonal scripting, describing partners who assisted the development of the interest. Both men and women, but particularly men, explained their interests by asserting that everyone has hidden desires about spanking. . . .

[R]esearch on SM has documented gender gaps. [Breslow, Evans & Langley] (1985) surveyed 130 men and 52 women, self-identified SM practitioners. They found that 90% of the men and 60% of the women had acknowledged SM interests by their early twenties. But by age 14, more than 50% of men had identified an SM interest. In Damon's study of 342 male SM participants, the overwhelming majority of the sample (93%) reported having childhood/adolescent SM related fantasies (2002). As an impression management strategy to neutralize stigma, essentializing culturally-defined deviance is not uncommon, as in, "I was born this way, this is hard-wiring, I have no choice, so don't discriminate against me."

Some did offer stories of having been spanked as children, and having made a connection at those early moments between sexual arousal and the punishment being received. This neutralization strategy seems designed to imply that the individual has not consciously orchestrated or chosen this sexual interest. . . . Others were never spanked as children but asserted a longstanding interest in spanking nonetheless. Christina told me her "coming-out" story, as she called it. Ever since she could remember, she thought about spanking (as a five-year-old, for example) and wanted to be spanked. She thought she was weird and thought it best to keep it to herself for most of her life. Preston recalled vividly the first time he developed an interest in spanking: He was 12 years old and saw an ad depicting "a beautiful woman's bottom." He looked at it and thought, "That's ripe for a spanking."

But the narratives differed slightly from person to person and encompassed broader aspects of the interest. Jim had been married for over 30 years. He could not precisely pinpoint the development of his interest in spanking, and although he had started a related business, in his private life there was a disjuncture. His wife knew that he enjoyed spanking but refused to participate and did not attend parties. Jim, Christina, and other participants described spanking relationships that did not include intercourse or other stereotypically sexual activities. These relationships were forged with trust—female participants noted that trust was essential for a good scene—and comfort. The focus was on playing out fantasy scenes and men providing erotic/sexual discipline. However, Christina and Belinda had confessed their interests to the men whom they later married. These husbands were able to adapt their sexual scripts to include spanking and discipline along with more "vanilla" sexual practices. Including spanking in these relationships enabled these and other women participants to feel much less alone, "less freakish," as Christina said.

Outside the context of relationships, it was difficult for participants to fully accept and understand themselves. Initially, Michael thought that he was the only person in the world who was into this "bizarre perversion." Once he had "been in the scene" for 4 or 5 years and discovered publications on spanking, he felt that he was not alone. . . .

Several participants combed more general publications for mentions of spanking. Jim was extremely knowledgeable about popular culture references to spanking, even nonsexualized but seemingly sexually-charged references. He situated his interest by arguing that everyone needs to try sexualized spanking, and that there is nothing "deviant" about his interests. About spanking aficionados, he did say, "We wonder about ourselves and our 'perversion' endlessly."

Newer participants were especially prone to these musings. Andrew said, "You know, I can't believe that I'm here. I look around and wonder what the hell I'm doing here. I mean, I'm not like these other people. This isn't all I do or anything." He was trying to neutralize any stigma to himself by comparing himself to the other party-goers. He implied that the others had a single-minded focus on spanking—but he was "normal," his interest in spanking was just a small piece of his identity. . . .

Another stigma neutralization followed this path, an attempt to broaden spanking parties beyond the ostensible reason for gathering. . . . Michael said, "Especially among the men, there's this tendency to talk about sports, politics—anything but spanking." In dancing around . . . the subject that had drawn the group together, participants could diminish its seeming importance and, like Andrew, present the impression that they have interests and identities beyond spanking.

Another stigma neutralization strategy was common among spanking aficionados. Many men took care to mention that those interested in spanking were "different" from those who were interested in SM more generally. There is a spectrum of activities included in SM, including play with whips, bondage devices, clothing (e.g., latex, leather), and role playing. . . . [P]articipants generally defined SM as "truly kinky" and "where the real weirdos go." In this strategy, one group denigrates another "fringe" group in order to mitigate the stigmatizing effects: "We are more normal than they are; they are the true deviants."

The Party and Subcultural Rules

. . . [The party described in this reading] was a social event where people of like minds could meet; some planned rendezvous with people they had only corresponded with previously. Some planned scenes with people who were essentially regular spanking dates. Rendezvous and planned scenes tended to be focused on spanking and fantasies only. Penile-vaginal and oral intercourse were limited to marital and dating partners, according to most participants. One married couple described their spanking scenes as separate from but also integral to intercourse.

Party organizers had leeway in terms of how much planning to do. Men tended to simply arrange the time, place, and some basic snacks, while women tended to make more elaborate preparations, including decorating and organizing public spankings and demonstrations. Occasionally, partygoers would provide their own public demonstrations, playing out a scene in the main gathering space while attendees watched avidly.

The organizer of this particular party had planned a "Bid-A-Swat" auction. The women at the party would bid on men with the number of swats they wanted to receive. The men were expected to display forearms, biceps, and handspans. The female auction host demonstrated her handspan for comparison, so that bidding women could assess the spanking potential of the men. Finally, each man was told to say, in his sternest possible voice, "Young lady, get over my knee now!" The most stereotypically attractive men, the men with the largest handspans, and two men who were known to be "good spankers" were bid on the most.

A group of six women monopolized the bidding. Many of the women made comments about one particular woman, Annalisa, because of her bidding behavior. She had won a cute young man with a high bid of 600 swats, after already having won a large-handed man with a bid of 400 swats. When two other women grouped their bid to get a total of 500 swats from Michael (known as a "good spanker," someone with just the right touch, sternness, and trustworthiness), they asked Annalisa if she was splitting her 600-swat bid with anyone.

"No," she responded emphatically, and seemed offended at the suggestion that she would share her swats with anyone. Behind Annalisa's back, the other women were moved to judge her behavior. One said, "There's no way she can do all that! She's going to need a pillow on the plane back!" The other women who had been bidding whispered to each other, "Wow, she's crazy," and looked at her disdainfully.

These women attributed her apparent desire to receive over 1000 swats from several men as simply a function of masochism—vaguely defined as, "a person who specifically enjoys receiving pain" (Wiseman, 1996, p. 372). The women at the party did not link spanking with masochism, pain, or SM. Belinda told me, "It's more about knowing that someone cares enough to discipline me, to keep me in line when I act like a brat." In other words, the women's desire to be spanked was seen as an emotionally-laden activity within a caring context, not as a desire for pain or humiliation. One man captured the group's shared distinction between SM and spanking:

> It's tough for male first-timers to get to spank anyone, because there is a shortage of women and they like to go with men they know they can trust. It's also difficult to know a woman's limits the first few times you spank, because there she is crying out "No, no, stop," and your natural inclination is to heed her cries.

This hints at a presumed difference between sadism and spanking, with participants believing that men who spank do so for the emotional fulfillment of women—not to hurt them. . . . Male participants did admit that there was an erotic charge in having "a squirming, bare-bottomed woman over your knee," as Cooper explained. Thus the apparently unspoken "Goldilocks" rule was revealed: There is a just-right amount of spanking to administer or receive, a just-right amount of discipline to desire, and a just-right amount of eroticism. . . .

Other apparently unspoken rules were revealed when one woman dared to offer to spank men. Since this party was billed and constructed as a gathering of women who liked to be spanked and men who liked to do the spanking, most of the women were offended by this act of switching. Only four men ended up bidding on the woman's services; she looked uncomfortable throughout the mini-auction. She refused to say, "Young man, get over my knee, now!" Finally, she offered to let all the men come to her room, so she could line them up and spank them all.

Some of the party-goers were in awe of this woman's offer, but most seemed disdainful of the fact that she was switching, knowing that she would spank men and also be spanked herself. "She doesn't even know what she is," one woman said. The woman who switched did have her limits, however. Melanie asked if she would spank women too and the very cold response was "No." While she was clearly seen as deviant in this particular setting, she remained resolutely heterosexual, in accordance with broader cultural scripts about sexual orientation.

However, in line with the subcultural scripting in this particular community, all of the behavior described above was transgressive. A woman wanting too many swats, from more than one man, all of whom were strangers to her—this was outside the unspoken rules. A woman offering to spank men at an event that had been constructed with specific roles and rules—only men spank women—was also deviant for this community. Before the party, a male participant had said, "Women who want to spank are borderline with being tops in the SM scene. Most [heterosexual] men in the spanking scene would be loathe to admit an interest in being spanked, as opposed to men in the SM scene." The most bitter judgment was reserved for transgressive women and not levied on the men who offered their bottoms or their multiple swats. . . .

Discussion

The Cultural Context of Sexualized Spanking

The participants . . . delighted in publicizing and analyzing public and pop cultural references to spanking, as a way to inscribe the "normality" of their interests. Particularly pleasing were anecdotes that participants thought hinted at the sexualized component of the activity, even if one needed to split hairs to find the sexual symbolism. . . . [S]everal participants recounted the spanking activities in the household of all-American singer and entertainer Pat Boone. One said, "There was far too much spanking going on in that house for it to lack any sexual charge for him." Many knew that page 37 of Cherry Boone O'Neill's autobiographical account of anorexia nervosa (1982) contains the following:

> I knew disobedience would result in swift, sure punishment. For the most part I was compliant, so spankings were relatively infrequent. I was strangely thankful for the uncommon spanking I did receive because it created a kind of penitential release for me—a victory over the nagging, inner torment of guilt. There would be a time of praying, crying, and hugging after the punishment and this seemed to give me a new lease on life.

This was precisely the kind of anecdote my informants enjoyed most, because they interpreted it to mean that Cherry actually enjoyed this form of punishment. However, it is a stretch to interpret this passage as having sexual symbolism. Chances are that the average reader would not have seen this as an example of erotic, sexual(ized) punishment. Rather, the average reader would probably see this as a child reflecting on a parent's corporal punishment.

More contemporary cultural references to more sexualized spanking were recounted by participants. Did you know that a London politician raved about the joy of spanking children on a popular morning television program (Wheen, 1996)? Or that the

British Chancellor of the Exchequer rented his basement to a dominatrix who said, "I'll test your limits with caning. There are two ways of hitting—where you leave a mark and where you don't" (Barber, 1991). Or that a Maryland lawyer spanked secretaries and clients, making one teenaged employee write, "If I continue to make stupid, no-brainer mistakes . . . I will have to be turned over Mr. Goldsborough's knee" (Roberts, Grove, Hendrickson, & Harden, 1992). A dean at Louisiana State University spanked a professor, chanting "You're a bad girl," while another dean apparently watched and laughed (Ruark, 1999).

Madonna's casual and favorable treatment of spanking in a song also delighted participants (Madonna & Leonard, 1990), and around that time, sparked a wave of celebrity references to spanking. The *Arsenio Hall Show,* an early 1990s late-night talk show hosted by a comedian/actor, twice had guests who extolled the virtues of a good spanking. Actor Robert Pastorelli of *Murphy Brown,* a popular early 1990s sitcom depicting a stubborn, clever female television journalist, commented that actor Candice Bergen (who played Murphy Brown) could use a good spanking. When Hall asked him if all assertive women ought to be spanked, and if Pastorelli did this sort of thing often, Pastorelli said that he had never spanked a woman who didn't deserve it. Singer Johnny Gill commented that singer Bobby Brown (both formerly of the 1980s pop band New Edition) would have to get a spanking if he did not stop challenging Gill to public singing competitions. Participants also pointed out that FM radio talk show host and "shock jock" Howard Stern mentioned spanking quite a bit in his autobiography, *Private Parts,* and that actors Ryan O'Neal and Farrah Fawcett had made veiled references to her being spanked during their long-term relationship. Stern had also tried to get NBC to broadcast him spanking a woman on host Jay Leno's late-night television variety show, but censors refused.

Popular references to spanking seemed to spring up everywhere. In New York, an SM restaurant opened in 1997, offering patrons spankings from the "Special Fare" menu . . . (Marin, 1998). Commentators noted that SM-related themes had become trendy. "Does naughty fashion need a spanking?"

asked Guy Trebay in a report on the spring designer collections, which were influenced by leather and fetishwear (2000, p. 12). A 2003 episode of MTV's *The Real World* featured some of the cast of the Las Vegas season spanking each other in a public skit in a nightclub.

What is the significance of these widely available references to an activity that may have clear sexual meanings to some but only punitive meanings to others, and both to still others? For spanking aficionados, these references are like unpolished gems, indicative of the larger social context of their particular sexual interests. They believe that the more casual and nonsexual anecdotes show an overwhelming cultural fascination with corporal punishment in all forms, and offer these anecdotes as proof that they are neither alone nor deviant in their interests. The efforts within the spanking community to delineate themselves from and disavow SM practices are offered as proof, again, that they are not deviant or, at the least, not as deviant as others. . . .

So what does this brief foray into one sexual subculture suggest about sexual scripts, neutralization of stigma, impression management, and the development of the sexual self? First, we might conclude that social norms are pervasive, even in a sexually radical subculture. This subculture's participants compared themselves to each other, made microlevel distinctions about the just-right, or Goldilocks, amount of spanking, and offered justifications for their interests. There were within-group judgments, redefinitions, and stigma neutralization techniques. This echoes the discourses that surround us in the cultural scripting of "normal" and "deviant" (e.g., Simon, 1996).

As for the development of both adaptive sexual scripts and the sexual self, it is harder to make conclusive statements based on these minimal data. It is safe to say that sexualities are enormously complex. The sexual self is clearly fluid, variable, and is simultaneously individually and culturally contextualized. Sexual scripts are basic blueprints, yes, but clearly they can be adapted and revised for the user. Sexual spanking should be viewed as one of the many sexual adaptations individuals make, based on interactions and changes to intrapsychic and interpersonal scripts. An expanded view of sexualities, seen as the potent interaction between cultures and individuals instead of as a series of "rights and wrongs," can only benefit all who seek to find sexual paths of comfort, pleasure, and pain.

It is inadequate to ask about the justifications and self stories of those who participate in sexualized spanking. We need to ask larger questions. Why does anyone do what they do sexually? Why be so concerned about "normal" or "abnormal" sexuality involving consenting adults? Ultimately, there is far more work to be done in this and other subcultures, and, as importantly, in the wide open "mainstream" of sexualities.

REFERENCES

Barber, L. (1991, April 21). Lynn Barber's base thoughts. *The Independent,* p. 21.

Brame, G. G., Brame, W. D., & Jacobs, J. (1993). *Different loving: An exploration of the world of sexual dominance and submission.* New York: Villard Books.

Brekhus, W. (1996). Social marking and the mental coloring of identity: Sexual identity construction and maintenance in the United States. *Sociological Forum,* 11, 497–522.

Breslow, N., Evans, L., & Langley, J. (1985). On the prevalence and roles of females in the sadomasochistic subculture: Report on an empirical study. *Archives of Sexual Behavior,* 14, 303–317.

Damon, W. D. (2002). Patterns of power: A test of two approaches to understanding sadomasochistic sexual behavior in heterosexual men. Unpublished manuscript. University of Illinois, Chicago.

Gagnon, J. H. & Simon, W. (1973). *Sexual conduct: The social sources of human sexuality.* Chicago: Aldine Publishing Company.

Goffman, E. (1963). *Stigma: Notes on the management of spoiled identity.* New York: Touchstone/Simon & Schuster.

Laumann, E. O., Gagnon, J. H., Michael, R. T., & Michaels, S. (1994). *The social organization of sexuality: Sexual practices in the United States.* Chicago: University of Chicago Press.

Madonna, & Leonard, P. (1990). Hanky panky. On I'm breathless: Dick Tracy, music from and inspired by the film [CD]. Los Angeles: Warner Brothers.

Marin, R. (1998, January 5). Lick me, flog me, buy me! *Newsweek,* p. 85.

O'Neill, C. B. (1982). *Starving for attention.* New York: Continuum.

Roberts, R., Grove, L., Hendrickson, P., & Harden, B. (1992, December 31). Whatever happened to . . . ? *The Washington Post,* p. C1.

Ruark, J. (1999, January 29). LSU professor charges that dean spanked her. *Chronicle of Higher Education,* p. A16.

Simon, W. (1996). *Postmodern sexualities.* London: Routledge.

Taylor, G. W. & Ussher, J. M. (2001). Making sense of s&m: A discourse analytic account. *Sexualities,* 4, 293–314.

Trebay, G. (2000, October 31). A detour into naughty for last season's nice girls. *The New York Times,* p. 12.

Wheen, F. (1996, October 31). Swish of the big stick. *The Guardian,* p. T2.

Wiseman, J. (1996). *SM101: A realistic introduction.* San Francisco: Greenery Press.

chapter 7

Sexual Disease

Spotlight on Research

An interview with . . .

Claire Sterk

Claire Sterk, Ph.D., is Charles Howard Candler Professor in Public Health in the Department of Behavioral Sciences and Health Education at the Rollins School of Public Health of Emory University in Atlanta, Georgia. Her research interests include HIV/AIDS, mental health and drug use, sexuality, and women's health. In addition to being the author of *Fast Lives: Women Who Use Crack Cocaine* (Temple University Press, 1999) and *Tricking and Tripping: Prostitution in the Era of AIDS* (Social Change Press, 1999), Dr. Sterk has written numerous journal articles about these issues.

What led you to begin studying sexuality?

My initial interest was triggered less by scientific curiosity to learn more about the topic, and more by the way in which scholars interested in sexuality are viewed. When studying sexuality, researchers are expected to justify their interest, and if they don't, they may be accused of being "deviant" or even "perverse." Growing up in the Netherlands, a country where prostitution has been legalized, I frequently encountered challenges of why I, as a social scientist, would be interested in the sex industry. An answer often was not expected, as the persons asking the question also volunteered answers such as, "you must have been involved in the sex industry," or "you use scholarship to satisfy your own sexual curiosity."

Which of your projects have you found most interesting?

Maybe because it was one of my first research endeavors in the area of sexuality, but a study of street prostitutes in the 1980s left an incredible impact on me. At that time, prostitution as a victimless crime was being challenged, the connection between prostitution and drug use was accentuated by the emerging crack cocaine epidemic, and the role of prostitution in the spread of HIV/AIDS was discussed. Prostitution reveals a society's views on gender and sexuality. In our society, prostitution traditionally was associated with social pathology and only in the last few decades have theories emerged that address the impact of gender role expectations, power differences, social constraints, and social policies on the lives of women. Through in-depth life history interviews with women involved in prostitution, I learned that their sexual behavior largely was determined by social, and not individual, factors. For example, trading sex for money or other material goods had little or no connection with the women's sexual desires. More important were factors such as economic opportunities, survival, and discrimination based on gender, race, and class.

Why is it important to do sex research?

Sex is an important part of human behavior and it is much more complex than often assumed. For instance, sex serves more than reproductive purposes. Sex research also requires an interdisciplinary approach and it forces students and researchers to look beyond their own disciplinary boundaries. As Foucault pointed out, sexuality needs to be understood in its sociohistorical context and is socially constructed. Such a perspective allows for placing sex research in the larger context of the social and behavioral sciences and it forces a continued discussion of sex as well as gender and its influence on people's lives. More recently, sex research has gained popularity among public health scholars. This is largely driven by the HIV/AIDS epidemic. A key route of transmission for the virus causing AIDS is through unprotected sex. Not only has this interest made sex research more respectable, it also has shown the complexities of linking sexual identity and sexual behaviors.

What ethical dilemmas have you faced? How did you resolve them?

When using a qualitative research paradigm, combined with a feminist orientation, studying sex and sexuality raises a multitude of ethical dilemmas. To mention a few: the woman who realizes that she has been prostituting herself without recognizing it; the man who describes his views on sex and in the process starts realizing that he is homosexual; the woman who reflects on her first sexual encounter, which happened to have been abusive; or, the man who knows he has a sexually transmitted disease, maybe even AIDS, but who refuses to use a condom. There is no simple solution to such situations. When people encounter sexual discoveries, it is important to remain a researcher who is supportive and willing to assist, but who does not pretend to be a social worker or psychotherapist. When dealing with abuse situations, either with the person who was abused or the abuser, it is important to withhold judgment. At the same time, there is the legal obligation of having to report certain types of abuse. When discovering that a person might cause others to become sick, in the case of AIDS—a disease for which there is no cure—it might be difficult to adhere to the promise of confidentiality. The key is to be honest to yourself and the study participants.

How do people react when they discover you are a sex researcher?

As I mentioned earlier, when presenting myself as a sexuality researcher, people assume there is some hidden reason. I can't count how many times I have been asked if I study prostitution because I am a prostitute, maybe was one in the past, or maybe want to become one. Typically, the more uncomfortable people feel with sex and sexuality, the more negatively they will react to the discovery of me doing sexuality research. A response that works well is to turn the tables and to indicate that the response reveals a lot about the person in question. It either creates silence or opens the door for a more constructive dialogue.

If you could teach people one thing about sex, what would it be?

You need to look at it from an interdisciplinary perspective. It is biology, psychology, sociology, and much more.

—Interviewed by Denise Donnelly

Tracking the Hidden Epidemics

Centers for Disease Control and Prevention

STDs are one of the most under-recognized health problems in the country today. Despite the fact that STDs are extremely widespread, have severe and sometimes deadly consequences, and add billions of dollars to the nation's healthcare costs each year, most people in the United States remain unaware of the risks and consequences of all but the most prominent STD—the human immunodeficiency virus or HIV.

While extremely common, STDs are difficult to track. Many people with these infections do not have symptoms and remain undiagnosed. Even diseases that are diagnosed are frequently not reported and counted. These "hidden" epidemics are magnified with each new infection that goes unrecognized and untreated. . . .

Magnititude of the Epidemics Overall

More than 25 diseases are spread primarily through sexual activity, and the trends for each disease vary considerably, but together these infections comprise a significant public health problem.

The latest estimates indicate that there are 15 million new STD cases in the United States each year (Cates, 1999). Approximately one-fourth of these new infections are in teenagers. And while some STDs, such as syphilis, have been brought to all time lows, others, like genital herpes, gonorrhea, and chlamydia, continue to resurge and spread through the population.

Because there is no single STD epidemic, but rather multiple epidemics, discussions about trends

From "Tracking the Hidden Epidemics: Trends in STDs in the United States, 2000" by Centers for Disease Control and Prevention. Retrieved from www.cdc.gov.

over time and populations affected must focus on each specific STD. More is known about the frequency and trends of some STDs than others, since many of the diseases are difficult to track. Not including HIV, the most common STDs in the U.S. are chlamydia, gonorrhea, syphilis, genital herpes, human papillomavirus, hepatitis B, trichomoniasis and bacterial vaginosis. . . .

Answers to the Most Frequently Asked Questions

Are STDS Increasing or Decreasing in the United States?

It depends on the disease. The latest scientific data suggest that chlamydia has declined in areas with screening and treatment programs, but remains at very high levels. For the first time in nearly two decades, gonorrhea is on the rise, increasing more than nine percent from 1997 to 1999, after a 72 percent decline from 1975 to 1997. An increase in drug-resistant gonorrhea has been seen in Hawaii and in small clusters in other states. Syphilis, in both adults and infants, has declined overall and is now at an all time low, presenting an opportunity for elimination of the disease. In October 1999, CDC launched the National Plan to Eliminate Syphilis in the United States. Chancroid also has declined steadily since 1987 (DSTDP, CDC, 2000).

Genital herpes continues to increase, spreading across all social, economic, racial and ethnic boundaries, but most dramatically affecting teens and young adults (Fleming, 1997). With an estimated 20 million people in the United States currently infected with human papillomavirus (HPV), this viral STD also continues to spread. An estimated 5.5 million people become newly infected with HPV each year (Cates, 1999).

What Are the Most Serious STDs in Women?

By far, women bear the greatest burden of STDs, suffering more frequent and more serious complications than men. Ten to 20 percent of women with gonorrhea and chlamydia develop one of the most serious complications, pelvic inflammatory disease (PID). PID can lead to chronic pelvic pain, infertility, and potentially fatal ectopic pregnancy. Many different organisms can cause PID, but most cases are associated with gonorrhea and chlamydia.

HPV also can result in severe consequences for women. Infection with certain types of HPV place women at increased risk for cervical cancer.

In addition, women who are infected with an STD while pregnant can have early onset of labor, premature rupture of the membranes, or uterine infection before and after delivery. STD-related syndromes—like bacterial vaginosis—may cause harm to infants through their association with premature birth. Preterm birth is the leading cause of infant death and disability in the United States, and there has been no reduction in more than 20 years. It is estimated that 30 to 40 percent of excess preterm births and infant deaths are due to STDs and bacterial vaginosis (Goldenberg, 1997).

Can the Most Serious STDs Infect Babies?

Many STDs can be passed from an infected woman to fetus, newborn, or infant, before, during or after birth. Some STDs—like syphilis—cross the placenta and infect the fetus during its development. Other STDs—like gonorrhea, chlamydia, genital herpes, and genital HPV infection—are transmitted from mother to child as the infant passes through the birth canal. HIV infection can cross the placenta during pregnancy, can infect the newborn during the birth process, or unlike other STDs, can infect a child as a result of breast feeding.

If an STD in a pregnant woman is detected soon enough, precautions can often be taken so that the disease is not spread to the baby. Newborns infected with syphilis and herpes may suffer severe consequences not completely relieved by treatment, including neurologic damage and death. Gonorrhea and chlamydia can cause prematurity, eye disease, and pneumonia in infants.

What Are the Most Common STDs among Teens?

Teens are at high behavioral risk for acquiring most STDs. Teenagers and young adults are more likely than other age groups to have multiple sex partners, to engage in unprotected sex, and, for young women, to choose sexual partners older than themselves. Moreover, young women are biologically more susceptible to chlamydia, gonorrhea and HIV.

Chlamydia and gonorrhea are the most common curable STDs among teens. Curable STDs are typically caused by bacteria that can be killed with antibiotics. However, if these diseases remain undetected and untreated, they can result in severe health consequences later in life. Among teens, it is not uncommon to see more than five percent of young men and five to 10 percent of young women infected with chlamydia (Mertz, CDC, 1998). Rates of gonorrhea are highest in females 15 to 19 years of age and in males 20 to 24 years of age.

The prevalence of herpes increases with age. Since this disease stays within the body once acquired, the older people are, the more likely they have been infected. The rate of new infections for herpes and HPV—both viral STDs—is typically highest during the late teens and early twenties. Among women under the age of 25, studies have found that 28 to 46 percent are typically infected with HPV. Between 15 to 20 percent of young men and women have become infected with herpes by the time they reach adulthood.

What Are STD Trends in Teens?

Syphilis, hepatitis B, and chancroid are declining among teens and other age groups. Chlamydia is likely going down in areas where there is screening and treatment among teens at family planning clinics and school-based screening programs. In areas where these services are not available, the disease may be increasing. Herpes was increasing among teens through the early 1990s. Currently, the data are not available to tell us whether HPV, trichomoniasis, or bacterial vaginosis are increasing, but these diseases are extremely widespread.

What Are the Most Common STDs among Men Who Have Sex with Men?

Researchers estimate that men who have sex with men (MSM) still account for 42 percent of new HIV infections annually in the United States and for 60 percent of all new HIV infections among men. Several recent studies have pointed to high, and increasing, levels of other STDs among MSM.

One 26-city study, the Gonococcal Isolate Surveillance Project, reported that from 1994 to 1999, the proportion of gonorrhea cases among MSM more than doubled from six to 13 percent. An STD clinic in Washington, D.C., serving a large number of gay and bisexual men reported that gonorrhea cases increased 93 percent from 1993 to 1996, with 82 percent of these cases among MSM.

In King County, Washington—which includes the city of Seattle—researchers reported marked increases in both gonorrhea and syphilis cases among MSM. Most notably, while the county had no cases of early syphilis in 1996, 88 cases were reported between 1998 and the first half of 1999, 85 percent of which were in gay and bisexual men. These men reported having multiple partners and frequently engaging in unprotected anal intercourse.

What Areas of the Country Have the Greatest Problems with STDs?

Herpes and HPV are widespread throughout the nation, showing very little regional variation. Chlamydia is also extremely common across geographic boundaries, but is on the decline in regions where effective screening and treatment programs are in place. Chlamydia remains most widespread among women in the southern region of the country. The south also faces the highest rates of both gonorrhea and syphilis. The high rates of STDs in the south may be due to high rates of poverty and lack of access to quality health care.

Are STDS More Common among Racial and Ethnic Minorities? If So, Why?

Although STDs like chlamydia, HPV, and herpes are widespread across racial and ethnic groups, STD rates tend to be higher among African Americans than white Americans. Reported rates of some STDs, like gonorrhea and syphilis, are as much as 30 times higher for African Americans than for whites. This disparity is due, in part, to the fact that African Americans are more likely to seek care in public clinics that report STDs more completely than private providers. However, this reporting bias does not fully explain these differences. Other important factors include the distribution of poverty, access to quality health care, health-seeking behaviors, the level of drug use, and sexual networks with high STD prevalence.

Moreover, the level of prevention education may vary widely across communities. In some areas, community-based efforts may be widespread across social, educational, and religious organizations, but in others, STD prevention may not yet be a high priority. Efforts are underway to increase both public and private sector HIV and STD prevention efforts in communities at risk throughout the nation. Yet, research demonstrates that some groups at very high risk still lack even basic information about STD prevention (Bunnell, CDC, 1998).

What Are the Economic Costs of STDS in the United States?

STDs are associated with both direct and indirect costs. Direct costs include expenditures for medical and non-medical services and materials, such as physician services, laboratory services, hospitalization, transportation, and medical supplies. Indirect costs mainly include lost wages due to illness or premature death. STDs also result in intangible costs related to pain, suffering, and diminished quality of life. In 1994, the direct and indirect costs of the major STDs and their complications were estimated to total almost $17 billion annually.

REFERENCES

Bunnell R, Dahlberg L, Stone K, et al. Misconceptions about STD Prevention and Associations with STD Prevalence and Incidence in Adolescent Females in a Southeastern City [abstract]. In: Program and Abstracts of the 1998 National STD Prevention Conference; December 1998.

Cates W et al. Estimates of the Incidence and Prevalence of Sexually Transmitted Diseases in the United States. *Sex Trans Dis* 1999;26 (suppl):S2–S7.

Division of STD Prevention. Sexually Transmitted Disease Surveillance, 1999. U.S. Department of Health and Human Services, Atlanta: Centers for Disease Control and Prevention (CDC), September 2000.

Fleming DT, McQuillan GM, Johnson RE, et al. Herpes Simplex Virus Type 2 in the United States, 1976 to 1994. *N Engl J Med* 1997;337(16):1105–11.

Goldenberg RL, Andrews WW, Yuan AC, et al. Sexually Transmitted Diseases and Adverse Outcomes of Pregnancy. *Clinics in Perinatalogy* 1997;24:23–41.

Mertz KJ, Trees D, Levine WC, et al. Etiology of Genital Ulcers and Prevalence of Human Immunodefiency Virus Coinfection in 10 U.S. Cities." *Journal of Infectious Diseases* 1998;178: 1795–1798.

Venereal Disease:

Sin versus Science

Elizabeth Fee

Ways of perceiving and understanding disease are historically constructed. Our social, political, religious, and moral conceptions influence our perceptions of disease, just as do different scientific and medical theories. Indeed, these different elements often cannot be easily separated, as scientists and physicians bring their own cultural ideas to bear in the construction of scientific theories. Because these cultural ideas may be widely shared, their presence within medical and scientific theory may not be readily apparent. Often, such cultural conceptions are more obvious when reviewing medical and scientific theories of the past than they are in contemporary medical practice.[1]

Just as cultural conceptions of disease may be embodied in the framing of scientific theories, so these theories also influence popular perceptions of disease. At times such scientific theories may reinforce, or contradict, other cultural conceptions, such as religious and moral ideas or racial stereotypes.

In the case of the venereal diseases, it is clear that our attitudes embody a fundamental cultural ambivalence: are venereal diseases to be studied and treated from a purely biomedical point of view—are they infectious diseases like any others—or are they to be treated as social, moral, or spiritual afflictions?[2] As the name implies, venereal diseases are inevitably associated with sexuality—and therefore our perceptions of these diseases tend to be entangled with our ideas about the social meanings and moral evaluation of sexual behaviors. In the case of syphilis, a major killer in the first half of the twentieth century, health officials could decide that the true "cause" of syphilis was the microorganism *Treponema pallidum,* or they could define the "underlying cause" as "promiscuous sexual behavior." Each claim focuses on a different part of social reality, and each carries different messages of responsibility and blame. Each is part of a different language in which the disease may be described and defined. The first suggests the primacy of the medical clinic for treating disease; the second, the primacy of moral exhortation.

Throughout the twentieth century struggles have been waged over the meaning and definition of the venereal diseases. At times these diseases have been blanketed in silence, as though they belonged to a "private" realm, not open to public discussion. Wars, however, have tended to make venereal diseases visible, to bring them out of the private sphere and into the center of public policy discussions; this has highlighted the struggles over their proper definition and treatment. In World War I, for example, the American Social Hygiene Association consistently equated venereal disease with immorality, vice, and prostitution.[3] Its members thus tried to close down brothels and taverns, to arrest prostitutes, and to advocate continence and sexual abstinence for the soldiers. The Commission on Training Camp Activities tried to suppress vice and liquor and also to organize "good, clean fun": sports events, theatrical entertainments and educational programs.[4] The Army, however, quietly issued prophylactic kits to the soldiers and made early treatment after possible exposure compulsory. Any soldier who failed to get treatment could face trial and imprisonment for neglect of duty. . . .

From "Sin vs. Science: Venereal Disease in Baltimore in the Twentieth Century" by Elizabeth Fee (1988), *Journal of the History of Medicine and Allied Sciences,* 43, 141–164. Reprinted by permission of Oxford University Press.

When dealing with major disease problems, we often try to find some social group to "blame" for the infection. During the war, educational materials clearly presented the fighting men as the innocent victims of disease; prostitutes were the guilty spreaders of infection. Indeed, prostitutes were often presented as implicitly working for the enemy against patriotic American soldiers.[5] In many communities prostitutes would be the focus, and often the victims and scapegoats, of the new attention to venereal infections. Prostitutes—the women responsible for the defilement of the heroic American soldier—would be regularly rounded up, arrested, and jailed in the campaign against vice.

The end of the war, however, brought a waning of interest in venereal disease and a return to "normal life," freed of the restrictions and regulations of military necessity. The energetic public discussion of venereal disease again lapsed into a public silence. Prostitutes and their customers were again permitted to operate without much official harassment; health departments quietly collected statistics on venereal disease but avoided publicity on the subject.[6]

This [reading] will examine the subsequent history of venereal disease, and especially syphilis, by focusing on a major industrial city, Baltimore, to see how the struggle between the moral and biomedical views of disease was played out in the context of city politics in the 1930s and 1940s. Although syphilis is no longer a significant public health problem, this account should be useful in helping us to reflect on the . . . problem of AIDS (acquired immune deficiency syndrome) today.

Treatment for Veneral Disease: The Public Health Clinics

In Baltimore in the 1920s a great social silence surrounded the problem of syphilis. Since venereal diseases carried such negative social stigma, only a small proportion of cases were ever reported. Deaths from syphilis were often attributed to other causes as physicians endeavored to save patients and their families from possible embarrassment. A social conspiracy of silence resulted: patients did not talk about their

diseases, physicians did not report them, the health department did not publicize them, and the newspapers never mentioned them. The diseases were thus largely invisible. Most hospitals and some physicians refused to treat patients with venereal diseases; some physicians specialized in these diseases and made a great deal of money from private patients.[7] Many patients, however, could not afford private medical care.

In the aftermath of the war, the city health department began quietly to treat venereal diseases in its public clinics. The first such clinic, opened in 1922, had 13,000 patient visits in its first year of operation. The clinic population grew so fast that the city soon opened a second clinic, and then a third. These patients, brought to the public clinics through poverty, were recorded in health department files as venereal disease cases. Like all the diseases of the poor, these cases attracted little public attention.

The venereal disease problem in Baltimore was, however, made publicly visible by a survey conducted by the United States Public Health Service in 1931.[8] The survey defined syphilis as a major problem in Baltimore, and as a problem of the black population. The reported "colored" rate was 22 per 1,000 males and 10 per 1,000 women; this contrasted with a reported white rate of 4 per 1,000 men and 1.3 per 1,000 women. Of course, whites were more likely to be seeing private physicians and thus less likely to have their disease reported to the health department. Syphilis, originally perceived as a disease of vice and prostitution, was now a black disease. . . .

The Depression: Restricting Treatment

During the Depression public clinics became more crowded than ever, with over 84,000 visits in 1932 alone. The city health department, already burdened with tight budgets and increasing health problems of every kind, complained that the hospitals in town were dumping poor patients on the city clinics.[9] . . .

In 1933 the problem of overcrowding became so acute that the city health department decided to treat only patients at the infectious stage of syphilis. They discontinued treatment to any patients who had received sufficient drugs to render them noninfectious to others, even though they had not been cured.[10] . . .

Venereal Disease and Racism

In the 1930s as today, health statistics were gathered by race but not by income. The statistics on venereal diseases confirmed the definition of syphilis as predominantly a black or "colored" problem. In fact almost all infectious diseases were far more prevalent among blacks than whites, reflecting the effects of poverty, poor housing, and overcrowding. . . .

While [Ferdinand] Reinhard [the head of the bureau of venereal diseases] described the black venereal disease problem as an effect of economics and social conditions, most whites saw venereal disease simply as a question of sexual morality. Blacks were popularly perceived as highly sexual, uninhibited, and promiscuous. . . . White doctors saw blacks as "diseased, debilitated, and debauched," the victims of their own uncontrolled or uncontrollable sexual instincts and impulses. . . . [11] [H]ealth officials were certainly convinced that the main issue was sexual behavior, and they were equally convinced that it was the sexual behavior of the black population that had to be changed.

Since the problem was clearly understood as one of sexual behavior, the city health department began an energetic public education project aimed at changing sexual attitudes—by persuasion or by fear. In 1934 the department directed a new program on sex hygiene at the black population. They gave talks at the Colored Vocational School and the Frederick Douglass High School, and organized exhibits for Negro Health Week and for the National Association of Teachers in Colored Schools. They distributed nearly 14,000 pamphlets on venereal diseases. A "social hygiene motion picture" with the discouraging title *Damaged Lives* played in twenty-three theaters, thus reaching over 65,000 people, one-tenth of Baltimore's adult population.[12]

The main aim of this health propaganda was to stress the dangers of sexual promiscuity, but it also emphasized the need for early detection and treatment of disease. . . . Pamphlets distributed by the Social Hygiene Association and the city health department continued to urge chastity before marriage and sexual fidelity within marriage as the proper solutions to syphilis.

In 1935 syphilis was by far the most prevalent of the communicable diseases occurring in the city, with 5,754 reported cases; the next most prevalent disease was chickenpox—not a disease considered of much importance—with 3,816 reported cases.[13] . . . The facilities for actually treating syphilis were still completely inadequate.

Syphilis deaths were now running at between 110 and 150 per year. As Reinhard complained, "Any other group of diseases scattered throughout the community to this extent would be considered to have taken on epidemic proportions and would be cause for alarm on the part of health authorities.[14] . . .

Reinhard continued for several years to struggle against the partial treatment plan and to advocate extended clinic facilities, sufficient for all syphilis patients, and staffed with black physicians, nurses, and social workers. It seemed, at the time, to be a one-man campaign. Most physicians approved of the fact that the health department was not offering treatment, the proper domain of fee-for-service medicine. Particularly during the depression years, when many physicians found it difficult to make a living on patient fees, the medical profession was antagonistic to efforts by public health officers to offer free treatments to any patients, whatever their illness.

Syphilis as Everyone's Disease: A National Campaign

In 1936 Reinhard's "one-man campaign" against syphilis in Baltimore suddenly became part of a major national effort. Thomas Parran, Surgeon General of the United States Public Health Service, now lent the full weight of his authority to a campaign against venereal diseases. A forceful and dynamic man, Parran decided to break through the wall of silence and make the public confront the magnitude of the problem. To do this, he redefined syphilis as a disease that struck "innocent" victims: the educated, respectable, white population. . . . Parran called syphilis "the great

American Disease" and declared: "we might virtually stamp out this disease were we not hampered by the widespread belief that nice people don't talk about syphilis, that nice people don't have syphilis, and that nice people shouldn't do anything about those who *do* have syphilis."[15] Parran's point was that nice people *did* have syphilis; he never tired of pointing out that respectable physicians, innocent children, and heads of industry were among those infected.[16] . . .

Parran declared that half the victims of syphilis were "innocently infected": "Many cases come from such casual contacts as the use of [a] recently soiled drinking cup, a pipe or cigarette; in receiving services from diseased nursemaids, barber or beauty shop operators, etc., and in giving services such as those of a dentist, doctor or nurse to a diseased person."[17] Syphilis was just another contagious disease, although a highly threatening and dangerous one. The point was to find syphilis cases and to treat them; the state should be obliged to provide treatment, said Parran, and the patient should be obliged to endure it. Syphilis would be the next great plague to go—as soon as the public broke with the old-fashioned and pre-scientific notion that syphilis was "the wages of sin." . . .

[W]hile the city health department was consolidating the new biomedical approach to syphilis, it was suddenly challenged with a resurgent moral crusade against vice and prostitution, led by none other than the redoubtable J. Edgar Hoover.

Medical Treatment or Crusade against Vice?

"Captives Taken in Weekend Drive Against City's White Slave Traffic," declared the headlines of the Baltimore *Sun* on May 17, 1937.[18] . . . The raids generated great excitement and controversy, magnified when local prostitutes implicated a number of high level police officers and at least one state senator in Baltimore's "white slave trade."[19] The local newspapers took delight in reporting the activities of this organized racket, playing up Baltimore as a notorious center of vice and iniquity. . . .

State Senator Raymond E. Kennedy now implied that the city health department, like the police department, was implicitly involved in condoning vice. He demanded that all prostitutes being treated in city clinics be immediately incarcerated. Parran was called to appear as a witness before a Grand Jury investigation. On his arrival in Baltimore, however, Parran managed to turn this into a public relations coup for the health department. He announced a state survey of venereal diseases, suggested that Baltimore follow the successful Swedish model of disease control, including the provision of free drugs, and he declared to enthusiastic mass meetings that Maryland would take the lead in the fight against "social diseases."[20] . . .

Thanks to citywide publicity and political pressure on Mayor Jackson, Williams was able to expand his budget and open the Druid Hill Health Center for black patients in west Baltimore—the first time that adequate public health facilities had been available in this area of the city.[21]

The city health department now tackled the problem of syphilis in industry. At the time, industrial workers were being fired (or never hired in the first place) if they were found to have positive blood tests for syphilis. Employers fired infected workers on the grounds that they were more likely to be involved in industrial accidents, and thus would increase the costs of workmen's compensation and insurance premiums. The health department started to provide free laboratory blood tests for industrial workers; the test results were kept confidential and those infected were referred for appropriate therapy. The health department followed individual workers to make sure they were receiving treatment but, at least in theory, no worker who accepted treatment could be fired. The fact that no guarantees were offered workers refusing therapy meant, however, that syphilis treatment was essentially made compulsory for industrial workers participating in the plan.[22] . . .

The Impact of War

In the late 1930s there were considerable grounds for optimism that the campaign against the venereal diseases was beginning to show results. The more open public health attitude toward syphilis as a problem of disease rather than of morality seemed to be successful. . . . The numbers of reported cases of syphilis were decreasing each year, despite increased screening efforts and more effective reporting mechanisms. In 1938, 8,236 new cases were reported; in 1939, 7,509; and in 1940, only 6,213. . . . These records of syphilis incidence and prevalence may have been quite unreliable from an epidemiological point of view, but this was the first time that syphilis rates had even seemed to be declining; it was a natural conclusion that health department efforts were finally showing demonstrable results.

In the midst of this optimism, however, came the prospect of war and, with it, the fear that war mobobilization and an influx of 60,000 soldiers would upset all previous gain.[23] In 1941, with the institution of selective service examinations, reported venereal disease rates began to climb. In Baltimore that year, 1.7 percent of the white enlistees had positive blood tests for syphilis, as had twenty-four percent of the black recruits.[24] Baltimore City won the dubious distinction of having the second highest syphilis rate in the country, second only to Washington, D.C. Baltimore's rate was 101.3 cases per 1,000 men examined, more than twice the national rate.[25] In an effort to justify these statistics, the city health department blamed the situation on the nonwhite population: the relatively high proportion of blacks to whites "explained" why Baltimore had the second highest venereal disease rate among the country's largest cities.[26] . . .

Such justifications were hardly likely to be sufficient for a country at war. With the war mobilization had come renewed national attention to protecting the health and fighting efficiency of the soldiers. As during World War I, the first concern was with the control or suppression of prostitution in the vicinity of army camps and with "social hygiene" rather than treatment programs. The May Act passed by Congress made prostitution a federal offense in the vicinity of military camps. . . .

[T]he Baltimore police seemed determined to prove their dedication to the attack on prostitution. By early 1943 they claimed to have closed most of Baltimore's brothels and to have driven prostitutes from the streets.[27] Police Commissioner Stanton demanded statewide legislation to allow police officers to arrest prostitutes and force them to submit to medical examination and, if infected, medical treatment.[28]

Dr. Nels A. Nelson, head of the state venereal disease control program, declared that these arrests of prostitutes and compulsory medical examinations were completely ineffective: only a few prostitutes could be arrested at any one time, and as soon as they were treated and released, they would immediately return to the streets to become reinfected and to continue to spread infection until their next arrest. The only real control of venereal disease, concluded Nelson, depended on the complete "repression of sexual promiscuity."[29] Meanwhile, the reported cases of syphilis were rapidly increasing. In 1942 the selective service records showed that almost three percent of the white draftees and over thirty-two percent of the black soldiers had syphilis.[30] . . . Between 1940 and 1942 new cases of syphilis had almost doubled, from 6,213 to 11,293, and gonorrhea rates were also climbing. . . .

Nelson of the state health department had . . . abandoned the fight against prostitution. He was busily distributing free drugs for syphilis control to private physicians, while he publicly declared the city venereal disease clinics "little more than drug pumping stations in dirty, unattractive quarters."[31] Nelson told the press he was tired of hearing the VD rate discussed as though it were only a Negro problem: "Negroes are plagued by venereal diseases because of their economic and social position."[32] . . .

The Army was also under attack for failing to organize an effective VD program.[33] Its programs and policies were plagued by contradictions; publicly, it advocated chastity, while privately, it provided prophylactics for the men. . . . The Army finally adopted a pragmatic approach and attempted to reduce the sources of infection as much as possible. The pragmatic approach lacked the fervor of a purity crusade, but tried to steer some middle course between laissez-faire attitudes and moral absolutism.

In Baltimore the new acting directors of the city's venereal disease program, Ralph Sikes and Alexander Novey, shared this pragmatic position. . . . Under their leadership health officers cooperated with the armed services in distributing prophylactic kits throughout the city: in police stations, fire houses, transportation terminals, hospitals, and clinic.[34] Implicitly, the VD control officers had thus accepted the idea that this was a campaign *against* disease, rather than a campaign *for* sexual morality; they concentrated on a fairly mechanical (if effective) approach to prevention while leaving the struggle around prostitution to social hygiene reformers, the police, and the courts.

Sex Education during the War

During the war the city health department and a research group at the Johns Hopkins School of Hygiene and Public Health undertook a daring task—to teach "sex hygiene" in the public schools. They gave talks to groups of high school students (separated by sex), showed plaster models of male and female reproductive systems, and gave simple explanations of "menstruation, conception, pregnancy, nocturnal emissions and masturbation, but omitting intercourse and childbirth."[35] . . .

Having been assured that sex was both exciting and dangerous, students were then given a brief description of male reproductive physiology, ending with a caution against masturbation. Masturbation was not dangerous, students were told, merely unnecessary and possibly habit-forming. . . . A brief description of the female reproductive system was followed by a discussion of morals and ethics, warning of the need for judgment, but avoiding specific advice. . . . Students were urged to discuss their questions with parents and teachers and to read a social hygiene pamphlet on "Growing Up in the World Today."[36]

The third part of the presentation, on venereal diseases, emphasized the dangers of sex. Intimacy brought the germs of syphilis: sexual intercourse was the most threatening, but even kisses could carry disease. The best strategy was to avoid any possible contact with these sexual germs:

> They can be caught only from an infected person and therefore, we should avoid intimate contact with an infected person. But we cannot tell by looking at a person whether he or she, is infected or not; the answer is to avoid intimate contact with all persons except in marriage. This is the only sure way of avoiding these diseases.[37]

At least for these high school students, the link between sexual morality and venereal disease was clear: sexual intimacy led to syphilis and was therefore to be avoided except in marriage. Why marital sex should be "safe" was never explained, nor was congenital syphilis ever mentioned.

After the War: The New Penicillin Therapy

By the end of World War II, the problem of syphilis was beginning to recede, both in public consciousness and in statistical measures. Part of this was the normal relaxation in the immediate aftermath of war, the return to home and family, the desire for stability, and a reluctance to confront social and sexual problems or to dwell on their existence. Even more important, however, was the success of the new drug, penicillin: at last, venereal diseases could, it seemed, be quickly and effectively treated. Many felt it was only a matter of time before the venereal diseases were finally eliminated with the aid of modern medicine's "miracle cures."

By 1940 the new "miracle drug" penicillin had been discovered and purified; in 1943 it was first used against syphilis, but it was not yet generally available; supplies were still strictly rationed.[38] Soon, it would completely transform the old methods of treating venereal diseases. On December 31, 1944, the Baltimore City Hospitals opened the first Rapid Treatment Center for treating syphilis with penicillin. Penicillin doses for syphilis were given over eight days; since supplies of the drug were then very limited, only cases judged to be highly infectious were sent for "an eight-day cure, or what is for the present considered to be a cure."[39] From all initial reports the new experimental treatment was remarkably effective.

On June 20, 1945, Mayor Theodore R. McKeldin approved a new city ordinance making treatment for venereal diseases compulsory for the first time. Those suspected of having syphilis or gonorrhea were required to take penicillin therapy at the Rapid Treatment Center.[40] Those refusing treatment could be quarantined and isolated in the Baltimore City hospitals. . . .

The ordinance was, however, rarely invoked. Most patients were eager to go to the Rapid Treatment Center when diagnosed. In 1946 nearly 2,000 people with infectious syphilis received treatment; most were reported as completely cured. (Before penicillin, only an estimated twenty-five percent of patients completed the lengthy treatments considered necessary for a full cure.[41]) In 1947 the Baltimore *Sun* reviewed the city's experience with the new ordinance:

> *On the basis of this experience (over the last 16 months), it is clear that the protection of the public against persons carrying the disease and refusing to be treated more than outweighs the sacrifice of individual rights by so small a number. . . . Under the circumstances, the enactment of a permanent ordinance seems fully justified.*[42]

The state health department in 1947 announced that "for the first time in history any resident of Maryland who contracts syphilis can obtain treatment resulting in prompt and almost certain cure."[43]

Conclusion: The End of the Struggle?

The biomedical approach to venereal diseases had apparently been stunningly successful. Diseases that only ten years before had been described as the most serious of all the infectious diseases had now been tamed by chemotherapy with a simple, safe, and effective cure. Diseases that twenty years previously had been guilty secrets, virtually unmentionable in the public press and quietly ignored by health departments, were now glorious examples of the triumph of modem medicine in overcoming ancient plagues. The ideological struggle between those who had seen the fight against venereal disease as a battle for sexual morality and those who had seen it as simply another form of bacteriological warfare was now over. The social hygiene reformers had to concede defeat to the public health officers, epidemiologists, and laboratory researchers. Or did they?

In 1947 the Maryland State Department of Health, announcing the success of the rapid treatment program, concluded its press bulletin with the warning: "To decrease the number of repeat patients and prevent venereal diseases it will be necessary to reduce sexual promiscuity. If fear of disease is a less

powerful restraining factor the problem must be attacked more strongly through moral training and suppression of prostitution."[44] . . .

Even those most committed to the bacteriological view of disease seemed uneasy about the decoupling of venereal disease from sin and promiscuity: How would sexual morality be controlled if not by the fear of disease? Would "rampant promiscuity" defeat the best efforts of medical treatment?

A brief review of health statistics in the years since the discovery of penicillin suggests that syphilis has, in the main, been effectively controlled. New cases of syphilis are reported each year, and doubtless others go unreported, but the rates are relatively low. In 1986 a total of 373 cases of primary, secondary, and early latent cases were reported in Baltimore; in 1987, a total of 364 cases. Although these cases are of continuing concern to health department officials, at least from the perspective of the 1930s and 1940s, the miracle of control really has occurred. . . .

As we have since discovered, the fear and underlying ambivalence toward sexuality were only lying dormant. Public concern, horror, and fear about AIDS have recently reignited the older social hygiene movement in a new form. The once prevalent description of the black population as sexually promiscuous, sexually threatening, and a reservoir of disease has now been applied to the gay male population. AIDS is popularly seen as "caused" by gay promiscuity and, even more broadly, as a punishment for unconventional or unapproved sexual behavior, rather than simply as the result of infection by a microorganism. Venereal disease is again perceived as the "wages of sin," or, as the Reverend Jerry Falwell says: "A man reaps what he sows. If he sows seed in the field of his lower nature, he will reap from it a harvest of corruption." . . .

Both the biomedical and moral perspectives on venereal disease highlight specific aspects of a complex social reality. Venereal diseases, like all other diseases, are experienced and reproduced in a social context. We may separate the biological and social aspects for analysis, but any complete understanding of a disease problem must involve both, as interrelated parts of a single social reality.

Social and cultural ideas offer a variety of ways in which diseases can be perceived and interpreted. The germ theory provides an explanation of disease that largely—but not completely—isolates it from this social context, robbing it of some of its social (and in this case, moral) meaning. But the purely "scientific" interpretation is never wholly victorious, for social and cultural meanings of disease reassert themselves in the interstices of science and prove their power whenever the biomedical sciences fail to completely cure or solve the problem. Only when a disease condition is completely abolished do social and cultural meanings cease to be relevant to the experience and perception of human illness.

NOTES

1. For a fascinating analysis of the history of cultural and scientific conceptions of syphilis, see Ludwig Fleck, *Genesis and Development of a Scientific Fact* (1935, rpt., Chicago: 1979).

2. For an excellent recent history of the controversies around venereal diseases in the United States, see Allan Brandt, *No Magic Bullet: A Social History of Venereal Diseases in the United States Since 1880* (New York: 1985).

3. National Academy of Sciences, *Scientific and Technical Societies of the United States and Canada,* 8th ed. (Washington, D.C.: 1968), 62.

4. Edward H. Beardsley, "Allied Against Sin: American and British Responses to Venereal Disease in World War I," *Medical History* 20 (1976): 194.

5. As one widely reprinted article, said to have reached eight million readers, described 'The Enemy at Home': "The name of this invisible enemy is Venereal Disease— and there you have in two words the epitome of all that is unclean, malignant and menacing. . . . Gonorrhea and syphilis are 'camp followers' where prostitution and alcohol are permitted. They form almost as great an enemy behind the lines as do the Huns in front." "V. D.: The Enemy at Home," as cited by William H. Zinsser, "Social Hygiene and the War: Fighting Venereal Disease a Public Trust," *Social Hygiene* 4 (1918): 519–20.

6. In 1920 William Travis Howard, a member of the city health department, complained: "The Baltimore health department has never inaugurated a single administrative measure directed at the control of the venereal diseases . . . the Baltimore health department has contented itself with receiving such reports as were made and with lending its power, when called upon, to force a few recalcitrant patients to appear at the venereal disease clinic established by the United States Government." Howard, *Public Health*

Administration and the Natural History of Disease in Baltimore, Maryland: 1797–1920 (Washington, D.C.:1924): 154–55.

7. Baltimore City Health Department, Annual Report (1930).

8. Taliaferro Clark and Lida Usilton, "Survey of the Venereal Diseases in the City of Baltimore, Baltimore County, and the Four Contiguous Counties," *Venereal Disease Information* 12 (Washington, D.C.:20 October 1931): 437–56.

9. Baltimore City Health Department, Annual Report (1932), 62.

10. Baltimore City Health Department, Annual Report (1933), 93.

11. James H. Jones, *Bad Blood. The Tuskegee Syphilis Experiment* (New York: 1981), 16–29.

12. Baltimore City Health Department, Annual Report (1934), 107.

13. Baltimore City Health Department, Annual Report (1935), 115.

14. Ferdinand O. Reinhard, "The Venereal Disease Problem in the Colored Population of Baltimore City," *American Journal of Syphilis and Neurology* 19 (1935): 183–95.

15. Thomas Parran, "Why Don't We Stamp Out Syphilis?" *Reader's Digest* (July 1936), reprinted in Baltimore *Health News* (August 1936): 3.

16. *E.g.* Parran, *Shadow on the Land: Syphilis* (New York: 1937). 207, 230.

17. Parran, "Why Don't We Stamp Out Syphilis?" *Reader's Digest,* 65–73.

18. "G-Men's Haul in Vice Raids Totals 47," *Baltimore Sun,* 17 May 1937.

19. "Vice Witness Names Police Lieutenant," *Baltimore Sun,* 18 May 1937; "Vice Arrests May Total 100; Bierman Named," *Sunday Sun,* 19 May 1937.

20. "Starts to Survey Venereal Disease," *Baltimore Sun,* 29 July 1937; "Venereal Disease Fight is Planned," *Baltimore Sun,* 22 August 1937; "Fight Opens Here on Social Disease," *Baltimore Sun,* 25 August 1937; "Syphilis Control Unit Begins Work," *Baltimore Sun,* 21 October 1937; "Over 2,000 Attend Talks on Syphilis," *Baltimore Sun,* 26 October 1937.

21. Baltimore City Health Department, Annual Reports (1938), 159; (1939), 159.

22. Baltimore City Health Department, Annual Report (1938); 16; "21 Employers Asked in Drive on Syphilis," *Baltimore Sun,* 27 March 1938; "Syphilis Control is Under Way Here," *Baltimore Sun,* 22 May 1938; W. M. P., "We Join the Anti-Syphilis Crusade," *The Kalends* (June 1938),

reprinted in *Baltimore Health News* 15 (July 1938): 53–54; Baltimore City Health Department, "Syphilis in Industry" (Baltimore: n.d.).

23. Baltimore City Health Department, Annual Report (1940), 149–51.

24. Baltimore City Health Department, Annual Report (1941), 139.

25. "City Shown Second in Syphilis Survey," *Baltimore Sun,* 22 October 1941.

26. "High Syphilis Rate Laid to Race Ratio," *Baltimore Sun,* 26 October 1941.

27. "Says Vice Control Has Improved Here," *Baltimore Sun,* 27 January 1943.

28. "State Law Held Needed in War on Vice," *Baltimore Sun,* 28 January 1943.

29. "Stanton Idea for Examination of Prostitutes Is Denounced," *Baltimore Sun,* 29 January 1943.

30. "Venereal Picture Dark: Dr. Huntington Williams Says No Improvement Is Expected for Some Time," *Baltimore Sun,* 21 January 1943.

31. "Clinics Here Under Fire," *Baltimore Sun,* 30 March 1943.

32. "Venereal Disease Rate High in State," *Baltimore Sun,* 15 June 1943.

33. Parran and Vonderlehr, *Plain Words About Venereal Disease,* especially 96–120.

34. Baltimore City Health Department, Annual Report (1943), 148.

35. C. Howe Eller, "A Sex Education Project and Serologic Survey in a Baltimore High School," *Baltimore Health News* 21 (November 1944): 83.

36. Emily V. Clapp, *Growing Up in the World Today* (Boston: n.d.).

37. *Ibid.,* 14.

38. For the development of penicillin therapy, see Harry F. Dowling, *Fighting Infection: Conquests of the Twentieth Century* (Cambridge: 1977): 125–57.

39. Baltimore City Health Department, Annual Report (1945), 29.

40. Baltimore City Health Department, Annual Report (1945), 145–46; "Venereal Law Made Specific," *Baltimore Sun,* 26 August 1945.

41. "End of VD—Cure Center Seen as Calamity," *Evening Sun,* 12 June 1946.

42. "A Temporary Power Made Permanent," *Baltimore Sun,* 9 January 1947.

43. "Rapid Treatment," Press Bulletin No. 1043, Maryland State Department of Health, (27 January 1947) Enoch Pratt Library, Maryland Room, Baltimore.

44. *Ibid.*

Damaged Goods: Women Managing the Stigma of STDs

Adina Nack

The HIV/AIDS epidemic has garnered the attention of researchers from a variety of academic disciplines. In contrast, the study of other sexually transmitted diseases (STDs) has attracted limited interest outside of epidemiology and public health. In the United States, an estimated three out of four sexually active adults have human papillomavirus infections (HPV—the virus that can cause genital warts); one out of five have genital herpes infections (Ackerman 1998; Centers for Disease Control and Prevention [CDC] 1998a). In contrast, the nation-wide rate of HIV infection is approximately 1 out of 300 (CDC 1998b). Current sociological research on the interrelationships between sexual health, stigma, and the self has focused overwhelmingly on HIV/AIDS (Sandstrom 1990; Siegel and Krauss 1991: Weitz 1989). . . .

This article focuses on how the sexual self-concept is transformed when the experience of living with a chronic STD casts a shadow of disease on the health and desirability of a woman's body, as well as on her perceived possibilities for future sexual experiences. The term *sexual self* means something fundamentally different from *gender identity* or *sexual identity*. Invoking the term *sexual self* is meant to conjure up the innately intimate parts of individuals' self-concepts that encompass how they think of themselves with regards to their experienced and imagined sensuality. Components of a sexual self may include the following: level of sexual experience, emotional memories of sexual pleasure (or lack thereof), perception of one's body as desirable, and perception of one's sexual body parts as healthy. . . .

To understand the individual-level experience of living with a chronic STD, it is important to take into account how these infections are symbolically constructed in American culture. The meanings that Americans give to being infected with an STD are intersubjectively formed during interactions. Individuals' experiences of health, illness, and medical care "are connected to the particular historically located social arrangements and the cultural values of any society" (Conrad and Kern 1994:5). Present American social values reflect the longstanding connections between sexual health and morality: Interactions with medical practitioners and lay people are the conduit through which the stigma of STDs is reinforced (Brandt 1987). Pryce (1998) pointed to a critical gap—the "missing" sociology of sexual disease—and asserted that this application of sociology should focus on the social construction of the body as central in the medical and social iconography of STDs.

In answer to Pryce's (1998) challenge, this research . . . sociologically analyz[es] the impact of genital herpes and HPV on women's sexual selves. This study adds to this research area by examining sexual self-transformation, starting from the point of how individuals' sexual selves are transformed by the lived experiences of being diagnosed and treated for chronic STDs. Beginning from a premise that the majority of people grow up feeling sexually invincible, a variety of traumas have the capacity to disrupt a positive sexual self-concept (e.g., molestation, rape, and illness). Social–interactional traumas also transmit messages that can damage sexual selves: Some physical bodies are undesirable; some sexual preferences are unacceptable; some levels of sexual experience are immoral.

Setting and Method

The motivation for this study stems from my personal experience with STDs. My "complete membership role" (Adler and Adler 1987) stems from legitimacy and acceptance by other women with STDs as a member of this unorganized and stigmatized group. At 20, sexual health became the center of my world when I was diagnosed with mild cervical dysplasia, the result of an HPV infection. I began an informal self-education process that helped me manage the stress of my treatments. My commitment to managing my sexual health status would become the foundation for this research project and provide me with the personal insights needed to connect with others facing STDs and the clinical knowledge necessary to be a sexual health researcher.

As a campus sexual health educator, I began to question what sexual health services were not provided. Seeing that women and men were being diagnosed and treated for STDs without receiving follow-up education and counseling, I developed a women-only support group for individuals dealing with STDs. Because of the topic's sensitive nature, I chose a gender-segregated approach to the support group and, ultimately, to the research. . . .

Unfortunately, only one woman used the support group. Initially disheartened, I began to question why people flocked to other support groups that were based on shared stigma (e.g., eating disorders and alcoholism) but failed to use this sexual health support group. Even persons living with HIV and AIDS used support groups to collectively manage their stigma. . . .

To investigate the failure of this support group, I conducted a survey among patients using a local women's health care clinic. During a month chosen at random, clinic staff gave each patient who came in for an appointment an anonymous survey about a new service being offered: a women's sexual health support group. In all, 279 completed surveys were collected. . . . Owing to the population from which the sample was drawn, generalizability is restricted to the population of women who receive women's health care services from this clinic. . . .

I performed a multiple regression analysis on the data, the results of which supported the hypothesis that a person who has been diagnosed with an STD is less likely to be interested in a sexual health support group. . . . One of the most revealing findings was that only 23.3 percent of the women were definitely interested ("yes") in a sexual health support group. . . .

I interpreted this finding to reflect that the stigma of having an STD is so severe that the perceived cost of disclosing this sexual health status to strangers outweighs the possible benefits. Because there has yet to be a moral entrepreneurial campaign to destigmatize STDs in our society, the norm remains secrecy (Brandt 1987). . . .

On the basis of these findings, I determined that in-depth interviews were my best chance for obtaining valid data. I constructed my research methods to reflect a reciprocal intention: As the women gave their stories to me, I would offer my support and resources as a sexual health educator. . . .

My first hurdle was to achieve approval from the campus Human Research Committee. . . . Because of the confidential nature of individuals' STD diagnoses, I was not allowed to directly recruit participants. Rather, they had to approach me, usually after hearing about my research project from other participants or women's health care practitioners with whom I had consulted. . . . I used snowball sampling to generate interviews.

I conducted 28 conversational, unstructured interviews with consensual participants, who ranged in age from 19 to 56. . . . I conducted the interviews in participants' preferred locations: their homes, my home, or other private settings. The interviews lasted from 1 to 2 hours and were tape recorded with the participants' permission. When appropriate, I concluded the interview with offers to provide sexual health information and resources, either in the form of health education materials or referrals to resources.

I then analyzed the data according to the principles of grounded theory (Glaser and Strauss 1967). . . . With each interview, I started to cluster participants' experiences around particular stages to check the validity of my initial model. The six stages of sexual self-transformation [that emerged from the interviews] in chronological order, are as follows: sexual invincibility, STD suspicion, diagnostic crisis, damaged goods, healing/treatment, and integration. . . .

Stigma and the Sexual Self

For all but 1 of the 28 women, their STD diagnoses radically altered the way that they saw themselves as sexual beings. Facing both a daunting medical and social reality, the women used different strategies to manage their new stigma. Each stigma management strategy had ramifications for the transformation of their sexual selves.

Stigma Nonacceptance

Goffman (1963) proposed that individuals at risk for a deviant stigma are either "the discredited" or "the discreditable." The discrediteds' stigma was known to others either because the individuals revealed the deviance or because the deviance was not concealable. In contrast, the discreditable were able to hide their deviant stigma. Goffman found that the majority of discreditables were "passing" as nondeviants by avoiding "stigma symbols," anything that would link them to their deviance, and by using "disidentifiers," props or actions that would lead others to believe they had a nondeviant status. Goffman (1963) also noted that individuals bearing deviant stigma might eventually resort to "covering," one form of which he defined as telling deceptive stories. To remain discreditable in their everyday lives, 19 of the women used the individual stigma management strategies of passing and/or covering. In contrast, 9 women revealed their health status to select friends and family members soon after receiving their diagnoses.

Passing

The deviant stigma of women with STDs was essentially concealable, though revealed to the necessary inner circle of health care and health insurance providers. For the majority, passing was an effective means of hiding stigma from others, sometimes even from themselves.

Hillary, a 22-year-old White college senior, recalled the justifications she had used to distance herself from the reality of her HPV infection and to facilitate passing strategies.

> At the time, I was in denial about it. I told myself that that wasn't what it was because my sister had had a similar thing happen, the dysplasia. So, I just kind of told myself that it was hereditary. That was kinda funny because I asked the nurse that called if it could be hereditary, and she said "No, this is completely sexually transmitted"—I really didn't accept it until a few months after my cryosurgery.

Similarly, Gloria, a Chicana graduate student . . . was not concerned about a previous case of gonorrhea she had cured with antibiotics or her chronic HPV "because the warts went away." Out of sight, out of her sex life: "I never told anybody about them because I figured they had gone away, and they weren't coming back. Even after I had another outbreak, I was still very promiscuous. It still hadn't registered that I needed to always have the guy use a condom."

When the women had temporarily convinced themselves that they did not have a contagious infection, it was common to conceal the health risk with partners because the women themselves did not perceive the risk as real. Kayla, a . . . White college senior, felt justified in passing as healthy with partners who used condoms, even though she knew that condoms could break. Cleo, a White 31-year-old . . . , had sex with a partner after being diagnosed with HPV.

> So at the time I had sex with him, yes, I knew but, no, I hadn't been treated yet. That gets into the whole "I never told him," and I didn't. Part of me thought I should, and part of me thought that having an STD didn't fit with my self-concept so much that I just couldn't disclose.

Francine, a White 43-year-old professional . . . , had never intended to pass as healthy, but she did not get diagnosed with herpes until after beginning a sexual relationship with her second husband.

> I think there was all the guilt: What if I bring this on you? So, I felt guilt in bringing this into the relationship. Because he had not been anywhere near as sexually active as I had. . . .

Similarly, Tasha, a White graduate student, found out that she might have inadvertently passed as healthy when her partner was diagnosed with chlamydia. "I freaked out—I was like, 'Oh my God! I gave you chlamydia. I am so sorry! I am so sorry!' I felt really horrible, and I felt really awful." . . . Even if the passing is done unintentionally, it still brings guilt to the passer.

The women also tried to disidentify themselves from sexual disease in their attempts to pass as being sexually healthy. Rather than actively using a verbal or symbolic prop or action that would distance them from the stigma, the women took a passive approach. Some gave nonverbal agreement to putdowns of other women who were known to have STDs. For example, Hillary recalled such an interaction.

> It's funny being around people that don't know that I have an STD and how they make a comment like "That girl, she's such a slut. She's a walking STD." And how that makes me feel when I'm confronted with that, and having them have no idea that they could be talking about me.

Others kept silent about their status and tried to maintain the social status of being sexually healthy and morally pure. . . . Putting up the facade of sexual purity, these women distanced themselves from any suspicion of sexual disease.

Covering

When passing became too difficult, some women resorted to covering to deflect family and friends from the truth. Cleo summed up the rationale by comparing her behavior to what she had learned growing up with an alcoholic father. " . . . I learned that's what you do. Like you don't tell people those things that you consider shameful, and then, if confronted, you know, you lie."

Hillary talked to her parents about her HPV surgery, but never as treatment for an STD. She portrayed her moderate, cervical dysplasia as a precancerous scare, unrelated to sex. . . . When Tasha's sister helped her get a prescription for pubic lice, she actually provided the cover story for her embarrassed younger sister. "She totally took control, and made a personal inquiry: 'So, how did you get this? From a toilet seat?' And, I was like, 'a toilet seat,' and she believed me." . . . For Anne, a 28-year-old . . .

graduate student, a painful herpes outbreak almost outed her on a walk with a friend. She was so physically uncomfortable that she was actually waddling. Noticing her strange behavior, her friend asked what was wrong. Anne told her that it was a hemorrhoid; that was only a partial truth because herpes was the primary cause of her pain. As Anne put it, telling her about the hemorrhoid "was embarrassing enough!"

Deception and Guilt

The women who chose to deny, pass as normal, and use disidentifiers or cover stories shared more than the shame of having an STD—they had also told lies. With lying came guilt. Anne, who had used the hemorrhoid cover story, eventually felt extremely guilty. Her desire to conceal the truth was in conflict with her commitment to being an honest person. . . . Deborah, a 32-year old White professional . . . , only disclosed to her first sexual partner after she had been diagnosed with HPV; she passed as healthy with all other partners. Deborah reflected, "I think my choices not to disclose have hurt my sense of integrity." However, her guilt was resolved during her last gynecological exam when the nurse practitioner confirmed that after years of "clean" pap smear results Deborah was not being "medically unethical" by not disclosing to her partners. In other words, her immune system had probably dealt with the HPV in such a way that she might never have another outbreak or transmit the infection to sexual partners.

When Cleo passed as healthy with a sexual partner, she started "feeling a little guilty about not having told." However, the consequences of passing as healthy were very severe for Cleo:

> No. I never disclosed it to any future partner. Then, one day, I was having sex with Josh, my current husband, before we were married, and we had been together for a few months, maybe, and I'm like looking at his penis, and I said, "Oh, my goodness! You have a wart on your penis! Ahhh!" All of a sudden, it comes back to me.

Cleo's decision to pass left her with both the guilt of deceiving and infecting her husband.

Surprisingly, those women who had unintentionally passed as being sexually healthy (i.e., they had no knowledge of their STD status at the time) expressed a similar level of guilt as those who had been purposefully deceitful. Violet, a middle-class, White 36-year-old, had inadvertently passed as healthy with her current partner. Even after she had preventively disclosed to him, she still had to deal with the guilt over possibly infecting him.

> It hurt so bad that morning when he was basically furious at me thinking I was the one he had gotten those red bumps from. It was the hour from hell! I felt really majorly dirty and stigmatized. I felt like "God, I've done the best I can: If this is really caused by the HPV I have, then I feel terrible."

When using passing and covering techniques, the women strove to keep their stigma from tainting social interactions. They feared . . . rejection from their social circles of friends, family, and, most important, sexual partners. For most of the women, guilt surpassed fear and became the trigger to disclose. Those who had been deceitful in passing or covering had to assuage their guilt: Their options were either to remain in nonacceptance, disclose, or transfer their guilt to somebody else.

Stigma Deflection

As the women struggled to manage their individual stigma of being sexually diseased, real and imaginary social interactions became the conduit for the contagious label of damaged goods. Now that the unthinkable had happened to them, the women began to think of their past and present partners as infected, contagious, and potentially dangerous to themselves or other women. The combination of transferring stigma and assigning blame to others allowed the women to deflect the STD stigma away from themselves.

Stigma Transference

. . . Stigma is neither an emotion nor an impulse; rather, it is a formal concept that captures a relationship of devaluation (Goffman 1963). Although the participants attributed their devalued relationship with sexual health ideals to real and imaginary others, they were not controlling unacceptable feelings. Rather, stigma transference manifests as a clear expression of anger and fear, and the women did not connect this strategy to a reduction in their levels of anxiety; in fact, several discussed it in relation to increased anxiety.

Cleo remembered checking her partner's penis for warts after her doctor told her that she could detect them by visual inspection. It became a habit for Kayla to check her partner for any visible symptoms of an STD. Gloria was more careful about checking future partners and asking if they had anything. Tasha explained, "I just felt like I was with someone who was dirty." In all four cases, the women were only sure of their own STD infections, yet in their minds these partners had become diseased.

Transference of stigma to a partner became more powerful when the woman felt betrayed by her partner. When Hillary spoke of the "whole trust issue" with her ex-partner, she firmly believed he had lied to her about his sexual health status and that he would lie to others. Even though she had neither told him about her diagnosis nor had proof of him being infected, she fully transferred her stigma to him. . . .

Kayla also transferred the stigma of sexual disease to an ex-partner, never confronting him about whether he had tested positive for STDs. The auxiliary trait of promiscuity colored her view of him: "I don't know how sexually promiscuous he was, but I'm sure he had had a lot of partners." Robin, a 21-year-old White undergraduate, went so far as to tell her ex-partner that he needed to see a doctor and "do something about it." He doubted her ability to pinpoint contracting genital warts from him and called her a slut. Robin believed that he was the one with the reputation for promiscuity and decided to trash him by telling her two friends who hung out with him. Robin hoped to spoil his sexual reputation and scare off his future partners. In the transference of stigma, the women ascribed the same auxiliary traits onto others that others had previously ascribed to them. . . .

In all cases, it was logical to assume that past and current sexual partners may also have been infected. However, the stigma of being sexually diseased had far-reaching consequences in the women's imaginations. The traumatic impact on their sexual selves led most to infer that future, as yet unknown partners were also sexually diseased. . . . They had already been damaged by at least one partner. Therefore, they expected that future partners, ones who had not yet come into their lives, held the threat of also being damaged goods.

For Hillary, romantic relationships held no appeal anymore. She had heard of others who also had STDs but stayed in non-acceptance and never changed their lifestyle of having casual, unprotected sex:

> I just didn't want to have anything to do with it. A lot of it was not trusting people. When we broke up, I decided that I was not having sex. Initially, it was because I wanted to get an HIV test. Then, I came to kind of a turning point in my life and realized that I didn't want to do the one-night-stand thing anymore. It just wasn't worth it. It wasn't fun.

At this stage in her sexual self-transformation, Hillary imagined the world of possible partners having been polluted with contagion.

Anne's lesbian friends [told her] . . . future partners should be suspected of being dangerous. . . . Anne recalled [one] friend's reaction. "Those rotten men! You should just leave them alone. It's clear that you should be with women, and it's safer and better that way. Women don't do this kind of thing to each other." Her friends' guidance was an overt attempt to encourage Anne to believe that only potential male partners bore the stigma.

Instead of going by gender, Gloria, a self-identified Chicana, made a distinction based on ethnicity as a predictor of sexual health status:

> Now, if it was a White man, I made 'em wear a condom because I got it from a White man, and so I assumed that there had to be something with their culture—they were more promiscuous. But, one thing I do know culturally and with the times is that Chicano men were more likely to have a single partner.

These women felt justified in their newfound attitudes about sexual partners. What was only supposed to happen to "bad" women had happened to them. Overall, these women transitioned from blaming their own naivete to blaming someone else for not being more cautious or more honest.

Blame

The women's uses of stigma transference techniques were attempts to alleviate their emotional burdens. First, the finger of shame and guilt pointed inward,

toward the women's core sexual selves. Their sexual selves became tainted, dirty, damaged. In turn, they directed the stigma outward to both real and fictional others. Blaming others was a way for all of the women to alleviate some of the internal pressure and turn the anger outward. This emotional component of the damaged goods stage externalized the pain of their stigma.

Francine recalled how she and her first husband dealt with the issue of genital warts. . . . Francine's husband had likely contracted genital warts from his wild fraternity parties: "We really thought of it as, that woman who did the trains [serial sexual intercourse]. It was still a girl's fault kind of thing." By externalizing the blame to the promiscuous women at fraternity parties, Francine exonerated not only herself but also her husband. . . .

For Violet, it was impossible to neatly deflect the blame away from both herself and her partner.

> I remember at the time just thinking, "Oh man! He gave it to me!" While he was thinking, "God, [Violet]! You gave this to me!" So, we kind of just did a truce in our minds. Like, OK, we don't know who gave it—just as likely both ways. So, let's just get treated. We just kind of dropped it.

Clearly, the impulse to place blame was strong even when there was no easy target.

Often, the easiest targets were men who exhibited the auxiliary traits of promiscuity and deception. Tasha wasn't sure which ex-partner had transmitted the STD. However, she rationalized blaming a particular guy. "He turned out to be kind of a huge liar, lied to me a lot about different stuff. And, so I blamed him. All the other guys were, like, really nice people, really trustworthy." Likewise, when I asked Violet from whom she believed she had contracted chlamydia, she replied, "Dunno, it could've been from one guy, because that guy had slept with some unsavory women, so therefore he was unsavory." . . .

The actual guilt or innocence of these blame targets was secondary. What mattered to the women was that they could hold someone else responsible.

Stigma Acceptance

Eventually, every woman in the study stopped denying and deflecting the truth of her sexual health status by disclosing to loved ones. The women disclosed for either preventive or therapeutic reasons. That is, they were either motivated to reveal their STD status to prevent harm to themselves or others or to gain the emotional support of confidants.

Preventive and Therapeutic Disclosures

The decision to make a preventive disclosure was linked to whether the STD could be cured. Kayla explained,

> Chlamydia went away, and I mean it was really bad to have that, but I mean it's not something that you have to tell people later 'cause you know, in case it comes back. Genital warts, you never know.

Kayla knew that her parents would find out about the HPV infection because of insurance connections. Before her cryosurgery, Kayla decided to tell her mom about her condition.

> . . . [I]t was kind of hard at first. But, she wasn't upset with me. Main thing, she was disappointed, but I think she blamed my boyfriend more than she blamed me.

. . . Preventive disclosures to sexual partners, past and present, were a more problematic situation. The women were choosing to put themselves in a position where they could face blame, disgust, and rejection. For those reasons, the women put off preventive disclosures to partners as long as possible. For example, Anne made it clear that she would not have disclosed her herpes to a female sexual partner had they not been about to have sex. After "agonizing weeks and weeks and weeks before trying to figure out how to tell," Diana, a 45-year-old African American professional, finally shared her HPV and herpes status before her current relationship became sexual. Unfortunately, her boyfriend had a negative reaction: "He certainly didn't want to touch me anywhere near my genitals." . . .

For Summer, a 20-year-old Native American administrative assistant, and Gloria, their preventive disclosures were actually a relief to their sexual partners. Summer decided to disclose her genital warts to a new boyfriend after they had been "getting hot n' heavy." Lying in bed together, she said, "I need to tell you something." After she disclosed, he lay there, staring at the ceiling for a couple of minutes before deeply exhaling, "I thought you were going to tell me you had AIDS." Similarly, one of Gloria's partners sighed in relief when she revealed that she had herpes; he thought she was going to say she was HIV positive.

Many of the therapeutic disclosures were done to family members. The women wanted the support of those who had known them the longest. . . . Tasha disclosed to her mother right after she was diagnosed with chlamydia.

> My family died—"Guess what, mom, I got chlamydia." She's like, "Chlamydia? How did you find out you got chlamydia?" I'm like, "Well, my boyfriend got an eye infection." [laughter] "How'd he get it in his eye?" [laughter] So, it was the biggest joke in the family for the longest time!

. . . The women often unburdened their feelings of shame and guilt onto their close friends. Cleo shared her feelings with her roommate: "I told her that I was feeling weird about having had sex with this second guy, knowing that I had an STD." Kayla's therapeutic disclosure was reciprocal with her best friend. "At that time, she was also going through a similar situation with her boyfriend, so I felt okay finally to talk about it." . . . In Anne's case, her therapeutic disclosure to a friend was twofold: both to seek support and to apologize for initially having used the hemorrhoid cover story. Anne explained to her friend that she had felt too uncomfortable to tell the truth. . . .

Consequences of Disclosure

With both therapeutic and preventive disclosure, the women experienced some feelings of relief in being honest with loved ones. However, they still carried the intense shame of being sexually diseased women. The resulting emotion was anxiety over how their confidants would react: rejection, disgust, or betrayal. Francine was extremely anxious about disclosing to her husband. "That was really tough on us because I had to go home and tell Damon that I had this outbreak of herpes . . . I was really fearful—I didn't think that he would think I had recently had sex with somebody else—but, I was still really afraid of what it would do to our relationship." . . .

Overall, disclosing intensified the anxiety of having their secret leaked to others in whom they would never have chosen to confide. In addition, each disclosure brought with it the possibility of rejection and ridicule from the people whose opinions they valued most. For Gloria, disclosing was the right thing to do but had painful consequences when her partner's condom slipped off in the middle of sexual intercourse.

> I told him it doesn't feel right. "You'd better check." And, so he checked, and he just jumped off me and screamed, "Oh fuck!" And, I just thought, oh no, here we go. He just freaked and went to the bathroom and washed his penis with soap. I just felt so dirty.

The risk paid off for Summer, whose boyfriend asserted, "I don't ever want to be *that guy*—the one who shuns people and treats them differently." He borrowed sexual health education materials and spent over an hour asking her questions about various STDs. Even in this best-case scenario, the sexual intimacy in this relationship became problematized (e.g., having to research modes of STD transmission and safe-sex techniques). Disclosures were the interactional component of self-acceptance. The women became fully grounded in their new reality when they realized that the significant people in their lives were now viewing them through the discolored lenses of sexual disease.

Conclusion

The women with STDs went through an emotionally difficult process, testing out stigma management strategies, trying to control the impact of STDs on both their self-concepts and on their relationships with others. . . .

Ironically, most of the women first tried to deny this deviant health status—one that was virtually secret through the protection of doctor–patient confidentiality laws. Although many used passing and covering techniques that relied on deceiving others, self-deception was impossible to maintain. The medical truth began to penetrate their sexual self-conceptions as soon as they fabricated their first lie. To strategize a successful ruse, it was necessary to know the scope of what they were trying to hide.

When guilt caught up with them, making it hard to pass as healthy, their goal shifted to stigma deflection.

. . . However, this only delayed the inevitable—a deviant sexual self that penetrated the women's prior conceptions of their sexual selves.

After mentally transferring their stigma to real and imaginary others, all of the women finally accepted their tainted sexual health status through the reflexive dynamics of disclosure. . . . The women's sexual selves moved along a deviant career path by means of the interactive dynamics of their stigma management strategies.

. . . As the women made choices on which stigma management strategies to use, they grappled with the ramifications of internalizing this new label. Choosing passing and covering techniques meant they could remain in non-acceptance and put off stigma internalization. When they deflected the stigma onto others by means of stigma transference, the women glimpsed the severity of an STD stigma as reflected in the presumed sexual selves of real and imaginary others. Finally, the women's disclosures confirmed the new story of their tainted sexual selves.

. . . Unlike the stigma of HIV/AIDS—which carries the threat of life-changing illness, death, and contagion beyond the scope of sexual behaviors—the STD stigma lends itself to compartmentalization. The women were able to hide their shame, guilt, and fear (of further health complications, of contaminating others, of rejection, etc.) in the sexual part of their self-concept. They recognized that this part of their self-concept did not have to affect their entire identity. . . . If the impact of the STDs on their sex lives ever became too emotionally painful, the women could always decide to distance themselves from this role: choosing temporary or permanent celibacy. . . .

A narrative model of the self proposes that personal myths create the self and become "the stories we live by" (McAdams 1996:266). I propose that we seek to understand the significance of the stories we choose not to live by. Personal STD "stories" are rarely told in American mass culture. McAdams (1996:22) proposed that "carrying on affairs in secret"—maintaining a discreditable stigma—is a way to keep stigmatizing stories from occupying center stage in people's personal myth. However, these data suggest that individuals manage identity transformations, especially transformations into deviant identities, by constructing and sharing self-narratives through disclosure interactions. Although the women do not maintain secrecy, they do keep their STD stories from center stage. . . .

REFERENCES

Ackerman, Sandra J. 1998. "HPV: Who's Got It and Why They Don't Know." *HPV News* 8(2):1, 5–6.

Adler, Patricia A. and Peter Adler. 1987. *Membership Roles in Field Research.* Newbury Park, CA: Sage.

Brandt, Allan M. 1987. *No magic bullet: A social history of venereal disease in the United States since 1880.* New York: Oxford University Press.

Centers for Disease Control and Prevention. 1998a. "Genital Herpes." *National Center for HIV, STD & TB Prevention.* Retrieved from the World Wide Web February 4, 1998: URL.

———. 1998b. "HIV/AIDS Surveillance Report." *National Center for HIV, STD & TB Prevention.* Retrieved from the World Wide Web February 4, 1998: URL.

Conrad, Peter, and Rochelle Kern, eds. 1994. *The Sociology of Health & Illness: Critical Perspectives.* 4th ed. New York: St. Martin's Press.

Glaser, Barney G. and Anselm L. Strauss. 1967. *The Discovery of Grounded Theory: Strategies for Qualitative Research.* Chicago: Aldine.

Goffman, Erving. 1963. *Stigma.* Englewood Cliffs, N. J.: Prentice Hall.

McAdams, Dan P. 1996. *The stories we live by: Personal myths and the making of the self.* New York: Guilford Press.

Pryce, Anthony. 1998. "Theorizing the Pox: A Missing Sociology of VD." Presented to the International Sociological Association.

Sandstrom, Kent L. 1990. "Confronting Deadly Disease: the Drama of Identity Construction among Gay Men with AIDS." *Journal of Contemporary Ethnography,* 19(3):271–94.

Siegel, Karolynn and Beatrice J. Krauss. 1991. "Living with HIV Infection: Adaptive Tasks of Seropositive Gay Men." *Journal of Health and Social Behavior* 32(1):17–32.

Weitz, Rose. 1989. "Uncertainty and the Lives of Persons with AIDS." *Journal of Health and Social Behavior* 30(3):270–81.

Lesbian Women and Sexually Transmitted Infections

Kathleen Dolan and Phillip W. Davis

Many people believe lesbian women are not at risk for sexually transmitted infections (STIs) and HIV, but several studies have found that, similar to heterosexual people, about one in four have a lifetime history of at least one STI.[1] Reported infections include herpes, gonorrhea, hepatitis A, genital warts, HIV, and bacterial vaginosis. Risk factors for lesbian women are similar to those for other groups. These factors include drug and alcohol use, having unprotected sex with men, and having sex with men who have sex with men. You may wonder why sex with men is a risk factor for lesbians. People are often surprised to learn that many lesbian women had sex with men prior to coming out, and that some of them continue to do so. This is important when discussing lesbian sexual health because women with infections such

as herpes often say that they contracted them from a man, and it is possible to then transmit them to another woman. Transmission of herpes (and several other STIs) only requires skin to skin contact, and genital to genital rubbing (sometimes called *tribadism*) is common among lesbian women.

Other potentially risky behaviors include performing oral sex on a menstruating partner and sharing sex toys. Infections can also be transmitted if women have cuts on their fingers when they use their hands to stimulate their partner's genitals. One thing that can help is wearing latex gloves, although some women believe that gloves are cumbersome and offensive. Another thing that can help is the use of a dental dam during oral sex. Dams are sheets of latex about 8 inches square that can prevent or inhibit transmission. Some women prefer to use plastic kitchen wrap instead. Needless to say, taking these kinds of precautions can be a delicate and complex matter, especially in a community in which the risk of STIs is often unacknowledged and in which members often do not receive adequate sexual health information, treatment, and services.

To find out more about the topic, we surveyed an especially diverse sample of 162 self-identified lesbian women in a large southeastern city in 1998 and 1999. One third were African American, Latina, and Asian, and two thirds were white. Consistent with other studies, our participants reported an overall infection rate of 23 percent. Eight out of ten had had vaginal sex with a man at some point in their lives, and one out of three had had sex with a man in the last year. Our study found relatively high rates of fisting (placing the entire hand in a partner's vagina), which can tear the vaginal lining, leaving small abrasions where viruses or bacteria could enter the bloodstream (thirty percent had fisted, twenty-three percent had been fisted). Half of the women reported performing oral sex on a menstruating partner.

When it comes to subjective perceptions of risk, the women generally fell into three groups. One group viewed themselves as essentially invulnerable. In other words, they felt protected from infection by virtue of being lesbian, believing that only heterosexuals were at risk. Most participants fell into a second group that viewed lesbian women as "socially inoculated." This view was based on a woman's familiarity with her partner's sexual history and her faith in her partner's honesty. A third group viewed themselves as fundamentally vulnerable, or at least as vulnerable as anyone else. They were very cautious when having sex. They used dental dams for oral sex and they put condoms on their sex toys. These three views were not fixed and static, and over time many women shifted in their views in response to new information, to their partners' beliefs and preferences, and to their own infections. Many of these patterns, beliefs, and practices are likely to change as health care providers become more knowledgeable, as health activism spreads in the lesbian community, and as lesbian women's sexual health becomes a higher priority in research, medical, and policy arenas.

For more information on this topic, see our article, "Nuances and shifts in lesbian women's constructions of STI and HIV vulnerability," in *Social Science and Medicine* (2003).

NOTE

1. Solarz (ed.) *Lesbian health: Current assessment and directions for the future.* 1999. Washington, D.C.: National Academy Press.

Showdown in Choctaw County

Jacob Levenson

David deShazo is chain-smoking Marlboros as he drives north out of Mobile on a bright November morning. A garbage bag stuffed with blankets, baby clothes, and toys takes up most of the backseat of the Pontiac. The car is chilly because deShazo's heater is busted, and he doesn't have the two hundred bucks it will cost to get it fixed. He's headed up to Choctaw County to find two sisters, Sara and Rebecca Jackson, who are infected with HIV. They live with their mother and their two baby sons down a dirt road somewhere outside of Gilbertown, near the Mississippi border. The girls haven't been heard from in seven months. He takes another draw off his cigarette, squints through his bug-smeared windshield at the two-lane highway, and tries to resist a flickering current of anxiety.

DeShazo hadn't really known what to expect when he was hired to work in the poor counties of southern Alabama to search out people infected with HIV, to convince the at-risk to get tested, and to warn community leaders about the threat of AIDS. In the 18 months since he took the job, he's driven more than 60,000 miles talking about the virus to just about anyone who will listen. He's caught hateful stares at general stores and gas stations. A county commissioner over in Wilcox attacked him verbally at a church meeting for talking about AIDS without permission. And he's heard comments that the "niggers" and "faggots" are just getting what they deserve. None of these things has really surprised deShazo. What's unsettling is the silence that surrounds him in these towns. When he talks to people it often seems as though he is shouting across an unbridgeable chasm.

From "Showdown in Choctaw County" by Jacob Levenson (2002), *Utne Reader* 111(May/June), 73–80. Reprinted by permission.

The Alabama that deShazo has been traveling for a year and a half ceased to exist in the minds of most Americans after the Civil Rights movement. Somehow it was never remade into the New South of Ted Turner, Emeril Live, and urban sprawl. There remains an expansive, aching beauty to these counties. The countryside, with its forests of hickory, oak, and pine, its cotton fields and tangles of green creeks and rivers, feels timeless. A procession of churches lines every road: NEW PROVIDENCE BAPTIST, JESUS IS LORD OLD ZION MISSIONARY, LITTLE ZION BAPTIST.

All of this lends the region a sense that it is somehow insulated from the perils of modern life. But now the greatest epidemic of recent times is spreading slowly and quietly through the black communities of rural Alabama. In the years since AIDS hit the headlines, the disease gradually has become a black epidemic. In 2000, according to the Centers for Disease Control, 54 percent of all new AIDS cases were African Americans. The disease is now the number-one killer of both black men and black women between the ages of 22 and 45. What's perhaps even more surprising is that the South is the new epicenter of AIDS in the United States. More people are living with AIDS in this region than in any other part of the country. And while the disease is still concentrated in Southern cities, there are warning signs that it is creeping into the countryside. The number of rural cases in the South more than doubled in seven years.

DeShazo and his co-workers represent a thin line of defense against this brewing public health crisis. Impoverished patients already have overburdened Alabama's small network of AIDS agencies. Mobile AIDS Support Services (MASS), for which deShazo works, has five caseworkers for roughly 800 clients in Mobile and the surrounding six rural counties. Most of their patients don't have private insurance,

Medicaid, or direct access to the new drug cocktails. The caseworkers spend the bulk of their time just trying to get medicine for their clients. MASS needs to hire more staff, but as it is can only afford to pay people like deShazo a salary of $23,000.

As deShazo crosses Choctaw County, a couple of logging trucks stacked with clear-cut pine trees rush by in the opposite direction. The last cotton plantations disappeared in the 1960s, and paper mills are pretty much the only industry now. The county is home to 16,000 people, roughly half of whom are black, with 22 percent of the population living in poverty. And there are no hospitals or infectious-disease doctors in Choctaw County.

DeShazo drives through Gilbertown, which isn't much more than a stoplight, a cemetery, a grocery, a pharmacy, and a dollar store, and makes a right turn down a narrow, unmarked dirt road. He saw the Jackson sisters once before, as a favor to the social worker in Selma who is supposed to be in charge of their case. A part of him is pissed off that they've dropped off the agency's radar since then. At the same time, he's not surprised, given the patchwork nature of AIDS care in Alabama. As worried as he is about these girls, he seems charged up about the case, confident that he has the skills to work through the welfare system so that the sisters can get the medications, doctors, and care that might save their lives. It's a sense of purpose that he has rarely felt in other social work jobs, which mostly left him feeling weak and hopeless.

DeShazo pulls over in front of a trailer home, steps out, climbs three rickety steps, and knocks. A female voice yells to come on in.

DeShazo opens the door and feels a wave of heat. The first person he sees is Sara, who is sitting on a couch changing a 2-year-old boy on her lap. She's wearing a Michael Jordan T-shirt and her hair is in long cornrows. He is relieved to see that she has full cheeks and looks healthy. Another child in blue pajamas is giggling and waddling back and forth on the floor. Piles of clothes, empty soda cans, and an overturned tricycle litter the living room. A raspy cough comes from the kitchen, where Sara's sister, Rebecca, is slumped over a chair facing an open oven, trying to keep warm. She must have fever chills because the trailer is stifling, almost too hot to

breathe in. DeShazo sets his bag of clothes and toys down on the floor. "Hi, I'm David deShazo from Mobile AIDS Support Services," he says. "How y'all doing?"

Rebecca doesn't move. Sara looks up from the couch and says hi. He had been worried about how they would receive him. White men who work for the government aren't always greeted warmly around here. But there is a loose confidence to Sara's smile, and the casual way she continues changing her son's diaper puts him at ease. DeShazo says that he's brought some supplies and then sits down and asks Sara if she's got any income.

"Nothing but food stamps," she says, seemingly unfazed.

"How about Rebecca?"

"She got a disability check."

"How long has Rebecca been like that?" deShazo asks, nodding toward the kitchen.

"She's been real sick for three days now," Sara answers. "Something's messing with her eyes."

DeShazo feels a twinge of fear. He thinks that she probably has contracted CMV, normally a relatively benign virus, but one that can blind AIDS patients.

"You getting any medicine, Sara?" deShazo asks.

"I get medicine while I'm pregnant, but I save it," she says. "I ain't going to get no more when I have the baby."

DeShazo's head starts to spin. "You pregnant again, Sara?" he asks. He was so relieved to see her carrying weight.

Sara smiles, shakes her head as if she can't believe he couldn't tell, and says, "Seven months."

DeShazo's questions begin to tumble out faster and with more urgency. "Y'all still seeing those doctors in Waynesboro?" he asks.

"Yeah, but I missed my last two appointments because I didn't have no way to get there," she says.

Rebecca still hasn't uttered a word. She coughs again—a coarse hack. Sara tells deShazo that she was turned down for Medicaid before she got pregnant. He figured as much. In Alabama you have to be over 65 years old or prove you are blind or disabled. In his experience, most people aren't able to get the help they need unless a lawyer or a professional advocate is working their case. Rebecca stumbles into the room and collapses on a couch next to the door. She has white flecks of spittle on her mouth and chin.

Sara's pregnancy has deShazo worried that she might have infected others. He asks Sara if her boyfriend has been tested. He tested negative a year ago, she says, but he hasn't been retested since she got pregnant again. (He's now in prison.) And, as far as she knows, Rebecca's boyfriend hasn't been tested at all. "My boyfriend takes some of my medicine," Sara says, "just to be careful." DeShazo feels a flush of anger. He can't believe these sisters are having unprotected sex and that they think feeding them AZT is going to keep their boyfriends safe. They could be starting a small epidemic.

As for the toddlers, Benny and William, Sara tells deShazo that they were tested a few months ago. This is good news, but it doesn't mean they are all right. Small children need to be tested repeatedly before it can be absolutely determined that they didn't contract the disease from their mothers. . . .

DeShazo was hired along with seven community outreach workers to canvas 32 of Alabama's poorest rural counties, which based on their sexually transmitted disease and teen pregnancy rates appear most vulnerable for AIDS. A year and a half into the three-year project, deShazo estimates that he's approached 300 people for testing. Only two have agreed to get into his aging blue Pontiac and head down to the local health department. This isn't unusual. There is a long-standing shortage of doctors and health facilities in black Southern communities. And many blacks in the region distrust doctors—a legacy of the infamous Tuskegee Syphilis Study, in which black test subjects were denied treatment for decades as part of a long-term health experiment. What is mentioned less often is that, compared with gay communities, much of black America—and particularly the rural South—has been relatively ignored in the campaign to educate people about AIDS.

DeShazo was hired in part because he had an idea about how to navigate the socially conservative, religious, and racially fractured landscape of rural Alabama. He was raised in Clark County, 50 miles north of Mobile, where his father was a country doctor. His understanding of the culture, the spiritual convictions of the people, and even the subtle rhythms of their speech have allowed him to penetrate his territory more deeply than any of his fellow workers. But growing up in the segregated world of 1950s Alabama did not prepare him for the rural black world this job has allowed him to enter. . . .

Alabama, which has always had a relatively low rate of AIDS, now seems primed for a burgeoning epidemic. Crack—which often breeds a sex-for-drugs trade and seems inevitably to show up just ahead of AIDS—has moved in from Florida and Texas and made its way into even the most rural counties. Already black women in the South are 26 times more likely than white women to have HIV. DeShazo is armed with these facts, but they seem somehow abstract in places like Gilbertown. The threat of AIDS here feels deeply entwined with poverty and the lingering effects of segregation. . . .

Every spring, Sara and Rebecca Jackson's high school holds a blood drive. It's always been a popular event with the students. Giving a pint of blood helps the sick, and it's an easy excuse to get out of afternoon classes. At least that's how 16-year-old Sara and her 14-year-old sister, Rebecca, felt one afternoon when they volunteered to have their blood drawn.

Sara was the more rebellious of the two sisters. Always using her quick wit to get her way with her mother, she had declared her independence by marrying her boyfriend and moving out of the house. As soon as she graduated she planned to join the army so she could earn enough money to pay for college and become a lawyer. Rebecca, the baby of the family, was more sensitive and even as a youngster wanted to become a nurse. Their father—who had been in and out of prison for drug offenses when the girls were young—worked as a logger and was making enough money to allow their mom to stay home with Rebecca. On a warm Wednesday afternoon about two months after the blood drive, Sara came home for a visit and greeted her mother, who absently handed her a plain white envelope from the county health department. Simple and straightforward, the letter thanked her for her donation but said that her blood was contaminated with HIV. Sara was stunned. She didn't know anything about the disease except that it was deadly.

Three days later an identical letter arrived for Rebecca.

Sara and Rebecca dropped out of high school. Sara's marriage didn't last, and the girls' father was soon back in prison. . . . Their mother has tried to care for the girls and her grandsons as best she can but has avoided asking welfare workers or AIDS agencies for help.

DeShazo is talking to Rebecca and Sara's aunt in the kitchen. He has been at the trailer for about an hour now. He is worried that he is not going to be able to keep these girls alive without help. He wants to enlist family and neighbors who can drive Rebecca two hours to Mobile to see a specialist. That is going to be tough as long as the sisters keep their illness secret. When he comes back into the living room, he says to Sara, "I know the doctors in Waynesboro have been good to you, but it may be time for you guys to see a specialist. How do you feel about that?"

"I'll do anything that'll keep me healthy like I am 'cause I don't want to leave my children like this," Sara says. But when he asks if she would consider telling her grandparents or the host of cousins and in-laws who live in the area that she's infected with HIV, she is silent. All the MASS case workers have heard stories about clients getting discriminated against at their jobs, frozen out by their churches, and abandoned by their families. Occasionally, the social worker who handles the agency's rural cases must deliver medications to clients at "secret" locations like a grocery store parking lot. . . .

Needing a break, [deShazo] offers to go down to the pharmacy in Gilbertown and pick up Rebecca's medication. . . .

AIDS can move relatively quickly through a rural county. HIV spreads mainly through what epidemiologists call "sexual networks," social groups in which people are sleeping together. On paper they can be traced like genealogical trees. When HIV is introduced into a small town where a significant number of people belong to a single tree, there is a real risk of an epidemic. (When two girls in a rural Mississippi town were diagnosed with AIDS several years ago, the state health department found a heterosexual network of 44 people, of whom 34 were tested and seven were found to be HIV positive. When the Centers for Disease Control followed up several months later, only two of the seven were receiving medical care.)

When deShazo gets back to the trailer, Sara has put the place together: The tricycle has been righted, and the clothes that were on the floor have been put away. Rebecca is sitting up, talking on the phone. She flashes a smile and for an instant looks like any other teenager. DeShazo sits down in front of her. She puts down the phone and is holding William tightly in her arms on the couch.

"Do you ever feel like there's no reason to live, Rebecca?" deShazo asks.

William's head is buried in her breast, and she is rocking him back and forth. "Sometimes," she says and stares at the ground.

"Is there anybody you can go to when you feel like that?" he asks.

"There ain't nobody but myself," she says and clenches her jaw. Her eyes fill with tears, but she stops herself just short of crying. . . .

If Sara is denied benefits, deShazo says, he will apply for free medications from one of the pharmaceutical companies. He also wants to get the sisters on a program that will help pay for electricity and heat without exposing that they have HIV. He carries a generic business card that says he works for the United Way. Maybe he can use it to cut a deal with the local utility company. He would like to find a nurse in the area with some HIV experience who will check up on Rebecca, but that will involve getting Rebecca approved for Alabama's home health program, which requires a medical history from her doctor and the cooperation of the Choctaw County health department. She might be dead by then. . . .

The job of getting AIDS patients like Rebecca and Sara Jackson the drug cocktails that have been popularly heralded as a panacea will ultimately fall on the shoulders of community-based organizations like MASS. In 2000, MASS, which operates on an annual budget of $600,000, had to "professionally beg" pharmaceutical companies for $1.8 million in medications for uninsured clients. The Alabama legislature has been unwilling to fully match federal funds to help the poor pay for expensive drugs, which can cost anywhere from $10,000 to $18,000 a year. And during any given month, about 400 infected Alabamians—mostly black, all living below the poverty line—can be on a waiting list to get on the federal government's drug assistance program.

The next Tuesday morning deShazo drives out to see Rebecca and Sara. He has been thinking about them all weekend. "I wasn't going to cry, and then I had all this stuff dammed up inside and the tears just came," he says. "Then the anger started. I've got to channel that anger. This girl ain't going to die. She ain't going to die. These girls are going to have a chance."

When he arrives at the Jacksons' trailer, there is no sign of anyone. A late-'70s Chevrolet drives up the road. Sara is in the backseat with her son, Benny. "Where's Rebecca?" he asks. Sara says Rebecca collapsed on Saturday. Just stopped breathing. She's in the hospital in Waynesboro. . . .

Waynesboro is a city of around 6,000. DeShazo passes a cluster of single-story brown cinder-block buildings—a housing project that seems out of place in a small town. After a couple of wrong turns, he finds the hospital. In the elevator heading up to Rebecca's room, deShazo looks tired and stares nervously up at the blinking floor numbers.

He finds Rebecca's door. Inside, she is in the fetal position facing a single window. She's alone. A movie is playing on a television bolted to the wall. Rebecca has her arms pulled up close to her face. An IV is hooked up to her right arm, and she's clinging to her blanket like a small child. DeShazo walks around to the side of her bed. He leans up against the radiator next to the window. "How you feeling, Rebecca?" he asks. "I'm going to have surgery tomorrow," she says, her voice raspy.

"What for?" deShazo asks.

"My gallbladder," she says before being seized by a fit of heavy coughing.

"How old are you, Rebecca?" deShazo asks.

"Nineteen," she answers.

"You know, Rebecca," deShazo says, "there's a lady in Mobile who does nothing but check on children whose parents are infected."

"He ain't infected," Rebecca says. This is the strongest statement she has ever made to him.

"I know," he says, "but it may be wise for William to see her anyway."

"My mama's with him," Rebecca says softly.

"Yeah, I know your mama's there doing a real good job." Realizing that there's nothing he can do or say at this moment to make the situation better, he decides to leave.

In the coming month deShazo will dedicate almost all of his time to this case. Rebecca's doctor will drop her for failing to take her medications. It will turn out that the doctor never even prescribed protease inhibitors, the most powerful lifesaving drugs, because he didn't believe she would take them. DeShazo will drive Rebecca to a specialist two hours away in Mobile, who will diagnose her with pneumonia, CMV, and thrush. When he tries to get home health care for her, an anonymous caller will warn the Choctaw County health department not to send a nurse to the Jacksons' because Rebecca plans to bite and infect as many people as she can before she dies. Sara will go into labor a month prematurely. The hospital in Waynesboro, saying they don't have the facilities to handle a premature birth, will refuse to admit her and opt instead to drive her to Mobile. Forty-eight hours after she gives birth, the hospital in Mobile, citing policy for mothers on public assistance, will attempt to discharge her with a bus ticket back to Gilbertown. DeShazo will get her another day in the hospital. But when Sara gets back to her trailer, the electricity will be shut off.

All of this is still in front of them though. On the drive back from the hospital in Waynesboro, the harsh reality hits deShazo: Keeping Rebecca alive with what few resources are available is unlikely. He passes a hand painted sign for Pine Grove Cemetery on the corner of a dirt road leading into the forest. He is smoking another cigarette. Along the highway the sweet gum trees have turned flaming orange and the oaks a sunflower yellow, "She's going to die," he says. "She's going to die, and there ain't one goddamn f-ing thing I can do about it."

EPILOGUE: DeShazo angles the blue Pontiac in front of Rebecca Jackson's trailer and kills the engine. It's spring, 2002. Their wooden porch has collapsed. He's stopped by to see Rebecca. For the past year, his work and much of his life has been centered around keeping her alive. Gradually, he's seen Rebecca's own desire to survive grow. Last spring, her boyfriend, John, proposed. And as soon as Rebecca is strong enough, they plan to have a wedding. Officially, deShazo was supposed to hand off the case to another social worker months ago. But he can't. Rebecca needs him (especially since Sara had pneumonia over the summer). In a sense he's kin to the Jacksons now. DeShazo hears the sound of wheels on the gravel road. He turns. It's John and he has Rebecca in the car. She's thinner than deShazo has ever seen her. John helps her out of her seat. She's too weak to walk so John lifts her into his arms and carries her into the trailer. A few days later, she'll be back in the hospital.

HIV/AIDS and People with Disability

Nora Ellen Groce

Although AIDS researchers have studied the disabling effects of HIV/AIDS on previously healthy people, little attention has been given to the risk of HIV/AIDS for individuals who have a physical, sensory, intellectual, or mental health disability before becoming infected. It is commonly assumed that disabled individuals are not at risk. They are incorrectly thought to be sexually inactive, unlikely to use drugs, and at less risk for violence or rape than their non-disabled peers. Yet a growing body of research indicates that they are actually at increased risk for every known risk factor for HIV/AIDS. For example, in a recent article, S Blumberg and W Dickey[1] analyze findings from the 1999 US National Health Interview Survey and show that adults with mental health disorders are more likely to report a medium or high chance of becoming infected with HIV, are more likely to be tested for HIV infection, and are more likely to expect to be tested within the next 12 months than are members of the general population. . . .

[D]espite the assumption that disabled people are sexually inactive, those with disability—and disabled women in particular—are likely to have more sexual partners than their non-disabled peers. Extreme poverty and social sanctions against marrying a disabled person mean that they are likely to become involved in a series of unstable relationships.[2] Disabled individuals (both male and female) around the world are more likely to be victims of sexual abuse and rape than their non-disabled peers. Factors such as increased physical vulnerability, the need for attendant care, life in institutions, and the almost universal belief that disabled people cannot be a reliable witness on their own behalf make them targets for predators.[3,4] In cultures in which it is believed that HIV-positive individuals can rid themselves of the virus by having sex with virgins, there has been a significant rise in rape of disabled children and adults. Assumed to be virgins, they are specifically targeted.[5] . . . Individuals with disability are at increased risk of substance abuse and less likely to have access to interventions. It is estimated that 30% of all street children have some type of disability and these young people are rarely reached by safe-sex campaigns.[6]

Furthermore, literacy rates for disabled individuals are exceptionally low (one estimate cites an adult literacy rate of only 3% globally[6]), thus making communication of messages about HIV/AIDS all the more difficult. Sex education programmes for those with disability are rare,[7–9] and almost no general campaigns about HIV/AIDS target (or include) disabled populations.[10] . . .

The future for disabled individuals who become HIV positive is equally grim. Although little is known about access to HIV/AIDS care, disabled citizens receive far fewer general health-services than others.[11,12] Indeed, care is not only often too expensive for impoverished disabled persons, but it can also be physically inaccessible . . .

Currently, little is known about HIV/AIDS and disability. Only a few studies have estimated prevalence[13,14] and no prevalence data exist for any disabled populations from sub-Saharan Africa, Asia, Europe, Central and South America, or the Caribbean. However, a growing number of stories from disability advocates worldwide point to significant unreported rates of infection, disease, and death.[15] Over the past decade there have be a handful of articles on HIV/AIDS pilot programmes and interventions for intellectually disabled adults or services for deaf adolescents.[16,17] Many of these projects are innovative but almost all are small and underfunded. There is a real need to understand the issue of HIV/AIDS in disabled people in global terms and to design and implement programmes and policy in a more coherent and comprehensive manner. The roughly

600 million individuals who live with a disability are among the poorest, least educated, and most marginalised of all the world's peoples. They are at serious risk of HIV/AIDS and attention needs to be focused on them. . . .

NOTES

1. Blumberg SJ, Dickey WC. Prevalence of HIV risk behaviors, risk perceptions, and testing among US adults with mental disorders. *J Acquir Immune Defic Syndr* 2003; 32: 77–79.

2. Economic and Social Commission for Asia and the Pacific. Hidden sisters: women and girls with disabilities in the Asian Pacific region. New York: United Nations, 1995.

3. Nosek MA, Howland CA, Hughes RB. The investigation of abuse and women with disabilities: going beyond assumptions. *Violence Against Women* 2001; 7: 477–99.

4. Chenoweth L. Violence and women with disabilities: silence and paradox. *Violence Against Women* 1996; 2: 391–411.

5. UNICEF. Global survey of adolescents with disability: an overview of young people living with disabilities: their needs and their rights. New York: UNICEF Inter-Divisional Working Group on Young People, Programme Division, 1999.

6. Helander E. Prejudice and dignity: an introduction to community-based rehabilitation. New York: UNDP, 1993.

7. Collins P, Geller P, Miller S, Toro P, Susser E. Ourselves, our bodies, our realities: an HIV prevention intervention for women with severe mental illness. *J Urban Health* 2001; 78: 162–75.

8. Gaskins S. Special population: HIV/AIDS among the deaf and hard of hearing. *J Assoc Nurses AIDS Care* 1999; 35: 75–78.

9. Robertson P, Bhate S, Bhate M. AIDS: education and adults with a mental handicap. *J Mental Def Res* 1991; 35: 475–80.

10. UNAIDS. Report on the global HIV/AIDS epidemic 2002. New York: Joint UN Programme on HIV/AIDS, 2002.

11. Altman BM. Does access to acute medical care imply access to preventive care: a comparison of women with and without disabilities. *J Disabil Policy Stud* 1997; 8: 99–128.

12. Lisher D, Richardson M, Levine P, Patrick D. Access to primary health care among persons with disabilities in rural areas: a summary of the literature. *Rural J Health* 1996; 12: 45–53.

13. Van Biema D. AIDS and the deaf. *Time Magazine* 1994; 143: 76–78.

14. Cournos F, Empfield M, Howarth E, Schrage H. HIV infection in state hospitals: case reports and long-term management strategies. *Hosp Comm Psychiatry* 1990; 41: 163–66.

15. Moore D. HIV/AIDS and deafness. *Am Ann Deaf* 1998; 143: 3.

16. Gaskins S. Special population: HIV/AIDS among the deaf and hard of hearing. *J Assoc Nurses AIDS Care* 1999; 10: 75–77.

17. McGillivray J. Level of knowledge and risk of contracting HIV/AIDS amongst young adults with mild/moderate intellectual disability. *J Appl Res Intellect Disabil* 1999; 12: 113–26.

Structural Violence, Poverty and the AIDS Pandemic

Joia S. Mukherjee

Introduction

Three and a half decades into the AIDS epidemic, prevention programmes are focused on information, education and communication about behaviours that put people at risk for HIV—a sexually transmitted disease. AIDS can be prevented, it is reasoned, through behaviour change. Yet despite prevention efforts, AIDS has continued to spread, particularly among the poor. Today, of the 40 million people worldwide living with HIV, 90 percent of them live in resource-poor countries.

What can be done about the AIDS epidemic? The answer is often simply stated as prevention and treatment. HIV prevention can be viewed as two interrelated entities: risk avoidance such as abstaining from sex and drug use; and harm reduction that is minimizing risk while conducting behaviours that are associated with HIV (this specifically refers to the use of clean injecting needles for drug users and the use of condoms if one is having sex). Prevention is often presented as "life-style choices," within the control of the individual. Yet those who live in poverty have severely constrained choice. The systematic exclusion of a group from the resources needed to develop their full human potential has been called "structural violence" (Galtung, 1969). The concept of structural violence is useful to understand the barriers that prevent risk mitigation in the HIV epidemic.

Lack of access to treatment is also intertwined with poverty. 1995 saw the advent of active antiretroviral therapy (ART), after which a combination of

Reprinted by permission from Macmillan Publishers Ltd: *Development,* 50(2), pp. 115–121, copyright © 2007, published by Palgrave Macmillan.

drugs or "cocktail," taken daily, could return even the sickest people with advanced immune deficiency to normal health. Availability of treatment, however, actually worsened inequality in AIDS outcomes between the rich and the poor. The poor were systematically excluded from ART as the drugs were thought to be too expensive, too complicated and not sustainable to use in resource-poor settings. This combination of factors has led to a global pandemic in which the poor have excess risk of acquiring HIV and, once infected, have less access to lifesaving ART. As a result, the most heavily HIV-burdened countries have become further impoverished due to the epidemic.

AIDS and Structural Violence

As mentioned above, 90 percent of the HIV epidemic is concentrated in developing countries. In poor countries, many people are trapped in wage slavery. This type of economic victimization is one of the major factors in the spread of HIV. Girls are often sent to cities to be domestic servants and, as such, are often forced to have sex with their masters. Women unable to support themselves and their children often become reliant on men who are neither economically reliable nor faithful. Finally, prostitution and the sex trade reflects a reality that has been most widely documented in South and Southeast Asia, now home to 6.5 million HIV-positive persons, but that likely occurs everywhere in the world (World Health Organization, 2004a). Women are less likely to be educated and less likely to find paying work. When working, women earn two-thirds of what men earn. Women also bear the enormous burden of uncompensated work, including caring for children and sick relatives, feeding the family and managing the home. As a result, women spend twice as much time performing unpaid work than do men (International Labour Organization, 2004, http://www.ilo.org/public/english/bureau/inf/download/women/pdf/factssheet.pdf, accessed 10 December 2004). Men are far from immune, however, to the crushing poverty of the developing world. They, too, suffer from desperation, depression, anger and emasculation, all of which have been linked with resultant so-called "social ills" such as substance abuse, domestic violence and other criminal activities (Kawachi and Kennedy, 1997). But we must ask: what really is the fundamental "social ill"? Such social ills are rooted in poverty and inequality. Structural violence, defined as the physical and psychological harm that results from exploitive and unjust social, political and economic systems, is the shadow in which the AIDS virus lurks. . . .

Gender Inequality

Young women have been recognized to be especially vulnerable to infection and the largest number of new cases comes from this group. The 2004, UNAIDS' AIDS Epidemic Update reported that women constitute half of the 37.2 million adults (aged 15–49) globally who are living with HIV. Close to 60 percent of adults living with HIV on the most heavily burdened continent, Africa, are women (World Health Organization, 2004b). Every region of the world has seen an increase in the number of women living with HIV during the past two years (World Health Organization, 2004b).

The differences between the rates of incident HIV infection between boys and girls are staggering. Girls under the age of 15 are five times more likely to be HIV-positive than boys of the same age group. Part of this vulnerability is biologic, for every sex act, an HIV-negative woman is at least twice as likely to become infected by an HIV-positive man, than an HIV-negative man is to become infected from an HIV-positive woman. We would make a critical mistake, however, to view this heightened threat to women as solely a matter of biology. While part of the greater transmissibility of HIV from men to women can be explained by basic science, biological vulnerability adds little to our understanding of the disproportionate

suffering borne by poor women across the globe at the hands of the AIDS epidemic.

When we take a step back from statistics and biology, the bigger picture reveals that AIDS affects women who are struggling under the overarching epidemic of *poverty,* have little control against the factors that put them at risk for this deadly disease. This link, between the economic conditions in which women live, those which make them more vulnerable to all facets of the pandemic, has not been translated into policies to remediate this vulnerability or mitigate the impact of HIV on women even in countries where ART is available. In the United States and western Europe, success stories of the late 1990s, when highly active antiretroviral therapy restored life to the dying, leave poor women in the darkened corner of statistical outliers, victims of the gross inequalities in rich countries. Among new AIDS cases in the United States, approximately half occur in African-Americans; representing only 12 percent of the population, this group's HIV prevalence is eleven times higher than among whites. African-American women, both urban and rural, account for an increasing proportion of new infections, and AIDS is now the leading cause of death for African-American women aged 25–34 in the United States and Canada.

In resource-poor settings the situation is more dire. Clearly, there is a role for AIDS prevention; particularly that which is evidence based such as the use of antiretroviral drugs in pregnant women to prevent HIV transmission to their infants; the treatment of sexually transmitted diseases; the use of harm-reduction strategies such as condom distribution and needle exchange; and most recently, male circumcision. However, in the last five years, HIV prevention has been co-opted by groups promoting moral or religious agendas—particularly in the United States. Today more than half of international funding for AIDS prevention comes from the United States' State Department and relies on a prevention education strategy given the epithet "ABC" for promoting abstinence, being faithful and condom use. All of these prevention strategies rely on personal choice and the agency to carry out such choices.

Abstinence relies on the ability to say "no" and to have it be heard. Such personal agency is robbed by violence of both the structural and physical varieties. Gender inequality through laws or practices from unequal access to education, housing, paying work or inheritance continue to place more women than men into destitution. Infidelity more commonly stems from the male partner and is worsened by a shortage of wage-earning jobs available. In such a state, women are more likely to be victimized by rape, or forced to use sex as a tradable commodity for survival. Trumpeting calls for abstinence and fidelity without addressing the economic roots of the commoditization of women's bodies is a cynical dismissal of the lives of the most vulnerable in the epidemic. Such an approach fails to address the fact that violence and brutality rather than love, trust or sexual activity are the forces that put women at risk for AIDS, death and unplanned pregnancy.

Rape is a major factor driving the AIDS epidemic. In political conflicts, rape is a common crime and can even be used purposefully as a tool of war. For example, in Rwanda, the systemic sexual molestation, rape and mutilation of women and girls were an integral part of the Hutu plan to annihilate the Tutsi population (Donovan, 2002; Amnesty International, 2004, http://web.amnesty.org/library/Index/ENGAFR4700 72004?open&of=ENG-RWA, accessed 13 December 2004). As a result, a total 70 percent of the 250,000 women who survived the genocide but were raped are now HIV-positive (Human Rights Watch, 2004: 7; http://www.avega.org.rw, accessed December 13, 2004). Similarly, studies by the United Nations Children's Fund concluded that over 75 percent of girls and young women abducted by rebel forces during times of armed conflict in Sierra Leone were sexually abused (Amnesty International, 2000: 2). In Uganda, the Lord's Resistance Army (LRA) continues to abduct children; in this 15-year conflict, thousands of children have been raped and HIV-infected by the LRA. Ninety percent of northern Uganda's 1.8 million people have been internally displaced and are now crowded into refugee camps. Forty thousand children routinely walk up to several kilometres each night to schools, hospitals and shelters in the town of Gulu to protect themselves from abduction. Not surprisingly, the HIV prevalence rate in northern Uganda is at least twice that of the rest of the country. . . .

A similar lack of real choice or agency faces women in monogamous relationships who are encouraged to rely on "being faithful" as their means to prevent HIV infection. This strategy, of course, withers against the backdrop of structural violence, as most women are infected as a result of their partners' infidelities, not their own. In fact, in many locations, the main HIV risk factor for a woman is the simple fact of having a stable sexual partner (World Health Organization, 2004b: 7–12). One study reports that HIV infection rates were 10 percent higher for married than for sexually active unmarried girls aged 15–19 years in Kenya and Zambia (Glynn *et al.*, 2001). A study in rural Uganda found that 88 percent of HIV-infected women aged 15–19 years were married (Kelly *et al.*, 2003). Because young women in many societies often have significantly older men as their partners, the men are more likely to have had other partners and are therefore more likely to have been exposed to HIV. Additionally, while infidelity is as old as the human species, structural violence often forces men living in poverty to leave their homes to search for work in cities, factories and mines where there are no provisions for family life. Such necessary migration for meagre wages, resulting in long absences from the family, sets the stage for multiple sexual partners.

Condom use is rarely under the control of women and access is limited in resource-poor settings. While "success stories" of commercial sex worker labour unions demanding condom use of their clients do exist, few would argue that a society that affords women no option but prostitution should be considered a "success" (Crossette, 1995; Hanenberg and Rojanapithayakorn, 1996; AIDS Weekly Plus, 1999; Cohen, 2003, 2004). Collective bargaining around the terms of the commercial exchange of sex only highlights the marginalization of women in a society where sex is their only marketable resource. Women in stable relationships may fare even worse than single women in terms of their ability to use condoms for HIV prevention. Many couples decrease condom use because of greater trust, or in an attempt to conceive children, or because the man holds economic sway and refuses to use a condom. Often, if a woman within a stable union demands that her partner use a condom, she is accused of infidelity, physically abused or even thrown out of the house (van der Straten *et al.*, 1995; De Zoysa *et al.*, 1996; Piot, 1999, http://www.thebody.com/unaids/women_violence.html, accessed 3 December 1999).

Worsening Poverty

AIDS is making the world's poorest countries poorer. One only needs to look at the salient economic indicators of family income, food, security, education and health care to see the impact of AIDS in sub-Saharan Africa. In Zambia, two-thirds of families who lose the head of the household experience an 80 percent drop in monthly income. In the Ivory Coast, families who lose an adult to HIV experience a 50 percent decrease in household income. Agricultural productivity in Burkina Faso has fallen by 20 percent because of AIDS. In Ethiopia, HIV-positive farmers spend between 11.6 and 16.4 hours a week farming compared with 33.6 hours weekly for healthy farmers (FAO, 2001).

As more adults perish, the education of children is compromised. In Swaziland, school enrollment fell by 36 percent, mainly because girls left school to care for sick relatives. The International Labour Organization estimated that in sub-Saharan Africa, 200,000 teachers will die from AIDS by 2010 (Bennell *et al.*, 2002). A report from the Ivory Coast indicated that in the 1996–1997 academic year, more than 50 percent of deaths among elementary school teachers were from AIDS and 280 teaching hours a year were lost because of teacher absences (Dzisah, 1999, www.aegis.com/news/ips/1999/IP990103.html, accessed 16 Oct 2003). HIV is also having an effect on healthcare workers. In Malawi and Zambia, the death rate of healthcare workers has increased six-fold since the early 1990s. In Southern Africa, 25–40 percent more doctors and nurses will need to be trained during 2001–2010 to compensate for deaths from AIDS.

Access to Treatment

Current global inequalities are often the legacies of oppression, colonialism and slavery, and are today perpetuated by radical, market-driven international financial policies that foment poor health. Neo-liberal economic "reforms" imposed on poor countries by international financial institutions such as the International Monetary Fund and the World Bank force poor governments, as the recipients of qualified loans, to decrease their public sector budgets, privatize health services and, when they would rather invest their minuscule capital to protect their vulnerable citizens and educate their children, these recipient countries are instead forced to march in lock step toward the "free" market, enforcing policies such as user fees for health and primary education.

In poor countries, revitalizing the public health infrastructure and improving the delivery of essentials such as vaccination, sanitation and clean water are critical aspects to remediating the structural violence that underlies disease. It is only with ongoing, large-scale international assistance that poor governments will be able to address the right to health in a sustained way. Advocacy to redress the violations of the basic right to health must recognize that more money is needed for health now, and for decades to come. Furthermore, the coercion by international financial institutions of poor governments to restrict health spending only serves to deepen inequalities in health care and perpetuate social injustice.

The advent of highly active antiretroviral therapy (HAART, now called ART) in 1996 has caused AIDS mortality to plunge sharply in industrialized countries. The results of ART in the initial studies in 1995 and 1996 were nothing short of miraculous. People who were nearly dead became healthy and strong in a matter of months. So commonly did patients "rise from the dead" that ART, it was said, had the "Lazarus effect." In this time of great promise, the theme of the XI International Conference on AIDS held in Vancouver in 1996 was "One World, One Hope." However, while the miracle of Lazarus, a poor leper, was invoked, the poor, who constituted 90 percent of the global AIDS sufferers even then, were not considered for the miracle. In fact, in resource-poor settings, the prospect of initiating ART was summarily dismissed. In effect, once effective therapy for HIV was introduced, treatment and prevention began to be presented as discrete and dichotomous interventions; the argument of limited resources was used to support a prevention-only approach even in the face of the destabilization of families, communities and economies.

Finally, five years and at least 15 million unnecessary deaths later, Kofi Annan, the Secretary General of the United Nations, held a General Assembly Special Session on AIDS (UNGASS). At UNGASS, the Secretary called for the creation of a novel funding mechanism to slow the rapid decimation of the African continent. This multilateral mechanism is called the Global Fund to Fight AIDS, Tuberculosis and Malaria (GFATM). Since 2003, the GFATM has dispersed three billion dollars to prevent and treat AIDS to more than 150 projects in low- and middle-income countries.

Drugs and Intellectual Property

While treatment costs were upwards of ten thousand dollars per patient per year in 1998, that same year in which the Global Fund was called for saw the entry of generic antiretroviral drugs onto the market. Advocacy by groups of people living with AIDS, as well as by international groups such as Medicines Sans Frontiers (MSF) and Partners In Health (PIH), was critical in assuring generic companies that if the drugs were cheaper, more patients could be started on therapy. The call for the money assured companies that there would be a "market" for such drugs. However, efforts at the rapid scale-up were hampered. Pharmaceutical companies, concerned about protecting their intellectual property, invoked patents as well as the World Trade Organization (WTO) agreements that bound signatories to respect patents from any country in which they were issued. AIDS activists, most notably the Treatment Action Campaign (TAC) in South Africa, MSF, Gay Men's Health Crisis and ACT-Up, have continued to fight for the protection of intellectual property in the climate of this global emergency. Within the WTO language, a clause called TRIPS (trade-related aspects of intellectual property) outlines the mandated adherence to intellectual property with a provision for national emergencies that allows for (1) parallel importing— importing the generic version of patented drugs and (2) compulsory licensing—the local development of

drugs through a low-cost licensure agreement with the proprietary company. After many rounds of trade talks, it appears finally that this clause will be allowed for countries facing a national emergency due to the AIDS epidemic.

The road block to accepting that AIDS was indeed a national emergency for heavily affected countries was led by the United States under both the Clinton and Bush administrations. Most recently, the President's Emergency Plan for AIDS Relief has mandated that the billions of dollars pledged by President Bush to a US-based programme, rather than the international GFATM, should be used only for branded drugs. Most countries, thankfully, have been able to avoid this issue and purchase generic drugs through other sources. Generic competition has now led to a 100-fold reduction in the price of antiretroviral therapy. Now, at just $150 per patient per year, treatment can be greatly expanded.

Conclusion

Poverty is intimately connected with the HIV epidemic. Structural violence connected with a large variety of factors including economic privation, gender inequality, lack of opportunity for education and work, and migration for work increases the risk of contracting HIV and makes prevention strategies less actionable. Meanwhile, effective, life-prolonging treatment has been available for 12 years, yet the access to this treatment, while being scaled up in resource-poor settings, is yet to reach the poorest. The approach to AIDS therefore must be targeted at the addressing the root causes of the epidemic. New funding through multilateral and bilateral agencies for treatment and prevention must also address economic and educational opportunities, the lack of which will continue to foment the epidemic.

REFERENCES

AIDS Weekly Plus (1999) "Anti-AIDS Program to be Expanded Throughout Cambodia," 10 March.

Amnesty International (2000) *Sierra Leone. Rape and Other Forms of Sexual Violence Against Girls and Women,* London, UK: Amnesty International.

Amnesty International (2004) "Rwanda: 'Marked for Death,' Rape Survivors Living with HIV/AIDS in Rwanda," available online.

Bennell, Paul, Nicola Swainson and Karin Hyde (2002) *The Impact of the HIV/AIDS Epidemic on the Education Sector in Sub-Saharan Africa: A Synthesis of Findings and Recommendations of Three Country Studies,* Brighton: University of Sussex.

Cohen, Jon (2003) "Two Hard-Hit Countries Offer Rare Success Stories: Thailand and Cambodia," Science 301(5640): 1658–1662.

Cohen, Jon (2004) "Sonagachi Sex Workers Stymie HIV," *Science* 304(5670): 23.

Crossette, Barbara (1995) "UN Fields Odd Allies as it Wages AIDS Battle," *New York Times,* 3 December A4.

De Zoysa, Isabelle, Michael D. Sweat and Julie A. Denison (1996) "Faithful but Fearful: Reducing HIV transmission in stable relationships," *AIDS* 10(A): S197–S203.

Donovan, Paula (2002) "Rape and HIV/AIDS in Rwanda," *Lancet* 360(S1): S17–S18.

Dzisah Melvis (1999) "Cote d'Ivoire: AIDS is the Main Cause of Death Among Teachers," Inter Press Service, 22 January, available online.

Galtung, Johan (1969) "Violence, Peace and Peace Research," *Journal of Peace Research* 6(3): 167–191.

Glynn, Judith R., Michel Caraël, Jane Chege, Bertran Auvert, Maina Kahindo, Rosemary Musonda, Fad Kaona and Anne Buv (2001) "Why Do Young Women Have a Much Higher Prevalence of HIV Than Young Men? A Study in Kisumu, Keynya and Ndola, Zambia," *AIDS* 15 (Suppl 4): S51–S60.

Hanenberg, Robert and Wiwat Rojanapithayakorn (1996) "Prevention as Policy: How Thailand reduced STD and HIV transmission," *Aidscaptions* 3(1): 24–27.

Human Rights Watch (2004) "Struggling to Survive: Barriers to Justice for Rape Victims in Rwanda," *Human Rights Watch* 16(10)(A) New York.

International Labour Organization (2004) Facts on Women at Work, p. 1, Geneva: International Labor Organization, available online.

Kawachi, Ichiro and Bruno P. Kennedy (1997) "Health and Social Cohesion: Why care about income inequality?" *British Medical Journal* 314: 1037.

Kelly, Robert J., Ronald H. Gray, Nelson K. Sewankambo, David Serwadda, Fred Wabwire-Mangen, Tom Lutalo and Maria J. Wawer (2003) "Age Differences in Sexual Partners and Risk of HIV-1 Infection in Rural Uganda," *Journal of Acquired Immune Deficiency Syndrome* 32: 446–451.

Piot, Peter (1999) "HIV/AIDS and Violence Against Women," Presented at the Panel on Women and Health 43rd Session, New York, 3 March, United Nations Commission on the Status of Women, available online.

van der Straten, Ariane, Rachel King, Olga Grinstead, Antoine Serufilira and Susan Allen (1995) "Couple Communication, Sexual Coercion and HIV Risk in Kigali, Rwanda," AIDS 9(8): 935–944.

World Health Organization (2004a) *Joint United Nations Program on HIV/AIDS, Report on the Global AIDS Epidemic,* Geneva: World Health Organization.

World Health Organization (2004b) *Joint United Nations Programme on HIV/AIDS, AIDS Epidemic Update: December,* Geneva: World Health Organization.

Aging and HIV—The Changing Face of AIDS

David M. Latini and David W. Coon

The face of HIV is changing. More older adults are becoming infected and more people who have become infected before their 50th birthdays are now aging with HIV/AIDS. These changing faces create new challenges for health educators, medical providers, and clinical researchers.

Even among Americans age 50 and older, the face of HIV is diverse. In San Francisco, the HIV epidemic has primarily impacted white men who have sex with men. In contrast, according to the Florida Department of Health, older Floridians diagnosed with HIV are primarily African-American (47.4%), with Latinos (16.1%) and women (18%) making up sizable proportions of the epidemic.

Older adults are more frequently diagnosed with HIV at a later stage of the disease and they are likely to die sooner than their younger counterparts. Among seniors, AIDS-related symptoms, such as fatigue, weight loss, and diminished appetite, are often misdiagnosed by health care professionals as age-related conditions rather than symptoms of HIV/AIDS. "It is difficult for me to think that HIV is why I feel old or have the problems of aging; and, it is difficult to think entirely otherwise," says Paul Quin, age 60 who was diagnosed with HIV 17 years ago. "I feel unable to track symptoms or monitor my health. I no longer understand what might be normal for a man my age and what might come with HIV—what might be a warning."

The picture is further complicated by the fact that there is little research regarding the safety and efficacy of AIDS medications in older adults, including accurate understandings of dosage and frequency. Medical providers also appear to have a limited understanding of how AIDS medications may interact with medications for other conditions common in older adults, such as diabetes, heart disease, and arthritis. All-too-common stereotypes about the sexuality of older adults persists among professionals and the public at large, making HIV prevention efforts more difficult. The myth that, "grandparents aren't interested in sex, and if they are interested in sex, no one is interested in them," continues to be a prevalent assumption in the general public. Debunking this myth is AARP's 1999 survey reporting that over 50% of 45–59 year olds, and over 25% of those 60–74, had sex at least once if not more, times a week.

Another common misperception is that older adults only have sex within the context of a heterosexual monogamous relationship. According to Florida's Senior HIV Intervention Project (SHIP), the ratio of men to women in South Florida is 1 to 7. This gender imbalance may make women more likely to have unprotected sex in order to secure a male partner. SHIP also reports that older males may frequent sex workers, particularly near the time that pension checks arrive.

It is also assumed that older adults do not use or abuse illicit drugs, or if they have used drugs, their use was so long ago that it does not carry any risk of HIV infection. Even the use of prescribed medications may carry HIV risk. Because seniors often live on a fixed income, they may be more likely to reuse and exchange needles for prescribed medications such as insulin. Healthcare providers may also share these misperceptions and may not assess older patients for sexual and drug use risks, or counsel them about safer sex practices. . . .

Seniors may hold their own misperceptions about their risk for HIV. In the early years of the HIV epidemic, research with at-risk groups such as heterosexual adolescents found that many teens who engaged in risky sexual practices did not believe themselves to be at risk because they saw HIV/AIDS as a gay man's disease. Some seniors still view HIV/AIDS as a younger person's disease and do not consider themselves to be at risk, regardless of their sexual behaviors.

"Post menopausal women and their sexual partners won't automatically consider using condoms, since they are past childbearing age," Dea reported. Even among older adults who would like to use condoms, the subject can be difficult to discuss. Because the reason for condom use would clearly be to prevent disease, the implication is that there is a lack of trust in a current partner. . . .

According to Dea, sexual behavior for seniors has also changed because of an increase in the use of Viagra. "Viagra is passed around like candy and middle-aged and older adults are continuing to get infected." Viagra has permitted men who have not been recently sexually active to reenter the dating and mating arena, perhaps in an environment of HIV/AIDS risk they do not understand and for which they are not prepared. . . .

Overcoming the taboos that older adults may hold about discussing their sexual behavior with their partners and healthcare providers, and dismantling ageist assumptions, are critical steps in effective HIV/AIDS education for older people. Among the stereotypes about older people, lies a particularly dangerous one—"You can't teach an old dog new tricks." This adage fuels the assumption that older adults are unwilling or unable to change their behavior. However, decades of gerontological research demonstrates that older adults can and will change their behavior when provided with appropriate education and interventions that target specific health concerns and provide support for skill development for seniors' real-world concerns. . . .

chapter 8

Social Control of Sexuality

An interview with . . .

Roderick Ferguson

Dr. Roderick Ferguson is Associate Professor of Race and Critical Theory and Chair of the Department of American Studies at the University of Minnesota. He studies issues of race, sexuality, culture, and social theory. The author of over ten articles and one monograph, *Aberrations in Black: Toward a Queer of Color Critique,* he is currently working on a book entitled *The Re-Order of Things: The Birth of the Interdisciplines.*

What led you to begin studying sexuality?

Well, it was a long route. As a graduate student at University of California San Diego, I was around all these folks who studied sexuality.

Over time, I got to know Judith Halberstam and Gayatri Gopinath. They had written significant articles on queer ethnic sexuality. My roommate, Chandan Reddy, was also doing a dissertation at the time, and he wrote one of the very first pieces on queer of color critique. So, I had some very fruitful exchanges with all these folks.

I wanted to intervene in queer studies and make it speak to race, political economy, and culture. I wanted to bring folks into queer studies who had been shut out before, and also go beyond the narrow focus of sociology, using literature—a fictional form—to critique sociology. There was very little work at the time doing this.

So, how do people react when they find out that you study sexuality?

I've had mainly positive reactions, but it really depends on the person. If I read them as queer, I tell them more. If they seem to like categories, I say that I study race, sexuality, and gender. When I say I do work in queer studies, I've had reactions like "oh, that's what they call it now?" (This reaction came from an older feminist. If I had said I did gay and lesbian studies, she would have understood what I meant.) Some people think that queer is a bad term, and I have to explain it is a re-articulation of the term. At times, reactions have been surprisingly positive. I have a friend who is not an academic, who is a very smart African American woman, and in the course of our friendship, I told her about my work. She is in her 70s and didn't grow up with queer studies, but was very heartened that these things were on the table now. I also wrote this piece called "Sissies at the Picnic" and I remember my cousin telling me that she shared the piece with one of my former English teachers, and the teacher was so moved that she asked to read anything else that I'd written (and this was in rural Georgia!).

What ethical dilemmas have you faced in studying sexuality?

I haven't really faced any. I do work with archival and textual materials—cultural texts, literature, visual art—so I don't have to deal with dilemmas around disclosure.

What do you think is most challenging about studying sexuality?

For me, it has to do with making connections that people don't think exist . . . between race and sexuality, sexuality and capitalism. This is difficult because you run into people's fixed ideas about sexuality and what it does and does not have to do with. I work in the tradition of Foucault, in renewing sexuality's association with power. I ask questions such as what does sexuality have to do with bureaucracy or institution building, and these are hard questions that aren't asked very often.

Why is sex research so important?

For me, it is important as a way to undermine nationalism. Nationalism has been so predicated on who constitutes a nation or group, whether we're talking about countries or minority groups, and so much of that effort involves the regulation of sexuality. If you're trying to undermine that regulation, you have to undermine the effort at nationalism—romantic notions of community and identity. This means working against the limits of identity, even as we recognize its importance. The emphasis on the non-normative, the "perversions" are a key ingredient in undermining the claim to respectability of organized movements such as the gay movement. These organized movements try to regulate their members. For example, Blacks try to regulate women and queers, and gays strive for marriage and children in a very heteronormative manner. People who don't fit are disciplined, or even excluded from the movement.

If you could teach people one thing about sexuality, what would it be?

Sexuality is a story of power. It focuses on who gets regulated, what practices are regulated, how things are affirmed and under [what] conditions, what things are left out . . . all of that is about power. For example, people say, "I'll endorse the gay lifestyle under these conditions . . . if they marry, have babies, and live like heterosexuals. . . ."

Is there anything else that you'd like to add?

I'd want students to know not only to see the different types of queer folks, but also the emerging group of heterosexual students who are unashamed about their interests in queer sexuality. They see it as an ethical and political move, and want to know how they can use it in their activism and scholarship. People can be allied both in terms of political issues and in terms of the subject matter. They're unlike the coalitions that come out of identity-based politics, and are different from those that came before.

The Social Control
of Adult–Child Sex

Jeffery S. Mullis and Dawn M. Baunach

In a New Jersey suburb, July 29, 1994, 7-year-old Megan Kanka was raped and strangled to death by Jesse Timmendequas, a 33-year-old twice-convicted sex offender who lived across the street from the Kanka residence. When questioned by police the next day, Timmendequas confessed and led them to a nearby park to show where he had hidden the body. The victim's mother told reporters that if she had known a sex offender lived nearby, her daughter would still be alive.

Three years later a jury found Timmendequas guilty and recommended the death penalty. In the three-year period between the crime and the sentencing, Megan Kanka's parents led a nationwide movement calling for local authorities to notify residents whenever a sex offender moves into the community. Their efforts were highly successful: today, every state in the United States has adopted some version of community notification—also known as "Megan's Law." Similar procedures designed to monitor the whereabouts of sex offenders, such as the requirement that offenders register their current addresses with local police, have also been implemented in Canada, England, Wales, and Australia (Lieb, Quinsey, and Berliner 1998; Plotnikoff and Woolfson 2000; Hinds and Daly 2001).

These and other recent developments in the handling of sex crimes against children are the impetus behind the present reading. Our main goals are, first, to place these developments in historical and cross-cultural perspective and, second, to identify underlying commonalities in the wide range of responses to adult–child sex in modern society.[1] Such responses can be understood as *social control;* that is, they are part of a larger process by which deviant behavior is defined and counteracted and conformity is encouraged. Social control is ubiquitous in human groups, and it manifests itself in a complex variety of ways.

Whenever people express any kind of disapproval over the actions of others—whether they do so informally or formally, individually or collectively, peacefully or violently—social control is present. People may even respond to their own actions with disapproval, a phenomenon known as "social control of the self" (Black 1993: 65). Social scientists study social control in order to better understand all its manifestations and effects. In this reading we use the theory of social control developed by Donald Black (1976, 1993) to classify responses to adult–child sex into four different categories of control—penal, therapeutic, compensatory, and preventive—each one a distinctive method of handling all manner of deviant behavior.

Unlike prior research on the regulation of sex crimes, we are not concerned here with whether the social response is disproportionately severe relative to the actual incidence of such crimes, nor do we focus on the functions of social control for maintaining moral boundaries in society. Excellent work has already been done along these lines. For example, Sutherland (1950) argues that the widespread passage of sexual psychopath laws between 1937 and 1949 was based on unfounded fears generated by the news media. And Jenkins (1998) shows how past "moral panics" over the welfare of children were defensive reactions against large-scale social changes such as those occurring in gender roles and sexual mores during the twentieth century. Although we recognize that the social construction of social problems is a process not always commensurate with objective conditions and that moral panics serve important functions for group solidarity, we set these issues aside and concentrate instead on simply describing and classifying variation in the social control of adult–child sex.[2] Although our purpose is mainly descriptive and classificatory, we also present some explanations of the observed variation. Finally, we examine the unintended consequences of the notification laws enacted in the wake of Megan Kanka's tragic death.

Modern and Premodern Views

From the standpoint of contemporary Western norms, *child molester* is one of the most stigmatizing labels that can be applied to a person. Disgust and outrage are evoked in almost everyone at the mere contemplation of such people (Finkelhor 1984; Holmes 1991; Pryor 1996). Even in prisons—within a society of sinners, so to speak—other inmates single out the child molester as particularly depraved and deserving of punishment (e.g., see Siewers 1994).[3]

The wrath reserved for child molesters is a product of our cultural construction of childhood. We will return to this subject shortly; for now we note that despite the popularized views of Sigmund Freud, who saw even infants as highly sexual beings, and despite the wealth of research that documents the existence of childhood sexuality,[4] children are commonly seen as innocently devoid of sexual motivation. This image, by extension, casts sex offenders of children as exploitive, corruptive, and blameworthy. Modern law codifies this image by portraying children as mentally incapable of consenting to sexual relations and as guiltless in criminal procedures. Thus predisposed with these cultural directives, jurors find it difficult to be impartial in deciding the facts of child sexual assault cases: "[T]hat the defendant is charged with sexual assault against a child will cause the juror to consider the defendant probably guilty, or, at the very least, the burden will be placed on that defendant to prove his or her innocence" (Vidmar 1997: 6). Defendants themselves will sometimes report feeling guilty, angry, and shocked by their own actions, as indicated in the following statements from four convicted offenders (all male):[5]

I realized that it was wrong. Normal people don't do these things. (O'Brien 1986: 46)

When I look into myself [I feel] anger, hatred for myself, sorrow, and hurt. . . . I feel disgustingly dirty, and wonder what makes me feel that I have the right to live after what I've caused. (Ingersoll and Patton 1990: 71)

I thought, oh God, all kinds of things. Like "God, what have I done?" . . . Before [the molestation] happened this was something I would read about. And the first thing that would come to my mind was, "They ought to take that sucker out and cut his nuts off and kill him. He doesn't deserve a trial." And that's the way I felt. Then it happened to me and that's what I thought about myself. I ought to be taken out and shot. . . . But that didn't stop me from doing it. (Pryor 1996: 166)

When I touched her the first time on her behind . . . almost every time I touched her, I said, "This isn't right." I knew it wasn't right. . . . After the first episode . . . I got mad. I picked a chair up and tossed it across the room. (Pryor 1996: 167)

Whether these men are sincere or merely providing the socially desirable response is unknown. The more relevant point is that they echo in their sentiments the larger societal reaction—as if they realize their acts are indefensible and therefore require appropriate self-condemnation. It is interesting to note that not all sex offenders against children are similarly self-condemning. Indeed, some are adamantly unrepentant and deny that anything is wrong with the behavior. This contrary view is most clearly expressed by the handful of organizations, such as the North American Man/Boy Love Association and the René Guyon Society, dedicated to justifying and normalizing adult–child sex. The slogan of the latter organization is "Sex by year eight or else it's too late" (De Young 1988: 584).

Such views are, of course, extremely disreputable and rare. Even so, the negative reaction that currently prevails is far from a cross-cultural universal. Excluding cases of father–daughter and mother–son incest (prohibitions against which are found in almost all known societies), the world-historical evidence contains numerous examples of adult–child sex as part of normal cultural life; these examples include both same-sex and opposite-sex behaviors involving sexually mature and immature or maturing persons. But nowhere is adult–child sex the predominant form of sexual interaction, and in those times and places where it is accepted it tends to be, like all sexual behavior, highly regulated. Perhaps the best-known example is the ancient Greek system of *pederasty* ("love of boys"), in which sexual relationships between upper-class men and boys were embedded in an educational context designed to further the younger males' social and emotional development. The sexual component of these mentor–student relationships was socially accepted, but only under certain conditions. For example, the man was expected to always be the dominant partner (penetrator) and the boy the submissive partner (penetrated) in anal and intercrural (between the thighs) sex. In addition, the boy was not supposed to actually enjoy the sexual interaction because it was considered improper for a future Athenian leader to desire taking a submissive role in any dealings with other males (Dover 1978; Halperin 1990). The boy also needed to be pubescent, for grown men who pursued sex with prepubescent boys were potentially subject to harsh legal punishment (Tannahill 1992). The onset of puberty thus appears to have been an important boundary dividing the acceptable from the unacceptable in adult–child sex among Grecian males. This "puberty standard" extended to upper class Grecian girls as well, as evidenced by their average age at marriage being between 14 and 18 and usually to a male around age 30 (Blundell 1995).

Beyond Ancient Greece, sexual contact between adults and children has served developmental goals elsewhere, such as the South Pacific, where ethnographers in the twentieth century documented adult–child sex rituals in several island societies. For instance, the Sambian tribe, located in the eastern mountains of Papua New Guinea, believed as late as the 1970s that the fellated semen of an older male "masculinizes" a prepubescent boy, allowing the boy to mature into a fierce warrior. Thus, around age 7, boys would begin a prolonged rite-of-passage characterized by frequent oral-sexual contacts with older, sexually mature males. Again, a reversal of dominant/submissive roles here was forbidden, and fully mature men were expected to live a heterosexual existence (Herdt 1984).

On Kolepom, an island located on the south coast of Irian Jaya/West Papua, a prepubescent girl of the Kiman Papuan would engage in sexual intercourse with multiple men as part of an elaborate semen-centered ritual. The semen produced by the intercourse would be collected in a banana leaf and rubbed on the girl's future husband, himself either prepubescent or pubescent. The cultural meaning of this custom was twofold: intercourse with several older men was intended to test the girl's suitability for marriage, and the rubbing of the semen helped facilitate the boy's entrance into manhood (Serpenti 1984).

On the Polynesian island of Mangaia, boys and girls both would be initiated into adulthood through explicit instruction and practical experience in how to sexually satisfy the opposite sex. A pubescent boy, for example, would first be instructed by an older man on such techniques as cunnilingus and how to achieve simultaneous mutual orgasm with a female partner. This formal instruction would be followed by a practical application in which the boy would have sex with a mature, sexually experienced woman. Of particular importance here was teaching the boy how to delay ejaculation. Emphasis was placed on the female orgasm, which was seen as a pleasurable end unto itself for Mangaian males. Failure to induce orgasm in a future female partner might also result in a loss of social status for men, as the news would spread through gossip. Consequently, for men (and presumably for women, too), the ideal ratio of female-to-male orgasms was at least two to one (Marshall 1971).

In addition to historical and ethnographic accounts, age of consent laws are another source of information on attitudes toward adult–child sex. The legal age of sexual consent is the minimum age at which a person is considered, by the particular government in question, to be capable of consenting to sexual activity. Although minimum age statutes may apply to both male and female children, such laws have tended to be written with specific reference to females only, reflecting the historical view of females as property in need of special protection (Oberman 1994) and also suggesting a greater tolerance of young male sexuality.

Following English common law, most jurisdictions in colonial America considered a 10-year-old girl to be old enough to give valid consent to sexual intercourse. If the girl was younger than 10, the act was defined as felony rape or carnal abuse (Jenkins 1998). A notable exception to the common law tradition was Delaware, which, curiously, set its age of consent at 7. Prepubescent ages such as these remained on the books in most U.S. states until the late 1800s, at which time a popular "social purity" movement began to pressure state legislatures and Congress to raise minimum ages. The moral justification for changing the laws was to prevent men from corrupting young girls and luring them into a life of prostitution, decried by purity activists as a major urban problem of the day. From 1886 to 1895, in response to the purity movement's campaign, the age of sexual consent was raised to between 14 and 18 years in the majority of states (Pivar 1973; D'Emilio and Freedman 1997).

At present, the age of sexual consent is 16 to 18 throughout most of the United States. Worldwide, whenever legislation specifies a minimum age, it is typically at least 14. Throughout contemporary Europe, for example, it tends to range from 14 to 16, although in a handful of European locales it is still as low as 12 (e.g., Malta, Spain, Vatican City) (Graupner 2000).[6] During the same time span that the legal age for sex has risen, the average age at puberty has fallen (see Jenkins 1998: 24), creating a category of people we might call *sexually mature legal minors*—youth in their mid-adolescent years caught in a limbo of hormonal urges and legal constraints.[7]

Why is adult–child sex taboo in the modern world? Why was it a culturally actionable option in earlier times and other places but not here and now? A number of factors have given shape to the current taboo, some more directly than others. Here we briefly sketch the influence of three historical developments: the spread of Christian thought, the "invention" and lengthening of childhood, and the advent of compulsory schooling. First and oldest among these is the spread of Christianity—now the leading religion of the Western world. Early Christian tenets strictly forbade all nonprocreative sex, a view that can still be found among many Christian moralists and one that clearly prohibits sexual intercourse with prepubescents at the same time that it prohibits masturbation and homosexuality. Christianity also has long emphasized the innocent and vulnerable nature of children and the need to protect them from "the harsh and sinful world" (see Conrad and Schneider 1992: 146). This view of childhood as an innocent, precious stage of life began to gain wider favor through the

1700s in Western Europe and the 1800s in the United States. Children increasingly became seen as "fragile creatures of God" (Ariès 1962: 133) who have special needs of their own, and parents increasingly became concerned with attending to those needs by applying appropriate childrearing practices, more benevolent and nurturing in style. Some scholars (e.g., Ariès 1962; Stone 1977) claim this general period of history marks a dramatic turning point in family life— the "invention" of childhood—the implication being that children prior to the Enlightenment were not recognized as fundamentally different from adults. This was certainly true in several key respects. For example, both adults and children were expected to make economic contributions to the family—most children in poorer families were put to work as early as age six. However, it is likely that there was more underlying continuity than dramatic change in attitudes toward and treatment of the very young in particular (Pollock 1983). For present purposes, the most important change from the eighteenth century onward is the gradual lengthening of that period of life referred to as "growing up," so that these ideas about the preciousness of childhood began to be applicable over a wider age range. Put differently, children remained *childlike*—relatively innocent and free from adult obligations—for a longer period of time than in earlier eras. We see this in the notion of the "teenager," which by the mid-1900s had become entrenched in popular thought and custom as a distinct age category characterized by continued development and dependency. A facilitating factor behind the lengthening of childhood was the expansion of laws requiring formal schooling during the late nineteenth and early twentieth centuries. Compulsory education from ages 6 to 16 helped solidify the separation of children from adults by creating a distinct role for children outside of the home economy and the paid labor market. Compulsory education also acted latently as an additional constraint on sexuality: Students were not supposed to have families of their own because of the heavy burden this would place on both the student and the educational system (Killias 1991).

These historical changes provide a normative backdrop against which the social purity agenda and other child-saving reforms become possible. To a greater degree than in centuries past, children and adults have come to live under separate social expectations, governmentally mandated and divinely ordained, with children as protected and adults as protector. Because adult–child sex, embodied by the child molester, defiles the sanctity of childhood, the child molestor has become "the most evil social type in our society" (Davis 1983: 110–111). How do we respond to this evil?

Varieties of Social Control

Human societies have developed a diverse repertoire of responses to deviant behavior. Adult–child sex provokes a number of these responses. For example, it is prosecuted in criminal courts as statutory rape and treated in psychiatric hospitals as pedophilia. Drawing on Black's theoretical framework, we classify these and other examples according to the general method of social control they illustrate, whether penal, therapeutic, compensatory, or preventive. These represent different strategies for defining and handling deviant behavior. They are not necessarily mutually exclusive strategies, however. Some of the specific examples described next combine the different methods of control in ways that make our classification somewhat arbitrary. In such cases our decision to classify in one category and not another is based on the primary type of social control in evidence.

Penal Control

In the application of penal control, the deviant is defined as an offender and punishment is seen as the logical response (Black 1976). The criminal justice system exemplifies the formal (i.e., governmental) variety of this type of social control. From the standpoint of criminal law, sexual contact between adults and minors may be prosecuted under any number of different sex offenses, including statutory rape, sexual assault, crimes against nature, defilement of a minor, carnal knowledge of a child, and indecent liberties with a child. In modern society it is the adult who is held accountable for these offenses. The minor is not charged with any crime and is in fact perceived as the victim of criminal wrongdoing, but the extent of perceived victimization will vary directly with situational characteristics such as the age difference between those involved and whether the act is mutually consensual versus coerced. Mutual consent, however, can have complex effects, sometimes absolving the older party of wrongdoing and sometimes resulting in a form of collective liability where both old and young are punished. For example, consider the following:

> *A priest by the name of Johann Arbogast Gauch, who for ten years (1735–1744), while serving as village parson in the former principality of Fürstenberg (Germany), had sexual relations with a number of boys and a few girls. The sexual acts were restricted to masturbation and, with the girls, displaying of the genitals. Some of the children were willing participants; many seem to have resisted at first but were compelled to give in. It seems that the whole village had been well aware of what had been going on, but for a long time nobody interfered. After ten years, i.e., after a change on the throne of Fürstenberg, however, Gauch was finally prosecuted and sentenced to death. The children were kept in a subterranean prison for several months and the boys, as accessories to the crimes, were beaten and whipped. The oldest of the boys barely escaped death sentences. The girls only received ecclesiastical penalty for unchaste behavior. Since the sexual activities in which they had been involved were heterosexual, they were thus not considered as being too serious. (Killias 1991: 42)*

Imprisonment and torture of the younger parties and capital punishment of the adult are evidenced in this example from eighteenth-century Germany. Today, in the United States, life imprisonment of the adult, without the possibility of parole, is the most severe formal punishment meted out for child sexual abuse.[8] But if murder is also committed, as in the case of Megan Kanka mentioned at the outset of this reading, then capital punishment may be imposed with the sexual act and the age of the victim regarded as aggravating circumstances justifying the harsher penalty.

In contrast to imprisonment and other officially authorized actions, ordinary citizens have been known to apply their own brand of punishment to child molesters. These informal measures vary from covert acts apparently perpetrated by lone individuals to more organized and collective responses, and they have become more common in the wake of community notification laws. For example, the home of a convicted child molester was burned to the ground after his name and address were released to the public (van Biema 1993). In another case, a convicted molester's car was firebombed within days of the community being notified of his release (Chiang, Gaura, and Lee 1997). In yet another case, five gunshots were fired at the home of a known molester, injuring no one but narrowly missing a woman in an upstairs room (Hajela 1999). In one community, 100 neighbors of a known molester protested outside his apartment building and collected signatures in a campaign to persuade his landlord to evict him (DelVecchio 1997). In some instances the actions of neighbors have forced molesters to move to a new location in the community or to move out of town altogether (see Anderson 1997).

It may seem incongruous to classify these informal and sometimes criminally violent acts together with official governmental sanctions. In particular, how can crimes such as arson and assault with a deadly weapon be equated with legitimate legal responses such as arrest and imprisonment? Although these acts would seem to be diametrically opposed—the difference between lawful and unlawful—Black's theory of social control leads us to consider the characteristics they share in common:

> *Far from being an intentional violation of a prohibition, much crime is moralistic and involves the pursuit of justice. . . . To the degree that it defines or responds to the conduct of someone else—the victim—as deviant, crime is social control. . . . This implies that many crimes belong to the same family as gossip, ridicule, vengeance, . . . and law itself. . . . In other words, for certain theoretical purposes we might usefully ignore the fact that crime is criminal at all. (Black 1993: 27, 41–42)*

Paradoxically, then, the molester might be both the perpetrator of crime and the victim of crime, depending on whether public officials or private citizens are acting against him. In either case, penal social control is present.

Therapeutic Control

One of the most significant trends in the social control of deviance is the increasing use of a thera-

peutic model to understand behaviors that might otherwise be seen as immoral or criminal, a trend referred to as the *medicalization of deviance* (Conrad and Schneider 1992). Therapeutic social control entails viewing the deviant as a patient, sick and in need of help (Black 1976). The impulse behind therapy is not to punish but to treat and ideally cure the deviant, thereby restoring normalcy to the mind or body. Psychiatric treatment exemplifies this type of social control. In psychiatry and related mental health fields, sexual contact between an adult and a child (whether real or imagined contact) indicates a potential mental disorder in the adult, namely pedophilia, defined clinically as "recurrent, intense, sexually arousing fantasies, sexual urges or behaviors" involving a prepubescent child, in which the individual with the disorder is at least 16 years old and five years older than the child (American Psychiatric Association 1994: 527–528). Pedophilia is distinguished from ephebophilia, which refers to an adult's sexual attraction to pubescent children or young teenagers. Ephebophilia is not widely recognized in professional therapeutic doctrine as a mental disorder. This may reflect the well-documented preference among human and other primate males for sexually mature younger partners (Ames and Houston 1990; Okami 1990), making ephebophilia perhaps more readily comprehensible as a biocultural norm than as a psychiatric problem.

The therapeutic control of pedophilia includes such techniques as social skills training, victim role-taking, aversion therapy, orgasmic reconditioning, surgical castration, libido-reducing drugs, and a host of other behavioral, cognitive, and pharmacological treatments (Howitt 1995; Stone, Winslade, and Klugman 2000). The sheer variety underscores the psychiatric belief that there is no single cause of pedophilia and that no single treatment is effective for all cases. Courts frequently order or provide such treatments as part of the criminal sentence, a practice that illustrates institutional cooperation between the criminal justice and mental health care systems in the control of deviant behavior (see Szasz 1963). This cooperation is further illustrated by U.S. Supreme Court rulings that allow states to confine "sexual predators" for psychiatric treatment *after* they have served their prison sentences (Greenhouse 2002).[9]

Of the different treatments for pedophilia, the most controversial are surgical castration and so-called *chemical castration*. Both reduce the level of testosterone in the body, which in turn reduces sexual desire. The controversy revolves around the ethics and efficacy of castration, some claiming it is simply barbaric (especially the surgical variety) and others questioning the validity of the theory that pedophilia is in fact caused by sexual desire. In surgical castration the testes are removed, permanently reducing testosterone. Chemical castration yields a temporary reduction in testosterone via the injection of antiandrogen drugs such as Depo-Provera. Historically, castration has served both penal and therapeutic ends. It has been used throughout history as punishment for sex crimes such as rape and adultery but is intended in modern society as a medical deterrent to sexual deviance. The first European country to legalize surgical castration was Denmark in 1929, followed by Germany, Iceland, Sweden, and other countries (Heim and Hursch 1979). A growing number of U.S. states authorize both surgical and chemical castration as a condition of parole for convicted child molesters. Because neither form has been shown to unambiguously reduce recidivism, some critics have speculated that therapists and lawmakers who advocate castration are actually seeking punishment by medical means (see Heim and Hursch 1979; Stone et al. 2000).

Compensatory Control

In compensatory social control, the deviant is defined as a debtor who has failed to fulfill an obligation. Payment is the solution (Black 1976), though punishment may be a byproduct. Compensatory control is seen most clearly and familiarly in civil lawsuits, in which offenders are asked to pay damages to remedy the wrongs they allegedly committed. It is also seen in lesser-known victim compensation programs, in which the government provides payment to victims, a provision partly based on social welfare ideology and partly on the argument that the government is liable because it has failed to prevent crime (Henderson 1985; Greer 1994). Although both civil lawsuits and governmental funds are options available to victims of sex crimes, we focus here on lawsuits only, specifically, lawsuits against the Roman Catholic Church.

In recent years the Catholic Church has been embroiled in public scandal over pedophilic priests, who might be more aptly termed "ephebophilic priests" because most of their known sexual activities have involved adolescents (Jenkins 1998; Ripley 2002). Reliable statistics are lacking on the total number of lawsuits and amount of paid compensation, but a national survey of Catholic dioceses suggests that, since the early 1960s, over 850 priests in the United States have been accused of child sexual abuse, and an estimated one billion dollars has been paid to the accusers in court-ordered and out-of-court settlements (Cooperman and Sun 2002). Approximately 40 percent of the accused priests were removed from their ministerial positions. Only 6 percent of these were actually defrocked (removed from the priesthood altogether) (Cooperman and Sun 2002). The Church apparently failed to promptly remove all the priests that were known to be abusers, thus enabling them to become repeat offenders:

> *At the same time that Church officials denied that clergy engaged in sexual activities with children, they privately assured complainants that the "problem" would be investigated and resolved immediately. In actuality, the Church began to transfer perpetrators either to active ministry in other parishes or to church-affiliated treatment centers. The international scope of the Catholic Church allowed the official hierarchy to relocate offending individuals to distant geographical locations. For Church officials, such moves [temporarily] solved the problem. (Krebs 1998: 19, citation omitted)*

However, the accumulating claims of abuse and the accompanying media scrutiny eventually forced the Church to take additional steps—the drafting of a zero-tolerance policy, "Charter for the Protection of Children and Young People." This is a truly remarkable title considering that the protection being referenced is *protection from priests*, in other words, from the Church itself.

Despite the number of civil claims against wayward priests, very few criminal charges have been brought to date (Pfeiffer and Cullen 2002). Why? In some cases the statute of limitations has expired, while other cases may prove to be unfounded. But, in general, the high number of civil claims and the low number of criminal charges reflects the social structure of these cases: When the accused ranks relatively high in social status, as priests do as individuals and the Catholic Church does as an organization, then compensatory control becomes more likely and penal control becomes less likely (see Black 1993: 53–55).

Preventive Control

In preventive social control deviants are defined in terms of past transgressions and the likelihood of future offending. Prevention might be attempted by placing deviants under closer surveillance or by restricting their freedom of movement, and by potential victims taking steps to reduce their vulnerability (see Black 1993: 8; Horwitz 1990). Corresponding examples in the preventive control of adult–child sex are registration and notification systems, electronic monitoring devices that alert authorities when the target has ventured beyond permitted boundaries, and the informal method of avoidance, curtailing interaction with the deviant. Next we describe registration and notification as implemented in the United States. We then address the unanticipated consequences of notification.

Beginning in the mid-1990s, all fifty states became federally required to maintain sex offender registries. On release into the community, offenders are ordered to provide local law enforcement with such data as their home address, photograph, criminal history, fingerprint identification, social security number, place of employment, vehicle registration, and DNA profile. The purpose is to maintain a record of the whereabouts and characteristics of offenders. If a sex crime occurs in the vicinity of a known offender, the police have an immediate suspect. Thus the lag between the commission of the crime and apprehension/arrest is potentially shortened (Finn 1997). Updated registries are needed for states to fulfill a second federal requirement of the 1990s, community notification (or Megan's Law), signed in 1996. Although roughly half of the fifty states had implemented notification systems before 1996, the federal version of Megan's Law required the remaining states to do so. All now have. States achieve

notification in several ways, ranging from active to passive. For example, officers may distribute fliers with the offender's photo, address, and criminal history, or a centralized database may be made available to the public via the internet (Adams 1999). In some jurisdictions, the offender may be required to notify neighbors personally, going door-to-door. Judges have also required offenders to place warning signs in their yards and bumper stickers on their cars. As Jenkins notes, such procedures have seldom been seen in Anglo-American law, "at least not since the days when thieves, adulterers, and blasphemers were branded or otherwise mutilated in order that they be identifiable by their crimes" (1998: 199).

Consequences of Community Notification

Notification transforms a "discreditable" neighbor into a "discredited" one (Goffman 1963; Pryor 1996), the secret stigma now publicly known. As a result, the neighborhood at large is placed in a heightened state of uneasy awareness:

> [W]hat few facts residents already had about their new neighbor—his chattiness, his bike rides, reports of his playing with children with water balloons—took on sinister implications after the police alert. (DelVecchio 1997)

As mentioned previously, the results of notification include vandalism, assault, protest demonstrations, and subsequent migration or banishment of the offender, none of which notification was intended to produce. Notification is premised on the "parents' right to know." The information is intended to be used as part of an avoidance-prevention strategy, with parents warning their children not to go near the offender's home or walk alone in the neighborhood. Vigilantism was an unintended consequence, but states are now fully aware of its possibility. In fact, many Internet-based registries now specifically warn citizens against using the information to commit a crime. The criminal actions of notified citizens may encourage child molesters to "go underground," not registering with local law agencies, thus thwarting notification. This in turn may allow them to continue molesting, only now with greater anonymity. In this sense, notification potentially creates the crime it is designed to control.

But how common are these informal responses? Are they in fact driving large numbers of child molesters underground? Even if uncommon, it plausibly takes only a few well-publicized incidents to get the attention of numerous molesters, who may read or watch the story with great interest and then choose to act upon it by moving, not registering, and so on. We investigated these issues by conducting a Lexis-Nexis search of incidents reported in newspapers nationwide during the years 1994 to 2001. The results are presented in Figure 40.1, which shows the nature and extent of informal responses occurring before and after the federal notification statute.[10] As shown in Figure 40.1, the number of incidents increased from 1994 through 1999. This increase very likely reflects (a) the enactment of notification, as those states without it began to comply with the federal statute, and (b) the novelty of notification (i.e., people initially responded with greater outrage on learning that a pedophile lived nearby). Over time, however, as people across the country became accustomed to the laws (and perhaps resigned to their neighbors), outrage diminished, as suggested by the decrease in events from 1998 through 2001.

Perhaps the most striking finding in Figure 40.1 is the seemingly low number of incidents—115 in all—surely far fewer incidents than there were notifications in this time period. The low number, however, is consistent with the findings of other studies. For example, surveys of law enforcement specialists who routinely work with sex offenders find that name calling, verbal threats, graffiti, protest demonstrations, and minor vandalism sometimes do occur, but not nearly as frequently as expected (see Finn 1997: 13–14 for an overview of these studies). In our data, the most common type of incident is what we call "miscellaneous protest," a category consisting mainly of scattered complaints to the police, landlords, and employers. There were forty-eight such incidents described in newspaper articles from 1994 through 2001. The second most common type of event is the comparatively organized protest demonstration (or picket), most of which occurred in front of offenders' homes. Overall, there were thirty-one pickets from 1994 through 2001. Also included in this second category are three instances of petitioning in 1996 through 1997 and two instances of petitioning in 2000 through 2001, in which individuals collected

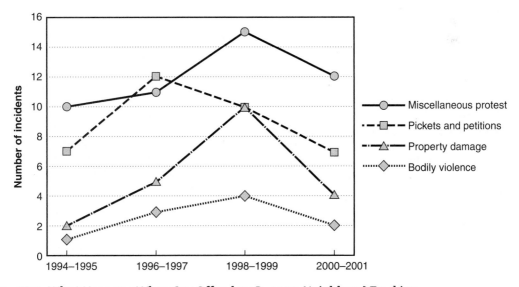

Figure 40.1 What Happens When Sex Offenders Become Neighbors? Tracking the Consequences of Community Awareness, 1994–2001

signatures supporting the ousting of offenders from their homes or jobs. We grouped these with picketing because of a tendency for petitioning and picketing to occur together. The third most common type of event is property damage, including firebombed cars, threats spray-painted on cars and lawns, homes set ablaze, and bricks and eggs thrown at homes. There were twenty-one instances of property damage. The least common event is actual physical violence inflicted on offenders. There were only ten such incidents reported in newspapers from 1994 through 2001. Two of these incidents were cases of mistaken identity in which residents beat the wrong man. In three of the ten cases the molester inflicted the violence on himself by committing suicide shortly after notification was made to the neighborhood. Finally, not shown in Figure 40.1 is the number of offenders evicted or otherwise compelled to relocate as a result of community actions. Overall, there were thirty-nine reported relocations, and these tended to occur during the height of the other activity, becoming less frequent from 1998 onward.

Summary and Conclusion

A wide range of social control is directed toward adult–child sex in modern society: imprisonment, hospitalization, castration, drug treatment, civil litigation, surveillance, assault, banishment, and even suicide, a type of self-applied social control. Extreme deviance brings forth the extremes in social control. We have sought to place these modern responses to adult–child sex in a world-historical context. Ancient Greece was examined in this regard, together with South Pacific examples and the changing legal age of sexual consent. Further, we have attempted to identify Blackian commonalities among the different responses, focusing on penal, therapeutic, compensatory, and preventive social control.

Regarding the consequences of community notification, we anticipate a continued drop in confrontational and violent social control, at least until the next moral panic over child sexual abuse. Then it seems reasonable to expect an increase in violence against child molesters. Community notification laws, unlike many other laws, appear to be a written rule that

actually has some consequence for the way people behave, for better or worse.

NOTES

1. In the scientific literature and the news media alike, adult–child sex is often referred to as *child sexual abuse, child molestation,* and *pedophilia. Pedophilia* denotes a psychiatric disorder found in some, but not all, sex offenders of children (Freund, Watson, and Dickey 1991). Depending on the context, we use each of these alternative terms, but for general sociological purposes we prefer the more neutral term *adult–child sex* because contemporary evaluative notions of abuse, molestation, and disorder do not always fit the empirical record of this behavior. For discussion of the normative character of research on adult–child sex and how it impedes a scientific understanding of the subject, see Ames and Houston (1990), Okami (1990), and Rind, Tromovitch, and Bauserman (2000).

2. Unless otherwise indicated, what follows is intended to apply to both incestuous and nonincestuous adult–child sex.

3. The early French sociologist Emile Durkheim suggests that even within a perfect "society of saints," certain acts inevitably will be defined as deviant, albeit to the average person the acts in question would probably be considered trifling ([1895] 1938: 68–69). Likewise, even within a society of sinners (such as a prison), there exists a moral ranking of acts from bad to worse. The fact that child molestation is considered one of the more loathsome crimes within the prison subculture—where tolerance levels for deviance are comparatively high—indicates the gravity of the stigma attached to the act in ordinary society.

4. Most college textbooks on human sexuality provide overviews of this research, and most rightly caution against equating early childhood sexuality with adult sexuality. The pleasure-seeking behavior of young children is not the same thing, subjectively at least, as the learned eroticism experienced later in life (e.g., see Rathus, Nevid, and Fichner-Rathus 2000: 386–392; Kelly 2001: 163–166). . .

5. Almost all convicted child molesters are male. Female offenders may be more prevalent, however, than the gender profile of the convicted would suggest. For example, compared to other offending scenarios, when an adult female sexually engages an underage male the event may be less likely construed as an unwelcome advance and hence less likely to be reported to the police. It can even become a source of pride and status for the boy (see Pryor 1996: 36–37). If it is reported, others will consider it less serious than cases involving male offenders, with arrest,

prosecution, and conviction being comparatively unlikely. In one case, a father remarked that his son "should consider himself lucky to have had a sexual experience with an older woman" (Holmes 1991: 34).

6. In the Philippines and in Thailand, where the child sex industry thrives, the ages of sexual consent are 12 and 15, respectively, except in cases of prostitution, whereupon it is raised to 18 in both countries in an attempt to curtail the exploitation of children (Graupner 2000).

7. This term has an analogue in the healthcare context, where the *mature minor doctrine* enables older adolescents to bypass parental consent and make their own decisions regarding medical treatment. The term *minor* in this doctrine refers to those under the age of full majority rather than those specifically under the age of sexual consent.

8. On sentencing outcomes and rates of incarceration, see Cheit and Goldschmidt (1997).

9. In the most recent ruling, *Kansas v. Crane* (decided January 22, 2002), the Supreme Court specified that postprison confinement is appropriate if offenders have a mental disorder that undermines their self-control.

10. We read newspaper articles with an eye toward counting the number of separate informal incidents resulting from notification. Newspapers tend to report more violent or organized incidents, hence minor insults and harassments are undoubtedly underrepresented. Considering the enormous media attention paid to the Kanka case and to notification legislation generally, when more visible events did occur (e.g., picketing), the news media probably were keen to report them (see Best and Horiuchi 1985 for a similar point regarding their newspaper analysis of Halloween sadism). Overall, from the period of January 1994 through December 2001, there were 1,401 articles generated by our inclusive keyword searches. The articles were generated from the Lexis-Nexis database of 219 different newspaper sources, including major city, regional, and national newspapers, and Associated Press and state/local wire reports. During the period observed, 128 separate incidents involving 85 different molesters were reported in these sources. Figure 40.1 presents a subset of these cases (n=115) classified according to the type of incident. The vast majority of incidents were directed at child molesters even though notification applies to other kinds of sex offenders too. Some incidents received coverage in multiple papers and on multiple days; these were counted only once. In addition, some offenders were targets in multiple incidents; these were counted as separate events. The complete details of the analysis are available on request.

REFERENCES

Adams, Devon B. 1999. *Summary of State Sex Offender Registry Dissemination Procedures.* Washington, D.C.: Department of Justice, Bureau of Justice Statistics.

American Psychiatric Association. 1994. *Diagnostic and Statistical Manual of Mental Disorders* (4th edition). Washington, D.C.: American Psychiatric Association.

Ames, M. Ashley, and David A. Houston. 1990. "Legal, Social, and Biological Definitions of Pedophilia." *Archives of Sexual Behavior* 19: 333–342.

Anderson, Nick. 1997. "Convicted Molester Will Find New Home." *Los Angeles Times,* March 13, p. B1.

Ariès, Philippe. 1962. *Centuries of Childhood: A Social History of Family Life.* New York: Vintage Books.

Best, Joel, and Gerald T. Horiuchi. 1985. "The Razor Blade in the Apple: The Social Construction of Urban Legends." *Social Problems* 32: 488–499.

Black, Donald. 1976. *The Behavior of Law.* New York: Academic Press.

———. 1993. *The Social Structure of Right and Wrong.* San Diego, CA: Academic Press.

Blundell, Sue. 1995. *Women in Ancient Greece.* Cambridge, MA: Harvard University Press.

Cheit, Ross E., and Erica B. Goldschmidt. 1997. "Child Molesters in the Criminal Justice System." *New England Journal of Criminal and Civil Commitment* 23: 267–301.

Chiang, Harriet, Maria Alicia Gaura, and Henry K. Lee. 1997. "Disclosure of Molesters Brings Fear of Vigilantism." *San Francisco Chronicle,* July 12, p. A1.

Conrad, Peter, and Joseph W. Schneider. 1992. *Deviance and Medicalization: From Badness to Sickness.* Philadelphia: Temple University Press.

Cooperman, Alan, and Lena H. Sun. 2002. "Crisis in the Church: Survey Finds 218 Priests Have Been Removed This Year." *Boston Globe,* June 9, p. A34.

Davis, Murray S. 1983. *Smut: Erotic Reality/Obscene Ideology.* Chicago: University of Chicago Press.

De Young, Mary. 1988. "The Indignant Page: Techniques of Neutralization in the Publications of Pedophile Organizations." *Child Abuse and Neglect* 12: 583–591.

DelVecchio, Rick. 1997. "Residents Want Molester Out of Santa Rosa." *San Francisco Chronicle,* July 7, p. A13.

D'Emilio, John, and Estelle B. Freedman. 1997. *Intimate Matters: A History of Sexuality in America* (2nd edition). Chicago: University of Chicago Press.

Dover, K. J. 1978. *Greek Homosexuality.* Cambridge, MA: Harvard University Press.

Durkheim, Emile. [1895] 1938. *The Rules of Sociological Method.* New York: Free Press.

Finkelhor, David. 1984. *Child Sexual Abuse: New Theory and Research.* New York: Free Press.

Finn, Peter. 1997. *Sex Offender Community Notification.* Washington, D.C.: Department of Justice, Office of Justice Programs.

Freund, Kurt, Robin Watson, and Robert Dickey. 1991. "Sex Offenses against Female Children Perpetrated by Men Who Are Not Pedophiles." *Journal of Sex Research* 28: 409–423.

Goffman, Erving. 1963. *Stigma: Notes on the Management of Spoiled Identity.* Englewood Cliffs, NJ: Prentice-Hall.

Graupner, Helmut. 2000. "Sexual Consent: The Criminal Law in Europe and Overseas." *Archives of Sexual Behavior* 29: 415–461.

Greenhouse, Linda. 2002. "Court Sets Limit on Detaining Sex Offenders after Prison." *New York Times,* January 23, p. A1.

Greer, Desmond S. 1994. "A Transatlantic Perspective on the Compensation of Crime Victims in the United States." *Journal of Criminal Law and Criminology* 85: 333–401.

Hajela, Deepti. 1999. "Linden Man Gets 10-Year Terms in Vigilante Shooting." *The Record,* February 20, p. A3.

Halperin, David M. 1990. "Why Is Diotima a Woman? Platonic Eros and the Figuration of Gender." In *Before Sexuality: The Construction of Erotic Experience in the Ancient Greek World,* edited by David M. Halperin, John J. Winkler, and Froma I. Zeitlin (pp. 257–308). Princeton, NJ: Princeton University Press.

Heim, Nikolaus, and Carolyn J. Hursch. 1979. "Castration for Sex Offenders: A Review and Critique of Recent European Literature." *Archives of Sexual Behavior* 8: 281–304.

Henderson, Lynne. N. 1985. "The Wrongs of Victim's Rights." *Stanford Law Review* 37: 937–1021.

Herdt, Gilbert H. 1984. "Semen Transactions in Sambian Culture." In *Ritualized Homosexuality in Melanesia,* edited by Gilbert H. Herdt (pp. 167–210). Berkeley: University of California Press.

Hinds, Lyn, and Kathleen Daly. 2001. "The War on Sex Offenders: Community Notification in Perspective." *Australian and New Zealand Journal of Criminology* 34: 256–276.

Holmes, Ronald M. 1991. *Sex Crimes.* Thousand Oaks, CA: Sage.

Horwitz, Allan V. 1990. *The Logic of Social Control.* New York: Plenum Press.

Howitt, Dennis. 1995. *Paedophiles and Sexual Offences against Children.* New York: Wiley.

Ingersoll, Sandra L., and Susan O. Patton. 1990. *Treating Perpetrators of Sexual Abuse.* Lexington, MA: Lexington Books.

Jenkins, Philip. 1998. *Moral Panic: Changing Concepts of the Child Molester in Modern America.* New Haven, CT: Yale University Press.

Kelly, Gary F. 2001. *Sexuality Today* (7th edition). New York: McGraw-Hill.

Killias, Martin. 1991. "The Historic Origins of Penal Statutes Concerning Sexual Activities Involving Children and Adolescents." *Journal of Homosexuality* 20: 41–46.

Krebs, Theresa. 1998. "Church Structures That Facilitate Pedophilia among Roman Catholic Clergy." In *Wolves within the Fold: Religious Leadership and Abuses of Power,* edited by Anson Shupe (pp. 15–32). New Brunswick, NJ: Rutgers University Press.

Lieb, Roxanne, Vernon Quinsey, and Lucy Berliner. 1998. "Sexual Predators and Social Policy." In Michael Tonry (ed.) *Crime and Justice: A Review of Research,* 23: 43–114.

Marshall, Donald S. 1971. "Sexual Aspects of the Life Cycle." In *Human Sexual Behavior: Variations in the Ethnographic Spectrum,* edited by Donald S. Marshall and Robert C. Suggs (pp. 103–162). New York: Basic Books.

Oberman, Michelle. 1994. "Turning Girls into Women: Reevaluating Modern Statutory Rape Law." *Journal of Criminal Law and Criminology* 85: 15–79.

O'Brien, Shirley J. 1986. *Why They Did It: Stories of Eight Convicted Child Molesters.* Springfield, IL: Thomas Books.

Okami, Paul. 1990. "Sociopolitical Biases in the Contemporary Scientific Literature on Adult Human Sexual Behavior with Children and Adolescents." In *Pedophilia: Biosocial Dimensions,* edited by J. R. Feierman (pp. 91–121). New York: Springer-Verlag.

Pivar, David J. 1973. *Purity Crusade: Sexual Morality and Social Control, 1868–1900.* Westport, CT: Greenwood Press.

Pfeiffer, Sacha, and Kevin Cullen. 2002. "Crisis in the Church: D. A. Seeks to Lift Time Limit on Rape Cases." *Boston Globe,* June 27, p. A23.

Plotnikoff, Joyce, and Richard Woolfson. 2000. *Where Are They Now: An Evaluation of Sex Offender Registration in England and Wales.* Police Research Series, Paper 126: Crown.

Pollock, Linda. 1983. *Forgotten Children: Parent–Child Relations from 1500–1900.* Cambridge: Cambridge University Press, 1983.

Pryor, Douglas W. 1996. *Unspeakable Acts: Why Men Sexually Abuse Children.* New York: New York University Press.

Rathus, Spencer A., Jeffrey S. Nevid, and Lois Fichner-Rathus. 2000. *Human Sexuality in a World of Diversity* (4th edition). Boston: Allyn and Bacon.

Rind, Bruce, Philip Tromovitch, and Robert Bauserman. 2000. "Condemnation of a Scientific Article: A Chronology and Refutation of the Attacks and a Discussion of Threats to the Integrity of Science." *Sexuality and Culture* 4: 1–62.

Ripley, Amanda. 2002. "Inside the Church's Closet." *Time,* May 20, p. 60.

Serpenti, Laurent. 1984. "The Ritual Meaning of Homosexuality and Pedophilia among the Kiman-Papuans of South Irian Jaya." In *Ritualized Homosexuality in Melanesia,* edited by Gilbert H. Herdt (pp. 292–317). Berkeley: University of California Press.

Siewers, Alf. 1994. "Prisoners Also Judge and Jury; Heinous Crimes Can Make Some Inmates a Special Target." *Chicago Sun-Times,* November 29, p. 7.

Stone, Lawrence. 1977. *The Family, Sex, and Marriage in England, 1500–1800.* New York: Harper and Row.

Stone, T. Howard, William J. Winslade, and Craig M. Klugman. 2000. "Sex Offenders, Sentencing Laws, and Pharmaceutical Treatment: A Prescription for Failure." *Behavioral Sciences and the Law* 18: 83–110.

Sutherland, Edwin H. 1950. "The Diffusion of Sexual Psychopath Laws." *American Journal of Sociology* 56: 142–148.

Szasz, Thomas. 1963. *Law, Liberty, and Psychiatry.* New York: Macmillan.

Tannahill, Reay. 1992. *Sex in History.* New York: Scarborough House.

van Biema, David. 1993. "Burn Thy Neighbor." *Time,* July 26, p. 58.

Vidmar, Neil. 1997. "General Prejudice and the Presumption of Guilt in Sex Abuse Trials." *Law and Human Behavior* 21: 5–25.

Too Young to Consent?

Elizabeth Cavalier and Elisabeth O. Burgess

In contemporary U.S. society, most sexual activity is between two people of similar ages. Approximately 74% of the first male sexual partners of adolescent females are the same age or one to three years older and only 8% of teen females have first partners 6 or more years older (Abma, Martinez, Mosher, & Dawson, 2004). But the legal and cultural significance of age difference is variable over the life course. The fifteen year gap between a 55-year-old man and his 40-year-old wife is less significant than the three year age difference between a 18- and 15-year-old having sex under the bleachers at their high school. In some states, that 18-year-old could be arrested for statutory rape, even if both parties agree the sex was consensual. Change the scenario and now the 18-year-old is engaging in sex acts with a 10-year-old. Most people in the U.S. would agree that 10 is too young to consent to sex. So, where do we draw the line? Who

gets to decide and why? How are these moral values legislated and prosecuted?

England developed the first known laws proscribing an age limit on consent to sexual activity in 1275. By 1576, the age limit was codified at 10 years old and sex between individuals above and below the age of consent became a felony. Colonial America adopted these laws defining ages of consent ranging from age 10 to 12 (Cocca, 2004). Traditionally, these laws were enacted to protect the virginity of white girls and, in fact, were only enforced if the victim was a white female who was a virgin prior to the sexual act in question. These crimes were prosecuted as property crimes—premarital virginity was treated as a valuable commodity.

Since Colonial times, laws about age of consent[1] have become more complicated, the age of consent has steadily risen, and the statute has expanded to include both female and male victims. Regulations around adolescent sexual activity in modern history have generally been couched in three different, and sometimes overlapping, areas of social concern. The first is a concern about potentially coercive sex. The second is a morality-based concern about sex between unmarried sexual partners. The third is an economically-based argument, which posits that adolescent sex leads to out-of-wedlock births which pose a drain on society via the welfare system (Cocca, 2004). Depending on specific social conditions, laws around age of consent have been more or less rigidly enforced. Since the 1970s, the United States has seen a steady tightening of control around issues of adolescent sex and age of consent.

Currently, the majority of states (33 and the District of Columbia) use 16 as the age of consent. Six states have 17 as the age of consent, and another 11 have 18 as the legal age of consent. However, in the United States, the laws vary widely and can be based on a number of factors. While 12 states have a single age of consent and individuals cannot consent to sex under any circumstances below this age, other states use a more complex formula (Lewin Group, 2004). These state laws are a combination of four factors: the age of consent, the minimum age of victim (the age below which an individual cannot consent to sex under any circumstances), the age differential between victim and perpetrator (the maximum difference in age between a victim and defendant where an individual can legally consent, assuming the victim is above the minimum age), and the minimum age of the defendant in order to prosecute (the age below which an individual cannot be prosecuted if the victim is above the minimum age (Lewin Group, 2004).[2] All of these laws focus on sexual intercourse—the laws about sexual contact (including oral and anal sex) are more complicated and unevenly enforced. Such variety in laws and enforcement creates a problem whereby sexual activity between consenting adolescents and young adults may be legal in one state, a misdemeanor in another, and a felony in a third state. In addition to legal disparities between states, enforcement differs based on the sex of the victim and defendant, the race of the victim and defendant, and the type of sexual activity in question (i.e. oral and anal sex rather than intercourse or heterosexual sex rather than homosexual sex).

Public perception and media coverage of age of consent cases do not coincide with actual rates of crime, particularly concerning the sex of perpetrators and victims. The National Incidents Based Reporting System (NIBRS) reports that 95% of the victims in statutory rape cases are female and 99% of the offenders of female victims are male (Troup-Leasure and Snyder, 2005). Yet popular press reports emphasize female perpetrators (often teachers) with younger male victims, such as the case of Mary Kay LeTourneau, who had two children with a student she began a sexual relationship with when she was 34 and the student was 13 (Caruso, 2006). Despite representing fewer than 5% of the cases of statutory rape and significantly less of the prosecutions (Cocca, 2004), female perpetrator/male victim statutory rape cases are sensationalized on the news and talk shows. This media coverage perpetuates the myth that there is an epidemic of older women preying on younger adolescent boys. One particularly sensational report labeled this as a "sexpidemic spreading across the planet" (WorldNet Daily, 2005). The disproportionate coverage of male victims is especially ironic considering that statutory rape laws were originally enacted to protect young girls. It was not until the early 1990s that the language of statutory rape laws was changed to include gender-neutral language allowing for the potential for male victims (Cocca, 2004). From the 1960s to the 1990s, public debate around legal and social policies about statutory rape often centered around rhetoric about protecting young girls from predatory older men. Adolescents, girls in particular, were seen as not having the legal capacity or emotional maturity to consent to sexual activity. Yet during the same time period, the juvenile justice system was also undergoing a profound shift, seeing a steady decline in treating defendants, primarily males, as juveniles and instead prosecuting them as adults, particularly for violent crimes (Schaffner, 2005). This sexual double standard illustrates a peculiar dichotomy whereby girls are treated as innocent, virginal children without the ability to be autonomous decision-makers about their sexual lives, while boys are treated as adults with the intellectual capacity to commit a crime and be held legally culpable.

Race of the victim and perpetrator is the second area where there are significant disparities in enforcement of statutory rape laws. Similar to other crimes, men of color, particularly African-American men, are more likely to be arrested and prosecuted and disproportionately sentenced (Criminal Justice Policy Foundation, 2005). The case of Marcus Dixon, a black 18-year-old male who had consensual sex with a white girl who was three months shy of her 16th birthday, received national coverage and illustrated a major problem with existing laws. Although he was acquitted of rape, battery, assault, and false imprisonment, he was convicted of statutory rape, and because of her age, aggravated child molestation. He was sentenced to ten years in prison, although his sentence was overturned and he was released after a year after public outcry about the case (Melby, 2006). Disproportionate prosecuting and sentencing of black men for statutory rape reflects remnants of historical racism predicated on white fears about black men having sex with white women.

A third area of differential enforcement of consent laws is based on types of sexual behavior. Matthew Limon was released from prison in 2005 after serving almost six years in prison for consensual gay sex when he had just turned 18 and his partner was 14, nearly 15. He was convicted of criminal sodomy because Kansas's "Romeo and Juliet" law, which reduced penalties for consensual sex between two teenagers, only applied to heterosexual sex. He was sentenced to 17 years in prison, and would have only been sentenced to 15 months had his partner been female. The case went all the way to the Supreme Court, which overturned the conviction, but by that time Limon had served nearly six years in prison (Melby, 2006). In another state, Gernarlow Wilson was convicted of aggravated child molestation for receiving oral sex from a 15-year-old girl when he was 17. He was sentenced to ten years in prison. Because of a loophole in the Georgia law at the time (which has since been closed), if he had engaged in sexual intercourse rather than oral sex with the girl he would have been guilty of a misdemeanor, punishable by up to 12 months. He served nearly three years in prison before his conviction was overturned (Jarvie & Fausset, 2007). In many states, the statutory rape laws do not apply to married partners. As a result, those who do not have access to marriage—gay couples or adolescents without parental consent for marriage—will be more likely to face criminal prosecution for sexual activity.

Age of consent and statutory rape laws are not designed to catch and punish persistent child sexual offenders; states have separate legislation that prohibits child molestation and pedophilia. Statutory rape laws, with their uneven and often discriminatory enforcement, have primarily served to criminalize adolescent sexual exploration. NIBRS (2005) reports that three out of 10 reported cases of statutory rape involving juveniles involve people who considered themselves "boyfriend/girlfriend," and six out of 10 involve people who considered each other "acquaintances or friends" (Troup-Leasure

and Snyder, 2005). Such laws do not prevent adolescents from having sex. The Centers for Disease Control and Prevention (CDC) (2008) report that in 9th grade 27.4% of girls have ever engaged in sexual intercourse and by 12th grade that percentage increases to 66.2%. For boys, 38% have engaged in sexual intercourse by 9th grade, but the percentage increases to 62.8% by 12th grade. The CDC also reports that over half (52.6%) of high school seniors have been sexually active in the past three months. Adolescents are having sex—the threat of criminal prosecution for sexual exploration adds unnecessary fear and anxiety over something that even adults disagree (as evidenced by the wide disparity across states in age of consent laws).

In the end, an arbitrary age limit on age of consent has often served to punish adolescent sexual exploration. Perhaps, we should focus our attention on defining and enforcing laws that address coercive sexual behavior.

NOTES

1. Age of consent laws traditionally define the age below which you are too young to consent to sexual behavior. These laws may stipulate exceptions to the law. Statutory rape laws (or related statutory offenses) define the criminal punishment for those who engage in sexual behavior that violates age of consent laws.

2. A list of the state-by-state laws about age of consent can be found at www.lewin.com/content/publications/3068.pdf. The lowest minimum age of victim in the United States is 10, in South Dakota, and the highest age is 18, in California, Idaho, and Wisconsin. Most states have between 14 and 16 years of age as the age below which individuals cannot consent to sex for any reason.

REFERENCES

Abma, J. C., Martinez, G. M., Mosher, W. D., & Dawson, B. S. 2004. "Teenagers in the United States: Sexual Activity, Contraceptive Use, and Childbearing, 2003." National Center for Health Statistics. *Vital Health Stat 23*(24).

Caruso, Michelle. 2006. "Vilified & Blissful: Mary Kay Marriage Milestone." *Daily News.* February 19, p. 16.

Centers for Disease Control and Prevention. 2008. Youth Risk Behavior Surveillance System—United States, 2007. *MMWR, 57* (SS-4).

Cocca, Carolyn. 2004. *Jailbait: The Politics of Statutory Rape Laws in the United States.* Albany: State University of New York Press.

Criminal Justice Policy Foundation. 2005. "Criminal Justice Policy Foundation: Sentencing Policy." Retrieved January 13, 2009. (www.cjpf.org/sentencing/racialdisparity.html)

Jarvie, J., and Fausset, R. 2007. "After Teen Sex Reading, He's Free." *Los Angeles Times,* October 27, p. A9.

The Lewin Group. 2004. "Statutory Rape: A Guide to State Laws and Reporting Requirements." Retrieved January 13, 2009. (www.lewin.com/content/publications/3068.pdf)

Melby, Todd. 2006. "When Teens Get Arrested for Voluntary Sex: Laws Designed to Punish Adult Offenders Sometimes Trap Kids." *Contemporary Sexuality 40*(2), 1–6.

National Incident-Based Reporting System (NIBRS). 2005. Washington, DC: Federal Bureau of Investigation.

Schaffner, Laurie. 2005. "Capacity, Consent, and the Construction of Adulthood." Pp. 189–205 in *Regulating Sex: The Politics of Intimacy and Identity,* edited by Elizabeth Bernstein and Laurie Schaffner. New York: Routledge.

Troup-Leasure, Karyl, and Howard N. Snyder. 2005. "Statutory Rape Known to Law Enforcement." Juvenile Justice Bulletin No. NJC 208803. Washington DC: Office of Juvenile Justice & Delinquency Prevention. Retrieved January 13, 2009. (www.ncjrs.gov/pdffiles1/ojjdp/208803.pdf)

WorldNet Daily. 2005. "Sextra Credit: U.S. Teacher Sexpidemic Spreading across Planet." Retrieved on January 13, 2009. (http://worldnetdaily.com/news/article.asp?ARTICLE_ID=47895)

reading 41

The Sexual Politics

of Black Womanhood

Patricia Hill Collins

Even I found it almost impossible to let her say what had happened to her as she perceived it. . . . And why? Because once you strip away the lie that rape is pleasant, that children are not permanently damaged by sexual pain, that violence done to them is washed away by fear, silence, and time, you are left with the positive horror of the lives of thousands of children . . . who have been sexually abused and who have never been permitted their own language to tell about it.

—*Alice Walker 1988, 57*

In *The Color Purple* Alice Walker creates the character of Celie, a Black adolescent girl who is sexually abused by her stepfather. Writing letters to God and forming supportive relationships with other Black women help Celie find her own voice, and her voice enables her to transcend the fear and silence of her childhood. By creating Celie and giving her the language to tell of her sexual abuse, Walker adds Celie's voice to muted yet growing discussions of the sexual politics of Black womanhood. But when it comes to other important issues concerning Black women's sexuality, U.S. Black women have found it almost impossible to say what has happened.

As Evelynn Hammonds points out, "Black women's sexuality is often described in metaphors of speechlessness, space, or vision; as a 'void' or empty space that is simultaneously ever-visible (exposed) and invisible, where black women's bodies are already colonized" (1997, 171). In response to this portrayal, Black women have been silent. One important factor

that contributes to these long-standing silences both among African-American women and within Black feminist thought lies in Black women's lack of access to positions of power in U.S. social institutions. Those who control the schools, news media, churches, and government suppress Black women's collective voice. Dominant groups are the ones who construct Black women as "the embodiment of sex and the attendant invisibility of black women as the unvoiced, unseen—everything that is not white" (Hammonds 1997, 171).

Critical scholarship also has approached Black women's sexuality through its own set of assumptions. Within U.S. Black intellectual communities generally and Black studies scholarship in particular, Black women's sexuality is either ignored or included primarily in relation to African-American men's issues. In Black critical contexts where Black women struggle to get gender oppression recognized as important, theoretical analyses of Black sexuality remain sparse (Collins 1993; 1998a, 155–83). . . . Everyone [else] has spoken for Black women, making it difficult for us to speak for ourselves.

But suppression does not fully explain African-American women's persistent silences about sexuality. U.S. Black women have been discouraged from analyzing and speaking out about a host of topics. Why does this one remain so difficult? In response, Paula Giddings identifies another important factor, namely, the "last taboo" of disclosing "not only a gender but a sexual discourse, unmediated by the question of racism" (Giddings 1992, 442). Within this taboo, to talk of White racist constructions of Black women's sexuality is acceptable. But developing analyses of sexuality that implicate Black men is not—it violates norms of racial solidarity that counsel Black women always to put our own needs second. Even within these racial boundaries, some topics are more acceptable

405

than others—White men's rape of Black women during slavery can be discussed whereas Black men's rape of Black women today cannot. . . .

[C]ertain elements of Black women's sexuality can be examined, namely, those that do not challenge a race discourse that historically has privileged the experiences of African-American men. The cost is that other elements remain off-limits. Rape, incest, misogyny in Black cultural practices, and other painful topics that might implicate Black men remain taboo.

Yet another factor influencing Black women's silences concerns the potential benefits of remaining silent. . . . [W]here regulating Black women's bodies benefited systems of race, class, and gender alike, protecting the safe spaces for Black women's self-definitions often required public silences about seemingly provocative topics. This secrecy was especially important within a U.S. culture that routinely accused Black women of being sexually immoral, promiscuous jezebels. In a climate where one's sexuality is on public display, holding fast to privacy and trying to shut the closet door becomes paramount. Hine refers to this strategy as a culture of dissemblance, one where Black women appeared too outgoing and public, while using this facade to hide a secret world within. As Hine suggests, "only with secrecy, thus achieving a self-imposed invisibility, could ordinary black women accrue the psychic space and harness the resources needed to hold their own in the often one-sided and mismatched resistance struggle" (Hine 1995, 382). In contexts of violence where internal self-censorship was seen as protection, silence made sense.

The convergence of all of these factors—the suppression of Black women's voice by dominant groups, Black women's struggles to work within the confines of norms of racial solidarity, and the seeming protections offered by a culture of dissemblance—influences yet another factor shaping patterns of silence. In general, U.S. Black women have been reluctant to acknowledge the valuable contributions of Black lesbian feminist theory in reconceptualizing Black women's sexuality. Since the early 1980s, Black lesbian theorists and activists have identified homophobia and the toll it takes on African-American women as an important topic for Black feminist thought. "The oppression that affects Black gay peo-

ple, female and male, is pervasive, constant, and not abstract. Some of us die from it," argues Barbara Smith (1983, xlvii). Despite the increasing visibility of Black lesbians as parents (Lorde 1984, 72–80; Williams 1997), as academics (Davenport 1996), as activists (Gomez and Smith 1994), within lesbian history (Kennedy and Davis 1993, 113–31), and who have publicly come out (Moore 1997), African-Americans have tried to ignore homosexuality generally and have avoided serious analysis of homophobia within African-American communities.

In this context, Black lesbian theorizing about sexuality has been marginalized, albeit in different ways, both within Black intellectual communities and women's studies scholarship. As a result, Black feminist thought has not yet taken full advantage of this important source of Black feminist theory. As a group, heterosexual African-American women have been strangely silent on the issue of Black lesbianism. Barbara Smith suggests one compelling reason: "Heterosexual privilege is usually the only privilege that Black women have. None of us have racial or sexual privilege, almost none of us have class privilege, maintaining 'straightness' is our last resort" (1982, 171). In the same way that White feminists identify with their victimization as women yet ignore the privilege that racism grants them, and that Black men decry racism yet see sexism as being less objectionable, heterosexual African-American women may perceive their own race and gender oppression yet victimize lesbians, gays, and bisexuals. Barbara Smith raises a critical point that can best be seen through the outsider-within standpoint available to Black lesbians—namely, that intersecting oppressions of sexuality, race, gender, and class produce neither absolute oppressors nor pure victims. . . .

Treating race, class, gender, and sexuality less as personal attributes and more as systems of domination in which individuals construct unique identities, Black feminist analyses routinely identify multiple oppressions as important to the study of Black women's sexualities. For example, Black feminist thinkers have investigated how rape as a specific form of sexual violence is embedded in intersecting oppressions of race, gender, and class (Davis 1978, 1981, 1989; Crenshaw 1991). Reproductive rights issues such as access to information on sexuality and birth control, the struggles for abortion rights, and patterns of forced sterilization require attention to how nation-state policies affect U.S. Black women (Davis 1981; Roberts 1997; Collins 1999). Black lesbians' work on homophobia investigates how heterosexism's impact on African-American women remains embedded in larger social structures (Lorde 1982, 1984; Clarke 1983; Shockley 1983; Smith 1983, 1998). This contextualization in power relations generates a particular kind of social constructionist argument, one that views Black women's sexualities as being constructed within an historically specific matrix of domination characterized by intersecting oppressions. In understanding these Black feminist contextualizations, it may be more appropriate to speak of the *sexual politics of Black womanhood,* namely, how sexuality and power become linked in constructing Black women's sexualities.

Black Women, Intersecting Oppressions, and Sexual Politics

Due in large part to the politicized nature of definitions themselves, questions of sexuality and the sexual politics in which they participate raise special concerns. What is sexuality? What is power? Both of these questions generate wide-spread debate. Moreover, analyzing questions of sexuality and power within an interpretive framework that takes intersecting oppressions into account can appear to be a daunting task.

Whereas sexuality is part of intersecting oppressions, the ways in which it can be conceptualized differ. Sexuality can be analyzed as a freestanding system of oppression similar to oppressions of race, class, and gender. This approach views heterosexism as a system of power that victimizes Black women in particular ways. Within heterosexism as a system of oppression, African-American women find that their distinctive group placement within hierarchies of race, class, and gender shape the experiences of Black women as a collectivity as well as the sexual histories of individual Black women.

A second approach examines how sexualities become manipulated *within* class, race, nation, and gender as distinctive systems of oppression and draw upon heterosexist assumptions to do so. Regulating Black women's sexualities emerges as a distinctive feature of social class exploitation, of institutionalized racism, of U.S. nation-state policies, and of gender oppression. In essence, this approach suggests that both the sexual meanings assigned to Black women's bodies as well as the social practices justified by sexual ideologies reappears across seemingly separate systems of oppression.

Yet another approach views sexuality as a specific site of intersectionality where intersecting oppressions meet. Studying Black women's sexualities reveals how sexuality constitutes one important site where heterosexism, class, race, nation, and gender as systems of oppression converge. For Black women, ceding control over self-definitions of Black women's sexualities upholds multiple oppressions. This is because all systems of oppression rely on harnessing the power of the erotic. In contrast, when self-defined by Black women ourselves, Black women's sexualities can become an important place of resistance. Just as harnessing the power of the erotic is important for domination, reclaiming and self-defining that same eroticism may constitute one path toward Black women's empowerment.

Heterosexism as a System of Power

One important outcome of social movements advanced by lesbians, gays, bisexuals, and transgendered individuals has been the recognition of heterosexism as a system of power. In essence, the political and intellectual space carved out by these movements challenged the assumed normality of heterosexuality (Jackson 1996; Richardson 1996). These challenges fostered a shift from seeing sexuality as residing in individual biological makeup, to analyzing heterosexism as a system of power. Similar to oppressions of race or gender that mark bodies with social meanings, heterosexism marks bodies with sexual meanings. Within this logic, *heterosexism* can be defined as the belief in the inherent superiority of one form of sexual expression over another and thereby the right to dominate.

When it comes to thinking about Black women's sexualities, what is needed is a framework that not only analyzes heterosexism as a system of oppression, but also conceptualizes its links to race, class, and gender as comparable systems of oppression. Such a framework might emphasize two interdependent dimensions of heterosexism, namely, its symbolic and structural dimensions. The symbolic dimension refers to the sexual meanings used to represent and evaluate Black women's sexualities. For example, via the "hoochie" image, Black women's sexualities are seen as unnatural, dirty, sick, and sinful. In contrast, the structural dimension encompasses how social institutions are organized to reproduce heterosexism, primarily through laws and social customs. For example, refusing to prosecute Black women's rapists because the women are viewed as sexual "freaks" constitutes a social practice that reinforces and shapes these symbolic structures. While analytically distinct, in actuality, these two dimensions work together.

In the United States, assumptions of heterosexuality operate as a hegemonic or taken-for-granted ideology—to be heterosexual is considered normal, to be anything else is to become suspect. The system of sexual meanings associated with heterosexism becomes normalized to such a degree that they are often unquestioned. For example, the use of the term *sexuality* itself references *hetero*sexuality as normal, natural, and normative.

The ideological dimension of heterosexism is embedded in binary thinking that deems heterosexuality as normal and other sexualities as deviant. Such thinking divides sexuality into two categories, namely, "normal" and "deviant" sexuality, and has great implications for understanding Black women's sexualities. Within assumptions of normalized heterosexuality, two important categories of "deviant" sexuality emerge. First, *African* or *Black* sexuality becomes constructed as an abnormal or pathologized heterosexuality. Long-standing ideas concerning the excessive sexual appetite of people of African descent conjured up in White imaginations generate gender-specific controlling images of the Black male rapist and the Black female jezebel, and they also rely on myths of Black hypersexuality. Within assumptions of normalized heterosexuality, regardless of individual behavior, being White marks the normal category of heterosexuality. In contrast, being Black signals the wild, out-of-control hyperheterosexuality of excessive sexual appetite.

Within assumptions of normalized heterosexuality, *homosexuality* emerges as a second important category of "deviant" sexuality. In this case, homosexuality constitutes an abnormal sexuality that becomes pathologized as heterosexuality's opposite. Whereas the problem of African or Black sexual deviancy is thought to lie in Black hyperheterosexuality, the problem of homosexuality lies not in an excess of heterosexual desire, but in the seeming absence of it. Women who lack interest in men as sexual partners become pathologized as "frigid" if they claim heterosexuality and stigmatized as lesbians if they do not.

Under Eurocentric ideologies, normalized heterosexuality thus becomes constructed in contrast to two allegedly deviant sexualities, namely, those attributed to people of African descent and those applied to lesbians and gays, among others. The binary fundamental to heterosexism, namely, that dividing alleged normal sexuality from its deviant other dovetails with binaries that underlie other systems of oppression. [Other] important binaries . . . —white/black, male/female, reason/emotion, and mind/body—now become joined by a series of sexual binaries: madonna/whore, real woman/dyke, real man/faggot, and stud/sissy. These sexual binaries in turn receive justification via medical theories (normal/sick), religious beliefs (saved/sinner), and state regulation (legal/illegal).

All of this influences the actual system of sexual regulation in the United States, where ideas about normalized heterosexuality permeate a range of social institutions. Despite the similarities that characterize constructions of African/Black sexuality and homosexuality, these sexualities differ in their characteristic modes of regulation. Black people experience a highly visible *sexualized racism,* one where the visibility of Black bodies themselves reinscribes the hypervisibility of Black men and women's alleged sexual deviancy. Because U.S. understandings of race rely on biological categories that, while renegotiated, cannot be changed—skin color is permanent—Black hypersexuality is conceptualized as being intergenerational and resistant to change.

The seeming intractability of the stigma of Blackness in turn shapes possible responses to this socially constructed yet highly visible deviancy. . . . Because biological traits are conceptualized as permanent, reformist strategies are unlikely to work. In this context, containment strategies of all sorts rise in importance. For example, racial segregation in housing, schools, employment, and public facilities not only benefit some groups of Whites economically—it also keeps allegedly hypersexual Blacks separated from Whites. Maintaining physical distance need not be the sole strategy. Blacks have long worked in close proximity to Whites, but Blacks and Whites alike were discouraged from seeing one another as friends, neighbors, lovers, and, most important, legal sexual partners. In a context where Black bodies signal sexual deviancy, laws against intermarriage and other components of racial segregation ensured that the deviancy could be simultaneously exploited yet contained.

Because the nature of the threat is deemed different, forms of control for lesbians, gays, and other sexually stigmatized groups differ from those of sexualized racism. *Homophobia* flourishes in a context where the invisibility of the alleged deviancy is perceived to be the problem. Whereas the fears associated with racism lie in ideas projected upon highly visible, objectified Black bodies, the fears underlying homophobia emerge from the understanding that *anyone* could be gay or lesbian. Reminiscent of the proximate racism of anti-Semitism, one where, for example, Nazi scientists spent considerable time trying to find ways to identify Jewishness, homophobia constitutes a proximate fear that anyone could at any time reveal himself or herself as gay or lesbian.

The panoply of responses to the alleged deviancy of homosexuality also match the nature of the perceived threat. Containment also operates, but differently. For example, the medical profession has been assigned the reformist strategy of counseling gays and lesbians to better cope with normalized heterosexuality. Hate crimes punish individuals, but such crimes make an example of a visible homosexuality in order to drive the rest back into the closet. Recognizing that homosexuality most likely cannot be eliminated, the intended effect is to remove it from public and thereby legitimated space. Laws forbidding gay and lesbian marriages coupled with resistance to gays

and lesbians having and raising children seem designed to stop the "spread" of homosexuality. Within this logic of the proximate threat, efforts to keep gays, lesbians, and other sexual minorities "in the closet" and "hidden" seem designed to contain the threat within.

Making heterosexism as a system of oppression more central to thinking through Black women's sexualities suggests two significant features. First, different groups remain differentially placed within heterosexism as an overarching structure of power. . . . African-American women's group history becomes crafted in the context of the specificity of the U.S. matrix of domination. Black women's particular group history within heterosexism intersects with that of other groups. For example, constructions of Black male and female sexuality are linked—they are similar yet different. Similarly, middle-class White women's sexuality could not be constructed as it is without corresponding controlling images applied to U.S. Black women. Moreover, this collective U.S. Black women's history does not eliminate further specification of group histories within the larger collectivity of African-American women, e.g., Black lesbians, adolescent Black women, older Black women, Black women who must rely on social welfare programs, and so on. Instead, it specifies the contours of sexual meanings that have been attributed to Black women. Considerable diversity exists among U.S. Black women as to how the symbolic and structural dimensions of heterosexism will be experienced and responded to.

A second significant feature concerns the space created for Black women's individual agency. Because African-American women express a range of sexualities, including celibate, heterosexual, lesbian, and bisexual, with varying forms of sexual expression changing throughout an individual's life course, Black women's self-definitions become essential. It is important to stress that both the symbolic and structural dimensions of heterosexism are always contested. Individual African-American women construct sexual meanings and practices within this overarching structure of heterosexual power relations. Thus, the individual agency of any one U.S. Black woman emerges in the context of larger institutional structures and particular group histories that affect many others. For individual Black women, the struggle lies in rejecting externally defined ideas and practices, and claiming the erotic as a mechanism for empowerment.

Sexuality within Distinctive Systems of Class, Race, Gender, and Nation

Analyzing how heterosexism as a system of oppression victimizes Black women constitutes one major approach to examining sexuality. A second approach explores how sexualities constructed in conjunction with an unquestioned heterosexism become manipulated within class, race, gender, and nation as distinctive systems of oppression. For example, the controlling image of jezebel reappears across several systems of oppression. For class oppression, the jezebel image fosters the sexual exploitation of Black women's bodies through prostitution. The jezebel image reinforces racial oppression by justifying sexual assaults against Black women. Gender ideology also draws upon the jezebel image—a devalued jezebel makes pure White womanhood possible. Overseeing these relationships are nation-state policies that because they implicitly see Black women as jezebels, deny Black women equal treatment under the law. Unmarried Black mothers have struggled to gain social welfare benefits long available to White women (Amott 1990), Black adolescents are more likely than White women to receive Norplant and other contraceptive methods that assume they cannot control their sexual libidos (Roberts 1997, 104–49), and as Anita Hill found out, Black women's claims of being sexually harassed and raped are often discounted. Thus, each system has a vested interest in regulating sexuality and relies on symbolic and structural practices to do so.

Examining how regulating Black women's sexuality functions to support each system constitutes one way of investigating these relationships. Controlling Black women's bodies has been especially important for capitalist class relations in the United States. When it comes to U.S. Black women's experiences, two features of capitalism remain noteworthy. First, Black women's bodies have been objectified and commodified under U.S. capitalist class relations.

The objectification of Black women . . . and the subsequent commodification of those objectified bodies are closely linked—objectifying Black women's bodies turns them into commodities that can be sold or exchanged on the open market. Commodified bodies of all sorts become markers of status within class hierarchies that rely on race and gender. For example, healthy White babies are hot commodities in the U.S. adoption market, while healthy Black babies often languish in foster care. A second feature of U.S. capitalist class relations concerns how Black women's bodies have been exploited. Via mechanisms such as employment discrimination, maintaining images of Black women that construct them as mules or objects of pleasure, and encouraging or discouraging Black women's reproduction via state intervention, Black women's labor, sexuality, and fertility all have been exploited.

Not only are commodification and exploitation linked, patterns of exploiting Black women's sexuality have taken many forms. In some cases, the entire body itself became commodified. For example, slave auctions brokered the commodified bodies of both Black women and men—bodies could be bought and sold on the open market. In other cases, parts of the body could be commodified and sold for profitability. Barbara Omolade introduces this notion of specialized commodification where "every part of the black woman" was used by the White master. "To him she was a fragmented commodity whose feelings and choices were rarely considered: her head and her heart were separated from her back and her hands and divided from her womb and vagina" (Omolade 1994, 7). Black women's sexuality could be reduced to gaining control over an objectified vagina that could then be commodified and sold. The long-standing interest in Black women's genitalia within Western science seems apt here in that reducing Black women to commodified genitalia and vaginas effectively treats Black women as potential prostitutes. Similarly, current portrayals of Black women in popular culture—reducing Black women to butts—works to reinscribe these commodified body parts. Commodifying and exploiting Black women's wombs may be next. When a California judge rejected African-American Anna Johnson's claim that the White baby she had carried in her womb entitled her to some rights of motherhood, the message seemed clear—storage lockers and wombs constitute rental property (Hartouni 1997).

Regulating Black women's sexuality has certainly been significant within racist discourse and practice. In the United States, because race has been constructed as a biological category that is rooted in the body, controlling Black sexuality has long been important in preserving racial boundaries. U.S. notions of racial purity, such as the rule claiming that one drop of Black "blood" determines racial identity, required strict control over the sexuality and subsequent fertility of Black women, White women, and Black men. Although explicitly a means to prevent Blacks and Whites from associating in public accommodations, racial segregation in the South rested upon a deep-seated fear that "social mixing would lead to sexual mixing" (d'Emilio and Freedman 1988, 106). These mechanisms of control affected diverse population groups differently. Affluent White men typically enjoyed access to the bodies of all women and removed other men from sexual competition. The creation of a class of "angry White men" in the aftermath of social reforms of the 1960s and 1970s reflects, in part, the deterioration of White supremacist practices that gave White men such power (Ferber 1998). Wealthy White women were valued for a premarital virginity that when "lost" in the context of heterosexual marriage, ensured that all children would be biologically "White." Regardless of social class, Whites were encouraged to fear racial amalgamation, believing that it would debase them to the status of other races (d'Emilio and Freedman 1988, 86). In this context, Black men were constructed as sexually violent beasts, a view that not only justified their persecution by the state (Berry 1994), but was used to deny them access to White women's bodies. Black women's sexuality found no protections. Thus, notions of White supremacy relied on a notion of racial difference where "difference would be largely based on perceptions of sexual difference, and . . . the foundation of sexual difference lay in attitudes about black women" (Giddings 1992, 447).

Regulating Black women's sexuality also constituted a part of gender oppression. Dividing women into two categories—the asexual, moral women to be protected by marriage and their sexual, immoral counterparts—served as a gender template for constructing ideas about masculinity and femininity. The major archetypal symbols of women in Western thought construct women's sexuality via a tightly interwoven series of binaries. Collectively, these binaries create a sexual hierarchy with approved sexual expression installed at the top and forbidden sexualities relegated to the bottom. Assumptions of normal and deviant sexuality work to label women as good girls or bad girls, resulting in two categories of female sexuality. Virgins are the women who remain celibate before marriage, and who gain license to engage in heterosexual sexual practices after marriage. In contrast, whores are the unmarried women who are willingly "screwed." Whether a woman is an actual virgin or not is of lesser concern than whether she can socially construct herself as a "good" girl within this logic. Racializing this gender ideology by assigning all Black women, regardless of actual behavior, to the category of "bad" girls simplifies the management of this system.

It is important to remember that what appear to be natural and normal ideas and practices concerning sexuality are in fact carefully manufactured and promoted by schools, organized religions, the news media, and, most importantly, government policies. The local, state, and federal branches of the U.S. government may appear to be removed from issues of sexuality, but via their taxation, social welfare, and other policies, the U.S. nation-state in effect regulates which sexualities are deemed legitimate and which are not. For example, U.S. nation-state policies shape understandings of which citizens shall be afforded privacy. Affluent families living in suburban gated communities are provided with far more privacy and government protection than are poor families who live in urban public housing, where police intrude on family privacy more often than they protect it. In a similar fashion, Black women's sexuality has been constructed by law as public property—Black women have no rights of privacy that Whites must observe. As Barbara Omolade suggests, "White men used their power in the public sphere to construct a private sphere that would meet their needs and their desire for black women, which if publicly admitted would have undermined the false construct of race they needed to maintain public power. Therefore, the history of black women in America reflects the juncture where the private and public spheres and personal and political oppression meet" (Omolade 1994, 17).

Regulating Black Women's Bodies

Sexuality can be conceptualized as a freestanding system of oppression similar to oppressions of race, class, nation, and gender, as well as part of each of these distinctive systems of oppression. A third approach views sexuality as one important social location that joins these distinctive systems of oppression. This conceptualization views sexuality as conceptual glue that binds intersecting oppressions together. Stated differently, intersecting oppressions share certain core features. Manipulating and regulating the sexualities of diverse groups constitutes one such shared feature or site of intersectionality.

In this context, investigating efforts to regulate Black women's bodies can illuminate the larger question of how sexuality operates as a site of intersectionality. Within this larger endeavor, Black women's experiences with pornography, prostitution, and rape constitute specific cases of how more powerful groups have aimed to regulate Black women's bodies. These cases emphasize the connections between sexual ideologies developed to justify actual social practices and the use of force to maintain the social order. As such, these themes provide a useful lens for examining how intersecting oppressions rely on sexuality to mutually construct one another.

Pornography and Black Women's Bodies

. . . Contemporary pornography consists of a series of icons or representations that focus the viewer's attention on the relationship between the portrayed individual and the general qualities ascribed to that class of individuals. Pornographic images are iconographic in that they represent realities in a manner determined by the historical position of the observers and by their relationship to their own time and to the history of the conventions which they employ (Gilman 1985). The treatment of

Black women's bodies in nineteenth-century Europe and the United States may be the foundation upon which contemporary pornography as the representation of women's objectification, domination, and control is based. Icons about the sexuality of Black women's bodies emerged in these contexts. Moreover, as race and gender-specific representations, these icons have implications for the treatment of both African-American and White women in contemporary pornography. . . .

One key feature about the treatment of Black women in the nineteenth century was how their bodies were objects of display. In the antebellum American South, White men did not have to look at pornographic pictures of women because they could become voyeurs of Black women on the auction block. A chilling example of this objectification of the Black female body is provided by the exhibition, in early-nineteenth-century Europe, of Sarah Bartmann, the so-called Hottentot Venus. Her display formed one of the original icons for Black female sexuality. An African women, Sarah Bartmann was often exhibited at fashionable parties in Paris, generally wearing little clothing, to provide entertainment. To her audience she represented deviant sexuality. At the time European audiences thought that Africans had deviant sexual practices and searched for physiological differences, such as enlarged penises and malformed female genitalia, as indications of this deviant sexuality. Sarah Bartmann's exhibition stimulated these racist and sexist beliefs. After her death in 1815, she was dissected, with her genitalia and buttocks placed on display (Gilman 1985). . . .

The pornographic treatment of the bodies of enslaved African women and of women like Sarah Bartmann has since developed into a full-scale industry. Within pornography, all women are objectified differently by racial/ethnic category. Contemporary portrayals of Black women in pornography represent the continuation of the historical treatment of their actual bodies (Forna 1992). African-American women are usually depicted in a situation of bondage and slavery, typically in a submissive posture, and often with two White men. A study of fifty-four videos found that Black women more often were portrayed as being subjected to aggressive acts and as submitting after initial resistance to a sexual encounter. Compared with White women, Black women were shown performing fellatio on their knees more often (Cowan and Campbell 1994). Russell (1993, 45–49) reports that Black women are equated with snakes, as engaging in sex with animals, as incestuous, and as lovers of rape, especially by White men. As Bell observes, these settings remind us of "the trappings of slavery: chains, whips, neck braces, wrist clasps" (1987, 59). White women and women of color have different pornographic images applied to them. The image of Black women in pornography is almost consistently one featuring them breaking from chains. The image of Asian women in pornography is almost consistently one of being tortured (Bell 1987, 161). . . .

This linking of views of the body, social constructions of race and gender, pornography's profitability, and conceptualizations of sexuality that inform Black women's treatment as pornographic objects promises to have significant implications for how we assess contemporary pornography. Pornography's significance as a site of intersecting oppressions promises new insights toward understanding social injustice. . . .

While the sexual and racial dimensions of being treated like an animal are important, the economic foundation underlying this treatment is critical. Under capitalist class relations, animals can be worked, sold, killed, and consumed, all for profit. As "mules," African-American women become susceptible to such treatment. The political economy of pornography meshes with this overarching value system that objectifies, commodifies, and markets products, ideas, images, and actual people. Pornography is pivotal in mediating contradictions in changing societies (McNall 1983). It is no accident that racist biology, religious justifications for slavery and women's subordination, and other explanations for nineteenth-century racism and sexism arose during a period of profound political and economic change. Symbolic means of domination become particularly important in mediating contradictions in changing political economies. The exhibition of Sarah Bartmann and Black women on the auction block were not benign intellectual exercises—these practices defended real material and political interests. Current transforma-

tions in international capitalists require similar ideological justifications. Contemporary pornography meshes with late-twentieth-century global transformations of postcolonialism in a fashion reminiscent of global changes associated with nineteenth-century colonialism (Dines 1998). . . .

The treatment of all women in contemporary pornography has strong ties to the portrayal of Black women as animals. In pornography women become nonpeople and are often represented as the sum of their fragmented body parts. Scott McNall observes:

> *This fragmentation of women relates to the predominance of rear-entry position photographs. . . . All of these kinds of photographs reduce the woman to her reproductive system, and, furthermore, make her open, willing, and available—not in control. . . . The other thing rear-entry position photographs tell us about women is that they are animals. They are animals because they are the same as dogs—bitches in heat who can't control themselves. (McNall 1983, 197–98)*

This linking of animals and women within pornography becomes feasible when grounded in the earlier debasement of Black women as animals.

Developing a comprehensive analysis of Black women's placement in pornography and of pornography itself as a site of intersecting oppressions offers possibilities for change. Those Black feminist intellectuals investigating sexual politics imply that the situation is much more complicated than that advanced within Western feminism in which "men oppress women" because they are men. Such approaches implicitly assume biologically deterministic views of gender and sexuality and offer few possibilities for change. In contrast, the willingness of Black feminist analyses of sexual politics to embrace intersectional paradigms provides space for human agency. Women are not hard-wired as victims of pornography, nor are men destined uncritically to consume it. . . .

A changed consciousness is essential to social change. If Black men can understand how pornography affects them, then other groups enmeshed in the same system are equally capable of similar shifts in consciousness and action. . . .

Prostitution and the Exploitation of Black Women's Bodies

. . . All Black women are affected by the widespread controlling image that African-American women are sexually promiscuous. . . . Not just White men, but Black men have been involved in finding ways to profit from Black women's bodies. During an interview with Brother Marquis from the group 2 Live Crew, Black cultural critic Lisa Jones realizes that "hoochie mama" and other songs by this group actually constitute "soft porn." Jones's interview with Brother Marquis reveals the important links among pornography, the marketing of Black women's images, and the exploitation of Black women's bodies. In defending the misogynist lyrics of 2 Live Crew's music, Brother Marquis states:

> I'm not gonna try to disrespect you and call you all those names like I do on those records. I would never do that to a young lady, especially a sister. I'm degrading you to try to get me some money. . . . And besides, you let me do that. You got pimps out here who are making you sell your body. Just let me talk about you for a little while, you know what I'm saying? And make me a little money. (Jones 1994, 243)

Brother Marquis's explanation displays familiar rationalizations. He divided women into two categories of good girls and "hoochies." In his mind, if Black women are devalued within prostitution already, what harm can it do to *talk* about debasing Black women, especially if he can profit from such talk?

Within Brother Marquis's logic, images of Black women as jezebels and "hoochies" do little harm. Yet this controlling image has been vital in justifying the negative treatment that Black women encounter with intersecting oppressions. Exploring how the image of the African-American woman as prostitute has been used by selected systems of oppression illustrates how sexuality links the three systems. But Black women's treatment also demonstrates how prostitution operates as a site of intersectionality.

Yi-Fu Tuan (1984) suggests that power as domination involves reducing humans to animate nature in order to exploit them economically or to treat them condescendingly as pets. Domination may be either cruel and exploitative with no affection or may be ex-

ploitative yet coexist with affection. The former produces the victim—in this case, the Black woman as "mule" whose labor has been exploited. In contrast, the combination of dominance and affection produces the pet, the individual who is subordinate and whose survival depends on the whims of the more powerful. . . .

African-American women simultaneously embody the coexistence of the victim and the pet, with survival often linked to the ability to be appropriately subordinate. Black women's experiences as unpaid and paid workers demonstrate the harsh lives victims are forced to lead. While the life of the victim is difficult, pets experience a distinctive form of exploitation. . . . Pets are treated as exceptions and live with the constant threat that they will no longer be "perfect in his sight," that their owners will tire of them and relegate them to the unenviable role of victim.

Prostitution represents the fusion of exploitation for an economic purpose—namely, the commodification of Black women's sexuality—with the demeaning treatment afforded pets. Sex becomes commodified not merely in the sense that it can be purchased—the dimension of economic exploitation—but also in the sense that one is dealing with a totally alienated being who is separated from and who seemingly does not control her body: the dimension of power as domination (McNall 1983). Commodified sex can then be appropriated by the powerful. . . . Both pornography and prostitution commodify sexuality and imply . . . that all African-American women can be bought.

Prostitution under European and American capitalism thus exists within a complex web of political and economic relationships. Gilman's (1985) analysis of the exhibition of Sarah Bartmann as the "Hottentot Venus" suggests another intriguing connection between race, gender, and sexuality in nineteenth-century Europe—the linking of the icon of the Black woman with the icon of the White prostitute. While the Hottentot woman stood for the essence of Africans as a race, the White prostitute symbolized the sexualized woman. The prostitute represented the embodiment of sexuality and all that European society associated with it: disease as well as passion. . . . These connections between the icons of Black women and White prostitutes demonstrate the interdependence of race, gender, and sexuality in shaping European understandings of social class.

In the American antebellum South both of these images were fused in the forced prostitution of enslaved African women. The prostitution of Black women allowed White women to be the opposite; Black "whores" make White "virgins" possible. This race/gender nexus fostered a situation whereby White men could then differentiate between the sexualized woman-as-body who is dominated and "screwed" and the asexual woman-as-pure-spirit who is idealized and brought home to mother (Hoch 1979, 70). The sexually denigrated woman, whether she was made a victim through her rape or a pet through her seduction, could be used as the yardstick against which the cult of true womanhood was measured. Moreover, this entire situation was profitable.

The image of the lesbian can also be linked with that of the prostitute and with images of Black women as the embodiment of the Black "race." Christian notes that Black women writers broadened the physical image of lesbians: "The stereotypical body type of a black lesbian was that she looked mannish; . . . she was not so much a woman as much as she was a defective man, a description that has sometimes been applied to any Negroid-looking or uppity-acting black woman" (1985, 191). Note Christian's analysis of the links among gender, race, and sexuality. Lesbianism, an allegedly deviant sexual practice, becomes linked to biological markers of race and looking "mannish." These links also reinforce constructions of Black women's sexualities as deviant—the co-joining of Black heterosexual women's sexual deviancy as lying in their excess sexual appetite with the perceived deviancy of Black lesbians as lying in their rejection of what makes women feminine, namely, heterosexual contact with men.

Rape and Sexual Violence

Force was important in creating African-American women's centrality to American images of the sexualized woman and in shaping their experiences with both pornography and prostitution. Black women did not willingly submit to their exhibition on

Southern auction blocks—they were forced to do so. Enslaved African women could not choose whether to work—they were beaten and often killed if they refused. Black domestics who resisted the sexual advances of their employers often found themselves looking for work where none was to be found. Both the reality and the threat of violence have acted as a form of social control for African-American women (Collins 1998b).

Rape has been one fundamental tool of sexual violence directed against African-American women. . . . Rape and other acts of overt violence that Black women have experienced, such as physical assault during slavery, domestic abuse, incest, and sexual extortion, accompany Black women's subordination in intersecting oppressions. These violent acts are the visible dimensions of a more generalized, routinized system of oppression. Violence against Black women tends to be legitimated and therefore condoned while the same acts visited on other groups may remain nonlegitimated and non-excusable. Historically, this violence has garnered the backing and control of the state (James 1996). Specific acts of sexual violence visited on African-American women reflect a broader process by which violence is socially constructed in a race- and gender-specific manner. Thus Black women, Black men, and White women experience distinctive forms of sexual violence. As Angela Davis points out, "It would be a mistake to regard the institutionalized pattern of rape during slavery as an expression of white men's sexual urges. . . . Rape was a weapon of domination, a weapon of repression, whose covert goal was to extinguish slave women's will to resist, and in the process, to demoralize their men" (1981, 23).

Angela Davis's work (1978, 1981, 1989) illustrates this effort to conceptualize sexual violence against African-American women as a site of intersecting oppressions. Davis suggests that depicting African-American men as sexually charged beasts who desired White women created the myth of the Black rapist. Lynching emerged as the specific form of sexual violence visited on Black men, with the myth of the Black rapist as its ideological justification. The significance of this myth is that it "has been methodically conjured up when recurrent waves of violence and terror against the black community required a convincing explanation" (Davis 1978, 25). Black women experienced a parallel form of race- and gender-specific sexual violence. Treating African-American women as pornographic objects and portraying them as sexualized animals, as prostitutes, created the controlling image of jezebel. Rape became the specific act of sexual violence forced on Black women, with the myth of the Black prostitute as its ideological justification.

Lynching and rape, two race/gender-specific forms of sexual violence, merged with their ideological justifications of the rapist and prostitute in order to provide an effective system of social control over African-Americans. Davis asserts that the controlling image of Black men as rapists has always "strengthened its inseparable companion: the image of the black woman as chronically promiscuous. And with good reason, for once the notion is accepted that black men harbor irresistible, animal-like sexual urges, the entire race is invested with bestiality" (1978, 27). A race of "animals" can be treated as such—as victims or pets. "The mythical rapist implies the mythical whore—and a race of rapists and whores deserves punishment and nothing more" (Davis 1978, 28).

Black women continue to deal with this legacy of the sexual violence visited on African-Americans generally and with our history as collective rape victims. One effect lies in the treatment of rape victims. Such women are twice victimized, first by the actual rape, in this case the collective rape under slavery. But they are victimized again by family members, community residents, and social institutions such as criminal justice systems which somehow believe that rape victims are responsible for their own victimization. Even though current statistics indicate that Black women are more likely to be victimized than White women, Black women are less likely to report their rapes, less likely to have their cases come to trial, less likely to have their trials result in convictions, and, most disturbing, less likely to seek counseling and other support services.

Another effect of this legacy of sexual violence concerns the significance of Black women's continued silences concerning rape. But Black women's silence about rape obscures an important issue: Most Black women [who are raped] are raped by Black men. While the historical legacy of the triad of pornography, prostitution, and the institutionalized rape of Black women may have created the larger social context within which all African-Americans reside, the unfortunate current reality is that many Black men have internalized the controlling images applied to Black women. Like Brother Marquis, they feel that if they as individuals do not rape women, they contribute little to the overall cultural climate that condones sexual violence. These beliefs allow them to ignore Black women's rape by other Black men, their own culpability in fostering Black women's objectification as pornographic objects, and, in some cases, their own behavior as rapists. For example, Black women and men often disagree as to whether Nola Darling, the sexually liberated heroine in Spike Lee's acclaimed film *She's Gotta Have It,* was raped. Men disbelieve Nola's protestations and see her protest as serving to heighten the sexual pleasure of her male partner. In contrast, many women see her reaction as typical for those of a rape victim. Recognizing that it is useless to protest, Nola Darling submits. Was Nola Darling raped? Do the sexual politics of Black womanhood that construct jezebels and "hoochies" have any grounding in reality? The answers to both questions may lie in who has the power to define.

REFERENCES

Amott, Teresa L. 1990. "Black Women and AFDC: Making Entitlement Out of Necessity." In *Women, the State, and Welfare,* ed. Linda Gordon, 280–98. Madison: University of Wisconsin Press.

Bell, Laurie, ed. 1987. *Good Girls/Bad Girls: Feminists and Sex Trade Workers Face to Face.* Toronto: Seal Press.

Berry, Mary Frances. [1971] 1994. *Black Resistance, White Law: A History of Constitutional Racism in America.* New York: Penguin.

Christian, Barbara. 1985. *Black Feminist Criticism, Perspectives on Black Women Writers.* New York: Pergamon.

Clarke, Cheryl. 1983. "The Failure to Transform: Homophobia in the Black Community." In *Home Girls: A*

Black Feminist Anthology, ed. Barbara Smith, 197–208. New York: Kitchen Table Press.

Collins, Patricia Hill. 1993. "It's in Our Hands: Breaking the Silence on Gender in African-American Studies." In *Understanding Curriculum as Racial Text,* ed. William F. Pinar and Louis Castenall, 127–41. Albany: SUNY Press.

———. 1998a. *Fighting Words: Black Women and the Search for Justice.* Minneapolis: University of Minnesota Press.

———. 1998b. "The Tie That Binds: Race, Gender and U.S. Violence." *Ethnic and Racial Studies* 21 (5): 918–38.

———. 1999. "Will the 'Real' Mother Please Stand Up?: The Logic of Eugenics and American National Family Planning." In *Revisioning Women, Health and Healing: Feminist, Cultural and Technoscience Perspectives,* ed. Adele Clarke and Virginia Olesen, 266–82. New York: Routledge.

Cowan, Gloria, and Robin R. Campbell. 1994. "Racism and Sexism in Interracial Pornography." *Psychology of Women Quarterly* 18: 323–38.

Crenshaw, Kimberle William. 1991. "Mapping the Margins: Intersectionality, Identity Politics, and Violence Against Women of Color." *Stanford Law Review* 43 (6): 1241–99.

Davenport, Doris. 1996. "Black Lesbians in Academia: Visible Invisibility." In *The New Lesbian Studies: Into the Twenty-First Century,* ed. Bonnie Zimmerman and Toni A. H. McNaron. New York: Feminist Press.

Davis, Angela Y. 1978. "Rape, Racism and the Capitalist Setting." *Black Scholar* 9(7): 24–30.

———. 1981. *Women, Race and Class.* New York: Random House.

———. 1989. *Women, Culture, and Politics.* New York: Random House.

D'Emilio, John, and Estelle Freedman. "Race and Sexuality." In *Intimate Matters. A History of Sexuality in America,* 85–108. New York: Harper and Row.

Dines, Gail. 1998. *Pornography: The Production and Consumption of Inequality.* New York: Routledge.

Ferber, Abby. 1998. *White Man Falling: Race, Gender, and White Supremacy.* Lantham, MD: Rowman & Littlefield.

Forna, Aminatta. 1992. "Pornography and Racism: Sexualizing Oppression and Inciting Hatred." In *Pornography: Women, Violence, and Civil Liberties,* ed. Catherine Itzin, 102–12. New York: Oxford University Press.

Giddings, Paula. 1992. "The Last Taboo." In *Race-ing Justice, En-gendering Power,* ed. Toni Morrison, 441–65. New York: Pantheon.

Gilman, Sander L. 1985. "Black Bodies, White Bodies: Toward an Iconography of Female Sexuality in Late Nineteenth-Century Art, Medicine, and Literature." *Critical Inquiry* 12 (1): 205–43.

Gomez, Jewell, and Barbara Smith. 1994. "Taking the Home Out of Homophobia: Black Lesbian Health." In *The Black Women's Health Book: Speaking for Ourselves,* ed. Evelyn C. White, 198–213, Seattle: Seal Press.

Hammonds, Evelynn M. 1997. "Toward a Genealogy of Black Female Sexuality: The Problematic of Silence." In *Feminist Genealogies; Colonial Legacies, Democratic Futures,* ed. M. Jacqui Alexander and Chandra Talpade Mohanty, 170–81. New York: Routledge.

Hartouni, Valerie. 1997. "Breached Birth: Anna Johnson and the Reproduction of Raced Bodies." In *Cultural Conceptions. On Reproductive Technologies and the Remaking of Life,* 85–98. Minneapolis: University of Minnesota Press

Hine, Darlene Clark. 1995. "For Pleasure, Profit, and Power: The Sexual Exploitation of Black Women." In *African American Women Speak Out on Anita Hill-Clarence Thomas,* ed. Geneva Smitherman, 168–77. Detroit: Wayne State University Press.

Hoch, Paul. 1979. *White Hero Black Beast: Racism, Sexism and the Mask of Masculinity.* London: Pluto Press.

Jackson, Stevi. 1996. "Heterosexuality and Feminist Theory." In *Theorising Heterosexuality,* ed. Diane Richardson, 21–38. Philadelphia: Open University Press.

James, Joy. 1996. *Resisting State Violence: Radicalism, Gender, and Race in U.S. Culture.* Minneapolis: University of Minnesota Press.

Jones, Lisa. 1994. *Bulletproof Diva: Tale of Race, Sex, and Hair.* New York: Anchor.

Kennedy, Elizabeth Lapovsky, and Madeline Davis. 1993. *Boots of Leather, Slippers of Gold: The History of a Lesbian Community.* New York: Penguin.

Lorde, Audre. 1982. Zami, *A New Spelling of My Name.* Trumansberg, NY: Crossing Press.

———. 1984. *Sister Outsider.* Trumansberg, NY: Crossing Press.

McNall, Scott G. 1983. "Pornography: The Structure of Domination and the Mode of Reproduction." In *Current Perspectives in Social Theory Volume 4,* ed. Scott McNall, 181–203. Greenwich, CT: JAI Press.

Moore, Lisa C., ed. 1997. *Does Your Mama Know? An Anthology of Black Lesbian Coming Out Stories.* Decatur: Red Bone Press.

Omolade, Barbara. 1994. *The Rising Song of African American Women.* New York: Routledge.

Richardson, Diane. 1996. "Heterosexuality and Social Theory." In *Theorising Heterosexuality,* ed. Diane Richardson, 1–20. Philadelphia: Open University Press.

Roberts, Dorothy. 1997. *Killing the Black Body: Race, Reproduction, and the Meaning of Liberty.* New York: Pantheon.

Russell, Diane E. H. 1993. *Against Pornography: The Evidence of Harm.* Berkeley: Russell Publications

She's Gotta Have It. 1986. Directed by Spike Lee. 40 Acres and a Mule Filmworks.

Shockley, Ann Allen. 1983. "The Black Lesbian in American Literature: An Overview." In *Home Girls: A Black Feminist Anthology,* ed. Barbara Smith, 83–93. New York: Kitchen Table Press.

Smith, Barbara. 1982. "Toward a Black Feminist Criticism." In *But Some of Us Are Brave,* ed. Gloria T. Hull, Patricia Bell Scott, and Barbara Smith, 157–75. Old Westbury, NY: Feminist Press.

———. 1983. "Introduction." In *Home Girls: A Black Feminist Anthology,* ed. Barbara Smith, xix–lvi. New York: Kitchen Table Press.

———. 1998. *The Truth That Never Hurts: Writings on Race, Gender and Freedom.* New Brunswick: Rutgers University Press.

Tuan, Yi-Fu. 1984. *Dominance and Affection: The Making of Pets.* New Haven, CT: Yale University Press.

2 Live Crew. 1995. "Hoochie Mama." Friday Original Soundtrack: Priority Records.

Walker, Alice. 1988. *Living by the Word.* New York: Harcourt Brace Jovanovich.

Williams, Rhonda. 1997. "Living at the Crossroads: Explorations in Race, Nationality, Sexuality, and Gender." In *The House That Race Built: Black Americans, U.S. Terrain,* ed. Wahneema Lubiano, 136–56. New York: Pantheon.

Punishing Drug Addicts Who Have Babies:
Women of Color, Equality, and the Right of Privacy

Dorothy E. Roberts

The Devaluation of Black Motherhood

The systematic, institutionalized denial of reproductive freedom has uniquely marked Black women's history in America. An important part of this denial has been the devaluation of Black women as mothers. A popular mythology that degrades Black women and portrays them as less deserving of motherhood reinforces this subordination. This mythology is one aspect of a complex set of images that deny Black humanity in order to rationalize the oppression of Blacks.[1]

In this [reading], I will discuss three manifestations of the devaluation of Black motherhood: the original exploitation of Black women during slavery, the more contemporary, disproportionate removal of Black children from their mothers' custody, and sterilization abuse. Throughout this [reading], I will also show how several popular images denigrating Black mothers—the licentious Jezebel, the careless, incompetent mother, the domineering matriarch, and the lazy welfare mother—have reinforced and legitimated their devaluation.

The Slavery Experience

The essence of Black women's experience during slavery was the brutal denial of autonomy over reproduction. Female slaves were commercially valuable to their masters not only for their labor, but also for their capacity to produce more slaves.[2] Henry Louis Gates, Jr., writing about the autobiography of a slave

named Harriet A. Jacobs, observes that it "charts in vivid detail precisely how the shape of her life and the choices she makes are defined by her reduction to a sexual object, an object to be raped, bred or abused."[3] Black women's childbearing during slavery was thus largely a product of oppression rather than an expression of self-definition and personhood.

The method of whipping pregnant slaves that was used throughout the South vividly illustrates the slaveowners' dual interest in Black women as both workers and childbearers. Slaveowners forced women to lie face down in a depression in the ground while they were whipped.[4] This procedure allowed the masters to protect the fetus while abusing the mother. It serves as a powerful metaphor for the evils of a fetal protection policy that denies the humanity of the mother. It is also a forceful symbol of the convergent oppression inflicted on slave women: they were subjugated at once both as Blacks and as females.

From slavery on, Black women have fallen outside the scope of the American ideal of womanhood.[5] Slave owners forced slave women to perform strenuous labor that contradicted the Victorian female roles prevalent in the dominant white society. Angela Davis has observed: "judged by the evolving nineteenth-century ideology of femininity, which emphasized women's roles as nurturing mothers and gentle companions and housekeepers for their husbands, Black women were practically anomalies."[6] Black women's historical deviation from traditional female roles has engendered a mythology that denies their womanhood.

One of the most prevalent images of slave women was the character of Jezebel, a woman governed by her sexual desires.[7] As early as 1736, the *South*

From "Punishing Drug Addicts Who Have Babies: Women of Color, Equality, and the Right of Privacy" by Dorothy E. Roberts (1991), *Harvard Law Review,* 104, 1419–1482. Reprinted by permission.

Carolina Gazette described "African Ladies" as women "of 'strong robust constitution' who were 'not easily jaded out' but able to serve their lovers 'by Night as well as Day.'"[8] This ideological construct of the licentious Jezebel legitimated white men's sexual abuse of Black women.[9] The stereotype of Black women as sexually promiscuous helped to perpetuate their devaluation as mothers.

The myth of the "bad" Black woman was deliberately and systematically perpetuated after slavery ended.[10] For example, historian Philip A. Bruce's book, *The Plantation Negro as a Freeman*, published in 1889, strengthened popular views of both Black male and Black female degeneracy.[11] Bruce traced the alleged propensity of the Black man to rape white women to the "wantonness of the women of his own race" and "the sexual laxness of plantation women as a class."[12] This image of the sexually loose, impure Black woman that originated in slavery persists in modern American culture.[13]

Black women during slavery were also systematically denied the rights of motherhood. Slave mothers had no legal claim to their children.[14] Slave masters owned not only Black women, but also their children. They alienated slave women from their children by selling them to other slaveowners and by controlling childrearing. . . .

Black women struggled in many ways to resist the efforts of slave masters to control their reproductive lives. They used contraceptives and abortives, escaped from plantations, feigned illness, endured severe punishment, and fought back rather than submit to slave masters' sexual domination.[15] Free Black women with the means to do so purchased freedom for their daughters and sisters.[16] Black women, along with Black men, succeeded remarkably often in maintaining the integrity of their family life despite slavery's disrupting effects.[17]

The Disproportionate Removal of Black Children

The disproportionate number of Black mothers who lose custody of their children through the child welfare system is a contemporary manifestation of the devaluation of Black motherhood.[18] This disparate impact of state intervention results in part from Black families' higher rate of reliance on government welfare.[19] Because welfare families are subject to supervision by social workers, instances of perceived neglect are more likely to be reported to governmental authorities than neglect on the part of more affluent parents.[20] Black children are also removed from their homes in part because of the child welfare system's cultural bias and application of the nuclear family pattern to Black families.[21] Black childrearing patterns that diverge from the norm of the nuclear family have been misinterpreted by government bureaucrats as child neglect.[22] For example, child welfare workers have often failed to respect the longstanding cultural tradition in the Black community of shared parenting responsibility among blood-related and non-blood kin.[23] The state has thus been more willing to intrude upon the autonomy of poor Black families, and in particular of Black mothers, while protecting the integrity of white, middle-class homes.[24]

This devaluation of Black motherhood has been reinforced by stereotypes that blame Black mothers for the problems of the Black family. This scapegoating of Black mothers dates back to slavery, when mothers were blamed for the devastating effects on their children of poverty and abuse of Black women. . . .

The scapegoating of Black mothers has manifested itself more recently in the myth of the Black matriarch, the domineering female head of the Black family. White sociologists have held Black matriarchs responsible for the disintegration of the Black family and the consequent failure of Black people to achieve success in America.[25] Daniel Patrick Moynihan popularized this theory in his 1965 report, *The Negro Family: The Case for National Action.*[26] According to Moynihan:

> *At the heart of the deterioration of the fabric of the Negro society is the deterioration of the Negro family. It is the fundamental cause of the weakness of the Negro community. . . . In essence, the Negro community has been forced into a matriarchal structure which, because it is so out of line with the rest of the American society, seriously retards the progress of the group as a whole.*[27]

Thus, Moynihan attributed the cause of Black people's inability to overcome the effects of racism largely to the dominance of Black mothers.

The Sterilization of Women of Color

Coerced sterilization is one of the most extreme forms of control over a woman's reproductive life. By permanently denying her the right to bear children, sterilization enforces society's determination that a woman does not deserve to be a mother. Unlike white women, poor women of color have been subjected to sterilization abuse . . . for decades.[28] The disproportionate sterilization of Black women is yet another manifestation of the dominant society's devaluation of Black women as mothers.

Sterilization abuse has taken the form both of blatant coercion and trickery and of subtle influences on women's decisions to be sterilized.[29] In the 1970s, some doctors conditioned delivering babies and performing abortions on Black women's consent to sterilization.[30] In a 1974 case brought by poor teenage Black women in Alabama, a federal district court found that an estimated 100,000 to 150,000 poor women were sterilized annually under federally-funded programs.[31] Some of these women were coerced into agreeing to sterilization under the threat that their welfare benefits would be withdrawn unless they submitted to the operation.[32] Despite federal and state regulations intended to prevent involuntary sterilization, physicians and other health care providers continue to urge women of color to consent to sterilization because they view these women's family sizes as excessive and believe these women are incapable of effectively using other methods of birth control.[33]

Current government funding policy perpetuates the encouragement of sterilization of poor, and thus of mainly Black, women. The federal government pays for sterilization services under the Medicaid program . . . while it often does not make available information about and access to other contraceptive techniques and abortion.[34] In effect, sterilization is the only publicly-funded birth control method readily available to poor women of color.

Popular images of the undeserving Black mother legitimate government policy as well as the practices of health care providers. The myth of the Black Jezebel has been supplemented by the contemporary image of the lazy welfare mother who breeds children at the expense of taxpayers in order to increase the amount of her welfare check.[35] This view of Black motherhood provides the rationale for society's restrictions on Black female fertility. . . . It is this image of the undeserving Black mother that also ultimately underlies the government's choice to punish crack-addicted women.

Prosecuting Drug Addicts as Punishment for Having Babies

Informed by the historical and present devaluation of Black motherhood, we can better understand prosecutors' reasons for punishing drug-addicted mothers. . . .

It is important to recognize at the outset that the prosecutions are based in part on a woman's pregnancy and not on her illegal drug use alone.[36] Prosecutors charge these defendants not with drug use, but with child abuse or drug distribution—crimes that relate to their pregnancy. Moreover, pregnant women receive harsher sentences than drug-addicted men or women who are not pregnant.[37]

The unlawful nature of drug use must not be allowed to confuse the basis of the crimes at issue. The legal rationale underlying the prosecutions does not depend on the illegality of drug use. Harm to the fetus is the crux of the government's legal theory. Criminal charges have been brought against women for conduct that is legal but was alleged to have harmed the fetus.[38]

When a drug-addicted woman becomes pregnant, she has only one realistic avenue to escape criminal charges: abortion.[39] Thus, she is penalized for choosing to have the baby rather than having an abortion. In this way, the state's punitive action may coerce women to have abortions rather than risk being charged with a crime. Thus, it is the *choice of carrying a pregnancy to term* that is being penalized.[40]

There is also good reason to question the government's justification for the prosecutions—the concern for the welfare of potential children. . . .

When a society has always closed its eyes to the inadequacy of prenatal care available to poor Black women, its current expression of interest in the health of unborn Black children must be viewed with suspicion. The most telling evidence of the state's disregard of Black children is the high rate of infant death in the Black community. . . . The government has chosen to punish poor Black women rather than provide the means for them to have healthy children.

The cruelty of this punitive response is heightened by the lack of available drug treatment services for pregnant drug addicts.[41] Protecting the welfare of drug addicts' children requires, among other things, adequate facilities for the mother's drug treatment. Yet a drug addict's pregnancy serves as an *obstacle* to obtaining this treatment. Treatment centers either refuse to treat pregnant women or are effectively closed to them because the centers are ill-equipped to meet the needs of pregnant addicts.[42] Most hospitals and programs that treat addiction exclude pregnant women because their babies are more likely to be born with health problems requiring expensive care.[43] Program directors also feel that treating pregnant addicts is worth neither the increased cost nor the risk of tort liability.[44]

Moreover, there are several barriers to pregnant women who seek to use centers that will accept them. Drug treatment programs are generally based on male-oriented models that are not geared to the needs of women.[45] The lack of accommodations for children is perhaps the most significant obstacle to treatment. Most outpatient clinics do not provide child care and many residential treatment programs do not admit children.[46] . . . Predominantly male staffs and clients are often hostile to female clients and employ a confrontational style of therapy that makes many women uncomfortable.[47] Moreover, long waiting lists make treatment useless for women who need help during the limited duration of their pregnancies. . . .

Finally, and perhaps most importantly, ample evidence reveals that prosecuting addicted mothers may not achieve the government's asserted goal of healthier pregnancies; indeed, such prosecutions will probably lead to the opposite result. Pregnant addicts who seek help from public hospitals and clinics are the ones most often reported to government authorities.[48] The threat of prosecution based on this reporting forces women to remain anonymous and thus has the perverse effect of deterring pregnant drug addicts from seeking treatment.[49] For this reason, the government's decision to punish drug-addicted mothers is irreconcilable with the goal of helping them.

Pregnancy may be a time when women are most motivated to seek treatment for drug addiction and make positive lifestyle changes.[50] The government should capitalize on this opportunity by encouraging drug-addicted women to seek help and providing them with comprehensive treatment. Punishing pregnant women who use drugs only exacerbates the causes of addiction—poverty, lack of self-esteem, and hopelessness.[51] Perversely, this makes it more likely that poor Black women's children—the asserted beneficiaries of the prosecutions—will suffer from the same hardships. . . .

The Intersection of Privacy and Equality

. . . The singling out of Black mothers for punishment combines in a single government action several wrongs prohibited by constitutional doctrines. Black mothers are denied autonomy over procreative decisions because of their race. The government's denial of Black women's fundamental right to choose to bear children serves to perpetuate the legacy of racial discrimination embodied in the devaluation of Black motherhood. . . .

Poor crack addicts are punished for having babies because they fail to measure up to the state's ideal of motherhood. Prosecutors have brought charges against women who use drugs during pregnancy without demonstrating any harm to the fetus.[52] Moreover, a government policy that has the effect of punishing primarily poor Black women for having babies evokes the specter of racial eugenics, especially in light of the history of sterilization abuse of women of color. . . . These factors make clear that these women are not punished simply because they may harm their unborn children. They are punished because the combination of their poverty, race, and drug addiction is seen to make them unworthy of procreating. . . .

Denying someone the right to bear children—or punishing her for exercising that right—deprives her of a basic part of her humanity.[53] When this denial is based on race, it also functions to preserve a racial hierarchy that essentially disregards Black humanity.

The abuse of sterilization laws designed to effect eugenic policy demonstrates the potential danger of governmental standards for procreation. During the first half of the twentieth century, the eugenics movement embraced the theory . . . that intelligence and other personality traits are genetically determined and therefore inherited.[54] This hereditarian belief, coupled with the reform approach of the progressive era, fueled a campaign to remedy America's social problems by stemming biological degeneracy. Eugenicists advocated compulsory sterilization to prevent reproduction by people who were likely to produce allegedly defective offspring. Eugenic sterilization was thought to improve society by eliminating its "socially inadequate" members.[55] Many states around the turn of the century enacted involuntary sterilization laws directed at those deemed burdens on society, including the mentally retarded, mentally ill, epileptics, and criminals.[56]

In a 1927 decision, *Buck v. Bell,* . . . the Supreme Court upheld the constitutionality . . . of a Virginia involuntary sterilization law.[57] The plaintiff, Carrie Buck, was described in the opinion as "a feeble minded white woman" committed to a state mental institution who was "the daughter of a feeble minded mother in the same institution, and the mother of an illegitimate feeble minded child."[58] The Court approved an order of the mental institution that Buck undergo sterilization. Justice Holmes, himself an ardent eugenicist, . . . gave eugenic theory the imprimatur of constitutional law in his infamous declaration: "Three generations of imbeciles are enough."[59]

The salient feature of the eugenic sterilization laws is their brutal imposition of society's restrictive norms of motherhood. Governmental control of reproduction in the name of science masks racist and classist judgments about who deserves to bear children. It is grounded on the premise that people who depart from social norms do not deserve to procreate. . . . Carrie Buck, for example, was punished by sterilization not because of any mental disability, but because of her deviance from society's social and sexual norms. . . .

Fourteen years after *Buck v. Bell,* the Court acknowledged the danger of the eugenic rationale. Justice Douglas recognized both the fundamental quality

of the right to procreate and its connection to equality in a later sterilization decision, *Skinner v. Oklahoma.* . . . *Skinner* considered the constitutionality of the Oklahoma Habitual Criminal Sterilization Act . . . authorizing the sterilization of persons convicted two or more times for "felonies involving moral turpitude."[60] An Oklahoma court had ordered Skinner to undergo a vasectomy after he was convicted once of stealing chickens and twice of robbery with fir[e]arms. . . . The statute, the Court found, treated unequally criminals who had committed intrinsically the same quality of offense. For example, men who had committed grand larceny three times were sterilized, but embezzlers were not. The Court struck down the statute as a violation of the equal protection clause. Declaring the right to bear children to be "one of the basic civil rights of man,"[61] the Court . . . held that the government failed to demonstrate that the statute's classifications were justified by eugenics or the inheritability of criminal traits. . . .

Although the reasons advanced for the sterilization of chicken thieves and the prosecution of drug-addicted mothers are different, both practices are dangerous for similar reasons. Both effectuate ethnocentric judgments by the government that certain members of society do not deserve to have children. As the Court recognized in *Skinner,* the enforcement of a government standard for childbearing denies the disfavored group a critical aspect of human dignity. . . .

The history of compulsory sterilization demonstrates that society deems women who deviate from its norms of motherhood—in 1941, teenaged delinquent girls like Carrie Buck who bore illegitimate children, today, poor Black crack addicts who use drugs during pregnancy—"unworthy of the high privilege" of procreation. The government therefore refuses to affirm their human dignity by helping them overcome obstacles to good mothering. . . . Rather, it punishes them by sterilization or criminal prosecution and thereby denies them a basic part of their humanity. When this denial is based on race, the violation is especially serious. Governmental policies that perpetuate racial subordination through the denial of procreative rights, which threaten both racial equality and privacy at once, should be subject to the highest scrutiny. . . .

Conclusion

Our understanding of the prosecutions of drug-addicted mothers must include the perspective of the women whom they most directly affect. The prosecutions arise in a particular historical and political context that has constrained reproductive choice for poor women of color. The state's decision to punish drug-addicted mothers rather than help them stems from the poverty and race of the defendants and society's denial of their full dignity as human beings. Viewing the issue from their vantage point reveals that the prosecutions punish for having babies women whose motherhood has historically been devalued.

A policy that attempts to protect fetuses by denying the humanity of their mothers will inevitably fail.[62] We must question such a policy's true concern for the dignity of the fetus, just as we question the motives of the slave owner who protected the unborn slave child while whipping his pregnant mother. Although the master attempted to separate the mother and fetus for his commercial ends, their fates were inextricably intertwined. The tragedy of crack babies is initially a tragedy of crack-addicted mothers. Both are part of a larger tragedy of a community that is suffering a host of indignities, including, significantly, the denial of equal respect for its women's reproductive decisions.

It is only by affirming the personhood and equality of poor women of color that the survival of their future generation will be ensured. The first principle of the government's response to the crisis of drug-exposed babies should be the recognition of their mothers' worth and entitlement to autonomy over their reproductive lives. A commitment to guaranteeing these fundamental rights of poor women of color, rather than punishing them, is the true solution to the problem of unhealthy babies.

NOTES

1. . . . For a discussion of the hegemonic function of racist ideology, see Crenshaw, *supra note*, at 1370–81 (1988). *See generally* G. Fredrickson, The Black Image in the White Mind 256–82 (1071) . . . ; J. Williamson, The Crucible of Race: Black-White Relations in the American South Since Emancipation 111–51 (1984). . . .

2. *See* A. Davis, Women, Race, and Class 7 (1981); J. Jones, Labor of Love, Labor of Sorrow: Black Women, Work and the Family from Slavery to the Present 12 (1985). Legislation giving the children of Black women and white men the status of slaves left female slaves vulnerable to sexual violation as a means of financial gain. *See* P. Giddings, When and Where I Enter: The Impact of Black Women on Race and Sex in America 37 (1984). . . .

White masters controlled their slaves' reproductive capacity by rewarding pregnancy with relief from work in the field and additions of clothing and food, punishing slave women who did not give birth, manipulating slave marital choices, forcing them to breed, and raping them. *See* J. Jones, *supra,* at 34–35; We Are Your Sisters: Black Women in the Nineteenth Century 24–26 (D. Sterling ed. 1984); Clinton, *Caught in the Web of the Big House: Women and Slavery,* in The Web of Southern Social Relations 19, 23–28 (W. Raser, R. Saunders & J. Wakelyn eds. 1985).

3. Gates, *To Be Raped, Bred or Abused,* N. Y. Times Book Rev., Nov. 22, 1987, at 12 (reviewing H. Jacobs, Incidents in the Life of a Slave Girl (J. Yellin ed. 1987)).

4. *See* J. Jones, *supra note,* at 20; Johnson, *supra note* 1, at 513.

5. *See* A. Davis, *supra note* 2, at 5; D. White, Ar'n't I a Woman? Female Slaves in the Plantation South 16, 27–29 (1985). . . .

6. A. Davis, *supra note* 91, at 7.

7. *See* D. White, *supra note* 5, at 28–29.

8. *Id.* at 30.

9. *See* E. Fox-Genovese, *supra note*, at 292; D. White, *supra note* 94, at 61.

10. *See* Black Women in White America 163–71 (G. Lerner ed. 1173); P. Giddings, *supra note* 91, at 85–89; B. Hooks, *supra note* 17, at 55–60.

11. *See* Gresham, *supra note*, at 117.

12. P. Bruce, The Plantation Negro as a Freeman 84–85 (1889).

13. *See* b. hooks, *supra note*, at 65–68; Omolade, *Black Women, Black Men and Tawana Brawley: The Shared Condition,* 12 Harv. Women's L. J. 12, 16 (1989).

14. *See* Allen, *Surrogacy, Slavery, and the Ownership of Life,* 13 Harv. J. L. & Pub. Pol'y 139, 140 n.9 (1990). . . .

15. *See* P. Giddings, *supra note* 2, at 46; We Are Your Sisters, *supra note* 2, at 25–26, 58–61; D. White, *supra note* 5, at 76–90.

16. *See* Black Women in White America, *supra note* 10, at 40–42 . . . Black Women in Nineteenth-Century American Life 329 (B. Loewenberg & R. Bogin eds. 1976).

17. *See generally* H. Gutman, The Black Family in Slavery and Freedom, 1790–1925 (1976) (describing the life of the Black family during slavery); Jones, *"My Mother*

Was Much of a Woman": Black Women, Work, and the Family Under Slavery, 8 Feminist Stud. 235, 252–61 (1982). . . .

18. *See* Gray & Nybell, *Issues in African-American Family Preservation,* 69 Child Welfare 513, 513 (1990) (noting that about half of the children in foster care are Black); Hogan & Sin, *Minority Children and the Child Welfare System: An Historical Perspective,* 33 Soc. Work 493 (1988). Once Black children enter foster care, they remain there longer and receive less desirable placements than white children; they are also less likely than white children to be returned home or adopted. *See* B. Mandell, Where Are the Children? A Class Analysis of Foster Care and Adoption 36 (1973); Gray & Nybell, *supra,* at 513–14; Stehno, *Differential Treatment of Minority Children in Service Systems,* 27 Soc. Work 39, 39–41 (1982). These realities have led some Blacks to deem foster care a system of legalized slavery. *See* B. Mandell, *supra,* at 60. . . .

19. *See* Wald, *supra* note, at 629 n.22.

20. See Faller & Ziefert, *supra* note, at 47; Wald, *supra* note 53, at 629 n. 21. . . . Jenkins, *Child Welfare as a Class System,* in Children and Decent People 3–4 (A. Schorr ed. 1974).

21. *Cf.* Santosky v. Kramer, 455 U.S. 745, 763 (1982) (noting that termination proceedings "are often vulnerable to judgments based on cultural or class bias"); Gray & Nybell, *supra* note 18, at 515–17; Stack, *Cultural Perspectives on Child Welfare,* 12 N. Y. U. Rev. L. & Soc. Change 539, 541 (1983–84) *See generally* A. Billingsley & J. Giovannoni, Children of the Storm (1972) (tracing the history of Black children in the American child welfare system).

22. *See* Gray & Nybell, *supra* note 18, at 515–17; Stack, *supra* note 21, at 541. . . .

23. *See* Stack, *supra* note 112, at 539–43.

24. *See id.* at 547.

25. *See* P. Giddings, *supra* note 2, at 325–35; b. hooks, *supra* note 17, at 70–83; R. Staples, The Black Woman in America 10–34 (1976); Bennett & Gresham, *supra* note, at 117–18.

26. Office of Planning & Policy Research, U.S. Dep't of Labor, The Negro Family: The Case for National Action (1965).

27. *Id.* at 5.

28. *See* A. Davis, *supra* note 2, at 215–21; Nsiah-Jefferson, *Reproductive Laws, Women of Color, and Low-Income Women,* in Reproductive Laws for the 1990s, at 46–47 (S. Cohen & N. Taub eds. 1988). One study found that 43% of women sterilized in 1973 under a federally funded program were Black, although only 33% of the patients were Black. . . . Spanish-speaking women are twice as likely to be sterilized as those who speak English. *See*

Levin & Taub, *Reproductive Rights,* in Women and the Law § 10A.07[3][b], at 10A-28 (C. Lefcourt ed. 1989). The racial disparity in sterilization cuts across economic and educational lines, although the frequency of sterilization is generally higher among the poor and uneducated. Another study found that 9.7% of college-educated Black women had been sterilized, compared to 5.6% of college-educated white women. Among women without a high school diploma, 31.6% of Black women and 14.5% of white women had been sterilized. *See id.*

29. *See* Clarke, *Subtle Forms of Sterilization Abuse: A Reproductive Rights Analysis,* in Test-Tube Women 120, 120–32 (R. Arditti, R. Klein & S. Minden eds. 1984); Nsiah-Jefferson, *supra* note, at 44–45; Petchesky, *supra* note 124, at 32.

30. *See* Nsiah-Jefferson, *supra* note, at 46–47.

31. *See* Relf v. Weinberger, 372 F. Supp. 1196, 1199 (D.D.C. 1974), *on remand sub nom.* Relf v. Mathews, 403 F. Supp. 1235 (D.D.C. 1975), *vacated sub nom.* Relf v. Weinberger, 565 F.2d 722 (D.C. Cir. 1977).

32. *See id.*

33. *See* Nsiah-Jefferson, *supra* note, at 47- 48; . . . In contrast to the encouragement of minority sterilization, our society views childbearing by white women as desirable. . . . *See* Colker, *Feminism, Theology, and Abortion: Toward Love, Compassion, and Wisdom,* 77 Calif. L. Rev. 1011, 1067 n.196 (1989). . . .

34. *See* Nsiah-Jefferson, *supra* note 125, at 45–46; Petchesky, *supra* note, at 39; . . .

35. *See* Harrington, *Introduction* to S. Sheehan, A Welfare Mother at x–xi (1976); Milwaukee County Welfare Rights Org., Welfare Mothers Speak Out 72–92 (1972).

36. At Jennifer Johnson's sentencing, the prosecutor made clear the nature of the charges against her: "About the end of December 1988, our office undertook a policy to begin to deal with mothers like Jennifer Johnson . . . as in the status of a child abuse case, Your Honor. . . . *We have never viewed this as a drug case.*" Motion for Rehearing and Sentencing at 12, State v. Johnson, No. E89–890-CFA (Fla. Cir. Ct. Aug. 25, 1989) (emphasis added).

37. The drug user's pregnancy not only greatly increases the likelihood that she will be prosecuted, but also greatly enhances the penalty she faces upon conviction. In most states, drug use is a misdemeanor, while distribution of drugs is a felony. *See* Hoffman, *supra* note, at 44.

38. Pamela Rae Stewart, for example, was charged with criminal neglect in part because she failed to follow her doctor's orders to stay off her feet and refrain from sexual intercourse while she was pregnant. *See* People v. Stewart, No. M508197, slip op. at 4 (Cal. Mun. Ct. Feb. 26, 1987);

Bonavoglia, *The Ordeal of Pamela Rae Stewart,* Ms., Jul./Aug. 1987, at 92, 92.

39. Seeking drug treatment is not a viable alternative. First, it is likely that the pregnant addict will be unable to find a drug treatment program that will accept her. . . . Second, even if she successfully completes drug counseling by the end of her pregnancy, she may still be prosecuted for her drug use that occurred during pregnancy before she was able to overcome her addiction.

40. I recognize that both becoming pregnant and continuing a pregnancy to term are not necessarily real "choices" that women—particularly women of color and addicted women—make. Rape, battery, lack of available contraceptives, and prostitution induced by drug addiction may lead a woman to become pregnant without exercising meaningful choice. Similarly, coercion from the father or her family, lack of money to pay for an abortion, or other barriers to access to an abortion may force a woman to continue an unwanted pregnancy. . . .

Nevertheless, these constraints on a woman's choice do not justify the government's punishment of the reproductive course that she ultimately follows. While we work to create the conditions for meaningful reproductive choice, it is important to affirm women's right to be free from unwanted state intrusion in their reproductive decisions.

41. *See* Chavkin, *Drug Addiction and Pregnancy: Policy Crossroads,* 80 Am. J. Pub. Health 483, 485 (1990); McNulty, *supra* note, at 301–02. . . .

42. *See* Cusky, Berger & Densen-Gerber, *Issues in the Treatment of Female Addiction: A Review and Critique of the Literature,* 6 Contemp. Drug Probs. 307, 324–26 (1977); McNulty, *supra* note, at 301–02; Suffet, Hutson & Brotman, *Treatment of the Pregnant Addict: A Historical Overview,* in Pregnant Addicts and Their Children: A Comprehensive Care Approach 13, 21 (R. Brotman, D. Hutson & F. Suffet eds. 1984); Alters, *supra* note 30, at 1, col. 1; Freitag, *Hospital Defends Limiting of Drug Program,* N. Y. Times, Dec. 12, 1989, at B9, col. 1.

43. *See* McNulty, *supra* note, at 301; Teltsch, *supra* note 30, at A14, col. 1.

44. *See* Chavkin, *Drug Addiction and Pregnancy: Policy Crossroads, supra* note 147, at 485; McNulty, *Combatting Pregnancy Discrimination in Access to Substance Abuse Treatment for Low-Income Women,* 23 Clearinghouse Rev. 21, 22 (1989).

45. *See* Cuskey, Berger & Densen-Gerber, *supra* note 44, at 312–14; Alters, *supra* note, at 1, col. 1.

46. *See* McNulty, *supra* note 150, at 22; *Substance Abuse Treatment for Women: Crisis in Access, supra* note 147, at 9.

47. *See* Chavkin, *Drug Addiction and Pregnancy, Policy Crossroads, supra* note 41, at 485; *see also* National Institute on Drug Abuse, Drug Dependency in Pregnancy 46 (1978) (describing pervasive negative attitudes toward pregnant addicts).

48. *See* Berrien, *Pregnancy and Drug Use: The Dangerous and Unequal Use of Punitive Measures,* 2 Yale J. L. & Feminism 239, 247 (1990).

49. *See* American Medical Association, *Report of the Board of Trustees on Legal Interventions During Pregnancy: Court Ordered Medical Treatments and Legal Penalties for Potentially Harmful Behavior by Pregnant Women,* 264 J. A. M. A. 2663, 2669 (1990). The reaction of pregnant women in San Diego to the 1997 arrest of Pamela Rae Stewart for harming her unborn child illustrates the deterrent effect of prosecution. Health care professionals reported that their pregnant clients' fear of prosecution for drug use made some of them distrustful and caused others to decline prenatal care altogether. *See* Moss, *supra* note, at 1411–12.

50. . . . Chavkin, *Help, Don't Jail, Addicted Mothers, supra* note 147 at A21, col. 2.

51. *See* Escamilla-Mondanaro, *Women: Pregnancy, Children and Addiction,* 9 J. Psychedelic Drugs 59, 59- 60 (1977); *see also* Zuckerman, Amaro, Bauchner & Cabral, *Depressive Symptoms During Pregnancy: Relationship to Poor Health Behaviors,* 160 Am. J. Obstetrics & Gyn. 1107, 1109 (1989). . . .

52. In the *Johnson* trial, for example, the prosecution introduced no evidence that Johnson's children were adversely affected by their mother's crack use. Indeed, there was testimony that the children were healthy and developing normally. *See* Trial Transcript, *supra* note 4, at 46–47, 120 (testimony of Dr. Randy Tompkin and Clarice Johnson, Jennifer's mother). A law proposed in Ohio makes drug use during pregnancy grounds for sterilization. . . . Similarly, several states have enacted statutes that make a woman's drug use during pregnancy by itself grounds to deprive her of custody of her child. *See supra* note 50.

53. *See* Karst, *supra* note, at 32; Stefan, *Whose Egg Is It Anyway? Reproductive Rights of Incarcerated, Institutionalized and Incompetent Women,* 13 Nova L. Rev. 405, 454 (1989); . . . Asch, *Reproductive Technology and Disability,* in Reproductive Laws for the 1990s, *supra* note, at 106–07. . . .

I recognize that there are women who choose not to have children or are incapable of having children and that this choice or inability does not make them any less human. . . . It is not the act of having children that makes an individual fully human; it is society's view of whether she deserves to have children.

54. For a discussion of the eugenic sterilization movement in the early twentieth century, see Burgdorf & Burgdorf, *The Wicked Witch Is Almost Dead: Buck v. Bell and the Sterilization of Handicapped Persons,* 50 Temp. L.Q. 995, 997–1005 (1977); and Cynkar, Buck v. Bell: *"Felt Necessities" v. Fundamental Values?,* 81 Colum. L. Rev. 1418, 1425–35 (1981). . . .

The discrediting of eugenic theory, the development of the constitutional doctrine of reproductive autonomy, and the changing view of mental retardation spurred a major reform of sterilization law. . . . Reports of Nazi Germany's program of racial eugenics achieved through widespread sterilization precipitated the modern rejection of these laws. *See* Scott, *supra* note, at 811–12.

55. One report written by a leading scholar of the eugenic movement defined the "socially inadequate" as:

"(1) feeble-minded; (2) insane (including the psychopathic); (3) criminalistic (including the delinquent and wayward); (4) epileptic; (5) inebriate (including drug-habitués); (6) diseased (including the tuberculous, the syphilitic, the leprous, and others with chronic, infectious and legally segregable diseases); (7) blind (including those with seriously impaired vision); (8) deaf (including those with seriously impaired hearing); (9) deformed (including the crippled); and (10) dependent (including orphans, ne'er-do-wells, the homeless, tramps and paupers)."

Cynkar, *supra* note 54, at 1428 (quoting H. Laughlin, The Legal Status of Eugenical Sterilization 65 (1929)).

56. As late as 1966, 26 states still had eugenic sterilization laws. . . . It has been estimated that over 70,000 persons were involuntarily sterilized under these statutes.

57. 1924 Va. Acts 394. For a discussion of the history of the Virginia sterilization law's enactment, see Lombardo, *Three Generations, No Imbeciles: New Light on* Buck v. Bell, 60 N.Y.U.L. Rev. 30, 34–48 (1985).

58. *Bell,* 274 U.S. at 205. Subsequent research has revealed that the Court's factual statement was erroneous. Although Carrie Buck became pregnant out of wedlock, the finding that she was "feeble minded" was based on insubstantial testimony. *See* Gould, *Carrie Buck's Daughter,* 2 Const. Commentary 331, 336 (1985); Lombardo, *supra* note 57, at 52.

59. *Bell,* 274 U.S. at 207.

60. *Id.* § 173.

61. *Id.* at 541.

62. I hear this false dichotomy in the words of Muskegon, Michigan, narcotics officer Al Van Hemert: "'If the mother wants to smoke crack and kill herself, I don't care.' . . . 'Let her die, but don't take that poor baby with her.'" Hoffman, *supra* note 5, at 34.

From Contraception to Abortion: A Moral Continuum

Wendy Simonds

I've spent over two decades doing sociological research on procreative matters; I've focused mostly on investigating ways in which women seek to prevent procreation. These methods include abortion (both surgical and medical—with mifepristone, commonly known as RU-486), and emergency contraception (higher dosages of the same drugs in birth control pills, which, when taken within seventy-two hours of unprotected heterosex, can be 80 percent effective at preventing a pregnancy) (Simonds and Ellertson 2004, Simonds et al. 1998, Simonds 1996, Simonds 1991, Ellertson et al. 1999). I've become fascinated by the ways in which health care workers and the women they serve think and speak about abortion and contraception as a moral issue, within a politicized climate in which anti-abortionists and pro-choice activists do rhetorical battle over women's rights and fetal status.

Each side refutes the other's language: anti-abortionists call themselves "pro-life," and refer to their enemies as "pro-abortion," whereas those who support abortion rights counter with "pro-choice," and refer to their opponents as "anti-choice," or more simply, as "antis." Each side seeks to ally itself with what the general public defines as *truly* moral, offering judgments about what the opposing value system threatens. Pro-choice activists proclaim the endangerment of individual rights, especially those of women. Anti-abortionists predict the destruction of the patriarchal heterosexual family unit by selfish (or sadly misguided) aborting women and evil profit-mongering doctors and clinic workers—all of whom they label "baby killers" (see, e.g., Ginsburg's 1989 and Luker's 1984 ethnographies of activists on both sides of the issue).

Carole Joffe writes that early anti-abortionist rhetoric in the United States in the late nineteenth century included the views that "abortion represents a threat to male authority and the 'traditional role' of women; abortion is a symbol of uncontrolled female sexuality and an 'unnatural' act. Above all, the aborting woman is selfish and self-indulgent" (1995: 29). In 1871, the AMA Committee on Criminal Abortion wrote of "the" aborting woman: "She becomes unmindful of the course marked out for her by Providence. . . . She yields to the pleasures—but shrinks from the pains and responsibilities of maternity" (Joffe 1995: 29). Today, with the popularization of sonography, and high-tech enhanced medical photography techniques (like Lennart Nilsson's film, *The Miracle of Life*), embryonic and fetal images have become ubiquitous; anti-abortionists take advantage of this technology in their quest to personify the fetus. This relatively recent fetal fetish means that women are increasingly absent from quite a lot of anti-abortion visual rhetoric (see, e.g., Petchesky 1987), and their absence may well go unnoticed the more accustomed people become to this manner of seeing fetuses.

Pro-choice rhetoric and representations, in contrast, are distinctly woman centered. Legal framing of the issue is more neutral: defining the right to abortion as a right to privacy, though sexual privacy remains *another* deeply contested issue in our culture. Pro-choice rhetoric draws on both liberalism and capitalism: As Barbara Katz Rothman (1989) points out, women are portrayed as individual self-owners entitled to control over our bodies. If I "own" my body, it is mine; anything within it counts as my property, thus abortion becomes an exercise in unarguably justifiable individualism. This rhetoric sidesteps an overt discussion of sexuality, but viewing sexuality through this lens clearly means seeing women as free choosers of what they want.

Pro-choice rhetoric includes endorsements of motherhood as a *chosen* activity; the decision to abort serves as testimony to how seriously women take motherhood. As Elizabeth Karlin writes, "I am an abortion practitioner because of my utmost respect for motherhood, which I refuse to believe is punishment for a screw. I do what I do because I am convinced that being a mother is the hardest job there is" (1998: 287).

In years spent talking with health care workers and their clients, I've found that a particular moral continuum emerges that shows how anti-abortionist views of sex as shameful and women as frivolous shape aspects of the pro-choice view, too. This moral continuum is particular to our time: Bear in mind that it is only recently (the late twentieth century) that contraception has not shared the same stigma as abortion, and that abortion was not considered a moral issue until the mid-1800s. On "our" current moral continuum, late abortion is the worst, and responsible heterosex is the best. (*No sex* is another matter altogether: the anti-abortionists' ultimate moral category for unmarried women, seen as unrealistic or nonsensical by pro-choice activists.) Women who have heterosex should be "responsible"—this means, basically, that they should use contraception. So an unanticipated pregnancy that happens because a condom breaks is morally superior to an unanticipated pregnancy that occurs without any contraception; using contraception during actual sex is better than using emergency contraception the next day or the day after that; having an abortion in the first trimester is better than having one later on; and so forth. Yet at least one dominant cultural script for sex endorses being carried away (especially for women wooed by men) and another discourages women from planning for sexual encounters, because to do so indicates slutty intent (according to the script, to be prepared equates being "loose").

Poll data show that people buy the moral dilemma approach promulgated by anti-abortionists. According to various polls, public support for first-trimester abortion is strongest (ranging between 60 and 70%). A significant minority (vacillating between 36 and 43%) have said they support "stricter limits" on abortion since 1989, even as stricter limits have been imposed (since the Supreme Court's *Webster* decision in 1989 gave states the right to impose various limitations on abortion (Goldberg 1998, pollingreport.com 2009). The most popular restrictions, according to poll data, are parental notification and parental consent laws. A large majority supports abortion when a pregnant woman's life is endangered by the pregnancy, when her pregnancy resulted from rape or incest, or when the fetus is "defective." Support wanes (ranges from less than half to one quarter of those polled) if a woman "cannot afford any more children"; if she "does not want to marry the man"; and if the "pregnancy would interfere with [her] work or education." These poll data indicate the power of cultural attitudes about sexually active women as untrustworthy and immoral. Antiabortionists perpetuate these attitudes in their legal assaults on abortion rights. The *Gonzales v. Carhart* 2007 Supreme Court decision made a particular late-term abortion procedure illegal. The procedure, called "intact dilation and extraction" by doctors and "partial-birth abortion" by antiabortionists, accounted for fewer than 1% of all abortions in the U.S.

In sum, depending on societal attitudes about women's sexuality, the freedom to use contraception and abortion may be conceptualized as dangerous and immoral or as an essential aspect of individual liberty. Both the legal and moral future of abortion—and other methods of limiting procreation—remain at stake.

REFERENCES

Ellertson, Charlotte, Wendy Simonds, Kimberly Springer, and Beverly Winikoff. "Providing Mifepristone-Misoprostol Medical Abortion: The View from the Clinic." *Journal of the American Women's Medical Association* 54 (Spring, 1999): 91–96, 102.

Ginsburg, Faye D. *Contested Lives: The Abortion Debate in an American Community.* Berkeley: University of California Press, 1989.

Goldberg, Carey, with Janet Elder. "Public Still Backs Abortion, But Wants Limits, Poll Says." *New York Times* (January 16, 1998): A1, A16.

Joffe, Carole. *Doctors of Conscience: The Struggle to Provide Abortion before and after Roe v. Wade.* Boston: Beacon, 1995.

Karlin, Elizabeth. "'We Called it Kindness': Establishing a Feminist Abortion Practice." In *Abortion Wars: A Half Century of Struggle, 1950–2000,* Rickie Solinger, ed. Berkeley: University of California Press, 1998.

Luker, Kristin. *Abortion and the Politics of Motherhood.* Berkeley: University of California Press, 1984.

Petchesky, Rosalind Pollack. "Fetal Images: The Power of Visual Culture in the Politics of Reproduction." *Feminist Studies,* v. 13, no. 2 (Summer, 1987): 263–292.

Pollingreport.com. Accessed in January, 2009. http://www.pollingreport.com/abortion.htm.

Rothman, Barbara Katz. *Recreating Motherhood: Ideology and Technology in a Patriarchal Society.* New York: W.W. Norton, 1989.

Simonds, Wendy. *Abortion at Work: Ideology and Practice in a Feminist Clinic.* New Brunswick, NJ: Rutgers University Press, 1996.

———. "At an Impasse: Inside an Abortion Clinic." In *Current Research on Occupations and Professions* 6, Helena Z. Lopata and Judith Levy, eds. Greenwich, CT: JAI Press, 1991: 99–116.

Simonds, Wendy, and Charlotte Ellertson. "Emergency Contraception and Morality: Reflections of Health Care Workers and Clients." *Social Science & Medicine* 58 (2004): 1285–1297.

Simonds, Wendy, Charlotte Ellertson, Kimberly Springer, and Beverly Winikoff. "Abortion, Revised: Participants in the U.S. Clinical Trials Evaluate Mifepristone." *Social Science & Medicine* 46 (1998): 1313–1323.

Dude, You're a Fag:

Masculinity and Sexuality in High School

C. J. Pascoe

The sun shone bright and clear over River High's annual Creative and Performing Arts Happening, or CAPA. During CAPA the school's various art programs displayed students' work in a fairlike atmosphere. . . . Teachers released students from class to wander around the quads, watch performances, and look at the art. This freedom from class time lent the day an air of excitement because students were rarely allowed to roam the campus without a hall pass, an office summons, or a parent/faculty escort. In honor of CAPA, the school district bussed in elementary school students from the surrounding grammar schools to participate in the day's festivities.

Running through the rear quad, Brian, a senior, yelled to a group of boys visiting from the elementary schools, "There's a faggot over there! There's a faggot over there! Come look!" Following Brian, the ten-year-olds dashed down a hallway. At the end of the hallway Brian's friend Dan pursed his lips and began sashaying toward the little boys. As he minced, he swung his hips exaggeratedly and wildly waved his arms. To the boys Brian yelled, "Look at the faggot! Watch out! He'll get you!" In response, the ten-year-olds raced back down the hallway screaming in terror. Brian and Dan repeated this drama throughout the following half hour, each time with a new group of young boys.

Making jokes like these about faggots was central to social life at River High. Indeed, boys learned long before adolescence that faggots were simultaneously

predatory and passive and that they were, at all costs, to be avoided. Older boys repeatedly impressed upon younger ones through these types of homophobic rituals that whatever they did, whatever they became, however they talked, they had to avoid becoming a faggot.

Feminist scholars of masculinity have documented the centrality of homophobic insults and attitudes to masculinity (Kimmel 2001; Lehne 1998), especially in school settings (Burn 2000; Kimmel 2003; Messner 2005; Plummer 2001; G. Smith 1998; Wood 1984). They argue that homophobic teasing often characterizes masculinity in adolescence and early adulthood and that antigay slurs tend to be directed primarily at gay boys. This chapter both expands on and challenges these accounts of relationships between homophobia and masculinity. Homophobia is indeed a central mechanism in the making of contemporary American adolescent masculinity. A close analysis of the way boys at River High invoke the faggot as a disciplinary mechanism makes clear that something more than simple homophobia is at play in adolescent masculinity. The use of the word *fag* by boys at River High points to the limits of an argument that focuses centrally on homophobia. Fag is not only an identity linked to homosexual boys but an identity that can temporarily adhere to heterosexual boys as well. The fag trope is also a racialized disciplinary mechanism.

Homophobia is too facile a term with which to describe the deployment of *fag* as an epithet. By calling the use of the word *fag* homophobia—and letting the argument stop there—previous research has obscured the gendered nature of sexualized insults (Plummer 2001). Invoking homophobia to describe the ways boys aggressively tease each other overlooks the powerful relationship between masculinity and this sort of insult. Instead, it seems incidental, in this conventional line of argument, that girls do not harass each other and are not harassed in this same manner. This framing naturalizes the relationship between masculinity and homophobia, thus obscuring that such harassment is central to the formation of a gendered identity for boys in a way that it is not for girls.

Fag is not necessarily a static identity attached to a particular (homosexual) boy. Fag talk and fag imitations serve as a discourse with which boys discipline themselves and each other through joking relationships. Any boy can temporarily become a fag in a given social space or interaction. This does not mean that boys who identify as or are perceived to be homosexual aren't subject to intense harassment. Many are. But becoming a fag has as much to do with failing at the masculine tasks of competence, heterosexual prowess, and strength or in any way revealing weakness or femininity as it does with a sexual identity. This fluidity of the fag identity is what makes the specter of the fag such a powerful disciplinary mechanism. It is fluid enough that boys police their behaviors out of fear of having the fag identity permanently adhere and definitive enough so that boys recognize a fag behavior and strive to avoid it.

An analysis of the fag discourse also indicates ways in which gendered power works through racialized selves. The fag discourse is invoked differently by and in relation to white boys' bodies than it is by and in relation to African American boys' bodies. While certain behaviors put all boys at risk for becoming temporarily a fag, some behaviors can be enacted by African American boys without putting them at risk of receiving the label. The racialized meanings of the fag discourse suggest that something more than simple homophobia is involved in these sorts of interactions. It is not that gendered homophobia does not exist in African American communities. Indeed, making fun of "negro faggotry seems to be a rite of passage among contemporary black male rappers and filmmakers" (Riggs 1991, 253). However, the fact that "white women and men, gay and straight, have more or less colonized cultural debates about sexual representation" (Julien and Mercer 1991, 167) obscures varied systems of sexualized meanings

among different racialized ethnic groups (Almaguer 1991). Thus far male homophobia has primarily been written about as a racially neutral phenomenon. However, as D. L. King's (2004) recent work on African American men and same-sex desire pointed out, homophobia is characterized by racial identities as well as sexual and gendered ones.

What Is a Fag? Gendered Meanings

"Since you were little boys you've been told, 'Hey, don't be a little faggot,'" explained Darnell, a football player of mixed African American and white heritage, as we sat on a bench next to the athletic field. Indeed, both the boys and girls I interviewed told me that *fag* was the worst epithet one guy could direct at another. Jeff, a slight white sophomore, explained to me that boys call each other fag because "gay people aren't really liked over here and stuff." Jeremy, a Latino junior, told me that this insult literally reduced a boy to nothing, "To call someone *gay* or *fag* is like the lowest thing you can call someone. Because that's like saying that you're nothing."

Most guys explained their or others' dislike of fags by claiming that homophobia was synonymous with being a guy. For instance, Keith, a white soccer-playing senior, explained, "I think guys are just homophobic." However, boys were not equal-opportunity homophobes. Several students told me that these homophobic insults applied only to boys and not to girls. For example, while Jake, a handsome white senior, told me that he didn't like gay people, he quickly added, "Lesbians, okay, that's *good*." Similarly Cathy, a popular white cheerleader, told me, "Being a lesbian is accepted because guys think, 'Oh that's cool.'" Darnell, after telling me that boys were warned about becoming faggots, said, "They [guys] are fine with girls. I think it's the guy part that they're like ewwww." In this sense it was not strictly homophobia but a gendered homophobia that constituted adolescent masculinity in the culture of River High. It is clear, according to these comments, that lesbians were "good" because of their place in heterosexual male fantasy, not necessarily because of some enlightened approach to same-sex relationships. A popular trope in heterosexual pornography depicts two women engaging in sexual acts for the purpose of male titillation. The boys at River High are not unique in making this distinction; adolescent boys in general dislike gay men more than they dislike lesbians (Baker and Fishbein 1998). The fetishizing of sex acts between women indicates that using only the term *homophobia* to describe boys' repeated use of the word *fag* might be a bit simplistic and misleading.

Girls at River High rarely deployed the word *fag* and were never called fags. I recorded girls uttering *fag* only three times during my research. In one instance, Angela, a Latina cheerleader, teased Jeremy, a well-liked white senior involved in student government, for not ditching school with her: "You wouldn't 'cause you're a faggot." However, girls did not use this word as part of their regular lexicon. The sort of gendered homophobia that constituted adolescent masculinity did not constitute adolescent femininity. Girls were not called dykes or lesbians in any sort of regular or systematic way. Students did tell me that *slut* was the worst thing a girl could be called. However, my field notes indicate that the word *slut* (or its synonym *ho*) appeared one time for every eight times the word *fag* appeared.

Highlighting the difference between the deployment of *gay* and *fag* as insults brings the gendered nature of this homophobia into focus. For boys and girls at River High *gay* was a fairly common synonym for "stupid." While this word shared the sexual origins of *fag,* it didn't consistently have the skew of gender-loaded meaning. Girls and boys often used *gay* as an adjective referring to inanimate objects and male or female people, whereas they used *fag* as a noun that denoted only unmasculine males. Students used *gay* to describe anything from someone's clothes to a new school rule that they didn't like. For instance, one day in auto shop, Arnie pulled out a large older version of a black laptop computer and placed it on his desk. Behind him Nick cried, "That's a gay laptop! It's five inches thick!" The rest of the boys in the class laughed at Arnie's outdated laptop. A laptop can be gay, a movie can be gay, or a group of people can be gay. Boys used *gay* and *fag* interchangeably when they referred to other boys, but *fag* didn't have the gender-neutral attributes that *gay* frequently invoked.

Surprisingly, some boys took pains to say that the term *fag* did not imply sexuality. Darnell told me, "It doesn't even have anything to do with being gay." Similarly, J. L., a white sophomore at Hillside High (River High's cross-town rival), asserted, "*Fag,* seriously, it has nothing to do with sexual preference at all. You could just be calling somebody an idiot, you know?" I asked Ben, a quiet, white sophomore who wore heavy-metal T-shirts to auto shop each day, "What kind of things do guys get called a fag for?" Ben answered, "Anything . . . literally, anything. Like you were trying to turn a wrench the wrong way, 'Dude, you're a fag.' Even if a piece of meat drops out of your sandwich, 'You fag!'" Each time Ben said, "You fag," his voice deepened as if he were imitating a more masculine boy. While Ben might rightly *feel* that a guy could be called a fag for "anything . . . literally, anything," there were actually specific behaviors that, when enacted by most boys, could render them more vulnerable to a *fag* epithet. In this instance Ben's comment highlights the use of *fag* as a generic insult for incompetence, which in the world of River High, was central to a masculine identity. A boy could get called a fag for exhibiting any sort of behavior defined as unmasculine (although not necessarily behaviors aligned with femininity): being stupid or incompetent, dancing, caring too much about clothing, being too emotional, or expressing interest (sexual or platonic) in other guys. However, given the extent of its deployment and the laundry list of behaviors that could get a boy in trouble, it is no wonder that Ben felt a boy could be called fag for "anything." These nonsexual meanings didn't replace sexual meanings but rather existed alongside them.

One-third (thirteen) of the boys I interviewed told me that, while they might liberally insult each other with the term, they would not direct it at a homosexual peer. Jabes, a Filipino senior, told me, "I actually say it *[fag]* quite a lot, except for when I'm in the company of an actual homosexual person. Then I try not to say it at all. But when I'm just hanging out with my friends I'll be like, 'Shut up, I don't want [to] hear you any more, you stupid fag.'" Similarly J. L. compared homosexuality to a disability, saying there was "no way" he'd call an actually gay guy a fag because "there's people who are the retarded people who nobody wants to associate with. I'll be so nice to those guys, and I hate it when people make fun of them. It's like, 'Bro do you realize that they can't help that?' And then there's gay people. They were born that way." According to this group of boys, gay was a legitimate, or at least biological, identity.

There was a possibility, however slight, that a boy could be gay and masculine (Connell 1995). David, a handsome white senior dressed smartly in khaki pants and a white button-down shirt, told me, "Being gay is just a lifestyle. It's someone you choose to sleep with. You can still throw around a football and be gay." It was as if David was justifying the use of the word *fag* by arguing that gay men could be men if they tried but that if they failed at it (i.e., if they couldn't throw a football) then they deserved to be called a fag. In other words, to be a fag was, by definition, the opposite of masculine, whether the word was deployed with sexualized or nonsexualized meanings. In explaining this to me, Jamaal, an African American junior, cited the explanation of the popular rap artist Eminem: "Although I don't like Eminem, he had a good definition of it. It's like taking away your title. In an interview they were like, 'You're always capping on gays, but then you sing with Elton John.' He was like 'I don't mean gay as in gay.'" This is what Riki Wilchins (2003) calls the "Eminem Exception. Eminem explains that he doesn't call people 'faggot' because of their sexual orientation but because they're weak and unmanly" (72). This is precisely the way boys at River High used the term *faggot.* While it was not necessarily acceptable to be gay, at least a man who was gay could do other things that would render him acceptably masculine. A fag, by the very definition of the word, could not be masculine.

This distinction between fag as an unmasculine and problematic identity and gay as a possibly masculine, although marginalized, sexual identity is not limited to a teenage lexicon; it is reflected in both psychological discourses and gay and lesbian activism. Eve Sedgwick (1995) argues that in contemporary psychological literature homosexuality is no longer a problem for men so long as the homosexual man is of the right age and gender orientation. In this literature a homosexual male must be an adult and

must be masculine. Male homosexuality is not pathologized, but gay male *effeminacy* is. The lack of masculinity is the problem, not the sexual practice or orientation. . . . This concern with both straight and gay men's masculinity not only reflects teenage boys' obsession with hypermasculinity but also points to the conflict at the heart of the contemporary "crisis of masculinity" being played out in popular, scientific, and educational arenas.

Becoming a Fag: Fag Fluidity

"The ubiquity of the word *faggot* speaks to the reach of its discrediting capacity" (Corbett 2001, 4). It's almost as if boys cannot help shouting it out on a regular basis—in the hallway, in class, or across campus as a greeting. In my fieldwork I was amazed by the way the word seemed to pop uncontrollably out of boys' mouths in all kinds of situations.[1] To quote just one of many instances from my field notes: two boys walked out of the PE locker room, and one yelled, "Fucking faggot!" at no one in particular. None of the other students paid them any mind, since this sort of thing happened so frequently. Similar spontaneous yelling of some variation of the word *fag,* seemingly apropos of nothing, happened repeatedly among boys throughout the school. This and repeated imitations of fags constitute what I refer to as a "fag discourse."

Fag discourse is central to boys' joking relationships. Joking cements relationships among boys (Kehily and Nayak 1997; Lyman 1998) and helps to manage anxiety and discomfort (Freud 1905). Boys both connect with one another and manage the anxiety around this sort of relationship through joking about fags. Boys invoked the specter of the fag in two ways: through humorous imitation and through lobbing the epithet at one another. Boys at River High imitated the fag by acting out an exaggerated "femininity" and/or by pretending to sexually desire other boys. As indicated by the introductory vignette in which an older boy imitated a predatory fag to threaten little boys, male students at River High linked these performative scenarios with a fag identity. They also lobbed the *fag* epithet at each other in a verbal game of hot potato, each careful to deflect the insult quickly by hurling it toward someone else. These games and imitations made up a fag discourse that highlighted the fag not as a static but rather as a fluid identity that boys constantly struggled to avoid.

In imitative performances the fag discourse functioned as a constant reiteration of the fag's existence, affirming that the fag was out there; boys reminded themselves and each other that at any moment they could become fags if they were not sufficiently masculine. At the same time these performances demonstrated that the boy who was invoking the fag was *not* a fag. Emir, a tall, thin African American boy, frequently imitated fags to draw laughs from other students in his introductory drama class. One day Mr. McNally, the drama teacher, disturbed by the noise outside the classroom, turned to the open door, saying, "We'll shut this unless anyone really wants to watch sweaty boys playing basketball." Emir lisped, "I wanna watch the boys play!" The rest of the class cracked up at his imitation. No one in the class actually thought Emir was gay, as he purposefully mocked both same-sex sexual desire (through pretending to admire the boys playing basketball) and an effeminate gender identity (through speaking with a lisp and in a high-pitched voice). Had he said this in all seriousness, the class most likely would have responded in stunned silence. Instead, Emir reminded them he was masculine by immediately dropping the fag act. After imitating a fag, boys assure others that they are not a fag by instantly becoming masculine again after the performance. They mock their own performed femininity and/or same-sex desire, assuring themselves and others that such an identity deserves derisive laughter.

Boys consistently tried to force others into the fag position by lobbing the *fag* epithet at each other. One day in auto shop, Jay was rummaging through a junk-filled car in the parking lot. He poked his head out of the trunk and asked, "Where are Craig and Brian?" Neil responded with "I think they're over there," pointing, then thrusting his hips and pulling his arms back and forth to indicate that Craig and Brian might be having sex. The boys in auto shop laughed. This sort of joke temporarily labeled both Craig and Brian as faggots. Because the fag discourse was so familiar, the other boys immediately understood that Neil was indicating that Craig and Brian were having sex.

However, these were not necessarily identities that stuck. Nobody actually thought Craig and Brian were homosexuals. Rather, the fag identity was fluid—certainly an identity that no boy wanted but that most boys could escape, usually by engaging in some sort of discursive contest to turn another boy into a fag.

In this way the fag became a hot potato that no boy wanted to be left holding. One of the best ways to move out of the fag position was to thrust another boy into that position. For instance, soon after Neil made the joke about Brian having sex with Craig, Brian lobbed the fag epithet at someone else, deflecting it from himself, by initiating a round of a favorite game in auto shop, the "cock game." Brian said quietly, looking at Josh, "Josh loves the cock," then slightly louder, "Josh loves the cock." He continued saying this until he was yelling, "JOSH LOVES THE COCK!" The rest of the boys laughed hysterically as Josh slunk away, saying, "I have a bigger dick than all you motherfuckers!" These two instances show how the fag could be mapped, for a moment, onto one boy's body and how he, in turn, could attach it to another boy, thus deflecting it from himself. In the first instance Neil made fun of Craig and Brian for simply hanging out together. In the second instance Brian went from being a fag to making Josh into a fag through the "cock game." Through joking interactions boys moved in and out of the fag identity by discursively creating another as a fag.

Given the pervasiveness of fag jokes and the fluidity of the fag identity, it is difficult for boys to consistently avoid the brand. As Ben stated, it almost seemed that a boy could get called a fag for "anything." But most readily acknowledged that there were spaces, behaviors, and bodily comportments that made one more likely to be subject to the fag discourse, such as bodily practices involving clothing and dancing.

According to boys at River, fags cared about the style of their clothes, wore tighter clothes, and cared about cleanliness. Nils explained to me that he could tell that a guy was a fag by the way he dressed: "Most guys wear loose-fitting clothing, just kind of baggy. They [fags] wear more tight clothes. More fashionable, I guess." Similarly, nonfags were not supposed to care about dirtying their clothes. Auto shop was a telling example of this. Given that the boys spent two hours working with greasy car parts, they frequently ended up smudged and rumpled by the end of class. While in the front of the classroom there was a room boys could change in, most of them opted not to change out of their school clothes, with a few modifying their outfits by taking their shirts off and walking around in their "beaters." These tank tops were banned at River High because of their association with gang membership. Auto shop was the one place on campus where boys could wear them with impunity. Like most of the boys in auto shop, Ben never changed out of his jeans or heavy-metal T-shirts. After working on a particularly oily engine he walked [into] the classroom with grease stains covering his pants. He looked down at them, made a face, and walked toward me laughing, waving his hands around with limp wrists, and lisping in a high-pitched sing-song voice, "I got my good panths all dirty!" Ben's imitation indicated that only a fag would actually care about getting his clothes dirty. "Real" guys didn't care about their appearance; thus it didn't matter if they were covered in grease stains. Of course, to not care about one's clothes, or to make fun of those who care about their clothes, ironically, is to also care about one's appearance. In this sense, masculinity became the carefully crafted appearance of not caring about appearance.

Indeed, the boys' approach to clothing and cleanliness mirrored trends in larger society and the ascendance of the "metrosexual." *Metrosexual* is the recently coined label for straight men who care about their appearance, meticulously piecing together outfits, using product in their hair, and even making manicure appointments (for clear polish, of course). Because these sorts of grooming practices are associated with gay men, straight men developed a new moniker to differentiate themselves from other straight men and from gay men.

Dancing was another practice that put a boy at risk of being labeled a fag. Often boys would jokingly dance together to diffuse the sexualized and feminized meanings embedded in dancing. At dances white boys frequently held their female dates tightly, locking their hips together. The boys never danced with one another unless they were joking or trying to embarrass one another. The examples of boys jok-

ingly dancing together are too numerous to discuss, but the following example was particularly memorable. Lindy danced behind her date, Chris. Chris's friend Matt walked up and nudged Lindy aside, imitating her dance moves behind Chris. As Matt rubbed his hands up and down Chris's back, Chris turned around and jumped back, startled to see Matt there instead of Lindy. Matt cracked up as Chris turned red and swore at his friend.

A similar thing happened at CAPA as two of the boys from the band listened to another band play swing music. These two boys walked toward each other and began to ballroom-dance. Within a second or two they keeled over in laughter, hitting each other and moving away. This ritualized dance, moving closer and then apart, happened again and again when music played at River High. Boys participated in this ritualized exchange to emphasize that indeed they weren't fags. . . .

The constant threat of the fag regulated boys' attitudes toward their bodies in terms of clothing, dancing, and touching. Boys constantly engaged in repudiatory rituals to avoid permanently inhabiting the fag position. Boys' interactions were composed of competitive joking through which they interactionally created the constitutive outside and affirmed their positions as subjects.

Embodying the Fag: Ricky's Story

Through verbal jockeying, most boys at River continually moved in and out of the fag position. For the one boy who permanently inhabited the fag position, life at River High was not easy. I heard about Ricky long before I met him. As soon as I talked to any student involved with drama, the choir, or the Gay/Straight Alliance, they told me I had to meet Ricky. Ricky, a lithe, white junior with a shy smile and downcast eyes, frequently sported multicolored hair extensions, mascara, and sometimes a skirt. An extremely talented dancer, he often starred in the school's dance shows and choreographed assemblies. . . . While other boys at River High engaged in continual repudiatory rituals around the fag identity, Ricky embodied the fag because of his homosexuality and his less normative gender identification and self-presentation.

Ricky assumed (rightly so in this context) that other people immediately identified him with his sexuality. . . .

Ricky lived at the margins of school, student social life, and society in general. His mother died when he was young. After her death, he moved around California and Nevada, alternately living with his drug-addicted father, a boyfriend's family, his aunt, his sister, and his homophobic grandmother (who forbade him to wear nail polish or makeup). The resulting discontinuities in his education proved difficult in terms of both academics and socialization:

> It's really hard to go to a school for a period of time and get used to their system and everything's okay. Then when all of a sudden you have to pick up and move the next week, get into a new environment you have no idea about, you don't know how the kids are gonna react to you. You don't know what the teachers are like and you don't know what their system is. So this entire time I have not been able to get used to their system and get used to the environment at all. That's why I had to say, "Fuck it," cause for so long I've been going back and going back and reviewing things I did in like fifth grade. I'm at a fourth-grade math level. I am math illiterate, let me tell you.

In addition to the continual educational disruptions, Ricky had to contend with intense harassment. Figuring out the social map of the school was central to Ricky's survival. Homophobic harassment at the hands of teachers and students characterized his educational experience. When he was beat up in a middle school PE class, the teacher didn't help but rather fostered this sort of treatment:

> They gave them a two-day suspension and they kind of kept an eye on me. That's all they could do. The PE coach was very racist and very homophobic. He was just like "faggot this" and "faggot that." I did not feel comfortable in the locker room and I asked him if I could go somewhere else to change, and he said, "No, you can change here."

Sadly, by the time Ricky had reached River High he had become accustomed to the violence.

> In a weird sense, in a weird way, I'm comfortable with it because it's just what I've known for as long as I can remember. I mean, in elementary school, I'm talking

like sixth grade, I started being called a fag. Fifth grade I was called a fag. Third grade I was called a fag. I have the paperwork, 'cause my mom kept everything, I still have them, of kids harassing me, saying "Gaylord," at that time it was "Gaylord."

Contrary to the protestations of boys earlier in the chapter that they would never call someone who was gay a fag, Ricky experienced this harassment on a regular basis, probably because he couldn't draw on identifiably masculine markers such as athletic ability or other forms of dominance to bolster some sort of claim on masculinity.

Hypermasculine environments such as sporting events continued to be venues of intense harassment at River High. "I've had water balloons thrown at me at a football game. Like, we [his friends Genevieve and Lacy] couldn't have stayed at the homecoming game. We had to go." The persecution began immediately at the biggest football game of the year. When he entered with his friend Lacy, "Two guys that started walking up to get tickets said, 'There's the fucking fag.'" When Ricky responded with "Excuse me?" the boy shot back, "Don't talk to me like you know me." The boy and his friends started to threaten Ricky. Ricky said, "He started getting into my face, and his friends started saying, 'Come on, man, come on, man'" as if they were about to hit Ricky. Ricky felt frustrated that "the ticket people are sitting there not doing a damn thing. This is right in front of them!" He found Ms. Chesney, the vice principal, after the boys finally left. While Ms. Chesney told him, "We'll take care of it," Ricky said he never heard about the incident again. Later at the game he and Lacy had water bottles thrown at them by young boys yelling, "Oh look, it's a fag!" He said that this sentiment echoed as they tried to sit in the bleachers to watch the half-time show, which he had choreographed: "Left and right, 'What the fuck is that fag doing here?' 'That fag has no right to be here.' Blah blah blah. That's all I heard. I tried to ignore it. And after a while I couldn't take it and then we just went home." While many of the boys I interviewed said they would not actually harass a gay boy, that was not Ricky's experience. He was driven out of the event he had choreographed because of the intense homophobic harassment.

Ricky endured similar torment at CAPA, the event at which Brian and Dan socialized the young boys to fear faggots by chasing them. Boys reacted with revulsion to Ricky's dance performances while simultaneously objectifying the girls dancing on the stage. The rear quad served as the stage for CAPA's dancers. The student body clustered around the stage to watch the all-female beginning jazz dance class perform. Mitch, a white senior, whose shirt read, "One of us is thinking about sex. It must be me," muttered, "This is so gay" and began to walk away. Jackson yelled after him, "Where are you going, *fag?*" As Mitch walked away, Jackson turned back to the dancing girls, who now had their backs to the boys, gyrating their behinds in time to the music, and shouted, "Shake that ass!" Jackson reached in his pocket to grab his glasses. Pablo commented, "He's putting on his glasses so he can see her shake her ass better." Watching the girls' behinds, Jackson replied, as he pointed to one of them, "She's got a *huge* ass." Mitch turned to Pablo and asked, seriously, "Why are there no guys?" Pablo responded, "You're such a fag."

The advanced dance troupe took the stage with Ricky in the center. Again, all the dancers sported black outfits, but this time the pants were baggy and the shirts fitted. Ricky wore the same outfit as the girls. He danced in the "lead" position, in the front and the center of the dance formation. He executed the same dance moves as the girls, which is uncommon in mixed-gender dance troupes. Usually the boys in a mixed-gender dance troupe perform the more "physical" moves such as flips, holding up the girls, and spinning them around. Ricky, instead, performed all the sexually suggestive hip swivels, leg lifts, arm flares, and spins that the girls did.

Nils and his group of white male friends made faces and giggled as they stared at Ricky. Soon Nils turned to Malcolm and said, "It's like a car wreck, you just can't look away." Both shook their heads in dismay as they continued to watch the "car wreck" with what can only be described as morbid absorption. Other boys around the stage reacted visibly, recoiling at Ricky's performance. One of them, J. R., a hulking junior and captain of the football team, shook his head and muttered under his breath, "That's disgusting." I asked him, "What?" J. R. turned to me

with his nose wrinkled in revulsion and responded, "That guy dancing, it's just disgusting! Disgusting!" He again shook his head as he walked off. Soon afterward an African American boy turned to his friend and admiringly said of Ricky, "He's a better dancer than all the girls! That takes talent!" He turned to me and said, "Can I wiggle my hips that fast?" and laughed as he tried. The white boys' revulsion bordering on violence was common for boys when talking about Ricky and his dancing. More surprising was the African American boys' admiration, if tinged with humor, of these skills. In these moments boys faced a terrifying, embodied [object], not just some specter of a fag.

Even though dancing was the most important thing in his life, Ricky told me he didn't attend school dances because he didn't like to "watch my back" the whole time. Meanings of sexuality and masculinity were deeply embedded in dancing and high school dances. Several boys at the school told me that they wouldn't even attend a dance if they knew Ricky was going to be there. In auto shop, Brad, a white sophomore, said, "I heard Ricky is going in a skirt. It's a hella short one!" Chad responded, "I wouldn't even go if he's there." Topping Chad's response, Brad claimed, "I'd probably beat him up outside." K. J. agreed: "He'd probably get jumped by a bunch of kids who don't like him." Chad said, "If I were a gay guy I wouldn't go around telling everyone." All of them agreed on this. Surprised and somewhat disturbed by this discussion, I asked incredulously, "Would you really not go to prom because a gay guy would be in the same room as you all?" They looked at me like I had two heads and said again that of course they wouldn't. Ricky's presentation of both sexual preference and gender identity was so profoundly threatening that boys claimed they would be driven to violence.

Ricky developed different strategies to deal with the fag discourse, given that he was not just *a* fag but *the* fag. While other boys lobbed the epithet at one another with implied threats of violence (you are not a man and I am, so watch out), for Ricky that violence was more a reality than a threat. As a result, learning the unwritten rules of a particular school and mapping out its social and physical landscape was literally a matter of survival. He found River High to be one of the most homophobic schools he had attended: "It's the most violent school I think that I've seen so far. With all the schools the verbal part about, you know the slang, 'the fag,' the 'fuckin' freak,' 'fucking fag,' all that stuff is all the same. But this is the only school that throws water bottles, throws rocks, and throws food, ketchup, sandwiches, anything of that nature."[2]

While there is a law in California protecting students from discrimination based on sexual identity, when Ricky requested help from school authorities he was ignored, much as in his interaction with the vice principal at the homecoming game. Ricky responded to this sort of treatment with several evasion strategies. He walked with his eyes downcast to avoid meeting other guys' eyes, fearing that they would regard eye contact as a challenge or an invitation to a fight. Similarly he varied his route to and from school:

> I had to change paths about three different times walking to school. The same people who drive the same route know, 'cause I guess they leave at the same time, so they're always checking something out. But I'm always prepared with a rock just in case. I have a rock in my hand so if anything happens I just chuck one back. I always walk with something like that.

Indeed, when I was driving him home from the interview that day, boys on the sidewalk glared at him and made comments I couldn't hear. He also, with the exception of the homecoming football game, avoided highly sexualized or masculinized school events where he might be subject to violence.

Soon after my research ended, Ricky dropped out of River High and moved to a nearby city to perform in local drag shows. While other boys moved in and out of the fag position, Ricky's gendered practices and sexual orientation forced him to bear all that the other boys cast out of masculinity. His double transgression of sexual and gender identity made his position at River High simply unlivable. The lack of protection from the administration meant facing torture on a daily basis. The abuse that was heaped on him was more than one person, certainly more than one parentless, undereducated, sweet, artistic adolescent, could bear.[3]

Racializing the Fag

While all groups of boys, with the exception of the Mormon boys, used the word *fag* or fag imagery in their interactions, the fag discourse was not deployed consistently or identically across social groups at River High. Differences between white boys' and African American boys' meaning making, particularly around appearance and dancing, reveal ways the specter of the fag was racialized. The specter of the fag, these invocations reveal, was consistently white. Additionally, African American boys simply did not deploy it with the same frequency as white boys. For both groups of boys, the *fag* insult entailed meanings of emasculation, as evidenced by Darnell's earlier comment. However, African American boys were much more likely to tease one another for being white than for being a fag. Precisely because African American men are so hypersexualized in the United States, white men are, by default, feminized, so *white* was a stand-in for *fag* among many of the African American boys at River High. Two of the behaviors that put a white boy at risk for being labeled a fag didn't function in the same way for African American boys.

Perhaps because they are, by necessity, more invested in symbolic forms of power related to appearance (much like adolescent girls), a given African American boy's status is not lowered but enhanced by paying attention to clothing or dancing. Clean, oversized, carefully put together clothing is central to a hip-hop identity for African American boys who identify with hip-hop culture. Richard Majors (2001) calls this presentation of self a "cool pose" consisting of "unique, expressive and conspicuous styles of demeanor, speech, gesture, clothing, hairstyle, walk, stance and handshake," developed by African American men as a symbolic response to institutionalized racism (211). Pants are usually several sizes too big, hanging low on the hips, often revealing a pair of boxers beneath. Shirts and sweaters are similarly oversized, sometimes hanging down to a boy's knees. Tags are frequently left on baseball hats worn slightly askew and perched high on the head. Meticulously clean, unlaced athletic shoes with rolled-up socks under the tongue complete a typical hip-hop outfit.

In fact, African American men can, without risking a fag identity, sport styles of self and interaction frequently associated with femininity for whites, such as wearing curlers (Kelley 2004). These symbols, at River High, constituted a "cool pose."

The amount of attention and care given to clothing for white boys not identified with hip-hop culture (that is, most of the white boys at River High) would certainly cast them into an abject, fag position, as Ben indicated when he cried, jokingly, "I got my good panths all dirty!" White boys were not supposed to appear to care about their clothes or appearance because only fags cared about how they looked. However African American boys involved in hip-hop culture talked frequently about whether their clothes, specifically their shoes, were dirty. In drama class both Darnell and Marc compared their white Adidas basketball shoes. Darnell mocked Marc because black scuff marks covered his shoes, asking incredulously, "Yours are a week old and they're dirty, I've had mine for a month and they're not dirty!" Both laughed. Monte, River High's star football player, echoed this concern about dirty shoes. Looking at the fancy red shoes he had lent to his cousin the week before, he told me he was frustrated because after his cousin used them the "shoes are hella scuffed up." Clothing, for these boys, did not indicate a fag position but rather defined membership in a certain cultural and racial group (Perry 2002). Especially for poor African American boys (as most were at River High), clean clothing was an indicator of class status. If one had enough money to have clean shoes one was not "ghetto," in the parlance of the students at River. . . .

Because African American boys lacked other indicators of class such as cars and the ability to leave campus during lunch, clean expensive basketball shoes took on added symbolic status.

Dancing was another arena that carried distinctly fag-associated meanings for white boys but masculine meanings for African American boys who participated in hip-hop culture. White boys often associated dancing with fags. However, dancing did not carry this sort of sexualized gender meaning for all boys at River High. For African American boys dancing demonstrates membership in a cultural community (Best 2000). At River, African American boys frequently danced together in single-sex groups, teaching each other the latest dance moves, showing off a particularly difficult move, or making each other laugh with humorous dance moves. In fact, while in drama class Liam and Jacob hit each other and joked through the entire dancing exercise, Darnell and Marc seemed very comfortable touching one another. They stood close to one another, heel to toe, as they were supposed to. Their bodies touched, and they gently and gracefully moved the other's arms and head in a way that was tender, not at all like the flailing of the two white boys.

Dancing ability actually increased an African American boy's social status. Students recognized K. J., along with Ricky, as the most talented dancer at the school. K. J. was a sophomore of mixed racial descent, originally from the Philippines, who participated in the hip-hop culture of River High. He continually wore the latest hip-hop fashions. His dark complexion and identification with hip-hop culture aligned him with many of the African American boys at River High. Girls hollered his name as they walked down the hall and thrust love notes folded in complicated designs into his hands as he sauntered to class. For the past two years K. J. had won first place in the talent show for dancing. When he danced at assemblies the auditorium reverberated with screamed chants of "Go K. J.! Go K. J! Go K. J.!" Because dancing for boys of color, especially African American boys, placed them within a tradition of masculinity, they were not at risk of being labeled a fag for engaging in this particular gendered practice. Nobody called K. J. a fag. In fact, in several of my interviews boys of multiple racial/ethnic backgrounds spoke admiringly of K. J.'s dancing abilities. Marco, a troublemaking white senior, said of K. J., "Did you know he invented the Harlem Shake?" referring to a popular and difficult dance move. Like Ricky, K. J. often choreographed assembly dance routines. But unlike Ricky, he frequently starred in them at the homecoming and Mr. Cougar rallies.

None of this is to say that participation in dancing made boys less homophobic. K. J. himself was deeply homophobic. But like the other boys, it was a gendered homophobia that had to do with masculine gender transgressions as much as sexuality. His sister, for instance, identified as a lesbian, and he looked up to and liked her. But he loathed Ricky. Because of their involvement with dance, the two came into contact relatively frequently. Stylistically, they mirrored one another. Both sported long hair: K. J.'s in cornrows and Ricky's lengthened with highlighted extensions. Both wore elaborate outfits: K. J. favored oversized matching red and white checked shorts and a button-down shirt over a white tank top, while Ricky sported baggy black pants, combat boots, and a white tank top. Both were thin with delicate facial features and little facial hair. But the meanings associated with what might seem like gender transgressions by both of them were mediated by their racial and sexual identities, leading to K. J.'s popularity and Ricky's debasement. K. J.'s appearance identified his style as hip-hop, a black, masculine cultural style, whereas Ricky's style identified him as gender transgressive and feminine.

Not surprisingly, K. J. and Ricky were the stars of the dance show at River High. As the day of the show arrived, K. J. asked me for what must have been the hundredth time if I was planning to attend. He said, "Everyone is sayin' that Ricky is my competition, but I don't think so. He's not my competition." K. J. continued to tell me that he was very upset with Ricky because the night before at the dress rehearsal Ricky had walked up to him, saying, "Hey, K. J., awesome dance." Ricky had put his hand on K. J.'s back when he said this. Angry and red, K. J. said to me, "I wanted to hit him hella bad! Then he came up again. I was like 'Oh My God!' Ugh!" Trying to identify exactly who Ricky was, another boy said, "I think that's the same guy who is in our history class. The guy who looks like a girl?" K. J., wanting to make sure the other boys knew how repulsive Ricky was, said, "You know how you look at girls like they are hella fine? That's how he looks at guys, dude! He could be looking at you!" All the boys groaned. K. J. expressed relief that he was "safe," saying Ricky "only checks out white guys." K. J. took pains to differentiate himself from Ricky by saying that Ricky wasn't his competition and that Ricky didn't even look at him as a sexual object because of his race. The respect K. J. commanded at River was certainly different from the treatment Ricky received because the meanings

associated with African American boys and dancing were not the same as the ones associated with white boys and dancing. K. J.'s dancing ability and carefully crafted outfits bolstered his popularity with both boys and girls, while Ricky's similar ability and just as carefully chosen outfits placed him, permanently, in a fag position.

None of this is to say that the sexuality of boys of color wasn't policed. In fact, because African American boys were regarded as so hypersexual, in the few instances I documented in which boys were punished for engaging in the fag discourse, African American boys were policed more stringently than white boys. It was as if when they engaged in the fag discourse the gendered insult took on actual combative overtones, unlike the harmless sparring associated with white boys' deployments. The intentionality attributed to African American boys in their sexual interactions with girls seemed to occur as well in their deployment of the fag discourse. One morning as I waited with the boys on the asphalt outside the weight room for Coach Ramirez to arrive, I chatted with Kevin and Darrell. The all-male, all-white wrestling team walked by, wearing gold and black singlets. Kevin, an African American sophomore, yelled out, "Why are you wearing those faggot outfits? Do you wear those tights with your balls hanging out?" The weight-lifting students stopped their fidgeting and turned to watch the scene unfold. The eight or so members of the wrestling team stopped at their SUV and turned to Kevin. A small redhead whipped around and yelled aggressively, "Who said that?!" Fingers from wrestling team members quickly pointed toward Kevin. Kevin, angrily jumping around, yelled back as he thrust his chest out, "Talk about jumping me, nigger?" He strutted over, advancing toward the small redhead. A large wrestler sporting a cowboy hat tried to block Kevin's approach. The redhead meanwhile began to jump up and down, as if warming up for a fight. Finally the boy in the cowboy hat pushed Kevin away from the team and they climbed in the truck, while Kevin strutted back to his classmates, muttering, "All they know how to do is pick somebody up. Talk about jumping me . . . weak-ass wrestling team. My little bro could wrestle better than any of those motherfuckers."

It would seem, based on the fag discourse scenarios I've described thus far, that this was, in a sense, a fairly routine deployment of the sexualized and gendered epithet. However, at no other time did I see this insult almost cause a fight. Members of the white wrestling team presumably took it so seriously that they reported the incident to school authorities. This in itself is stunning. Boys called each other fag so frequently in everyday discussion that if it were always reported most boys in the school would be suspended or at least in detention on a regular basis. This was the only time I saw school authorities take action based on what they saw as a sexualized insult. As a result Mr. J. explained that somebody from the wrestling team told him that Kevin was "harassing" them. Mr. J. pulled Kevin out of weight-lifting class to discuss the incident. According to him, Kevin "kept mouthing off" and it wasn't the first time he had been in trouble, so they decided to expel him and send him to Hillside.

While Kevin apparently had multiple disciplinary problems and this interaction was part of a larger picture, it is important that this was the only time that I heard any boy (apart from Ricky) tattle on another boy for calling him gay or fag. Similarly it was the only time I saw punishment meted out by the administration. So it seems that, much as in the instance of the Bomb Squad at the Dance Show, intentionality was more frequently attributed to African American boys. They weren't just engaging in the homophobic bantering to which teachers like Mr. Kellogg turned a blind eye or in which Mr. McNally participated. Rather, they were seen as engaging in actual struggles for dominance by attacking others. Because they were in a precarious economic and social position, the ramifications for African American boys for engaging in the fag discourse were more serious. Precisely because some of them were supposed to be attending, not River High, but the "bad" school, Chicago, in the neighboring school district, when they did encounter trouble their punishment was more severe. . . .

Reframing Homophobia

Homophobia is central to contemporary definitions of adolescent masculinity. Unpacking multilayered meanings that boys deploy through their uses of homophobic language and joking rituals makes clear that it is not just homophobia but a gendered and racialized homophobia. By attending to these meanings, I reframe the discussion as a fag discourse rather than simply labeling it as homophobia. The fag is an "abject" (Butler 1993) position, a position outside masculinity that actually constitutes masculinity. Thus masculinity, in part, becomes the daily interactional work of repudiating the threatening specter of the fag.

The fag extends beyond a static sexual identity attached to a gay boy. Few boys are permanently identified as fags; most move in and out of fag positions. Looking at fag as a discourse in addition to a static identity reveals that the term can be invested with different meanings in different social spaces. *Fag* may be used as a weapon with which to temporarily assert one's masculinity by denying it to others. Thus the fag becomes a symbol around which contests of masculinity take place.

Researchers who look at the intersection of sexuality and masculinity need to attend to how racialized identities may affect how *fag* is deployed and what it means in various social situations. While researchers have addressed the ways in which masculine identities are racialized (Bucholtz 1999; Connell 1995; J. Davis 1999; Ferguson 2000; Majors 2001; Price 1999; Ross 1998), they have not paid equal attention to the ways *fag* might be a racialized epithet. Looking at when, where, and with what meaning *fag* is deployed provides insight into the processes through which masculinity is defined, contested, and invested in among adolescent boys.

Ricky demonstrates that the fag identity can, but doesn't have to, inhere in a single body. But it seems that he needed to meet two criteria—breaking both gendered and sexual norms—to be constituted as a fag. He was simultaneously the penetrated fag who threatened psychic chaos (Bersani 1987) and the man who couldn't "throw a football around." Not only could he not "throw a football," but he actively flaunted his unmasculine gender identification by dancing provocatively at school events and wearing cross-gendered clothing. Through his gender practices Ricky embodied the threatening specter of the fag. He bore the weight of the fears and anxieties of the boys in the school who frantically lobbed the *fag* epithet at one another.

The *fag* epithet, when hurled at other boys, may or may not have explicit sexual meanings, but it always has gendered meanings. When a boy calls another boy a fag, it means he is not a man but not necessarily that he is a homosexual. The boys at River High knew that they were not supposed to call homosexual boys fags because that was mean. This, then, has been the limited success of the mainstream gay rights movement. The message absorbed by some of these teenage boys was that "gay men can be masculine, just like you." Instead of challenging gender inequality, this particular discourse of gay rights has re-inscribed it. Thus we need to begin to think about how gay men may be in a unique position to challenge gendered as well as sexual norms.

NOTES

1. In fact, two of my colleagues, both psychotherapists, suggested that the boys exhibited what we could think of as a sort of "Fag Tourette's Syndrome."

2. Though River was not a particularly violent school, it may have seemed like that to Ricky because sexuality-based harassment increases with grade level as gender differentiation becomes more intense. As youth move from childhood into adolescence there is less flexibility in terms of gender identity and self-presentation (Shakib 2003).

3. There were two other gay boys at the school. One, Corey, I learned about after a year of fieldwork. While he wasn't "closeted," he was not well known at the school and kept a low profile. The other out gay boy at the school was Brady. While he didn't engage in the masculinity rituals of the other boys at River High, he didn't cross-dress or engage in feminine-coded activities as did Ricky. As such, when boys talked about fags, they referenced Ricky, not Brady or Corey.

REFERENCES

Almaguer, Tomas. 1991. "Chicano Men: A Cartography of Homosexual Identity and Behavior." *Differences* 3, no. 2:75–100.

Baker, Janet G., and Harold D. Fishbein. 1998. "The Development of Prejudice towards Gays and Lesbians by Adolescents." *Journal of Homosexuality* 36, no. 1:89–100.

Bersani, Leo. 1987. "Is the Rectum a Grave?" *AIDS; Cultural Analysis/Cultural Activism*, no. 43:197–222.

Best, Amy. 2000. *Prom Night: Youth, Schools, and Popular Culture.* New York: Routledge.

Bucholtz, Mary. 1999. "You Da Man: Narrarating the Racial Other in the Production of White Masculinity." *Journal of Sociolinguistics* 3, no. 4:443–60.

Burn, Shawn Meghan. 2000. "Heterosexuals' Use of 'Fag' and 'Queer' to Deride One Another: A Contributor to Heterosexism and Stigma." *Journal of Homosexuality* 40, no. 2:1–11.

Butler, Judith. 1993. *Bodies That Matter: On the Discursive Limits of "Sex."* New York: Routledge.

Connell, R. W. 1995. *Masculinities.* Berkeley: University of California Press.

Corbett, Ken. 2001. "Faggot = Loser." *Studies in Gender and Sexuality* 2, no. 1:3–28.

Davis, James Earl. 1999. "Forbidden Fruit: Black Males' Constructions of Transgressive Sexualities in Middle School." In *Queering Elementary Education: Advancing the Dialogue about Sexualities and Schooling,* edited by William J. Letts IV and James T. Sears, 49–59. Lanham, MD: Rowan and Littlefield.

Ferguson, Ann. 2000. *Bad Boys. Public Schools in the Making of Black Masculinity.* Ann Arbor: University of Michigan Press.

Freud, Sigmund. 1905. *The Basic Writings of Sigmund Freud.* Translated by A. A. Brill. New York: Modern Library.

Julien, Isaac, and Kobena Mercer. 1991. "True Confessions: A Discourse on Images of Black Male Sexuality." In *Brother to Brother: New Writings by Black Gay Men,* edited by Esses Hemphill, 167–173. Boston: Alyson Publications.

Kehily, Mary Jane, and Anoop Nayak. 1997. "'Lads and Laughter': Humour and the Production of Heterosexual Masculinities." *Gender and Education* 9, no. 1:69–87.

Kelley, Robin D. G. 2004. "Confessions of a Nice Negro, or Why I Shaved My Head." In *Men's Lives,* edited by Michael Kimmel and Michael Messner, 335–41. Boston: Allyn and Bacon.

Kimmel, Michael S. 1999. "'What about the Boys?' What the Current Debates Tell Us—and Don't Tell Us—about Boys in School." *Michigan Feminist Studies* 14:1–28.

———. 2001. "Masculinity as Homophobia: Fear, Shame, and Silence in the Construction of Gender Identity." In *The Masculinities Reader,* edited by Stephen Whitehead and Frank Barrett, 266–87. Cambridge: Polity Press.

————. 2003. "Adolescent Masculinity, Homophobia, and Violence: Random School Shootings, 1982–2001." *American Behavioral Scientist* 46, no. 10:1439–58.

King, J. L. 2004. *On the Down Low: A Journey into the Lives of Straight Black Men Who Sleep with Men.* New York: Broadway Books.

Lehne, Gregory. 1998. "Homophobia among Men: Supporting and Defining the Male Role." In *Men's Lives,* edited by Michael Kimmel and Michael Messner, 237–49. Boston: Allyn and Bacon.

Lyman, Peter. 1998. "The Fraternal Bond as a Joking Relationship: A Case Study of the Role of Sexist Jokes in Male Group Bonding." In *Men's Lives,* edited by Michael Kimmel and Michael Messner, 171–93. Boston: Allyn and Bacon.

Majors, Richard. 2001. "Cool Pose: Black Masculinity and Sports." In *The Masculinities Reader,* edited by Stephen Whitehead and Frank Barrett, 208–17. Cambridge: Polity Press.

Messner, Michael. 2005. "Becoming 100% Straight." In *Gender through the Prism of Difference,* edited by Maxine Baca Zinn, Pierrette Hondagneu-Sotelo, and Michael Messner, 227–32. New York: Oxford University Press.

Perry, Pamela. 2002. *Shades of White: White Kids and Racial Identities in High School.* Durham: Duke University Press.

Plummer, David C. 2001. "The Quest for Modern Manhood: Masculine Stereotypes, Peer Culture and the Social Significance of Homophobia." *Journal of Adolescence* 24, no. 1:15–23.

Price, Jeremy. 1999, "Schooling and Racialized Masculinities: The Diploma, Teachers and Peers in the Lives of Young, African American Men." *Youth and Society* 31, no. 2:224–63.

Riggs, Marlon. 1991. "Black Macho Revisited: Reflections of a Snap! Queen." In *Brother to Brother: New Writings by Black Gay Men*, edited by Essex Hemphill, 253–60. Boston: Alyson Publications.

Ross, Marlon B. 1998. "In Search of Black Men's Masculinities." *Feminist Studies* 24, no. 3:599–626.

Sedgwick, Eve Kosofsky. 1995. " 'Gosh, Boy George, You Must Be Awfully Secure in Your Masculinity!' " In *Constructing Masculinity,* edited by Maurice Berger, Brian Wallis, and Simon Watson, 11–20. New York: Routledge.

Shakib, Sohaila. 2003. "Female Basketball Participation: Negotiating the Conflation of Peer Status and Gender Status from Childhood through Puberty." *American Behavioral Scientist* 46, no. 4:1405–22.

Smith, George W. 1998. "The Ideology of 'Fag': The School Experience of Gay Students." *Sociological Quarterly* 39, no. 2:309–35.

Wilchins, Riki. 2003. "Do You Believe in Fairies?" *Advocate,* February 4, 72.

Wood, Julian. 1984. "Groping Towards Sexism: Boy's Sex Talk." In *Gender and a Generation,* edited by Angela McRobbie and Mica Nava, 54–84. London: Macmillan.

In the Closet

Steven Seidman

Heterosexual domination may have a long history, but the closet does not.[1] As I use the term, the closet will refer to a life-shaping pattern of homosexual concealment. To be in the closet means that individuals hide their homosexuality in the most important areas of life, with family, friends, and at work. Individuals may marry or avoid certain jobs in order to avoid suspicion and exposure. It is the power of the closet to shape the core of an individual's life that has made homosexuality into a significant personal, social, and political drama in twentieth-century America.

The closet may have existed prior to the 1950s, but it was only in the postwar years that it became a fact of life for many gay people.[2] At this time, there occurred a heightened level of *deliberateness and aggressiveness* in enforcing heterosexual dominance. A national campaign against homosexuality grew to an almost feverish pitch in the 1950s and 1960s. . . .

The attack on gays accompanied their social visibility. After the war years, many gay individuals moved to cities where they expected to find other people like themselves and at least enough tolerance to put together something like a gay life. My sense is that gay visibility was less the cause than the justification of an anti-gay campaign. A growing public homosexual menace was invoked to fuel an atmosphere of social panic and a hateful politic. But why the panic around homosexuality?

Despite popular images of domestic tranquility on television and in the movies, the 1950s and early 1960s was a period of great anxiety for many Americans.[3]

There was a feeling of change in the air that evoked new hopes as well as new dangers. For example, as the war ended America emerged as a true superpower. However, it now faced what many considered to be a growing Soviet threat. Hysteria around the red scare narrowed social tolerance. Dissent and nonconventional lifestyles were associated with political subversion. Communists and homosexuals were sometimes viewed as parallel threats to "the American way of life." As invisible, corrupting forces seducing youth, spreading perversion and moral laxity, and weakening our national will, communists and homosexuals were to be identified and ruthlessly suppressed. And ruthlessly suppressed they were.[4]

Moreover, though the war was over and America was victorious, this nation was changing in ways that were troubling to many of its citizens. For example, women now had some real choices. Their social independence during the war gave many women a sense of having options; some wanted only to return to being wives and mothers, but others wished to pursue a career or remain single. Set against the happy homemaker on television shows such as *I Love Lucy, Leave It to Beaver,* and *Ozzie and Harriet* was the "new woman" in *Cosmopolitan* or Helen Gurl[e]y Brown's *Sex and the Single Girl.* The Cosmo girl may have been heterosexual, but she was also educated, career-minded, and sexy.

Men were also restless. During the war they had been exposed to different types of people, places, and ideas. While many men wanted little more than a job, wife, and a home, the world they returned to offered them many choices—a bounty of well-paying jobs, free higher education, and "good" women who did not necessarily believe that sex had to lead to marriage. Hugh Hefner's playboy lifestyle may not have expressed men's actual lives, but it tapped into a reality and a wish for expanded sexual choice.

It was not just adults who were restless. There was a growing population of young people who were becoming downright unruly. The popularity of rock 'n' roll expressed something of their restless spirit. Many young people wished to fashion lives that expressed their individual desires and wants rather than the social scripts of their parents and society. The panic over "juvenile delinquents" and "loose girls" expressed Americans' fears that the family, church, and neighborhood community had lost control of their youth.

So, while changes in the postwar period created a sense of expanded choice for many Americans, it also stirred up fears of disorder and social breakdown. Many citizens looked to the government and cultural institutions like television and magazines such as *The Reader's Digest* to be reassured about what this nation stood for. On the global front, protecting what came to be thought of as "the American way of life" meant flexing our military muscle to ward off the communist threat. On the domestic front, moral order was thought to require stable families—and such families were to be built on the exclusive foundation of heterosexuality, marriage, monogamy, and traditional dichotomous gender roles. In this context, the homosexual stepped forward as a menacing figure, invoked to defend a narrow ideal of respectable heterosexuality. In popular culture and in the psychiatric establishment, the homosexual came to symbolize a threat to marriage, the family, and civilization itself; he or she was imagined as predatory, seductive, corrupting, promiscuous, and a gender deviant. The moral message of this campaign against homosexuality was clear: anyone who challenges dominant sexual and gender norms risks homosexual stigma and social disgrace. The homosexual was not alone in symbolizing social disorder and deviance; there was also the "loose woman," "the delinquent," and "the sex offender." All these menacing figures served to reinforce a narrow norm of the respectable sexual citizen—heterosexual, married, monogamous, gender conventional, and family oriented.

By the end of the 1960s, the idea of a rigid division between the pure heterosexual and the polluted, dangerous homosexual began to take hold in American culture. The state and other institutions were given the moral charge to protect America from the homosexual menace. Gay men and lesbians were to be excluded from openly participating in respectable society. They were demonized, and any trace of them in public was to be repressed. The world of the closet was created.

The Closet as Social Oppression

. . . If the concept of the closet is to be sociologically useful, it should not be used casually to cover any and all acts of homosexual concealment. The closet is a historically specific social pattern. This concept makes sense only if there is also the idea of homosexuality as a core identity. Viewed as an identity, homosexuality cannot be isolated and minimized as a discrete feeling or impulse; choosing to organize a public heterosexual life would create a feeling of betraying one's true self. The closet may make a respectable social status possible but at a high price: living a lie. Not surprisingly, the closet is often likened to "a prison," "an apartheid," "a coffin-world," or to "lives led in the shadows."[5] It is said to emasculate the self by repressing the very passions that give life richness and vitality. . . .

In short, the closet is about social oppression. Among its defining features are the following. First, to be in the closet means that individuals act to conceal who they are from those that matter most in their lives: family, friends, and sometimes spouses and children. Being in the closet will shape the psychological and social core of an individual's life. Second, the closet is about social isolation. Individuals are often isolated from other homosexually oriented individuals and are often emotionally distant from the people they are closest to—kin and friends.[6] Third, secrecy and isolation are sustained by feelings of shame, guilt, and fear. The closeted individual often internalizes society's hatred of homosexuals; if he or she manages to weaken the grip of shame, the fear of public disgrace and worse enforces secrecy and isolation. Finally, secrecy, isolation, shame, and fear pressure individuals to conduct a life involving much deception and duplicity.[7] To be in the closet is, then, to suffer systematic harm—to lack basic rights and a spectrum of opportunities and social benefits; to be denied respect and a feeling of social belonging; and more than likely to forfeit the kinds of intimate companionship and love that make personal happiness possible.

This notion of the closet makes sense only in relation to another concept: *heterosexual domination.*[8] The closet is a way of adjusting to a society that aggressively enforces heterosexuality as the preferred way of life. In the era of the closet, heterosexual dominance works not only by championing a norm of heterosexuality but also by demonizing homosexuality. The making of a culture of homosexual pollution is basic to the creation of the closet. Enforcing the exclusion of homosexuals from public life also involves aggressive institutional repression. Homosexuals are suppressed by means of laws, policing practices, civic disenfranchisement, and harassment and violence. The state has been a driving force in the making of the closet. To the extent that heterosexual privilege is enforced by keeping homosexuals silent and invisible, we can speak of a condition of heterosexual domination.

The closet does not, however, create passive victims. Too often, critics emphasize only the way the closet victimizes and strips the individual of any sense of integrity and purposefulness. But closeted individuals remain active, deliberate agents. They make decisions about their lives, forge meaningful social ties, and may manage somewhat satisfying work and intimate lives, even if under strained circumstances.

Passing is not a simple, effortless act; it's not just about denial or suppression. The closeted individual closely monitors his or her speech, emotional expression, and behavior in order to avoid unwanted suspicion. The sexual meaning of the things (for example, clothes, furniture) and acts (for example, styles of walking, talking, posture) of daily life must be carefully read in order to skillfully fashion a convincing public heterosexual identity. For closeted individuals, daily life acquires a heightened sense of theatricality or performative deliberateness. The discrete, local practices of "sexual identity management" that is the stuff of the closet reveals something of the workings of heterosexual domination but also of how gays negotiate this social terrain.

Accommodating to the closet is only part of the story. Rebellion is the other. For individuals to rebel against the closet they must be seen as active, thoughtful, and risk-taking agents. Passive victims do not rebel; they surrender to things as they are. To reject the closet, individuals must view the disadvantages and indignities of the closet as illegitimate and changeable. They must have the inner resources and moral conviction to contest heterosexual domination. As sociologists have put it, rebellion is propelled less by utter despair and victimization than by "relative deprivation." Individuals rebel when social disadvantages feel unjust but changeable—which is to say, when they don't feel only like victims.

Finally, it is perhaps more correct to speak of multiple closets. The experience and social pattern of being in the closet vary considerably depending on factors such as age, class, gender, race, ability or disability, region, religion, and nationality. In this [reading] I convey something of the negotiated and varied texture of the closet through a series of case studies. These examples are not intended to capture the full spectrum of closet experiences, but to show something of its oppressive, negotiated, and varied character. . . .

Social Class and the Closet: Bill's Story

Bill (b. 1958) is a baby boomer. . . . He grew up in a small town. Bill recalls feeling sexual desire for boys at an early age. "I probably started thinking about my homosexuality around the time I was ten. I guess it was when other boys were becoming interested in girls and dating and I wasn't. That's when I started to see that I've got to hide who I am and I've got to pretend that I like girls." . . . Bill remembers being exposed to a public culture of homophobia. Family and friends referred to homosexuals in demeaning ways. Bill was very religious and quickly learned from his church minister that "God hates homosexuals." . . . Bill grew up in a culture that not only viewed heterosexuality as an ideal, but also aggressively enforced its compulsory status by defiling the homosexual.

Bill felt overwhelming pressure to be heterosexual. His parents encouraged dating and expected him to marry and have a family. Kin, friends, church, and the media likewise celebrated an adult life organized around heterosexuality. For virtually all Americans born after 1950, there was a clear, often explicit expectation that adults should marry and raise a family.

Bill didn't want to disappoint those who mattered to him. While being socialized into an ideal of heterosexuality motivated him to adopt a public heterosexual identity, fear drove Bill into the closet. "Fear is the biggest thing. Fear of the people that might find out, fear of what will happen if they did." Fear, for Bill, translated into an anxiety that he would lose his family, livelihood, and the respect of his community.

The closet provided Bill with a strategy to resolve the conflict between social expectations and his homosexuality. He decided to present a consistently heterosexual public identity. This entailed managing his homosexual feelings and negotiating a public identity that avoided suspicion. From the standpoint of being in the closet, Bill experienced social life as filled with risk, a world where others read the sexual meaning of his behavior. To navigate this scary world, Bill had to learn the skills to successfully project a heterosexual identity. . . .

From childhood to his coming out in his midthirties, Bill relied on several strategies to sustain the closet. At the heart of the closet was self-control. At times, this meant that Bill simply had to suppress any homosexual feeling. "I didn't act on it at all for many years." At other times, Bill threw himself into work and his marriage to control his homosexuality. "I channeled my energies into work and our marriage. I wanted a family, a house. I just worked and worked. I was so closeted." Even after he was married, Bill describes a life of intense self-control to a point of self-estrangement. "I've always been aware of what I say and how I act, how I hold my cigarette, how I laugh, I mean anything. When I was living in the closet, I had a mask that I presented to anybody. It was tailored to the person or people that I was around. I didn't know who I was really." Self-control meant carefully regulating his behavior. Bill dressed to avoid homosexual suspicion. "I didn't wear anything that looked like it could be gay." Finally, self-control involved social distance. Bill had few friends after high school, and they were kept at arm's length to avoid possible exposure. Although his family was

close, Bill kept aloof from his parents. "I couldn't be as open to them as I wanted to be."

In Bill's closet world, everyone potentially suspected. Despite his considerable efforts to avoid suspicion, including marriage, enlisting in the marines, and a seamless masculine self-presentation, Bill believed that his wife suspected. Perhaps, he thinks, she interpreted his lack of sexual passion symptomatically. Bill believes that his parents suspected as well. Asked why, Bill referred to a cluster of behaviors that might signal homosexuality. "The people I hung around with, the way I dressed, and [after marriage] the absence of a girl in my life." Bill thought that his mother suspected because he didn't date after his divorce. Bill threw himself into work and parenting in part to avoid suspicion. "I was hoping that my mother would figure that I didn't have time for a relationship, but I think that's when she started to question [my sexual identity]." In this world of pervasive suspicion, Bill began to suspect others. For example, he wondered about his father. "I always had an idea that he might be gay. He was very gentle. He tried real hard to get everybody to like him, and everybody did."

Bill described his closet world in theatrical terms. "My whole life until recently has been being the actor, pretending I'm somebody I'm not." Invoking the image of the actor to describe his life tellingly acknowledges that Bill had in fact acquired considerable social skill in order to succeed at passing. Of course, this heterosexual identity performance meant, as he says, living an inauthentic life. Bill passed successfully, but to do so he married, had children, joined the marines, became dependent on alcohol, and distanced himself from his own inner life as well as from family and friends. In short, the closet was a way to accommodate being the bearer of a polluted identity but at a considerable psychic and social cost. . . .

Homosexuality presented a real symbolic and economic threat. . . . In . . . working-class culture, family was the corner-stone of life. Getting married and having a family was expected and celebrated. Men were expected to present a more or less seamless masculine self. Homosexuality threatened humiliation—for themselves and their families. Exposure risked isolation from their kin and their blue-collar community of kin, peers, and neighbors. . . .

[His] fear of exposure was also economically based. The financial interdependence between the individual and family is central to working-class life. For example, as a wage earner Bill was economically independent. Yet he was aware that his material well-being was never secure. Growing up, he had seen adults lose jobs as industry migrated from his hometown. He saw kin sustaining their own when brothers, cousins, aunts, and uncles were out of work for long periods of time. Bill considered his family a potential source of material support; he also expected that at some point his family would ask for his financial help.

Class shapes closet patterns.[9] The extent of economic interdependence between the individual and his or her family varies between blue- and white-collar workers. This class difference shapes how individuals manage their homosexuality.

For the middle class, economic independence is valued and expected. This provides a material base for coming out and organizing a public gay life. At a minimum, middle-class individuals have options. They can move to avoid exposure; they can afford to establish a workable double life; and they can sustain themselves if estranged from their families. Moreover, because of the high value placed on individualism, middle-class individuals anticipate a considerable disengagement from their family and the community they were brought up in. They can also expect a relatively smooth integration into a middle-class gay life as compensation for any estrangement from family and friends resulting from coming out.

For working-class individuals, economic interdependence with kin is a lifelong expectation. Exiting the closet as a working-class lesbian or gay man carries serious economic risks—for themselves and their kin. Blue-collar workers expect that at some point they will either turn to kin for economic help or their family will turn to them. Additionally, estrangement from kin carries the threat of losing a primary source of community. There is no anticipation of an immediate compensation for lost community because of the middle-class character of the gay institutionalized world.

The closet is not, then, the same experience for all individuals. To understand its workings, we have to pay close attention to . . . social class.

Race and the Closet: Robert's Story

Bill's . . . strong economic ties to [his family] made exiting the closet difficult and potentially more risky than for the economically independent middle class. But [his] white racial status made it relatively easy for [him] to identify as gay. The gay world— at least the institutionalized world of bars, social and political organizations, and cultural institutions (newspapers, magazines, publishers, theater groups)— was and still is overwhelmingly white. Moreover, American public cultures, both white and nonwhite, associate being gay with being white. Accordingly, race is a key factor shaping the dynamics of homosexuality, including the closet. . . .

To illustrate, consider the implications for blacks of an overwhelmingly white gay community. No matter how accepting some individuals may be, blacks often feel like outsiders in the gay community. The culture, the leadership, the organizations, and the political agenda of the institutionalized gay world have been and remain dominated by whites. Blacks often report encountering an inhospitable gay world, one that until recently participated in the racism of straight America. For example, through the early 1990s, black men tell of being carded at gay bars or objectified as exotic sexual selves; black women describe being silenced or ignored in decisions about social events and politics. Despite a deliberate commitment to a multicultural gay community, blacks continue to feel that they have to negotiate a somewhat foreign social terrain.

White privilege in the gay world means that blacks manage their homosexuality somewhat differently than whites. Whites may come out to an unfriendly world of kin and friends, but they anticipate an easy integration into a gay world that will affirm their sense of self and offer an alternative type of community. By contrast, if blacks exit from the closet they expect a struggle for acceptance not only in the straight but also in the gay world. To state the contrast sharply, whites expect a trade-off when they come out: estrangement from the straight world in exchange for social integration and acceptance in the gay community. Blacks do not expect such compensation for their anticipated disapproval and diminished status in the straight world. Given their more ambivalent relationship to the gay community, blacks may be more likely than their white counterparts to manage their homosexuality within the framework of the closet.

If an inhospitable or at least uncertain reception in the gay world gives pause to blacks as they consider coming out, so too does the central role that a race-based community plays in their lives. Many blacks have a fundamental personal and social investment in maintaining integration into a race-based community. This community offers protection and material sustenance in the face of the bodily and economic threats of racism; it provides a positive culture of racial pride and solidarity. Maintaining strong ties with kin and a race-based community is a cornerstone of black identity in a way that is obviously not true for whites. If whites grow up with a sense of racial entitlement and a feeling that it is their America, many blacks experience and expect an inhospitable reception in the larger society. Experience and kin have taught them that their personal and social well-being depends on maintaining solidarity with a black community. For many blacks, America is two nations, and it's only in the black world that they feel a sense of integrity and social belonging.

In short, blacks—straight or gay—are heavily invested in their racial identity and in their membership in the black community in a way that is generally not true of whites. Coming out, then, risks not merely estrangement from kin and community but potentially the loss of a secure sense of identity and social belonging. In other words, leaving the closet threatens social isolation from both the straight and gay worlds. It risks being cast adrift in a society that does not recognize or value being black and gay; it jeopardizes a secure sense of belonging and protection (physical and economic) in exchange for an outsider status. . . .

The absence, at least until recently, of a politically assertive public gay and straight culture supporting black gay men and women has made the wager of coming out risky and potentially too costly for many

individuals. Moreover, as black communities have continued to struggle with a sense of being under assault by racism, poverty, and family instability, tolerance for a public gay life is shaky. The closet presents a credible option, especially if, as some evidence suggests, a more relaxed or flexible closet pattern than that experienced by . . . Bill is possible in many black communities. Moreover, as black gay networks developed in the 1980s and 1990s, some blacks now have an alternative to the closet. However, to the extent that these networks remain small and institutionally insecure, establishing an independent gay life remains much more difficult for many blacks than for whites.

Some of these dynamics and dilemmas of being black and gay in America surface in Robert's story. His is a story of a black gay man trying to navigate between a black world that is not seen as particularly hostile nor especially friendly and a somewhat welcoming white-dominated gay world but one that doesn't feel quite like home. In the end, Robert tries to forge a satisfying life by becoming part of a small, fragile black gay world that is not solidly part of a gay or a black community. . . .

Anticipation of disapproval and rejection underpins Robert's emotional and social distancing from the straight world. Fear prevented Robert from disclosing to his family as a young person. Fear also shaped his public school experience. Although he grew up in a predominantly black community in Brooklyn, Robert went to high school in what he described as a small all-white town in upstate New York. He lived in an almost constant state of fear during these years. Negotiating his racial difference was hard enough. The prospect of being viewed as sexually deviant terrified him. Robert managed by maintaining social distance. He avoided any contact with classmates that might be suspected of being gay. He remained silent in the face of an openly homophobic school culture. Robert tried to fit in by lying about having a girlfriend back home. Despite excelling in sports and enjoying athletics, Robert refused to participate in any school team sports. He was afraid that he'd "get a hard-on in the shower." . . .

After high school, Robert joined the navy, where exposure would have meant a discharge as well as social disgrace. He managed to pass by being a loner and by excessive drinking during his years in the service.

After leaving the navy, Robert worked as an electrician in Los Angeles. Away from home, economically independent, and in a liberal social environment, Robert began to participate in gay life. He dated and soon had a boyfriend.

Robert did not, however, disclose his sexual identity to any of his coworkers. He preferred to keep personal matters out of his work life. Although his coworkers often talked about their boyfriends, girlfriends, marriages, and children, Robert never shared any of his personal life. Robert remained aloof. Although he worked at this job for six years, he did not become friends with any of his coworkers. In order to sustain social distance, Robert avoided any meaningful social ties with his coworkers. As a result of being closeted, Robert's workplace experience resembled the impersonal, dehumanizing world that Karl Marx and Max Weber described in their chilling portraits of modern industrial life.

At the age of twenty-three, Robert came out to his mother, who told his father and his siblings. Robert has never discussed specific aspects of his gay life with any family member. They all know, but it's not talked about. Robert interprets the absence of hostile behavior and rejection on the part of his family as indicating acceptance. Asked why he keeps his gay life separate from his family, Robert says that his homosexuality is personal and doesn't need to be shared. Accordingly, his family knew nothing of his boyfriend or any other aspect of his personal life. Much to his regret, but hardly surprising, Robert speaks of a weakening of his family bond. Today, he's not close to his mother or anyone in his family. His visits with his family are infrequent and lack the emotional spontaneity and richness of past family interactions. For these reasons, Robert has not told his family that he is HIV positive. . . .

Cheap housing led Robert to live in a predominantly black neighborhood. His contacts with his neighbors are formal and lack emotional depth. In fact, he has never come out to any straight black person, aside from his mother. Robert says matter-of-factly that no black person ever asked him if he

was gay. He admits, though, that many blacks disparage being gay. "Many blacks think . . . it's already dangerous out there for a black man, why would you want to add another danger to your life? Besides, being gay was viewed for a long time as equivalent to having AIDS. So, most of the conversations [among blacks] about being gay . . . is about having sex and death. Because they perceive the lifestyle as being very painful . . . not many people are going to be accepting of the lifestyle." . . .

Today, Robert's life is divided between a gay and a straight world. The former provides emotional and social sustenance; the latter is a somewhat risky terrain he navigates to do what he has to do. He speaks, as is typical of those speaking from a closeted standpoint, of a heterosexual dictatorship. Robert's closetedness entails such a narrowing of his world that intimate expression and bonding are possible only within a very small social circle. His closet world is not built on pretense (as was true of Bill), but a fear and distrust so deeply felt that his social distancing has cost him his family, meaningful ties to a black community, a satisfying work life, and has resulted in a pervasive loneliness. . . .

Gender and the Closet: Renee's Story

Despite their . . . differences, . . . Bill and Robert relied heavily on being more or less conventionally masculine men to avoid suspicion. Fortunately, a masculine self-presentation and social roles expressed their spontaneous sense of themselves. However, not all lesbians and gay men can manage a conventional gender presentation so effortlessly. For some individuals, their sense of self can be poignantly at odds with gender norms. If these individuals are to avoid coming out, they must find ways to be gender nonconventional without eliciting suspicion.

These remarks highlight an obvious point: managing gender has been and still is at the heart of managing sexual identity. This is true for men and women. To the extent that men and masculinity are socially privileged, however, the dynamics of managing gender and sexual identity are somewhat different for men and women.[10]

For men, exhibiting the conventional signs of masculinity confers social authority and privilege. Although factors such as class, ethnicity, or ableness create inequalities among men, their masculinity establishes them as a privileged group in relation to women. Masculine men are also presumed to be heterosexual. Of course, if men fail to exhibit those behaviors that serve as conventional markers of masculinity, their dominant status is threatened. And if men depart considerably from masculine norms, they risk losing the privileges associated with being a man and being heterosexual. For men whose inner sense of self is emphatically feminine, passing presents a huge challenge because of the scarcity of acceptable social identities and roles for feminine men. Accordingly, gay men who wish to successfully pass must effectively manage a routine performance of masculinity. But—and here's the key point—when gay men pass by means of exhibiting a conventional masculine persona they share fully in men's gender privilege. Closeted gay men are given the same support straight men receive to conform to masculine gender roles and can claim its considerable social benefits.

For women, the gender managing of sexual identity is somewhat different. Although a conventional feminine self-presentation confers a status as normal and straight, it also positions women as subordinate to men. Respectable women are expected to take up social identities and roles that are consistent with feminine gender expectations. In contemporary America, these roles do not carry the authority, status, and material advantage of masculine roles. Women who wish to assume the social roles and claim the privileges associated with masculine men risk disapproval and may forfeit the benefits of being a normal woman. Lesbians who wish to pass but also to appropriate masculine roles that confer authority and material advantage risk exposure. This is a dilemma that men don't experience. Men who claim masculine power are rewarded as men, and as presumptively straight; women who claim the same privileges associated with masculinity are gender rebels and risk stigma and social harm.

One way that lesbians manage this dilemma is to take on social roles that may be considered mascu-

line (for example, as an athlete, a member of the military service, an office manager) but are viewed as marginally legitimate for straight women. Although there are such roles, they are few and are not free of risk. The story of Renee illustrates this particular closet strategy.

Renee describes herself as a masculine woman. She was born in 1970 and grew up in a small southern town. Her Baptist family and community did not accept homosexuality. Growing up, she became aware of her strong feelings for women while learning that others considered homosexuality to be immoral. She was confused about what these feelings meant for her sense of self. She decided to keep them secret. "I was brought up hearing the statement that you can grow up to be anything you want except a faggot. And it was engrained in me that this was not an accepted lifestyle. It was sinful and it was a way that God was telling you that your life is not good." Renee "feared rejection. I mean, nobody wants to be rejected." Exposure would put her at risk of losing her family "emotionally and financially. . . . The biggest thing that I feared was they wouldn't love me anymore because it was so engrained that this [homosexuality] was not an acceptable lifestyle."

It was not only the homophobia of her family and community that worried Renee. The world of her kin, neighbors, and church was heterosexual—it was both the reality and the unquestioned ideal. Renee was expected to marry and have a family. "My father talked all the time about how much he was looking forward to walking me down the aisle and that I should have lots of children so that they could have lots of grandchildren." Renee retreated into the closet to avoid social rejection and to manage the conflict between what was expected of her and her desires.

Because Renee is not a feminine woman, the closet has been a difficult adjustment. As long as she can remember, Renee felt more comfortable as part of a masculine male culture. As a young person, she was thought of as a tomboy. She says that in the town where she grew up in the 1970s and early 1980s, the tomboy did not evoke homosexual suspicion. Girls could be tomboys but only, as she came to learn, as a young person. The same masculine self-presentation in an adult would evoke suspicion. . . .

Renee felt that a masculine-gendered self was basic to who she was. It could not be denied or changed, but perhaps its social meaning could be managed. As the tomboy identification lost credibility in high school, she tried to fashion a public identity as an athlete. Renee thought that participating in school sports might minimize suspicion or at least create ambiguity around the sexual meaning of her masculine presentation. It was as if being identified as a female athlete, like her earlier identity as a tomboy, would allow Renee to safely express her masculinity. In short, as Renee moved closer to an adult world, it was harder to control the social meaning of her masculine self-presentation; it became difficult to avoid being read, by herself and others, as a lesbian.

In a last-ditch effort to find a legitimate social role for her masculinity Renee joined the military. She encountered a fairly open network of lesbians. She came to accept herself as a lesbian in the course of her military duty.

She believes that today people look at her and see a lesbian. "There's no doubt in my mind that because of my masculine way of dress and look that this signals to people that I am a lesbian. . . . The way I walk, dress, wear my hair. . . . I look like a dyke." Renee feels the weight of a society that collapses gender and sexual nonconformity. Indeed, since Renee believes that her masculinity expresses something basic to who she is, the choice she confronted was stark: to be spontaneous and honest, and therefore to be read as a lesbian; or to pass, which would require a considerable effort at refashioning her public persona. Because gender nonconventionality was at the core of her sense of self, the closet proved a tough accommodation. For a time, the availability of social roles for masculine but presumed straight women (tomboy, athlete, soldier) allowed Renee to avoid exposure. However, as she became an adult civilian, the lack of such roles put pressure on her to either escalate gender management in order to pass or come out. Renee eventually came out.

While there are no unambiguous markers of sexual identity in contemporary America, gender has served as perhaps the chief sign. Masculine men and feminine women are typically assumed to be heterosexual. Emphatically feminine men and masculine

women would likely surrender this presumption. As one twenty-four-year-old gay man told me, "You assume straight men are more masculine, a little rough looking, hair's not perfect. So when you see a guy whose dress is perfect, the hair's perfect, everything is, you know, picture perfect, that's gay." Managing gender presentation has then been at the heart of managing sexual identity. To the extent, moreover, that gender is thickly coded, passing may entail considerable effort. Describing herself as having a forceful, take-charge personality as well as preferring a no-makeup, jeans-and-sweatshirt look, Rachel, a forty-three-year-old lesbian, says that passing required a virtual makeover of her public self. She groomed and dressed in a self-consciously feminine style and crafted a public persona that deemphasized her masculine personality. "I try to look and act very feminine so people won't look at me or take notice."

Gender is not, however, an unambiguous sign of sexual identity. Albert is a twenty-six-year-old gay black man. His soft and high-pitched voice and the meticulous attention he pays to grooming and dress could have marked him as gay during high school. However, Albert thinks that his high profile as an athlete and the absence of explicit homosexual disclosure created ambiguity around his sexual identity. Being black reinforced uncertainty about the sexual meaning of his gender nonconformity. "A lot of people see being gay as a white issue."

The indeterminate character of a homosexual sign system is in sharp contrast to the way racial and gender identities are socially coded. In the United States, race is in most instances unambiguously conveyed by skin color. And gender is so thickly coded by the sexed body and by our behaviors that it's almost impossible to avoid publicly flagging a clear gender identity.[11] Sexual identity, however, is thinly and ambiguously coded. In the age of the closet, there were efforts to thicken the code by identifying specific behaviors as marking heterosexual and homosexual identities. In particular, gender served as a master code of sexual identity, but it remained somewhat ambiguous as a sexual signifier. A prolonged single status, a lack of interest in the opposite sex, a steady gaze at a person of the same sex, or a fastidiousness about grooming (men) or the lack thereof (women) have also functioned as part of a historically specific grammar of sexual identity.

Neither Victims nor Heroes

The closet is a condition of social oppression. To be in the closet is to live with shame, guilt, and fear. Individuals carefully manage daily life in order to avoid suspicion. Some individuals may make life-shaping decisions about love and intimacy, or work and friends, that are motivated by the wish to avoid detection. The closet makes integration possible but at a considerable personal cost: passionless marriages, loveless lives, estrangement from family and peers, and, sometimes, a paralyzing isolation that leaves individuals depressed and suicidal.

The closet didn't just happen. The aggressive enforcement of heterosexuality as an identity and way of life produced it. Specifically, the closet took shape in response to a culture that polluted homosexuality and policed behavior by stigmatizing gender nonconformity as a sign of homosexuality. And, through the repressive (censoring, criminalizing, and disenfranchising) practices of the state, the homosexual was driven from public life. By the 1950s the closet had become the defining reality for many gay Americans.

The closet is a strategy of accommodating to heterosexual domination. Individuals choose the closet to manage what is considered a deviant identity; it makes possible social respect and integration, even if it may cost the individual his or her sense of personal integrity and well-being. There is enormous variation in closet patterns. . . .

[The] shift in the emotional, moral, and social texture of the closet after Stonewall is evident in the stories of Bill, Robert, and Renee. . . . They each grew up in a world organized around heterosexuality. But there was a well-organized visible movement and gay subcultures in many cities that celebrated being gay as good. Despite the weight of society pressuring them to live heterosexually, the decision to live as a "heterosexual" wasn't a foregone conclusion. Individuals coming of age after the 1970s had a sense of choice that was for all practical purposes absent [before]. But the flip side was that choosing to be closeted was likely much more anguished and difficult

for these later generations. . . . Being in the closet was now associated with living a false, inauthentic life. . . .

Stonewall likely had the effect of driving many individuals deeply into the closet. Indeed, many homosexuals who came of age in the 1950s and early 1960s thought that this new social assertiveness and visibility would bring about greater social repression; it would also create considerable turmoil for many homosexuals who had managed a more or less comfortable social adjustment in the closet. They were in some ways right. While the closet doors may have tightened for some, they were loosened, even unhinged, for many others. "Out of the closet" became the slogan of the new gay liberationist movement.

The closet is an unstable social condition. While its purpose is to keep homosexuals silent and invisible, its very creation causes a heightened public awareness of homosexuality. Laws criminalizing homosexuality, police harassing and arresting homosexuals, and newspapers publishing their names in order to shame them have the effect of both enforcing heterosexual domination and heightening public awareness of the pervasive presence of homosexuals. The closet may expel real, living homosexuals from visible public life, but it makes this sexual personage into a haunting symbolic presence.[12] The status of the closeted homosexual as both omnipresent but unseen shapes a culture of homosexual suspicion. In principle, no one is to be spared. No matter how impeccable an individual's heterosexual credentials, he or she is not entirely free of suspicion. A flawless heterosexual presentation may, after all, be taken as masking a latent homosexual self.

The closet has another ironic effect. It creates a heightened self-awareness on the part of homosexually oriented individuals. The social pressure to methodically conceal rivets attention precisely on that which is proscribed: homosexuality. For some closeted individuals, homosexuality becomes a core self-identity as daily life centers on either avoiding suspicion of homosexuality or coming out. And the fashioning of homosexuality into a core social identity makes rebellion against the closet possible—and likely. At an individual level, rebellion often meant coming out, affirming a gay self, and becoming part of a gay community. At a political level, a movement took shape—gay liberationism and lesbian feminism—that challenged the institutional and cultural supports of the closet; that is, the culture of pollution and the state-backed policy of repression. This movement has, by all accounts, been enormously successful even if so many battles have been lost and so many remain to be waged.

The era of the closet is hardly over. Yet the present is a world apart from that of just one or two decades ago. The universe of the butch, the queen, the normal straight, the culture of camp, the seamless and open homophobic culture, and uniform state and institutional repression are taking on the character of a historical era. The closet has not disappeared, but there are today more people choosing to live beyond the closet.

NOTES

1. Consider this description of the world of a middle-class lesbian living in the late 1920s and 1930s: "During the 1920s and 1930s Boyer Reinstein was an active lesbian within a community of lesbian friends. She had few, if any, negative feelings about being a lesbian, and she was 'out' to her immediate family. . . . Yet, she did not publicly disclose being gay. She was always discreet." The author, Elizabeth Kennedy, cautions against using the concept of the closet to depict Reinstein's social world. "I am afraid using the term 'closet' to refer to the culture of the 1920s and 1930s might be anachronistic." Elizabeth Kennedy, "'But We Would Never Talk about It': The Structures of Lesbian Discretion in South Dakota, 1928–1933," in *Inventing Lesbian Cultures in America*, ed. Ellen Lewin (Boston: Beacon Press, 1996). Similarly, George Chauncey describes a working-class gay culture in which gays and straights openly mingle in saloons, cafeterias, rent parties, and speakeasies. The gay world before World War I is said to be very different from the era inaugurated by the Stonewall rebellions. For example, the language and concept of "coming out of the closet" was foreign to this gay world. "Gay people in the prewar years . . . did not speak of coming out of what we call the gay closet but rather of coming out into what they called homosexual society or the gay world, a world neither so small, nor so isolated, nor . . . so hidden as closet implies." George Chauncey, *Gay New York Gender, Urban Culture, and the Making of the Gay Male World, 1890–1940* (New York: Basic Books, 1994).

2. For descriptions of homosexual life in the 1950s and 1960s, *The Mattachine Review* and *The Ladder,* respectively published by the Mattachine Society and the Daughters of Bilitis, are superb sources. For examples of personal testimony, see Peter Nardi, David Sanders, and Judd Marmor, eds., *Growing up before Stonewall: Life Stories of Some Gay Men* (New York: Routledge, 1994); Donald Vining, *A Gay Diary,* 5 vols. (New York: Pepys Press, 1979–93); Martin Duberman, *Cures: A Gay Man's Odyssey* (New York: Dutton, 1991); Robert Reinhart, *A History of Shadows: A Novel* (Boston: Alyson, 1986); Audre Lorde, *Zami: A New Spelling of My Name* (New York: Crossing Press, 1982); Andrea Weiss and Greta Schiller, *Before Stonewall; The Making of the Gay and Lesbian Community* (New York: Naiad Press, 1988); Jonathan Ned Katz, *Gay American History* (New York: Meridian, 1976) and *Gay/Lesbian Almanac* (New York: Harper and Row, 1983); and Eric Marcus, *Making History: The Struggle for Gay and Lesbian Equal Rights: An Oral History* (New York: HarperCollins, 1992). For informative popular and academic work of the time, see Daniel Webster Cory [psuedonym Edward Sagarin], *The Homosexual in America* (New York: Peter Nevill, 1951); Evelyn Hooker, "Male Homosexuals and Their Worlds," in *Sexual Inversion,* ed. J. Marmor (New York: Basic Books, 1965); Martin Hoffman, *The Gay World* (New York Basic Books, 1968); Del Martin and Phyllis Lyon, *Lesbian/Woman* (San Francisco: Bantam, 1972); Sidney Abbott and Barbara Love, *Sappho Was a Right-On Woman: A Liberated View of Lesbianism* (New York: Stein and Day, 1972); John Gagnon and William Simon, "The Lesbians: A Preliminary Overview," in *Sexual Deviance,* ed. William Simon and John Gagnon (New York Harper and Row, 1967). For some current scholarly perspectives on gay life in the immediate postwar years, see John D'Emilio, *Sexual Politics, Sexual Communities: The Making of a Homosexual Minority in the United States, 1940–1970* (Chicago: University of Chicago Press, 1983); Lillian Faderman, *Odd Girls* and *Twilight Lovers: A History of Lesbian Life in Twentieth-Century America* (New York: Columbia University Press, 1991); Elizabeth Kennedy and Madeline Davis, *Boots of Leather, Slippers of Gold: The History of a Lesbian Community* (New York: Roudedge, 1993); Leila J. Rupp, "'Imagine My Surprise': Women's Relationships in Mid-Twentieth-Century America," in *Hidden from History,* ed. M. Duberman, M. Vicinus and G. Chauncey Jr. (New York: Meridian, 1990); Rochella Thorpe, "'A House where Queers Go': African-American Lesbian Nightlife in Detroit, 1940–1975," in *Inventing Lesbian Cultures in America,* ed. Ellen Lewin (Boston: Beacon Press, 1996); and Marc Stein, *City of Sisterly*

and Brotherly Loves: Lesbian and Gay Philadelphia, 1945–72 (Chicago: University of Chicago Press, 2000).

3. To understand the social context of the 1950s as a time of both change and anxiety, especially regarding gender and intimate life, I have drawn on the following: Wini Breines, *Young, White, and Miserable: Growing up Female in the Fifties* (Boston: Beacon Press, 1992); Stephanie Coontz, *The Way We Never Were: American Families and the Nostalgia Trap* (New York: Basic Books, 1992); Barbara Ehrenreich, *Hearts of Men: American Dreams and the Flight from Commitment* (Garden City, N.Y.: Anchor Books, 1983); Elaine Tyler May, *Homeward Bound: American Families in the Cold War Era* (New York: Basic Books, 1988); Jessica Weiss, *To Have and to Hold: Marriage, the Baby Boom, and Social Change* (Chicago: University of Chicago Press, 2000); Cynthia Enloe, *The Morning after: Sexual Politics and the End of the Cold War* (Berkeley: University of California Press, 1993); and Robert Corber, *In the Name of National Security: Hitchcock, Homophobia, and the Political Construction of Gender in Postwar America* (Durham, N.C.: Duke University Press, 1993).

4. On the making of the closet in the 1950s, see John D'Emilio, "The Homosexual Menace: The Politics of Sexuality in Cold War America," in *Making Trouble: Essays on Gay History, Politics, and the University* (New York: Routledge, 1992), and *Sexual Politics, Sexual Communities;* Allan Berube and John D'Emilio, "The Military and Lesbians during the McCarthy Years," *Signs* 9 (Summer 1984): 759–75; Barbara Epstein, "Anti-Communism, Homophobia, and the Construction of Masculinity in the Postwar U.S." *Critical Sociology* 20 (1994): 21–44; Faderman, *Odd Girls;* Robert Corber, *Homosexuality in Cold War America: Resistance and the Crisis of Masculinity* (Durham, N.C.: Duke University Press, 1997); and Gerard Sullivan, "Political Opportunism and the Harassment of Homosexuals in Florida, 1952–1965," *Journal of Homosexuality* 37 (1999): 57–81.

5. Chauncey, *Gay New York,* p. 6; William Eskridge Jr., *Gaylaw: Challenging the Apartheid of the Closet* (Cambridge, Mass.: Harvard University Press, 1999), p. 13; Paul Monette, *Becoming a Man: Half a Life Story* (New York: HarperCollins, 1992), p. 2; Joseph Beam, "Leaving the Shadows Behind," in *In the Life: A Black Gay Anthology,* ed. Joseph Beam (Boston: Alyson, 1986), p. 16.

6. In his memoir, Mel White, the former ghostwriter for Billy Graham and Jerry Falwell, movingly describes his experience of isolation: "I was isolated, not by bars or guards in uniforms, but by fear. I was surrounded by my loving family and close friends, but there was no way to explain to them my desperate, lonely feelings even when we were together. I wasn't tortured by leather straps or cattle prods, but my guilt and fear kept me in constant torment. . . . I was starving for the kind of human intimacy that would satisfy my longing, end my loneliness." White says that this isolation made him "feel like an alien who had been abandoned on a strange planet. . . . Living rooms and dining rooms, restaurants and lobbies, became foreign, unfriendly places. [I grew] weary of pretending to be someone I was not, tired of hiding my feelings. . . . My once lively spirit was shriveling like a raisin in the sun. . . . Desperation and loneliness surged. . . . I felt trapped and terrified." Mel White, *Stranger at the Gate: To Be Gay and Christian in America* (New York: Plume, 1995), pp. 123, 177–78.

7. Allan Berube describes the closet as a "system of lies, denials, disguises, and double entendres—that had enabled them to express some of their homosexuality by pretending it didn't exist and hiding it from view." Berube, *Coming Out under Fire,* p. 271.

8. My research suggests that the category of the closet initially appeared in the writing of gay liberationists. The earliest reference I've found was an "editorial" statement in the short-lived newspaper *Come Out!* in 1969. By the early 1970s the concept of the closet was widely circulating in liberationist writings; e.g., Signo Canceris, "From the Closet," *Fag Rag* 4 (January 1973); Bruce Gilbert "Coming Out," *Fag Rag* 23/24 (1976); Morgan Pinney, "Out of Your Closets," *Gay Sunshine* 1 (October 1970); Ian Young, "Closet Wrecking," *Gay Sunshine* 28 (Spring 1976); Jennifer Woodhul, "Darers Go First," *The Furies* 1 (June/July 1972); and Allen Young, "Out of the Closets, into the Streets," in *Out of the Closets,* ed. Karla Jay and Allen Young. The closet underscored a condition of oppression. Gays were not merely discriminated against but dominated. And the closet was not a product of individual ignorance or prejudice but a social system of heterosexual domination. The core institutions and culture of America were said to be organized to enforce the norm and ideal of heterosexuality. In short, the closet underscored the way a system of compulsory heterosexuality creates a separate and oppressed homosexual existence. By arguing that the very organization of American society compels homosexuals to live socially isolated, inauthentic lives, the category of the closet served both as a way to understand gay life and as a critique of America.

By the mid-1970s, as liberationism gave way to a politics of minority rights, the concept of the closet was in wide use. However, its meaning began to change. Within the minority rights discourse that triumphed in the late 1970s, the closet was viewed as an act of concealment in response to actual or anticipated prejudice; it was seen as a matter of individual choice. By, the late 1970s and 1980s, some gays were arguing that America had become a much more tolerant nation; the risks of coming out were greatly diminished. Being in or out of the closet was now seen as an individual choice rather than an adjustment to heterosexual domination. In fact, gays began to feel considerable pressure to come out, as many came to believe that visibility was both more possible and a key to challenging prejudice. For example, David Goodstein, the owner and editor of *The Advocate* from roughly the mid-1970s through the mid-1980s, gravitated to a view of the closet as almost self-imposed, as a product of "low self-esteem" or "cowardice." "I truly believe that there is no reason for you to be closeted and hide who you are" (*The Advocate,* 1983, p. 6). Goodstein blamed social intolerance in part on the cowardice of those who choose to be closeted. "I take a dim view of staying in the closet. . . . What brings up my irritation at this time . . . is the price we uncloseted gay people pay for the cowardice and stupidity of our [closeted] brothers and sisters" ("Opening Spaces," *The Advocate,* 1981, p. 6).

I have stated my preference for a liberationist approach. If the concept of the closet is to help us to understand changes in gay life, it should be used in a way that indicates more than an act of concealment. In this regard, the liberationist idea of the closet as a condition of social oppression is persuasive. Explaining gay subordination, at least from the 1950s through the 1980s, as a product of individual prejudice or ignorance makes it hard, if not impossible, to understand its socially patterned character. It was not simply that gays were disadvantaged in one institution or only by isolated acts of discrimination or disrespect, but gay subordination occurred across institutions and culture. Heterosexual privilege was aggressively enforced by the state, cultural practices, daily acts of harassment and violence, and by institutions such as marriage, the wedding industry, and a dense network of laws covering taxes, family, immigration, military policy, and so on. At least during the heyday of the closet, the social risks of exposure were so great that it is naive to speak of the closet as an individual choice. In short, the concept of the closet helps us to understand the way heterosexuality functioned as an "institution" or a "system" that oppressed gay people.

A liberationist approach requires, however, some modification. In particular, the closet should be approached as a product of historically specific social dynamics; in particular, a culture of homosexual pollution and state repression. Furthermore, liberationists tend to read heterosexual domination as so closely and deeply intertwined with a whole system of gender, racial, economic, and political domination that

America is viewed as irredeemably repressive. Such totalizing views are not credible.

9. Class is absent from much of queer social analysis. There are theoretical and rhetorical appeals to the importance of class, but little social research that addresses class patterns of concealment and coming out, gay and lesbian identification, and workplace dynamics. I have made use of the following work: Nicole Field, *Over the Rainbow: Money, Clans, and Homophobia* (London: Pluto Press, 1995); Steve Valocchi, "The Class-Inflected Nature of Gay Identity," *Social Problems* 46 (1999): 207–44; Katie Gilmartin, "We Weren't Bar People: Middle Class Identities and Cultural Space," *Gay and Lesbian Quarterly* 3 (1996): 1–5; Roger Lancaster, *Life Is Hard: Machismo, Danger, and the Intimacy of Power in Nicaragua* (Berkeley: University of California Press, 1992); and David Evans, *Sexual Citizenship: The Material Construction of Sexualities* (London: Routledge, 1993). Joshua Gamson's *Freaks Talk Back: Tabloid Talk Shows and Sexual Nonconformity* (Chicago: University of Chicago Press, 1998) and Chrys Ingraham's *White Weddings: Romancing Heterosexuality in Popular Culture* (New York: Routledge, 1999) weave class into an analysis of sexual identities in interesting ways. Lillian Faderman's *Odd Girls, Twilight Lovers* and Kennedy and Davis's *Boots of Leather, Slippers of Gold* are indispensable sources for understanding the role of class in early postwar lesbian life.

10. There is a substantial theoretical and research literature on the role of gender in shaping patterns of sexual identification and dynamics of the closet and coming out. The literature of gay liberationism and lesbian feminism is crucial. On the tradition of lesbian feminism, see Nancy Myron and Charlotte Bunch, eds., *Lesbianism and the Women's Movement.* (Baltimore: Diana Press, 1975). For gay liberationism, see Karla Jay and Allen Young, eds., *Out of the Closets: Voices of Gay Liberationism,* (New York: New York University Press, 1992 [1972]). For more recent theoretical and empirical statements, see Judith Butler, *Gender Trouble: Feminism and the Subversion of Gender* (New York: Routledge, 1990); Biddy Martin, "Sexualities without Genders and Other Queer Utopias," *Diacritics* 24 (Summer 1994): 104–21; Chrys Ingraham, "The Heterosexual Imaginary: Feminist Sociology and Theories of Gender," in *Queer Theory/Sociology,* ed. Steven Seidman (Cambridge: Blackwell, 1996); Peggy Reeves Sanday, *Fraternity Gang Rape: Sex, Brotherhood, and Privilege on Campus* (New York: New York University, 1990); Christine Williams and Arlene Stein, eds., *Sexuality and Gender* (Maiden, Mass.: Blackwell, 2002); and Kath Weston, *Render Me, Gender Me: Lesbians Talk Sex, Class, Color,*

Nation, Studmuffins (New York: Columbia University Press, 1996).

It is interesting to note that the term *the closet* was initially developed in liberationist texts, which, though a mid-gender movement, was shaped considerably by men. By contrast, the chief architects of lesbian feminism such as Charlotte Bunch, Rita Mae Brown, Ti Grace Atkinson, the Furies Collective, and New York Radicalesbians did not place the concept of the closet at the center of their thinking and politics. To the extent that being a lesbian was understood as a political act of resistance to male dominance and compulsory heterosexuality, it was the struggle against sexism and the development of a women-centered culture that was the political focus. With the decline of lesbian feminism, along with the gradual development of a gender-integrated gay movement, the closet and issues of coming out became more prominent in lesbian writing as well.

11. For a wonderful illustration of the thickness of gender codes in contemporary America, see Deirdre McCloskey's description of gender passing in her memoir, *Crossing* (Chicago: University of Chicago Press, 1999), pp. 160–62.

12. For approaches to the closet that emphasize dynamics of knowledge/ignorance, presence/absence and its haunting power, see Sedgwick, *The Epistemology of the Closet,* Diana Fuss, "Inside/Out," in *Inside/Out: Lesbian Theories, Gay Theories* (New York: Routledge, 1991); Michael Moon, "Flaming Closets," in *Out in Culture: Gay, Lesbian, and Queer Essays on Popular Culture,* ed. Corey Creekmur and Alexander Doty (Durham, N.C.: Duke University Press, 1995); and Lee Edelman, "Tearooms and Sympathy, or, The Epistemology of the Water Closet," in *The Lesbian and Gay Studies Reader,* ed. Henry Abelove, Michele Aina Barale, and David Halperin (New York: Routledge, 1993).

LGBTQ Politics in America: An Abbreviated History

Chet Meeks

The lesbian, gay, bisexual, transgender, queer (LGBTQ) community has been the target of systematic, institutionalized forms of regulation in American society since at least the middle of the 20th century. This means that LGBTQ people are not merely discriminated against by particular individuals, but that a social norm making heterosexuality superior is embedded in and informs the logics of all of America's core social institutions: the state, the criminal justice system, the media, education, and the family. American social institutions have worked to make any sexuality deviating from the heterosexual norm criminal and deviant. When a group of individuals is systematically regulated in such a way, they sometimes organize to create social changes in the areas of law, public opinion, or social policy. Sometimes they try to revolutionize how we think of and practice sex itself. This is what we mean by "sexual politics," and here I offer an abbreviated history of LGBTQ politics in America.

The first rumblings of LGBTQ resistance could be felt in the 1950s. Harry Hay and Rudi Gernreich organized a group called the Mattachine Society. Del Martin and Phyl-

lis Lyon organized the Daughters of Bilitis at almost the same time. Some others were ONE, and The Society for Individual Rights. These early groups called themselves "homophile" organizations. They emerged in response to the state-sponsored harassment and criminalization of homosexuality in America. America in the 1950s was a place where homosexuality, like communism, had come to be associated with evil and moral bankruptcy. Homophile organizations were fledgling groups, and only ever partially visible in the mainstream public sphere. They spoke through heterosexual proxies, like tolerant doctors or lawyers, in order to make their case about a given issue. Homophile groups had some successes, though. For example ONE sued the American postal service in 1958 for refusing to mail their monthly magazine. But in reality, a strong, vocal, and truly organized LGBTQ politics did not really get underway until the late 1960s.

On June 28, 1969, a brawl broke out between New York City police officers and some drag queens at a Greenwich Village bar called the Stonewall. The Stonewall riots marked the beginning of a new era in LGBTQ politics. From the spirit of rebellion at Stonewall, two LGBTQ organizations were born: The Gay Liberation Front and The

Gay Activist Alliance. Although these organizations are no longer around, the spirit and worldview that animated their respective political actions remain very much present in contemporary forms of LGBTQ struggle.

The Gay Liberation Front was organized by Martha Shelley, Craig Rodwell, and Jim Fourrat three weeks after the Stonewall riots. As their name suggests, the Gay Liberation Front espoused a liberationist worldview. According to liberationists, America is a society that systematically demonizes, criminalizes, and ghettoizes all forms of sexual and gender expression that do not conform to a very narrow standard of heterosexual "normality." Struggle and resistance, in a world like this, cannot be limited to demanding civil rights, reform, or tolerance. Rather, revolution—sexual revolution in particular—is the only viable option. Borrowing an idea from feminism, liberationists argued that "the personal is political," and they believed that only by transforming sexuality could the broader social fabric be revolutionized. They encouraged their members to experiment with new forms of "liberated" sexuality and social relationships—like non-monogamy and communal living. Liberationists, moreover, viewed the plight of LGBTQ people as indelibly linked to the problems faced by black Americans, third world people and refugees, the victims of American and European military aggression, and the working classes. They struggled alongside the Black Panthers and critics of the Vietnam War demanding justice for all oppressed people.

Although the Gay Activist Alliance emerged at nearly the same time and in the same political climate as the Gay Liberation Front, they possessed a worldview that was very different than that of the liberationists. They did not believe that the plight faced by lesbians and gay men was necessarily linked to other forms of oppression, like race or class status. Neither did they believe that American society was systematically anti-queer, in the way suggested by liberationists. Rather, they believed that, at bottom, America was a tolerant and just society, one that had successfully integrated a large number of minority groups. American institutions, they argued, are copious and open to change. The problem was that this tolerance had not yet reached lesbians, gay men, transgender people, and bisexuals.

Sexual revolution was not the answer, according to the Gay Activist Alliance. They were not liberationists, but reformists. They believed that tolerance and respect for LGBTQ people had to be won through the slow, incremental reform of existing institutions. They believed that,

just as black Americans and women had fought to gain civil rights reforms in the 1960s and 1970s, lesbians and gay men must fight to be recognized as respectable Americans. They fought to pass civil rights ordinances in cities like New York. Unlike the liberationists, they focused much less on the sexual lives of activists themselves, and they eschewed attempts to connect lesbian and gay justice to the struggles of other groups.

Although the Gay Liberation Front and the Gay Activist Alliance have long since disbanded, the worldviews that animated their activism are very much alive. The liberationist worldview was reborn in the radical sexual politics of the 1980s and 1990s, in groups like Act-Up and Queer Nation. The Reagan Administration of the 1980s had completely ignored the growing AIDS epidemic, largely because gay men were the most visible victims of the disease. Also, large pharmaceutical companies were making the drugs used to treat AIDS symptoms so expensive that only the very wealthy could afford them. Against this stifling climate, Act-Up shouted "Silence equals Death," and against the growing stigmatization of gay and queer people due to AIDS, Queer Nation shouted "We're Here, We're Queer, Get Used to It!" Like liberationists, Act-Up and Queer Nation linked notions of social revolution to self-transformation. And they believed that nothing would ever truly change until queer people had put an end to "straight tyranny." More recently, the National Lesbian and Gay Task Force took a vocal stance against the Bush Administration's decision to declare war on Iraq. Echoing the earlier liberationist worldview, they argued that the heightened patriotism and nationalism of wartime often results in heightened violence toward minorities, including gays and lesbians, who are perceived to be "anti-American."

As for the Gay Activist Alliance, their reformist spirit remains central to many of the most visible contemporary LGBTQ organizations. Coming to power largely in the 1990s, the Human Rights Campaign, the Lambda Legal Defense and Education Fund, and the Gay and Lesbian Alliance Against Defamation all borrow from the worldview of the Gay Activist Alliance. The Human Rights Campaign has become an extremely successful lobbying organization in Washington, DC. It has over 600,000 members, and they lobby Congress continually for Federal hate crimes legislation and other legal reforms to make LGBTQ people safe and equal citizens. Both the Human Rights Campaign and the Lambda Legal Defense and Education Fund have been slowly but surely making inroads in the fight toward lesbian and gay equality in the arena of marriage. Lambda was the first organization to successfully take a marriage lawsuit to a state Supreme Court in the famous *Baehr v. Lewin* case in Hawaii in 1993. GLAAD was declared by *Entertainment Weekly* to be one of the most successful media organizations in the country. GLAAD came into existence in an era when LGBTQ people were only vilified on television and in the media, when they were represented at all. Today, the GLAAD awards (given for fair, accurate, and positive portrayals of LGBTQ people) are coveted by many of Hollywood's most elite actors, actresses, directors, and producers.

A lot has changed in American society since the 1950s and 1960s, when the postal service refused to carry LGBTQ publications, when cities like New York still had laws requiring that everyone wear at least "three articles of gender appropriate clothing," and when police would frequently raid bars like the Stonewall in order to harass their patrons. We live in the world of *Will and Grace, Queer as Folk,* and

Lawrence v. Texas.[1] LGBTQ inequality nonetheless persists, as does the norm of heterosexuality, even if in more subtle forms. LGBTQ people still face violence in their everyday lives, and second-class status in most areas of social policy. It will be up to tomorrow's LGBTQ political organizations to tackle these problems—but in doing so, they will likely borrow from the tactics and worldviews of their historical predecessors.

NOTE

1. *Lawrence v. Texas* was decided in 2003. This case struck down the ruling in an earlier case, *Bowers v. Hardwick,* decided in 1986, in which the Supreme Court ruled that homosexuals had no Constitutional protections against laws that criminalized sodomy. With *Lawrence v. Texas,* an era where homosexuality could be made officially criminal was finally over. The case was remarkable because the Supreme Court very rarely goes against its previous decisions, and because it provides LGBTQ people with a new legal precedent when battling for other rights such as marriage.

The "Pinking" of Viagra Culture: Drug Industry Efforts to Create and Repackage Sex Drugs for Women

Heather Hartley

The year 2003 marked both the 5th anniversary of Viagra's launch and the release of two prominent new competitors to Viagra's multi-billion-dollar annual market share: Levitra and Cialis. The makers of these products, Bayer HealthCare Pharmaceuticals/Glaxo-SmithKline (Levitra) and Lilly ICOS (Cialis) promote the ideology that *more* is better. Both products are advertised as "lasting longer" than Viagra, with Cialis even nicknamed "the weekender" because of its alleged 36-hour range of effectiveness. In general, of course, the pharmaceutical industry embraces the philosophy that "more is better," especially when the topic is profit. The success of the blockbuster drug Viagra—and the concomitant spread of a "Viagra culture"—prompted the industry both to develop other drugs to treat male sexual problems, and served as an incentive for it to espouse a medical approach to women's sexual problems and develop new sex drugs to treat those problems. Just as happened with men's problems, women's sexual problems became increasingly medicalized—defined and understood as a largely physiologically based set of conditions called "female sexual dysfunction" (FSD).

That the annual market for medical treatments for women's sexual woes is estimated at about $1.7 billion creates tremendous incentives for pharmaceutical companies to develop a specific, FDA-approved "Viagra for women" (Leland, 2000). At the time of writing (January 2006), despite a huge outlay of expense and effort, there is no drug approved for FSD—currently, the only FDA-approved prescription treatment is a mechanical clitoris-stimulator called EROS-CTD. Proctor and Gamble's testosterone patch, Intrinsa, was the first (and so far, only) drug to be considered by the FDA, and it did not receive FDA-approval. But a variety of other products for women—pills, patches, creams, sprays—are being developed and tested by over a dozen pharmaceutical companies (Enserik, 2005).

The heart of this [reading] focuses on two interrelated aspects of Viagra culture playing out in drug industry efforts to create and expand a market for sex drugs for women. These industry efforts concentrate along two main strategies: (1) a "hunt for the Pink Viagra" to treat the "disease" of FSD, the chronology of which involved an almost unnoticed shift from development of products to treat arousal problems to those intended for desire problems, and (2) the increasing promotion and normalization of off-label uses of men's sex drugs for women.

Since the late 1990s, the drug industry has increased its power to shape definitions of women's sexual problems and has built institutional capacity enabling it to develop and promote sex drugs for women. Events and activities of particular significance include the mass dissemination of estimates of disease prevalence; the institutionalization of FSD in academic circles; and public-relations stimulated mainstream media coverage.

Industry Consolidation of Power and Building of Capacity

Inflated Epidemiology Promotes a Medicalized View of Women's Sexuality

No accounting of drug industry interest in FSD would be complete without reference to the "43–31" study, shorthand for the widely-cited study published in *JAMA* (Journal of the American Medical Association) that concluded that more than 4 out of 10 women (43%) have sexual problems, a rate of sexual dysfunction higher than that of men (31%) (Laumann et al., 1999). The critiques of this statistic are widespread (see Moynihan, 2003a), and even Laumann himself has gone on record saying his findings were appropriated to promote the medicalization of sexual problems (O'Connor, 2005), yet both mass media and professional literature constantly cite this figure. The pharmaceutical industry in particular has used this "inflated epidemiology" to expand a medicalized perspective on women's sexual problems (Tiefer, 2002). Subsequent studies indicating lower prevalence rates and supporting social-psychological rather than physical factors as primary determinants of women's sexual problems (e.g. Bancroft, 2002; Bancroft et al., 2003) receive almost no media attention.

The Institutionalization of FSD

FSD has become institutionalized in academic circles in a manner that solidifies pharma-medical control over the naming and treatment of women's sexual problems. Key milestones in the institutionalization process include: development of systems of disease classification amenable to medical approaches; creation of a legitimized infrastructure for disseminating supporting research and education; formation of an attendant professional organization; and establishment of an appropriate medical specialty.

The American Psychiatric Association's *Diagnostic and Statistical Manual of Mental Disorders* (DSM) is the most widely used system for classifying women's sexual problems, specifying four categories: lack of desire, lack of arousal, pain during intercourse, and lack of orgasm (APA, 1994; see Tiefer, 2004 for a critique). In 1998, a consensus conference, consisting of a group of 19 sexuality researchers and clinicians (18 of whom had financial ties to the pharmaceutical industry) was convened to revise the DSM nomenclature. Ultimately, the system was revised in a manner that facilitates a platform for a new area of physical medicine (for details, see Basson et al., 2000; Tiefer, 2000). . . .

Strategy I: Securing FDA Approval for a Woman's Sex Drug

Pfizer determined that clinical trials of Viagra in women showed that it is no more effective than a placebo, and the company stopped the trials in February 2004 (Harris, 2004). While some drug companies are still developing products that follow a "Viagra model" by targeting genital blood flow (e.g. alprostadil), and others are developing products like PT-141 that aim to augment dopamine-like brain chemicals (Enserik, 2005), arguably the main focus in drug development now is on products specifically intended to enhance sexual desire, mainly through the administration of testosterone. At least seven drug companies are developing testosterone products for women (NAMS, 2005).

When Viagra was being tested in women, the targeted condition was "female sexual arousal disorder" (FSAD). When these trials came up empty, not only did the focus in drug development shift to testosterone but also the intended targeted condition changed to "hypoactive sexual desire disorder" (HSDD). Just months after Pfizer pulled the plug on the Viagra trials because the drug did not enhance arousal, Proctor and Gamble (P&G) announced plans to seek FDA approval later that year for its Intrinsa testosterone patch to treat desire problems. This shift from FSD "being about" an arousal problem to FSD "being about" a desire problem seems to have gone largely unnoticed by most cultural commentators. Yet the shift in focus from FSAD to HSDD is a dramatic illustration of active drug industry "disease mongering" tactics (Payer, 1992; Tiefer, 2006)—the change seems to indicate an effort to match up some drug (*any drug?*) with some subcomponent (*any subcomponent?*) of the DSM classification. Did women's problems with arousal suddenly go away? Of course not, but mainstream media, following the P&G marketing spin, proclaimed the failure of the Viagra trials to be evidence of women's "more complex" sexuality, and they moved on to the "next big thing."

The "Hormone of Desire"

And the "next big thing" was the focus on testosterone as the "hormone of desire." A dominant medical explanation for "hypoactive sexual desire disorder"

(HSDD) is that it is a product of "androgen insufficiency syndrome" (Fishman, 2004). This linkage has fueled development and promotion of androgen replacement therapies for women's sexual problems—primarily prescription-only testosterone and over-the-counter dehydroepiandrosterone (DHEA) treatments (see Hartley, 2003). In spite of the known risks of such therapies (Basson et al., 2001; Fourcroy, 2001), the paucity of data on the efficacy of such treatments, and even prominent articles that demonstrate *no linkage* between low sexual desire and low testosterone levels (Davis et al., 2005), drug development efforts increasingly concentrate in this area and growing numbers of physicians are prescribing testosterone off-label to women.

With hopes of being the first to win FDA approval (key to dominating the market), P&G sought approval for its Intrinsa testosterone patch in December 2004. The FDA advisory committee determined that the benefit of the drug (an average of one additional sex act per month) was overshadowed by the patch's potential health risks. The recent drug safety scandals surrounding Vioxx and hormone replacement therapy (HRT) likely influenced the FDA advisors to be more risk-adverse than in the past, and they *unanimously* voted against approval of Intrinsa. Critics were also particularly concerned that were Intrinsa approved for its target population—surgically menopausal women also taking estrogen—that marketing surrounding the drug would also target and drive up off-label prescriptions for women outside that main group.[1] Ironically, P&G tried to use the existence of off-label prescribing of testosterone to its advantage. Especially for prescription testosterone products, determining off-label dosage for women is a guessing game, and P&G has argued that its patch would insure more consistent and accurate dosage (Neff, 2003).

Strategy II (The New Game): Off-Label Prescribing of Men's Sex Drugs to Women

The two erectile dysfunction drugs approved in the US after Viagra, Levitra and Cialis, represent only the tip of the iceberg, as a wide variety of other products are in development for men, including drugs for premature ejaculation and PT-141, a nasal spray intended to act as an aphrodisiac. Additionally, testosterone replacement products such as AndroGel and Testim are increasingly promoted as treatments for men's sexual problems. While none of these drugs approved for use in men—Viagra, Levitra, Cialis, AndroGel, and Testim—has been sufficiently tested or proven for use in women, increasingly, when women discuss their sexual problems with their doctors, they are given "off-label" prescriptions for one or another of these products. Testosterone researcher Dr. Jan Shifren estimates that one-fifth of all the prescriptions of testosterone products approved for men are actually written (off-label) for women (Kantrowitz and Wingert, 2005).

The Federal Drug Administration Modernization Act (FDAMA) of 1997 loosened the restrictions on the type of information that drug companies could share with physicians regarding off-label uses for their drugs (Conrad and Leiter, 2004), thus facilitating a general growth in off-label prescribing. Although drug companies are not allowed officially to market drugs for off-label uses, the companies are largely able to circumvent this law by "merely informing" doctors of these uses at "educational" CME [continuing medical education] conferences (Angell, 2004). A key reason why numbers of physicians are writing these off-label prescriptions for women is their exposure to presentations at CME conferences on FSD (such as those hosted by ISSWSH [International Society for the Study of Women's Sexual Health]) that have promoted a biomedical perspective on sexual problems, conceptualized women's sexual problems as largely based in "androgen deficiencies," and reported "anecdotal" stories of success in treating female patients with testosterone (Fishman, 2004; Hartley, 2003; Hartley and Tiefer, 2003; Loe, 2004). Such off-label prescribing is also becoming increasingly normalized in mainstream media accounts of FSD. For example, the 3 May 2004 *CBS Evening News* ran a segment showing two women being treated with testosterone for their libido problems (CBSNEWS, 2004).

Five years ago, it seemed that such off-label prescribing practices represented a "side game" in the larger effort to pharmacologically manage women's sexual problems—a way to prescribe a little something to women until they got their own FDA-approved "Pink Viagra." Today, however, it is becoming increasingly clear that off-label prescribing represents something much larger: a way to circumvent the FDA-approval process altogether in some cases. Why bother to conduct expensive clinical trials and risk having a drug denied approval in the end? . . .

Controversy and Critique: Public Health Advocacy and Challenges to Medicalization

The medicalization of women's sexual problems is being met with growing resistance and critique. For example, in January 2003, Australian journalist and pharmaceutical-industry gadfly Ray Moynihan published an article in the *British Medical Journal* (*BMJ*) that generated an impressive number of responses from both critics and supporters of the pharmaceutical industry's development of an FSD drug. The take-home message of the piece, entitled "The Making of a Disease: Female Sexual Dysfunction," is that FSD is a prime example of "the corporate-sponsored creation of a disease" (Moynihan, 2003a: 45). As core evidence, Moynihan presents data on the significant levels of industry sponsorship of key FSD conferences . . . arguing that the companies funded the meetings to create a "clearly defined medical diagnosis with measurable characteristics to facilitate credible clinical trials" (Moynihan, 2003a: 45. See Hartley, 2003 and Hartley and Tiefer, 2003 for similar observations). As evidence of the fear the article generated in the drug industry, an unnamed pharmaceutical company—Pfizer, Bayer and Lilly-ICOS are the likely candidates—even hired a public relations company to launch a global campaign to counter the charges made in the piece (Moynihan, 2003b).

Critical viewpoints on FSD have also been appearing in a growing number of mainstream publications. For example, in 2005, the *Seattle Times* ran several stories exploring the process of disease-mongering for its series entitled "Suddenly Sick," featuring FSD as one of its prime examples (Kelleher, 2005). As

another example, the *Los Angeles Times* published a critical piece later that year on Jennifer Berman's new Rodeo Drive practice (O'Connor, 2005). And as discussed . . . by Leonore Tiefer, an activist/advocacy group called the New View Campaign has used a variety of tactics to challenge the disease-mongering of FSD for over five years.[2] Since its 2000 inception, the New View has emphasized the *prevention* of women's sexual problems and has called for resituating women's sexuality within the *political* domain (away from the health-and-treatment domain). Several New View members testified against Intrinsa approval at the FDA hearing, and the group assembled and made available a range of educational materials for that hearing (FSD-Alert.org, 2004–2006). Other central events of the New View Campaign have included: the formulation of a classification system to compete with that in the DSM (see Kaschak and Tiefer, 2001); a 2000 press conference; publication of a book (Kaschak and Tiefer, 2001); the creation of a web site; the creation of a teaching manual; the creation and maintenance of a listserve; the creation of a CME course, released on Medscape; and the organization of two professional conferences on the topic.[3] The campaign has been covered in major US newspapers, including the *Washington Post,* the *Chicago Tribune,* the *Boston Globe,* the *Los Angeles Times,* and the *Wall Street Journal;* in newsmagazines, including *Time* and *Newsweek;* and in television news programs on all three main networks.

The increasing promotion and prescription of lifestyle drugs, coupled with the aging of the baby boom population, suggests that the medicalization of sexual function is likely to expand. Even though Intrinsa was denied FDA approval, the media are monitoring the development of a growing avalanche of FSD drugs, many currently in the later stages of the clinical trial process. And pharmaceutical companies are backing up this product development with serious PR and marketing campaigns—for example, it was estimated that P&G would provide a marketing launch budget of as much as $100 million for Intrinsa were it approved (Neff, 2003).

Resistance to this expansion, however, is also growing rapidly. Recent drug scandals, such as those involving the Vioxx brand pain reliever and hormone replacement therapy (HRT), have inflamed public concerns about potentially unsafe drugs being approved for market. The critiques—both academic and popular—of the drug industry are increasing (see, e.g., Abramson, 2004; Angell, 2004; Kassirer, 2005). Moreover, these drug industry critiques can be read as just one example of a broad public health advocacy movement intent on challenging harmful corporate practices (Freudenberg, 2005); earlier in this issue, Tiefer called the work of the New View campaign "part of a new public health advocacy movement dealing with corporate practices that affect health, such as those in the tobacco, automobile, and food industries." It seems that this tension—between growing biocorporate power (medicalization being one process facilitating that growth) and resistance to that power—will become more pronounced in the coming years.

NOTES

1. See FSD-Alert.org (2004–2006) for a variety of critical positions on Intrinsa.

2. See FSD-Alert.org (2004–2006) for full documentation of the campaign.

3. The group's first conference, held in San Francisco in March 2002, drew close to 140 participants. The second conference, held in Montreal, Quebec in July 2005, drew about 200 attendees.

REFERENCES

Abramson, J. (2004) *Overdosed America: The Broken Promise of American Medicine*. New York: HarperCollins.

APA (American Psychiatric Association) (1994) *Diagnostic and Statistical Manual of Mental Disorders* (4th edn). Washington, DC: APA.

Angell, M. (2004) *The Truth about the Drug Companies*. New York: Random House.

Bancroft, J. (2002) "The Medicalization of Female Sexual Dysfunction: The Need for Caution," *Archives of Sexual Behavior* 31: 451–5.

Bancroft, J., Loftus, J. and Long, J. (2003) "Distress About Sex: A National Survey of Women in Heterosexual Relationships," *Archives of Sexual Behavior* 32: 193–208.

Basson, R., Berman, J., Burnett, A., Derogatis, L. Ferguson, D., Fourcroy, J., et al. (2000) "Report of the International Consensus Development Conference on Female Sexual Dysfunction: Definitions and Classifications," *Journal of Urology* 163: 888–92.

Basson, R., Bourgeois-Law, G., Fourcroy, J., Heiman, J., Priestman, A., Rowe, T., Stevenson, R., Thomson, S. and Tiefer, L. (2001) "Androgen 'Deficiency' in Women is Problematic," *Medical Aspects of Human Sexuality*, pp. 45–7, URL (accessed 18 March 2002) http://www.medicalsexuality.org

CBSNEWS (2004) "Women's Sexual Woes Get Attention," URL (accessed 6 May 2004) www.cbsnews.com/sections/eveningnews/main3420.shtml

Conrad, P. and Lieter, V. (2004) "Medicalization, Markets and Consumers," *Journal of Health and Social Behavior* 45 (extra issue): 158–76.

Davis, S., Davison, S., Donath, S., Bell, R. (2005) "Circulating Androgen Levels and Self-Reported Sexual Function in Women," *Journal of the American Medical Association* 294: 91–6.

Enserik, M. (2005) "Let's Talk about Sex—and Drugs," *Science* 308(10 June): 1578–80.

Fishman, J. A. (2004) "Manufacturing Desire: The Commodification of Female Sexual Dysfunction," *Social Studies of Science* 34: 187–218.

Fourcroy, J. (2001) "Androgen Deficiency Syndrome in Women: Implications, Mechanisms and Treatments," paper presented at the Female Sexual Function Forum (FSFF) conference 25–28 October, Boston, MA.

Freudenberg, N. (2005) "Public Health Advocacy to Change Corporate Practices: Implications for Health Education Practice and Research," *Health Education and Behavior* 32: 1–22.

FSD-Alert.org (2004–2006) "FDA Hearing on Intrinsa, New View Resources," URL (accessed March 2006): www.fsd-alert.org/intrinsa.html

Harris, G. (2004). "Pfizer Gives up Testing Viagra on Women," *New York Times* (28 February), URL (accessed 1 March 2004): www.nytimes.com/2004/02/28/business/28viagra.html

Hartley, H. (2003) "'Big Pharma' in our Bedrooms: An Analysis of the Medicalization of Women's Sexual Problems," *Advances in Gender Research* 7: 89–129.

Hartley, H. and Tiefer, L. (2003) "Taking a Biological Turn: The Push for a 'Female Viagra' and the Medicalization of Women's Sexual Problems," *Women's Studies Quarterly* 31(1/2): 42–6.

Kantrowitz, B. and Wingert, P. (2005) "Inside the Struggle to Treat Women with Dwindling Sex Drives," *Newsweek* (4 October), URL (accessed 4 October 2005): http://msnbc.msn.com/id/9546806/site/newsweek

Kaschak, E. and Tiefer, L. (eds) (2001) *A New View of Women's Sexual Problems.* New York: The Haworth Press.

Kassirer, J. P. (2005) *On the Take: How Medicine's Complicity with Big Business Can Endanger Your Health.* New York: Oxford University Press.

Kelleher, S. (2005) "Clash Over 'Little Blue Pill' for Women," *Seattle Times* (30 June), URL (accessed 4 July 2005): http://seattletimes.nwsource.com/news/health/suddenlysick

Laumann, E., Paik, A. and Rosen, R. (1999) "Sexual Dysfunction in the United States: Prevalence and Predictors," *Journal of the American Medical Association* 281: 537–44.

Leland, J. (2000) "The Science of Women and Sex," *Newsweek* (29 May): 48–55.

Loe, M. (2004) *The Rise of Viagra: How the Little Blue Pill Changed Sex in America.* New York: New York University Press.

Moynihan, R. (2003a) "The Making of a Disease: Female Sexual Dysfunction," *British Medical Journal* 326: 45–7.

Moynihan, R. (2003b) "Company Launches Campaign to Counter BMJ Claims," *British Medical Journal* 326: 120.

NAMS (North American Menopause Society) (2005) "The Role of Testosterone Therapy in Postmenopausal Women: A Position Statement of the North American Menopause Society," *Menopause: The Journals of the North American Menopause Society* 12: 497–511.

Neff, J. (2003) "P & G Sex Patch to Get $100 Million Advertising Push," URL (accessed 15 December 2003): www.adage.com/news

O'Connor, A. (October 2, 2005) "Dr. Berman's Sex Rx," *Los Angeles Times* (2 October), URL (accessed 25 January 2006): www.latimes.com/features/health/medicine/la-tm-sexresearch40oct02,1,7694520.story

Payer, L. (1992) *Disease-Mongers: How Doctors, Drug Companies, and Insurers Are Making You Feel Sick.* New York: Wiley & Sons.

Tiefer, L. (2000) "The 'Consensus' Conference on Female Sexual Dysfunction: Conflicts of Interest and Hidden Agendas," *Journal of Sex and Marital Therapy* 27: 227–36.

Tiefer, L. (2002) "'Female Sexual Dysfunction': Where'd It Come From and Where's It Going?" paper presented at the conference *The New Female Sexual Dysfunction: Promises, Prescriptions, and Profits.* San Francisco, CA. 9 March 2002.

Tiefer, L. (2004) *Sex is Not a Natural Act* (2nd edn). Boulder, CO: Westview.

Tiefer, L. (2006) "Female Sexual Dysfunction: A Contemporary Care Study of Disease Mongering and Activist Resistance," paper presented at the Inaugural Conference on Disease-Mongering, 11–13 April, Newcastle, Australia.

9

Sexual Violence

An interview with...

Diana E. H. Russell

Diana E. H. Russell, Ph.D., is one of the foremost experts on sexual violence against women and girls. For the last thirty-eight years she has been engaged in research and activism on this massive social problem. She has authored, co-authored, edited, or co-edited seventeen books, which have become authoritative sources on rape (including wife rape), incest, femicide (the misogynist murder of women), and pornography.

What led you to begin studying rape and sexual assault?

In 1971, I was outraged by a typically sexist rape trial that occurred in San Francisco in which it appeared that the victim, not the accused, was on trial. After participating in a feminist protest outside the courthouse, I realized how little I knew about women's experiences of rape. A review of the rape literature revealed that it was riddled with sexist woman-blaming, so I decided to embark on an interview-based study of rape survivors. My book, The Politics of Rape _(1975), which includes twenty-one of these interviews, was among the first feminist analyses of this woman-hating crime. I was not aware at the time that I was also motivated by my own experiences of childhood_ *incestuous abuse and an attempted rape when I was 20 years old. I am now convinced that the most traumatic of these experiences (the incestuous abuse) caused me to dedicate my life to research and writing about many different forms of sexual violations perpetrated by males on females, including incestuous abuse.*

Which of your projects have you found most interesting? Why?

I found working on incestuous abuse to be most interesting. My research on this topic culminated in my book, The Secret Trauma: Incest in the Lives of Girls and Women *(1986), which was a co-recipient of the 1986 C. Wright Mills Award for books that exemplify outstanding social science research on a significant social problem. Completing this book was cathartic for me, particularly because I had been told by many social science researchers that it would be impossible to provide a sound estimate of the prevalence of incest on the basis of a scientific probability sample. Furthermore, it was very gratifying to know that it would be helpful to many incest survivors.*

What ethical dilemmas have you faced in studying rape and sexual assault?

One of my ethical dilemmas was caused by my being a white South African (South Africa is the country of my birth) who wanted to study rape and incest there, so as to raise awareness about the shocking magnitude of these problems in that country. Despite the tremendous need for research on sexual violence against women and girls in South Africa, particularly in the black community (black is the term used for all people of color in South Africa), the long history of apartheid resulted in very few black women researchers having the time, motivation, or qualifications to tackle this form of terrorism against females. Since approximately 85 percent of the South African population was black (mainly Africans, Indians, and "coloreds") when I conducted my study, this meant that the majority of my informants would be black. Had this been the case, some black South Africans, like people of color in the United States would have resented my doing this research on their lives. In addition, accounts about black men's violence toward black women and children would likely have reinforced many white people's racist stereotypes about black men. I would probably have been considered racist had 85 percent of my respondents been black. Therefore, I limited my research for a book on incestuous abuse to white South Africans (see Behind Closed Doors in White South Africa: Incest Survivors Tell Their Stories *[1997]). However, in my effort to avoid contributing to racist stereotypes, I again risked being viewed as racist for confining my research to the white ruling class minority in South Africa. I was . . . caught between a rock and a hard place whatever decision I made about the racial composition of my respondents.*

What do you think is the most challenging thing about studying [researching, writing, speaking about] rape and sexual assault?

I am most challenged by the fact that—as a researcher and author on rape and other sexual assault—I am often unable to have an impact on those whom I most want to affect. For example, I, and other feminist rape researchers, have made several determined efforts to point out the appalling inadequacies in the research methodology of the National Crime Victimization Surveys (NCVS) conducted annually by the Federal Government's Bureau of Justice Statistics (BJS).

Why is it important to do this kind of research?

Choosing from several different research studies that I have conducted on rape and child sexual abuse, I will focus here on the importance of conducting rigorous scientific studies on the prevalence of different forms of violence against women and girls. By prevalence, as distinct from incidence, I am referring to the percentage of women who were victims of rape or child sexual abuse at some time in their lives, or during a specified period of time. (The incidence of rape typically refers to the number of rapes that occurred within the prior year.) It is vital to know the approximate magnitude of a problem before theorizing about it or trying to ascertain the most effective ways to combat it. For example, before my study of the prevalence of incestuous abuse was published, there was no scientific basis for estimating the prevalence of this mostly hidden crime. One psychiatrist estimated that only one in a million females had been so victimized. However, my study found that 16 percent of a probability sample of adult women in San Francisco had been the victims of sexual abuse before they turned 18, and 4.5 percent of them had been sexually abused by a biological, step-, or adoptive father—also before they turned 18. These findings—still an underestimate—revolutionized the contemporary understanding of incestuous abuse in the United States.

If you could teach people one thing about sexuality, what would it be?

I would teach people that sexuality is socially constructed. In our patriarchal society, sexuality is shaped by male domination and sexism: For example, many men view having sex with women as conquest—a notch on their belts. They see it as proof of their "manhood." The more notches they have on their belts, the more status they have among their male peers. They brag with their male friends about whether or not they "got to first base" or made a "home run." For such men, sex is often devoid of caring, respect, love, or tenderness—as is the pornography they use. Sexual equality cannot be achieved without gender equality.

—Interviewed by Denise Donnelly

"I Wasn't Raped, but . . .": Revisiting Definitional Problems in Sexual Victimization

Nicola Gavey

When a woman says she wasn't raped but describes an experience of forced, unwanted sexual intercourse, what are we to think? Was she "really" raped, despite disowning that label for her experience? Or does her refusal of the label suggest that her interpretation of the experience as other than rape makes it so? And what does it say about our culture(s) that there can be so much ambiguity over the differential diagnosis of rape versus sex? How should we conceptualize and judge the myriad coercive sexual acts that lie somewhere between rape and consensual sex? Finally, is being the object of violence or coercion always the same thing [as] being the *victim* of such violence or coercion?

In this [reading] I begin to explore some of the convoluted layers of issues in which such questions are embedded. . . . In thinking through and around these questions, I find I can't settle comfortably into a straightforward, unitary position from which to craft an argument. . . . I have concluded . . . that there are indeed murky issues at the interface between (hetero)sex and sexual victimization. Even at the most basic level, I want to talk about and against rape and sexual victimization (as though these are straightforward terms) at the same time as I destabilize these categories, in the belief that this is an important part of the same fight at a different level.

I trace some of the changes in research on rape and sexual victimization over the past two decades and consider some of the implications of the new feminist social science approach. In particular, I consider

three points that raise the need to revisit current conventions for conceptualizing sexual victimization. These points concern the concept of the unacknowledged rape victim, the loose distinction between rape and attempted rape, and the use of the term *sexual victimization* to refer to a broad range of arguably normative coercive heterosexual practices. . . .

A Starting Point

In the title of this [reading], I refer back to Martha Burt and Rhoda Estep's 1981 paper "Who Is a Victim? Definitional Problems in Sexual Victimization." In their . . . article, Burt and Estep mapped the nascent influence of 1970s feminism on a redefinition and reconceptualization of sexual assault. They endorsed the more inclusive definition of sexual assault that was emerging from feminism at the time, drawing attention to the similarity between rape and other coercive sexual practices. Moreover, they argued strongly for the benefits for all women who have been sexually assaulted to claim the victim role. Although aware of what they called the "negative social value" and the "obligations" of the victim role, they proposed that the benefits would include "the right to claim assistance, sympathy, temporary relief from other role responsibilities, legal recourse, and other similar advantages." (p. 16).

. . . [Using] the language of victimization was imposed as a way of making sense of and opposing the moral injustice of women's oppression in the forms of violence and harassment.

The "New" Feminist Research on Sexual Victimization

Since 1981, . . . both feminist activism and feminist social science have been instrumental in promoting a major rethinking of rape—and sexual victimization in

From "'I Wasn't Raped, but . . .': Revisiting Definitional Problems in Sexual Victimization" by Nicola Gavey, in *New Versions of Victims: Feminists Struggle with the Concept* (1999, 57–81), edited by Sharon Lamb. Reprinted by permission of New York University Press.

many western societies. . . . In a very short time we moved from a climate in which rape was widely regarded as rare to one in which rape is regarded as a widespread social problem. . . .

[F]eminist empirical research was specifically designed to overcome the limitations of previous estimates of rape prevalence (which relied on reports of rape to the police or reports in national crime surveys). . . . This work introduced an important methodological point of departure from any previous attempts to measure the scope of rape. Women were asked not whether they had been raped[1] but rather whether they had had any experiences that matched behavioral descriptions of rape. For example, they were asked whether they had ever had sexual intercourse when they didn't want to because a man threatened or used some degree of physical force to make them do so (e.g., Koss et al. 1987). Moreover, this question was one among many such specific questions that women would be asked about a range of coercive sexual experiences. Such methodological refinements were designed to be sensitive to women's reluctance to report rape. They were seemingly successful, and the body of research produced shocking new data showing widespread rape and sexual victimization.

At the same time, two other important changes to the picture of rape emerged from this research. First, Diana Russell (1982; 1984)—and later, others—showed that women were far more likely to be raped by husbands, lovers, boyfriends, and dates than by strangers. Not only were the cultural blinkers that had enabled this to be regarded as "just sex" lifted, but it was found that such rapes were far more common than the stereotypical rape by a stranger. Second, . . . while rape [was] the extreme act, it [was] regarded as being on a continuum with more subtle forms of coercion, from an unwanted kiss to unwanted sexual intercourse submitted to as a result of continual verbal pressure. . . .

[These changes] have two important effects: (1) They construe experiences that would have previously fallen within the realm of sex as forms of sexual *victimization;* and 2) they implicitly invite a critical examination of the whole realm of normal heterosexual practice. . . .

Against a backdrop where rape was considered to be rare—and where complaints of rape were commonly regarded to be lies, distortions of normal sex, harmless, or provoked by the victim—the call to broaden the definition of sexual assault and victimization has been an important feminist move. Similarly, the way in which we have elaborated on the understanding of rape as a form of *victimization* has arguably contributed to more widespread concern about rape as a serious social problem. These moves [were] one part of increased focus during the 1980s on many forms of victimization, and of widespread social concern for understanding their extent and dynamics and for ameliorating and preventing their harm.

"Victimization" in Crisis

[By] the late 1990s, the concept of victimization [was] arguably in crisis. Joel Best (1997) opened a . . . *Society* commentary with the unfavorable verdict that "victimization has become fashionable" (p. 9). As Richard Feldstein (1997) . . . observed, the term *victim* . . . has been targeted for critique by neoconservatives in the United States. . . . As part of more general conservative campaigns against research and services relating to victimization, there has been critical dispute over the new feminist research on rape—especially that on "date rape." It has been claimed that the issue has been exaggerated or that it has no validity as a concept (e.g., Gilbert 1994; Paglia 1992; Roiphe 1993; see also Denfeld 1995; Sommers 1994; Newbold 1996). . . .

Are Victims Created by a Victimization Framework?

There are many ways to victimize people. One way is to convince them that they are victims.
—(Hwang 1997, p. 41)

One strand of public concern at the moment is the fear that talk about victimization is needlessly creating victims. Moreover, critics of the movement against date rape have implied that it violates "assumptions of women's basic competence, free will, and strength of character" (Roiphe 1993, p. 69; see also Paglia 1992). . . .

There are various ways in which the language of sexual victimization can have material cultural effects. . . . For example, it may reinforce and perpetuate images of women as weak, passive, and asexual and images of men as sexually driven, unstoppable, and potentially dangerous. These gendered ways of being may be further enhanced by the exacerbation of women's fears about rape through media reportage and through warnings about violent sexual attacks that emphasize women's vulnerability to rape over their potential for resistance. . . . A rapist's moral infringement prescribes an experience of victimization for the rape *victim* . . . [and a] particular psychological outcome is preconfigured by calling the violence "victimization."

. . . [H]ow valid is the sort of seductive public warning in Karen Hwang's point? Are victims really created out of thin air? When feminists and other social critics name certain practices as victimization, they are drawing attention to the relationships of power that systematically privilege the experiences of some groups of people over those of others. Is the hysterical anxiety behind the suggestion that talking about victimization creates victimization a sort of head-in-the-sand approach to unpleasant social conditions—a naive hope that if a phenomenon is not seen and not heard, then it does not exist? . . . [C]ommentators such as Katie Roiphe suggest that "prior to the discourse of date rape, the experience itself did not occur, or at least not with such traumatizing after-effects as we now associate with rape" (p. 16). . . .

In light of the backlash crisis of representation of victimization . . . , it is perhaps time to revisit Martha Burt and Rhoda Estep's (1981) contention that it is in a woman's best interests to be perceived as a victim when she has experienced sexual coercion or violence. It is difficult to know how to evaluate this claim, and our attempts may benefit from some empirical analysis of women's accounts of their experiences of coercion, abuse, and violence. Few would deny that what we refer to as rape, sexual assault, sexual coercion, and sexual abuse can be victimizing. That is, they can be horrific events that traumatize

women[2] and produce victims. Moreover, abusive and coercive practices can produce victims in a more subtle and less horrific ways, through undermining a woman's confidence and eroding her agency over time. In the fight against rape, public feminist rhetoric has tended to privilege one of the many contradictory broader cultural meanings of rape—that is, its power to cause severe and irrevocable psychological harm to the victim. Those of us drawn to activism against rape often have firsthand knowledge of the effects of rape on friends, family members, women we have worked with, or ourselves. The potential trauma and devastating harm of rape, silenced and hidden for so many years, has now come to be almost automatically signified by the term *rape* (although not without exceptions). . . .

Unacknowledged Rape Victims

As discussed earlier, the new research on rape has tended not to rely on asking women whether or not they have ever experienced "rape." Some studies have included this direct question along with the more specific behavioral questions about forced, unwanted sex. It has been found that only around 30 to 50 percent of women who affirm they have had an experience that meets a narrow definition of rape identify that they have experienced "rape" (e.g., Koss 1988; Gavey 1991a; 1991b). . . . [T]his research paradigm has . . . categorize[d] women as victims of rape if they report having had an experience consistent with the predetermined behavioral description that researchers define as rape when the questionnaires or structured interview data are analyzed. If these women do not report that they have experienced "rape" (when asked directly), then they are considered "unacknowledged" rape victims by the researchers (e.g., Koss 1985). . . .

[S]ocial critics have targeted this feature of the feminist empirical work on rape prevalence as a major weakness of the whole body of research.[3] Neil Gilbert (1994), for example, cites as a problem of Koss's rape prevalence estimates that "almost three-quarters of the students whom Koss defined as victims of rape did not think they had been raped" (p. 23). . . . Ironically, this methodological approach is totally consistent with the positivist conventions of social and behavioral psychology . . . , where it is considered good research practice to use operational definitions for specifying precise categories of behavior that can be reliably measured. . . . For instance, it would be considered valid to classify a person as "depressed" if he or she answered a range of questions on a depression inventory in the predicted ways, even if the individual did not affirm the statement "I am depressed."

Let us consider an example of the sort of experience that could be described as an unacknowledged rape. One woman I interviewed described an experience, which occurred when she was nineteen, of waking to find her thirty-year-old male apartment mate in her bed, "groping" her (Gavey 1990; 1992). She had no prior sexual or romantic relationship with this man, but on this night he got into her bed while she was asleep and had intercourse with her, with no apparent consideration of her lack of interest. She explained:

> **Ann:** . . . it all happened quite quickly really, but I remember thinking quite clearly, "Well if I don't—If I try and get out of the bed, perhaps if I run away or something . . . he might rape me [pause] so I had better just . . ."
>
> **Nicola:** If you try and run away you mean?
>
> **Ann:** If I tried it, if I'd resisted, then he might rape me, you know. So he did anyway, sort of thing, really, when you think about it, when I look back.

This man was rough and left her bleeding. Later, she was frightened, "confused," "nervous within the house," and hypervigilant about making sure she was never asleep before he'd gone to bed. . . . Nevertheless, Ann did not conceptualize this event as rape at the time.

Technically, this encounter may not count as rape in a narrow legal sense, because it is unclear how explicitly Ann communicated her nonconsent. Most feminist analyses, however, would point out the restraints on her being able to do this, such as being only just awake and fearing that her resistance might lead to worse treatment. Feminists would also highlight the absence of reasonable grounds for this man assuming consent (e.g., Pineau 1989). That is . . . it [is not] reasonable for a man to assume that a woman approached when she is asleep in her own bed by a man with whom she had no prior sexual or romantic relationship would be consenting to sex, in the absence of some active communication of this consent. Consequently, many feminists would describe this incident as rape or, at the very least, sexual assault. Clearly, in spite of Ann's resistance to the identity of rape victim, the experience had a negative psychological impact on her. It is impossible to know how, if at all, the effects would have been different had she viewed what happened as rape. There is some indication in her account that to have had an experience she would have called "rape" would have been worse—"if I'd resisted, then he might rape me." Indeed, it would have been a different experience and one that may have more powerfully signaled her lack of control and her vulnerability. Psychologically, she perhaps maintained more control (a meager but significant amount) and risked losing less by choosing not to "run away or something" than if she had resisted as hard as she could and been raped anyway.

During our interview several years after this incident, Ann moved toward retrospectively understanding it as rape—after explaining that she did not resist because "he might rape me," she said "So he did anyway, sort of thing . . . when I look back." . . . I . . . struggle with the validity and ethics of labeling Ann a "rape victim" at the time when she did not choose this label herself. However, . . . ambiguity . . . arises in talking about Ann's experience and how to make sense of it in the research context. . . . If this woman's experience is not considered to be rape or some form of sexual assault very close to rape (by her *or* by the man involved *or* by police, judges, and juries *or* by researchers and social theorists), then what is it? Sex? If it can be accepted as just part of the realm of sex, then it redirects a critical spotlight onto heterosexuality itself.

It is worth noting that although Ann "resisted" seeing herself as a rape victim, this did not enable her to resist the assault physically. This illuminates how it would be misleading to assume that *not* being positioned in an overt discourse of rape or victimization somehow protects a woman from sexual assault. In a situation such as that Ann faced, the mark of gender difference imposed on what is a physical contest of sorts already incites certain responses, such as immobility and fear, that aid a rapist in his attack. . . . [T]his suggests that [we need] . . . ways of understanding heterosex that don't leave room for ambiguity over a woman's entitlement to refuse unwanted sex.

A Feminist Response—The Methodology

With critical reflection on the research strategy of classifying some women as unacknowledged rape victims, what do we want to say in response to the critics but also as part of ongoing . . . research practice? There is probably no straightforward answer, but I think it is important that we approach it as an open question rather than with formulaic answers. Why do so many women who have bad experiences consistent with a legal definition of rape label resist the label of "rape victim" (e.g., Koss 1985)? And how should feminist research respond to these women's rejection of the "rape" label? These questions raise complicated issues that are at the heart of feminist theory about research practice. If we see our role as giving women voice, then it may not be legitimate to "put words in their mouths," to describe experiences as rape that women themselves do not describe in that way. However, feminist research increasingly seeks to go beyond giving women voice and reporting on women's experiences, to offer analyses and critiques that help make sense of women's experiences as they are shaped and constrained by power relations in social contexts. When women's voices don't always tell "our story," it can be troubling to know how to proceed. (See also Fine 1992; Kitzinger and Wilkinson 1997.)

Evaluated in this light, the feminist empirical research on rape prevalence occupies an interesting position. In its use of traditional methods to produce conventional data dressed in the language of science rather than that of feminist politics, this research has been an important part of wider feminist action. This action has had some important successes—most notably, changes to rape laws, in many English-speaking countries and in portions of the United States, to recognize rape within marriage as a crime. Widespread publicity about date rape has also led to rape prevention programs on many university campuses. Despite the limited effectiveness of these changes so far (for instance, convictions for wife rape are extremely rare), this body of research has nevertheless had a subversive and transformative role in the changing representations of rape. It has generated a profound shift in the meaning of rape, to the extent that it is no longer impossible to think of man raping his wife or a sporting hero raping a woman he dated (although this possibility is still more likely to be readily accepted if the man is black). . . .

Research and Complexity

. . . [R]esearch . . . has yielded the findings discussed above at a cost. It has forced closure on definitions of various forms of victimization and classified women's experiences into readymade categories of victims. This style of methodology necessitates disregard for nuanced and possibly contradictory meanings. Moreover, researchers seem to find it reasonably unproblematic that answers to such basic questions as whether or not a particular experience counts as "rape" are constructed through the research process. The resulting certainty that can be projected about the extent and nature of rape and sexual victimization may eventually undermine the authority of the findings, when it is found that the reductive and universalizing features of this style of research don't "speak to" the experience of all women whom it ostensibly represents. Not only are decisions about who is and who is not a rape victim not always straightforward, but the partiality of new truths about the effects of rape is sometimes overlooked.

In some instances, women's reactions may be contradictory and not consistent with either dominant traditional or dominant feminist constructions of rape. One woman participating in my research (Gavey 1990) described a situation with her boyfriend, whereby she said she wanted to say to him, "The very first time we had sex you raped me." However, she didn't always view the forced sex as rape, and she continued her relationship with this man for more than two years. She detailed a complex set of contradictory, ambivalent, and changing reactions to this and other coercive sexual experiences in the relationship. She also discussed how the usual feminist analyses of rape, such as those she later encountered at a rape crisis center, were not entirely helpful. Her reactions were not consistent with what she was hearing about how women, respond to rape—because she loved the man who raped her, remembered some of their sex as "wonderful," and so on—she went through a stage of feeling that she must be a "sick" and "masochistic" person. . . .

Feminist accounts of rape need to be able to take account of such women's experiences without, in effect, dismissing them as the result of false consciousness. Carefully listening to and theorizing such ambivalent and confusing experiences may illuminate the complex relationship between heterosexuality and rape. Moreover, it may produce feminist analyses of rape that are sympathetic to all women who are raped, no matter how they experience it.

Although there may be short-term political costs, embracing a more complex and less certain position on the ways in which rape can and does affect women may ultimately be an effective political strategy. By this I mean that psychologists, therapists, and activists should continue to work on understanding, helping, and speaking about the trauma of rape but at the same time be open to accepting, for example, that not all women are traumatized by rape. . . . The notion that it may be possible to experience rape and suffer no lasting devastating psychological effects is less often articulated than is the discourse of harm. But this "finding" about the effects of rape begs the question of whether such research, which once again must compress and order experience into finite categories, is adequate to perceive more subtle, idiosyncratic, and unpredictable psychological effects of rape. . . .

Is Attempted Rape Sometimes Very Different from Completed Rape?

While some experiences of sexual coercion (and presumably most, if not all, experiences of sexual coercion that fit a narrow definition of rape) are surely victimizing, some possibly are not. Is it possible that our framework for conceptualizing *all* instances of sexual assault, and many instances of unwanted sex, as victimization actually helps constitute some of these experiences as victimizing, when they might

otherwise have had effects that were less disabling? Although this question shares the anxiety typical of the backlash positions, it is an important question for feminists. In particular, are experiences of attempted rape and attempted sexual assault *sometimes* very different from actual experiences of rape and sexual assault?

I can think of a personal experience, when I was sixteen, that was probably attempted rape. This episode involved being tricked into stopping at an older male co-worker's place on the way to a party after we had finished work past midnight on New Year's Eve. I was thrown onto a bed that was just across from the front door of the flat, and he proceeded to jump on top of me and attempt to remove my pants. He was a relatively small man, and I was relatively physically strong from sports, and I remember having to struggle as hard as I could to prevent him [from] removing my pants, with the intention (it seemed to me at the time) of having intercourse with me. (This point also reminds me how it is difficult to judge when a man's actions become "attempted rape" when a man and woman are acquainted and, at some stretch of the imagination, a mutual sexual encounter could be appropriate.) Despite the fact that both of us had been drinking alcohol with other workers at the restaurant where we worked before we left, I was never in any doubt as to my lack of sexual interest in this man—at all, let alone on this occasion. I was not ambivalent in my communication with him and told him clearly, verbally, that I did not want to have sex with him, and I resisted him physically as hard as I could. Yet he seemed to have one goal on his mind, which was unchanged by my refusal. I think it was my relative physical strength that enabled me to resist him vigorously and successfully, to the point that he possibly decided not to keep trying.

Ten years later, when I was working at a sexual abuse counseling agency, the subcultural milieu encouraged me to think back on and identify this experience as attempted rape and to wonder about its negative effects on me. While this was not a totally new way of interpreting this experience, it did sediment it with more certainty. And it did induce me to scrutinize my past to look for psychological effects of this experience. I recall that I was subsequently worried about this man's "interest" in me and arranged for my mother to pick me up from work on some of the following nights. I also recall that being able to successfully prevent a forceful attempt at unwanted sex left me feeling strong, determined, and invulnerable. Although I can't remember enough of the detail of what followed to be sure there were not also subtle negative effects on my identity and sexuality, it strikes me that such experiences of attempted rape that [are] successfully repelled are extremely different from experiences of completed rape, in terms of their effect on women. In my case, I did not feel like a victim. I despised his actions, but I did not feel I had been harmed. To the contrary, the effects of his attempt had probably been as empowering as they were disempowering. Was what happened "victimization"? Or is there a better way of describing it that recognizes and celebrates the power of this kind of physical resistance, of fighting back . . . ?

. . . [A]t the time I was imagining the possibility of identifying as an attempted rape victim, it seemed important to join together with women who had been sexually victimized by men, in part to make a political show of solidarity in the face of oppressive acts of male sexuality. However, I never really felt like I properly "belonged," in the sense that I didn't share the legacy of pain that some of the women around me had suffered. Moreover, it backed me into a speaking position that did not fully represent my recollected experience. That adopting an identity as an attempted rape victim would have silenced my different kind of story, which included traces of empowerment, seemed (and still seems) a relatively trivial concern in relation to the political and interpersonal importance of standing alongside women who *had* been harmed. However, perhaps there is more at stake here than some notion of making room for the "authenticity" of experiences like my own. Perhaps there is some political advantage in being able to tell lots of different stories about diverse experiences of sexual violence. In making room for a respectful plurality, we may be able to acknowledge the oppressiveness and potential pain of rape at the same time as igniting discourses that disrupt the possibilities of rape. . . .

Clearly, not all attempted rapes are the same. Some experiences will involve violent and terrifying attacks, where a woman may literally fear for her life. However, the use of behavioral descriptions in surveys to measure the extent of sexual victimization does not distinguish these discrepant possibilities.

Emphasizing Women's Strength

. . . [T]he normative practices of therapy for rape and sexual abuse victims may inadvertently help reinforce some of the effects of victimization through their concern with trauma, recovery, and healing. Again, a particular kind of psychological subject is assumed by such therapy approaches, and arguably, this "recovering" subject is always already constituted as lacking and in need of "betterment."

. . . Sharon Marcus (1992) considers how particular constructions of rape affect the very possibility of rape. . . . Marcus argues that in order to resist rape culture, we need to deny a necessary conflation between the act of rape and irrevocable harm. Marcus's feminist approach to rape is radically different from the approach of Susan Brownmiller's (1975) classic feminist analysis of rape. Marcus (1992) considers that "such a view takes violence as a self-explanatory first cause and endows it with an invulnerable and terrifying facticity which stymies our ability to challenge and demystify rape" (p. 387). She, in contrast, argues that

> in its efforts to convey the horror and iniquity of rape, such a view often concurs with masculinist culture in its designation of rape as a fate worse than, or tantamount to, death; the apocalyptic tone which it adopts and the metaphysical status which it assigns to rape implies that rape can only be feared or legally repaired, not fought. (p. 387)

Marcus instead argues for the need to "envision strategies which will enable women to sabotage men's power to rape, which will empower women to take the ability to rape completely out of men's hands" (p. 388). It is sometimes difficult to understand exactly how this sort of transformation could take place, but Marcus's . . . argument is at least suggestive that it may be possible to conceptualize rape differently, in a way that somehow renders it less powerful without trivializing it.

I suggest that a small step in this sort of transformative direction would be the opening up of all sorts of narratives of resistance—by making room for stories about how potential rape was successfully fought, about how some women who are raped do not experience overwhelming psychological despair, and so on. As I suggested earlier, the potential cost of this strategy is that it may do violence to the experience of women who are victimized and traumatized by rape. Sensitivity to this possibility is necessary so that stories of particular kinds of resistance don't come to be privileged in ways that contribute once again to a silencing of women's experiences of victimization.

Apart from concern about the . . . effects of the language of victimization, there are other questions that should be on the minds of feminists. . . . [W]e may need to observe critically the effects of backlash discourse around "victimization." In the ensuing battle over the meaning of victimization, we may need to question which sorts of tactics are most likely to be effective in the political fight against rape. For instance, will the . . . strategy of simply speaking a victim-advocacy position more loudly be sufficient, or will we need to . . . contest the very terms of the debate? . . . [Moreover,] I suggest that an unwanted kiss or touch doesn't always make a *victim,* and the effect of this rhetorical excess in the context of backlash activity may be to weaken the whole struggle against rape by acquaintances, dates, husbands, and so on. . . . [We must recognize that we live in] a culture of heterosexuality in which power is allowed to infuse sex in different ways for women and men—ways that consistently foreground men's rather than women's rights and desires. . . .

Another problem with the way the framework of victimization is used is that it may implicitly require us to establish psychological harm in order to take a moral stand against violence and against heterosexual practice that is offensive or disrespectful without necessarily being violent (in the usual sense). That is, the injustice of sexual coercion and sexual violence may become too closely tied with the "proof" of psychological damage. . . .

Supplementing the Language of Victimization

The new feminist research has come a long way, since Burt and Estep's article (1981), in describing the widespread problem of sexual victimization. But has it both gone too far and not gone far enough? Positivist methodologies have required us to iron out complexity, ambivalence, and contradiction. Public expectations of science have reinforced this drive for certainty in the form of concrete, definitive "findings." But when we peep behind the positivist mask, all sorts of discomforting questions arise: Are all instances of sexual coercion always victimizing? Do they always cause harm? For instance, in the arena of attempted sexual assaults, are women sometimes warriors, fighters, heroes? What are the effects of using these different kinds of language? Are the more subtle forms of sexual coercion, argued to be contiguous with rape by some feminists, best conceptualized on a continuum of sexual victimization? Or are there other ways of critiquing heterosexual practice, which routinely privileges men's sexual interests over women's? Or should both strategies be adopted simultaneously?

In case I've overstated my concerns about the language of victimization, I emphasize that I am not arguing for an abandonment of the victimization framework. Rather, I am suggesting that we need to question whether it is always appropriate or wise to talk about all the different forms and occasions of sexual coercion, sexual assault, sexual abuse, and sexual violence as *victimization.* Making connections between everyday sexual practices (such as sexual pressure in a marriage) and sexual violence has been important for highlighting the role of normative culture in sustaining problems such as rape. However, we have not always maintained a distinction between the theorization of, say, a continuum of sexual victimization and the implications for how we then understand men's and women's actions and experiences at the more normative end of the continuum. Using the language of victimization to discuss this territory of the continuum may be theoretically valid yet at the same time (wrongly?) give the impression that we believe every act that falls along the continuum is an act of "victimization," that it makes "victims." I don't think I want to insist every time a woman experiences some unwanted sexual contact, it is an experience of victimization. But far from dismissing such experiences, it seems to me the challenge is to find different ways of critiquing the ways in which our culture(s) can tolerate all sorts of injustices, inequalities, and plain unfairness in the name of normative heterosexuality.

I close this [reading] in a mood of uncertainty. I worry that my questions could lead to unnecessary and undermining problems for the feminist analyses of rape and sexual coercion that I value. Yet I raise these points in a desire to help strengthen and sharpen our critique of victimizing forms of sexual coercion, in ways that help prevent victimization and ameliorate the effects of potentially victimizing acts for individual women. If we don't ask these questions about the victimization framework, I sense we may risk leaving a fertile gap for backlash discourse to take hold. At the same time, this kind of move should create spaces for developing supplementary ways to critique both normative and violent forms of heterosexual practice—without losing sight of the possibility for both rape and more normative forms of sexual coercion to be victimizing. That is, it may enable us to issue new and more varied moral arguments against the cultural acceptance of a form of heterosexual practice in which it can be hard to tell the difference between "just sex" and rape.

NOTES

1. In some of Koss's studies women were asked this direct question in addition to many more of the specific behavioral questions.

2. Of course, men are also raped and sexually abused, but not usually by women. As I am writing largely about the rape and sexual coercion of women in heterosexual relationships, I refer to those who rape as men and those who are raped as women.

3. Another common criticism of this work centers on the ambiguity of questions about unwanted sexual intercourse and unwanted attempts that occurred "because a man gave you alcohol or drugs." Due to the ambiguity of the question, the validity of scoring affirmative

responses as "rape" has been questioned. Discussion of this problem with the research is beyond the scope of this [reading].

REFERENCES

Best, J. May/June 1997. Victimization and the victim industry. *Society,* 9–17.

Brownmiller, S. 1975. *Against our will: Men, women and rape.* Harmondsworth: Penguin.

Burt, M. R., and Estep, R. E. 1981. Who is a victim? Definitional problems in sexual victimization. *Victimology: An International Journal* 6, 15–28.

Denfeld, R. 1995. *The new Victorians: A young woman's challenge to the old feminist order.* New York: Warner Books.

Feldstein, R. 1997. *Political correctness: A response from the cultural left.* Minneapolis: University of Minnesota Press.

Fine, M. 1992. *Disruptive voices: The possibilities of feminist research.* Ann Arbor: University of Michigan Press.

Gavey, N. 1990. Rape and sexual coercion within heterosexual relationships: An intersection of psychological, feminist, and postmodern inquiries. Unpublished doctoral thesis, University of Auckland.

———. 1991a. Sexual victimization prevalence among Auckland university students: How much and who does it? *New Zealand Journal of Psychology* 20, 63–70.

———. 1991b. Sexual victimization prevalence among New Zealand university students. *Journal of Consulting and Clinical Psychology* 59, 464–466.

———. 1992. Technologies and effects of heterosexual coercion. *Feminism and Psychology* 2, 325–351.

Gilbert, N. 1994. Miscounting social ills. *Society* 31 (3),18–26.

Hwang, K. 1997. Excerpt from *The Humanist,* July/ August 1997. Cited in Talking stick. *Utne Reader,* (84), 41.

Kitzinger, C., and Wilkinson, S. 1997. Validating women's experience? Dilemmas in feminist research. *Feminism and Psychology* 7, 566–574.

Koss, M. P. 1985. The hidden rape victim: Personality, attitudinal, and situational characteristics. *Psychology of Women Quarterly* 9, 193–212.

———. 1988. Hidden rape: Sexual aggression and victimization in a national sample of students in higher education. In A. W. Burgess (ed.), *Rape and sexual assault,* Vol. 2 (pp. 3–25). New York and London: Garland.

Koss, M. P., Gidycz, C. A., and Wisniewski, N. 1987. The scope of rape: Incidence and prevalence of sexual aggression and victimization in a national sample of higher education students. *Journal of Consulting and Clinical Psychology* 55, 162–170.

Marcus, S. 1992. Fighting bodies, fighting words: A theory and politics of rape prevention. In J. Butler and J. W. Scott (eds.), *Feminists theorize the political* (pp. 385–403). New York: Routledge.

Newbold, G. 1996. Commentary on Professor Mary Koss's keynote address: Redefining rape. In J. Broadmore, C. Shand, and T. Warburton (eds.), *The proceedings of 'Rape: Ten years' progress? An interdisciplinary conference,'* Wellington, New Zealand, 27–30 March 1996 (pp. 144–146). Doctors for Sexual Abuse Care.

Paglia, C. 1992. Sex, art, and American culture. New York: Vintage Books.

Pineau, L. 1989. Date rape: A feminist analysis. *Law and Philosophy* 8, 217–243.

———. 1996. A response to my critics. In L. Francis (ed.), *Date rape: Feminism, philosophy, and the law* (pp. 63–107). University Park, PA: Pennsylvania State University Press.

Roiphe, K. 1993. *The morning after: Sex, fear, and feminism.* London: Hamish Hamilton.

Russell, D. E. H. 1982. *Rape in marriage.* New York: Macmillan.

———. 1984. *Sexual exploitation: Rape, child sexual abuse, and workplace harassment.* Beverly Hills: Sage.

Sommers, C. H. 1994. *Who stole feminism? How women have betrayed women.* New York: Simon & Schuster.

BDSM or Intimate Violence: How Do You Tell the Difference?

Denise Donnelly

What if I told you that a neighbor of yours had bitten, slapped, pinched, or verbally demeaned their partner? Would you be shocked? Outraged? Would you conclude that this person had committed intimate violence or partner abuse? Careful . . . what seems so simple at first glance may not be. What if I then told you that these actions took place during sex and with the consent of the partner? Would you still think of it as intimate violence?

Those who practice BDSM (bondage, discipline, dominance, submission, and/or sadomasochism) note that pain, humiliation, and dominance can be powerful sexual aphrodisiacs, and if practiced by two or more consenting adults, they are viable sexual choices. They argue that so long as consent is present, rules are agreed on beforehand, and safe sex is practiced, no abuse has taken place. They go on to point out that unlike most abusive relationships (in which a woman is victimized), often it is the male partner who is dominated, bound, humiliated, or made to feel pain in a BDSM relationship.

Advocates for battered women, on the other hand, argue that abusive relationships often masquerade as "alternative sexuality," allowing the batterers to justify the abuse and elude arrest. They note that battered women (and men) may go along with this explanation— all the while insisting the actions are consensual— because of reasons as diverse as love, fear of losing the other person, or the risk of being seriously injured or killed. Finally, they also point out that adults abused as children may be acting out old familiar scenarios where violence masquerades as love, and that they may not be able to recognize "healthy" sexual and intimate relationships.

So, how does one tell the difference between BDSM and intimate violence? It's not that easy. One writer[1] offered this suggestion: If it leaves one or both partners feeling trapped, used, angry, or afraid, then it is probably coercive and exploitive. If, on the other hand, it leaves them feeling free, creative, valued, and trusting, it is likely consensual sex play.

NOTE

1. Eckhart, T. J. (2005). "BDSM and Feminism: An Insider's View." Retrieved October 27, 2005, from www.columbia.edu/cu/sister/BDSM.html.

All That Sheltering Emptiness

Mattilda Bernstein Sycamore

I always liked hotel lobbies, the chandeliers and so much ceiling I'd yawn like I was oblivious really I was trying not to go in the wrong direction. If I made a mistake then the key was to act like it was the funniest thing, oh I'm so relaxed! I developed fantasies about what the receptionist did and did not know, fantasies that might involve mischief if our eyes met in a certain way—I wanted something like understanding, I'm not sure I would have called it that.

This particular hotel was the Hyatt or one of those chains, right on Central Park and the lobby wasn't on the ground level—more exclusive that way, the place was fancier than I'd expected. The mirrors sparkled and everything looked freshly-designed—camel, auburn, amber—a little different from the standard beige. I imagined the views were spectacular since the hotel was right on Central Park but tricks always have their curtains drawn, they don't want anyone to see anything not even the trees. This guy had the features of someone very popular in the '80s, swept-back hair and still a walled muscularity, disdain in his eyes he wanted to give me a massage, sure. He rubbed the hotel lotion into my back, something awful and floral-scented—strong hands I always needed a massage.

Of course then he was grinding on top of me, dick teasing my asshole—this was no surprise. Then his dick slid in, so easy and dangerous this was also familiar. I allowed a few thrusts so I could relax, then I said oh I need you to put on a condom. I was thinking about the lotion, what good would the condom do with lotion—maybe I should get a washcloth. His dick remained in my ass, so different when it slides in smoothly like foreplay instead of that desperation, push push push. I started to push myself upright, he was heavy on top of me, still thrusting as I struggled to get onto my knees I'll admit it was hot then he slammed me down on the bed. Oh. This is what's happening: his weight on my back he's holding me down I'm not sure I can get him off me.

I thought about screaming but what would that do—hotel security, they have ways of dealing with situations but nothing that would help me. Maybe no one would arrive at all, bruises or blood and more rage directed my way. At least I wasn't in pain, my asshole was relaxed I

was still hard he was fucking me faster I didn't want him to come in my ass, that was the important thing. Come on my face, I said—pull out and come on my face, I want your come on my face I want to eat your come. I wasn't sure if he was listening but then he did pull out and I rolled onto my back, he straddled me with shit on his dick in my face, jerking fast and moaning I could feel his come in between my chin and neck I closed my eyes.

The bathroom was always where I'd go to breathe; in the shower I was shaking, soft towel, just hurry up I need cocktails. Studying myself in the mirror before opening the door, do my eyes look okay? Back to the trick, he had his clothes on he wasn't smiling or frowning I wondered how often he did this. He handed me $250 in three crisp bills, I smiled and said thanks, I was glad for the money I wanted to think it was worth it.

Back into the elevator, it opened automatically at the lobby so the staff could pretend not to stare in, then downstairs to the ground level past those spotless mirrors, glass doors and then I was outside. Walking fast through the wind like everything and nothing mattered I wanted safety; I hailed a cab.

If I say that cocktails cleared my head, then you know that all my analysis failed me: I didn't tell anyone, I felt stupid; I thought it was my fault. Yes, there was force; no, he didn't pull out when I asked him to—but otherwise how was this trick different from every other guy who just slid it in? Every guy who assumed that if his dick was near my asshole and I was enjoying that gentle tease, the security of arousal—then forget about words, my consent had arrived.

New York is a lonely place, it was a lonely place for me eight years ago. I felt stupid because I couldn't use language to help—I was nervous that my friends would think I was someone to worry about. I thought maybe this was a trauma to push aside, with bigger issues in the picture, from a childhood of my father splitting me open to the overwhelm of the everyday. If consent was already assumed in the public sexual cultures where I searched for beauty amid the ruthlessness of objectification without appreciation, then what about the rooms where I swallowed cock for cash? I didn't want to call it rape because it felt so commonplace. Except for the shaking afterwards, desperation mixed with a determination to escape.

Sexual Assault on Campus: A Multilevel, Integrative Approach to Party Rape

Elizabeth A. Armstrong, Laura Hamilton, and Brian Sweeney

A 1997 National Institute of Justice study estimated that between one-fifth and one-quarter of women are the victims of completed or attempted rape while in college (Fisher, Cullen, and Turner 2000).[1] College women "are at greater risk for rape and other forms of sexual assault than women in the general population or in a comparable age group" (Fisher et al. 2000:iii).[2] At least half and perhaps as many as three-quarters of the sexual assaults that occur on college campuses involve alcohol consumption on the part of the victim, the perpetrator, or both (Abbey et al. 1996; Sampson 2002). The tight link between alcohol and sexual assault suggests that many sexual assaults that occur on college campuses are "party rapes."[3] A recent report by the U.S. Department of Justice defines party rape as a distinct form of rape, one that "occurs at an off-campus house or on- or off-campus fraternity and involves . . . plying a woman with alcohol or targeting an intoxicated woman" (Sampson 2002:6).[4] While party rape is classified as a form of acquaintance rape, it is not uncommon for the woman to have had no prior interaction with the assailant, that is, for the assailant to be an in-network stranger (Abbey et al. 1996).

Colleges and universities have been aware of the problem of sexual assault for at least 20 years, directing resources toward prevention and providing services to students who have been sexually assaulted. Programming has included education of various kinds, support for *Take Back the Night* events, distri-

bution of rape whistles, development and staffing of hotlines, training of police and administrators, and other efforts. Rates of sexual assault, however, have not declined over the last five decades (Adams-Curtis and Forbes 2004:95; Bachar and Koss 2001; Marine 2004; Sampson 2002:1).

Why do colleges and universities remain dangerous places for women in spite of active efforts to prevent sexual assault? While some argue that "we know what the problems are and we know how to change them" (Adams-Curtis and Forbes 2004:115), it is our contention that we do not have a complete explanation of the problem. To address this issue we use data from a study of college life at a large midwestern university and draw on theoretical developments in the sociology of gender (Connell 1987, 1995; Lorber 1994; Martin 2004; Risman 1998, 2004). Continued high rates of sexual assault can be viewed as a case of the reproduction of gender inequality—a phenomenon of central concern in gender theory.

We demonstrate that sexual assault is a predictable outcome of a synergistic intersection of both gendered and seemingly gender neutral processes operating at individual, organizational, and interactional levels. The concentration of homogenous students with expectations of partying fosters the development of sexualized peer cultures organized around status. Residential arrangements intensify students' desires to party in male-controlled fraternities. Cultural expectations that partygoers drink heavily and trust party-mates become problematic when combined with expectations that women be nice and defer to men. Fulfilling the role of the partier produces vulnerability on the part of women, which some men exploit to extract non-consensual sex. The party scene also produces fun, generating student investment in it.

From "Sexual Assault on Campus: A Multi-Level, Integrative Approach to Party Rape" by Elizabeth A. Armstrong, Laura Hamilton, and Brian Sweeney (2006), *Social Problems,* 53, 483–499.

Rather than criticizing the party scene or men's behavior, students blame victims. . . .

Approaches to College Sexual Assault

Explanations of high rates of sexual assault on college campuses fall into three broad categories. The first tradition, a psychological approach that we label the "individual determinants" approach, views college sexual assault as primarily a consequence of perpetrator or victim characteristics such as gender role attitudes, personality, family background, or sexual history (Flezzani and Benshoff 2003; Forbes and Adams-Curtis 2001; Rapaport and Burkhart 1984). While "situational variables" are considered, the focus is on individual characteristics (Adams-Curtis and Forbes 2004; Malamuth, Heavey, and Linz 1993). . . .

The second perspective, the "rape culture" approach, grew out of second wave feminism (Brownmiller 1975; Buchward, Fletcher, and Roth 1993; Lottes 1997; Russell 1975; Schwartz and DeKeseredy 1997). In this perspective, sexual assault is seen as a consequence of widespread belief in "rape myths," or ideas about the nature of men, women, sexuality, and consent that create an environment conducive to rape. . . .

A third approach moves beyond rape culture by identifying particular contexts—fraternities and bars—as sexually dangerous (Humphrey and Kahn 2000; Martin and Hummer 1989; Sanday 1990, 1996; Stombler 1994). Ayres Boswell and Joan Spade (1996) suggest that sexual assault is supported not only by "a generic culture surrounding and promoting rape," but also by characteristics of the "specific settings" in which men and women interact (p. 133). Mindy Stombler and Patricia Yancey Martin (1994) illustrate that gender inequality is institutionalized on campus by "formal structure" that supports and intensifies an already "high-pressure heterosexual peer group" (p. 180). This perspective grounds sexual assault in organizations that provide opportunities and resources.

We extend this third approach by linking it to recent theoretical scholarship in the sociology of gender. Martin (2004), Barbara Risman (1998; 2004),

Judith Lorber (1994) and others argue that gender is not only embedded in individual selves, but also in cultural rules, social interaction, and organizational arrangements. This integrative perspective identifies mechanisms at each level that contribute to the reproduction of gender inequality (Risman 2004). Socialization processes influence gendered selves, while cultural expectations reproduce gender inequality in interaction. At the institutional level, organizational practices, rules, resource distributions, and ideologies reproduce gender inequality. Applying this integrative perspective enabled us to identify gendered processes at individual, interactional, and organizational levels that contribute to college sexual assault. . . .

Method

Data are from group and individual interviews, ethnographic observation, and publicly available information collected at a large midwestern research university. Located in a small city, the school has strong academic and sports programs, a large Greek system, and is sought after by students seeking a quintessential college experience. . . .

The bulk of the data presented in this [reading] were collected as part of ethnographic observation during the 2004–05 academic year in a residence hall identified by students and residence hall staff as a "party dorm." While little partying actually occurs in the hall, many students view this residence hall as one of several places to live in order to participate in the party scene on campus. This made it a good place to study the social worlds of students at high risk of sexual assault—women attending fraternity parties in their first year of college. . . .

With at least one-third of first-year students on campus residing in "party dorms" and one-quarter of all undergraduates belonging to fraternities or sororities, this social world is the most visible on campus. As the most visible scene on campus, it also attracts students living in other residence halls and those not in the Greek system. Dense pre-college ties among the many in-state students, class and race homogeneity, and a small city location also contribute to the dominance of this scene. Of course, not all students . . .

participate in the party scene. To participate, one must typically be heterosexual, at least middle class, white, American-born, unmarried, childless, traditional college age, politically and socially mainstream, and interested in drinking. Over three-quarters of the women . . . we observed fit this description.

There were no non-white students among the first and second year students on the floor we studied. This is a result of the homogeneity of this campus and racial segregation in social and residential life. African Americans (who make up 3 to 5% of undergraduates) generally live in living-learning communities in other residence halls and typically do not participate in the white Greek party scene. We argue that the party scene's homogeneity contributes to sexual risk for white women. . . .

We . . . conducted 16 group interviews (involving 24 men and 63 women) in spring 2004. These individuals had varying relationships to the white Greek party scene on campus. Groups included residents of an alternative residence hall, lesbian, gay, and bisexual students, feminists, re-entry students, academically-focused students, fundamentalist Christians, and sorority women. . . .

We also incorporated publicly available information about the university from informal interviews with student affairs professionals and from teaching (by all authors) courses on gender, sexuality, and introductory sociology. Classroom data were collected through discussion, student writings, e-mail correspondence, and a survey that included questions about experiences of sexual assault.

Unless stated otherwise, all descriptions and interview quotations are from ethnographic observation or interviews. Passages in quotation marks are direct quotations from interviews or field notes. Study participants served as informants about venues where we could not observe (such as fraternity parties).

Explaining Party Rape

We show how gendered selves, organizational arrangements, and interactional expectations contribute to sexual assault. We also detail the contributions of processes at each level that are not explicitly gendered. We focus on each level in turn, while attending to the ways in which processes at all levels depend upon and reenforce others. We show that fun is produced along with sexual assault, leading students to resist criticism of the party scene.

Selves and Peer Culture in the Transition from High School to College . . .

Non-Gendered Characteristics Motivate Participation in Party Scenes

Without individuals available for partying, the party scene would not exist. All the women on our floor were single and childless, as are the vast majority of undergraduates at this university; many, being upper-middle class, had few responsibilities other than their schoolwork. Abundant leisure time, however, is not enough to fuel the party scene. Media, siblings, peers, and parents all serve as sources of anticipatory socialization (Merton 1957). Both partiers and non-partiers agreed that one was "supposed" to party in college. This orientation was reflected in the popularity of a poster titled "What I Really Learned in School" that pictured mixed drinks with names associated with academic disciplines. As one focus group participant explained:

> You see these images of college that you're supposed to go out and have fun and drink, drink lots, party and meet guys. [You are] supposed to hook up with guys, and both men and women try to live up to that. I think a lot of it is girls want to be accepted into their groups and guys want to be accepted into their groups.

Partying is seen as a way to feel a part of college life. Many of the women we observed participated in middle and high school peer cultures organized around status, belonging, and popularity (Eder 1985; Eder, Evans, and Parker 1995; Milner 2004). Assuming that college would be similar, they told us that they wanted to fit in, be popular, and have friends. Even on move-in day, they were supposed to already have friends. When we asked one of the outsiders, Ruth, about her first impression of her roommate, she replied that she found her:

> Extremely intimidating. Bethany already knew hundreds of people here. Her cell phone was going off from day one, like all the time. And I was too shy to ask anyone to go to dinner with me or lunch with me or anything. I ate while I did homework.

Bethany complained to the RA on move-in day that she did not want to be roommates with Ruth because she was weird. A group of women on the floor—including Bethany, but not Ruth—began partying together and formed a tight friendship group. Ruth noted: "There is a group on the side of the hall that goes to dinner together, parties together, my roommate included. I have never hung out with them once . . . And, yeah, it kind of sucks." Bethany moved out of the room at the end of the semester, leaving Ruth isolated.

Peer Culture as Gendered and Sexualized

Partying was also the primary way to meet men on campus.[5] The floor was locked to non-residents, and even men living in the same residence hall had to be escorted on the floor. The women found it difficult to get to know men in their classes, which were mostly mass lectures. They explained to us that people "don't talk" in class. Some complained they lacked casual friendly contact with men, particularly compared to the mixed-gender friendship groups they reported experiencing in high school.

Meeting men at parties was important to most of the women on our floor. The women found men's sexual interest at parties to be a source of self-esteem and status.[6] They enjoyed dancing and kissing at parties, explaining to us that it proved men "liked" them. This attention was not automatic, but required the skillful deployment of physical and cultural assets (Stombler and Padavic 1997; Swidler 2001). Most of the party-oriented women on the floor arrived with appropriate gender presentations and the money and know-how to preserve and refine them. While some more closely resembled the "ideal" college party girl (white, even features, thin but busty, tan, long straight hair, skillfully made-up, and well-dressed in the latest youth styles), most worked hard to attain this presentation. They regularly straightened their hair, tanned, exercised, dieted, and purchased new clothes.

Women found that achieving high erotic status in the party scene required looking "hot" but not "slutty," a difficult and ongoing challenge (West and Zimmerman 1987). Mastering these distinctions allowed them to establish themselves as "classy" in contrast to other women (Handler 1995; Stombler

1994). Although women judged other women's appearance, men were the most important audience. A "hot" outfit could earn attention from desirable men in the party scene. A failed outfit, as some of our women learned, could earn scorn from men. One woman reported showing up to a party dressed in a knee length skirt and blouse only to find that she needed to show more skin. A male guest sarcastically told her "nice outfit," accompanied by a thumbs-up gesture.

The psychological benefits of admiration from men in the party scene were such that women in relationships sometimes felt deprived. One woman with a serious boyfriend noted that she dressed more conservatively at parties because of him, but this meant she was not "going to get any of the attention." She lamented that no one was "going to waste their time with me" and that, "this is taking away from my confidence." Like most women who came to college with boyfriends, she soon broke up with him.

Men also sought proof of their erotic appeal. As a woman complained, "Every man I have met here has wanted to have sex with me!" Another interviewee reported that: "this guy that I was talking to for like ten/fifteen minutes says, 'Could you, um, come to the bathroom with me and jerk me off?' And I'm like, 'What!' I'm like, 'Okay, like, I've known you for like, fifteen minutes, but no.'" The women found that men were more interested than they were in having sex. These clashes in sexual expectations are not surprising: men derived status from securing sex (from high-status women), while women derived status from getting attention (from high-status men). These agendas are both complementary and adversarial: men give attention to women en route to getting sex, and women are unlikely to become interested in sex without getting attention first.

University and Greek Rules, Resources, and Procedures

Simply by congregating similar individuals, universities make possible heterosexual peer cultures. The university, the Greek system, and other related organizations structure student life through rules, distribution of resources, and procedures (Risman 2004).

Sexual danger is an unintended consequence of many university practices intended to be gender neutral. The clustering of homogeneous students intensifies the dynamics of student peer cultures and heightens motivations to party. Characteristics of residence halls and how they are regulated push student partying into bars, off-campus residences, and fraternities. While factors that increase the risk of party rape are present in varying degrees in all party venues (Boswell and Spade 1996), we focus on fraternity parties because they were the typical party venue for the women we observed and have been identified as particularly unsafe (see also Martin and Hummer 1989; Sanday 1990). Fraternities offer the most reliable and private source of alcohol for first-year students excluded from bars and house parties because of age and social networks.

University Practices as Push Factors

The university has latitude in how it enforces state drinking laws. Enforcement is particularly rigorous in residence halls. We observed RAs and police officers (including gun-carrying peer police) patrolling the halls for alcohol violations. . . . As a consequence, students engaged in only minimal, clandestine alcohol consumption in their rooms. In comparison, alcohol flows freely at fraternities.

The lack of comfortable public space for informal socializing in the residence hall also serves as a push factor. A large central bathroom divided our floor. A sterile lounge was rarely used for socializing. There was no cafeteria, only a convenience store and a snack bar in a cavernous room furnished with big-screen televisions. Residence life sponsored alternatives to the party scene such as "movie night" and special dinners, but these typically occurred early in the evening. Students defined the few activities sponsored during party hours (e.g., a midnight trip to Wal-Mart) as uncool.

Intensifying Peer Dynamics

The residence halls near athletic facilities and Greek houses are known by students to house affluent, party-oriented students. White, upper-middle class, first-year students who plan to rush request these residence halls, while others avoid them. One of

our residents explained that "everyone knows what [the residence hall] is like and people are dying to get in here. People just think it's a total party or something." . . .

The homogeneity of the floor intensified social anxiety, heightening the importance of partying for making friends. Early in the year, the anxiety was palpable on weekend nights as women assessed their social options by asking where people were going, when, and with whom. One exhausted floor resident told us she felt that she "needed to" go out to protect her position in a friendship group. At the beginning of the semester, "going out" on weekends was virtually compulsory. By 11 p.m. the floor was nearly deserted.

Male Control of Fraternity Parties

The campus Greek system cannot operate without university consent. The university lists Greek organizations as student clubs, devotes professional staff to Greek-oriented programming, and disbands fraternities that violate university policy. Nonetheless, the university lacks full authority over fraternities; Greek houses are privately owned and chapters answer to national organizations and the Interfraternity Council (IFC) (i.e., a body governing the more than 20 predominantly white fraternities).

Fraternities control every aspect of parties at their houses: themes, music, transportation, admission, access to alcohol, and movement of guests. Party themes usually require women to wear scant, sexy clothing and place women in subordinate positions to men. During our observation period, women attended parties such as "Pimps and Hos," "Victoria's Secret," and "Playboy Mansion"—the last of which required fraternity members to escort two scantily-clad dates. Other recent themes included: "CEO/Secretary Ho," "School Teacher/Sexy Student," and "Golf Pro/Tennis Ho."

Some fraternities require pledges to transport first-year students, primarily women, from the residence halls to the fraternity houses. From about 9 to 11 p.m. on weekend nights early in the year, the drive in front of the residence hall resembled a rowdy taxi-stand, as dressed-to-impress women waited to be carpooled to parties in expensive late-model vehicles. By allowing party-oriented first-year women to cluster in particular residence halls, the university made them easy to find. One fraternity member told us this practice was referred to as "dorm-storming."

Transportation home was an uncertainty. Women sometimes called cabs, caught the "drunk bus," or trudged home in stilettos. Two women indignantly described a situation where fraternity men "wouldn't give us a ride home." The women said, "Well, let us call a cab." The men discouraged them from calling the cab and eventually found a designated driver. The women described the men as "just dicks" and as "rude."

Fraternities police the door of their parties, allowing in desirable guests (first-year women) and turning away others (unaffiliated men). . . .

Fraternities are constrained . . . by the necessity of attracting women to their parties. Fraternities with reputations for sexual disrespect have more success recruiting women to parties early in the year. One visit was enough for some of the women. A roommate duo told of a house they "liked at first" until they discovered that the men there were "really not nice."

The Production of Fun and Sexual Assault in Interaction

Peer culture and organizational arrangements set up risky partying conditions, but do not explain *how* student interactions at parties generate sexual assault. At the interactional level we see the mechanisms through which sexual assault is produced. As interactions necessarily involve individuals with particular characteristics and occur in specific organizational settings, all three levels meet when interactions take place. Here, gendered and gender neutral expectations and routines are intricately woven together to create party rape. Party rape is the result of fun situations that shift—either gradually or quite suddenly—into coercive situations. . . .

College partying involves predictable activities in a predictable order (e.g., getting ready, pre-gaming,[7] getting to the party, getting drunk, flirtation or sexual interaction, getting home, and sharing stories). It is characterized by "shared assumptions about what constitutes good or adequate participation." . . . A fun partier throws him or herself into the event, drinks,

displays an upbeat mood, and evokes revelry in others. Partiers are expected to like and trust partymates. Norms of civil interaction curtail displays of unhappiness or tension among partygoers. . . . Drinking assists people in transitioning from everyday life to a state of euphoria.

Cultural expectations of partying are gendered. Women are supposed to wear revealing outfits, while men typically are not. As guests, women cede control of turf, transportation, and liquor. Women are also expected to be grateful for men's hospitality, and as others have noted, to generally be "nice" in ways that men are not (Gilligan 1982; Martin 2003; Phillips 2000; Stombler and Martin 1994; Tolman 2002). The pressure to be deferential and gracious may be intensified by men's older age and fraternity membership.[8] The quandary for women, however, is that fulfilling the gendered role of partier makes them vulnerable to sexual assault.

Women's vulnerability produces sexual assault only if men exploit it. Too many men are willing to do so. Many college men attend parties looking for casual sex. A student in one of our classes explained that "guys are willing to do damn near anything to get a piece of ass." A male student wrote the following description of parties at his (non-fraternity) house:

> Girls are continually fed drinks of alcohol. It's mainly to party but my roomies are also aware of the inhibition-lowering effects. I've seen an old roomie block doors when girls want to leave his room; and other times I've driven women home who can't remember much of an evening yet sex did occur. Rarely if ever has a night of drinking for my roommate ended without sex. I know it isn't necessarily and assuredly sexual assault, but with the amount of liquor in the house I question the amount of consent a lot.

Another student—after deactivating—wrote about a fraternity brother "telling us all at the chapter meeting about how he took this girl home and she was obviously too drunk to function and he took her inside and had sex with her." Getting women drunk, blocking doors, and controlling transportation are common ways men try to prevent women from leaving sexual situations. Rape culture beliefs, such as the belief that men are "naturally" sexually aggressive, normalize these coercive strategies. Assigning women the role of sexual "gatekeeper" relieves men from responsibility for obtaining authentic consent, and enables them to view sex obtained by undermining women's ability to resist it as "consensual" (e.g., by getting women so drunk that they pass out).[9]

In a focus group with her sorority sisters, a junior sorority woman provided an example of a partying situation that devolved into a likely sexual assault.

> *Anna:* It kind of happened to me freshman year. I'm not positive about what happened, that's the worst part about it. I drank too much at a frat one night, I blacked out and I woke up the next morning with nothing on in their cold dorms, so I don't really know what happened and the guy wasn't in the bed anymore, I don't even think I could tell you who the hell he was, no I couldn't.
>
> *Sarah:* Did you go to the hospital?
>
> *Anna:* No, I didn't know what happened. I was scared and wanted to get the hell out of there. I didn't know who it was, so how am I supposed to go to the hospital and say someone might've raped me? It could have been any one of the hundred guys that lived in the house.
>
> *Sarah:* It happens to so many people, it would shock you. Three of my best friends in the whole world, people that you like would think it would never happen to, it happened to. It's just so hard because you don't know how to deal with it because you don't want to turn in a frat because all hundred of those brothers . . .
>
> *Anna:* I was also thinking like, you know, I just got to school, I don't want to start off on a bad note with anyone, and now it happened so long ago, it's just one of those things that I kind of have to live with.

This woman's confusion demonstrates the usefulness of alcohol as a weapon: her intoxication undermined her ability to resist sex, her clarity about what happened, and her feelings of entitlement to report it (Adams-Curtis and Forbes 2004; Martin and Hummer 1989). . . .

Amanda, a woman on our hall, provides insight into how men take advantage of women's niceness, gender deference, and unequal control of party resources. Amanda reported meeting a "cute" older guy, Mike, also a student, at a local student bar. She explained that, "At the bar we were kind of making out a little bit

and I told him just cause I'm sitting here making out doesn't mean that I want to go home with you, you know?" After Amanda found herself stranded by friends with no cell phone or cab fare, Mike promised that a sober friend of his would drive her home. Once they got in the car Mike's friend refused to take her home and instead dropped her at Mike's place. Amanda's concerns were heightened by the driver's disrespect. "He was like, so are you into ménage à trois?" Amanda reported staying awake all night. She woke Mike early in the morning to take her home. Despite her ordeal, she argued that Mike was "a really nice guy" and exchanged telephone numbers with him.

These men took advantage of Amanda's unwillingness to make a scene. Amanda was one of the most assertive women on our floor. Indeed, her refusal to participate fully in the culture of feminine niceness led her to suffer in the social hierarchy of the floor and on campus. It is unlikely that other women we observed could have been more assertive in this situation. That she was nice to her captor in the morning suggests how much she wanted him to like her and what she was willing to tolerate in order to keep his interest.[10]

. . . [M]en can control party resources and work together to constrain women's behavior while partying in bars and at house parties. What distinguishes fraternity parties is that male dominance of partying there is organized, resourced, and implicitly endorsed by the university. Other party venues are also organized in ways that advantage men.

We heard many stories of negative experiences in the party scene, including at least one account of a sexual assault in every focus group that included heterosexual women. Most women who partied complained about men's efforts to control their movements or pressure them to drink. Two of the women on our floor were sexually assaulted at a fraternity party in the first week of school—one was raped. Later in the semester, another woman on the floor was raped by a friend. A fourth woman on the floor suspects she was drugged; she became disoriented at a fraternity party and was very ill for the next week.

Party rape is accomplished without the use of guns, knives, or fists. It is carried out through the combination of low level forms of coercion—a lot of liquor and persuasion, manipulation of situations so that women cannot leave, and sometimes force (e.g., by blocking a door, or using body weight to make it difficult for a woman to get up). These forms of coercion are made more effective by organizational arrangements that provide men with control over how partying happens and by expectations that women let loose and trust their party-mates. This systematic and effective method of extracting non-consensual sex is largely invisible, which makes it difficult for victims to convince anyone—even themselves—that a crime occurred. Men engage in this behavior with little risk of consequences.

Student Responses and the Resiliency of the Party Scene

The frequency of women's negative experiences in the party scene poses a problem for those students most invested in it. Finding fault with the party scene potentially threatens meaningful identities and lifestyles. The vast majority of heterosexual encounters at parties are fun and consensual. Partying provides a chance to meet new people, experience and display belonging, and to enhance social position. Women on our floor told us that they loved to flirt and be admired, and they displayed pictures on walls, doors, and websites commemorating their fun nights out.

The most common way that students—both women and men—account for the harm that befalls women in the party scene is by blaming victims. By attributing bad experiences to women's "mistakes," students avoid criticizing the party scene or men's behavior within it. Such victim-blaming also allows women to feel that they can control what happens to them. . . . When discussing the sexual assault of a friend, a floor resident explained that:

> She somehow got like sexually assaulted . . . by one of our friends' old roommates. All I know is that kid was like bad news to start off with. So, I feel sorry for her but it wasn't much of a surprise for us. He's a shady character.

Another floor resident relayed a sympathetic account of a woman raped at knife point by a stranger in the bushes, but later dismissed party rape as nothing to worry about " 'cause I'm not stupid when I'm drunk." Even a feminist focus group participant explained that her friend who was raped "made every single mistake and almost all of them had to with alcohol. . . . She got ridiculed when she came out and said she was raped." These women contrast "true victims" who are deserving of support with "stupid" women who forfeit sympathy (Phillips 2000). Not only is this response devoid of empathy for other women, but it also leads women to blame themselves when they are victimized (Phillips 2000).

Sexual assault prevention strategies can perpetuate victim-blaming. Instructing women to watch their drinks, stay with friends, and limit alcohol consumption implies that it is women's responsibility to avoid "mistakes" and their fault if they fail. Emphasis on the precautions women should take—particularly if not accompanied by education about how men should change their behavior—may also suggest that it is natural for men to drug women and take advantage of them. . . .

Victim-blaming also serves as a way for women to construct a sense of status within campus erotic hierarchies. As discussed earlier, women and men acquire erotic status based on how "hot" they are perceived to be. Another aspect of erotic status concerns the amount of sexual respect one receives from men (see Holland and Eisenhart 1990:101). Women can tell themselves that they are safe from sexual assault not only because they are savvy, but because men will recognize that they, unlike other women, are worthy of sexual respect. For example, a focus group of senior women explained that at a small fraternity gathering their friend Amy came out of the bathroom. She was crying and said that a guy "had her by her neck, holding her up, feeling her up from her crotch up to her neck and saying that I should rape you, you are a fucking whore." The woman's friends were appalled, saying, "no one deserves that." On other hand, they explained that: "Amy flaunts herself. She is a whore so, I mean . . ." They implied that if one is a whore, one gets treated like one. [11]

Men accord women varying levels of sexual respect, with lower status women seen as "fair game" (Holland and Eisenhart 1990; Phillips 2000). On campus the youngest and most anonymous women are most vulnerable. High-status women (i.e., girlfriends of fraternity members) may be less likely victims of party rape.[12] Sorority women explained that fraternities discourage members from approaching the girlfriends (and ex-girlfriends) of other men in the house. Partiers on our floor learned that it was safer to party with men they knew as boyfriends, friends, or brothers of friends. . . .

Opting Out

While many students find the party scene fun, others are more ambivalent. Some attend a few fraternity parties to feel like they have participated in this college tradition. Others opt out of it altogether. On our floor, 44 out of the 51 first-year students (almost 90%) participated in the party scene. Those on the floor who opted out worried about sexual safety and the consequences of engaging in illegal behavior. For example, an interviewee who did not drink was appalled by the fraternity party transport system. She explained that:

> All those girls would stand out there and just like, no joke, get into these big black Suburbans driven by frat guys, wearing like seriously no clothes, piled on top of each other. This could be some kidnapper taking you all away to the woods and chopping you up and leaving you there. How dumb can you be?

. . . Her position was unpopular. She, like others who did not party, was an outsider on the floor. Partiers came home loudly in the middle of the night, threw up in the bathrooms, and rollerbladed around the floor. Socially, the others simply did not exist. A few of our "misfits" successfully created social lives outside the floor. The most assertive of the "misfits" figured out the dynamics of the floor in the first weeks and transferred to other residence halls.

However, most students on our floor lacked the identities or network connections necessary for entry into alternative worlds. Life on a large university campus can be overwhelming for first-year students. Those who most needed an alternative to the social world of the party dorm were often ill-equipped to actively seek it out. They either integrated themselves into partying or found themselves alone in their

rooms, microwaving frozen dinners and watching television. . . .

Discussion and Implications

We have demonstrated that processes at individual, organizational, and interactional levels contribute to high rates of sexual assault.[13] Some individual level characteristics that shape the likelihood of a sexually dangerous party scene developing are not explicitly gendered. Party rape occurs at high rates in places that cluster young, single, party-oriented people concerned about social status. Traditional beliefs about sexuality also make it more likely that one will participate in the party scene and increase danger within the scene. This university contributes to sexual danger by allowing these individuals to cluster.

However, congregating people is not enough, as parties cannot be produced without resources (e.g., alcohol and a viable venue) that are difficult for underage students to obtain. University policies that are explicitly gender-neutral—such as the policing of alcohol use in residence halls—have gendered consequences. This policy encourages first-year students to turn to fraternities to party. Only fraternities, not sororities, are allowed to have parties, and men structure parties in ways that control the appearance, movement, and behavior of female guests. Men also control the distribution of alcohol and use its scarcity to engineer social interactions. The enforcement of alcohol policy by both university and Greek organizations transforms alcohol from a mere beverage into an unequally distributed social resource.

Individual characteristics and institutional practices provide the actors and contexts in which interactional processes occur. We have to turn to the interactional level, however, to understand *how* sexual assault is generated. Gender neutral expectations to "have fun," lose control, and trust one's party-mates become problematic when combined with gendered interactional expectations. Women are expected to be "nice" and to defer to men in interaction. This expectation is intensified by men's position as hosts and women's as grateful guests. The heterosexual script, which directs men to pursue sex and women to play the role of gatekeeper, further disadvantages women, particularly when virtually *all* men's methods of extracting sex are defined as legitimate.

The mechanisms identified should help explain intra-campus, cross-campus, and over time variation in the prevalence of sexual assault. . . . We would expect to see lower rates of sexual assault on campuses characterized by more aesthetically appealing public space, lower alcohol use, and the absence of a gender-adversarial party scene. Campuses with more racial diversity and more racial integration would also be expected to have lower rates of sexual assault because of the dilution of upper-middle class white peer groups. . . .

This perspective may also help explain why white college women are at higher risk of sexual assault than other racial groups. Existing research suggests that African American college social scenes are more gender egalitarian (Stombler and Padavic 1997). African American fraternities typically do not have houses, depriving men of a party resource. The missions, goals, and recruitment practices of African American fraternities and sororities discourage joining for exclusively social reasons (Berkowitz and Padavic 1999), and rates of alcohol consumption are lower among African American students (Journal of Blacks in Higher Education 2000; Weschsler and Kuo 2003). The role of party rape in the lives of white college women is substantiated by recent research that found that "white women were more likely [than non-white women] to have experienced rape while intoxicated and less likely to experience other rape" (Mohler-Kuo et al. 2004:41). . . .

Our analysis also provides a framework for analyzing the sources of sexual risk in non-university partying situations. Situations where men have a home turf advantage, know each other better than the women present know each other, see the women as anonymous, and control desired resources (such as alcohol or drugs) are likely to be particularly dangerous. Social pressures to "have fun," prove one's social competency, or adhere to traditional gender expectations are also predicted to increase rates of sexual assault within a social scene.

This research has implications for policy. The interdependence of levels means that it is difficult to enact change at one level when the other levels remain unchanged. Programs to combat sexual assault currently focus primarily or even exclusively on education (Bachar and Koss 2001; Leaning 2003). But as Ann Swidler (2001) argued, culture develops in response to institutional arrangements. Without change in institutional arrangements, efforts to change cultural beliefs are undermined by the cultural commonsense generated by encounters with institutions. Efforts to educate about sexual assault will not succeed if the university continues to support organizational arrangements that facilitate and even legitimate men's coercive sexual strategies. Thus, our research implies that efforts to combat sexual assault on campus should target all levels, constituencies, and processes simultaneously. Efforts to educate both men and women should indeed be intensified, but they should be reinforced by changes in the social organization of student life.

Researchers focused on problem drinking on campus have found that reduction efforts focused on the social environment are successful (Berkowitz 2003:21). Student body diversity has been found to decrease binge drinking on campus (Weschsler and Kuo 2003); it might also reduce rates of sexual assault. Existing student heterogeneity can be exploited by eliminating self-selection into age-segregated, white, upper-middle class, heterosexual enclaves and by working to make residence halls more appealing to upper-division students. Building more aesthetically appealing housing might allow students to interact outside of alcohol-fueled party scenes. Less expensive plans might involve creating more living-learning communities, coffee shops, and other student-run community spaces.

While heavy alcohol use is associated with sexual assault, not all efforts to regulate student alcohol use contribute to sexual safety. Punitive approaches sometimes heighten the symbolic significance of drinking, lead students to drink more hard liquor, and push alcohol consumption to more private and thus more dangerous spaces. Regulation inconsistently applied—e.g., heavy policing of residence halls and light policing of fraternities—increases the power of those who can secure alcohol and host parties. More consistent regulation could decrease the value of alcohol as a commodity by equalizing access to it.

Sexual assault education should shift in emphasis from educating women on preventative measures to educating both men and women about the coercive behavior of men and the sources of victim-blaming. Mohler-Kuo and associates (2004) suggest, and we endorse, a focus on the role of alcohol in sexual assault. Education should begin before students arrive on campus and continue throughout college. It may also be most effective if high-status peers are involved in disseminating knowledge and experience to younger college students.

Change requires resources and cooperation among many people. Efforts to combat sexual assault are constrained by other organizational imperatives. Student investment in the party scene makes it difficult to enlist the support of even those most harmed by the state of affairs. Student and alumni loyalty to partying (and the Greek system) mean that challenges to the party scene could potentially cost universities tuition dollars and alumni donations. Universities must contend with Greek organizations and bars, as well as the challenges of internal coordination. Fighting sexual assault on all levels is critical, though, because it is unacceptable for higher education institutions to be sites where women are predictably sexually victimized.

NOTES

1. Other studies have found similar rates of college sexual assault (Abbey et al. 1996; Adams-Curtis and Forbes 2004; Copenhaver and Grauerholz 1991; DeKeseredy and Kelly 1993; Fisher et al. 1998; Humphrey and White 2000; Koss 1988; Koss, Gidycz, and Wisniewski 1987; Mills and Granoff 1992; Muehlenhard and Linton 1987; Tjaden and Thoennes 2000; Ward et al. 1991).

2. While assaults within gender and by women occur, the vast majority involve men assaulting women.

3. Other forms of acquaintance rape include date rape, rape in a non-party/non-date situation, and rape by a former or current intimate (Sampson 2002).

4. On party rape as a distinct type of sexual assault, see also Ward and associates (1991). Ehrhart and Sandler (1987) use the term to refer to group rape. We use the term to refer to one-on-one assaults. We encountered no reports of group sexual assault.

5. This is consistent with Boswell and Spade's (1996) finding that women participate in dangerous party scenes because of a lack of "other means to initiate contact with men on campus" (p. 145).

6. See also Stombler and Martin (1994). Holland and Eisenhart (1990) discuss a "culture of romance" in which women derive status from boyfriends. Among the first-year women we observed, status revolved more around getting male attention than male commitment. Focus group interviews with junior and senior sorority women suggest that acquiring high-status fraternity men as boyfriends occurs after women are integrated into Greek life.

7. Pre-gaming involved the clandestine consumption of alcohol—often hard liquor—before arriving at the party.

8. Stombler and Martin (1994:156) found that fraternity men demanded "niceness" from women with whom they partied. They selected "little sisters" on the basis of physical beauty and "charm, friendliness, and outgoingness."

9. In ongoing research on college men and sexuality, Sweeney (2004) and Rosow and Ray (2006) have found wide variation in beliefs about acceptable ways to obtain sex even among men who belong to the same fraternities. Rosow and Ray found that fraternity men in the most elite houses view sex with intoxicated women as low status and claim to avoid it.

10. Holland and Eisenhart (1990) and Stombler (1994) found that male attention is of such high value to some women that they are willing to suffer indignities to receive it.

11. Schwalbe and associates (2000) suggest that there are several psychological mechanisms that explain this behavior. *Trading power for patronage* occurs when a subordinate group accepts their status in exchange for compensatory benefits from the dominant group. *Defensive othering* is a process by which some members of a subordinated group seek to maintain status by deflecting stigma to others. Maneuvering to protect or improve individual position within hierarchical classification systems is common; however, these responses support the subordination that makes them necessary.

12. While "knowing" one's male party-mates may offer some protection, this protection is not comprehensive. Sorority women, who typically have the closest ties with fraternity men, experience more sexual assault than other college women (Mohler-Kuo et al. 2004). Not only do sorority women typically spend more time in high-risk social situations than other women, but arriving at a high-status position on campus may require one to begin their college social career as one of the anonymous young women who are frequently victimized.

13. Our recommendations echo and extend those of Boswell and Spade (1996:145) and Stombler and Martin (1994:180).

REFERENCES

Abbey, Antonia, Lisa Thomson Ross, Donna McDuffie, and Pam McAuslan. 1996. "Alcohol and Dating Risk Factors for Sexual Assault among College Women." *Psychology of Women Quarterly* 20:147–69.

Adams-Curtis, Leah and Gordon Forbes. 2004. "College Women's Experiences of Sexual Coercion: A Review of Cultural, Perpetrator, Victim, and Situational Variables." *Trauma, Violence, and Abuse: A Review Journal* 5:91–122.

Bachar, Karen and Mary Koss. 2001. "From Prevalence to Prevention: Closing the Gap between What We Know about Rape and What We Do." Pp. 117–42 in *Sourcebook on Violence against Women,* edited by C. Renzetti, J. Edleson, and R. K. Bergen. Thousand Oaks, CA: Sage.

Berkowitz, Alan. 2003. "How Should We Talk about Student Drinking—And What Should We Do about It?" *About Campus* May/June:16–22.

Berkowitz, Alexandra and Irene Padavic. 1999. "Getting a Man or Getting Ahead: A Comparison of White and Black Sororities." *Journal of Contemporary Ethnography* 27:530–57.

Boswell, A. Ayres and Joan Z. Spade. 1996. "Fraternities and Collegiate Rape Culture: Why Are Some Fraternities More Dangerous Places for Women?" *Gender & Society* 10:133–47.

Brownmiller, Susan. 1975. *Against Our Will: Men, Women, and Rape*. New York: Bantam Books.

Buchward, Emilie, Pamela Fletcher, and Martha Roth, eds. 1993. *Transforming a Rape Culture*. Minneapolis, MN: Milkweed Editions.

Connell, R. W. 1987. *Gender and Power*. Palo Alto, CA: Stanford University Press.

———. 1995. *Masculinities*. Berkeley, CA: University of California Press.

Copenhaver, Stacey and Elizabeth Grauerholz. 1991. "Sexual Victimization among Sorority Women: Exploring the Link between Sexual Violence and Institutional Practices." *Sex Roles* 24:31–41.

DeKeseredy, Walter and Katharine Kelly. 1993. "The Incidence and Prevalence of Women Abuse in Canadian University and College Dating Relationships." *Canadian Journal of Sociology* 18:137–59.

Eder, Donna. 1985. "The Cycle of Popularity: Interpersonal Relations among Female Adolescents." *Sociology of Education* 58:154–65.

Eder, Donna, Catherine Evans, and Stephen Parker. 1995. *School Talk: Gender and Adolescent Culture*. New Brunswick, NJ: Rutgers University Press.

Ehrhart, Julie and Bernice Sandler. 1987. "Party Rape." *Response* 9:205.

Fisher, Bonnie, Francis Cullen, and Michael Turner. 2000. "The Sexual Victimization of College Women." Washington, DC: National Institute of Justice and the Bureau of Justice Statistics.

Fisher, Bonnie, John Sloan, Francis Cullen, and Lu Chunmeng. 1998. "Crime in the Ivory Tower: The Level and Sources of Student Victimization." *Criminology* 36:671–710.

Flezzani, James and James Benshoff. 2003. "Understanding Sexual Aggression in Male College Students: The Role of Self-Monitoring and Pluralistic Ignorance." *Journal of College Counseling* 6:69–79.

Forbes, Gordon and Leah Adams-Curtis. 2001. "Experiences with Sexual Coercion in College Males and Females: Role of Family Conflict, Sexist Attitudes, Acceptance of Rape Myths, Self-Esteem, and the Big-Five Personality Factors." *Journal of Interpersonal Violence* 16:865–89.

Gilligan, Carol. 1982. *In a Different Voice: Psychological Theory and Women's Development*. Cambridge, MA: Harvard University Press.

Handler, Lisa. 1995. "In the Fraternal Sisterhood: Sororities as Gender Strategy." *Gender & Society* 9:236–55.

Holland, Dorothy and Margaret Eisenhart. 1990. *Educated in Romance: Women, Achievement, and College Culture*. Chicago: University of Chicago Press.

Humphrey, John and Jacquelyn White. 2000. "Women's Vulnerability to Sexual Assault from Adolescence to Young Adulthood." *Journal of Adolescent Health* 27:419–24.

Humphrey, Stephen and Arnold Kahn. 2000. "Fraternities, Athletic Teams, and Rape: Importance of Identification with A Risky Group." *Journal of Interpersonal Violence* 15:1313–22.

Journal of Blacks in Higher Education. 2000. "News and Views: Alcohol Abuse Remains High on College Campus, But Black Students Drink to Excess Far Less Often Than Whites." *The Journal of Blacks in Higher Education*. 28:19–20.

Koss, Mary. 1988. "Hidden Rape: Incidence and Prevalence of Sexual Aggression and Victimization in a National Sample of Students in Higher Education."

pp. 4–25 in *Rape and Sexual Assault*, edited by Ann W. Burgess. New York: Garland.

Koss, Mary, Christine Gidycz, and Nadine Wisniewski. 1987. "The Scope of Rape: Incidence and Prevalence of Sexual Aggression and Victimization in a National Sample of Higher Education Students." *Journal of Counseling and Clinical Psychology* 55:162–70.

Leaning, Jennifer. April 2003. "Committee to Address Sexual Assault at Harvard: Public Report." Cambridge, MA: Harvard University.

Lorber, Judith. 1994. *Paradoxes of Gender*. New Haven, CT: Yale University Press.

Lottes, Ilsa L. 1997. "Sexual Coercion among University Students: A Comparison of the United States and Sweden." *Journal of Sex Research* 34:67–76.

Malamuth, Neil, Christopher Heavey, and Daniel Linz. 1993. "Predicting Men's Antisocial Behavior against Women: The Interaction Model of Sexual Aggression." Pp. 63–98 in *Sexual Aggression: Issues in Etiology, Assessment, and Treatment*, edited by G. N. Hall, R. Hirschman, J. Graham, and M. Zaragoza. Washington, DC: Taylor and Francis.

Marine, Susan. 2004. "Waking Up from the Nightmare of Rape." *The Chronicle of Higher Education*. November 26, p. B5.

Martin, Karin. 2003. "Giving Birth Like a Girl." *Gender & Society*. 17:54–72.

Martin, Patricia Yancey. 2004. "Gender as a Social Institution." *Social Forces* 82:1249–73.

Martin, Patricia Yancey and Robert A. Hummer. 1989. "Fraternities and Rape on Campus." *Gender & Society* 3:457–73.

Merton, Robert. 1957. *Social Theory and Social Structure*. New York: Free Press.

Mills, Crystal and Barbara Granoff. 1992. "Date and Acquaintance Rape among a Sample of College Students." *Social Work* 37:504–09.

Milner, Murray. 2004. *Freaks, Geeks, and Cool Kids: American Teenagers, Schools, and the Culture of Consumption*. New York: Routledge.

Mohler-Kuo, Meichun, George W. Dowdall, Mary P. Koss, and Henry Weschler. 2004. "Correlates of Rape While Intoxicated in a National Sample of College Women." *Journal of Studies on Alcohol* 65:37–45.

Muehlenhard, Charlene and Melaney Linton. 1987. "Date Rape and Sexual Aggression: Incidence and Risk Factors." *Journal of Counseling Psychology* 34:186–96.

Phillips, Lynn. 2000. *Flirting with Danger: Young Women's Reflections on Sexuality and Domination*. New York: New York University.

Rapaport, Karen and Barry Burkhart. 1984. "Personality and Attitudinal Characteristics of Sexually Coercive College Males." *Journal of Abnormal Psychology* 93:216–21.

Risman, Barbara. 1998. *Gender Vertigo: American Families in Transition*. New Haven, CT: Yale University Press.

———. 2004. "Gender as a Social Structure: Theory Wrestling with Activism." *Gender & Society* 18:429–50.

Rosow, Jason and Rashawn Ray. 2006. "Getting Off and Showing Off: The Romantic and Sexual Lives of High-Status Black and White Status Men." Department of Sociology, Indiana University, Bloomington, IN. Unpublished manuscript.

Russell, Diana. 1975. *The Politics of Rape*. New York: Stein and Day.

Sampson, Rana. 2002. "Acquaintance Rape of College Students." Problem-Oriented Guides for Police Series, No. 17. Washington, DC: U.S. Department of Justice, Office of Community Oriented Policing Services.

Sanday, Peggy. 1990. *Fraternity Gang Rape: Sex, Brotherhood, and Privilege on Campus*. New York: New York University Press.

———. 1996. "Rape-Prone versus Rape-Free Campus Cultures." *Violence against Women* 2:191–208.

Schwalbe, Michael, Sandra Godwin, Daphne Holden, Douglas Schrock, Shealy Thompson, and Michele Wolkomir. 2000. "Generic Processes in the Reproduction of Inequality: An Interactionist Analysis." *Social Forces* 79:419–52.

Schwartz, Martin and Walter DeKeseredy. 1997. *Sexual Assault on the College Campus: The Role of Male Peer Support*. Thousand Oaks, CA: Sage Publications.

Stombler, Mindy. 1994. " 'Buddies' or 'Slutties': The Collective Reputation of Fraternity Little Sisters." *Gender & Society* 8:297–323.

Stombler, Mindy and Patricia Yancey Martin. 1994. "Bringing Women In, Keeping Women Down: Fraternity 'Little Sister' Organizations." *Journal of Contemporary Ethnography* 23:150–84.

Stombler, Mindy and Irene Padavic. 1997. "Sister Acts: Resisting Men's Domination in Black and White Fraternity Little Sister Programs." *Social Problems* 44:257–75.

Sweeney, Brian. 2004. "Good Guy on Campus: Gender, Peer Groups, and Sexuality among College Men." Presented at the American Sociological Association Annual Meetings, August 17, Philadelphia, PA.

Swidler, Ann. 2001. *Talk of Love: How Culture Matters*. Chicago: University of Chicago Press.

Tjaden, Patricia and Nancy Thoennes. 2000. "Full Report of the Prevalence, Incidence, and Consequences of Violence against Women: Findings from the National Violence against Women Survey." Washington, DC: National Institute of Justice.

Tolman, Deborah. 2002. *Dilemmas of Desire: Teenage Girls Talk about Sexuality.* Cambridge, MA: Harvard University Press.

Ward, Sally, Kathy Chapman, Ellen Cohn, Susan White, and Kirk Williams. 1991."Acquaintance Rape and the College Social Scene." *Family Relations* 40:65–71.

Weschsler, Henry and Meichun Kuo. 2003. "Watering Down the Drinks: The Moderating Effect of College Demographics on Alcohol Use of High-Risk Groups." *American Journal of Public Health.* 93:1929–33.

West, Candace and Don Zimmerman. 1987. "Doing Gender." *Gender & Society* 1:125–51.

Linking Sexual Aggression and Fraternities

Mindy Stombler and Marni Kahn

"It was her first fraternity party. The beer flowed freely and she had much more to drink than she had planned. It was hot and crowded and the party spread out all over the house, so that when three men asked her to go upstairs, she went with them. They took her into a bedroom, locked the door and began to undress her. Groggy with alcohol, her feeble protests were ignored as the three men raped her. When they finished, they put her in the hallway, naked, locking her clothes in the bedroom."[1]

This scenario is more typical than you might think, regularly repeated on college and university campuses across the country. Why do fraternity membership and sexual aggression seem to be related? Researchers have explored these connections, using qualitative studies of predominantly white fraternities,[2] and have come up with some interesting findings.[3] They describe a fraternity context in which the structure, culture, and the nature of rushing and pledging often encourage sexual aggressiveness and even gang rapes. Researchers also suspect that fraternity men's narrow conceptualizations of masculinity, comprising "competition, athleticism, dominance, winning, conflict, wealth, material possessions, willingness to drink alcohol, and sexual prowess vis-à-vis women," play a major role in sexual aggression. Alcohol and drugs, combined with intense pressure to have sex with women, create a "party rape" culture in which these substances are used as "weapons against sexual reluc-tance."[4] The ultimate goal is to "work out a yes"[5] with available young women (who often lack power to escape the situation because of social pressure, brute force, and/or their own alcohol or drug use). Researchers also point to the consumption of pornography that degrades women as contributing to an atmosphere more accepting of sexual violence. Pornography is often celebrated in fraternity culture. While rapes are prevalent, generally, on college campuses, the numbers rise disproportionately when fraternity members and fraternity houses are taken into consideration.[6]

However, not all fraternities and their members buy into this culture or engage in sexual exploitation or assault.[7] Much depends on their traditions, guiding ideologies, relative level of prestige, and interpersonal dynamics. In addition, some fraternity men have tried to change fraternity culture by attending rape prevention programs and rethinking what it means to be a man. Universities and colleges have also begun to crack down on sexual offenses, and to require that fraternities be educated on sexual assault and familiar with the laws in their particular areas. In the process, fraternities are changing the ways in which they treat women and are revising traditional fraternity versions of masculinity.

NOTES

1. Sanday, Peggy Reeves. 1990. *Fraternity Gang Rape: Sex, Brotherhood, and Privilege on Campus.* New York: New York University Press, p. 3.

2. Researchers have not yet produced in-depth analyses of predominantly black fraternities and rape behaviors.

3. Martin, Patricia Yancey, and Robert A. Hummer. 1989. "Fraternities and Rape on Campus." *Gender & Society* 3(4): 457–473.; Sanday; Stombler, Mindy. 1994. " 'Buddies' or 'Slutties': The Collective Sexual Reputation of Fraternity Little Sisters." *Gender & Society* 8(3): 297–323.

4. Bleeker, E. T., and K. S. Murnen. 2005. "Fraternity Membership, the Display of Degrading Sexual Images of Women, and Rape Myth Acceptance." *Sex Roles* 53(7/8): 487–493; Carr, J. L., and K. M. VanDuesen. 2004. "Risk Factors for Male Aggression on College Campuses." *Journal of Family Violence* 19(5): 279–289; Martin and Hummer 1989, 460, 464.

5. Koss, Mary P., and Hobart H. Cleveland III. 1996. "Athletic Participation, Fraternity Membership, and Date Rape." *Violence Against Women* 2(2): 180–190; Martin and Hummer 1989, 464; Sanday 1990.

6. Carr and Van Duesen 2004; Bleeker and Murnen 2005.

7. Humphrey, Stephen E., and Arnold S. Kahn. 2000. "Fraternities, Athletic Teams, and Rape: Importance of Identification with a Risky Group." *Journal of Interpersonal Violence* 15(2): 1313–1322.

Effects of Rape on Men:
A Descriptive Analysis

Jayne Walker, John Archer, and Michelle Davies

Introduction

The occurrence of male rape outside of institution-alized settings, such as prisons, is an issue that has been neglected by society and the research literature (Stermac, Sheridan, Davidson, & Dunn, 1996). It is estimated that the help and support for male victims of rape is more than 20 years behind that of female victims (Rogers, 1998). . . . [A]lthough the reporting of male sexual assault is increasing year by year, recorded sexual offences against men are much lower than those recorded against women. In 2002, 4,096 indecent assaults and 852 rapes were recorded against men [in the U.K.] compared with 24,811 indecent as-saults and 11,441 rapes recorded against women.[1] However, official figures are grossly misleading when evidence from victimization surveys are con-sidered. Stermac et al. (1996) found that 7.2% of men in a general household sample of the U.S. population had experienced some form of sexual assault. Some research (e.g., Mezey & King, 1989) has found that gay and bisexual men are more likely to report sexual assault by other men than heterosexual men. Hickson et al. (1994) found that 27.6% of a sample of 930 British gay and bisexual men had experienced some form of sexual assault. In 45% of these cases, the as-sault committed was anal rape.

Few male rapes appear in police files or other offi-cial records. Very few male rape victims report their assault to the police because they think that they will experience negative treatment, be disbelieved, or blamed for their assault (e.g., Hodge & Cantor, 1998;

King & Woolett, 1997; Mezey & King, 1989). Fur-ther, fear of negative reactions . . . prevents men in many cases from seeking medical attention after rape. Frazier (1993) studied 74 male and 1380 female rape victims reporting to a United States hospital emer-gency department within three days of being raped. The men had more severe physical injuries and were significantly more likely to have been sexually as-saulted by more than one perpetrator than the women were. Frazier suggested that men might only report rape to medical services under extreme circumstances, such as gang rape. In some cases, male victims ap-proach medical services for help with physical injuries while concealing the sexual context of their assault (Kaufman, Divasto, Jackson, Voorhees, & Christy, 1980). This means that many male rape victims do not receive testing for sexually transmitted diseases that they may have contracted during their rape. . . .

Previous research has suggested that gay and bi-sexual men are more at risk of rape than heterosexual men for two reasons (Davies, 2002). The first is that they are at risk of being raped by dates or while in re-lationships with men. Hickson et al. (1994) found that current or ex-sexual partners were responsible for 65% of the assaults in their study of gay and bisexual men. Likewise, women who spend more time with men are more likely to be sexually assaulted than those who do not (Tewksbury & Mustaine, 2001). The second reason that gay and bisexual men are more at risk is through homophobic sexual assaults; for example, Comstock (1989) found that 10% of anti-gay attacks involved sexual assault.

Most . . . research on effects of post-rape trauma has focused on female victims, using either the character-istics of the victim (e.g., the victim's age) or the assault (e.g. the severity of the assault) as correlates of trauma and recovery (Frazier & Schauben, 1994). Frazier

From "Effects of Rape on Men: A Descriptive Analysis" by Jayne Walker, John Archer, and Michelle Davies (2005), *Archives of Sexual Behavior,* 34, 69–80. Reprinted with kind permission from Springer Science and Business Media.

(1993) found some differences in the ways that male and female victims coped immediately after the rape. In Frazier's study, male victims reported significantly more hostility, anger, and depression than females did. Frazier concluded that men were more likely to react with anger immediately after rape because anger is a "masculine" way to deal with trauma. However, many male victims reacted with a "controlled" style of coping exemplified by subdued acceptance, minimization of the assault, or denial (Kaufman et al., 1980; Walker, 1993). Kaufman et al. suggested that a controlled reaction reflects one aspect of male socialization, to be emotionally inexpressive to aversive situations. Furthermore, Rogers (1998) suggested that this type of coping strategy renders male victims prone to long-term psychological problems as it makes help-seeking less likely, and denial undermines men coming to terms with their rape.

After rape, most victims experience an increased sense of vulnerability. Some victims become overly concerned with taking safety precautions (Mezey & King, 1989) or change their lives drastically to avoid the possibility of rape happening again. In addition, victims may change the perceptions they have of themselves after rape. They may feel ashamed or blame themselves for their assault. In order to regain their sense of controllability of the world, they may think that they were raped because something they did caused the rape or they were raped because of the type of person they are. Although making sense of the event can be constructive, self-blame can be detrimental to the victim's recovery (Frazier & Schauben, 1994). Self-blaming also affects how people respond to the victim. For example, those who blame themselves are perceived as less well-adjusted and more responsible for the rape than those who do not (Thornton et al., 1988). . . .

[S]ome negative attributions occur in males above and beyond those expected of victims generally. Many male victims become confused about their sexual orientation (e.g., Mezey & King, 1989). . . . Lockwood (1980) showed that some of the stress associated with male rape within prison related to the victim's horror of appearing gay or not masculine. For heterosexual victims, the rape may be their first experience of homosexual contact. They may question the extent to which they may have "contributed" to the assault, making attributions such as, "I must be gay" for "letting" the assault

occur. McMullen (1990) suggested that it is not unusual for heterosexual victims to seek out homosexual contact after rape or, in contrast, manifest irrational loathing or hatred of all gay men (because they assumed the perpetrator(s) to be homosexual). Walker (1993) reported that 80% of the heterosexual victims in her study reported experiencing long-term crises over their sexual orientation. One victim stated:

> Since the assault I have trouble relating to my wife. I have found myself in homosexual relationships that disgust me afterwards . . . it is almost as if I am punishing myself for letting the assault happen in the first place. (p. 26)

Gay male victims may also experience problems with their sexual orientation. When behavior that is formerly associated with consensual sexual activity becomes associated with violence, gay men can experience difficulty in defining their sexuality in a positive way. They might, for example, experience internalized homophobia or interpret the assault as "punishment" for their sexuality (Garnets, Herek, & Levy, 1990). As in the case of female victims, male victims may perceive consensual sex after rape as "dirty" or they may lose trust in their partners or in men in general. Walker (1993), for example, reported that all of the gay men in her study experienced long-term problems with their sexuality. One victim stated: "Before the assault I was proud to be a homosexual; however, now I feel 'neutered.' I feel sex is dirty and disgusting and I have a real problem with my sexual orientation" (p. 27).

Sexual dysfunction is common in male rape victims, as in females (e.g., Mezey & King, 1989) and can continue for years after the assault. This may cause problems in existing relationships, with partners of the victim having to come to terms with the realities of living with a rape victim. . . . [S]exual problems ranged from complete inactivity to promiscuity or . . . problems with the sexual act, such as fear of "re-creating" the assault either as a victim or perpetrator.

Some male victims perceive a loss of masculinity directly, feeling less of a man. In others, it results in destructive or violent behavior towards others. Anger, revenge fantasies towards the perpetrator(s), or at society in general for being insensitive to him as a male victim are common (Anderson, 1982; Myers, 1989; Walker, 1993). . . .

The aim of the current research was to provide a detailed descriptive analysis of the nature and effects of rape on a non-clinical sample of men who had been anally raped as adults (over the age of 16 years). Men were recruited from a variety of sources, mainly from press advertisements from around the United Kingdom. . . .

Method

Participants

. . . A total of 52 responses were received and 73% returned questionnaires. . . . [Two] responses were received from [patients recruited in genitourinary departments] making the total sample 40.

At the time of the study, respondents had a mean age of 34 years (range, 19–75 years). At the time of the assault, most victims (70%) were between 16 and 25 years of age. . . . The mean age at the time of the assault was 24 years, and the mean time between the assault and participation in the study was 10 years. All respondents reported that they were white and of British nationality. . . .

The majority of respondents were employed at the time of the study: 3% as unskilled workers, 15% as semi-skilled workers, 12% as skilled workers, and 28% in professional occupations; 35% of respondents were unemployed at the time of the study.

Of the 40 respondents, 21 (53%) . . . identified as gay, 4 (10%) as bisexual, 13 (32%) as heterosexual, and 2 (5%) as asexual. Sixty percent of respondents were not in a relationship at the time of the study; however, 17% reported that they were in a heterosexual relationship and 23% in a homosexual relationship at the time of the study. Regarding their past experiences of sexual abuse, six (15%) reported to have been raped on more than one occasion, and three (7.5%) to have experienced childhood sexual abuse as well as rape as an adult. . . .

Results

Characteristics and Nature of the Assault

. . . Victims were asked to indicate several characteristics of the assaults. . . . Table 48.1 details [these]. . . .

Table 48.1 *Assault Characteristics*

CHARACTERISTIC	N	%
Victim's age at time of assault		
16–25	28	70.0
26–30	4	10.0
31–40	5	13.0
41–50	2	5.0
Over 50	1	2.0
Location of assault		
Victim's home	8	20.0
Perpetrator's home	18	45.0
Vehicle	2	5.0
Street	4	10.0
Other	8	20.0
Use of Violence		
No force	4	10.0
Physical force	21	52.5
Violent force	11	27.5
Weapon used	4	10.0
Number of Perpetrators		
One	25	62.5
Two	10	25.0
Three or more	5	12.5
Victim-perpetrator relationship		
Male family member	4	10.0
Brief acquaintance	8	20.0
Well established acquaintance	7	17.5
Lover or ex-lover	6	15.0
Person in position of trust	5	12.5
Stranger	10	25.0
Sexual acts performed during assault		
Anal penetration	40	100.0
Anal and oral penetration of victim	22	55.0
Victim masturbated	20	50.0
Victim penetrated by object(s)	6	15.0
Sadomasochistic practices	7	17.5
Victim forced to penetrate perpetrator(s)	17	42.5
Forced to masturbate perpetrator(s)	4	10.0
Forced to watch sexual assault on another person	1	2.5

Location of Assaults

The highest proportion of assaults took place in the perpetrator's home. In one instance, the perpetrator had offered to put the victim up for the night. The victim was awoken in the early hours of the morning being assaulted by the perpetrator. Assaults were also carried out in the victim's home or in a vehicle. For example, one victim was given a lift by the perpetrator. During the course of the ride, the perpetrator offered a sum of money to have sex with the victim. When he refused, the perpetrator produced a knife and made the victim get in to the back seat of the car where he was both orally and anally raped.

The remaining assaults were carried out in the street, public toilets, in the workplace, a party, and, in one case, a health club. In the last instance, five men whom the victim did not know came in to the sauna where the victim was relaxing and took it in turns to anally rape him. The victim was also forced to perform oral sex on all of the perpetrators.

Level of Coercion

Some form of coercion was reported in most cases. Physical force (e.g., kicking, punching, and slapping) was used in more than half the cases. Four also involved the use of a weapon (e.g., knife, baseball bat, and in one case, a gun). In addition, the threat of HIV infection was used against six of the victims. The majority of the victims experienced physical injuries during the assault, including anal lacerations and bleeding, bruises, broken bones, knife wounds, and burns. Only 14 of the victims sought medical treatment for their injuries and, and only a minority (five) disclosed the sexual nature of the assault during medical treatment (see also below). In seven cases, a non-sexual crime was also committed at the time of the rape (e.g., kidnapping, robbery, and criminal damage). In one of the most violent cases, the victim was attacked with a knife, his body was badly cut and then a noose was put around his neck. His rapists stripped him down to his underpants, poured petrol over his genital area and then set fire to him. He was later anally raped several times by the gang of men and left for dead. In another particularly violent case, the victim was anally raped by three men he met at a party. In between each assault the victim was held down and the assailants took it in turns to burn him with a cigarette lighter. The victim was so severely injured he was hospitalised for one month, spending several days in intensive care.

Type and Number of Perpetrators

Someone known to the victim (e.g., acquaintance, lover, or family member) was responsible for most of the assaults, although strangers carried out a significant number (25%). In most cases (62.5%), one perpetrator raped the victim, although in 25% there were two perpetrators. Three or more perpetrators were involved in the assault in 12.5% of cases.

Type of Assaults Committed

In addition to being anally raped, 55% of victims had also experienced oral penetration by one or more of the perpetrators. In half of the cases, the victim had been masturbated by the perpetrator(s), and, in four cases forced to masturbate the perpetrator(s). In six cases, objects had been used to penetrate the victim.

Victims' Perceptions during the Assault

Victims were asked to recall certain details of the assault. . . . Table 48.2 shows victims' perceptions of the assault and of the perpetrators.

Perceived Characteristics of Perpetrators

The majority of victims (92.5%) recalled the perpetrator(s) being white. Only three perpetrators were nonwhite. Most victims knew or perceived the perpetrator(s) to be gay (42.5%) or bisexual (12.5%). A total of 22.5% believed the perpetrator(s) to be heterosexual, and the remaining 22.5% said that they did not know the perpetrator's sexual orientation.

Remarks during the Assault

Victims were asked whether the perpetrator(s) made remarks during the assault. A quarter of the men were asked whether they were enjoying the rape. For example, one man was told: "Be a good boy and you will enjoy it." In some cases, attackers told the victim how much they were enjoying the experience, as this man explained:

> One said how physically attractive I was and told me how many orgasms he had and how much he enjoyed it.

Table 48.2   *Victims' Perceptions of the Assault*

CHARACTERISTIC	N	%
Perpetrator Ethnicity		
White	37	92.5
Black	1	2.5
Moroccan	2	5.0
Perceived sexual orientation of perpetrator		
Heterosexual	9	22.5
Homosexual	17	42.5
Bisexual	5	12.5
Unknown	9	22.5
Victim responses during assault		
Frozen fear, helplessness, submission	35	87.0
Able to fight back	11	27.0
Fear for life	26	65.0
Remarks made by perpetrator(s) during assault		
Said nothing or not remembered	13	32.5
Threats if tell anyone	2	5.0
Victim asked if enjoying it	10	25.0
Taunts and insults from onlookers	9	22.5
Pretence of love or consensual sex	7	17.5
Homophobic comments	2	5.0
Instructions on what sexual acts to perform	3	7.5
Perpetrator(s) claimed to have raped other men	1	2.5

Note: The total N does not equal 40 in some categories due to some men reporting more than one response to the question.

> Another talked to me while anally penetrating me and masturbating me about how he and his partner did this and similar awful things to men . . .

It was also common for perpetrators to verbally abuse the victim during the rape, using misogynistic (e.g., slut, bitch, whore) or anti-gay language (e.g., "you filthy queer"). This man explained how his attacker intimidated him . . .

> He called me a bitch and a cunt—then called me filthy for sucking his penis—which he had forced me to do. He repeatedly said I wanted it.

Another man was subjected to homophobic comments during the assault. The attackers told him that:

> I was a filthy queer and that I deserved all I got and he knew I was secretly enjoying it. To each other they shouted out encouragement and egged each other on to do more brutal things to me.

In other instances, the perpetrator(s) tried to act as if the assault was a consensual activity. . . .

> He told me how much he loved me and that I could never leave him.

Responses to the Assault

When asked what their responses were at the time of the assault, the majority of victims said that they reacted with frozen fear, helplessness or submission. However, 27% said that they were able to put up at fight at some point during the assault. A total of 65% said that they feared for their lives. When asked their responses in the hours and days after the assault, the majority (78%) said that they reacted in a "controlled" style (e.g., calm, composed or subdued). A total of 72% also reported that the sense of helplessness and loss of control during the assault was worse than the sexual aspects of the encounter.

Disclosure of the Assault to Other People

The men were asked to identify the first person to whom they disclosed their assault. The majority (60%) stated that it was someone they knew, including friends (54%), partners (29%), and family members (17%). Of the remaining 40%, 11 (27.5%) said that it was a professional, such as a work colleague, health care professionals, social workers, therapist or the police (only five men ever reported their assault to the police; see below). The remaining five (12.5%) said that they had never told anyone until they participated in this study.

The length of time that passed before victims disclosed their assault ranged from a few hours to 20 years. In many instances, there was a long time between the assault and disclosure. . . . When asked about reactions that they received from the people to whom they disclosed, many reported positive reactions, such as offers of help and support. Others reported lack of support, such as insensitive remarks, or homophobic victim-blaming. . . .

Reporting to the Police

Only five men ever reported their assault to the police. Of those who did report, only one man said that the police were responsive and helpful. The other four found the police to be unsympathetic, disinterested, and homophobic. They felt that their complaint was not taken seriously and all four regretted their decision to tell the police. Only one perpetrator was subsequently convicted (and sentenced to 10 years imprisonment). However, having gone through a court case, this victim was distressed at the way he was treated in court. He stated that he was made to feel that he . . . was the assailant, and that his ordeal in court probably had a worse effect on him than the rape itself. In the other four cases, the police did not press charges.

Medical and Psychological Treatment

Medical services were utilized by 14 (35%) of the men. However, of these, only five reported the sexual context of the assault, the others only disclosing their physical injuries. . . . All of these men reported that the attitudes of the medical staff were helpful, understanding, and supportive.

Over half (58%) of the men sought psychological treatment at some point after the assault. However, in most cases help was not sought until long after the assault occurred. . . . Issues dealt with included sexuality, anger, guilt and shame, and relationship problems. All of the men who sought treatment reported that it was beneficial to some degree. In general, the most helpful aspects of the treatments included being told that it was not their fault, having someone to talk to, and someone to listen and express care and concern. However, even though the men said that the attitudes of therapists were helpful and supportive, they also felt that the professionals lacked the expertise to deal with male sexual assault issues. In addition to psychological treatment, 11 men were prescribed medication, such as anti-depressants, sleeping tablets, or anti-psychotic drugs.

Other Issues Concerning Reporting

The men were asked what advice they would offer to the police and other professionals dealing with male rape victims. The most common responses were to offer the same support to male as to female victims, such as to listen to and believe the victim, and to offer more publicity that men can become victims of rape. . . . [T]he men felt that professionals should be more empathic to men, and that work should be done to eliminate homophobia within professional services. When asked what support services they would like to see available, the men said that services such as male rape crisis centres, and support groups in all major towns, 24-hour help-lines, more easily available therapy services, and the police specially trained to deal with male rape victims.

When asked why they had participated in the study, responses focused on promoting informed publicity about male rape. For example, men said that they responded to the advertisement to try to help professionals understand male rape and what victims experience, to bring male rape to the attention of the public, to help future victims, and to establish support for male victims. . . .

Long Term Effects of the Assault

All of the men experienced long term negative psychological and behavioral effects after the assault. Table 48.3 shows the range of effects that the men reported. The following victim-reports highlight some of the specific reactions to the assaults.

Depression, Anxiety, and Anger

Almost all the men reported depression in the weeks and months following their assaults. This man stated that in the six years after his rape he suffered from periods of severe depression:

> I have felt like I have been living in a void since the assault. I suffer panic attacks, mood swings, total depression, but the medical profession have given up on me and said I am too damaged to help. I feel I have no future.

Some form of anxiety was felt by almost all the men after the assault. In some cases, anxiety focused on their interactions with men. As the following man stated:

> I am extremely anxious around straight men, especially in social situations. What often can be genuine friendliness on their part can put me on edge and I think they are going to make a move on me.

Table 48.3 *Long Term Effects of the Assault*

REACTION	N	%
Depression	39	97.5
Fantasies about revenge and retaliation	38	95.0
Flashbacks of the assault	37	92.5
Feelings of anxiety	37	92.5
Loss of self respect/damaged self image	36	90.0
Increased sense of vulnerability	36	90.0
Emotional distancing from others	34	85.0
Fear of being alone with men	33	82.5
Guilt and self-blame, e.g. for not being able to prevent the assault	33	82.5
Increased anger and irritability	32	80.0
Low self esteem	31	77.5
Intrusive thoughts about the assault	30	75.0
Withdrawal from family and friends	29	72.5
Impaired task performance	28	70.0
Long term crisis with sexual identity	28	70.0
Damaged masculine identity	27	68.0
Increased use of tobacco	27	67.5
Abuse of alcohol	25	62.5
Increased security consciousness	23	57.5
Suicide ideation	22	55.0
Abuse of drugs	21	52.5
Self harming behaviors	20	50.0
Suicide attempts	19	47.5
Eating disorders, e.g. bulimia, anorexia	11	27.5

Another common response to the assaults was anger. This man was still struggling to deal with feelings of anger and revenge fantasies:

> In an attempt to deal with my anger, I am attending anger management classes and I also see a psychiatrist. My need for revenge is so strong that it is as damaging as the rape itself. My anger has led me to be a psychological abuser and a bully.

Almost all the men reported that they had fantasized about gaining revenge or retaliation against the perpetrator(s). Some fantasized about killing them. . . .

Confusion about Sexuality and Masculinity

A total of 70% of the men reported experiencing long-term crises with their sexual orientation and 68% with their sense of masculinity after the assault. This man stated that since he felt that he was capable

of handling confrontational situations, being raped was a shock both to his self-image and masculinity:

> The sense of powerlessness I experienced during the assault totally surprised me. I thought I was pretty good at handling potentially violent situations as I worked in a night shelter for men. However, I never imagined I could be so vulnerable and become a victim. It was a big shock to my male ego.

The following man similarly wrote of the shock and long-term effects on his self-image and masculinity:

> The assault was a threat to my male pride and dignity. It was a shock to find that a so-called "strong man" could become a helpless victim of sexual assault at the hands of another man. My sense of who I was (ex-army) was destroyed for about 10 years.

Another man equated his perceived loss of masculinity with his inability to prevent his assault. He also stated that negative reactions from others reinforced this view:

> For a long time after the assault, I felt a failure as a man for not being able to protect myself. Other people's attitudes reinforced my feelings of inadequacy, so to compensate for my feelings I became aggressive and a bully.

Changes in Sexual Behavior

Several men reported changes in their sexual behavior after the assault. Some became promiscuous, while others refused to have sexual relations with either men or women for a considerable time after the assault. Sexual problems included erectile failure and lack of libido. One described his sexual experience after his assault as one of promiscuity and sexual compulsion:

> Before the assault I was straight; however, since the assault I have begun to engage in voluntary homosexual activity. This causes me a great deal of distress as I feel I am not really homosexual but I cannot stop myself having sex with men. I feel as if having sex with men I am punishing myself for letting the assault happen in the first place.

Unlike this man, since his assault the following had not engaged in sexual relations with anyone:

> Since the assault I believe I no longer have a sexual orientation. I no longer want a sexual relationship with a man or a woman. I feel sex is a horrible act and just an excuse for an individual to experience self-satisfaction.

Some of the men also expressed confusion and disgust about their sexual responses during the assault. Several of the men reported getting erections and ejaculating during the assault. These men reported that prior to the assault they had equated sexual responses with pleasure; however, after experiencing sexual responses during sexual assault, they felt that, although they were disgusted at the thought of the assault, they must have enjoyed it really because they responded sexually. This (heterosexual) man stated:

> If I really thought that the sexual acts I was subjected to during the assault were so degrading and perverse, why did I ejaculate? For a long time I thought I must have really enjoyed it, therefore, I must have homosexual tendencies. I was confused for a very long time.

Loss and Grief Reactions

Almost all of the men reported feeling a loss of self-respect or self-worth after the assault. Some of the men equated losses to their self-image or their feelings of powerlessness as grief. For example, this man wrote:

> I don't care about myself any more, if someone could assault me in such a way *[he was anally and orally raped]* how can I be worth anything? The pain I feel is like grieving over the death of a loved one . . . now a big chunk of me is missing.

Another similarly stated:

> The loss of dignity can be quite overwhelming. The very essence of one's character and being has been invaded and treated as worthless, just there for the taking.

Guilt and Self-Blame

Over 80% of the men reported that they experienced profound feelings of guilt and self-blame following the assault. Commonly, these feelings focused on failure to prevent the assault or inability to fight back. Some of the men blamed themselves for willingly putting themselves in a situation where they were vulnerable to assault. For example, this man stated:

> For me, the worst part of the assault was I put myself at his hands. I willingly went to his house; hence, I put myself in a vulnerable position. So the blame will always be on my shoulders and the guilt will never go away.

Suicide Ideation and Self-Harm

Many of the men reported partaking in self-destructive behaviors as a consequence of the assault, such as self-harming, suicide ideation or attempts, or abuse of alcohol, drugs, tobacco or food. . . . This man stated:

> I dream of killing myself to forget what happened.

Another man reported that his attempt at suicide was at the location where the assault took place (a public toilet):

> In an attempt at killing myself, I drove my car into a wall next to the toilets where the assault took place.

Another reported that since the assault he has had both alcohol and eating problems, as well as experiencing mood swings and problems interacting with others:

> Since the assault I have developed bulimia and an alcohol problem. I avoid physical contact with people and I have become withdrawn and moody.

Another stated that he self harms and has severe mood swings in an attempt to cope with his problems with sex and relationship difficulties following his assault:

> I have a distaste for sex and sexual acts hence I no longer have a full relationship. This has led me to self harm, have violent outbursts and severe mood swings.

Resolution

The men were asked how much they felt they had recovered from the assault. Only one man recorded his recovery as complete; 18 (45%), however, said that they had "mostly" recovered. Thirteen (32.5%) described their recovery as "somewhat complete," and 8 (20%) said that they had not recovered at all.

Discussion

This study provided a descriptive analysis of the experiences of 40 British male rape victims. . . .

The demographic characteristics of the men were consistent with previous research . . . that has found that gay and bisexual men are more likely to report sexual assault by other men than are heterosexual men (e.g., Mezey & King, 1989). Previous research has [also] found that gay and bisexual men are more at risk of rape than heterosexual men are, because they are at risk of sexual assault by dating men, and because they are more likely to find themselves victims of anti-gay violence (Davies, 2002). The use of anti-gay language by some perpetrators in the current study denoted the homophobic context of some of these rapes. . . .

The majority of the men were young, between the age of 16 and 25 (mean age, 24) at the time of assault. . . . The figures in this study are consistent with other studies (e.g., Mezey & King, 1989; Stermac et al., 1996), and with routine activity theory, in that young men are more likely to put themselves in situations where sexual assault may occur than older men are (Tewsbury & Mustaine, 2001). It is possible that young men are more likely to report sexual assaults, but are no more at risk than older men. Further research is needed to investigate this possibility.

All of the men in this study were white and of British nationality. It is not clear whether this was because white men are more likely to be sexually assaulted than non-whites, because men of ethnic minorities are not as likely to report it as white men are, or because the recruitment method was inadvertently discouraging to ethnic minorities. . . .

The majority of assaults took place indoors, namely in the perpetrator's or the victim's home, and someone the victims knew carried out most assaults. This is consistent with research on female rape victims. The locations in which assaults took place are also consistent with routine activity theory. The circumstances of the male rapes described in this study are inconsistent with people's perceptions of what is considered the "stereotypic rape" (Krahé, 2000). Most people view rape as a crime that takes place outdoors, as a violent assault between two strangers (Krahé, 2000). . . . [T]he majority of the assaults . . . involve[d] some form of violence. Physical force (e.g., kicking, punching, and slapping) was used in more than half the cases. The majority of the victims experienced physical injuries during the assault, including anal lacerations and bleeding, bruises, broken bones, knife wounds, and burns. Frazier (1993) suggested that men were more likely to report rape if

they had been seriously injured. Thus, the relatively high number of violent assaults could be a result of reporting bias. . . . In a considerable minority, more than one perpetrator carried out the assault. This is consistent with Frazier's research in which it was found that male victims were more likely to have been assaulted by more than one man than females were.

When asked what their responses were at the time of the assault, the majority of victims said that they reacted with frozen fear, helplessness, or submission; however, just over a quarter of the men said that they were able to put up at fight at some point during the assault. . . . [M]en (like women) react to extreme personal threat with frozen helplessness. The belief that men should be able to fight back during sexual assault contributes to secondary victimization (Williams, 1984). . . . As the majority of male rape victims cannot fight back, self blame for not being able to do so may contribute to the victim failing to seek help from the police, medical sources or friends and family.

Socialization can also explain the gender difference reported in initial reactions to rape. The majority of female victims are said to display an emotional "expressive" reaction to rape (Burgess & Holstrom, 1974); however, a "controlled" reaction was reported by the majority of men in this study. . . . It reflects a gender role expectation that it is unmanly for men to express negative emotion even in the face of physical and emotional trauma. . . . [T]he reluctance of male victims to tell anyone about the assault, coupled with the lack of counseling and support for male victims, could explain . . . [why] many male victims suffer deep and long lasting psychological and behavioral effects. Although each victim has a different set of long term consequences, common reactions reported include emotional disruption manifested by depression and increased anger. There is also disturbed cognitive functioning taking the form of flashbacks to, or preoccupation with, memories of the assault and increased thoughts of suicide. Psychologically, the victims reported feeling devalued with regard to their identity and self-esteem, and they experienced a disruption in social relations due to feelings of emotional distancing. Victims also reported long-term crises with their sexual orientation, with sexual dysfunction, and suicide attempts.

How representative this sample is of all male rape victims is difficult to determine because the present research is based on victims who responded to media advertising. However, it does offer a valuable insight into the experiences of male rape victims of non-clinical origin, which to date has been missing from the research literature. Future studies might extend the current work to investigate differences between men who have been anally raped, as in the present study, compared with those sexually assaulted in other ways, such as oral rape. Future studies might also investigate the effects of repeat sexual victimization in men, such as those repeatedly sexually victimized in the course of relationship violence, and the effects of sexual violence compared with physical abuse.

NOTE

1. At the end of 2003, the legal categorization of sexual offences in the United Kingdom was subject to major change. The Sexual Offences Act 2003 includes non-consensual oral as well as anal and vaginal penile penetration as rape. The offence of indecent assault is no longer in statute and has been replaced by two offences: assault by penetration and sexual assault. Assault by penetration includes non-consensual sexual penetration by any object other than the penis while sexual assault covers every other non-consensual sexual act. Because the data for this study were collected before the changes in law, our definition of rape includes non-consensual anal penetration only.

REFERENCES

Anderson, C. L. (1982). Males as sexual assault victims: Multiple levels of trauma. *Journal of Homosexuality, 7,* 145–162.

Burgess, A. W., & Holmstrom, L. L. (1974). Rape trauma syndrome. *American Journal of Psychiatry, 131,* 981–986.

Comstock, G. D. (1989). Victims of anti-gay/lesbian violence. *Journal of Interpersonal Violence, 4,* 101–106.

Davies, M. (2002). Male sexual assault victims: A selective review of the literature and implications for support services. *Aggressive and Violent Behavior, 7,* 203–214.

Frazier, P. A. (1993). A comparative study of male and female rape victims seen at a hospital-based rape crisis program. *Journal of Interpersonal Violence, 8,* 64–76.

Frazier, P. A., & Schauben, L. (1994). Causal attributions and recovery from rape and other stressful life events. *Journal of Social and Clinical Psychology, 13,* 1–14.

Garnets, L., Herek, G., & Levy, B. (1990).Violence and victimization of lesbians and gay men: Mental health consequences. *Journal of Interpersonal Violence, 5,* 366–383.

Hickson, F. C. I., Davies, P. M., Hunt, A. J., Weatherburn, P., McManus, T. J., & Coxon, A. P. M. (1994). Gay men as victims of non-consensual sex. *Archives of Sexual Behavior, 23,* 281–294.

Hodge, S., & Cantor, D. (1998). Victims and perpetrators of male sexual assault. *Journal of Interpersonal Violence, 13,* 222–239.

Kaufman, A., Divasto, P., Jackson, R., Voorhees, H., & Christy, J. (1980). Male rape victims: Non-institutionalized assault. *American Journal of Psychiatry, 137,* 221–223.

King, M., & Woolett, E. (1997). Sexually assaulted males: 115 men consulting a counselling service. *Archives of Sexual Behavior, 26,* 579–583.

Krahé, B. (2000). Sexual scripts and heterosexual aggression. In T. Eckes & H. M. Trautner (Eds.), *The developmental social psychology of gender* (pp. 273–292). Hillsdale, NJ: Erlbaum.

Lockwood, D. (1980). *Prison sexual violence.* New York: Elsevier.

McMullen, R. J. (1990). *Male rape: Breaking the silence on the last taboo.* London: GMP Publishers Ltd.

Mezey, G., & King, M. (1989). The effects of sexual assault on men. *Psychological Medicine, 19,* 205–209.

Myers, M. F. (1989). Men sexually assaulted as adults and sexually abused as boys. *Archives of Sexual Behavior, 18,* 205–209.

Rogers, P. (1998). Call for research into male rape. *Mental Health Practice, 1,* 34.

Stermac, L., Sheridan, P. M., Davidson, A., & Dunn, S. (1996). Sexual assault of adult males. *Journal of Interpersonal Violence, 11,* 52–64.

Tewksbury, R., & Mustaine, E. E. (2001). Life-style factors associated with the sexual assault of men: A routine activity theory analysis. *Journal of Men's Studies, 9,* 153–182.

Thornton, B., Ryckman, R., Kirchner, G., Jacobs, J., Laczor, L., & Kuehnel, R. (1988). Reactions to self-attributed victim responsibility: A comparative analysis of rape crisis counsellors and lay observers. *Journal of Applied Social Psychology, 18,* 409–422

Walker, J. L. (1993). *Male rape: The hidden crime.* Unpublished honors thesis, University of Wolverhampton, UK.

Williams, J. E. (1984). Secondary victimization: Confronting public attitudes about rape. *Victimology, 9,* 66–81.

Women Raping Men

Denise Donnelly

In their article entitled "Sexual Molestation of Men by Women," P. M. Sarrel and W. H. Masters recount this story of a 27-year-old male, 178-pound truck driver, who was held captive for more than 24 hours. When he was released, he did not tell others about his experience, fearing ridicule. He experienced erectile dysfunction following the rape.

"[Sam] had been drinking and left a bar with a woman companion he had not known previously. They went to a motel where he was given another drink and shortly thereafter fell asleep. He awoke to find himself naked, tied hand and foot to a bedstead, gagged, and blindfolded. As he listened to voices in the room, it was evident that several women were present. When the women realized that he was awake, he was told to "have sex with all of them." He thinks that during his period of captivity four different women used him sexually, some of them a number of times. Initially he was manipulated to erection and mounted. After a very brief period of coitus, he ejaculated. He was immediately restimulated to erection and the performance was repeated . . . it became increasingly difficult for him to maintain an erection. When he couldn't function well, he was threatened with castration and felt a knife held to his scrotum. He was terrified that he would be cut and did have some brief improvement in erectile quality."[1]

NOTE

1. Sarrel, P. M., and W. H. Masters. 1982. "Sexual Molestation of Men by Women." *Archives of Sexual Behavior,* 11(2): 117–181.

Rape and War: Fighting Men and Comfort Women

Joane Nagel

Sexuality has always been an important, though often disregarded aspect of all militaries and military operations. Throughout history women have been among "camp followers" providing services such as laundry, nursing, companionship, and sex to soldiers on military missions during peace and war.[1] Sometimes these women have been wives, relatives, or girlfriends, but always among their ranks have been prostitutes as well. Women who have had sex with servicemen around the world, however, have not always been volunteers. Throughout history local women have been involuntarily "drafted" in the sexual service of militaries as rape victims and sexual slaves.[2]

Rape in war is at its core an ethnosexual phenomenon. Whether a war is fought across national borders or inside state boundaries, the military front is typically an ethnosexual frontier. Differences in nationality, race, or ethnicity separate the combatants and identify the targets of aggression in military operations. Whether violence in war is from combat or sexual attack, and whether it is guns or bodies that are used as weapons, those who are physically or sexually assaulted almost always are different in some ethnic way. Men at war do not, as a rule, rape their "own" women unless, of course, those women are suspected of disloyalty, especially sexual disloyalty or "collaboration."

Sexual exploitation and abuse are important weapons of war, and rape is perhaps the most

common component of war's sexual arsenal. Susan Brownmiller documents the routine practice of rape, especially gang rape, in war.[3] Moving or occupying armies use the rape of "enemy" women and girls as both a carrot and a stick: raping local women is a spoil of war for the troops to enjoy, and rape is also a technique of terror and warfare designed to dominate and humiliate enemy men by sexually conquering their women. Rape in war, as in many other ethnosexual settings, is best understood as a transaction between men, where women are the currency used in the exchange. Sexually taking an enemy's women amounts to gaining territory and psychological advantage. In countries around the world, rape often is defined as a polluting action, a way to soil the victim, her kin, and her nation physically and symbolically. Sexual warfare can extend beyond the moment of violation in situations where victims are reputationally smeared, physically mutilated, or when pregnancies or births result from sexual assaults. For instance, the widespread rape of mainly Muslim and some Croatian women by Serbian men in Bosnia in the early 1990s was partly intended to impregnate the women so that they would bear Serbian babies, "little Chetniks."[4] In order to guarantee that these rape victims could not obtain abortions, the Serbs set up concentration camps where pregnant women were imprisoned until they gave birth.[5]

Probably the best-known instance of rape in war is the so-called Rape of Nanking that occurred during the Japanese invasion of China in the winter and spring of 1938–1939, when Japanese soldiers raped an estimated eighty thousand Chinese women and girls.[6] A less well-known instance of Japanese wartime sexual exploits was the sexual enslavement of thousands of mainly Asian women by the Japanese

Imperial Army during World War II. Sexual slavery in war is a variation on the theme of wartime rape. Slavery extends the tactic of rape as a short-term strategy of a military mission into a permanent feature of military operations. The Japanese military established camps of so-called military comfort women *(Jugun Ianfu)* in Japan and other countries where Japanese troops were stationed. While there were some mainly lower-class Japanese women forced into sexual slavery, most of the estimated 200,000 women enslaved by the Japanese army were ethnic or national. Others were brought from Korea, China, Taiwan, Indonesia, Malaysia, and the Philippines to sexually service the troops.[7] Kazuko Watanabe reports that in such settings a woman's worth as a sexual commodity was based on her class and her ethnicity:

> *The Japanese Imperial Army divided comfort women into a hierarchical order according to class, race, and nationality. . . . Korean and most other Asian women were assigned to lower-class soldiers. Japanese and European women went to high-ranking officers. Most of the European women were Dutch [often of mixed ancestry] who were imprisoned in a prisoner of war camp in the Netherlands East Indies.[8]*

Soldiers' rankings of and preferences for women of particular races and nationalities enslaved in rape camps were not unique to the Japanese military.[9] Japan was not the only country that established large-scale organized operations of forced sexual servitude during World War II. The Nazis used concentration camps in Germany and other occupied countries for more than industrial and war-related labor, their program of genocide against the Jews, and the mass deportation and killing of Roma (gypsies) and other "non-Aryan" peoples. Sexual labor was also demanded of women internees, and both men and women prisoners were used for sexual experimentation by Nazi scientists and physicians. German concentration camps were sites of forced prostitution and sexual assault, and as was the case with Japan, not all women in the German camps were treated as "equal" when it came to sexual abuse. A woman's age, youth, and physical appearance made her more or less likely to be the target of Nazi sexual aggression.[10] And, as in so many areas of social life, even (especially) in

wartime concentration camps, ethnicity mattered. There were official prohibitions against German soldiers having sex with Jewish women, though these rules often were not enforced. Many Jewish women survivors reported extensive sadistic sexual torture, as well as rape, and these assaults often were accompanied by a barrage of racial and anti-Semitic verbal abuse.[11]

The Allies also were involved in sexual violence and exploitation during World War II. Some was in the form of mass rapes, such as those committed against German women by the Soviet army.[12] In other cases, sexual abuse and exploitation resulted when military personnel capitalized on the vulnerability of women who faced economic hardship, malnourishment, or starvation because of the war's disruption of local economies and food production. Many women in occupied or liberated countries found sexual liaisons or prostitution preferable to the grim alternatives available for themselves and their dependent families. U.S. troops also committed rapes during the war and the occupation that followed. In her examination of U.S. Army records, Brownmiller found 947 rape *convictions,* not simply charges or trials of American soldiers in Army general courts-martial during the period from January 1942 to July 1947.[13]

Wartime rape did not stop at the end of World War II, nor did its ethnosexual character change after 1945. The practice of rape in war extended into major and minor conflicts during the second half of the twentieth century—in civil wars, wars of independence, and military invasions, interventions, and operations in countries and regions around the world including Bangladesh, Vietnam, Iraq, Kuwait, Bosnia, Croatia, Serbia, Rwanda, Liberia, Kashmir, and Sierra Leone.[14] The logic of rape in war is always the same: rapes are committed across ethnosexual boundaries, and rape is used by both sides for the familiar time-honored reasons—to reward the troops, to terrorize and humiliate the enemy, and as a means of creating solidarity and protection through mutual guilt among small groups of soldiers. Ethnic loyalty and ethnic loathing join hands in rape in war.

In the post-Soviet era East European nationalist conflicts, the use of rape as a weapon of war has begun to move from the shadows more fully into view. For instance, during the 1990s warfare occurred along a number of ethnic and national borders in the former Yugoslavia—between Croats and Serbs, Christians and Muslims, and against Roma, among others. The most notorious of these ethnic conflicts was in Bosnia; the conflict's notoriety stemmed in part from its sexual character, especially the mass rape of Bosnian Muslim women by Orthodox Christian Serbian men. Many of these men and women were former neighbors. Muslims and Christians had lived side by side in the city of Sarajevo and elsewhere in Bosnia for decades and many had intermarried. That peace was shattered in 1992 when "ethnic cleansing" began.

Ethnic cleansing, or the removal of one ethnic group from a territory claimed by another, followed a common pattern across the region. Groups of armed Serbian men (sometimes uniformed troops and sometimes "irregulars" who were not officially in the military and not in uniform) roamed Bosnian towns and villages in groups, opportunistically looting and pillaging houses and businesses, raping and killing mainly unarmed Muslims they encountered along the way. Survivors reported that the Serbs came through the same towns several times in waves. During the first wave, typically, some of the Muslim men were killed and the rest were rounded up to be killed later or to be interned in concentration camps. Muslim women, children, and the elderly were left behind. It was during the next waves of Serbs passing through the towns that they raped local non-Serbian girls and women.

Munevra was a forty-eight-year-old widow with three sons ranging in age from fourteen to twenty-four, ages that made them targets for the Serbs to kill or deport to concentration camps. She kept the young men hidden in the cellar as small groups of armed Serbian men repeatedly came through the town. In the spring of 1992, two men came to her house and sexually assaulted her. . . .

I was afraid my sons would hear me. I was dying of fear 'cause of my sons. They're decent people. . . . Then this man touched my breasts. He pulled up my blouse and took out my breasts. . . . He said, "For a woman your age your breasts aren't bad." Then they brought me to

the other room. . . . I begged him and cried, and I crossed my legs. Then he took out his thing, you know, and he did it and sprayed it on me. When he was done the other one came and did the same thing. . . . When they left, my sons came out and . . . they asked me what happened: "What'd they do to you?" I said, "Nothing." I couldn't tell them about it. . . . I'd rather die than have them find out about it.[15]

Women's and families' shame about such incidents were part of the process of victimization and violations.[16] Munevra's experience occurred relatively early in the nationalist conflict; far worse sexual violations were in store for women as the war escalated.

The scene in Serbian so-called rape camps was a longer, more brutal nightmare for Muslim and other non-Serbian women and girls. Twenty-six-year-old Ifeta was arrested by Serbian soldiers, most of whom she knew, and taken to a women's camp in Doboj:

Three drunken [Serbian army] soldiers . . . dragged her into a classroom . . . here she was raped by all three men "at the same time," says Ifeta, pointing to her mouth and backside. "And while they were doing it they said I was going to have a baby by them". . . . After that the rapes were a part of Ifeta's daily life. . . . It was always a gang rape, they always cursed and humiliated her during it, and the rapists very frequently forced her to have oral sex with them.[17]

Another camp internee, Kadira, described the weeks she spent at Doboj:

"They pushed bottle necks into our sex, they even stuck shattered, broken bottles into some women. . . . Guns too. And then you don't know if he's going to fire, you're scared to death". . . . Once she was forced to urinate on the Koran. Another time she and a group of women had to dance naked for the Serbian guards and sing Serbian songs. . . . She has forgotten how many times she was raped.[18]

The same pattern of sexual terror, torture, and rape used by the Serbs in their campaigns of ethnic cleansing and warfare in Bosnia was repeated in Kosovo, Yugoslavia, in 1998–1999. Once again groups of Serbian men—police, soldiers, irregulars—swept through villages invading homes and raping Kosovar Albanian (mainly Muslim) female occupants, sexually attacking Kosovar Albanian women refugees fleeing combat zones, and sexually assaulting Kosovar Albanian women who were being held hostage or detained. The Kosovo conflict ended when NATO troops entered Kosovo in June 1999.[19]

In spring 2000, the UN convened the *International Criminal Tribunal for the Former Yugoslavia* in The Hague, Netherlands, to investigate and prosecute those ordering mass killing and mass rape in the various ethnic conflicts in the former Yugoslavia.[20] This investigation raised the issue of whether rape and sexual slavery are "crimes against humanity." Enloe argues that this question reflects a new awareness and public airing of what has been a long hidden history of sexual assault, torture, and exploitation of women during war:

> [T]he rapes in Bosnia have been documented by women's organizations . . . [that] have helped create an international political network of feminists who are making news of the Bosnian women's victimization not to institutionalize women as victims, not to incite men to more carnage, but to explain anew how war makers rely on peculiar ideas about masculinity. . . . [F]eminist reporters are using news of wartime sexual assaults by male soldiers to rethink the very meanings of both sovereignty and national identity. . . . If they succeed, the construction of the entire international political arena will be significantly less vulnerable to patriarchy.[21]

As the reports of human rights hearings and organizations document every year, it is not only enemy women who are the targets of sexual abuse and torture in war. I have not seen reported the establishment of rape camps with men as sexual slaves, however, men often are assaulted sexually as part of intimidation, torture, and combat in international conflicts and wars, as well as in military or paramilitary operations against internal political or ethnic insurgents. For instance, in Bosnia, there were numerous reports of cases in which Muslim and Croatian men were castrated or forced to castrate one another:

> In villages, towns, cities, the countryside, and concentration camps, male and female adults and children are raped as part of more extensive torture. Many of the atrocities committed are centered on the genitalia. . . . [T]estimonies of castrations enforced on Bosnian-Herzegovinian and Croatian prisoners, and in particular of orders under threat of death that they castrate

> each other with various instruments and at times with their teeth, are widely available, as the [United Nations] Bassiouni Report makes clear.[22]

Men also can be vulnerable to sexualized warfare in more indirect ways. In her critique of Japan's patriarchal Confucianist view of all women and racist treatment of non-Japanese men and women, Kazuko Watanabe also identifies a danger for men. She argues that in many countries men are trapped in masculinist roles, and forced to act out patriarchal and sexual scripts that commodify and endanger them as well as the women they victimize:

> Men's bodies and sexualities are also victims of militarist and consumerist capitalist societies. Men are, supposedly, unable to control their sexual impulses and are in need of prostitutes. [In World War II] Male soldiers were dehumanized to make them good fighters then stimulated by sexual desire that was fulfilled by comfort women. . . . Both the soldiers who were forced to die for the emperor on the battlefields and today's businessmen who die for their companies from karoshi (overwork) have often been rewarded with prostitutes.[23]

Watanabe's analysis suggests that although they are perpetrators of the rape and sexual abuse of both women and other men in times of war, men pay a psychological, social, and physical price for their complicity in patriarchal masculinist systems of sexual and ethnosexual violence. For instance, many soldiers display varying degrees of post-traumatic stress or "shell shock" following combat. Michael Kimmel reports that during World War I officers and doctors tended to view such disorders as "failures to conform to gender demands":

> Most psychiatric treatments for shell shock involved treating the disease as the result of insufficient manliness. T. J. Calhoun, assistant surgeon with the Army of the Potomac, argued that if the soldier could not be "laughed out of it by his comrades" or by "appeals to his manhood," then a good dose of battle was the best "curative."[24]

Although modern-day soldiers suffering from post-traumatic stress are viewed with more sympathy than their historical counterparts, many, including those working in the health care industry, still view soldiers exhibiting symptoms arising from combat and military operations with some suspicion, as malingerers, frauds, or weaklings.[24]

NOTES

1. See for instance, Butler, *Daughters of Joy, Sisters of Misery.*

2. For a recent overview see Barstow, *War's Dirty Secret.*

3. Brownmiller, *Against Our Will.*

4. Allen, *Rape Warfare,* 96.

5. Ibid., 96.

6. See Iris Chang, *The Rape of Nanking: The Forgotten Holocaust of World War II* (New York: Basic Books, 1997); James Yin and Shi Young, *The Rape of Nanking: An Undeniable History in Photographs* (Chicago: Innovative Publishing Group, 1997).

7. Japan has yet to make satisfactory restitution to Korean and Filipina "comfort women" who were sexually enslaved during World War II, and some former victims have come forward to demand a public apology and accounting for their treatment; see Seth Mydans, "Inside a Wartime Brothel: The Avenger's Story," *New York Times,* November 12, 1996:A3; Maria Rosa Henson, *Comfort Woman: A Filipina's Story of Prostitution and Slavery under the Japanese Military* (Lanham, MD: Rowman and Littlefield Publishers, 1999); Sangmie Choi Schellstede, *Comfort Women Speak: Testimony by Sex Slaves of the Japanese Military* (New York: Holmes and Meier, 2000); for discussions of Japan's system of brothels, see George L. Hicks, *The Comfort Women: Japan's Brutal Regime of Enforced Prostitution in the Second World War* (New York: W.W. Norton, 1995); Keith Howard, *True Stories of the Korean Comfort Women* (London: Cassell, 1995); Sayoko Yoneda, "Sexual and Racial Discrimination: A Historical Inquiry into the Japanese Military's 'Comfort' Women System of Enforced Prostitution," in *Nation, Empire, Colony: Historicizing Gender and Race,* ed. Ruth Roach Pierson and Nupur Chaudhuri (Bloomington: Indiana University Press, 1989), 237–50; for a discussion of restitution in general and specifically as it relates to the women enslaved by Japan during World War II, see Elazar Barkan, *The Guilt of Nations: Restitution and Negotiating Historical Injustices* (New York: W.W. Norton, 2000), especially chapter 3.

8. Watanabe, "Trafficking in Women's Bodies," 503–504.

9. Both sexual and nonsexual labor were also demanded of women enslaved by the Japanese (ibid., 503); the Japanese also used rape as an instrument of terror and domination, most infamous is the "rape of Nanking" in which thousands of women were raped and killed; see Brownmiller, *Against Our Will,* 53–60.

10. Brownmiller, *Against Our Will,* 61–62.

11. For firsthand accounts of women's treatment in the camps, see Sarah Nomberg-Przytyk, *Tales from a Grotesque Land* (Chapel Hill: University of North Carolina Press, 1985), 14–20; Livia E. Bitton Jackson, *Elli: Coming of Age in the Holocaust* (New York: Times Books, 1980) 59–61; Cecile Klein, *Sentenced To Live* (New York: Holocaust Library, 1988), 73–77; Lore Shelley, *Auschwitz: The Nazi Civilization* (Lanham, MD: University Press of America, 1992).

12. See Cornelius Ryan, *The Last Battle* (New York: Simon and Schuster, 1966); Barstow, *War's Dirty Secret.*

13. Brownmiller, *Against Our Will,* 76–77; these 947 convictions are only part of a much greater universe of sexual assault by U.S. troops for several reasons: most rape is not reported and when it is, convictions are relatively rare even today, much less back in the 1940s during a state of war and/or military occupation; further, these were *convictions* where the soldier was found guilty, and did not include what could only have been a much larger number of charges filed and trials conducted; further still, these records were only for convictions of Army and Air Force personnel, and did not include data on the U.S. Navy or Marine Corps; finally, these records did not include information on charges, trials, or convictions for lesser sexual crimes than rape, such as sodomy or assault with the intent to commit rape or sodomy.

14. See Americas Watch and the Women's Rights Project, *Untold Terror: Violence against Women in Peru's Armed Conflict* (New York: Americas Watch, 1992); Asia Watch and Physicians for Human Rights, *Rape in Kashmir: A Crime of War* (New York: Asia Watch, 1993); Ximena Bunster, "Surviving beyond Fear: Women and Torture in Latin America," in *Women and Change in Latin America,* ed. June Nash and Helen Safa (South Hadley, MA: Bergin & Garvey, 1986), 297–325; Samir al-Khalil, *Republic of Fear: The Politics of Modern Iraq* (Berkeley: University of California Press, 1989).

15. Stiglmayer, "The Rapes in Bosnia-Herzegovina," 101.

16. See Elizabeth Bumiller, "Deny Rape or Be Hated: Kosovo Victims' Choice," *New York Times,* June 22, 1999:1; Peter Finn, "Signs of Rape Sear Kosovo; Families' Shame Could Hinder Investigation," *Washington Post,* June 27, 1999:1.

17. Stiglmayer, "The Rapes in Bosnia-Herzegovina," 117–18.

18. Ibid., 118–19.

19. Human Rights Watch reports that although both sides committed sexual assault during the conflict, rates of rape by Serbian men far outnumbered instances of sexual abuse by Kosovar Albanian men during the conflict; see Human Rights Watch Report, "Kosovo: Rape as a Weapon of 'Ethnic Cleansing' " (March 21, 2000); my thanks to Hsui-hua Shen, Department of Sociology, University of Kansas, for bringing this report to my attention.

20. For early reports on the hearings and judgments of that tribunal, see Marlise Simons, "Bosnian Serb Trial Opens: First on Wartime Sex Crimes," *New York Times,* March 21, 2000:3; John-Thor Dahlburg, "Bosnian Witness Says She Endured Series of Rapes; Courts: Victim No. 50 Testifies in The Hague," *Los Angeles Times,* March 30, 2000:1; Chris Bird, "UN Tribunal Told of Bosnian Rape Camp Horrors," *Guardian,* April 21, 2000:1; Roger Thurow, "A Bosnian Rape Victim Suffers from Scars that Do Not Fade," *Wall Street Journal,* July 17, 2000:18.

21. Cynthia Enloe, "Afterword: Have the Bosnian Rapes Opened a New Era of Feminist Consciousness?" in *Mass Rape,* 219–30; progress continues to be made, slowly, in the shift toward defining rape as a human rights violation and in the prosecution of those responsible for the sexual assaults in the former Yugoslavia: on June 29, 2001, the Serbian government turned over former Yugoslavian president Slobodan Milosevic to the United Nations war crimes tribunal in The Hague, Netherlands; Marlise Simons with Carlotta Gall, "Milosevic Is Given to U.N. for Trial in War-Crime Case," *New York Times,* June 29, 2001:1; it is important to note that at about the same time the rapes and killings were happening in Yugoslavia and Bosnia, millions of men, women, and children were being raped, mutilated, and murdered in Rwanda; while Western governments dithered and delayed responding to both the Yugoslavian and Rwandan massacres and atrocities, and while an international tribunal was established in 1994 to prosecute Rwandans for their war crimes, the issue of rape as a war crime came to the fore in Yugoslavia, but not in the much larger-scale Rwandan case; perhaps it required reports of the mass rapes and sexual enslavement of white women, albeit Muslim white women, for the "civilized" world to take notice of ethnosexual violence in war.

22. Allen, *Rape Warfare, 78;* the "Bassiouni Report" is the result of an October 1992 decision by the Secretary-General of the United Nations to appoint a commission of experts "to examine and analyze information gathered with a view to providing the Secretary-General with its conclusions on the evidence of grave breaches of the Geneva Conventions and other violations of international humanitarian law committed in the territory of the former Yugoslavia" (ibid., 43).

23. Watanabe, "Trafficking in Women's Bodies," 506–507.

24. Kimmel, *Manhood in America,* 133–34.

chapter 10

Commercial Sex

Spotlight on Research

An interview with...

Jacqueline Boles

Jacqueline Boles, Ph.D., is a professor emeritus of sociology at Georgia State University in Atlanta, Georgia. Her research interests include sex work and sex workers, prostitution and HIV transmission, and deviant behavior. Dr. Boles is the author of over 40 articles and book chapters.

How did you get involved in the study of sexuality?

My dissertation advisor said, "Why don't you study strippers?" He knew my husband and I had been in show business and that I knew people familiar with the business. I thought, "Why not?" The great fan dancer, Sally Rand, was in town. I interviewed her and then began interviewing strippers in Atlanta clubs. About a year after I finished my dissertation, the police asked me to find out why so many prostitutes were coming to Atlanta. A colleague and I started interviewing prostitutes in the vice squad office, hooking bars, massage parlors, and on the street. That's how it all got started.

Which of your projects have you found most interesting?

In 1987, Kirk Elifson and I received a grant from the CDC to investigate HIV risk factors among male prostitutes (hustlers). We interviewed and drew blood from over 300 male prostitutes. We found that hustlers self-identified as heterosexual, homosexual, and bisexual. A hustler's self-identification was a strong predictor of HIV seropositivity. For example, heterosexual identified hustlers refused to engage in anal receptive sex, which is a major risk factor for contracting HIV. Consequently, heterosexual identified sex workers had the lowest rate of HIV seropositivity.

What have you found most challenging about studying sexuality?

A person can be HIV seropositive for 10 years without exhibiting any symptoms. When we began our research, we needed to look at the sexual history of the hustlers over a 10-year period. How do you ask these men to account for all their sex acts over 10 years? We needed to know how many partners they had, the gender of the partners, what kinds of sex acts were performed, and whether a condom was used. We faced a similar problem with drug use. Intravenous drug use is a risk factor for HIV, so we needed a history. We had to develop a workable strategy for getting accurate histories, and this took a great deal of experimentation and pre-testing of our instruments.

What have you learned from your years of research?

Too bad that sexual behavior in humans is not instinctive. If it were, we would all behave similarly, and life would be less complicated. Unfortunately, behaving sexually (or not) is associated with a number of problems: low self-esteem, jealousy and rage, sexually transmitted diseases, psychosocial adjustment issues, etc. We cannot help solve these problems unless we understand sexual behavior: what people do and how they feel about what they do. Simply asserting that a behavior is "wrong" or "immoral" will not prevent the behavior from occurring.

Have you encountered any ethical dilemmas in your research? How did you resolve these?

In our hustler study, we guaranteed the anonymity of all our study participants. They were given a patient identification number that they could use to receive their HIV serostatus from the health department. Even though we knew their serostatus, we were not allowed to inform them. Many times we knew that an HIV-positive hustler was living with an HIV-negative lover. We could not warn the uninfected person; all we could do is stress to lovers that they "get their test results." When we started our study, we did not want any thing we did to have a negative impact on our study participants. We declined interviews with the media so that our results would not be sensationalized. The sex workers we studied were constantly harassed by police, and we did not want to do anything that would increase that harassment.

How do people react when they find that you are a sex researcher?

A few years ago, I was asked to substitute for a well-known prostitute/activist on a panel. After the program ended, a woman (who had come late and did not know that I was not a sex worker) came up to me and gushed, "I always wanted to meet one; now I can say I have finally met a woman of the night." I did not have the heart to disappoint her! Most people are curious about the people I have met and interviewed. They enjoy hearing about the strip clubs, massage parlors, hooking bars, and other disreputable places I frequent. I try to humanize sex workers by sharing favorite stories.

If you could teach people one thing about sex, what would it be?

I may be swimming against the current, but I would like to suggest that we are asking sex to carry too big a burden. "Good sex will make me happy; if I'm not successful sexually, then I'm a failure; there's nothing worse than a sexual loser." Sex is designed to give pleasure, but so are swimming in a clear lagoon, viewing Monet's garden, eating an ice-cream cone, and cuddling one's child. Good sex (whatever that means) is but one component of a life well lived.

—Interviewed by Denise Donnelly

Sex Work for

the Middle Classes

Elizabeth Bernstein

By the end of the 1990s in postindustrial cities such as San Francisco, a burgeoning internet economy was in full swing, and media stories abounded which suggested that technology was pushing contemporary culture towards new frontiers of sexual tolerance by eliminating the biggest obstacles to the buying and selling of sexual services: shame and ignorance. Commentators highlighted the ease and efficiency of the new technologies and the ways in which online sexual commerce had shifted the boundaries of social space, blurring the differences between underworld figures and "respectable citizens" (Droganes, 2000; *Economist,* 2000; Prial, 1999).

Less frequently commented upon were the broader cultural underpinnings of new forms of technologized sexual exchange. Nor was there much discussion of the socioeconomic transformations that linked seemingly disparate cultural phenomena together. What were the underlying connections between the new "respectability" of sexual commerce and the new classes of individuals who were participating in commercial sexual transactions? What was the relationship between the overwhelmingly white, native-born and class-privileged women (and men) who were finding their way into sex work and more generalized patterns of economic restructuring? How did the emergence of new communications technologies transform the meaning and experience of sexual commerce for sex workers and their customers?

My discussion in this essay derives from ethnographic fieldwork carried out in five US and Euro-pean postindustrial cities between 1994 and 2002, a period of rapid technological growth and expansion.[1] Fieldwork consisted of on-site observations and informal interviews with participants in a variety of erotic work spaces and at sex workers' support groups; 15 in-depth, face-to-face interviews of 2–6 hours in length and an immersion in sex workers' own writings and documentary films (Bernstein, 2007). In this article, I focus on the experiences of sex workers who exemplify the ways that middle-class sex work has been facilitated by—and itself facilitates—new technologies of sexual exchange. . . .

Economic Concerns in Sexual Labour

In postindustrial cities of the West, sex workers who are white and middle class have sometimes been hard pressed to defend themselves against critics who maintain that they are atypical and unfit spokeswomen for the majority of women engaged in sexual labour, whose "choice of profession" is made under far greater constraints. Although middle-class sex workers may not be speaking for the majority when they seek to reframe sexual labour in terms of a respectable and esteem-worthy profession (Leigh, 2004; Nagle, 1997), some of the most sociologically interesting questions go unasked and unanswered if we limit ourselves to the non-majoritarian critique. Why are middle-class women doing sex work? Can sex work be a middle-class profession? Most crucially, if sexual labour is regarded as, at best, an unfortunate but understandable choice for women with few real alternatives, how are we to explain its apparently increasing appeal to individuals with combined racial, class, and educational advantages?[2]

The research that I conducted during the internet boom years of the late 1990s suggests that economic considerations, in fact, remain highly relevant to middle-class sex workers' erotic and professional decision-making. . . . Even during the peak years of the internet economy, well-paid, part-time work—especially for women of these "creative classes"—was, more often than not, difficult to come by. Despite the huge expansion of jobs in postindustrial dot-com economies, patterns of gendered inequality within the high technology sector meant that even white, college-educated women were likely to be excluded from the highest-paying positions.

Compared to men with similar forms of educational capital and class provenance, middle-class women in postindustrial economies are much more likely to find themselves working in the lowest-paid quarters of the temporary help industry, in the service and hospitality sectors, or in other poorly remunerated part-time jobs (McCall, 2001; Milkman and Dwyer, 2002; Sassen, 2002). Jenny Scholten and Nicki Blaze (2000) have written about their experiences living in San Francisco during the dot-com boom years and supporting their nascent writing careers by working as strippers, coining the term "digital cleavage" to refer to a gender-specific version of the more frequently remarked upon "digital divide" (the class-based gap in access to high technology). . . .

Given the gendered disparities of postindustrial economic life, the relatively high pay of the sex industry (compared to other service sector jobs) provides a compelling reason for some women from middle-class backgrounds to engage in sexual labour. Girl-X's narrative of her decision to become a phone sex worker, which appeared in a special Sex Industry issue of the alternative parenting magazine *Hip Mama*, exemplifies one common route of passage into the Bay Area sex industry in the late 1990s:

> *I had gotten bored with my day job, which was—and still is—unworthy of mention . . . The idea [of doing phone sex] excited me . . . I would no longer be subject to the indignities that came along with my previous jobs in the service industry, slinging espresso, records, books, or trendy clothes. I could barricade myself in my cave-like studio apartment all day and all night if I*

> *wanted, leaving only for special occasions, like the appearance of a Japanese noise band at one of those divey punk clubs. (Girl-X, 1997: 20)*

Where Girl-X exemplifies the transition from low-end service work into sexual labour, Zoey's account of trying to support a middle-class lifestyle on $17.75 an hour (despite holding bachelor's and master's degrees) exemplifies another. Zoey was a 30-year old former social worker who was working as an erotic masseuse when I met her. During a conversation over tea in her apartment, she described her transition into sexual labour this way:

> A year out of school I was very burnt out on the low pay, and really wanted to make more money . . . My boyfriend at the time had a good friend who had been doing sensual massage for many years and had found it tremendously lucrative . . . And so, I thought, oh, this would be a great ground for me to, you know, skip over years of torturous low pay [laughter] and actually then, to practice things that were truly dear to my heart. . . .

Sex Work and Distinction

Economic factors also served to shape middle-class sex workers' choices in other ways, ways which were not directly related to the pursuit of material sustenance in a high-tech economy but which pertained more generally to members' class-specific cultural dispositions. In *Distinction,* Pierre Bourdieu's analysis of the material and social underpinnings of taste, he describes "the new petite bourgeoisie" as composed of individuals with two primary class trajectories—on the one hand "those who have not obtained from the educational system the qualifications that would have enabled them to claim the established positions their original social position promised them"—women like Anna, a sex worker I met from an affluent suburb in Colorado, who had just completed her BA but had yet to pursue an advanced degree—and on the other hand, "those who have not obtained from their qualifications all they felt entitled to"—women like Zoey or Elise, who were dismayed that their educational credentials had not lifted them to greater heights (Bourdieu, 1984: 357). . . .

Middle-class sex workers' frequent embrace of an ethic of sexual experimentation and freedom must thus be seen not only in ideological terms, but as a particular strategy of class differentiation as well. Not incidentally, many of the middle-class sex workers that I interviewed were unpartnered and without children, and the majority described themselves as non-monogamous, bisexual, and experimental. Some sex workers even espoused an ideology of sexual fluidity that (along with the necessary economic capital) enabled them to serve as both sellers and occasional *buyers* of sexual services. In contrast to the old petit-bourgeois values of upwardly mobile asceticism and restraint (which served to distinguish this class from the working class, whose ethos rejects "pretense" and striving), the new petite bourgeoisie regards fun, pleasure, and freedom as ethical ideals worthy of strenuous pursuit. The embrace of these ideals serves as a means for members of the new petite bourgeoisie to distinguish themselves from the old petite bourgeoisie, an invisible boundary separating classes of individuals who might seem, at first glance, to exist in close proximity.

Organizing the Exchange for Authenticity

Middle-class sex workers' sense of distinction vis-à-vis their work could also be found in the types of work situation that they favored. As researchers Melissa Ditmore and Juhu Thukral (2005) have observed, the goal for most indoor sex workers (of whatever class background) who remain in the business is usually to be able to work independently. A common trajectory is to enter the industry working for someone else and to gradually build up one's own clientele. While professional autonomy was indeed desirable for the middle-class sex workers that I spoke with, there were other organizational criteria that were important to them as well. During whatever period of time that they might spend engaged in brothel-based work with third-party management, they were inclined to remove themselves from locales that seemed to foster a purely instrumentalist relationship to the labour. . . .

I worked at a place once in a sort of gourmet neighbourhood in Berkeley—alternative but ritzy . . . But even though they acted like we were a co-op—they expected us to do all of the cleaning and answering the phones, and required us to do the laundry during our shifts, stuff that a madam would normally do—all they did was come in and collect the money . . . They also made us come to staff meetings in addition to our regular schedule. These meetings were unpaid, a waste of our time . . . I finally left when I got a chance to open my own place in the City. (Amanda, 38) . . .

The Role of New Technologies

Despite the broader structural trend which situates women of most social classes on the wrong side of the "digital cleavage," the internet has reshaped predominant patterns of sexual commerce in ways that many middle-class sex workers have been able to benefit from. As various commentators have noted, the internet has enabled sexual commerce to thrive not only by increasing clients' access to information but also by facilitating community and camaraderie amongst individuals who might otherwise be perceived (and perceive themselves) as engaging in discreditable activity (Lane, 2000; Sharp and Earle, 2003).[3] For women who are able to bring technological skill and experience to sex work, it is increasingly possible to work without third-party management, to conduct one's business with minimal interference from the criminal justice system, and to reap greater profits by honing one's sales pitch to a more elite and more specialized clientele (Sanders, 2005a).

During our interview, Amanda was quite explicit about the ways that the new technologies had revolutionized her practice. She recounted how, after her brief stint working in a Berkeley brothel in which she was consistently "passed up" by the predominantly working-class clientele "in favor of younger, bustier, blonde women," she decided to give sex work another try when a friend suggested to her that she could advertise on the internet and work out of her own space:

Now, I only advertise on the internet. It insures me a reliable pool of well-educated, professional men with predictable manners and predictable ways of talking. When they make appointments, they keep them. My ad attracts a lot of first timers. I seem "safe," like someone they would already know, since it's clear that I have the same kind of background as they do and I seem easy to talk to. White educated women like me have a lot of appeal to professional white men. . . .

Professionalizing Sexual Labour

As Bourdieu observes, one way that members of the new petite bourgeoisie have found to embrace a sense of social distinction is via the adoption of "re-conversion strategies," in which cultural capital is employed to "professionalize" marginal spaces within the labour market and to invest them with a sense of personal meaning and ethical value (1984: 368). At the meetings of sex worker activists that I attended in San Francisco, members made efforts to professionalize their trade through activities such as the demonstration of "penetration alternatives," discussions of novel and tested safe-sex techniques, and presentations of statistical studies documenting the incidence of HIV in body fluids. Meetings were also a common place for members to make referrals to one another and to circulate written materials such as "dirty trick" lists (featuring the names and phone numbers of clients who were suspected of being dangerous); legal, investment, and tax advice; and safer sex guidelines. . . .

For the middle-class sex worker I spoke with, the performance of sex work often implied a distinctive skill set that could be elaborated through education and training. Many spoke explicitly about their deliberate pursuit of special skills as a means of enhancing both their experience of doing sex work and their earning power. The forms of training that they pursued ranged from massage certification to yogic breathwork (useful, one woman explained, with clients who were interested in tantric sex) to sexual surrogacy courses to the self-conscious embellishment of skills left over from prior careers. Zoey, for example, who had completed graduate school and an internship in social work, considered her earlier training as a therapist to be vital to her current work as an erotic masseuse:

> The model that I have always chosen in doing this work has actually been a psychotherapy model . . . As a therapist, in order to continue working with repetitively traumatized children, I had to be doing a ton of behind-

the-scenes work so I could hold my ground and have something to give them of value . . . Because of my training as a therapist I knew, intimately, how to do that; so, I brought that to sex work too. . . .

In addition to the acquisition of skills and training, the strategic deployment of educational and cultural capital came into play for middle-class sex workers in other ways. Lisa got her job at a Sausalito massage parlour when she "faked a French accent and answered an ad for a European blonde." Sybil, like other women, described screening her clients closely, and could restrict her practice to powerful businessmen once she knew "how to ask the right questions." Whereas on the streets, many women describe their previous private-sphere heterosexual relations as constituting sufficient technical preparation to engage in sex work (Bernstein, 2007; Høigård and Finstad, 1992; Maher, 1997), for middle-class women, cultural capital, work experience and special training often constitute vital components of sexual labour.

"Bounded Authenticity" and the Single Self

Ironically, it is precisely amongst the middle-class women and men, who are the most strident purveyors of the normalizing term "sex work," that sexual labour is most likely to implicate one's "private" erotic and emotional life. Those who have fought hardest for the social and political recognition of prostitution as "work" (as opposed to a uniquely degrading violation of self) are also those for whom the paid sexual encounter is likely to include emotionally engaged conversation as well as a diversity of sexual activities (bodily caresses, genital touching, cunnilingus and even occasional mouth-to-mouth kisses, rather than simply intercourse or fellatio), requires a larger investment of time with each client (typically at least an hour, as opposed to 15 minutes for streetwalkers), and is more likely to take place within the confines of one's own home (see also Lever and Dolnick, 2000). Since middle-class sex workers generally charge by the hour rather than for specified acts, their sexual labour is diffuse and expansive, rather than delimited and expedient.

During the era of industrial capitalism in which the institution of modern prostitution in the West was consolidated, what was typically sold and bought in the prostitution encounter was an expedient and emotionally contained exchange of cash for sexual release (Corbin, 1990; Rosen, 1982; Walkowitz, 1980). Although more intimate encounters still occurred, the expansion of the brothel system during this period led to the emergence of a new paradigm of efficiently Taylorized, commercialized sex. In contrast to this, within the postindustrial paradigm of (new) middle-class sex work that I have been describing, what is bought and sold frequently incorporates a great deal more emotional, as well as physical labour within the commercial context. . . .

In my own research, evidence of middle-class sex workers' efforts to manufacture authenticity resided in their descriptions of trying to simulate—or even produce—genuine desire, pleasure and erotic interest for their clients. Whereas in some cases this involved mere "surface acting" (as with Amanda, in the next extract) it could also involve the emotional and physical labour of manufacturing *authentic* (if fleeting) libidinal and emotional ties with clients, endowing them with a sense of desirability, esteem or even love. In contrast to the "counterfeit intimacy" that some sociological researchers have presumed to occur in the commercial sexual encounter (Foote, 1954; Ronai and Ellis, 1989; Sanders, 2005b), many sex workers' depictions of their work exemplified the calling forth of genuine feeling that Arlie Hochschild (2003) has termed "deep acting" and that Wendy Chapkis (1997) has described as the "emotional labour" of sex. Hochschild distinguishes between the practices of "surface acting" and "deep acting" in emotional life (2003: 92–3), noting that middle-class jobs typically call for "an appreciation of display rules, feeling rules," while working-class jobs "more often call for the individual's external behaviour and the products of it" (2003: 102).

> When I first started out, I enjoyed the sex. I'd go to work and "have sex." Now, I don't have that association as much. But my clients seem to think that being a nice guy means being a good lover. They do things to me that they should do with a girlfriend. Like they ask me what

I'm into, and apologize for coming too soon! So I need to play along. They apparently have no idea that the best client is the one that comes immediately. (Amanda) . . .

In addition to satisfying their clients' desires for bounded authenticity, many sex workers placed a premium upon ensuring that the labour felt meaningful to *themselves*. Through the recent development of blogging, a growing number of middle-class women have taken to writing about their experiences doing sex work and the satisfactions and disappointments that they have encountered. . . . [One] woman spoke to me about creating meaning and authenticity for herself in sex work by offering her clients only the kinds of erotic experiences that she herself enjoyed giving: "I don't go into those sessions teaching my clients how to pleasure me like a lover, but I *do* teach them how to pleasure me by receiving the service that I offer." For these sex workers, emotional authenticity is incorporated explicitly into the economic contract, challenging the view that commodification and intimacy constitute "hostile worlds," which has often prevailed in sociological discussions of the subject (Zelizer, 2005). . . .

Conclusion

The contingent of postindustrial, middle-class sex workers that I have been describing call into question a number of common presuppositions about what is necessarily entailed by the commercial sexual encounter and the likely impact of such transactions upon the body and psyche of the sex worker. These sex workers bring a constellation of subjective meanings and embodied practices to commercial sexual exchange that would not have been possible at earlier historical junctures. . . .

I have argued that the meanings with which they have endowed their labour are connected to new and historically specific conditions of possibility. These conditions include a technologically driven, postindustrial economy that has rapidly driven up the cost of living in desirable urban centers, while at the same time creating a highly stratified occupational sector (one with a limited number of time-intensive, highly paid, and hard-to-acquire professional positions, but with poorly paid temporary and part-time "junk" jobs that exist in ample quantities). These economic developments are intricately connected to some of the ways that increasing numbers of young, urban middle-class people are restructuring their intimate lives—either by delaying marriage and childbearing until these are more economically viable options, or by defying the expectations of heterosexual monogamy entirely.

NOTES

1. A fuller elaboration of some of these themes is presented in Elizabeth Bernstein, *Temporarily Yours* (2007).

2. See a recent article in *The Independent,* which notes that some 40,000 university students in France (or nearly 2%) admitted to funding their studies through the sex trade (Duval Smith, 2006).

3. When I did a count of web-based advertisements in San Francisco in 2001, there were approximately 3000. By 2005, there were some 5000 advertisements on one popular website alone—one crude indication of the expanding scope of online sexual commerce in the city.

REFERENCES

Bernstein, Elizabeth (2007) *Temporarily Yours: Intimacy, Authenticity, and the Commerce of Sex.* Chicago, IL: University of Chicago Press.

Bourdieu, Pierre (1984) *Distinction: A Social Critique of the Judgement of Taste* (trans. Richard Nice). Cambridge, MA: Harvard University Press.

Chapkis, Wendy (1997) *Live Sex Acts: Women Performing Erotic Labor.* New York: Routledge.

Corbin, Alain (1990) *Women for Hire: Prostitution and Sexuality in France After 1860.* Cambridge: MA: Harvard University Press.

Ditmore, Melissa and Thukral, Juhu (2005) *Behind Closed Doors: an Analysis of Indoor Sex Work in New York City.* New York: Urban Justice Center.

Droganes, Constance (2000) "Toronto the Naughty," *National Post* 22 January.

Duval Smith, Alex (2006) "40,000 French Students Join Sex Trade to Fund Degrees," The *Independent* 31 October (EUROPE): 20.

Economist (2000) "Sex, News, and Statistics: Where Entertainment on the Web Scores," *The Economist Online,* URL (accessed 19 October 2000): www.economist.com

Foote, Nelson (1954) "Sex as Play," *Social Problems* 1(4): 159–63.

Girl-X (1997) "Will Moan for Rent Money," *Hip Mama: The Parenting Zine,* Special Issue on the Sex Industry (13): 20–4.

Hochschild, Arlie Russell (2003) *The Commericalization of Intimate Life: Notes from Home and Work.* Berkeley: University of California Press.

Høigård, Cecilie and Finstad, Liv (1992) *Backstreets: Prostitution, Money, and Love.* University Park: Pennsylvania State University Press.

Lane, Frederick (2000) *Obscene Profits: The Entrepreneurs of Pornography in the Cyber Age.* New York: Routledge.

Leigh, Carol (2004) *Unrepentant Whore: Collected Works of Scarlot Harlot.* San Francisco: Last Gasp.

Lever, Janet and Dolnick, Deanne (2000) "Clients and Call Girls: Seeking Sex and Intimacy," in Ronald Weitzer (ed.) *Sex for Sale: Prostitution, Pornography, and the Sex Industry,* pp. 85–103. New York: Routledge.

McCall, Leslie (2001) *Complex Inequality: Gender, Class, and Race in the New Economy.* New York: Routledge.

Maher, Lisa (1997) *Sexed Work: Gender, Race and Resistance in a Brooklyn Drug Market.* Oxford: Oxford University Press.

Milkman, Ruth and Dwyer, Rachel E. (2002) *Growing Apart: the "New Economy" and Job Polarization in California, 1992–2000,* URL (accessed 22 February 2003): http://repositories.cdlib.org/ile/scl2002/Milkman Dwyer

Nagle, Jill (1997) *Whores and Other Feminists.* New York: Routledge.

Prial, Dunstan (1999) "IPO Outlook: 'Adult' Web Sites Profit, Though Few are Likely to Offer Shares," *The Wall Street Journal* 8 March: B10.

Ronai, Carol Rambo and Ellis, Carolyn (1989) "Turn-ons for Money: Interactional Strategies of the Table Dancer," *Journal of Contemporary Ethnography* 18(3): 271–98.

Rosen, Ruth (1982) *The Lost Sisterhood: Prostitution in America, 1900–1918.* Baltimore, MD: Johns Hopkins University Press.

Sanders, Teela (2005a) *Sex Work: a Risky Business.* Devon: Willan Publishing.

Sanders, Teela (2005b) " 'It's Just Acting': Sex Workers' Strategies for Capitalizing on Sexuality," *Gender, Work, and Organization* 12(4): 319–42.

Sassen, Saskia (2002) "Global Cities and Survival Circuits," in Barbara Ehrenreich and Arlie Russell Hochschild (eds) *Global Woman: Nannies, Maids, and Sex Workers in the New Economy,* pp. 254–75. New York: Metropolitan Books.

Sharp, Keith and Earle, Sarah (2003) "Cyberpunters and Cyberwhores: Prostitution on the Internet," in Yvonne Jewkes (ed.) *Dot.cons: Crime, Deviance, and*

Identity on the Internet, pp. 36–52. Devon: Willan Publishing.

Walkowitz, Judith R. (1980) *Prostitution and Victorian Society: Women, Class, and the State.* Cambridge: Cambridge University Press.

Zelizer, Viviana (2005) *The Purchase of Intimacy.* Princeton, NJ: Princeton University Press.

Strip Clubs and Their Regulars

Katherine Frank

Sexual services and products have long been a part of the U.S. entertainment and leisure industries. In a 1997 article for *U.S. News & World Report,* Eric Schlosser reported that in the prior year Americans spent "more than $8 billion on hard-core videos, peep shows, live sex acts, adult cable programming, sexual devices, computer porn, and sex magazines." The number of major strip clubs catering to heterosexually identified men nearly doubled between 1987 and 1992, and an estimate for late 1998 puts the number of clubs at around 3000 with annual revenues ranging from $500,000 to more than $5 million.

While some men dislike strip clubs or find them boring, there is a significant population of heterosexual American males who are willing to spend their money on the kind of public, voyeuristic (although interactive) fantasy available in a no-contact strip club. Despite popular beliefs to the contrary, strippers are generally not selling sex to their customers in this type of club—although they are selling sexualized and gendered services. Rather than fulfilling a biological need for sexual release, as some pop sociobiological accounts suggest, or serving a masculine need for domination, strip clubs provide a kind of intermediate space (not work and not home, although related to both) in which men can experience their bodies and identities in particular pleasurable ways. . . .

Strip clubs are stratified in terms of luxury, status, and other distinguishing features. Whereas strip clubs were once primarily located in "red light" areas of towns and cities associated with crime and prostitution, the upscale clubs are now often quite visible and work to develop reputations for safety, comfort, and classiness. Drawing on cultural markers of status—such as luxury liquors, fine dining, valet parking, and private conference rooms—upscale clubs advertise themselves as places for businessmen to entertain clients or for middle class professionals to visit after work. Dancers may be advertised as refined, well-educated women. Sophisticated sound and lighting equipment, multiple stages, large video screens, and multi-million dollar construction budgets make many contemporary strip clubs into high-tech entertainment centers. This is not to say that smaller or "seedier" clubs have disappeared. The clubs in any locale, however, are categorized through their relationships to one another and this system of relationships helps inform both the leisure experiences of the customers and the work experiences of the dancers.

The proliferation and upscaling of strip clubs during the 1980s needs to be situated in late capitalist consumer culture as well as within a variety of social changes and developments. In many ways it makes sense that strip clubs should multiply during the last several decades, along with the panic about AIDS and fears about the dissolution of "the family." The process of upscaling in strip clubs, with a promise of "clean" and respectable interactions, alleviated fears about contamination and disease. The fact that sexual activity is not generally expected or offered in strip clubs also fit well with a growing emphasis on monogamy and marriage for heterosexuals after the sexual experimentation (and ensuing disillusionment for many) of the 1970s. There are other social changes which may be influencing this rapid increase in strip clubs as well: women's increased presence in the workforce, continuing backlashes against feminism, on-going marketing efforts to sexualize and masculinize particular forms of consumption ("sports, beer, and women," for example), changing patterns of mobility which influence dating practices and intimate relationships, and increased travel for businessmen and more anonymous opportunities to purchase commodified sexualized services, to name just a few.

Despite their prevalence and popularity, strip clubs are still often the subject of intense public scrutiny. Local ordinances have been drafted across the nation to harass, limit or eradicate strip clubs—often citing "adverse secondary effects" such as increased crime and decreased property values in neighborhoods that house such venues as justifications for these legislative actions. Many such ordinances seem to be based on conjectures about just what the men (and women) are up to when they set foot in a strip club. There is endless speculation about drug use, prostitution, and crime—by customers, lawmakers, and people who have never even entered a strip club. . . . While these activities surface at times, in often scandalous ways—as they do in many industries— I came away from my research with a belief that most of the customers were in search of something completely different through their interactions.

Media and scholarly attention to the customers of strip clubs has been far less pervasive than that focused on the dancers or the clubs themselves. But what is it, exactly, that the customers are seeking in these venues? After all, without enough men willing to open their wallets each night the industry would cease to exist. As a cultural anthropologist dedicated to participant observation—that is, becoming immersed in the community you study—I selected five strip clubs in one city, sought employment as an entertainer, and interviewed the regular male customers of those clubs. For regulars, visits to strip clubs are a significant sexualized and leisure practice; these are not men who have wandered into a club once or twice or visit only for special occasions like bachelor parties. The majority of the regulars were men middle-aged or older with enough disposable income and free time that they could engage in this relatively private and often expensive leisure practice. I also interviewed dancers, club managers and other club employees, advertisers, and men who preferred other forms of adult entertainment.

Most of the regular customers claimed that they knew where to get sex if they wanted it, and that they chose no-contact strip clubs (or clubs that offered table-dancing rather than lap dancing) precisely because they knew that sex would not be part of the experience. While watching the dancers perform on the stages was certainly appealing, many of the regulars were also interested in the conversations that they could have with dancers. Unlike burlesque performers of years past, contemporary exotic dancers "perform" not just onstage but individually for

the customers as they circulate amongst the crowd selling table-dances. Dancers are thus also selling their personalities, their attentions, and conversation to the customers. Some of the regulars returned repeatedly to see a particular dancer; others enjoyed briefer interactions with a number of dancers. Either way, talk was one of the important services being provided and conversations would focus on work, family, politics, sports, sexual fantasies, or any number of other topics.

Whether visiting a small neighborhood bar or a large, flashy gentleman's club, the customers repeatedly told me that they visited strip clubs to relax. Part of the allure of strip clubs for their patrons lies in part in their representation as somewhere out of the ordinary, somewhere proscribed and perhaps a bit "dangerous"—yet as a safe space of play and fantasy where the pressures, expectations and responsibilities of work and home can be left behind.

In many ways, then, strip clubs were seen as relaxing because they provided a respite from women's demands or expectations in other spheres, as well as the possibility (not always actualized) of avoiding competition with other men for women's attention. Strip clubs also offered the customers an opportunity for both personal and sexual acceptance from women, a chance to talk about their sexual desires without reproach or to fantasize that they were attractive enough to gain the interest of a dancer regardless of whether or not they paid her. Some customers wanted an ego boost. As one man said: "It's just absolutely an ego trip because you go in there, and if you're a warthog, bald, and got a pot belly, some good looking girl's gonna come up and go, 'Hey, do you want me to dance for you?' Seducing women is something all men wish they were better at . . . this seems like you're doing it, and it's easy!"

Strip clubs were also relaxing because they provided a safe space in which to be both married or committed and interacting with women in a sexualized setting, and the services offered fit well with these particular men's desires to remain sexually monogamous. Customers are also not expected to perform sexually or to provide any pleasure to the dancer (beyond paying her for her time), and this was also seen as relaxing by many of the men. . . .

However, because they provided a space in which many everyday expectations are inverted (by featuring public nudity, for example), the clubs were still seen as "taboo," as dangerous and exciting, by the regulars as well as safe and predictable. Many of the interviewees discussed their experiences in the language of "variety," "travel," "fun," "escape" and "adventure" and described themselves as "hunters" or "explorers" despite the fact that their experiences in the clubs were highly regulated by local ordinances, club rules, and club employees. Some customers enjoyed the fact that their visits to strip clubs took them to marginal areas of the city. Further, visits to the clubs often were unacceptable to the married regulars' more "conservative" wives or partners. Significantly, then, strip clubs are also dangerous enough to be alluring, a bit "less civilized" and rowdier than the places these middle-class customers would ordinarily enter. This balance between safety and excitement was very important, for if strip clubs lose their edge for a particular customer, or conversely, become too transgressive, he may lose interest and seek a different form of entertainment.

Understanding the motivations of the men who frequent no-contact strip clubs can help quell some of the fears that tend to drive oppressive regulation. There are indeed problems with strip clubs as they currently exist, often rooted in material inequalities between different classes of laborers, in the poor working conditions found in many clubs, in the stigma that surrounds sex work, and in double standards for men's and women's sexualities, for example. However, eradicating or more tightly regulating strip clubs does little to combat these problems, which are related to the organization of labor in late capitalism, to systemic inequalities and prejudices, and to the stigmatization and fear that still surrounds issues of sex and sexuality in the United States.

Source: "Strip Clubs and Their Regulars" by Katherine Frank. *American Sexuality Magazine 1*(4). Copyright 2003, National Sexuality Resource Center/San Francisco State University. Reprinted by permission.

Overcome: The Money Shot in Pornography and Prostitution

Lisa Jean Moore

For a few years in the early 1990s, I worked on a national sex information switchboard. Much to my surprise, a majority of the callers were men, and their two most common questions were "What is the normal penis size?" and "Where is the clitoris?" Trained to provide anonymous, nonjudgmental, and accurate information to callers, I would respond that most penises, when erect, were between 5 and 7 inches. I would receive immediate thanks for this information, and as they hung up I remember thinking their relief was palpable. Their penises, presumably, were "okay."

As for the clitoris question, I instructed callers to place their hands in a praying position, bend their knuckles slightly and imagine this as the vagina. If the area between the thumbs was the vagina opening, the clitoris was roughly located in the place above the tips of their thumbs, in the triangular area. This answer was not as successful as the first. Many callers fumbled with or even dropped the phone while trying to follow my instructions. Some callers were clearly confused by the model itself, asking, "So it's a hole?" or "But what does the vagina really look like?" Furthermore, I was increasingly alarmed by the steady stream of female callers who asked for instructions on how to find their own clitorises or, somewhat paradoxically, wanted suggestions on how to experience orgasms exclusively though vaginal penetration. "Is there something wrong with me?" they inquired when discussing their dissatis-

faction with penis-vagina penetration, often explaining that they had never experienced an orgasm during sex. Clearly, there is something baffling and mysterious about the clitoris. Even though size doesn't matter, location and purpose do. Where is it? What does it do? These callers rarely hung up with the same sense of relief as the first set of callers. The former found answers; the latter continued to question.

I use these examples to illustrate the conventional wisdom on male and female anatomy and sexual responses. In contrast to women, and whether or not each man experiences it to be true, conventional wisdom holds that men's sexuality is fairly simple. It isn't difficult to make men come, and it isn't difficult to know whether or not they have come. The phenomenon of men faking orgasm, though possible, doesn't often get discussed. Semen is, of course, the reason for this; it is thought to be the irrefutable evidence.

Although male callers rarely asked about their semen, in our training, we were instructed to provide them with these facts. Spermatogenesis, or the production of the sperm cell, takes approximately 72 days. Both Cowper's and Littre's glands, which are located in the genital area, contribute secretions in the processes of ejaculation. The prostate also adds fructose and liquefying enzymes.[1] When a man comes, a range of 2–10 milliliters of fluid is produced though his ejaculation at about 10 miles per hour. Between 200 and 500 million sperm cells are contained in most ejaculates, the equivalent of about 5–15 calories. It is estimated that a man ejaculates 5,000 times in his lifetime.[2] Theoretically any man could repopulate the United States with just a few ejaculates (and the participation of 290 million women or less if multiple births occur).

Growing Up: From Innocence to Debauchery

. . . Ejaculation is taken as external proof that a man has experienced an orgasm, despite evidence that men can ejaculate without orgasm, technically known as anorgasmic ejaculation.[3] The physical presence of the ejaculate, the seminal fluid, is a material reality that confirms men's pleasure.[4] Most pornographic entertainment reinforces this belief, as ejaculation, or the "money shot" in porn parlance, is the raison d'être of sexual encounters. The money shot signals the end of the male sexual act—cue the drum roll, he has come. Cindy Patton, an activist and scholar of human sexuality, points out that in Western culture male sexual fulfillment is "synonymous with orgasm" and that the male orgasm is "an essential and essentialist punctuation of the sexual narrative. No orgasm, no sexual pleasure. No cum shot, no narrative closure."[5] In other words, the cum shot is the period at the end of the sentence. Case closed. Alternatively, with the rare exception of anorgasmic ejaculation, both the female anatomy and orgasm are more complex, even elusive—for both men and women. That being the case, in pornography the sex act itself is centered around the male penis and orgasm. Only when that happens does conventional wisdom tell us that sex has occurred.[6]

There is an entire lexicon for the release of semen from the body; terms like ejaculation, premature ejaculation, nocturnal emissions, wet dreams, and shooting your wad are just a few. With such a wide variety of ways to describe ejaculates and the act of ejaculating, it would seem that many men are preoccupied with ejaculation, and especially measurements of it. From the record books to website legends, claims about the feats of men and their ejaculations abound. For example, the world record for number of male orgasms is 16 in one hour. According to several unsubstantiated reports on websites, the greatest distance of an ejaculate is 18 feet 9 inches, which was achieved by Horst Schultz, who apparently also holds the record for the greatest height of ejaculate (12 feet 4 inches).

Not all ejaculates are created equal. Each time ejaculation occurs, semen contains varying proportions of ingredients. These variations are affected by diet, age, how the ejaculation was achieved (through masturbation or partner sexual stimulation, whether anal, oral, or vaginal), level of arousal, physical fitness, and number of ejaculations in the past 72 hours. The age of first conscious ejaculation, known as "oigarche," is generally between 10 and 15 years old. Nocturnal emissions, or wet dreams that are generally erotic or sexual, are accompanied by the release or ejaculation of semen. Roughly 50 percent of boys between the ages of 10 and 20 experience wet dreams, possibly as a way for the reproductive system to get rid of excess semen, although most agree that semen is reabsorbed back into the body.

But sometimes men are not physiologically in control of when and how their semen emerges. Premature ejaculation, recently renamed "rapid ejaculation" . . . is increasingly considered a medically diagnosable condition for men under 40. It is defined as ejaculation prior to the desires of both sexual partners. Although rapid ejaculation maybe underreported, the National Health and Social Life Survey suggests that its prevalence is roughly 30 percent. Sex therapy, antidepressants, and lidocaine cream or related topical anesthetic agents have all demonstrated success at treating rapid ejaculation.

Regardless of the quantity of semen or the quality of its delivery during ejaculation, in the world of sex entertainment the release of semen signifies the successful conclusion of the sex act. The appearance of semen is the proof of sexual fulfillment, so the more the more better, right? It turns out that the equation is not so simple when we consider the layered meanings of sperm and semen across the worlds of pornography, prostitution, and popular culture.

Fetishizing Semen

Members of the specifically heterosexual[7] sex entertainment industry, sex workers and pornographic filmmakers in particular, contribute to our understanding of sperm in important ways. From ideas about what constitutes sex or sex acts to what is considered sexy, to how men and their penises can perform, the sex industry—even if covertly—has greatly influenced popular notions of sex. Pornographic filmmakers specialize in representing a variety of techniques to animate ejaculation and semen, thereby fetishizing it. Within sex entertainment settings, semen is worshiped as a magical substance of both supernatural arousal and erotic achievement. It is depicted in films and printed media as a substance that has extraordinary power over humans. The male actors seem repeatedly shocked by the force, volume, and desirability of their semen, while the female actors can't control themselves in the presence of this semen and must slather it all over their bodies, even drink it down as if dying of thirst. Different cultures vary the themes of seminal ejaculate in their pornography. For example, in the late 1990s, *bukkake,* a style of pornography that was popularized in Japan, depicts multiple men ejaculating on a woman or group of women.[8] The use of ejaculation is part of a humiliation ritual and generally does not involve any of the female characters experiencing orgasm.

So although semen is presented as the end product of a sexual experience, it is also an object manipulated by the directors, cameras, lighting, scripts, and actors to elicit arousal. The camera lens focuses on the glory of seminal expression and encourages the viewer to witness the money shot as the reward of spectatorship. . . .

But semen does not exist in a vacuum; rather, it is a bodily fluid that is deeply implicated in history and epidemiology. At least for the past 30 years, unprotected seminal ejaculation brings to mind disease transmission—including HIV, hepatitis B and C, and sexually transmitted diseases (STDs). Being such a dangerous vector of infection, semen has become increasingly seen as grotesque—something feared and unwanted. Unprotected seminal ejaculation during vaginal or anal sex is not the only dangerous practice; semen ejaculated into the mouth, eyes, and nose can transmit herpes, chlamydia, syphilis, and gonorrhea.

As a result of these risks, exposure to semen is evermore regulated within the sex entertainment industry. California's Division of Occupational Safety and Health (CAL-OSHA) oversees and regulates

workers in the adult film industry; most porn films are produced in southern California. The agency provides adult film workers with safety guidelines and employment protection from work practices that might expose them to blood and "other potentially infectious material (OPIM)."[9] According to CAL-OSHA's website, "semen and vaginal fluid are always considered OPIM." The website also provides examples of "engineering and work practice controls" used in the adult film industry. . . .

In the sex entertainment industry, some film studios demand regular HIV tests. Adult Industry Medical Health Care Foundation (AIM), a nonprofit health-care foundation concerned with sex worker mental and physical health, provides on-site testing services for performers and encourages the responsible sharing of test results between working partners. Yet there have been HIV transmission cases within the pornography industry. As reporter Ann Regentin explains:

> *In 1986, John Holmes contracted the virus and continued to work without telling anyone until 1988, when he died of AIDS. In 1998, a rash of HIV cases seemed to point to Marc Wallice, who tested positive for the virus and had been caught working with faked HIV test results. In 1999, Tony Montana tested positive and immediately stopped working. As far as anyone knows, he did not infect anyone else.[10]*

Recently, on April 12, 2004, porn star Darren James, who contracted the virus while shooting in Brazil, infected others through work, leading to a brief shutdown of production within the San Fernando Valley. Clearly, there are occupational risks to working in the porn industry, but these can be mitigated through precautions and regulations. Within the sex entertainment industry, then, this bodily fluid straddles the line between being supremely erotic and a lethal weapon.

Each sex worker must develop methods, practices, and professional expertise to avoid exposure to potential diseases or lethal toxins. Furthermore, fertile female sex workers must also try to limit their risk of pregnancy, an occupational hazard of frequent contact with semen. As one of my informants related to me, sex work includes aspects of "hazardous waste material" management. There are different risks associated with exposure to semen by sex workers in the porn industry. Reviewing a working partner's HIV tests is one industry standard. With the advantage of not performing sex in real time, actors and actresses in the porn industry are able to manipulate some exposure to seminal ejaculation. For example, a porn star can appear to swallow ejaculate without actually doing so. During an interview, Raylene, a porn star, stated, "I don't swallow that often because I really don't like the taste. I mean I have, but I don't really like it."[11] . . .

The Money Shot

Some recent mainstream films use semen in a different way: as props for gags or as symbols of alienation. The actual appearance of sperm in mainstream films is a relatively new phenomenon and perhaps can be seen, in some ways, as an extension of the increasingly graphic and "realistic" images of the body that are so commonplace today, especially in television crime and medical dramas. Here severed limbs, burnt bodies, and gaping wounds are regularly featured, but we often even "go inside" the body to see the actual source of the disease, parasite, or infected organ.

Given the intensely graphic nature of such shows, and given that sperm has long been readily seen and featured in pornographic films, it perhaps not surprising that the once-taboo substance now makes its appearance in mainstream movies. In the film *Magnolia,* for example, protagonist Frank Mackey (played by Tom Cruise), is a motivational speaker for a seminar series, "Seduce and Destroy," which includes a session entitled "How to turn your 'friend' into your sperm receptacle," encouraging insecure men to use their sperm as a means of conquering and depositing waste into the female body. Taking this a step further, films like *There's Something About Mary* and *The Squid and the Whale* use sperm as, in the former, hair gel and, in the latter, a means for acting out adolescent angst. Such material would once have been considered obscene but is now enough of a novelty in mainstream film that it is capable of grabbing the audience's attention and eliciting somewhat shocked laughs. . . .

Such treatment of semen is a far cry from its standard depiction in pornographic films. Far from providing comedic relief, semen . . . often has a star-

ring and very important role to play in these features . . . the man's ejaculation is the raison d'être for these films. The money shot, where a man ejaculates on screen, is the compulsory display of semen in most pornographic films and a number of pornographic magazines as well. Ejaculation, the release of seminal fluid often with astounding force, authenticates the pornographic film in that the sexual desire, the arousal, and the performance are seemingly based on "real" desire. As a male friend quipped to me during a more explosive money shot, "Now you can't fake that." The cum shot is typically defined where a man ejaculates onto a woman, usually onto her face (referred to as a facial) or sometimes onto her sex organs. To be classified as a money shot, the semen must be clearly visible. The "money" refers to the money the actor receives as payout for making the film, which sometimes includes a bonus for the act of ejaculation. . . .

When seminal ejaculation is the denouement of a film, there is a presumption about those watching the film. As Patton states, "Even though not everyone in this culture has a penis, the cinematic conventions which position the viewer as the person coming are fairly seamless, and it is quite easy to imagine that this is your penis, regardless of your anatomical configuration."[12] In the porn film, we are each beckoned to identify with that penis and to experience the rush of relief as ejaculate spews forth. Furthermore, Patton has argued that after the wild abandon of pornographic sex, seminal ejaculation enables the man to be responsible for the restoration of sexual order.[13] The stylized repetition of money shots is alluring in that it signals release of control, pleasure, achievement, and success.

It is not clear at what historical moment the money shot emerged as a cinematic convention, but Patton suggests that it has at least existed in the United States since the 1930s as "handmade gay male pornographic drawings from the interwar years."[14] The male orgasm demonstrated through ejaculation indicates the completion of a sex act, the scene, the movie, the book, and the encounter. It instructs the audience that the activity is over and has been successful. As an industry standard of pornographic films, the money shot was fairly commonplace after World War II.[15] . . .

Girls Gone Wild for Sperm

There is a new niche market of seminal ejaculate films that expand on the glorification of men's ejaculate. Unlike other pornographic genres, these movies focus on semen as the central theme of the narrative and the action, not solely the denouement. Titles such as *Semen Demons, Desperately Seeking Semen, The Cum Cocktail, We Swallow, Sperm Overdose* (volumes 1–6), *Sperm Dreams, Sperm Burpers* (volumes 1–5), *A Splash of Sperm,* and *Feeding Frenzy* (volumes 1–3) venture beyond the money shot toward eroticizing seminal ingestion. The contents of the promotional descriptions of the videos, as well as the videos themselves, depict a variety of women drinking and bathing in semen from diverse male partners. Women appear to be insatiable and competitive about their desire for ingesting the semen as they rush to get to the ejaculating penis, the full shot glass, or residual ejaculate on a sheet. What does it mean to see women completely overcome with their desire to drink semen? To smear it all over their bodies? What does this say about male desire and masculinity? Here is a sampling of promotional descriptions of a few films:[16]

Promo for the movie Semen Shots 2

> *There's nothing that a pretty girl likes more at the end of a sexual encounter than to drink her lover's cum out of a shot glass. That's the premise behind this developing series, anyway. Delilah Strong entertains five young men and takes two cocks in her pussy before swigging multiple shots of their hot spunk. Jasmyn Taliana whimpers a lot before downing her two shots. Mason Storm enjoys a bit of anal before laughing her way through two fingers of warm sperm. Rio Mariah takes a double penetration and then squeezes the contents of her pussy and ass into a glass for savoring. Monica Sweetheart looks pretty in a sheer nightie with sparkly flowers during her anal and still looks cute while tossing back some of Brian Pumper's love cocktail. . . .*

Promo for Wad Gobblers, Volume 13

> *This video begins with an amazing wild montage of twelve or fourteen chicks all taking it in the face with gobs of splashing semen, a dozen or more beauties being blasted with emissions so powerful it shoots up their nostrils. Their tongues snake out to lap up every drop and the overflow bubbles like lava out of their mouths.*

These descriptions of money shots use sensational linguistic cues to entice the reader to purchase or rent these videos. It is obvious that seminal ejaculation is the main attraction in each video, the star of the show. Women's bodies are the surfaces for seminal display or the containers to ingest semen. Using the props of shot glasses and cocktail accessories, women literally become drunk on semen, often losing control in the presence of such powerful and intoxicating fluids.

Ironically, this genre of pornography is being produced against a cultural backdrop in which semen is directly associated with risk. Warnings about HIV/AIDS and STDs are plastered on bus stops, broadcast through public service announcements on radio and television, and echoed in health-care interactions. We are told to avoid semen to lessen our risk of pregnancy, disease, and death. Some industries, such as health care and forensics, have worked to imbue the raw material of semen with risk. Similarly, fertility enterprises and spouse or partner surveillance companies market their services by both reminding us of the risk of seminal ejaculate and claiming to mitigate that risk for us.

But the constant messages about risk and danger from seminal ejaculate have likely affected men's own relationship to their semen, as well as amplified a sense of it as forbidden. These pornographic videos then capitalize on recovering and eroticizing the raw material of semen as safe, natural, organic, whole. The commodification of semen in these videos relies on a specific form of consumption in the narrative arc. Taking the action a moment beyond the money shot, the triumph of these videos is actually the expression of reverence for semen as it is placed either in a shot glass or on a woman's face, buttocks, or breasts. The absence of, or disregard for, risk is also a saleable dimension of these videos. They sell the image of sperm as not embodying risk or, even if risky, then certainly worth that risk. In these films, these female actors are depicted as willing to debase themselves, put themselves at risk, and even become sick in order to please their men. . . .

[T]he taste of semen is not as delicious as the videos portray. Some have compared the scent of semen to bleach, household cleanser, or swimming pool water. The taste has been described as salty and bitter, which may explain why Semenex, a patented, all-natural powder drink has been created to sweeten semen. Semenex, with an advertised price of $54.95 for a 30-serving container, relies on testimonials similar to this one: "Tasty! I've never really had a problem with semen, except when it gets really bitter, but this product really makes drinking a man down a treat!" so says, Jenni from Mesa, Arizona. As an online ad in *Maxim* magazine claims, "Semenex is where to go for delicious sperm guaranteed. Finally, an answer to the 'I don't like the taste' argument."[17] Interviewed as part of the 2005 documentary *Inside Deep Throat* about the infamous porn movie, Helen Gurley Brown, *Cosmopolitan* editor in chief and author of the 1962 best seller *Sex and the Single Girl,* extols the benefits of semen, saying, "Women have known for years that ejaculate is good for the skin because it is full of babies . . . it's full of protein. Just rub it all over your face, and skin and chest."

While semen may get mixed reviews from actual women, in the world of pornographic films semen is no longer something that is gross, yucky, smells bad, or brings disease—rather, it is something delicious, desired, and needed. Perhaps only the bold fantasy of a world dominated by men, and their need for sexual pleasure, could provide the scenario where women actually fight with each other for the pleasure of guzzling down ounces of semen. . . .

Within the sex industries of prostitution and pornography, sperm maintains contradictory meanings. It is referred to as a dangerous, if not lethal, weapon and, alternatively, as the crowning achievement of human interaction. For sex workers who perform sex acts with actual people (as opposed to pornography film actors), seminal ejaculation is a hazardous waste material to be managed and avoided for fear of pregnancy or disease. Sex workers do not have the benefit of reviewing their partners' HIV test results before a scene. Nor are there multiple takes to "get it right." And since many male clients are socialized by pornographic videos that do not depict safe sex, many sex workers find that, while they must use latex devices to protect themselves, at the same time they must eroticize their safe sex practices or risk failing to perform the job they are being paid for.

"Dealing with the Jizz": Stories from Sex Workers

Most sex workers handle men as if they are dangerous; they can be violent, deceiving, and vectors of disease. Despite this belief about men, most sex workers will take on the risk of intimate physical contact as long as the men have the money to pay for it. This, of course, assumes that men can afford an average $200 an hour sexual experience. In an ironic twist, sex workers and sperm banks have an inverse relationship with regard to sperm and money. Men pay sex workers for their services, which includes managing their potentially dangerous semen, while people pay sperm banks to store or purchase certifiably healthy semen. Semen banks pay donors between $40 and $60 per ejaculate. Each ejaculate can be divided up into between two and three vials, which cost roughly $150 each. So one ejaculate divided into two samples is $(150 \times 2) - 60 = 240 profit per ejaculate. This is $40 more than the typical sex worker makes.

The analysis that follows is based on interviews conducted over a five-year period (1991–1996) with well-paid, in-call, consenting sex workers. Sex workers occasionally reject clients who use heavy drugs or alcohol, are on the bad trick list, or simply give them the creeps. A bad trick list circulates within communities of sex workers and has the names and descriptions of previously delinquent or violent male clients. Perhaps through personal stigma and immersion in an AIDS/HIV culture, sex workers view all bodily products as having degrees of toxicity. In the pursuit of self-preservation and profit, semen is treated as a carrier of pathogens, germs, and sperm that may debilitate, kill, or impregnate the worker. All sex workers interviewed about their safer sex practices stated they always use a condom for each act of vaginal and anal intercourse. Here are some of their comments about men and their sperm:

> I personally do not want to have any contact with fluids that come out of a man's dick. So like today I saw somebody who had a little pre-ejaculate on his belly and what I do is I take a piece of tissue and I wipe it off, then I take another piece of tissue and I apply nonoxynol nine. (Bonny, 54; 20-year professional dominant) . . .

My party line is rubbers for fucking and rubbers for sucking. I have always been strict about it. (Hadley, 55; 25-year veteran stripper, prostitute, professional dominant) . . .

Men and their semen are viewed here as universally dangerous, distrustful, and dirty. Semen is something that must be managed. No matter how it is represented, as good or bad, or somewhere in between, at the time of its ejaculation, semen has to be dealt with. As Quincy, a 45-year-old sex worker who has been in the industry since her late 20s states,

> The guys want me to really like their cum. I think many of them would like to see me roll around in it and drink it and basically bathe in it. Maybe like they see on the movies they watch. But, I can't really do that. So I just sort of pretend. There would be something nice about being able to wallow in body fluids but I am not even going to go there.

As discussed, this desire to "wallow in body fluids" is promoted in almost all pornographic videos, but it is only risk free for the jizzee, not the jizzed upon. Quincy empathizes with her clients about semen, telling them, "I really love sperm and I wish I could swallow it. But we can pretend and I bet you will not even notice the difference." In her sex work career and as a practitioner of latex devices, Quincy claims that men do not know the difference between safer sex and unprotected sex when things are done by a professional. She claims when safer sex is seamlessly accomplished, her male clientele (and perhaps men in general) accept its use: "So it's like a Pavlovian trick to get people more comfortable with and more turned on to the possibility of safe sex. The snap of the glove or smell of condoms means something fun is going to happen."

Sex workers create safety standards for dealing with semen. They use male and female condoms, gloves, and finger cots (small latex coverings for individual fingers), as actual physical barriers that inhibit the semen from making contact with unexposed body surfaces. Safer sex, as a collection of symbols, practices, and technological innovations, both protects sex workers from contamination and assures the client of standard operating procedures that reduce their own exposure to the "hazardous waste material"

of previous clients. As Michelle, a 38-year-old petite blonde, states, "When my clients get a little strange about my safer sex stuff, I will say, 'Well, this might bug you a little bit, but I promise to keep you safe' and then I will smile all sweet."

In addition to manipulations for safety purposes, sex workers have crafted techniques to make semen perform more predictably, to make this recalcitrant substance more workable. Sex workers train their clients in techniques for semen control and manipulation. For example, many sex workers instruct their clients on how to put on a condom. They can instruct men in how to maintain erections and delay ejaculation through practicing sex acts and talking about their bodies. By bringing an erect man close to orgasm and then delaying the ejaculation, sex workers talk about building a man's endurance and self-control during sex acts. They work with their clients, talking to them and coaxing them to understand their own bodies and sexual responses. Several of the women I interviewed have developed symbolic rituals of performance to promote pleasurable semen control. They place a variety of male condoms in special places on a night table or at an altar with candles and incense, "To honor the act they know will be coming soon," as Olivia put it. Most sex workers opened up male condoms during our interviews to demonstrate different techniques for placing condoms on imaginary penises using their mouth and hands, coaching men through the safer sex requirements with statements like, "Now comes the fun part," and, "I can't wait. Can you?"

When I was interviewing Michelle at her apartment, she invited me to look at an album of erotic photographs of herself in full makeup and dressed in lingerie. "This is how I look when my clients come over," she explained as we explored the ironies of attempting to be sexy and available while assiduously managing men's ejaculate. Michelle knows that in her work she cannot use the universal precautions of the health-care industry to protect herself. Rather, she must maintain her sexy, available, and pleasurable image while ensuring her survival:

> I mean going to see my dentist becomes—I feel like a hazardous waste material myself. First he had some new

goggles, well then he got a shield, you know, and next I expect him to come in just like—you know, a space suit next time. It's so funny. But that's what we're having to do. See the medical profession has the luxury of looking like they're in this space suit. I can't look like I'm in a space suit. I have got to look like I'm being very intimate and everything, and yet really I am trying to have my own little space suit going on here.

Ana, a 38-year-old petite, brunette sex worker, explained one of the ways she flatters men while retrieving used condoms:

> It's funny because I started doing this thing with the condoms. When I take them off the guy, before I throw them away or flush them down the toilet, I show them to the guy. . . . I mean most guys because a couple of my guys might be out the door before I get a chance. But when I show them to the guy, I say something like, "Wow you must really like me a lot" or "I have never seen this much before." Lots of guys seem to really like that when you tell them that they have a lot [of semen]. They kind of get off on it.

This verbal acknowledgement and visual display of seminal volume echoes the penis size concerns explored at the beginning of this [reading]. Ana is exploiting a man's concern with size, density, and volume as a way to praise men and continue the pleasurable (safer) sexual experience. If seminal ejaculate were not contained in a condom, how else might a man know how virile he apparently is?

In spite of the acknowledged risks, sex workers are handling semen and managing men. In many instances, sex workers innovate containment strategies to limit exposure to semen while also making men feel good about their semen and their expressions of masculinity. Through the use of flattery, men are encouraged to believe they measure up or exceed other men's performances and bodies. Sex workers' (like Ana's) use of male condoms enables them to capture semen. In this context, semen is used to compliment a man on his potency. By empathizing with men about the "good old days," sex workers can enforce rules about seminal exposure, while making men feel that their semen is not hazardous. Sex workers' expertise at using latex devices enables them to make men feel taken care of, while assuring their own safety from exposure.

The Essence of (Every)Man

With the proliferation of movies and videos that glorify the money shot, the sex entertainment industry provides an avenue for men to be spectators in the celebration of unprocessed, carnal, natural semen. Unlike other industries that manage semen, such as scientific laboratories, fertility clinics, and forensics enterprises, male bodily products do not need to be technologically enhanced or scientifically manipulated to be useful or understood. Unlike the workers in these industries, porn stars do not use universal precautions of covering their bodies with latex gloves, goggles, and face masks when handling semen. In real life, most sex workers, particularly the successful ones, are not entirely cloaked in thin layers of plastic, rigidly carrying out state-regulated mandates for handling body fluids. Sex workers, in films and real life, are either very minimally dressed or naked and do not shrink away from intimate contact with seminal fluid.

As other industries that manage sperm have established, not all men are created equal. For example, a majority of men who attempt to donate sperm are rejected from sperm banks. And even outside of the fertility clinics, there are multiple reminders that most men produce semen that is gross, diseased, genetically inferior, incompetent, lazy, and unwanted. To some extent, then, the pornography industry produces images that address the needs and desires of these men. That is, since men are socialized to believe that their semen is undesirable and even disgusting to women, and possibly perceived as a health hazard, it is a relief to see representations of their semen as cherished. The raw material of male desire, seminal fluid, is produced directly from the source, and it is wanted and desperately desired in its purest form.

In these videos, there is still power associated with the man's characteristics, but power and social desirability is also assigned to the color, amount, and image of the semen itself—and the woman's positive reaction to it. No one is running to the bathroom to spit out the ejaculate, and everyone swallows with a smile. Semen, in these videos, is not abstracted into a characterization—it is not anthropomorphized—yet it is still desirable. Furthermore, the fairly recently established niche genres that focus on the consumption of semen depict women who can't get enough. They have no fear and no disgust for the substance in its natural state. No technological manipulation of semen is necessary.

While this process of appreciating everyman's sperm may seem liberating, it is still occurring within systems of male domination. The forces of hegemonic masculinity act to subjugate some men to the control of other men deemed more worthy, esteemed, or powerful. These fantasies about seminal consumption sell subjugated men the belief that they are the epitome of traditionally masculine power when they may rank quite low. While some men may opt out of a traditionally masculine set of behaviors and work to redefine masculinity, other men will literally buy in to the images and tropes of pornography. Those men who are still participating in and consenting to a process that devalues them become perfect consumers of films that bolster the story of male dominance. This means that, even though these men may not directly benefit from hierarchal relations of masculine power, they will support films that depict male domination because they identify with the male protagonist. Porn becomes one of the many opiates of the wimpy men who cannot take a stand against the ultimate nonconsensual subordination of others because they themselves are so subordinated. In this way, hegemonic masculinity maintains its dominance by providing commodities that work to placate those oppressed by activities that are in reality disempowering.

My analysis of semen as represented, consumed, and manipulated within industrial and commercial sex markets further establishes sperm's elasticity of meaning. While individual men may be aware of their social worth as subordinate to other men, commercial sex work is one arena in which men can retain hope that their seminal ejaculate, their essence of manhood, is enjoyed, powerful, and spectacular.

NOTES

1. Vivien Marx, *The Semen Book* (London: Free Association, 2001).

2. Caroline Aldred, *Divine Sex: The Art of Tantric and Taoist Arts of Conscious Loving* (San Francisco: Harper-Collins, 1996).

3. For recent scientific explorations of ejaculatory disorders, see David J. Ralph and Kevan Wylie, "Ejaculatory Disorders and Sexual Function," *British Journal of Urology* 95:9 (2005): 1181–1186.

4. Kalyani Premkumar, *The Massage Connection: Anatomy and Physiology.* (Philadelphia: Lippincott, Williamson and Wilkins, 436.

5. Cindy Patton, "Hegemony and Orgasm: Or the Instability of Heterosexual Pornography," *Screen* 30:4 (1989): 1–34.

6. For example, Laura M. Carpenter, *Virginity Lost: An Intimate Portrait of First Sexual Experiences* (New York: New York University Press, 2005).

7. Due to methodological constraints, this chapter primarily relies on heterosexually produced pornography and heterosexually oriented sex workers. That is not to say that viewers or participants in these industries are heterosexual, but it is to bracket the data as produced primarily for a presumed heterosexual audience. Clearly, gay porn or porn featuring men who have sex with men would be a robust site for research about semen and the eroticization of ejaculation.

8. Pamela Paul, *Pornified: How Pornography Is Transforming Our Lives, Our Relationships and Our Families* (New York: Holt, 2005).

9. *Vital Information for Workers and Employers in the Adult Film Industry,* CAL-OSHA, 2003, available at http://www.dir.ca.gov/dosh/adultfilmindustry.html (accessed October 14, 2006).

10. Ann Regentin, *What We're Really Watching,* May 26, 2004, available at http://www.cleansheets.com/articles/regentin_05.26.04.shtml (accessed October 14, 2006).

11. Interview with Raylene by Max Gunner, "Seven Inches of Pleasure," *Popsmear Online Magazine,* available at http://www.popsmear.com/lovemaking/seveninches/15.0/index.html (accessed October 14, 2006).

12. Patton, "Hegemony and Orgasm," 105.

13. Cindy Patton, "The Cum Shot: Three Takes on Lesbian and Gay Studies," *Out/Look* 1:3 (1988): 72–76.

14. Ibid., 106.

15. For a history of pornography in the United States, see Joseph Slade, *Pornography in America: A Reference Handbook* (Santa Barbara, Calif.: ABC-CLIO, 2000). As Slade states on page 323: "After the war, the cum shot, the penis ejaculating out of the vagina, became nearly universal."

16. These are a collection of descriptions taken from *Reviews,* 2004, available at www.avn.com (accessed October 14, 2006).

17. *Come Again, and Again . . . ,* available at http://www.semenex.com/maximwebguide4th.jpg (accessed October 14, 2006).

Human Rights, Sex Trafficking, and Prostitution

Alice Leuchtag

Despite laws against slavery in practically every country, an estimated twenty-seven million people live as slaves. . . .

A Life Narrative

Of all forms of slavery, sex slavery is one of the most exploitative and lucrative with some 200,000 sex slaves worldwide bringing their slaveholders an annual profit of $10.5 billion. Although the great preponderance of sex slaves are women and girls, a smaller but significant number of males—both adult and children—are enslaved for homosexual prostitution. The life narrative of a Thai girl named Siri . . . illustrates how sex slavery happens to vulnerable girls and women. Siri is born in northeastern Thailand to a poor family that farms a small plot of land, barely eking out a living. Economic policies of structural adjustment pursued by the Thai government under the aegis of the World Bank and the International Monetary Fund have taken former government subsidies away from rice farmers, leaving them to compete against imported, subsidized rice that keeps the market price artificially depressed.

Siri attends four years of school, then is kept at home to help care for her three younger siblings. When Siri is fourteen, a well-dressed woman visits her village. She offers to find Siri a "good job," advancing her parents $2,000 against future earnings. This represents at least a year's income for the family. In a town in another province the woman, a trafficker,

From "Human Rights, Sex Trafficking, and Prostitution" by Alice Leuchtag (2003), *Humanist 63*(1): 10–15. Reprinted by courtesy of Alice Lechtag and *The Humanist.*

"sells" Siri to a brothel for $4,000. Owned by an "investment club" whose members are business and professional men—government bureaucrats and local politicians—the brothel is extremely profitable. In a typical thirty-day period it nets its investors $88,000.

To maintain the appearance that their hands are clean, members of the club's board of directors leave the management of the brothel to a pimp and a bookkeeper. Siri is initiated into prostitution by the pimp who rapes her. After being abused by her first "customer," Siri escapes, but a policeman—who gets a percentage of the brothel profits—brings her back, whereupon the pimp beats her up. As further punishment, her "debt" is doubled from $4,000 to $8,000. She must now repay this, along with her monthly rent and food, all from her earnings of $4 per customer. She will have to have sex with three hundred men a month just to pay her rent. Realizing she will never be able to get out of debt, Siri tries to build a relationship with the pimp simply in order to survive.

The pimp uses culture and religion to reinforce his control over Siri. He tells her she must have committed terrible sins in a past life to have been born a female; she must have accumulated a karmic debt to deserve the enslavement and abuse to which she must reconcile herself. Gradually Siri begins to see herself from the point of view of the slaveholder—as someone unworthy and deserving of punishment. By age fifteen she no longer protests or runs away. Her physical enslavement has become psychological as well, a common occurrence in chronic abuse.

Siri is administered regular injections of the contraceptive drug Depo-Provera for which she is charged. As the same needle is used for all the girls, there is a high risk of HIV and other sexual diseases from the injections. Siri knows that a serious illness threatens her and she prays to Buddha at the little shrine in her room, hoping to earn merit so he will protect her from dreaded disease. Once a month she and the others, at their own expense, are tested for HIV. So far Siri's tests have been negative. When Siri tries to get the male customers to wear condoms—distributed free to brothels by the Thai Ministry of Health—some resist wearing them and she can't make them do so.

As one of an estimated 35,000 women working as brothel slaves in Thailand—a country where 500,000 to one million prostituted women and girls work in conditions of degradation and exploitation short of brothel slavery—Siri faces at least a 40 percent chance of contracting the HIV virus. If she is lucky, she can look forward to five more years before she becomes too ill to work and is pushed out into the street.

Thailand's Sex Tourism

Though the Thai government denies it, the World Health Organization finds that HIV is epidemic in Thailand, with the largest segment of new cases among wives and girlfriends of men who buy prostitute sex. Viewing its women as a cash crop to be exploited, and depending on sex tourism for foreign exchange dollars to help pay interest on the foreign debt, the Thai government can't acknowledge the epidemic without contradicting the continued promotion of sex tourism and prostitution.

By encouraging investment in the sex industry, sex tourism creates a business climate conducive to the trafficking and enslavement of vulnerable girls such as Siri. In 1996 nearly five million sex tourists from the United States, Western Europe, Australia, and Japan visited Thailand. These transactions brought in about $26.2 billion—thirteen times more than Thailand earned by building and exporting computers.

In her 1999 report *Pimps and predators on the internet: Globalizing the sexual exploitation of women and children,* published by the Coalition Against Trafficking in Women (CATW), Donna Hughes quotes from postings on an Internet site where sex tourists share experiences and advise one another. The following is one man's description of having sex with a fourteen-year-old prostituted girl in Bangkok:

> *Even though I've had a lot of better massages . . . after fifteen minutes, I was much more relaxed. . . . Then I*

> *asked for a condom and I fucked her for another thirty minutes. Her face looked like she was feeling a lot of pain. . . . She blocked my way when I wanted to leave the room and she asked for a tip. I gave her 600 bath. Altogether, not a good experience.*

Hughes says, "To the men who buy sex, a 'bad experience' evidently means not getting their money's worth, or that the prostituted woman or girl didn't keep up the act of enjoying what she had to do . . . one glimpses the humiliation and physical pain most girls and women in prostitution endure."

Nor are the men oblivious to the existence of sexual slavery. One customer states, "Girls in Bangkok virtually get sold by their families into the industry; they work against their will." His knowledge of their sexual slavery and lack of sensitivity thereof is evident in that he then names the hotels in which girls are kept and describes how much they cost!

As Hughes observes, sex tourists apparently feel they have a right to prostitute sex, perceiving prostitution only from a self-interested perspective in which they commodify and objectify women of other cultures, nationalities, and ethnic groups. Their awareness of racism, colonialism, global economic inequalities, and sexism seems limited to the way these realities benefit them as sex consumers.

Sex Traffickers Cast Their Nets

According to the *Guide to the new UN trafficking protocol* by Janice Raymond, published by the CATW in 2001, the United Nations estimates that sex trafficking in human beings is a $5 billion to $7 billion operation annually. Four million persons are moved illegally from one country to another and within countries each year, a large proportion of them women and girls being trafficked into prostitution. The United Nations International Children's Emergency Fund (UNICEF) estimates that some 30 percent of women being trafficked are minors, many under age thirteen. The International Organization on Migration estimates that some 500,000 women per year are trafficked into Western Europe from poorer regions of the world. According to *Sex trafficking of women in the United States: International and domestic trends,* also published by the CATW in 2001, some 50,000 women and children are trafficked into the United States each year, mainly from Asia and Latin America.

Because prostitution as a system of organized sexual exploitation depends on a continuous supply of new "recruits," trafficking is essential to its continued existence. When the pool of available women and girls dries up, new women must be procured. Traffickers cast their nets ever wider and become ever more sophisticated. The Italian Camorra, Chinese Triads, Russian Mafia, and Japanese Yakuza are powerful criminal syndicates consisting of traffickers, pimps, brothel keepers, forced labor lords, and gangs which operate globally.

After the breakdown of the Soviet Union, an estimated five thousand criminal groups formed the Russian Mafia, which operates in thirty countries. The Russian Mafia traffics women from African countries, the Ukraine, the Russian Federation, and Eastern Europe into Western Europe, the United States, and Israel. The Triads traffick women from China, Korea, Thailand, and other Southeast Asian countries into the United States and Europe. The Camorra traffics women from Latin America into Europe. The Yakuza traffics women from the Philippines, Thailand, Burma, Cambodia, Korea, Nepal, and Laos into Japan.

A Global Problem Meets a Global Response

Despite these appalling facts, until recently no generally agreed upon definition of trafficking in human beings was written into international law. In Vienna, Austria, during 1999 and 2000, 120 countries participated in debates over a definition of trafficking. A few nongovernmental organizations (NGOs) and a minority of governments—including Australia, Canada, Denmark, Germany, Ireland, Japan, the Netherlands, Spain, Switzerland, Thailand, and the United Kingdom—wanted to separate issues of trafficking from issues of prostitution. They argued that persons being trafficked should be divided into those who are forced and those who give their consent, with the burden of proof being placed on persons being trafficked. They also urged that the less explicit

means of control over trafficked persons—such as abuse of a victim's vulnerability—not be included in the definition of trafficking and that the word exploitation not be used. Generally supporters of this position were wealthier countries where large numbers of women were being trafficked and countries in which prostitution was legalized or sex tourism encouraged.

The CATW—140 other NGOs that make up the International Human Rights Network plus many governments (including those of Algeria, Bangladesh, Belgium, China, Columbia, Cuba, Egypt, Finland, France, India, Mexico, Norway, Pakistan, the Philippines, Sweden, Syria, Venezuela, and Vietnam)—maintains that trafficking can't be separated from prostitution. Persons being trafficked shouldn't be divided into those who are forced and those who give their consent because trafficked persons are in no position to give meaningful consent. The subtler methods used by traffickers, such as abuse of a victim's vulnerability, should be included in the definition of trafficking and the word exploitation be an essential part of the definition. Generally supporters of this majority view were poorer countries from which large numbers of women were being trafficked or countries in which strong feminist, anti-colonialist, or socialist influences existed. The United States, though initially critical of the majority position, agreed to support a definition of trafficking that would be agreed upon by consensus.

The struggle—fed by the CATW to create a definition of trafficking that would penalize traffickers while ensuring that all victims of trafficking would be protected—succeeded when a compromise proposal by Sweden was agreed to. A strongly worded and inclusive UN Protocol to Prevent, Suppress, and Punish Trafficking in Persons—especially women and children—was drafted by an ad hoc committee of the UN as a supplement to the Convention Against Transnational Organized Crime. The UN protocol specifically addresses the trade in human beings for purposes of prostitution and other forms of sexual exploitation, forced labor or services, slavery or practices similar to slavery, servitude, and the removal of organs. The protocol defines trafficking as:

The recruitment, transportation, transfer, harboring or receipt of persons, by means of the threat or use of force or other forms of coercion, of abduction, of fraud, of deception, of the abuse of power or of a position of vulnerability or of the giving or receiving of payments or benefits to achieve the consent of a person having control over another person, for the purpose of exploitation.

While recognizing that the largest amount of trafficking involves women and children, the wording of the UN protocol clearly is gender and age neutral, inclusive of trafficking in both males and females, adults and children.

In 2000 the UN General Assembly adopted this convention and its supplementary protocol; 121 countries signed the convention and eighty countries signed the protocol. For the convention and protocol to become international law, forty countries must ratify them.

Highlights

Some highlights of the new convention and protocol are:

- For the first time there is an accepted international definition of trafficking and an agreed-upon set of prosecution, protection, and prevention mechanisms on which countries can base their national legislation.
- The various criminal means by which trafficking takes place, including indirect and subtle forms of coercion, are covered.
- Trafficked persons, especially women in prostitution and child laborers, are no longer viewed as illegal migrants but as victims of a crime.
- The convention doesn't limit its scope to criminal syndicates but defines an organized criminal group as "any structured group of three or more persons which engages in criminal activities such as trafficking and pimping."
- All victims of trafficking in persons are protected, not just those who can prove that force was used against them.
- The consent of a victim of trafficking is meaningless and irrelevant.

- Victims of trafficking won't have to bear the burden of proof.
- Trafficking and sexual exploitation are intrinsically connected and not to be separated.
- Because women trafficked domestically into local sex industries suffer harmful effects similar to those experienced by women trafficked transnationally, these women also come under the protections of the protocol.
- The key element in trafficking is the exploitative purpose rather than the movement across a border.

The protocol is the first UN instrument to address the demand for prostitution sex, a demand that results in the human rights abuses of women and children being trafficked. The protocol recognizes an urgent need for governments to put the buyers of prostitution sex on their policy and legislative agendas, and it calls upon countries to take or strengthen legislative or other measures to discourage demand, which fosters all the forms of sexual exploitation of women and children. . . .

Refugees, Not Illegal Aliens

In October 2000 the U.S. Congress passed a bill, the Victims of Trafficking and Violence Protection Act of 2000, introduced by New Jersey republican representative Chris Smith. Under this law penalties for traffickers are raised and protections for victims increased. Reasoning that desperate women are unable to give meaningful consent to their own sexual exploitation, the law adopts a broad definition of sex trafficking so as not to exclude so-called consensual prostitution or trafficking that occurs solely within the United States. In these respects the new federal law conforms to the UN protocol.

Two features of the law are particularly noteworthy:

- In order to pressure other countries to end sex trafficking, the U.S. State Department is to make a yearly assessment of other countries' anti-trafficking efforts and to rank them according to how well they discourage trafficking. After two years of failing to meet even minimal standards, countries are subject to sanctions, although not sanctions on humanitarian aid. "Tier 3" countries—those failing to meet even minimal standards—include Greece, Indonesia, Israel, Pakistan, Russia, Saudi Arabia, South Korea, and Thailand.

- Among persons being trafficked into the United States, special T-visas will be provided to those who meet the criteria for having suffered the most serious trafficking abuses. These visas will protect them from deportation so they can testify against their traffickers. T non-immigrant status allows eligible aliens to remain in the United States temporarily and grants specific non-immigrant benefits. Those acquiring T-1 non-immigrant status will be able to remain for a period of three years and will be eligible to receive certain kinds of public assistance—to the same extent as refugees. They will also be issued employment authorization to "assist them in finding safe, legal employment while they attempt to retake control of their lives."

A Debate Rages

A worldwide debate rages about legalization of prostitution fueled by a 1998 International Labor Organization (ILO) report entitled *The sex sector: The economic and social bases of prostitution in Southeast Asia.* The report follows years of lobbying by the sex industry for recognition of prostitution as "sex work." Citing the sex industry's unrecognized contribution to the gross domestic product of four countries in Southeast Asia, the ILO urges governments to officially recognize the "sex sector" and "extend taxation nets to cover many of the lucrative activities connected with it." Though the ILO report says it stops short of calling for legalization of prostitution, official recognition of the sex industry would be impossible without it.

Raymond points out that the ILO's push to redefine prostitution as sex work ignores legislation demonstrating that countries can reduce organized sexual exploitation rather than capitulate to it. For example, Sweden prohibits the purchase of sexual services with punishments of stiff fines or imprisonment, thus declaring that prostitution isn't a desirable economic and labor sector. The government also helps women getting out of prostitution to rebuild their lives. Venezuela's Ministry of Labor has ruled that prostitution can't be considered work because it lacks the basic elements of dignity and social justice. The Socialist Republic of Vietnam punishes pimps, traffickers, brothel owners, and buyers—sometimes publishing buyer's names in the mass media. For women in prostitution, the government finances medical, educational, and economic rehabilitation.

Raymond suggests that instead of transforming the male buyer into a legitimate customer, the ILO should give thought to innovative programs that make the buyer accountable for his sexual exploitation. She cites the Sage Project, Inc. (SAGE) program in San Francisco, California, which educates men arrested for soliciting women in prostitution about the risks and impacts of their behavior.

Legalization advocates argue that the violence, exploitation, and health effects suffered by women in prostitution aren't inherent to prostitution but simply result from the random behaviors of bad pimps or buyers, and that if prostitution were regulated by the state these harms would diminish. But examples show these arguments to be false.

In the pamphlet entitled *Legalizing prostitution is not the answer: The example of Victoria, Australia,* published by the CATW in 2001, Mary Sullivan and Sheila Jeffreys describe the way legalization in Australia has perpetuated and strengthened the culture of violence and exploitation inherent in prostitution. Under legalization, legal and illegal brothels have proliferated, and trafficking in women has accelerated to meet the increased demand. Pimps, having even more power, continue threatening and brutalizing the women they control. Buyers continue to abuse women, refuse to wear condoms, and spread the HIV virus—and other sexually transmitted diseases—to their wives and girlfriends. Stigmatized by identity cards and medical inspections, prostituted women are even more marginalized and tightly locked into the system of organized sexual exploitation while the state, now an official party to the exploitation, has become the biggest pimp of all.

The government of the Netherlands has legalized prostitution, doesn't enforce laws against pimping, and virtually lives off taxes from the earnings of prostituted women. In the book *Making the harm visible* (published by the CATW in 1999), Marie-Victoire Louis describes the effects on prostituted women of municipal regulation of brothels in Amsterdam and other Dutch cities. Her article entitled "Legalizing Pimping, Dutch Style" explains the way immigration policies in the Netherlands are shaped to fit the needs of the prostitution industry so that traffickers are seldom prosecuted and a continuous supply of women is guaranteed. In Amsterdam's 250 officially listed brothels, 80 percent of the prostitutes have been trafficked in from other countries and 70 percent possess no legal papers. Without money, papers, or contact with the outside world, these immigrant women live in terror. Instead of being protected by the regulations governing brothels, prostituted women are frequently beaten up and raped by pimps. These "prostitution managers" have practically been given a free hand by the state and by buyers who, as "consumers of prostitution," feel themselves entitled to abuse the women they buy. Sadly and ironically the "Amsterdam model" of legalization and regulation is touted by the Netherlands and Germany as "self-determination and empowerment for women." In reality it simply legitimizes the "right" to buy, sexually use, and profit from the sexual exploitation of someone else's body.

A Human Rights Approach

As part of a system of organized sexual exploitation, prostitution can be visualized along a continuum of abuse with brothel slavery at the furthest extreme. All along the continuum, fine lines divide the degrees of harm done to those caught up in the system. At the core lies a great social injustice no cosmetic reforms can right: the setting aside of a segment of people whose bodies can be purchased for sexual use by others. When this basic injustice is legitimized and regulated by the state and when the state profits from it, that injustice is compounded.

In her book *The prostitution of sexuality* (New York University Press, 1995), Kathleen Barry details a feminist human rights approach to prostitution that points the way to the future. Ethically it recognizes prostitution, sex trafficking, and the globalized industrialization of sex as massive violations of women's human rights. Sociologically it considers how and to what extent prostitution promotes sex discrimination against individual women, against different racial categories of women, and against women as a group. Politically it calls for decriminalizing prostitutes while penalizing pimps, traffickers, brothel owners, and buyers.

Understanding that human rights and restorative justice go hand in hand, the feminist human rights approach to prostitution addresses the harm and the need to repair the damage. As Barry says:

> *Legal proposals to criminalize customers, based on the recognition that prostitution violates and harms women, must . . . include social-service, health and counseling and job retraining programs. Where states would be closing down brothels if customers were criminalized, the economic resources poured into the former prostitution areas could be turned toward producing gainful employment for women.*

With the help of women's projects in many countries—such as Buklod in the Philippines and the Council for Prostitution Alternatives in the United States—some women have begun to confront their condition by leaving prostitution, speaking out against it, revealing their experiences, and helping other women leave the sex industry.

Ending the sexual exploitation of trafficking and prostitution will mean the beginning of a new chapter in building a humanist future—a more peaceful and just future in which men and women can join together in love and respect, recognizing one another's essential dignity and humanity. Humanity's sexuality then will no longer be hijacked and distorted.

Sexuality and Militarism

Cynthia Enloe

Through wartime mobilization, postwar demobilization, and peacetime preparedness maneuvers, sexuality and militarism have been intertwined. They have been constructed and reconstructed together, usually with the help of deliberate policy decisions. *Together,* ideologies of militarism and sexuality have shaped the social order of military base towns and the lives of women in those towns. . . .

Conditions that promote organized prostitution:

1. When large numbers of local women are treated by the government and private entrepreneurs as second-class citizens, a source of cheapened labor, even while other women are joining the newly expanded middle class. . . .
2. When the foreign government basing its troops on local soil sees prostitution as a "necessary evil" to keep up their male soldiers' fighting morale
3. When tourism is imagined by local and foreign economic planners to be a fast road to development
4. When the local government hosting those foreign troops is under the influence of its own military men, local military men who define human rights violations as necessary for "national security." . . .

The [Status of Forces Agreement] (SOFA) is a major vehicle for cementing and sustaining a military alliance between the U.S. government and its international partners. A SOFA spells out in minute detail the conditions under which American troops can be stationed on the host government's territory. Health, surveillance, policing, finances—all are subjects of the intense government-to-government negotiations that result in these formal diplomatic agreements. The fine print of these alliance agreements is not open to public scrutiny. In behind-closed-door negotiations over a SOFA, governments' officials hammer out the sexual politics of militarization.

The actual implementation of any SOFA is left to American base commanders. Anyone wanting a realistic sense of how a government-to-government alliance works needs to keep an inquisitive eye on base commanders. A base commander for a U.S. force overseas is not merely an instrument of the policy makers in the White House or the State Department. He (rarely have U.S. women officers been promoted to base commander) is not even simply a cipher for Defense Department senior officials' designs. A base commander has his own concerns and his own career aspirations. Typically, he is a colonel. That is, he (and now occasionally, on some small bases, she) is at a very delicate point in his military career. In all militaries there are fewer slots for generals (or admirals) than there are for colonels. Not all colonels will be promoted. A colonel is a person who hopes to be a general. So much depends on how his superiors assess his performance as a base commander. A base commander has his own sources of information, his own social circles.

The base commander and his deputy commander (in the 1990s more American women officers are gaining assignments as deputy base commanders) are likely to have a stake in creating smooth working relationships with local host-country officials and with local business owners. It is standard procedure for American base commanders in South Korea, for example, to develop mutual relationships with the local Korean Chamber of Commerce, many of whose members are the proprietors of the bars and discos that are at the heart of the prostitution industry. Some American military officers, women and men, have reported feeling quite uneasy with this part of their jobs as deputy base commanders. On the other hand, their performance—and thus their own chances for future promotion—will depend on how trouble-free they can keep these base-local business relations. . . .

Prostitution and Peacekeeping. . . .

Many future military peacekeeping operations will look like the peacekeeping missions launched in Cambodia in 1992–1994, in Bosnia in 1996–1998, and in Kosovo in 1999: "victory" will be elusive; a variety of governments will contribute soldiers of their own, many of them trained to be combat troops; the UN Secretariat's own Peace Keeping Organization (UNPKO) will be able to run military training programs, but only for officers and only for those officers whose governments have the funds and the will to pay for their officers' UNPKO training; coordination between governments and the UN will be delicate; NATO will be directly involved; civilian businesses will win contracts to provide support services for the troops; humanitarian aid agencies will be trying to operate without being too reliant on militaries and too deeply sucked into militarized cultures; rival domestic politicians will be competing in the rearranged public arena; local residents will be trying to recover from war-produced trauma while at the same time creating political organizations to compete in the postwar public space; pro-democracy activists will be seeking lasting reforms. Each of these processes will be gendered, will be shaped by how femininity and masculinity are imagined and deployed.

There is nothing inherent in international peacekeeping operations as currently structured that makes their soldiers immune to the sort of sexism that has fueled military prostitution in wartime and peacetime. As in every other military operation conducted by every other government, the extent of future military peacekeeping operations' reliance on the prostitution of some women will be determined by decisions made at the top and in the middle of military organizations. . . .

Source: Enloe, Cynthia. 2000. "The Prostitute, the Colonel, and the Nationalist." In *Maneuvers: The International Politics of Militarizing Women's Lives* (pp. 49–107). Reprinted by permission of the University of California Press.

Marketing Sex: U.S. Legal Brothels and Late Capitalist Consumption

Barbara G. Brents and Kathryn Hausbeck

Selling sex is business. In addition to all else it may be, it is also situated in the specific forms of production and consumption at particular locales and time periods. The economic and cultural context in which sex is sold has changed significantly. Since the Second World War, a globally integrated economic system has developed, whose engine has changed from production to consumption, making service the core industrial sector (Harvey, 1989; Jameson, 1991). These forces have driven the development of new commodities, new forms of labour and new forms of consumption.[1] Most recently, travel and tourism have become the world's largest industries employing 11 per cent of all workers world wide, and producing 10 per cent of the world's gross domestic product (Wonders and Michalowski, 2001: 549). Simultaneously, the non-tourist service industry has become increasingly "touristic"—that is, rather than selling services with specific outcomes, services sell experience, spectacle, fantasy, adventure, escapism and personal interactions (Urry, 2002).

These economic changes have had profound effects on cultural practices, especially intimacy, sex and sexuality. Late capitalist mass consumption has encouraged, according to some studies, a pornographication of culture, more liberal and egalitarian sexual attitudes, and an acceptance of fleeting, temporary relationships (Bauman, 2003; Giddens, 1992; Hawkes, 1996; McNair, 2002). Studies also demonstrate an increasing commodification of intimacy and

a heightened sexualization of work (Adkins, 2002; Zelizer, 2005). An important empirical question emerges: In this context, how has the sex industry changed? . . .

Shifting Sexual Services: Tourist and Touristic Industries

We also choose to situate the sex industry in a larger context of tourism and touristic services (Wonders and Michalowski, 2001). A growing global tourist economy has spurred a growth in sex industry businesses.[2] . . . The media have made much of an apparent growth in size and respectability of the sex industries (*Economist,* 1998). The *Economist* notes "a handful of well run, imaginative businesses" are increasingly profitable, upscale, and exploiting market niches. Where this kind of growth has occurred, it has been executed in part through the use of the same marketing tactics as businesses in other tourist and touristic industries; for instance, marketing to wider audiences via upscaling, expanding services, market specialization, and expanding markets (Frank, 2002: 25). For example, the seedy, dark, secluded sex shops and strip joints of the past are being replaced by large, glitzy, and upscale adult stores and gentlemen's clubs, many with upscale restaurants. In Antwerp, in Belgium, a new upscale, chic "super brothel" has opened decorated by superstar architects and designers (Castle, 2006).

Some of these businesses are also adopting mainstream business organizational forms such as corporate structures and diversified holdings. Some legal sex industry businesses are partnering with multinational corporations, such as adult video distribution partnerships with General Motors, America Online/

Time Warner, AT&T, Marriott, Hilton, Hyatt and Westin. In the USA, while small private firms still dominate the legal sex industry, there is a trend toward larger national and international corporate chains. Adult businesses are even opening mainstream business enterprises such as the Vivid nightclub at the Venetian, a Las Vegas casino resort, where holographic images of adult film stars are projected onto the dance floor.

This mainstreaming has not occurred in all sectors of the adult sex industry. Just as in the non-sex industry workforce, there is labour market segmentation with primary (higher wages, more stable) and secondary (lower paying, less stable) labour markets. . . . In the secondary labour markets the pay is likely to be lower and labour conditions worse. There is deep stratification among workers in the global sex industry. The nature of the product sold is evolving, too.

Along with the growth of tourism in mainstream sectors, there has been a trend toward more touristic services. Traditionally, service work has sold emotion as much as a specific service. Research on service-providers such as restaurant servers, airline hostesses, and various salespeople has shown that managers and workers have rationalized the service product by applying assembly line principles. This "McDonaldization" of services relies on rationalized work processes, centralized work places, controlled environments, interactive scripts, standardized employment contracts and highly predictable production/consumption rituals to increase efficiency and profit and standardize emotional services (Hochschild, 1983; Leidner, 1993; Ritzer and Liska, 1997). However, as the service industry has become more touristic, these rationalized outcome-oriented approaches have given way to decentralized, do-it-yourself workers compelled to sell uniqueness, variety and individuality. In essence, the product in these tourist/touristic leisure services becomes more an individualized, interactive experience with less rationalized and scripted outcomes (Beck, 1992; Holyfield, 1999; Sharpe, 2005). . . .

In this article, we . . . examine these changing structures and practices by looking at sex-industry organization and marketing at one local site of consumption, Nevada's legal brothels. In doing so, we emphasize that local sites may respond to global processes in different ways. We choose the legal brothels in Nevada as our site for several reasons. First, brothels sell sexual contact, sex acts, and sexual release rather than sexualized fantasies or non-contact services. . . . Prostitution remains among the most stigmatized segment of the sex industry, and research in this field has frequently conceptualized this business as deviant and fundamentally different from other service industries. Thus, brothels are exceedingly interesting place[s] to examine changes in how sex acts become touristic products. Second, while the informal economy has been dramatically affected by globalization and the growth of late capitalist tourist economies and culture, we choose to focus on legal businesses. Legal businesses are potentially more stable and more embedded in institutionalized business systems than independent prostitutes.

We are feminist sociologists who live in Las Vegas. Our research stems from a larger project on the social organization of Nevada brothels involving nearly 10 years of ethnographies, observations, formal and informal interviews with workers, managers, owners and policymakers, participation in public debates, and analysis of historical and contemporary documents, websites, media stories, and newspaper articles.[3] . . . In particular we look at changes in business forms and marketing strategies.

Shifting Consumption and Nevada Brothels

Nevada's sex industry exists within the context of a state whose primary source of income is tourism. Las Vegas draws more than 38 million tourists annually to more than 133,000 hotel rooms (Las Vegas Convention and Visitors Authority, 2006). . . .

The marketing of sexuality has been central to Las Vegas' growth as a global tourist resort. Despite marketing itself implicitly as a place where sexual fantasies may come true, with slogans such as "what happens here stays here," and unlike many Asian or European resort centers, prostitution itself is not explicitly marketed. . . . And as the casinos have become larger, more corporate, and answer to stockholders from around the globe, it has become important to them to look legitimate. In the large resort centers of Las Vegas and Reno, then, where prostitution of any kind is illegal, the resort industry works hard to prevent its visible forms.

Yet there are estimates that up to 3500 illegal prostitutes work in Las Vegas' underground economy at any given time (Hausbeck et al., 2006). Illegal independent prostitutes evade casino security and discreetly work the bars and/or advertise via alternative weekly newspapers or the internet. There are highly informal and discreet systems at a few hotels where concierges independently retain lists of preferred upscale prostitutes who can be made quickly available to the wealthiest guests. There are also thriving legal outcall entertainment businesses operating call centers that dispatch nude dancers to hotel rooms for an agency fee, and dancers may provide sexual services illegally for tips. Despite concerted efforts by the resort industry to control public spaces around the resorts and eliminate these outcall businesses, outcall agencies advertise heavily through billboards, stands containing flyers and through individuals leafletting tourists on the sidewalks. Street prostitution is the most heavily surveilled, and police and the resort industry are vigilant in keeping obviously working-class prostitutes away from highly visible resort areas. There are also a few businesses operating legally as Asian massage parlors, where the predominantly Asian women provide "happy endings" illegally. Thus, sex tourism in the resort zones is an informal industry. While scantily clothed cocktail waitresses, partially nude shows, and sexy nightclubs lure tourists to resorts with the illusion of sexuality, the sale of sex acts is discouraged to the extent that it takes tourists away from time gambling or shopping in the casinos.

Nevada's legal brothel industry . . . helps to maintain the illusion of a sexual playground, yet the casino industry works hard to officially distance itself from the brothels both physically and politically. Brothels are a minimum of one hour's drive from any of the major resort areas and cannot market themselves as international sex tourist destinations because it is illegal to advertise. Compared to the money spent on illegal prostitution in Las Vegas and Reno, and compared to legal brothels in Amsterdam's highly

concentrated urban red-light district, or even Australia's legal brothels, Nevada's brothel industry is small and geographically dispersed.

At most, 500 women work legally at any time in the entire state. While there are licenses for about 36 brothels, only about 25 to 30 are currently operating. There are 8 to 10 large brothels, housing 15 to 50 workers each, clustered about an hour's drive from Las Vegas and Reno. The rest are along the 850 miles of relatively remote stretches of desert highway linking Las Vegas to Reno, or connecting San Francisco, California, to Salt Lake City, Utah, a route that passes through Nevada. The smallest legal brothels house from 1 to 5 workers, and these tend to be several hours' drive from major resort centers. The midsize brothels are just outside of the smaller towns of Winnemucca, Carlin, Elko, Wells and Ely, with 5 to 12 workers in each. Brothels are legal in only 10 of Nevada's 17 counties. . . .

[I]t is doubtful that, without the tourist industry, the brothels would have remained legal here while the rest of the USA outlawed prostitution. Prostitution has been a part of the state's economic development since mining and railroads populated the state in the early 1900s. Mining booms and busts kept the population of the state under 80,000 until large federal dam projects around Las Vegas brought workers in the 1930s. By 1940, the state's population began climbing to 110,000 and gambling and quick divorces drove an increase in tourism. During the 1940s, some well-known writers moved to Virginia City, a gold rush town outside of Reno. From there they filled the pages of the *Saturday Evening Post, Ladies Home Journal, Gentlemen's Quarterly, the New Yorker, Gourmet* and *Town and Country Life* with articles that created our current myths about the wild and woolly west, and its legendary "soiled dove" prostitutes (Taylor, 1998). Nevada's small towns drew on these images to bolster sagging mining economies and build profitable tourism.

In the years after the Second World War, the growing urban casino industry distanced itself from prostitution as casinos struggled to gain legitimacy. Efforts to outlaw brothels by casino owners and local officials in the 1970s met with strong resistance from rural county governments, resulting in a law which technically legalized them outside of Las Vegas (Brents and Hausbeck, 2001; Hausbeck and Brents, 2000). Throughout the 1980s and early 1990s, casinos occasionally worked to shut down the rural brothels. As Las Vegas population growth pushed the state's population to nearly 2 million in 2000, the political clout of the urban casino industry has grown. But they have been unable and perhaps increasingly unwilling to close the brothels. Lately, visible players such as the mayor of Las Vegas and the owners of the Hard Rock Casino have publicly expressed desires to open brothels in Las Vegas itself.

Brothel Business Practices: Rationalized Past to Touristic Present

. . . To understand recent changes in the brothels we must first understand past organizational and marketing trends. Rural brothels historically had two major customer bases, the temporary and mobile male labour force (from the mining, construction and ranching industries) and male tourists, and they have primarily marketed themselves to the former. Since it is illegal for brothels to advertise, the primary mechanism for learning about the brothels, especially prior to the internet, has been word of mouth and independently published book-length guides to the brothels. These methods have worked well for local temporary workers, and for regular customers.

Most brothels have provided sexual gratification in McDonaldized contexts where the provision of sex acts is highly rationalized through line-ups (where women literally form a line to allow a customer to choose among all women at once), timers (to mark the beginning and end of a timed "party"), and often a "get it in, get off and get out" mindset among workers (Hausbeck and Brents, 2002). Brothels rationalize the negotiation process and closely monitor monetary exchanges (Brents and Hausbeck, 2005). Despite the existence of bars in many brothels, most owners discourage men from hanging out without purchasing sex. Some smaller rural brothels market themselves as a sexual home away from home for nomadic working men, a marketing strategy that is not directed at tourists or is itself touristic. The few services offered in addition to sex acts include what they call the

"comforts of home" (free coffee, a shower, living-room-like atmosphere, and other homey amenities). These are designed mostly to get men in the door, and those who partake in these services without purchasing sex are typically frowned upon (Hausbeck and Brents, 2000). Those brothels that do market to tourists market their "old west" experience, with western-sounding names like The Old Bridge Ranch, Kit Kat Guest Ranch, Donna's Ranch, or the Stardust Ranch.

Most of the brothels, especially those located inside the city limits of small towns, are so non-distinct that they are hardly recognizable as brothels. Low key, under-the-radar marketing is part owner choice, and part legal necessity. While the rural economy became dependent on the licensing fees, taxes, work-card fees, and secondary income, the towns have only come to accept and normalize the brothels by also embracing the notion that the sexuality is hidden and not to be encountered as one goes about daily business. Many brothel owners live in fear that any increased visibility could motivate a community backlash, or inspire local politicians to legislate them out of existence.

In the past several years, however, some larger brothels located close to tourist cities have shifted notably in marketing strategies. They are trying to appeal to broader audiences, using more mainstream business forms and selling individualized touristic experiences instead of McDonaldized standardization. They are relying on the internet and other forms of creative marketing to get around advertising restrictions. Several of the larger brothels have invested in renovating their facilities, moving away from western or homey interiors to more upscale, stylish, and even elegant aesthetics. The Sagebrush Ranch near Reno, for example, recently added a mahogany bar with granite countertops and red overhead lights. Themed fantasy rooms are increasingly commonplace, and even the smaller brothels are adding hot tub rooms, dungeon rooms, bachelor party rooms and other specialty spaces. Several brothels are expanding their services by adding souvenir shops, larger bars, restaurants, coffee shops and small strip clubs. While most brothels remain oriented to male customers, some are welcoming couples.

While these changes are happening in many brothels, we want to focus on two that best exemplify the shift toward touristic brothel marketing: the Resort at Sheri's Ranch, owned by Resort Entertainment Company, a corporation, and the Moonlite Bunny Ranch, owned by individual entrepreneur Dennis Hof.

The Resort at Sheri's Ranch

Sheri's Ranch began around 1982 as a small trailer home with a few wings later added for more rooms. In January 2001, Sheri's was purchased by new corporate owners who immediately began a $7 million renovation, expanded the services offered, integrated it with a hotel, and altered marketing strategies to attract more and different customers. The name was changed to The Resort and Spa at Sheri's Ranch, and the atmosphere became more elegant. They built freestanding fantasy bungalows with themes such as a Roman bacchanal, the Middle Ages, an African safari and the 1960s, and they provided new amenities for workers including a pool, a gym, facial room, full beauty salon and computer room. According to a newspaper article, the main goal in redoing Sheri's was to "draw the mainstream attention that the Nevada brothel industry has always avoided . . . [the new owner] wants the brothels to be seen as just another business in the community" (Abowitz, 2001). Sheri's has accomplished this in several ways. First, their doors are always unlocked, and one opens directly to a new $500,000 sports bar. . . .

Second, the business welcomes anyone of any gender. Unlike other brothels, where two women entering may be a novel and unusual event, here senior citizens, families and groups of friends eating and drinking, with no pressure to consume any of the services sold by the attached brothel, are commonplace. Sheri's also markets itself to swingers, organizations of couples who exchange partners for sex, receiving recommendations at various swingers' websites.

Third, Sheri's is marketing to mainstream audiences in other ways. They offer brothel tours to groups as diverse as Elderhostel and the Red Hat Society (organizations for retired citizens), university classes, and Asian tourists on outings from Las Vegas.

Fourth, the corporation is opening mainstream businesses in and near the brothel, as well as two strip clubs in Las Vegas. Sheri's added a separate 10-room, non-brothel resort hotel with a heated pool and waterfall, volleyball court, spa and a golf course. The non-brothel resort hotel markets itself to semi-adventurous couples who want to spend the night "at a brothel" without necessarily purchasing any sexual services. Inside the brothel, the décor in a hot tub party room was provided by Budweiser, a large US beer producer, allowing them to claim "sponsorship" of the room. Budweiser has helped sponsor other brothel parties and public concerts.

Fifth, the nature of the sales interaction is less McDonaldized. Working women will line up when a customer wants to purchase sex, but a customer can bypass the line-up; managers say up to 50 per cent of business is through interactions with customers by women working the bar. The setting encourages a more open, "party" atmosphere and a more individualized, less rationalized interaction. Unlike most brothels in Nevada, workers negotiate with customers a price for activities rather than charging for time spent—a significant shift in the nature of the product sold in Nevada brothels, allowing for a much more individualized and less rationalized interaction than before.

The Moonlite Bunny Ranch

Up until the mid 1990s, the Moonlite Bunny Ranch was a mid-sized brothel with fewer than a dozen or so women working, located just outside of Reno and Carson City, the state capital. In the last few years, the owner, Dennis Hof, began getting adult video stars to work at his brothel, and now he markets the Moonlite Bunny Ranch as a sexualized fantasy land where you can sleep with your dream porn star. With renovations, additions, and several new business practices, it has become a large, modern, luxury brothel.

The Moonlite Bunny Ranch is not only embracing more mainstream business organization but is also more explicitly touristic in selling personalized, interactive experience and spectacle in its marketing and workplace organization. First, to the great consternation of the rest of the industry, Hof has a flamboyant and visible media style. He and several of the working women have appeared regularly on Howard Stern, various TV talk shows, a number of radio shows, and Hof has an ongoing series, *Cathouse,* on the popular cable channel HBO. He works hard to be very high profile and sees himself as bringing a message to the public that legalized prostitution is good and here to stay. Hof told us, "I'm singlehandedly trying to sanitize this vice," he said, "I'm on a mission." And as he told one reporter, "A high-profile approach brings higher-quality girls and better-quality customers" (Tanner, 2006).

Second, Hof explicitly markets his brothel as a sexualized touristic destination, or, in his words, a "singles bar, except the odds are real good." Hof markets voyeuristic transgression by making sure to tell interviewers that "Everybody comes here—every rock star, athlete and a few politicians that you'd love to know about but I can't tell you" (Cosby, 2005). Hof argues that he is able to get more money from customers by approaching the "product" customers are buying as more of an experience rather than a sex act, maintaining that the customer "doesn't want to go to the room unless he feels close to you, or feels like you're friends, or there's some inner personal action going on there, okay?"

Third, like Sheri's, Hof still has women line up for customers entering the brothel but also encourages client–worker interactions in the bar area, and non-McDonaldized, personalized exchanges. As Violet from the Moonlite Bunny Ranch says,

> part of my day is spent working the bar and just kinda hanging out talking to people. I don't get picked out of a line up a whole lot, so I have to work the bar if I want to make any money. And a lot of people will just go with me because they like my personality.

Fourth, his choice to employ porn stars is also designed to develop the fantasy experience. Customers are likely to spend $5000 to $10000 to have an experience with, for example, the most photographed *Playboy* Playmate in the world. "I know a guy that drove half way across the United States to lose his virginity to [adult film star] Sunset Thomas because she was his favorite." Hof explains,

> I don't want that mentality of "come in, get it up, get off, get the fuck out." Moonlight has a mentality that the

> girls believe they're worth the money . . . When you can look somebody in the eye with conviction and say, "great, you know, I understand oral sex, I am the best at it, and it's gonna be five hundred [dollars]," perception is reality. If you can build a perception that you're the best sexual partner in the world, and the experience that I'm gonna have with you is gonna be the ultimate experience, well, then it is.

Fifth, Hof tells us that he has expanded his relationships with the casino industry in Reno as casinos need to distance themselves from illegal prostitution,

> The casino business is kind of between a rock and hard place. They're not privately owned anymore. They're all corporate entities. They have stock holders to answer to. They can't supply prostitution, but they love to send the guys to me because it solves both things. It gets the guy laid, and it keeps the casino from having any problems.

Finally, Hof like Sheri's owners, also hopes to appeal to women who want to buy sex.

> Women are a new market. It's a new emerging market, if you will, and women are just now to the point where they, they consider spending money for something like that . . . It's interesting to watch, so, uh, we don't flaunt it, but we do it. And I like that because I think it is good business.

Conclusions

. . . The largest of Nevada's brothels with the capital to do so are beginning to adopt marketing strategies that are more like mainstream businesses. They are up-scaling, expanding services, clientele and markets and using business forms similar to mainstream businesses, including corporate forms and diversification, as they try to integrate into the tourist economy. The nature of the product sold involves less of a McDonaldized rationalization of outcome-oriented sexual gratification than in the past, and is aimed more at providing individualized, interactive, touristic experiences. . . .

What some researchers have documented in other parts of the global sex industry, we are witnessing in Nevada brothels. There is a slow but noticeable convergence between some legal brothels and mainstream tourist and touristic businesses.

This is likely to make significant impacts on the industry. As some adult sex businesses become structurally integrated with "legitimate" businesses, their economic and political power are likely to increase. Las Vegas' gaming industry went through a similar mainstreaming process as they went from control by organized crime to corporate structures (Moehring, 2000). While the legal brothels are still highly stigmatized businesses, this kind of mainstreaming has already made it harder for local governments to close or increase sanctions against profitable businesses. Working conditions are also likely to improve somewhat, at least approximating other service industry jobs, in sectors that become more structurally similar to mainstream businesses. This is largely because these more upscale, touristic businesses are increasingly competing with mainstream service industries for skilled workers. . . .

Research on the sex industries can tell us much about the effects of the economic infrastructure of mass consumption and the values and attitudes of consumer culture. Employing a framework grounded in economic and cultural shifts promises to add much to analyses of sex work. It historicizes our understandings, situates changes in the economic contexts and the cultural meaning of sex in which sex work occurs, and invites examination of the social construction and material conditions of gender, sex and sexuality. . . . Only within these broader contexts of economic and cultural, political and legal change can we effectively assess the potentially empowering, exploitative, humane or inhumane elements of labour in late capitalist tourist and service industries, including sex work.

NOTES

1. In this article we use the term late capitalism to refer to general economic and cultural trends, based on the works of Agger (1989), Bell (1976), Jameson (1991), Lash and Urry (1994) and Mandel (1975).

2. This growth in the sex industry includes legal and illegal enterprises, formal and informal. The sex industry includes all businesses that sell explicit sexual fantasies, sexual products, sexual services and/or sexual contact, for profit. It includes prostitution, pornography, strip dancing, phone sex, internet sex, adult video industries and a host of other sexual services.

3. We conducted research in 13 Nevada brothels, interviewing prostitutes, management and owners between 1996 and 2002. Much of our information on changes in the brothels comes from further interviews conducted between 2002 and 2006.

REFERENCES

Abowitz, Richard (2001) "Cathouse Dreams: A Day in the Life of a Ranch—Nevada Style," *Las Vegas Weekly* 31 May: 29–34.

Adkins, Lisa (2002) *Revisions: Gender and Sexuality in Late Modernity.* Buckingham, UK and Philadelphia, PA: Open University Press.

Agger, Ben (1989) *Fast Capitalism: A Critical Theory of Significance.* Urbana: University of Illinois Press.

Bauman, Zygmunt (2003) *Liquid Love: On the Frailty of Human Bonds.* Malden, MA: Blackwell.

Beck, Ulrich (1992) *Risk Society: Towards a New Modernity.* London and Newbury Park, CA: Sage.

Bell, Daniel (1976) *The Cultural Contradictions of Capitalism.* New York: Basic Books.

Brents, Barbara G. and Hausbeck, Kathryn (2001) "State Sanctioned Sex: Negotiating Informal and Formal Regulatory Practices in Nevada Brothels," *Sociological Perspectives* 44(3): 307–32.

Brents, Barbara G. and Hausbeck, Kathryn (2005) "Violence and Legalized Brothel Prostitution in Nevada: Examining Safety, Risk, and Prostitution Policy," *Journal of Interpersonal Violence* 20(3): 270–95.

Castle, Stephen (2006) "Passports and Panic Buttons in the Brothel of the Future," *The Independent* 23 September.

Cosby, Rita (2005) "Bunny Ranch," in MSNBC (ed.) *Rita Cosby Live and Direct.* MSNBC. URL (accessed 10 October 2006): http://video.msn.com/v/us/ msnbc.htm?g= d174f457–7af1–46a6–8cff-172a7c381b3f&f=00%20

Economist (1998) "Giving the Customer What He Wants," *The Economist* 14 February: 21–3. URL (accessed 26 October 2006): http://www.economist.com/background/ displaystory.cfm?story_id=113208.

Frank, Katherine (2002) *G-Strings and Sympathy: Strip Club Regulars and Male Desire.* Durham, NC: Duke University Press.

Giddens, Anthony (1992) *The Transformation of Intimacy: Sexuality, Love, and Eroticism in Modern Societies.* Stanford, CA: Stanford University Press.

Harvey, David (1989) *The Condition of Postmodernity: An Enquiry into the Origins of Cultural Change.* Oxford, UK and Cambridge, MA: Blackwell.

Hausbeck, Kathryn and Brents, Barbara G. (2000) "Inside Nevada's Brothel Industry," in R. Weitzer (ed.) *Sex for Sale*, pp. 217–38. New York: Routledge.

Hausbeck, Kathryn and Brents, Barbara G. (2002) "Mc-donaldization of the Sex Industries? The Business of Sex," in G. Ritzer (ed.) *Mcdonaldization: The Reader*. Thousand Oaks, CA: Pine Forge Press.

Hausbeck, Kathryn, Brents, Barbara G. and Jackson, Crystal (2006) "Sex Industry and Sex Workers in Nevada," in D. Shalin (ed.) *Social Health of Nevada: Leading Indicators and Quality of Life*. University of Nevada, Las Vegas: Center for Democratic Culture Publications. URL (accessed June 2007): http://www.unlv.edu/centers/cdclv/mission/index2.html [click *Leading Indicators*].

Hawkes, Gail (1996) *A Sociology of Sex and Sexuality*. Philadelphia, PA: Open University Press.

Hochschild, Arlie Russell (1983) *The Managed Heart: Commercialization of Human Feeling*. Berkeley: University of California Press.

Holyfield, L. (1999) "Manufacturing Adventure: The Buying and Selling of Emotions," *Journal of Contemporary Ethnography* 28(1): 3–32.

Jameson, Fredric (1991) *Postmodernism, or, the Cultural Logic of Late Capitalism*. Durham, NC: Duke University Press.

Lash, Scott and Urry, John (1994) *Economies of Signs and Space*. London and Thousand Oaks, CA: Sage.

Las Vegas Convention and Visitors Authority (2006) *Visitor Statistics*. Las Vegas: Las Vegas Convention and Visitors Authority. URL (accessed 13 October 2006): http://www.lvcva.com/press/statistics-facts/visitor-stats.jsp

Leidner, Robin (1993) *Fast Food, Fast Talk: Service Work and the Routinization of Everyday Life*. Berkeley: University of California Press.

Mandel, Ernest (1975) *Late Capitalism*. London: Humanities Press.

McNair, Brian (2002) *Striptease Culture: Sex, Media and the Democratization of Desire*. London and New York: Routledge.

Moehring, Eugene P. (2000) *Resort City in the Sunbelt: Las Vegas, 1930–2000*. Reno: University of Nevada Press.

Ritzer, George and Liska, Allen (1997) " 'McDisneyization' and 'Post Tourism': Complementary Perspectives on Contemporary Tourism," in C. Rojek and J. Urry (eds) *Touring Cultures: Transformations of Travel and Theory*, pp. 96–112. London and New York: Routledge.

Sharpe, Eric (2005) "'Going Above and Beyond': The Emotional Labor of Adventure Guides," *Journal of Leisure Research* 37(1): 29–50.

Tanner, Adam (2006) "Nevada's Legal Brothels Given Timid Embrace," *Washington Post* 12 March: A8.

Taylor, Andria Daley (1998) "Girls on the Golden West," in R.M. James and C. Elizabeth Raymond (eds) *Comstock Women: The Making of a Mining Community*, pp. 265–82. Reno: University of Nevada Press.

Urry, John (2002) *The Tourist Gaze*. London and Thousand Oaks, CA: Sage.

Wonders, Nancy A. and Michalowski, Raymond (2001) "Bodies, Borders, and Sex Tourism in a Globalized World: A Tale of Two Cities—Amsterdam and Havana," *Social Problems* 48(4): 545–71.

Zelizer, Viviana A. Rotman (2005) *The Purchase of Intimacy*. Princeton, NJ: Princeton University Press.

Elroi J. Windsor and Elisabeth O. Burgess[1]

The title of this book, *Sex Matters*, is a double entendre. First, the book presents issues related to sex, the matters of sex, for readers to consider. Each chapter addresses the numerous contexts for understanding sexuality in contemporary society. We hope that these diverse topics have offered readers a greater appreciation for studies of sexuality. By applying a sociological lens to sex matters, readers can begin to understand the complex ways that social factors shape human sexuality. In addition to relaying these issues about sex, the book's title compels readers to take sex more seriously. We believe that sex *matters*. Sex and sexuality are meaningful subjects that require attention, both scholarly and personal. Our epilogue explores why sex matters and how we talk about the matters of sex. By deconstructing examples of how sexuality has become especially significant in recent times, we set the stage for an alternative perspective. In the end, we identify the potential for productive change in the matters of sex by envisioning a more sex-positive society.

Americans live in a sex-saturated society. Few would refute this claim. But the visibility of sexual imagery does not speak to the meanings and messages they illustrate. When we examine what sex topics actually enter the public discourse and how social structures manage these topics, it is evident that this saturation promotes a narrow framework of acceptable sexuality. We illustrate that the information about sexuality available to the general public does not represent quality information or diverse perspectives.

Since the first edition of *Sex Matters* was published in 2004, America has been exposed to many sex controversies. These topics shape the public discourse of sex. When people's private matters become fodder for public consumption, sex becomes sensationalized. But the *public,* in the form of numerous social institutions, has always constructed and controlled our notions of appropriate sexuality. It is only when these instances challenge dominant ideology that sex scandals become the top stories on television talk shows and news reports. By recounting some of these stories, we illustrate how controversies continue to regulate American sexuality. Consider how the following hot topics—which reflect some themes within this book—construct certain sexualities as remarkable.

Challenging Sexuality Norms

Scientists and social analysts enjoy debating the origins of sexual identity,[2] but marginalized categories of sexuality have recently enjoyed increased visibility in media. For decades, television has propagated heterosexual romance through game shows and reality television, such as *The Newlywed Game, The Dating Game,* and *The Bachelor.* Today, television showcases much more than these heteronormative fairytales. In 2007, MTV launched a new kind of dating show in *A Shot at Love with Tila Tequila.* Lesbian women and straight men competed for the attention of Tila, the bisexual bachelorette.[3] This show debuted as the number one cable show in its time slot among 18–34 year olds. The season finale attracted 6.2 million viewers, making it the highest rated MTV show in two years.[4] MTV continued to promote the concept in a second season, *A Shot at Love 2* with Tila Tequila,[5] and *A Double Shot at Love,* with bisexual identical twins.[6] In 2008, MTV aired *Transamerican Love Story* on its sister network Logo, "the channel for Gay America."[7] This series was the first dating show where men competed to win the heart of an openly transgender woman, Calpernia Addams.[8]

Shows like these broadcast non-normative sexuality to mass audiences, expanding the televised scope of love and lust on reality TV.

None of this niche "reality" programming caused as much of a stir, however, as reports about "the pregnant man." In April 2008, Thomas Beatie, a female-to-male transgender man, wrote about his process of becoming pregnant.[9] As the first transman to publicly discuss his pregnancy, his experiences garnered incredible media attention, including an appearance on *The Oprah Winfrey Show*. His story shocked and confused many people.[10] Although Beatie was assigned a female sex at birth, he passes as a man in his daily interactions and became legally male after medically transitioning with testosterone and chest surgery. He has not had genital reassignment surgery, but hormones have developed his body so that he is able to have intercourse with his wife.[11] These details of Beatie's life raised many questions about gender and sex. His account introduced novel conversations to national audiences.

These examples of televised media delivered new ideas about categorizing sex to mainstream audiences. Although some audiences appear to have thrilled at the dating exploits of sexual nonconformists, procreation was still sacrosanct. At first blush, the promotion of diverse identities and practices seems progressive. The media appear willing to feature marginalized groups. A closer analysis of these representations, however, exposes their underlying adherence to traditional sexual norms. These stories send strong messages about when, where, and by whom sex and gender norms can be challenged. Like tabloid television talk shows of the 1980s and 90s,[12] these portrayals of non-heteronormative pairings serve both to challenge and reify what is normative. The transgressions featured in these stories become a spectacle to be consumed. Non-normative narratives become fascinating. What makes them so exciting to viewers is their queerness, their strangeness, which cannot exist without the notion of normality. By sensationalizing non-normative representations, the media assuage viewers' fears about their own normalcy. The public can examine these complex scenarios with great interest, while ignoring their own potentially complicated sexualities. The media reify normative practices by allowing them to be taken for granted.

Defining "Marriage"

Another controversial issue related to sexuality has actually been breaking news for over a decade. As of early 2009, Connecticut and Massachusetts are the only states that issue marriage licenses to same-sex couples. Nine other states and the District of Columbia legally recognize same-sex relationships in other ways.[13] But the battle over same-sex marriage recognition took an unexpected turn recently. After permitting same-sex couples to marry for six months, California residents voted to ban same-sex marriage in the state's constitution in 2008. Although about 18,000 lesbian and gay couples married under the state Supreme Court's previous decision to legalize their unions, the narrow passage of Proposition 8 threatens to rescind their spousal rights. Lawsuits challenging the passage of the proposition await hearing.[14]

The controversy over marriage is a clear example of both social construction and social control. While American society inches toward granting marital rights to same-sex couples, the meanings of marriage change. As a longstanding social institution, marriage bears much symbolic and legal importance. Meanings of marriage, however, have changed throughout history. The current effort to extend marital rights and responsibilities beyond heterosexual couples is not new, and marriage is not the stable foundation that conservative commentators tout.[15] Different social forces stake claims in the battle over same-sex marriage. Religious groups, government agencies, political organizations, and grassroots social movements struggle for power in shaping the marriage agenda. With each legislative move, and subsequent opposition or celebration, the process of social control becomes more transparent. By regulating marriage, society enforces norms regarding the legitimacy of sexual relationships. The process of redefining marriage illustrates how social construction works, and the simultaneous regulation of this institution demonstrates social control.

Policing Public Officials

Other powerful examples of social control occur in the political arena. Although sex scandals about politicians are nothing new, two recent incidents highlight the power of violating normative notions of appropriate sexual behavior. These stories also expose how whiteness affords politicians a certain advantage throughout the scandals. In the first case, Idaho Senator Larry Craig was arrested for lewd conduct in a men's bathroom at the Minneapolis-St. Paul airport. In the second case, New York Governor Eliot Spitzer was accused of patronizing a high-class escort service. Both men's political careers diminished following the scandals.

Normative notions of sexuality emphasize monogamy, heterosexuality, romance, and privacy. Anonymous same-sex hook-ups in public venues directly challenge our traditional images of sexuality. In the case of Senator Craig, the arresting officer observed the senator tapping his foot and using hand signals in a public restroom.[16] The public became fascinated with this supposed secret code of "gay" public sex. Reports about men's cruising culture flooded the national news circuit.[17] For a moment, it seemed that people could not hear enough about men anonymously hooking up with each other in public places. This scandal exposed a hidden sexual practice. It allowed people to consider the relevance of space, and how private sexual acts may discreetly occur in innocuous public spaces. A politician brought kinky sex to Middle America, albeit in an unintended way that cost him his career.

But throughout the debacle, few observed the similarities between the accusations against Craig and the "down low" phenomenon.[18] Like others before him who endured similar dishonors, Craig enjoyed one privilege throughout the shame. Craig is white. Although men have been secretly having sex with each other throughout history, the down low label is typically reserved for Black men.[19] Discussions of Craig's sexuality were never about race. White privilege enabled Craig to be accused of leading a double life without acquiring a special stigmatizing label. White privilege also kept Craig from being blamed for

rampant HIV infection. Despite the devastation of the charge, his actions were not viewed as emblematic of an entire race of people. This incident demonstrates how race and racism affect the social construction of heterosexually-identified men who have sex with other men.

Senator Craig is certainly not the only politician to experience a sex scandal. In America, the basic idea of commercial sex is controversial. Selling sex violates multiple social norms. So when officials accused New York Governor Eliot Spitzer of patronizing a high-class escort service in 2008, public outcry was swift.[20] The scandal resulted in Spitzer's resignation and public apology for his failings.[21] His escort, Ashley Dupré, shared her story in an interview with Diane Sawyer on *20/20*.[22]

The scandal illuminates multiple matters. On the surface, the illegal act of paying for sex appears to be the main issue. But deeper concerns propelled the controversy through the public discourse. Some scoffed at Spitzer's apparent ethical hypocrisy because he vigilantly guarded against corruption during his tenure in office. Others lamented the infidelities of yet another married public figure. Lying beneath the exposé of a prominent public official was the woman blamed for his fall. After learning about Ashley Dupré, people wondered how a nice, middle-class, white girl could end up in such a deplorable position. Her girl-next-door good looks did not match most people's image of a prostitute. Ultimately, the Spitzer scandal highlighted what happens when normative sexuality becomes tainted by sex work. A tenacious and powerful politician and a pretty young woman from New Jersey maintained model images of wholesomeness. Their sex lives betrayed their blameless façades. The public interrogated the private transactions between one customer and his service provider. They violated a dominant norm in society: sexual transactions should be free.

In both cases, prominent white male politicians took a hit for violating social norms about when and where sex is appropriate. They were eventually punished in very public ways for their indiscretions. Exposés of fringe sexual practices alert normative Americans about the sexual deviancy of others.

Consequently, these accounts also reify sexual norms. But even as the American public revels in learning juicy tidbits about sex, these salacious details are always informed by the systematic practices of social structures.

Why Sex Matters

Sex scandals exemplify how American society manages sexuality. People who violate sexual norms become ridiculed social pariahs. They can lose their families, careers, and freedoms for their sexual transgressions. By sensationalizing sexual transgressions as shocking and appalling, the public discourse of sex constructs and maintains a narrow framework of normative sexuality. This discourse positions certain sexualities as deviant anomalies worthy of intense public scrutiny. Simultaneously, the discourse renders other forms of sexuality unremarkable and mundane. It prevents normative sexuality from being examined and questioned. Consequently, normative sexualities become stabilized and difficult to dislodge. As the discourse castigates many forms of "deviant" sex, it curiously ignores the intricacies of "normal" sex.

The passion and furor that surrounds sex scandals demonstrate that sex does indeed matter—to many different people, in many different ways. Through the narratives of controversy, people realize the importance of adhering to sexual norms. And although controversy sends us clear messages about what *not* to do, Americans still struggle with defining healthy sexuality. The public discourse constructs healthy sex as free of disease and dysfunction. Beyond that limited scope, it is notably silent.

Toward a Sex-Positive Society

As sexuality scholars, we believe that dominant sexual attitudes of Americans suffer from an overly negative outlook. Positive messages about sex are few and are typically found within sexual minority communities like those catered to swinging, BDSM, and polyamory.[23] To conclude this book, we want to present readers with new ways of thinking about sexuality. We want to promote sex as important for

individuals and our larger society. To achieve these goals, we describe what it means to be sex-positive.

Sex-positivity asserts, at its core, that people benefit from holding positive attitudes about sexuality. It is not a simple assertion that sex is good,[24] nor does it mean that sex should pervade every part of life. Despite the proliferation of sex in American media, the United States is not a sex-positive society.[25] An abundance of messages about sex is not the same as being sex-positive. A positive sexuality can help us become more physically, emotionally, and psychologically healthy. To be sex-positive is to recognize that sex can be enriching. It is to affirm that sex matters.

Celebrating Sexual Diversity

An important tenet of a sex-positive ideology is appreciation for sexual diversity. Sex-positivity rejects the notion that there is such a thing as "normal" sex.[26] People experience pleasure in numerous ways. Our bodies provide us with unique sensations worthy of exploration, and we each have our own boundaries. Sexual enjoyment is different for everyone. Sex-positivity recognizes that sexual norms are socially controlled by constraining sexual agendas. Without this restrictive management, people might have fuller sex lives. The ideology of sex-positivity recognizes that the public discourse of sex is oppressive. Social inequalities based on gender, race, sexual identity, class, size, age, and ability affect how people relate to each other, including sexual relationships. Our sexualities intersect with these oppressions, and sex is a site where erotic power converges.[27] Embracing sex-positivity would mean practicing equality, even within relationships that choose to play with power dynamics.

Sex-positivity also strives to represent sexuality in diverse ways. In the media, people encounter limited depictions of sexuality that lack variety. Instead of censoring sex from media, sex-positive approaches advocate creating more varied representations of sexuality.[28] People also have the right to choose to engage with or abstain from these representations without persecution. Similarly, sex-positivity acknowledges that sexually explicit material is important for some people.[29] Commercial sex can be entertaining and empowering for both producers and consumers.[30] The economy of sex in pornography, strip clubs, and prostitution has the potential to overcome its current exploits. Sex work could be more sex-positive if it included the fair pay, benefits, security, and safety features characteristic of more conventional forms of employment.

Consenting to Sex

Consent is another core feature of sex-positivity. This ideology stresses the importance of sex that is consensual and voluntary, not coerced or required.[31] In practicing sex-positive sex, people need to understand and respect each other's boundaries, and understand that feelings can change in any given situation. Practicing sex-positivity recognizes that sex can be intoxicating without using inebriating substances. In addition to affecting performance and satisfaction, alcohol and drugs can confuse our limits.[32]

In promoting consent, it is also important to consider legal "age of consent" issues. Sex-positivity realizes that it is difficult to assign a numerical value to the ability to consent to sex. It is also hard to define sexually appropriate behavior for youth of all ages. While many youth are sexually and emotionally immature, so are some adults. In the current climate of sex-negativity—which includes sexual violence against children—American society must find ways to ensure that children are not exploited. Protecting children, however, can also restrict their sexual agency.[33] Respecting young people's developing sexualities means equipping them with knowledge about their bodies, helping them establish personal boundaries, and empowering them to decide when and how to become sexually active.[34]

Issues of consent become more complicated for people with limited cognitive abilities. A sex-positive approach acknowledges the rights of all people to sexual agency[35] and to sexual education.[36] It also appreciates that people with cognitive disabilities, particularly young women, face a high risk of victimization. Additionally, stereotypes about persons with cognitive disabilities or dementia may cause others to label them as problems in need of management, such as through sterilization or institutionalization.[37] Moreover, for some older adults, the onset or progression of dementia may lead to changes in sexual behavior,

including misinterpreting the actions of others.[38] Overall, a sex-positive approach values the sexual agency of all individuals, regardless of age or cognitive ability, and strives to create a society where sex is always consensual and voluntary.

Promoting Sexual Health

Practicing sex-positivity begins with oneself. By exploring our own bodies, we can understand our likes and dislikes. Masturbation is a healthy part of sexuality. It can be an effective way to explore our sexualities so that we can have more satisfying sex with our partners.[39] Through partnering, we can further practice sex-positivity by finding people to share in our sexual desires. Partnering can enhance our sexual growth. For some people, sex is best in monogamous relationships. For others, polyamory is ideal. A sex-positive approach to sexual exploration respects the partnering choices people make, including an acceptance of asexuality as a legitimate choice for some people.[40]

Promoting sexual health is crucial in a sex-positive society. Regardless of health status, a sex-positive approach to partnering aims to reduce both risks of transmitting STIs and the stigma associated with having STIs. Sexual health also seeks effective ways to address people's sexual problems. Treating sexual "dysfunction" should extend beyond prescriptions for assorted pharmaceutical drugs. Sex therapies should move beyond focusing on rote genital performance, understanding that sex is about emotions, attraction, and desire. In managing sexual health, people need access to comprehensive, nonjudgmental healthcare. Fostering sexual health includes safe, affordable access to contraceptive and procreative choices. Sex-positivity maintains that sexuality information should be made available to people who live in institutions and require care from attendants. Sexual health should be enjoyed by people with disabilities and disease, and people who have physical and psychosocial disadvantages in the socio-sexual arena.[41]

Educating the People

Education is an important means to a sex-positive society. Sex education is appropriate at all levels of life because learning about sex is a lifelong process.[42]

Information about sex and sexuality should be age appropriate, accessible, and comprehensive. Sex-positive sex education does not limit discussion to harmful consequences of sex. Instead, it emphasizes the benefits of healthy, consensual sex. To become sex-positive, people need to know about bodies. Education should include details about sexual anatomy and non-genital erogenous zones. It should focus on strategies for staying sexually healthy—mentally and physically. Sex-positive sex education would affirm that good sex is not just about skill, but also a result of open communication about desires and limits.

Educating about sex is a big responsibility. Social institutions already manage information about sex, and people learn about sex from numerous individuals like peers and family members. A sex-positive approach to education recognizes that multiple agents can effectively deliver healthy information about sex. Ultimately, supportive sex education would allow individuals to learn about and explore their sexualities based on their own personal and spiritual values.[43]

In addition, quality research on sexuality is essential to educating the people. We believe that before we can accurately teach about sexuality, we must be able to understand and critique sexuality from multiple perspectives. Unfortunately, contemporary sexualities research is marginalized, published in specialty journals by isolated scholars, and ignored by academia and mainstream media. A sex-positive model of sexualities research recognizes not only that sexuality applies to many disciplines including sociology, anthropology, psychology, medicine, art, and history, but also that research on sexualities may be interdisciplinary and not easily regimented into narrow academic boxes. Sex research of diverse sexualities from multiple perspectives must be valued and promoted by academic departments and funding agents.[44] In addition, researchers need to become versed in conveying their findings to media.[45] Effective sex research informs effective sex education.

In writing this epilogue, we aspired to provide readers with new ways of thinking about sexuality. As we have shown, the meanings and implications of sex and sexuality are hotly contested in American society. Sex remains a source of controversy and scandal. We believe that this discourse has the potential to change, not through censoring sensational sex stories, but by producing more varied perspectives. President Obama's lift of the global gag rule on abortion is one discreet example of promoting multiple viewpoints.[46] Ultimately, we advocate using a sex-positive approach to sexuality. This ideology involves multiple micro- and macro-level contributions to help foster sexual liberation. Although our discussion of sex-positivity is not exhaustive, we hope that this concluding section allowed readers to seriously consider the role of sex in society. Some people will undoubtedly reject this philosophy, and we respect their right to do so. Our assertion that sex matters allows for different viewpoints. But for us, it is impossible to idly accept the sexual status quo. We need change in the sociology of sexuality. Ultimately, our presumption that *sex matters* begs some kind of action. What does "sex matters" mean to you?

NOTES

1. The authors would like to thank Amy Palder, Mindy Stombler, and Dawn Baunach for their helpful comments in constructing this article.

2. Gross, Larry and James D. Woods. 1999. "Causes and Cures: The Etiology Debate." Pp. 185–9 in *The Columbia Reader on Lesbian and Gay Men in Media, Society, and Politics*, edited by L. Gross and J. D. Woods. New York: Columbia University Press.

3. MTV. "A Shot at Love with Tila Tequila." Retrieved January 9, 2009 (http://www.mtv.com/ontv/dyn/tila_tequila_1/series.jhtml).

4. James, Susan Donaldson. 2008. "'A Shot at Love' Explores (and Exploits) Bisexuality." *ABC News*, January 5. Retrieved January 25, 2009 (http://a.abcnews.com/Entertainment/WinterConcert/story?id=4088351&page=1).

5. MTV. 2008. "A Shot at Love 2 with Tila Tequila." Retrieved January 25, 2009 (http://www.mtv.com/ontv/dyn/tila_tequila/series.jhtml).

6. MTV. 2009. "A Double Shot at Love." Retrieved January 29, 2009 (http://www.mtv.com/ontv/dyn/a_double_shot_at_love/series.jhtml).

7. Logo Online. "Frequently Asked Questions: What Is Logo?" Retrieved January 19, 2009 (http://www.logoonline.com/about/faq.jhtml).

8. Logo Online. "Transamerican Love Story." Retrieved January 9, 2009 (http://www.logoonline.com/shows/dyn/transamerican_love_story/series.jhtml).

9. Beatie, Thomas. 2008. "Labor of Love: Is Society Ready for This Pregnant Husband?" *The Advocate*, April 8. Retrieved January 11, 2009 (http://www.advocate.com/issue_story_ektid52664.asp).

10. Trebay, Guy. 2008. "He's Pregnant. You're Speechless." *The New York Times,* June 22. Retrieved January 11, 2009 (http://www.nytimes.com/2008/06/22/fashion/22pregnant.html?pagewanted=1&_r=1).

11. Oprah.com. 2008. "First TV Interview: The Pregnant Man." *The Oprah Winfrey Show,* April 3. Retrieved January 11, 2009 (http://www.oprah.com/media/20080601_tows _222020001DRAPPTocom_O_VIDEO_1) and (http://www.oprah.com/dated/oprahshow/oprahshow_20080403).

12. Gamson, Joshua. 1998. *Freaks Talk Back: Tabloid Talk Shows and Sexual Nonconformity*. Chicago, IL: University of Chicago Press.

13. Human Rights Campaign. 2008. "Relationship Recognition in the U.S." Washington, D.C.: Human Rights Campaign. Retrieved January 20, 2009 (http://www.hrc .org/documents/Relationship_Recognition_Laws_Map .pdf).

14. Egelko, Bob. 2008. "Same-sex Marriage Issue Back to State Top Court." *San Francisco Chronicle*, November 6. Retrieved January 20, 2009 (http://www.sfgate.com/cgibin/article.cgi?f=/c/a/2008/11/05/BA3B13UM63.DTL).

15. Chauncey, George. 2005. *Why Marriage? The History Shaping Today's Debate*. New York: Basic Books.

16. 2007. "Senator, Arrested at Airport, Pleads Guilty." *The New York Times,* August 28. Retrieved January 19, 2009 (http://www.nytimes.com/2007/08/28/washington/28craig.html?_r=1).

17. For one example, see "Secret Signals: How Some Men Cruise for Sex." 2007. *ABC News*, August 28. Retrieved January 19, 2009 (http://abcnews.go.com/US/Story?id=3534199&page=1).

18. Robinson, H. Alexander. 2007. "NBJC Responds to Sen. Larry Craig Restroom Incident." *The Bilerico Project*, August 29. Retrieved January 19, 2009 (http://www .bilerico.com/2007/08/nbjc_responds_to_sen_larry_craig_restroo.php).

19. Boykin, Keith. 2005. *Beyond the Down Low: Sex, Lies, and Denial in Black America*. New York: Carroll and Graf Publishers.

20. Hakim, Danny and William K. Rashbaum. 2008. "Spitzer Is Linked to Prostitution Ring." *The New York Times*, March 10. Retrieved January 9, 2009 (http://www .nytimes.com/2008/03/10/nyregion/10cnd-spitzer.html).

21. Grynbaum, Michael M. 2008. "Spitzer Resigns, Citing Personal Failings." *The New York Times*, March 12. Retrieved January 20, 2009 (http://www.nytimes.com/2008/03/12/nyregion/12cnd-resign.html).

22. Launier, Kimberly and Katie Escherich. 2008. "Ashley Dupré Exclusive: 'My Side of the Story.'" *ABC News*, November 19. Retrieved January 20, 2009 (http://abcnews .go.com/2020/story?id=6280407&page=1).

23. Society for Human Sexuality. 2007. "A New Look at Sex." Retrieved January 24, 2009 (http://www.sexuality .org/book/index.pdf).

24. Glickman, Charlie. 2000. "The Language of Sex Positivity." *Electronic Journal of Human Sexuality* 3, July 6. Retrieved January 23, 2009 (http://www.ejhs.org/volume3/sexpositive.htm).

25. Moore, Thomas. 1997. "Sex (American Style)." *Mother Jones* 22 (5):56–64.

26. Glickman, Charlie. 2000. "The Language of Sex Positivity." *Electronic Journal of Human Sexuality* 3, July 6. Retrieved January 23, 2009 (http://www.ejhs.org/volume3/sexpositive.htm).

27. Collins, Patricia Hill. 2000. *Black Feminist Thought: Knowledge, Consciousness, and the Politics of Empowerment*. New York and London: Routledge.

28. Office of the Surgeon General. 2001. *The Surgeon General's Call to Action to Promote Sexual Health and Responsible Sexual Behavior*. Rockville, MD: Office of the Surgeon General.

29. 2005. "Mission, Goals, and History: Basic Sexual Rights." The Institute for Advanced Study of Human Sexuality. Retrieved January 23, 2009 (http://www.iashs.edu/rights.html).

30. Frank, Katherine. 2002. "Stripping, Starving, and the Politics of Ambiguous Pleasure." Pp. 171–206 in *Jane Sexes It Up: True Confessions of Feminist Desire,* edited by Merri Lisa Johnson. New York and London: Four Walls Eight Windows; Hartley, Nina. 1987. "Confessions of a Feminist Porno Star." Pp. 142–4 in *Sex Work: Writings by Women in the Sex Industry*, edited by Frédérique Delacoste and Priscilla Alexander. Pittsburgh, PA: Cleis Press.

31. Society for Human Sexuality. 2007. "A New Look at Sex." Retrieved January 24, 2009 (http://www.sexuality .org/book/index.pdf).

32. Society for Human Sexuality. 2007. "A New Look at Sex." Retrieved January 24, 2009 (http://www.sexuality .org/book/index.pdf).

33. Egan, R. Danielle and Gail L. Hawkes. 2008. "Imperiled and Perilous: Exploring the History of Childhood Sexuality." *Journal of Historical Sociology* 21 (4):355–67.

34. Melby, Todd. 2001. "Childhood Sexuality." *Contemporary Sexuality* 35 (12):1–5.

35. Wilkerson, Abby L. 2002. "Disability, Sex Radicalism, and Political Agency." *NWSA Journal* 14 (3):33–57.

36. Rurangirwa, Jacqueline, Kim Van Naarden Braun, Diana Schendel, and Marshalyn Yeargin-Allsopp. 2006.

"Healthy Behaviors and Lifestyles in Young Adults with a History of Developmental Disabilities." *Research in Developmental Disabilities* 27 (4):381–99. References and further reading may be available for this article. To view references and further reading you must *purchase* this article.

37. Wilkerson, Abby L. 2002. "Disability, Sex Radicalism, and Political Agency." *NWSA Journal* 14 (3):33–57.

38. LoboPrabhu, Sheila, Victor Molinari, Kimberly Arlinghaus, Ellen Barr, and James Lomax. 2005. "Spouses of Patients with Dementia: How Do They Stay Together 'Till Death Do Us Part?'" *Journal of Gerontological Social Work* 44 (3/4):161–74; Tabak, Nili and Ronit Shemesh-Kigli. 2006. "Sexuality and Alzheimer's Disease: Can the Two Go Together?" *Nursing Forum* 41 (4):158–66.

39. Society for Human Sexuality. 2007. "A New Look at Sex." Retrieved January 24, 2009 (http://www.sexuality.org/book/index.pdf).

40. Petchesky, Rosalind Pollack. 1999 (2001). "Sexual Rights: Inventing a Concept, Mapping an International Practice." Pp. 118–39 in *Sexual Identities, Queer Politics,* edited by Mark Blasius. Princeton, NJ: Princeton University Press.

41. 2005. "Mission, Goals, and History: Basic Sexual Rights." The Institute for Advanced Study of Human Sexuality. Retrieved January 23, 2009 (http://www.iashs.edu/rights.html).

42. Office of the Surgeon General. 2001. *The Surgeon General's Call to Action to Promote Sexual Health and Responsible Sexual Behavior*. Rockville, MD: Office of the Surgeon General.

43. SIECUS. "Position Statements: Sexuality Education." Retrieved January 25, 2009 (http://www.siecus.org/index.cfm?fuseaction=Page.viewPage&pageId=497&grandparentID=472&parentID=494).

44. Office of the Surgeon General. 2001. *The Surgeon General's Call to Action to Promote Sexual Health and Responsible Sexual Behavior*. Rockville, MD: Office of the Surgeon General.

45. McBride, Kimberly R., Stephanie A. Sanders, Erick Janssen, Maria Elizabeth Grabe, Jennifer Bass, Johnny V. Sparks, Trevor R. Brown, and Julia R. Heiman. 2007. "Turning Sexual Science into News: Sex Research and the Media." *Journal of Sex Research* 44 (4):347–58.

46. Meckler, Laura. 2009. "Obama Intends to Lift Family-Planning 'Gag Rule.'" *The Wall Street Journal*, January 23. Retrieved January 26, 2009 (http://online.wsj.com/article/SB123267481436808735.html).

Name Index

Subject Index